AQUATIC PLANTS FOR WATER TREATMENT AND RESOURCE RECOVERY

AQUATIC PLANTS FOR WATER TREATMENT AND RESOURCE RECOVERY

Edited by

K.R. Reddy
University of Florida
Institute of Food and Agricultural Sciences
Central Florida Research and Education Center
Sanford, Florida 32771

W.H. Smith
University of Florida
Institute of Food and Agricultural Sciences
Center for Biomass Energy Systems
Gainesville, Florida 32611

1987

Magnolia Publishing Inc.
Orlando, Florida

LIBRARY OF CONGRESS CATALOGING IN PUBLICATION DATA

Conference on Research and Applications of
Aquatic Plants for Water Treatment and Resource Recovery
(1986, Orlando, Florida)

Aquatic Plants for Water Treatment and Resource Recovery

"Proceedings of the conference on Research and Applications of
Aquatic Plants for Water Treatment and Resource Recovery, held
July 20-24, 1986, in Orlando, Florida.

Bibliography: P.
Includes index.
1. Water treatment - Congresses. I. Reddy, K. R. II. Title.

ISBN 0-941463-00-1

Library of Congress Catalog Card Number: 87-61397

Printed in the United States of America

EDITORS

K. RAMESH REDDY is a Professor in the Soil Science Department at Gainesville, and the Central Florida Research and Education Center (Sanford) of the University of Florida's Institute of Food and Agricultural Sciences. His research activities include: i) biogeochemical cycling of nutrients in poorly drained soils, flooded rice soils, wetlands and lake sediments, in relation to plant nutrition and water quality, ii) physiological characteristics of aquatic macrophytes used in water treatment, in relation to growth, pollutant assimilation and root zone environment, iii) development of design criteria for optimization of artificial wetlands and retention ponds used for water treatment and resource recovery and iv) impact of aquatic macrophytes on water and sediment biochemistry in eutrophic lakes. Dr. Reddy co-teaches a graduate level course on flooded soil biochemistry at the University of Florida and supervises graduate students and post-doctorals in the areas of his research. He received a Ph.D. in Soil Biochemistry in 1976 from Louisiana State University after his MS and BS degrees from Andhra Pradesh Agricultural University, Hyderabad, India. Dr. Reddy has served as member of several national and international committees, and chaired sessions at national and international conferences. Currently, he serves as Associate Editor for the Journal of Environmental Quality. Dr. Reddy has authored more than 120 scientific papers in his research area.

WAYNE H. SMITH is a Professor of Forestry Department and Director, Center for Biomass Energy systems at the University of Florida's Institute of Food and Agricultural Sciences. His research activities have included the physiology of nutrition in relation to pine reproduction, nutrition of forest species and nutrient cycling in forests, and waste recycling in forest ecosystems. He co-taught a course on Forest Soils and supervised graduate students in these topical areas. Dr. Smith served as the Director of Center for Environmental and Natural Resources, where he developed research programs in waste management, non-point source pollution, management of natural resources and water treatment systems. As Director of the Center for Biomass Energy Systems he has developed research and education programs in biomass production, conversion to useful energy and bioenergy product utilization from waste, residues, and energy crops. He received a Ph.D. in Forest Soils in 1965 from Mississippi State University after earning a M.S. degree from same institution in Agronomy and Forestry and a B.S. degree in Agronomy from the University of Florida. Dr. Smith has served on numerous national and international committees dealing with the biomass energy development, and has been an invited lecturer and session chair at national and international conferences. He is currently the North American editor of the international journal, Biomass. Dr. Smith has authored over 110 scientific papers in his research area and was the editor or coedited four books.

DEDICATION

JOHN F. GERBER

The ecological roles of aquatic plants in wetland environments in processing nutrients at the aquatic/terrestrial interface have been long recognized. Using these processes to solve anthropogenic environmental problems, however, is a recent development. Probably, the pioneering investigations on the use of macrophytes in water treatment were conducted by Dr. Kathie Seidel and co-workers in the early 1950s at the Max Planck Institute in Germany. In Florida, attention was focused on aquatic plants in the 1960s because certain exotics were becoming "weed" problems, especially in nutrient-enriched reservoirs. Dr. John F. Gerber, in 1971, while Assistant Dean for Research in the University of Florida's Institute of Food and Agricultural Sciences (IFAS), was among the earliest to observe that the rapid growth properties of aquatic plants in eutrophic waters could be used beneficially. Early success by projects encouraged by Dr. Gerber suggested that there was much to be gained if a comprehensive, coordinated effort could be organized for addressing such environmentally wise topics. This innovative thinking contributed substantially to the establishment in 1973 of the Center for Environmental and Natural Resources Programs in IFAS at the University of Florida with Dr. Gerber as the first Director.

John Gerber, a native of Missouri, received his academic degrees at the University of Missouri in Climatology and Soil Science. Afterwards he joined the IFAS Fruit Crops Department and established a distinguished record of research, teaching and extension in the area of agricultural meteorology. His research on energy balances, water behavior and use, and cold hardiness of plants led to numerous successful cold protection schemes for citrus. His research eventually led to an on-line computer meditated freeze forecasting system which made use of thermal data transmitted from satellites. Because of breath of knowledge and scientific expertise, he was selected to serve on three National Research Council Panels of the National Academy of Sciences, on the Scientific Advisory Panel for Walt Disney Enterprises which advised on EPCOT and its pavilion, THE LAND, and the various pollution abatement projects such as the water hyacinth wastewater/resource recovery system at Disney's Reedy Creek Utilities site, and numerous other important national, state and university committees.

Dr. Gerber gave leadership to widely-acclaimed programs on land-spreading of wastewaters, recycling sludges in agricultural and forested ecosystems, management of aquatic plants, including their use to renovate waste streams and utilization of the biomass for beneficial products. Also, in 1973, the Center for Wetlands was formed at the University of Florida to explore the use of natural systems for renovating wastewater. These center programs along with the departmental research on conventional wastewater treatment systems combined to give comprehensive coverage of water treatment opportunities.

The magnitude of the program on aquatic plants that Dr. Gerber was able to develop expanded until a new Center was warranted. Thus, in 1978, the Center for Aquatic Plants Research was formed in IFAS. Later, as renewable energy and water quality and quantity programs in Florida became critical and the programs in these areas grew in the Center for Environmental and Natural Resources Programs, the Centers for Biomass Energy Systems, Natural Resources, and Environmental Toxicology were spawned in IFAS to comprehensively address the family of related problems. All except the latter Center jointly initiated planning for this conference.

Planning for this conference began as an opportunity to synthesize the near 20 years of research performed by all these Centers and to review the success of applications made of the research relative to aquatic plants for water treatment and resource recovery. Contacts made early on quickly revealed to us that interest in this topic was widespread and that a forum for broader participation was needed. As new sponsors and cooperators were identified, the conference scope and participation expanded until conference participants at the meeting referred to it as the First International Conference on Aquatic Plants for Water Treatment and Resource Recovery. Dr. John Gerber probably did not stimulate the work he started in Florida with an international conference in mind, nor did we in our initial planning. But, it is fitting that the conference and these proceedings become a tribute to Professor John F. Gerber for his innovation, futuristic planning and leadership.

CONTENTS

PART IV. AQUATIC PLANT MANAGEMENT

PREFACE

Aquatic and wetland plants are important components of lake, pond, river and stream ecosystems throughout the world. Much of the attention focused on vascular aquatic plants has been directed primarily toward their elimination from water bodies, since rapid proliferation can present impedments to navigation and threat to the balance of biota in the aquatic system. In spite of their nuisance characteristics, the ecological and environmental significance of these plants, especially their capability to improve water quality, has created substantial interest in their photosynthetic and physiological activities, and their potential use for beneficial purposes.

Material cycling and water treatment by aquatic plants, the special conditions that these plants create in aquatic environment, and the potential use of the biomass resource for beneficial purpose encourage design and development of integrated systems. There is growing interest in managing aquatic plants in various types of systems (e.g., natural and artificial or constructed wetlands, ponds, channels, lakes, streams and rivers) for purpose of water treatment (e.g., municipal, industrial, agricultural and non-point sources) and resource recovery (for water and nutrient reuse, wildlife habitat creation, and maintenance and biomass production for energy, feeds and fiber, etc.).

Sufficient biological, engineering, economic, ecologic and environmental data are now emerging to make possible the design and operation of water treatment/resource systems using aquatic plants. This book contains papers selected by review panel from those presented at an International Conference on Research and Applications of Aquatic Plants for Water Treatment and Resource Recovery, held in Orlando, Florida, 20-24 July 1986. About 400 participants representing 22 countries from universities, nonprofit institutions, industry and government agencies attended the conference. Twenty-five were synthesis papers invited from international experts and 120 papers were contributed on current research and applications. Complete text of the 25 invited papers and 57 contributed papers are included in this volume. Abstracts of 65 additional papers presented at the conference are also included. The papers are divided into six specific topical groups: 1) overview of global issues, 2) model systems -- natural and artificial wetlands, and constructed floating macrophyte systems, 3) critical process dynamics, 4) aquatic plant management, 5) systems evaluation and 6) research and development needs. The research and development needs were developed by a panel of scientists and engineers of international repute selected to evaluate the papers presented at the conference and to prepare a synthesis of the oversights and opportunities for aquatic plant water treatment/resource recovery systems.

The financial assistance provided by the sponsors for this conference made it possible to tap the international pool of experts, support conference operations and compile this book. The editors wish to acknowledge the financial support by the **University of Florida-Institute of Food and Agricultural Sciences (IFAS); Florida Department of Natural Resources; Florida Department of Environmental Regulation; South Florida Water Management District; Amasek, Inc; Camp Dresser and McKee, Inc; Gas Research Institute; U. S. Army Corps Engineers** -- Waterways Experiment Station; **Tennessee Valley Authority** -- Southeastern Regional Biomass Energy Program; **U. S. Environmental Protection Agency; National Science Foundation; U. S. Department of Energy** -- Solar Energy Research Institute; **U. S. Department of Interior** -- Fish and Wildlife Service and Geological Survey; **U. S. Department of Agriculture** -- Soil Conservation Service; **National Aeronautics and Space Administration** -- National Space Technology Laboratories. In addition, the assistance of the following cooperating organizations is also duly acknowledged; American Society of Agricultural Engineers, American Society of Agronomy, Soil Science Society of America, Crop Science Society of America, American Water Works Association, American Society of Civil Engineers, Weed Science Society of America, Freshwater Foundation, UNDP-World Bank Integrated Resource Recovery Project, Electric Power Research Institute, Aquatic Plant Management Society, North American Lake Management Society, the Centers for Water Resources and Wetlands -- University of Florida and the Florida Governor's Energy Office.

The editors also wish to thank K. R. Tefertiller, Vice President for Agricultural Affairs, University of Florida-IFAS, J. M. Davidson, Dean for Research, University of Florida-IFAS, and J. F. Darby, Director (now retired), Central Florida Research and Education Center (CFREC) IFAS, Sanford for their administrative support and encouragement for this effort.

Compiling this volume is the result of the efforts from a number of people. We wish to acknowledge the efforts of the Steering Committee and Program Committee, who helped to lay the groundwork for the conference, identified the sponsors, helped plan the program, and identified the highly qualified speakers to invite. Members of the Steering Committee, in addition to ourselves, were: Harold Draper, Florida Governor's Energy Office; Joe Joyce, Center for Aquatic Plant Research, Arnett Mace, Center for Natural Resources, William Bowden, Office of Conferences and Institutes of the University of Florida-IFAS; Larry Nall, Florida Department of Natural Resources; and G. J. Thabaraj, Florida

Department of Environmental Regulation. The members of the Program Committee include: Robert Bastian (Chairman), U. S. Environmental Protection Agency, Ramesh Reddy (Co-chairman), University of Florida-IFAS, Frank Coley, U. S. Department of Interior/Geological Survey, Lewis Decell, U. S. Army Corps. Engineers, Tom Hayes, Gas Research Institute, Robert Kadlec, University of Michigan, Wiley Kitchens, U. S. Department of Interior/Fish & Wildlife Service, G. Lakshman, Saskatchewan Research Council, Nicholas Lailas, U. S. Department of Energy, Cecil Martin, California State Water Resources and Control Board, Curtis Richardson, Duke University and Allen Stewart, Amasek, Inc. The Publication Committee members functioned as Associate Editors to assure high quality manuscripts. Members of this committee in addition to ourselves include: Phillip Badger, Tennessee Valley Authority; G. R. Best, University of Florida; Larry Nall, Florida Department of Natural Resources; Donna Johnson, Solar Energy Research Institute; and G. J. Thabaraj, Florida Department of Environmental Regulation. We especially wish to acknowledge the authors who chose to prepare manuscripts in accordance with reviewer requirements and to share their technical knowledge and experience.

The editors would like to thank the staff at CFREC-Sanford, Center for Biomass Energy Systems and the IFAS Office of Conferences and Institutes, who assisted in many ways during the conference planning, developing and staging and in producing this book. Special appreciation goes to Brenda Clutter who played a major role in every step of the process from preparing program announcements and calls for papers, communicating with interested participants and developing the final typed, reviewed and edited manuscripts ready for the publisher. She worked effectively and tirelessly with each of the over 145 conference presenters and 85 authors for the past eighteen months. The assistance provided by Linda LaClaire in proofreading the manuscripts is greatly appreciated. Finally, the editors would like to thank their wives, Sulochana Reddy and Midge Smith, for their interest, tolerance, and support during this two year period.

Any opinions, findings, conclusions or recommendations expressed in this publication are those of the authors and do not necessarily reflect the views of the Institute of Food and Agricultural Sciences, University of Florida or Magnolia Publishing Inc.

K. R. Reddy and W. H. Smith
Editors

FOREWORD

In the USA, the Federal Clean Water Act has led to thousands of new wastewater treatment facilities being constructed or expanded across the country to help control municipal and industrial sources of water pollution. In the future it is clear that additional processes will be needed to upgrade many of these treatment facilities while more attention will need to be given to controlling many of the non-point sources of water pollution as well if any significant improvements in water quality are to be realized.

Over the years a wide range of treatment technologies have been used in an effort to restore and maintain the chemical, physical and biological integrity of the water bodies. Yet during the past 15 years or so, considerable interest has been expressed in the potential use of a variety of aquatic plant systems to help remove contaminants from wastewater while effectively recycling many of these previously unwanted materials - in a manner not unlike that which can result from land treatment of wastewater.

Some of the earliest efforts to explore the capabilities of specific aquatic plant systems to help treat wastewater were undertaken in various European countries by Seidel, Kickuth, de Jong and others, and were mainly focused on reeds and rushes. Related studies were eventually undertaken by Spangler, Sloey, Small, Gersberg, Goldman and others in several locations in the United States. Kadlec, Odum, Valiela and others have undertaken longterm assessments of the capabilities of several types of natural wetlands to handle wastewater additions. While Ryther and others undertook some early assessments of the possibility of culturing marine species in wastewater, Wolverton, McDonald, Dinges, Reddy, and many others have developed a comprehensive information base on the capabilities of floating aquatic plants to help treat wastewater. Early studies in the USA supported by National Science Foundation, National Aeronautics and Space Administration, Environmental Protection Agency, United States Department of the Interior and other agencies have played an important role in stimulating the development of more recent detailed studies of the mechanisms involved in aquatic plant treatment systems. Similar efforts have been sponsored by counter part agencies throughout the world. Basic biomass production, harvesting, processing and conversion studies supported by the U.S. Department of Energy, Gas Research Institute and other groups have also played an important role in providing valuable information for use in designing and operating such systems.

Many aquatic plants are widely dispersed, highly productive forms of life which can effectively use solar energy to fix C while absorbing nutrients and other chemicals from water to produce more plant biomass. The biomass produced can serve as surface area to enhance bacterial decay of organic pollutants, habitat for wildlife, and when harvested as raw material for the production of energy, animal feeds, fiber, chemical feedstocks, etc. As a result, aquatic plants systems offer considerable potential for use in water treatment and resource recovery.

Many of the potential benefits to be gained by treating and recycling the organic matter and nutrient resources in wastewater using aquatic plant systems have been well demonstrated and documented, and should lead to an increase in such uses in the future. The conference which lead to this publication was designed to help assess the status of managing various types of aquatic plant systems for treating water to remove pollutants from a variety of sources while producing biomass and other products that can be used as a resource. It provided a forum for the synthesis and interpretation of current research and an opportunity to analyze case studies of operating systems. Nearly 400 people participated, including registrants from 22 countries. These included a balanced mixture of researchers from scientific, engineering and socio-economic disciplines, consultants, facility managers and regulatory officials, many meeting together for the first time, reflecting the truly interdisciplinary nature of the subject.

Both full scale, operating projects and research studies based on managing naturally occurring and constructed systems involving various configurations were covered. Projects involving a wide range of aquatic plant species to help treat a variety of municipal and industrial wastewaters as well as runoff from mining, agricultural and urban areas were discussed. The experience in managing various types of natural wetlands to provide advanced treatment of secondary effluents, designing and operating constructed wetlands to achieve either secondary or advanced treatment, as well as culturing cattails, reed, rushes, water hyacinths, duckweed, algae and other aquatic plants in ponds or channels designed to facilitate both water treatment and plant harvesting were covered in detail. Many of the critical processes involved in regulating pollutant removal rates and limiting aquatic plant biomass production in such systems were covered with biomass production, harvesting, handling and conversion. Experiences with such systems in Europe, Asia, Australia, Africa, as well as North, South and Central America were presented.

Wetlands and various waterways which are often filled with naturally occurring aquatic plants have been inadvertently used for water treatment for many years both in the United States and overseas. At the same time, considerable effort has gone into the development of cost-effective techniques for controlling unwanted aquatic weed growths in waterways, harvesting and transforming aquatic biomass from such areas into useful products. Only in recent years, however, have the necessary research and monitoring studies been undertaken in an attempt to develop sound guidelines for the meaningful management of aquatic plant systems designed to treat and recycle wastewater. Appropriate management practices are only now being developed to allow some of these systems to be properly designed and operated from an environmental standpoint.

Of course aquatic plant systems must still be closely examined in terms of protection of the environment, human health and biomass quality. As discussed during the conference, the various existing regulations, criteria and guidelines and others currently being developed under various regulatory authorities will help provide the necessary mechanisms to properly control the implementation of aquatic plant treatment and resource recovery systems.

The functional role of wetlands in achieving water quality improvement (through such processes as nitrification, denitrification, volatilization, sorption, and plant uptake) that has been well demonstrated in numerous locations provides a compelling argument for both wetland preservation and creation. Consistent and predictable N removals (e.g., 75% or more on a mass loading basis) over a substantial range of loadings, but variable P retention capacities which are dependent on site specific factors can be expected for natural wetlands. Further, work on constructed wetlands (mainly using cattails, reeds and rushes) designed for treating wastewater in various locations in Europe, Canada and the United States also suggests that if properly designed and controlled to avoid overloading, such systems can remove or process significantly higher concentrations of BOD, SS and N and also remove a large mass of P from wastewater than can be expected by most natural wetland systems. Induced changes in hydrology as a result of wastewater additions to natural wetlands may well be the major factor controlling impacts on flora and fauna in these systems which are among the issues of greatest concern facing increased use of managed natural wetlands for water quality and biomass production purposes.

The culture of aquatic organisms (especially water hyacinths, duckweed, algae, aquatic ferns - and fish) has been a traditional way of improving water quality and facilitating nutrient recovery from wastes in many parts of the world, but especially in India, China and S.E. Asia. But only recently have serious efforts been taken in these areas as well as in the United States to optimize the design of such systems for the purpose of water treatment and biomass recovery. Aquatic plant systems (especially water hyacinths) have been evaluated at least experimentally to treat a wide range of industrial as well as municipal wastewaters (e.g., dairy, pulp and paper, textile, sugar refinery, tannery, palm oil, electroplating, metal works, distillery, munitions, etc.) and have been effective in the removal of such constituents as phenols, pesticides, heavy metals, flouride, radionuclides, bacteria and viruses. In certain cases the plants serve primarily as living substrates for microbial activity and as a cover resulting in significant reductions of BOD, SS and N in the effluent. For other treatment purposes, such as the removal of some organic chemicals, heavy metals and P, plant uptake can play a major role in these systems. Certain species can produce a substantial standing crop of biomass, in some cases (especially water hyacinths) in excess of the most productive terrestrial plant systems.

The sizable quantity of biomass that can be produced from aquatic plant systems (generally in the form of algae and/or macrophytes) can potentially be used for fiber products, chemical production, livestock feed or converted to energy or soil amendments. While considerable progress has been made in recent years to identify possible uses for the aquatic biomass, further research and demonstration are still needed to improve the overall efficiencies of available harvesting and processing systems to make aquatic biomass harvesting/utilization systems more cost-effective. Integration of wastewater treatment with anaerobic digestion of harvested biomass and sewage sludge appears to be one of the more attractive conversion options for utilization aquatic biomass at this time. Based on the results of recent pilot scale operations, improvements to anaerobic digestion reactor designs appear to be able to realize relatively high gas conversion yields under proper conditions.

The operational experience and research results reported here suggest that the growing interest in managing aquatic plants as a part of water treatment and resource recovery systems offers considerable opportunity for realizing sizable future savings in wastewater treatment costs and resource recovery opportunities at the same time. Clearly the technical feasibility of using various aquatic plants for the treatment of water and recovery of beneficial resources is well established. Yet, although there are a considerable number of full-scale aquatic plant treatment systems operating in countries around the world, it is also clear that there is still a way to go before such systems will be considered for general routine use in the United States. While existing projects have demonstrated the potential for future use of these concepts, there is an obvious need for further study to improve our understanding of the internal components of these aquatic systems, their responses and interactions, in order to allow for more optimum project designs.

Robert K. Bastian
U. S. Environmental Protection Agency
Washington, D.C. 20460

PART I
OVERVIEW OF GLOBAL ISSUES

AQUATIC PLANTS FOR WASTEWATER TREATMENT: AN OVERVIEW

B. C. Wolverton
National Aeronautics and Space Administration
National Space Technology Laboratories
NSTL, Mississippi 39529

Humans, like all other animals, depend upon a symbiotic relationship between green plants and microorganisms for existence on earth. Photosynthesizing plants produce O_2 and regulate its atmospheric concentration while transforming radiant energy into useful chemical energy. In the process, CO_2 and other gaseous chemicals produced by humans, animals, and microorganisms during their metabolic processes are used and their atmospheric concentrations mediated. Plants in conjunction with microorganisms therefore produce food for humans and also recycle their waste. These fundamental facts have been known for a long time and taken for granted. What has not been known, but is beginning to be realized, is the potential of plants in conjunction with microorganisms for correcting environmental imbalances caused by industrial development and environmental abuse.

With the exception of rice, aquatic plants have received little recognition for their contributions to the environment or other human needs. The value attributed to aquatic plants in the past has been restricted to their aesthetic or ornamental qualities or usefulness to wildlife. The more aggressive aquatic plants such as water hyacinths (Eichhornia crassipes [Mart] Solms), however, have caused serious problems in some parts of the world as nuisance weeds that clog slow moving streams and lakes.

Only during the past 20 years has the benefit of aquatic plants in improving water quality been widely recognized. Boyd (1970), Cornwell et al. (1977), Sheffield (1967), Steward (1970), Wooten and Dodd (1976) and Yount (1964) were among the first scientists to demonstrate the nutrient removal potential of aquatic plants. Seidel (1976), Wolverton and Harrison (1973), Wolverton and McDonald (1975,1976,1981b), Wolverton et al. (1984a,c) and Wolverton and McKown (1976) demonstrated the importance of aquatic plants in removing organic chemicals from aquatic environments. The importance of aquatic plants in wastewater treatment has grown significantly since the early

Aquatic Plants for Water Treatment
and Resource Recovery
K.R. Reddy and W.H. Smith (Eds.)

ISBN 0-941463-00-1

research conducted starting in the 1960's. Only during the past 15 years has the ecology of natural wetlands been studied extensively (Odum, 1976; Kadlec and Kadlec, 1978).

The first international conference on biological control of water pollution was held at the University of Pennsylvania in 1976. Although only six papers on aquatic plants and wastewater treatment were published from this conference, the overall concepts were established (Tourbier and Pierson, 1976). The work of Seidel (1976) at the Max Plank Institute in Germany with bulrush along with that of Wolverton et al. (1976) of the National Aeronautics and Space Administration (NASA) at the National Space Technology Laboratories (NSTL) in south Mississippi with water hyacinth was presented at that conference.

The continued rapid growth of technology in this area led to another conference on aquaculture systems for wastewater treatment at the University of California at Davis in September 1979 (Bastian and Reed, 1979). The Davis Conference was the first introduction of wastewater engineers to aquatic plants as a potential tool in wastewater treatment. Their participation in this conference added a new and important dimension to aquatic plant applications since engineers primarily design and approve wastewater treatment systems. Since the Davis conference, a large amount of additional data has accumulated on the use of aquatic plants in wastewater treatment, as evidenced in the number of papers and their references contained in this book.

NASA has been one of the leaders in developing this technology because of its potential importance in future Closed Ecological Life Support Systems (CELSS) for space applications (Wolverton, 1980). Although NASA's primary goal in plant research is to develop technology utilizing plants as a component of a CELSS for a future space station (Figure 1), most of the NSTL research has been funded through the NASA Technology Utilization Office (TU). This office supports the utilization of space developed technology for applications directed toward solving earthly problems such as wastewater treatment (see Figure 2).

SCIENTIFIC BASIS FOR USING AQUATIC PLANTS IN WASTEWATER TREATMENT

The scientific basis for waste treatment in a vascular aquatic plant system is the cooperative growth of both the plants and the microorganisms associated with the plants. A major part of the treatment process for degradation of organics is attributed to the microorganisms living on and around the plant root systems.

Once microorganisms are established on aquatic plant roots, they form a symbiotic relationship in most cases with the higher plants. This relationship normally produces a synergistic effect resulting in increased degradation rates and removal of organic chemicals from the wastewater surrounding the plant root systems. Microbial degradation products of the organics are produced which

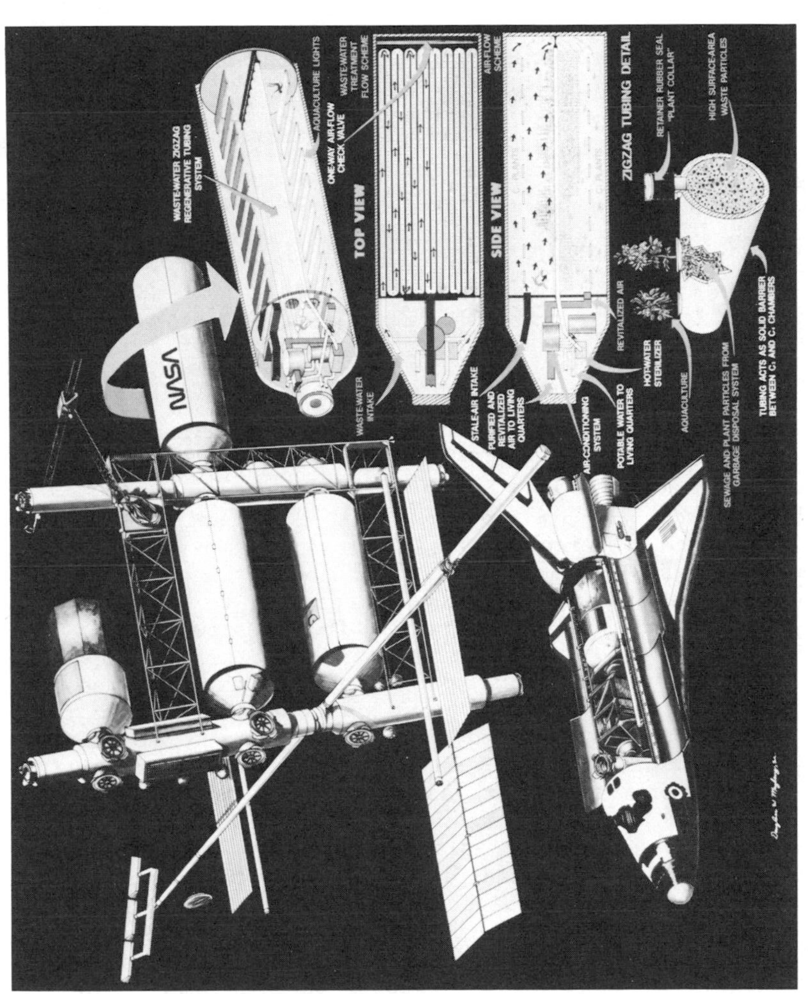

FIGURE 1. Space station bioregenerative life-support module.

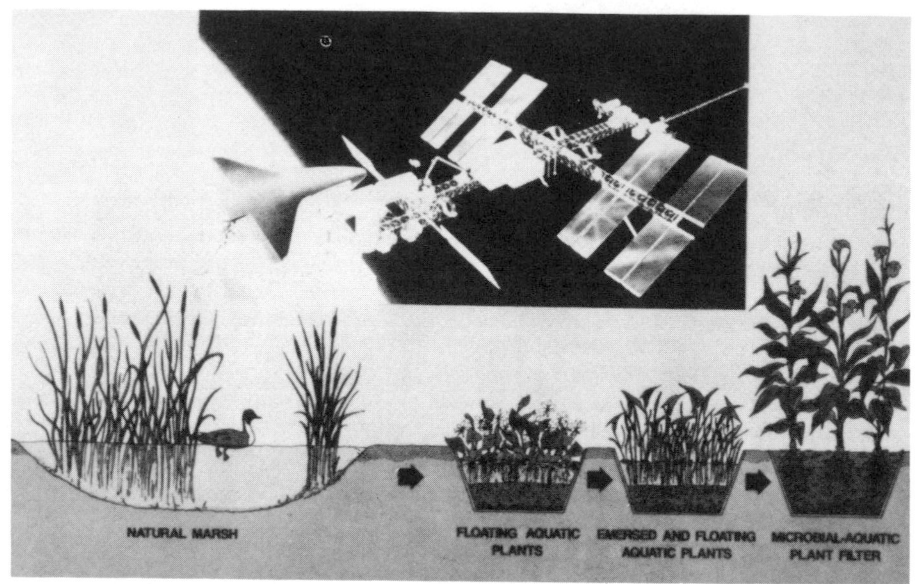

FIGURE 2. Plants for pollution abatement: past and present.

the plants absorb and utilize along with N, P, and other minerals as a food source. Microorganisms also use some or all metabolites released through plant roots as a food source. By each using the others waste products, this allows a reaction to be sustained in favor of rapid removal of organics from wastewater. Electric charges associated with aquatic plant root hairs also react with opposite charges on colloidal particles such as suspended solids causing them to adhere to the plant roots where they are removed from the wastewater stream and slowly digested and assimilated by the plant and microorganisms. Aquatic plants have the ability to translocate O_2 from the upper leaf areas into the roots producing an aerobic zone around the roots which is desirable in domestic sewage treatment. Aquatic plant roots are also capable of absorbing, concentrating, and in some cases, translocating toxic heavy metals and certain radioactive elements, therefore, removing them from the water system (McDonald, 1981; Wolverton, 1975; Wolverton and McDonald, 1975,1977). In addition, aquatic plants have demonstrated the ability to absorb certain organic molecules intact where they are translocated and eventually metabolized by plant enzymes as demonstrated with systemic insecticides (Wolverton and Harrison, 1973).

The biological reactions that take place between environmental pollutants, plant and microorganisms are numerous and complex, and to date are not fully understood. But there is enough information available to demonstrate that aquatic plants serve more of a function than simply supplying a large surface area for microorganisms as some scientists and engineers have suggested. Several of the papers in this volume add to the knowledge of these fundamental processes important to the use of aquatic plant systems.

FLOATING, EMERGENT AQUATIC PLANTS WITH EMPHASIS ON OPERATIONAL SYSTEMS

Water Hyacinth

The water hyacinth has been one of the most studied aquatic plants because of its detrimental and as well as beneficial effects on the environment. An astounding growth in the number and extent of research projects since the first work in the '60's involving the water hyacinth has occurred in recent years (Dinges, 1978; Gersberg et al., 1986; Haller, 1970; McDonald and Wolverton, 1980; Ornes and Sutton, 1975; Reddy and DeBusk, 1984,1985a,b; Rogers and Davis, 1972; Scarsbrook and Davis, 1971; Stephenson et al., 1980; Wolverton and McDonald, 1976,1978,1979a). A review was published by Pieterse (1978) and Gopal and Sharma (1981) which covered all aspects of water hyacinth research that had been accomplished up to 1980.

The first operational water hyacinth wastewater treatment system for treating domestic sewage was installed at NSTL in 1976 and has been functioning effectively for the past 10 years (Wolverton and McDonald, 1979b). The system consists of a single cell lagoon with a surface area of 2.02 ha and an average depth of 1.22 m. The average flow rate was 473 m^3 d^{-1} in 1976 and approximately 606 m^3 d^{-1} in 1985 (Wolverton, unpublished data). The BOD_5 loading rate in 1976 averaged 24.6 kg ha^{-1} d^{-1} but has increased to approximately 33.7 kg ha^{-1} d^{-1} today (Wolverton, unpublished data).

The first operational water hyacinth system for treating photographic and laboratory chemical wastewater was also installed at NSTL in 1975 (Wolverton and McDonald, 1977). Although this water hyacinth system has been effective in treating chemical wastewater during the past 11 years, it was recently upgraded with a rock-plant microbial filter system designed according to the concept described by Wolverton et al. (1981) using more cold-tolerant aquatic plants such as the reed (*Phragmites communis* Trin.) and cattail (*Typha latifolia* L.).

In 1978, a tertiary wastewater treatment system was designed for the Coral Springs Improvement District at Coral Springs, Florida, using water hyacinths to treat 378.5 m^3 d^{-1} of secondary effluent from an activated sludge wastewater treatment plant (Swett, 1979). The system consists of a series of 5 ponds with total water surface area of 0.50 ha and average water depth of 0.38 m. The total retention time for all five ponds was 6 d. In this case, the water quality parameters of primary concern were total N and P. Total N levels into the ponds were reduced by 91% from 10.12 mg L^{-1} to 0.94 mg L^{-1}. Total P concentrations were reduced by 38% from 6.12 mg L^{-1} to 3.77 mg L^{-1} which indicates that nutrient uptake by the water hyacinth was N limited. During several months of the year there was a 50% reduction in volume from influent to effluent due to high evapotranspiration rates. If the N and P concentrations were adjusted for water loss, the effluent P concentration would have been approximately 1 mg L^{-1} as required for advanced wastewater treatment. The total N was well below the 3 mg L^{-1} level required.

In 1979, a joint project involving NSTL, EPA and the Reedy Creek Improvement District (Disney World at Orlando, Florida) was initiated to evaluate the use of water hyacinths for treating primary effluent from the wastewater reclamation plant at Disney World (Kruzic, 1979). The wastewater was pumped from a primary clarifier with a 2 h detention time. The average BOD_5 and TSS leaving the clarifier were 150 and 80 mg L^{-1}, respectively. Channels, 8.84 m W x 0.61 m D x 109.73 m L, were constructed to contain the water hyacinths. A detention time of approximately 5 d was maintained. After 5 d in the water hyacinth channels, both the monthly average BOD_5 and TSS had been reduced to 20 mg L^{-1} or below. Over the past several years, emphasis for this system has shifted from just waste treatment to a combination waste treatment/biomass energy production due to support from the Department of Energy and the Gas Research Institute (GRI).

One of the most ambitious wastewater treatment systems in the United States is located in San Diego, California. The present system, which went into operation in July 1984, is designed to convert raw sewage into potable water with water hyacinths being used as the major wastewater treatment component of this system.

Duckweed

Duckweed (*Lemna*, *Spirodela*, and *Wolffia* sp.) has had limited investigation compared to the water hyacinth for use in wastewater treatment (Culley and Epps, 1973; Reddy and DeBusk, 1985a; Sutton and Ornes, 1977). However, this plant has a much wider geographic range in the United States than water hyacinths because it can vegetate at temperatures as low as 1° to 3° C which makes it more suitable for temperate climates. This small, floating plant can be easily harvested using a continuous belt skimmer similar to those used for removing oil from water surfaces. Because these plants are so small, wind and wave action hinder maintaining a continuous mat of plants on large surface areas without floating barriers. A continuous mat of duckweed cover will prevent algal growth in wastewater but also, severely reduces the exchange of O_2 between the atmosphere and water. Therefore, a shallow water depth should be used with duckweed systems to prevent total anaerobic conditions from developing (Culley and Epps, 1973). A duckweed mat will also prevent mosquito breeding and development which sometimes causes problems with water hyacinth systems that become anaerobic.

In May 1979, NASA assisted Cedar Lake Development in North Biloxi, Mississippi in evaluating a two cell lagoon wastewater treatment system which had become infested with a mixed duckweed culture of Lemna, Spirodela and Wolffia sp. (Wolverton, 1979). This system which receives 52.8 m^3 of domestic sewage consists of a primary lagoon with a surface area of 0.083 ha and a depth of 2.4 m followed by a duckweed-covered lagoon. The duckweed lagoon has a surface area of 0.075 ha and a depth of 1.5 m. The average BOD_5 influent and effluent levels were 31 and 15 with TSS concentrations of 94 and 18 mg L^{-1}, respectively. Because of the depth of the duckweed lagoon, the discharged effluent dissolved oxygen (DO) level averaged 1 mg L^{-1}. The DO increased to an average concentration of 5.3 mg L^{-1} after being discharged over a 0.9 m drop into a receiving ditch. Papers in this volume update the reader on the status of developed systems.

ROOTED, EMERGENT AQUATIC PLANTS WITH EMPHASIS ON OPERATIONAL SYSTEMS

Artificial Wetlands

Although the floating water hyacinth is effective in wastewater treatment, its usefulness is limited to tropical and semi-tropical climate zones for year-round effectiveness and survival. To extend the useful temperature range of vascular aquatic plant systems and eliminate the need for restocking of plants in the spring when extended winter freezes killed the floating plants, NASA at NSTL is studying the use of more temperate vascular aquatic plants in artificial wetlands. A system designed as an artificial wetland is currently being installed at the NSTL to upgrade the effluent from one of NSTL's facultative lagoon systems. This artificial wetland will be stocked with giant bulrush [Scirpus californicus (C. A. Mey.) Steud] and duckweed. Bulrush for waste treatment was previously studied by DeJong (1976) and Seidel (1976). The retention time is 5 to 7 d and the maximum depth 38 cm. Another artificial wetland which uses a shallow reservoir with a maximum depth of 38 cm and total surface area of 4 ha was recently installed at Collins, Mississippi to treat 1325.5 m^3 d^{-1} of effluent from a facultative sewage lagoon. The City of Arcata in California conducted a pilot wetland wastewater treatment study for several years where oxidation pond effluent was used as the influent to artificial wetland channels (Inouye, 1986). When hard-stem bulrush (Scirpus acutus Muhl.) was used as the only aquatic plant in the wetland system, average influent BOD_5 levels of 50 mg L^{-1} were reduced to 10 mg L^{-1} in the effluent. Such promising results from unharvested wetland systems with 6-7 d retention times are very encouraging and demonstrate a wide geographic potential application for such systems.

Vascular Plant/Microbial Filters

The integration of emergent aquatic plants with microbial filters has produced one of the most promising wastewater treatment technologies since development of the trickling filter process in 1893 (Wolverton, 1982; Wolverton et al., 1983). This process, a lateral flow system containing rooted aquatic plants with microbial communities on rocks serving as a trickling filter, represents a different biological process. Once the microorganisms are established on the rocks and plant roots, a symbiotic relationship develops between them which enhances the wastewater treating capability of both processes.

By using long, shallow (<60 cm in depth) rock-plant filters with hydraulic retention times of 6-24 h, mean cell residence times of several hundred days can be maintained within the plant-rock filter. Operational data with small systems have demonstrated the importance of maintaining DO levels within the filter of 1.5 mg L^{-1} or greater (Wolverton, 1982; Wolverton et al., 1983). This O_2 level is required to achieve odor free, low BOD_5 (<10 mg L^{-1}) levels in the discharged effluent. This method of treatment has been used in conjunction with existing waste treatment facilities as discussed below as well as small septic tank systems (Wolverton et al., 1984c).

This type system can be designed to achieve the desired maximum level of BOD_5 and TSS, ranging from secondary levels of 30 mg L^{-1} each to tertiary levels of 5 mg L^{-1} each. The plant-rock filters can also be planted with more aesthetically desirable plants such as the canna lily (*Canna flaccida* Salisb.), pickerelweed (*Pontederia cordata* L.) and arrowhead (*Sagittaria latifolia* Willd.). Two rock-plant wetland systems capable of treating approximately 1326 m^3 d^{-1} of effluent from facultative lagoons will begin operation at Benton and Haughton, Louisiana in May 1987. A 15,151 m^3 d^{-1} system at Denham Springs, Louisiana will be put on line by late 1987 to upgrade facultative lagoon effluent to advanced secondary levels. The retention time of each of the above systems is 24 h.

BIOMASS: A RESOURCE

Biomass removal required for sustained functioning of aquatic plant treatment by the large number of aquatic plant wastewater treatment systems projected to be in operation within the next several years represents a vast potential resource. The conversion of plant material into energy, feed and fertilizer has already been demonstrated (Culley and Epps, 1973; Ghosh and Klass, 1976; Parra and Hortenstein, 1974; Taylor et al., 1971; Taylor and Robbins, 1968; Wolverton and McDonald, 1978,1981a,1983). Most biomass energy research to date has focused on CH_4 production using water hyacinth. Animal feed studies also have been conducted with both water hyacinth and duckweed. As more aquatic plant wastewater treatment systems become operational, additional research is expected to expand the uses of harvested plant material. Several papers in this volume report results from research on some of the biomass utilization opportunities.

NEW OPPORTUNITIES

The technology developed using aquatic plants to treat wastewater is now being expanded to include houseplants and indoor air pollution abatement.

Recent studies by the U. S. Environmental Protection Agency (EPA) identified more than 350 volatile organic chemicals inside modern energy-efficient buildings (Gammage and Kay, 1984; Wallace et al., 1984). The numbers and types of these organics demonstrate the serious potential health hazards associated with indoor air pollution in tightly sealed facilities such as future space stations and well-insulated homes. Recent research by NASA at NSTL has demonstrated the potential indoor air pollution abatement characteristics of various houseplants (Wolverton et al., 1984b,1985). The ability of a large number of common houseplants to remove formaldehyde, benzene and carbon monoxide from sealed experimental chambers has been demonstrated.

The technology developed using aquatic plants to treat wastewater is now being extended to other contaminated media. Specifically, contained atmospheres such as space vehicles and well-insulated home environments with little air exchange can be benefited by plants. NASA, NSTL, has recently explored the potentials for using plants, especially epiphytes, for cleaning air of pollutants contributed by fossil fuel combustion and other human activities.

SUMMARY

1. The technology for using water hyacinth to upgrade domestic sewage effluent from lagoons and other wastewater treatment facilities to secondary and advanced secondary standards has been sufficiently developed to be used where the climate is warm per year round.
2. Systems of using emergent plants such as bulrush combined with duckweed are also sufficiently developed to make this a viable wastewater treatment alternative. This system is suited for both temperate and semi-tropical areas found throughout most of the U.S.
3. The newest approach in artificial marsh wastewater treatment involves the use of emergent plant roots in conjunction with high surface area rock filters. Smaller land areas are required for these systems because of the increased concentration of microorganisms associated with the rock and plant root surfaces than is required for a strict artificial wetland to achieve the same level of treatment.

4. The future opportunities extend beyond the use of biological organisms to treat wastewater but the use of plants also to treat contained atmospheric environments contaminated by space conditioning and incident human activities.

REFERENCES

Bastian, R. K., and S. C. Reed (ed.). 1979. Aquaculture systems for wastewater treatment: Seminar Proceedings and Engineering Assessment. U. S. Environmental Protection Agency, EPA 430/9080-006. 495 pp.

Boyd, C. E. 1970. Vascular aquatic plants for mineral nutrient removal from polluted waters. Econ. Bot. 24:95-103.

Cornwell, D. A., J. Zoltek, Jr., C. D. Patrinely, T. S. Furman, and J. I. Kim. 1977. Nutrient removal by water hyacinths. J. Water Pollut. Control Fed. 49:57-65.

Culley, Jr., D. D., and A. E. Epps. 1973. Use of duckweed for waste treatment and animal feed. J. Water Pollut. Control Fed. 45:337-347.

DeJong, J. 1976. The purification of wastewater with the aid of rush or reed ponds. p. 133-139. In J. Tourbier and R. W. Pierson, Jr. (ed.) Biological Control of Water Pollution. University of Pennsylvania Press, Philadelphia, PA.

Dinges, R. 1978. Upgrading stabilization pond effluent by water hyacinth culture. J. Water Pollut. Control Fed. 50:833-845.

Gammage, R. B., and S. V. Kaye (ed.). 1984. Indoor air and human health. Proceedings of the Seventh Life Sciences Symposium, Knoxville, TN, October 29-31, 1984. Lewis Publishers, Inc., Chelsea, MI.

Gersberg, R. M., B. V. Elkins, S. R. Lyon, and C. R. Goldman. 1986. Role of aquatic plants in wastewater treatment by artificial wetlands. Water Res. 20:363-368.

Ghosh, S., and D. L. Klass. 1976. SNG from refuse and sewage sludge by the biomass process. p. 123-182. In Proc. Clean Fuel from Biomass, Sewage, Urban Refuse and Agricultural Wastes.

Gopal, B., and K. P. Sharma. 1981. Water hyacinth. Hindasia, Delhi, India. 128 pp.

Haller, W. T. 1970. Phosphorus absorption by and distribution in water hyacinths. Proc. Soil Crop Sci. Soc. Fla. 30:64-69.

Inouye, T. 1986. Wetland bacteria speciation and harvesting effects on effluent quality. Final Report. Project No. 3-154-500-00. State Water Resources Control Board, Sacramento, CA. 114 pp.

Kadlec, R. H., and J. A. Kadlec. 1978. Wetlands and water quality. In P. E. Greeson, J. R. Clark, and J. E. Clark (ed.) Wetland Functions and Values: The State of Our Understanding. Am. Water Res. Assoc. Tech. Pub. No. TPS 69-2. Minneapolis, MN.

Kruzic, A. P. 1979. Water hyacinth wastewater treatment system at Disney World. p. 257-271. In R. K. Bastian and S. C. Reed (ed.) Aquaculture Systems for Wastewater Treatment: Seminar Proceedings and Engineering Assessment. U.S. Environmental Protection Agency, EPA 430/9-80-006.

McDonald, R. C. 1981. Vascular plants for decontaminating radioactive water and soils. NASA Technical Memorandum TM-X-72740.

McDonald, R. C., and B. C. Wolverton. 1980. Comparative study of wastewater lagoons with and without water hyacinth. Econ. Bot. 34:101-110.

Odum, H. T. 1976. In H. T. Odum and K. C. Ewel (ed.) Cypress Wetlands for Water Management, Recycling and Conservation. Annual Report, Center for Wetlands, University of Florida, Gainesville, FL.

Ornes, W. H., and D. L. Sutton. 1975. Removal of phosphorus from static sewage effluent by water hyacinth. Hyacinth Control J. 13:56-58.

Parra, J. V., and C. C. Hortenstein. 1974. Plant nutritional content of some Florida water hyacinths and response by pearl millet to incorporation of water hyacinths in three soil types. Hyacinth Control J. 12:85-90.

Pieterse, A. H. 1978. The water hyacinth (*Eichhornia crassipes*) - a review. Department of Agricultural Research, Royal Tropical Institute, Amsterdam.

Reddy, K. R., and W. F. DeBusk. 1984. Growth characteristics of aquatic macrophytes cultured in nutrient-enriched water: I. Water hyacinth, water lettuce, and pennywort. Econ. Bot. 38:229-239.

Reddy, K. R., and W. F. DeBusk. 1985a. Growth characteristics of aquatic macrophytes cultured in nutrient-enriched water: II. Azolla, duckweed, and salvinia. Econ. Bot. 39:200-208.

Reddy, K. R., and W. F. DeBusk. 1985b. Nutrient removal potential of selected aquatic macrophytes. J. Environ. Qual. 14:459-462.

Rogers, H. H., and D. E. Davis. 1972. Nutrient removal by water hyacinth. Weed Sci. 20:423-428.

Scarsbrook, E., and D. E. Davis. 1971. Effect of sewage effluent on growth of five vascular aquatic species. Hyacinth Control J. 9:26-30.

Seidel, K. 1976. Macrophytes and water purification. p. 109-121. In J. Tourbier and R. W. Pierson, Jr. (ed.) Biological Control of Water Pollution. University of Pennsylvania Press, Philadelphia, PA.

Sheffield, C. W. 1967. Water hyacinth for nutrient removal. Hyacinth Control J. 6:27-30.

Stephenson, M., G. Turner, P. Pope, J. Colt, A. Knight, and G. Tchobanoglous. 1980. The use and potential of aquatic species for wastewater treatment. Appendix A. In The Environmental Requirements of Aquatic Plants. Publication

No. 65, California State Water Resources Control Board, Sacramento, CA.

Steward, K. K. 1970. Nutrient removal potential of various aquatic plants. Hyacinth Control J. 8:34-35.

Sutton, D. L., and W. H. Ornes. 1977. Growth of Spirodela polyrhiza in static sewage effluent. Aquat. Bot. 3:231-237.

Swett, D. 1979. A water hyacinth advanced wastewater treatment system. p. 233-255. In R. K. Bastian and S. C. Reed (ed.) Aquaculture Systems for Wastewater Treatment: Seminar Proceedings and Engineering Assessment. U.S. Environmental Protection Agency. EPA 430/9-80-006.

Taylor, K. G., and R. C. Robbins. 1968. The amino acid composition of water hyacinth (Eichhornia crassipes) and its value as a protein supplement. Hyacinth Control J. 7:24-25.

Taylor, K. G., R. P. Bates, and R. C. Robbins. 1971. Extraction of protein from water hyacinth. Hyacinth Control J. 9:20-22.

Tourbier, J., and R. W. Pierson, Jr. (ed.). 1976. Biological Control of Water Pollution. University of Pennsylvania Press, Inc., Philadelphia, PA. 340 pp.

Wallace, L., S. Brombert, E. Pellizzari, T. Hartwell, H. Zelon, and L. Sheldon. 1984. Plan and preliminary results of the U. S. Environmental Protection Agency's indoor air monitoring program (1982). In Indoor Air, Swedish Council for Building Research, Stockholm, Sweden. 1:173-178.

Wolverton, B. C. 1975. Water hyacinths for removal of cadmium and nickel from polluted waters. NASA Technical Memorandum TM-X-72721.

Wolverton, B. C. 1979. Engineering design data for small vascular aquatic plant wastewater treatment systems. p. 179-182. In R. K. Bastian and S. C. Reed (ed.) Aquaculture Systems for Wastewater Treatment: Seminar Proceedings and Engineering Assessment. U.S. Environmental Protection Agency. EPA 430/9-80-006.

Wolverton, B. C. 1980. Higher plants for recycling human waste into food, potable water, and revitalized air in a closed life support system. NASA/ERL Report No. 192.

Wolverton, B. C. 1982. Hybrid wastewater teratment system using anaerobic microorganisms and reed (Phragmites communis). Econ. Bot. 36:373-380.

Wolverton, B. C., and D. D. Harrison. 1973. Aquatic plants for removal of mevinphos from the aquatic environment. J. MS Acad. Sci. 19:84.

Wolverton, B. C., and R. C. McDonald. 1975. Water hyacinths and alligator weeds for removal of lead and mercury from polluted waters. NASA Technical Memorandum TM-X-72723.

Wolverton, B. C., and R. C. McDonald. 1976. Don't waste waterweeds. New Scientist 71:318-320.

Wolverton, B. C., and R. C. McDonald. 1977. Wastewater treatment utilizing water hyacinths (Eichhornia crassipes) (Mart) Solms. p. 205-208. In Treatment and Disposal of Industrial

Wastewaters and Residues. Proceedings of the National Conference on Treatment and Disposal of Industrial Wastewaters and Residues, Houston, TX.

Wolverton, B. C., and R. C. McDonald. 1978a. Nutritional composition of water hyacinths grown on domestic sewage. Econ. Bot. 32:363-370.

Wolverton, B. C., and R. C. McDonald. 1978b. Water hyacinths productivity and harvesting studies. Econ. Bot. 33:1-10.

Wolverton, B. C., and R. C. McDonald. 1979a. The water hyacinth from prolific pest to potential provider. AMBIO 8:2-9.

Wolverton, B. C., and R. C. McDonald. 1979b. Upgrading facultative wastewater lagoons with vascular aquatic plants. J. Water Pollut. Control Fed. 51:305-313.

Wolverton, B. C., and R. C. McDonald. 1981a. Energy from vascular plants wastewater treatment systems. Econ. Bot. 35:224-232.

Wolverton, B. C., and R. C. McDonald. 1981b. Natural processes for treatment of organic chemical waste. The Environ. Prof. 3:99-104.

Wolverton, B. C., and R. C. McDonald. 1983. Aquatic vascular plant food. p. 263-272. In Miloslav Rechcigl, Jr. (ed.) Handbook of Nutrition Supplements, Vol. 1. Human Uses. CRC Press, Inc., Boca Raton, Florida.

Wolverton, B. C., and M. M. McKown. 1976. Water hyacinths for removal of phenols from polluted waters. Aquat. Bot. 30:29-37.

Wolverton, B. C., R. C. McDonald, and J. Gordon. 1975. Water hyacinths and alligator weeds for final filtration of sewage. NASA Technical Memorandum TM-X72724.

Wolverton, B. C., R. C. McDonald, and W. R. Duffer. 1983. Microorganisms and higher plants for wastewater treatment. J. Environ. Qual. 12:236-242.

Wolverton, B. C., R. C. McDonald, and L. K, Marble. 1984a. Removal of benzene and its derivatives from polluted water using the reed/microbial filter technique. J. MS Acad. Sci. 29:119-127.

Wolverton, B. C., R. C. McDonald, and E. A. Watkins, Jr. 1984b. Foliage plants for removing indoor air pollutants from energy efficient homes. Econ. Bot. 38:224-228.

Wolverton, B. C., R. C. McDonald, C. C. Myrick, and K. M. Johnson. 1984c. Upgrading septic tanks using microbial/plant filters. J. MS Acad. Sci. 29:19-25.

Wolverton, B. C., R. C. McDonald, and H. H. Mesik. 1985. Foliage plants for the indoor removal of the primary combustion gases carbon dioxide and nitrogen dioxide. J. MS Acad. Sci. 30:1-8.

Wooten, J. W., and J. D. Dodd. 1976. Growth of water hyacinth in treated sewage effluent. Econ. Bot. 30:29-37.

Yount, J. L. 1964. Aquatic nutrient reduction potential and possible methods. Rep. 35th Ann. Meet., FL Anti-mosquito Assoc. p. 83-85.

ECOLOGICAL/ENVIRONMENTAL PERSPECTIVES ON THE USE OF WETLANDS IN WATER TREATMENT

W. A. Wentz
National Wildlife Federation
Washington, DC 20036

ABSTRACT

As natural values and potential uses of wetland systems are better understood, ecologists and engineers will face significant new opportunities and problems. A high potential for the use of natural and artificial wetlands for treating wastewater and enhancing wildlife production exists. Such uses are in early design stages and we must better define the assimilative capacities of wetland types and the impact of their utilization. Recent experiences have shown that wetlands and their biological components can be seriously damaged by uncontrolled delivery of wastewater. These experiences should cause us to exercise caution in the utilization of wetlands. The experience of wildlife managers in creating and manipulating wetlands, combined with appropriate engineering design holds promise for the construction of wetlands to provide multiple public benefits. Great strides have been made in educating the public and decision makers to the values of wetlands. As a result, many people question the use of wetland systems for such purposes as cleansing wastewaters. Continuing to educate the public on the values of wetlands, protecting these natural values, and developing a better understanding of the range of possible uses for both natural and artificial wetlands, while maintaining public credibility, are crucial challenges to ecologists and engineers.

Keywords: Wildlife, wastewater, water quality, ecology of wetlands, aquatic plants, artificial wetlands, public education, conservationists.

INTRODUCTION

All wetlands are of concern to the National Wildlife Federation (NWF). Our interests in this area are broad, but they are based on the philosophy that wetlands are one of the most valuable components of the natural landscape, and we need to do everything in our power to prevent any further loss or degradation

ISBN 0-941463-00-1

of this important habitat type. NWF lobbies for wetlands protection, goes to court to enforce wetlands laws, publishes educational materials on wetlands, works with citizen's groups to educate people about wetlands and methods to protect them, cooperates with state and federal agencies on wetland projects, opposes agencies that would harm or destroy wetlands, and initiates many other wetland activities. Given our protective attitude toward wetlands, most people would likely think that NWF would oppose the use of wetlands in wastewater treatment.

But NWF supports the need to develop appropriate technology to utilize wetland systems to treat wastewater, and we are excited about the possibility that this topic offers to help educate the public on values of wetlands and to result in positive benefits to the environment. For instance, we have cooperated with the Tennessee Valley Authority in developing a demonstration project to use artificial wetlands to treat municipal effluents from small communities in western Kentucky. Also, NWF has promoted the concept in testimony before Congress, in publications, and in numerous public forums. To be sure, we have some reservations about the whole idea, but we see some extremely significant opportunities here.

WETLANDS VALUES AND LOSSES

Wetlands have only recently been recognized as a valuable component of our natural landscape (Wentz, 1986). While conservationists have long valued wetlands, the general public has only recently learned that these areas are highly desirable habitat types.

The problem of wetlands loss in the U.S. has been widely documented. The Fish and Wildlife Service found that wetlands were being destroyed at the rate of 185,353 ha yr^{-1} in the United States from the mid-1950s to the mid-1970s, and by the mid-1970s only 46% of the original 87 million ha of wetlands in the lower 48 states remained (Frayer et al., 1983; Tiner, 1984). The root of this problem comes from the mindset of governments and individuals that wetlands are not of value, and that they are in fact dangerous because of disease and other unknown biological factors.

Duck hunters and most other conservationists have long known that wetlands are not worthless. Their concern over the rapidly dwindling supply of wetlands in the U.S. ignited a movement in the 1930s, when organizations such as NWF and Ducks Unlimited were founded, that continues today. As scientific evidence of wetlands loss accumulated, these conservationists were motivated to prevent this loss. Their concern has been translated into a grassroots movement that is rapidly educating the public. In the last two decades scientists have refined the information on losses and, more importantly, they have begun the accumulation of knowledge on the many values of wetlands and how these important habitats affect the lives of literally millions of Americans.

Most scientists and much of the public have concluded that the rate of wetlands loss in this country is unacceptable (Wentz, 1986). Numerous polls have shown that the public wants wetlands protected. I suspect that most of our citizens would also be concerned over the lowered quality of our wetlands and would oppose the degradation of wetlands by pollution with nutrients and toxic chemicals, partial dredging and filling, the introduction of exotic organisms, or other forms of degradation.

Much research has been done on wetland values, but it is only a beginning. This mass of information is now being delivered to the public and they are beginning to understand that wetlands are valuable for wildlife, water quality, flood control, recreation, and many other purposes. They recognize that coastal wetlands provide seafood, prairie potholes raise ducks, and bottomlands grow timber. In short, people are beginning to like wetlands.

I do not want to overstate how much we know about the values of wetlands because our scientific understanding of wetlands is in its infancy with only the surface scratched. More scientists, economists, and sociologists working at understanding wetlands and their values to our society are needed. We also need policy analysts, attorneys, and engineers doing more basic analysis work with this important habitat type. More money and time should be devoted to the careful study of this important natural resource.

KNOWLEDGE LEADS TO OPPORTUNITIES AND PROBLEMS

As the values of wetlands are better understood, ecologists and engineers have begun to see new and creative ways of utilizing their services. Because wetlands and their plant components have considerable capability to treat wastewaters and recover a variety of resources, they can potentially provide a very valuable service.

The idea of wastewater disposal in wetlands is not a new one, as literally hundreds of communities have utilized wetlands as a dumping ground for effluents (EPA, 1985). In most cases, of course, the reasoning behind this use was disposal, rather than treatment. I suspect few of the engineers who designed effluent disposal systems that dump into wetlands had any idea that they were in the forefront of a new technology. In most cases the wetland simply served as a convenient receptacle that was closer than the nearest river or other waterway. Of course, now we are looking at purposefully using wetlands for this function.

As with any new technology there are both significant opportunities and problems here. Some people see the opportunity to utilize the services of wetlands as a low-cost, low-tech way of cleaning up various wastewaters. In addition, the optimist will see a combination of an alternative to other forms of disposal when appropriate surface waters or land disposal areas are not available, the opportunity for advanced treatment that will help the environment, and even a possible mechanism to restore altered wetlands and enhance wildlife habitats. Others may see the potential degradation and destruction of nature's natural wetland systems as a result of wastewater filled with toxic industrial compounds that threaten sensitive pristine areas, unique wetlands, or other wetland types that would be damaged by any such use and where there is no method for mitigating the damage. There is some truth in each point of view, but we can all agree that we will face new challenges in the development of this technology.

Natural versus Artificial

It is important to make a distinction between the use of natural and artificial wetlands. Natural wetlands are waters of the United States and subject to a variety of protective measures and regulations under the Clean Water Act. Artificial wetlands are not covered by the Clean Water Act and are much less subject to regulation. Conservationists will look quite favorably on increasing our wetland inventory by creating artificial wetlands for wastewater treatment, but they will take some convincing that a similar use of large numbers of natural wetlands is a good idea.

In my opinion, the real future of this technology lies in our ability to create new wetlands or to restore previously altered wetlands to their former levels of productivity. While the use of natural wetlands will continue and increase in the long-term, it seems that artificial wetlands specifically created for this use and other benefits are the most desirable option.

Wildlife Management

In some situations we can expect to enhance the production of wildlife on natural wetlands by the proper management of wastewater treatment systems. Certainly the construction of artificial wetlands has great potential to enhance wildlife. Many people have noted the way waterfowl flock to artificial wetlands and even to sewage lagoons, but enhancement is more than just providing a spot for ducks to rest. If we handle the development of these systems correctly, the potential exists to add artificial wetlands to a region with the result of improving diversity of the overall wildlife habitat in the area. Knowledge of how to better manipulate the excess water and its accompanying nutrient load could improve on the diversity and productivity of existing wetlands. In some situations the selective manipulation of water and nutrients might change certain individual wetlands to create a wider diversity of wetland types in a single region.

Engineers and ecologists who are involved in this issue would do well to examine the literature of wildlife management to better understand what wildlife managers already have discovered about designing and manipulating wetland systems (Kadlec and Wentz, 1974; Linde, 1969; Weller, 1981; Wentz et al., 1974). Many wildlife managers have considerable experience in creating and manipulating wetlands and this experience should provide essential guidance in developing systems designed to treat wastewater. Properly constructed wastewater treatment systems should provide multiple public benefits.

In some areas wildlife managers have developed techniques to manipulate water levels in order to change the type of vegetation present (Kadlec, 1962; Meeks, 1969). Even minor changes in water regime can be enough to cause drastic changes in the biological communities of a wetland. The uncontrolled addition of water to a wetland is likely to produce rapid changes and it potentially could alter the hydrology of the wetland. Most wetland systems are characterized by changing water levels, but the amount and timing of water level changes can be critical to the health of the biological community.

Changed water levels combined with nutrient additions may present a situation difficult to control. For instance, the addition of nutrient-rich waters to a nutrient limited environment will often result in enhanced productivity and eventually vegetation change (Wentz, 1976), but additions to an existing nutrient rich wetland are less likely to cause such a change.

Nonpoint Pollution Control

Wetland systems offer great potential for the control of effluent problems from point sources, but their potential for control of non-point pollution may be even greater. Non-point pollution problems have mostly been ignored until recently due to a lack of knowledge. Today non-point problems are better documented, but what to do about them is still poorly understood. Certainly there are practices that can help to control such problems.

Utilization of artificial wetlands would seem to hold some promise for controlling non-point water pollution problems. Wetlands would be part of a land management system to help control pollution problems in an entire watershed. This would be accomplished by strategic placement of numerous small wetlands in locations where they would intercept runoff from farm fields and other drainages. Establishment of one or more experimental watersheds should be attempted where small artificial wetlands are created in abundance for the purpose of improving water quality to demonstrate this concept. For instance, major land disruption sites, such as surface mined lands, should be looked upon as opportunities to create new wetland complexes during restoration of the area in general (Brooks 1986; Robertson, 1986). It is time for some agency or private concern to move forward and establish one or more major demonstration watersheds to determine if artificial wetlands can be part of an effective solution to non-point pollution. This problem is one that would benefit greatly from some innovative thinking by ecologists and engineers.

CAUTION NECESSARY

The natural ecological processes of wetlands are very complex. Engineering problems that are encountered in the utilization of wetlands increase this complexity. The problems of a poorly-known type of environment, difficult engineering tasks, water sources with highly variable components, and the need to separate the effects of nutrients, toxic compounds, and water on the natural ecosystem, combined with the great variability among wetland types and individual wetlands and their site-specific biological and hydrological processes, make for situations that demand research investigation.

But we must exercise caution with the application of this technology. The public, conservationists, and regulatory agencies have a variety of concerns about the utilization of natural wetlands for wastewater treatment (EPA and FWS, 1984). All of the functions and values of wetlands are likely to come into consideration anytime such utilization is proposed. The natural functions and values of wetlands are important to people and, as a result, few people will be willing to tolerate adverse changes in those functions and values.

There are limits to what you can expect a wetland to clean up. An example of how bad it can be is the Kesterson National Wildlife Refuge. This is an uncontrolled problem rather than an accident resulting from an attempt to utilize a wetland, but it is an instructive situation. Reports about the Kesterson problem and how it will impact agriculture are numerous. The impacts that have been documented on the Kesterson National Wildlife Refuge are the result of drainage from several hundred thousand acres of irrigated lands in the western San Joaquin Valley. The problem was brought into focus by high concentrations of selenium delivered in irrigation water that have harmed birds and other vertebrates.

The Kesterson situation has been followed by numerous reports of other, similar problems at other sites throughout the West (investigations conducted by The Sacramento Bee indicate the problem is widespread in the West around irrigation projects). The Fish and Wildlife Service (FWS, 1986) has documented problems with agricultural drainwaters on at least 42 National Wildlife Refuges (about 10% of all refuges) and the number of such problems probably is much higher. Considering that this analysis looked only at Federal refuges, it is not unreasonable to expect the problem to be extremely widespread on other types of lands that are not subject to the intense scrutiny given National Wildlife Refuges. The Kesterson problem has convinced many conservationists that a real crisis exists. Unfortunately, this crisis has the potential of slopping over into the considerations of using natural, and even artificial, wetlands for the treatment of wastewaters. While this may slow development of this new technology, it also probably will be beneficial to the public interest because fewer mistakes will be made and final techniques that are not harmful to the environment will result.

The evidence shows that wetlands and their biological components can be seriously damaged by the uncontrolled delivery of wastewater and significant uncertainties and risks are associated with the controlled delivery of wastewater (summarized in Freshwater Wetlands for Wastewater Management Environmental Assessment Handbook, by Region IV of the Environmental Protection Agency, EPA, 1985). Much of their volume is devoted to methods and techniques to reduce the chance of problems from such utilization of wetlands. The list of areas in which EPA believes uncertainty and risk exists deserves emphasis. The areas are:

1. Assessing the short and long term assimilative capacity of a wetland.
2. Predicting short and long term impacts to the wetland from wastewater loadings.
3. Engineering design criteria enhancing short and long term wastewater assimilation and wetlands protection.
4. Establishing effluent limits to meet standards or other protective guidelines.
5. Evaluating environmental impacts to the watershed, other wetland uses and wildlife.
6. Determining downstream impacts.
7. Defining the scope of monitoring programs.

All of these considerations must be evaluated in any plan to use wetlands for wastewater treatment. In a more general sense these areas also are an outline of needed comprehensive research that could potentially reduce the risks of using wetlands.

SUMMARY

Great strides in educating the public and public decision makers about the values of wetlands have been made. Twenty years ago few people would have recognized the term "wetland," but today the term is well understood in many parts of the country. People know that wetlands are a valuable part of our landscape.

The water quality function of wetlands is one of the significant values that has been promoted. Mostly the public has heard about wetlands that, in their natural state, are said to be worth tens of thousands of dollars in water purification costs. This probably leaves an image in most people's minds that these areas shouldn't be tampered with. We must take people beyond the idea that because wetlands are valuable they cannot and should not be "managed." It is very important that people understand that manipulation of wetlands is not necessarily a bad thing. Many people will question the purposeful "use" of wetlands for such things as cleaning up wastewaters, but that, in itself, may not be bad because it will require those who advocate such uses to better understand what they are doing and its impacts in order to satisfy critics, and, in the end, we will have a better outcome and better public policy.

Conservationists have created the atmosphere that will allow the possibility of doing creative things with wetlands, but the education can not stop now. People have to be carried to that next step where they begin to understand that wetlands can be improved, used, created, restored, and otherwise managed without destroying their essential character and, in some cases, creating and improving on natural values.

Continuing to educate the public on values, protection, and the range of possible uses for both natural and artificial wetlands, while maintaining public credibility, is a crucial challenge to ecologists and engineers. That means each of us, including researchers, engineers, and conservationists, has to be sure to inform the public and decision makers about what we are doing with wetlands and what it means, not only to the economy and our ability to control such things as water pollution, but also impacts on the wetland system. Extra caution should be exercised any time we begin to do something in a natural wetland by being sure that the concerns and curiosity of local citizens, conservation groups, civic groups, and state and federal authorities in addition to our own colleagues are satisfied.

I believe it is especially important that all those involved with this subject devote more time to keeping the conservation community informed of the progress of this technology and what it means for the environment. Conservation organizations place wetlands protection high on their list of issues and they are quick to attack anything that is likely to have an adverse impact on wetlands. Using natural wetlands for treatment of wastewater is a subject that will soon fall under the scrutiny of many of the major conservation organizations. Because these organizations can help to form the opinion of their millions of members and much of the rest of the public, it is critical that they be well informed on this topic so they develop their opinions on the best scientific knowledge. Conservation organizations are critical to this effort and the only way to obtain their support is be sure they are kept informed about what such activities mean.

If we are willing to be careful and not damage ecosystems as a result of our actions, we stand the chance of succeeding in overall efforts at better utilization of wetlands. The use of wetlands in wastewater management is not a panacea for the nation's water quality problems, but it does offer significant potential benefits to water quality and the environment.

REFERENCES

Brooks, R. P. 1986. Wetlands as a compatible land use on coal surface mines. National Wetlands Newsletter 8(2):4-6.

Environmental Protection Agency. 1985. Freshwater wetlands for wastewater management environmental assessment handbook. U.S. E.P.A., Region IV, Atlanta, GA. EPA 904/9-85-135.

Environmental Protection Agency and Fish and Wildlife Service. 1984. The ecological impacts of wastewater on wetlands - An annotated bibliography. EPA Region V, Chicago, IL, FWS, Eastern Energy and Land Use Team, Kearneysville, WV. EPA-905/3-84-002.

Fish and Wildlife Service. 1986. Preliminary survey of contaminant issues of concern on National Wildlife Refuges. U.S. Fish and Wildlife Service, Washington, DC. 163 pp.

Frayer, W. E., T. J. Monahan, D. C. Bowden, and F. A. Graybill. 1983. Status and trends of wetlands and deepwater habitats in conterminous United States, 1950s to 1970s. 34 pp.

Kadlec, J. A. 1962. Effects of a drawdown on a waterfowl impoundment. Ecology 43:267-281.

Kadlec, J. A., and W. A. Wentz. 1974. Evaluation of marsh plant establishment techniques: Induced and natural. Tech. Paper of the Coastal Engineering Research Center and the Waterways Experiment Station, U.S. Army Corps of Engineers, NTIS Report #A012837, Vol. I. 266 pp.

Linde, A. F. 1969. Techniques for wetlands management. Wisconsin Department of Natural Resources, Report 45. 156 pp.

Meeks, R. L. 1969. The effect of drawdown date on wetland plant succession. J. of Wildlife Management 33:817-821.

Robertson, D. J. 1986. Freshwater wetland reclamation by the Florida phosphate industry. National Wetlands Newsletter 8(3):9-12.

Tiner, R. W., Jr. 1984. Wetlands of the United States: Current status and recent trends. U.S. Fish and Wildlife Service, Washington, DC. 59 pp.

Weller, M. W. 1981. Freshwater marshes: Ecology and wildlife management. University of Minnesota Press, Minneapolis, MN. 146 pp.

Wentz, W. A. 1976. The effects of simulated sewage effluents on the growth and production of peatland plants. Ph.D. Dissertation, The University of Michigan. 112 pp.

Wentz, W. A. 1986. Functional status of the nation's wetlands. International Symposium on the Ecology and Management of Wetlands, Charleston, SC (16-20 June 1986 - in press).

Wentz, W. A., R. L. Smith, and J. A. Kadlec. 1974. Annotated bibliography on aquatic and marsh plants and their management. Tech. Paper of the Coastal Engineering Research Center and the Waterways Experiment Station, U.S. Army Corps of Engineers, NTIS Report #A012837. Vol. II. 206 pp.

AQUATIC PLANT SYSTEMS FOR WASTEWATER TREATMENT: ENGINEERING CONSIDERATIONS

G. Tchobanoglous
Department of Civil Engineering
University of California
Davis, California 95616

ABSTRACT

Important engineering considerations in the design of aquatic plant systems used for the treatment of wastewater include characteristics of the wastewater, required effluent quality, type of aquatic system, operative contaminant removal mechanisms, local environmental factors, process design parameters, physical design features, and process reliability. Although all of these engineering considerations are important and are reviewed, special attention is focused on odor control techniques, mosquito control strategies, and contaminant removal kinetics as they affect the physical design and management of aquatic plant-based wastewater treatment systems. Based on an assessment of these and other considerations, some alternative physical designs and operating strategies are proposed.

Keywords: Aquatic treatment systems, wastewater characteristics, odor control, mosquito control, treatment process kinetics, process design parameters.

INTRODUCTION

The technical feasibility of using aquatic plants for the treatment of wastewater is well established. Nevertheless, aquatic treatment systems are often not considered as viable treatment alternatives. One of the reasons has been the lack of useable engineering design data and information. The purpose of this paper is to present and discuss the important engineering and related considerations that must be addressed in the design of these systems. The topics considered in this paper include 1) characteristics of wastewater, 2) required effluent quality, 3) contaminant removal mechanisms, 4) types of aquatic systems, 5) process selection, 6) environmental factors, 7) process design, 8) physical design features, and 9) process reliability. To provide a basis for understanding the material to be presented, the characteristics of aquatic systems are first reviewed.

Aquatic Plants for Water Treatment
and Resource Recovery
K.R. Reddy and W.H. Smith (Eds.)

ISBN 0-941463-00-1

CHARACTERISTICS OF AQUATIC TREATMENT SYSTEMS

Most aquatic treatment systems consist of one or more shallow ponds in which one or more species of aquatic macrophytes (water tolerant vascular plants such as cattails, bulrushes, and water hyacinths) are grown. The shallower depths and the presence of aquatic macrophytes in place of algae are the major differences between aquatic treatment systems and stabilization ponds. The presence of plants is of great practical significance as the effluent from aquatic systems is of significantly higher quality than the effluent from stabilization pond systems for equivalent or shorter detention times.

In aquatic systems, wastewater is treated principally by means of bacterial metabolism and physical sedimentation, as is the case in conventional activated sludge and trickling filter systems. The aquatic plants, themselves, bring about very little actual treatment of the wastewater. Their function is to provide components of the aquatic environment that improve the wastewater treatment capability and/or reliability of that environment. Some specific functions of aquatic plants in aquatic treatment systems are summarized in Table 1. The morphology of some typical aquatic plants is shown schematically in Figure 1.

The fundamental difference between conventional and aquatic systems is that in conventional systems, wastewater is treated rapidly in highly managed, energy intensive environments (i.e., reactors); whereas in aquatic systems, treatment occurs at a comparatively slow rate in essentially unmanaged natural environments. The consequences of the above differences are: 1) conventional systems require more construction and equipment but less land than aquatic systems; and 2) conventional processes are subject to greater operational control and less environmental influence than aquatic processes.

Aquatic treatment systems should not be confused with other types of systems that may also involve the application of waste-

TABLE 1. Functions of plants in aquatic treatment systems[+].

Plant parts	Function
Roots and/or stems in water column	Uptake of pollutants. Surfaces on which bacteria grow. Media for filtration and adsorption of solids.
Stems and/or leaves at or above water surface	Attenuate sunlight; thus can prevent growth of suspended algae. Reduce effects of wind on water (e.g., roiling of settled matter). Reduce transfer of gases and heat between atmosphere and water.

[+]Adapted from Stowell et al., 1981.

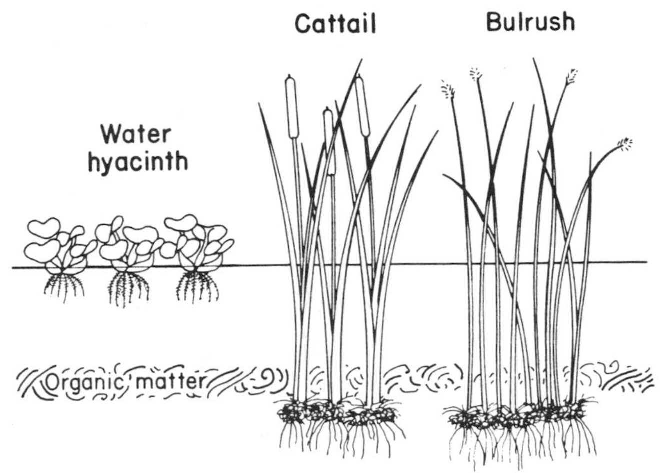

FIGURE 1. Morphology of some common aquatic plants used in aquatic treatment systems (adapted from Stowell et al., 1981).

water to wetlands but for reasons other than wastewater treatment such as: 1) aquaculture (growth of organisms having economic value; 2) environmental enhancement (creation of habitat for wildlife); and 3) wetlands effluent disposal (nonpoint source disposal of treated wastewater). The wetlands environments needed for each type of project are quite varied. Thus, a wetlands system designed to treat wastewater will be different from one designed for any of these other purposes.

CHARACTERISTICS OF WASTEWATER

The characteristics of wastewater that are of general concern in the design of aquatic treatment systems are:

* Carbonaceous biochemical oxygen demand ($CBOD_5$)
* Suspended solids (SS)
* Nitrogen compounds
* Phosphorus compounds
* Heavy metals
* Refractory organics
* Pathogenic bacteria
* Pathogenic virus

Although $CBOD_5$ and SS are the parameters used most commonly to characterize wastewater, it should be recognized that they are nonspecific (lumped) parameters. In most cases, the nature of the constituents that comprise the $CBOD_5$ and SS are usually unknown. Consequently, the development of sophisticated treatment process models using these parameters is unwarranted, although the practice continues. The use of these parameters continues because of their use as water quality standards and enforcement limits.

In addition to the above constituents, two other constituents must also be considered:

* Sulfate
* Toxicity

The presence of SO_4^{2-} is important because it serves as an electron acceptor in the reduction of SO_4^{2-} to H_2S. The presence of H_2S can cause odor problems and is lethal at low concentrations to fish used for mosquito control. If the SO_4^{2-} concentration is greater than about 50 mg L^{-1}, the potential for the production of H_2S must be considered. The development and control of odors is considered further in the sections dealing with environmental factors and design.

Toxicity is a characteristics of the wastewater that is often associated with the presence of refractory organics although other constituents such as heavy metals can, and do, contribute to the toxicity. If it is suspected that the wastewater may be toxic, toxicity bioassay tests should be conducted using the mosquito control fish. A pretreatment program may be required to eliminate or significantly reduce the toxicity.

REQUIRED EFFLUENT QUALITY

The required effluent quality is an important consideration in assessing the use of aquatic systems. Typical effluent quality requirements are summarized in Table 2. Based on actual field data, it has been found that the effluent $CBOD_5$ and SS from well designed aquatic treatment systems will be on the order of 10 mg L^{-1}. Effluent $CBOD_5$ values below 10 mg L^{-1} are difficult to achieve because of the residual leakage of organic matter from the plants themselves. Although effluent SS values considerably below 10 mg L^{-1} have been reported, an effluent with 10 mg L^{-1} of SS is a reasonable design expectation.

TABLE 2. Typical water quality characteristics and effluent requirements.

Treatment	Value, mg L^{-1}			
	CBOD	SS	N^{+}	P^{++}
Untreated wastewater	220	220	30	8
Primary	150	80	25	7
Advanced primary	80	50	20	6
Secondary	≤ 30	≤ 30	20	6
Advanced secondary	≤ 10	≤ 10	18	5
Tertiary	≤ 5	≤ 5	≤ 1	≤ 1

+Total (org. N, NH_3, NO_2^-, NO_3^- expressed as N).
++Total (org. P, PO_4^{3-} expressed as P).

CONTAMINANT REMOVAL MECHANISMS

The physical, chemical and biological contaminant removal mechanisms that are operative in aquatic treatment systems include:

* Physical
  - Sedimentation
  - Filtration
  - Adsorption
  - Volatilization
* Chemical
  - Precipitation
  - Adsorption
  - Hydrolysis reactions
  - Oxidation-reduction
  - Photochemical reactions
* Biological
  - Bacterial metabolism
  - Plant metabolism
  - Plant absorption
  - Natural die-off

Each of the above removal mechanisms must be considered in the design of aquatic treatment systems. The relative importance of these removal mechanisms will depend on the type of aquatic system and the treatment objectives. For example, photochemical reactions will be less important in systems where the surface is covered with plants such as in a water hyacinth system. As noted, sedimentation and bacterial metabolism are the principal removal mechanisms with respect to $CBOD_5$ and SS (Stowell et al., 1981).

TYPES OF AQUATIC TREATMENT SYSTEMS

The types of aquatic treatment systems considered in this paper include: 1) floating aquatic plants, 2) emergent plants, and 3) packed-bed systems with emergent plants. Because of the limited scope of this paper, the primary focus is on aquatic treatment systems used for the secondary treatment of wastewater.

Systems with Floating Plants

The most common floating aquatic plant used for the treatment of wastewater is the water hyacinth. The general physical characteristics of water hyacinth based treatment systems are presented graphically in Figure 2. Of the systems shown in Figure 2, the most commonly used are systems 2a through 2d. The step-feed system with recycle (See Figure 2f) is now used at the San Diego aquaculture treatment facility; this system is considered further in the section dealing with the design of aquatic treatment systems. Systems 2g through 2i are recommended to reduce the organic loading to the front end of the treatment

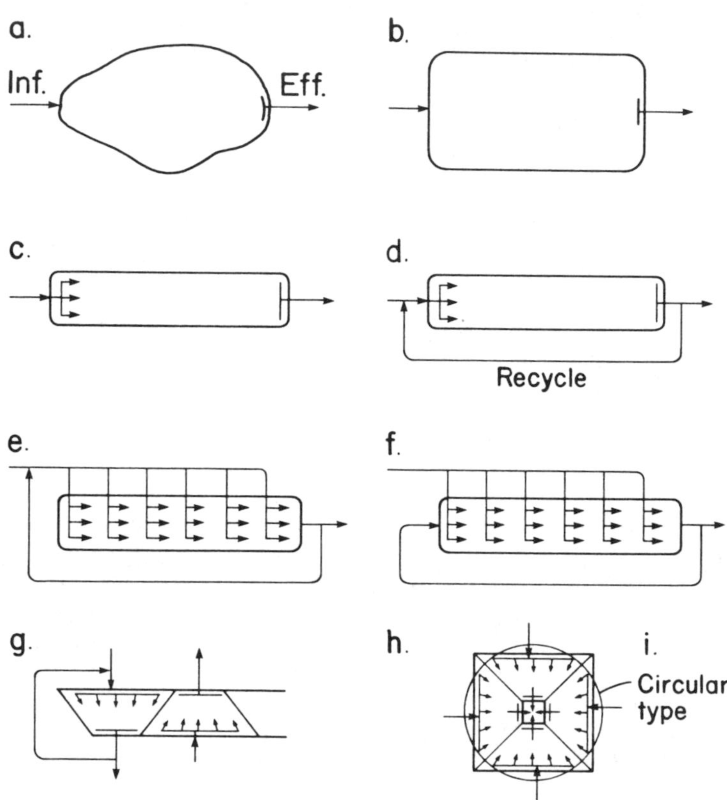

FIGURE 2. Typical configurations for aquatic treatment systems employing both floating and emergent aquatic plants: a) arbitrary flow, b) semi plug-flow, c) plug-flow, d) plug-flow with recycle, e) semi plug-flow with step feed and recycle-type 1, f) semi plug-flow with step feed and recycle-type 2, g) variable geometry semi plug-flow without (with) recycle-type 1, h) variable geometry semi plug-flow without (with) recycle-type 2, i) variable geometry semi plug-flow without (with) recycle type-3.

process. Variants of system 2h have been used elsewhere in the world (Abwasserreiniguug mit Hilfe von Wasserplanzen, 1983).

Typical physical characteristics for the aquatic systems shown in Figure 2 are summarized in Table 3. Water depths as great as 2400 mm have been used with the arbitrary flow reactor (see Figure 2a), but are not recommended. The best working depth for most of the systems shown in Figure 2 is between 500 and 700 mm. The reason for using this range of depths is considered later in this paper. Depending on the application, the bottom of the reactor may be sloped towards the effluent end.

TABLE 3. Typical physical dimensions for aquatic treatment systems.

Type of treatment system	Figure reference	Value	
		Range	Typical
<u>Floating Aquatic</u>			
Depth of water, mm	2a	600-2400	900
	2b	600-1000	900
	2c-2i	350-1000	500-700
Aspect ratio (length:width)	2a	1-2	-
	2b	1-3	-
	2c-2f	4-15	8
	2g-2i	1-1.5	1.25
<u>Emergent Aquatic</u>			
Depth of water, mm	2a-2i	250-750	300-600
Aspect ratio	2a-2b	1-3	
	2c-2f	4-10	
	2g-2i	1.5-2	
<u>Packed-bed</u>			
Depth of bed, mm	3a-3e	600-1000	900
Depth of water, mm	3a-3e	450-900	850
Aspect ratio	3a-3b	4-10	6
	3c	1-1.5	1.25
	3d	1-1.5	1.25
Gravel Type	3a-3e		
Gravel layer			
Depth, mm		700-800	
Size, mm		12.5-37.5	
Cover layer			
Depth, mm		100-200	
Size, mm		2.5-12.5	
Rock Type	3a-3e		
Rock layer			
Depth, mm		700-800	
Size, mm		25-75	
Cover layer			
Depth, mm		100-200	
Size, mm		2.5-12.5	

Systems with Emergent Plants

Cattails, bulrush, and various sedges are the emergent plants used most commonly in aquatic treatment systems. The physical characteristics of aquatic treatment systems designed for use with emergent plants are similar to those shown in Figure 2.

Trench (Packed-Bed) Systems with Emergent Plants

In packed-bed systems, plants including cattails, bulrush, native sedges, and other local species are planted in unlined and lined trenches or basins filled with a granular porous medium, usually gravel. The physical configuration of trench systems is shown in Figure 3.

PROCESS SELECTION

Process selection involves selecting one or more aquatic treatment systems (ATSs) to achieve a specific treatment objective.

Aquatic Treatment System (ATS)

An ATS is a reactor containing an assemblage of plants (and possibly animals) designed to achieve a specific treatment

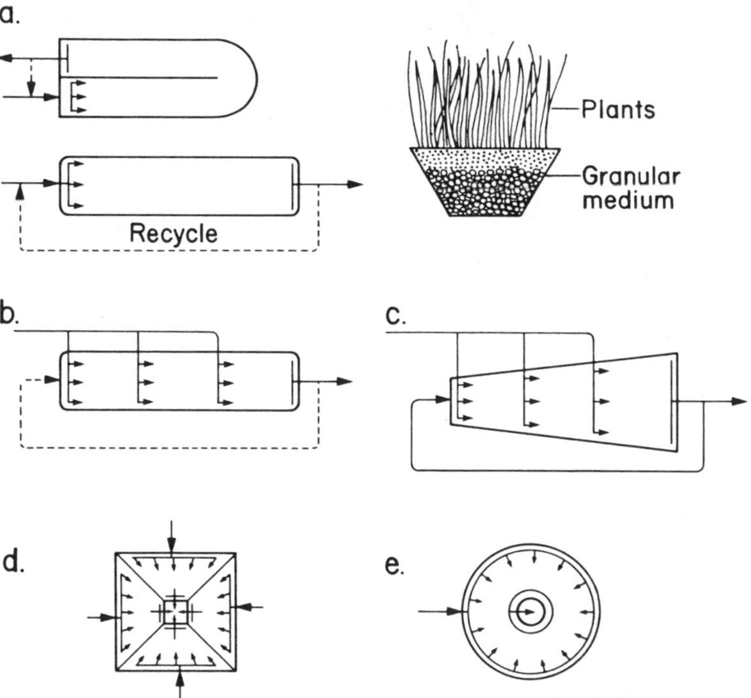

FIGURE 3. Typical configuration for trench type (packed bed) aquatic treatment systems; a) plug-flow without (with) recycle, b) plug-flow with step-feed without (with) recycle, c) variable geometry plug-flow with step-feed with recycle, d) variable geometry semi plug-flow without (with) recycle-type 1, e) variable geometry semi plug-flow without (with) recycle-type 2.

objective (Stowell et al., 1981). As shown in Figure 4, one or more ATSs will be used in conjunction with more conventional unit operations and processes in most complete treatment process flowsheets. Design considerations for the secondary treatment applications shown in Figure 4 are considered in the following sections.

Typical Flowsheets for Small Communities

Typical flowsheets that can be used to achieve secondary treatment in which an ATS is incorporated, are shown in Figure 5. Summary information on the function of the various components shown in Figure 5 is presented in Table 4.

ENVIRONMENTAL FACTORS

Environmental impacts that could result from the presence of an aquatic treatment system include odors, increased disease vector organism populations, and introduction of nuisance organisms to the local environment. The potential for significant environmental impact from any of these or other factors must be evaluated and mitigating measures taken as necessary.

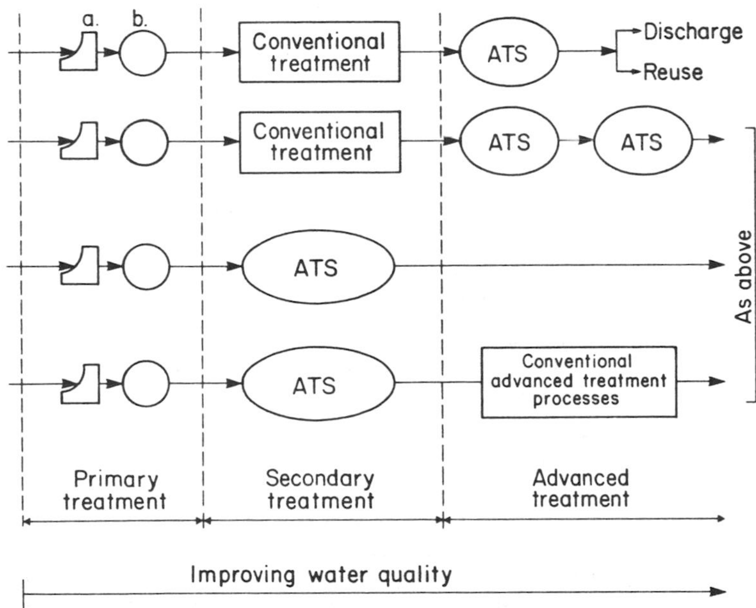

FIGURE 4. Typical applications of aquatic treatment systems for the treatment of municipal wastewater (adapted from Stowell et al., 1981).

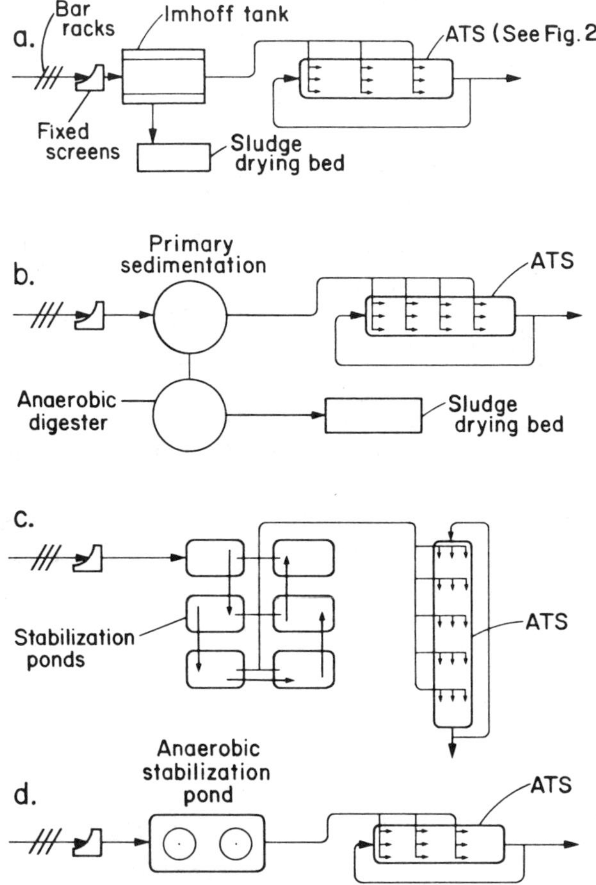

FIGURE 5. Typical flowsheets using aquatic treatment systems designed to achieve secondary treatment: a) for very small communities used in conjunction with Imhoff tank, b) for small communities used in conjunction with primary sedimentation, c) for small communities used in conjunction with stabilization ponds, d) for small communities used in conjunction with deep anaerobic stabilization ponds.

Odors in Aquatic Treatment Systems

The odors identified most commonly in aquatic treatment systems are associated with organic compounds containing S, such as mercaptans and skatoles and with H_2S. Hydrogen sulfide is

TABLE 4. Recommended components for flowsheets with ATSs.

Unit operation or process	Function
Very small communities: 40-400 m^3 d^{-1}	
Screens: bar racks alone or followed by fixed parabolic screens	Removal of coarse solids
Community septic tank(s)	Reduction of $CBOD_5$ and SS concentrations in wastewater
Imhoff tank	Reduction of $CBOD_5$ and SS concentrations in wastewater and sludge storage and digestion
Sludge drying bed	Drying of sludge from septic or Imhoff tank
Small communities: 400-4000 m^3 d^{-1}	
Screens	As above
Imhoff tank	As above
Primary sedimentation	Reduction of $CBOD_5$ and SS concentrations in wastewater
Anaerobic digester	Digestion of sludge from primary clarifier
Sludge drying beds	Drying of sludge from Imhoff tank or anaerobic digester
Stabilization ponds	Reduction of $CBOD_5$ and SS concentrations in wastewater and sludge storage and digestion

TABLE 5. Electron acceptors in bacterial metabolism.

Environment	Electron acceptor	Process
Aerobic	O_2	Aerobic metabolism
Anaerobic	NO_3^-	Denitrification
	SO_4^{2-}	Sulfate reduction
	CO_2	Methanogenesis

produced by obligate anaerobic organisms capable of reducing SO_4^{2-}. As shown in Table 5, in the absence of O_2, and NO_3^-, SO_4^{2-} will serve as an electron acceptor and is reduced to H_2S in the process. Thus, the presence of SO_4^{2-} in the wastewater can lead to the formation of H_2S in the bottom sludge accumulations. The organic matter in the sludge accumulation serves as a C source for the anaerobic process. The incomplete oxidation of other organic materials containing S will also lead to the development of odors.

Anaerobic conditions develop when the treatment process is overloaded organically. Most commonly, anaerobic conditions develop near the influent end of an aquatic treatment system. The reason for this occurrence can be explained easily by considering Figure 2c. For a length to width ratio equal to 10, an organic process loading rate of 100 kg ha^{-1} based on the total surface area corresponds to an actual loading rate of 1000 kg ha^{-1} on the first tenth of the system. From this simple analysis, it is easy to see why odors can develop in the immediate vicinity of the process inlet.

Strategies that can be used to control the development of odors include:

1. More effective pretreatment to reduce the total organic loading on the aquatic treatment system.
2. More effective influent distribution.
3. Step-feed of influent waste stream with effective influent distribution.
4. Step-feed of influent waste stream with recycle (see Figure 2f).
5. Supplemental aeration.

Mosquitos and Their Control

In many parts of the United States, especially in California, the growth of mosquitos in aquatic treatment systems may be the critical factor in determining whether the use of such systems will be allowed. Typically, mosquito problems develop when aquatic systems are overloaded organically and anaerobic conditions develop (Stowell et al., 1983). Under these conditions, most, if not all, of the fish (typically Gambusia affinis) used as biological control agents die, and the mosquito larvae mature into adults. Another condition that develops in organically overloaded water hyacinth systems is plant bridging, in which the plants grow together so closely that isolated water pockets form. Because the mosquito fish cannot get to these pockets of water, mosquito larvae that may be present also mature. In systems with emergent plants, mats of decaying plant matter can develop if the plants are not harvested. Because the fish used for mosquito control cannot penetrate the mats effectively, mosquito larvae found in these mats will usually mature.

The objective of mosquito control is to suppress the mosquito population below the threshold level required for disease transmission or nuisance tolerance level. Strategies that can be used to control mosquito populations include:

1. More effective pretreatment to reduce the total organic loading on the aquatic system.
2. Step-feed of influent waste stream with effective influent distribution.
3. Step-feed of influent waste stream with recycle (see Figure 2f).

4. More effective vegetation management in conjunction with the above techniques.

5. Use of natural controls, principally mosquito fish in conjunction with the above measures.

6. Application of man-made control agents.

Although the application of man-made agents is relatively inexpensive, most local health agencies will not approve their continued use because of a fear that a resistant strain of mosquitos will develop. Man-made agents that have been used with considerable success include BTI and a light oil such as GB 1111. In general, it is best if natural controls can be used. Man-made agents can be used periodically if unforeseen problems develop.

PROCESS DESIGN

Process design for aquatic processing units involves consideration of 1) operating water depths, 2) process loading rates, 3) process kinetics, 4) temperature effects, and 5) plant harvesting.

Operating Water Depths

The operating water depths for aquatic systems are extremely important with respect to process performance and in defining the hydraulic detention time.

ATSs with Floating Plants. To achieve effective treatment when using floating aquatic plants, particularly water hyacinths, the bulk of wastewater flow should be below, rather than through the floating plants. With water hyacinths, treatment performance is dependent on the contaminant flux to the root and petiole zones (See Figure 6). If the clear water zone hydraulics are such that contaminant flux to the root zone is less than its microbial metabolic oxidation potential, the process is not being used effectively. If the contaminant flux from the clear water zone is in excess of the treatment potential of the root-petiole complex, plant health may suffer. In addition, such loading conditions favor the development of odors and the production of nuisance levels of mosquitos. Thus, the clear water zone hydraulics should be engineered, so that the hydraulic conveyance of contaminants to the root-petiole complex matches the treatment potential of the system.

Results of a study (Stowell and Tchobanoglous, 1983) to determine the effects of clear water zone depth and turbulence on the performance of a water hyacinth process receiving primary effluent is presented in Figure 7. Three water depths were studied: 180-200, 460-500, and 760-800 mm. The clear water zone Reynolds numbers (Re) for the laminar, transitional, and turbulent studies were estimated to be 500, 2,000, and 3,000 respectively. In this study, the hyacinths extended about 200 mm into the water column (See Figure 6).

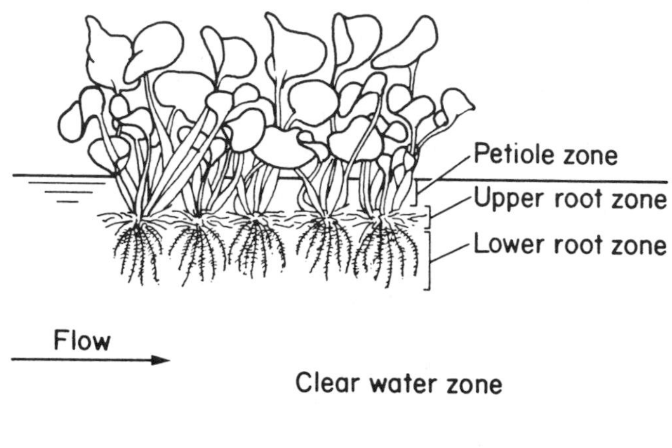

FIGURE 6. Section through a typical water hyacinth aquatic treatment system (adapted from Stowell and Tchobanoglous, 1983).

At the shallowest water depths, 180-200 mm, wastewater flowed through the root and petiole zones. At these depths, the total oxygen demand (TOD) reduction rates were reduced as a result of 1) hydraulic short circuiting (particularly through the petiole zone as the root zones became congested with wastewater particulates), and 2) scouring of particulates from the petiole and upper root zone at higher water turbulences.

In the 460-500 mm water depth studies, the clear water zone was about 200 mm deep. Because of the relatively shallow depth of the clear water zone, it was concluded that the clear water zone was well mixed, even under "laminar" conditions. Consequently, the grouping of the study results at the estimated TOD reduction rate potential (180 kg ha^{-1} d^{-1} at 25°C) was not surprising.

In the 760-800 mm deep studies, when the clear water zone hydraulics were turbulent (Re 3,000), TOD reduction rates were near the estimated TOD reduction rate potential of the media. In this case, the hydraulic conditions were such that contaminant flux to, and conveyance within, the root/petiole complex were sufficient to result in virtually complete utilization of its oxidation potential. Reducing the clear water zone turbulence (Re value reduced from 3,000 to 2,000) lowered the TOD removal rate by about 20 kg ha^{-1} d^{-1}. Reducing clear water zone turbulence further (Re value reduced from 2,000 to 500) lowered the TOD removal rate an average of 30 kg ha^{-1} d^{-1}.

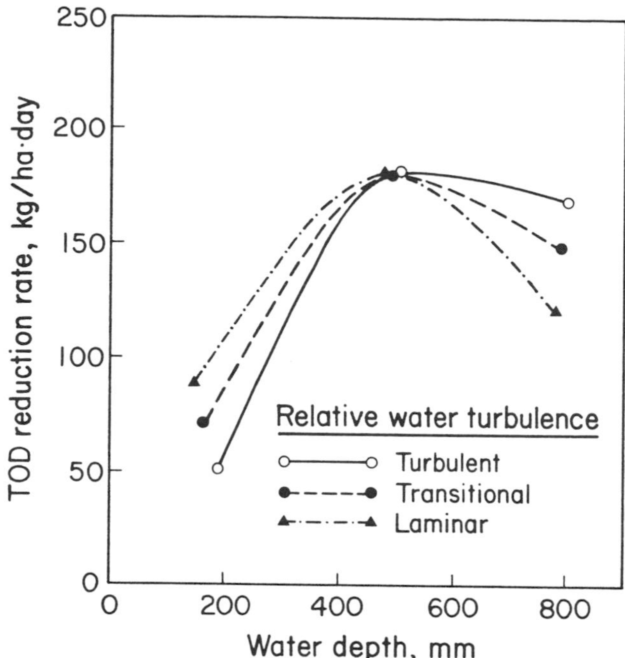

FIGURE 7. Effect of water depth and clear water zone turbulence on the performance of a water hyacinth treatment system (adapted from Stowell and Tchobanoglous, 1983).

Based on the results of the studies discussed above and reported in Figure 7, the recommended depth for water hyacinth systems is in the range from 500 to 700 mm. The deeper depths with turbulent flow, are favored because it is easier to insure that the bulk wastewater flow will be below the plants in the clear water zone.

ATSs with Emergent Plants. The depth of flow in emergent plant systems will, to a large extent, depend on the type of emergent plants. Cattails and bulrush depths typically range from 300 to 600 m. Where sedge is used as the emergent plant, water depths will usually be in the range from 250 to 450 mm.

Process Loading Rates

The most commonly used loading parameter for aquatic processing units is based on surface area and is expressed as kg $CBOD_5$ ha^{-1} d^{-1}. Typical design values for the aquatic processing units shown in Figure 2 are reported in Table 6. Based on recent data from the San Diego Aquaculture project (Black & Veatch, 1986), the most effective configuration for ATSs with water

TABLE 6. Typical organic loading rates for various aquatic treatment systems to achieve secondary treatment of wastewater following primary treatment.

ATS	Figure reference	Value, kg $CBOD_5$ ha^{-1} d^{-1} Range	Typical+
Semiplug-flow reactor without recycle	2b	50-200	60++
Plug-flow reactor without recycle	2c	50-200	60++
Plug-flow reactor with recycle	2d	50-200	60++
Semiplug-flow reactor with step-feed and 2:1 recycle	2f	100-200	150
As above with supplemental aeration	2f	150-300	200
Semiplug-flow variable geometry reactor without recycle	2g	50-200	80+++

+Typical loading values based on an odor free system. Higher loading rates can be used if odors and mosquitos are not an environmental issue.
++Limited by influent distribution.
+++With experience, a higher rate may be feasible.

hyacinths appears to be that of Figure 2f. Although not as well defined, it appears that a reactor with step-feed and recycle will also be most effective for use with ATSs with emergent plants.

Process Kinetics

For plug-flow reactors without and with recycle, it has been found that the removal kinetics for $CBOD_5$ can be described adequately with a first order model.

$$C = C_o e^{-k_T(t \text{ or } x)} \qquad [1]$$

Where C = $CBOD_5$ concentration at time t (or distance x), mg L^{-1}
C_o = $CBOD_5$ concentration at time t = 0 (or at distance x = 0), mg L^{-1}
k_T = removal rate constant at temperature T, t^{-1} or x^{-1}
t = time, h
x = distance, m

Because of the variable nature of ATSs, k_T values tend to be quite site specific. The effect of temperature is considered later in this section. In trying to arrive at k_T values from field measurements, an interesting observation has been made. In most cases, it has been found that the removal of $CBOD_5$ and SS occurs far more rapidly than would be expected (see Figure 8). In San

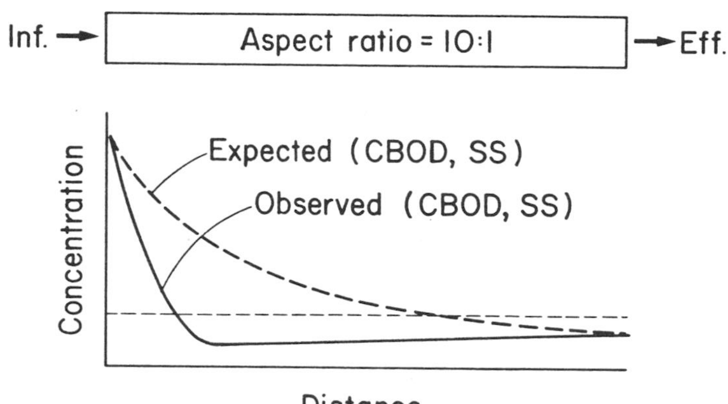

FIGURE 8. Observed $CBOD_5$ and SS removal in long plug-flow aquatic treatment systems.

Diego, in plug-flow reactors with length to width ratios of 10, essentially all of the $CBOD_5$ and SS removal took place in the first 10 to 15% of the length (Black & Veatch, 1986). This finding led to the use of the semi-plug flow reactor with step-feed and recycle (See Figure 2f). Typical $CBOD_5$ and SS performance data for one of the semi plug-flow ponds at San Diego are presented in Figure 9.

For the purpose of analysis, assume that a semi plug-flow reactor with step-feed (8 points) and recycle (See Figure 10a), can be described adequately as a cascade (series of CFSTRs (continuous-flow stirred-tank reactors) as shown in Figure 10b. The steady-state materials balance for the first reactor assuming first order kinetics is:

$$\text{accum} = \text{inflow} - \text{outflow} + \text{generation} \quad [2]$$

$$0 = Q_r(C_8) + 0.125Q(C_o) - (Q_r + 0.125Q)(C_1) - k_T(C_1)V_1 \quad [3]$$

where Q_r = recycle flow, $m^3\ d^{-1}$
C_8 = $CBOD_5$ concentration in effluent from reactor number 8 in series, mg L^{-1} = g m^{-3}
Q = inflow, $m^3\ d^{-1}$
C_o = $CBOD_5$ concentration in influent, mg L^{-1} = g m^{-3}
C_1 = $CBOD_5$ concentration in effluent from reactor number 1 in series, mg L^{-1} = g m^{-3}
k_T = first order reduction rate constant at temperature, T, 1 d^{-1}
V_i = volume of individual reactor, m^3

Using the actual flow and volume data, the effluent quality that would have been expected at the end of each segment is plotted on

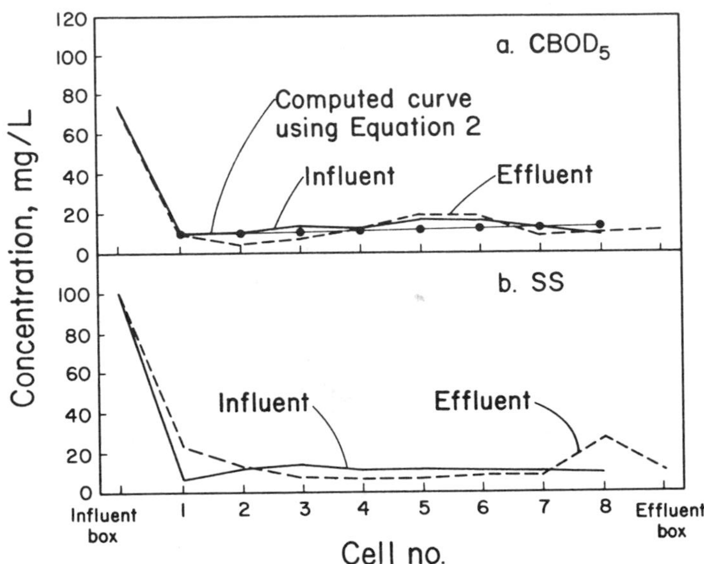

FIGURE 9. Performance data for a semi plug-flow water hyacinth pond with step-feed and recycle (see Figure 2f). Data are for pond 3 at the San Diego aquaculture project (Black & Veatch, 1986).

Figure 9. The corresponding k value based on the first segment is 1.95 d^{-1}. Clearly, a cascade CFSTR model can be used to model the performance of the San Diego step-feed ponds.

Configuration of ATSs

Although plug-flow reactors (See Figure 2c) have been used in the past, the results of recent studies show that a step-feed system with recycle is a more optimum configuration. It is most interesting to note the beneficial effect achieved by the step-feed combined with the recycle flow. In the plug-flow reactor with recycle (see Figure 2c), the recycle flow of 2Q results in a recycle ratio of 2:1, whereas in the step-feed recycle flow configuration (see Figure 10a), an overall recycle flow of 2Q results in a recycle ratio of 16:1 for the first segment. Assuming the effluent quality from each segment is essentially the same, the recycle ratio to the last segment is about 23:1 (See Figure 10b). The recycle flow is also important in maintaining turbulent flow conditions in the clear water zone below the plant roots. The use of segmented systems with recycle is also recommended for emergent plant ATSs.

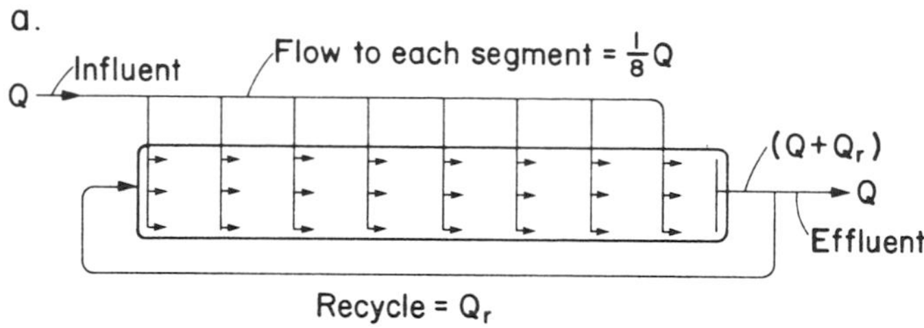

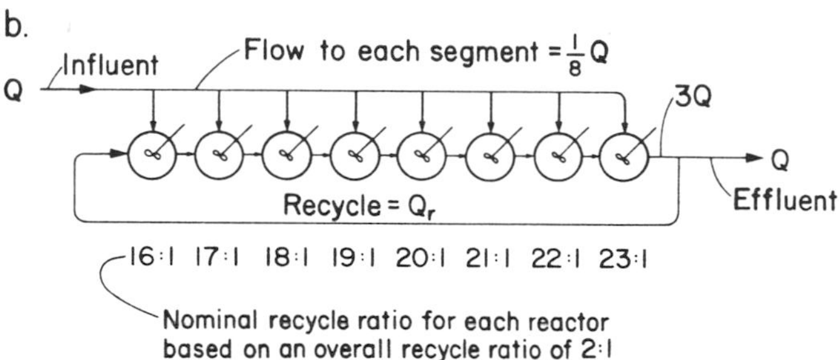

FIGURE 10. Definition sketch for the analysis of a semi plug-flow pond with step-feed and recycle: a) actual system, b) equivalent reactor system.

Temperature Effects

The performance of all aquatic treatment systems is temperature dependent. Based on both experimental studies and an analysis of data presented in the literature, it appears that a modified van't Hoff-Arrhenius temperature relationship, as presented below, can be used to estimate the effect of temperature on wastewater treatment using aquatic systems.

$$k_t = k_{20} \quad (T-20) \qquad [4]$$

Where k_T = removal rate constant at water temperature T, d^{-1}
k_{20} = removal rate constant at 20°C, d^{-1}
= empirically derived temperature coefficient
T = operating water temperature, °C

Based on experimental studies with water hyacinth and emergent plant systems, it has been found that the value of the temperature coefficient is about 1.09. The effect of temperature on the detention time requirements for a typical aquatic system is illustrated in Figure 11 for wastewater with varying characteristics.

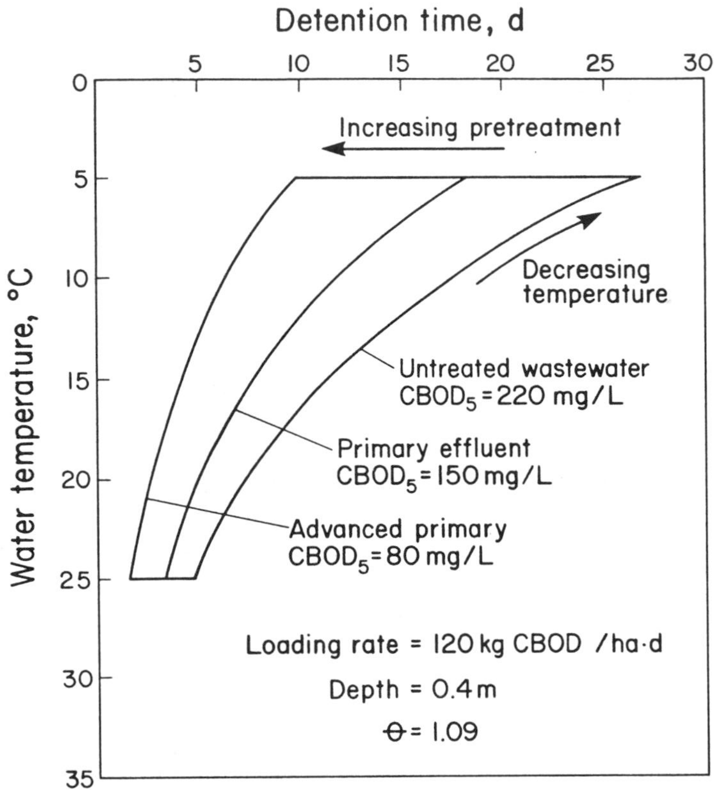

FIGURE 11. Effect of temperature on the required detention time for a typical aquatic treatment system (Adapted from Stowell et al., 1985)

A complete discussion of the effects of temperature on aquatic plants is beyond the scope of this paper. Temperature effects are considered in greater detail in Stephenson et al. (1980), Stowell et al. (1981), and Tchobanoglous (1979). Because of the adverse effect of temperature on water hyacinths, their use should be limited to the more temperate climates where the changes in both the water and air temperature between summer and winter are within a limited range. Cattail systems, however, have been used in Canada the year round with great success.

Plant Harvesting

The necessity of harvesting the plants grown in a given ATS will be a function of climatic factors, the plant species being grown, and the specific wastewater treatment objectives to be achieved. Harvesting plants to remove wastewater contaminants taken up by the plants is, as noted previously, inefficient. However, harvesting plants can have an appreciable affect on the wastewater treatment performance of an ATS by altering the effect that plants have on the aquatic environment (as described in Table 1). Further, because harvesting reduces plant congestion at the water surface, the control of mosquito larvae using Gambusia (mosquito fish) is enhanced.

In ATSs with floating aquatic plants, the ATS should be divided into segments as shown in Figure 10a. When harvesting is required, the load to the segment to be harvested is diverted to the remaining segments, while the plant biomass is removed and the process is allowed to restabilize. In emergent systems with cattail/bulrush, a segmented system should also be used. It must also be possible to drain each segment separately so that harvesting equipment can be used. Depending on the location, it may be possible to burn the dried plant mass in place. If a step-feed system were used, burning could occur every other year.

PHYSICAL DESIGN FEATURES

The physical design features of aquatic treatment systems are very site specific. Nevertheless, it is recommended that the following general features be incorporated in the design of aquatic treatment systems using floating or emergent plants.

1. Plug-flow channels should be divided into segments that can be operated and drained separately (see Figure 10a).
2. Provision for step-feeding the influent waste.
3. Provision for effluent recycling.
4. Provision for supplemental aeration.

PROCESS RELIABILITY

Properly designed aquatic systems are as reliable as conventional systems for the removal of CBOD, SS, and N compounds assuming the reduced rate of treatment during winter is accounted for in the design. The reliability of removing other wastewater contaminants by aquatic treatment processes is not as well established.

Causes of aquatic process upsets and the nature, magnitude, and duration of disruption of treatment have not been studied extensively, but most upsets seem to be related to either climatic events or plant damage caused by insects or diseases. Aquatic systems are comparatively insensitive to variations in influent wastewater quality. At the San Diego Aquaculture project, regardless of the condition of the plug-flow ponds, the effluent $CBOD_5$ and SS are consistently below the requirements for secondary treatment.

FUTURE CHALLENGES

Although much is now known about the operation of aquatic treatment systems, much remains to be learned. Subject areas where additional information is needed include:

* Alternative physical configurations
* Improved pretreatment
* Improved influent distribution
* Improved odor control techniques
* Improved supplemental aeration systems
* Improved vegetation management
* Improved mosquito management techniques

As more information is developed on the application and operation of aquatic treatment systems it is anticipated that the use of these systems will become more commonplace in the future.

REFERENCES

Abwasserreiniguug mit Hilfe von Wasserplanzen, Nol. 1983. Technische Universitat Hamgurg-Harburg, Hamburg West Germany.

Black & Veatch, Engineers-Architects. 1986. Interim Progress Report San Diego Aquaculture Project, Kansas City, MI. October, 1986.

Stephenson, M., G. Pope, P. Pope, J. Colt, A. Knight, and G. Tchobanoglous. 1980. The use and potential of aquatic species for wastewater treatment, Appendix A. The environmental requirements of aquatic plants. Publication No. 65, California State Water Resource Control Board, Sacramento, CA.

Stowell, R., and G. Tchobanoglous. 1983. Design of water hyacinth systems. Unpublished manuscript. Department of Civil Engineering, University of California, Davis, CA.

Stowell, R., R. Ludwig, J. Colt, and G. Tchobanoglous. 1981. Concepts in aquatic treatment system design. J. Environ. Eng. Div., Proc. Amer. Soc. Civil Engineers, Vol. 107, No. EE5, October. 1981.

Stowell, R., S. Weber, G. Tchobanoglous, B. A. Wilson, and K. R. Townzen. 1985. Mosquito considerations in the design of wetland systems for the treatment of wastewater. In P. J. Godfrey, E. R. Kaynor, S. Pelczarski, and J. Benforado (ed.) Ecological Consideration in Wetlands Treatment of Municipal Wastewaters. Van Nostrand Reinhold Co., New York, NY.

Tchobanoglous, G. 1979. Wetland systems for wastewater treatment in cold climates: An engineering assessment. Prepared for United States Army Cold Regions Research and Engineering Laboratory, Hanover, NH.

ECOTECHNOLOGICAL OPPORTUNITIES FOR AQUATIC PLANTS - A SURVEY OF UTILIZATION OPTIONS

G. Lakshman
Saskatchewan Research Council
15 Innovation Blvd.
Saskatoon, Saskatchewan
CANADA S7N 2X8

ABSTRACT

Utilization of conventional food crops for the production of energy and chemical feedstocks is usually untenable because of the unreliable economic future and the possible food-feed-energy conflicts. Aquatic plants, which can be established in vast untapped non-agricultural lands and wetlands, present a viable and alternative resource base for exploitation.

Aquatic plant systems can produce protein and fiber for animal feed, cellulose and starch for ethanol production and C for direct combustion in systems also designed for tertiary treatment of wastewaters. Further prospects for producing polyunsaturated oils, plant growth hormones, pharmaceutical components, drug principles, paper pulp, fabric and insulation from some of these aquatic plants represent new utilization options. This has special significance to the Third World countries in terms of job creation, sewage treatment and development of small-scale industries.

Keywords: Aquatic plants, biomass, sewage treatment, bioenergy, feedstock, plant chemicals, combustion, ethanol, drug principles, systems approach, commercial potential.

WHY AQUATIC BIOMASS?

The energy situation of the 70's stimulated the development of biofuels and the commercial utilization of agricultural and forest biomass for feedstock chemicals. Although the development of sugar and starch crops for ethanol production made global impact it was not an unequivocal success. The political and economic climate created in many countries to encourage biofuel development also generated a false economic viability for biomass processes. Serious appraisal of the presumed dependability of the

ISBN 0-941463-00-1

agriculture-biofuel relationship (Carruthers and Spedding, 1985) indicated that it was possible only under well-defined scenarios of energy demand, environmental impact and opportunity costs which are clearly country-specific parameters.

It appears that we need alternative, perhaps unconventional, sources of biomass which can economically sustain the production of energy and feedstocks under the scenarios where the conventional sources failed. Preferably the economic strategy should focus on the complete utilization of the resources through the generation of multiple-product streams and minimize adverse environmental impacts. It should be more compatible with the country's economic and social issues than the earlier efforts for long term stability. Aquatic biomass, including macrophytes and microalgae, appears to offer an attractive opportunity throughout the world for commercial development. In most countries non-agricultural areas, peatlands and wetlands are available for selective development into "managed" aquatic biomass resources which can also exploit their unique biological advantages.

Aquatic plants can assimilate nutrients from treated and untreated sewage for their rapid growth. The land and the fertilizer costs are minimal. Insects and diseases affecting the aquatic plants have been rarely reported in northern climates reducing the requirement for pesticides. Because of their high productivities the aquatic biomass systems lend themselves to a variable-scale operation. Managed aquatic plant cultivation does not disturb traditional agriculture; rather it supplies additional economic opportunity for the entrepreneur to pursue production, processing and marketing of new products.

A SYSTEMS VIEW

A systems approach to the utilization of aquatic biomass links the availability of feedstock to the production processes and ensures the comprehensive utilization of the biomass for economic viability. Different parameters control the production, processing and manufacturing operations and it is important that they are understood and managed for maximum efficiency. This includes proper species selection, optimizing growing conditions, harvesting and utilization (Figure 1). Achieving multiple harvests and densifying the biomass reduce operating costs. Most aquatic plants can be densified into pellets, briquettes or cubes without using any thermoplastic binders.

Most aquatic plants contain several chemical constituents which make them useful as a feedstock in more than one process. Reliable data on these specific parameters can help to establish the technical feasibility of converting them into marketable products.

A biomass species exhibiting a broad spectrum of properties can offer a variety of opportunities for commercialization. A simple utilization model cannot deal with the product development

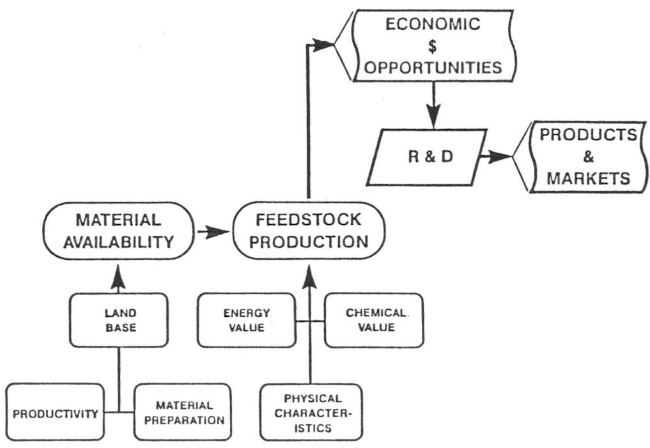

FIGURE 1. Systems approach to biomass utilization.

in a competitive market. A systems approach can improve feedstock supply, initiate appropriate R&D schemes and develop products. Mission-oriented research can develop scientific data relevant to these utilization opportunities. These are examined here to draw attention to promising areas where innovative schemes and exploratory research are needed.

MATERIAL AVAILABILITY

Establishing a new industry requires adequate supplies of biomass at an affordable cost. Supply is determined by the productivity and the area available; cost is determined by land prices and the value of inputs for production.

Land Availability

Agriculturally marginal or unusable lands such as wetlands, saline soils and peatlands can be used to produce naturally or artificially established aquatic plant systems. In North America there are about 200 million ha of wetlands potentially available for intensive aquatic biomass production. If one-half of some 20 million ha of marshland in the U.S. were used for emergent biomass energy plantations, approximately 5% of the present total energy requirements in the U.S. might be met (Kresovich et al., 1982). Canada has the largest wetland area in the world and parts of this are available for biomass production without endangering the waterfowl or wildlife habitats (Lakshman, 1984). Globally, the aquatic biomass productivity is established at about 3.7 times the

TABLE 1. Global perspective: Aquatic biomass and cultivated crops (Callaghan et al., 1985).

Total Plant Production Area	149 x 10^8 ha
Annual Production	133 x 10^9 Mg
Aquatic Plants: Area	2 x 10^8 ha (1.34%)
Annual Production	7 x 10^9 Mg (5.5%)
Cultivated Land: Area	16 x 10^8 ha (10.7%)
Annual Production	15 x 10^9 Mg (11.3%)
Productivity:	
Aquatic Areas	3.7 kg m^{-2}
Cultivated Lands	<1.0 kg m^{-2}

TABLE 2. Wetland areas available for aquatic biomass production.

Location	Area (ha)
U.S.A.	20 x 10^6
Canada	170 x 10^6
Romania	3 x 10^6
Sudan	0.3 - 1 x 10^6
EEC	1 x 10^6
France	>2.5 x 10^4

productivity of cultivated lands (Table 1). Cultivated lands, requiring enormous energy input, achieve less than 27% of the aquatic biomass production. This highlights the efficiency of aquatic communities under normal conditions. The potential availability of wetland areas in some countries is shown in Table 2.

Productivity

Aquatic plants generally are more productive than terrestrial communities and agricultural crops because they do not suffer from water deficit, have high tolerance for environmental fluctuations and exhibit high photosynthetic efficiencies. The photosynthetic apparatus and the morphological advantage for capturing solar radiation in aquatic plants have been examined in detail (McNaughton, 1970; Dykyjova, 1971,1978). Several aquatic plants adapting C_3 pathway are more efficient than those operating with the C_4 pathway. Photosynthetic rates and ranges in environmental conditions for some aquatic species are given in Table 3. Cattails and reeds can tolerate a wide pH range including pH's associated with industrial and mining effluents. For a C_3 plant, cattail photosynthetic rates are high. Its value can be as high as 13.6% with average values between 6.1 and 10.9% depending upon the growing conditions (McNaughton, 1970; Dykyjova, 1971,1978).

TABLE 3. Growth characteristics - aquatic plants (Kadlec and Tilton, 1979; Reed et al., 1981; EPA, 1979,1980; Stephenson et al., 1980).

Plant	Soil/water pH	Photosynthetic rate	Water salinity %
Cattail	4.7 - 11.0	39.1 mg CO_2 g^{-1}	0.0 - 2.5
Reeds	2.0 - 8.5		1.0 - 4.0
Rushes and sedges	4.8 - 7.5	3.5 mg C $m^{-2}d^{-1}$	0.8 - 2.5
Bulrush	5.0 - 9.0		0.0 - 3.2
Pondweed	7.0 - 8.3		0.0 - 3.6
Watermilfoil	7.2 - 8.9		0.0 - 0.2

The annual biomass yields from aquatic plants are impressively high (Table 4). Emergent plants provide two types of biomass, shoots from aboveground, and roots and rhizomes from below ground. The shoots normally contain more cellulose, hemicellulose and protein than the roots and rhizomes. The below ground biomass contains more sugars and starch than the shoots. Biomass utilization schemes will determine which part is more valuable and incorporate appropriate harvesting schemes.

Material Preparation

Aquatic biomass contains a large amount of water which frequently must be removed before processing. Dewatering requirements vary among the plant species and depend upon the time of harvest. Dewatering, drying and densification are often essential for handling and storage before processing. The cost of the final product is very sensitive to these costs. Natural conditions can be used to accomplish drying under favorable circumstances, however, the cost of pelleting or briquetting, when required, are considerable. In addition to optimizing the annual biomass yields and supplying biomass in a convenient form for processing, the identification of the specific characteristics of the biomass is important in determining the potential for commercialization.

FEEDSTOCK PRODUCTION

Aquatic plants exhibit more interesting physiological adaptations than most terrestrial plants. Many of them sustain their innate ability to switch on alternate metabolic pathways when challenged for survival under adverse conditions. For example, some aquatic plants, as some terrestrial plants, when subjected to prolonged periods of flooding depriving their roots of O_2 for respiration develop an anaerobic metabolism to produce

TABLE 4. Annual productivity (Kresovich et al., 1982; Stephenson et al., 1980) of selected aquatic plants.

Type & Species	Aboveground	Below ground	Total
	Mg (dry wt) ha^{-1}		
Emergent Plants			
Phragmites communis (Common Reed)	3.8 - 4.0	3.7 - 88.9	8.2 - 122.9
Typha	3.8 - 52.7	1.6 - 48.7	9.7 - 101.4
Juncus roemerianus Rush)	2.3 - 16.0	97.0 - 124.0	---
Carex (Sedge)	2.2 - 22.3	1.5 - 11.7	---
Scirpus (Bulrush)	2.0 - 24.3	12.0 - 18.7	2.5 - 25.0
Spartina alterniflora (Saltwater Cord Grass)	5.4 - 30.2	112.0	---
Floating Plants			
Eichhornia crassipes (Water Hyacinth)	4.6 - 212.0		
Lemna (Duckweed)	0.3 - 90.0		
Azolla pinnata (Water Fern)	0.25 - 22.0		
Pistia stratiotes (Water Lettuce)	4.6 - 146.0		
Salvinia spp. (Water Fern)	40.0 - 67.0		
Submerged Plants			
Potamogeton (Pondweed)	2.0 - 9.3		
Elodea	13.0 - 47.0		
Ceratophyllum (Coontail)	7.0 - 10.0		
Myriophyllum (Watermilfoil)	1.2 - 11.5		

energy from a reaction of the following type,

$$CH_3CHO + NADH + H^+ \leftrightarrow CH_3CH_2OH + NAD^+$$

where the alcohol dehydrogenase converts acetaldehyde to ethanol in the presence of nicotinamide adenine dinucleotide (NAD) (Hutchinson, 1975). The ethyl alcohol thus produced is stored in the rhizomes but in some aquatic plants the anaerobic metabolic pathway is driven to produce and store malate which is far less toxic than ethanol. Biosynthesis of chemicals in aquatic plants taking advantage of these mechanisms is an area for further research.

Highly efficient photosynthetic rates and carbohydrate metabolism in some aquatic plants result in a large storage of sugars and starch in the rhizomes as a part of their winter reserve. Translocation of photosynthetic products from leaves to rhizomes and vice versa varies through the growing season but will be mostly unidirectional towards the rhizomes during the later part of the growing season. The winter survival of seedheads in cattail requires an essential lipid storage in the seeds which prevents them from freezing.

Aquatic plants are known to produce a large number of alkaloids, a group of chemical compounds which exhibit a wide variety of interesting properties such as antibacterial, antiviral and antifungal agents. Some of them have been implicated in allelopathic interactions with respect to their own species, other plants and specific algae (Van Allen et al., 1985; Cutler, 1985; Anderson, 1985).

Ethanol Production

The storage of structural and nonstructural carbohydrates in aquatic plants presents an opportunity to use them as feedstock for ethanol production via hydrolysis and fermentation. Typically the leaves contain about 30 to 35% cellulose, similar amounts of hemicellulose and about 6-15% lignin (Table 5). Cattail, with its thick, rhizomatous growth, stores large amounts of carbohydrates as starch and sugars in the rhizomes through the winter. Cellulose and hemicellulose upon enzymatic or acid hydrolysis, provide fermentable sugars. Sugars and starch can be fermented after a mild hydrolysis.

Cattails grown in sewage-discharge areas contain less cellulose and more hemicellulose than cattails grown in freshwater (Lakshman, 1984). The mean cellulose content in samples from sewage-fed cattail marshes was 23.4% compared with about 32.1% for freshwater samples. In the same study the mean hemicellulose content in the samples from sewage-discharge areas was about 30.3% compared with 19.6% in the freshwater samples. The reducing sugars and starch content in the freshwater rhizomes ranged from 7.0 to 24.9% and from 6.3 to 27.6%, respectively. Starch and sugar values in the sewage-discharge areas ranged from 6.4 to 19.8% and from 5.0 to 13.8%, respectively. The unlimited availability of nutrients results in reduced sugar and starch accumulation in the rhizomes. We need more studies to determine the effect of nutrient-rich growing media on carbohydrate metabolism in these plants.

TABLE 5. Carbohydrate distribution in cattail (Lakshman, 1984).

	Cellulose	Hemi cellulose	Starch	Sugars	Fermentable material
	%				
Leaves	30 - 35	19 - 37	--	4	>11
Rhizomes	10 - 40	25	>35	25	>40

The potential of cattail as a viable feedstock for ethanol production has been investigated in detail under Canadian conditions and the study suggests that it is possible to produce ethanol from a well managed cattail crop using the current techniques of hydrolysis and fermentation (Lakshman, 1984). Several laboratory trials in the U.S. (Dyck and Ladisch, 1979; Gabrielson, 1981; Gless, 1980; Ladenburg, 1981) show that up to 80% of cattail rhizomes can be converted to fermentable sugars. From 24 to 54% of the substrate by weight can be converted to ethanol. Rough estimates of ethanol production from cattail and conventional crops are shown in Table 6. The estimate assumes 30-50% conversion to fermentable sugars and about 30-40% fermentation efficiency. Rhizomatous species such as cattail are prime candidates as energy crops for ethanol production which should be seriously investigated.

Energy by Direct Combustion

Wood and other terrestrial biomass have been traditionally used as fuel in furnaces, fireplaces and stoves. Pelleted wood chips, sawdust and a variety of pelleted refuse materials have been sold in the U.S., Canada and Europe as home heating fuel. The competitive potential from the aquatic biomass comes from the fact that their yields are high, they can be harvested during fall which reduces or eliminates the drying costs and they can be developed in areas where the forests do not exist. Calorific values for many of the aquatic species equal or excel the values for wood or refuse-based fuels (Table 7). Aquatic biomass can compete favorably with the values obtainable for the conventional fuel sources such as lignite coal (15.9 GJ Mg^{-1}), municipal waste (13.9 GJ Mg^{-1}), poplar wood (19.3 GJ Mg^{-1}) and sugarcane bagasse (19.3 GJ Mg^{-1}).

Fuel pellets from aquatic biomass such as cattail compete at U.S. $42 to U.S. $56 per Mg which amounts to about U.S. $3.20/GJ to U.S. $4.20/GJ for delivered heat at the present time, taking

TABLE 6. Ethanol production potential from grain crops and cattail (Lakshman, 1984).

Crop	Yield	Potential alcohol conversion	Alcohol yield	Landbase
	Mg ha^{-1}	--L Mg^{-1}--	L ha^{-1}	
Corn	6.8	390	2,650	Agricultural
Wheat	2.1	360	756	Agricultural
Sugarbeet	50.0	92	4,600	Agricultural
Sugarcane	88.7	70	6,200	Agricultural
Cattail	20-40		1,500-5,000	Wetland

TABLE 7. Energy content for direct combustion (Stephenson et al., 1980).

Plant	Calorific value
	-----GJ Mg^{-1}-----
Emergent Species	
Cattail	15.4 - 19.6
Reeds & rushes	16.7 - 20.7
Sedges	15.4
Bulrush	17.7 - 18.4
Grasses	16.6 - 19.2
Floating Species	
Water hyacinth	15.9 - 19.0
Duckweed	10.3 - 13.4
Giant duckweed	15.4 - 17.0
Submerged Species	
Pondweed	12.8 - 17.9
Elodea	8.6 - 17.6
Coontail	15.5 - 17.8
Watermilfoil	7.2 - 16.5

into account the furnace efficiency and favorable land base costs. On the Canadian prairies, a typical home requires an estimated 4.5 to 9.0 Mg of cattail pellets to provide fuel through the heating season (Lakshman, 1986b). The demonstration study conducted in Saskatchewan also successfully tested a pellet-burning furnace, Viking Eagle 150, manufactured by the Viking Heating Division of the Fabridyne Inc., at Litchfield, Minnesota. This furnace has efficient heat exchangers and the overall furnace efficiency exceeds 72% during the high-fire mode of operation.

Wastewater Treatment

The use of aquatic plants for sewage treatment has attracted global attention in recent years. The reasons are simple. Towns and small communities simply cannot afford the vast expenses involved in setting up physico-chemical treatment plants to provide advanced secondary or tertiary treatment to municipal wastewaters. The conventional treatment methods are less flexible in terms of design modifications and are targeted primarily for removing BOD and to lesser extent for reducing P and N levels. The presence of heavy metals, hydrocarbons and toxic chemicals are not affected by most treatment plants. The communities in the developing and the industrialized countries are moving towards greater material recycling and water re-use schemes as a means of addressing the water-crisis and saving capital and operating costs. Establishment of artificial and natural wetlands to provide various levels of water treatment is aesthetically economical and environmentally acceptable and compatible. Demonstration studies at Humboldt, Saskatchewan (Lakshman, 1983) operating in the northern climate and a number of case studies (Kadlec and Tilton, 1979; Reed et al., 1981; EPA, 1979,1980; Stephenson et al., 1980) document the efficiency of artificial or natural wetlands for wastewater treatment.

Aquatic plants have the ability to remove and accumulate heavy metals such as Cd, Ni, Cu, Zn, Va and Hg and even radionuclides from water and sediments. Many floating, submerged and emergent species can concentrate heavy metals in their tissues up to 100,000 times the ambient concentration. Plants have been known to contain simple peptides, termed phytochelatins, which bind heavy metals and thus participate in metal detoxification (Grill et al., 1985). Short-chain peptides similar to the sulphur-rich metallothionein proteins may be involved in the rhizomes of many of the aquatic emergents for uptake and accumulation of heavy metals. Typha, Phragmites and many floating species have been observed to concentrate high levels of heavy metals. The use of selected aquatic species for revegetating abandoned mines and for treating mine effluents is being actively pursued in Saskatchewan and Ontario in Canada. The use of specific phytochelatins extracted from aquatic plants for adsorbing heavy metals from tailings and contaminated waters should open new opportunities.

Animal Feed

Aquatic plants are a source of fiber, protein and minerals. The concentrations of these substances vary through the growing season. In the emergent plants the protein content in the leaves reaches a maximum level sometime during June-July under Canadian conditions before inflorescence. As the plants reach maturity the fiber content increases. In the case of cattails the above-ground biomass should be harvested at inflorescence to achieve the best combination of protein, lipid and fiber. Aquatic plants grown in nutrient-rich environments (Lakshman, 1979,1982) such as sewage discharge areas are high in crude protein and digestible organic matter (DOM) which are the important constituents of good animal feed (Table 8). Cattail seedheads from freshwater areas contain up to 18% crude protein. Feeding trials conducted with sheep and cattle using a combination of crested wheat grass - cattail ration indicate that cattail inclusion at a level less than 50% of total ration would provide optimal animal feed (Mir and Lakshman, 1986). In these trials freshwater cattail leaves were used with a mean protein value of about 9% (dry weight basis) which were harvested at less than optimal conditions. However, it is suggested that cattails grown in nutrient-rich areas or harvested just before inflorescence from freshwater wetlands can, in fact, produce better results. The feeding trials also showed that cattail diets did not pose any problems as to their palatibility, voluntary intake or weight gain.

TABLE 8. Animal feed values of aquatic plants as a function of nutrient supply (Lakshman, 1982). DOM = digestable organic matter.

	Fresh Water			Sewage Fed		
	Protein	DOM	Fiber	Protein	DOM	Fiber
	%					
Cattail						
Leaves	6-11	27-44	26-38	13-26	35-58	15-25
Rhizomes	7- 9	53-56	11-14	6- 9	38-41	16-26
Bulrush						
Leaves	6-11	23-45	27-33	14-25	27-62	20-30
Rhizomes	5- 8	43-54	16-23	8-10	47-50	19-21
Alfalfa	18-20	55-60				
Straw	3- 5	30-45				

BOTANOCHEMICALS

Allelochemicals

Aquatic plants produce a variety of chemical substances which often exhibit strong properties as bactericides, fungicides, algicides, growth promoting hormones and drug components. Some plants store lipids and hydrocarbons. These plants can be produced under intensive cultivation as sources of botanochemicals and offer excellent opportunities for commercial exploitation. Some examples of types of allelochemicals produced by aquatic plants are shown below:

1. Growth inhibitors
   - *Ambrosia*
   - *Peltandra*
   - *Bidens*
   - *Typha*
2. Fungicides, bactericides and larvicides
   - *Xanthium*
   - *Scirpus*
   - *Typha*
   - *Phragmites*
3. Growth stimulating hormones
   - *Typha*
   - *Eleocharis*
4. Selective algicides
   - *Xanthium*
   - *Asclepias*
   - *Typha*
   - *Eleocharis*

Broadly, the botanochemicals can be grouped under different categories depending upon their potential use as a commercial product. The broadspectrum allelochemicals secreted by plants contain compounds which interfere with the growth of other plants or its own species by affecting seed germination or the metabolic pathways as growth inhibitors or promoters. Experimental data are available for some plants, although in some cases only sketchy and merely observational information are available.

Studies conducted almost 37 years ago (Hasler and Jones, 1949) showed that Potamogeton foliosus and Anacharis canadensis could inhibit the growth of blue-green algae and the root-exudates had a definite inhibitory effect on other phyto- and zooplanktons. More recent investigations (Banasera et al., 1979) have shown that leachates from Ambrosia, Bidens, Peltandra and Typha exhibit strong growth inhibitory and growth stimulatory effects in bioassays with lettuce, radish, cucumber and tomatoes. Percentage increase or decrease in the growth of treated plants compared with the control (Table 9) show the stimulatory properties of Typha root leachates to be impressive and deserving of further investigation. Oxygenated fatty acids produced from some plants including Eleocharis have been identified as the allelopathic agents which can selectively inhibit algal growth (Van Allen et al., 1985; Cutler, 1985; Anderson, 1985).

Algal blooms resistant to copper sulfate treatment have been found to be on the increase in farm ponds and lakes in North America. Many of these algae produce toxins which kill animals and produce harmful side-effects in humans. Natural algicides produced by promising aquatic plants open up new commercial opportunities. Larvicidal and bacteriostatic properties of root exudates from some aquatic species should be explored further.

A new plant growth hormone has been extracted from cattail pollen (Schneider et al., 1983). The component is 2-deoxy-castasterone, termed typhasterol, a steroidal plant hormone similar in activity to brassinolide extracted from rape pollen. Bioassays with celery have confirmed the biostimulatory properties of this hormone but its commercial potential, however, awaits evaluation.

TABLE 9. Allelopathic potential of leachates (Bonasera et al., 1979).

	Growth Reduction (%) Leachates from		Growth Stimulation (%) Leachates from		
	Leaf	Stem	Leaf	Stem	Root
Ambrosia trifida	48- 80	37- 70	115	--	--
Bidens laevis	27- 78	20- 60	--	--	--
Peltandra virginica	44-100	23-100	--	--	--
Typha latifolia	24- 60	41- 48	--	--	128-141

Feedstock Chemicals

Apart from producing a variety of allelochemicals and hormones the aquatic plants also produce and store feedstock chemicals such as hydrocarbons and fatty acids. Over 500 species of plants, including a few aquatic species, were screened for their potential for producing hydrocarbons, oils, polyphenols and proteins by the Northern Regional Research Centre at Peoria, Illinois (Buchanan et al., 1979,1980; Bagby et al., 1980; Roth et al., 1982). Several aquatic species such as swamp milkweed (*Asclepias incarnata*), canarygrass (*Phalaris canadiensis*), common reedgrass (*Phragmites communis*) and cordgrass (*Spartina pectinata*) were identified as hydrocarbon producers. Hydrocarbon fractions extracted from these plants and the data from mole plant (*Euphorbia lathyrus*) which has been identified as the most promising hydrocarbon-producing plant are shown in Table 10. The aquatic species compare favorably and when the annual yields are taken into account they appear economically attractive. Despite the initial encouraging results the aquatic plants have not received the serious investigation they deserve.

Cattail was extensively used in the United States during the first and second world wars as a substitute for kapok, insulation for jackets, parachute material and a source of pulp. Oil extracted from cattail seeds contains saturated and polyunsaturated fractions, similar in profile to the sunflower seed oil. The oil yield is about 20% by weight (Lakshman, 1986c). Total unsaturated fraction exceeds 85% and most of the oil is concentrated as linolcic acid (Table 11). The oil contains many long chain fatty acids, saturated and polyunsaturated, up to C24.

TABLE 10. Hydrocarbon-producing aquatic plants (Buchanan, et al, 1979,1980; Bagby et al., 1980; Roth et al., 1982).

	Polyphenol fraction	Oil fraction	Polymeric hydrocarbons	Triglycerides	Hydrocarbons
	%				
Asclepias incarnata (Swamp Milkweed)	11.5	3.0	1.9	13	7
Phalaris canariensis (Canary Grass)	4.9	2.1	1.2	--	1.22
Phragmites communis (Common Reed Grass)	6.4	1.2	--	--	1.27
Spartina pectinata (Cord Grass)	5.8	2.0	--	--	0.47
Euphorbia lathyris (Mole Plant)	7.6	9.9	0.40	3.0	7

TABLE 11. Fatty acid profile of cattail seeds compared with sunflower (Lakshman, 1986 unpublished results).

Fatty acid	Cattail seed oil	Sunflower oil
	--------------%	--------------
C16 Palmitic	6.6	3.0
C18 Stearic	2.2	0.6
C18:1 Oleic	12.2	34.0
C18:2 Linoleic	71.2	58.5
C18:3 Linolenic	0.7	--
C20 to C24:1	5.2	0.4
Total Unsaturates	88.3	95.9
Total Polyunsaturates	74.0	60.6

The fatty acid profile, in terms of chain length and degree of unsaturation, is affected by the nutrient status of the growing medium and the time of harvest. When seeds are allowed to go through the winter the elongation of C chain occurs at the expense of shorter chain fatty acids with an increase in the degree of unsaturation (Lakshman, 1986d).

A preliminary estimate indicates that approximately 400 to 850 L of oil can be produced per ha of cattail stands in natural, unmanaged wetlands. Data from a short field study involving cattails in roadside ditches and wetlands in Saskatchewan were compiled in Table 12. The theoretical oil yield potential compares favorably with the oil production from commercial sunflower and canola crops. Extraction and refinement requirements and methods to enhance the specificity of fatty acids and the total yields are topics for further study.

Pharmaceutical Compounds

The pharmaceutical importance of plant alkaloids, although sporadically exemplified by some well known applications, has been largely of academic interest. Aggressive efforts to evaluate and

TABLE 12. Oil yield from cattail seeds (Lakshman, 1986 unpublished results).

Oil Yield (by weight)	5-10% of Seedhead Wt. 20% of Seed Wt.
Seedhead Density (Natural Wetlands)	40-60 m^{-2}
Average Seedhead Wt.	8-13 g
Oil Yield (estimate)	430-840 L ha^{-1}
Sunflower Oil (production)	560 L ha^{-1}
Canola Oil (production)	550 L ha^{-1}

exploit the numerous plant species which are known to accumulate pharmacologically active compounds are conspicuously absent. The case of aquatic plants is no exception. Cultivation of special aquatic species in the vast aquatic environments for the production of economically important chemicals could develop a new generation of renewable resources; and advances in biotechnology could hasten this development.

In 1980, American consumers paid about $8 billion for prescription drugs derived solely from higher plants (Balandrin et al., 1985). From 1959 to 1980, the drugs derived solely from higher plants represented a constant 25% of all new and refilled prescriptions in the U.S. Extracts from several marsh plants including *Juncus roemerianus*, *Spartina cynosuroides* and *Scirpus americanus* showed statistically significant anti-tumor activity against P388 lymphocytic leukemia in BDF mice (Miles and de la Cruz, 1976). These tests conducted on the basis of survival time and tumor weight inhibition showed that 10 out of 17 marsh plants that were screened for activity exhibited an activity level greater than the control by 125 to 148% (Table 13). Further examination of the extract from *Juncus roemerianus* has resulted in the isolation of a new tumor inhibitor called Juncusol. In addition, further fractionation and extraction of *Spartina cyanosuroides* showed significant activity up to 172%, at a dosage of 400 μg kg^{-1} (Table 14).

Extracts from cattail pollen have been found to have significant anticoagulant effects on human plasma. Studies of the mechanisms of the anticoagulant effect indicate that polysaccharides from the pollen inhibit the rate of release of fibrinopeptides by thrombin and also the aggregation of fibrin monomers (Gibbs et al., 1983). The polysaccharides, in this study, increased the thrombin times by a factor of approximately 2.0. Addition of polysaccharides at 750 μg mL^{-1} increased the thrombin time from 14.1 s to 26.0 s and the reptilase time from

TABLE 13. Anti-tumor activity of aquatic plant extracts (Miles and dela Cruz, 1976).

Plant	Sample	Dose (μg kg^{-1})	% T/C
Spartina alterniflora (Shoots)	B	400	148
Juncus roemerianus	A	400	147
(Roots)	B	200	138
Spartina patens (Roots)	A	300	141
Sigittaria falcata (Roots)	A	100	139
Phragmites communis (Roots)	B	300	133

15.0 s to 28.0 s. The polysaccharides acted as a procoagulant at concentrations less than 100 μg mL^{-1}.

Cattail pollen has also been shown to have potential in the prevention and treatment of atherosclerosis. Traditional Chinese medicine has used cattail pollen to activate circulation and disperse stasis and for alleviating the clinical symptoms of angina pectoris. Experimental data are now available to show its usefulness in the control of atherosclerosis (Ji et al., 1983). The pollen significantly inhibited the proliferation of aortic smooth muscle cells _in vitro_ and reduced the adhesiveness and aggregation of platelets as well as the release reaction of platelets. In a related study, cattail pollen was shown to reduce the size of atherosclerotic plaques and lower the serum cholesterol level. Available data indicate that the rapid growth of aortic smooth muscles in the intima of the arteries and the factors released by the platelets contribute to a rapid progress of atherosclerosis. The usefulness of cattail pollen in inhibiting these trends is yet to be evaluated.

Data from studies (Su and Staba, 1973) focused on a number of aquatic plants show that _Nuphar_, _Sagittaria_, _Carex_, _Myriophyllum_ and _Nymphea_ produce alkaloids which have anticoagulent effects.

Development of Products

The fuzzy cotton from cattail seedheads is an excellent material for producing home insulation. It is not combustible in the absence of an open flame and its thermal characteristics are under study (Lakshman, 1986a). Substitution for expensive down in sleeping bags, parkas, pillows and jackets is an economically attractive opportunity. Fibers from cattail leaves after processing through a Hollander beater can be used to produce paper. Plants such as _Phragmites_, _Asclepias_ and _Scirpus_ are also good sources of pulp for paper. In Romania, over 125,000 Mg of dry common reeds (_Phragmites communis_) are mechanically harvested annually to produce about $10 million worth of paper pulp.

The dry stem biomass of _Phragmites communis_, _Spartina cynosuroides_ and _Typha latifolia_ contain 38, 33 and 30% pulp respectively (Cruz and Lightsey, 1981). The strength properties

TABLE 14. Anti-tumor activity of _Spartina cynosuroides_ (Miles and dela Cruz, 1976) -- after secondary extraction.

Sample	Dosage (μg kg^{-1})	% T/C
A	264	139
	400	139
B	400	172
	200	162

of paper sheets made from marsh plant pulps are comparable to wood pulp either because of similarities in fiber length or due to the good interfiber bonding quality of marsh plant fibers. Marsh plant pulp can be blended with wood pulp for bulk or to increase paper strength or texture quality. Spartina cynosuroides had the highest cellulose content (35%) and Phragmites communis the highest concentration of six-carbon sugars (70%). The feasibility of farming the wetlands for pulp, cellulose or alcohol exists.

There are other products which can be produced from aquatic plants through innovative research and development. Cattail fluff, after separating the seeds, can be spun and blended with synthetic fibers to produce fabrics. Production of fish food for aquaculture operations, soil conditioner for upgrading the fertility of agriculturally marginal lands, production of handicrafts, thatched furniture and cat litter are some examples of other potential uses (Lakshman, 1986a).

CONCLUSIONS

Aquatic biomass presents unique opportunities for commercial exploitation. High annual productivities, wide tolerance for environmental variations, and their physical and chemical characteristics are sufficiently attractive for careful consideration. Particularly in the developing countries where the traditional agricultural land base is limited, the aquatic biomass offers an alternative resource base.

Utilization of aquatic plants for wastewater treatment, energy, animal feed and for the production of a variety of products presents commercial opportunities which can result in increased local economic growth, jobs and the development of resource based industries. However, the economic viability of these processes can only be assured by targeted research and developmental programs designed to evaluate the technical feasibility of various biomass utilization options. A systems approach helps to maximize the benefits for a site-specific operation and to develop innovative utilization schemes.

REFERENCES

Anderson, L. W. J. 1985. Use of bioassays for athelochemicals in aquatic plants. p. 351-370. In A. C. Thompson (ed.) Chemistry of Allelopathy. ACS Symposium Series.

Bagby, M. O., R. A. Buchanan, and F. H. Otey. 1980. Multi-use crops and botanochemical production. In Biomass as a Non Fossil Fuel Source. ACS Symposium Series. No. 144. pp. 125-136.

Balandrin, M. F., et al. 1985. Natural plant chemicals: Sources of industrial and medicinal materials. Science 228:1154-1160.

Bonasera, J., J. Lynch, and M. A. Leck. 1979 . Comparison of the allelopathic potential of four marsh species. Bull. The Torrey Botanical Club 106:217-222.

Buchanan, R. A., et al. 1979. Gutta-producing grasses. Phytochemistry 18:1069-1071.

Buchanan, R. A., F. H. Otey, and M. O. Bagby. 1980. Botanochemicals. Recent Advances in Phyto-chemistry. Plenum, NY. 14:1-22.

Callaghan, T. V., G. J. Lawson, and R. Scott. 1985. Natural vegetation as a world resource. Bioenergy '84 2:150-158.

Carruthers, S. P. and C. R. W. Spedding. 1985. Practical and commercial limitations on using agricultural crops as an energy source. Bioenergy 84 1:91-121.

Cutler, H. T. 1985. Secondary metabolites from plants and their allelochemic effects. In Bioregulations for Pest Control. Amercian Chemical Society. pp. 456-468.

Cruz, A. A., dela and G. R. Lightsey. 1981. Pulping characteristics and paper making potential of non-wood wetland plants. Mississippi-Alabama Sea Grant Consortium, Ocean Springs. MS (USA). April 1981.

Dyck, K. and M. R. Ladisch. 1979. Cattails: A novel cellulosic substrate. Laboratory of Renewable Resources Engineering, Purdue University, Lafayette. Indiana Publication No. 7763.

Dykyjova, D. 1971. Productivity and solar energy conversion in reedswamp stands. Photosynthetica 5:329-340.

Dykyjova, D. 1978. Determination of energy content and net efficiency of solar energy conversion by fishpond helophytes. Pond Littoral Ecosystems. Springer-Verlag, New York.

EPA. 1980. Aquaculture systems for wastewater treatment - An engineering assessment. EPA 430/9-80-007, MCD-68. June 1980.

EPA. 1979. Aquaculture systems for wastewater treatment seminar proceedings. EPA 430/9/-80-006, MCD-67. September, 1979.

Gabrielson, J. E. 1981. Cattail rhizome - derived alcohol interim report. U.S. Dept. of Energy, Alcohol Fuels Technology Grant DE-FG02-81. AF92016.

Gibbs, A., C. Green, and V. M. Doctor. 1983. Isolation and anticoagulent properties of polysaccharides of Typha angustata and Daemonorops species. Thrombosis Research 32:97-108.

Glass, R. L. 1980. Chemical compounds in cattail useful as an energy source. Final Report to the Minnesota Energy Agency on Alternate Energy Research. University of Minnesota, St. Paul, MN.

Grill, E., E. L. Winnacker, and M. H. Zenk. 1985. Phytochelatins: The principal heavy-metal complexing peptides of higher plants. Science 230:674-676.

Hasler, A. D. and E. Jones. 1949. Demonstration of the antagonistic action of large aquatic plants on algae and rotifers. Ecology 30:359-364.

Hutchinson, G. E. 1975. A treatise on limnology. John Wiley & Sons 3:207-214.

Ji, Z., Z. Caiyang, and X. Demin. 1983. Preventive effects of pollen Typhae and Radix Salviae Miltiorrhizae in Atherogenesis inhibition on proliferation of aortic smooth muscle cells in culture. J. Traditional Chinese Medicine 3:177-183.

Kadlec, R. H. and D. L. Tilton. 1979. The use of freshwater wetlands as a tertiary wastewater treatment alternative. CRC Critical Reviews in Environmental Control. November, 1979. p. 185-212.

Kresovich, S. et al. 1982. The utilization of emergent aquatic plants for biomass energy systems development. Report to Solar Energy Research Institute, Golden, Colorado, Aquatic Species Program. NTIS. SERI/TR-98281-03.

Ladenburg, K. 1981. Cattails, a potential energy source. Contract Report to the South Carolina Sea Grant Consortium. Agricultural Energy Dept., Clemson University, Clemson, NC.

Lakshman, G. 1979. An ecosystem approach to the treatment of wastewaters. J. Environ. Qual. 8:353-361.

Lakshman, G. 1982. Utilization of aquatic biomass for wastewater treatment. In Biomass Utilization, Wilfred A. Cote, Ed. Proceedings of NATO Advanced Study Institute on Biomass Utilization. Plenum Press, NY. p. 233-239.

Lakshman, G. 1983. A demonstration project at Humboldt to provide tertiary treatment to the municipal effluent using aquatic plants. Saskatchewan Research Council Technical Report. Publication No. E-904-1-B-83.

Lakshman, G. 1984. A study to evaluate the potential of cattail as an energy crop. Saskatchewan Research Council Technical Report No. 162 E-901-28-B-84.

Lakshman, G. 1986a. Current and potential economic benefits from cattail utilization. Saskatchewan Research Council, Publication No. E-901-2-B-86.

Lakshman, G. 1986b. Demonstration of cattail pellets as alternative home heating fuel. Saskatchewan Research Council. Publication E-901-9-C-86.

Lakshman, G. 1986c. Fatty acid profile of oil extracted from cattail seedbeds. (unpublished results).

Lakshman, G. 1986d. Effects of nutrients and environment on the fatty acid composition of cattail seed oil. (unpublished results).

McNaughton, S. J. 1970. Photosynthesis and photorespiration in *Typha latifolia*. Plant Physiol. 45:703-707.

Miles, D. H. and A. A. dela Cruz. 1976. Phermacological potential of marsh plants. In Estuarine Processes, M. Wiley, Ed. Academic Press 1:267-276.

Mir, Z. and G. Lakshman. 1986. Voluntary intake and digestibility of complete diet containing varying levels of cattails (*Typha latifolia* L.) by sheep and cattle. (To be published).

Reed, S. C., R. K. Bastian, and W. J. Jewell. 1981. Engineers Assess Aquaculture Systems for Wastewater Treatment. Civil Engineering - ASCE. July, 1981. pp. 64-67.

Roth, W. B., et al. 1982. Whole plants as renewable energy resources: Checklist of 508 species analyzed for hydrocarbon, oil, polyphenol and protein. Trans. Illinois Academy of Sciences 75:217-231.

Schneider, J. A., K. Yoshihara, and K. Nakanishi. 1983. Typhasterol (2-deoxycastasterone): A new plant growth regulator from cattail pollen. Tetrahedron Letters 24:3859-3860.

Stephenson, M., et al. 1980. The environmental requirements of aquatic plants publication no. 65 - Appendix A. Agreement No. 8-131-499-9. A report prepared for The State Water Resources Control Board, State of California. Sacramento, California.

Su, K. L. and E. J. Staba. 1973. Toxicity, anti-neoplastic and coagulation effects of aquatic plants from Minnesota. Lloydia 36:99-102.

Van Allen, R. T., et al. 1985. Oxygenated fatty acids: A class of allelochemicals from aquatic plants. In The Chemistry of Allelopathy, A. C. Thompson, Ed. American Chemical Society, Washington, D.C.

EPA's REGULATORY AND POLICY CONSIDERATIONS ON WETLANDS AND MUNICIPAL WASTEWATER TREATMENT

D. G. Davis and J. C. Montgomery
Office of Federal Activities
U.S. Environmental Protection Agency
Washington, DC 20002

ABSTRACT

Through its program under Section 404 of the Clean Water Act EPA seeks to preserve wetlands in its review of Army Corps of Engineers or state permits for discharge of dredged or fill material to waters of the U.S., including wetlands. Among the wetlands values which EPA has identified, is the ability of wetlands to utilize nutrients which would otherwise pollute streams, rivers and lakes. Wetlands are also particularly valuable as buffers for non-point sources of water pollution. EPA also supports artificial wetland-type land treatment systems as part of its Innovative and Alternative wastewater construction grants program. When properly designed in appropriate situations, these can be cost-effective treatment systems, which have the effect of expanding wetland-type habitats. One concern is the possible effect of pathogens on wildlife and contamination of aquifers. Finally, EPA regulates wastewater discharges to "natural" wetlands (those defined as waters of the U.S.) through the Clean Water Act National Pollutant Discharge Elimination System permit program. Municipal dischargers to these wetlands must meet minimum technology requirements and conform with applicable state water quality standards. In the current absence of water quality criteria and water quality standards for wetlands, a conservative case-by-case approach to municipal discharges is the most appropriate one, combined with research and more work on developing applicable standards.

Keywords: Wetlands, waters of the United States, wastewater treatment, Clean Water Act.

INTRODUCTION

In the last few years the U.S. Environmental Protection Agency (EPA) has become aware of an increased interest in using aquatic plants for treatment of wastewater. As the Agency steps

Aquatic Plants for Water Treatment and Resource Recovery
K.R. Reddy and W.H. Smith (Eds.)

ISBN 0-941463-00-1

up its program for municipal compliance, and more smaller systems are required to meet more stingent effluent limits, there will probably be more proposals for discharges to natural as well as artificial wetlands. It will be important for EPA to make sure that its regulatory program in this area is consistent and well understood.

Clearly the scope of the topic addressed in this paper is broader than wetlands and wastewater treatment. Wastewater may be applied to wetlands for purposes other than, or in addition to, treatment, such as enhancement or restoration of degraded or limited wetlands, creation of new wetlands, or the reclamation of wastewater for uses such as irrigation. Likewise wastewater may be applied to systems other than "wetlands" in the ecological sense, such as monoculture of water hyacinth or duckweed with the primary or additional objective of biomass production or the harvest of particular products. Many of the same cost, engineering, and environmental factors will apply to these situations as well. However, it is in the area of wetlands and wastewater treatment that the policy and regulatory issues have received the most attention at EPA, and this will be our focus.

The purpose of this paper is to provide an overview of the relevant regulatory and policy considerations that govern, or at least affect, the use of wetlands for wastewater treatment. The focus is on discharges of municipal wastewater but wetlands may play an important role in water quality improvement involving other classes of discharge such as runoff, mine drainage, or industrial wastewater.

The Agency generally supports increased attention to these treatment methods since they may prove to be cost-effective and, at the same time, may have environmentally positive aspects. EPA has provided construction grant or research financial support for numerous natural and constructed wetland treatment systems. At least 25 such systems out of over 400 land treatment systems have received higher levels of grant funding than conventional systems (such as activated sludge systems) under EPA's Innovative and Alternative (I&A) wastewater treatment grants program since 1977. However, EPA's main responsibility in this area is--and will continue to be--protecting and improving the quality of the Nation's waters. As a result, the Agency must take an especially careful look at any proposed treatment system which is designed to take advantage of natural wetlands' abilities to assimilate higher nutrient loads than other water bodies. It is important to note that wetlands protection is a high priority program in EPA and therefore any potential impacts (including wastewater discharge) to natural wetlands will be evaluated very carefully.

Therefore, in looking at the regulatory and policy considerations involved in utilizing aquatic plants for waste treatment, it is important to understand the basic goals of environmental legislation which EPA is charged with implementing. There is a tendency to view all waste treatment applications involving use of aquatic plants solely in terms of their effectiveness in removing nutrients and toxic materials. While this aspect obviously has to be considered, it is critical that engineers, planners, public officials and others involved in developing wastewater treatment systems also understand the legal framework which has been set up to protect U.S. water bodies and the impact of this framework on evaluating treatment options. The main elements of EPA's regulatory program which must be considered in looking at possible uses of aquatic plants and wetlands for treatment will be reviewed.

REGULATORY FRAMEWORK

The legislative authority which is applicable to discharge of wastewater to U.S. waters, including wetlands, is the Clean Water Act. Its goal is quite clear: to restore and maintain the chemical, physical, and biological integrity of the Nation's waters. There are two main features of this law which have the strongest impact on proposals for using aquatic plants for waste treatment.

All municipal wastewater treatment systems, except for certain ocean discharges and aquaculture systems, must meet a minimum technology requirement of secondary treatment prior to discharge into waters of the U.S. Further, these discharges must also comply with applicable State water quality standards, which are designed to protect water body uses and which may require more stringent controls. In the majority of cases, the delegated States issue National Pollutant Discharge Elimination System (NPDES) permits for water discharges to ensure compliance with these requirements.

Second, EPA provides construction grants funding to support localities in the construction of municipal wastewater treatment plants.* In doing this, EPA must comply with a large number of requirements, including the National Environmental Policy Act (NEPA) and Executive Order 11990 on protection of wetlands. Under EPA's construction grant NEPA regulations, for example, an EIS is required whenever a major part of a treatment plant will be located in a wetland. In another example, reviews of groundwater effects could have an impact on whether use of aquatic plants for

*At the time of this manuscript preparation, reauthorization of the Clean Water Act was still pending in the Congress. While the specifics of any future program remain unknown, most observers believe that the program will continue at some level, and funding in the pipeline may provide for some construction over the next several years. For purposes of this paper, however, the construction grants aspects of wastewater treatment in the context of the program as it has existed over the last decade are assumed.

treatment is acceptable or not. In addition, EPA construction grants regulations require that the most cost-effective treatment systems be selected.

Given this regulatory framework, it is necessary to divide the concept of using aquatic plants for wastewater treatment into two distinct categories. The first category would cover utilization of aquatic plants in constructed or artificial wetland-type settings which do not involve impoundment or other modification of natural water bodies. The second category would cover discharge of wastewater to natural wetlands which are defined as water of the U.S. and protected under the Clean Water Act. These two categories must comply with very different regulatory requirements.

ARTIFICIAL SYSTEMS

The main EPA regulatory requirements on these systems relate to whether the effluents from the artificial wetland meet minimum technology requirements or applicable water quality standards prior to discharge into waters of the United States. Such systems must also go through all of the reviews related to construction-grant awards, including NEPA.

However, the key point here is that wetland-type areas constructed for wastewater treatment are ordinarily <u>not</u> waters of the U.S. and therefore are not themselves water bodies which are regulated under the Clean Water Act. In these systems there are no EPA water quality limitations directly applicable to the effluent entering the created wetland-type area. This allows designers to focus primarily on utilizing the treatment, removal, storage and transformation capacity of the constructed wetland ecosystem since there are no prior "existing uses and characteristics" of a water body to be considered.

EPA's experience indicates that artificial wetland-type land treatment systems can be cost-effective, particularly for small communities, without creating environmental harm. This technology also has the advantage of expanding wetland-type habitats, although these systems rarely are at the same level of biological complexity as natural wetlands systems, and their ecological values are correspondingly less than for natural systems. There are a number of examples of projects where constructed wetlands have enhanced wetland habitats, including small constructed wetlands which polish pretreated wastewater effluents and provide the equivalent of advanced treatment (Bastian, 1982). A California project totaling around 10 ha, discharges into Suisun Bay and includes structures designed to provide diverse wildlife habitats--including open water, vegetated islands, and areas planted with grasses and bullrushes to provide food for migratory waterfowl. As a result, a wide variety of waterfowl, small mammals, amphibians, reptiles and fish have become established in this project, while the effluent quality has been greatly improved prior to discharge into the Bay.

However, there are several possible environmental concerns which should be considered with such artificial systems -- most of which are also of concern in some conventional wastewater treatment systems such as lagoons. First, since the wetland-type area may not be receiving effluent which has been treated at a secondary level, it is possible that pathogens or toxic materials could be transmitted to birds and other wildlife which might use the area. Second, there could be transfer of pathogens or toxics to groundwater. Also, the potential for insect (e.g. mosquito) and odor problems needs to be considered.

In general, however, the current EPA regulatory and construction grants policies do not create any significant problems for consideration of constructed wetlands as a treatment option. Since an artificial wetland constructed for wastewater treatment is not a regulated water body under the Clean Water Act (part of waters of the U.S.), there is no need to consider protection of existing uses. From a regulatory point of view, this gives the use of artificial wetlands as a treatment method a considerable advantage over the use of natural wetlands for treatment. Operational controls can be designed to regulate flow, application rates, and detention time to meet desired seasonal variations in operation and treatment needs. Plant species can be selected and utilized on various bases such as nutrient uptake efficiency, ease of culturing or harvesting, value as biomass, etc. Finally, land purchases for artificial wetland systems are clearly eligible under EPA's construction grants program.

NATURAL SYSTEMS

Despite the relative advantages of artificial wetland treatment systems, there is also an increasing interest in utilizing the treatment, removal, storage, and transformation capacity of natural wetlands (which are generally classified as waters of the U.S.) particularly in cases where this can serve as a low cost alternative to advanced (but <u>not</u> secondary) wastewater treatment prior to discharge into a lake, river, or estuary. Since both artificial and natural systems involve wetland vegetation, there is a tendency to view them as similar. While there are clearly environmental differences between these two types of systems, from a regulatory point of view the differences are even more striking. The primary difference is that, in looking at a natural wetland, it is not only necessary to consider the efficacy of pollutant removal or conversion, but potential project planners must also address complex regulatory requirements in which protection of existing wetland values is the primary consideration.

It must be strongly emphasized that waters of the United States, including most wetland areas, are protected under the

Clean Water Act, and the act includes a strong presumption against the use of waters of the United States as treatment systems. This means that discharge of pollutants to them, as with any other water body, must be limited in order to protect their uses and values. At a minimum, effluent discharges into the wetland must meet applicable technology limits (that is, secondary treatment). Discharges must also comply with applicable State water quality standards. This may limit the flexibility designers have to make optimum use of aquatic vegetation for uptake and disposal of nutrients and toxics.

As an example, the changes in wetland plant species due to a wastewater discharge would have to be evaluated in terms of impact on overall wetland functions and fauna. The practice of harvesting vegetation, which has been mentioned in some papers on extending capacity nutrient removal, would usually not be compatible with protection of natural wetlands.

If a proposed discharge involves alteration of a natural wetland by channeling or building dikes, it may be necessary to obtain a permit for the discharge of dredged or fill material from the Army Corps of Engineers (or appropriate State Agency) under Section 404 of the Clean Water Act before such construction would be allowed. The Corps or State review for the Section 404 permit will require determination that the impacts of the dredged or fill material on the wetland do not constitute significant degradation; that there are no practicable, environmentally preferable alternatives; that unavoidable impacts have been minimized; and a determination that the proposed wetland alteration is in the public interest. The proposed modification will also require a review under the National Environmental Policy Act (NEPA), consideration of other applicable Federal laws and executive orders (such as the Endangered Species Act), and any applicable State laws governing wetland filling or other alteration. (Please note carefully that these reviews are for the physical modifications, not the wastewater discharge).

All of this is not intended to suggest that such wastewater discharges are prohibited under the Clean Water Act, but to emphasize that the law does not view a protected wetland as simply a "treatment process." Indeed, EPA's Region IV office has found over 400 discharges to wetlands in the Southeast, and the Chicago region has found 100 in the Midwest (EPA Region IV, 1985; EPA Region V, 1983,1984). All of these (except those in Florida) were under State-issued NPDES permits which require secondary treatment or compliance with levels set under site-specific water quality standards. (Those not currently meeting these levels are under compliance schedules requiring attainment of them in the future). Although they were for the most part small systems which had been historically discharging into the wetland area, there were some examples of planned discharges. For example, at the Royal Lakes Wastewater Treatment Plant near Jacksonville, FL, an extensive study of alternatives determined that discharge of 2574 m^3 d^{-1} of secondarily treated wastewater into a 182 ha mixed hardwood wetland (Pottsburg Creek Swamp) was the most cost-effective treatment option, and would not result in harmful impacts to the wetland (CH2M Hill, 1981). Discharge began in 1981, and nutrient removal goals have been met. Interestingly, this was not an EPA-funded project.

Another factor which may create difficulties for potential use of natural wetlands for treatment is that very few states have water quality standards specifically applicable to wetlands. Although effluents which meet secondary standards or water quality standards for adjacent waterbodies would still be able to receive NPDES permits, the appropriateness of these limits might need to be reviewed in the construction grants NEPA process, in applying for a 404 permit, and in response to public concerns. In addition, water quality standards are a key mechanism in the Clean Water Act for protection of water bodies, and these would appear to offer a logical and consistent way to develop and implement a policy on wastewater application to wetlands. Florida is clearly in the lead on this, having established standards this year for the use of wetlands for treatment. Wisconsin is also in the process of developing standards for wetlands. Under the Clean Water Act, State water quality standards should provide the crucial guidance which potential dischargers must have: what kind and how much change, if any, is allowed in a wetland as a result of a discharge. Given the great diversity of wetlands this is not easy guidance to develop. Yet, without overall State standards, it may be necessary to develop site-specific standards in order to permit a given discharge to a wetland, which can be an extensive, resource intensive task.

RECENT EPA ACTIONS

As a result of this situation, a recent EPA Task Force, in an internal Agency report, endorsed development of EPA water quality criteria for wetlands which would receive wastewater discharges (EPA, Office of Federal Activities, 1985). In a subsequent effort, EPA is now beginning to look at the need for and feasibility of developing water quality criteria for wetlands, which would serve as the basis for establishing State water quality standards. This effort is just beginning, however, and there are questions about the technical feasibility, as well as the resource needs required for such an undertaking.

In another follow-up activity related to the Task Force effort, the EPA Water Policy Office will be examining NPDES permitting and construction grants policies which affect wastewater discharge to wetlands in order to identify problems and possible alternatives in this area. As with the effort on standards, this is just getting underway, and no conclusions have been reached.

Therefore, for the time being, EPA will continue to review requests for treatment systems involving discharges (treated to secondary levels) to natural wetlands using a conservative, case-by-case approach. EPA Region IV has developed a handbook for municipalities in the Southeast, and EPA's Region V continues to look into the use of wetlands to treat as well as receive fully-treated effluent discharges in the upper Midwest (EPA Region IV, 1985; EPA Region V, 1983,1984). Outputs of these Regional efforts are recommended for anyone who wants to see the detailed elements which should be considered. The main steps which have been recommended in the Region IV handbook for the construction grants program are presented below.

EVALUATION PROCESS

First, the wastewater must be characterized in terms of what hydrological and pH changes would be created in the wetland. It should be determined if any toxics will be present; EPA discourages discharge of wastewater containing harmful levels of heavy metals or other toxic pollutants, and does not recommend this practice to municipal treatment plants which receive industrial effluents lacking adequate pretreatment. The impact of effluent chlorination without dechlorination prior to discharge on wetland biota and the possible need for supplement aeration in the wetland may also need to be assessed.

Second, the wetland type must be characterized and its sensitivity to discharges determined. Important factors would include drainage in the wetland, whether it is a unique type, and whether the discharge would affect endangered species. Size, topography, and hydrology need to be well understood in order to assess the impact of a proposed discharge. It is worth noting that, for specific situations, discharges to wetlands meeting secondary treatment limits might still be environmentally unacceptable due to hydrological or other impacts.

Once the discharge and wetland type are well understood, it is necessary to consider the wetland values which may be affected by a wastewater discharge. It must be determined to what extent the discharge will affect the plant and animal species which are associated with the wetland type as a result of hydrological changes, nutrient loading, and possible toxic or pathogenic impacts. It has been suggested that wastewater discharges should perhaps be limited to "degraded wetlands" where wastewater loadings may not contribute significant additional damage but may actually enhance or help restore the previously degraded wetland. Accordingly, the Region IV handbook encourages consideration of wetlands which have been modified before looking at possible use of high quality or "pristine" wetlands. Even in the case of degraded wetlands, the potential benefits of wastewater discharge must be balanced against potential additional degradation.

Once this review is completed and a wetland discharge is determined to be environmentally acceptable, loading criteria must be determined and effluent limits established. EPA's regional experience is that there is an especially great need for better models of wetland processes which allow these calculations to be made.

In some specific situations, discharges which meet secondary standards or which meet State water quality standards might still cause unacceptable impacts on wetlands values. This is because many States apply water quality standards which have been set for open water systems such as streams and which may be under-protective of vegetated wetlands. Likewise, the effects of changing the hydrology (rate, volume, or period) of the system must be considered since such physical changes may be more important to the ecological health of the wetland than the chemical parameters considered in an NPDES permit. NEPA and Executive Order 11990 (Wetlands Protection) create a requirement for EPA to consider these broader factors when EPA construction grant funds are involved. Conversely, there may be cases where a discharge could replace nutrients or water which have been lost to a wetland as a result of nearby development or other factors. In this case the discharge might have an environmentally beneficial impact. For example, in Hilton Head, S.C., the 24 ha Boggy Gut wetland had been drained, and sources of water inflow had been diverted as a result of development. Following a study (CH2M Hill, 1986) by the State of South Carolina, it was decided to use wastewater discharge to restore this wetland area. In 1983, application was started at 1136 m^3 d^{-1}, which should eventually be expanded to 3785 m^3 d^{-1}. EPA will be very interested in the results of this project, since it offers a clear case where the focus is on wetland enhancement as well as wastewater treatment.

In some cases it may be possible that effluents which meet applicable, but inappropriate, levels of treatment might be harmful to a wetland. For example, there are reports that mine drainage discharges to certain naturally acidic wetlands, when treated to meet EPA's effluent limits, are more harmful than untreated discharges would be. This is because EPA's limits require higher pH levels than are found in the natural wetland. EPA has no information on whether any similar problems have been encountered with municipal wastewater discharges. As mentioned earlier, EPA is just beginning to look at this whole question of wetlands water quality standards, and one of the Agency's concerns will be to determine whether this is an extensive problem.

RESEARCH

As mentioned earlier, EPA has funded major generic studies of this problem in two of the EPA regions, totaling $1 million over three years. While they do not answer all of the questions, these two efforts may provide a basis for planners to evaluate potential wetland discharges of municipal wastewater, as well as a framework for EPA to carry out site-specific evaluations. They also provide a starting point for developing water quality criteria for wetlands.

Also, starting this year, EPA has initiated a small research effort specifically directed at wetlands. While the purpose of this effort is to support EPA's responsibilities under section 404 of the Clean Water Act related to wetlands filling, the research will undoubtedly be useful in evaluating applications for discharge of wastewater to wetlands as well. One of the 3 major information needs to which this research effort is directed is quantifying the water quality functions of freshwater wetlands. This should improve efforts to better understand the basic functioning of wetlands in the following areas:

- processes which effect transformation and removal of nutrients (particularly N and P) in wetlands; and
- storage and transformation of metals and organic chemicals

EPA's research plan specifically mentions use of data from studies of wastewater in wetlands to help determine the impact of alterations on water quality functions within a wetland. In addition, EPA will use its own and other facilities for carrying out mesocosm studies and studies using artificial systems. The Agency will be developing models which will facilitate the assessment of the role of wetlands in altering water quality in receiving water. This will cover nutrients, organic chemicals and metals. Again, while this is primarily oriented to understanding wetland values, in particular the role of wetlands in filtering non-point pollution prior to entry into other water bodies, this type of tool may be of use in dealing with water releases to wetlands as well.

Another main focus, research on mitigation, will be somewhat more indirectly useful in dealing with wastewater. However, it may provide useful data on optimizing wetland values in building artificial wetlands for treatment. Information on restoring hydrology and nutrient loadings might also be useful for assessing possible beneficial uses of wastewater discharge to wetlands.

SUMMARY

In conclusion, the protective regulatory system set up under the Clean Water Act offers a necessarily stringent level of protection to U.S. water bodies, including wetlands. While this may complicate efforts to utilize the treatment capacities of these areas to receive wastewaters, the degree of caution built into the law is, on balance, desirable. Discharge limits under the Clean Water Act must always be based on protecting and enhancing water quality, and a clear distinction between "treatment systems" and protected wetlands must always be made.

REFERENCES

Bastian, R. K. 1982. National treatment system in wastewater treatment and sludge management. Civil Engineering-ASCE, May 1982. p. 62-67.

CH2M Hill. 1981. The assimilation of secondarily treated sewage effluent by Pottsburg Creek Swamp. August 1981, Prepared for Jacksonville Suburban Utilities, Jacksonville, Florida. p. 1-1.

CH2M Hill. 1986. Boggy Gut Wetlands treated effluent disposal system Hilton Head Island, South Carolina. January 1986, Prepared for Sea Pines Public Service District. ES1,ES2.

EPA Region IV. 1985. Freshwater wetlands for wastewater management handbook. EPA 904/9-15-135, September 1985, Atlanta, Georgia. 493 pp.

EPA Region V. 1983. The Effects of wastewater treatment facilities on wetlands in the midwest. EPA 905/3-83-002, September 1983, Chicago, Illinois.

EPA Region V. 1984. Literature review of wetland evaluation methodologies. EPA 905/3-84-002, September 1984.

EPA. 1986. Office of Federal Activities, Internal Report. August 1986, Washington, DC. 12 pp.

PART II
MODEL SYSTEMS

NORTHERN NATURAL WETLAND WATER TREATMENT SYSTEMS

R. H. Kadlec
Wetlands Ecosystem Research Group
Department of Chemical Engineering
The University of Michigan
Ann Arbor, Michigan 48109-2136

ABSTRACT

The performance of northern natural wetlands in the treatment of secondary municipal wastewater is described. Results from nine systems are compared to the Houghton Lake system, which is presented in greater detail. The hydrology of these systems is shown to be a controlling factor in operation, although wastewater need not seriously disrupt the water regime. Water quality is improved by passage through the wetland, but some mechanisms are temporary. Areal requirements are site specific, and increase with time. Winter operation is possible, but at a reduced level, since mechanisms of water and pollutant transport change considerably from summer. Sediments are filtered by the wetlands, but also generated by microorganisms. Biomass increases several-fold, and changes in species composition, usually to cattail-dominant. Animal species composition also changes, and usually becomes less diverse.

Keywords: Wetland treatment, nutrient removal, water quality, vegetation, animals.

INTRODUCTION

Natural wetlands have been used intentionally for wastewater polishing in northern North America for the past decade. Most have not been comprehensively studied, but some performance trends are emerging. Water quality improvement is achieved for N, suspended solids and BOD; and at least some P is removed. The hydrologic and nutrient effects are significant, resulting in alteration of the wetland. Winter operation is less common, and less effective than summer operation. The cost effectiveness of this treatment system warrants the careful consideration of both positive and negative aspects.

ISBN 0-941463-00-1

SYSTEM DESCRIPTION

The Houghton Lake wetland wastewater treatment system has been described in some detail elsewhere (Kadlec, 1979); only a summary is given here. Research at the wetland from 1971-1974, prior to discharge of wastewater, provided background data on natural circumstances. In 1973 and 1974, plot fertilization studies were conducted, followed by pilot scale wastewater irrigation in 1975, 1976 and 1977 (360 m^3 d^{-1}). The full scale (10,000 m^3 d^{-1}) system was constructed and placed in operation in 1978, and has run successfully since.

The community of Houghton Lake, located in the central lower peninsula of Michigan, has a seasonally variable population, averaging approximately 5000. A sewage treatment plant was built in the early 1970's to protect the large shallow recreational lake. Wastewater from this residential community is collected and transported to two aerated lagoons, which provide initial treatment. Effluent is then stored in a 12 ha pond for summer disposal to the 700 ha peatland. Provision for chlorination is available, but not presently in use because of low levels of fecal coliform indicator organisms.

Wastewater from this pond is pumped through a 30 cm diameter underground force line to the edge of the Porter Ranch peatland. There the transfer line surfaces and runs along a raised platform for a distance of 800 m to the discharge area in the wetland. The wastewater may there be split between two halves of the discharge pipe which runs 500 m in each direction. The water is distributed across the width of the peatland through small gated openings in the discharge pipe. Each of the 100 gates discharge approximately 100 m^3 d^{-1} under typical conditions and the water spreads slowly over the peatland. The branches are not used equally, depending on operational goals, but distribution has been about equal on average over nine years.

The peatland irrigation site originally supported two distinct vegetation types. The sedge-willow community included predominantly sedges (*Carex* spp.) and willows (*Salix* spp.). The second community was leatherleaf-bog birch, consisting of mostly *Chamaedaphne calyculata* (L.) Moench and *Betula pumila* L., respectively. Standing water was present at most times throughout most years, with lower levels in late summer (Richardson et al., 1976). Soil in the sedge-willow community is 1 to 2 m of a highly decomposed sedge peat, while in the leatherleaf-bog birch there is 2 to 5 m of medium decomposition sphagnum peat.

Small, natural water inflows occur on the north and east margins of the wetland. Overland flow proceeds from northeast down a 0.02% gradient to a stream outlet (Deadhorse Dam) and beaver dam seepage outflow (Beaver Creek), both located 3 km from the discharge. Wastewater adds to the surface sheet flow.

The cost of construction was $397,900 and operation of the wetland portion of the system costs $12,600 per year. It should be noted that the dechlorination pond has proven unnecessary, and thus the 1978 construction cost could have been $206,100. Similarly, operating costs are inflated by a research cost, unique to wetland systems. The current balance of operating cost is $2,600 per year. However, maintenance of the wetland structures is soon expected, at projected costs of 2 to 3 dollars per m of distribution pipe.

WATER MOVEMENT

The hydrology of the Houghton Lake wetland is described in detail by Hammer and Kadlec (1986) and Kadlec (1986a). This wetland is sealed underneath by an impervious clay layer (Haag, 1979). Water movement is by overland flow through a complete vegetative cover. Spring runoff from the surrounding watershed is important in some years, but there are no significant watershed inputs during the summer. Rainfall and evapotranspiration are normally about equal during the summer months, although evaporative losses are a function of cover type (Kadlec et al., 1986). Outflow exists at two locations, subject to the control of a beaver dam and of a man-made dam.

Overland flow has been found to be channelized on a local basis, with only about 15% of the surface water sheet being in motion. Hummocks and depressions form sinuous channels, and deer create walking-trail channels both parallel and inclined to the flow direction. The water sheet is relatively flat, with the storage volume exceeding the flow volume. Thus, the nominal residence time is several times higher than actual.

The functional dependence of water velocity on depth and gradient at this site has been determined (Kadlec et al., 1981). Flow rate depends on the square of the depth and on the gradient. As a result, the wetland is strongly resistant to large water depth increase. The coefficient is dependent on vegetation density (Kadlec, 1986a). Lateral underground flow is not significant for this peat soil, except possibly during dry conditions, when capillary wicking can occur.

The water depth is uniform during the summer irrigation season (Figure 1). But, on closer examination, complicated flow phenomena are found to be present. A pump shut-off can result in three different simultaneous flow directions.

Because of the dynamic nature of flows and depths, and distance variability, a complicated water budget equation is needed. The required information includes precipitation, evapotranspiration, pumped additions, inflows, storage proposities, degree of channelization, a friction law, and boundary conditions.

WATER QUALITY

Many aspects of the Houghton Lake system performance were reported by Kadlec and Hammer (1984). A brief reiteration and update follows.

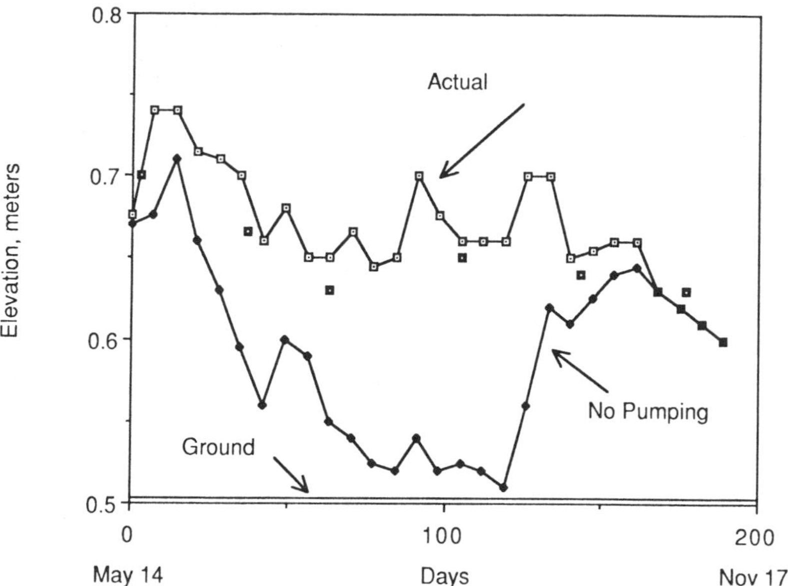

FIGURE 1. Water elevation at 250 m from discharge, Houghton Lake 1983. Solid squares represent data; the actual and no-pumping points are calculated from a water budget.

Transect data collected in 1985 is representative of water chemistry under steady irrigation conditions. Variations of TDP concentrations occur with downgradient distance from the pipeline (Figure 2). Profiles obtained from similar transect samples during previous years are also shown for comparison. A P concentration front has advanced over the years. This phenomena may be due to saturation of the fast mechanisms for nutrient immobilization, such as physical adsorption and algal uptake. A similar N front is apparent. A lesser backgradient movement of nutrients was observed.

The disappearance of the pollutants in the wetland raises questions of their ultimate fate. Using a nutrient balance approach, a greatly simplified model of wastewater/wetland interactions has been presented elsewhere (Hammer and Kadlec, 1986). In this model, the removal of dissolved nutrients from surface waters is considered to be a two step process--consisting of delivery and consumption. Delivery is accomplished by convective mass transfer within surface waters or by downward flow due to water infiltration. Consumption occurs principally at the surfaces of the soil, litter, plant stems and the algal mat. Four principal processes, biomass expansion, adsorption on peat solids, soil building, and microbial activity, collectively provide the consumption mechanisms. Adsorption will reach an equilibrium in the upper soil horizons, reducing the average areal uptake rate.

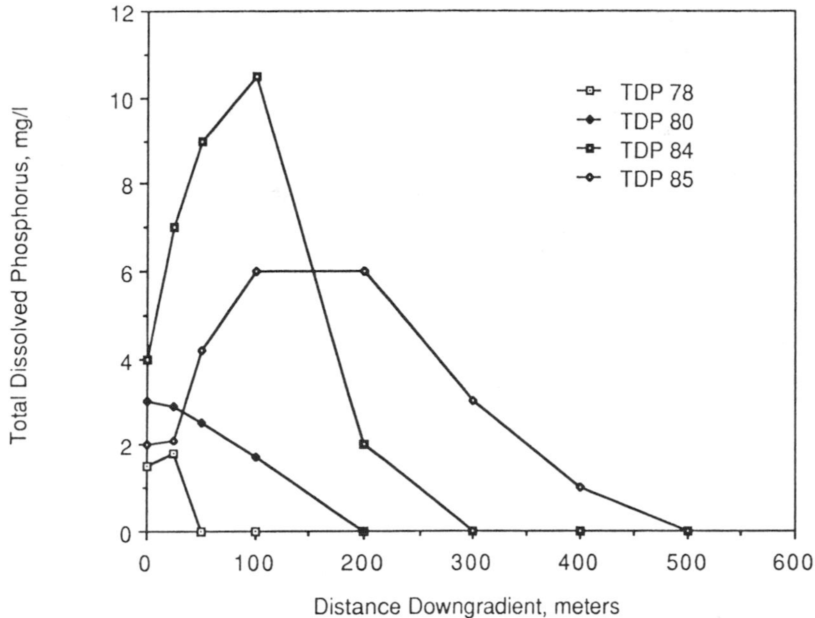

FIGURE 2. Phosphorus concentration profiles parallel to flow, Houghton Lake.

Similarly, biomass expansion, which offers a sink for nutrients, will also reach a saturation condition, when the release of nutrients due to biomass decay offsets any uptake in new growth. Woody biomass production allows longer immobilization of nutrients and constitutes a relatively permanent removal mechanism. Soil production represents a long-term removal process, but is quite slow.

Thus, two treatment zones will exist in an older wetland system. In the vicinity of the wastewater discharge a saturated region will exist. Here component removal rates will be quite slow, comprised of the uptake rates due to 1) adsorption deep in the soil column, 2) incorporation of material into new soil and woody plants, and 3) microbial release of gases to the atmosphere. Outside this saturated region, surface water concentrations of wastewater components will drop exponentially with distance. In this latter zone of rapid removal, it is the transport of dissolved components through the water sheet and uptake by microflora and microfauna which limits the overall rate. The amount of wetland area needed for this zone of rapid removal will be determined by mass transfer and microbiological considerations, and for constant operating conditions (i.e., depth, velocity, microbial populations, etc.), will not change. In the saturated zone, removal of nutrients will continue at a rate which is slow but insensitive to modest changes in water flow or depth. The expansion of this saturated region will continue until the area is sufficient to allow all incoming wastewater components to be removed by infiltration flows, incorporation into new soil or woody biomass, or release to the atmosphere. If the available area is less than that required for total retention of pollutants, breakthrough will occur. Then only a portion of the wastewater components fed to the wetland will be retained and the collection efficiency will drop sharply. This is illustrated in Figure 3, for the Bellaire wetland (Kadlec, 1985).

The dissolved O_2 status of the wetland in the irrigation area is erratic. Levels are depressed to about 1 mg L^{-1} peak on some dates, but on other dates, the discharge area is O_2-rich, about 14 mg L^{-1}. Most often, conditions are anoxic but not anaerobic. The most probable cause is the thick duckweed mat, which is a barrier to O_2 transfer and to photosynthesis in the water column.

The background BOD of this wetland is about 1.5 mg L^{-1}, and that of the wastewater is about 13 mg L^{-1}. Removal to background occurs within the first 400 m of water travel.

Ten northern sites have been compared in terms of water quality (Table 1). Distance versus water quality data from either the reference given or the primary data base were used to estimate the distance at which the level of a pollutant reached one-half the discharge value. This is the 'half-distance' for the site. This distance is expected to vary with depth, flow rate, channelization, micro populations, and other site-specific

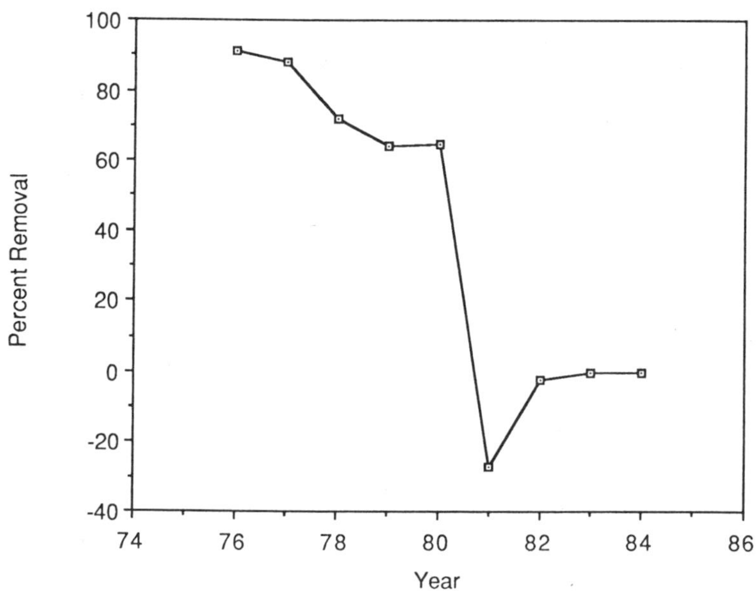

FIGURE 3. Phosphorus removal in the Bellaire wetland.

factors. An order of magnitude spread in values occurs with the 'engineered' sites having low values and the old, point discharge sites having high values (Table 1).

The performance of these sites was compared for NH_4^+-N, total P and BOD removals (Figure 4). Percent remaining is plotted versus a scaled distance, obtained by dividing distance by half-distance. Not all data are shown; only a few representative points for each site. There is of course still scatter in the data, because of high intra-site variability. At Houghton Lake, replicate samples show standard deviations of one-third to one-half the mean. Two facts emerge from this comparison: a single line appears to represent the general behavior of N, P and BOD; and that is a straight line on semi-log coordinates. The later implies a first order removal process, with the rate proportional to concentration.

There are, however, several data points at the 100% level at several distances, which implies that removal mechanisms have been saturated in that zone. Thus the Kincheloe site shows no P removal, and a later Bellaire data set would not either.

The wetland is an active participant in S cycling. Accordingly, all compartments, inputs and outputs were measured for S content. There is clear evidence of altered S cycling in the discharge zone, with removal occurring from the water within 400 m. Extra S in the discharge area is the result of irrigation, accumulated over the project history.

The overall (regulatory) performance of the Houghton Lake system is given in Table 2. Background data from pre-irrigation was used to set target regulatory values at an internal distance of 800 m, thus providing a safety factor of 4 on distance. This internal point is the 'outflow' in Table 2. It is noteworthy that most parameters have wetland values in the discharge zone which are higher than the entering wastewater. The process of

TABLE 1. Natural wastewater treatment sites in the northern environment. Estimated half distances are given.

	Meters	Comments	Reference
Drummond, WI	60	Distribution pipe	Shaw and Reinecke, 1983
Bellaire, WI	80	Distribution pipe	Kadlec, 1985
Houghton Lake, MI	90	Distribution pipe	Kadlec, 1986b
Listowel, Ont.	140	Constructed	Black et al., 1981
Fontanges, Que.	220	Point discharge	Dubuc et al., 1986
Seneca, NY	300	Old	Bouwkamp et al., 1984
Great Meadows, MA	340	Old	Yonika et al., 1979
Kincheloe, MI	400	Point discharge	Kadlec and Bevis, 1981
Hay River, NWT	600	Point discharge	Hartland-Rowe and Wright, 1975
Brillion, WI	840	Old	Fetter et al., 1978

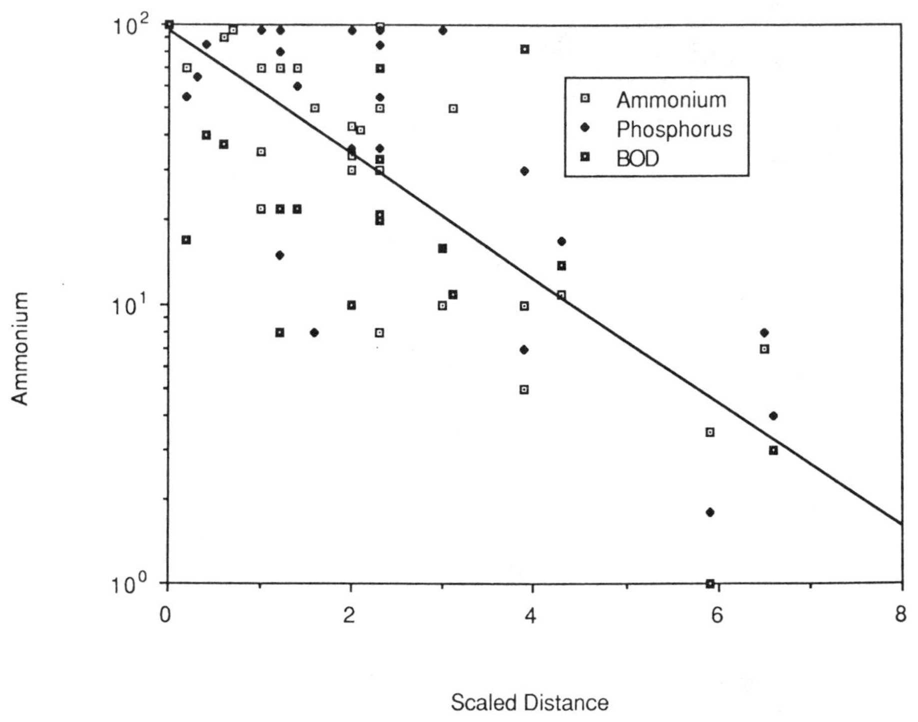

FIGURE 4. Nutrient removal versus distance, selected data points from 10 wetland systems.

TABLE 2. Overall water quality performance of the Houghton Lake system.

Parameter	Waste-water	Peak in wetland	Wetland "outflow"	Permit target	Back-ground
	mg L^{-1}				
Total Dissolved P	4	12	0.08	0.15	0.05
Ammonium N	8	9	0.13	3.0	0.70
BOD	13	12	5.0	--	--
Suspended Solids	20	40	5.0	--	--
Sulfate Sulfur	8	25	1.0	--	--
Chloride	100	160	95.0	--	28.0

evaporation concentrates inactive species such as chloride, and biologically active substances are amplified by internal cycling.

WINTER

The November freeze-up (earlier further north) causes many wetland processes to slow or stop The Houghton Lake system does not operate a discharge in the winter, but other sites have done so. The Listowel (Black et al., 1981; Reed et al., 1984; and Herskowitz and Black, 1986) and Great Meadows (Yonika et. al., 1979) sites both show water quality improvement in winter, as does Kincheloe (Kadlec and Bevis, 1981). Phosphorus removal continues in winter even at Hay River.

Even in the absence of a discharge, winter still causes alteration of water quality. Nutrient levels decrease under the ice compared to summer values, but remain higher than background. Ice and water have about the same nutrient concentrations, but biologically inactive solutes such as chloride partition selectively to the water.

Typically, wetland vegetation traps a good deal of snow, which insulates the water sheet and allows only thin ice to form. Flow can continue under the ice. If there is sufficient resistance under the ice, an over-ice flow may occur, which carries high nutrient waters slightly downgradient before refreezing (Kadlec, 1984). Spring melt waters usually run off with little communication with under-ice water. Those systems with a winter discharge have not had 'freeze-up' problems of pipes and structures.

SEDIMENTS

The overall performance of natural systems for suspended solids removal has traditionally been reported in terms of inputs, outputs, and percent removal. In general, wetlands discharge low amounts of solids in summer, more in winter. However, these input-output data miss almost all of the solids-related phenomena.

Internal measurements of vertical sediment flux show a very large cycle of sedimentation and resuspension occurring in the irrigation zone at Houghton Lake (Kadlec, 1986, Univ. of Michigan, unpublished results). The dry weight depositing is comparable to leaf litterfall. The source of these sediments is the detritus from invertebrates and other microflora and microfauna, created mostly within the wetland. A mass balance derived from field data (Figure 5) shows that the influence of wastewater solids is minimal. However, the influence of wastewater nutrients is very large, since it stimulates a ten-fold increase in suspendable solids generation in the discharge zone.

Detailed mass balances may be used to estimate the fate of wastewater incoming solids when subjected to the processes of settling, filtration, and resuspension, coupled with lateral transport. This may in total be termed sloughing, and occurs at velocities of 1 to 2 m d^{-1} at Houghton Lake. The inferred location of these entering wastewater solids remains close to the discharge. Thus the output solids from the wetland are currently

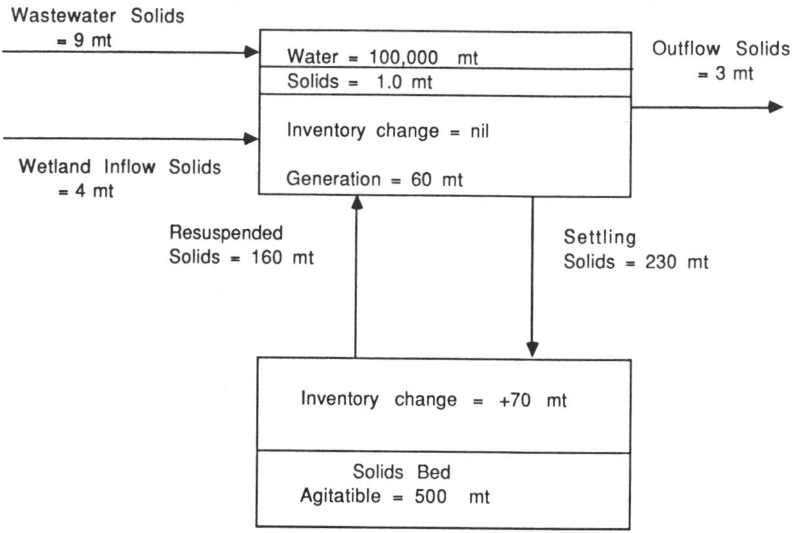

FIGURE 5. Estimated solids budget for the Houghton Lake wetland irrigation zone, May through August, 90 ha zone.

of different origin than input solids, and percent removals based on contemporaneous measurements are meaningless.

VEGETATION RESPONSE

The details of the Houghton Lake vegetation response may be found in Kadlec (1986c). Response of the peatland vegetation to repeated additions of treated wastewater has been slow but large. Some of the initial changes have not been sustained in later years. All abundant species have been affected by the discharge.

Algal biomass varies with season, distance, and duration of discharge. The amounts of chlorophyll and pheophytin in the surface water near the discharge are orders of magnitude higher than controls. Similar results have been updated by Sanders and Kuenzler (1979). This creates a large, semi-mobile nutrient sink, because these plants are first in line for the added nutrients.

A large Lemna biomass, created by nutrient additions, has also been reported elsewhere (Price, 1975). The availability of open water with little wind reach, together with N and P, combine to encourage this species. The thickness of the duckweed mat at Houghton Lake is unusual. The presence of living plants deep in the mat indicates abnormal growth conditions. The reproductive capacity of this plant gives it the second-best advantage in the short term. In unshaded areas, its presence is a good visual indicator of high nutrient levels in the surface water. This mat probably causes the erratic O_2 status of the surface water sheet. It also acts as a substrate for periphyton, a filter for microorganism detritus, and as a substrate for cattail seedlings.

The sedge-willow cover type originally occupied about 50% of the area near the discharge line. The ecosystem in the vicinity of the discharge has been drastically altered due to the wastewater addition. The first response was an enhancement of the sedge to standing crops which were many times the background level (Figure 6). This was an unstable situation, evidenced by subsequent large oscillations in the biomass of this species.

The cattail cover type did not exist in enough abundance (1.76% of the peatland area) to warrant study in pre-irrigation years, but was present in many locations (17% of all test plots) (Wentz, 1976). The expected growth patterns are present for living and standing dead aboveground material, with a much larger peak standing crop in the pipeline area (Figure 6). The 1983 relative low standing crop was attributable to muskrat activity, which resulted in large herbivory losses. There is also a backgradient enhancement of growth, including more roots, due to hydrological effects. The standing dead varies in the expected manner, with high end-of-season values.

Root biomass is not as heavily developed in the irrigation area. This is presumably due to two factors: the newness of the irrigation area roots and rhizomes, and the availability of

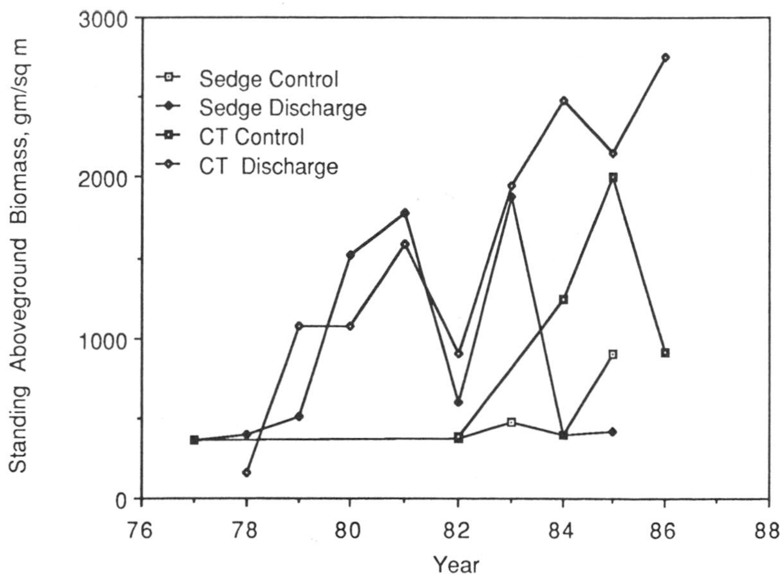

FIGURE 6. Aboveground biomass in sedge and cattail areas discharge and control zones, Houghton Lake.

nutrients. The amount of cattail litter is variable, but generally much larger in the irrigation area. The winter season brings about a locally very thick mat of fallen plant parts, compared to backgradient locations. The other northern sites display very similar increases in cattail biomass.

The woody shrubs were all able to utilize the added nutrients, and to survive several years of altered water regime. The alder (Alnus spp.) communities of the peatland edges are flourishing and expanding, but it is probable that the woody shrubs cannot permanently survive the altered water regime, as evidenced by increased mortality. The death of the aspen island communities was anticipated, since that species cannot tolerate continued inundation (Teskey and Hinckley, 1978). The damage to trees on the edges of the peatland was not foreseen. It is apparent that relatively minor sustained increases in water depth were enough to kill these trees in previously marginal habitat.

Other instances of tree mortality due to water additions have been observed. Apparent drowning of spruce (Picea spp.) at the Kincheloe, Michigan wetland (Kadlec and Bevis, 1981), was probably due to beaver dams and wastewater addition. Several tree species at the Roscommon, Michigan wetland have not survived the seasonal addition of seepage bed effluent (Williams, 1985). Root zone erosion, followed by uprooting, was a result of lagoon effluent irrigation at Bellaire, Michigan (Kadlec, 1985).

Both color and color infrared aerial photographs reveal the general patterns of influence of the wastewater discharge. The infrared reflectance of the wetland shows the more dramatically altered portions of the wetland. Regions of increased biomass and chlorophyll--and generally better health status of the upper canopy--show clearly on color infrared. The measured areas are shown as a time progression in Figure 7.

The species composition within this affected area is changing with each year. In general terms, cattail areas are spreading; and cattail (Typha spp.) is intruding into other communities. In the leatherleaf-bog birch community, grasses (primarily Calamagrostis canadensis) are the intruders, bog birch (Betula pumila) is increasing in biomass but decreasing in stem density. In the sedge-willow community, grasses and duckweed (Lemna spp.) have intruded. Some root-mat floating has occurred there. Immediately adjacent to the discharge duckweed mats are several cm thick.

All of the added nutrients were retained in the wetland. The fate of these nutrients is a complicated question, which has been addressed elsewhere (Hammer and Kadlec, 1986). The nutrient requirements for the aboveground peak standing crops are representative of this transient (saturable) sink. The entire amount of N added in one year would be found in 10 ha of aboveground cattail or sedge community vegetation increase if no other mechanisms were operative. The entire amount of P added would be found in 60 ha of aboveground cattail or sedge community

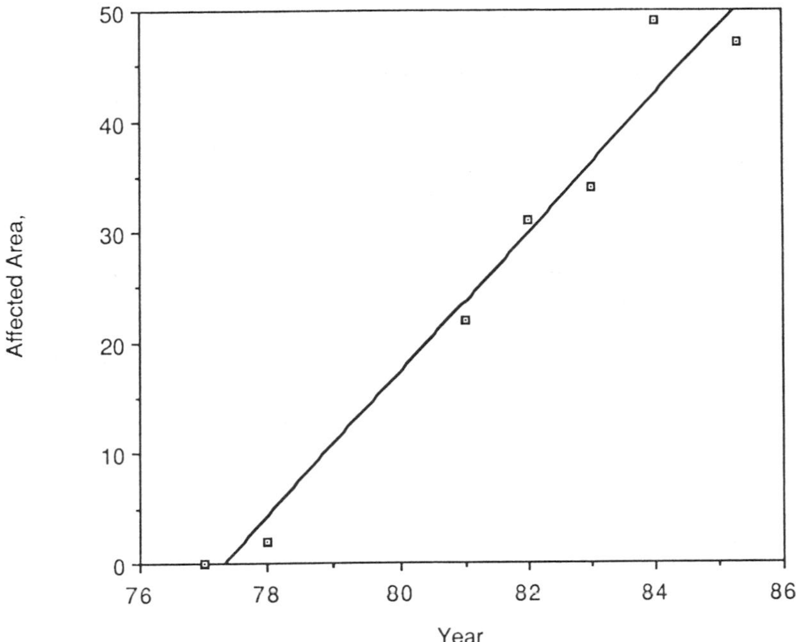

FIGURE 7. Affected area expansion with time. Houghton Lake, from color IR photos.

vegetation if no other mechanisms were operative. The storage capacity in the new cattail community was approximately triple that for the original sedge community. Other temporary, saturable sinks are present in the expanded woody shrubs, duckweed, and root structures. The combination of all the physical and biological sinks was adequate to absorb all the added nutrients, but with an annual increase in the required wetland area. The ultimate area needed to absorb added nutrients depends on the non-vegetative processes of sorption, burial, and gasification.

ANIMALS

This is perhaps the least studied aspect of wetland wastewater treatment systems. Results from Houghton Lake are presented in a series of reports, including Rabe and Rabe (1985). A brief summary is given here.

Diversity of the microflora and microfauna decrease with the addition of wastewater. This is true for zooplankton at Hay River, and for the invertebrate communities at Houghton Lake. Amphibian species composition remains the same, with shifts in relative abundance. Fish populations are depressed near the discharge, but enhanced elsewhere with shifts in relative abundance. This is likely the result of a deeper water regime, in areas of no nutrient impact.

Small mammal abundance and diversity have increased near the discharge area. Meadow voles, water shrews and meadow jumping mice are all more abundant there. This is in contrast to Seneca Lakes, where small mammals are reported to be virtually absent (Bouwkamp, 1984).

Bird species composition and abundance is also changing. Swamp sparrows and yellow throats were the dominant pre-irrigation species. A shift to redwing blackbirds, sora and Virginia rails, ducks and herons has occurred, with impressive populations developing. Hundreds of rails utilized the wetland irrigation area in 1984 (Rabe and Rabe, 1985). As a result, duck hunting is a new wetland use.

Large mammal patterns are also changing. Muskrats have increased, and trapping is a new wetland use. Deer continue to frequent the peatland, and deer hunting there continues. Beavers continue to use the wetland fringes. The first bobcat sighting occurred in 1986.

Older systems, such as Kincheloe, do not have similar species numbers. Cover type there is all cattail-lemna, with few internal boundaries or open areas. Such conditions are not conducive to species richness.

SUMMARY

Natural wetlands can provide advanced wastewater treatment in the northern environment. The Houghton Lake system continues to work well, and is qualitatively comparable to other northern sites. Many wetland values are altered, some negatively and some positively. Such systems are cheaper to build and operate than other alternatives if low cost land is available. Flow distribution can be a problem in a natural wetland, as can short residence times. Some mechanisms for pollutant removal can be saturated, while others continue indefinitely. Wetlands can produce some pollutants, such as sediments and dissolved organics. Winter operation is possible, but less effective than summer. Biomass increases several-fold, with a shift to duckweed and cattail. Animal species composition changes, and diversity goes down. A complicated combination of land availability, economics, public opinion, wildlife values, and treatment alternatives will determine the desirability of such a system in a given setting.

REFERENCES

Black, S. A., I. Wile, and G. Miller. 1981. Sewage effluent treatment in an artificial wetland. Paper at WPCF Conference, Detroit, MI.

Bouwkamp, C. A., T. A. Gallagher, and T. Battaglia. 1984. Innovative wetlands wastewater treatment project two year evaluation, Seneca Army Depot, New York. p. 947-961. In Proceedings of the Water Reuse Symposium III, San Diego, CA.

Dubuc, Y., P. Janneteau, R. Labonte, C. Roy, and F. Briere. 1986. Domestic wastewater treatment by peatlands in a northern climate: A water quality study. Water Res. Bul. V22, p. 297-303.

Fetter, C. W., Jr., W. E. Sloey, and F. L. Spangler. 1978. Use of a natural marsh for wastewater polishing. J. Water Pollut. Control Fed., Feb. 1978, p. 290-307.

Haag, R. D., Jr. 1979. The hydrogeology of the Houghton (Lake) Wetland. M.S. Thesis, The University of Michigan, Ann Arbor.

Hammer, D. E., and R. H. Kadlec. 1986. A model for wetland surface water dynamics. Water Resources Research, accepted.

Hartland-Rowe, R., and P. B. Wright. 1975. Effects of sewage effluent on a swampland stream. Verh. Int. Ver. Limnol. 19:1575.

Herskowitz, J., and S. A. Black. 1986. Listowel artificial marsh project. In K. R. Reddy and W. H. Smith (ed.) Aquatic Plants for Water Treatment and Resource Recovery. Magnolia Publishing, Inc., Orlando, FL.

Kadlec, R. H. 1979. Wetland tertiary treatment at Houghton Lake, Michigan. In R. K. Bastian and S. C. Reed (ed.) Proc. of the Seminar on Aquaculture Systems for Wastewater Treatment. USEPA Publication No. MCD-67.

Kadlec, R. H. 1984. Freezing-induced vertical solute movement in peat. Seventh International Peat Congress Proceedings, Dublin, Ireland. 4:248-257.

Kadlec, R. H. 1985. The Bellaire Wetland: Wastewater alteration and recovery. Wetlands 3:44-63.

Kadlec, R. H. 1986a. The hydrodynamics of wetland water treatment systems. In K. R. Reddy and W. H. Smith (ed.) Aquatic Plants for Water Treatment and Resource Recovery. Magnolia Publishing, Inc., Orlando, FL.

Kadlec, R. H. 1986b. Wetland utilization for management of community wastewater. 1985 Operations Summary. WERG Internal Report.

Kadlec, R. H. 1986c. Wetlands and wastewater: Vegetation response. Proc. SREL Wetlands Meeting, Charleston, SC.

Kadlec, R. H., and D. E. Hammer. 1984. Wastewater renovation in wetlands: Six years at Houghton Lake. p. 596-616. In Proc. of the Water Reuse Symposium III. San Diego, CA.

Kadlec, R. H., and D. E. Hammer. 1986. Modeling nutrient behavior in wetlands. Ecol. Modeling (accepted for publication).

Kadlec, R. H., and F. B. Bevis. 1981. The condition and effectiveness of a wetland after 20 years of wastewater. Presented at the Water Pollution Control Federation Meeting, Detroit, MI.

Kadlec, R. H., R. B. Williams, and R. D. Scheffe. 1986. Evaporation and transpiration in wetlands in temperate and acid climates. Proc. Int. Conf. on Wetlands, Charleston, SC.

Kadlec, R. H., D. E. Hammer, I-S. Nam, and J. O. Wilkes. 1981. The hydrology of overland flow in wetlands. Chemical Engineering Communications 9:331-344.

Price, D. 1975. The role of duckweed in recycling sewage effluent in a cypress swamp. In H. T. Odum, K. C. Ewel, and M. K. Johnston (ed.) Cypress Wetlands for Water Management, Recycling and Conservation. Univ. of Florida, Center for Wetlands.

Rabe, M. L., and D. L. Rabe. 1985. Impact of wastewater discharge upon a northern Michigan wetland wildlife community. Report to HLSA and MDNR.

Reed, S., R. Bastian, S. Black, and R. Khettry. 1984. Wetlands for wastewater treatment in cold climates. p. 962-972. In Proc. of the Water Reuse Symposium III, San Diego, CA.

Richardson, C. J., J. A. Kadlec, W. A. Wentz, J. P. M. Chemie, and R. H. Kadlec. 1976. Background ecology and the effects of nutrient additions on a central Michigan wetland. p. 34-42. In M. W. LeFor, W. C. Kennard, and T. B. Helfgott (ed.) Proc. of the Third Wetland Conference. Institute of Water Resources, The Univ. of Connecticut. Report No. 26.

Sanders, J. G., and E. F. Kuenzler. 1979. Phytoplankton population dynamics and productivity in a sewage-enriched tidal creek in North Carolina. Estuaries 2:87-96.

Shaw, B. H., and L. Reinecke. 1983. Chemistry and ecology of an acid bog receiving municipal wastewater at Drummond, Wisconsin. Report to USFWS, U. Wis. Stevens Point.

Teskey, R. O., and T. M. Hinckley. 1978. Impact of water level changes on woody riparian and wetland communities. Vol. 4. Eastern deciduous forest region. FWS/OBS-78/87, U. S. Fish and Wildlife Service, Biological Services Program, Columbia, Missouri.

Wentz, W. A. 1976. Growth and production of Carex subjected to simulated sewage effluents. p. 24-26. In J. A. Kadlec, R. H. Kadlec and C. J. Richardson (ed.) The Effects of Sewage Effluent on Wetland Ecosystems. Report to NSF.

Williams, D. 1985. Aerial photographics analysis of wastewater treatment plant impacts wetlands. USEPA Report TS-AMD-83122/83531.

Yonika, D., D. Lowry, G. Hollands, W. Mulica, G. Smith, and S. Bigelow. 1979. Feasibility study of wetland disposal of wastewater treatment plant effluent. Final Report to the Commonwealth of Massachusetts Water Resources Commission, Division of Water Pollution Control. Research Project #78-04. 134 p.

NATURAL WETLANDS - SOUTHERN ENVIRONMENT: WASTEWATER TO WETLANDS, WHERE DO WE GO FROM HERE?

G. Ronnie Best
Center for Wetlands
University of Florida
Gainesville, Florida 32611

ABSTRACT

Disposal of waste products into wetlands is not a new practice. Societies have been discharging waste products into wetlands for centuries. Only recently, especially with the advent of recognizing the multifaceted values of wetlands, have we started to evaluate the effect of waste disposal into these valuable ecosystems. In fact, in the early 1970s, researchers began to assess the possibility of managing wastewater discharge to wetlands. The concept being the use, but not abuse, of wetlands for treatment of wastewater. When considered within the context of environmental effects, energy demands, and economic effects of other wastewater treatment/discharge alternatives, the low-energy wastewater treatment capacity of wetlands is in reality, especially if managed properly, an alternative well worth serious consideration. The purpose of this paper is to review wastewater-to-wetlands research conducted in the southeastern U.S., with emphasis on research in Florida. The review will include 1) an assessment of response of wetland biota to increased nutrient loading, 2) a discussion of treatment efficiencies and long-term treatment potential of wetlands and 3) management recommendations for increasing management of wetlands for wastewater treatment/discharge.

Keywords: Low-energy wastewater treatment, heavy metals, disposal, vegetation, recycling, nutrients, wetlands, wildlife.

INTRODUCTION

Actions and frequently reactions regarding environmental issues, especially at the implementation level, are generally based only on consideration of a small, related set of possible alternatives. For example, environmental and/or regulatory actions regarding what should be the broad topic of wastewater treatment/discharge may instead become focused on some specific

Aquatic Plants for Water Treatment
and Resource Recovery
K.R. Reddy and W.H. Smith (Eds.)

ISBN 0-941463-00-1

permit request, not on an equitable consideration of all possible alternatives. Although environmental policy makers generally attempt to integrate the broad concept into the rule-making process, that concept is often lost in day-to-day implementation of existing rules/policies. This paper not only discusses the alternative of wastewater treatment/discharge through wetlands, but does so within the context of comparison to other treatment/ discharge alternatives. The emphasis of the discussion relates primarily to direct and indirect effects of treatment/disposal alternatives on natural ecosystems.

A brief discussion is presented of several of the more common alternatives for treatment/discharge of wastewater. Then a brief discussion of the broad concept of wastewater treatment by wetlands in general is followed by specific examples of wastewater-to-wetlands research results in the southern environment (especially research by the Center for Wetlands in Florida). The last section attempts to transcend the current dogma of treating wastewater as a waste product, to treating wastewater, especially high quality wastewater, as a possible resource. Properly managed, this water resource can be used for restoring overly drained wetlands, and/or for creating wetlands with multifunctional roles as wastewater treatment/discharge areas as well as functional wetland wildlife habitat.

OVERVIEW OF WASTEWATER TREATMENT/DISPOSAL ALTERNATIVES

First, consider the primary components of typical secondary-treated wastewater discharged from municipal wastewater treatment facilities. At the simplest level, there are two basic components in secondary treated municipal wastewater -- the waste constituent and the medium of transport, water. Principal "waste" constituents in wastewater are nutrients (especially N and P) and total suspended solids with resultant increased biological demand (BOD), and pathogens (generally treated through chlorination or other sanitizing processes). Both the waste (especially nutrients) and water must be considered in developing treatment and/or discharge alternatives. When considering wastewater treatment/disposal alternatives, "remember everything has got to go somewhere!"

An additional item that often is not considered when evaluating wastewater treatment/discharge alternatives is the total impact of different alternatives on the environment. Direct impacts of specific treatment/disposal alternatives are often considered. However, indirect impacts, especially increase in energy consumption, generally do not enter into consideration often because these "hidden" impacts are difficult to quantify, especially at the "single" permit level. Alternatives that require an increase in energy consumption generally enter the review process only from the perspective of increase in costs, not from the perspective of indirect effects on the environment. It is this increase in demand for energy (which always translates to increased costs) that can contribute indirectly to environmental degradation of terrestrial and aquatic systems. Briefly summarized, an increase in energy demand means an increase in use of fossil (or nuclear) fuel. Some direct environmental problems caused by increased coal use include, for example, mining impacts (surface mining means degradation or loss of native habitat), acid mine drainage, increased energy use in transportation, "acid rain", CO_2 and particulate production (contributing to potential for greenhouse effect), and others. Until the cost for energy becomes "environmentally" inexpensive, indirect impacts of energy consumption must be considered when evaluating wastewater treatment/discharge alternatives.

The most common wastewater treatment/discharge alternatives are discharge to aquatic systems (rivers and lakes), deep-well injection, ocean outfall, technological advanced waste treatment (AWT) and reuse, land application, and wetlands treatment/ recycling. These alternatives are presented below with emphasis, where appropriate, on the overall effect (direct and indirect) of the alternative on functioning of natural ecosystems.

Eutrophication of aquatic systems, in part caused directly by discharge of wastewater, has lead to strict state and federal guidelines regulating wastewater discharge directly to rivers or lakes. Future wastewater disposal directly into rivers or lakes must first meet strict water quality standards where the receiving aquatic system will be used for discharge of the "water" component minus most of the "waste" in wastewater. In essence, continued degradation of aquatic systems is not acceptable. Therefore, discharge of wastewater directly into rivers and lakes is not a good alternative for wastewater disposal unless the water is advanced treated to high water quality standards.

Injection of wastewater into non-potable aquifers, salt water lenses, or discharge through ocean outfall appears on the surface to be a viable disposal alternative. However, in many places where these alternatives are practiced, especially in coastal areas, the water portion of wastewater is a valuable freshwater resource, often too valuable to simply be discarded. In addition, there are areas (e.g., Florida) where secondary or advanced-secondary treated wastewater is discharged indirectly, and in some cases, directly into freshwater aquifers. Serious problems will be faced if a mistake is made in disposing wastewater into a groundwater supply. If a mistake is made, it would be far more difficult to correct the problems in below ground than aboveground systems.

At first thought it appears as if the solution to wastewater treatment is simply a technological problem to be solved with advanced wastewater treatment facilities. And, it is true that technological solutions for advanced treatment of secondary effluent are yielding very high quality wastewater treated to the point where the water is suitable, as far as nutrient levels are concerned, for indirect reuse. But what it takes to achieve advanced secondary or tertiary effluent treatment is energy. Energy to build as well as run the advanced waste treatment facility. Energy to supply chemicals to precipitate P. Energy to dispose of the enormous amount of sludge. Add to this the problem of sludge disposal. Should it be put in landfills, spread across the landscape? After all, the sludge is simply a concentrate of the "waste" products of wastewater.

There are various methods for disposal of wastewater through land application with the more common disposal methods including spray irrigation, overland flow, and rapid infiltration basins. Although land application is generally a good alternative for wastewater disposal, there are potentially three major environmental costs that may be related to land application -- alteration of natural ecosystems, moderate-to-high energy demand and potential for increase in public health hazard.

Land application is most ideally suited for situations where the landscape has been altered, e.g. pasture, crops, golf courses, abandoned farm land, etc. In addition, it may be possible to reuse wastewater to reduce and/or replace demand for irrigation water. However, even reuse of wastewater for irrigating golf courses, parks or other municipal areas, and/or residential areas has the hidden environmental costs associated with increased use of energy, especially where considerable distances may require increased piping and pumping costs. And, finally, there is a potential for environmental health liability associated with pathogens in wastewater sprayed in areas generally accessible to the public.

Land disposal of wastewater is not, except at very low hydraulic loading rates, compatible with natural ecosystems. Since natural ecosystems generally will not process the needed or desired volume of water, the most common practice is, unfortunately, to purchase a parcel of land and alter the landscape to fit some land application disposal method (Figure 1). This results in a complete loss of all original functions, especially wildlife (plant and animal) of the natural ecosystem. For example, a common practice on upland, dry, sandy soils in Florida is to clear away natural communities and construct rapid infiltration basins or spray irrigation fields.

The question should be, "If alternatives being considered for wastewater treatment/disposal are going to involve natural ecosystems, are there natural ecosystems that can tolerate an increase in hydraulic loading, yield an increase in water quality, yet still retain all or most of their natural functions?" An additional question to be asked: "Is there a low-energy alternative for treatment/discharge/recycling of wastewater?" The answer to both of these questions is, "yes, wetlands." If properly managed within functional tolerance limits, wastewater can be effectively treated and recycled through wetlands without

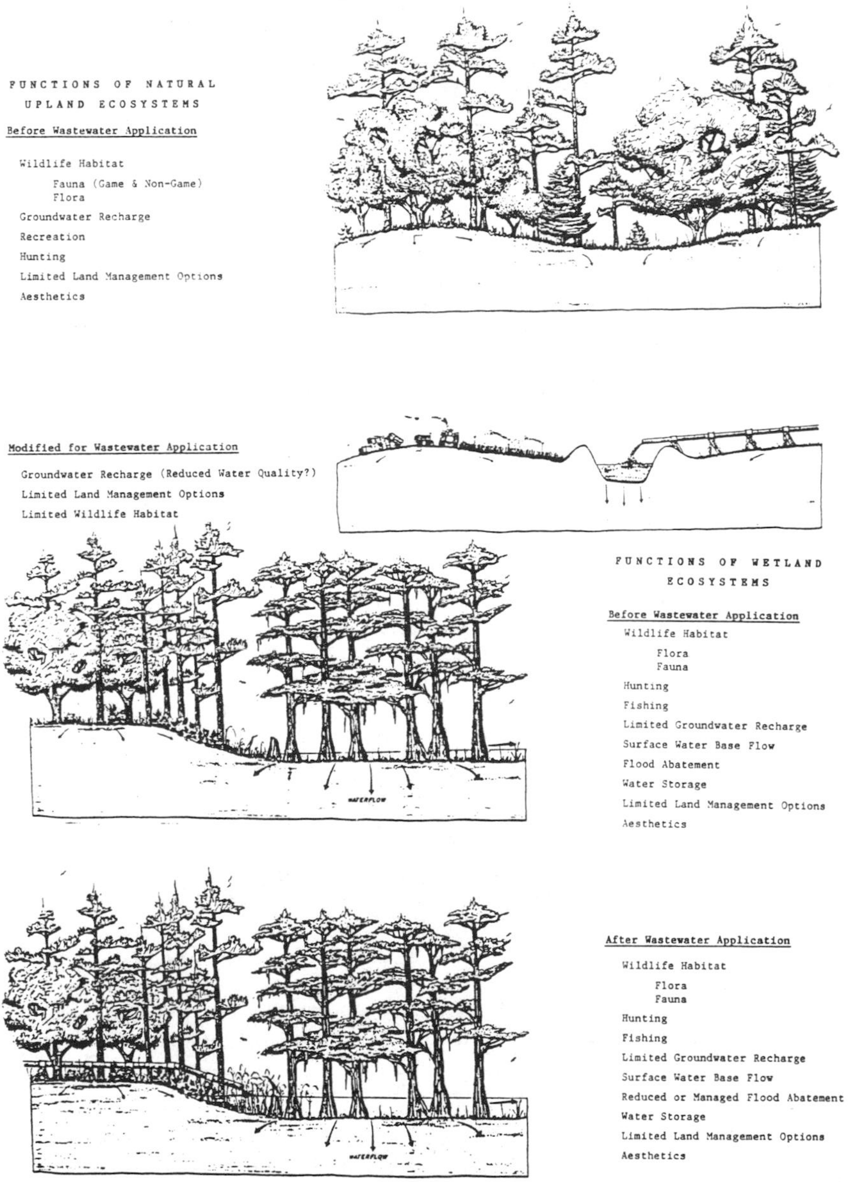

FUNCTIONS OF NATURAL UPLAND ECOSYSTEMS

Before Wastewater Application

Wildlife Habitat
- Fauna (Game & Non-Game)
- Flora

Groundwater Recharge

Recreation

Hunting

Limited Land Management Options

Aesthetics

Modified for Wastewater Application

Groundwater Recharge (Reduced Water Quality?)

Limited Land Management Options

Limited Wildlife Habitat

FUNCTIONS OF WETLAND ECOSYSTEMS

Before Wastewater Application

Wildlife Habitat
- Flora
- Fauna

Hunting

Fishing

Limited Groundwater Recharge

Surface Water Base Flow

Flood Abatement

Water Storage

Limited Land Management Options

Aesthetics

After Wastewater Application

Wildlife Habitat
- Flora
- Fauna

Hunting

Fishing

Limited Groundwater Recharge

Surface Water Base Flow

Reduced or Managed Flood Abatement

Water Storage

Limited Land Management Options

Aesthetics

FIGURE 1. Alterations of functions of natural ecosystems used for wastewater treatment and recycling.

adversely affecting type, nature, function, or flora and fauna of the wetland (Figure 1). And, if federal and state water quality standards are applied to waters exiting the wetland, rather than to waters entering wetlands, reasonable water quality standards could be met.

WETLANDS - A LOW ENERGY ALTERNATIVE FOR WASTEWATER TREATMENT AND RECYCLING

Although wetlands, like aquatic systems, have been used for many years for disposal of wastewater, the idea of properly managing wetlands for treatment and discharge of wastewater is a relatively new concept. In the late 1960's, H. T. Odum proposed and directed research studying the fate of wastewater discharged in a North Carolina estuary (Copeland et al., 1972; Odum, 1985). Concepts proposed in this original wastewater-to-wetlands study lead to Rockefeller Foundation, National Science Foundation and Environmental Protection Agency funding in the early to mid-seventies for research assessing the utility of this new concept of low energy wastewater treatment by wetlands. Research focused on both ecological and water quality aspects of the wastewater-to-wetlands alternative (Odum et al., 1974,1975a,b,1976,1978,1980; Richardson and Marshall, 1986; Richardson et al., 1975,1976,1978; Tilton et al., 1976,1977; Valiela and Vince, 1976; Kadlec et al., 1977,1979; Tilton and Kadlec, 1979; Kadlec and Tilton, 1979; Ewel and Odum, 1984). Over the last twenty years more than 1,100 articles have been published dealing wholly or partly, with some aspect of wastewater-to-wetlands (an annotated bibliography published in 1984 listed 1,097 publications) (EPA, 1984). These publications cover the gamut of research from "absorption" to "zooplankton". Several excellent overviews of the wastewater-to-wetlands concept from national and regional perspectives have been published (e.g., Kadlec and Tilton, 1979; Ewel and Odum, 1984; Richardson and Marshall, 1986).

Much of the wealth of information regarding wastewater-to-wetlands has been generated by research conducted at the Center for Wetlands, University of Florida, again under initial leadership and direction of H. T. Odum. Much of the original "classical" wetlands research in the South is published in Cypress Swamps (Ewel and Odum, ed., 1984). The remainder of this article will present a brief overview of results of selected wastewater-to-wetlands case studies conducted in Florida by the Center for Wetlands.

Nutrients

Potential for use of isolated cypress wetlands (cypress domes), common in Florida, for advance treatment of wastewater was studied for several years (Odum et al., 1974,1975a,b,1976,1978, 1980; Ewel and Odum, 1984). In the study, "typical" secondary treated wastewater (treatment through package plant and holding pond) was applied for five years to the cypress wetland at a rate of 2.5 cm wk^{-1}. Outflow from the cypress dome wetland was restricted to groundwater flow except at rare high-water periods when flooding occurred in adjacent pine flatwoods is possible. Nitrogen removal efficiency during the five year study was 92% (Table 1). Phosphorus was reduced from about 8 mg L^{-1} in effluent to less than 0.5 mg L^{-1} in groundwater (Dierberg and Brezonik, 1983b). Even surface water within the wetland from the center (point of application) to edge decreased in total N by 33-44% and P by 29-31% indicating that even for wetlands without surface outflow, water quality can be enhanced within the system. Dierberg and Brezonik (1983b) concluded that "...effectiveness of cypress domes in removing high percentages (greater than 90%) of organic matter, nutrients and minerals is more obvious when concentrations of these substances in the shallow water table aquifer below the sewage-enriched domes are examined. Concentrations of these parameters in shallow wells in and around the sewage domes were at background levels throughout the (five year) study." They went on to conclude that even after almost two years after cessation of sewage inputs to the cypress domes "...parameters associated with organic matter (BOD) and with the reducing environment of the sewage-enriched domes ... displayed a rapid return to background levels."

Similar removal efficiencies were observed in another wetland system near Wildwood, Florida, that had been receiving for over 20 years about 570 m^3 d^{-1} advanced primary-treated wastewater. The wetland system (size about 200 ha) consisted of a small marsh that flowed into two connecting mixed hardwood forest wetlands. Even after 20 years of wastewater inflow, 96-98% of the ammonia was still being removed. Nitrogen removal ranged from 75 to 85%; P removal averaged 87% (Table 1) (Boyt et al., 1977). During the study, the high nutrient wastewater was contained within about 3% of the total wetland area.

An experiment was conducted in a freshwater marsh near Clermont, Florida (Zoltek et al., 1979; Dolan et al., 1981), to test fate and effect on P dynamics of secondarily treated effluent applied at different loading rates. The marsh was dominated by rooted emergent herbaceous macrophytes (principally _Sagittaria lancifolia_, _Pontederia cordata_, _Panicum_ spp.) and the semi-woody _Hibiscus_ sp. Study plots received 1.3, 3.8, and 10.2 cm wk^{-1} of secondary wastewater while a control plot received 3.8 cm wk^{-1} of freshwater. Discharge from study plots through groundwater revealed that the marsh and peat complex was over 97% efficient in P removal even at the high application rate. Of the 38.03 g P applied per m^2 at the 10.2 cm wk^{-1} application rate, 69% (26.31 g P), 23% (8.81 g P), and 5% (1.97 g P) were stored in the peat, roots and rhizomes, and litter respectively (Zoltek et al., 1979; Dolan et al., 1981). One suggested drawback to using wetlands for wastewater treatment relates to potential for reduced uptake/ storage of nutrients during the dormant season. During the

TABLE 1. Wastewater Treatment Efficiency of Various Wetlands in Florida.

Type of System	Principal discharge from System	Wetland Treatment Efficiency	Study Location	Reference
Cypress Dome	Groundwater	BOD >90%	Gainesville, FL	Odum & Ewel, 1984; Odum et al., 1974,1975a,b,1976,1978,1980; Dierberg & Brezonik, 1983a,b, 1984
		N 2%		
		P 98%		
Marsh/Mixed Hardwood	Surface	N 75-85%	Wildwood, FL	Boyt et al., 1977
		P 87%		
Marsh	Groundwater	BOD 90%	Clermont, FL	Zoltek & Bayley, 1979; Dolan et al., 1981
		N 98%		
		P 97%		
Shrub/Forest	Surface	BOD 75%	Apalachicola, FL	Best et al., 1983,1987b; Pezeshki, 1987
		NO_3+NO_2 98%		
		NH_3 92%		
		TKN 72%		
		TP 96%		
		Ortho-P 99%		
Oligohaline Marsh	Surface	BOD 70%	Kennedy Space Center, FL	Best et al. 1987a; Owens-Mion et al., 1985,1987; Owens-Mion, 1986
		N 94%		
		Ortho-P 97%		
		P 99%		
		Cu 100%		
		Zn 88%		
Forest	Surface	Cd 82%	Waldo, FL	Best et al., 1982; Tuschall, 1981
		Cu 78%		
		Mn 68%		
		Zn 77%		

Clermont marsh study, there was no observed flushing of P during winter or early spring. Apparently, mild Florida winters, coupled with relatively warm temperature of wastewater may maintain biological and chemical functions essential for continued assimilation of nutrients (Zoltek et al., 1979; Dolan et al., 1981).

In an attempt to remove sewage disposal generated by the small town of Apalachicola, Florida, from Apalachicola Bay, one of the nation's leading shellfish production area, Florida legislators appropriated seed-money through Florida Department of Environmental Regulation to investigate the wetlands alternative. A new secondary wastewater treatment facility was constructed with discharge (started spring 1985) to a shrub wetland. The idea was to use the shrub swamp for advance treatment of the secondary-treated wastewater with flow from the swamp into a freshwater creek, and ultimately to Apalachicola River. After about one year of operation, the wetland has been effective in significant improvement of wastewater to near-background water quality levels (Table 1) (Best et al., 1987b). Although preliminary indications suggest that partial treatment of nutrients is possible even when the predominant discharge from the wetland is surface flow, additional data from the five-year study required by the "wastewater-to-wetland experimental exemption" (see Florida Statute Chapter 17-4.243 (4)) will allow for evaluating long-term efficiency of the wetland to treat wastewater in this critically important region.

An oligohaline coastal marsh at Kennedy Space Center was studied to evaluate potential of a flow-through marsh for nutrient removal. _Juncus roemerianus_, _Spartina bakeri_, _Typha domingensis_, _Bacopa monnieri_, and _Distichlis spicata_ comprise the dominant vegetation in the marsh. Secondary effluent was pumped continuously for about a year from a holding pond to study plots at rates of 2.54 and 10.16 cm wk^{-1}. Results from this short-term project indicate that the marsh is effective in removing over 95% of nutrients from wastewater (Table 1) without altering wetland function and character.

Heavy Metals

Municipal wastewater may contain trace metals (EPA, 1984) which could cause problems with potential toxicity because of the tendency to accumulate in the food chain. Two preliminary studies were conducted to investigate fate of selected heavy metals in forested and marsh wetlands in Florida.

Primary effluent was spiked with concentrations of select heavy metals to emulate levels typically found in municipal wastewater. The heavy metal-spiked wastewater was piped to small study plots in a forested wetland near the small town of Waldo, Florida. Results indicate that a large portion of the added metals were immobilized by the swamp. In all cases, levels of metals declined significantly (Table 1) in surface water discharged from the flow-through study plots, indicating metal immobilization in the peat surface (Best et al., 1982; Tuschall, 1981). Rates of immobilization were calculated to be a minimum of 7.2, 36, 72, and 72 g metal ha^{-1} d^{-1} for Cu, Cd, Mn and Zn. Dissolved organic C, Fe, Ca, and especially sulfide and pH greatly affected metal immobilization rates (Best et al., 1982; Tuschall, 1981).

Copper and Zn dynamics, in addition to typical water quality parameters, were studied in the marsh at Kennedy Space Center. Secondary-treated effluent, spiked with Cu and Zn for total effluent concentrations of 1.57 and 4.66 mg L^{-1} respectively, was pumped into marsh study plots. Mean removal efficiencies in surface water were 100% for Cu and 88% for Zn (Table 1). A significant correlation between metal concentration and distance from effluent source suggests that heavy metals are being assimilated by the marsh ecosystem. In portions of study plots near the inflow pipe, plant tissue Cu concentration rose from 3.67 to 36.25 µg g^{-1} and Zn concentration went from 13.00 to 160.33 µg g^{-1}. However, there was a significant decrease in metals concentration in plant tissue from inflow to outflow portions of the study plots. To test the fate of Cu and Zn under more controlled conditions, laboratory microcosms were constructed and planted with dominant marsh species (Owens-Mion, 1986; Owens-Mion et al., 1985,1987). These microcosms received various applications of Cu and Zn with the high level treatments equivalent to 50-plus years of Cu (225 mg) and about 15 years of Zn (225 mg) accumulation from "typical" municipal effluent. Although metals were applied to microcosms in forms apparently readily available for plant uptake, no detrimental effects on the microcosm vegetation from the high concentration of metals were observed. In fact the plants seemed to flourish. *Bacopa* took up 74.2% of Cu while other plant species accounted for 2.6 to 8.8%. *Bacopa* also incorporated 46.2% of the Zn compared to 8.2 to 13.8% for other plants. There were species specific patterns for above- and below-ground allocation of the metals with a slight predominance of below-ground allocation of metals (Owens-Mion, 1985,1986; Owens-Mion et al., 1987). Very little Cu or Zn was retained by microcosm sediments.

Wetlands Vegetation

A major advantage to using wetlands for recycling wastewater is that vegetation in wetlands are already adapted to periodically flooded conditions. Brown (1981) demonstrated increased photosynthesis rates in cypress in wetlands receiving wastewater effluent. In fact, increases were observed in nutrient uptake by foliage (Boyt et al., 1977; DeBusk, 1984; Dierberg et al., 1986) and tree growth (Nessel et al., 1982). Cypress tress in a swamp receiving wastewater accumulated 1% of incoming P in aboveground tissue (Dierberg and Brezonik, 1983a) with 63% of total P in vegetation in root biomass (Lugo et al., 1984). Not only do these increases in nutrient accumulation and growth account in part for some of the long-term storage of wetlands, but these increases also point out that the vegetation community is responding positively to wastewater application. Similar trends of increased plant biomass production were observed for marsh communities (Zoltek et al., 1979; Dolan et al., 1981; Owens-Mion, 1986). However, although no dramatic changes were observed in marsh community structure in these short-term experimental studies (Zoltek et al., 1979; Dolan et al., 1981; Owens-Mion, 1986), marshes may shift in species dominance as a result of wastewater application (Kadlec and Tilton, 1979).

Wetlands Wildlife

Effect of wastewater on wetlands fauna depends in part on faunal dependance on the aquatic phase of wetlands flooding and dissolved O_2 levels. Forested wetlands receiving wastewater acted as a sink for leopard frogs (Odum et al., 1976) with significant increases in migration into enriched wetlands. Insect species abundance and species diversity were greater in cypress domes receiving wastewater than in control domes (Harris and Vickers, 1984). Davis (in Odum et al., 1978) found no significant differences in mosquito populations (medically or economically important species) between control and wastewater-treated cypress domes. The response of amphibians was much the same as insects. Part of the increase in amphibian abundance appears to have resulted from increased perching area provided by floating duckweed and increased food supplies in wastewater domes (Harris and Vickers, 1984). In addition, increased numbers of water treaders (Mesoveliidae) provided a concentrated food resource for overwintering passerine birds (Harris and Vickers, 1984). This resulted in bird sightings in wastewater domes 150% greater than control domes (Jetter and Harris in Odum et al., 1976).

A controlled microcosm study of response of select marsh fish species to wastewater revealed that although Gambusia and Poecilea had LC-50's (lethal concentration to 50% of individuals after 96 h exposure in laboratory) of 73 and 64% respectively, both species avoided effluent concentrations greater than 15% (Sargent, 1986; Best et al., 1987a). The reality is, except for zones immediately adjacent to outfall pipes, that the percentage of wastewater in wetlands should be less than either LC-50 or avoidance levels, especially in flow-through wetlands properly managed for wastewater discharge. However, surface waters of isolated wetlands with restricted inflow may have effluent concentration levels somewhere between avoidance and LC-50 levels especially in zones near discharge.

WASTEWATER-TO-WETLANDS: WHERE DO WE GO FROM HERE?

There are considerable data to support the conclusion that wetlands may be used for enhancing water quality and recycling wastewater without adversely affecting type, nature, function, and flora and fauna of wetland ecosystems. However, much of the research reported herein and in published literature deals with wastewater application to wetlands at research-scale time-durations and application levels, or from opportunistic, historical-type (that is, after-the-fact), small discharges. Very limited data exist for wastewater recycling through wetlands from properly managed, long-term, large-scale applications (say application rates in excess of 4,000-12,000 m^3 d^{-1}. Additional research is necessary to evaluate long-term functioning of wetlands properly managed to receive larger application rates.

If, as the overwhelming volume of data suggest, it is possible to use natural wetlands for wastewater treatment and recycling, then is it also possible to manage wastewater as a resource for use in restoring overly drained wetlands while at the same time enhancing water quality? A significant percentage of wetlands has been lost through drainage and development. For example, in Florida alone it is estimated that from 1950's to 1970's wetland acreage declined from 6.9 to 4.6 million ha (Mitsch and Gosselink, 1986), a net loss of over 30% of wetland habitat. Proper reuse of wastewater as a resource could be used for enhancing recovery of overly drained wetlands. To that end, when the Florida Department of Environmental Regulation (FDER) adopted a set of wastewater-to-wetland rules in 1986 (Florida Statutes 17-6.055--Wetlands Application), FDER policy makers had the foresight to include "hydrologically altered" wetlands in the rule (Schwartz, 1987). However, permitting practicality for reusing wastewater for restoration of wetlands depends, in significant part, on current state and federal policy regarding where in the wetland-to-aquatic zone water quality standards for regulated water bodies are required to be met. If, for example, US-EPA (or some state regulatory agency) policy interprets that water quality standards for "waters of the nation (or state)" must be met at the landward extent of those "waters," then it may be almost impossible to permit reuse of wastewater for restoration of altered wetlands. The question really is, "Is it possible to reuse wastewater to restore altered wetlands while at the same time balancing the net gain of wetland habitat with meeting water quality standards in aquatic systems?"

Perhaps one of the most ideal wastewater reuse alternatives (while also achieving treatment and discharge) is to reuse wastewater for creating multifunctional wetland habitat. Creation of artificial wetlands for wastewater treatment is not a new concept (Richardson and Davis, 1987). However, most artificial wetlands created for wastewater treatment are designed to preform one primary function -- wastewater treatment (Richardson and Davis, 1987). These artificial wetland "facilities" bear little resemblance to functional natural wetlands. Generally, they are simply constructed and managed facilities which use wetland plants to enhance water quality. The question is, or should be, "Is it possible to create wetlands that not only achieve the primary purpose of water quality enhancement and wastewater discharge, but also create additional wetland functions (especially wildlife)?"

One such wetland system was designed (Figure 2) (and is currently under construction) for the City of Orlando, Florida (designed by G. R. Best and M. T. Brown of the Center for Wetlands for Post, Buckley, Schuh and Jernigan, Inc., and R. Havens, Utilities Director, City of Orlando). The created wetland system is approximately 500 ha in size and is conservatively designed to treat between 62,000-93,000 $m^3 d^{-1}$ of wastewater with ultimate capacity depending upon documented long-term treatment efficiency of the created wetland ecosystem. The created wetland system is relatively simple in design. Wetlands were divided into three functional classes. The first one-third of the system is designed to be the managed ("facilities") portion of the system allowing for various management options (e.g., harvesting, fire management, etc.). Although the first system is presently scheduled for planting of cattails for maximizing nutrient removal, the system could be planted and managed for almost any wetland plant. Treated effluent from the first system is then discharged into the second one-third of the created wetland. Although the second system, the mixed emergent marsh wetland, is divided into two discrete cells to allow for some management options, the plan presently is to limit management and allow the system to function as a "natural marsh." The "mixed emergent marsh" wetland is to be planted with several marsh species with various diverse functions (Table 2). The final one-third of the system is to provide final polishing of water, serve as a buffer, and provide floral and faunal habitat. This final polishing wetland is to be planted with both mixed emergent marsh plants, to provide an initial diverse cover, and several wetland tree species (Table 2). Ultimately, the final one-third of the created wetland area will become a multi-functional forested wetland.

It may be possible and desirable to combine use of created and natural wetlands to treat and recycle wastewater. One such system was designed (Figure 3) for the Public Utilities Division of Orange County, Florida (designed by G. R. Best and Camp Dresser & McKee, Inc. -- the system has been constructed and is scheduled for operation in early 1987.) Again, the system is relatively simple in design. The wetland treatment systems essentially consist of created wetlands (planted with select wetland herbaceous plants and trees) integrated with natural wetlands. The treatment system is divided into two major halves. The first half consists of an overland-flow type created wetland integrated with an "isolated" natural wetland. Wastewater from the first half is collected and redistributed into the second half of the system. The second half of the system consists of an overland-flow type created wetland integrated with a "jurisdictional" wetland. Recycled wastewater will ultimately discharge from the system into a small creek. The 120 ha system will initially be operated at 11,600 $m^3 d^{-1}$ with an ultimate design capacity of 23,000 $m^3 d^{-1}$.

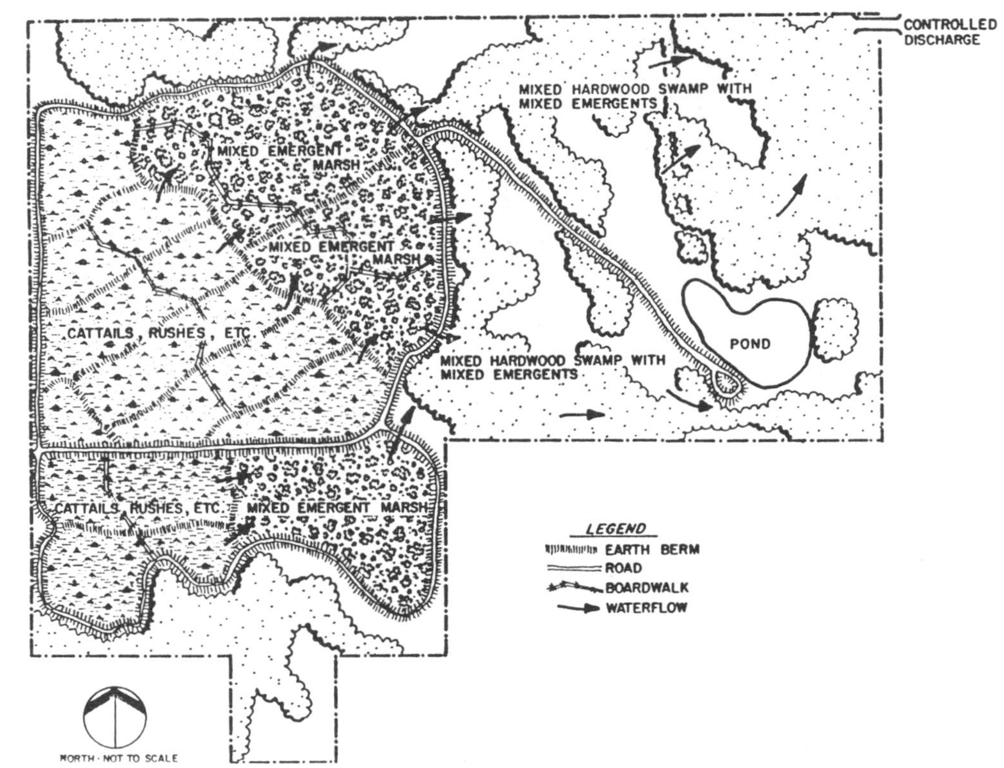

FIGURE 2. Planned view of created multifunctional wetland ecosystem designed primarily for advanced treatment and reuse of wastewater (approximate size 500 ha [1200 ac]). (Conceived and designed by G. R. Best and M. T. Brown [Center for Wetlands] and engineered by Post, Buckley, Schuh & Jernigan, Inc., for the City of Orlando, Florida).

TABLE 2. Food and cover value to wildlife of wetland species proposed for use in artificial wetlands.

Species	Common Name	Food value	Cover value	Primary users
HERBACEOUS SPECIES				
Echinochloa walteri	Water millet	H	M	Waterfowl, marsh birds
Juncus effusus	Soft rush	L	M-H	Waterfowl
Leersia oryzoides	Rice cutgrass	M	M	Waterfowl, marsh birds
Nuphar luteum (*macrophyllum*)	Spatter-dock	H	L	Waterfowl
Nymphaea odorata	Water-lily	L-M	H	Waterfowl
Panicum hemitomon	Maiden-cane	M	M	Waterfowl, small mammals, marsh birds
Polygonum punctatum	Smartweed	H	M	Waterfowl, songbirds, marsh birds
Pontederia cordata	Pickerelweed	M	M	Waterfowl, small mammals, marsh birds
Sagittaria lancifolia		H	L-M	Waterfowl
Scirpus spp.	Bulrush	M	M	Waterfowl
Typha latifolia	Southern cattail	L	M	Waterfowl, marsh birds
Zizania aquatica	Wild rice	H	M	Wide variety wildlife
Zizaniopsis miliacea	Southern wild rice	H	M	Wide variety wildlife
WOODY SPECIES				
Acer rubrum	Red maple	M	M	Songbirds, game mammals, small mammals
Fraxinus caroliniana	Popash	H	M	Game mammals, songbirds, small mammals

TABLE 2 (cont'd.)

Species	Common Name	Food value	Cover value	Primary users
Nyssa sylvatica var. *biflora*	Swamp black gum	H	M	Wide variety wildlife fruit readily consumed by birds and mammals
Quercus laurifolia	Laurel oak	H	M	Game birds, game mammals
Salix caroliniana	Coastal plain willow	M	M	Songbirds, game mammals, game birds
Sabal palmetto	Cabbage palm	M	M	Wide variety wildlife
Taxodium distichum	Bald cypress	L	M	Songbirds use structure as perches
Ulmus americana var. *floridana*	Florida elm	L-M	M	Songbirds, game birds

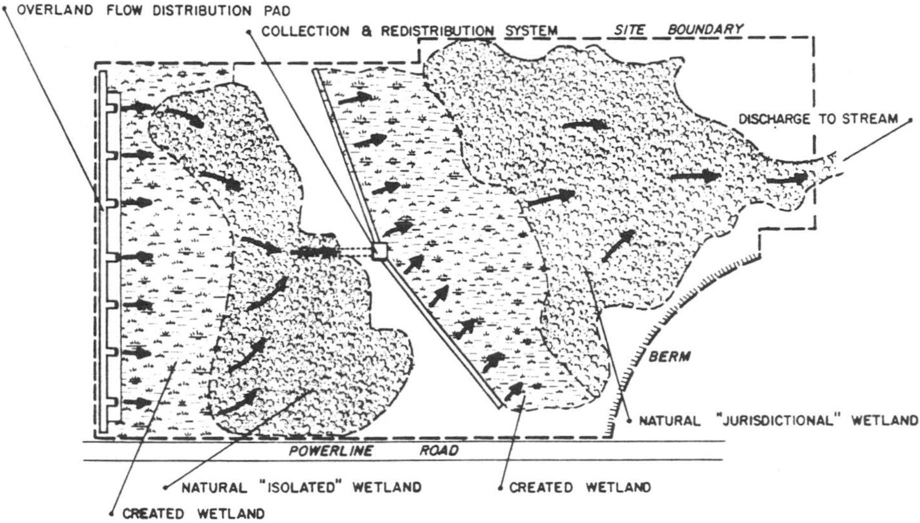

FIGURE 3. Planned view for integrating created and natural wetlands for treatment and recycling of wastewater (approximate size 130 ha [320 ac]). (Conceived by G. R. Best [Center for Wetlands] and designed and engineered by Camp, Dresser & McKee, Inc. for Orange County, Florida.

SUMMARY

Treatment efficiency of southern wetlands (Table 1) is consistent with or slightly exceeds efficiencies reported for wetlands of other regions (see for comparison Kadlec and Tilton, 1979: Table 1, p. 194). In addition, if properly managed, use of wetlands for recycling wastewater is, much unlike that for natural upland ecosystems, compatible with maintaining most, if not all, primary natural functions, especially wildlife habitat functions.

The ultimate challenge is to integrate the "wastewater-to-wetlands" concept firmly and fairly into the "list of possible alternatives" for wastewater treatment/disposal. Presently, since wetlands are simply treated as an extension of aquatic systems and fall under strict "waters of the nation (state)" type water quality restrictions, it is far more difficult to secure a permit for recycling wastewater through wetlands than for almost any other alternative. Should regulatory "policy" encourage equitable consideration of all "reasonable" wastewater treatment/disposal alternatives? When reviewing wastewater treatment/disposal alternatives, do not simply ask, "How effective is the wetland in removal of nutrients?" Ask, instead, "How effective is the wetland alternative as compared to other alternatives (land application, groundwater injection, etc.)?" If a natural resource (native wildlife habitat, surface and/or subsurface water resource, etc.) is being used in the treatment/disposal alternative, be sure to evaluate how much the resource will be altered from its natural state. And, most importantly, be especially cognizant of hidden environmental/ecological costs! Do not lose sight of the fact that high energy alternatives for wastewater treatment/disposal not only carry a higher economic cost, but equally as important, high energy alternatives also carry the increased environmental costs associated with increased energy consumption.

ACKNOWLEDGMENTS

This work was supported in part by grants to the Center for Wetlands (G. R. Best, Principal Investigator), University of Florida, from U.S. Environmental Protection Agency (EPA-R-806286020), Florida Department of Environmental Regulation (FDER-LR-46 & WM-156), Kennedy Space Center/Bionetics Corp. (BIO-1-82-0240); contracts to G. R. Best from Camp Dresser & McKee, Inc., and Post, Buckley, Schuh and Jernigan, Inc.; with support for G. R. Best by the College of Engineering to Center for Wetlands.

The author acknowledges the "work well done" on the various aspects of the research by graduate students (especially W. DeBusk, A. Hernandez, P. Owens-Mion, C. Pezeshki, W. Sargent, L. Schwartz, K. Sibley, and J. Tuschall). Dr. M. T. Brown assisted on various projects plus offered much useful advice on the manuscript.

Center for Wetlands Publication No. CFW-87-04.

REFERENCES

Best, G. R., J. R. Tuschall, P. L. Brezonik, J. R. Butner, W. F. DeBusk, K. C. Ewel, A. Hernandez, and H. T. Odum. 1982. The state of selected heavy metals in a forested wetland ecosystem. Report to U.S. Environmental Protection Agency. Center for Wetlands, Univ. of Florida, Gainesville, FL.

Best, G. R., L. N. Schwartz, L. Sonnenberg, S. Kidd, and J. McCreary. 1983. Low-energy wastewater recycling through wetlands ecosystems: Apalachicola study -- experimental use of a freshwater shrub swamp. Summary Progress Report to the Department of Environmental Regulation. Center for Wetlands, Univ. of Florida, Gainesville, FL. 105 pp.

Best, G. R., P. Owens-Mion, W. Sargent, and C. Ross Hinkle. 1987a. Low energy wastewater recycling through wetland ecosystems: experimental use of a marsh ecosystem at J.F. Kennedy Space Center. Final Report to Bionetics Corp. and

J. F. Kennedy Space Center. Center for Wetlands, Univ. of Florida, Gainesville, FL (in preparation).

Best, G. R., L. N. Schwartz, C. Pezeshki, K. Sibley, and J. J. Delfino. 1987b. Low-energy wastewater recycling through wetland ecosystems: Apalachicola Study - Experimental Use of a Freshwater Shrub Swamp. Progress Report to Florida Department of Environmental Regulation (in preparation).

Boyt, F. L., S. E. Bayley, and J. Zoltek Jr. 1977. Removal of nutrients from treated municipal wastewater by wetland vegetation. J. Water Pollut. Control Fed. 789-799.

Brown, M. T. 1981. Energy basis for hierarchies in urban and regional landscapes. Proceedings of a Symposium Sponsored by the International Symposium of Energy Ecological Modelling. p. 517-534. In W. J. Mitsch, R. W. Bosserman, and J. M. Klopatek (ed.): Energy and Ecological Modelling: Developments in Environmental Modelling 1. Elsevier Scientific Publ. Co., New York, NY.

Copeland, B. J., H. T. Odum, and D. C. Cooper. 1972. Water quality for preservation of estuarine ecology. p. 107-126. In Conflicts in Water Resources Planning. Water Resource Symp. 5. Univ. of Texas, Austin, Texas.

DeBusk, W. F. 1984. Nutrient dynamics in a cypress strand receiving municipal wastewater effluent. MS Thesis. Univ. of Florida, Gainesville, FL. 103 pp.

Dierberg, F. E., and P. L. Brezonik. 1983a. Nitrogen and phosphorus mass balance in natural and sewage enriched cypress domes. J. Appl. Ecol. 20:323-337.

Dierberg, F. E., and P. L. Brezonik. 1983b. Tertiary treatment of municipal wastewater by cypress domes. Water Resour. 17:1027-1040.

Dierberg, S. E., and P. L. Brezonik. 1984. Nitrogen and phosphorus mass balances in a cypress dome receiving wastewater. In K. C. Ewel and H. T. Odum (ed.) Cypress Swamps. Univ. Presses of FL, Gainesville, FL.

Dierberg, F. E., P. A. Straub, and C. D. Hendry. 1986. Leaf-to-twig transfer conserves nitrogen and phosphorus in nutrient poor and enriched cypress swamps. Forest Sci. 32:900-913.

Dolan, T. J., S. E. Bayley, J. Zoltek, Jr., and A. J. Hermann. 1981. Phosphorus dynamics of a Florida freshwater marsh receiving treated wastewater. J. Appl. Ecol. 18:205-219.

EPA. 1984. The ecological impacts of wastewater on wetlands: an annotated bibliography. Environmental Protection Agency, Chicago, IL. EPA-905-84-002.

Ewel, K. C., and H. T. Odum (ed.). 1984. Cypress Swamps. Univ. Presses of FL, Gainesville, FL. 427 pp.

Harris, L. D., and C. R. Vickers. 1984. Some faunal community characteristics of cypress ponds and the changes induced by perturbations. In K. C. Ewel and H. T. Odum (ed.) Cypress Swamps. Univ. Presses of FL, Gainesville, FL. p. 171-185.

Kadlec, R. H., and D. L. Tilton. 1979. The use of freshwater wetlands as a tertiary wastewater treatment alternative. CRC Critical Reviews in Environmental Control 9:185-212.

Kadlec, R. H., D. L. Tilton, and J. A. Kadlec. 1977. Feasibility of utilization of wetland ecosystems for nutrient removal from secondary municipal wastewater treatment plant effluent. Semi-Annual Report No. 5 to the National Science Foundation. Univ. of Michigan, Ann Arbor, MI.

Kadlec, R. H., D. L. Tilton, and B. R. Schwegler. 1979. Wetlands for tertiary treatment: a three-year summary of pilot scale operations at Houghton Lake. Report to the National Science Foundation. Univ. of Michigan, Ann Arbor, MI. 101 pp. (NTIS No. PB 295 965).

Lugo, A. E., J. K. Nessel, and T. M. Hanlon. 1984. Root distribution in a north-central Florida cypress strand. p. 279-285. In K. C. Ewel and H. T. Odum (ed.) Cypress Swamps. University Presses of FL, Gainesville, FL.

Mitsch, W. J., and J. G. Gosselink. 1986. Wetlands. Van Nostrand Reinhold Company Inc., New York, NY. 539 pp.

Nessel, J. K., K. C. Ewel, and M. S. Burnett. 1982. Wastewater enrichment increases mature pond cypress growth rates. Forest Sci. 28:400-403.

Odum, H. T. 1985. Self organization of ecosystems in marine ponds receiving treated sewage. (UNC Sea Grant, Pub.# UNC-SG 85-04). Center for Wetlands, Univ. of Florida, Gainesville, FL. 250 pp.

Odum, H. T., K. C. Ewel, J. W. Ordway, M. K. Johnston, and others. 1974. Cypress wetlands for water management, recycling and conservation. First Annual Report to the National Science Foundation and The Rockefeller Foundation. Center for Wetlands, Univ. of Florida, Gainesville, FL. 948 pp.

Odum, H. T., K. C. Ewel, W. J. Mitsch, and J. W. Ordway. 1975a. Recycling treated sewage through cypress wetlands in Florida. Presented at "Rockefeller Conference on Waste Recycling on Land, Bellagio, Italy. Center for Wetlands, Univ of Florida, Gainesville, FL. 14 pp.

Odum, H. T., K. C. Ewel, J. W. Ordway, M. K. Johnston, and others. 1975b. Cypress wetlands for water management, recycling and conservation. Second Annual Report to the National Science Foundation and The Rockefeller Foundation. Center for Wetlands, Univ. of Florida, Gainesville, FL. 817 pp.

Odum, H. T., K. C. Ewel, J. W. Ordway, M. K. Johnston, and others. 1976. Cypress wetlands for water management, recycling and conservation. Third Annual Report to the National Science Foundation and The Rockefeller Foundation. Center for Wetlands, Univ. of Florida, Gainesville, FL. 879 pp.

Odum, H. T., K. C. Ewel, J. W. Ordway, M. K. Johnston, and others. 1978. Cypress wetlands for water management, recycling and conservation. Fourth Annual Report to the National Science Foundation and The Rockefeller Foundation. Center for Wetlands, Univ. of Florida, Gainesville, FL. 945 pp.

Odum, H. T., K. C. Ewel, J. W. Ordway, M. K. Johnston, and others. 1980. Cypress wetlands for water management, recycling, and conservation. Fifth Annual and Final Report to the National Science Foundation and The Rockefeller Foundation. Center for Wetlands, Univ. of Florida, Gainesville, FL. 284 pp.

Owens-Mion, P. 1986. Low-energy wastewater recycling through an oligohaline coastal marsh ecosystem. MS Thesis. Univ. of Florida, Gainesville, FL. 148 pp.

Owens-Mion, P., W. B. Sargent, G. R. Best, and C. R. Hinkle. 1985. Low energy wastewater recycling through wetland ecosystems: experimental use of a marsh ecosystem at J. F. Kennedy Space Center. Progress Report to Bionetics Corp. and J. F. Kennedy Space Center. Center for Wetlands, Univ. of Florida, Gainesville, FL. 47 pp.

Owens-Mion, P., G. R. Best, and C. R. Hinkle. 1987. Low-energy wastewater recycling through wetland ecosystems: study of copper and zinc in wetland microcosms. Proceedings of Freshwater Wetlands and Wildlife, Savannah River Ecology Lab., Charleston, SC.

Pezeshki, C. 1987. Response of benthic macroinvertebrates of a shrub swamp to discharge of treated wastewater. MS Thesis. Univ. of Florida, Gainesville, FL.

Richardson, C. J., and J. A. Davis. 1987. Natural and artificial wetland ecosystems: ecological opportunities and limitations. In K. R. Reddy and W. H. Smith (ed.) Aquatic Plants for Water Treatment and Resource Recovery. Magnolia Publishing Inc., Orlando, FL.

Richardson, C. J., P. E. Marshall. 1986. Processes controlling movement, storage, and export of phosphorus in a fen peatland. Ecological Monographs 56:279-302.

Richardson, C. J., J. Z. Kadlec, W. A. Wentz, J. P. M. Chamie, and R. H. Kadlec. 1975. Background ecology and the effects of nutrient additions on a central Michigan wetland. Publ. No. 4. Univ. of Michigan, Ann Arbor, Michigan. 64 pp.

Richardson, C. J., W. A. Wentz, J. P. M. Chamie, J. A. Kadlec, and D. L. Tilton. 1976. Plant growth, nutrient accumulation and decomposition in central Michigan peatland used for effluent treatment. p. 77-118. In D. L. Tilton, R. H. Kadlec, and C. J. Richardson (ed.) Proceedings of a National Symposium on Freshwater Wetlands and Sewage Effluent Disposal. Univ. of Michigan, Ann Arbor, MI.

Richardson, C. J., D. L. Tilton, J. A. Kadlec, J. P. Chamie, and W. A. Wentz. 1978. Nutrient dynamics in northern wetland ecosystems. p. 217-241. In R. E. Good, D. F. Whigham, and R. L. Simpson (ed.) Freshwater Wetlands: Ecological Processes and Management Potential. Academic Press, Inc., New York, NY.

Sargent, W. 1986. Avoidance of wastewater treatment plant effluent by selected fish and macrobenthos. MS (Non Thesis Paper). Univ. of Florida, Gainesville, FL. 32 pp.

Schwartz, L. N. 1987. Regulation of wastewater discharge to Florida wetlands. In K. R. Reddy and W. H. Smith (ed.) Aquatic Plants for Water Treatment and Resource Recovery. Magnolia Publishing Inc., Orlando, FL.

Tilton, D. L., and R. H. Kadlec. 1979. The utilization of a freshwater wetland for nutrient removal from secondarily treated wastewater effluent. J. Environ. Qual. 8:328-334.

Tilton, D. L., R. H. Kadlec, and C. J. Richardson (ed.). 1976. Proceedings of a National Symposium on Freshwater Wetlands and Sewage Effluent Disposal. Univ. of Michigan, Ann Arbor, MI. 343 pp.

Tilton, D. L., R. H. Kadlec, and J. Linde. 1977. Surface water chemistry and element budgets of a wetland used for wastewater treatment. p. 53-126. In R. H. Kadlec, D. L. Tilton, and J. A. Kadlec (ed.) Feasibility of Utilization of Wetland Ecosystems for Nutrient Removal from Secondary Municipal Wastewater Treatment Plant Effluent. Semi-Annual Report No. 5. Univ. of Michigan, Ann Arbor, MI.

Tuschall, Jr., J. R. 1981. Heavy metal complexation with naturally occurring organic ligands in wetland ecosystems. Ph.D. Dissertation. Univ. of Florida, Gainesville, FL. 212 pp.

Valiela, I., and S. Vince. 1976. Assimilation of sewage by wetlands. In M. Wiley (ed.) Estuarine Processes, Vol. 1. Uses, Stresses and Adaptation to the Estuary. New York, N.Y. 541 pp.

Zoltek, Jr., J. and S. E. Baley. 1979. Removal of nutrients from treated municipal wastewater by freshwater marshes. Final Report to the City of Clermont, Florida. Center for Wetlands, Univ. of Florida, Gainesville, FL. 325 pp.

WATER HYACINTH SYSTEMS FOR WATER TREATMENT

T. D. Hayes and H. R. Isaacson
Gas Research Institute
Chicago, Illinois 60631

K. R. Reddy
Central Florida Research and Education Center
University of Florida, IFAS
Sanford, Florida 32771

D. P. Chynoweth
Agricultural Engineering Department
University of Florida, IFAS
Gainesville, Florida 32611

R. Biljetina
Institute of Gas Technology
Chicago, Illinois 60632

ABSTRACT

The long-range potential of hyacinth aquaculture technology in the treatment of municipal wastewater rests upon the performance and cost of all of the major components of an integrated system. A conceptual design and analysis of a hyacinth facility employing anaerobic digestion for solids disposal and energy generation is presented in this chapter. The technical information serving as the basis for this economic analysis was provided by an experimental hyacinth treatment/anaerobic digestion system located at the Community Waste Research Facility of the Walt Disney World Resort Complex.

The integrated concept consists of primary settling of the sewage, secondary treatment to Federal EPA effluent quality standards in elongated water hyacinth channels sized at 0.75 ha per 1000 m^3 of wastewater flow per day, a harvesting system that collects an average of 1360 Mg of wet hyacinths (5.0% total solids) from each hectare of pond area per year, and a vertical flow anaerobic digestion system capable of a total solids reduction of more than 60% and CH_4 yields of 0.47 m^3 kg^{-1} volatile solids (VS) added when operated on a typical 1:1 hyacinth/sludge blend at a solids loading of 3.2 kg VS m^3 d^{-1}.

ISBN 0-941463-00-1

Major revenues for the facility include wastewater treatment service charges and CH_4 sales to local natural gas distributors.

Using municipal utility financing and assuming that the gas from the digesters could be upgraded to 97% CH_4 and sold to a local natural gas distributor for $2.00/GJ, the costs for secondary treatment with the integrated hyacinth/anaerobic digestion concept range from $61/1000 m³ for a community of 500,000 to $239/1000 m³ for a town of 10,000; these estimates represent a 15 to 20% reduction in treatment cost compared to conventional technology. The sensitivity of component costs to system performance and new concepts that may have significant impact on the economics of integrated hyacinth aquaculture treatment systems are discussed.

Keywords: Primary sewage effluent, secondary treatment, biomass, anaerobic digestion, methane, natural gas.

INTRODUCTION

The water hyacinth process has gained increased attention as an "alternate and innovative" method for wastewater treatment (US EPA, 1978). The long-range commercial success of the technology, however, rests upon the performance and cost of the entire integrated aquaculture system, and not the hyacinth process alone. The major components of the water hyacinth system include: 1) the water hyacinth treatment channel, 2) water hyacinth harvesting and handling, and 3) solids disposal. Each of these process categories can comprise a substantial portion of the capital and O&M costs of an entire facility. Attention, therefore, must be directed towards the development of an integrated system, rather than just the hyacinth process alone.

Since 1978, research directed toward an integrated system has been conducted at Walt Disney World Resort Complex, Florida, employing anaerobic digestion to convert water hyacinth biomass produced at this site in channels and primary sludge to low cost methane (CH_4). This research involved the combination of at least three technologies: 1) aquaculture treatment of wastewater to meet federal, state and local standards, 2) biomass management for achieving optimum yields, and 3) anaerobic digestion. Specific experimental activities conducted in each of these areas are detailed in this book by other investigators (Biljetina et al., 1987; Chynoweth, 1987; DeBusk and Reddy, 1987a,b; Moorhead et al., 1987; Reddy and DeBusk, 1987; Srivastava et al., 1987). The next steps required to meet full integration is the incorporation of MSW, locally grown energy crops, and recycling of the digester sludge. The purpose of this chapter is to present the major accomplishments to date of the project within the context of the integrated system and to discuss the implications of these results on treatment costs projected for systems of various sizes.

Most investigations conducted to date have been of a proof-of-concept and demonstration nature (Bastian and Reed, 1979;

Duffer and Moyer, 1978; Reed et al., 1980; Tchobanoglous et al., 1979). Pilot-scale hyacinth systems have typically achieved removals of 75-90% of biochemical oxygen demand (BOD_5) and suspended solids (TSS) under sewage loadings of 20-150 kg ha^{-1} d^{-1} (Bastian and Reed, 1979; Dinges, 1978; Hauser, 1984; Kruzic, 1979; Wolverton and McDonald, 1979). Nutrient removal reported for these systems has been moderately successful, with most reporting high N but low P removal efficiencies (Bastian and Reed, 1979; DeBusk and Reddy, 1987a; Dinges, 1978; Hauser, 1984; Ryther et al., 1979). These observations of performance mostly relate to non-stressed systems which have not been optimized for pollutant removal and hyacinth productivity. Nevertheless, hyacinth systems continue to be tested and implemented by municipalities as an "innovative and alternate" technology for the cost-effective treatment of sewage, with the majority of these pilot plants being applied to wastewater polishing and N removal. Information needs for these new systems include: 1) strategies for process improvement based on a sound understanding of plant growth and pollutant removal mechanisms; 2) a data base for rational scale up and design approaches; and 3) operational procedures that minimize cost and stabilize process performance.

Equally important is the need to identify low cost methods for the disposal and/or utilization of the large amounts of solids that can be generated by the water hyacinth treatment process. In many applications, the production of hyacinths (5% total solids content) could equal or exceed sludge output from a treatment facility, about 11-14 Mg (wet) d^{-1} per 10,000 population served (Hayes et al., 1985). Anaerobic digestion has the potential of converting this community waste problem into an energy production benefit when effectively integrated into the water hyacinth treatment system. Advantages include: 1) a long history of dependable performance in the reduction of municipal sludges (Wastewater Engineering, 1972); 2) process compatibility with high and low moisture feedstocks; 3) the potential for the direct production of high-energy CH_4 gas (22,330-35,356 kJ m^{-3}) (Chynoweth et al., 1984; Hayes and Isaacson, 1986; Klass and Ghosh, 1981; Ryther et al., 1979; Vaidyanathan et al., 1985); and 4) economy of scale at low processing capacities (Hayes et al., 1985).

Fermentation research conducted at the Community Waste Research Facility (CWRF) of the Walt Disney World Resort Complex has been directed toward the development of an advanced conversion system that is capable of achieving high CH_4 yields through improved solids management while decreasing mixing requirements to reduce power consumption and maintenance costs. This work is described in another chapter of this book (Biljetina et al., 1986).

INTEGRATED AQUACULTURE/ANAEROBIC DIGESTION CONCEPT

In the system concept (Figure 1), effluent from the primary settler is passed through the water hyacinth channel where pollutants such as organic matter (biochemical oxygen demand or BOD_5), suspended solids (SS), nitrogen (NH_3 and NO_3^-) are removed by the root system through mechanisms of direct plant uptake, microbial conversion, physical entrapment and sedimentation. Hyacinths growth rapidly on the wastewater and are periodically harvested, combined with sewage sludge from the primary settler and introduced into the anaerobic digester. As the feed passes through the digester, bacteria convert complex organic matter to biogas, a mixture of CH_4 (60-65%) and CO_2, which can be upgraded to a product gas (95% CH_4) suitable for introduction into the pipeline.

Three technical objectives aimed at reducing the cost of CHF produced from a blend of hyacinths and sludge were emphasized in the development of the biomass wastewater treatment energy conversion scheme. These included: 1) optimizing biomass yields on the sewage treatment channels; 2) maximizing wastewater treatment efficiency; and, 3) increasing CH_4 yields from anaerobic digestion under high solids loading conditions. These objectives were covered under the work of three research organizations participating in the project, the Institute of Food and Agricultural Sciences (IFAS), the Institute of Gas Technology

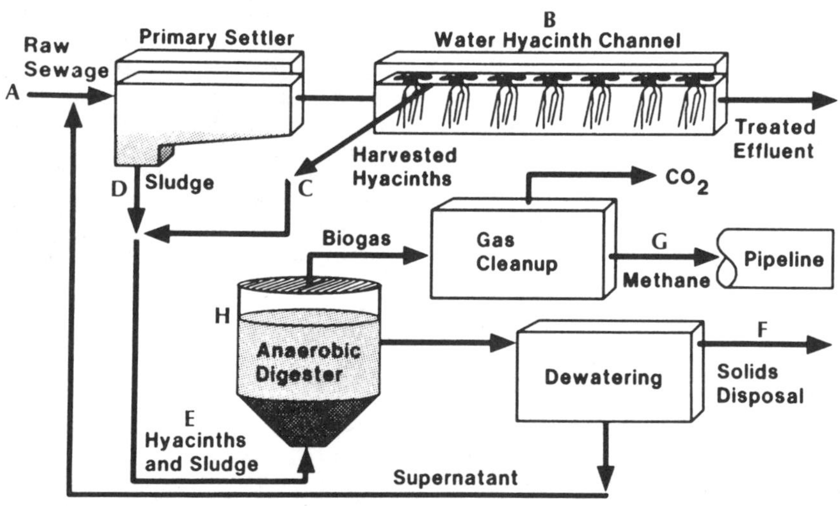

FIGURE 1. Integrated water hyacinth wastewater treatment/ anaerobic digestion concept.

(IGT), and several subsidiary companies of Walt Disney Productions. Much of the cost analysis and systems evaluation was provided by an architectural and engineering A&E) firm, Black and Veatch, under contract to the Gas Research Institute (GRI). The current sponsor is the Gas Research Institute (GRI). Previous sponsors have included United Gas Pipeline, the U.S. Environmental Protection Agency and the U.S. Department of Energy.

WASTEWATER TREATMENT AND WATER HYACINTH PRODUCTIVITY

Hyacinth wastewater treatment studies and hyacinth productivity research were conducted in five 0.1 ha^{-1} hyacinth test channels, each with dimensions of 8.8 m x 110 m x 0.35 m deep, constructed of reinforced concrete blocks and lined with 20-mil PVC sheet. Previous studies on these channels showed that secondary effluent standards could be achieved under low sewage feed rates (BOD_5 loadings) typically applied to aerobic ponds without hyacinths, amounting to about 70-90 kg BOD_5 ha^{-1} d^{-1}). In 1983 and 1984, four channels were fed with primary sewage (obtained from the Walt Disney World wastewater treatment settling basins) at loadings of 55, 110, 220 and 440 kg BOD_5 ha^{-1} d^{-1} corresponding to channel hydraulic retention times of 24, 12, 6, and 3 days, respectively. The technical objective was to achieve desirable BOD_5 and SS removal efficiencies under high sewage loading conditions. Wastewater treatment data collected from the channels included influent and effluent BOD_5, SS, pH, temperature, dissolved O_2 and various forms of N and P.

Results over a 12-month test period (November 1983 through October 1984) indicate that a single hyacinth channel is capable of removing 72-90% of the BOD_5 (81% average) and 70-90% of the SS (80% average) in the wastewater at loading rates as high as 440 kg BOD ha^{-1} d^{-1} (3 days HRT). Concentrations of BOD_5 and TSS in hyacinth pond effluents (Table 1) satisfied federal standards for BOD_5 ($\leq$30 mg L^{-1}) and TSS ($\leq$30 mg L^{-1}) at loadings up to 220 kg BOD_5 (6 days HRT) during all but two of the coldest months of the test period during which time secondary effluent standards were met at the 110 kg BOD_5 ha^{-1} d^{-1} loading rate. The average BOD_5 removal performances of the channels are compared to the performances of pilot scale channels reported in 17 other studies in the plot (Figure 2) of BOD_5 removed versus BOD_5 loading (Dinges, 1978; Hauser, 1984; Tchobanoglous et al., 1979). The dots in Figure 2 represent literature values of a linear plot with good correlation (R^2=0.98) and for a wide range of loadings from 110 to 220 kg BOD_5 ha^{-1} d^{-1} and the BOD_5 removal efficiency approximates 80%. Interestingly, the Walt Disney World points (triangle symbols) fall very close to this same line; even at loadings as high as 440 kg ha^{-1} d^{-1} BOD_5 removal efficiencies were approximating 80%. This strongly suggests that the channels were

TABLE 1. Hyacinth wastewater treatment performance summary.

Sewage loading	Hydraulic retention time	Average Percent Removals†	
		BOD_5	Suspended Solids
kg ha^{-1} d^{-1}	----d----		
55	24	89	71
110	12	87	72
220	6	84	83
440	3	81	80

†Based on a 12-month operation from November 1983 through October 1984, and an influent BOD_5 concentration of 200-260 mg L^{-1} and an influent TSS concentration of 50-90 mg L^{-1}.

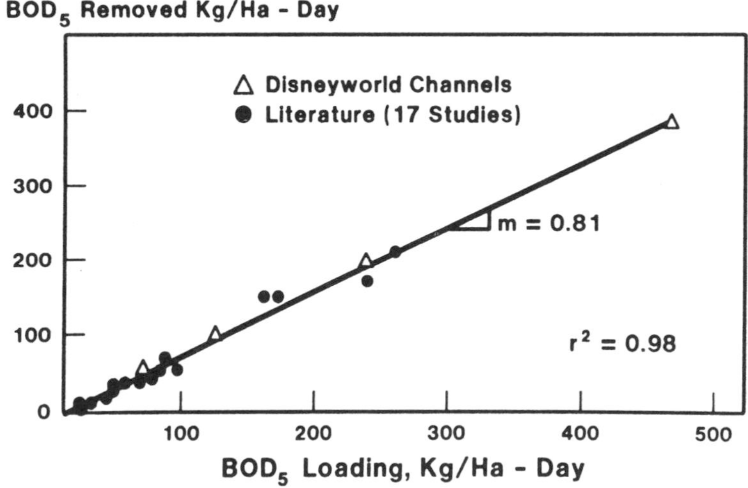

FIGURE 2. Effect of BOD_5 loading on the BOD_5 removal rate in water hyacinth treatment ponds.

not stressed with respect to BOD_5 loadings and that the limits of the hyacinth channel for secondary treatment has yet to be determined.

A statistical analysis of the influent, effluent, and channel profile data from four years of operation was performed and a wastewater treatment model was developed. Effluent BOD_5 and total suspended solids (TSS) concentrations in mg L^{-1} are primarily related to pond hydraulic retention time, t (d), according to the following equations:

(i) Effluent BOD_5 = 0.9 x TSS + Influent BOD_5/(1+1.215 t)
(ii) Effluent TSS = 10.75 + 0.645 t

The equation for total suspended solids (Figure 3) reflects the low concentration of TSS (<20 mg L^{-1}) achieved in all channel effluents throughout the year. This model shows that for a hyacinth pond receiving settled sewage of a BOD_5 typical for municipal wastewaters (120-150 mg L^{-1}), an effluent BOD_5 of 30 mg L^{-1} could be achieved at a retention time of 6 to 7 days or at a BOD_5 loading of about 220 kg ha^{-1} d^{-1}. The plot in Figure 3 also suggests that although treatment efficiencies may be improved by extending hyacinth pond retention time, the use of staging unit processes while keeping the total retention time constant may be a cost-effective means of improving secondary treatment efficiency while avoiding expansion of pond volumes. Experiments with a high-through-put, two-stage hyacinth system are underway.

A test of tertiary treatment in one of the channels receiving secondary effluent indicated that N and P removals of 50-70% and 20-30%, respectively, could be achieved in systems where hyacinths are well managed and harvested on a regular basis. Annual N and P uptake rates of hyacinths grown in tertiary treatment channels were in the range of 1,170-1,200 kg N ha^{-1} yr^{-1} and 320-390 kg P ha^{-1} yr^{-1}, respectively.

Hyacinth productivity in the large channels under unoptimized conditions ranged from 45 to 58 Mg ha^{-1} yr^{-1}. Methods used in measuring water hyacinth yields in these channels have been detailed by Reddy (1984) and Reddy et al. (1985). The use of a harvesting schedule that provides an optimum plant density of 20-36 kg m^{-2}, however, has increased hyacinth yields to 60-70 Mg

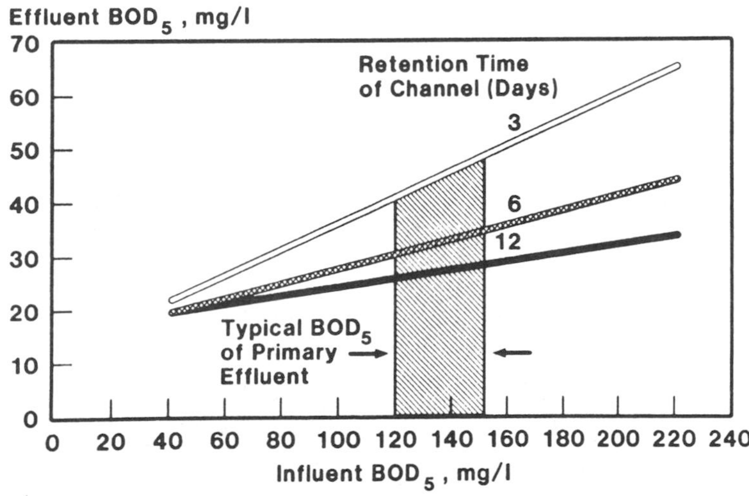

FIGURE 3. Wastewater treatment performance model for the hyacinth channel operating at the CWRF: effluent BOD_5 versus influent BOD_5.

ha^{-1} yr^{-1}. Preliminary tests in small field units suggest that additional yield increases of 30-50% are possible through the discretionary use of aeration and foliar spray applications of plant growth hormone, gibberellic acid.

ANAEROBIC DIGESTION PROCESS DEVELOPMENT

The technical objective of this R&D effort was to develop an optimized system for the biogasification of hyacinth and sludge and to integrate this process with the hyacinth wastewater treatment facility. Hyacinth was regarded as a model feedstock for a process design expected to be applicable to other types of cellulosic community wastes. The strategy used for this work consisted of evaluating conventional and advanced reactor concepts at the bench scale, selection of a reactor design on the basis of the laboratory data, and the testing of the selected reactor at an experimental test unit (ETU) under actual field conditions next to the water hyacinth channels at Walt Disney World.

Laboratory Studies

Details of the laboratory studies and the kinetic analysis of the results are presented by Srivastava et al. (1987) and Chynoweth (1987) in this book. Laboratory units tested included the conventional continuous stirred tank reactor and the non-mixed vertical flow reactor (VFR) which was designed to promote a long solids retention time under high hydraulic loadings. A VFR shown in the schematic (Figure 1) of the integrated system employs little or no mixing and can be fed at the top or at the bottom (which ever is advantageous from a solids management standpoint).

In laboratory trials, the VFR was fed from the bottom and liquid effluent was withdrawn at the top. Both the VFR and the CSTR control were fed with a 3:1 blend of hyacinths and primary sludge at loadings between 1.6 and 6.4 kg VS m^{-3} d^{-1}, corresponding to HRT's between 31 and 8 days. Steady state data (Figure 4) show that in side-by-side tests, the VFR operated in the upflow solids mode (USR) consistently achieved 15-30% greater CH_4 yields over a wide range of HRTs. The superior performance of the USR was attributed to the reactor's ability to increase the solids and microorganism residence time significantly above the HRT through sedimentation of particulate solids. Thus, the USR reactor achieved greater CH_4 production with substantially less mixing. These results provided the basis for the selection of the VFR design for testing at the ETU scale.

Biogasification Experimental Test Unit

In 1983, a 4.5 m^3 vertical flow reactor ETU was designed and constructed beside the five existing hyacinth channels at Walt Disney World. The technical objective of the first phase of the

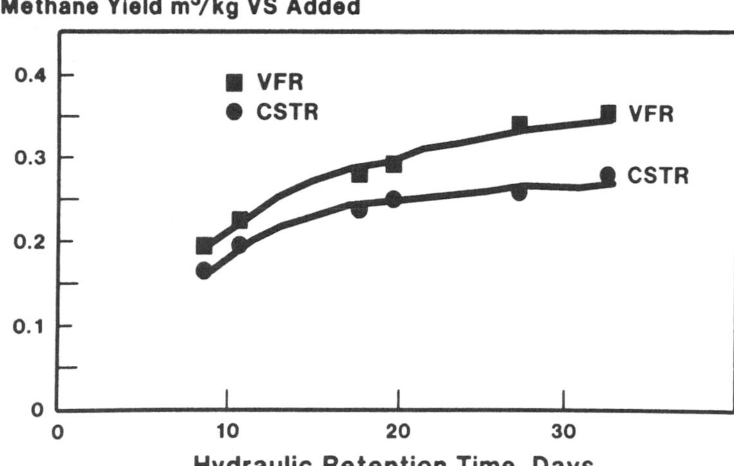

FIGURE 4. Methane yield versus hydraulic retention time for bench scale upflow solids reactor (USR) and continuous stirred tank reactor (CSTR) units operated on a 3:1 hyacinth/sludge feed blend.

ETU study was to evaluate reactor performance, scale-up, and materials handling parameters at several different mixtures of hyacinth/sludge blends. The ETU facility is capable of processing up to 910 kg (1.0 wet ton) of hyacinth/sludge feed blend (5% total solids) each day. The ETU is sized to ensure that the demand for biomass feedstock does not exceed the availability of hyacinths from the channels during the coldest months of the winter when hyacinth productivity is at its lowest. Major components of the facility include two feed tanks for short-term storage of sludge and chopped hyacinth, a feed blend tank, the vertical flow reactor, an effluent storage tank, and gas compression and storage.

The ETU was tested in the upflow and downflow modes on 1:1 and 2:1 feed blends of ground hyacinths and sewage sludge. Organic loadings applied to the reactor were maintained at 3.2 kg VS m^{-3} d^{-1} (HRT = 10-12 days) for most of the operation of the ETU. At the annual hyacinth production yields of 56-67 Mg ha^{-1} yr^{-1} achieved from the channels at Walt Disney World, the hyacinth to sludge ratio fed to the reactor on a large scale would be expected to approximate 1:1 on the average and 2:1 during the peak hyacinth production periods during the year. At each feed condition in the ETU, the steady state performance parameters (Table 2) of the ETU was evaluated.

TABLE 2. ETU evaluation parameters.

Performance Parameters	Engineering Parameters
Methane yield	Materials balance
Methane production rate	Solids
Gas composition	Carbon
Volatile fatty acids	Nitrogen
Temperature	Phosphorus
Alkalinity	Materials handling
Organic matter reduction	Scale-up of laboratory performance

Results from four steady state conditions, summarized by Biljetina et al. (1987), illustrate the effect of feedstock blend ratio and feed mode on CH_4 yield performance. Operated in the upflow mode at a loading of 3.2 kg VS m^{-3} d^{-1}, the VFR reactor achieved good CH_4 yields on 1:1 and 2:1 blends averaging 0.26 and 0.4 m^3 kg^{-1} VS added, respectively. This performance exceeded the performance of the completely mixed control operated at the same feed condition by 10 to 15%. Solids profile data taken from the reactor revealed that a large float of solids of a thickness of more than 1.2 m had been maintained during the steady state upflow reactor runs. On the basis of this information, it was decided that improved solids retention might be realized if the reactor feed mode were to be changed to a downflow mode.

When the feed mode was shifted from upflow to downflow, CH_4 yields increased to 0.45 and 0.35 m^3 kg^{-1} VS added for the 1:1 and 2:1 feed blend. This represents a solids destruction efficiency of nearly 70% which approximates the anticipated average performance expected from a large production scale facility. The CH_4 yields observed with the VFR operated in the down-flow mode are compared with CH_4 yields achieved with the conventional digester control (CSTR) (Figure 5).

Carbon balances conducted on the ETU during each steady state condition showed that at an HRT of 10-12 days, the solids retention time (SRT) of the VFR was maintained at 17-21 days in the upflow mode and at 24-35 days in the downflow mode. Laboratory and ETU data clearly show that higher CH_4 yields are associated with reactors that maintain high SRTs. This ability to maintain SRTs at double or triple the HRT represents a marked advantage over conventional digestion (CSTR) in which HRT and SRT are virtually equal. This means that high CH_4 yields can potentially be maintained in a vertical flow reactor at less than half the digester volume required for conventional digestion.

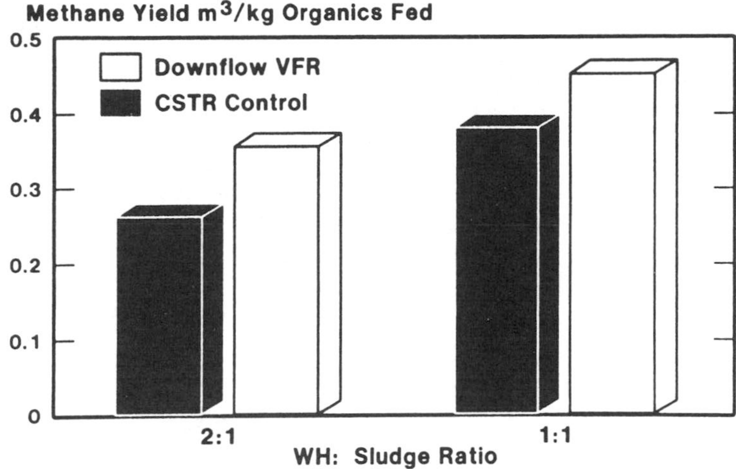

FIGURE 5. Methane yield achieved with the 4.0 m^3 vertical flow reactor fed with 1:1 and 2:1 hyacinth/sludge blends at a 3.2 kg VS m^{-3} d^{-1} loading (35°C).

Systems Analysis

Systems evaluations of the integrated waste conversion concept have been continually performed to assess progress in the research effort and to identify promising new research directions. Early in the project, a preliminary A&E economic feasibility analysis was conducted on a conceptual secondary treatment water hyacinth system employing conventional anaerobic digestion and gas upgrading to pipeline quality. Revenues assumed for wastewater treatment in that analysis were in the range of conventional secondary treatment: about $72 per 1000 m^3 and $100 per 1,000 m^3 (1985 dollars), respectively, for the 500,000 and 100,000 population facilities. Results from this study indicated that a significant amount of CH_4 could be generated with the water hyacinth concept at a cost of $2.40-4.60 GJ^{-1} at treatment plant sizes of 190 x 10^3 to 38 x 10^3 m^3 d^{-1} corresponding to populations of 500,000 to 100,000. These costs were based on some key assumptions of system performance which became the goals of the project. The A&E assumptions included:

- Water hyacinth yields of 110 Mg ha^{-1} yr^{-1} in wastewater treatment channels.
- Methane yields from the conversion of the water hyacinth/ sludge blend of 0.28 m^3 kg^{-1} VS added achieved with a 28-d reactor retention time

- Water hyacinth pond sizes of about 0.75 ha per 1000 $m^3\ d^{-1}$ capacity of sewage treatment

Over the last two years, the performance of the integrated experimental test unit at the CWRF has met or exceeded virtually all of these goals, as shown in Table 3, largely due to the unique, vertical flow design of the reactor (VFR). On the basis of these results, mass flow diagrams were constructed for the concept at capacities of 10,000, 100,000 and 500,000 population equivalents. In all cases, a climate similar to that of central Florida was assumed in the estimation of water hyacinth yields and net energy production. Mass flows through the concept diagram (Figure 1) sized for a 500,000 population are described in Table 4. Mass flows, kinetic models, and solids handling information

TABLE 3. Summary of project accomplishments.

	A&E Projections (goals)	ETU system performance
Methane yield $m^3\ kg^{-1}$ VS added†	0.28	0.47
Hydraulic retention time, d	28	11
Water hyacinth production $Mg\ ha^{-1}\ yr^{-1}$	114	68
Pond area required for secondary treatment ha per 1000 $m^3\ d^{-1}$	0.75	0.75

†1.0 $m^3\ CH_4$ = 0.0367 GJ.

TABLE 4. Mass flow through an integrated hyacinth sewage treatment anaerobic digestion facility sized for a community of 500,000. Units of C, D, E and F are on dry wt basis.

Location on the schematic of Figure 1	Description	Units	Performance
A	Sewage flow	$m^3\ d^{-1}$	190,000
B	Hyacinth pond area	ha	142
C	Harvested hyacinths	$Mg\ d^{-1}$	25
D	Primary sludge	$Mg\ d^{-1}$	23
E	Digester feed blend of hyacinths and sludge	$Mg\ d^{-1}$	48
F	Digester effluent to disposal	$Mg\ d^{-1}$	19
G	Net CH_4 produced	GJ/d	550
H	Reactor volume	$m^3 \times 10^{-3}$	11.4

were used to calculate the required capacity and probable performance of each unit process in the integrated hyacinth system.

The project results and mass flow analyses were then translated into system costs. A&E cost curves constructed for each unit process were used to relate process throughput capacity requirements to capital and annual O&M expenditures. Capital and operating costs (in 1985 dollars) for a 500,000 population system are broken out for all of the major cost components in Table 5. The major capital and O&M costs (Table 5) are associated with wastewater treatment. Not obvious from the table is the effect that the performance of one system component can have on another. For example, the rate of nutrient removal, the capacity of hyacinth harvesters, the volume of the digesters and the amounts of the digested sludge requiring dewatering and disposal will be significantly affected by the growth rate of hyacinths propagating in the treatment ponds. Likewise, conversion efficiency of the digester will have a large impact on the amounts of effluent solids requiring disposal. These relationships illustrate the need to perform R&D on the total system to gain the most effective cost improvement.

Financial analysis of costs for a 500,000 population facility, assuming municipal utility financing, is summarized in Table 6. A similar analysis was conducted for systems sized for 10,000 and 100,000 populations. In this cost analysis, only two principle revenue streams were considered, the service charge for wastewater treatment and the sale of pipeline quality CH_4 to a gas utility. The levelized costs (inflation-corrected amortized costs) of all three sizes of systems are presented in Table 7. In this table, costs of wastewater treatment are calculated for all three sizes of plants on the basis of being able to obtain a price of \$2.00 GJ^{-1} for CH_4 sold to a local gas utility. The break-even price of wastewater renovation is affected by the price charged to the gas utility for the CH_4 produced (Figure 6).

TABLE 5. Capital and O&M costs for the major components of an integrated water hyacinth/anaerobic digestion facility sized for a 500,000 population.

Systems component	Costs (millions of 1985 dollars)	
	Capital	Annual O&M
Wastewater treatment	11.9	1.05
Water hyacinth harvesting	4.1	1.23
Anaerobic digestion	2.8	0.21
Sludge disposal	3.9	0.33
Gas cleanup	1.3	0.29
Total	24.0	3.11

TABLE 6. Summary of economics for the integrated water hyacinth/anaerobic digestion facility sized for 500,000 population.

Assumptions

Return to debt	9.2%	Construction period	2 yr
Return to equity	13.7%	Book life	
Fraction to debt	0.65	Concrete structures	50 yr
Working capital fraction	0.10	All other	20 yr
Inflation	6.0%	Tax life	10 yr
Methane price charged to utilities, $ GJ^{-1}	2.00	Net CH_4 output	50 GJ d^{-1}

Costs (1985 $)

Total capital	$24 million
Total annual O&M	$3.1 million yr^{-1}
Annual CH_4 sales revenue	$0.40 million yr^{-1}
Cost of wastewater treatment	$61 per 1000 m^3

The levelized cost results presented in Table 7 (in constant 1985 dollars) indicate that if the performance of the hyacinth treatment pilot system can be duplicated at a community scale, secondary wastewater treatment can be provided at a cost of $61 to $85 per 1000 m^3 for populations of 500,000 and 100,000 respectively if a gas price of $2.00 GJ^{-1} is obtained for the CH_4 sold to the utility. These wastewater treatment costs represent a 15 to 20% reduction in cost when compared to conventional secondary treatment technology. Equally important, the economics showed that hyacinth aquaculture could remain cost effective for communities with populations as low as 10,000.

Overall, research and development on the entire integrated system reduced annualized facility costs (amortized capital plus O&M) by about 20% below the annual costs projected by the initial

TABLE 7. Methane costs from the integrated water hyacinth/anaerobic digestion concept.

Population of community	Wastewater flow 1000's m^3	Net methane output GJ d^{-1}	Revenue from methane sales to a gas utility, $ GJ^{-1}	Cost of hyacinth water treatment $ per 1000 m^3
500,000	190	550	2.00	61
100,000	38	110	2.00	85
10,000	3.8	11	2.00	239

*All costs are in 1985 dollars.

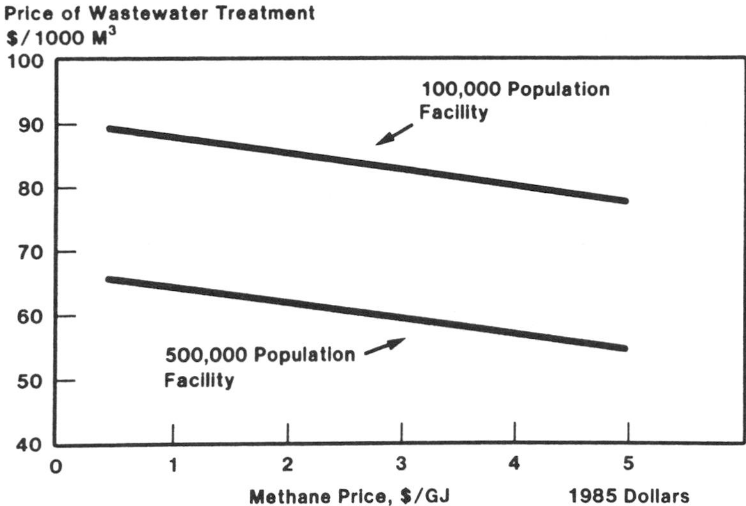

FIGURE 6. Relationship between wastewater treatment and CH_4 production economics for a hyacinth system sized for a 500,000 population.

A&E study based upon the original performance goals. Major factors contributing to this reduction of cost included the following:

- The achievement of secondary effluent quality standards at the target wastewater loading of 224 kg BOD_5 ha^{-1} d^{-1} at hyacinth yields of 67 Mg ha^{-1} yr^{-1}, 40% less than the projected hyacinth yield, effectively reduced hyacinth harvesting and handling requirements;
- Total solids output was reduced by 27% and digester hydraulic retention time was reduced from 25 to 11 days which led to a 60% decrease in digester volume and a 45% reduction in the overall cost of digestion;
- Despite the lower throughput of solids through the anaerobic digester, the CH_4 yield per gram of feed organics added was increased by 59% causing the net CH_4 output from the facility to increase by 33%;
- Sludge generation was reduced by 57% through the improved solids destruction efficiency of the vertical flow reactor which led to a 35-45% reduction in sludge disposal costs.

These cost results indicate that the integration of the vertical flow reactor into aquaculture operations markedly improved the economics of the hyacinth wastewater treatment and that both cost-effective wastewater renovation and low-cost pipeline-quality CH_4 can be obtained as benefits for the community using the design and operating methods developed by CWRF project.

FUTURE DIRECTIONS

Significant cost reductions have been made through empirical design improvements and optimization of major parameters controlling system performance. Further reductions in cost may be achieved through a better understanding of the biological, chemical and physical mechanisms that mediate pollutant removal and conversion of waste solids to CH_4. Research that looks beyond the surface of the "black box" will no doubt lead to greater reliability of performance and economy of design. This kind of approach is needed to provide the kinds of diagnostic, design and operational information that will be needed in the future to support a growing number of municipal aquaculture projects.

Investigations into the mechanisms of removal of pollutants such as nutrients, suspended solids, BOD_5, heavy metals, chlorinated organics and pathogens, would provide a rational basis for process design and operation. Initial observations on a mechanistic level of nutrient uptake have revealed that plant growth and N uptake rates can be improved as much as 50% when a 1:1 molar balance exists between the cationic (NH_4^+) and anionic (NO_2^- and NO_3^-) forms of N. This would suggest a number of nitrification and nutrient management schemes that would maintain a favorable nutrient balance to optimize nutrient removal throughout the hyacinth channels. These strategies will be tested at the CWRF. Furthermore, understanding the role of plant hormones in the growth of water hyacinth could suggest novel approaches to the stimulation of greater levels of nutrient removal from wastewater in aquaculture systems. Other channel operating techniques employing staged processing, freeze control via intermittent spraying and plant density control to optimize pollutant removal performance will also be investigated at the CWRF. Future plans also include research on cold-tolerant nutrient film technique systems that would extend the application of the integrated concept to colder regions of the U.S.

Equally important, the CWRF is concentrating on the development of advanced features in anaerobic digestion that have the potential of expanding the benefits of this technology to the community. Monoclonal antibody and cell-wall lipid analysis techniques have allowed the rapid characterization and quantification of active bacterial species in the digestion process making it possible to determine the distribution and dynamics of the key microorganisms that control the digestion process. This work will undoubtedly lead to sensors and feedback control systems that can be used to improve optimization strategies, increase solids destruction performance and enhance reliability. Experiments have also been initiated on the use of flotation to achieve better solids retention and CH_4 yields per kg of organic feed in the digester. This concept would involve the periodic recycle of digester gas to spargers strategically placed in the digester to control the solids concentration in the liquid effluent. Research on the action of enzymes in the micro-environment of the bacterial film coating particulate matter in the digester may suggest low cost techniques to increase conversion efficiency. Development at the CWRF will also focus on the operation of the anaerobic digestion process to maximize the solubilization of CO_2 in the liquid fraction in order to produce high-energy gas directly from the reactor. This would reduce gas cleanup costs by more than 80%.

CONCLUSIONS

The results from this comprehensive research project indicate that the integrated hyacinth/anaerobic digestion system can be of substantial benefit to the community as well as the gas rate payer in terms of providing: 1) a cost-effective technology for wastewater renovation for communities as small as 10,000 population, 2) a method of waste volume reduction that could, if applied to the total community organic waste stream, extend landfill life by a factor of 5 to 7 times, and 3) a stable, local supply of CH_4 gas to supplement natural gas supplies.

REFERENCES

Bastian, R. K., and S. C. Reed. 1979. Aquaculture systems for wastewater treatment: Seminar proceedings and engineering assessment/MCD-67. Available from General Services Administration, Denver, CO, Document No. EPA 430/9-80-006.

Biljetina, R., V. J. Srivastava, D. P. Chynoweth, and T. D. Hayes. 1987. Anaerobic digestion of water hyacinth and sludge. In K. R. Reddy and W. H. Smith (ed.) Aquatic Plants for Water Treatment and Resource Recovery. Magnolia Publishing Inc., Orlando, FL.

Chynoweth, D. P. 1987. Biomass conversion process options. In K. R. Reddy and W. H. Smith (ed.) Aquatic Plants for Water Treatment and Resource Recovery. Magnolia Publishing Inc., Orlando, FL.

Chynoweth, D. P., et al. 1984. Biogasification of water hyacinth and primary sludge. Proceedings of the International Gas Research Conference, Government Institutes, Inc., Rockville, MD.

DeBusk, T. A., and K. R. Reddy. 1987a. Wastewater treatment using floating aquatic macrophytes: Management strategies. In K. R. Reddy and W. H. Smith (ed.) Aquatic Plants for Water Treatment and Resource Recovery. Magnolia Publishing Inc., Orlando, FL.

DeBusk, W. F., and K. R. Reddy. 1987b. Density requirements to maximize the productivity of water hyacinth (Eichhornia crasssipes). In K. R. Reddy and W. H. Smith (ed.) Aquatic Plants for Water Treatment and Resource Recovery. Magnolia Publishing Inc., Orlando, FL.

Dinges, R. 1978. Upgrading stabilization pond effluents by water hyacinth culture. J. Water Pollut. Control Fed. 50:833.

Duffer, W. R., and J. E. Moyer. 1978. Municipal wastewater aquaculture. Available from the National Technical Information Service, Springfield, VA, EPA Report No. EPA-600/2-78-110.

Hauser, J. R. 1984. Use of water hyacinth aquatic treatment systems for ammonia control and effluent polishing. J. Water Pollut. Control Fed. 56:219-225.

Hayes, T. D., and H. R. Isaacson. 1986. Advanced concepts for methane enrichment in anaerobic digestion. p. 205-212. Proceedings of the 21st Intersociety Energy Conversion Engineering Conference. Amer. Chem. Soc., Washington, DC.

Hayes, T. D., D. P. Chynoweth, K. R. Reddy, and B. Schwegler. 1985. The integration of biogas production with wastewater treatment. p. 189-200. In M. Z. Lowenstein (ed.) Energy Application of Biomass, Elsevier Applied Science Publishers, New York, NY.

Innovative and alternative technology assessment manual/MCD-53. 1978. United States Environmental Protection Agency Report No. EPA 430/9-78-009.

Klass, D. L., and S. Ghosh. 1981. Methane production by anaerobic digestion of water hyacinth (Eichhornia crassipes). p. 129-149. In Fuels from Biomass and Wastes. Institute of Gas Technology, Chicago, IL.

Kruzic, A. P. 1979. Water hyacinth wastewater treatment system at Walt Disney World. In Aquaculture Systems for Wastewater Treatment/MCD 67. Available from General Services Administration, Denver, CO, Document No. EPA 430/9-80-006.

Moorhead, K. K., K. R. Reddy, and D. A. Graetz. 1987. Nitrogen cycling in an integrated "biomass for energy" system. In K. R. Reddy and W. H. Smith (ed.) Aquatic Plants for Water Treatment and Resource Recovery. Magnolia Publishing Inc., Orlando, FL.

Reddy, K. R. 1984. Water hyacinth biomass production in Florida. Biomass 6:167.

Reddy, K. R., and W. F. DeBusk. 1987. Plant nutrient storage capabilities. In K. R. Reddy and W. H. Smith (ed.) Aquatic Plants for Water Treatment and Resource Recovery, Magnolia Publishing Inc., Orlando, FL.

Reed, S., R. Bastian, and W. Jewell. 1980. Engineering assessment of aquaculture systems for wastewater treatment: An overview. p. 1. In Aquaculture Systems for Wastewater Treatment/MCD 68. Available from General Services Administration, Denver, CO, Document No. EPA 430/9-80-007.

Ryther, J. H., et al. 1979. Biomass production by marine and freshwater plants. p. 13-23. In Proceedings of the Third Annual Biomass Energy Systems Conference Proceedings/DOE, Golden, CO.

Srivastava, V. J., K. F. Fanin, R. Biljetina, D. P. Chynoweth, and T. D. Hayes. 1987. Development of an advanced anaerobic digester design and a kinetic model for biogasification of water hyacinth/sludge blends. In K. R. Reddy and W. H. Smith (ed.) Aquatic Plants for Water Treatment and Resource Recovery. Magnolia Publishing Inc., Orlando, FL.

Tchobanoglous, G., R. Stowell, R. Ludwig, J. Colt, and A. Knight. 1979. The use of aquatic plants and animals for the treatment of wastewater: An overview. p. 35. In Aquaculture Systems for Wastewater Treatment/MCD 68. Available from General Services Administration, Denver, CO, Document No. EPA 430/9-80-006.

Vaidyanathan, S., K. M. Kavadia, K. C. Shroff, and S. P. Mahajan. 1985. Biogas production in batch and semicontinuous digesters using water hyacinth. Biotechnology and Bioengineering 27:905-908.

Wastewater engineering. 1972. Metcalf & Eddy, Inc., McGraw-Hill Book Company, New York, NY.

Wolverton, B. C., and R. McDonald. 1979. Upgrading facultative wastewater lagoons with vascular aquatic plants. J. Water Poll. Control Fed. 51:305.

ARTIFICIAL MARSHES FOR WASTEWATER TREATMENT

B. C. Wolverton
National Aeronautics and Space Administration
National Space Technology Laboratories
NSTL, Mississippi 39529

ABSTRACT

A promising natural means of wastewater treatment has been developed by NASA at the National Space Technology Laboratories (NSTL) in South Mississippi during the past 15 years. This biotechnology involves the use of marsh plants, microorganisms and high surface area support media such as rocks. The symbiotic relationship that exists between microorganisms and plant roots can result in synergistic action toward degradation and removal of biochemical oxygen demanding (BOD) substances from domestic sewage and toxic chemicals from industrial wastewaters.

When plants such as reed (*Phragmites communis*), cattail (*Typha* spp.), canna lily (*Canna flaccida*), arrowhead (*Sagitaria latifolia*), arrow-arum (*Peltandra virginica*), pickerelweed (*Pontederia cordata*) and green taro (*Colocasia esculenta*) are planted in rock filters, artificial marshes are produced which are highly biologically active. These filters can reduce BOD_5 levels in septic tank and oxidation lagoon effluents from 110-50 mg L^{-1} to 10-2 mg L^{-1} in 12 to 24 h. These marsh filters can also reduce toxic organic chemicals such as benzene from 9 mg L^{-1} to 0.05 mg L^{-1} in 24 h in addition to removing toxic heavy metals and radioactive elements from contaminated waters.

Keywords: Aquatic plants, sewage effluent, industrial effluents, artificial wetland, gravel bed system.

INTRODUCTION

The treatment of domestic sewage and removal of hazardous chemicals from contaminated water is a problem confronting communities and cities throughout the United States and other countries. Wastewater treatment is an integral part of the water crisis that is emerging throughout the world. Even areas of the U.S. and other parts of the world with a plentiful supply of water are facing problems because the water is becoming contaminated with sewage and/or hazardous chemicals. Therefore, one of the

ISBN 0-941463-00-1

most urgent environmental needs in the world today is a simple, low cost means of wastewater treatment and water reuse. A promising means of utilizing vascular aquatic plants for wastewater treatment has been investigated by NASA and other scientists during the past 15 years (Bastian and Benforado, 1983).

Much success has been achieved in utilizing higher plants and microorganisms in developing low cost wastewater treatment and recycling processes. The use of artificial marshes for treating both domestic and industrial wastewater is discussed in this report.

DOMESTIC SEWAGE TREATMENT

The first phase of research conducted by NASA in wastewater treatment utilizing aquatic plants was begun at NSTL in 1971, and involved the use of water hyacinth (*Eichhornia crassipes*) and duckweed (*Lemna*, *Spirodela*, and *Wolffia* sp.) floating aquatic plants (Wolverton and McDonald, 1976a,b; 1977a,b; 1978a,b; 1979a,b,c,; 1980; 1981a,b; Wolverton and McKnown, 1976; Wolverton et al., 1976). These plants were used to upgrade sewage lagoons at NSTL in 1975. By using water hyacinths and duckweed in lieu of conventional activated sludge processes, NASA has realized cost savings at NSTL of several million dollars over the past 11 years of operation.

Although the water hyacinth/duckweed combination has been effective for treating wastewater for the past 11 years at NSTL, severe hyacinth kill-back during several cold winters has occurred. Water hyacinth was completely eliminated from one small marsh system and was replaced with water pennywort (*Hydrocotyle umbellata*), a more cold-tolerant plant. For the past six years the pennywort/duckweed system has worked very effectively without any plant harvesting. Other researchers have also demonstrated the value of these and other aquatic plants in treating wastewater (Culley and Epps, 1973; Dinges, 1982; Reddy, 1983; Reddy and DeBusk, 1984, 1985a,b; Reddy et al., 1983).

In an effort to increase the geographical range and effectiveness of floating aquatic plant systems, an advanced hybrid system was developed which combined emersed, cold-tolerant and salt-tolerant plants with microbial filter technology. The first hybrid system consisted of an anaerobic sludge collecting and digesting chamber followed by an up-flow rock filter in which reed (*Phragmites communis*) or rush (*Juncus effusus*) was grown (Wolverton, 1982; Wolverton et al., 1983).

The hybrid system has changed over the past several years by adding aerobic and facultative lagoons to collect and digest sludge. The reeds and rushes have also been replaced in most cases by more aesthetically desirable plants such as the canna lily, arrowhead, arrow-arum, elephant ears, pickerelweed and water iris which performed equally well (Table 1). The canna lily,

TABLE 1. Artificial marsh filters for removing BOD_5 from domestic sewage.†

Marsh plants	Concentration before and after exposure to marsh filter	
	Initial	After 24 h
	------------mg L^{-1}------------	
Reed	306.0‡	36.0
(*Phragmites communis*)	71.7	2.8
Cattail	80.1	8.3
(*Typha latifolia*)		
Arrowhead	75.0‡	5.0
(*Sagittaria latifolia*)		
Arrow Arum	53.0	2.0
(*Peltandra virginica*)		
Canna Lily	116.0‡	12.0
(*Canna flaccida*)	64.0	3.0

†Three (3) or more different replicates were performed.
‡Two initial ranges.

arrowhead, pickerelweed and water iris also produce beautiful yellow, red, orange, white and blue flowers.

Although microbial rock filters have been used to treat sewage for over 90 years and the ability of aquatic plants to enhance sewage treatment in natural marshes has been recognized for many years, only recently have the two processes been combined. The combination and optimization of microbial filters and higher plants into an artificial marsh has produced one of the most promising wastewater treatment technologies since development of the trickling filter process in 1893.

Although this technology is relatively simple, it is very important that sound engineering practices be used in the design of these filters. It is also important that filter depth be considered, especially in the last section of the filter, to assure that aerobic conditions are achieved before discharge. A dissolved O_2 level of 1.5 mg L^{-1} or more is required to achieve low BOD_5 effluent levels (<10 mg L^{-1}).

Since the application of the microbial-plant filter is new and only a limited number of small systems have been in operation over the past several years, engineering design data is still being generated. Several small systems, 0.74-3.78 m^3 d^{-1}, have been in operation in Mississippi for several years (Wolverton et al., 1984). There have been seven microbial-plant filter systems ranging in size from 7.6 to 1325 m^3 d^{-1} designed for use in Louisiana in the past year. Several of these systems are now under construction and scheduled to be operational by late 1986. These filters were designed to treat wastewater discharged from septic tanks (Figures 1 and 2) and sewage lagoons (Figure 3).

FIGURE 1. Single home wastewater treatment system using plants.

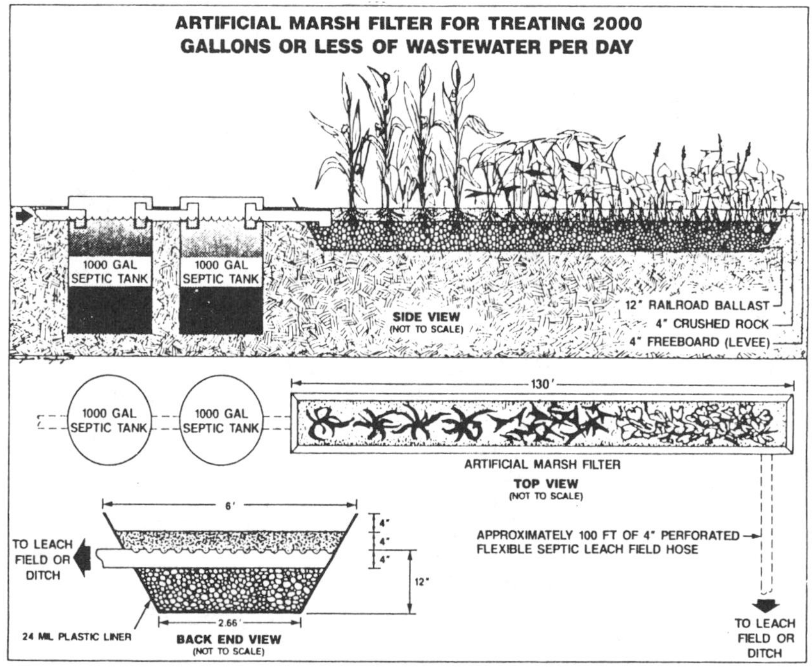

FIGURE 2. Artificial marsh filter for treating 7.57 m^3 d^{-1} or less of wastewater.

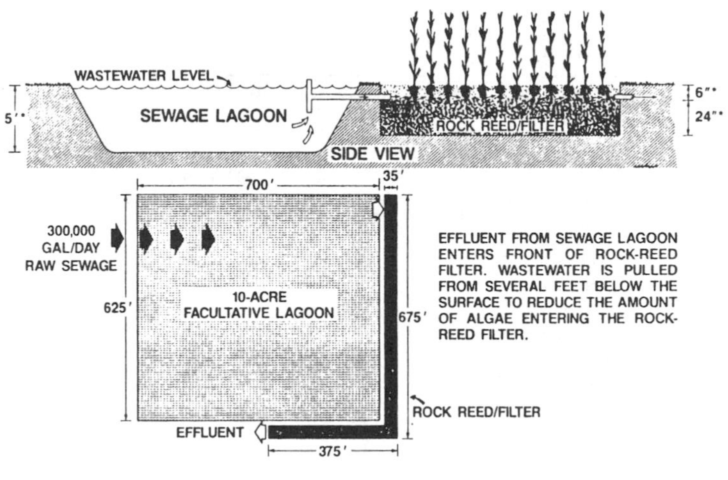

FIGURE 3. The use of artificial marshes (rock-reed filters) to upgrade sewage lagoons to meet advanced wastewater treatment standards.

Marsh filters are also capable of treating wastewater discharged from any system provided sludge is removed to prevent filter clogging. Marsh filters can be designed to achieve various levels of BOD_5 and TSS removal, ranging from secondary levels of 30 mg L^{-1} to tertiary levels of 5 mg L^{-1} or less.

INDUSTRIAL WASTEWATER TREATMENT

The ability of microorganisms to degrade organic chemicals is well documented (Bouwer and McCarty, 1981,1983a,b; Bouwer et al., 1981; Eaton and Ribbons, 1982; Gibson, 1977,1980; Haber et al., 1983; Kellogg et al., 1981; Keyser et al., 1976; Kilbane et al., 1982; Klecka and Maier, 1985; Rittman and McCarty, 1980; Tabak et al., 1981; Wilson and Wilson, 1985; Wolverton and McDonald, 1977, 1981,1986; Wolverton et al., 1981,1984; McDonald, 1981) (Tables 2 and 3). Microorganisms can adapt to utilizing carbon sources from various organic chemical structures. This adaptation occurs through recruiting various genes from existing plasmids to make new plasmids. The new plasmids then code for enzymes necessary to convert the C sources into compounds useful for energy and cell mass synthesis (Kellogg et al., 1981).

Biological processing techniques have been developed which enable adapted microorganisms to be retained in the biological treatment unit or filter for periods much greater than the hydraulic retention time. Mean cell residence times of approximately 100 d can be achieved with short hydraulic retention

TABLE 2. Artificial marsh filters containing reed (Phragmites communis) for removing toxic organics from domestic sewage and tap water.†

Organic	Solution	Concentration Before and After Exposure to Marsh Filter			
		Initial	Final		
			3 h	6 h	24 h
		mg L^{-1}			
Benzene	Tap water	9.33	0.95	0.39	0.05
Benzene	Domestic sewage	9.59	0.85	0.60	0.23
Toluene (methyl benzene)	Tap water	6.60	0.78	0.22	0.005
Toluene (methyl benzene)	Domestic sewage	7.13	0.66	0.49	0.12
p-Xylene (p-dimethyl-benzene)	Tap water	4.07	0.65	0.43	0.14
p-Xylene (p-dimethyl-benzene)	Domestic sewage	4.34	0.69	0.65	0.35

†An average of 12 replicates were performed with each solution.

TABLE 3. Artificial marsh filter containing reed (Phragmites communis) for removing chlorinated hydrocarbons from contaminated river water.†

Organics	Concentration Before and After Exposure to Marsh Filter		
	Initial	4 h	24 h
	µg L^{-1}		
Chloroform	837.7	387.5	263.2
Tetrachloroethylene	457.3	161.7	112.4

†Forty-eight (48) replicates were performed.

times. This characteristic of the microbial filter process makes it very appealing for treating domestic sewage and industrial chemical wastewater.

The efficiency and versatility of the microbial filter process has undergone significant improvement recently with the addition of vascular aquatic plants to the system (Wolverton and McDonald, 1981,1986; Wolverton et al., 1984). The ability of plant roots to absorb, translocate and metabolize organic chemicals was recognized in the early 1930's. This phenomenon made possible the development of systemic pesticides and opened up a new industry. A highly biologically active artificial marsh filter can be developed by the use of plant roots and rocks. Nutrient-enriched waters such as domestic sewage should be used to condition the artificial marsh filter before adding wastewater containing organic chemicals. Once the microorganisms are established on and around the plant roots, they form a symbiotic relationship with the plants which results in synergistic actions toward degradation and removal of organic chemicals from the wastewaters exposed to this filter. These reactions are very complex and are not fully understood.

During microbial degradation of the organics, certain fragments (metabolites) are produced which the plants absorb and utilize along with minerals as a food source. The microorganisms also utilize certain metabolites produced by plant roots as a food source. By each removing the others waste products, this allows a reaction to be sustained in favor of rapid removal of organics from the wastewater stream. The plants also add to the microbial filter the capability of removing toxic heavy metals and radioactive elements from the wastewater stream flowing through the artificial marsh (Wolverton et al., 1976; Wolverton and McDonald, 1977; McDonald, 1981). The plants remove the soluble metals and radioactive elements from the wastewater by absorption and concentration.

PLANT MANAGEMENT REQUIREMENTS

When plants are used to concentrate non-biodegradable substances and remove them from wastewater, a plant harvesting and storage process must be developed. One scheme that has been in use for over 10 years at NSTL is the use of a clay-lined pit. The harvested plants containing heavy metals such as silver are stored in the clay-lined pit which has an overflow outlet back into the front end of the marsh filter. Most aquatic plants are over 90% water, therefore, their volume is reduced to 5-10% of the original volume after decomposition.

There are several options available for managing plants grown in wastewater containing domestic sewage and/or industrial wastewater that contains biodegradable organics and non-toxic elements. The simplest method involves no harvesting as occurs in natural marshes. Another possible option is the controlled burning of dead plant material during late winter or early spring before the appearance of new plant shoots. The use of animals such as goats for controlled grazing of the marsh plants is an interesting alternative to burning or mechanical harvesting (Figure 4). This method can only be used after assurance that the plants are free of toxic chemicals.

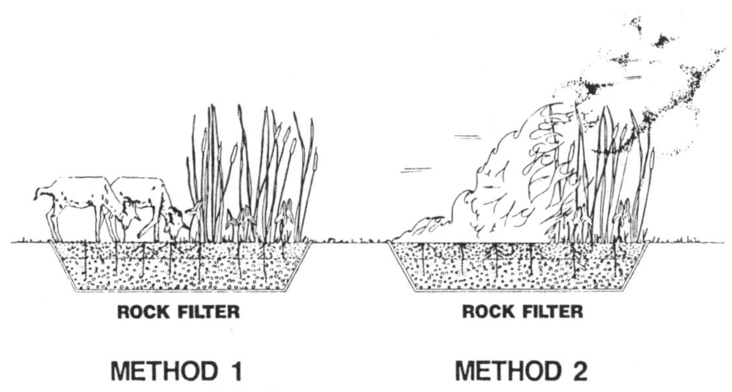

FIGURE 4. Marsh plant harvesting methods.

ADVANTAGES AND DISADVANTAGES OF USING ARTIFICIAL MARSHES FOR WASTEWATER TREATMENT

The artificial marsh concept for treating and recycling wastewater is, in most cases, a viable alternative to conventional mechanical treatment systems.

Advantages of the artificial marsh treatment process over mechanical systems are: 1) less costly to install in most locations; 2) lower operational and maintenance costs; 3) non-technical personnel can operate and maintain; 4) more flexibility and less susceptibility to shockloading; 5) less energy required to operate, and 6) greater reliability. The major disadvantage of the artificial marsh process is the increased land area required.

DISCUSSION AND RECOMMENDATION

Artificial marshes can be designed and constructed in several different configurations. The most effective marshes for treating domestic and industrial wastewaters include rock filters. Each filter should be designed in accordance with the receiving wastewater stream. Large rocks should be used in the front portion of marsh filters receiving algal laden discharge water from sewage lagoons during the summer months to minimize filter clogging. An area of 1.6-2.0 ha of marsh filter is required to treat 3,800 m^3 of sewage lagoon effluent per day. Marshes installed in colder climates will require a longer retention time in the filter, different types of plants, and increased land area. Different types of wastewater may also require different retention times and different types of marsh plants.

REFERENCES

Bastian, R. K., and J. Benforado. 1983. Waste treatment: Doing what comes naturally. Technology Review. Feb/Mar:59-66.

Bouwer, E. J., and P. L. McCarty. 1981. Biofilm degradation of trace chlorinated organics. Proceedings of the 1981 National Conference on Environmental Engineering. p. 196-202.

Bouwer, E. J., and P. L. McCarty. 1983a. Transformations of 1- and 2-carbon halogenated aliphatic organic compounds under methanogenic conditions. Appl. Environ. Microbiol. 45:1286-1294.

Bouwer, E. J., and P. L. McCarty. 1983b. Transformations of halogenated organic compounds under denitrification conditions. Appl. Environ. Microbiol. 45:1291-1299.

Bouwer, E. J., B. W. Rittmann, and P. L. McCarty. 1981. Anaerobic degradation of halogenated 1- and 2-Carbon organic compounds. Environ. Sci. Technol. 15:596-599.

Culley, D. D., Jr., and A. E. Epps. 1973. Use of duckweed for waste treatment and animal feed. J. Water Poll. Control Fed. 45:337-347.

Dinges, R. 1982. Natural systems for water pollution control. Published by Van Nostrand Reinhold Co., New York, NY. pp. 252.

Eaton, R. W., and D. W. Ribbons. 1982. Metabolism of dimethylphthalate by _Micrococcus_ sp. strain 12B. J. Bacteriol. 151:465-467.

Gibson, D. T. 1977. Biodegradation of aromatic petroleum hydrocarbons. p. 39-46. _In_ D. S. Wolfe (ed.) Fate and Effects of Petroleum Hydrocarbons in Marine Ecosystems and Organisms. Pergamon Press, New York, NY.

Gibson, D. T. 1981. The microbial oxidation of aromatic hydrocarbons. Crit. Rev. Microbiol. 1:199-223.

Haber, C. L., L. N. Allen, S. Zhao, and R. S. Hanson. 1983. Methylotrophic bacteria: Biochemical diversity and genetics. Science 221:1147-1153.

Kellogg, S. T., D. K. Chatterjee, and A. M. Chakrabarty. 1981. Plasmid-assisted molecular breeding: New techniques for enhanced biodegradation of persistent toxic chemicals. Science 214:1133-1135.

Keyser, P., B. C. Pujar, R. W. Eaton, and D. W. Ribbons. 1976. Biodegradation of phthalates and their esters by bacteria. Environ. Health Perspect. 18:159-166.

Kilbane, J. J., D. K. Chatterjee, J. S. Karns, S. T. Kellogg, and A. M. Chakrabart. 1982. Biodegradation of 2,4,5-trichlorophenoxyacetic acid by a pure culture of _Pseudomonas cepacia_. Appl. Environ. Microbiol. 44:72-78.

Klecka, G. M., and W. J. Maier. 1985. Kinetics of microbial growth on pentachlorophenol. Appl. Environ. Microbiol. 49:46-53.

McDonald, R. C. 1981. Vascular plants for decontaminating radioactive water and soils. NASA Tech. Memorandum, TM-X-72740. NSTL, MS.

McDonald, R. C., and B. C. Wolverton. 1980. Comparative study of wastewater lagoon with and without water hyacinth. Econ. Bot. 34:101-110.

Reddy, K. R. 1983. Fate of nitrogen and phosphorus in a wastewater retention reservoir containing aquatic macrophytes. J. Environ. Qual. 12:137-141.

Reddy, K. R., and W. F. DeBusk. 1984. Growth characteristics of aquatic macrophytes cultured in nutrient-enriched water: I. Water hyacinth, water lettuce, and pennywort. Econ. Bot. 38:225-235.

Reddy, K. R., and W. F. DeBusk. 1985a. Growth characteristics of aquatic macrophytes cultured in nutrient-enriched water: II. Azolla, duckweed, and salvinia. Econ. Bot. 39:200-208.

Reddy, K. R., and W. F. DeBusk. 1985b. Nutrient removal potential of selected aquatic macrophytes. J. Environ. Qual. 14:459-495.

Reddy, K. R., D. L. Sutton, and G. E. Bowes. 1983. Biomass production of freshwater aquatic plants in Florida. Proc. Soil Crop Sci. Soc. Fla. 42:28-40.

Rittman, B. E., and P. L. McCarty. 1980. Model of steady-state biofilm kinetics. Biotech. and Bioeng. 22:2343-2357.

Rusoff, L. L., and B. C. Wolverton. 1978. Vascular aquatic plants - a source of foodstuff for animals and man. I. Water hyacinth. Presented at the XI International Congress of Nutrition, Rio de Janerio, Brazil.

Wilson, J. T., and B. H. Wilson. 1985. Biotransformation of tricholorethylene in soil. Appl. Environ. Microbiol. 49:242-243.

Wolverton, B. C. 1979a. Water hyacinth. Maxingira (United Kingdom) 11:59-65.

Wolverton, B. C. 1979b. Engineering design data for vascular aquatic plant wastewater treatment systems. Aquaculture systems for wastewater treatment. EPA 430/9-80-006.

Wolverton, B. C. 1980. Water hyacinth for controlling water pollution. Water Pollution and Management Reviews. Jawaharlal Neru University, New Delhi, India. 9 pp.

Wolverton, B. C. 1982. Hybrid wastewater treatment system using anaerobic microorganisms and reed (Phragmites communis). Econ. Bot. 36:373-380.

Wolverton, B. C., and R. C. McDonald. 1976a. Water hyacinths, (Eichhornia crassipes) (Mart.) Solms, a renewable source of energy. Proceedings of a Conference on Capturing the Sun Through Bio-conversion, coordinated by Washington Center for Metropolitan Studies, Washington, DC. p. 240-252.

Wolverton, B. C., and R. C. McDonald. 1976b. Water hyacinths: A natural biological filtration system. Proceedings of the Association for Rational Environmental Alternatives, Wellsboro, PA.

Wolverton, B. C., and R. C. McDonald. 1977a. Wastewater treatment utilizing water hyacinth (*Eichhornia crassipes*) (Mart.) Solms. *In* Treatment and Disposal of Industrial Wastewaters and Residues. Proceeding of the National Conference on Treatment and Disposal of Industrial Wastewaters and Residues, Houston, TX. p. 205-208.

Wolverton, B. C., and R. C. McDonald. 1977b. Wastewater treatment utilizing water hyacinths, (*Eichhornia crassipes*) (Mart.) Solms. *In* Treatment and Disposal of Industrial Wastewaters and Residue, Houston, TX, April 26-28, 1977.

Wolverton, B. C., and R. C. McDonald. 1978a. Water hyacinths productivity and harvesting studies. Econ. Bot. 33:1-10.

Wolverton, B. C., and R. C. McDonald. 1978b. Nutritional composition of water hyacinths grown on domestic sewage. Econ. Bot. 32:363-370.

Wolverton, B. C., and R. C. McDonald. 1979a. Bio-accumulation and detection of trace levels of cadmium in aquatic systems using *Eichhornia crassipes*. Presented at the National Institute of Environmental Health Sciences Workshop on Higher Plant Systems as Monitors of Environmental Mutagens, Orlando, FL. Env. Health Persp., U.S. Department of HEW 27:161-164.

Wolverton, B. C., and R. C. McDonald. 1979b. The water hyacinth from prolific pest to potential. AMBIO 8:2-9.

Wolverton, B. C., and R. C. McDonald. 1979c. Upgrading facultative wastewater lagoons with vascular aquatic plants. J. Water Poll. Control Fed. 51:59-65.

Wolverton, B. C., and M. M. McKnown. 1976. Water hyacinths for removal of phenols from polluted waters. Aquatic Bot. 2:191-201.

Wolverton, B. C., and R. C. McDonald. 1980. Vascular plants for water pollution control and renewable sources of energy. Proceedings Bio-Energy '80, Atlanta, GA. p. 120-122.

Wolverton, B. C., and R. C. McDonald. 1981a. Energy from vascular plant wastewater treatment systems. Econ. Bot. 35:224-232.

Wolverton, B. C., and R. C. McDonald. 1981b. Natural processes for treatment of organic chemical waste. The Environ. Prof. 3:99-104.

Wolverton, B. C., and R. C. McDonald-McCaleb. 1986. Biotransformation of priority pollutants using biofilms and vascular plants. J. Miss. Acad. of Sci. 31:79-89.

Wolverton, B. C., R. M. Barlow, and R. C. McDonald. 1976. Application of vascular aquatic plants for pollution removal, energy, and food production in a biological system. Biological Control of Water Pollution, University of Pennsylvania Press, Philadelphia, PA. p. 141-149.

Wolverton, B. C., R. C. McDonald, and W. R. Duffer. 1983. Microorganisms and higher plants for wastewater treatment. J. Environ. Qual. 12:236-242.

Wolverton, B. C., R. C. McDonald, and L. K. Marble. 1984. Removal of benzene and its derivatives from polluted water using the reed/microbial filter technique. J. Miss. Acad. of sci., 29:119-127.

Wolverton, B. C., C. C. Myrick, and K. M. Johnson. 1984. Upgrading septic tanks using microbial/plant filters. J. of Miss. Acad. of Sci. 29:19-25.

THE USE OF PHRAGMITES FOR WASTEWATER TREATMENT BY THE ROOT ZONE METHOD: THE UK APPROACH

P. F. Cooper and A. G. Boon
Water Research Centre, Processes - UK
Stevenage Laboratory
Elder Way, Stevenage
Hertfordshire SG1 1TH
UNITED KINGDOM

ABSTRACT

The Root Zone Method (RZM) of wastewater treatment developed by Prof. Reinhold Kickuth in West Germany is being evaluated in the United Kingdom. The treatment process based on bacterial activity in the rhizosphere of *Phragmites* (common reed) is described and compared with similar wetland processes. The RZM process may have significant benefits in relation to operational costs and performance for the treatment of sewage from small populations especially in rural areas. Capital costs may be reduced for populations below 10,000 if the claims made by Prof. Kickuth are substantiated. A coordinated national program of research and development is being carried out on RZM in the UK -- the key features of this program are described. It is planned to expand the UK data collection to an international scale by forming links with fellow researchers and national organizations in Germany, Denmark, France, Spain, Holland, Canada, and the USA.

Keywords: Root Zone Method, wastewater treatment, *Phragmites*, National Program of Work in UK, design, evaluation.

INTRODUCTION

The use of wetlands for treatment of wastewaters has been practiced in the UK for more than a century. In 1877, it was reported (Stanbridge, 1976) that 6 m^3 of sewage was being applied daily per m^2 of land resulting in the production of an offensive-smelling swamp which produced a highly-polluting effluent. By providing suitable underdrainage, at a depth of about 1.8 m, it was possible to treat effectively about 0.05 m^3 of sewage daily per m^2 of land without the soil becoming clogged (Stanbridge, 1976). Such systems of treatment are still used in some rural areas of the UK today where land is cheap and consists of sandy

ISBN 0-941463-00-1

loam soils. To prevent clogging of the soil, which would result in overland flow of sewage and hence deterioration of effluent quality, the area used for treatment has been increased to allow a proportion (about 25 to 35%) to be 'rested' for about three months, then ploughed and replanted with grass. This rejuvenation is carried out sequentially at approximately 1, 2 or 3 yr intervals so that a works would need at least three or four separate beds of which two or three would be in use while one was being rested. This method of treatment involves the use of microorganisms (bacteria and protozoa) in the soil to treat biochemically (aerobically and anaerobically) the impurities in the sewage. Grass, planted in the topsoil, serves little purpose other than to assist with penetration of water, to avoid overgrowth with weeds, and to improve appearance. The possibility of using aquatic species of plants to assist with treatment by maintaining aerobic conditions in the soil and to improve the structure of the water-saturated soil was not understood until studies were started in Europe, USA and Canada about 15 to 20 years ago.

Reeds (Phragmites) can be used to improve the hydraulic conductivity of soils and to increase the rate at which atmospheric oxygen can be supplied to the soil microorganisms. A method, termed Root Zone, has been developed by Professor Reinhold Kickuth at the University of Hessen in Germany (GFR). Application rates of about 0.1 m^3 m^{-2} d^{-1} have been used to treat screened and degritted sewage at Othfresen since 1974 (Kickuth, 1984), at works which have been extended in stages from an original design population of 2,700 to 10,000 in 1985. Kickuth has claimed that the works have produced a fully-nitrified effluent of very high quality, although others (Ebling, 1985) have disputed such claims on the basis that the area used for treatment is much larger (22.5 ha) so that the application rate would be much lower (0.03 m^3 m^{-2} d^{-1}). Ebling (1985) has also claimed that the discharge values quoted by Kickuth relate to the effect of the unpolluted rainfall over the entire 22.5 ha extent of the wetland, but this can be refuted on the basis of detailed data related to rainfall and discharge rates made available by representatives of the local authorities (Boon, 1986a).

Interest in the Root Zone Method (RZM) was first aroused in the UK following a 2 d visit made to Germany in December 1984, by staff of WRc, Wessex Water and Oceans International Services (OIS)*. A report of the visit (Boon et al., 1985) concluded that RZM could be cost-effectively used to treat screened and degritted sewage to produce an effluent of high quality (including nitrification, denitrification and removal of P). Initial estimates, based on data provided by the local authority in

*OIS is a UK-based commercial company that has a contract with Professor Reinhold Kickuth for design, construction and operation details of the RZM in the UK.

Germany (Boon et al., 1985) and on costs in the UK and USA (Boon, 1986a), indicate that capital costs are likely to be from 25 to 75% of conventional treatment works (for populations below 10,000) and operating costs could be 10 to 25% of conventional processes.

In July 1985, a group of 29 people representing most of the UK Water Authorities, a firm of UK Consultants, OIS, and WRc made a 5 d visit to three sites in Germany (GFR) where RZM is being used to treat sewage (two sites) and wastewater from a textile finishing and dyeing factory (one site). It was the unanimous opinion of all the representatives of UK Water Authorities who made the visit that RZM should be fully evaluated in the UK. This should be achieved by WRc coordinating the studies planned by each of the Authorities particularly with respect to design, installation, operation and monitoring. A report of the visit was produced in September 1985 and was revised and reprinted in February 1986 (Boon, 1986a).

As part of the studies planned by WRc, it was arranged to coordinate the information available on the treatment of wastewaters using wetlands and marshes from other countries including Denmark, Germany, France, Spain, Holland, Canada and the USA. Published data indicated that wetlands treatment has been researched and developed for at least 10 years in both Canada and the USA. A visit to Denmark in October 1985, confirmed that there were then about 65 RZM works serving populations of about 1000 with indications that perhaps 300 to 400 more works might be constructed during the next two to three years. A visit made to Canada and the USA verified that wetlands, both natural and man-made, have been used effectively for up to 10 years to treat wastewaters and secondary effluents to produce final effluents of high quality, including removal of P (Boon, 1986b). Data obtained for the design, operation and performance of wetlands gave limited support to RZM; no direct evidence was found to contradict the claims made by Professor Kickuth. A report of the visit has been published (Boon, 1986b).

In the UK, a Coordination Group, consisting of senior representatives of the UK Water Authorities, has been set up to coordinate the design, construction and operation of all works to be built in the UK for the next three to four years. At present, there are plans to construct about 25 works serving populations from about 50 to 1500. The first works (to serve 1300 people) was constructed by Anglian Water in September/October 1985, at a capital cost of about $140,000. *Phragmites* planted at that time are now growing so that treatment should now be possible, including removal of phosphorus. The prime objective of the group is to produce a design guide and operations manual by 1989/90 based on data already published (Boon, 1986a) and to be obtained from practical experience of operating works.

In this paper, three methods of sewage treatment, involving the use of wetlands which are currently being used in Europe, are described together with the studies planned to evaluate fully these methods. No analytical data are given as much of the existing literature contains contradictory results particularly related to RZM.

WETLAND METHODS OF WASTEWATER TREATMENT

Root Zone Method (RZM)

To make the maximum effective use of the natural ability of a wetland to purify wastewater that may be applied to it, Kickuth developed an engineered process which he termed Root Zone Method.

The ability of marsh vegetation to assimilate nutrients (N and P) and hence to aid directly the purification of wastewater is not important to the success of the process. The system is claimed by Kickuth to maximize the biochemical processes of oxidation in the vicinity of the rooting system (rhizosphere) and of anaerobic fermentation in the 'porous' soil structure surrounding the roots and rhizomes. BOD is satisfied by oxidation and also by reduction (anaerobic fermentation); NH_4-N is oxidized by autotrophic bacteria (growing in the rhizosphere) to NO_2^- and then NO_3^- which in turn is reduced to N under anaerobic conditions by facultative anaerobic bacteria in the surrounding soil; and phosphate is removed by chemical combination with cations normally present in soils (Fe, Ca and Al) provided aerobic conditions are maintained in the zones where precipitation has occurred.

Key features of RZM are summarized below:

- Rhizomes of reeds (normally *Phragmites*) provide a 'hydraulic pathway' through the rhizosphere (the annular space between rhizomes and roots and surrounding soil) along which wastewater can flow;
- Wastewater is treated by bacterial action (aerobic in actively growing rhizospheres and anaerobic in dead and decaying rhizospheres and in the surrounding soil);
- Atmospheric O_2 is provided to the rhizosphere via the leaves and stems through the hollow rhizomes and roots;
- Aerobic composting of sludges in wastewaters occurs in the aboveground layer of 'straw' derived from dead leaves and stems.

To provide maximum porosity of the bed in which the reeds are to be grown, it is necessary to select a soil which has a composition from which a stable structure can evolve so that wastewater can flow freely around living rhizomes and roots and also through the 'tubes' created by dead and decaying rhizomes. Initial studies in the UK indicate (Reading Agricultural Consultants Ltd., 1985) that soils classed as sandy clay loam, clay loam, silty clay loam, sandy clay, silty clay and the lighter part of clay may be suitable. Further work is in progress, and is planned, to determine the most suitable types of soil that could be used and the circumstances for their use. To improve soil structure and to strengthen pores and 'tubes' which develop in the soil, Kickuth has recommended that the Ca content of the soil should be at least 2 to 2.5% by weight; chalk or hydrated lime may be added as required to achieve the minimum content. Initially the hydraulic conductivity of the replaced soil should be about 10^{-3} to 10^{-5} m s^{-1}. Kickuth claims that conductivity will increase as the bed matures, and roots and rhizomes develop, so that within two to four years (depending on rate of growth of reeds) the value should reach 10^{-3} m s^{-1}. This claim has been disputed by Bucksteeg (1985) on the basis of calculations he has made using Kickuth's assumptions and on the data available from some existing works. Clearly, there is a need to evaluate fully this aspect of conflicting claims and this will form part of the research and development project planned by WRc.

To achieve such a high conductivity within an engineered bed which has a soil depth of about 0.6 m it is very important to encourage deep penetration of roots and rhizomes. Kickuth claims that this is achieved by reducing the water level in the bed for about three months each year (for the first three years following planting) during the months of August, September and October when the leaves start to die-back and below-ground growth would be at maximum rate. To be able to vary the depth of water, the bed should be constructed on a suitable sealant of clay (hydraulic conductivity of less than 10^{-8} m s^{-1}), bentonite, synthetic fabric (with a smooth surface and about 2 mm thickness to prevent penetration of rhizomes), asphalt or even concrete. In such a sealed 'tank', the water level can be varied by lowering the outlet so as to drain the bed when required. By this technique, Kickuth claims that the deep-lying horizontal rhizomes of the reeds will create a porous structure which will contain a mosaic of aerobic and anaerobic zones.

At the inlet and outlet ends of each bed, trenches should be left into which media of stones, granite, or slag can be placed. The nominal diameter of the medium should be about 60 to 100 mm. Each trench should be sited across the width of a bed and should be about 0.35 m wide and 0.65 m deep. Final effluent can be collected into the outlet trench and flow out via a 200 mm diameter pipe situated at the bottom of the trench so that the discharge level of water can be varied to fill or drain the bed. The inlet trench serves to distribute the incoming wastewater into the bed throughout its depth, particularly during the initial few years until the vertical and horizontal conductivity has reached its maximum value (about 10^{-3} m s^{-1}). However, if the conductivity were lower than 10^{-3} m s^{-1}, substantial overland flow would occur, for example if the conductivity were 10^{-4} m s^{-1}, 90% of the wastewater would overflow the bed with detrimental effect on effluent quality.

To avoid compaction of the soil during construction, heavy vehicles should not be allowed onto the bed. Subsequently, it is essential to avoid damage to the porous soil structure and rhizomes (dead and alive) so that access to the bed to harvest reeds must be excluded.

At no time can reeds be cut as a crop as it would reduce the rate of O_2 supply to the rhizosphere and there might be insufficient 'straw' to achieve effective composting of sludge, and to make use of the straw layer to provide a trickling filter effect to overland flows.

To avoid damage to the 'structure' of the soil in an established RZM bed, the cross-sectional area of the bed is designed so that the maximum 'horizontal' flow-rate does not exceed 10^{-4} m s^{-1}. Such a high velocity would normally not be achieved without construction of a bed with a slope of about 10% (0.1 m m^{-1}) unless the hydraulic conductivity of the fully developed bed exceeded 10^{-3} m s^{-1}.

Kickuth has recommended that the slope of the bed should normally be in the range of 2 to 6% and that steeper slopes (7 to 9%) should only be used where combined drainage systems result in short periods of excessively high flow-rates of diluted sewage. The claim will need examination, particularly if the conductivity of soil in the bed remains low and overland flow occurs at average flow rates. In addition, it may prove impossible to grow Phragmites on a bed with such steep slopes except at the outlet end of the bed. The cross-sectional area (Ac) can be calculated from the application of Darcy's Law:

$$Ac = \frac{Qs}{kf\ dH/ds} \quad (m^2)$$

where: Qs is the average flow-rate of sewage (m^3 s^{-1}). Data related to variations in flow-rate should be examined to establish the average flow-rate under wet-weather conditions so that it can be used in the equation if such conditions were to exist frequently for periods greater than 12 h each 'wet-day' and then the slope would be increased to avoid the high cost of constructing a wide bed of short length; kf is the hydraulic conductivity (m^3 m^{-2} s^{-1}) of the fully developed RZM bed (i.e. kf is claimed by Kickuth to be equal to about 10^{-3} m^3 m^{-2} s^{-1}) and dH/ds is the slope of the bed (m m^{-1}).

Based on the data from Othfresen and other sites, Kickuth has claimed (Boon, 1986a; Kickuth, 1984) that the area of a bed (Ah) can be calculated from the equation:

$$Ah = 5.2\ Qd\ (\ln.Co - \ln.\ ct)\ (m^2)$$

where: Qd is the daily average flow-rate of wastewater (m^3 d^{-1}) Co is the average BOD of the wastewater (mg L^{-1}) and Ct is the required average BOD of the effluent (mg L^{-1}).

The value of the factor depends on the depth of the bed and the biodegradability of the wastewater. For sewage and readily biodegraded wastewaters the value is 5.2, but it may increase up to 15 for difficult to biodegrade wastewaters being treated in shallow (0.3 m) beds. Variations in temperature of wastewater appear to have little affect on effluent quality even when the temperature changes from just above freezing in winter to 25°C in summer. This is presumably because the total number of active bacteria in the soil and rhizosphere increase in winter months, which allows increased concentrations of substrate away from the inlet end of the bed, with the effect that the concentrations of bacteria can increase in the middle and outlet zones of a bed as a result of reduced activity of individual bacteria.

To distribute the wastewater onto the inlet of the bed, particularly when treating screened and degritted sewage, Kickuth has advocated the construction of a distribution channel with a V-notch side-weir which could be fabricated in reinforced concrete, plastic-coated steel, glass-reinforced plastic, or other suitable material. Such a system (made of reinforced concrete) was used for the first RZM works constructed in the UK and was used at Othfresen in Germany (Boon et al., 1985; Boon, 1986a). However, it is likely that a suitable plastic pipe, laid on the inlet trench, with several outlets across the bed will be used for subsequent beds in the UK, particularly when treating settled sewage or for tertiary treatment of effluents.

When treating raw sewage, the overflow level of the inlet should be at least 0.5 m above the top of the soil initially so that sludge and straw could accumulate for at least 35 years before the top layer of composted sludge (which has the appearance of peat) needs to be removed. From calculations and observations, the rate of sludge accumulation would tend to be about 10 mm per annum (with up to 20 mm per annum near to the inlet) and of straw (when treating settled sewage or effluent) would be about 4 mm per annum.

Because the initial hydraulic conductivity of the soil in a newly-planted bed is likely to be very low (10^{-4} to 10^{-6} m s^{-1}), it would be impossible to allow the design flow-rate to be applied for the first two or three years without the danger of overland flow which could erode some of the topsoil and would produce an effluent of poor quality. To avoid such difficulties and to permit rapid drainage of the bed at the appropriate times of year, a layer of pea-gravel (about 5 to 10 mm depth) could be installed at the bottom of the bed, on top of the sealant, through which water could flow at a high rate for the first two or three years before the rhizomes and roots have fully developed. Clearly, the quality of effluent would be poor during this initial stage - although data from Denmark indicate that at least a 60% reduction of BOD could be expected within the first year. This gravel layer would have to be sealed by the end of the third year to prevent further short-circuiting and this could be achieved by pouring sealant into the gravel down vertical pipes installed for the purpose at intervals at the inlet end of the bed.

In addition to the treatment of sewage and sludges, the RZM has been used since 1974 to treat wastewaters from a textile factory (Windel Textil GmbH) (Boon, 1986a). Successful treatment of 2000 to 2500 m^3 of wastewater daily (about 34% of the total flowrate) is achieved by an extensive system of RZM works on a total area of about 20 ha. The factory uses various processes to finish cloth including dyeing, coating, bleaching and printing. Liquors from the dye-house contain sulphides, sulphur compounds, and chromium salts (hexavalent) and are fully treated without apparent ill-effects on the reeds (Phragmites) or the RZM process. At this site, the beds were constructed using existing grass plots (previously used for land treatment of the wastewater) which were only 0.3 m deep. As a result, a proportion of the applied wastewater overflows the bed and is treated on the submerged stems by a 'trickling-filter' effect.

Max Planck Institute Process (MPIP)

The MPIP or 'Krefeld' process was developed by Seidel (1976) and others (Lakshman, 1979; Lewis et al., 1982; Pope, 1981; Seidel and Hapel, 1981). It relies on the growth of wetland plants to achieve treatment in a 'constructed' marsh. It is used to treat settled wastewater (and in some cases, raw wastewater after grit removal) in trenches (often constructed from reinforced concrete) which may be 2 to 4 m wide, up to 100 m length; and between 0.5 and 1 m depth.

Hydraulic conductivity is not regarded as important and the ability of Phragmites to produce a soil/root/rhizome 'structure' with a hydraulic conductivity of 10^{-3} m s^{-1} is not essential for success. This is probably because the beds are filled with stones and gravel of high conductivity. It does not require 'management' of water levels to achieve deep penetration of roots and rhizomes. Most of the MPIP beds have the reeds harvested at least once every year.

Performance of a MPIP, installed at the Moulton Nigiel Water District, Laguna Niguel, California, was carefully monitored for nearly 12 months by an EPA contractor (Pope, 1981). Two trenches each 25 m length, 4 m width and 1.3 m depth were filled with three layers of gravel. At the bottom of the bed was placed 150 mm depth of 50 mm diameter gravel in the middle section was 225 mm depth of 19 mm gravel, and on top was 75 mm of 'pea' gravel. A 75 mm deep layer of sand was spread over the surface of the bed in which reeds (Phragmites) or bulrush (Scirpus) were planted. Effluent quality did not comply consistently with the standards required particularly with respect to removal of N; P removal was erratic and never exceeded about 15%. The 'standard' for effluent quality was to achieve average values (30 d period) for BOD and SS concentrations not exceeding 30 mg L^{-1}. This standard was achieved for five months at flow rates of 95 m^3 d^{-1} but at 133 m^3 d^{-1} the BOD values were not within the standard for five out of the six months.

The MPIP process has been used in various different designs of works with a number of wetland plants including Phragmites, Scirpus, and Typha. A series of gravel trenches planted with various wetland species were used to treat settled sewage to produce an effluent of fairly consistent quality (but without complete nitrification and removal of phosphate). While results of this method have been good (Lewis et al., 1982), there remain some operational difficulties with clogging and ponding (overflow of water in wet weather) and the need to completely replace the bed and to replant with reeds every 10 to 15 years when the bed finally becomes totally blocked by debris and accumulated biological sludges (Lewis et al., 1982).

The process has been claimed (Banks, Biological Water Purification, Inc., private communication) to have been successfully used to treat sludges (waterworks sludge and aerobically and anaerobically digested sewage sludges) at several sites in New Jersey (Boon, 1986b). For treatment of sludges, the MPIP has been constructed on sludge drying-beds of conventional design which would normally have under-drainage with a gravel layer (15 to 25 mm diameter size) on the surface and a top layer of sharp sand (0.5 to 2 mm diameter grain size) on which the sludge would be poured. To adapt conventional drying beds, the side-walls were increased in height to about 1 m and rhizomes of _Phragmites_ planted in the surface sand in the spring or autumn. The 'density' of planting was about five to six rhizomes per m^2. Initially the plants are watered with effluent or water with added nutrients (N and P). Four to eight weeks after planting, a layer of sludge (about 5 to 10 cm deep) was added to the bed avoiding submergence of the reeds. Further sludge would be added at approximately bi-weekly intervals (depending on the rate at which the previously added sludges were 'dewatered') so that each year about 2 to 3 m of sludge could be 'treated'; more sludge might be added in summer months compared with winter and more added if the rates of evapotranspiration were high. Essentially, the process dewaters the sludge by evapotranspiration (1.5 to 2 m water loss per annum) and improved drainage (resulting from the development of roots and rhizomes in the sand and gravel), and treats the sludge by biochemical oxidation and fermentation to remove residual organic substances. It can produce a friable 'soil' with a 30 to 40% content of suspended solids which need only be removed from the treatment works once every 10 to 15 years when the bed is 'full'. At that time, replanting should not be necessary as sufficient rhizomes and roots should remain in the sand and gravel at the bottom of the bed provided care is taken in removal of the top layers of accumulated sludge and that such removal is carried out in the early spring before reed growth starts.

In the USA there are patents related to the MPIP (No. 3770623, 6 November 1973) and RZM (No. 4331538, 25 May 1982) for which Biological Water Purification Inc., Denville, New Jersey, has exclusive licenses to use. At present, several MPIP works are in operation in New Jersey to treat sludges from conventional water and wastewater treatment; there are no RZM works in the USA.

Lelystad Process

The IJsselmeerpolders Development Authority started to use wetlands for the treatment of sewage in 1967 (deJong, 1976). The process has evolved from the MPIP although studies by de Jong et al. (1977) were not able to establish differences between *Scirpus* and *Phragmites*. The first marsh (about 1 ha area and 0.4 m deep) was planted with *Scirpus* and was used to treat sewage from a camping site which was only occupied during the summer months. In 1969, additional ditches were constructed (about 3 m wide) and dams (of similar width) built in parallel both of which were about 400 m in length to give a retention time of about 10 d (similar to that of RZM).

The importance of soil composition has been described, particularly in relation to removal of P (Greiner and de Jong, 1982). The ability of clay soil, containing Al and Fe compounds, to adsorb and precipitate P is recognized. Nitrification and denitrification are attributed to bacterial activity with little effect of N removal attributed directly to uptake by the plants.

The importance of rhizomes and root growth (essential for RZM) are not considered in the Lelystad Process so that encouraging their growth initially and avoiding destruction of 'secondary structures' through high velocities of water through the bed during subsequent operation are ignored. The effect of both inadequate root and rhizome growth, combined with excessively high velocities, is that a significant proportion of the sewage/ effluent flows aboveground over the bed, resulting in potential problems with flies and mosquitoes, unpleasant odors, short-circuiting, and freezing in the winter.

Data from the literature indicate that about twice the marsh area per unit volume of sewage treated (or people served) is required for the Lelystad Process compared with RZM to produce a similar effluent quality; both processes appear capable of producing a high quality, fully-nitrified effluent with a significant proportion of P being removed.

Although results indicate a slight deterioration of effluent quality in winter months this was not important at the site selected as the maximum load was treated successfully during the summer.

A larger (15 ha) marsh has been constructed to give tertiary treatment to a secondary effluent from a population of about 70,000. Data from this site are encouraging with only slight decrease in performance in winter (Greiner and deJong, 1982).

Potential Applications of Wetlands Processes to Treatment of Wastewaters and Sludges

At this time, while few published data are available to give a clear guide as to the best wetland process which can be applied in given circumstances, it is possible to suggest which of the above processes might be most successful for a given purpose.

Below are given the authors' views on selection of the process based on their knowledge of published data and the results of their experience to date.

Process	Application	Reasons
RZM	Industrial wastewaters, leachate, raw sewage	Relatively intensive process on a relatively small area of land which may be capable of producing a high-quality fully-nitrified effluent.
RZM	Primary sewage sludge	Capable of producing a treated sludge with a good quality filtrate without odor problems.
MPIP	Settled sewage and sludge liquors	Can be constructed using gravel and sand to enable rapid start-up with high horizontal velocities to produce reasonable effluent quality (30 SS and 20 BOD on average).
MPIP	Aerobically and anaerobically digested sewage sludges; Waterworks sludges	Simple construction with rapid start-up and good results. Drainage liquors would need further treatment.
Lelystad	Seasonal treatment of settled sewage Tertiary treatment of secondary effluents	Simple construction and operation. Capable of removing solids but not as effective for BOD and nitrification.

THE UNITED KINGDOM'S NATIONAL PROGRAM FOR DEVELOPING ROOT ZONE TREATMENT

Following the visit of the WRc and Water Authorities staff to Germany (Boon, 1986a), all showed great enthusiasm for trying RZM in the UK for sewage and sludge treatment. Under the umbrella of the Water Authorities Association a national coordinating group was established to draw together all the development work which was proposed. The group comprises representatives from all the Water Authorities plus a representative of the Scottish Regional Councils (responsible for works and effluent treatment in Scotland) and a representative of the Department of the Environment's Northern Ireland Water Service. WRc act as group coordinators and provide the secretarial services.

The aim of the group is to be able to produce a design and operational manual for root zone treatment by 1989. To this end, the research and development work done by the individual Water

Authorities are being carefully coordinated and monitored to cover the range of treatment options offered by RZM and other wetland treatments.

WRc have established a data-base for logging the design details of all the RZM units built and their performance when they come into operation in the UK. Two were built in Fall 1985, and planted at the beginning of November 1985. Another was planted in March 1986, and a further three have just been completed in June/July 1986. There are proposals for a further 24 RZM to be constructed in Fall 1986, and Spring 1987. The data collected will be used to verify and refine the existing design equations derived in Germany by Prof. Kickuth and colleagues. The UK group has already contacted colleagues in West Germany and in Denmark with the idea of forming a European group for exchanging data and experience of RZM-type plants. It is hoped that this grouping can be further extended by making contacts in the USA, Canada, France, Spain, Belgium and Holland.

Common Features of RZM Systems

In order to avoid duplication of the work already done in West Germany, Denmark, Holland, USA, Canada and elsewhere, the following features have been accepted initially:

a) The common reed (Phragmites australis) appears to be the most effective plant for wetland treatment processes in that they are resistant to a wide range of substances, produce an extensive root system which aids water transfer, and are capable of transferring O_2 into the soil at a high rate.
b) The bed will be about 0.6 m deep after initial settlement.
c) The inlet distributor and outlet collector will contain stones of nominal size 60 to 100 mm. The trench containing these stones will be about 0.35 m wide across the full width and for its total depth.
d) For best survival rate reeds should be planted in Spring (March/April) or Fall (September/October) avoiding frosts.
e) The excavated site or 'tank' must be fully sealed. This may be done with "puddled" clay or bentonite but will more normally be done with a smooth synthetic material such as HDPE.
f) The slope of the bed will normally be in the range 2 to 6%.
g) After the reeds have been planted the bed should be flooded with water or sewage effluent. The water level should be kept about 25 mm below the surface of the bed.
h) The water level in the bed should be dropped between August and October for the first three years to encourage the downward penetration of the roots and rhizomes.
i) The newly-planted reeds should not be kept under water because it can lead to rotting of the plants.

A typical Root Zone-type bed will look like Figure 1.

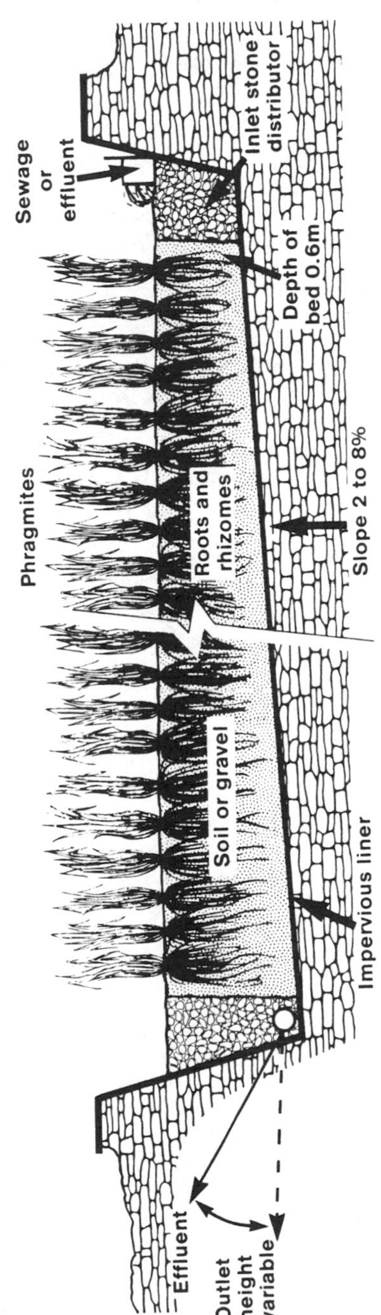

FIGURE 1. Typical arrangements for a Root Zone-type works.

National Program of Research and Development

Tables 1 and 2 show the status of the various plants that are being constructed in the UK and design details where available. The features that will be studied in the UK national program will be:

i) Waste to be treated

The majority of proposals relate to the treatment of screened crude sewage but present proposals cover: a) septic tank effluent; b) screened crude sewage; c) settled sewage; d) secondary effluent; e) sludges; and f) sludge liquors. As yet there is no proposal to treat an industrial waste or leachate but proposals are likely at a later date.

ii) Selection of soils and their conditioning

In most cases it is likely that the existing soil will be used but in many places it may need conditioning (e.g., by addition of Ca) to improve its structure and improve the ability to pass water. This parameter is one in which we have the least knowledge. Advice and practical help has been sought from consultants and from UK Government's soil experts: The Soil Survey of England and Wales. RZM-type systems have already been built using different soil types including: a) low conductivity - Acle; b) high conductivity (gravel) - Gravesend; c) sandy soil - Castleroe; d) recovered grit - may be used at Warton; and e) mining dross - may be used at Radstock. Chalk (calcium carbonate) has been added at Acle, Holtby, Marnhull and Gravesend to improve the soil structure.

iii) Design of the beds

Some of the beds have been "DIY designs" based upon the design relationships in the visit report (Boon, 1986a) involving joint work between Water Authority staff and WRc. One bed (Holtby) was designed entirely by OIS. One bed (Marnhull) was built by Water Authority staff with OIS consultancy.

Features to be examined will be: a) rates of treatment (area required/people); b) horizontal flow velocity; c) design kf value; d) bed shape (length to width ratio). Design to take account of flow patterns; and e) slope - does the top of the bed need to slope?

iv) Construction Details/Methods

Features include: a) different liner types; b) no liner -- rolled clay; and c) inlet arrangements -- stones + weir -- stones + slotted pipe; d) outlet arrangements -- stones + slotted pipe; e) controllable underdrain system -- used at Holtby; and f) methods of soil handling.

v) Plants and methods of planting

All RZM systems will use *Phragmites*. Different methods of planting will be examined. The WRc, on behalf of the WAA Coordinating Group, commissioned the Institute of Terrestrial

TABLE 1. Root Zone Works Status - July 1986.

Site	Authority	Feed	Flow	Population equivalent	Status/planting time	
			$m^3\ d^{-1}$			
Acle	Anglian	Screened crude sewage	240	1260	Completed	November 1985
Woburn	Anglian	Screened crude sewage	320	1000	Possible	Fall 1986
Broxted	Anglian	Screened crude sewage		200	Firm	Fall 1986
Kirmington	Anglian	Screened crude sewage		800	Firm	Fall 1986
Reepham	Anglian	Screened crude sewage or humus tank effluent	154 or 463		Possible	Fall 1986
Freethorpe	Anglian	Screened crude sewage		900	Firm	Fall 1986
Yardley Hastings	Anglian	Screened crude sewage		1500	Possible	Fall 1986
Holtby	Yorkshire	Screened crude sewage	30	130	Completed	June 1986
Bishops Wilton	Yorkshire	Screened crude sewage		350	Possible	Fall 1986
Wheldrake	Yorkshire	Sludge		1143	Probable	
St. Pauls Walden	Thames	Screened crude sewage	11	50	Completed	November 1985
Bracknell	Thames	Sludge			Firm	Fall 1986
Windsor	Thames	Sludge or screened crude sewage			Possible	Fall 1986
Stormy Down	Welsh	Screened crude sewage	28	200	Firm	Fall 1986
Kingstone and Madeley	Welsh	Primary settled sewage (1st) Screened crude sewage (later)	215	1200	Probable	Fall 1986
Penparc	Welsh	Final effluent	75	500	Probable	Fall 1986
Wardle	North-West	Screened crude sewage	55	155	Probable	Fall 1986
Lustleigh	South-West	Screened crude sewage	200	500	Firm	Fall 1986
Black Dog	South-West	Septic tank effluent	6	40	Firm	Fall 1986

TABLE 1 (cont'd.)

Site	Authority	Feed	Flow	Population equivalent	Status/planting time	
			$m^3\ d^{-1}$			
West Buckland	South-West	Final effluent (after secondary settlement) (1st) Screened crude sewage (later)	33	180	Firm	Fall 1986
Warton	Severn-Trent	Screened crude sewage	Part of 200		Possible	
Middleton	Severn-Trent	Screened crude sewage	47		Firm	Fall 1986
Whittington	Severn-Trent	Secondary effluent	Aquifer recharge		Firm	
Fleckney	Severn-Trent	Sludge	1000 $m^3\ yr^{-1}$	4000	Possible	
"Sewer Dykes"	Severn-Trent	Sewage			Possible	
Marnhull	Wessex	Primary settled sewage and screened crude crude sewage	85	375	In construction	July 1986
Radstock	Wessex	Final effluent			Possible	
Milbourne St. Andrew	Wessex	Final effluent			Possible	
Gravesend	Southern	i) Sludge liquor	100		Completed	June 1986
		ii) Settled sewage	240			
		iii) Crude sewage	150			
	Northumbrian	- 3 sites under consideration				
	SADWASS	- 1 site under consideration				
Castleroe	DoE (NI)	Primary settled sewage	5	25	Completed	March 1986

Table 2. Root Zone Plants - Design/Construction Details

Site	Feed† BOD_5	Feed† SS	Effluent+ design BOD_5	Effluent+ design SS	Number of beds	Length	Breadth	Slope	Mean horizontal velocity	Bed area/ pe++
	mg L^{-1}					m	m	%	m s^{-1}	m^2/pe++
Acle	394		20		2	50	35	2	0.66×10^{-4}	2.8
Broxted	360		20		1	30	25	4	0.39×10^{-4}	3.3
Holtby	260	346	15	30	1	18	34	5	0.17×10^{-4}	4.7
St. Pauls Walden	250+++		8		1	20	10	2	0.21×10^{-4}	4.0
Stormy Down	350+++		20		2	13.5	18.5	1.5	0.15×10^{-4}	2.5
Wardle	150		18		1	25.7	17.8	2	0.62×10^{-4}	3.0
Marnhull	250	200	10	20	2	21	35	4	0.22×10^{-4}	3.9
Gravesend i)	1000	1500	180		1	35	35	2	0.55×10^{-4}	1.5
" ii)	250		120		1	35	35	2	1.30×10^{-4}	0.9
" iii)	380		120		1	35	35	2	0.83×10^{-4}	0.9
Castleroe	75	100	<20	<20	2	8	3.6	2	0.13×10^{-4}	2.2

+ = mean values.
++ = people.2
+++ = assumed.

Ecology to survey the literature on reed cultivation (Lawson, 1985) and have followed that up with a contract to examine different methods of propagation.

In the first RZM-type bed built at Acle, (Anglian Water) local reed-rhizomes were planted. This was also the case at Gravesend (Southern Water). At Holtby (Yorkshire Water) German rhizomes were planted. The Marnhull site (Wessex Water) will examine three different options. Two beds are being built at Marnhull. The front half of each bed will be planted with small clumps of reeds from nearby existing reed beds. The second halves of the Marnhull beds to be planted with a) plantlets from a nearby site and b) rhizomes imported from Germany with the batch used at Holtby.

At the present time, it is believed that the best and probably cheapest method is likely to be the transplantation of small clumps (say 20 cm square). Where rhizomes or plantlets are used it is felt that the planting density needed is 2 m^{-2} if planted in Fall or Spring, but if summer planting has to be done the density might have to rise to 4 to 6 m^{-2} to achieve the same survival rate.

The WAA monitoring program will attempt to assess the effects of planting: a) local rhizomes; b) specially-bred rhizomes from Germany; c) plantlets; and d) clumps.

The monitoring program will also attempt to assess differences relating to time of planting and density of planting.

vi) The possible effects of a number of other parameters have been identified but have not yet been scheduled for testing.

Temperature. It is appreciated that the performance of the system may be affected by temperature. There is no plan at the present to do other than monitor the air and water temperatures at a number of the RZM sites.

Pests (parasites). Nothing has been planned but general observation at RZM sites is expected.

Fire. Nothing has been planned as yet to study the performance recovery of a bed which has been burned. However, in a few years time when the process has been fully validated it is possible that a small bed on a site with several beds could be burnt in the interest of seeing how quickly it could recover.

Chemicals. No specific tests have been planned yet to see how the RZM process reacts to effluents containing heavy metals, organics or herbicides.

Removal of N and P. It is anticipated that the beds will remove a large proportion of N and P. This is a particular interest for the Acle system.

vii) Monitoring the RZM beds

The program of work is in its infancy with very little data on performance expected until the Fall of the year. However a monitoring program has been suggested and is to be gradually refined as more experience is gained.

The monitoring program is given in outline in Appendix 1.

Two other studies are being funded by members of the WAA RZM Coordination Group:

a) Wessex Water are part-funding a study by the University of Bath of the microbiology of the Root Zone Method. This study will examine the composition and activities of the microbial populations in the rhizosphere of *Phragmites australis*.
b) WRc-Processes have awarded a grant to Dr. W. Armstrong at the University of Hull to study the mechanism and rates of O_2 transfer in Root Zone Method systems. This will involve study on laboratory and full-scale systems.

SUMMARY

Based on observations made during visits to Germany, Denmark, USA and Canada during 1985 and 1986 by staff and members of WRc and on data published in the literature, the following advantages and disadvantages of the Root Zone Method can be described.

The RZM has the following benefits:

- environmentally acceptable (appearance, flies, and smells are not a problem) and it offers considerable wildlife conservation potential,
- simple construction with no mechanical or electrical equipment; therefore, reduced capital costs,
- robust process able to withstand a wide range of operating conditions (including wastewater compositions),
- low maintenance requirements,
- consistent effluent quality.

Potential problems could arise from the following although the risks are probably small and could be reduced to a very low and acceptable level:

- burning of the reeds (accidental or by vandals),
- need for a three year period to complete commisioning,
- effects of parasites, plant disease and severe chemical contamination (very slight risk),
- loss of O_2 supply to rhizomes if the bed became totally covered by ice.

It was the unanimous opinion of all the representatives of UK Water Authorities who made the visit to Germany (GFR) in July 1985 (Boon, 1986a) that the process should be fully evaluated in the UK. This should be achieved by WRcP coordinating the studies planned by each of the Authorities particularly with respect to design, installation, operation and monitoring.

REFERENCES

Boon, A. G. 1986a. Report of a visit by members and staff of WRc to Germany (GFR) to investigate the Root Zone Method for treatment of wastewaters. Report No. 376-S. Water Research Centre, Processes, Stevenage, Herts, UK.

Boon, A. G. 1986b. Report of a visit by A. G. Boon to Canada and the USA to investigate the use of wetlands for the treatment of wastewater (8-28 March 1986). Report No. 424-S. Water Research Centre, Processes, Stevenage, Herts, UK.

Boon, A. G., R. D. Davis, and R. J. Huggins. 1985. Report of a visit by Arthur G. Boon, Dr. Robert D. Davis, and Dr. Robert J. Huggins to Germany (GFR) to investigate the Root Zone Method. Report No. 328-S. Water Research Centre, Processes, Stevenage, Herts, UK.

Bucksteeg, K. 1985. Initial experience of the Root Zone Process in Bavaria. In Proc. Symposium held at the Technical University of Darmstadt, July 11, 1985.

Ebling, W. 1985. Practical experiences of the Othfresen root zone sewage treatment installation. Korrespondenz Abwasser 32(5):372-375.

de Jong, J. 1976. The purification of wastewater with the aid of rush or reed ponds. p. 123-132. In J. Tourbier and R. Pierson (ed.) Biological Control of Water Pollution. Philadelphia: Pennsylvania University Press.

de Jong, J., T. Kok, and A. H. Koridon. 1977. The purification of sewage with the aid of ponds containing bulrushes or reeds in the Netherlands. Rapport 1977 - 7 Bbw. Lelystad, Netherlands: Rijksdienst voor de IJsselmeerpolders.

Greiner, R. W., and J. de Jong. 1982. The use of marsh plants for the treatment of wastewater in areas designated for recreation and tourism. 35th International Symposium (Cebedeau), Liege. RIJP Report No. 225. Lelystad, Netherlands: Rijksdienst voor de IJsselmeer Polders.

Kickuth, R. 1984. Das Wurzelraumverfahren in der Praxis. Landsch. Stadt., 16:145-153.

Lakshman, G. 1979. An ecosystem approach to the treatment of wastewaters. J. Environ. Qual. 8:353.

Lawson, G. 1985. Cultivating reeds (Phragmites australis) for Root Zone Treatment of sewage. Contract report by Institute of Terrestrial Ecology for Water Research Centre, October 1985.

Lewis, R. F., L. Banks, and S. F. Davis. 1982. Wastewater treatment by rooted aquatic plants in sand and gravel trenches. In Abwasserreinigung mit Hilfe von Waserpflanzen, Veranstalter, Technishe Universitat Hamburg-Harburg in Zusammenarbeit mit der Stadt Ratzeburg, pp. 1-28.

Pope, P. R. 1981. Wastewater treatment by rooted aquatic plants in sand and gravel trenches. R. F. Lewis (Project Officer). EPA-600/S2-81-091. Cincinnati, Municipal Environmental Laboratory.

Reading Agricultural Consultants Ltd. 1985. Soil suitability and handling for the Root Zone Method. Contract report for WRc Processes, December 1985.

Seidel, K. 1976. Macrophytes and water purification. In J. Tourbier and R. W. Pierson (ed.) Biological Control of Water Pollution. Philadelphia, Pennsylvania University Press. p. 109-122

Seidel, K., and H. Hapel. 1981. Sewage treatment using plants according to the Krefeld systems. Sicherheit in Chemie und Umweld 1:127-129.

Stanbridge, H. H. 1976. History of sewage treatment in Britain. 5. Land Treatment. Inst. Wat. Pollut. Control, Maidstone, Kent, UK, p. 4.

Stanbridge, H. H. 1976. History of sewage treatment in Britain. 5. Land Treatment. Inst. Wat. Pollut. Control, Maidstone, Kent, UK, p. 16.

APPENDIX 1

WAA Coordination Group for Implementation of Root Zone Method in UK

Preliminary suggestions for monitoring program for Root Zone Beds

At the start of project ensure that basic feed data has been collected and recorded together with bed design data.

i.e. nature of feed (BOD, SS, NH_3-N)
flowrate (mean, peak and if possible the daily flow pattern)
type of soil and detailed analysis if possible
hydraulic conductivity if possible
bed slope
source of reeds
number of reeds planted m^{-2}.

1st Year

Analysis of liquid samples:

	Determinand	
*	BOD_5	
*	SS	
	NH_3-N	
	NO_3-N	
	NO_3-N	
	PO_4-P	Influent and effluent spot
	Cl^-	samples at monthly intervals
*	DO	
	Total Ca^{++}	
	pH value	
	Redox potential	
	Metals if appropriate	

Note: Spot samples may also be taken from sampling pipes installed in the bed to determine the regions of treatment and the degree of treatment achieved and where BOD removal, NH_4^+ oxidation and denitrification occur.

*Note:

1. It is not anticipated that all RZM plants will be monitored as intensively as above. The more important parameters are asterisked.
2. The above recommendations are primarily aimed at sewage and effluent treatment systems. When dealing with sludge treatment units more attention will need to be paid to (a) sludge loading rate and (b) bed depth.

Liquid flows:

* Feed flowrate) Cumulative if possible
* Effluent flowrate)
Rainfall - either on-site or from local weather station
(Calculate transpiration loss)
(Calculate k_f ms^{-1})

Measurements on bed:

Ground temperature - monthly average in bed and in surrounding fields (as control)
Humidity
Saturation deficiency
Water tension
* Monitor liquid level at inlet, outlet and intermediate points in bed in order to calculate hydraulic conductivity.

At end of 1st year:

* 1. Measure survival rate of reeds i.e., measure density (stems m^{-2})
* 2. Mean height of reeds
3. Measure bed depth i.e., height above datum
4. Dig out small section (1 m wide) and examine rhizome penetration, length, thickness, depth
5. Test soil structure.

2nd Year

As for the first year but increase the sampling frequency to 2/month. At the end of the year, dig out a different section of the bed for examination of the rhizomes. Test soil structure.

3rd Year

As for previous two years but increase sampling frequency to the desired level (suggest 1/week). 1/month may be appropriate for rural plants with more intensive analysis if there are any problems evident. At the end of the year dig out a different section of the bed for examination of the rhizomes. Test soil structure.

AQUATIC PLANT BASED WATER TREATMENT SYSTEMS IN ASIA

S. A. Abbasi
Water Quality & Environment Division
Centre for Water Resources Development & Management
Kerala, INDIA

ABSTRACT

Purification of biodegradable wastewaters through lagooning or 'ponding' is common in Asia, especially in India, China and the south-east Asian countries. Cultures of fish and aquatic plants have been traditionally used with lagooning to improve water quality and facilitate recovery of nutrients from wastes. While the traditional systems have been operated by farmers more or less intuitively, the interest in developing the science and technology of aquatic plant-based water treatment systems gathered momentum in the 1970s. Efforts have been made to study at laboratory scale the feasibility of treating a variety of domestic and industrial effluents with aquatic macrophytes. A few pilot plants for demonstration/research as well as a few full-scale treatment systems have been set up.

This review attempts to bring together information on aquatic plant-based water treatment systems in Asia. The review includes: 1) an assessment of research on the use of aquatic plants for water treatment in Asian countries, 2) typical case-studies of laboratory scale, pilot and full-scale systems with information on design, operation and maintenance, 3) biomass utilization efforts for cost recovery, 4) economics of these systems compared to conventional systems, 5) long-term implications of the past and present R&D efforts and 6) potential applications of the systems and future research needs.

Keywords: Aquatic plants, aquaculture, industrial effluents, ponds, sewage effluents, wastewater.

INTRODUCTION

Water treatment through lagooning or 'ponding' has been common in Asia, especially India, China and south-east Asian countries. The relative inexpensiveness, extreme simplicity in operation and maintenance, and appropriateness in treating low

Aquatic Plants for Water Treatment
and Resource Recovery
K.R. Reddy and W.H. Smith (Eds.)

ISBN 0-941463-00-1

volumes of waste effluents have all contributed to the popularity of lagooning. It has also been known for centuries that fish and vegetation if grown in ponds receiving human or agricultural wastes not only speed up the treatment of wastes but 'recover' the nutrients in the form of live biomass. Farmers in China and Southeast Asia have developed the recycling of nutrient-rich organic wastes into an art. It has been common to situate household latrines over the family fish ponds. In rural areas, barns are so built that the manure from dairy animals inside falls into a pond to fertilize aquatic plants. Harvested regularly, the plants provide feed for the animals (LeMare, 1952). The Bayan Lepas Farm near Penang (Malaysia) was organized in the 1950's to combine pig-rearing with fish-farming and vegetable growing. The centerpiece of this intensive system is a lagoon stocked with herbivorous fish and water spinach (*Ipomoea aquatica* or *I. reptans*). Wastes from pig sties are flushed into the lagoon to fertilize and maintain the water spinach crop. A portion of the crop is eaten by the fish and the rest is harvested for pig food. Yeoh (1983) reports that water hyacinth (*Eichhornia crassipes* (Mart) Solms) has long been grown in Malaysia by small-scale pig farmers in ponds receiving piggery washings. The hyacinths harvested from such ponds are used as an animal feed supplement. Simple systems like these that harness aquatic plants to recycle nutrients are reportedly common in Asia (Hara, 1951; NAS, 1976) but unfortunately little, if any, scientific information is available on the design basis and performance. Simple systems like these, though useful in recovering nutrients, are never free from the hazards of introducing pathogens into the human food chain. A large number of parasitic diseases prevalent in the East could have their origin in the practices of recycling human excreta and other animal-based biowastes as fertilizers (Pacey, 1978).

ALGAE BASED WATER TREATMENT SYSTEMS

Algae influence the biological, chemical and visual features of facultative waste stabilization ponds. The symbiotic relationship between the decomposer bacteria and algae -- the former producing CO_2, NH_4^+ and other nutrients while the latter utilizing these nutrients and generating O_2 through photosynthesis for maintaining the aerobic zone of the pond -- is essential for the functioning of facultative ponds. However, such ponds are not traditionally referred as 'algae-based' systems. Production of algae, though essential, is to be firmly kept under control. Excessive algal production can destabilize a facultative pond, and the problems associated with this phenomena are believed to be the biggest drawbacks of facultative pond systems. On the other hand, the 'high-rate ponds' concept, initiated in the 1950s in the United States (Oswald and Gotaas, 1955) and followed up in the Philippines, Israel, India, Singapore and other countries, lays emphasis on the maximization of algal growth. Such ponds are kept shallow (0.2-0.4 m) to aid in the penetration of light and increase the efficiency of solar conversion. The pond contents need to be mixed at low speed to keep the algae in suspension and in good contact with the wastewater nutrients. It is essential to prevent algae from getting into the final effluent.

In Asia, high-rate ponds have been built below ground level as well as aboveground level (Majid and Akhtar, 1980; Lee et al., 1980). Some ponds have been built into the roofs of animal housing units (Stanton, 1976). The ponds are stirred with pumps or paddle-wheel mixers. Innovative approaches include use of low-cost asbestos sheets for building ponds in Singapore and small windmills for stirring the ponds in India (NAS, 1981).

The prime objective of the high-rate ponds is algal production. The conventional systems in Asia have slanted towards maximizing biomass production rather than wastewater treatment. Attempts to develop optimal algae-based water treatment biomass production systems have been mostly made in Israel (Shelef et al., 1977,1978a,1978b,1980; Oron and Shelef, 1982).

Shelef et al. (1977) operated two 0.1 ha, 0.4 m deep, high-rate ponds with domestic wastewater. Mixing was provided by a paddle wheel. Detention times were 2 d during summer and 10 d during winter. Micractinium, Scendesmus, Oocystis and Euglena were the dominant algae genera at various times. The biomass was harvested by alum flocculation followed by dissolved air flotation. Subsequent to the harvest, 93% of the BOD and P and 50% of the N had been removed from the wastewaters. Extrapolation of the results of pilot scale studies indicated that the wastewaters produced by a community of 6000-8000 people received in a 1 ha high-rate stabilization pond system would yield about 100 Mg dry biomass per year. About 60% of the biomass would be of algal origin while the remainder would be mostly bacteria. Dried biomass can be used as an alternative protein source for chicken, fish and pig feed.

Shelef et al. (1978) operated a pond receiving domestic wastewaters at depths of 0.35-0.5 m. A horizontal caged rotor produced flow rates of 3-5 cm s^{-1} during the day and 7-12 cm s^{-1} during the night. The rotor also accomplished mixing of pond contents. Mean organic loading on the pond was 46.5 g m^{-2} d^{-1} and detention times varied from 1.8 d in summer to 7 d in the winter. Total biomass production was calculated to be 40.7 g m^{-2} d^{-1} with algal substance being produced at a rate of 35.1 g m^{-1} d^{-2}.

The biggest drawback of the algae-based wastewater treatment systems is the high cost of algae harvesting and drying. Shelef et al. (1978) estimated that the aeration-mixing required for a high-rate stabilization pond is only one-third that of an activated sludge plant. However, the total energy required exceeded that needed for separation and disposal of activated sludge due to the energy used for the concentration and drying of the biomass. Total construction and operating costs of a high-rate algae pond would approach that of an activated sludge treatment facility. Light availability is a critical factor controlling the algal growth and artificial light is not economically viable because at the very best an efficiency of only 20% may be obtained from the energy supplied. High-rate algae ponds have a light conversion efficiency of about 3% (Shelef et al., 1977); thus, sunshine is the only practical light source for algae production but illumination from the sun may often exceed light requirements for maximum algal photosynthesis and may damage exposed algal cells. Other recognized but yet to be overcome limitations of the algae-based systems include difficulties in maintaining desirable algal species in the ponds; sudden shifts in algal species composition occur as the result of weather or operational changes. Such shifts have an impact on the cost of harvesting. Genera such as *Micractinium* and *Scenedesmus* which are colonial and spine bearing, and *Spirulina* are readily harvested while species such as *Chlorella*, which are small coccoid or single-celled alga are difficult to harvest. Predators also pose problems. In Singapore, the cladoceran *Moina* is an intermittent predator; elsewhere *Daphne* and rotifers are common algal predators (Stanton, 1976). Such predators rapidly decimate the algal population and adversely affect the quality of the discharge water by adding soluble BOD.

Researchers in Israel are now focusing research on duckweed (Oron et al., 1984) in view of the above mentioned problems with algae, especially the high costs involved in harvesting and drying, while researchers elsewhere in Asia are trying to develop more economical harvesting and post-harvest processing techniques. In Singapore, research on a pilot-scale project with 2.9 ha high rate ponds involves continuous filtration using commercially viable fineweave filter fabrics (NAS, 1981). Attempts are also being made to develop a process in which the alum used in algae flocculation is recovered by acidification of the algal slurry and recycled. Success in these attempts will lead to reduction of residual alum in the algae and lower costs. Another alternative being explored is to pump the algal-bacterial slurry grown over a high-rate pond supplied with swine waste directly into the feeding troughs of the swine. Swine accept liquid food and dewatering of algal biomass may be avoided if the slurry can turn out to be as effective a feed as dewatered algae. Alternatively, harvested algal slurry can be cooked, preferably by steam, and fed in wet form to pigs. Cooking requires less energy than drying, but the product must be used immediately since it has poor stability. Feeding trials showed that steam cooked algae can replace half of the 16% soybean meal in the diet of growing pigs. When algae totally replaced the soybean meal, the growth performance of the pigs was only slightly depressed (Abito, 1986).

Researchers in the Philippines are evaluating a natural process of autoflocculation in algae culture as a means of preconcentrating the algae suspension and have achieved better than 90% algae recovery. Harvesting, therefore, may no longer be a major constraint to the broad application of high-rate pond technology. The potential impact of algal protein production (56-82 Mg ha^{-1} yr^{-1}) on livestock and poultry feed supply and the environmental benefit of wastewater treatment, justify continued efforts to develop algae-harvesting technology.

In a rare attempt to use algae in treating industrial wastewaters, John (1983) allowed algae to grow over pre-treated block rubber effluent, in a shallow (0.25 m) tank using retention times ranging from 2-10 d. No marked improvement in BOD and total solids removal was observed in the algal system but COD and suspended solids recorded an increase. This adverse effect was greater with higher retention times; at 10 d retention COD increased from 200 mg L^{-1} to 440 mg L^{-1} and suspended solids increased from 80 mg L^{-1} to 330 mg L^{-1}.

MACROPHYTE BASED WATER TREATMENT SYSTEMS

The traditional expertise of Asian farmers in recycling human and animal wastes through aquaculture and the practices intuitively developed by them for recovering nutrients from wastes by aquatic macrophytes propagated over waste-fed ponds (Hara, 1951; Yeoh, 1983), should place Asian researchers in the lead in developing macrophyte-based water treatment systems. However, while the lead in systematic research on the treatment of domestic wastewaters using aquatic macrophytes has come from the West -- mainly West Germany, USA and the Netherlands -- one of the first research reports on the treatment of industrial wastewater with aquatic macrophyte appeared in Asia. This publication (Sinha and Sinha, 1969) which preceded reports on this subject from other parts of the world by some years, describes experiments for evaluating the capacity of water hyacinth to purify digested sugar factory wastes. Treatment of septic tank effluents is also described. The anaerobically digested sugar factory waste with 258 mg L^{-1} of BOD, turbidity 150 mg L^{-1}, odor 24 mg L^{-1}, pH 7.05 and redox potential -129 mv was retained in containers with or without water hyacinth cover. At all retention times studied, varying from 1-7 d, water hyacinth facilitated waste treatment achieving reductions in BOD, 94%; turbidity, 97%; and odor, 96%. The redox potential changed to +784 mv and pH to 7.50. In containers without water hyacinth the corresponding changes were BOD, 54%; turbidity, 40%; odor, 92%; redox potential +431 mv; and pH, 7.35. Similar results were achieved with septic tank effluent. They also investigated the mechanism of the purifying action of water hyacinth and demonstrated the presence of enzyme dehydrogenase in the hyacinth roots to which they attributed the capability of the macrophyte to 'oxidize' the organic wastes. During absorption of water, the collodial particles of the waste possibly strike the surface of the hyacinth roots and get agglomerated after losing their electrical charges. While settling, the agglomerated particles possibly carried with them more suspended solids. Suspended solids removal was possibly facilitated by the absorption of natural peptising agents from the wastewater by the hyacinth roots. From the pattern of change of redox potential in water hyacinth covered wastewater from -129 mv to +784 mv, the authors suggested that facultative anaerobes and aerobes were operative. The fairly detailed and promising study, unfortunately, was not followed up with larger-scale trials.

In the late 1970s, there was a world-wide increase in interest in developing aquatic plant based wastewater treatment systems, and by the early 1980s, several studies were undertaken in Asia. Most of the work has centered around water hyacinth, with some reports on duckweed, salvinia and watercress -- water hyacinth combination.

TREATMENT OF INDUSTRIAL WASTEWATERS

Water Hyacinth

Water hyacinth has been explored for treating wastewaters from dairies, piggeries, tanneries, distillaries, sugar factories, pulp and paper industries, textile industries, palm oil mills, natural rubber factories, electroplating units and metal work industries. Efforts have also been made to assess the capability of water hyacinth to remove phenol, pesticides, bacteria, virus, fluoride and heavy metals (including radionuclides) from water. The studies carried out so far in Asia are summarized in Table 1. Most were done at the laboratory scale and even though in a large number of cases the presence of weeds significantly improved the treatment of wastewaters in tanks/ponds, very few attempts have been made at scale-up.

John (1984) conducted laboratory scale and pilot plant trials on the treatment of effluents from palm oil mills (POM). Water hyacinth was propagated on POM effluent and at a retention time of 25 d BOD was reduced from 4980 mg L^{-1} to 180 mg L^{-1} (96% reduction) while COD was reduced from 8850 mg L^{-1} to 1120 mg L^{-1} (87% reduction). Other pollutants were also significantly removed. However, the system was not successful when extended to ponds treating liquid wastes in the POM, as the plants were inhibited in their growth and tended to decay (John, 1986, personal communication). The experience of Yeoh (1983) has been similar: good results were obtained (Table 1) when POM effluent pretreated through anaerobic digestion and extended aeration was subjected to advanced treatment in 4000 L tanks with water hyacinth. When extended to ponds in a POM, the system did not function satisfactorily as the water hyacinth plants tended to wither and die. This was traced to higher (40 times) concentration of ammoniacal N in the mill effluent compared to the effluent used in pilot treatment plant. The mill was advised to reduce the ammoniacal N in the effluent by aeration before water

TABLE 1. Treatment of industrial wastewaters and some specific pollutants using water hyacinth.

Wastewater	Type and capacity/ dimensions of holding tanks/ containers	Retention time (days)	Influent conc., mg L^{-1} maximum removal shown in parenthesis	Remarks	Reference
1	2	3	4	5	6
Sugar refinery (predigested)	Beakers 2 L	0-7	BOD 258 (94%), turbidity 150 (97%), odor 24 (96%)		Sinha and Sinha, 1969
Sugar refinery	Fiberglass tanks 3m x 2m x 1m; 4000 L; operated at depth of 0.66 m	7	BOD 999 (43%), COD 1918 (36%), SS 32 (21%), TS 3163 (85%)	Plants tended to decay after 6 weeks	Yeoh, 1983
Dairy	Plastic containers 0.6 m dia., 0.21 m height; glass containers 0.30 m dia., 0.11 m high	1-14	BOD 1443 (84%), COD 1690 (88%), SS 1107 (40%), TS 3693 (50%), fats and grease 173 (85%)	Decayed plants were removed from time to time	Aowal and Singh, 1982
Dairy	Plastic tubs 0.33 m dia., 12 L	7,14	BOD 61 (87%), COD 120 (63%), total N 35 (60%), inorg. P 0.4 (50%), total P 3.5 (79%)	Maximum BOD, COD and total P removed was achieved at RT 7 d, for other pollutants RT 14 d was required. Plants tended to accumulate as well as leach out Ca, Mg & N.	Trivedy et al., 1983; Goel et al., 1985

TABLE 1 (cont'd.)

1	2	3	4	5	6
Distillery (diluted 24 times with water)	Cement, tanks 1 m x 1 m x 0.8 m	16,31,49	Ca 40 (6%) Mg 32 (11.6%), Available P 0.31 (19.4%), total dissolved P 0.75 (96%), total dissolved N 0.44 (87.4%)	Available P was removed by 19.4% in 31 d but increased thereafter; Total dissolved N removed by 75.5% in 16 d	Trivedy and Khomane, 1985
Piggery (sun-dried pig waste mixed with water)	Fiberglass tanks 200 L	1-7	BOD 70 (74%), 146 (61%), 196 (68%), 320 (67%), COD 245 (42%), 463 (32%), 675 (30%), 920 (21%)	In general water hyacinth was 20-30% more efficient than algae. Waste with BOD 320 and COD 920 caused plants to decay after 5 d	Yeoh, 1983
Palm Oil (pretreated by anaerobic digestion followed by extended aeration)	Fiberglass tanks 3 m x 2 m x 1 m; 4000 L; operated at depth of 0.66 m	5	BOD 82 (40%), COD 388 (35%), SS 116 (85%), NH_3-N 1.23 (54%), total N 32 (69%)	Field trials under actual mill operation conditions indicated that hyacinth plants tended to wither after a few days because of high NH_3-N in the wastewater; further trials are underway	Yeoh, 1983
Palm Oil (partially digested)	Concrete tanks 120 L, depth 0.3 m/0.6 m/1.2 m	10,20,25	BOD 4980 (96%), COD 8850 (87%), SS 3560 (96%), TS 8210 (45%),	Attempts to extend this system to ponds treating palm oil mill	John, 1983, 1984

TABLE 1 (cont'd.)

1	2	3	4	5	6
			total N 285 (77%), NH_4-N 120 (83%), oil and grease 660 (97%)	effluents were not successful as the plants tended to die soon after introduction	
Natural rubber (raw effluent)	--as above--	5,10,15	BOD 1430 (94%), COD 2480 (89%), TS 1420 (57%) SS 810 (89%), NH_4-N 100 (70%), total N 150 (67%)	At RT 10d, 85% BOD, 80% COD, 88% SS, 50% NH_4-N and 53% NH_4-N were removed. Optimum operating depth was 0.3 m. Plants grew best at pH 5.0-7.5.	John, 1984
Natural rubber (effluent from anaerobic lagoon)	Lagoons in remilling factories, generating 1 million L effluent per day	12-15	BOD 160 (89%), COD 380 (66%), TS 700 (72%), SS 255 (88%), NH_4-N 20 (70%), total N 30 (50%)	The plants were harvested periodically; average yield was 500 kg dry matter ha^{-1} d^{-1}	John, 1984
Tannery (diluted 10 times with water)	Plastic tubs 33 cm dia., 12 L	7,14	BOD 380 (35%), COD 800 (70%), total N 108 (72%), inorg. P 1.4 (86%), total P 4 (64%)	Addition of sewage hastened BOD & COD removal but slowed down the removal of N & P	Trivedy et al., 1983
Tannery (mixed with sewage)	Cement tanks 600 L	Up to 24	BOD 700 (80%), Cr 80 (100%)	With tannery waste (BOD 2000-2500 mg L^{-1} and Cr 150-200 mg L^{-1}) mixed with sewage	Prasad et al., 1983

TABLE 1 (cont'd.)

1	2	3	4	5	6
				in 1:4 ratio, BOD was reduced by 80% and Cr by nearly 100% in 16 d. Plants tended to decay after 4 weeks	
Tannery	Earthenware vessels 65 L	2	TS 12300 (absorption of metals and reduction of BOD & COD was observed; values not reported)	The plants wilted in 2 d	Haider et al., 1983
Pulp and paper (paper machine/ combined)	Pots 30 L for survivability and coverage studies; tanks 200 L for other studies. Batch as well as continuous process were studied	1-15	Combined effluent COD 485-655 and SS 174-300 were reduced by 70% and 80% respectively at RT 15 d in a continuous process. For paper machine effluent 90% COD was removed in 6 d	The plants exhibited excellent growth and survivability at pH 4-10	Behera et al., 1982
Pulp and paper	Vessels 1.5 L and 65 L	Up to 10	TS 5100	Wilting of the plants started after 3 d. Of the various parameters studied, significant reductions	Haider et al., 1983

TABLE 1 (cont'd.)

1	2	3	4	5	6
				were observed in COD (44%) and BOD (53%)	
Textile			TS 1185-1204, SO_4 719	Plants died within 4 d even when influent was diluted by 50%. At higher dilutions the plants could survive	Widyanto et al., 1975
Textile (diluted 3 times with water)	Cement tanks 1 m x 1 m x 0.8 m	16,31,49	Ca 45 (32%), Mg 12 (31%), available P 0.19 (42%), total dissolved P 0.4 (72%), total dissolved N 0.7 (31%), particulate N 0.5 (75%)	Significant reduction of Mg and particulate N occurred at RT 16 d	Trivedy and Khomane, 1985
Electroplating (chemically treated and diluted 2.5 times)	Cement tanks 700 L	1-5	TDS 3180 (72%), Cr 0.2 (100%), Cu 5 (60%), Ni 2.3 (22%)		Shroff, 1982
Electroplating (with pH adjusted	Cement tanks	1-3	Cu 5 (10%), Fe 62 (22%), Ni 70 (10%), Zn 13 (18%)	Plants began to wither after 24 h	Yeoh, 1983

TABLE 1 (cont'd.)

1	2	3	4	5	6
from 1.35 to 5.50)					
Metal work	Cement tanks 1 m x 1 m x 0.8 m	16,31,49	Ca 55 (52%), Mg 13 (16%), available P 0.25 (40%), total dissolved N 0.4 (32%), total dissolved P 0.5 (56%), particulate N 0.8 (79%)		Trivedy and Khomane, 1985
Engineering industry		1-3	Industrial waste was mixed with sewage in ratios of 3:7, 1:1, 7:3 (vol/vol)	In general, better removal of pollutants occurred in mixtures containing industrial waste and sewage in 7:3 ratio	Trivedy, 1986, Y. C. College of Science, Karad, India, personal communication
Mercury		--	--	Absorption of Hg from Hg solutions and Hg-bearing effluents was influenced by initial concentration of the metal and growth rate of the plants	Das, 1984

TABLE 1 (cont'd.)

1	2	3	4	5	6
Pesticide	Plastic buckets 10 L	1-4	Sodium pentachlorophenate 53 (64%), 30 (82%), 29 (76%)	Comparable treatment seen in controls where algae developed; the hyacinth plants tended to wilt	Gudekar et al., 1984
Formic acid (explosive manufacturing)				Formic acid concentration appropriate for treatment with water hyacinth was worked out	Vithal Rajan et al., 1983
Phenol	Circular vessels, height 0.24 m, diam. 0.6 m, 62 L	1.5-2	At flow rate 42 L d^{-1}: Phenol 25 (96%), 75 (89%); At flow rate 62 L d^{-1}: phenol 25 (93%), 75 (87%), 100 (78%), 125 (70%)	Nutrients were added to facilitate plant growth. A method was worked out for the designing of large scale systems	Vaidyanathan et al., 1983
Fluoride		30	Fluoride 6-26	Authors concluded that efficiency of uptake was too low to be of practical importance	Rao et al., 1973
Pathogenic bacteria and	Tanks 50 L	Up to 3	*E. coli* K 13 Vibre chloerae 04	Concentration of bacteria was signifi-	Gilman et al., 1983†

TABLE 1 (cont'd.)

1	2	3	4	5	6
virus† (in diluted sewage)				cantly reduced but there was no increase in die-off virus	
Heavy metals		Up to 3	Individually: Au 50 Cd/Ni 100; Pb 78-100; pH 6.9/4.6	Uptake was dramatic up to 24 h; thereafter plants began to wither and the uptake dropped. Pb showed least phyto-toxicity	Yeoh, 1983
Heavy metals	Plastic pots 4 L		Individually and in mixtures. Cd 3, Hg 3, Ni 3 in 12.5% Hoagland solution	Uptake of metals by hyacinth is rapid and is proportional to the concentrations present in the water. Maximum absorption took place at RT 3 d	Widyanto & Susilo, 1978; Widyanto &, Sopannata, 1979
Heavy metals	Containers 0.73 m x 0.45 m x 0.23 m		Individually: Pb 1/10; Cd 10; Cu 10; Mixtures: Pb + Cu, Pb + CD, Cu + Cd, Pb + Cu + Cd	Pb was taken up in the highest amounts followed by Cu and Cd. Uptake decreased with increase in the acidity and decrease in the temperature of the medium	Tatsuyama et al., 1977

TABLE 1 (cont'd.)

1	2	3	4	5	6
Heavy metals	Containers 2 L	Up to 7	Pb/Cd/Cu 1-160	Pb was absorbed up to 70 mg g^{-1} dry root. Stirring of medium increased metal uptake	Tatsuyama et al., 1979
Heavy metals	Plastic pots 2 L	Up to 16 at 25°C ± 2°C	Cd/Pb 1-8, Hg 0.5-2, individually and in mixtures	All metals were well absorbed by roots; the absorption increased exponentially with time	Muramoto & Oki, 1983
Heavy metals (in presence of anionic surfactants)	Plastic pots 2 L	12	Cd/Ni 1-8, Cd 1 plus Ni 1 with or without sodium dedecyl sulphate 25	In general the metal uptake was lesser in presence of the surfactant	Muramoto & Oki, 1984
Heavy metals (radio-nuclides)	Glass beakers 1 L	2	137 Cs specific activity 10^{-1} 10^{-3} Ci/mL; 90 Sr specific activity 1-5x10^{-3} Ci/mL	Both radionuclides were significantly absorbed; the bulk in the roots	Jayaraman Prabhakaran, 1982

†Duckweed was also explored but was found to have no significant impact.

hyacinth treatment. According to Yeoh (1986, personal communication, SIRI of Malayasia, Shah Alam, Selangor, Malaysia), currently several rubber processing factories and POM's in Malaysia are experimenting with the water hyacinth systems for polishing their effluents.

John (1984) developed an aquatic plant-based system for treatment of natural rubber factory effluents and at present, 10 factories are using these systems. The recommended ponding system consists of one anaerobic pond with 12-15 d hydraulic retention time (HRT) followed by two facultative ponds, each with HRT 10 d. The water hyacinth grew best in the second pond (i.e., first facultative pond). If the influent BOD is less than 1000 mg L^{-1} there is good growth of the plants even in the first (anaerobic) pond. However, if the BOD goes above this limit, the growth of the plants in the first pond is inhibited; the rate of inhibition being dependent on the BOD/COD levels of the influent. If the BOD of the influent is above 1500 mg L^{-1}, there is a near total inhibition in the first pond; however, the plants grow profusely in the second and third (first and second facultative) ponds. The ponds are not basically designed for the propagation of water hyacinth: they are typical lagoons with earthen base and sides. The anaerobic ponds are deeper (2.5 m) than the facultative ponds, the depth of which is limited to about 1.5 m. Cultivation of water hyacinth is only a secondary feature, which helps in upgrading the stabilization ponds and enables the effluents to meet the discharge standards (Table 2). In the ponds, water hyacinth doubled its weight in two weeks, and harvest is recommended for at least 1/3 of the pond every two weeks, followed by the 2nd and 3rd portions, taking care to spread out the plants into the vacant space after the harvest. The yield approximated 500 kg (dry matter) ha^{-1} d^{-1}. Harvested plants were used as mulch under rubber or oil palm. The economics have not been worked out

TABLE 2. Final treatment of natural rubber effluents with water hyacinth.†

Property		Raw effluent	Final Discharge Value	Final Discharge % reduction	Regulatory standards for discharge
pH		6.1	7.2	--	6-9
BOD	mg L^{-1}	160	17	89.4	50
COD	"	380	130	65.8	400
Total solids	"	700	195	72.1	--
Suspended solids	"	255	30	88.2	100
Ammoniacal N	"	20	6	70.0	40
Total N	"	30	15	50.0	60

†John (1984).

but are likely to be favorable because the running cost is limited to the wages of the persons harvesting the water hyacinth plants.

Behera et al. (1982) studied treatment of pulp and paper mill effluents in batch as well as continuous processes in experimental lagoons. For combined effluent, at an optimum of 75% water hyacinth coverage and 15 d retention, the COD (485-655 mg L^{-1}) was reduced by 80%. For paper machine effluent, 90% reduction in COD was achieved in 6 d retention. The water hyacinth had good growth and survivability in the effluents in the pH range 4-10, and tended to bring the effluent to neutral irrespective of the starting pH. The authors proposed two alternatives -- continuous process and batch process -- for large-scale treatment of the effluents. They estimated that for a wastewater flow of 3,785 m^3 d^{-1} the continuous process will require a 5.7 ha lagoon, 1 m deep, with retention time of 15 d. They also proposed an alternate lagoon for use when the first lagoon is to be cleared. For the batch process, three lagoons, each 2.3 ha and 1 m deep, were proposed. The effluent could be filled in the first lagoon over a period of 6 d and subsequently retained for 9 d. The effluent from the 7th to 12th d could be fed to the second lagoon and retained for 9 d. Similarly, effluent from the 13th to 18th d could be fed to the third lagoon. Thus, each lagoon would complete a 15 d cycle. During the remaining 3 d, the effluent in lagoon I could be discharged and the lagoon cleaned. The same may be repeated for other lagoons in sequence. The paper machine effluent which constitutes roughly 25% of the total effluent was proposed to be segregated and fed to a clarifier; after settlement of sludge the supernatant could be drained or recycled in the mill. The remaining effluent could be fed to a clarifier and then to the lagoons.

The economics were not worked out but were likely to be favorable. Except for the cost of land, no major capital or recurring expenses can be foreseen, and there is always the possibility of gains if water hyacinth harvested from the lagoons could be utilized as a source of biogas or animal feed. The studies appeared to hold promise but were not carried further. The main constraint has been the difficulty in acquiring land for the lagoons. The present protracted land acquistion policy, amongst other administrative factors, discourages adopting water hyacinth based systems.

Other Aquatic Macrophytes

Amongst aquatic macrophytes only African payal (*Salvinia molesta* Mitchell), apart from water hyacinth, appears to have been used in treatment of industrial wastewater in Asia. Of the several species of the aquatic fern (genus *Salvinia*), the species *S. molesta* is known to be the most competitive and fastest growing. It has colonized large tracts of freshwater in Sri Lanka, Thailand, Indonesia, Burma and several other regions in Asia, Africa, Australia and South America. The weed has established itself in Kerala (India) by outcompeting water hyacinth (Abbasi and Nipaney, 1986a).

Abbasi and Nipaney (1981a,1982,1985) have explored possibilities of using S. molesta in treating heavy metals, and effluents from dairies, tanneries, and industries producing rubber, pulp and paper, insecticides and fertilizers. They have simultaneously studied utilization of the weed in biogas production (Abbasi and Nipaney, 1981b,1984a,1984b). In general S. molesta is comparable with water hyacinth as a wastewater purifier. The water loss due to evapotranspiration by Salvinia is less than by water hyacinth.

TREATMENT OF DOMESTIC WASTEWATER

Water Hyacinth

After Sinha and Sinha (1969) reported that water hyacinth increases the rate of removal of BOD, turbidity, coliforms and odor from septic tank effluents, sporadic attempts have been made to utilize water hyacinths in improving treatment capability of stabilization ponds. Pachaiyapan (1986, personal communication, New Delhi, India) provided information on one such system of two oxidation tanks, 140 m x 21 m, at Phulpur (India) in which water hyacinth was introduced in October, 1979. The initial growth was poor but with the warming of weather, there was vigorous growth and 100% coverage was achieved. The plants helped in reducing the odors and the discharge from the tanks became quite clear and free from all suspensions and algal growth. No quantitative information is available on the upgrading achieved by water hyacinth or maintenance of the plant cover.

In recent years, efforts have been made to set up medium scale test facilities to evaluate and control the performance of macrophytes and to obtain basic design information for developing optimal wastewater treatment/resource recovery systems. At Sangli (India), Joglekar (1985, personal communication, Maharashtra, India) and coworkers have set up a test facility in which 0.5 million L d^{-1} of domestic wastewater is treated in a system of 10 oxidation ponds (total surface area 0.41 ha). The details are given elsewhere in this volume (Joglekar and Sonar, 1987).

Oki (1983) used a pilot plant set up in Okayama, Japan, designed to treat 20 m^3 d^{-1} of domestic wastewater. Monitoring conducted during April-November 1982, revealed the raw wastewater characteristics: BOD 1.81-48.04, COD 3.75-49.82, DO 0.4-8.4, TOC 4.94-61.75, SS 7.2-97.4, Total N 1.01-12.45, Total P 0.32-2.98 (all in mg L^{-1}). On an average, the influent BOD was reduced by 70.35%, COD by 45.57%, SS by 80.29%, TOC by 50.55%, Total-N by 60.44% and Total-P by 52.61%. The yield of water hyacinth from the first pond was 102 kg fresh wt m^{-2} compared with 63.7 kg m^{-2} from the fourth pond. The economics of the system were not evaluated (Oki, 1986, personal communication, Okayama Univ., Japan).

Kira (1986, personal communication, Lake Biwa Research Institute, Otsu, Shiga, Japan) provided information on a pilot plant set up at Shifa, Japan, to evaluate the performance of water hyacinth and watercress in treating domestic wastewater originating from a community of 256 persons. The wastewater is diluted with raw water from a spring and is passed through watercress and water hyacinth channels. Watercress channels have been incorporated in the system to facilitate treatment during winter when water hyacinth growth slackens or stops. Similar pilot plants are being tested in a number of other districts in Japan, mainly to develop criteria for design and operation of larger-scale systems.

An interesting package named 'Bio-Filter System' has recently been offered by Takaneka Komuten Company, Japan (Anonymous, 1986). The system was developed on the basis of a demonstration test plant operated in Doho Pond (3.4 ha) at Tsukuba Science City (Japan). The system consists of four main components, involving culture, recovery, processing and reuse of aquatic plants. A section of the Doho Pond is designated as an aquatic plant culture zone. Polluted water is pumped at a flow rate of 300-800 m^3 d^{-1} through the culture zone via a 'catalytic oxidation pathway'. The matured aquatic plants are vacuum picked into a 'recovery system' in which they are crushed and drained of excess water. The biomass is next dried in a solar drying system. The package includes a composting device and pelletization device; the solar-dried biomass can be composted and used as manure or pelleted and used either as solid fuel or livestock feed. A brochure provided by Deguchi (1986, personal communication, Takaneka Komuten Co., Tokyo, Japan) includes conceptual drawings and some specifications of the various units of the Bio-Filter, though no cost estimates are provided. The main distinguishing feature of the system is its reliance on portions of natural ponds or lakes, rather than separate basin, for culturing aquatic plants and purifying water. The system also provides a rather comprehensive package cultivation system, recovery and solar drying system, and composting and pelletization devices which should make it relatively easy to adopt.

Other Aquatic Macrophytes

Duckweed, watercress and African payal (*S. molesta*) have been explored. In Japan, watercress is mainly being evaluated as a standby to water hyacinth during winters. Oron et al. (1984;1986) screened three duckweed species; *Lemna gibba*, *Wolffia arrhiza* and *Spirodela polyrrhiza* for the treatment of domestic wastewater in miniponds. The main findings include: a) *Spirodela* had a slightly higher growth rate than *Lemna* but the latter appeared to be more competitive; *Wolffia* was unable to maintain itself as pure culture; b) at influent COD levels of 600/300/100 mg L^{-1}, N levels of 200/50 mg L^{-1} and detention time of 10/20 d, the removal of COD, uptake of N by the plant, specific growth rate of the plant, and overall N removal were inversely proportional to influent N concentration; c) removal efficiency of major pollutants approached 50-60%; d) duckweed yield was not dependent on COD concentration, and ranged 3-15 g m^{-1} d^{-1} (dry wt) with crude protein content of 30-45%; e) duckweed cover appeared to reduce water losses by 20-30% compared to free-surface waste treatment methods; and f) the cost of wastewater treatment can be reduced with the duckweed system by 33-13%. The authors list several advantages of duckweed over water hyacinth, the major ones being higher protein content of the duckweeds and the lesser temperature sensitiveness and lesser water losses of the duckweed based system.

In conclusion, the review of the studies presented on aquatic plant based water treatment systems have shown promise as an alternative to the conventional systems whenever tried in Asia, the science and technology of this option has been slow in developing in this region. While a large number of reports are available on the removal of one or more pollutants from wastewaters in laboratory-scale vessels with and without aquatic plant cover, there has been a dearth of attempts to understand and control the basic processes operative in such systems or to generate basic engineering data and design information appropriate to typical Asian situations. Research and development efforts based on medium and large scale experimental/demonstration systems need to be taken up on a priority basis to cover this knowledge gap.

ACKNOWLEDGMENTS

The authors are thankful to Dr. K. R. Reddy for valuable suggestions, Dr. P. C. Nipaney for technical help and Ms. V. Subaida for secretarial assistance. Financial support from the Department of Non-Conventional Energy Sources, Government of India, is gratefully acknowledged.

REFERENCES

Abbasi, S. A., and P. C. Nipaney. 1981a. Tolerance and growth of aquatic weed salvinia on waters treated with trace elements. Basic Data Report No. WQE/BD-8/81, CWRDM, Calicut, p. 1-51.

Abbasi, S. A., and P. C. Nipaney. 1981b. Biogas from different aquatic weeds and mixture of weeds. Basic Data Report No. WQE/BD-8/82, CWRDM, Calicut, p. 1-42.

Abbasi, S. A., and P. C. Nipaney. 1984a. The catalytic effect of copper (11), zinc (11), and nickel (11) on the anaerobic digestion of <u>Salvinia molesta</u> (Mitchell). p. 237-242. <u>In</u> F. A. Curtis (ed.) Energy Development: New Forms, Renewables, Conservation. Pergamon Press, Oxford.

Abbasi, S. A., and P. C. Nipaney. 1984b. Utilization of aquatic weeds relevant in irrigation and drainage management with special reference to salvinia. Proceedings of the First Regional Pan-American Conference of the ICID, Salvador (Brazil), p. 251-283.

Abbasi, S. A., and P. C. Nipaney. 1985. Wastewater treatment using aquatic plants. Survivability and growth of _Salvinia molesta_ over waters treated with zinc and the subsequent utilization of the harvested weeds. Resources and Conservation 12:47-55.

Abbasi, S. A., and P. C. Nipaney. 1986a. Aquatic fern of the genus _Salvinia_ -- its infestation and control. Environmental Conservation (in press).

Anonymous. 1986. Takaneka develops bio-filter system. News release from Takaneka Komutin Company, Ltd., Tokyo (March).

Aowal, A. F. S. A., and J. Singh. 1982. Water hyacinth for testing dairy waste. J. Inst. Eng. 62:73-75.

Chakraverty, R. K. 1983. Potentially of root extract of _Eichhornia crassipes_ (Mart) Solms on crop production. Int. Conf. Water Hyacinth, Hyderabad, Synopsis of Papers, p. 37.

Das, H. 1984. Mercury absorption capacity of the water hyacinth _Eichhornia crassipes_. Env. Eco. 2:338-340.

Edwards, P. 1983. Fish cultivation on water hyacinth: Int. Conf. Water Hyacinth, Hyderabad, Synopsis of Papers, p. 38.

Ghosh, S. R., T. Goswami, M. K. C. Nambiar, and B. P. Chaliha. 1983. Investigation on water hyacinth for making water hyacinth-cement boards: Int. Conf. Water Hyacinth, Hyderabad, Synopsis of Papers, p. 34.

Gilman, R. H., D. Mullick, B. D. Chatterjee, and K. Nath. 1983. Clearance of pathogenic bacteria and virus from the water column by aquatic plants. Int. Conf. Water Hyacinth, Hyderabad, Synopsis of Papers, p. 51.

Goel, P. K. R. K. Trivedy, and R. R. Vaidya. 1985. Accumulation of nutrients from wastewater by water hyacinth, _Eichhornia crassipes_. Geobios. 12:115-119.

Gotaas, H. B., W. J. Oswald, and G. Golueke. Algal-bacteria symbiosis in sewage oxidation ponds. Report, California Sanitary Engineering Laboratory, University of California, Berkeley, p. 1-71.

Gudekar, V. R., L. P. Borkar, K. M. Kavadia, and R. K. Trivedy 1984. Studies on the feasibility of removal of sodium pentachlorophenate (SPCP) with water hyacinth. Poll. Res. 3:71-75.

Haider, S. Z., K. M. A. Malik, M. M. Rahman, and M. A. Ali. 1983a. Pollution control by water hyacinth of waste effluents of pulp and paper mills and of tanneries. Int. Conf. Water Hyacinth, Hyderabad, Synopsis of Papers, p. 54.

Haider, S. Z., K. M. A. Malik, M. M. Rahman, and M. A. Ali. 1983b. Water hyacinth compost as a cheap fertilizer. Int. Conf. Water Hyacinth, Hyderabad, Synopsis of Paper, p. 35.

Hara, S. L. 1951. The water hyacinth problem and pig farming. Science and Culture 17(6):231-232.

Jayaraman, A. P., and S. Prabhakar. 1982. The water hyacinth's uptake of ^{137}Cs and ^{90}Sr and its decontamination potential as an approach to the zero-release concept. Environmental migration of long-lived radionuclides. International Atomic Energy Agency, Vienna, p. 557-569.

John, C. K. 1983. Use of water hyacinth in the treatment of effluents from rubber industry. Proc. Int. Conf. Water Hyacinth, Hyderabad, UNEP Nairobi, p. 699-712.

John, C. K. 1984. Treatment of agro-industrial wastes using water hyacinth. Wat. Sci. Tech. 17:781-790.

Joglekar, V. R., and Sonar, V. G. 1987. Application of water hyacinth for treatment of domestic wastewater, generation of biogas and organic manure. In K. R. Reddy and W. H. Smith (ed.) Aquatic Plants for Water Treatment and Resource Recovery. Magnolia Publishing, Inc., Orlando, FL.

Khan, N. M., M. A. Kashem, K. Sen, U. Das, and S. Islam. 1983. Management of water hyacinth: Utilization of water hyacinth for animal feed (Part I). Int. Conf. Water Hyacinth, Hyderabad, Synopsis of Papers. p. 29.

Lee, B. Y., K. W. Lee, M. G. McBarry, and M. Graham. 1980. Waste water treatment and resource recovery report of a workshop on high-rate algae ponds. Singapore International Development Research Centre, Ottawa, Canada.

LeMare, D. W. 1952. Pig rearing fish-farming and vegetable growing. Malayan Agricultural Journal 35(3):156-166.

Mara, D. 1976. Sewage treatment in hot climates. Wiley, New York, p. 77-81.

Majid, F. Z., and N. Akhtar. 1980. Use of aquatic algae and aquatic weeds as livestock feeds. Paper presented at a seminar on Maximum Livestock Production on Minimum Land. Bangladesh Agricultural University, Mymensingh, Bangladesh.

Muramoto, S., and Y. Oki. 1983. Removal of some heavy metals from polluted water by water hyacinth (Eichhornia crassipes). Bull. Environ. Contam. Toxicol. 30:170-171.

Muramoto, S., and Y. Oki. 1984. Influence of anionic surface-active agents on the uptake of heavy metals by water hyacinth (Eichhornia crassipes). Bull. Environ. Contam. Toxicol. 33:444-450.

Majumdar, A. K. M. A., K. A. Haque, A. K. M. K. Alam, and Z. Rahman. 1983. Study on making board from water hyacinth. Int. Conf. Water Hyacinth, Hyderabad, Synopsis of Papers, p. 33.

National Academy of Sciences. 1976. Making aquatic weeds useful: Some perspectives for developing countries. NAS, Washington, DC, p. 115-125.

National Academy of Sciences. 1981. Food, fuel and fertilizer from organic wastes. NAS, Washington, DC, p. 1-154.

Omar, K. I., and S. Farooq. 1983. Growth and fermentation studies of water hyacinth biomass. Int. Conf. Water Hyacinth, Hyderabad, Synopsis of Papers, p. 39.

Oron, G., and G. Shelef. 1982. Maximizing algal yield in high rate oxidation ponds. J. Environ. Eng. Div., ASCE 108: 730-738.

Oron, G., L. R. Wildschut, and D. Porath. 1984. Wastewater recycling by duckweed for protein production and effluent renovation. Wat. Sci. Tech. 17:803-817.

Oron, G., D. Porath, and L. R. Wildschut. 1986a. Wastewater treatment and renovation by different duckweed species. J. of the Environ. Eng. Div., ASCE 112:247-263.

Pacey, A. (ed.). 1978. Sanitation in developing countries. The Gresham Press, Ch 12.

Pillai, K. R., B. G. Unni, A. Borthakur, H. D. Singh, and J. N. Baruah. 1983. Production of biogas from water hyacinth. Int. Conf. Water Hyacinth, Hyderabad, Synopsis of Papers. p. 43.

Prasad, B. G. S., W. Madhavakrishna, and Y. Nayudamma. 1983. Utilization of water hyacinth in the treatment and disposal of tannery wastewater. Int. Conf. Water Hyacinth, Hyderabad, Synopsis of Papers, p. 56.

Rao, K. V., A. K. Khandekar, and D. Vaidyanadhan. 1973. Uptake of fluoride by water hyacinth *Eichhornia crassipes*. Ind. J. Exp. Biol. 11:68-69.

Shelef, G., R. Moraine, T. Berner, A. Levi, and G. Oron. 1977. Solar energy conversion via algal wastewater treatment and protein production. Proceedings of the Fourth International Congress on Photosynthesis, Great Britain. p. 657.

Shelef, G., G. Oron, and R. Moraine. 1978b. Economic aspects of microalgae production on sewage. Arch. Hydrobiol. Beih. Ergbn. Limnol. 11:281.

Shelef, G., Y. Azov, R. Maraine, and G. Oron. 1980. Algal mass production as an integral part of a wastewater treatment and reclamation system. p. 163-189. *In* G. Shelef and C. J. Soeder (ed.) Algae Biomass Production and Use. Elsevier/ North Holland Biomedical Press.

Shroff, K. C. 1983. Reuse of water and sludge for cultivation of variety of value added botanical species. ENPC-IIT Joint Workshop on Strategy and Technology for Water Quality Management. Indian Institute of Technology, Bombay, p. 379-425.

Sinha, S. N., and L. P. Sinha. 1969. Studies on use of water hyacinth culture in oxidation ponds treating digested sugar wastes and effluents of septic tank. Environmental Health 11:197-207.

Stanton, W. R. 1976. Algae in waste recovery. p. 129-135. *In* W. R. Stanton and E. J. DaSilva (ed.) Global Impacts of Applied Microbiology: State of the Art, 1976, and its Impact on Developing Countries. UNEP/UNESCO/ICRO Panel of Microbiology Secretariat, Kuala Lumpur. University of Malaya Press, Kyala Lumpur.

Tatsuyama, K., H. Egawa, H. Yamamoto, and M. Nahamura. 1979. Sorption of heavy metals by the water hyacinth from the metal solutions (11) some experimental conditions influencing the sorption. Weed Res. Japan 22:151-156.

Tatsuyama, K. H. Egawa, H. Yamamoto, and M. Nakamura. 1979. Sorption of heavy metals by the water hyacinth from the metal solutions (11) some experimental conditions influencing the sorption. Weed Res. Japan 24:260-263.

Trivedi, R. K., P. K. Goel, V. R. Gudekar, M. G. Kirpekar. 1983. Treatment of tannery and dairy wastes using water hyacinth. Indian J. Environ. Protection 3:106-111.

Trivedi, R. K., and B. V. Khomane. 1985. Water hyacinth for removal of nutrients from wastewater. Comp. Phiol. Ecol. 10:123-128.

Vaidyanathan, S., K. M. Kavadia, M. G. Rao, and S. Basu. 1983. Removal of phenol using water hyacinth in a continuous unit. Intern. J. Environ. Studies 21:183-191.

Venkataramanan, M. N., H. D. Singh, J. N. Baruah. 1983. Utilization of water hyacinth roots in biofertilization of agriculture fields. Int. Conf. Water Hyacinth, Hyderabad, India, Synopsis of Papers. p. 36.

Vithal R., R. Marayya, R. E. C. Venkateswara, and R. B. Basava. 1983. Water hyacinth treatment of formic acid and related studies. Int. Conf. Water Hyacinth, Hyderabad, India, Synopsis of Papers. p. 58.

Widyanto, L. S. 1975. The effect of industrial pollutants on the growth of water hyacinth (*Eichhornia crassipes*) tropical pest biology program BIOTROP, Bogor. Proc. Indonesian Weed Sci. Conf. 3:328-329.

Widyanto, L. S., and H. Susilo. 1978. Water hyacinth (*Eichhornia crassipes*) (Mart) Solms) as bioagent to absorb heavy metals and nitrogen in polluted water. 1st Symposium of the Federation of Asian and Oceanic Biochemists, Singapore.

Widyanto, L. S., and A. Sopannato. 1979. Water hyacinth (*Eichhornia crassipes* (Mart) Solms) as a potential plant in a paper factory. Annual Meeting of the Aquatic Plant Management Society, Chatanooga, Tennessee.

Yeoh, B. G. 1983. Use of water hyacinth in wastewater treatment. Terminal Report, Standards and Industrial Research Institute of Malaysia. p. 22.

EDAPHIC-PHYTODEPURATION: A NEW APPROACH TO WASTEWATER TREATMENT

E. Salati
University of Sao Paulo
Piracicaba, BRAZIL

ABSTRACT

From 1980, research has been conducted in Brazil on the possibility of decontaminating polluted waters using monoculture of water hyacinths (*Eichhornia crassipes*) or combination of several other species. The project addressed secondary and tertiary treatments (sometimes primary), for urban wastes, and the pre-treatment of polluted rivers and streams to feed water into conventional treatment stations. Aquatic plants were also associated with other processes for decontamination of polluted waters, especially filtering through soils planted to rice. The treatment facility utilized, as a first step, canals with aquatic plants. Subsequently, the water passed through the filtering soil planted to rice. Removals of up to 99% BOD were achieved when the influent BOD was in the range of 150 to 200 mg L^{-1}. In other systems, polluted water was allowed to flow once, twice or three times through filtering soils, planted with and without rice. Subsequent to this treatment, the effluent was placed in canals with aquatic plants for a final treatment. This arrangement is being tested especially in sugarcane, paper and cellulose industries (final treatment) and in eucalyptus fiber industries. Results have been promising, the removals have many times met the law requirements (this process has been called edaphic-phyto-depuration). Aquatic plants, for use in small communities, are under test in several areas of Brazil (Northeast, Center, South). The climatic variations have determined the types of plant associations and the prevailing species. A general discussion of the advantage of the system, BOD removal rates and handling problems are presented.

Keywords: Water treatment, industrial effluent, aquatic plant, Brazil.

Aquatic Plants for Water Treatment
and Resource Recovery
K.R. Reddy and W.H. Smith (Eds.)

ISBN 0-941463-00-1

INTRODUCTION

Treatment of sewage in cities of developing countries is becoming an increasingly critical problem. The lack of an economically feasible water purification process is the main reason why many lakes and rivers are now highly-polluted water resources. The valley of the Piracicaba River, Sao Paulo, Brazil, is a typical case. The Piracicaba River is a tributary of the Tiete River (Parana River basin) and flows through 48 municipalities of the Sao Paulo state and some municipalities of the Minas Gerais state.

The area surrounding this river basin is one of the richest Brazilian regions and some important cities such as Campinas, Rio Claro, Limeira, Americana and Piracicaba are located in this valley. Industrial activities in the region are among the most developed of the country and represent a great economic and social potential. Some example industries are: sugarcane (sugar and alcohol), cellulose and paper, textiles, and chemical industries.

There are 2.5 million inhabitants in the region, located mainly in the urban zones. Water for industrial and domestic purposes is supplied from the rivers which form the basis of the Piracicaba River. From April to September (dry season) the outflow of the river is considerably low, and under 30 $m^3\ s^{-1}$ at the city of Piracicaba. Of this outflow, about 5-6 $m^3\ s^{-1}$ is discharged from domestic sewage and industrial effluents without any treatment. This makes the Piracicaba River, in its lower part, an "open sky" sewage, causing serious problems to the inhabitants of the valley (Anonymous, 1985).

Health authorities are pressuring the industries to treat their effluents. Regulatory measures, such as penalties imposed by the government, along with loan programs for treatment of polluted industrial effluents have been successful in the control of over 90% industrial pollution. Nevertheless, industrial pollution, if measured in terms of BOD_5, is equivalent to domestic sewage pollution, i.e., the polluted organic charge corresponds to a population of approximately five million inhabitants.

This situation is causing critical problems to some cities regarding the supply of water to the population. Therefore, some cities are looking for new sources of water for their population from non-polluted or less polluted streams. This always requires high investment without guarantee that these sources will be preserved in the future. Today, 50% of the urban water for the city of Piracicaba comes from the Corumbatai River which is a tributary of the Piracicaba River. However, the level of pollution of this river which passes through cities under development is increasing rapidly.

The situation might become critical in the not too distant future (15 years), if measures are not taken immediately. The situation in the Piracicaba River Valley represents the general situation in Brazil, where domestic sewage is discharged into streams near the cities, polluting their water resources including important water reservoirs used to supply the cities and artificial lakes for recreation.

Special programs are being proposed for cleaning the water resources, but are not yet put into practice. As a matter of fact, new sewage systems are being built which discharge into streams passing through cities, and therefore, mixing with rain water. This situation exists in many areas of the country and the cities and surrounding regions suffer from unpleasant odors, proliferation of mosquitoes, and moreover, several diseases transmitted through city sewage.

A program has been developed which permits the study of several alternatives to solve the problem. Considering social-economic conditions of the country, purification of the water resources could be put into practice immediately with a small investment, later on, if necessary and when further resources are available, some improvement to the system might be introduced.

One alternative, edaphic-phytodepuration, aims at recycling nutrients from domestic sewage in agricultural systems and the use of the biomass for the production of energy. It consists of a simple process of cultivation of floating aquatic plants and filtering soils together with rice cultivation. This process is being tested in some pilot-plant facilities for treatment of industrial effluents and domestic sewage (Salati, 1984).

Basic ideas and some examples are given in the present paper and efficiency and management problems are also discussed.

METHODS

The process uses floating aquatic plants associated with terrestrial plants of economic interest. The type of plant species to be used depends on the effluent characteristics and climatic conditions.

Filtering Soils

The purification process of the soil involves three main factors:
a) Mechanical filtering activity, which depends essentially on the structure and other hydraulic properties of the soil; b) Physico-chemistry of the soil to retain anions and cations. This activity is closely linked to the pollutant adsorptive capacity of the soil; c) Biological activity, via four mechanisms: 1) activity of soil microorganisms during the decomposition of organic matter, 2) soil microorganisms acting in biogeochemical processes, 3) soil microorganisms acting on microorganisms existing in polluted waters, and 4) activity of plants that grow in the soil and remove nutrients at the same time that the root system improves the physicochemical soil conditions.

To be utilized for purification, the soil should have the following characteristics: high permeability, high cation exchange capacity, and high microbiological activity. The first and second characteristics are generally antagonistic. When a soil has a high permeability, normally it has a low cation exchange capacity. An attempt was made to change the characteristics of the soil in order to overcome this problem, through the combination of some products. The best results were obtained using expanded vermiculite and sugarcane bagasse which resulted in a soil with good permeability and high cation exchange capacity. In this process, the soil acts as a storage system for nutrients which are later taken up by the cultivated plants.

Aquatic Plants

In the initial studies several aquatic plants were tested for depurating properties. Many species, although having desirable qualities, good root development and rapid growth, died under the adverse conditions of the highly polluted river waters and industrial effluents. The first plant to survive was the water hyacinth (Eichhornia crassipes). The water hyacinth is a macrophyte of the Pontedericeae family. It is spread over many continents, and in Brazil has caused many problems to hydroelectric dams.

Attention has been drawn to the water hyacinth due to its basic characteristics, i.e. rapid growth and ability to adapt easily to different regions. This means that it is capable of resisting an adverse environment. It was noted that this plant can survive in waters with considerable pH variation, and is resistant to several pollutants.

The water purifying activity of the water hyacinth is due to: 1) rapid growth in polluted waters; 2) the capacity to absorb heavy metals; Wolverton and McDonald (1977) observed that after 6 wk of growth in water containing heavy metals, the plant had accumulated substantial concentrations of copper, lead, cadmium, mercury and chromium; and 3) great efficiency in reducing the Biological Oxygen Demand (BOD) of polluted waters (Wolverton and McDonald, 1979). This efficiency is due to the adsorption of organic matter, fractionated and dissolved by the root "curtain" of the water hyacinth, which under optimum conditions, forms a cluster of roots. These roots act as real filters through mechanical and biological activity. Mechanically, they remove suspended particles from the water, thus decreasing turbidity. Material adsorbed by the roots creates an excellent ecosystem for the development of fungi and bacteria that decompose organic matter. Products resulting from this mineralization process are in part absorbed as nutrients by the plant. This process also reduces the bad odor of polluted waters.

PILOT FACILITIES USING EDAPHIC-PHYTODEPURATION

The filtering soils and the floating aquatic plant channels can be arranged in different configurations according to the problem to be solved. Also, either filtering soils or water hyacinth channels can be used.

Water Hyacinth + Filtering Soil

The first and simplest configuration used in our experiments was a sequence of one Eichhornia crassipes channel and a set of filtering soils (Figure 1). The effluent to be treated passes through the water hyacinth channel and the retention time varies from 18 to 36 h. In sequence, the effluent overpasses the filtering soil no. 1. This filtering soil planted with rice operates for 10 d. When permeability is reduced, the effluent from the water hyacinth channel is directed to the filtering soil no. 2; the filtering soil no. 1 being temporarily discarded. After 10 d, the filtering soil no. 3 is used. At the end of the cycle (1 month), the filtering soil no. 1 is reused after surface plowing.

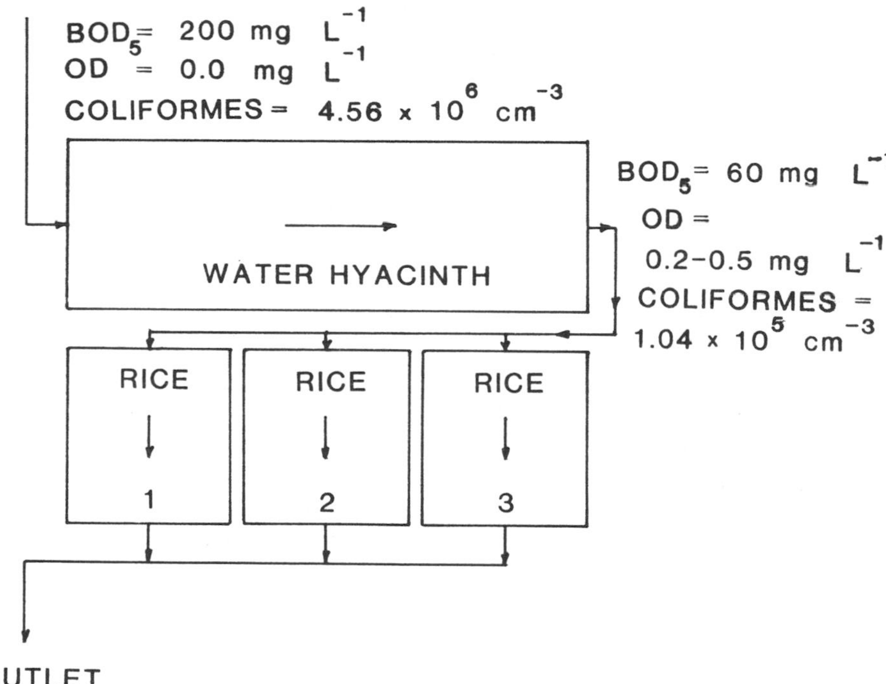

BOD$_5$ = 1-3 mg L^{-1}
OD = 2-4 mg L^{-1}
COLIFORMES = 0.36 x 10^5 cm^{-3}

FIGURE 1. System consisting of a sequence of floating aquatic plants and filtering soils cultivated with rice.

Rice is planted in the filtering soils, and depending on the phase of development of the crop, the level of water can be controlled to maintain maximum soil moisture, improve development of the rice crop and control weeds. Water level control can be accomplished by closing the drain exit or using reversed tubulation so that the height of the water in the reversed pipe corresponds to the level of desired groundwater. This is easily managed and after development of the radicular rice system, ploughing is no longer necessary.

The pilot plant used in this process had approximately 1000 m^2 of water hyacinth and three plots of 320 m^2 each with filtering soils. In this experiment the effluent came from a stream highly polluted with domestic sewage. In the dry season, BOD_5 values reached near 200 mg L^{-1}. The average efficiency obtained during several years of operation is shown in Figure 1 (Salati and Rodrigues, 1982; Saito, 1982).

In another experiment, water hyacinth + filtering soils were used to treat polluted river water (Figure 2). The effluent released from this system met drinking water standards or the

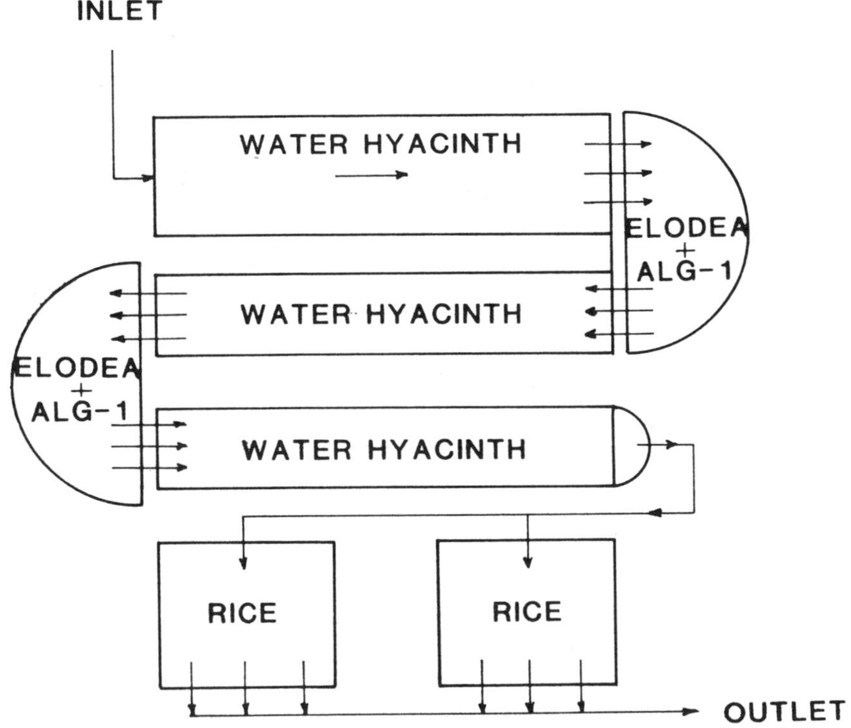

FIGURE 2. Water hyacinth channels (5000 m^2) and filtering soils cultivated with rice (5000 m^2). Retention time 1-2 d; water flow: 80 L s^{-1} ha^{-1}.

water was comparable to non-polluted rivers which are used as a source of water for conventional water treatment plants. The aquatic plants were stocked in three channels (15 m width x 100 m length) among which there was free surface water, cultivated with "elodea". The water remained in the channels for approximately 24 h which corresponds to an average flow of 80 L s^{-1} ha^{-1}.

The filtering soils consisted of two plots of approximately 1600 m^2 each. The flow through the filtering soils was equivalent to 100 L s^{-1} ha^{-1}. The excess water flowing through the water hyacinth ponds was returned to the river. The average treatment efficiency during three years was 99% removal of BOD_5 and fecal coliforms, 98% removal of TSS and turbidity.

The set-up, working mainly with water from polluted rivers with BOD_5 of 15 or less, did not cause problems with unpleasant odor or proliferation of mosquitoes. The basic idea is to use this technique to purify water of rivers or lakes which do not have high levels of pollution, but have somewhat poor water quality, as a pretreatment to pilot treatment facilities.

During the three years of operation of this pilot facility, the water coming out of the filtering soils was always quite clear in spite of the condition of the water flowing into the system. During the dry season, the water has a high level of organic pollution and coliform bacteria; however, during the rainy season, the biological quality of the water improves, while sediment, especially clay, greatly increases.

Filtering Soils + Water Hyacinth Channels

In order to purify industrial effluent with high amounts of BOD_5 and suspended solids, it was decided to set up a sequence of filtering soils (2 to 3 stages) followed by water hyacinth channels (Figure 3). The management system is similar to the previously mentioned arrangement with sequential lines of filtering soils operating in alternate periods varying from 1 wk to 15 d.

The system has been used in sugarcane industries without problems with rice cultivated on the filtering soils. A pilot facility built at a sugarcane industry located near Piracicaba has 12 plots of filtering soils with 360 m^2 each and two channels cultivated with <u>Eichhornia</u> <u>crassipes</u> in their final quarter. This system operates with flows equivalent to 80-100 L s^{-1} ha^{-1} and the retention time is from 4-10 d. The efficiency of the system during the first tests was 50 to 60% BOD_5 reduction for an initial charge of 4000 to 5000 BOD_5.

Alternate System of Filtering Soils and Aquatic Plant Channels

In cases of industrial effluents, when the BOD_5 is due to solutes, different geometries will have to be applied which will lead to a fermentation process in the various phases of the treatment. An experiment was conducted testing for treatment

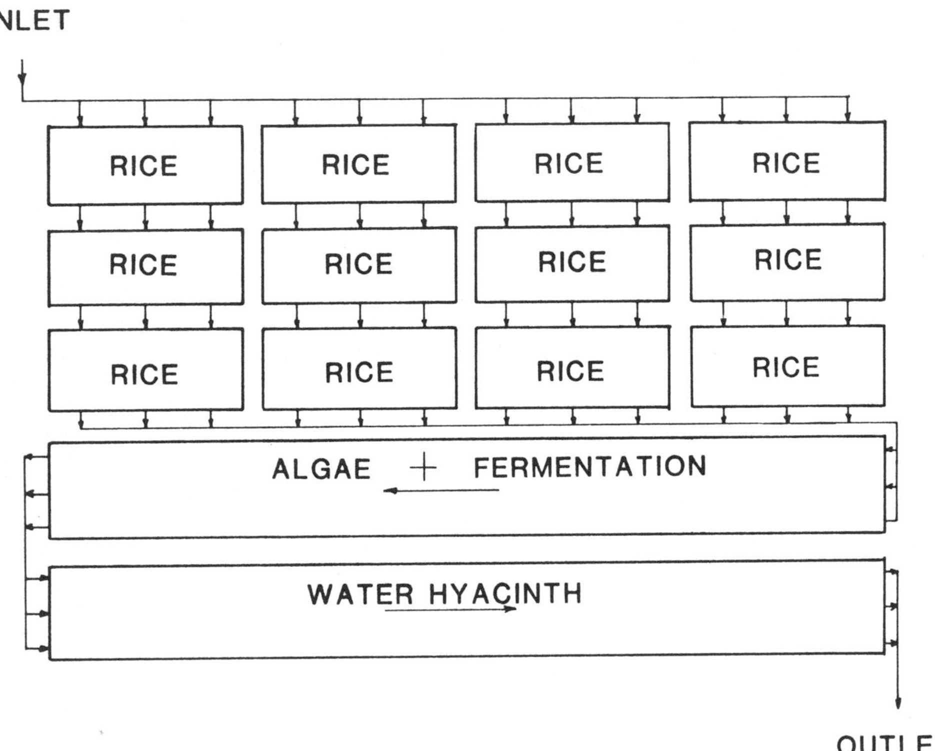

FIGURE 3. System using filtering soils planted with rice and later on channels with algae and fermentation, and finally water hyacinth channels.

efficiency (Figure 4). After passing through two homogenization lakes, the industrial effluent, in this case from the sugarcane and alcohol industry, enters in channel no. 1 (see Figure 4), and stays there for approximately three days. It then passes through filtering soil (FS) no. 1 and channel 2, filtering soil 2 and channel 3, and finally filtering soil 3. The filtering soils are planted with rice and the water level is maintained at 10-20 cm. The water flows through a channel containing half algae and half water hyacinth.

During the first month of operation the BOD_5 reduction was over 95% when the effluent had a BOD_5 varying from 2000 to 3000 mg L^{-1}. The flow through the soil was equivalent to 15-20 L s^{-1} ha^{-1} and retention time was 15-20 d.

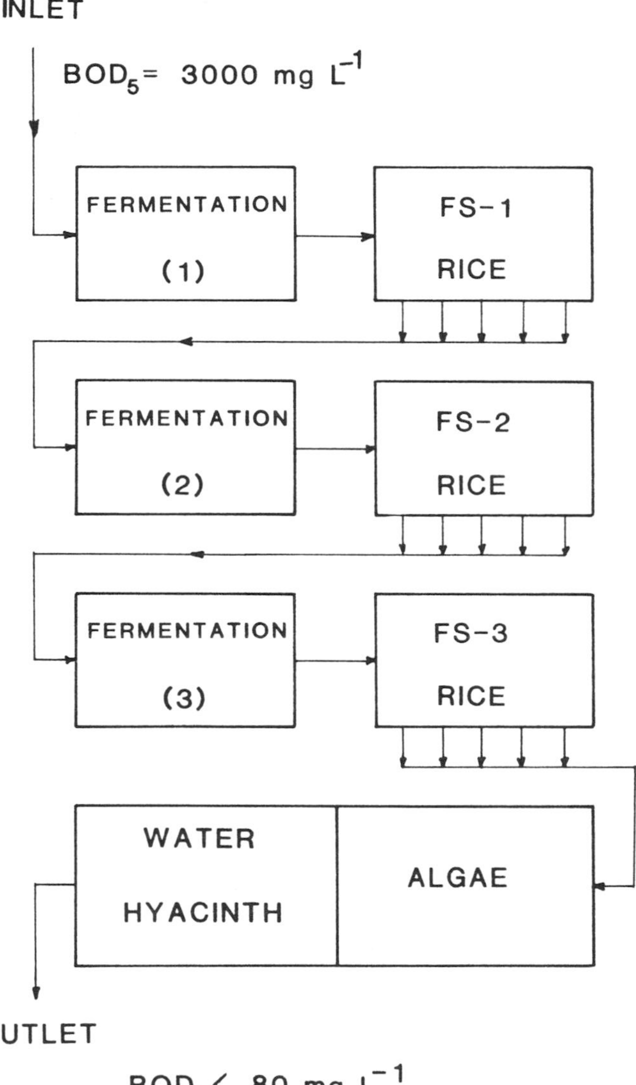

FIGURE 4. A sequence of fermentation ponds and filtering soils cultivated with rice. In the end the water passes through a channel containing algae and water hyacinth. BOD_5 removal efficiency was over 96% for a three week retention time.

CONCLUSIONS

Various experiments are being carried out in cities of Sao Paulo and other Brazilian states using aquatic plants for purification of domestic sewage. The results obtained are similar to those found in the literature. When clearing of primary sewage is tried, some problems arise; the most serious are the proliferation of mosquitoes and an unpleasant odor.

The association of aquatic plants and filtering soils and/or other traditional methods of sewage treatment, should be worthy of special attention, especially in countries with a hot climate. Nutrient recycling through cultivation of economically important plants, such as rice, on filtering soils appears to be an encouraging process; however, further research is still necessary to evaluate ecological health problems.

A practical pilot facility for domestic sewage treatment should consist of: biodigestors with ascendant flowing → filtering soils → aquatic plants. The biodigestors to be used should have a removal rate around 50 to 60% so that the process is economically feasible. Besides the tertiary treatment with nutrient recycling in agronomic productivity, the utilization of biomass for energy is also planned as a part of the systems.

Note: Patent has been requested (no. PI8503030) in Brazil for the Edaphic-Phytodepuration technique, including the different set-ups involved.

REFERENCES

Anonymous. 1985. Acao Integrada de controle da Poluicao na Bacia do Piracicaba. Relatorio Anual de 1985. CETESB-SP.

Saito, S. M. T., M. J. Valarine, and A. J. Oliveira. 1982. Exame bacteriologico em tratamentos de recuperacao de afluentes da Bacia do Piracicaba, 34.o Reuniao Anual da SBPC.

Salati, E. 1984. De-pollution of waters through intensive agriculture. In Spirit of Enterprise the 1984 Rolex Awards. Aurum Press Limited.

Salati, E., and N. S. Rodrigues. 1982. Do poluente a nutriente a descoberta do Aguape, Rev. Bras. Tecnol. Brasilia, Vol. 13(3).

Wolverton, B. C., and R. C. McDonald. 1977. Wastewater treatment utilizing water hyacinths (*Eichhornia crassipes*). Conference on treatment and disposal of industrial wastewater and residues. Houston, TX, EUA, 10 pp.

Wolverton, B. C., and R. C. McDonald. 1979. Water hyacinths of upgrading sewage lagoons to meet advanced wastewater standards. Part I. NASA Tech. Memoranda TM-X-72720.

START-UP AND OPERATION OF AN EVAPORATIVE WETLANDS FACILITY

R. B. Williams
Culp/Wesner/Culp, Consulting Engineers
P. O. Box 518
Cameron Park, California 95682

J. Borgerding and D. Richey
Incline Village General Improvement District
P. O. Drawer P
Incline Village, Nevada 89450

R. H. Kadlec
Department of Chemical Engineering
University of Michigan
Ann Arbor, Michigan 48109-2136

ABSTRACT

The Incline Village General Improvement District (IVGID) was faced with stringent discharge standards, which required nutrient removal. A facility plan was completed that recommended the construction of a nondischarging wetlands system in the Carson River Valley, north of Minden, Nevada. The selected site contained two existing warm water springs, which were to be preserved. Effluent was applied to the Wetlands Facility in September 1984. During the summer months, effluent is withdrawn by a local farmer for crop irrigation. When effluent is not discharged to the facility, the site dries up and the warm spring water is conveyed into portions of the wetlands to maintain the plant life. This paper describes the system design and the start-up and operation of the facility. Comparisons between design values and measured value of the evaporation rates are presented, and the project's operations concept is described. A discussion of operational problems is included. During the 1986 floods, this project experienced the worst storm in the 116 year period of record.

Keywords: Wetland treatment, evapotranspiration, water budget.

ISBN 0-941463-00-1

INTRODUCTION

The IVGID was faced with changing discharge standards that required higher levels of treatment (nutrient removal) for effluent discharged to the Carson River. A facility plant (CH2M Hill, 1979,1980) was completed that recommended the construction of a wetlands system in an area south of Carson City, Nevada. Construction was completed in September 1984. IVGID owns and operates wastewater collection, treatment and effluent pumping facilities around the northeast area of Lake Tahoe, Nevada. In addition, wastewater from the Crystal Bay General Improvement District (CBGID) is treated in the IVGID system. The effluent is exported out of the Lake Tahoe Basin via a 30 km pipeline, as required by state law, and discharged to the Carson River Basin. For the period April through October, the effluent is used to irrigate a ranch in Jack's Valley. For the remainder of the year, effluent is discharged to the Wetlands Facility.

DESIGN CONSIDERATIONS

An analysis of the existing and future wastewater flows was presented in the facility plan. However, the Regional Administrator, U.S. EPA, limited the capacity of the proposed wetlands system in accordance with the Tahoe Regional Planning (Bi-State) Compact (P.L. 96-551). Projected wastewater flows are estimated to be 6245 m^3 d^{-1} (Culp/Wesner/Culp, 1983). The monthly flows were projected to range from 0.158 to 0.229 m^3/mo. The wetlands project was designed on the basis that surface discharge to the Carson River would not occur. The zero surface discharge concept was achieved through the construction of new wetlands areas at the project site, and through evapotranspiration and percolation. The design estimate of required water area was 155 ha. An overall view of the site is shown in Figure 1. The Wetlands Facility has the following general features: 1) The created wetlands area contains four cells (Nos. 1 through 4) and normally operates in series. Each cell is divided into four subcells. Separate outlets to the cells allow for individual management of each cell as required. Water depths in the created wetlands range from 15 cm to about 1 m. 2) The overflow area (Cell 5) receives overflows from Cells 3 and 4 as well as directly from the effluent distribution system. The overflow area receives all effluent in excess of the capacity of the created wetlands. 3) The seasonal storage/wildlife cell (Cell 8) is used to store excess effluent during cold, wet seasons. This area contains an open body of water with three islands for wildlife use. Water is maintained around the islands. 4) The floodplain/effluent storage area (Cells 6 and 7) is used only for periods of excessive flow combined with inclement weather (precipitation). Typically, this will occur during the winter months. 5) The existing warm water wetlands have been isolated from the wetlands receiving effluent.

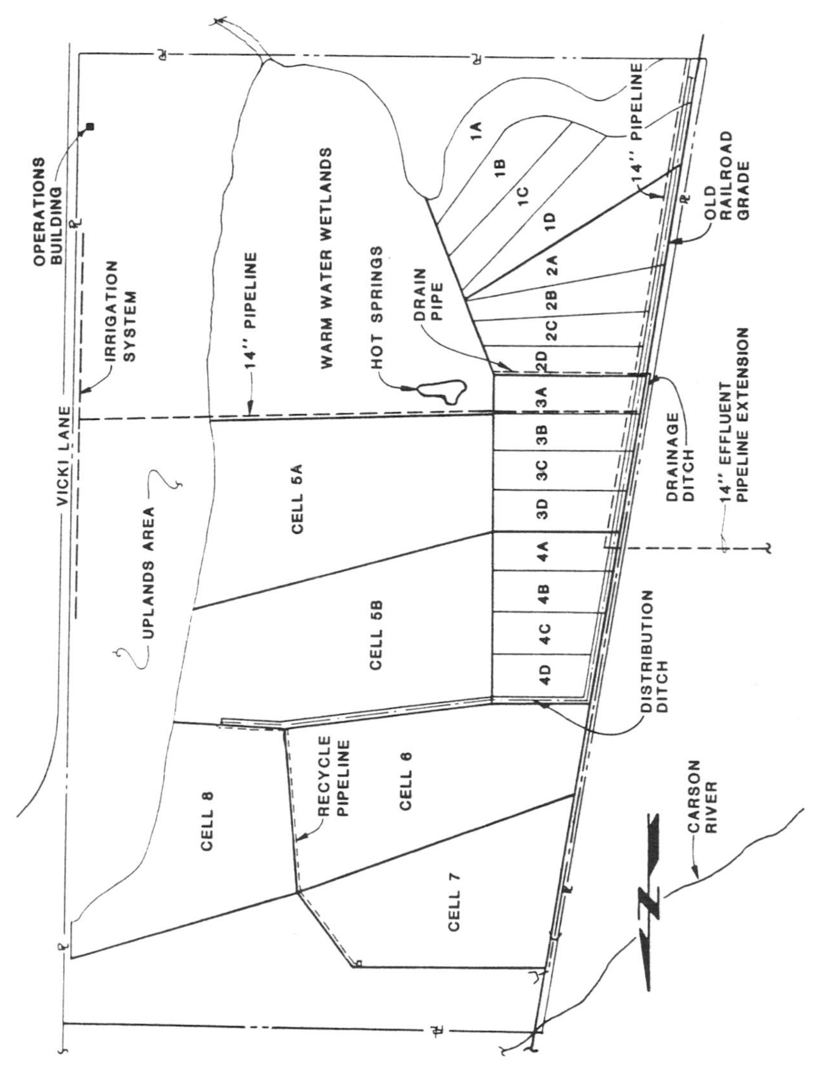

FIGURE 1. General layout.

Water entering this area is conveyed off-site in a drain pipe and released directly to the Carson River.

The area required for the evapotranspiration and percolation of applied effluent was determined by calculating water balances for five sets of conditions, including high and low infiltration, precipitation and effluent availability. Percolation had the most dramatic effect on land area requirements. The alternatives using percolation have area requirements of 71 ha or less. If percolation does not occur, area requirements range from 179 to 228 ha.

The piping system was designed to allow secondary effluent to discharge directly into the created wetlands (Cells 1 through 4), Cell 5A, and the east uplands area. Normally, flow is discharged into Cells 1 through 4 using valved, inlet pipes. Propeller flowmeters are provided for guiding day-to-day operation and totalizing. Effluent can be discharged in to Cell 5A if needs are satisfied in Cells 1 through 4. Effluent is conveyed to other cells by gravity flow and controlled with valved culverts or slide gates. The hydraulic profile across the wetlands site is steeply stepped, with the maximum fall across the proposed site about 4 m, and is adequate to direct the water to any of the lower cells (5 through 8).

The purposes of the District's Wetlands Facility are for effluent disposal and the creation of wildlife habitat. The biological components of the project are critical to both of these goals. The Wetlands Facility consists of about 42 ha of permanent wetlands, about 157 ha of seasonal wetlands, and about 81 ha of uplands. Seasonal wetlands are flooded by winter precipitation and the seasonally increased availability of effluent. These areas previously were vegetated with greasewood/saltgrass cover (Cells 5 through 8), but because of the seasonal inundation, the vegetation is changing to algae, rushes and cattail.

The uplands occur mostly on the eastern and southern edges of the site, and on high spots in cells. Vegetation is not expected to change in this area. Formerly, trees (cottonwood and willow) grew only along the banks of the Carson River, but this facility will expand the presence of this taller story of vegetation by planting. Avian usage of the site includes ducks, shorebirds, raptors, and field birds. The birds utilize the area for feeding, resting and nesting activities. Migratory waterfowl and some shorebirds travel through the Carson Valley. The Wetlands Facility has become an important feeding and resting ground for these migrants. Hundreds of waterfowl already nest in the new wetlands. Animals such as deer, coyote, jackrabbit, muskrat, and pack rats, utilize the site as well.

SYSTEM OPERATION: OBSERVATIONS AND RESULTS

Effluent was first discharged to the site on September 7, 1984. Discharges were made into Cell 1A and then allowed to fill

Cells 1 through 4 in serpentine fashion. During the process of filling Cells 1 through 4, adjustment of slideplates was required in the control structures to optimize water depths. Problems were anticipated due to the gypsum formations known to occupy the sites. The worst location was Cell 1A where the concrete inlet structure and a berm settled due to gypsum dissolution. Operation during the winter of 1984/1985 was difficult due to unusually cold temperatures. Cells 1 through 4 completely iced over and the only ice free area was at the effluent discharge points and at the control structures. Ice clogged all pipelines without flow, consequently the flowmeters jammed. After water was completely distributed to Cells 1 through 4, operators were able to maintain flows in all pipelines to prevent freezing.

The mountains west of the site affect the amount of wind and sunlight at the site and cause large variations in microclimate. Because of these effects, and due to the proximity of the hot springs, an on-site study was conducted (Culp/Wesner/Culp, 1986). Two weather stations were established at the wetlands: an evaporation station in Cell 1B, and a climatological station at the Operations Building. All the wetlands cells are equipped with staff gauges, and can be isolated from each other. During June and July, 1985, certain cells were isolated so that effluent did not enter or leave them, and further, Cell 8 was equipped with a level recorder.

The climatological factors for the area are characterized by moderate to average temperatures and low relative humidity. Solar radiation is high; the values represent 87% of the maximum, as determined from pyranograph records on cloudless days. Winds are strong in the late afternoon in summer, and are caused by thermal effects, brought on by the neighboring mountains. Precipitation was low in 1985, at only 13.3 cm, and normally is about 25.4 cm per year. Levels were monitored during June and July for 15 of the cells using staff gauges.

Two predictive equations were selected to correlate with available meterological data. These equations are needed to extrapolate to other years having different temperatures, insolation, humidity, and wind. Based on an earlier study (Guitjens, and Mahannah, 1975), the Penman (1948) equation appeared to be a reasonable predictor of pan evaporation data for an area located about 8 km south of the site. Penman's formula utilizes mass and energy balances. The Christiansen (Christiansen and Low, 1970) equation was chosen as the best purely empirical form available for wetlands at the same approximate latitude. In the present work, this equation was slightly modified to make use of pyranograph data, which includes cloud percentage. Monthly pan evaporation data were correlated with the Christiansen equation, with an average error of 9.5%. The ratio of evapotranspiration to pan evaporation was determined for the June-July period, during which both sets of data were available, resulting in an average multiplier of 0.80. These predictions of evapotranspiration are shown in Table 1. Both agree, within a few percent, on an evaporative loss of about 152.4 cm yr^{-1}, based on 1985 meteorological data. A more complete description of this study may be found in Kadlec et al. (1987).

During the design of the Wetlands Facility, infiltration allowances were included in the water balances. One amount used was 19.6 cm per month, which was based on preconstruction infiltration tests. Because effluent infiltration is required to balance applied effluent to the site, a brief study of infiltration rates was completed. Staff gauge readings indicate that some amount of infiltration is occurring, because the water level changes cannot be explained by predicted evaporation amounts. About 8 cm $month^{-1}$ appears probable.

The capacity of the Wetlands Facility may be determined from the predicted evaporation rates and the water surface areas in each of the cells. Assuming Cells 1 through 4 are full, and the remaining cells are partly full, the water surface area would be about 132 ha, and an estimate of the evaporation volume is 1.82 Mm^3. This amount is lower than the 2.3 Mm^3 projected to potentially enter the site. If a larger water surface area is maintained, higher evaporation rates will be achieved. By using the uplands area for the disposal of effluent, the complete facility has the capacity to handle the projected volume of water entering the site. This evaluation will be altered if infiltration takes place.

IVGID staff have analyzed grab samples of the water in the wetlands. The data available are summarized in Figure 2. Review of the data shows that the contaminants of concern for discharge to the Carson River are close to zero, except for the PO_4 in Cell 7, possibly due to evaporative concentration.

TABLE 1. Water losses from wetlands treatment site, 1985, cm.

Month	Cells 1A-4D	0.8 x Pan	Penman	Christiansen (modified)
January			3.5	1.1
February			8.1	3.8
March			13.3	6.4
April		15.3	17.6	17.0
May		20.5	24.0	22.0
June	25.6	24.9	24.1	23.6
July	25.9	26.3	24.4	24.7
August		24.0	20.6	22.4
September		12.3	12.4	10.8
October		9.5	8.7	6.8
November			4.5	3.0
December			1.9	1.8
TOTAL			163.7	143.4

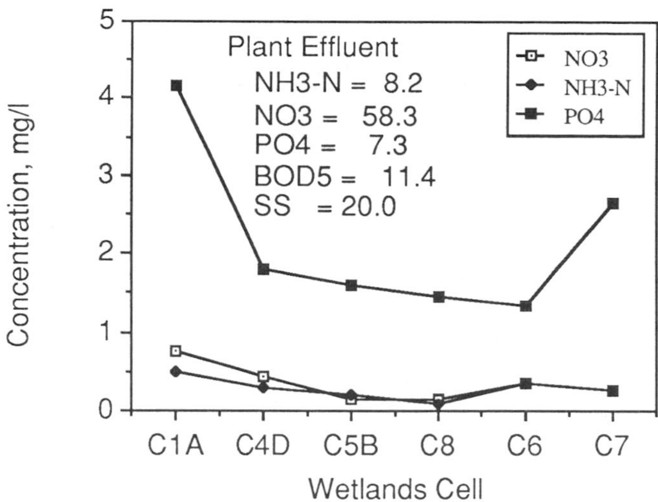

FIGURE 2. Concentrations of NH_4-N, NO_3-N and PO_4-P in the wetlands facility.

CONCLUSIONS

An evaporative wetland effluent disposal facility has been designed and built to deal with 2.3 million m^3 yr^{-1}. Evaporation and infiltration are the key processes, and have been studied. Evapotranspiration appears to be predictable, but infiltration is variable across the site. Water management has not been a problem, but some leaking dikes have required repair. Water quality is good in the wetlands, with improvements occurring in most cells. The wildlife habitat has attracted large numbers of waterfowl and shore birds. Over two years of operation, the project is meeting design and regulatory requirements.

REFERENCES

Christiansen, J. E., and J. B. Low. 1970. Water requirements of waterfowl marshlands in northern Utah. Utah Division of Fish and Game, Publication No. 69-12.

CH2M Hill. 1979 and 1980. Wastewater management facilities plan. Prepared for Incline Village General Improvement District, Incline Village, Nevada.

Culp/Wesner/Culp (Cameron Park, CA). 1983. Design memorandum - wetlands enhancement project. Prepared for Incline Village general Improvement District, Incline Village, Nevada.

Culp/Wesner/Culp (Cameron Park, CA). 1986. First annual operations report. Prepared for Incline Village General Improvement District, Incline Village, Nevada.

Guitjens, J. C., and C. N. Mahannah. 1975. Upper Carson River water study, water year 1974. University of Nevada, Reno, NV. Agricultural Experiment Station Report R107.

Kadlec, R. H., R. B. Williams, and R. D. Scheffe. 1987. Wetland evapotranspiration in temperature and arid climates. International Symposium on Wetlands, Charleston, SC.

Penman, H. L. 1948. Natural evaporation from open water, bare soil, and grass. Proc. R. Soc. Lond. 93:120-145.

NUTRIENT REMOVAL BY A FLORIDA HARDWOOD SWAMP RECEIVING SECONDARILY-TREATED EFFLUENT

B. H. Winchester and J. C. Higman
CH2M Hill, Inc.
P. O. Box 1647
Gainesville, Florida 32602

M. Sambamurthi
Jacksonville Suburban Utilities
P. O. Box 8004
Jacksonville, Florida 32239

ABSTRACT

Nutrient mass balance data were collected monthly from a mixed hardwood swamp which has continuously received secondarily-treated effluent for over 19 years. Over the two year study period, significant ($P < 0.05$) N and P removals occurred, even though the hydrologic balances indicated the swamp was receiving unmeasured groundwater inflows. Removal efficiencies of NH_4-N, (NO_3+NO_2)-N, and organic N averaged 72.8, 56.9, and 33.6%, respectively. Both NH_4-N and (NO_3+NO_2)-N removal efficiencies were related to temperature. Ammonia N removal efficiency was also related to inflow concentration. Total N removal averaged 0.39 kg ha^{-1} d^{-1} (54.7% removal) for all measurements combined. Removal efficiencies of total P were related to inflow concentration and total outflow volume. Total P removal averaged 0.15 kg ha^{-1} d^{-1} (41.4% removal).

Keywords: Nitrogen, phosphorus, wastewater, freshwater wetland, pollutant assimilation.

INTRODUCTION

Interest in using Florida's freshwater wetlands as receptors and treatment sites for municipal effluent recently has increased greatly. However, studies involving forested wetlands which have received effluent over substantial periods are relatively uncommon (Boyt et al., 1977; Tuschall et al., 1981; Nessel and Bayley, 1984; Knight, R. L., T. W. McKim, and R. Koh., 1986, unpublished results). Such research is important in assessing the long-term capability of swamp wetlands to remove nutrients, especially since

ISBN 0-941463-00-1

a saturation point can be reached after which wetland assimilative capacities for some nutrients show marked declines (Brinson, 1985; Kadlec, 1985; Richardson, 1985; Knight et al., 1986). In this study, current nutrient removal rates were examined in a Florida hardwood swamp which has continuously received effluent over the last 19 years.

METHODS

Study Area

Pottsburg Creek Swamp (PCS) is a 206 ha mixed hardwood swamp located south of Jacksonville, Florida. It is completely circumscribed by built-up roads so that significant surface inflows and outflows are restricted to specific points around the swamp perimeter. The amount of swamp inundated (i.e., the effective treatment area) typically averages around 100 ha on an annual basis, varying from 60 ha during the dry season to 135 ha during the wet season. The remainder of PCS is usually inundated only under peak flow events. The composition and structure of the swamp vegetation has been described previously (Winchester and Emenhiser, 1983).

Discharge from the Royal Lakes Wastewater Treatment Plant (WWTP) enters PCS via a partially channelized tributary east of the swamp. The release of secondary effluent into the tributary began in 1967 at a rate of approximately 190 $m^3\ d^{-1}$. In 1982, when regular water quality monitoring began, the rate of effluent discharge was 2650 $m^3\ d^{-1}$. By the end of the study period (February, 1986), effluent flows were 4550 $m^3\ d^{-1}$. Prior to 1984, treatment facilities consisted of two Sanitaire prefabricated steel contact stabilization treatment plants, with rated capacities of 1130 and 2270 $m^3\ d^{-1}$, respectively. By May 1984, a treatment unit with a capacity of 5680 $m^3\ d^{-1}$ had been added, bringing the total capacity of the WWTP up to 9080 $m^3\ d^{-1}$.

Station A represents the main surface inflow into PCS, located just downstream from the WWTP effluent discharge. The remainder of the surface inflow is contributed by six major tributaries. The major surface outflow from PCS occurs at the southern end of the swamp at Station D. The only other outflow is intermittent, located at the northern end of the swamp.

Sampling and Analytical Procedures

From January 1982 to February 1986, monthly water chemistry measurements were collected from all of the major surface inflows and outflows of PCS. Parameters measured included temperature, dissolved O_2, pH, specific conductance, Cl, (NO_3+NO_2)-N, NH_4-N, and TKN. In 1984, total P was added to the suite of parameters. Also in 1984, minor surface inflow stations were added to the program and monthly flow measurements began at all stations. Flows were measured with a portable Model 201, Marsh-McBirney current meter by the six-tenths or two-point method, depending on water depth (USDI, 1974). All laboratory analyses followed APHA (1985) or US EPA (1979). Statistical analyses utilized standard linear regressions and T Tests with $\alpha = .05$. Where percentages (i.e., removal efficiencies) were involved, data were transformed (arcsin) prior to testing.

RESULTS AND DISCUSSION

Water Balance

Measured total surface inflows to PCS varied from 7535 to 30,960 $m^3\ d^{-1}$ during the 26-month period and averaged 14,040 $m^3\ d^{-1}$. Measured surface outflows ranged from 2175 to 43,135 $m^3\ d^{-1}$, averaging 16,915 $m^3\ d^{-1}$. Consequently, measured surface inflows generally accounted for 83% of the total surface flows leaving PCS.

Based upon a long-term average local precipitation of 134 cm yr^{-1} (NOAA, 1985), rainfall directly over the 206 ha swamp could account for an additional 7580 $m^3\ d^{-1}$ of unmeasured inflow. Based upon a regional pan evaporation value of roughly 152.4 cm yr^{-1}, and a mean annual Class A pan coefficient of 76.5 (NOAA, 1982-1985), evapotranspiration could account for an estimated 6590 $m^3\ d^{-1}$ of this unmeasured outflow. The difference of 990 $m^3\ d^{-1}$ is a rough estimate of unmeasured net precipitation (inflow) to PCS which should show up in outflow measurements. The greatest disparity between surface inflows and outflows generally occurred in the period of July - September, which are also the 3 highest rainfall months in the Jacksonville area (NOAA, 1985).

However, even with corrections for precipitation and evapotranspiration, an appreciable portion of the inflow to PCS is still unaccounted for. One possible source is that lateral flow of groundwater is occurring from the upland sandy soils surrounding PCS. Another possibility is that upwelling is occurring from the underlying aquifer. This latter possibility is not altogether unlikely, for Healy (1975) found the potentiometric surface of the Floridan aquifer to be 9 to 12 m above msl (mean sea level) in the study area and classified the area as one of artesian flow. The floor of the central (i.e., deepest) portion of PCS is less than 5 m above msl.

Regardless of whether the unmeasured inflows are from rainfall, groundwater, or both, their impact upon calculated nutrient removal rates is to make them more conservative. If the unmeasured inflows have low nutrient levels, the calculated mass removal rates presented in the following section will be very close to actual removal rates. To the extent that unmeasured inflows contain appreciable amounts of N or P, the calculated removal rates will underestimate actual removal rates.

Concentration Reductions

The inflow and outflow concentrations of NH_4-N, (NO_3+NO_2)-N, organic N, total N, and total P, respectively, over the measurement period are depicted in Figures 1-5. Inflow concentrations presented are from Station A, which provides 93% of the total N and 96% of the total P mass entering PCS via surface flows. Outflow concentrations are from Station D, which accounts for approximately 86% of the total N and 91% of the total P mass outflows from PCS.

Ammonia N. Ammonia N inflow concentrations at Station A averaged 3.54 mg L^{-1} during the four year measurement period, compared with an average outflow concentration at Station D of 0.39 mg L^{-1} (Figure 1). During this period, NH_4-N concentrations were reduced by an average of 89%. The start-up of additional treatment capability at the WWTP in April 1984 was quickly followed by a dramatic decline in NH_4-N in the effluent and at Stations A and D. Prior to this time, inflow NH_4-N concentrations averaged 5.78 mg L^{-1} and outflow concentrations averaged 0.56 mg L^{-1} (a reduction of 90%). After April 1984, inflow concentrations averaged 0.68 mg L^{-1} and outflow concentrations averaged 0.17 mg L^{-1} (a reduction of 75%).

Nitrate-nitrite N. Prior to April 1984, (NO_3+NO_2)-N concentrations averaged 1.88 mg L^{-1} at Station A and 1.38 mg L^{-1} at Station D (Figure 2). After WWTP expansion and the substantial improvement in in-plant nitrification, (NO_3+NO_2)-N concentrations rose to a significantly higher average of 5.13 mg L^{-1} at Station A. Average outflow concentrations at Station D rose to 1.99 mg L^{-1}, though this was not significantly greater than Station D concentrations prior to the WWTP expansion. The swamp therefore received significantly higher (NO_3+NO_2)-N inflow concentrations (i.e. 172% higher) without a significant increase in outflow concentrations.

Organic N. During the four years of measurement, organic N concentrations at Stations A and D averaged 1.48 and 0.79 mg L^{-1}, respectively (Figure 3). This difference was significant, indicating that effective reduction of organic N concentrations was occurring within PCS. There was no apparent change in either inflow or outflow organic N concentrations with the expansion of the WWTP.

Total N. Inflow concentrations of total N at Station A averaged 8.28 mg L^{-1}, while outflow concentrations at Station D averaged 2.97 mg L^{-1} (Figure 4). On the average, total N concentrations declined 64% between Stations A and D. No seasonal patterns of concentration decline were apparent in total N or any of the N species.

Total P. Total P measurements within PCS began in February 1984. Both inflow and outflow concentrations were

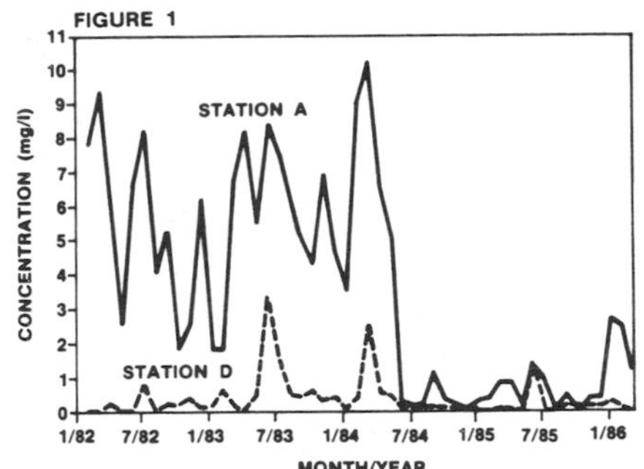

AMMONIA NITROGEN CONCENTRATIONS IN MAJOR INFLOWS (STATION A) AND OUTFLOWS (STATION D) OF POTTSBURG CREEK SWAMP, JAN. 1982 TO JAN. 1986.

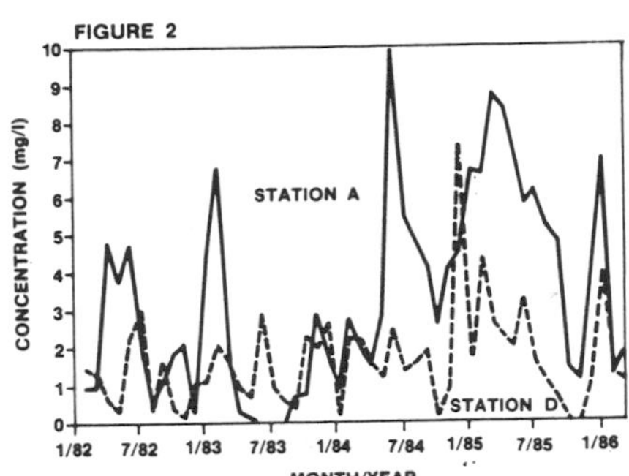

NITRATE-NITRATE NITROGEN CONCENTRATIONS IN MAJOR INFLOWS (STATION A) AND OUTFLOWS (STATION D) OF POTTSBURG CREEK SWAMP, JAN. 1982 TO JAN. 1986.

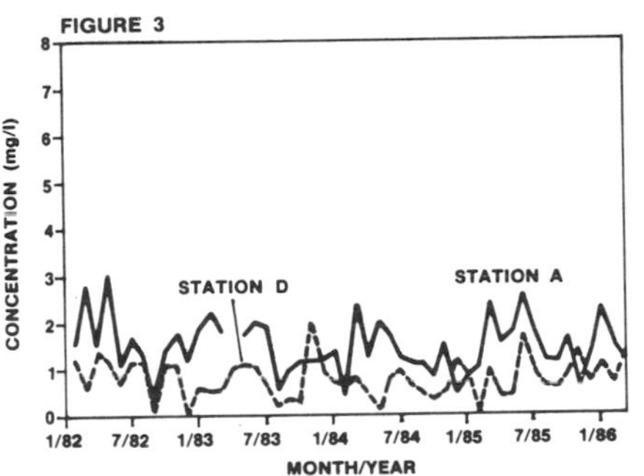

ORGANIC NITROGEN CONCENTRATIONS IN MAJOR INFLOWS (STATION A) AND OUTFLOWS (STATION D) OF POTTSBURG CREEK SWAMP, JAN., 1982 TO JAN., 1986.

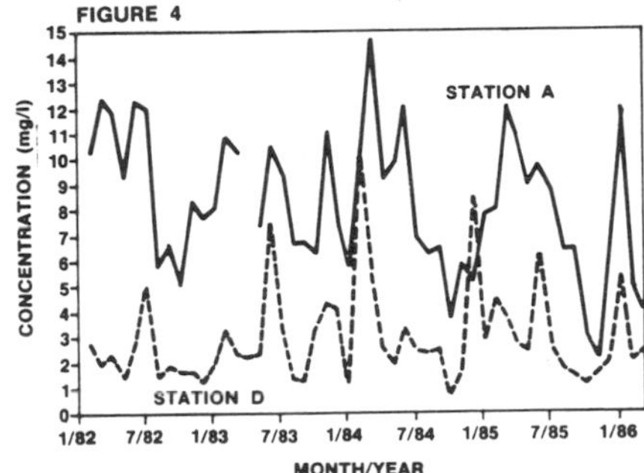

TOTAL NITROGEN CONCENTRATIONS IN MAJOR INFLOWS (STATION A) AND OUTFLOWS (STATION D) OF POTTSBURG CREEK SWAMP, JAN. 1982 TO JAN. 1986.

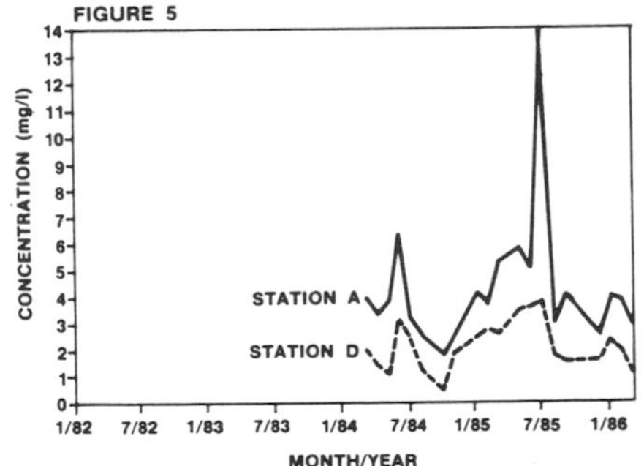

TOTAL PHOSPHOROUS CONCENTRATIONS IN MAJOR INFLOWS (STATION A) AND OUTFLOWS (STATION D) OF POTTSBURG CREEK SWAMP, JAN. 1982 TO JAN. 1986.

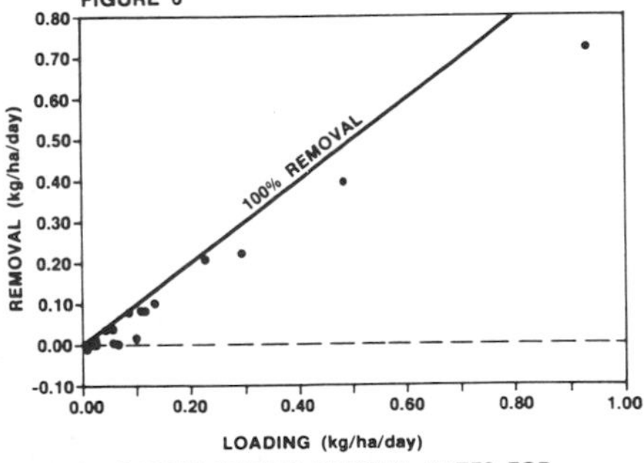

LOADING VERSUS REMOVAL RATES FOR AMMONIA NITROGEN IN POTTSBURG CREEK SWAMP, FOR THE PERIOD FEB. 1984 TO FEB. 1986.

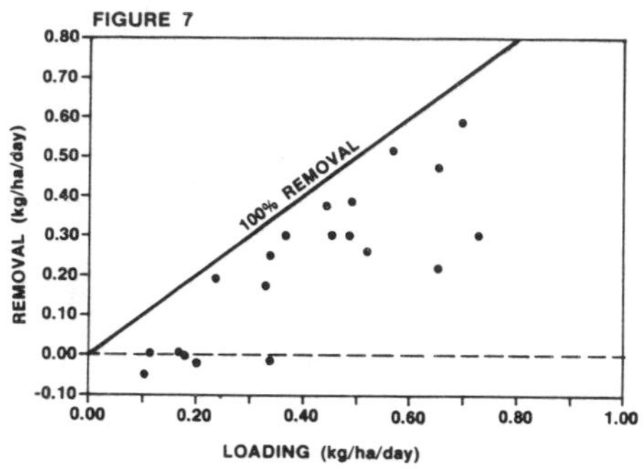

LOADING VERSUS REMOVAL RATES FOR NITRATE-NITRATE NITROGEN IN POTTSBURG CREEK SWAMP FOR THE PERIOD FEB. 1984 TO FEB. 1986.

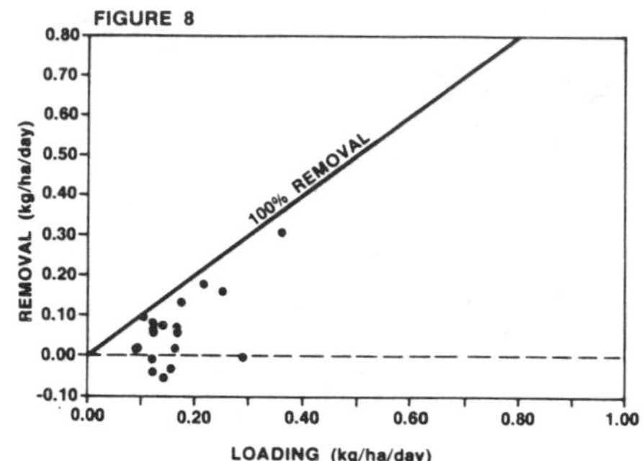

LOADING VERSUS REMOVAL RATES FOR ORGANIC NITROGEN IN POTTSBURG CREEK SWAMP FOR THE PERIOD FEB. 1984 TO FEB. 1986.

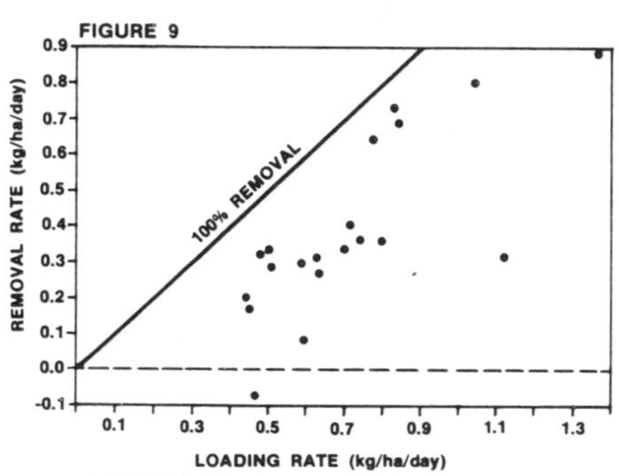

LOADING VERSUS REMOVAL RATES FOR TOTAL NITROGEN IN POTTSBURG CREEK SWAMP FOR THE PERIOD FEB. 1984 TO FEB. 1986.

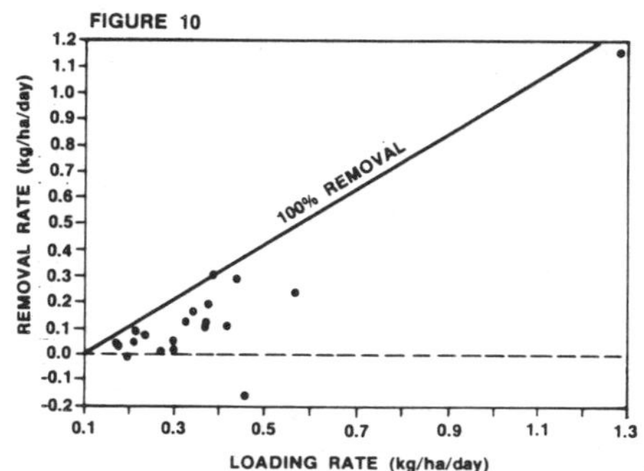

LOADING VERSUS REMOVAL RATES FOR TOTAL PHOSOHORUS IN POTTSBURG CREEK SWAMP FOR THE PERIOD FEB. 1984 TO FEB. 1986.

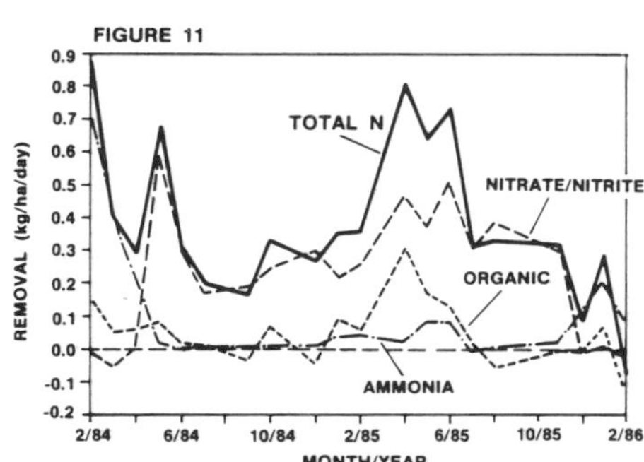

REMOVAL OF TOTAL NITROGEN AND NITROGEN SPECIES BY POTTSBURG CREEK SWAMP, FEBRUARY, 1984 TO FEBRUARY, 1986

variable with no apparent seasonal correlation (Figure 5). Inflow levels averaged 4.28 mg L^{-1} at Station A, and were significantly higher than the average outflow concentration of 2.12 mg L^{-1}.

Nutrient Removal

A summary of nutrient loading and removal rates is provided in Table 1 and Figures 6-10. Because flow measurements were not taken during the first two years of monitoring, mass balance calculations are possible only for the period from February 1984 to February 1986. Where the influence of inflow concentrations is considered, the concentrations referred to are flow-proportionalized for all inflows and are not single station concentrations as in the previous section.

Ammonia N. Total inflows and outflows of NH_4-N for PCS averaged 0.14 and 0.04 kg ha^{-1} d^{-1}, respectively, corresponding to an average removal efficiency of 73%. Removal rates were strongly correlated with loading rates (r^2 = 0.99, y = 0.80x - 0.011). Prior to WWTP expansion, loading and removal rates averaged 0.57 and 0.45 kg ha^{-1} d^{-1}, respectively (79% removal efficiency). After the expansion, average loading and removal rates dipped to 0.06 and 0.04 kg ha^{-1} d^{-1}, respectively (58% removal efficiency). This demonstrated that NH_4-N removal efficiency remained relatively high at both higher and lower loading rates (Figure 6).

A comparison of NH_4-N mass removal efficiencies with flow-proportionalized inflow concentrations showed a sharply curvilinear relationship with lower efficiencies at lower concentrations (Figure 11). Removal efficiencies averaged 81% and were never below 70% when inflow concentrations of NH_4-N were greater than 0.5 mg L^{-1}. Below 0.5 mg L^{-1} removal efficiencies had a significantly lower average of 30% and were much more variable.

TABLE 1. Nutrient inflow and outflow summaries for Pottsburg Creek Swamp February 1984-February 1986.

	Average inflow concen-tration	Average outflow concen-tration	% reduction	Average total inflow	Average total outflow	% removal
	-----mg L^{-1}-----			---kg ha^{-1} d^{-1}---		
Ammonia N	1.03	0.29	71.8	0.14	0.04	72.8
Nitrate-nitrite N	3.48	1.43	58.9	0.40	0.17	56.9
Organic N	1.29	0.71	45.0	0.16	0.10	33.6
Total N	5.81	2.43	58.2	0.71	0.32	54.7
Total P	3.03	1.70	43.9	0.37	0.22	41.4

Ammonia N removal efficiencies were generally higher when water temperatures in PCS were lower. When temperatures were less than 20°C, removals averaged 74% of total inflow. When water temperatures rose above 20°C, removals averaged 38% of total inflow. The difference, however, was not significant. No relationship was apparent between NH_4-N removal efficiencies and inflow or outflow volumes.

Nitrate-Nitrite N. Total inflows and outflows of (NO_3+NO_2)-N averaged 0.40 and 0.17 kg ha^{-1} d^{-1}, respectively, corresponding to an average removal efficiency of 57% (Figure 7). The correlation between loading and removal rates was not as strong as for NH_4-N, with r^2 equalling only 0.68 (y = 0.80x - 0.093). Prior to the WWTP expansion, inflow and outflow rates averaged 0.15 and 0.16 kg ha^{-1} d^{-1}, respectively, suggesting a small net export of (NO_3-NO_2)-N from PCS. However, if the additional input of (NO_3+NO_2)-N from bacterial nitrification of NH_4-N within the swamp is considered, actual removals of (NO_3+NO_2)-N would be substantially higher, depending on the relative proportions of NH_4-N being lost via plant uptake and transformed via nitrification. Volatilization is not considered to be a significant pathway of NH_4-N loss in PCS because water column pH's are generally below 7.5 (Reddy and Patrick, 1984). After the WWTP expansion, inflow and outflow rates of (NO_3+NO_2)-N averaged 0.44 and 0.27 kg ha^{-1} d^{-1}, a removal of 61%.

Percent removals of (NO_3+NO_2)-N were significantly greater when swamp water temperatures were higher (r^2 = 0.42, y = 6.592x - 107.333, where y = removal efficiency and x = water temperature). When water temperatures were below 20°C, an average of 13.5% of the (NO_3+NO_2)-N mass entering PCS was removed. Above 20°C, (NO_3+NO_2)-N removal averaged 63%. There was no apparent correlation between removal efficiencies of (NO_3+NO_2)-N and inflow or outflow volumes.

Organic N. Removal rates of organic N correlated poorly with loading rates (r^2 = 0.32, y = 0.80x - 0.077). Total inflow and outflows of organic N to PCS averaged 0.16 and 0.10 kg ha^{-1} d^{-1}, respectively, corresponding to a removal of 34% (Figure 8). However, the difference of inflow and outflow loads was significant, indicating that net removal of organic N did occur over the two year period. No relationship was apparent between percent removal of organic N and temperature, season, or inflow concentrations.

There was a relatively high positive correlation (r^2 - 0.82) between the total export of organic N (kg d^{-1}) and outflow volumes (m^3 d^{-1}). This is not unexpected considering the large volume of loosely consolidated organic soils in the deepest portion of the swamp and that entrainment of particulate organic matter would increase as discharge rates from the swamp increased.

Total N. Removals of total N within PCS correlated positively with total N loadings (r^2 = 0.57, y = 0.76x - 0.154).

Total N removals averaged 0.39 kg ha^{-1} d^{-1}, or 55% of the inflow loading of 0.71 kg ha^{-1} d^{-1} (Figure 9). Of the amount removed, 59% was from reduced outflows of (NO_3+NO_2)-N, 26% from reduced outflows of NH_4-N, and the remaining 15% from reduced outflows of organic N (Figure 11). The 55% removal efficiency was less than the 87% removal efficiency encountered by Knight et al. (1986) at a much higher loading rate of 1.99 kg ha^{-1} d^{-1}. It was also lower than the 69% removal efficiency measured by Tuschall et al. (1981) at a lower loading rate of 0.38 kg ha^{-1} d^{-1}.

Total P. Unlike other forested wetlands which have shown substantial declines in P removal capabilities after a few years (Kadlec, 1983; Brinson, 1985; Knight et al., 1986), PCS demonstrated P retention even after 19 years of receiving effluent. Inflows and outflows of total P averaged 0.37 and 0.22 kg ha^{-1} d^{-}, respectively, corresponding to an average removal of 41%. The inflows and outflows were significantly different, indicating that PCS was, in fact, effectively removing P.

The data also indicated generally higher P removal rates with higher loading rates, though the correlation was relatively weak ($r^2 = 0.34$, $y = 0.006x - 0.002$). Removal efficiencies of total P averaged 57.5% when inflow concentrations were above 3 mg L^{-1}, versus an average removal efficiency of 21% when inflow concentrations were below 3 mg L^{-1}. Removal efficiency of total P also declined as total outflow volume increased.

Accumulation of P in sediments is the major removal mechanism in wetlands and that microbial and vegetation uptake cannot be considered as major, long-term P sinks (Patrick and Khalid, 1974; Richardson, 1985; Richardson and Nichols, 1985; Brinson, 1985). Sediments in PCS apparently have not yet become saturated and appreciable P retention is still occurring.

The continuing ability of PCS to remove P may be related to the predominately mineral sediments which occur in all but the deepest portions of the swamp. Richardson (1985) showed much higher P adsorption potentials in mineral versus organic soils. Water in PCS is also consistently aerobic ($\geq$ 5.0 mg L^{-1} dissolved O_2) and moderate in pH ($\geq$ 6.5), which may also enhance the swamps' ability to retain P (Richardson and Nichols, 1985).

REFERENCES

American Public Health Association. 1985. Standard Methods for the Examination of Water and Wastewater, 17th ed. APHA, Washington, DC.

Brinson, M. M. 1985. Management potential for nutrient removal in forested wetlands. p. 405-416. In P. J. Godfrey et al. (ed.) Ecological Considerations in Wetlands Treatment of Municipal Wastewaters. Van Nostrand Reinhold Co., New York.

Boyt, F. L., S. E. Bayley, and J. Zoltek, Jr. 1977. Removal of nutrients from treated municipal wastewater by wetland vegetation. J. Water Pollut. Control Fed. 49:789-799.

Healy, H. G. 1975. Potentiometric surface and areas of artesian flow of the Floridan aquifer in Florida, May 1974. U.S. Geological Survey, Map Series No. 73.

Kadlec, R. H. 1985. Aging phenomena in wastewater wetlands. p. 338-347. In P. J. Godfrey et al. (ed.) Ecological Considerations in Wetlands Treatment of Municipal Wastewaters. Van Nostrand Reinhold Co., New York.

Kadlec, R. H. 1983. The Bellair wetland: Wastewater alteration and recovery. Wetlands 3:44-63.

National Oceanic and Atmospheric Administration. 1982-1985. Climatological Data Annual Summary, Florida, Vol. 86-89(13).

Nessel, J. K., and S. E. Bayley. 1984. Distribution and dynamics of organic matter and phosphorus in a sewage-enriched cypress swamp. p. 262-278. In K. C. Ewel and H. T. Odum (ed.) Cypress Swamps. University of Florida Press, Gainesville, Florida.

Patrick, W. H., Jr., and R. A. Khalid. 1974. Phosphate release and sorption by soils and sediments: Effects of aerobic and anaerobic conditions. Science 186:53-55.

Reddy, K. R., and W. H. Patrick, Jr. 1984. Nitrogen transformations and loss in flooded soils and sediments. CRC Crit. Rev. Environ. Cont. 13(4):273-309.

Richardson, C. J. 1985. Mechanisms controlling phosphorus retention capacity in freshwater wetlands. Science 228:1424-1427.

Richardson, C. J., and D. S. Nichols. 1985. Ecological analysis of wastewater management criteria in wetland ecosystems. p. 351-391. In P. J. Godfrey et al. (ed.) Ecological Considerations in Wetlands Treatment of Municipal Wastewaters. Van Nostrand Reinhold Co., New York.

Tuschall, J. R., P. L. Brezonik, and K. C. Ewel. 1981. Tertiary treatment of wastewater using flow-through wetland systems. Proceedings of 1981 Annual Conference of the American Society of Civil Engineers, Environmental Division.

U.S. Department of the Interior. 1974. Water Measurement Manual.

U.S. Environmental Protection Agency. 1979. Methods for Chemical Analysis of Water and Wastes. EPA-600/4-79-020.

Winchester, B. H., and T. C. Emenhiser. 1983. Dry season wastewater assimilation by a north Florida hardwood swamp. Wetlands 3:90-107.

NUTRIENT REMOVAL USING SHALLOW LAGOON-SOLID MATRIX MACROPHYTE SYSTEMS

H. J. Bavor, D. J. Roser, and S. McKersie
Water Research Laboratory
Hawkesbury Agricultural College
Richmond, N.S.W. AUSTRALIA

ABSTRACT

The design, operation, and performance of seven large-scale, shallow lagoon-macrophyte systems which receive secondary treated sewage effluent, is reported upon. The systems consist of lined, gravel filled trenches which have been designed to have dense macrophyte, unplanted gravel, and open water sections. Macrophytes used include Typha, Schoenoplectus, and Myriophyllum species. Effective removal of BOD and N has been achieved in the systems. The potential for P transformation or immobilization is discussed. Removal of indicator bacteria by the systems, with retention times of 3 to 7 d, has been equivalent to or greater than removal obtained in conventional oxidation ponds operating at much longer retention times.

Keywords: Wastewater treatment, macrophyte, artificial wetlands, nutrient transformation, nitrogen and phosphorus removal.

INTRODUCTION

The use of natural and artificial wetland systems for waste-water treatment has been described by Seidel (1976), Mitchell (1978), Bavor et al. (1981), Finlayson and Chick (1983), and Howard-Williams (1985). Wastewater in these studies was treated by flow through a heterogeneous system dominated by large aquatic plants rooted in a porous gravel substratum or an unconsolidated, peaty sediment. Significant nutrient removal could be achieved in these macrophyte systems; however, they emphasized that wetland systems could be more effectively utilized if internal removal mechanisms were better understood and could be optimized by appropriate design and management techniques.

Based on experience gained by the Hawkesbury Agricultural College (HAC), Water Research Laboratory and CSIRO-Centre for Irrigation Research (Griffith) in studying nutrient removal in

ISBN 0-941463-00-1

natural and artificial wetlands, a program was devised, in conjunction with the Sydney Water Board, to study these mechanisms in detail and test the overall concept in a full-scale system. This program will characterize a number of specifically constructed macrophyte systems in order to derive empirical design and operating criteria to achieve optimum removal of nutrients (C, N, P) and other sewage constituents under local loading and climatic conditions.

DESCRIPTION OF STUDY

A large-scale pilot study to investigate the use of aquatic macrophytes in removing nutrients from sewage was established jointly at HAC and CSIRO and the Metropolitan Water, Sewerage anu Drainage Board, Sydney.

Five macrophyte and two control trenches, each 100 m long, 4 m wide and 0.5 m deep, were constructed on HAC land adjacent to the Board's Richmond Water Pollution Control Plant (WPCP). The following macrophyte systems were evaluated: 1) an open lagoon planted with *Myriophyllum aquaticum* (parrot feather); 2) a gravel-filled trench planted with *Schoenoplectus validus* (bulrush); 3) a gravel filled trench planted with *Typha orientalis* (cumbungi), 4) two artificial wetland systems consisting of alternating sections of open water and gravel planted with *Typha orientalis*; and 5) two control trenches without plants, one of which contained gravel while the second contained open water.

All trenches have essentially vertical sides and horizontal inverts. Each trench is provided with inlet and outlet metering and sampling facilities. The trenches are lined with an impermeable membrane (U.V. resistant, double-coated PVC) to allow water and nutrient mass balances to be determined. A typical trench cross-sectional elevation is shown in Figure 1.

Secondary effluent (clarified effluent from a biological trickling filter) was pumped from Richmond WPCP to the macrophyte trenches. Characteristics of the effluent are shown in Table 1. Trench effluent was collected in a sump and pumped back to the tertiary maturation pond at WPCP. Physico-chemical and microbial parameters were measured for trench inlet and outlet flow, at the same time that samples were taken for nutrient analyses.

For the initial two months of operation, the trench inlet and outlet flow were manually adjusted daily. Wide fluctuations in flow were experienced and an improved ball-cock metering device was installed at the trench inlets, leading to much improved, less fluctuating flow. Both inlet and outlet water meters, cumulative volume type (Davies-Kent, NSW), on each trench, were read daily. Further flow improvement was achieved through use of an electronic level controller (pump actuator) at the outlet end of the systems.

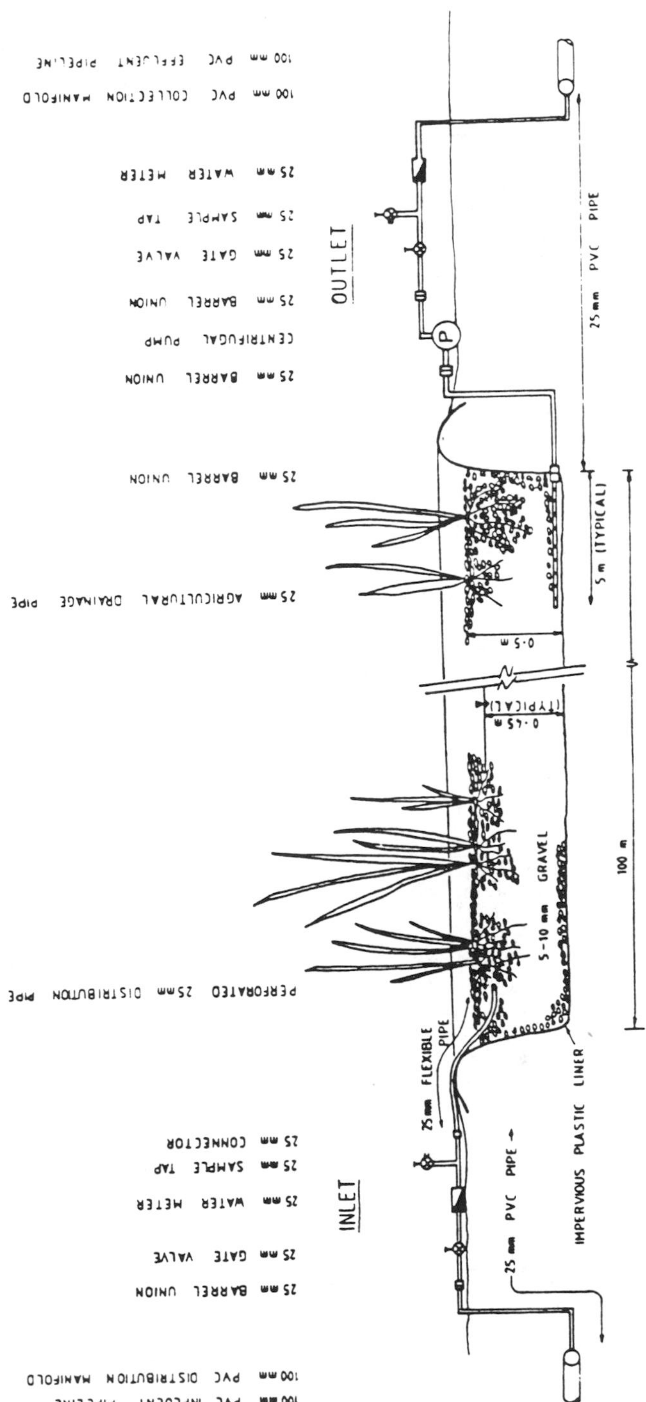

FIGURE 1. Typical trench cross section.

TABLE 1. Characteristics of inlet water for the shallow lagoon-macrophyte study system.

Characteristic	Units	Normal range
pH	units	7.2-7.8
Temperature	°C	16.8-27
BOD_5	mg L^{-1}	20-70
SS	"	30-130
NH_4-N	"	30-60
NO_2+NO_3-N	"	0.01-1.5
Total-P	"	7-14
Dissolved O_2	"	2.0-<1.0

RESULTS AND DISCUSSION

Estimated nutrient loading rates for the trench systems are presented in Table 2 and indicate the relatively high hydraulic and nutrient loadings imposed on the systems. The loads are more than double the loads normally placed on conventional lagoon systems.

Nitrogen removal rates during the macrophyte establishment period were in the range of 20 to 30% of input loads. These results were obtained in systems with poor plant cover and distinct hydraulic gradients, both situations which are not conducive to optimum system performance. Removal of the effluent components BOD, N, suspended solids and indicator bacteria has been striking. The latest results indicate that the trench systems are developing an increased capacity to consistently remove nutrients (Figures 2 and 3).

The different systems may be characterized by performance, into the following groups: open water systems (1 and 4), full

TABLE 2. Influent and effluent loading levels for trench 5 and 7 systems.

Parameter	Units	Influent	Trench 5 outlet	Trench 7 outlet
Suspended solids	mg L^{-1}	57	4.5 ± 3.3	5.3 ± 3.1
BOD_5	"	33	4.6 ± 2.7	3.8 ± 2.3
TKN	"	47	11.0 ± 2.0	7.6 ± 1.3
NH_4-N	"	35	10.6 ± 2.1	7.1 ± 1.1
Total P	"	10	6.8 ± 1.0	8.2 ± 0.6
TOC	"	43	9.8 ± 4.6	9.3 ± 6.2
Fecal Colif.	CFU 100 mL^{-1}	1.2 X 10E6	3.0 X 10E3	2.5 ± 10E1
Detention time	EP ha^{-1} d^{-1}	--	8.9 ± 1.7	7.5 ± 1.8
Loading rate	EP ha^{-1} d^{-1}	--	1100 ± 200	1700 ± 500

EP calculated at 240 L EP^{-1}. Influent--mean 1985 values; Outlet--mean Dec. 1985 to Feb. 1986, ± one std. dev.

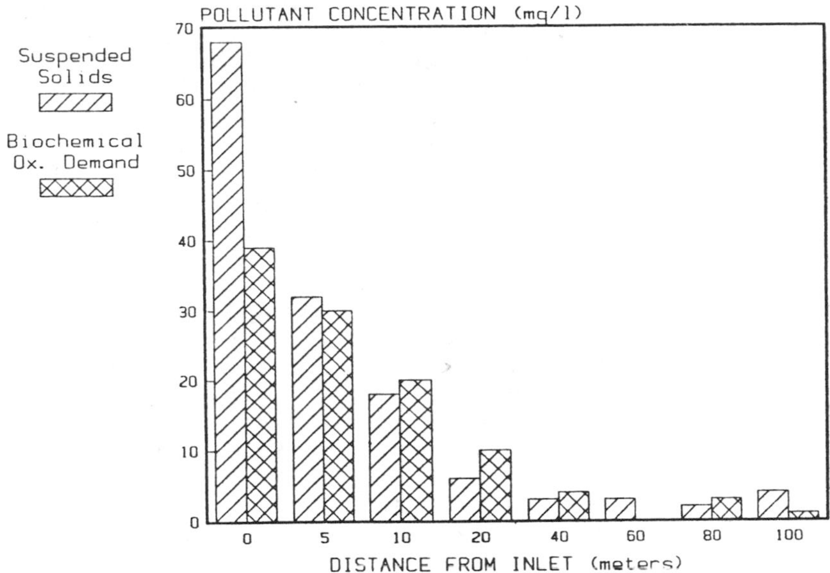

FIGURE 2. Removal of BOD_5 and suspended solids by a Typha/ Gravel system.

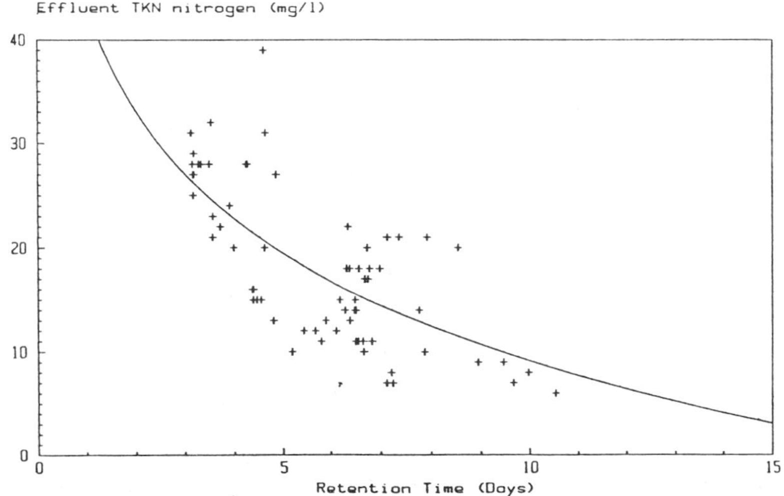

FIGURE 3. Regression curve of TKN (mg L^{-1}) versus retention time in the effluent of an alternating Typha/open water/gravel system. The curve is a logarithmic fit and has a correlation coefficient of 0.70.

length gravel systems (2, 3 and 5), alternating gravel/open water systems (artificial wetlands 6 and 7).

The open water trenches (the open control-1 and the floating macrophyte-4 trenches) showed the poorest performance. BOD, suspended solids, N and P removal were low. Generally, it may be considered that dissolved nutrients were converted to particulate solids in the form of algal biomass, with little net loss or immobilization of nutrient. Trenches 2, 3 and 5 were filled with gravel, with 3 and 5 planted with Typha and Schoenoplectus, respectively. The gravel control 2, has performed, in some instances, almost as well as the planted trenches. It was not unanticipated that the gravel control, actually an extended gravel-bed filter, would remove particulate solids quite well. It is anticipated that the improvement in the planted trenches will continue as the systems mature. The simulated wetland systems, trenches 6 and 7, have shown the most promising performance with BOD, N and suspended solids removal approaching 90% in the latest samplings. Intensive sampling has confirmed that the performance is consistent and related to the alternating zones within the systems. Both CSIRO (small-scale) bucket experiments and the Richmond trench results indicate that if O_2 can be moved into the trench system, then nitrification and denitrification will readily follow. Such a sequence appears to occur in trenches 6 and 7 and may be possible to induce in the fully planted trenches by altering flow patterns with baffle or recycle techniques. Carbon limitation of denitrification has not been demonstrated at the C:N input ratios used in these systems.

The removal of P in the trench systems is of particular interest. The results indicate that approximately 60 to 80% removal was occurring at times, but recorded values are typically less than 40%. It is well documented that P removal is inconsistent in other biological systems (including both macrophyte based and conventional schemes), and careful planning in the design and operation of such systems is required to achieve consistent removal. The P sink in these systems and in the Richmond macrophyte trenches, involves the immobilization and removal of P into sludge/sediments through chemical precipitation and bacterial action, in addition to adsorption onto the gravel (or other solid matrix) substratum, plant uptake and related physico-chemical pathways. The characterization of these compartments and operation of the system to allow physical entrapment of one or more of these compartments is required to achieve reliable P removal. This characterization will be a major part of continuing studies. The problem of P removal represents a significant challenge in the development of wetland treatment systems.

The results have shown that the macrophyte treatment systems achieve significantly greater reductions in bacterial populations than oxidation pond systems of similar retention time (and many chlorinated effluents). The artificial wetland trenches, 6 and 7- alternating zones of planted solid matrix, open water and unplanted solid matrix, exhibited the highest reduction, 99%, in which indicator bacterial counts were consistently reduced by 3 to 4 orders of magnitude. These results demonstrate the promise shown by macrophyte systems for the treatment of secondary effluents and the removal of potential pathogens (Figures 4 and 5).

CONCLUSIONS

The joint macrophyte project promises to provide technically simple solutions for problems of effluent treatment and water management. The studies performed at both Griffith and Richmond support the use of macrophyte systems and indicate that transformation processes occurring in natural wetlands and simulated in bench-scale experiments can be reproduced in large-scale artificial wetland systems.

In the Richmond systems, BOD, nutrients (particularly C and N) and suspended solids have been consistently removed with high efficiency even when the systems have operated at a retention time of only three days. Loadings have been applied at levels as high as twice that applied in conventional oxidation pond systems. Increasing retention time to six days has resulted in greatly enhanced ability of the systems to remove N and coliform bacteria.

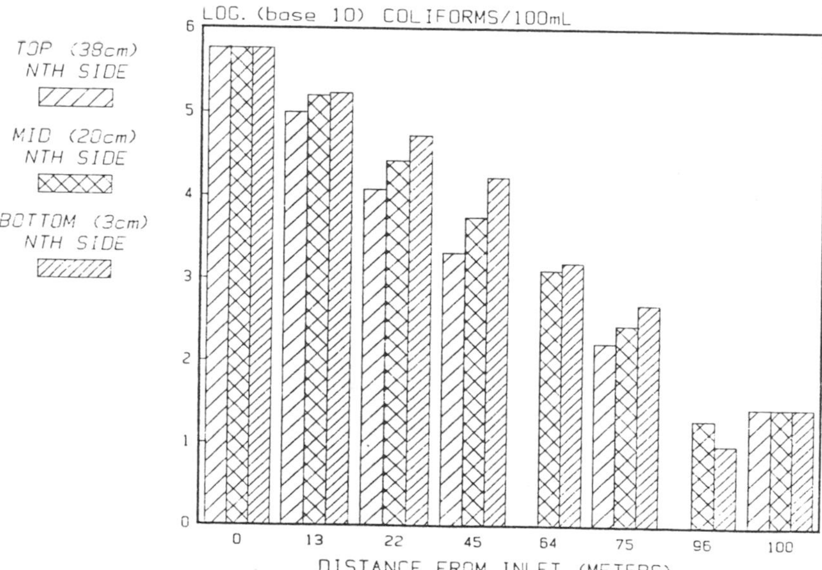

FIGURE 4. Fecal coliform populations in water extracted from different depths and increasing distance from the inlet of an alternating *Typha*/water/gravel system.

Removal of P has also occurred, giving effluent with less than 2 mg L^{-1} total P, but this performance has been inconsistent and related to the type of gravel used.

Seasonal variation was most evident in the removal of N. However, it was evident that there was significant removal, occurring even in late autumn, unlike the situation in the simulated oxidation pond. Little effect was observed in trench performance due to increased flow from heavy rains, slug inputs of toxic hypochlorite, or diurnal fluctuation in nutrient loadings. This would indicate that the systems have a significant buffering capacity to cope with fluctuating loads or toxic inputs.

Emergent plant biomass required harvesting, or cut-back, as a management technique. Because the cut-back is proposed as an infrequent, once per season, management technique and not as a regular nutrient removal/harvest system (as in floating macrophyte schemes) the resultant biomass does not represent as significant a utilization or disposal problem as that derived from a continuously harvested system.

Bacterial quality of effluent, after passage through the systems, was similar to that obtained in conventional chlorinated systems. These results demonstrate the promise shown by macrophyte systems for the treatment of secondary effluents and the removal of potential pathogens.

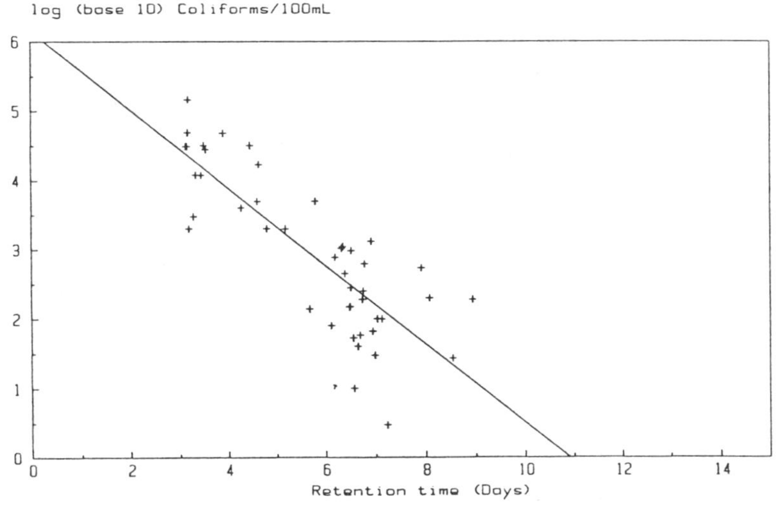

FIGURE 5. Regression curve of fecal coliform numbers versus retention time in an alternating _Typha_/open water/gravel system. The curve is a linear fit with a correlation coefficient of 0.82.

ACKNOWLEDGMENTS

The work reported upon in this paper is part of the Joint Study on Nutrient Removal Using Shallow Lagoon - Macrophyte Systems, a collaborative project involving the CSIRO Centre for Irrigation and Freshwater Research, Griffith, N.S.W., the Sydney Water Board, Sydney, N.S.W. and the Water Research Laboratory at Hawkesbury Agricultural College, Richmond, N.S.W. Project leaders for the above groups are Dr. David Mitchell, Mr. John Browne, and Dr. H. J. Bavor, respectively. Funding by the Sydney Water Board is gratefully acknowledged.

REFERENCES

Bavor, H. J. (ed.). 1986. Joint study on nutrient removal using shallow lagoon - macrophyte systems. Interim Rpt. Metropolitan Water, Sewerage and Drainage Boards, Sydney, Australia. 84 pp.

Bavor, H. J., N. F. Millis, and A. J. Hay. 1981. Assimilative capacity of wetlands for sewage effluent. Minist. for Conserv., Vict. Environ. Studies Prog. ESP 363.

Finlayson, C. M., and A. J. Chick. 1983. Testing the potential of aquatic plants to treat abattoir effluents. Wat. Res. 17:415-422.

Howard-Williams, C. 1985. Cycling and retention of nitrogen and phosphorus in wetlands: A theoretical and applied perspective. Freshwater Biol. 15:391-431.

Mitchell, D. S. 1978. The potential for wastewater treatment by aquatic plants in Australia. Water Aust. 5:15-17.

Seidel, K. 1976. Macrophytes and water purification. In J. Tourbier and R. W. Pierson (ed.) Biological Control of Water Pollution. Univ. Penn. Press, USA. 109 pp.

SURVIVAL OF BACTERIA AND VIRUSES IN MUNICIPAL WASTEWATERS APPLIED TO ARTIFICIAL WETLANDS

R. M. Gersberg
Graduate School of Public Health
San Diego State University
San Diego, California 92182

R. Brenner, S. R. Lyon and B. V. Elkins
San Diego Region Water Reclamation Agency
Santee, California 92071

ABSTRACT

Removal of chemical pollutants by wetland treatment is well documented, but there is relatively little information available on the removal of bacterial and viral pollution indicators in wetland ecosystems. In the present study, the survival of indigenous total coliform bacteria and seeded MS-2 bacteriophage was examined in artificial wetlands which received primary municipal wastewaters. At the hydraulic application rate of 5 cm d^{-1}, the mean influent total coliform level of 6.75×10^7 MPN 100 mL^{-1} was reduced 99.1% in the effluent of a vegetated (bulrush) bed, as compared to only 95.7% in the effluent of an unvegetated bed. This significant difference between the vegetated and unvegetated beds shows the important role that higher aquatic plants have in the removal of a bacterial indicator of pollution by wetlands. The concentration of seeded MS-2 bacteriophage, used as a viral indicator, was also greatly reduced by wetland treatment, with the mean influent level of MS-2 virus of 5.35×10^5 PFU mL^{-1} reduced by 98.3% in the effluent of a vegetated wetland bed. These results demonstrate the artificial wetlands may serve as low-cost alternatives to conventional treatment systems for reducing the load of disease-causing bacteria and viruses to the aquatic environment.

Keywords: Wastewater treatment, artificial wetlands, pathogen removal, aquatic plants.

INTRODUCTION

The use of wetlands for wastewater treatment offers an attractive approach for small to medium-sized communities to meet

Aquatic Plants for Water Treatment
and Resource Recovery
K.R. Reddy and W.H. Smith (Eds.)

ISBN 0-941463-00-1

their treatment needs in a cost-effective and environmentally sound manner. The removal of chemical contaminants by wetland treatment is well documented for both natural (Nichols, 1983) and artificial systems (Gersberg et al., 1984a,b); however, there is much less information available on the survival of bacterial and viral indicators of pollution in these wetland ecosystems.

Pathogens are removed in wetlands by both physical-chemical processes (e.g. filtration, adsorption) and biological inactivation and predation. Although there is some evidence that higher aquatic plants may serve an important function in removing bacterial pathogens (Seidel, 1976), there is no quantitative information available on the specific role of higher aquatic plants in overall pathogen removal by wetland ecosystems.

A primary objective of the present study was to determine the removal rates of total coliform bacteria of municipal wastewater origin in both vegetated and unvegetated artificial wetland beds, and to compare these values to those obtained for seeded F-specific bacteriophages, these used as indicators of enteric virus behavior in the environment.

MATERIALS AND METHODS

Total coliform bacteria were enumerated by the multiple-tube fermentation technique (presumptive and confirmed tests) as per "Standard Methods" (1985).

The host-strain used for our bacteriophage (MS-2) assay was *Salmonella typhimurium* strain WG 49 [phage type 3 Nal^r (F'42*lac*::Tn5)]. Bacteriophages were enumerated by the double agar layer method of Adams (1959) as modified by Havelaar and Hogeboom (1984). Large batches of high-titer MS-2 virus were prepared according to the method of Loeb and Zinder (1961) and Nathans (1968). By this method high titers of MS-2 ($5\text{-}10 \times 10^{11}$ PFU mL^{-1}) could be attained for enrichment of wetlands inflow.

The chlorination system consisted of a chlorine contact chamber (20.3 cm diam. PVC), a submersible pump to transfer the wetland effluent to the chlorinator, and a liquid metering pump which pumped the sodium hypochlorite (NaOCl) solution into the effluent stream. The chlorine residual was measured using the DPD colorimetric method ("Standard Methods", 1985). The chlorine contact chamber was designed to give a contact time of 2 h. Suitable aliquots for testing were neutralized with sodium thiosulfate after sampling to stop the chlorine reaction.

Samples for analyses were collected by pumping water from a standpipe reaching to the bottom at the effluent end of each bed. The beds were kept flooded throughout the period of study. The hydraulic application rate was adjusted to 5 cm d^{-1} (corresponding to a hydraulic residence time of about 5.5 d) by regulating inflow and outflow by control valves.

Tests for significant differences between treatments (vegetated versus unvegetated beds) were done by comparing the critical value for the Student's t-distribution with the test statistic for each treatment contrast.

The decay rates of total coliform bacteria were determined from plots of the log of the fractional decrease in bacteria concentration over time, $\ln(C_t/C_o)$ versus time. The slope of the line (fit by a linear regression) was equal to the decay rate, k. The larger the number, the greater the decay rate.

RESULTS AND DISCUSSION

The artificial wetland site was located at Santee, California. Each wetland bed consisted of a plastic-lined (Hypalon, 0.76 mm) excavation, 18.5 m long x 3.5 m wide x 0.76 m deep, containing emergent vegetation growing in gravel. Primary municipal wastewater from the Santee Water Reclamation Facility was used as the inflow to each vegetated bed, and to an unvegetated (control) bed.

The levels of total coliform bacteria in the inflow and outflow of a vegetated (bulrush) and unvegetated bed which received continuous applications of primary wastewater are shown in Figure 1. At the hydraulic application rate of 5 cm d^{-1}, the mean influent total coliform level of 6.75×10^7 MPN 100 mL^{-1} was reduced to 5.77×10^5 MPN 100 mL^{-1} in the vegetated bed. This latter value was significantly below ($P<0.01$) the effluent total coliform level of 2.89×10^6 MPN 100 mL^{-1} for the unvegetated bed.

The survival of total coliform bacteria in wetland ecosystems is affected by many factors. The population decline of coliforms we observed in the artificial wetlands is not only due to cell die-off, but also encompasses processes other than loss of viability, including sedimentation, filtration, and adsorption. Sunlight has been shown to have a lethal effect on coliforms. Predators, bacteriophages, and competition for limiting resources, as well as antibiosis may also exert bacteriocidal effects.

It has been shown that root excretions of certain aquatic plants, including *Scirpus lacustris* and *Phragmites communis* can kill fecal indicators (*E. coli*) and pathogenic (*Salmonella*) bacteria (Seidel, 1976). Indeed, several regions of the root are known to produce compounds which may leak from root cells or be actively pumped by metabolic processes and which may inhibit certain microorganisms (Bowen and Rovira, 1976). Additionally, the enhanced development of populations of bacteria (e.g. pseudomonads) in the rhizosphere (root zone) with antibiotic activity (Broadbent et al., 1971), may also account for coliform die-off. Palmateer et al. (1985) found that levels of coliform bacteria increased dramatically in artificial marshes when they became anoxic in summer, suggesting that the ability of plants to aerate an otherwise anaerobic substrate, through their ability to translocate O_2 from shoot to root (Armstrong, 1964) may also play an important role in explaining the enhanced coliform removal we observed in the vegetated as opposed to unvegetated bed.

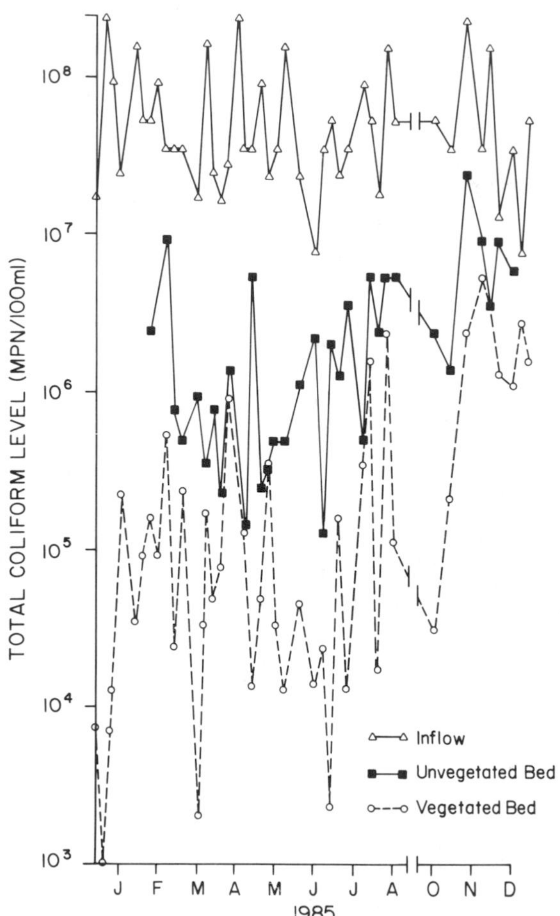

FIGURE 1. Concentration of total coliform bacteria in the applied primary municipal wastewater and in the effluent of a vegetated (bulrush) bed and an unvegetated bed. Hydraulic application rate was 5 cm d^{-1} for both beds.

For a bulrush bed containing sand instead of gravel at the effluent end (1/3 of bed), the mean effluent total coliform level of 5.09×10^5 MPN 100 mL^{-1} was not significantly below that for the bulrush bed without sand polishing. This indicates that filtration due to simple straining by the pore size of the substrate was not a major factor in total coliform bacteria removal. Rather, adsorption and inactivation are probably the major determinants in overall coliform removal by the wetlands.

The rate of inactivation of coliforms in the artificial wetlands was measured by incubating primary wastewaters (with the indigenous coliforms) _in situ_ in dialysis bags placed in depressions below the gravel surface of the wetlands. The decay of total coliform bacteria followed a first-order relationship described by Equation 1:

$$\ln(C_t/C_o) = -kt \qquad [1]$$

where k is the decay constant (h^{-1}), C_o is the initial total coliform concentration, and C_t is the total coliform concentration at time t. The rate constants for *in situ* decay of total coliforms were 0.018-0.022 h^{-1} (Table 1). For the flowing wetlands, coliform decay rates were calculated from the applied coliform concentration (C_o), the effluent coliform concentration (C_t), and the hydraulic residence time (t). The mean decay rate for the flowing wetlands was 0.036 h^{-1}, nearly twice that for the *in situ* incubations. The magnitude of this difference reflects both rhizosphere effects as well as bacterial adsorption to the root surfaces and substrate biofilm. The total coliform decay rate of 0.036 h^{-1} we measured for the flowing artificial wetlands was very similar to the value of 0.031 h^{-1} determined by Scheuerman et al. (1985) for total coliform (0.029 for fecal coliform) decay in a natural cypress wetlands.

In a study of artificial wetlands in Ontario, Canada, Palmateer et al. (1985) determined a fecal coliform removal efficiency of approximately 90% when operated at a 6-7 d residence time, while Gearheart et al. (1982) found a total coliform removal efficiency of 70-90% during winter and 0-50% during summer at 1.5-7 d retention times in artificial marshes in Arcata, California. These values are somewhat lower than the total coliform removal efficiencies of 99.1% we observed in artificial bulrush wetlands at the 5.5 d hydraulic residence time.

When the effluent from a bulrush bed was chlorinated, total coliform bacteria were reduced to very low levels (Table 2). Except for one value of 8 MPN 100 mL^{-1}, on all occasions levels

TABLE 1. Survival of total coliform bacteria incubated in artificial wetlands.

Date	Incubation time	Initial coliform level (C_o)	Coliform level after time, t (C_t)	Decay constant, k
		-------MPN 100 mL^{-1}-------		----h^{-1}----
2/10/86	0	$3.5x10^7$	--	
	48		$7.9x10^6$	
	192		$4.9x10^5$	0.019
5/5/86	0	$9.2x10^7$	--	
	96		$2.4x10^7$	
	216		$2.8x10^6$	0.018
6/18/86	0	$1.3x10^7$		
	48		$4.9x10^6$	
	120		$1.3x10^6$	
	168		$3.3x10^5$	0.022

TABLE 2. Survival of total coliform bacteria after chlorination† of the wetland effluent.

Date	Total chlorine residual	Total coliform inflow into wetlands	Total coliform level after chlorination	Overall log removal
	mg L^{-1}	---------MPN 100 mL^{-1}	---------	
3/4/86	1.5	$1.7x10^7$	<2	>7-log
3/12	20.0	$1.6x10^8$	<2	>8-log
3/18	20.0	$2.4x10^7$	<2	>7-log
3/27	7.0	$1.7x10^7$	<2	>7-log
3/30	4.5	$2.8x10^7$	<2	>7-log
4/8	9.1	$2.4x10^8$	<2	>8-log
4/16	>20.0	$3.5x10^7$	<2	>7-log
4/23	12.0	$3.5x10^7$	<2	>7-log
4/30	14.0	$9.2x10^7$	<2	>7-log
5/28	>20.0	$1.6x10^8$	<2	>8-log
6/3	>20.0	$2.4x10^7$	<2	>7-log
6/11	19.0	$2.2x10^7$	<2	>7-log
6/17	>20.0	$7.9x10^6$	<2	>6-log
6/25	18.3	$3.5x10^7$	<2	>7-log
7/2	>20.0	$5.4x10^7$	<2	>7-log
7/23	10.0	$2.4x10^7$	<2	>7-log
8/6	9.0	$5.4x10^7$	<2	>7-log
8/15	13.0	$1.8x10^7$	<2	>7-log
8/18	8.0	$3.5x10^7$	8	>6-log
8/29	9.5	$5.4x10^7$	<2	>7-log
10/31	9.0	$2.4x10^8$	<2	>8-log
11/12	3.0	$1.6x10^8$	<2	>7-log
11/22	3.0	$1.6x10^8$	<2	>8-log
12/23	13.0	$5.4x10^7$	2	>7-log

†Chlorine contact time was 2 h.

were reduced to 2.2 MPN 100 mL^{-1} or less, at all levels of chlorine (as hypochlorite) residual from 1-20 ppm. These data show the potential of wetlands treatment coupled with disinfection to produce waters suitable for unrestricted reuse applications.

Since viruses are in many cases more resistant to inactivation than are bacteria, we also evaluated the removal efficiency of an indicator of viral pollution in these wetland systems. Several investigators have suggested the suitability of bacterial viruses (bacteriophages) as indicators of human enteric virus survival in water treatment processes (Havelaar and Hogeboom, 1984). In particular, the F-specific RNA viruses such as MS-2 are attractive as models for the behavior of enteric viruses since they are nearly the same size as enteroviruses, both contain single-stranded RNA, and since MS-2 is more resistant to the effects of u.v. light (Kapucinski and Mitchell, 1983), heat

(Burge et al., 1981) and disinfection (Havelaar and Nieuwstad, 1985) than are most enteric viruses.

The level of MS-2 in the influent and effluent of a demonstration-scale ($800 m^2$) bulrush bed which received primary wastewater spiked with MS-2 virus is shown in Table 3. The influent level of 5.35×10^5 PFU mL^{-1} was reduced to 8.89×10^3 PFU mL^{-1} for a mean virus removal efficiency of 98.3%. Since raw wastewater contains as many human enteric viruses as 10^1-10^4 PFU L^{-1} (Rao et al., 1972), then in some cases further disinfection would be required to assure complete virus removal.

Artificial wetlands have previously been shown to be capable of removing a wide variety of wastewater contaminants, including BOD and suspended solids (Gersberg et al., 1984a), as well as NH_3 (Gersberg et al., 1986) and heavy metals (Gersberg et al., 1984b). The present study demonstrates that removal efficiency is equally high (99-99.9%) for several indicators of both bacterial and viral pollution, at hydraulic application rates similar to those used for land treatment of wastewater by rapid infiltration into soil (US EPA, 1981). Artificial wetlands may offer a low-technology approach for reducing the load of disease-causing bacteria and viruses to the aquatic environment.

TABLE 3. Removal of MS-2 bacteriophage in virus-enriched wastewater applied to artificial wetlands†.

Date	Level of MS-2 in inflow	Level of MS-2 in wetland effluent
	PFU mL^{-1}	
1/20/86	2.90×10^5	2.40×10^4
1/24	7.86×10^5	9.00×10^2
2/1	2.05×10^5	4.80×10^3
2/16	8.70×10^5	1.28×10^4
2/22	1.11×10^6	7.60×10^3
3/7	8.00×10^5	1.64×10^4
5/16	1.16×10^5	1.79×10^3
5/24	1.02×10^5	2.80×10^3
Mean	5.35×10^5	8.89×10^3

†Hydraulic application rate = 5 cm d^{-1} to a demonstration-scale ($800 m^2$) bulrush bed.

ACKNOWLEDGMENTS

This work was supported by Grant B-54835 from the California Department of Water Resources (R. Lindholm, Project Officer) and by the members of the San Diego Water Reclamation Agency. We also thank V. Bitter, C. Loss and the staff of the Santee Water Reclamation Facility (E. Houser, Manager) for assistance.

REFERENCES

Adams, M. H. 1959. Assay of phage by agar layer method. p. 450-454. In Bacteriophages. Interscience, New York.

Armstrong, W. 1964. Oxygen diffusion from the roots of some British bog plants. Nature 204:801-802.

Bowen, G. D., and A. D. Rovira. 1976. Microbial colonization of plant roots. Annual Review of Phytopathology 12:181-197.

Broadbent, P., K. F. Baker, and Y. Waterworth. 1971. Bacteria and actinomycetes antagonistic to fungal root pathogens in Australian soils. Aust. J. Biol. Sci. 24:925-944.

Burge, W. D., D. Colacicco, and W. N. Cramer. 1981. Criteria for achieving pathogen destruction during composting. J. Wat. Pollut. Control Fed. 53:1683-1690.

Gearheart, R. A., S. Wilbur, J. Williams, D. Hull, N. Hoelper, K. Wells, S. Sandberg, D. Salinger, D. Hendrix, C. Holm, L. Dillon, J. Morita, P. Grieshaber, N. Lerner, and B. Finney. 1981. City of Arcata, Marsh Pilot Project, Second Annual Progress Report. Project No. C-06-2270, State Water Resources Control Board, Sacramento, California.

Gersberg, R. M., B. V. Elkins, and C. R. Goldman. 1984a. Wastewater treatment by artificial wetlands. Wat. Sci. Technol. 17:443-450.

Gersberg, R. M., S. R. Lyon, B. V. Elkins, and C. R. Goldman. 1984b. The removal of heavy metals by artificial wetlands. Proceedings of Water Reuse Symposium III, AWWA Research Foundation, August 26-31, 1984, San Diego, California. p. 639-648.

Gersberg, R. M., B. V. Elkins, S. R. Lyon, and C. R. Goldman. 1986. Role of aquatic plants in wastewater treatment by artificial wetlands. Wat. Res. 20:363-368.

Havelaar, A. H., and W. M. Hogeboom. 1984. A method for the enumeration of male-specific bacteriophages in sewage. J. Appl. Bacteriol. 56:439-447.

Havelaar, A. H., and T. J. Nieuwstad. 1985. Bacteriophages and fecal bacteria as indicators of chlorination efficiency of biologically treated wastewater. J. Water Pollut. Control Fed. 57:1084-1088.

Kapuscinski, R. B., and R. Mitchell. 1982. Sunlight-induced mortality of viruses and *Escherichia coli* in coastal seawater. Environ. Sci. Technol. 17:1-6.

Loeb, T., and N. D. Zinder. 1961. A bacteriophage containing RNA. Proc. Natl. Acad. Sci. USA 47:282-289.

Nathans, D. 1968. Natural coding of bacterial protein snythesis. p. 787-788. In L. Grossman and K. Moldave (ed.) Methods in Enzymology, Vol. XII, Part B. Academic Press, New York and London.

Nichols, D. S. 1983. Capacity of natural wetlands to remove nutrients from wastewater. J. Water Pollut. Control Fed. 55:495-505.

Palmateer, G. A., W. L. Kutas, M. J. Walsh, and J. E. Koellner. 1985. Abstracts of the 85th Annual Meeting of the Am. Soc. for Microbiology. March 3-7, 1985. Las Vegas, Nevada.

Rao, V. C., V. Chandorkar, N. V. Rao, P. Kjmaran, and S. D. Lakhe. 1972. A simple method for concentrating and detecting viruses in wastewater. Water Res. 6:1565-1576.

Scheuerman, P. R., G. Bitton, S. R. Farrah, J. M. Bassart, and R. J. Dutton. 1985. Abstracts of the 85th Annual Meeting of the Am. Soc. for Microbiology. March 3-7, 1985. Las Vegas, Nevada.

Seidel, K. 1976. Macrophytes and water purification. p. 109-120. In J. Tourbier and R. W. Pierson, Jr. (ed.) Biological Control of Water Pollution. University of Pennsylvania Press, Philadelphia, PA.

Standard Methods for the Examination of Water and Wastewater. 1985. 16th Ed., Am. Public Health Assoc., Washington, D.C.

United States Environmental Protection Agency. 1981. Rapid infiltration process design. p. 5-1-1-49. In Process Design Manual for Land Treatment of Municipal Wastewater. US EPA, Center for Environmental Research Information. Cincinnati, Ohio.

LISTOWEL ARTIFICIAL MARSH TREATMENT PROJECT

J. Herskowitz, S. Black, and W. Lewandowski
Water Resources Branch
Ontario Ministry of Environment
135 St. Clair Ave., W.
Toronto, Ontario
CANADA M4V 1P5

ABSTRACT

Five separate cattail (Typha spp.) marsh treatment systems, occupying a total area of 8670 m^2, were operated for four years. Several different marsh designs and two pretreatment types, namely, complete-mix aeration cell effluent and lagoon effluent from the existing Town of Listowel sewage works, were tested. Marsh effluent quality achieved was at levels between conventional secondary and tertiary treatment. The marsh systems demonstrated large reductions in BOD, suspended solids and bacteria on a year-round basis. Effluent quality was highest when the O_2 supply was adequate to support aerobic metabolism in the marshes. Pilot study recommendations for marsh system design and operation have been implemented at a full-scale marsh treatment facility in Port Perry, Ontario.

Keywords: Wetlands, cattails, Typha, wastewater, municipal sewage.

INTRODUCTION

The study of marsh wastewater treatment systems was initiated by the Ontario Ministry of the Environment in response to reports that they may provide a viable and cost-effective alternative to conventional practices of wastewater treatment in rural communities and small urban centers. Marsh treatment has the advantages of being less land consumptive than retention lagoons and more economical and energy efficient than mechanical systems.

The primary objectives of the Listowel Artificial Marsh Project were 1) to investigate the efficiency and feasibility of year-round marshland wastewater treatment in cold climates and 2) to provide guidelines for the design and operation of marsh systems in Ontario. This paper describes the operating conditions and effluent quality achieved in Systems 3 and 4, channelized

Aquatic Plants for Water Treatment
and Resource Recovery
K.R. Reddy and W.H. Smith (Eds.)

ISBN 0-941463-00-1

marshes used to treat lagoon effluent and aeration cell effluent, respectively, as the channelled design yielded the highest treatment efficiencies.

DESCRIPTION OF SITE AND FACILITIES

The experimental facility was constructed adjacent to the existing 5455 m^3 d^{-1} sewage works in the Town of Listowel and was used to treat 4% of the town's sewage from 1980 to 1984. The existing sewage treatment at Listowel consisted of alum injection prior to a complete-mix aeration cell (3.5 d HRT) followed by two wastewater stabilization lagoons operated in series (combined retention 85 d). Alum treatment was withheld during the first two summers (May-October 1981 and 1982) as the town spray irrigated an adjoining property in summer. Wastewater was diverted from two stages of the existing system and distributed to the marsh systems as shown in Figure 1.

The marsh system designs included a channelized marsh with serpentine configuration (Systems 3 and 4), a shallow marsh (Systems 2 and 5) and a complex of shallow marsh, deep pond and channelized marsh (System 1). The channels, separated by earthen berms, were 4 m wide and 334 m long. Surface areas of Systems 1 through 5 were 4172, 909, 1324 and 941 m^2, respectively. The marsh basins were composed of compacted clay and filled to a depth of 15 cm with a combination of top soil and peat (10% by volume). Cattails (predominantly *Typha latifolia* with some *T. angustifolia* present), propagated from rhizomes planted at 1 m intervals, provided a complete cover which was maintained throughout the study. The pilot project is described in more detail in the final report (Herskowitz, 1986).

OPERATIONAL CONDITIONS AND PROCEDURES

Average hydraulic flow rates and loadings to the channelized systems were 17 m^3 d^{-1} (0.2 L s^{-1}) and 128 m^3 ha^{-1} d^{-1}, respectively, for most of the study period. Hydraulic loadings were increased (2-3 times initial levels) during the first year (beginning in winter) to prevent freezing. As the higher loadings resulted in reduced treatment efficiencies, in the following winter culvert aerators and effluent chamber heaters were installed instead to prevent flow blockage from ice formation. Average influent BOD_5 concentrations and annual loadings (following the first year) were 20 mg L^{-1} (range 3-69 mg L^{-1}) and 86 g m^{-2} (range 74-100 g m^{-2}), respectively, in System 3 and 56 mg L^{-1} (range 10-168 mg L^{-1}) and 294 g m^{-2} (range 239-359 g m^{-2}), respectively, in System 4.

Theoretical retention times were altered by evapotranspiration, ice formation and precipitation. In order to increase the rate of flow through the marshes in summer, the water depth was lowered to 5-20 cm. The presence of a 5 cm lip on the outflow

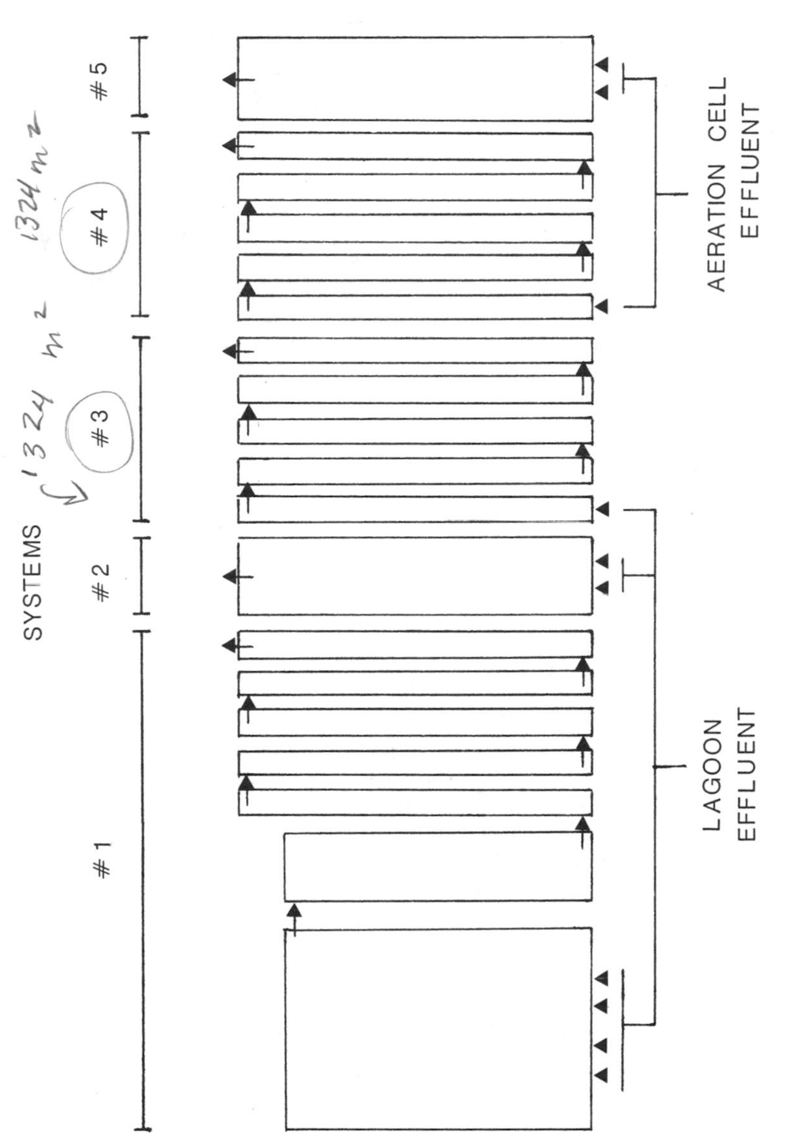

FIGURE 1. Design of Listowel marsh systems.

chambers prevented the complete drainage of the marshes in summer which would likely have increased the O_2 content of the sediment and contributed to greater contaminant removal in summer (Brinson, 1985). To maintain a water depth of 20 cm and counteract short-circuiting due to ice blockages, water levels were raised to $\geq$30 cm prior to the onset of winter. Heavy rains may have temporarily reduced the retention time but the resulting dilution tends to balance losses in treatment efficiency. Treatment efficiencies declined when retention time in the marshes deviated from the range of 7-14 d.

Monthly average temperatures of marsh effluents ranged between 0° and 19.6°C with average temperatures less than 2°C in December through March. Monthly average marsh effluent pH values generally fell within the range of 6.5-7.5 (measurements ranged between 6.3 and 8.9). Routine chemical parameters and fecal indicator bacteria were monitored weekly from April to November and biweekly from December to March. Tests for hydrogen sulfide, phenols and bacterial pathogens were conducted predominantly in winter. Analytical techniques are described elsewhere (MOE, 1981).

RESULTS AND DISCUSSION

Dissolved O_2 Levels and Sediment Redox Potential (Eh)

The Listowel marsh system demonstrated peak dissolved O_2 levels in spring and fall (monthly averages $\leq$11 mg L^{-1}) and varying degrees of O_2 depletion in the summer and winter. The lowest levels occurred in summer when O_2 concentrations in the marsh effluents were generally at or near zero for one or more months. There was a progressive decline in O_2 in the marsh systems during the winter period of ice cover (usually lasting from December through March). The winter decline was often followed by O_2 peaks resulting from spring algal blooms.

Most measurements of the sediment Eh were between -100 and +240 mV, the zone of facultative anaerobic respiration. A decline in Eh close to or below -100 mV (the range in which true anaerobes, e.g. sulfate-reducing bacteria, predominate) was measured in summer whereas decreases in Eh in winter were not as severe. Reductions in treatment efficiency (based on mass balances of wastewater constituents) were observed during the steep decline in redox potential (around -300 mV) in the summer of 1983 when the unusually high evapotranspiration rates caused the formation of stagnant pools of anoxic wastewater.

Both types of pretreatment had shortcomings with respect to the maintenance of aerobic metabolism in the marshes. The lagoon effluent was usually anoxic in winter due to the ice cover barrier to O_2 transfer, whereas the aeration cell lacked sufficient capacity to sustain adequate O_2 levels in the wastewater, particularly during the summer months, and the high solids levels increased the O_2 demand in the marsh. The growth of duckweed on the marsh water surface in summer and the ice cover in winter impeded diffusion of atmospheric O_2 into the marshes.

Suspended Solids

Monthly average suspended solids concentrations in the marsh system effluents were generally below 15 mg L^{-1} from fall through spring, often 5 mg L^{-1} or less for extended periods. Elevated concentrations of suspended solids occurred in one or more years in all systems in summer or late spring as a result of algae growth. This was compounded in summer by the concentration of suspended material resulting from evapotranspiration. The high suspended solids loadings from the complete-mix aeration cell effluent caused the development of sludge deposits at the influent end of System 4. These disrupted flows, caused die-back of the cattails and contributed to an elevated O_2 demand in the marsh, but did not significantly affect the marsh effluent levels of suspended solids which were comparable in both systems.

Five-Day Biological Oxygen Demand

Marsh effluent BOD_5 levels were generally less than 15 mg L^{-1} during the ice-free months, often between 5 and 10 mg L^{-1}. In the period of January through March, the monthly average BOD_5 levels in Systems 3 and 4 rose slightly in some years to maximum monthly average levels of 26 and 23 mg L^{-1}, respectively. Although low winter temperatures result in reduced microbial activity, substantial reductions in BOD_5 were achieved during the winter months. At loadings experienced in the last three years of the study, winter removal efficiencies ranged between 58 and 82% in System 3 and between 92 and 98% in System 4. Increases in BOD_5 levels occurred occasionally in one or more summer months, reaching maximum monthly concentrations of 32 and 34 mg L^{-1} in Systems 3 and 4, respectively, often coincident with increases in suspended solids concentrations.

Phosphorus

Marsh effluent levels of total P were generally below 1 mg L^{-1} and often below 0.5 mg L^{-1} in the period of fall through spring. Elevated total P levels occurred in summer (usually July) at which time 67-82% of the total P was in the soluble fraction. Monthly average total P values in System 3 exceeded 1 mg L^{-1} during the summer of 1981 (May-October) when alum treatment was suspended and in the summer of 1983 during a period of severe O_2 depletion. System 4 showed higher summer peak total P levels which occurred in all years and were sustained for more than one month.

Annual soluble P removal declined in Systems 3 and 4 with increases in cumulative soluble P loadings. Similar results have been reported in different types of natural wetlands used for wastewater treatment (Richardson, 1985). The decline in soluble P removal efficiency over the four years, and net annual soluble P export by the end of the study, suggests reduction in the P adsorption capacity of the sediment. Factors contributing to the decline in P retention were the extended periods of O_2 depletion and the high organic and P loadings in System 4. Reports indicate that a major mechanism of P retention in sediments is adsorption onto oxyhydroxides of Fe and Al. During the last summer when O_2 levels in System 3 remained above 2 mg L^{-1}, 84% soluble P removal was achieved and total P levels remained $\leq$0.2 mg L^{-1}.

Nitrogen

Marsh effluent total Kjeldahl N (TKN) concentrations were lowest in the spring and fall ($\leq$10 mg L^{-1}, often $\leq$5 mg L^{-1}). Increases occurred in winter ($\leq$15 mg L^{-1} in System 3 and $\leq$17 mg L^{-1} in System 4) and summer ($\leq$13 mg L^{-1} in System 3 and $\leq$23 mg L^{-1} in System 4). Ammonium N concentrations generally showed a similar pattern of variation in the marsh effluents. Monthly effluent NH_4-N levels declined to $\leq$1.0 mg L^{-1} for varying lengths of time in the spring and early summer in System 3, whereas NH_4-N levels in the effluent of System 4 decreased to $\leq$3.0 mg L^{-1} during this period.

Ammonium N treatment efficiencies were lowest in winter. Maximum monthly average concentrations were 13 mg L^{-1} and 16 mg L^{-1} in the effluent of System 3 and 4, respectively. System 4 showed little NH_4-N removal during influent peaks in summer and winter with effluent levels often exceeding influent levels. The data suggest that nitrification was inhibited in summer by an inadequate O_2 supply whereas in winter low water temperatures appear to have been the major limiting factor, although low O_2 levels may have also contributed to reduced nitrification.

Hydrogen Sulfide

Hydrogen sulfide (H_2S) levels in the marsh increased at the end of the winter and in summer when O_2 and NO_3^- were unavailable to satisfy the requirements of heterotrophic bacterial metabolism. Marsh effluent H_2S levels remained low (<0.5 mg L^{-1}) until February or March at which times concentrations rose to a maximum of 6 mg L^{-1} in Systems 3 and 4. However, the elevated H_2S levels in the lagoon effluent during the period of ice cover (maximum 12.1 mg L^{-1}) in almost all cases showed improvement after treatment in marsh System 3. Hydrogen sulfide production in summer was observed in all marsh systems in months when sampling was conducted. In Systems 3 and 4, monthly summer levels rose to a maximum of 7.1 mg L^{-1} and 14.5 mg L^{-1}, respectively.

Fecal Bacteria

Fecal bacteria reductions were high during most of the year with marsh effluent fecal coliform (FC) levels less than or equal to Ministry design objectives for disinfected secondary effluent (200 100 mL^{-1}). However, elevated monthly geometric mean levels occurred in summer and/or winter. Average monthly FC reductions in System 3 (influent range 10^2-10^4 per 100 mL^{-1}) were $\geq$94% in November through May with effluent FC levels exceeding influent levels in summer when influent levels were low ($\leq$376 100 mL^{-1}). Average FC reductions in System 4 (influent range 10^5 100 mL^{-1}) were $\geq$99% in all months. The detection of maximum levels of FC and bacterial pathogens in the winter months may result from longer bacterial survival at low temperatures (Berg, 1971), short-circuiting or the decline in sediment redox potential (Palmateer et al., 1985). FC levels in the effluent of Systems 3 and 4 were similar although the influent levels in System 3 were 0.1-2.0% of the levels in the influent of System 4.

TABLE 1. Average wastewater concentrations and treatment efficiencies in Systems 3 and 4 (1980-1984).

Parameters	Average Conc., mg L^{-1} Influent	Effluent	% Removal Based on Mass Balance, Years 1	2	3	4	Avg.
System 3: Channelized marsh receiving lagoon effluent							
Suspended Solids	22.8	9.2	40	75	53	73	61
BOD_5	19.6	7.6	57	56	63	62	59
Total P	1.0	0.5	53	39	47	45	46
Soluble P	0.37	0.26	59	1	-12	-10	9
Total Kjeldahl-N	12.0	6.1	32	41	54	46	43
NH_4-N	7.2	3.8	31	32	51	42	39
Unionized NH_3-N	0.13	0.01					
NO_3^--NO_2^--N	0.25	0.23					
H_2S†	1.8	1.0					
Unionized H_2S†	1.31	0.65					
System 4: Channelized marsh receiving aeration cell effluent							
Suspended Solids	111.1	8.0	90	93	93	94	93
BOD_5	56.3	9.6	78	80	88	81	82
Total P	3.2	0.6	79	76	84	78	79
Soluble P	0.40	0.34	59	37	-57	-138	-25
Total Kjeldahl-N	18.7	8.7	49	46	55	41	48
NH_4-N	8.6	6.1	28	22	35	5	23
Unionized NH_3-N	0.07	0.02					
NO_3^--NO_2^--N	0.38	0.21					
H_2S†	0.20	1.31					
Unionized H_2S†	0.13	0.81					

†The dates and frequency of H_2S analyses varied between years; most samples were collected in winter.

CONCLUSIONS

The marsh systems were capable of producing effluent of secondary to tertiary quality (Table 1). Large BOD_5 reductions were measured throughout the year despite the low wastewater temperature ($\leq 2°C$) in the winter months. Removal efficiencies for soluble P and NH_4-N were appreciably lower in System 4 indicating the importance of pretreatment method on marsh system performance.

The O_2 budget proved to be a major influence on the efficiency of wastewater renovation in the marsh systems. Elevated levels of NH_4-N, H_2S, phenols and soluble P in the marsh effluent were generally associated with anaerobic conditions in the marshes. However, low water temperatures appeared to be responsible for much of the reduction in NH_4-N removal during those winter months when O_2 levels were maintained above 2 mg L^{-1} and should have been adequate to support nitrification.

The data from the experimental systems suggested a number of improvements on marsh design and operation (primarily relating to changes that increase the O_2 supply and decrease the O_2 demand in the marsh) which have been incorporated into a full-scale marshland sewage treatment facility at Port Perry, Ontario. The major modification is the installation of an upgraded pretreatment unit. The effluent quality produced at Port Perry will provide a better indication of the potential for the application of this type of marshland sewage treatment in Ontario.

REFERENCES

Berg, G. 1971. Viruses and water quality occurrence and control. Proc. of the 13th Water Quality Conference, Univ. of Illinois, Urbana, IL.

Brinson, M. M. 1985. Management potential for nutrient removal in forested wetlands. p. 405-414. In P. J. Godfrey et al. (ed.) Ecological Considerations in Wetlands Treatment of Municipal Wastewaters. Van Nostrand Reinhold Co., NY.

Herskowitz, J. 1986. Listowel artificial marsh project report. Ontario Ministry of Environment. Water Resources Branch. 253 pp.

Ontario Ministry of Environment. 1981. Outlines of analytical methods. Laboratory Services Branch. 246 pp.

Palmateer, G., W. L. Kutas, M. J. Walsh, and J. E. Koellner. 1985. Recovery of pathogenic and indicator bacteria from wastewater following artificial wetland treatment of domestic sewage in Ontario. In Abstracts of the Annual Meeting of the American Society for Microbiology, Las Vegas.

Richardson, C. J. 1985. Mechanisms controlling phosphorus retention capacity in freshwater wetlands. Sci. 228:1424-1427.

ACID MINE WATER TREATMENT IN WETLANDS: AN OVERVIEW OF AN EMERGENT TECHNOLOGY

R. L. P. Kleinmann and M. A. Girts
U. S. Bureau of Mines
Pittsburgh Research Center
P. O. Box 18070
Pittsburgh, Pennsylvania 15236

ABSTRACT

Experimental wetlands are being constructed on mined lands in the United States as an inexpensive alternative to conventional acid mine water treatment facilities. The U.S. Bureau of Mines is conducting an inventory of these constructed wetlands as part of a long-term evaluative study. Preliminary results, based on the 20 sites surveyed to date, indicate that the wetlands dominated by emergent species are out-performing the *Sphagnum*-dominated wetlands, and that much of the water treatment is accomplished by other aspects of the wetland, including bacteria, algae, amendments and other plants. Iron concentrations as high as 85 mg L^{-1} are reduced to less than 3 mg L^{-1} after flow through the constructed wetlands. Manganese is also removed, though somewhat less efficiently.

Keywords: Iron, manganese, *Sphagnum*, *Typha*, cattails.

INTRODUCTION

Contamination of streams and rivers by acidic mine water is one of the most persistent industrial pollution problems in the United States. The acid lowers the pH of the water, making it corrosive and toxic to many forms of aquatic life. In Appalachia, over 8,000 km of streams and rivers are adversely affected by drainage from abandoned coal mines, and this pollution will likely continue unabated for decades (Kim et al., 1982).

However, the water quality in many streams and rivers of the region have improved, primarily due to enactment of the Surface Mining Control and Reclamation Act. At active mining operations and at sites where mining occurred after 1977, discharge water must now be treated to meet fairly stringent regulatory limits at a cost to the industry of over $1 million a day. The mine water is typically pumped to a collection pond, after which it is

ISBN 0-941463-00-1

neutralized with either lime ($Ca(OH)_2$), soda ash (Na_2CO_3) or sodium hydroxide (NaOH). The pH is usually adjusted to between 8.5 and 10 to facilitate rapid oxidation and precipitation of iron (Fe) and manganese (Mn), which in turn lowers the pH. Average effluent values of Fe and Mn cannot exceed 3 and 2 mg L^{-1}, respectively (U.S. Code of Federal Regulations, 1981). The treated water, although high in SO_4^{2-}, hardness, and total dissolved solids, can be legally discharged. State and Federal regulations require that this water treatment continue even after mining and reclamation is completed, for as long as acidity, Mn or Fe remain a problem.

Wetlands are a potential natural treatment system for small flows of acid mine water. The use of wetlands to treat acid mine water did not develop as an application of industrial or municipal water treatment with aquatic plants. Instead, two independent studies of _Sphagnum_ bogs, undertaken to determine what adverse effects acid mine water was having on the wetland vegetation, demonstrated a lack of adverse effects and, in fact, natural treatment of the mine water (Huntsman et al., 1978; Wieder et al., 1982). First, Huntsman et al. (1978) studied _Sphagnum recurvum_ that was found growing in water of pH 2.5. Iron, Mg, SO_4^{2-}, Ca, and Mn all decreased while the pH increased from 2.5 to 4.6 as the mine water flowed through the bog. A natural outcrop of limestone located at the downstream end provided sufficient neutralization to raise the effluent pH to between 6 and 7 (Huntsman et al., 1978). Wieder et al. (1982) in northern West Virginia found that acid drainage flowing into the wetland area rapidly improved in quality. In 20-50 m, pH rose from 3.05-3.55 to 5.45-6.05, while only 10-20 m of flow through the bog was needed to lower SO_4^{2-} concentrations from 210-275 mg L^{-1} to 5-15 mg L^{-1} and Fe from 26-73 mg L^{-1} to less than 2 mg L^{-1}. Water quality of the bog effluent was found to be equal to that of nearby streams unaffected by mine drainage.

In subsequent laboratory experiments, it was shown that 1 kg (wet weight) of _S. recurvum_ could remove up to 92% of the influent 50 mg L^{-1} of Fe in 15 L of pH 3.8 synthetic mine water solution by cation exchange (Harris et al., 1984). Laboratory work by Wieder and Lang (1986) indicated that this adsorption of Fe was independent of pH over the pH range of 3-6. In a natural wetland, bacterial action (oxidation and SO_4^{2-} reduction in the organic-rich bottom waters), metal adsorption by algae and other processes add to the Fe removal capability. These processes are summarized in Figure 1.

FIELD EVALUATION OF TREATMENT BY WETLANDS

Over 100 wetlands have been constructed in Ohio, Pennsylvania, Maryland, and West Virginia by mining companies for acid water treatment. The Bureau of Mines is facilitating monitoring and evaluation at many of these sites. The Bureau of

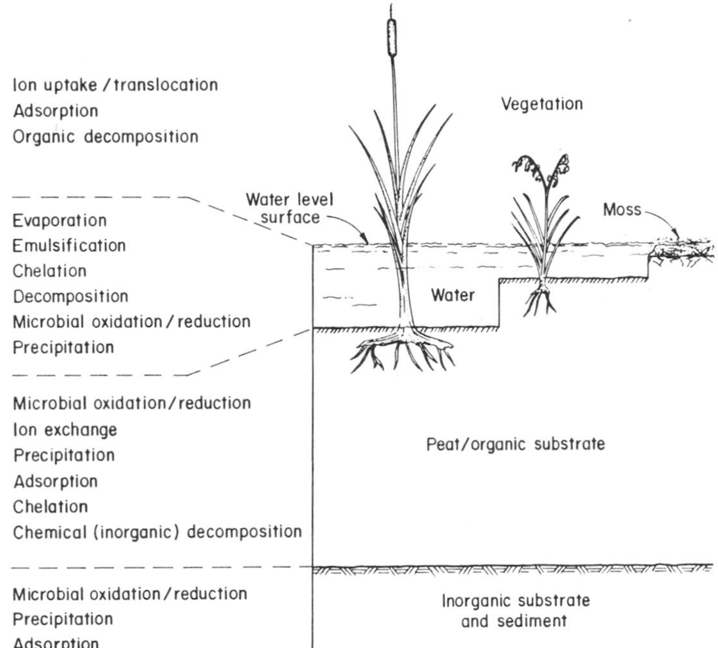

FIGURE 1. A complex and inter-related system of chemical transformations, much of which are biologically mediated, is responsible for the effective treatment of acid water in wetlands.

Mines is also cooperating with the National Park Service in constructing a wetland to treat extremely acid water (pH 2.6) from an abandoned mine at the Friendship Hill National Historic Site in southwestern Pennsylvania.

In addition, the Bureau of Mines is conducting an inventory of approximately 50 of these biological systems that were constructed for acid water treatment prior to 1986. Our intent is to characterize and evaluate wetland construction technology and to provide a data set from which we will select sites for intensive monitoring. To date, 20 wetlands have been inventoried (Table 1).

The constructed wetlands are either *Sphagnum*-dominated (simulating the previously-studied natural bogs) or dominated by emergent species (i.e., *Typha* and *Equisetum*). The emergent species were observed to volunteer on mined lands and to also have a beneficial effect on water quality; the earliest full-scale field tests were attempts to enhance this type of volunteer growth. At nine sites, the *Sphagnum* moss and emergent species have been combined, either by intergrowth or in sequenced wetted areas.

In general, constructed wetland treatment systems that have an influent Fe concentration less than 30 mg L^{-1} and an influent Mn concentration less than 15 mg L^{-1} reduce both Fe and Mn to less than 2 mg L^{-1}. At many sites, much higher Fe concentrations are

TABLE 1. Preliminary analysis of biological systems constructed for treatment of acid mine water, based on the first 20 inventoried sites.

	Mean	Range
Size (m^2)	1,550	93-6,070
Number of basins (ponds)	3	1-7
Size of basin (m^2)	795	19-6,070
Flow rate, L s^{-1}	1.3	0.06-12.6
Water depth, m	0.3	0-2
Water chemistry (n=11)		
Inflow:		
pH	4.9	3.1-6.3
Acidity, mg L^{-1}	170	ND-600
Fe, mg L^{-1}	33	0.4-220
Mn, mg L^{-1}	26	8.7-54
SO_4, mg L^{-1}	950	270-1,600
Outflow:		
pH	6.0	3.5-7.7
Acidity, mg L^{-1}	40	ND-140
Fe, mg L^{-1}	1.2	0.05-7.3
Mn, mg L^{-1}	15	0.3-52
SO_4, mg L^{-1}	740	160-1500
Construction cost	$10,000	$1,500-$65,000

ND = below detection limits.

being treated by the wetlands, but not necessarily well enough to meet the discharge criteria of 3 mg L^{-1}. The highest average Fe concentration being successfully treated at that level is 85 mg L^{-1}, though influent concentrations over 100 mg L^{-1} are being reduced to 10-20 mg L^{-1} (unpublished data).

Manganese is being reduced to, or near, effluent limits at many sites where the influent concentration is 15 mg L^{-1} or less and is typically reduced by 25-50% when influent concentrations are higher. Two sites with influent Mn concentrations above 35 mg L^{-1} are successfully meeting effluent criteria but at some other sites, influent and effluent Mn concentrations are virtually equal.

Manganese removal in the constructed wetlands appears to be related to biota, pH and effluent Fe values. As Fe concentrations fall to less than 5 mg L^{-1}, Mn removal becomes significant if the pH of the water in the pond is at 5 or above. Thus, additional ponds or wetland sections are often needed if both Fe and Mn are present. *Sphagnum*, while very effective in removing Fe, is ineffective in removing Mn (Harris et al., 1984; Kleinmann et al., 1985; Wieder and Lang, 1986). Algae and Mn-oxidizing bacteria appear to play a very important role (Gregory and Staley, 1982; Kleinmann et al., 1983). Manganese is also taken up by some emergent plants, such as Typha (Snyder and Aharrah, 1984) and Equisetum (Kepler, 1986).

Although the planted or transplanted vegetation represents only one aspect of the biological treatment system, failure to thrive is equivalent to failure of the system. Survival of cattails was high in mine water with a pH of 3 or above, with little replanting necessary and considerable spreading during the second growing season. The Sphagnum, in contrast, showed very low survival rates. Three sites had difficulty with Sphagnum mortality and had to be replanted at least once. At other sites, the Sphagnum was definitely stressed. Sphagnum is very sensitive to the water level fluctuations that are typical of disturbed lands and some species are also susceptible to "sunburn." It also appears that high levels of Fe (>100 mg L^{-1}) kill the transplanted moss, due to the high adsorption rate of the moss. On the positive side, Sphagnum tolerates lower pH conditions than the emergent species, though Fe adsorption diminishes rapidly below pH 2.5 (Harris et al., 1984; Kleinmann et al., 1983).

Hay bales or loose hay was used as an artificial substrate in six of the wetlands in conjunction with Sphagnum, and mixed with clay in another wetland. Spent mushroom compost was included in the substrate layers in three wetlands, while vegetation was planted in spoil or topsoil with clay layers at another three sites. Limestone was included as a 15 cm substrate layer in three cattail wetlands. [It should not be considered for use with Sphagnum moss since Ca would be preferentially adsorbed relative to Fe (Harris et al., 1984)]. Forest duff and manure were also used. Agricultural lime was added after construction on five sites and superphosphate was added in two cases. Reported maintenance included replacing limestone ditch rip-rap, embankments, grading to limit surface runoff inflow to the wetland, and establishment of hay bale dikes to limit channelization. Maintenance was generally viewed as inexpensive and not time-consuming. One mine operator estimated annual maintenance costs at $20/year and several reported that no maintenance had been done on the wetlands.

SUMMARY

Constructed wetlands represent an inexpensive alternative to conventional treatment of acid mine water and have, therefore, gained rapid acceptance amongst mine operators. Preliminary results of an inventory of constructed wetlands indicate that wetlands dominated by emergent species (especially cattails) outperform Sphagnum-dominated wetlands on mined lands. However, dominant vegetation is only one aspect of the water treatment process; algae, bacteria, sediment, amendments such as mulch and other plants all contribute to metal removal. It is hoped that long-term evaluation of wetlands will elucidate the relative importance of each of these factors and optimize water-treatment efficiency.

REFERENCES

Gregory, E., and J. T. Staley. 1982. Widespread distribution of ability to oxidize manganese among freshwater bacteria. Appl. Environ. Microbiol. 46:1073-1079.

Harris, R. L., T. O. Tiernan, J. Hinders, J. G. Solch, B. E. Huntsman, and M. L. Taylor. 1984. Treatment of mine drainage from abandoned mines by biological iron oxidation and limestone neutralization. Peer Consultants report prepared for Bureau of Mines under contract J0113033, 113 pp; available from Robert Kleinmann, BuMines, Pittsburgh, PA.

Huntsman, B. E., J. G. Solch, and M. D. Porter. 1978. Utilization of Sphagnum species dominated bog for coal acid mine drainage abatement. Geol. Soc. Am. (91st Annual Meeting) Abstracts, Toronto, Ontario, Canada. 322 pp.

Kepler, D. A. 1986. Manganese removal from mine drainage by artificial wetland construction. Proceedings, 8th Annual National Abandoned Mined Lands Conference, August 13-15, 1986, Billings, Montana (in press).

Kim, A. G., B. S. Heisey, R. L. P. Kleinmann, and M. Deul. 1982. Acid mine drainage: Control and abatement research. BuMines IC 8905. 22 pp.

Kleinmann, R. L. P., G. R. Watzlaf, and T. E. Ackman. 1985. Treatment of mine water to remove manganese. p. 211-217. In D. H. Graves (ed.) 1985 Proceedings, Symposium on Surface Mining, Hydrology, Sedimentology, and Reclamation. December 9-13, 1985, Lexington, KY.

Kleinmann, R. L. P., T. O. Tiernan, J. G. Solch, and R. L. Harris. 1983. A low-cost low maintenance treatment system for acid mine drainage using Sphagnum moss and limestone. p. 241-245. In D. H. Graves (ed.) 1983 Symposium on Surface Mining, Hydrology, Sedimentology, and Reclamation. Univ. of Kentucky, Lexington, KY.

Snyder, C. D., and E. C. Aharrah. 1984. The influence of the Typha community on mine drainage. p. 149-153. In D. H. Graves (ed.) Proceedings, 1984 Symposium on Surface Mining, Hydrology, Sedimentology, and Reclamation. Dec 5-7, 1984, Lexington, KY.

U.S. Code of Federal Regulations. 1981. Title 30--Mineral resources; Chapter VII--Office of Surface Mining Reclamation and Enforcement, Department of the Interior; Subchapter B--General Performance Standards; Part 715--General Performance Standards. July 1, 1981.

Wieder, R. K., and G. E. Lang. 1986. Fe, Al, Mn, and S Chemistry of Sphagnum peat in four peatlands with different metal and sulfur input. Water Air and Soil Pollution 29:309-320.

Wieder, R. K., G. E. Lang, and A. E. Whitehouse. 1982. Modification of acid mine drainage in a fresh water wetland. Paper in Proceedings, Acid Mine Drainage Research and Development, 3d WV Surface Mine Drainage Task Force

Symposium. WV Surface Mine Drainage Task Force, Charleston, WV, 1982. p. 38-62.

Wieder, R. K., G. E. Lang, and A. E. Whitehouse. 1985. Metal removal in *Sphagnum*-dominated wetlands: Experience with a man-made wetland system. p. 353-364. *In* R. P. Brooks, D. E. Samuel, and J. B. Hill (ed.) *Proceedings*, Wetlands and Water Management on Mined Lands. Pennsylvania State University, State College, PA, October 23-24, 1985.

DESIGN AND PERFORMANCE OF THE ARTIFICIAL WETLANDS WASTEWATER TREATMENT PLANT AT ISELIN, PENNSYLVANIA

J. T. Watson
Tennessee Valley Authority
270 Haney Building
Chattanooga, Tennessee 37401

F. D. Diodato and M. Lauch
Pennsylvania Bureau of Water Quality Management
P. O. Box 2063
Harrisburg, Pennsylvania 17120

ABSTRACT

The Tennessee Valley Authority (TVA) is demonstrating the use of a marsh/pond/meadow system for treatment of municipal wastewater as a low cost system for meeting National Pollutant Discharge Elimination System (NPDES) discharge limitations. The system is modeled after a small system at Iselin, Pennsylvania. The Iselin system was designed and constructed by the Pennsylvania Department of Environmental Resources, which has provided the design information and monitoring results to TVA. The Iselin wetlands system has a design capacity of 45.4 $m^3\ d^{-1}$ and consists of four key components: an aerated pond, a cattail (Typha) marsh, a stabilization pond, and a reed canary grass (Phalaris) meadow. Average effluent concentrations for key parameters for the first 31 months of operation are: BOD_5, 7.4 mg L^{-1}; total suspended solids, 19 mg L^{-1}; NH_4-N, 3.3 mg L^{-1}; total P, 2.6 mg L^{-1}; and fecal coliforms, 150/100 mL^{-1}.

Keywords: Marsh/pond/meadow treatment system, cattails (Typha), duckweed (Lemna), and reed canary grass (Phalaris), low cost system for NPDES permit compliance.

INTRODUCTION

In cooperation with the Kentucky Division of Water, TVA has initiated a project in Benton, Hardin, and Pembroke, Kentucky, to demonstrate how small communities can provide low cost, high quality sewage treatment with artificial wetlands. One of the difficulties TVA encountered during the planning and design of the

ISBN 0-941463-00-1

demonstration is the scarcity of design criteria and performance data in the literature for artificial wetlands. During TVA's search for information, the Pennsylvania Bureau of Water Quality Management (BWQM) informed TVA of the data they were collecting on a marsh/pond/meadow system at Iselin, Pennsylvania. The data base was provided to TVA, computerized and returned to the BWQM with an analysis and interpretation of the system's performance. This report summarizes the data analyses.

SYSTEM DESIGN

The system serves 158 persons. It consists of six components in series: pretreatment (comminution and bar screens), an aeration cell, a cattail marsh, a stabilization pond, a reed canary grass meadow, and a chlorination unit (Figure 1). The application rates for the marsh and meadow are 470 m^3 ha^{-1} d^{-1} and 940 m^3 ha^{-1} d^{-1}, respectively.

PERFORMANCE EVALUATION

Data are summarized (Table 1) for key parameters often regulated by NPDES permits: BOD_5, total suspended solids, fecal coliforms, NH_4-N, and P.

Performance is evaluated by parameter for each component and for the total system. Concentration, rather than loading, forms the primary basis for the evaluation because flow is monitored only on an instantaneous basis at the influent and effluent. When loadings are identified, they are based on the average daily effluent flow for the period of record [6,800 gpd (26 m^3 d^{-1})]. The design capacity of the system is 12,000 gpd. Since most of the time only one of the two parallel marsh and meadow cells were used to treat the flow, these components were typically operating near or slightly above their design hydraulic capacity. Cells were switched occasionally which complicates the evaluation. The aeration basis and pond were typically loaded at about half of design hydraulic capacity since there is only one of each.

Another key variable that must be considered in evaluating the performance of the marsh is the type and amount of vegetation that was present. Although cattails were planted in each cell, they did not reproduce very well. In Cell 1, the predominant type of vegetation was Kentucky Fescue 31 due to overseeding. In Cell 2, cattails were more abundant but still sparse overall. The poor stand of cattails may be caused by the inability to flood the cells and the toxic effect of high NH_4^+ concentrations (Gersberg et al., 1986). Consequently, the data for the marsh reflect a much less than ideal situation from a vegetation perspective.

Biochemical Oxygen Demand

The system reduces the BOD by an average of 97% (from 260 mg L^{-1} to 7.4 mg L^{-1}). Reduction rates are similar for winter (96%)

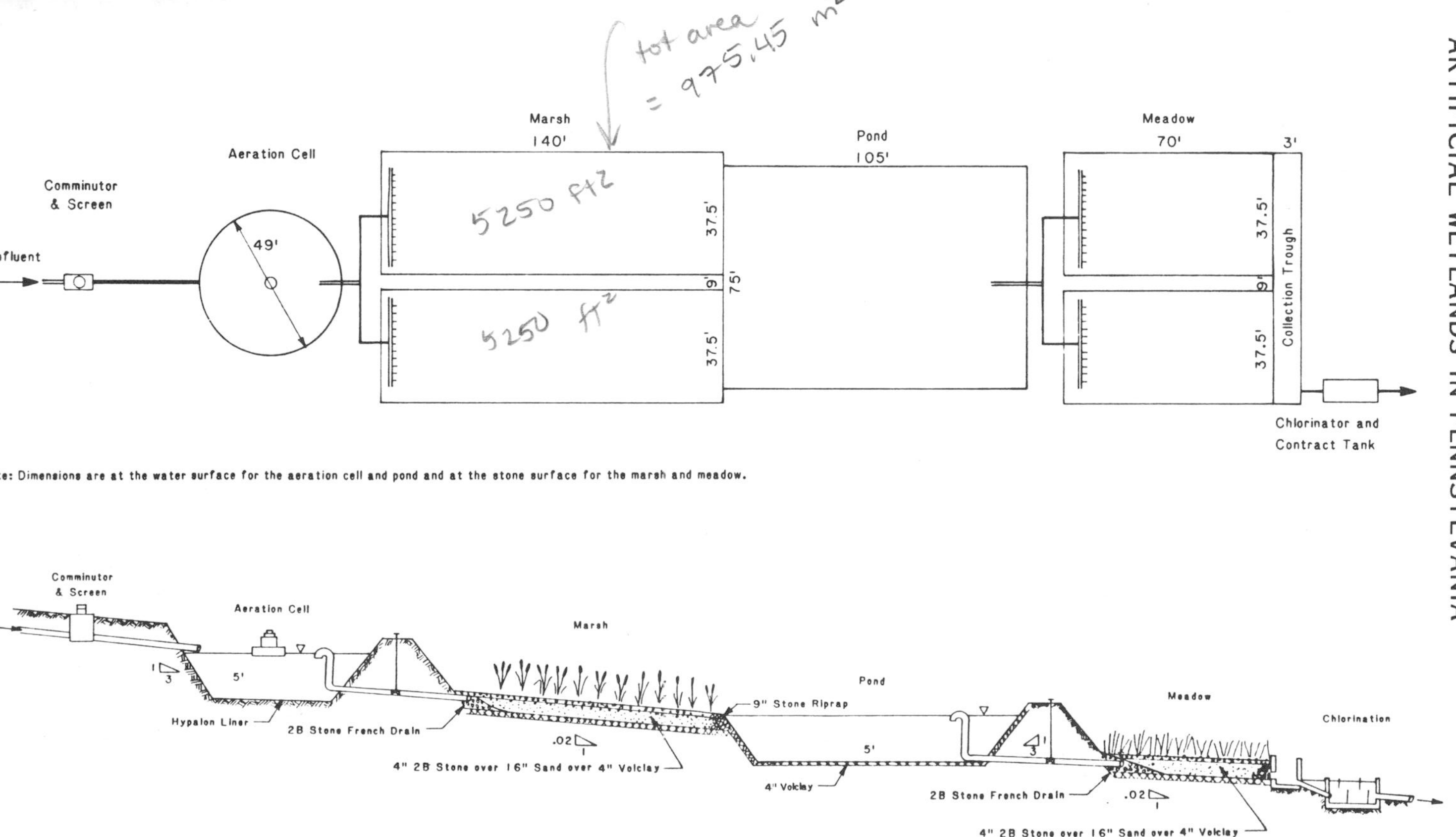

FIGURE 1. Iselin artificial wetlands treatment scheme.

TABLE 1. Performance data for the artificial wetlands at Iselin, Pennsylvania.†

Component	Season	Biochemical Oxygen Demand Influent	Biochemical Oxygen Demand Effluent	Total Suspended Solids Influent	Total Suspended Solids Effluent
		mg L^{-1}			
Aeration Basin	Winter	230	200 (15)	180	490 (-170)
	Summer	280	92 (67)	170	290 (-67)
	Total	260	140 (46)	180	380 (-120)
Marsh	Winter	200	15 (93)	490	33 (93)
	Summer	92	19 (79)	290	69 (76)
	Total	140	17 (88)	380	53 (86)
Pond	Winter	15	17 (-15)	33	38 (-16)
	Summer	19	23 (-22)	69	80 (-16)
	Total	17	20 (-20)	53	61 (-14)
Meadow	Winter	17	8.5 (50)	38	21 (45)
	Summer	23	6.5 (72)	80	18 (78)
	Total	20	7.4 (64)	61	19 (69)
System	Winter	230	8.5 (96)	180	21 (88)
	Summer	288	6.5 (98)	170	18 (90)
	Total	260	7.4 (97)	180	19 (89)

Component	Season	Ammonia Nitrogen Influent	Ammonia Nitrogen Effluent	Total Phosphorus Influent	Total Phosphorus Effluent
Aeration Basin	Winter	13	24 (-92)	12	11 (7.8)
	Summer	16	35 (-120)	16	15 (5.7)
	Total	14	30 (-110)	15	13 (7.0)
Marsh	Winter	24	12 (49)	11	7.1 (37)
	Summer	35	14 (61)	15	2.0 (87)
	Total	30	13 (56)	13	4.2 (69)
Pond	Winter	12	9.1 (27)	7.1	4.2 (42)
	Summer	14	1.9 (86)	2.0	2.8 (-36)
	Total	13	5.2 (60)	4.2	3.4 (20)
Meadow	Winter	9.1	5.8 (36)	4.2	3.9 (6.8)
	Summer	1.9	1.2 (38)	2.8	1.6 (43)
	Total	5.2	3.3 (36)	3.4	2.6 (23)
System	Winter	13	5.8 (54)	12	3.9 (68)
	Summer	16	1.2 (93)	16	1.6 (90)
	Total	14	3.3 (77)	15	2.6 (82)

TABLE 1 (cont'd.)

Component	Season	Fecal Coliforms	
		Influent	Effluent
		--------colonies 100 mL^{-1}--------	
Aeration Basin	Winter	1,200,000	1,700,000 (-48)
	Summer	2,600,000	1,000,000 (60)
	Total	1,800,000	1,400,000 (21)
Marsh	Winter	1,700,000	6,200 (100)
	Summer	1,000,000	720 (100)
	Total	1,400,000	3,700 (100)
Pond	Winter	6,200	3,200 (48)
	Summer	720	630 (12)
	Total	3,700	2,100 (43)
Meadow	Winter	3,200	240 (92)
	Summer	630	23 (96)
	Total	2,100	150 (93)
System	Winter	1,200,000	240 (100)
	Summer	2,600,000	23 (100)
	Total	1,800,000	150 (100)

†Numbers in parentheses are percent reduction.

NOTES: Period of record: March 1983-September 1985. Winter months include November through April. Summer months include May through October.

and summer (98%). Only one month showed an average BOD above mg L^{-1} (Feb. 1984, 32 mg L^{-1}), and this probably resulted from unrepresentative data because the concomitant BOD at the point of discharge to the receiving stream was very low. Consequently, the data indicate that the system is capable of meeting EPA's secondary treatment standard (30 mg L^{-1}) essentially 100% of the time. The average effluent quality exceeds secondary quality.

Each component of the system except for the pond significantly reduces BOD. The aeration basin and the marsh reduce BOD by about the same quantity [around 6.7 lbs d^{-1} (3000 g d^{-1}) and 7.0 lbs d^{-1} (3200 g d^{-1}), respectively, assuming an average flow of 6,800 gpd] but the marsh has the highest reduction percentage (88% versus 46%). The meadow has the second highest reduction percentage (64%). The pond typically increases BOD due to algal production.

Total Suspended Solids

The system removes an average of 89% of the suspended solids (from 180 mg L^{-1} to 19 mg L^{-1}). The reductions are similar for winter (88%) and summer (90%). The average effluent concentration for 6 of the 28 months of available data exceeded 30 mg L^{-1}; however, data at the final monitoring point prior to discharge to the receiving stream revealed that only one month exceeded 30 mg L^{-1} (August 1984, 36 mg L^{-1}). The high values for the meadow effluent probably result from the sampling procedure. Samples are obtained from weep holes, and solids may be scraped from the sides or resuspended within the rock media due to the sampling personnel walking over the cell. Consequently, the data indicate that the system meets EPA's secondary treatment standard (30 mg L^{-1}) more than 90% of the time (including the start-up period). The average effluent quality is much better than secondary quality. The remaining solids probably consist of algae and plant fragments rather than sewage particles. Concentrations are generally highest during spring and fall when the system's vegetative growth dynamics are in the greatest state of flux.

Like BOD, the marsh and the meadow are the two components that effectively reduce solids concentrations. The marsh removes an average of about 18 lbs d^{-1} (8,200 g d^{-1}) or 86% of the solids. The meadow removes about 2.4 lbs d^{-1} (1,100 g d^{-1}) or 69% of the remaining solids.

Fecal Coliforms

Reductions in fecal coliforms approach 100% (from 1,800,000/100mL^{-1} to 150/100mL). The system is highly effective during both winter and summer. Only one spike in excess of 1,000/100mL occurred in the monthly geometric means for the meadow effluent. Geometric means exceeded 200/100mL, which is a typical, average permit limit, during only 5 of the 29 months that were monitored. All of these occurrences were during fall and winter months and may be related to small mammals wintering within the system. Nests occasionally had to be removed from the meadow weep holes.

All components except the aeration basin effectively reduce fecal coliforms during each season. Most of the organisms are reduced in the marsh with the pond and meadow serving as polishing components for the remaining organisms. The reductions are attributed to natural die-off in an unfavorable environment and the toxic effect of root excretions on enteric organisms.

Ammonia Nitrogen

The system removes an average of 77% of the NH_4^+ (from 14 mg L^{-1} to 3.3 mg L^{-1}) contained in the raw sewage. Removal is better during the summer (93%) than winter (54%). However, these removal rates have little meaning because of the conversion of organic N to NH_4^+ in the aeration basin and marsh. The effectiveness of the system for NH_4^+ removal is based primarily on the effluent concentrations. The average effluent concentration is 3.3 mg L^{-1}. The concentrations vary seasonally. During the summer the average is 1.2 mg L^{-1} and during winter the average is 5.8 mg L^{-1}. During summer only one month exceeded 4 mg L^{-1} (October 1984, 6.0 mg L^{-1}). Only two months exceeded 10 mg L^{-1} (January 1984, 15 mg L^{-1}, and February 1984, 13 mg L^{-1}).

The components that effectively reduce NH_4^+ concentrations are the marsh, pond, and meadow. Ammonia in the marsh is converted to NO_2^- and NO_3^- (nitrification). Reductions amount to about 56% by concentration and 0.96 lb d^{-1} (4,400 g d^{-1}) by mass. In the pond, nitrification and volatilization (loss of NH_3 as a gas) both appear to be important. The average reduction in concentration is the highest in the pond (60%), but on a mass basis the reduction is only about half of that occurring in the marsh [0.44 lb d^{-1} (200 g d^{-1})]. Nitrification continues in the meadow with a 36% reduction in NH_4^+.

Total Phosphorus

Phosphorus is reduced by an average of 82% (from 15 mg L^{-1} to 2.6 mg L^{-1}). Reductions are attributed to three mechanisms: absorption onto bed substrate, compost, and liner (Volclay); plant uptake; and chemical precipitation. Reductions are higher during summer (90%) than winter (68%). Reduced effectiveness during winter has been reported in the literature and is caused in part by plant dormancy and decay and a net release of precipitated P (Black et al., 1981; Gearheart et al., 1984).

The effluent average was always under 6 mg L^{-1} except for one month, February 1985, when the average was 16 mg L^{-1}. Average concentrations were reduced in each component with the marsh being the most effective (69%) and the aeration basin the least effective (7%).

CONCLUSIONS

The marsh/pond/meadow system is capable of consistently meeting EPA's secondary treatment standards and even more stringent standards. High quality effluent was achieved without benefit of a thick stand of cattails, suggesting that the treatment mechanism for organic pollutants is primarily bacterial metabolism. An even greater degree of treatment therefore would be expected with the desired plant growth. The marsh component normally provides most of the treatment for the key parameters often regulated by NPDES permit. The meadow polishes the wastewater and serves as a safety net for meeting permit limits. Either component could be added as an upgrade to existing treatment facilities.

The aeration basin is effective primarily for BOD reduction. Of the key parameters that are often regulated by NPDES permits, the pond is effective in reducing NH_4-N and fecal coliforms.

A more detailed evaluation can be obtained from the primary author.

REFERENCES

Black, S. A., I. Wile, and G. Miller. 1981. Sewage effluent treatment in an artificial marshland. Paper presented at the 1981 WPCF Conference, Detroit, Michigan.

Gearheart, R. A., B. A. Finney, S. Wilbur, J. Williams, and D. Hull. 1984. The use of wetland treatment processes in water reuse. Future of Water Reuse, Volume 2. AWWA Research Foundation, Denver, Colorado.

Gersberg, R. M., B. V. Elkins, S. R. Lyon, and C. R. Goldman. 1986. Role of aquatic plants in wastewater treatment by artificial wetlands. Water Research 20:363-368.

AN EVALUATION OF THE LAKE JACKSON (FLORIDA) FILTER SYSTEM AND ARTIFICIAL MARSH ON NUTRIENT AND PARTICULATE REMOVAL FROM STORMWATER RUNOFF

B. J. Tuovila, T. H. Johengen, and P. A. LaRock
Department of Oceanography
Florida State University
Tallahassee, Florida 32306

J. B. Outland
Department of Environmental Regulation
Tallahassee, Florida 32301

D. H. Esry
Northwest Florida Water Management District
Havana, Florida 32333

M. Franklin
U. S. Geological Survey
Tallahassee, Florida 32301

ABSTRACT

Concern over pollution caused by stormwater runoff entering Lake Jackson from the city of Tallahassee culminated in the construction of a sediment filtration plant and artificial marsh to remove suspended solids and nutrients from the runoff prior to its discharge into the lake. Water samples collected during storm events were analyzed for a wide range of particulate and dissolved parameters, including suspended solids and various N and P species. Gauging stations, located at key points in the system, provided an accurate determination of water flow during sampling periods. Accurate flow data, rarely available in natural systems, permitted mass balance and removal efficiency calculations to be made. Results from the first year of study indicate that the system is capable of removing a large fraction of both suspended solids and dissolved and particulate nutrient material.

Keywords: Nutrient removal, pollution abatement, stormwater treatment, urban runoff.

ISBN 0-941463-00-1

INTRODUCTION

Non-point source pollution problems are among the most pervasive, persistent and diverse water quality problems facing the nation today (Peterson, 1985). Recent studies have indicated that pollution from urban runoff has caused major water quality problems with lakes, streams and reservoirs including nutrient enrichment, introduction of toxic materials, turbidity, depressed dissolved O_2 levels and heavy sediment deposition (Randall et al., 1978; Glandon et al., 1981; Baca et al., 1982). Non-point pollution can offset decreased nutrient loading obtained from improvement of point source treatment. Research directed under section 208 of the Clean Water Act determined that stormwater discharges were responsible for over half of the pollution loads entering Florida waters and, in some instances, stormwater discharges accounted for all the pollution loads (Livingston, 1985).

Comprehensive studies of the water quality of Lake Jackson, Leon County, Florida, have led to increased awareness of the significance of the pollution derived from stormwater runoff (Harris and Turner, 1974; Turner et al., 1977). Rapid urbanization in the Megginnis Arm watershed of Lake Jackson (white area, Figure 1) resulted in higher runoff with increased nutrient and sediment loads and subsequently began to visually accelerate the eutrophication of both Megginnis Arm and Lake Jackson itself. Working cooperatively, the Northwest Florida Water Management District and the Department of Environmental Regulation constructed a stormwater treatment facility along a natural inflow stream to Megginnis Arm (labeled Pond I and Marsh System, Figure 1). This facility, which began operation in the fall of 1983, incorporates both proven and innovative techniques for treatment of stormwater runoff entering Megginnis Arm.

Stormwater runoff enters a 163,000 m^3 detention pond (Figure 2), passes through a 1.8 ha intermittent underdrain filter to remove the majority of the sediment load and discharges into a triple box culvert running underneath Interstate 10. From there the stormwater enters a diversion impoundment, where it joins with direct runoff from I-10, and is channeled into an artificial marsh to remove nutrients. The 2.5 ha marsh has an average depth of 0.5 m, except for a 2.5 m deep settling basin near the outfall. The marsh is divided into three sections, and contains the emergent macrophyte *Typha* in the first section, *Scirpus* in the second section, and *Pontedaria* in the final section. A concrete spillway built into the impoundment dam, and a stoplog weir at the diversion impoundment leading into the marsh, permit runoff which exceeds the holding capacity of the system to bypass the filter and marsh and be discharged untreated into the receiving waters. An important feature of the system is the location of gauging stations at the inflow and outflow ends of both the impoundment and marsh. From the gauging data, the water Management District and US Geological Survey can calculate the flows entering, leaving and bypassing the various sections of the facility during a storm event.

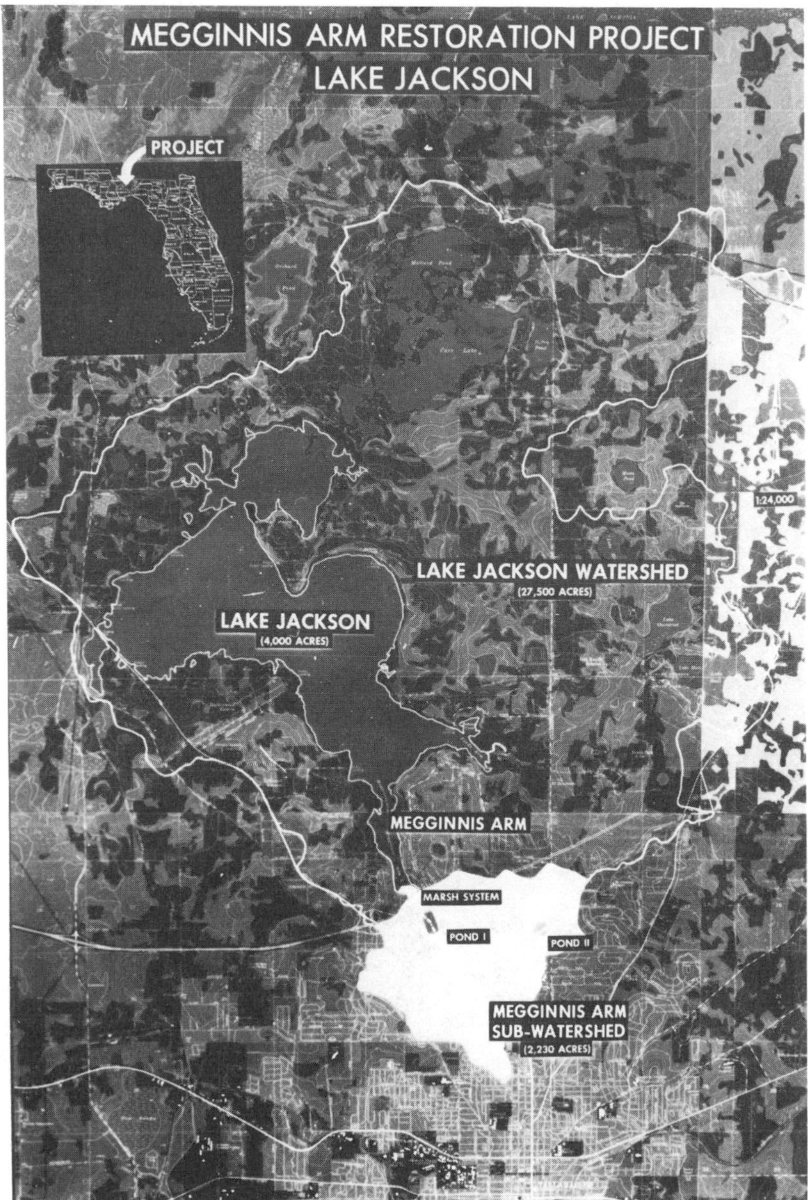

FIGURE 1. Location of project study area. The watershed for Megginnis Arm at the southern end of Lake Jackson is depicted in white. Stormwater drains into the impoundment and filtration system (Pond I) and the artificial marsh prior to discharge into Megginnis Arm.

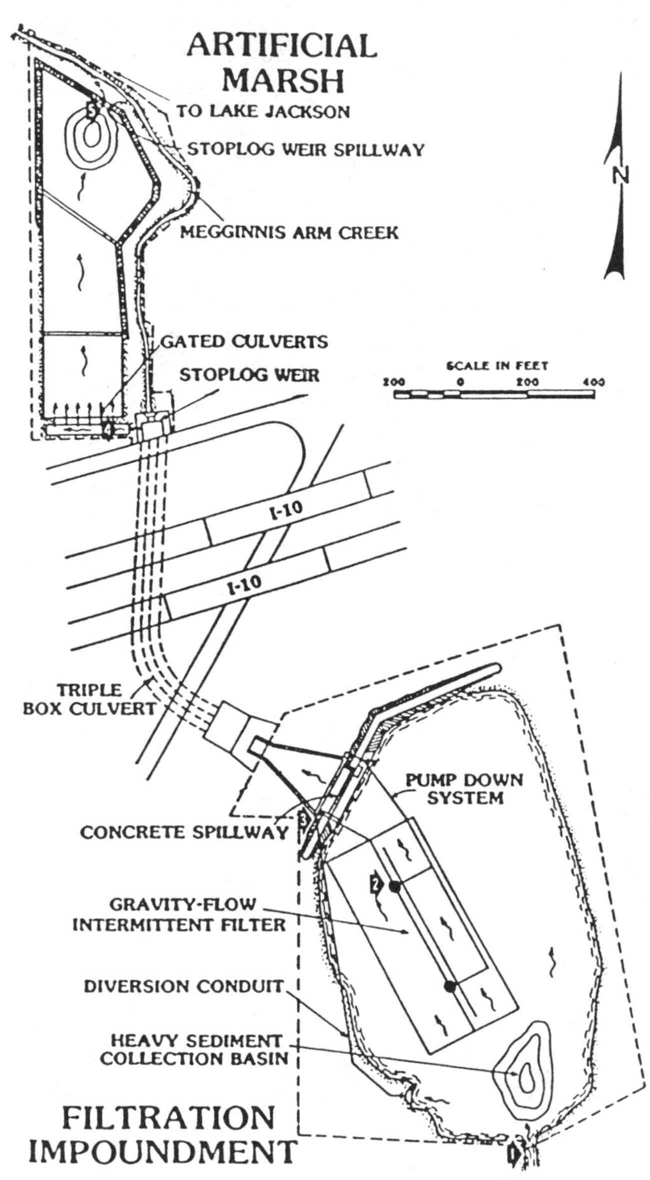

FIGURE 2. Detail of the treatment facility. Numbered arrows designate the location of sample stations.

MATERIALS AND METHODS

Water samples were collected at Stations 1-5 (Figure 2) using ISCO Model 1680 automatic samplers. Samples were taken at 15-30 min intervals during the initial flow period ("first flush") when flow rates and concentration values were changing most rapidly. The sample interval was gradually increased to 8-12 h during the remainder of the sampling period, which lasted from 3-14 d depending on the storm duration. Samples were analyzed for a variety of physical and chemical parameters including: inorganic and organic solids, Ca, Mg, chloride, NO_3^-, NO_2^-, NH_3, filtered and unfiltered phosphate, total N, and total P. All analyses were performed according to Standard Methods (APHA, 1985) and validated by an in-house quality assurance program. The flows into and out of the impoundment and marsh were calculated from weir equations and changes in pool elevation recorded during the storm. Bypass flow was also measured when it occurred. Loading values were calculated from the chemical concentrations of the samples, and the total volume of flow that occurred within the sample interval. The total loading for each parameter was the sum of the individual loadings integrated over the entire storm period. The efficiency of removal for each of the measured quantities was calculated as the percentage difference between the inflow and outflow mass in the impoundment, the marsh and the bypass canal.

RESULTS AND DISCUSSION

The feature of the Megginnis Arm treatment facility which most significantly affects its operational effectiveness is its holding capacity. Stormwater which exceeds the holding capacity of the impoundment flows over the spillway and receives little treatment other than settling of the heavier portion of its suspended solid load. In addition, due to unavoidable constraints on site location, a large volume of runoff from I-10 flows directly into the marsh diversion impoundment without passing through the main filtration impoundment. Since the diversion impoundment is relatively small, much of this runoff bypasses the marsh and flows untreated directly into Megginnis Arm. Thus, two modes of operation exist in this system resulting in significantly different levels of treatment of the stormwater--normal operation in which stormwater passes through the entire system and receives maximum treatment, and bypass operation in which a portion of the stormwater bypasses one or both sections of the facility and receives minimal treatment. Because of the configuration of the system, the location of sampling stations and the capability to determine inflow, outflow and bypass flow during a storm event, it is possible to calculate the mass balances for normal and bypass operation.

At several times during the monitoring period, bypass flow occurred at the impoundment spillway and the marsh diversion weir. A storm which was monitored for a period of 13 d beginning on June 11, 1985, provided an opportunity to determine the effects of bypassing complete treatment. The results of the mass balance calculations comparing the effectiveness of the facility under both normal and bypass operations (Table 1) showed that under normal operating conditions, the facility is capable of removing about 95% of the suspended solid load. When bypass occurs, this level is reduced to approximately 10%. Calcium and Mg, which both

TABLE 1. Comparison of pollutant loading changes under normal and bypass operating conditions† in the treatment facility during a storm on June 11, 1985.

Loading parameter	Normal operation	Bypass operation
	Mass Change in Total Loading	
Volume (m³)	-98310	$+1.029\ 10^{6}$
Inorg. Sol. (Kg)	-68449.7	-9140.1
Org. Sol. (Kg)	-13712.7	+259.9
Calcium (Kg)	+1222.3	+18057.5
Magnesium (Kg)	+286.5	+4705.6
Chloride (Kg)	-277.2	+1654.4
Total N (Kg)	-213.9	+364.3
Ammonia (Kg)	-2.9	+26.8
Nitrate (Kg)	-25.4	+128.2
Nitrite (Kg)	-2.2	+4.0
Total P (Kg)	-234.4	+137.3
Unfilt. Phos. (Kg)	-32.1	+244.3
Filt. Phos. (Kg)	-5.3	+14.2
	Percent Change in Total Loading	
Volume (%)	-31.2	+326.4
Inorg. Sol. (%)	-96.3	-12.9
Org. Sol. (%)	-94.1	+1.8
Calcium (%)	+58.6	+865.6
Magnesium (%)	+67.3	+1105.2
Chloride (%)	-51.9	+309.7
Total N (%)	-75.9	+129.4
Ammonia (%)	-37.4	+339.5
Nitrate (%)	-69.8	+352.5
Nitrite (%)	-75.3	+138.2
Total P (%)	-90.0	+52.7
Unfilt. Phos. (%)	-52.7	+401.7
Filt. Phos. (%)	-78.3	+211.5

†Under normal operating conditions, stormwater introduced into the impoundment flows through the filter bed and into the artificial marsh with discharge into Lake Jackson after receiving complete treatment. If the capacity of the system is exceeded, the excess stormwater will bypass the facility and discharge into the lake without treatment.

show moderate increases under normal operation due to leaching from the dolomitic limestone in the filter bed underdrain, increase as much as 1100% when bypass occurs. All other parameters measured show reductions ranging from 37 to 90% under normal operation; however, under bypass operation, increases ranging from 53 to 400% occur.

These results indicate that holding capacity and the amount of bypass permitted by a treatment facility of this type are crucial to its overall effectiveness. Under normal operating conditions, the Megginnis Arm treatment facility is capable of reducing most stormwater pollutant loadings by a large percentage. However, when bypass occurs, large increases in pollutant loading are noted, due probably to leaching from temporarily resuspended sediments and mixing with untreated runoff. Since holding capacity is so important to the effectiveness of this type of system, the initial design and construction of similar systems should match holding capacity as closely as possible with the maximum anticipated volume of storm runoff. Once in operation, maintaining this capacity is vital to the continued effectiveness of the system. In the Megginnis Arm treatment facility, heavy sedimentation in the main filtration impoundment has already begun and dredging will soon be necessary. Scraping the filter bed surface to remove accumulated silt and clay is essential to maintain a high flow rate through the filter to avoid excessive accumulation of stormwater in the impoundment during periods of multiple storm events. Likewise, the holding capacity of the marsh must be maintained by occasional dredging as well as harvesting of accumulated plant biomass, to prevent its decay and the resulting release of nutrients. Under normal operating conditions, this type of system has proven to be highly effective and relatively low in maintenance cost and can serve as a model for future systems designed to treat urban stormwater runoff.

REFERENCES

Baca, E., P. B. Bedient, and R. Olson. 1982. Urban impacts of water supply reservoir. J. Environ. Eng. Div., ASCE, Vol. 108, No. EE1. p. 73-87.

Glandon, R. P., F. C. Payne, C. D. McNabb, and T. R. Batterson. 1981. A comparison of rain-relayed phosphorus and nitrogen loading from urban, wetland and agricultural sources. Water Research, Vol. 15. p. 81-887.

Harris, R. C., and R. R. Turner. 1974. Job completion report, Lake Jackson investigations. Florida State University Marine Laboratory, Tallahassee, Florida. 231 pp.

Livingston, E. H., and J. H. Cox. 1985. Urban stormwater quality management: The Florida experience. p. 289-292. In Perspectives on Nonpoint Source Pollution. EPA 440/5-85-001.

Peterson, S. A., W. E. Miller, J. C. Greene, and C. A. Callahan. 1985. Use of bioassays to determine potential toxicity effects of environmental pollutants. p. 38-45. In Perspectives on Nonpoint Source Pollution. EPA 440/5-85-001.

Randal, C. W., T. J. Grizzard, and R. C. Hoehn. 1978. Effect of upstream control on a water supply reservoir. J. Water Pollut. Control Fed. 4812:2687-2702.

Turner, R. R., T. M. Burton, and R. C. Harris. 1977. Lake Jackson watershed study. p. 19-32. In D. L. Correl (ed.) Watershed Research in Eastern North America. A Workshop to Compare Results. Vol. 1. Chesapeake Bay Center for Environmental Studies. Edgewater, Maryland.

REVIEW OF OPERATIONS AND PERFORMANCE DATA ON FIVE WATER HYACINTH BASED TREATMENT SYSTEMS IN FLORIDA

E. A. Stewart III, D. L. Haselow, and N. M. Wyse
Amasek, Inc.
3708 N. U.S. 1
Cocoa, Florida 32926

ABSTRACT

Operational data are reviewed from five water hyacinth [*Eichhornia crassipes* (Mart) Solms] based wastewater treatment systems in Florida. Discussions are also presented regarding the impact of crop growth and viability upon system performance. A model developed around the Monod relationship provides performance projections which are compared to actual values. Model projections are sufficiently conservative for operational dependability, with N removal in particular being much more dependent upon removal mechanisms not associated with direct plant uptake. Information regarding system management as related to system performance, harvesting needs and pest/pathogen control is presented.

Keywords: Nutrient removal mechanisms, plant uptake, simulation model, wastewater, system management, harvesting.

INTRODUCTION

While the concept of using aquatic vegetation, particularly the water hyacinth [*Eichhornia crassipes* (Mart) Solms], for wastewater treatment has been extensively investigated and reviewed for nearly 20 years, there still remains little information regarding the operational needs associated with large scale applications. Work by Amasek, Inc., in Florida has been directed principally towards the commercial application of this technology for domestic wastewater treatment, a need which is most critical in Florida's regulation and management of surface waters. The purpose of this paper was: 1) to describe the model for predicting nutrient removal; 2) review operational data from five water hyacinth-based wastewater treatment systems; and 3) compare model predictions with operational data.

ISBN 0-941463-00-1

MODEL DESCRIPTION

In developing an operations and design approach to meet these practical demands, a model was developed from field studies (Stewart et al., 1984) in which nutrient removal was considered to be accomplished by two basic means; direct plant uptake and all other processes. The direct plant uptake fraction was expressed using the Monod relationship:

$$Uf = Ufmax\ [S/(Ks+S)] \qquad [1]$$

where Uf = specific field growth rate, d^{-1}; S = concentration of limiting factor mg L^{-1}; Ks = concentration of limiting factor when Uf = Ufmax; Ufmax = maximum potential field growth rate, d^{-1}.

This relationship was adjusted in accordance with the V.'ant Hoff Arrhenius relationship:

$$U_2/U_1 = \theta\ T_2 - T_1 \qquad [2]$$

where U_1, U_2 = specific field growth rate at temperatures T_1, T_2; T_1, T_2 = air temperatures in K°; θ = constant (1.04 - 1.09).

While other researchers (Musil and Breen, 1977), have evaluated hyacinth growth dynamics on a small scale finding U to approach 0.15 d^{-1}, it was felt that measurements from large scale operations would give a more practical value. Using the Lineweaver-Burke (1934) approach, it was determined (Stewart et al., 1984) that Ufmax of 0.06 d^{-1} was an appropriate value for field conditions, with total N serving as the limiting nutrient, at Ks = 5 mg L^{-1}.

In completing the model, a final nutrient concentration was expressed as a function of flow out, loads in and removal by direct uptake and other processes.

$$Cn = (QICi - Nu - NI)/Qo \qquad [3]$$

where, Cn = effluent nutrient concentration; Ci = influent nutrient concentration; QI = daily flow in; Qo = daily flow out; Nu = daily mass nutrient removal by plant uptake; NI = daily mass nutrient removal by incidental processes.

In final form the developed equation becomes:

$$Cn = \frac{(1-Km)\ Qf\ CI - Pw\ Pn\ Z\ [\exp\ (UfTaf) - 1]}{(1-Km)\ Qo} \qquad [4]$$

where Km = fraction of total nutrient removed not attributable to direct plant uptake; Pw = solids fraction of the crop; Pn = fraction of nutrients in dry weight of crop; Z = standing crop; Taf = temperature adjustment factor; Taf = $1/_{\theta}\ 298 - T_1$.

TESTING MODEL RELIABILITY

Amasek operated five hyacinth based systems in Florida and collected pertinent water quality and flow data for a one year period. Operational practices exercised during this period included maintenance through harvesting, control of pests and pathogens and to maintain a desired crop density maintenance between 12 to 19 kg (fresh wt) m^{-2} (Ryther et al., 1979) and addition of necessary macro and micronutrients (particularly Fe). Standing crop was measured weekly in each system, and plant nutrient content monitored regularly to permit a reasonable assessment of direct plant uptake.

Applied empirical parameter values were as follows: Kn for N 0.3 - 0.6; Kp for P 0 - 0.6; $\theta = 1.06$; Ufmax = 0.04 d^{-1} to 0.06 d^{-1}; Pn for N 0.025 - 0.04; Pp for P 0.005 - 0.008; and Pw = 0.05.

SITES OF INVESTIGATION

The five operating projects all varied in size and performance requirements (Table 1). Of the five systems, the City of Orlando and the Loxahatchee lagoons were sealed with a clay admix to prevent interface with the ground water. The Naval Training Center (NTC) facility and City of Kissimmee facility contained natural clay seals. The City of Melbourne system was constructed with underdrains. However, they were not used as part of this operation. Both the Melbourne and Kissimmee systems which had been previously used as wastewater polishing ponds were characterized by a highly organic sediment. The NTC facility lagoons occasionally received some solids from the contributing secondary systems. These solids were comprised largely of alum floc and organic material. Accumulation of this material was noted in the receiving area of the lagoons. Both the Iron Bridge and Loxahatchee lagoon sediments were largely inorganic, as they received a highly treated low solids effluent.

RESULTS AND DISCUSSION

System performance in terms of N and P influent and effluent concentration are noted in Figures 1 and 2. Desired effluent N and P goals were met at each system. In general, the model sufficiently tracked performance for operational purposes. A comparison of actual and model projected effluent values for N and P are presented in Table 2.

Kissimmee

Model projections for Kissimmee were notably optimistic for both N and P for the period of March 1985 through December 1985, even when relatively conservative values are used for Ufmax (0.04 d^{-1}) and the incidental loss coefficients (Kn = 0.3, Kp = 0). A more detailed review of the nutrient budget during this time period by Amasek (1986) revealed that large amounts of unmonitored nutrients were being contributed to the system from an extraneous source. Indications were that the underlying organic sediments served as an autochthonous nutrient source, although N_2 fixation may also have been a contributor. It was determined that nearly

TABLE 1. Description of five systems investigated.

Name	Flow	Influent BOD_5, TSS, TN, TP	Lagoon size and description	Effluent goals BOD_5, TSS, TN, TP	Comments
	$m^3\ d^{-1}$	---mg L^{-1}---		----mg L^{-1}----	
Orlando, NTC McCoy	3,024-4,536	10-20,10-20, 10-20,1-3	0.61 ha, detention time less than 24 h	0-10,0-5, 5-10,0.5-1	Lagoons added to increase permitted capacity
Orlando, Iron Bridge	30,240	2-6,2-6, 12-16,0.2-1	12.15 ha, detention time 3-5 d, 2 lagoons in paralled	2.5,2.5, 10.5-14.5,0.5	Require 45.4 kg-N removed per day. Lagoons added to increase permitted capacity.
Melbourne, David B. Lee	9,450-13,230	20-40,20-40, 20-60,2-6	4.86 ha, detention time 3 d or less 4 lagoons, 2 in series set as 2 parallel systems	20,20, 14-25,2-5	Require 62 kg-N removed per day. Lagoons are old perc ponds converted to hyacinth lagoons to increase permitted capacity.
Loxahatchee River Environmental Control District Jupiter, FL	7,560-11,340	1-6,1-6 1-3,0.5-1.5	3.44 ha, detention time 5-7 d. One lagoon	0-5,0-5, 3,1	Hyacinth originally introduced to control N during upset periods and control suspended solids prior to spray irrigation.
Kissimmee, Martin Street	588	6,20, 15,1.5	1.49 ha, detention time over 20 d, 2 lagoons in series	5,5, 2.5,0.5	Funded by State of Fla. to determine treatment capabilities of hyacinths.

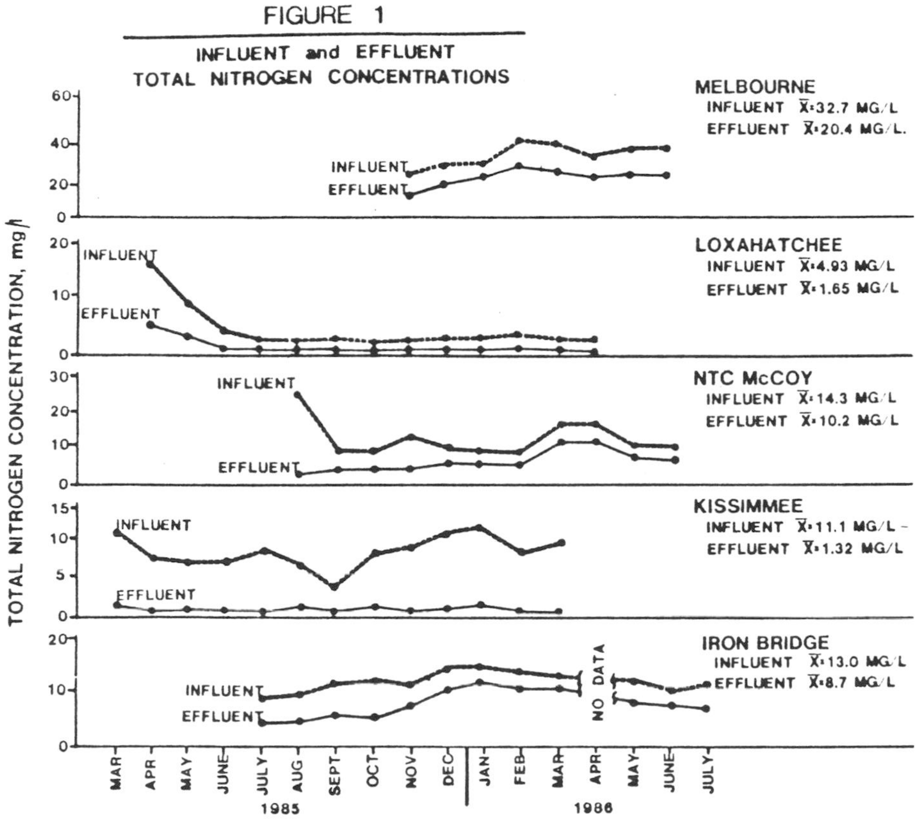

TABLE 2. Comparison of nutrient effluent values to projected values.

System	Influent N	Influent P	Actual effluent N	Actual effluent P	Projected effluent N	Projected effluent P	Model parameters Ufmax	Model parameters Kn	Model parameters Kp
	mg L^{-1}						d^{-1}		
Kissimmee	11.1	1.46	1.32	0.27	-3.6	-0.65	0.04	0.3	0
Iron Bridge	13.0	0.74	8.7	0.35	9.1	0.41	0.04	0.3	0
NTC McCoy	14.3	1.97	10.2	0.66	12.4	0.69	0.04	0.6	0.5
Loxahatchee	4.93	1.06	1.65	0.55	1.81	0.71	0.04	0.3	0
Melbourne	32.7	4.33	20.4	3.70	25.6	3.57	0.06	0.6	0

20% of the removed N and 23% of the removed P came from autochthonous sources. Of the removed N, 56% was accountable through direct plant uptake while 44% was attributed to incidental mechanisms (Kn = 0.44). Similarly, nearly 65% of the P removed

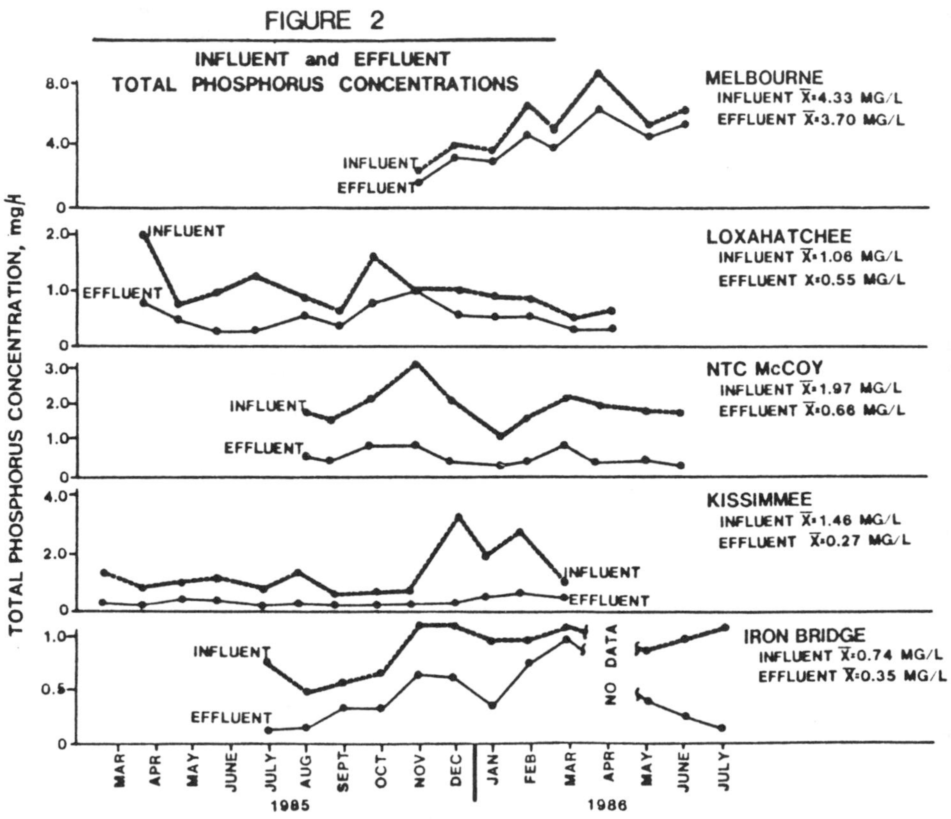

was accountable through direct plant uptake, while 35% was attributed to incidental mechanisms (Kp = 0.35)--in this case probably sedimentation within the receiving lagoon. The Kissimmee study clearly indicated the importance of sediment dynamics when low effluent concentrations are required. Subsequently, it is suggested that during design, considerations should be given to careful selection of pond sediments.

Iron Bridge

Performance at Iron Bridge followed the model projections rather closely, particularly for N, with Ufmax at 0.04 d^{-1}, Kn = 0.3 and Kp = 0.0. This system is of interest because of an upset condition that occurred between November 1985 and May 1986. The upset was characterized by a loss of standing crop due to infestation by the hyacinth weevil, encroaching aquatic vegetation, possible toxic influences and a following debilitating opportunistic infection by the water mold <u>Pythium</u> sp. The correlation between mass removal and standing crop which is shown in Figure 3, indicates that N removal, regardless of the mechanisms involved, is dependent upon standing crop viability and mass. At the Iron Bridge facility, the actual Kn value for the study period was about 0.6 with Kp being approximately 0.3. Accordingly, field growth was somewhat lower than projected, particularly during the upset period. Using the more conservative values of Kn = 0.3 and Kp = 0, however, provides the operation the necessary degree of safety for ensuring system performance.

NTC McCoy

The facility at NTC McCoy is characterized by a high hydraulic and nutrient loading rate. Incidental mechanisms played an important role in nutrient removal, with the model showing reasonable projections at Kn = 0.6 and Kp = 0.5. Phosphorus loss is largely due to precipitation as aluminum phosphate, which is carried over from the secondary clarifiers.

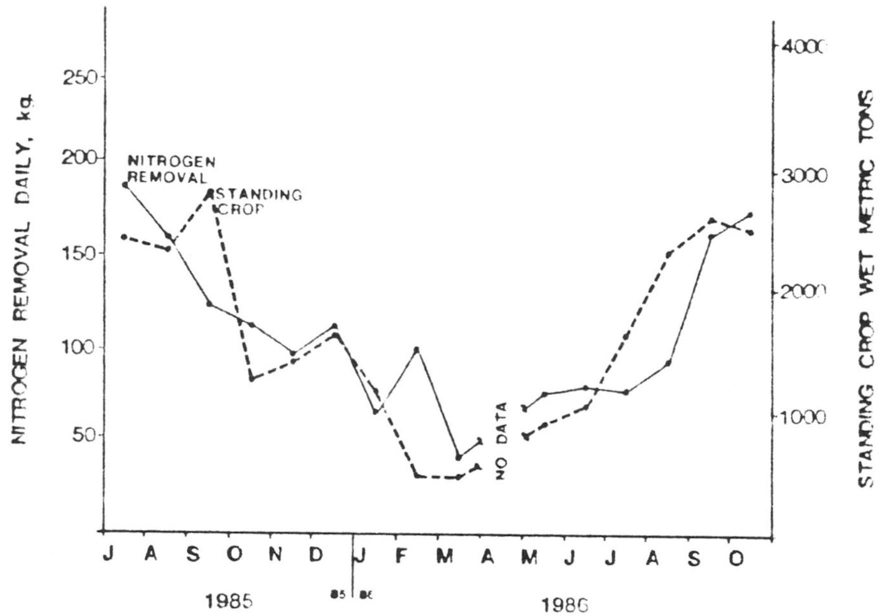

FIGURE 3. Standing crop and system N removal performance at Iron Bridge.

Loxahatchee

This system's response was adequately simulated by the model, even at lower concentrations of N (1.5 mg L^{-1}).

Melbourne

Incidental losses of N, as with NTC McCoy, were very influential at Melbourne. Even with Kn = 0.6 and Ufmax at 0.06 d^{-1}, projections were conservative. The actual average Kn value for the system over the study period was calculated at 0.90 with Kp averaging near zero. Some drop in system performance and growth rate was noted from March to May 1986, at a time in which encroachment by other aquatic species (principally, alligator weed, *Alternanthera* sp.), was most extensive. This problem was eliminated during June 1986. Observed growth rates were generally near those projected during most of the study period.

In establishing initial design criteria and operational parameters, the model as presented is appropriate, providing sufficient safety margin to ensure performance. It was observed that growth rate and plant uptake is a more predictable parameter, with other removal mechanisms showing wide variations, depending upon water quality, crop health, temperature, etc. Therefore, while it is tempting to suggest that system design and operation can be established upon processes other than direct plant uptake (DeBusk and Ryther, 1984; Weber and Tchobanoglous, 1985), until these processes can be properly identified, and their dynamics predicted, it may be precarious to depart from the more conservative uptake model. Using the values of Ufmax at 0.04 d^{-1} and a Kn at 0.3 and Kp at 0.0, can result in a safe design and operation. As research and development progresses, the impact of incidental processes should become more predictable. Significant work regarding the influences of nitrification and denitrification have already been conducted by Reddy (1984) and Weber and Tchobanoglous (1986) in hyacinth cultures. Other processes which need research attention are sediment influences, internal ecological influences, and the role of larval emergence and external predation.

One significant observation, as previously noted, is the importance of crop viability to overall performance. This suggests that the hyacinth crop itself directly facilitates the major nutrient removal processes. This has been suggested by Reddy (1984) and Weber and Tchobanoglous (1986), who noted that nitrification is probably supported within the root zone by active pumping of O_2 through the plant's vascular system to the nitrifying population.

In managing large-scale systems, while the concept of non-harvesting/non-management has some obvious appeal, it is not a practical approach to maintaining crop viability where heavy grazing by pests, such as the hyacinth weevil (*Neochetina eichhorniae*) is prevalent, or successional pressures from other aquatic plants are likely to occur. Consequently, some method of effective crop harvesting must be incorporated into design and operational programming. While it may not be needed to harvest at a level to optimize crop yield, sufficient plant material should be removed to maintain crop viability and control pest populations.

CONCLUSIONS

The importance of processes other than direct plant uptake for nutrient removal varied with the five systems studied. The direct correlation between the rate of areal loading and areal removal as noted in Figure 4, indicates that at least in the case of N that nutrient availability influences the rate of nutrient removal, and that direct plant uptake dominates at lower loading rates. In the case of P, this correlation is not so obvious. Except for the condition presented by the NTC data, areal removal rates do not appear to be influenced by influent loading rates. Based upon the data and findings presented, a need can be clearly seen to expand our ability to identify all of the nutrient removal

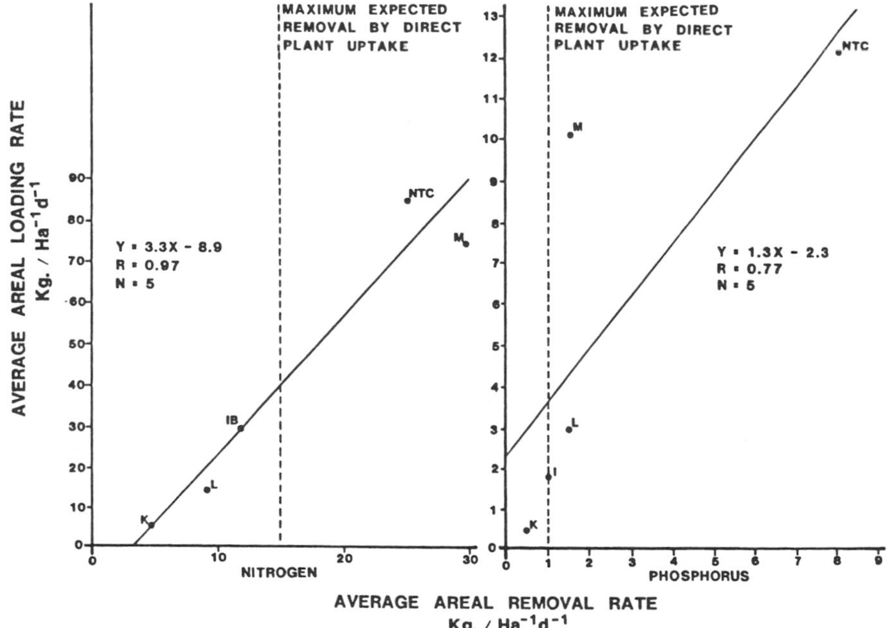

FIGURE 4. Relationship of areal loading and removal rates for N and P.

processes involved in hyacinth systems. At this time, establishing design and operations around direct plant uptake appears legitimate and adequately conservative to ensure system performance.

REFERENCES

Amasek, Inc. 1986. Assessment of OPERATIONS, Water Hyacinth Nutrient Removal Treatment Process Pilot Plant: City of Kissimmee. Florida Department of Environmental Regulation. FEID #59-6000348. Prepared for Briley Wild and Associates, Inc., Ormond Beach, FL.

DeBusk, T. A., and J. H. Ryther. 1984. Nutrient removal from domestic wastewater by water hyacinths. The importance of plant growth, detritus production, and denitrification. Future of Water Reuse. Proceedings: Water Reuse Symposium III. San Diego, CA. p. 713-723.

Lineweaver, H., and D. Burk. 1934. The determination of enzyme dissociation constants. J. Am. Chem. Soc. 56:658.

Musil, C. F., and C. M. Breen. 1977. The application of growth kinetics to the control of Eichhornia crassipes (Mart) Solms. through nutrient removal by mechanical harvesting. Hydrobiologia 53:165.

Reddy, K. R.. 1984. Nutrient transformations in aquatic macrophyte filters used for water purification. Future of Water Reuse Proceedings: Water Reuse Symposium III. San Diego, CA. p. 660-678.

Ryther, J. H., D. W. LaVergne, M. D. Banisak, and T. A. DeBusk. 1979. Biomass production by marine and fresh water plants. Proceedings Third Annual Biomass Energy Systems Conference. SERI/TP-33-285.

Stewart, E. A., D. L. Haselow, and N. M. Wyse. 1984. A practical model for water hyacinth based wastewater management. Design and Operation. Future of Water Reuse. Proceedings: Water Reuse Symposium III. San Diego, CA. p. 679-702.

Weber, A. A., and G. Tchobanoglous. 1985. Rational design parameters for ammonia conversion in water hyacinth treatment systems. J. Water Pollut. Control Fed. 57:316-323.

Weber, A. A., and G. Tchobanoglous. 1986. Prediction of nitrification in water hyacinth systems. J. Water Pollut. Control Fed. 58:376-380.

PENNYWORT AND DUCKWEED MARSH SYSTEM FOR UPGRADING WASTEWATER EFFLUENT FROM A MECHANICAL PACKAGE PLANT

B. C. Wolverton and R. C. McCaleb
National Aeronautics and Space Administration
National Space Technology Laboratories
NSTL, Mississippi 39529

ABSTRACT

A small artificial marsh system has been used to upgrade the effluent from a mechanical package plant for over seven years. The artificial marsh has a hydraulic retention time of 7 to 8 d. Although originally stocked with water hyacinth (Eichhornia crassipes), extremely cold winters shifted the predominant aquatic macrophyte from the water hyacinth to a dual system of pennywort (Hydrocotyle umbellata) in the summer and duckweed (Lemna, Spirodela, and Wolffia spp.) in the winter.

The artificial marsh system maintained the wastewater in aerobic conditions. The yearly average effluent BOD_5 was reduced from 35.5 mg L^{-1} to 6.2 and 3.0 mg L^{-1} with water hyacinth and pennywort/duckweed, respectively. The yearly average TSS were reduced from 47.7 mg L^{-1} to 5.8 and 11.5 mg L^{-1}, respectively. The artificial marsh system proved to be an effective and reliable post-treatment process to upgrade the effluent from a mechanical package treatment plant to secondary standards of 30 mg L^{-1} BOD_5 and TSS.

Keywords: Duckweed, water pennywort, Lemna, Spirodela, Wolffia, Hydrocotyle umbellata, artificial marsh, wastewater treatment.

INTRODUCTION

Floating vascular aquatic plants, particularly the water hyacinth (Eichhornia crassipes), have proved useful as an integral part of major domestic wastewater treatment systems (Dinges, 1978; McDonald and Wolverton, 1980; Wolverton and McDonald, 1979a,b). Other floating plants such as duckweed (Lemna minor, Spirodela polyrhiza and Wolffia sp.) and pennywort (Hydrocotyle umbellata) can be used in biological treatment systems to bridge the gap during the winter months when water hyacinth growth is reduced or

ISBN 0-941463-00-1

stopped (Boyd, 1969; Culley and Epps, 1973; Reddy and DeBusk, 1984,1985a,b).

The National Aeronautics and Space Administration (NASA) at the National Space Technology Laboratories (NSTL) has several vascular aquatic plant waste treatment systems. One is used to upgrade a mechanical package treatment plant which treats domestic sewage from 64-68 office workers. Comparative data from this system are presented here.

SYSTEM DESCRIPTION

The mechanical package plant at NSTL, Mississippi, is a small system, 2.1 m (7 ft) in diameter which treats approximately 7.57 m^3 of domestic sewage daily. Originally installed in 1965, no additional office space was tied into the system and total personnel fluctuated little during the study period 1977-1985. During the winter of 1978-79, effluent from the package plant was diverted into an artificial marsh system consisting of a reservoir 35 m L x 4.3 m W x 0.38 m D, lined with 20 mil PVC. Effluent from the package plant enters one end of the pond and is discharged through a tablet chlorinator at the other end. The flow rate is estimated to be 7.57 m^3 d^{-1} and has not significantly changed over the years.

The new reservoir was originally stocked with water hyacinths in February, 1979, with coverage reaching 100% during the first summer. After the first three years, extremely cold winters in the area caused the dominant aquatic vegetation to shift from water hyacinth to pennywort in the spring and summer and duckweed in late fall and winter. In the winter (December through March), pennywort covered 90% of the lagoon surface with duckweed filling in around the plants. By May of each year, pennywort coverage would naturally reduce to less than 20% of the lagoon surface and a thick duckweed cover over the entire surface would form. Water hyacinths were partially harvested once each summer during 1979 and 1980. After that no further plants have been removed from the system.

MONITORING AND ANALYSIS PROCEDURES

Grab samples were collected biweekly at the discharge point of the package plant prior to installing the reservoir for aquatic plants. After the artificial marsh system was included in the treatment train, a representative sample from the discharge of the package plant was no longer possible since the intake to the reservoir was submerged. At that time grab samples were taken biweekly at the discharge point of the artificial marsh.

Dissolved oxygen (DO) measurements were taken in the field using a portable YSI O_2 meter and probe. The samples were analyzed for 5 d biochemical oxygen demand (BOD_5), total suspended solids (TSS), and pH according to standard methods (APHA, 1971).

RESULTS AND DISCUSSION

There was little pH variation in the package plant effluent when treated with water hyacinth or pennywort/duckweed. All pH values were in the acceptable range of 6.0-9.0. Average pH values were 7.34 ± 0.37, 7.57 ± 0.31 and 7.24 ± 0.16, for package plant effluent and effluent treated with water hyacinth and pennywort/duckweed, respectively.

The DO measurements (Table 1) indicate that water hyacinth is more effective in reoxygenating the water than pennywort/duckweed. The yearly average effluent DO of 4.4 mg L^{-1} with water hyacinth was almost double the average DO with pennywort/duckweed. The most significant differential occurred during the winter months of December through March. Every DO measurement taken year-round was above 1.0 mg L^{-1}, indicating that the system remained aerobic throughout the year.

In general, the extent of the root system of water hyacinth was greater or equal to that of pennywort. Emergent hydrophytes *Menyanthes trifoliata* and *Eriophorum angustifolium*, *Oryza sativa*, and *Spartina alterniflora* reported to release O_2 from their root tips into an anaerobic environment. Oxygen was possibly emitted into the aqueous medium from the roots. Sculthorpe and Duncan (1967) reviewed this subject and concluded that linear gradients of O_2 concentration in shoots to roots support the hypothesis that underground organs derive their O_2 supply from the aerial or floating foliage. In addition, mature foliage which has ceased to

TABLE 1. Average dissolved oxygen (DO) for package plant effluent before and after the addition of an aquatic plant treatment system.

Month	Package plant effluent (1977-78)	Effluent Treatment: Water hyacinth (1979-80)	Effluent Treatment: Pennywort and Duckweed (1984-85)
	DO, mg L^{-1}		
June	3.1	2.3	1.5
July	3.7	3.8	3.1
August	3.3	4.1	1.9
September	3.7	2.3	1.6
October	4.5	1.9	1.7
November	4.1	3.4	2.4
December	2.6	7.4	2.8
January	4.7	7.0	2.6
February	4.7	7.2	3.0
March	3.8	6.0	3.0
April	3.5	3.7	1.9
May	2.7	3.9	1.8
Yearly Average	3.7	4.4	2.3

TABLE 2. Average 5 d biochemical oxygen demand (BOD_5) for package plant effluent before and after the addition of an aquatic plant treatment system.

Month	Package plant effluent (1977-78)	Effluent Treatment	
		Water hyacinth (1979-80)	Pennywort and Duckweed (1984-85)
	BOD_5, mg L^{-1}		
June	22.6	7.5	2.8
July	15.6	3.4	0.2
August	27.3	5.2	1.8
September	115.1	2.3	2.8
October	27.7	5.1	3.0
November	19.9	7.9	3.6
December	41.7	7.3	2.0
January	50.9	5.7	2.7
February	61.5	6.3	1.5
March	15.5	11.9	2.0
April	14.5	7.0	6.4
May	13.8	5.3	7.0
Yearly Average	35.5	6.2	3.0

TABLE 3. Average total suspended solids (TSS) for package plant effluent before and after the addition of an aquatic plant system.

Month	Package plant effluent (1977-78)	Effluent Treatment	
		Water hyacinth (1979-80)	Pennywort and Duckweed (1984-85)
	TSS, mg L^{-1}		
June	39.8	8.3	16.9
July	38.0	6.5	6.7
August	58.9	3.6	1.5
September	38.6	6.8	4.0
October	46.3	3.6	8.5
November	51.1	2.9	8.0
December	52.0	9.5	10.7
January	56.5	1.5	13.0
February	67.3	6.4	12.8
March	39.8	6.5	25.7
April	56.0	7.1	15.6
May	28.4	6.7	15.5
Yearly Average	47.7	5.8	11.5

grow supplied more O_2 to underground or submerged organs than young leaves do.

The BOD_5 reductions (Table 2) clearly indicate the benefit of having post-treatment with an artificial marsh system. The mechanical package plant alone provided secondary treatment approximately 66% of the time. After a 7 to 8 d detention in the artificial marsh system, the effluent BOD_5 averaged 6.2 mg L^{-1} with water hyacinth and 3.0 mg L^{-1} with pennywort/duckweed.

The mechanical package plant effluent contained over 30 mg L^{-1} total suspended solids (TSS) on a monthly average basis all but one month of the 12 month data period (Table 3). The artificial marsh system consistently brought the TSS concentrations below 30 mg L^{-1} as shown in Table 3. The TSS trend with water hyacinth and pennywort/duckweed was opposite to that for BOD_5. The pennywort/duckweed yearly average TSS of 11.5 mg L^{-1} was almost double the yearly average of 5.8 mg L^{-1} for water hyacinth.

The artificial marsh system in this application proved to be an effective and reliable system to upgrade effluent from a mechanical package plant. The system construction was simple and the yearly maintenance since its installation in early 1979 minimal. The system has operated since 1980 with no harvesting or external energy inputs. Mosquito breeding is not a problem due to a large population of mosquito fish (Gambusia sp.) which can survive due to the aerobic conditions.

REFERENCES

American Public Health Association (APHA). 1971. Standard methods for the examination of water and wastewater. 13th ed. APHA, Washington, DC.

Boyd, C. E. 1969. Vascular aquatic plants for mineral nutrient removal from polluted waters. Econ. Botany 23:95-103.

Culley, D. D., and E. A. Epps. 1973. Use of duckweed for waste treatment and animal feed. J. Water Pollut. Control Fed. 45:337-347.

Dinges, R. 1978. Upgrading stabilization pond effluent by water hyacinth culture. J. Water Pollut. Control Fed. 50:833-845.

McDonald, R. C., and B. C. Wolverton. 1980. Comparative study of wastewater lagoon with and without water hyacinth. Econ. Botany 34:101-110.

Reddy, K. R., and W. F. DeBusk. 1984. Growth characteristics of aquatic macrophytes cultured in nutrient-enriched water: I. Water hyacinth, water lettuce, and pennywort. Econ. Botany 38:229-239.

Reddy, K. R., and W. F. DeBusk. 1985a. Growth characteristics of aquatic macrophytes cultured in nutrient-enriched water. II. Azolla, duckweed, and salvinia. Econ. Botany 39:200-208.

Reddy, K. R., and W. F. DeBusk. 1985b. Nutrient removal potential of selected aquatic macrophytes. J. Environ. Qual. 14:459-462.

Wolverton, B. C, and R. C. McDonald. 1979b. Water hyacinths for upgrading sewage lagoons to meet advanced wastewater treatment standards. NASA Technical Memorandum TM-X-72720, October 1979.

Sculthorpe, C. D. 1967. The biology of aquatic vascular plants. Edward Arnold Ltd., London. p. 157-164.

Wolverton, B. C., and R. C. McDonald. 1979a. Upgrading facultative wastewater lagoons with vascular aquatic plants. J. Water Pollut. Control Fed. 51:305-313.

MUNICIPAL WASTEWATER PURIFICATION IN A VEGETATIVE FILTER BED: A DEMONSTRATION

A. A. Theisen
SaLUT, Inc.
P. O. Box 1153
Columbia, Maryland 21044

C. D. Martin
Town of Emmitsburg
P. O. Box 380
Emmitsburg, Maryland 21727

ABSTRACT

A limestone gravel bed (76.2 m x 9.1 m x 0.86 m) planted to cattail (Typha spp.) has been in operation for the treatment of municipal wastewater in the Town of Emmitsburg, northwestern Maryland, since September 1984. Approximately 110 m^3 d^{-1} of secondary wastewater was purified to 10 mg L^{-1} or less of TSS since mid-May 1985. Since late June 1985 and through March 1986, the BOD_5 content ranged from a low of 4 mg L^{-1} to a high of 20 mg L^{-1}.

Keywords: Constructed wetlands, cattail, gravel filter bed, secondary wastewater treatment, BOD_5, TSS, N removal.

INTRODUCTION

The ability of aquatic plants in natural wetlands to reduce BOD_5, pathogens, N and other impurities in wastewater has led to the planned use of wetlands for the secondary treatment of wastewater (Hyde et al., 1984). It has also led to the design of constructed aquatic systems for the treatment of wastewater (Seidel and Happel, 1978; Wolverton et al., 1983).

In greenhouse experiments, SaLUT observed that when raw sewage was circulated through test basins planted to common reed (Phragmites australis) and duck potato (Sagittaria latifolia), 90% of the suspended solids and 80% of the BOD_5 were removed. When clarified wastewater was applied, the common reed basins removed 85% of the TSS and 82% of the BOD_5 (SaLUT, 1984).

Aquatic Plants for Water Treatment
and Resource Recovery
K.R. Reddy and W.H. Smith (Eds.)

ISBN 0-941463-00-1

MATERIALS AND METHODS

In 1984, a vegetative filter bed (VFB) containing Pennsylvania 2B crushed rock (<=2,5 cm) (length = 76.2 m, width = 9.1 m and depth = 0.86 m) was designed by SaLUT for the Town of Emmitsburg in northwestern Maryland to treat 189 m^3 d^{-1} of secondary effluent (after passage through a clarifier and a very erratic trickling filter).

Bentonite, in the ratio of 562 kg m^{-2} of soil surface, was mixed with the top 25.4 cm of soil to render it impermeable. Perforated 20.3 cm pipes allow feeding of wastewater and draining of effluent. Flow valves control influent and effluent. The residence time, depending on the average daily load, varied from 2.5 d at 128.7 m^3 d^{-1} to 3.3 d at 96.5 m^3 d^{-1}.

Two-hundred cattail plants were planted in August 1984 and a further 200 were planted in July 1985. BOD_5, TSS, DO, SS, and pH measurements were made on composite samples collected once a week since September 1984. Since it was not possible to withdraw a composite sample from the influent end of the VFB, the composition of the total plant effluent is taken as an indication of what entered the VFB as influent.

RESULTS AND DISCUSSION

In the time period mid-January through June 1985, when the cattail population in the VFB was minimal (less than 20% of the VFB area was covered by immature cattail plants in May 1985), the VFB removed only 57% to 68% of the BOD_5. When the cattail population was more fully established and in full growth over 25% to 30% of the VFB area, the BOD_5 of the effluent dropped to an average of 11 mg L^{-1} in the summer and to less than 10 mg L^{-1} in the fall of 1985. In the winter of 1986, the concentration of BOD_5, in spite of the cold and very often freezing temperature, varied from a low of 7 mg L^{-1} to a high of 20 mg L^{-1} and averaged 11 mg L^{-1} (Table 1, Figure 1).

TABLE 1. Effect of the VFB on BOD_5, TSS and pH.

Period of year	# of observations	Average loading	BOD_5 In	BOD_5 Out	BOD_5 % Removal	TSS In	TSS Out	TSS % Removal	pH In	pH Out
		m^3 d^{-1}	mg L^{-1}			mg L^{-1}				
Fall 84	12	117	29	12	59	25	7	72	7.1	7.2
Win. 85	11	111	68	29	57	37	9	76	7.0	7.1
Spr. 85	12	130	117	38	68	37	13	65	7.1	7.1
Sum. 85	11	100	87	11	87	28	10	64	7.0	7.1
Fall 85	9	97	28	7	75	29	7	76	7.2	7.1
Win. 86	9	106	40	11	73	25	4	84	N.D.	N.D.

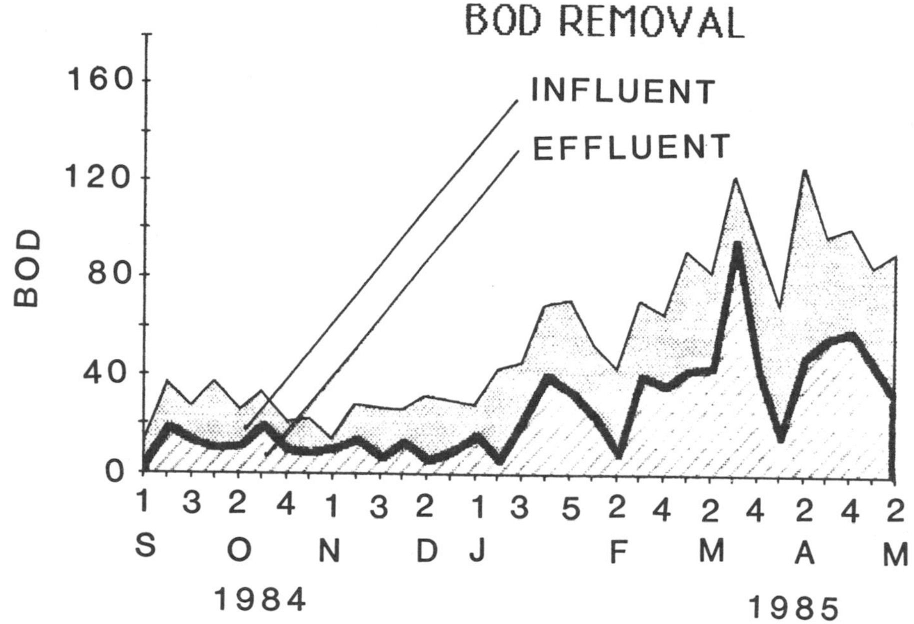

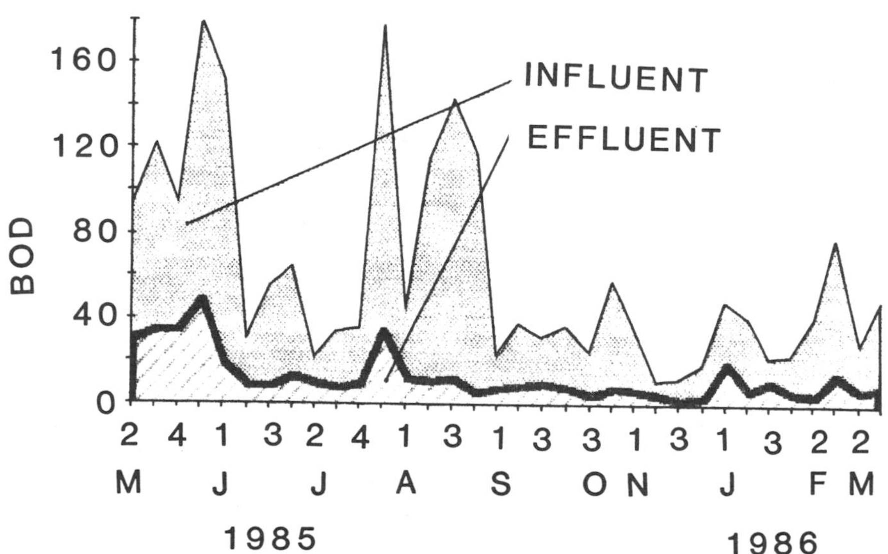

FIGURE 1. Weekly BOD_5 content in mg L^{-1} from week 1 of September 1984 through week 4 of March 1986.

The average TSS content of the effluent exceeded the discharge limit of 10 mg L^{-1} only in the spring of 1985 (Table 1). The best performance occurred in the fall of 1985 when 76% of TSS was removed and in the winter of 1986, when the removal amounted to 84% (Table 1).

The effect of the VFB on pH is negligible: pH remains near neutral in the effluent (Table 1). Settled Solids (SS) throughout the observation period remained below 0.1 mg L^{-1}. Odor in the immediate vicinity of the VFB was strong only when the bed was first activated in the fall of 1984.

Over a period of five weeks in October and November, 1984, with the cattail vegetation barely established, an average NO_3-N reduction of 25% and an average NH_4-N reduction of 39% were measured (D. J. Garry, 1984, unpublished report, Science Department of Mount Saint Mary's College, Emmitsburg, MD). An analysis (December 12, 1985) performed by the Maryland Department of Health and Mental Hygiene, yielded the following reductions: BOD_5 90%, COD 69%, TSS 99%, NH_4-N 51% and TKN-N 59%.

CONCLUSIONS

Very satisfactory removal of BOD_5 and TSS was obtained throughout the observation period. Removal levels improved in proportion to the area covered by and the amount of growth of the cattail plants. Most recently BOD_5 and TSS levels were achieved that were almost uniformly below the discharge limit of 10 mg L^{-1}, in spite of the real life operating conditions that result in periodic malfunctions of the trickling filter.

REFERENCES

Hyde, H. C., R. S. Ross, and L. Sturmer. 1984. Technology assessment of aquaculture systems for municipal wastewater treatment. Environmental Protection Agency, Municipal Environmental Research Laboratory, Cincinnati, Ohio.

Seidel, K., and H. Happel. 1981. Pflazenklaranlage "Krefelder System." Sicherheit in Chemie und Umwelt 1:127-129.

SaLUT, Inc. 1984. Advanced limnological systems for reclaiming wastewater for reuse. Phase I SBIR Report to the Department of Agriculture, Washington, D.C.

Wolverton, B. C., R. C. McDonald, and W. R. Duffer. 1983. Microorganisms and higher plants for wastewater treatment. J. Environ. Qual. 12:236-242.

ABSTRACTS

UTILIZATION OF WETLANDS AS A RELIABLE LOW COST WASTEWATER TREATMENT PROCESS.

R. A. Gearheart and B. A. Finney (Humboldt State University, Arcata, California 95521).

The use of macrophytes in wetland treatment systems has been shown to be an effective, reliable, and non-energy intensive alternative for treating domestic wastewater. The emphasis in the Clean Water Act of 1977 supports innovative and alternative treatment technologies, such as land treatment, wetland and marsh treatment, aquaculture, etc. The basic interest of the law makers was to force alternative treatment strategies to encourage creative processes which in many cases, are natural processes. The creation of new or enhanced beneficial uses of the receiving waters by reuse and recycling was an important element in this legislation. Research by the City of Arcata has shown that marshes and wetlands can be designed and managed to not only treat wastewater, but to create a new or compliment existing, beneficial water uses. A pilot project in the City of Arcata, CA, staffed by Humboldt State University personnel attempted to increase the understanding of these processes and to develop design criteria and management strategies for wetland treatment systems. In this project, 12 experimental marshes (6.1 x 61 m) received oxidation pond effluent continuously for 48 months. The hydraulic loading to the experimental cells varied from 187 to 2356 $m^3\ d^{-1}\ ha^{-1}$. The depth of water in the experimental marshes varied between 0.3 and 0.6 m. Macrophyte communities were allowed to establish themselves by natural succession after an initial planting of alkali bulrush and hardstem bulrush.

The influent and effluent BOD, COD, NFR, ammonia, nitrates, total phosphate, ortho-phosphate temperature, pH, alkalinity, total coliform, fecal coliform, and dissolved oxygen turbidity were monitored for each of the 12 cells. The frequency of analysis varied with the parameter from daily temperature and dissolved oxygen values to tri-weekly BOD and NFR measurements. For the entire project period, the average effluent BOD from the experimental marshes ranged from 9.0 to 15.3 mg L^{-1} with removal rates of 41 to 86%. The cells receiving the lower organic loads consistently produced effluent BOD values of less than 20 mg L^{-1}. The average effluent NFR concentration for the twelve cells ranged from 4.0 to 13.6 mg L^{-1}, with an overall average effluent concentration for all cells for two years of 5.3 mg L^{-1}.

ISBN 0-941463-00-1

Removal rates ranged from 80 to 89% with an overall average of 85%.

The marsh cells averaged 86% removal of fecal coliform organisms. Several of the cells consistently removed 90 to 97% of the fecal coliform over the two year study period. The fecal coliform removal rate varied from 0.33 d^{-1} in the summer to 0.23 d^{-1} in the winter as measured through baffled cells. A *Salmonella* spp. die-off experiment showed a 94 to 96% reduction with residence times of 23 to 52 h. Ammonia N removals varied from 9 to 33% with effluent values of 12.4 and 8.6 mg L^{-1}, respectively. Over 70% of the organic N was removed while 30% of Kjeldahl N (TKN) was removed. Filtered ortho-P removal varied from 0 to 12% over the study period.

In summary, the five year Arcata Marsh Pilot Project has demonstrated that wetland treatment systems can effectively and consistently remove BOD and NFR's from an oxidation pond effluent. Design criteria has been developed for BOD, NFR, fecal coliform, and total coliform removal. Effects of long-term solids loading and detritus accumulation have been documented on these pilot cells. The project also showed that these systems can reduce pathogen and public health indicator densities. These systems have proven to be effective and efficient with the ability to produce a constant effluent over a wide-range of hydraulic and organic loads. Wetland process can be managed to remove nutrients as demonstrated in the project.

UTILIZATION OF WETLANDS AS BMP'S FOR THE REDUCTION OF NITROGEN AND PHOSPHORUS IN AGRICULTURAL RUNOFF FROM SOUTH FLORIDA WATERSHEDS. A. L. Goldstein (South Florida Water Management District, West Palm Beach, Florida 33402).

As part of an overall strategy to evaluate the impacts of river channelization, the Florida Legislature funded a multi-year demonstration project. One of the objectives of the project was an evaluation of the effectiveness and efficiency of wetlands in the Kissimmee River Basin to act as nutrient removal sinks for nonpoint source runoff from upland agricultural watersheds. Results obtained from this study were compared with data collected from other Kissimmee basin wetlands during recent years. The abilities of these wetlands to remove nutrients were actively taken up while particulate-bound forms (mostly organics) were exported in amounts comparable to those measured in the inflows.

TREATMENT OF STORMWATER RUNOFF USING AQUATIC PLANTS. R. D. Blackburn, P. L. Pimentel, and J. E. Fensch (Joyce Environmental Consultants, Inc., 414 Live Oak Blvd., Casselberry, Florida 32707-3894).

The stormwater runoff from a 948 ha golf course - residential - commercial development, located in Palm Beach County, Florida,

U.S.A., is drained into a series of man-made marshes, canals and lakes. Aquatic marshes (36.6 ha) have been planted using native emergent and submersed aquatic plants. Aquatic plants utilized in the man-made marshes were required to be native plants, have the ability to filter stormwater runoff, be aesthetically pleasing and have a minimal maintenance cost. During periods of heavy rainfall, stormwater runoff is pumped from the man-made system into a natural retention marsh (120 ha). Before water is pumped from the man-made drainage system, water quality must meet state of Florida Class III Water Quality Standards (recreation water). Automatic water samplers have been installed to sample water as it is pumped into the natural retention system. Water that flows out of the natural retention system must meet Florida Class I Standards (drinking water). Design of marsh systems, aquatic plants selected and management of water levels in the man-made system have proven to be important factors in the success of the total system objective. These factors have also proven to be the key to management of the system for aesthetic value and wildlife resources. Water quality data show the system is working as designed. Water quality parameters that may be a problem in future years can be avoided by change in aquatic species and increasing marsh size.

BOTANICAL ASPECTS OF THE ROOT ZONE TREATMENT PLANT IN MANNERSDORF, AUSTRIA.

G. A. Janauer (University of Vienna, A-1091 Vienna, Althanstr. 14, AUSTRIA)

Under the authority of the Provincial Government of Lower Austria and the technical supervision of the Institute of Hydraulic Engineering, the construction of a root zone sewage treatment plant was accomplished in June 1983 in Mannersdorf on the Leitha, Lower Austria, about 50 km from Vienna. Matters concerning the plant's vegetation have been dealt with by the author. The plant's test fields are loaded with raw, mechanically treated, and biologically treated wastewater, respectively. After the initial growth of weeds had been controlled, the area densely covered by reed increased threefold to 86.1% of the total area of 450 m^2 in two years. The plant has proven its efficiency by reducing the BOD_5 by 90%, by retaining more than 50% of P and N, and by requiring a minimum area of 3 m^2 per person equivalent, when loaded with mechanically or biologically treated water. Transpiration values gained so far have corresponded to the difference between inflow and discharge. Biometrical studies of the above-ground and underground biomass initiated last year will be at the center of attention in 1986. At present, Mannersdorf is the only thoroughly examined root zone treatment plant in Austria. The results will serve as a basis for future subsidies granted by the Federal and Provincial Authorities.

HYACINTH WASTEWATER TREATMENT, THE FIRST STEP IN SAN DIEGO'S WATER RECLAMATION PROGRAM. G. R. Miller, G. E. Montgomery (Black & Veatch, P. O. Box 8405, Kansas City, Missouri), and F. Maitski (Water Utilities Dept., California).

The San Diego Total Resource Recovery Program was established to demonstrate an innovative/alternative wastewater treatment system with the additional cost effective recovery of water and energy. Conceptually, the program has four segments: Aquaculture Wastewater Treatment, Advanced Water Treatment, Energy Recovery, and a Health Effects Study. Raw wastewater is processed through water hyacinth ponds and then is to be treated to potable water quality for reuse, initially irrigation, in San Diego. The wastewater sludge and the hyacinths harvested from the wastewater treatment system are to be anaerobically digested to produce CH_4 gas. An extensive public health study is to be conducted, recognizing that the program will have to meet severe public scrutiny to gain acceptance. Prior to Advanced Water Treatment, the raw wastewater is treated in water hyacinth ponds with a three to four day detention time. A portion of the pond effluent is aerated and recycled to increase the dissolved oxygen concentration in the ponds. The hyacinth ponds have been tested at total flows of 379-757 $m^3\ d^{-1}$ since May 1984. The BOD and suspended solids concentrations in the pond effluent are usually below 30 mg L^{-1}, ranging from 5 to 50 mg L^{-1}. At times there is a slight yellow color in the effluent, possibly caused by humic acids from the hyacinth plants. The capacity of the ponds will be expanded to 3785 $m^3\ d^{-1}$ when the program is moved to a permanent site in Balboa Park.

REVIEW OF RESEARCH ON THE USE OF AQUATIC MACROPHYTES FOR TREATMENT OF AGRICULTURAL DRAINAGE AND EUTROPHIC LAKE WATERS. K. R. Reddy (University of Florida, P. O. Box 909, Sanford, Florida 32771).

About 8% (1.2 million ha) of the total surface area is occupied by freshwater. Most of the freshwater bodies in Florida are eutrophic either naturally or as a result of nutrient loading from urban and agricultural activities. One such example is Lake Apopka (12,500 ha surface area) located in central Florida which is currently highly eutrophic. Eutrophication of Lake Apopka is enhanced by nutrient loading from external and internal sources. External sources include drainage from vegetable farms, surface and sub-surface runoff from citrus groves, sewage effluent from the Winter Garden treatment plant, and precipitation. Internal sources include nutrient release from underlying sediment, and nitrogen and carbon fixation by algae. Nutrient loading from the discharge of drainage water from the adjacent 9000 ha organic soils (Histosols) planted to vegetable crops contributes a N and P loading of 30.3 and 4.6 kg $ha^{-1}\ yr^{-1}$. The water table in these soils is at the soil surface and the water holding capacity is high; therefore, drainage is often necessary before these soils can be planted with vegetable crops. During the periods of heavy rainfall, considerable amounts of drainage water must be pumped off the farms into adjacent Lake Apopka.

For the past few years, our research was aimed in developing techniques to reduce nutrient levels of agricultural drainage before discharge into adjacent Lake Apopka. These techniques utilize aquatic macrophytes cultured in retention ponds and artificial wetlands. Results show a net reduction of up to 80% in N and P, when drainage water is allowed to flow through aquatic macrophyte system. Second phase of this program evaluated the use of aquatic macrophytes for improving water quality of Lake Apopka. Results indicate that 50-60% of total N and P in lake water can be reduced when allowed to flow through a water hyacinth system at an hydraulic retention period of 36 h.

NUTRIENT AND BOD REMOVAL FROM HATCHERY AND OTHER EFFLUENTS USING WATERCRESS (RORIPPA NASTURTIUM-AQUATICUM).

B. Thomas (University of Washington, Seattle, Washington 98105).

Watercress (*Rorippa nasturtium-aquaticum*) has potential for treatment of sewage, feedlot, and aquaculture effluents. In cool climates, *Rorippa* has superior growth rates compared to water hyacinths (*Eichhornia crassipes*), and some other aquatic macrophytes used in water treatment projects. The morphological characteristics of *Rorippa* make it ideal for polyculture with floating plants or algae and it does not have the exotic, weedy reputation of *Eichhornia*. Effluent from the Steward Park Lake Washington trout hatchery is being treated in two 2.8 m x 1 m fiberglass troughs to compare water quality improvements after passing through 10 cm of gravel only or 10 cm of gravel and *Rorippa*. Water quality parameters analyzed include BOD, DO, NH_3-NH_4, pH, hardness, and temperature. Final harvests are scheduled for March and July 1986 to determine yield of *Rorippa*. The results of an earlier project using *Rorippa* to purify and recycle farm house sewage are discussed. These are the first projects to demonstrate *Rorippa* as a tool for wastewater treatment in cool climates.

UTILIZATION OF TRIPLOID GRASS CARP FOR CONTROL OF FLOATING VEGETATION IN WASTEWATER RETENTION PONDS.

J. L. Underwood, R. S. Hestand, III, and B. Z. Thompson (Florida Game and Fresh Water Fish Commission, P. O. Box 1903, Eustis, Florida 32727-1903).

Triploid grass carp (*Ctenopharyngodon idella*) were stocked into wastewater ponds covered by duckweed (*Lemna* sp.). Estimates of floating vegetative biomass and water chemistries were obtained on a regular basis. Tank studies determined that triploid grass carp (XTL=150 mm) would consume at least 2.5 times their body weight in duckweed per day; this information along with estimates of duckweed growth rates will allow a stocking model to be constructed. Such a model will permit wastewater treatment plant managers to reduce their budgets and time expenditures on controlling floating vegetation in retention ponds.

WASTEWATER TREATMENT IN FLOW-THROUGH AND BERMED CYPRESS DOMES IN POLK COUNTY, FLORIDA. R. W. Ogburn III and B. W. Breedlove (Breedlove, Dennis & Associates, Inc., 2412 Forsythe Road, Orlando, Florida 32807).

Approximately 1136 $m^3\ d^{-1}$ of secondarily treated domestic wastewater was discharged to a series of three connected cypress domes in Polk County, Florida for five years. The effluent subsequently was re-routed to a bermed 46.5 ha cypress dome that has been drained historically by man-made ditches. Nutrient chemistry was monitored for one year in each system to evaluate their effectiveness at nutrient uptake and storage. The flow-through system demonstrated phosphorus removal of about 75%; no significant reduction of total nitrogen was observed, but nitrate levels tended to decrease. No surface discharge from the bermed wetland occurred during the one year period. However, nutrient and conductivity increases in groundwater and a stream adjacent to the wetland indicated that subsurface seepage did occur. Potential mechanisms of nutrient removal and storage will be discussed.

SURFACE WATER QUALITY MODIFICATIONS THROUGH CREATED AND EXISTING WETLANDS IN AN URBAN DEVELOPMENT. J. L. Gilio (Wetlands Management, Inc., P. O. Box 1122, Jensen Beach, Florida 33457).

Impervious runoff from a 1 ha commercial and 25 ha residential area of 625 units flow through an engineered drainage system of interconnected lakes and a wet prairie. Lake littoral zones and the restored wet prairie designed and aquascaped with native vegetation have developed flourishing plant communities.

High nutrient runoff concentrations from the commercial center are reduced after flow through a small perched lake and a 2.5 ha wet prairie. Both these surface water management bodies receive impervious runoff from parking lots, roofs, and extensive sodded areas. A conservative fertilization management system reduces nutrient runoff. Weir discharge leaving this lake indicates high dissolved oxygen levels are maintained, nutrient levels are low to moderate but fecal coliform is high. The latter is probably due to residential owners dumping pet excrement into the lake. The drainage system provides visual/aesthetic enhancement as well as sustained recreational fishery.

USE OF WATER HYACINTH FOR THE POLISHING OF SECONDARY SEWAGE EFFLUENT AT THE CITY OF AUSTIN HYACINTH GREENHOUSE FACILITY. J. Doersam (City of Austin - Water and Wastewater Utility, 1524 South Ih 35, Suite 301, Austin, Texas 78704).

The City of Austin has been experimenting with the use of water hyacinths for the polishing of secondary wastewater effluent since the mid 1970's. In 1980, the City received an EPA Innovative Construction Grant to construct a 2 ha greenhouse enclosure containing three hyacinth basins having a total of four surface area acres. In October 1985, construction was complete and start up procedures began. The system receives influent from an existing oxidation pond at a centralized sludge treatment facility, therefore, many beneficial organisms were introduced into the hyacinth facility upon filling of the basins. Each basin was stocked with water hyacinths to about 50% coverage, and approximately five pounds of mosquito fish (Gambusia Affinis Minnows) were introduced. On February 3, 1986, the basins were nearly 80% covered and discharge from the facility began. Thus far, the facility has demonstrated promising results on TSS, BOD, NH_3-N and NO_3-N removal.

STUDIES ON FLOATING AQUATIC PLANTS IN FRANCE. P. Morand and G. Blake (AFME, 27, rue Louis Vicat, 75015 Paris, FRANCE)

The floating macrophytes are furnished by marshes, water depuration systems and hot waters enriched with nutrients. For water hyacinth (and other tropical plants), cultures in hot waters for the elimination of nutrients, organic loading or toxics (metals...), possibilities of valorisation by CH_4 generation or for animal feeding are the main scopes of the research. For the native species (*Lemna*, *Trasa*), the low values of productivity are balanced by small demands of energy. The productivity of floating macrophytes runs from 4 Mg ha^{-1} (*Lemna*, *Trasa*) in natural cultures to 50 Mg ha^{-1} in water treatment (*water hyacinth*). Some values of 150 Mg ha^{-1} have been noticed in enriched lagoons. For water hyacinth, the limits of concentration are close to a level of 5 g m^{-2} of BOD_5 and of 10 mg m^{-2} d^{-1} for Cd, while the percent removal are 80 in spring and 30 in autumn for organic loading and 70 for Cd. The aptitude for methanisation is better for water hyacinth than for *Trasa*.

EFFICACY OF TRIPLOID GRASS CARP IN CENTRAL FLORIDA LAKES. R. S. Hestand III, J. L. Underwood, and B. Z. Thompson (Florida Game and Fresh Water Fish Commission, P. O. Box 1903, Eustis, Florida 32727-1903).

Nineteen lakes ranging from 0.6 ha to 42.1 ha were stocked with triploid grass carp (*Ctenopharyngodon idella*) at rates of

8 fish ha^{-1} to 370 ha^{-1}. In the majority of lakes the target plant was hydrilla (Hydrilla verticillata). However, two lakes were primarily southern naiad (Najas guadalupensis) and two others were Brazilian elodea (Egeria densa). The higher stocking rates were successful while the lower rates gave mixed results. Several areas were stocked in conjunction with herbicide treatments in which all stocking rates used were successful.

AN INTEGRATED APPROACH FOR WASTEWATER TREATMENT USING AQUATIC PLANTS.

M. Hota and D. K. Biswas (Department of Environment, Bikaoer House, Shahjahan Road, New Delhi 110 011, INDIA).

Aquatic plants are known to have high uptake of toxic metals and organic matter. A number of plants have been identified as the potential pollutant removers from the wastewater. This paper outlines the possibilities of an integrated approach for wastewater treatment using aquatic plants. Considering the high order of investment as required in conventional techniques, it is imperative that aquatic plants should find a place in wastewater treatment to reduce the cost and control problems otherwise encountered.

GROUND-WATER AND SURFACE-WATER INTERACTIONS IN WETLANDS: COMPARISONS AND CONTRASTS.

R. G. Brown (U.S. Geological Survey, 702 Post Office Building, St. Paul, Minnesota 55101, G. L. Patterson (U.S. Geological Survey, Wisconsin), and J. R. Stark (U.S. Geological Survey, Minnesota).

The U.S. Geological Survey is studying the interaction between ground water and surface water in two wetlands as part of a larger study of the hydrologic, chemical, and biological effects of discharging secondarily treated municipal wastewater into wetlands as a method of tertiary treatment. The two wetlands are located near St. Joseph in central Minnesota and near Phelps in northeastern Wisconsin. The two wetlands were selected for study because their hydrologic settings are substantially different, particularly with respect to ground- and surface-water interactions.

The St. Joseph wetland consists of 6 ha of cattail marsh and tamarack bog located on the edge of a glacial-outwash plain and adjacent to a perennial stream. The wetland and stream receive ground-water discharge from the surfical outwash aquifer. The aquifer is unconfined regionally, but water in the aquifer is confined in the area of the wetland by organic deposits, including peat. The wetland receives surface-water from a municipal storm sewer (0 to 738 L s^{-1}) and from the St. Joseph wastewater-treatment plant (14-26 L s^{-1}). Outflow from the wetland (11-132 L s^{-1}) is through a small stream tributary to the adjacent perennial stream. Preliminary analysis of the hydrologic budget for July through September 1985 indicates that approximately 80% of the outflow from the wetland results from ground-water discharge to the wetland; the remaining 20% is from surface-water discharge.

The Phelps wetland consists of 12 ha of wooded bog situated between two steep-sided drumlins. The wetland is perched about 80 feet above the regional water table. A dense compacted clay underlies the wetland and inhibits downward leakage to the water table. A small stream (2.8-8.5 L s^{-1}) enters the northwest corner of the wetland and another small stream (5.7-11.4 L s^{-1}) drains the wetland to the south. Ground-water inflow to the wetland is limited to flow from thin, probably discontinuous, perched sandy lenses in the drumlins. In addition, the wetland receives an average of 2.5 L s^{-1} discharge from the wastewater-treatment facility. The St. Joseph wetland is a ground-water-discharge zone in which the interaction between ground water and surface water is a major component of the wetland's hydrology. The hydrology of the wetland is influenced primarily by ground-water discharge to the wetland. Surface-water discharges are of less importance in the hydrologic balance of the St. Joseph wetland compared to ground-water discharges in the summer, but may be more important during snowmelt events and in the chemical balance. In contrast, the most important water-balance components at the Phelps wetland are precipitation, evapotranspiration, and surface-water inflow and outlow. Except for minimal leakage through the clay layer into the underlying unsaturated zone, there is no ground- and surface-water interaction between the Phelps wetland and the regional water-table aquifer.

INNOVATIVE SLUDGE TREATMENT UTILIZING PHRAGMITES.

S. Davis (Biological Water Purification, Inc., P. O. Box 114, Denville, New Jersey 07834).

An innovative method of treating sewage sludge, chemical slimes and hydroxide colloids has been patented in the United States and Canada by the Max-Planck-Institute of West Germany, represented in North America by Biological Water Purification, Inc. of Denville, New Jersey. This new system combines the action of conventional drying beds with the effects of aquatic plants upon water-bearing substrates. While conventional drying beds are used to drain 20 to 25% of water content from sludge, the resulting residue must be hauled away for further treatment. By having the drying beds constructed in a specific manner and then planted with reeds (<u>Phragmites communis</u>) further desiccation is effected by the voracious demand for water by these plants. To satisfy this demand, the plants extend their root systems continually into the sludge deposits. Additionally this extended root system causes the establishment of a rich microflora which feeds upon the organic content of the sludge. This microflora is kept aerobic by the action of the plants. So effective is the degradation by the microflora that eventually more than 95% of sludge solids are converted into carbon dioxide and water with a corresponding volume reduction. The beneficial end result is that these planted drying beds can be operated for up to 10 years before the remaining sludge residues have to be removed. This paper will present operational data from three wastewater facilities utilizing this process for treatment of aerobically stabilized sludge (Avalon, N.J.), anaerobically stabilized sludge (Hightstown, N.J., Beverly, N.J.), and water works sludge; iron hydroxide in (Hightstown, N.J.).

PROPOSED APPLICATION OF AN AQUATIC PLANT - WASTEWATER LAGOON SYSTEM IN A HIGH ELEVATION ENVIRONMENT (LAKE TITICACA, PERU). R. U. Kistritz (R.U. Kistritz Consultants Ltd., 4420 Corless Road, Richmond, B.C., CANADA, V7C 1N3), P. Morales (Universidad Nacional del Altiplano, PERU), and T. G. Northcote (University of British Columbia, CANADA).

The recommendation to investigate the utilization of aquatic plants for wastewater treatment emerged from a four year water resources training program between the University of British Columbia and the Universidad Nacional del Altiplano funded by the Canadian International Development Agency. The problem focuses on a practical low-cost solution to the serious pollution of Inner Puno Bay connected to Lake Titicaca (elevation 3,800 m). The raw sewage contamination originates from the rapidly growing population of Puno (presently at ca. 80,000 inhabitants). Local conditions are conducive for the development of an aquatic plant - lagoon system because of the shallow, generally undeveloped shoreline, productive littoral plant community, and aquatic plant management which is an integral part of lakeshore farming practices. Current plans are to direct hydrobotanical, water quality and other studies aimed at developing design criteria, a pilot project, and ultimate full-scale application of an aquatic plant - wastewater lagoon system.

PART III
CRITICAL PROCESS DYNAMICS

PHYSIOLOGICAL PLANT PROCESSES: PHOTOSYNTHESIS

G. Bowes
Department of Botany and
Center for Aquatic Weeds
University of Florida, IFAS
Gainesville, Florida 32611

S. Beer
Department of Botany
Tel-Aviv University
Tel-Aviv 69978, ISRAEL

ABSTRACT

Photosynthesis is the process by which inorganic carbon (C) is converted to organic C, and radiant energy is stored as chemical energy in the form of biomass. Thus, it is the biochemical process most closely related to plant productivity. The environmental factors that most often limit this process, and hence growth, are light, N, P, C, or water availability, as well as temperature. In aquatic species, whether they photosynthesize under water or in air, is a major determinant of photosynthetic rate and productivity. Inherited factors are crucial. These include: sun versus shade photosynthetic characteristics, leaf and canopy architecture, and whether the species possesses the C_3, or more efficient C_4 pathway, which eliminates the wasteful process of photorespiration. Emergent and floating aquatic plants exhibit C_3 or C_4 photosynthesis, like terrestrial plants. However, submersed plants can alter their photosynthetic mode in response to environmental stress conditions by shifting to a C_4-like system or by utilizing bicarbonate ions, in addition to CO_2. Despite their plasticity, the photosynthesis and productivity of submersed macrophytes is much lower than that of other aquatic plants because of the diffusion resistance of water to movement of dissolved inorganic C, which greatly limits its availability; and to the shade nature of submersed macrophytes, as they live in generally low light energy habitats. Enrichment with CO_2 increases the biomass production of some C_3 aquatic plants, and causes the reallocation of C away from protein and into carbohydrates. The presence of lacunal gas channels in aquatic plants facilitates the oxidation of the root zone, thereby

Aquatic Plants for Water Treatment
and Resource Recovery
K.R. Reddy and W.H. Smith (Eds.)

ISBN 0-941463-00-1

allowing the roots access to virtually unlimited water supplies under otherwise anaerobic conditions, and thus maximizing productivity. In some plants, lacunae make sediment CO_2 available to the leaves for photosynthesis. The maximum theoretical production has been estimated to be 760 Mg ha^{-1} yr^{-1}, but this is about ten-fold higher than current systems achieve. The most efficient (C_4) plant canopies convert about 2% of the solar energy into stored chemical energy (biomass). Despite this low efficiency, annual global photosynthetic energy storage exceeds by ten-fold the total human energy use. An emergent or floating aquatic plant, with sun photosynthetic features, a high leaf area index, and in tropical regions preferably a C_4 species, should be the best biomass candidate.

Keywords: Canopy architecture, carbon limitation, photosynthetic efficiency, photorespiration, sun and shade aquatic plants.

INTRODUCTION

Plant growth and development is the net result of many interacting physiological and biochemical processes within the organism, of which photosynthesis is the one most directly related to growth and productivity. Its key role can be inferred even from a simple elemental analysis of plant tissues (Table 1) showing that C constitutes close to half the total plant biomass. Virtually all this C is in organic form, and is derived from the photosynthetic fixation of inorganic C. Similarly, the O and H content is largely a result of photosynthesis. These three elements account for some 95% of a plant's total dry weight.

Nitrogen and P, although required in much lesser amounts, are vital plant constituents. They are obtained as NO_3^- or NH_4^+, and PO_4^{3-} ions, respectively, generally via the roots, though also

TABLE 1. Elemental, water and organic composition of plants.

Macronutrients:	
C (44%)	from CO_2
O (44%)	from CO_2 and water
H (6%)	from water
N (4%)	from NO_3^- and NH_4^+
K, Ca, P, Mg, S, Fe	
Micronutrients:	
Cl, Cu, Mn, Zn, Mo, B, Na, Si	
Water:	
10-95% of fresh weight	
Inorganic nutrients:	
1-5% of fresh weight	
Organics (major):	
carbohydrates, lipids, proteins, nucleic acids	

through the leaves of some submersed species. These two elements have been considered as major limiting factors to growth. Their levels in the environment are often far below intracellular concentrations; which is not usually the case for other elements. For example, N and P in "typical" freshwater occur in concentrations of only 0.5 to 50 and 0.5 to 2 mmol m^{-3}, respectively (Raven, 1984), though in eutrophic or wastewaters the levels may be many times higher. The processing of inorganic N, whether as N_2 fixation by cyanobacteria and plant/bacteria symbiotic associations, or in its reduction and incorporation into organic form, is very costly in terms of energy. This is also true when performed by human technology to produce fertilizer. In plants, the acquisition and interconversion of N is driven by chemical energy derived from photosynthesis, and there is evidence to suggest that photosynthesis may limit N utilization, rather than vice-versa.

Because photosynthesis is so intimately linked to growth, the photosynthetic rate is used to estimate gross plant productivity. If measured often enough, and with sufficient care, and corrected for dark respiration losses, then the photosynthetic rate must closely correlate with the growth rate and productivity. However, short-term leaf or BOD bottle measurements are not always accurate predictors of productivity, and long-term extrapolations from them should be made with caution. Problems occur with short-term measurements of small subsamples, because it is difficult to duplicate the variety of environmental conditions that can influence the photosynthesis of a canopy or plant population during its growth season in the field. Despite this caveat, relatively short photosynthetic and dark respiration rate measurements can be used to estimate a plant's potential productivity under a given set of conditions.

Photosynthesis is an energy-dependent process which historically has been divided into two parts: the light and dark reactions. In the light reactions, radiant energy from the sun in the form of quanta (photons) from the wavelength range of approximately 400 to 700 nm (photosynthetically active radiation, PAR) is captured and converted to chemically bound energy (adenosine triphosphate, ATP) and a reducing agent (reduced nicotinamide adenine dinucleotide phosphate, NADPH), by two photochemical reactions linked through an electron transport system. Chlorophyll serves as the major antenna pigment for the capture of quanta, as well as the initial oxido-reductant. Electrons for the reduction are taken from water, and molecular O_2 is evolved as a by-product. The stored energy and reducing power generated by the light reactions are subsequently used in the dark (non-photochemical) reactions to form organic compounds, principally sugars, from CO_2. Radiant energy is thus finally stored as chemical energy in the form of carbohydrates and other organic compounds which are ultimately used for plant growth. The light reactions are located in the chloroplast membranes (grana stacks), while the dark reactions are located in the intra-membranal or stromal regions of the chloroplast. The chloroplast is also the site of other vital metabolic processes that rely on photosynthetically generated chemical energy and reductants. These include NO_3^- and SO_4^{2-} reduction, and also lipid and amino acid biosynthesis (Anderson, 1981). The dependence of these processes on photosynthesis, further emphasizes the key role that photosynthetic metabolism plays in biomass production and inorganic nutrient utilization.

In the last 20 years, some important variations in the CO_2 fixation reactions have become apparent. Consequently, we will briefly review the major biochemical, physiological, and ecological features of the different dark reaction pathways, and how they relate to freshwater plants, and the aquatic environment. Also, we will assess the efficiency of photosynthesis; how it affects productivity, including the theoretical maximum; and review some external and inherited factors that regulate or limit the photosynthetic process.

PHOTOSYNTHETIC CARBON FIXATION PATHWAYS

Photosynthesis in some aquatic plants differs from that in terrestrial species. A fundamental difference among aquatic species is whether photosynthesis occurs under water or in air. Submersed aquatic species, which include macrophytes (angiosperms, lower vascular plants, and bryophytes) and microphytes (algae, and cyanobacteria or blue-green algae) utilize dissolved inorganic carbon (DIC) from the water. In contrast, emergent and floating (emersed) aquatic species use air-CO_2 as their C source, and in this regard differ little from terrestrial plants. Amphibious aquatic species are those which have submersed and emersed leaves, sometimes on the same stem, and thus assimilate inorganic C both from the aqueous and gaseous phases. As will become evident later, whether or not a plant has direct access to air-CO_2 has important implications for its mechanism of C fixation, maximum photosynthetic capacity, and productivity.

In all plants, inorganic C is ultimately fixed into carbohydrate via the C_3 photosynthetic C reduction (PCR) pathway or cycle. In C_3 plants, this pathway includes the initial CO_2 fixation step. It is interesting to note that the PCR (or Calvin) cycle was initially elucidated in aquatic organisms, the unicellular algae Chlorella pyrenoidosa and Scenedesmus obliquus, in the 1950s, although most of the subsequent work on the C_3 pathway has been carried out with terrestrial plants (Robinson and Walker, 1981). Other methods for the initial acquisition of inorganic C are now well-established, including: Crassulacean Acid Metabolism (CAM), the C_4 pathway, and the systems operating in unicellular autotrophs such as green and blue-green algae, and submersed aquatic macrophytes (SAM). However, all of these initial acquisition methods are adjunct pathways or cycles which serve to enhance the operation of the basic C_3 PCR cycle (Lorimer and Andrews, 1981).

The C_3 Pathway

The C_3 pathway derives its name from the first stable organic compound formed by CO_2 fixation: a three-C compound, phosphoglycerate (PGA). In this cyclic pathway the five-C sugar phosphate, ribulose bisphosphate (RuBP), is carboxylated with CO_2 to form two molecules of PGA. Then in a series of reactions, PGA is phosphorylated and reduced by ATP and NADPH, respectively (derived from the light reactions), and the triose sugar phosphates so formed are condensed to more complex sugars, including the substrate for CO_2 fixation, RuBP. Because the regeneration of RuBP is a cyclic event, this pathway is also referred to as the C_3 PCR cycle. Stoichiometrically, for every three CO_2 molecules reacting with three RuBPs, six triose-phosphate molecules are produced; of these six, five are used to reform three RuBPs, while one triose phosphate represents the net organic carbon gain of the cycle.

The initial step of CO_2 fixation in C_3 plants is catalyzed by ribulose-1,5-bisphosphate carboxylase (RuBPcase). This enzyme is ubiquitous in green plants, and comprises a high proportion of the soluble protein within the chloroplasts, and thus of the total protein in a plant. In the early 1970s it was discovered that, in the presence of O_2, RuBPcase can also act as an oxygenase (Bowes et al., 1971), so that RuBP is oxidized to form a two-carbon compound, phosphoglycolate, in addition to PGA. This oxidation, and the subsequent metabolism of phosphoglycolate, comprise the photorespiratory C oxidation (PCO) cycle (Lorimer and Andrews, 1981), which for many plants results in the photorespiratory release of CO_2. From our present understanding of photorespiration, it appears to be a wasteful process, especially for C_3 crop and cultivated plants (Ogren and Chollet, 1982). Not only does the reaction of RuBP with atmospheric O_2 fail to gain any carbon for the plant, but CO_2 is actually lost during the operation of the PCO cycle. Also, during photorespiration, NH_3 is released from the amino acid glycine, and has to be recycled back to its organic form at considerable energetic cost. Thus, photorespiration, in contrast to mitochondrial or dark respiration, does not result in the net production of useful energy in the form of ATP, but rather consumes energy; it also differs in being very sensitive to light, temperature and O_2 concentrations above 2%. The CO_2 level is another influential factor. Because O_2 and CO_2 compete to react with the enzyme RuBPcase, photorespiration is reduced by elevating the CO_2 around the plant above ambient levels.

The presence of photorespiration is a major determinant of the photosynthetic, and hence growth rate, characteristics of C_3 plants. Some of these characteristics are listed in Table 2. Because of photorespiration, O_2 inhibits by 30 to 40% the photo-

TABLE 2. Photosynthetic and growth characteristics of C_3 plants.

1. First product of CO_2 fixation, via RuBPcase, is the C_3 compound (PGA)
2. Chloroplasts occur throughout the leaf mesophyll cells
3. Ambient CO_2 levels do not saturate photosynthesis
4. High CO_2 compensation points of 35-70 μL^{-1} L^{-1}
5. Photosynthetic rate inhibited 35-40% by atmospheric O_2
6. Photorespiratory CO_2 evolved
7. Usually low net photosynthetic rates of 0.4-1.1 mg CO_2 m^{-2} s^{-1}
8. Maximum light energy conversion efficiency of 3.5-4.5%
9. Includes sun and shade adapted species
10. Low optimum temperature for photosynthesis and growth of 15-25°C
11. Low water use efficiency of 450-950 g H_2O g^{-1} dry wt
12. Relatively high leaf N content
13. Low ^{13}C isotopic content
14. Lower potential productivity than C_4 plants
15. Includes most crop and temperate species; the majority of emergent and floating plants fall into this category

synthesis of C_3 plants growing at atmospheric CO_2 levels (0.034%). Thus under ambient O_2 conditions (21%) the potential biomass production by these species is considerably reduced. A high CO_2 compensation point in C_3 plants (Table 2) is also a consequence of photorespiration. The compensation point is the CO_2 concentration at which photosynthetic uptake of CO_2 is equivalent to photorespiratory CO_2 release, i.e. the CO_2 level at which no net photosynthesis occurs. High compensation points imply inefficient C fixation, especially at low CO_2 concentrations such as occur intracellularly if stomates are partially closed. Conversely, when the stomates are fully open to increase photosynthesis, much water is lost to the atmosphere by transpiration. Thus, C_3 plants feature lower water use efficiencies (water lost per CO_2 fixed), and this effect is magnified because the present atmospheric CO_2 levels are insufficient to saturate C_3 photosynthesis.

Because temperature has a greater effect on photorespiration than on photosynthesis, the temperature optimum for many C_3 plants is relatively low as compared to most other plant groups, and their photosynthetic quantum efficiency drops at temperatures above about 25°C (Table 2). It is thus not surprising to find that C_3 plants make up the major proportion of the flora in temperate regions. Because C_3 plants utilize the large and rather sluggish (in turnover time) RuBPcase enzyme for the initial fixation reaction, they have to invest substantial amounts of soluble protein in this one enzyme molecule in order to achieve reasonable photosynthetic rates. Consequently the leaves often show a relatively high protein, and organic-N content, and the plant may exhibit high N utilization; which is potentially a positive feature if the plant is used for wastewater treatment or as an animal feedstock. The converse of this is that, if used for biomass, they may have a lower N use efficiency than a typical C_4 plant.

Examples of common, terrestrial C_3 plants are: spinach (Spinacia oleracea), tobacco (Nicotiana tabacum), soybean (Glycine max), the majority of tree species, wheat (Triticum aestivum), barley (Avena sativa), and most other temperate grasses. Although they have been only poorly characterized, most of the emergent and floating aquatic plants that have been examined fall into the C_3 photosynthetic category, including: water hyacinth (Eichhornia crassipes (Patterson and Duke, 1979; Spencer and Bowes, 1986), cattail (Typha latifolia) (McNaughton and Fullem, 1970; Reddy et al., 1983), pennywort (Hydrocotyle umbellata), duckweed (Lemna minor), water lettuce (Pistia stratiotes), bulrushes (Scirpus species), elephant ear (Colocasia esculentum), and soft rush (Juncus effusus) (Garrard and Van, 1982; Wedge and Burris, 1982; Reddy et al., 1983).

The C_4 Pathway

A mode of C fixation differing from that in C_3 plants was discovered in the late 1960s. In this pathway, atmospheric CO_2 in the form of bicarbonate initially reacts with a three-C compound (phosphenolpyruvate, PEP) to form oxaloacetate (OAA), which is a four-C organic acid; thus giving rise to the epithet C_4 plants or pathway (Hatch and Slack, 1970; Black, 1973). This initial carboxylation occurs in the cytosol of the peripherally-arranged mesophyll cells of the leaf. OAA is rapidly transformed to the more stable four-C acids, malate and aspartate, which are transported out of the mesophyll and into the bundlesheath cells, where they are decarboxylated and the CO_2 released is finally fixed by RuBPcase and reduced via the C_3 PCR cycle in the bundlesheath chloroplasts. Thus in C_4 photosynthesis there are two sequential, and spatially separate carboxylation reactions that occur in the light.

The carboxylation enzyme catalyzing the initial fixation of CO_2 in the mesophyll cells of C_4 plants is phosphoenolpyruvate carboxylase (PEPcase). Unlike RuBPcase, this enzyme is not inhibited by O_2, and it has a more rapid turnover rate. Since the PEPcase and RuBPcase carboxylation enzymes are located in different cell types, C_4 plants show a different leaf anatomy to C_3 plants. It is termed Kranz (wreath) anatomy because each leaf bundle (or vein) is surrounded by concentric rings of mesophyll and bundlesheath cells, and the leaf chloroplasts are confined to these layers. The three-C compound (or a derivative of it), formed by decarboxylation of the transported C_4 acids, returns to the mesophyll cells where it is used to produce PEP, the substrate for the initial C fixation reaction. The C_4 pathway is cyclic, starting and finishing in the mesophyll cells, but with decarboxylation occurring in the bundlesheath cells. Thus C_4 plants utilize two linked biochemical cycles to assimilate inorganic C into carbohydrates: the C_4 acid and C_3 PCR cycles.

The decarboxylation step in the bundlesheath cells is very important. It differs among C_4 species and this involves whether malate or aspartate is the acid predominately transported. Thus C_4 plants are divided into three subcategories, depending on whether decarboxylation is catalyzed by NAD-malic enzyme in the mitochondria, PEP carboxykinase in the cytosol, or NADP-malic enzyme in the chloroplast (Edwards and Huber, 1981).

The double carboxylation processes in C_4 plants may seem to be redundant. However, the separate intercellular compartmentation of the two inorganic C fixation systems improves the photosynthetic capacity of C_4 plants in comparison with their C_3 counterparts. This occurs because the C_4 cycle, using the O_2 insensitive PEPcase, operates as a "CO_2 pump" to raise the CO_2 concentration above air-levels around the RuBPcase enzyme in the bundlesheath chloroplasts. This favors the carboxylation over the oxygenation reaction of RuBPcase, and thus virtually eliminates O_2 inhibition of the enzyme, and carbon flux through the PCO cycle. Furthermore, if photorespiratory CO_2 is produced, it is effectively recaptured by PEPcase in the surrounding mesophyll cells, and returned to the RuBPcase in the bundlesheath chloroplasts. The extra cycle in C_4 plants has energetic costs associated with it, but under many environmental conditions, this mechanism to reduce the negative effects of photorespiration appears to be a cost-effective measure.

The lack of O_2 inhibition and photorespiration is the basis for many of the photosynthetic and growth response characteristics of C_4 plants (Table 3). Because there is little or no photorespiratory CO_2 release to offset photosynthetic CO_2 uptake, the plants exhibit low CO_2 compensation points, and maximum photosynthetic rates occur at CO_2 levels below ambient. This provides the potential at atmospheric CO_2 levels for higher growth rates than most C_3 species can attain. It also permits high rates of C fixation when stomates are partially closed; which increases the water use efficiency, especially at higher temperatures. Elimination of the photorespiratory process gives C_4 species quite high temperature optima for photosynthesis and growth. The natural distribution reflects this characteristic, as they make up a much larger proportion of the flora in the tropics than in temperate regions. The CO_2 concentrating action reduces the need for large amounts of RuBPcase protein to achieve reasonable photosynthetic rates; and this in turn reduces the need for N by the plants, thereby improving N use efficiency.

It seems that C_4 plants have evolved mainly in subtropical and tropical regions, where high temperatures and light maximize the ecological benefits of the C_4 cycle. In cooler, lower light habitats, especially where water is not a limiting resource, C_4

TABLE 3. Photosynthetic and growth characteristics of C_4 plants.

1. First product of CO_2 fixation, via PEPcase in the mesophyll cells, is a C_4 acid (OAA). Decarboxylation in the bundlesheath cells rapidly provides CO_2 for refixation, via RuBPcase, into the C_3 PCR cycle
2. Dimorphic chloroplasts restricted to concentric rings of mesophyll and bundlesheath cells (Kranz anatomy)
3. Ambient CO_2 levels saturate photosynthesis
4. Low CO_2 compensation points of 0-10 μL^{-1} L^{-1}
5. Photosynthetic rate not inhibited by atmospheric O_2
6. No apparent photorespiratory CO_2 evolved
7. Usually high net photosynthetic rates of 1.1-3.0 mg CO_2 m^{-2} s^{-1}
8. Maximum light energy conversion efficiency of 5.0-5.8%
9. Includes mainly (but not only) sun adapted species
10. High optimum temperature for photosynthesis and growth of 30-45°C
11. High water use efficiency of 250-350 g H_2O g^{-1} dry wt
12. Relatively low leaf N content
13. High ^{13}C isotopic content
14. Higher potential productivity than C_3 plants
15. Includes some important crops; more abundant in the tropics; contains some emergent aquatic species

plants may have little advantage over C_3 species. Because C_4 species can be found in unrelated genera that also contain C_3 species, it appears that this biochemical strategy to improve competitiveness evolved more than once.

The major examples of C_4 plants among crop species are maize (*Zea mays*), sugarcane (*Saccharum officinarum*), millet (*Panicum milliaceum*), and sorghum (*Sorghum bicolor*); however, a number of the world's worst weeds are also examples, including crabgrass (*Digitalis sanguinalis*) and pigweed (*Amaranthus retroflexus*). A number of emergent aquatic species fall into the C_4 category: napier grass (*Pennisetum purpureum*), and several *Panicum* species including para grass (*P. purpurascens*), torpedograss (*P. repens*) and guinea grass (*P. maximum*) (Garrard and Van, 1982). Napier grass, in terms of biomass production, lives up to its C_4 reputation. Its production potential (85 Mg ha^{-1} yr^{-1}) is equivalent to that of sugarcane, and it exhibits a high solar energy conversion efficiency (Boardman, 1978). Occasionally emergent C_3 and C_4 grasses can be found growing together in similar aquatic or wetland habitats, and whether one has any ecological or competitive advantage over the other under these conditions is not known. At present, no floating or amphibious aquatic plants have been identified as C_4 species.

CAM

In Crassulacean Acid Metabolism (CAM) plants, atmospheric CO_2 in the form of bicarbonate is fixed via PEPcase during the night. Malic acid, being the stable product of this fixation, is then stored in the vacuoles for later metabolism. During the light period, malate is moved out of the vacuoles and decarboxylated. The CO_2 released is photosynthetically assimilated into carbohydrate via the C_3 PCR cycle, using ATP and NADPH from the light reactions. By performing the initial fixation at night, with the stomates open when the heat load is least, transpiration losses are minimized, and water use efficiency is maximized in arrid regions (Table 4). During the day, the stomates remain closed, which results in the retention of the CO_2 released from malate, and allows CO_2 to build-up within the leaf. In effect, this process concentrates CO_2 for RuBPcase and the PCR cycle,, when the light reactions can operate. CAM differs biochemically from C_4 photosynthesis by the PEPcase and RuBPcase carboxylation reactions being temporally separated by night and day, respectively, instead of spatially separated in different cells. Furthermore, PEP, which accepts inorganic carbon in the PEPcase reaction, is derived at night from carbohydrate degradation. As a result, CAM plants show opposite diel rhythms in acidity (malic acid) and carbohydrate levels (Table 4).

TABLE 4. Photosynthetic and growth characteristics of CAM plants.

1. CO_2 fixation of night (stomates open), via PEPcase, forms malic acid. Decarboxylation during the day (stomates closed), provides CO_2 for refixation, via RuBPcase, into the C_3 PCR cycle (diel fluctuations in acidity). CAM induced by growth conditions in some species
2. Chloroplasts occur throughout vacuolated mesophyll cells
3. Has high (1-2%) internal CO_2 levels during the day
4. Variable day/night CO_2 compensation points
5. Variable O_2 inhibition of photosynthesis
6. Photorespiratory CO_2 evolution difficult to detect
7. Low net photosynthetic rates of <0.3 mg CO_2 m^{-2} s^{-1}
8. Light energy conversion efficiency uncertain
9. Daytime photosynthesis saturated by less than full sun irradiance
10. High optimum temperature for photosynthesis and growth of 35°C
11. Very high water use efficiency of 50 g H_2O g^{-1} dry wt
12. Uncertain leaf N content; often high fresh/dry wt ratios
13. Variable ^{13}C isotopic content
14. Very low potential productivity in the CAM mode
15. Includes one important crop species; most abundant in arrid regions, but some submersed plants (isoetids) show a variation on this pathway

CAM tends to be associated with succulent plants, especially of desert regions (e.g. cactii). Some are obligate CAM species, whereas others are facultative, and are induced to change from C_3 to CAM under environmental stress conditions of low water, high salinity, or even an inappropriate photoperiod (Kluge and Ting, 1978). Low productivity values suggest that CAM is a strategy to maximize survival chances under extreme stress conditions, and not as in C_4 plants, a means to enhance the growth potential. It permits the acquisition of some CO_2 under temperature and water stress conditions that would prevent CO_2 fixation in other photosynthetic types. As might be anticipated from the low productivity, few crop species fall into this category; pineapple (*Ananas comosus*) being a notable exception.

In 1924, the submersed angiosperm hydrilla (*Hydrilla verticillata*) was reported to undergo diel fluctuations in acidity and malic acid levels, somewhat like cactii, during the summer (Bose, 1924). We rediscovered this surprising phenomenon half a century later, and suggested that it conserved inorganic C under conditions where this vital nutrient was severely limiting (Holaday and Bowes, 1980). Since then it has become apparent that some submersed isoetids undergo a form of CAM to a greater extent than hydrilla (Keeley and Bowes, 1982). This is obviously not a response to water stress, but rather to diurnal DIC limitations in the aquatic environment. Thus by fixing DIC at night when it is available, and then decarboxylating and refixing it into the PCR cycle during the day, when energy and reducing power are available, some submersed isoetids can significantly increase their net diel C uptake. No emergent or floating aquatic macrophytes belong to the CAM photosynthetic category, because of the access that this type of aquatic plant has to air-CO_2 and abundant water.

Algal CO_2 Concentrating Mechanisms

Unicellular algae and cyanobacteria feature photosynthetic gas exchange characteristics similar to those of C_4 plants. They have low CO_2 compensation points, lack photorespiratory CO_2 release and sensitivity to O_2, show a high temperature optimum for photosynthesis, and in some instances have high photosynthetic rates (Table 5). But, they fix DIC mainly via the C_3 PCR cycle, not the C_4 cycle (Table 5). This apparent anomaly can be explained by the organisms having DIC concentrating systems that operate, at least partially, at the membrane level. In some cases, DIC in the form of bicarbonate is actively transported across the cell and/or chloroplast membrane resulting in high internal concentrations. Alternatively, bicarbonate may be dehydrated to CO_2 at the cell surface; either by an active proton pump that creates a low pH in the unstirred boundary layer surrounding the cells, or by the extracellular secretion of carbonic anhydrase (CA), an enzyme that rapidly equilibrates the CO_2 and bicarbonate forms of DIC. In the latter cases, CO_2 would

TABLE 5. Photosynthetic and growth characteristics of unicellular algae and cyanobacteria.

1. CO_2 fixed first by RuBPCase, into the C_3 compound PGA; some C_4 acid production may occur in cyanobacteria
2. Cells exist in high- and low-CO_2 grown states, induced by growth at 1-2% or air CO_2 levels, respectively
3. High- and low-CO_2 grown cells appear C_3- and C_4-like, respectively, in their photosynthetic gas exchange characteristics
4. Low CO_2 compensation points in low-CO_2 grown state
5. No O_2 inhibition of photosynthesis in low-CO_2 grown state
6. No photorespiratory CO_2 evolution or glycolate release in low-CO_2 grown state
7. Very low $K_{1/2}$(DIC) values for photosynthesis in low-CO_2 grown state (>1 mmol CO_2 m^{-3})
8. High net photosynthetic rates in low-CO_2 grown state
9. Growth at low CO_2 induces carbonic anhydrase activity (not in cyanobacteria), and a DIC uptake mechanism
10. Ethoxyzolamide (a carbonic anhydrase inhibitor) causes the high- and low-CO_2 grown cells to become photosynthetically similar
11. High internal CO_2 levels in the low-CO_2 grown state (CO_2 concentrating mechanism) suppress photorespiration
12. Only a few species studied; ecological significance yet to be established

be the actual inorganic form of C crossing the membrane along a concentration gradient. In these mechanisms, irrespective of the form crossing the membrane, bicarbonate is the exogenous DIC source utilized. However, in the algae and all aquatic autotrophs, exogenous free CO_2, when readily available, can be assimilated. The energy to drive these "CO_2 pumping systems" is obtained from the photosynthetic light reactions. In addition to the "pump", an internal CA to rapidly interconvert the DIC forms, is apparently essential. As in C_4 plants, the elevated internal CO_2 concentration suppresses the oxygenase function of RuBPcase, thus alleviating the first step of photorespiration. Because the CO_2 is concentrated by a membrane-based transport system, rather than by the C_4 pathway, it has been termed a "biophysical CO_2 concentrating mechanism" (Raven et al., 1985).

Algae grown at high CO_2 (0.5 to 5%, gas phase) lose much of their capacity to actively concentrate DIC, and they show a marked reduction in CA activity. As a result, their ability to suppress photorespiration is very limited, and CO_2 compensation points and other gas exchange characteristics become similar to those of C_3 plants. Unicellular, as well as some filamentous algae, mainly among the greens and cyanobacteria, have been described as belonging to this efficient photosynthesis group (Spalding, 1987;

Colman, 1987). Recent work suggests that some macrophytic filamentous algae, for example lyngbya (*Lyngbya birgei*, a cyanobacterium that can form dense mats in freshwater lakes), also feature a similar photosynthetic mechanism (Beer et al., 1986). As this system has been discovered only in the last decade, its application to ecology and productivity in natural habitats is sparse. Initial data suggest that at least some filamentous algae exist naturally in the low photorespiration condition, as if "low-CO_2 grown" (Beer et al., 1986). Whether this condition is ubiquitous among freshwater algae is unknown. Certainly among marine macroalgae not all feature an effective bicarbonate utilization system, and they do not seem to show an induced growth response to the CO_2 level (Bowes, 1985). The "Algae" constitute a taxonomically very diverse assemblage of organisms, much more so than higher plants. Consequently, it would be surprising to find that they all operated in the same biochemical manner, and variations on the mechanism described here might be expected to be discovered over the next few years, as the various algal divisions are investigated in more detail.

Submersed Aquatic Macrophytes

One mode of C fixation, based on the metabolism of C_4 acids, which is present in some submersed aquatic macrophytes, has already been alluded to in the CAM section. However, others show no evidence of C_4 acid metabolism during photosynthesis, and perform *biochemically* more or less as C_3 plants (Bowes, 1985). Irrespective of whether or not they utilize C_4 acids in photosynthesis, all freshwater submersed macrophytes show the unusual ability to modify their gas exchange characteristics and, concomitantly the relative flux of C through the PCR and PCO cycles, in response to changes in growth conditions. Because of this physiological and biochemical plasticity, they have been placed in a novel photosynthetic category termed SAM (Holaday et al., 1983), and the different biochemical modes that produce this plasticity can be referred to as SAMM (submersed aquatic macrophyte metabolism).

Most SAM plants taken from the lake exhibit C_3-like gas exchange characteristics; i.e. the CO_2 compensation points and photorespiratory CO_2 release rates are relatively high, and the low photosynthetic rates are inhibited by O_2. However, during incubation under crowded, summer-like stress conditions (high temperature, long photoperiods, and low DIC concentrations), the compensation points decline to values close to those of terrestrial C_4 plants (Holaday et al., 1983). This lowering of the compensation point is associated with a decrease in photorespiration and an increase in net photosynthesis (Bowes, 1985). Although the high photorespiration state is most common, plants with low photorespiration do occur naturally; especially when subject to the stresses that develop in dense vegetation (Bowes et al., 1979).

To date, two different biochemical methods are known that enable plants with SAMM to achieve the low photorespiration state (Bowes, 1985). In species exemplified by hydrilla, the PEPcase/RuBPcase activity ratio and the activity of all C_4 metabolism enzymes increase, as the low photorespiration state is induced. Concomitantly, four-C acids are the predominant initial products in the light, and they rapidly pass the fixed C to the C_3 PCR cycle (Salvucci and Bowes, 1983a). There is no Kranz anatomy as in terrestrial C_4 plants, but the carboxylase enzymes appear to be separated by placement in the cytosol (PEPcase) and chloroplast (RuBPcase). It is hypothesized that decarboxylation occurs in the chloroplast via NADP-malic enzyme, and this leads to an elevation of the CO_2 level around the RuBPcase enzyme, thus reducing carbon flow to the PCO cycle (Salvucci and Bowes, 1983a). In a CAM-like variation on this theme, some SAMs such as *Isoetes howellii*, when faced with low daytime DIC levels, fix a substantial amount of C into C_4 acids (mainly malate) at night (Keeley and Bowes, 1982). The malate is decarboxylated during the day to provide CO_2 for the C_3 PCR cycle, and presumably elevates the internal DIC level. For some reason, these plants do not show such high PEPcase activities as occur in low photorespiration hydrilla (Farmer et al., 1986).

In the second biochemical method, typified by plants like watermilfoil (*Myriophyllum spicatum*), the decline in the CO_2 compensation point is not paralleled by a shift towards C_4 metabolism. Enzymatic, ^{14}C-labelling, and inhibitor studies suggest that a DIC concentrating mechanism, similar to that found in unicellular algae, is induced under stressful growth situations (Salvucci and Bowes, 1983a; 1983b). Many SAMs possess the ability to utilize exogenous bicarbonate for photosynthesis either by direct uptake (Lucas, 1983), or by dehydration at the cell surface (Prins et al., 1982); and the enzyme CA is an important component of the process. Measurements of internal DIC pools suggest that plants with SAMM can indeed concentrate DIC internally (Reiskind and Bowes, 1986), which in turn could suppress the oxygenase activity of RuBPcase. At this stage, more research is needed to quantitatively show that bicarbonate use increases the internal CO_2 sufficiently to alleviate photorespiration, and result in the low photorespiratory state. Conditions which induce the low photorespiratory state are typically found in dense plant stands during the summer, when DIC levels during the day are low due to high photosynthetic activity and temperatures. General photosynthetic and growth characteristics of SAM plants are listed in Table 6.

PHOTOSYNTHETIC CARBON FIXATION AND THE AQUATIC ENVIRONMENT

The Efficiency of Photosynthesis and Plant Productivity

The highest irradiance typically encountered at the surface of the earth is about 2,000 µmol PAR m^{-2} s^{-1}. If this area were

TABLE 6. Photosynthetic and growth characteristics of freshwater SAM plants.

1. Very low photosynthetic rates, and low enzyme activities.
2. Often have thin or dissected leaves; chloroplasts in epidermal cells; no Kranz anatomy or functional stomates; high fresh/dry wt ratios; may possess lacunal gas channels
3. Shade photosynthesis plants with low light saturation points
4. Require high DIC levels to saturate photosynthesis with high $K_{1/2}$ (DIC) values; photosynthesis and growth often very DIC limited
5. Prefer free CO_2 for photosynthesis, but able to use bicarbonate
6. Exhibit variable CO_2 compensation points, from high to low, depending on the growth conditions; summer-like, stress conditions can induce low (C_4-like) values
7. Plants with low CO_2 compensation points have higher net photosynthetic rates; lower photorespiration, O_2 inhibition of photosynthesis, and $K_{1/2}$ (DIC) values. The reverse is true for high CO_2 compensation point plants.
8. The low photorespiration state is due to the induction of either a C_4-like system (as in hydrilla), or increased utilization of bicarbonate (as in watermilfoil). Both seem to be CO_2 concentrating mechanisms, that alleviate the DIC limitation and O_2 inhibition effects
9. In hydrilla, transition to the low-photorespiration state involves:
   a) Induction of C_4 enzymes; the first fixation product is malate, by PEPcase in the cytosol; rapid decarboxylation provides CO_2 for fixation into the C_3 PCR cycle, via RuBPcase in the chloroplasts
   b) CO_2 fixation potentially in both light and dark, with diel acidity changes
   c) A reduced flow of carbon through the PCO cycle
10. In watermilfoil, transition to the low-photorespiration state involves:
   a) No induction of C_4 enzymes; RuBPcase remains the major carboxylase, and PGA is the initial fixation product
   b) Decreased carbon flow through the PCO cycle
   c) Increased bicarbonate utilization
   d) Increased carbonic anhydrase activity, and sensitivity to carbonic anhydrase inhibitors, which reverse the low-photorespiration state
11. Irrespective of the photorespiration state, productivity is low in comparison with terrestrial C_3 or C_4 plants.

covered with plants collecting all the available radiant energy for 12 h each day, and assuming a conversion efficiency of 1 mol CO_2 fixed per 10 mol photons absorbed, one might expect the production of about 760 Mg organic dry matter ha^{-1} yr^{-1} (Raven, 1984). This is more than 10 times the actual yields of highly productive ecosystems; for example: 40-60 Mg ha^{-1} yr^{-1} in tropical rain forests, 66 Mg ha^{-1} yr^{-1} for sugarcane, a semi-tropical crop, and 24 Mg ha^{-1} yr^{-1} for the temperate crop wheat (Beadle et al., 1985). It is apparent that factors other than irradiance _per se_ may limit plant productivity.

Of the radiant energy intercepted annually by the earth's surface (2×10^{24}J), only a small fraction (0.15%) is stored by photosynthesis as chemical energy; yet this fraction is still about ten-fold greater than the amount of energy annually expended by the earth's population. Furthermore, this photosynthetic stored energy provides all of the food energy, and via the fossil fuel reserves, 90% of the technological energy utilized by humans (Blaxter, 1978).

There are a number of reasons why only 0.15% of the incoming radiant energy is stored in photosynthesis, encompassing factors external to, as well as inherited by, the plant. Approximately 50% of the solar energy is comprised of photons with wavelengths outside of the PAR range (360-720 nm), and even for photons within the range many are intercepted by nonphotosynthetic surfaces, or are incompletely absorbed. Conversion of absorbed photons to excitation energy, and thence chemical energy, can result in a further 30% loss, while dark respiration and photorespiration can account for another 5 to 9% (Beadle et al., 1985). Thus, the highest net efficiency of photosynthesis theoretically attainable has been estimated to be about 5.8%. That light is not always the factor limiting the productivity of a region is clear when one considers that the highest solar irradiance occurs in the desert regions of Arizona and the Sahara, yet the highest productivities are encountered in wet, tropical areas, such as the Amazon basin and S.E. Asia.

With regard to aquatic plants, in general the emergent and floating forms, which by definition photosynthesize in an aerial environment and yet still have an abundant water supply, produce biomass at rates similar to, or higher than, highly productive terrestrial systems. For example, among emergent species, above-ground standing crop yields of 10 to 45 Mg ha^{-1} yr^{-1} have been reported for cattail (Reddy et al., 1983), and even higher amounts (85.3 Mg ha^{-1} yr^{-1}) for napiergrass in El Salvador (Boardman, 1978). For the floating plant water hyacinth, in natural stands in Florida, the standing crop ranged from 9 to 20 Mg ha^{-1}. However, in nutrient-enriched cultivated systems up to 64 g dry wt m^{-2} d^{-1} (equivalent to 234 Mg ha^{-1} yr^{-1}, assuming an extremely optimistic, optimal growing season of 365 days each year, and regular harvesting) has been attained with water hyacinth (Reddy et al., 1983). Not all floating plants do as well; water ferns

(Salvinia rotundifolia, and Azolla caroliniana), and duckweed (Lemna minor), cultivated in a similar manner to the water hyacinth above, had only about 10 to 15% of its productivity.

In contrast to some of the highly productive emergent and floating aquatic plants, submersed freshwater species are characterized by low biomass yields, ranging up to about 10 Mg ha^{-1} yr^{-1}, even in tropical regions. Although some SAMs, such as hydrilla, appear to be very prolific from the manner in which they can rapidly cover a body of water, on closer examination most of the biomass is confined within 0.5 m of the surface, and the plant composition includes about 95% water. Consequently, the dry matter produced on an area basis is usually very low. It is now clear that for any particular aquatic (or terrestrial) species, both external and internal (inherited) factors set the upper limits to gross photosynthesis, and hence potential productivity. Some of these factors will be examined in the last two sections.

External Factors

For an aquatic plant, a major determinant of the maximum photosynthetic rate is whether or not it has direct access to air-CO_2. Emergent, floating, and the aerial parts of amphibious species do have direct access; whereas submersed species do not. The importance of this is due to the fact that CO_2 diffuses some 10,000 times slower in aqueous solution than in air. Thus, in terms of CO_2, submersed leaves are subject to a massive diffusion resistance, which limits the availability of this resource to a far greater extent than for plants in air. This is probably the major reason why SAMs exhibit much lower photosynthetic rates than terrestrial (with the exception of CAM) or emergent aquatic species (Bowes, 1985).

The aqueous diffusion resistance has other implications. In dense, submersed vegetation during the day, it impedes the loss to the air of photosynthetically produced O_2, thus allowing this potentially inhibitory substance to build-up to levels in excess of 200% air-saturation (Bowes, 1985). Concomitantly, DIC levels decline dramatically, and pH values may rise to above 10. These conditions are not conducive to high photosynthetic rates, but in contrast actually facilitate loss of CO_2 through photorespiration. During the night, due to respiratory and decay processes, the reverse effects can be found. Flowing, as opposed to static, water can improve the situation, but even in rapidly flowing, shallow streams, localized microhabitats of high O_2 and low DIC can develop in dense stands of submersed plants during the day. A high flow rate will improve photosynthesis and growth because it decreases the thickness of the boundary layer around the leaves. This facilitates diffusion of DIC and other nutrients to the uptake sites (Smith and Walker, 1980). In nutrient-poor waters, high flow rates are especially important to ensure adequate resupply rates to the leaves following nutrient uptake.

A further implication that follows from the strongly limiting DIC availability, is that one might expect the productivity of submersed macrophytes to respond less to nutrient enrichment with N or P than emergent or floating species. This hypothesis requires testing, but it is consistent with the generally low protein and dry weight of submersed macrophytes. It would probably not apply to microphytes which usually possess large surface area to volume ratios, combined with very effective DIC utilization mechanisms. Nutrients such as NO_3^-, PO_4^{3-}, K and Fe may in SAMs, as in emergent and floating aquatic plants, be supplied via the roots. However, submersed plants usually have poorly developed phloem and xylem transport systems, and lack the active transpiration stream that facilitates the movement of nutrients from the roots to the leaves of emergent forms. To compensate, some submersed plants are capable of direct nutrient uptake by the leaves from the water column; which increased the surface area for absorption. Direct leaf uptake probably does not occur naturally to any great extent in emergent species, and it is not clear if floating aquatic plants can obtain nutrients through abaxial leaf surfaces in contact with the water.

Aerial plants require a substantial investment in structural components, such as polysaccharides and lignin (woody tissues), in order to support an effective photosynthetic canopy for the capture of solar energy. In contrast, the buoyancy provided by the dense, water medium obviates much of the need for support structure in submersed plants. Consequently, from a teleological viewpoint, submersed plants, or prostrate floating species should not "need" the biomass of their emergent counterparts.

In contrast to aerial leaves, the photosynthetic organs of SAMs are exposed to an external H^+ ion concentration, due to their immersion in water, a polar solvent. Few macrophytes can survive below pH 4, which is one reason why acid rain is so devastating, but many tolerate periods at pH 10 to 11 (Bowes, 1985). The pH of freshwater is variable from acid to alkaline, sometimes on a diel basis. Some SAMs regulate the microenvironment of the surrounding aqueous boundary layer by secreting H^+ and OH^- ions from the abaxial and adaxial leaf surfaces, respectively, such that the abaxial values may be below pH 5 (Prins et al., 1982). These large microenvironmental pH effects mean that gross measurements of water pH may not provide an accurate reflection of the pH to which the leaves are actually exposed. Although all SAMs must be able to compensate for the external pH, their tolerance varies. For example, the amphibious angiosperms limnophila (*Limnophila sessiliflora*) and hygrophila (*Hygrophila polysperma*) grow best at pH 5 to 7, and hardly at all at pH 9. In contrast, although hydrilla grows well at pH 5 to 7, its growth rate is tenfold higher at pH 9 (Spencer and Bowes, 1985). A wide pH tolerance may be a factor in the competitive success of an aquatic plant.

The pH indirectly affects the photosynthesis of submersed species by influencing the equilibrium between the various forms of DIC: free CO_2, H_2CO_3, HCO_3^-, and CO_3^{2-}. It is generally agreed that CO_3^{2-} ions are not used directly, and free CO_2 is preferred to HCO_3^-, while H_2CO_3 levels are insignificantly low. The concentration of dissolved CO_2 is a function of its partial pressure in the gas phase and its solubility coefficient. The latter is in turn a function of temperature and ionic strength. Since CO_2 is a very soluble gas, at 25°, its concentration in water that is in equilibrium with air is approximately 10 μM. However, aquatic habitats which are not air-equilibrated can have less or more CO_2.

When CO_2 dissolves, a small part hydrates to form carbonic acid which in turn dissociates to bicarbonate and carbonate ions. The equilibrium between dissolved CO_2 and its ionic forms thus depends on two equilibrium constants (that are a function of temperature, and ionic strength), and especially pH. The concentration of bicarbonate is much higher than that of CO_2 in many natural systems. For example, in waters of pH 8 and 9, the bicarbonate concentration would be 91 and 900 times, respectively, that of CO_2. Such pH values are commonly found in lakes. In dense plant stands, the slow equilibration of CO_2 with air in comparison with the rate of photosynthesis would further increase the HCO_3^-/CO_2 ratio. Given these conditions, the ability to utilize bicarbonate should be advantageous to SAMs as well as algae and cyanobacteria. The quantitative importance of bicarbonate use will depend on ambient concentrations of CO_2 and bicarbonate as well as the plant's affinity for each form. Although the capacity varies among species, and even within a species depending on growth conditions (Bowes, 1985,1986), only one group of aquatic plants, the bryophytes, is believed to be incapable of utilizing bicarbonate (based on a limited survey). Thus these plants are often restricted to habitats where the availability of free CO_2 is high.

For aquatic plants that photosynthesize in air, the bicarbonate in the water appears not to be a direct source of carbon. Some aphibious species are an exception in that their submersed leaves may utilize bicarbonate, while their aerial leaves rely on CO_2 (Bowes, 1986). There is no evidence that floating aquatic plants, such as water hyacinth, can absorb bicarbonate ions for photosynthesis via leaves on the water surface or roots in the water column.

Among aquatic plants that photosynthesize in air, and fall into the C_3 category, the present CO_2 levels (340 μL^{-1} L^{-1}) are insufficient to saturate photosynthesis. Thus, with all else being optimal, they normally photosynthesize at only 60 to 70% of their maximum, CO_2-saturated rate. Recently we have demonstrated that doubling the atmospheric CO_2 level during growth of water hyacinth (a C_3 plant) causes a transient increase in the photosynthetic rate. This leads to a sustained improvement in the leaf area index of the ramets, and a 40% increase in biomass production (Spencer and Bowes, 1986). The elevated CO_2 also results in a 40 to 50% shift in the allocation of C away from protein and into carbohydrates. The present CO_2 levels are saturating for most C_4 plants, and thus this nutrient is less of a limiting resource for emergent aquatic plants that fall into the C_4 category. It is unlikely that an increase in atmospheric CO_2 would affect them as much as it does C_3 aquatic plants.

Although there are negative aspects for a plant growing in an aquatic habitat, there are substantial benefits. An obvious and major benefit is that water rarely becomes a limiting resource. Thus emergent and floating plants, with their roots bathed in water, can photosynthesize at high rates throughout the day, without having to close the stomates to conserve water when the heat load and water loss become severe. This is probably a major reason why some emergent or floating plants, even with the potentially less productive C_3 pathway, can produce yields equivalent to terrestrial C_4 systems. A further consideration is that in eutrophic waters, with an abundant supply of N and P, C_3 emergent or floating plants can afford to invest large amounts of nutrients in RuBPcase and the associated components of the PCR cycle to maximize their CO_2 fixation capacity. Although not as elegant a strategy as the C_4 pathway, it can be an effective means to improve the maximum photosynthetic rate.

A final external factor to be mentioned is light. Emergent and floating plants have potentially better access to light, as irradiance is attentuated exponentially along any depth gradient. Furthermore, once an emergent plant has grown above the surface, it has a competitive edge in that it can shade SAMs that are obligately restricted to growth in the water column. In a similar manner, SAMs that elongate rapidly and place their photosynthetic canopy at the water surface, for example hydrilla and watermilfoil, can effectively outcompete benthic species, and usually have higher productivity. Although submersed plants adapt well to low light levels, insufficient light may set the lower depth penetration limit. This is the compensation depth, and it varies with species and water bodies of varying clarity. In addition to decreased irradiance, submersed plants are subjected to a selective attenuation of different wavelengths. In clear water, the PAR becomes enriched in the blue; because red photons are absorbed first while blue, having the highest energy per photon, penetrates deepest. In turbid waters, while red is still absorbed, blue is scattered by suspended particles, and therefore green light penetrates the deepest.

Plants, including submersed, adapt to reduced irradiance by increasing their total chlorophyll content, thereby increasing the antenna for more efficient capture of photons. Also, SAMs adapt to the changing spectrum with depth, by shifting their chlorophyll a/b ratio towards chlorophyll b, which is more complementary to the wavelengths at greater depths. However, the quantitative importance of this adaptation is questionable.

Inherited Factors

Aquatic plants, in addition to the physiological and biochemical characteristics endowed by their particular photosynthetic category, also show various genetic adaptations to the environment that influence photosynthesis and productivity. Certainly in submersed forms, many of the adaptations ameliorate the gas diffusion and light limitation problems.

Many aquatic plants feature longitudinal gas channels called lacunae. Although septae are present, they are gas permeable, and thus the lacunae often constitute continuous gas canals from the leaves to the roots. Photosynthetically produced O_2 can therefore diffuse from the leaves to the root system; which is important, since the roots and rhizomes of aquatic plants frequently grow in anaerobic sediments. This process in some plants not only facilitates root respiration, but also nutrient uptake by producing an oxidized sediment zone in the immediate vicinity of the root. Thus lacunae are an adaptation that enable some emergent and floating plants to have the best of both the aerial and aquatic worlds.

In certain SAMs (e.g. <u>Littorella uniflora</u>), lacunae serve to transport sediment CO_2 to the leaves for photosynthetic fixation, thereby alleviating some of the DIC limitation. It has been suggested that lacunae reduce photorespiration by accumulating photorespiratory CO_2 for subsequent refixation; but the validity of this hypothesis is questionable. Since lacunae are gas filled spaces, they are susceptible to pressure. At great depths insufficient O_2 may be produced to keep them inflated, thus obstructing O_2 transport to the roots. Therefore, hydrostatic pressure may limit the depth penetration of a SAM by crushing the lacunae, or preventing their formation, which may explain why plants do not always grow at the depth predicted from their diel light compensation points (Hutchinson, 1975).

Submersed macrophytes invariably can be categorized as shade plants, as leaf photosynthesis is saturated at an irradiance of less than half full sunlight, even for species that inhabit surface waters (Bowes, 1985). Thus individual leaves are genetically adapted to the lower radiant energy fluxes of the environment, not the high surface irradiance. However, a dense submersed canopy structure may show increasing light interception and growth up to full sunlight. In addition to low light saturation points for photosynthesis, other inherent shade features found in SAMs include: a relatively high chlorophyll content; reduced chlorophyll a/b ratios; low light compensation points; and low photosynthetic rates, even at light- and DIC-saturation. The latter is in part due to relatively low activities of photosynthetic enzymes such as RuBPcase.

In the leaves, chloroplasts are found mainly in the epidermis. Not only does this maximize exposure to light, but diffusion of nutrients such as CO_2 to the metabolic sites is enhanced by shortening the diffusion distance. The high surface area to volume ratio of the thin, dissected leaves found in many SAMs also has been viewed as an adaptation to improve access to nutrients. Although most of these features adapt somewhat to the higher irradiance at the water surface, SAMs are inherently limited by their shade characteristics to low photosynthesis and productivity, even under optimal environmental conditions. Consequently, they do not make good biomass candidates, except perhaps in polyculture with emergent species; though they may prove useful in absorbing nutrients from a water column.

Among emergent and floating aquatic plants, both sun and shade species occur. It was originally believed that C_3 and C_4 plants were composed of shade and sun species, respectively (Black, 1973). It is now known that sun and shade species can be found within either photosynthetic category, and furthermore, some plants adapt their light saturation point to the growth irradiance (Boardman, 1977). For example, water hyacinth belongs in the C_3 category, yet when grown in full sunlight it shows sun photosynthetic characteristics (Patterson and Duke, 1979), but under lower light conditions it exhibits a reduced light saturation point, and photosynthetic rate (Spencer and Bowes, 1986). Among other C_3 aquatic plants, cattails appear to be sun species, and the duckweeds shade plants; which coincides with their high and low productivities, respectively. For emergent and floating species especially, leaf architecture is a further important factor in the ability to intercept light, as it affects the leaf area index (LAI). The LAI is a measure of the photosynthetic leaf area which is subtended by a given ground area. Thus, plants with high LAIs have more photosynthetic antenna for photon capture per unit ground area, and can usually pack more biomass into a given area. Duckweeds and other prostrate floating species have low LAI values, and consequently show relatively low productivity per unit ground area, unless harvested frequently. In contrast, plants such as cattails and the rushes, because of their vertical leaf architecture have high LAI values. Under nutrient-rich, crowded conditions the otherwise prostrate plant, water hyacinth, produces large, upright leaves, thereby increasing both its ability to capture photons and its biomass per unit ground area.

From this overview it can be seen that emergent or floating aquatic plants that are sun species with high LAI values, and preferably C_4 plants in tropical areas, should be the best choice for biomass production. However, a high nutrient-utilization capacity must also be a consideration if the plant is to be used for water treatment.

ACKNOWLEDGMENTS

Supported in part by grant 82-CRCR-1-1147 from the Competitive Research Grants Office, Science and Education Administration, United States Department of Agriculture, and by a cooperative program between the Institute of Food and Agricultural

Sciences, University of Florida, and the Gas Research Institute, Chicago, entitled: "Methane from Biomass and Waste." Florida Agricultural Experiment Station Journal Series Number 7826.

REFERENCES

Anderson, J. W. 1981. Light-energy-dependent processes other than CO_2 assimilation. p. 473-500. In M. D. Hatch and N. K. Boardman (ed.) The Biochemistry of Plants, Vol. 8, Photosynthesis. Academic Press, New York.

Beadle, C. L., S. P. Long, S. K. Imbamba, D. O. Hall, and R. J. Olembo. 1985. Photosynthesis in Relation to Plant Production in Terrestrial Environments. Tycooly Publishing Ltd., Oxford, U.K. p. 1-156.

Beer, S., W. Spencer, and G. Bowes. 1986. Photosynthesis and growth of the filamentous blue-green alga *Lyngbya birgei* in relation to its environment. J. Aquat. Plant Manage. 24:61-65.

Black, C. C., Jr. 1973. Photosynthetic carbon fixation in relation to net CO_2 uptake. Annu. Rev. Plant Physiol. 24:253-286.

Blaxter, K. L. 1978. Energy flow in agriculture. p. 685-694. In D. O. Hall, J. Coombs, and T. W. Goodwin (ed.) Photosynthesis 77. Proceedings of the Fourth International Congress on Photosynthesis. The Biochemical Society, London, U.K.

Boardman, N. K. 1977. Comparative photosynthesis of sun and shade plants. Annu. Rev. Plant Physiol. 28:355-377.

Boardman, N. K. 1978. Solar energy conversion in photosynthesis and its potential contribution to world demand for liquid and gaseous fuels. p. 635-644. In D. O. Hall, J. Coombs, and T. W. Goodwin (ed.) Photosynthesis 77. Proceedings of the Fourth International Congress on Photosynthesis. The Biochemical Society, London, U.K.

Bose, J. C. 1924. The Physiology of Photosynthesis. Longmans, Green and Co., London, U.K.

Bowes, G. 1985. Pathways of CO_2 fixation by aquatic organisms. p. 187-210. In W. J. Lucas, and J. A. Berry (ed.) Inorganic Carbon Uptake by Aquatic Photosynthetic Organisms. Am. Soc. Plant Physiol., Rockville, Maryland.

Bowes, G. 1987. Aquatic plant photosynthesis: Strategies that enhance carbon gain. p. 77-96. In R. M. M. Crawford (ed.) Plant Life in Aquatic and Amphibious Habitats. British Ecolog. Soc. Spec. Pub. No. 5, Blackwell Scientific Publications Ltd., Oxford, U.K.

Bowes, G., W. L. Ogren, and R. H. Hageman. 1971. Phosphoglycolate production catalyzed by ribulose diphosphate carboxylase. Biochem. Biophys. Res. Commun. 45:716-722.

Bowes, G., A. S. Holaday, and W. T. Haller. 1979. Seasonal variation in the biomass, tuber density, and photosynthetic metabolism of hydrilla in three Florida lakes. J. Aquat. Plant Manage. 17:61-64.

Colman, B. 1987. Photosynthetic carbon assimilation and the suppression of photorespiration in the cyanobacteria. In G. Bowes (ed.) Photosynthesis and Photorespiration in Aquatic Organisms. Elsevier Science Publishers B.V. Amsterdam, The Netherlands. (In press).

Edwards, G. E., and S. C. Huber. 1981. The C_4 pathway. p. 237-281. In M. D. Hatch, and N, K. Boardman (ed.) The Biochemistry of Plants. Vol. 8, Photosynthesis. Academic Press, New York.

Farmer, A. M., S. C. Maberly, and G. Bowes. 1986. Activities of carboxylation enzymes in freshwater macrophytes. J. Exp. Botany 37:1568-1573.

Garrard, L. A., and T. K. Van. 1982. General characteristics of freshwater vascular plants. p. 75-85. In O. R. Zaborsky, A. Mitsui, and C. C. Black (ed.) CRC Handbook of Biosolar Resources. Vol. 1, Pt. 2, Basic Principles. CRC Press, Inc. Boca Raton, Florida.

Hatch, M. D., and C. R. Slack. 1970. Photosynthetic CO_2-fixation pathways. Annu. Rev. Plant Physiol. 21:141-162.

Holaday, A. S., and G. Bowes. 1980. C_4 acid metabolism and dark CO_2 fixation in a submersed aquatic macrophyte (*Hydrilla verticillata*). Plant Physiol. 65:331-335.

Holaday, A. S., M. E. Salvucci, and G. Bowes. 1983. Variable photosynthesis/photorespiration ratios in *Hydrilla* and other submersed aquatic macrophyte species. Can. J. Bot. 61:229-236.

Hutchinson, G. E. 1975. A treatise on limnology. Vol. 3, Limnological Botany. John Wiley & Sons, New York. p. 1-660.

Keeley, J. E., and G. Bowes. 1982. Gas exchange characteristics of the submerged aquatic crassulacean acid metabolism plant, *Isoetes howellii*. Plant Physiol. 70:1455-1458.

Kluge, M., and I. P. Ting. 1978. Crassulacean acid metabolism. Analysis of an ecology adaptation. Ecological Studies, Vol. 30. Springer-Verlag, New York. p. 1-209.

Lorimer, G. H., and T. J. Andrews. 1981. The C_2 chemo- and photorespiratory carbon oxidation cycle. p. 329-374. In M. D. Hatch, and N. K. Boardman (ed.) The Biochemistry of Plants. Vol. 8, Photosynthesis. Academic Press, New York.

Lucas, W. J. 1983. Photosynthetic assimilation of exogenous HCO_3^- by aquatic plants. Annu. Rev. Plant Physiol. 34:71-104.

McNaughton, S. J., and L. W. Fullem. 1970. Photosynthesis and photorespiration in *Typha latifolia*. Plant Physiol. 45:703-707.

Ogren, W. L., and R. Chollet. 1982. Photorespiration. p. 191-230. In Govindjee (ed.) Photosynthesis. Vol. II, Development, Carbon Metabolism, and Plant Productivity. Academic Press, New York.

Patterson, D. T., and S. O. Duke. 1979. Effect of growth irradiance on the maximum photosynthetic capacity of water hyacinth (Eichhornia crassipes [Mart] Solms). Plant & Cell Physiol. 20:177-184.

Prins, H. B. A., J. F. H. Snel, P. E. Zanstra, and J. Helder. 1982. The mechanism of bicarbonate assimilation by the polar leaves of Potamogeton and Elodea. CO_2 concentrations at the leaf surface. Plant, Cell and Environment 5:207-214.

Raven, J. A. 1984. Energetics and Transport in Aquatic Plants. MBL Lectures in Biology, Vol. 4. Alan R. Liss, Inc., New York. p. 1-587.

Raven, J. A., B. A. Osborne, and A. M. Johnston. 1985. Uptake of CO_2 by aquatic vegetation. Plant, Cell and Environment 8:417-425.

Reddy, K. R., D. L. Sutton, and G. Bowes. 1983. Freshwater aquatic plant biomass production in Florida. Soil and Crop Sci. Soc. Florida Proc. 42:28-40.

Reiskind, J. B., and G. Bowes. 1987. Inorganic carbon concentrating mechanisms from an environmental perspective. In J. Biggins (ed.) Proceedings of the VIIth International Congress on Photosynthesis. Martinus Nijhoff Publishers, Dordrecht, The Netherlands. (in press).

Robinson, S. P., and D. A. Walker. 1981. Photosynthetic carbon reduction cycle. p. 193-236. In M. D. Hatch, and N. K. Boardman (ed.) The Biochemistry of Plants. Vol. 8, Photosynthesis. Academic Press, New York.

Salvucci, M. E., and G. Bowes. 1983a. Two photosynthetic mechanisms mediating the low photorespiratory state in submersed aquatic angiosperms. Plant Physiol. 73:488-496.

Salvucci, M. E., and G. Bowes. 1983b. Ethoxyzolamide repression of the low photorespiration state in two submersed angiosperms. Planta 158:27-34.

Smith, F. A., and N. A. Walker. 1980. Photosynthesis by aquatic plants: effects of unstirred layers in relation to assimilation of CO_2 and HCO_3^- and to carbon isotopic discrimination. New Phytol. 86:245-259.

Spalding, M. H. 1987. Photosynthesis and photorespiration in freshwater green algae. In G. Bowes (ed.) Photosynthesis and Photorespiration in Aquatic Organisms. Elsevier Science Publishers B.V., Amsterdam, The Netherlands. (in press)

Spencer, W., and G. Bowes. 1985. Limnophila and hygrophila: A review and physiological assessment of their weed potential in Florida. J. Aquat. Plant Manage. 23:7-16.

Spencer, W., and G. Bowes. 1986. Photosynthesis and growth of water hyacinth under CO_2 enrichment. Plant Physiol. 86:528-533.

Wedge, R. M., and Burris, J. E. 1982. Effects of light and temperature on duckweed photosynthesis. Aquatic Bot. 12:133-140.

NUTRIENT STORAGE CAPABILITIES OF AQUATIC AND WETLAND PLANTS

K. R. Reddy and W. F. DeBusk
Central Florida Research and Education Center
University of Florida, IFAS
Sanford, Florida 32771

ABSTRACT

Floating aquatic macrophytes, such as Eichhornia crassipes, Hydrocotyle sp. and Pistia stratiotes, have demonstrated considerable potential for nutrient removal from wastewaters due to their rapid growth and high nutrient assimilative capacity. Because the turnover time for these plants is relatively brief, they can provide only short-term nutrient storage. Emergent macrophytes such as Typha spp., Phragmites sp., Scirpus sp., Panicum sp., Pontederia sp. and Sagittaria sp. also show potential for rapid nutrient uptake from wetlands used for water treatment, while providing a greater duration of nutrient storage. Efficiency of water treatment in these systems depends in part on the frequency of harvesting the plants. Forested wetlands dominated by such species as Taxodium distichum, Nyssa sp., Acer rubrum, Ulmus americana, Fraxinus sp., and Quercus sp. are characterized by lower rates of nutrient uptake, but provide long-term nutrient storage. Nutrient assimilation by aquatic and wetland plants is a function of several factors, including growth rate, standing crop, tissue nutrient content, and physico-chemical characteristics of sediment and water. Plant uptake typically accounts for 16 to 75% of total N removal and 12 to 73% of total P removal. In addition to plant uptake, nutrient removal in aquatic plant-based water treatment systems is affected by a number of biological, physical and chemical processes functioning in the water and sediment.

Keywords: Plant uptake, nitrogen, phosphorus, water treatment, nutrient assimilation.

INTRODUCTION

Wetland and aquatic plant-based systems, both natural and artificial, are increasingly popular alternatives for treatment of various types of wastewater (Boyd, 1969; Lakshman, 1979; Stowell

ISBN 0-941463-00-1

et al., 1981; Reddy et al., 1982,1985). The significance of macrophytes in contaminant removal varies according to the treatment system design which, in turn, depends on the desired contaminant-removal goals. Certain types of aquatic macrophyte-based treatment systems incorporate plants primarily as living substrates for microbial activity. There is evidence that this design strategy is effective for reduction of suspended solids, BOD and N (Boyd, 1969). For other treatment purposes, such as removal of P, metals and some organics, the preferred system designs are those which optimize conditions for plant uptake (Stowell et al., 1981; Reddy and Sutton, 1984). The basic functions of plants in the latter use are in assimilating, concentrating and storing contaminants on a short-term basis. Subsequent harvest of plant biomass results in permanent removal of stored contaminants from the treatment system.

Regardless of the design of an aquatic or wetland treatment system, the actual role and potential significance of plant uptake and storage of contaminants are poorly understood. This is, in large part, due to the "black box" approach frequently employed in studies of these types, for which inflows and outflows are monitored with little regard for internal nutrient fluxes and transformations. Evaluation of internal system processes, including plant uptake and storage, permits more efficient development and optimization of design parameters, and can greatly reduce the use of trial-and-error in designing an aquatic or wetland treatment system.

Although several researchers have examined the potential of natural or artificial wetlands for wastewater treatment, little is known of the nutrient storage capability and uptake rates of these plants in wastewater treatment applications. This paper provides an overview of the nutrient (N and P) uptake and storage capabilities of aquatic and wetland plants, reviews some of the basic information available on plants in natural communities, and relates this to the nutrient-removal potential of these plants.

ROLE OF PLANT UPTAKE IN NUTRIENT REMOVAL

The potential rate of nutrient uptake by a plant is limited by its net productivity (growth rate) and the concentration of nutrients in the plant tissue. Nutrient storage is similarly dependent on plant tissue nutrient concentrations, and also on the ultimate potential for biomass accumulation: that is, the maximum standing crop. Therefore, desirable traits of a plant used for nutrient assimilation and storage would include rapid growth, high tissue nutrient content, and the capability to attain a high standing crop (biomass per unit area).

A schematic representation of nutrient storage in aquatic macrophytes as a function of nutrient supply is shown in Figure 1. Plant growth is directly proportional to nutrient supply at low to moderate levels of nutrients. Further increases in nutrients

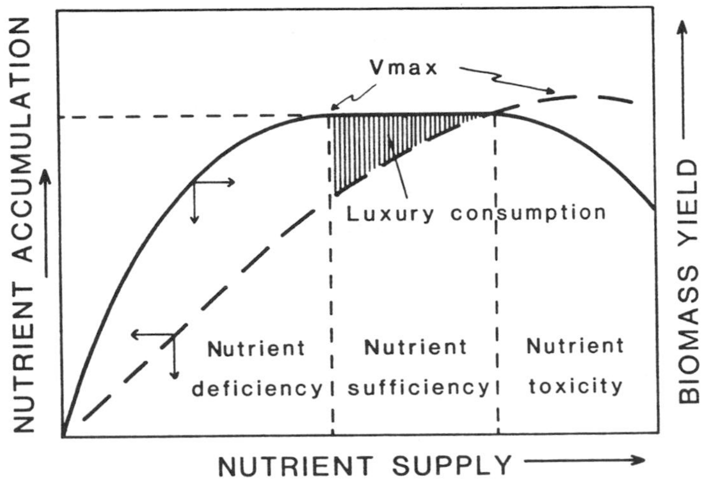

FIGURE 1. Schematic representation of the relationship between nutrient supply and biomass yield and nutrient accumulation of aquatic macrophytes.

supply do not increase the growth of the plant, but instead may result in luxury uptake of nutrients. Vmax for growth is typically attained at the lower range of nutrient supply, while Vmax for nutrient uptake is reached at much higher levels of nutrients. The difference between the two rates is an indicator of the nutrient-storage capability of the plant.

In addition to plant assimilation, nutrient removal in aquatic plant-based water treatment systems is affected by a number of biological, physical and chemical processes functioning in the water, sediment and rhizosphere (Reddy, 1984; Good and Patrick, 1987). In studies on the fate of N added to floodwater, mass balances indicated that plant uptake accounted for 13 to 67% of the total N removal, while unaccounted-for N was assumed to be lost through nitrification and denitrification or NH_3 volatilization (Reddy, 1983; Reddy and DeBusk, 1985). In a related study (Table 1), plant uptake accounted for 16 to 75% of total N removal, and for 12 to 73% of total P removal, indicating that other removal processes were functioning (Reddy and DeBusk, 1985).

Mass balance of N and P for a water hyacinth-based water treatment system indicated that 50% of the total N and 40% of the total P were lost through means other than plant uptake, presumably via biochemical processes and seepage (Reddy et al., 1982). For a water hyacinth system receiving secondary sewage effluent, 40 to 92% of the input N was estimated to be lost through denitrification (DeBusk et al., 1983). Results indicate that denitrification plays a significant role in N removal when water hyacinth plants are cultured in NO_3-rich waters. Similar results have been observed in emergent macrophyte systems. In a

TABLE 1. Potential N and P removal by aquatic macrophyte systems operated at a 7 d detention period (Reddy and DeBusk, 1985).

	Nitrogen				Phosphorus			
	Summer		Winter		Summer		Winter	
	A	B	A	B	A	B	A	B
	mg m^{-2} d^{-1}							
Eichhornia crassipes	1278	3276	254	551	243	371	49	252
Pistia stratiotes	985	2759	258	434	218	297	72	205
Hydrocotyle umbellata	365	2025	370	777	86	240	81	265
Lemna minor	292	946	70	450	87	234	18	205
Spirodela polyrhiza	151	740	135	353	34	139	34	248
Azolla caroliniana	108	--	48	--	33	128	10	135
Salvinia rotundifolia	406	873	96	208	105	217	32	203
Egeria densa	125	581	121	161	48	410	38	202

A = calculated using the growth rate in the linear phase of the growth curve and average tissue N and P content. This represents N and P removal due to plant uptake alone.

B = Calculated using the N and P concentrations in the water. This represents N and P removal due to plant uptake and nutrient transformations.

freshwater marsh containing *Typha latifolia*, about 25% of the added N was lost from the system, while 54% of the added N was recovered in the plant (Dean and Biesboer, 1986).

FLOATING MACROPHYTES

Floating macrophytes are commonly found in lakes and slow-moving streams. Many of these plants are highly productive, especially in eutrophic waters, making them attractive for possible utilization in water treatment. During rapid growth, these plants assimilate large quantities of pollutants into their tissue.

In natural systems, the most common management practice is to chemically control the growth of these plants by application of herbicides. Pollutants which are stored in the tissue are released back into the water upon decomposition of dead tissue, thus enhancing the overall eutrophication process. Harvesting plant biomass is an alternative which takes advantage of the nutrient-removal potential of aquatic plants, but harvesting technology has not been sufficiently developed for economical use (Reddy et al., 1983; Bagnall, 1986,1987).

A number of floating aquatic macrophytes have been evaluated for their possible use in treating nutrient-enriched water (Reddy et al., 1983). These include: water hyacinth (*Eichhornia crassipes*), water lettuce (*Pistia stratiotes*), pennywort (*Hydrocotyle umbellata*), duckweed (*Lemna* sp.), salvinia (*Salvinia* sp.) and azolla (*Azolla* sp.). The concept of using floating aquatic plants, primarily water hyacinth, for treating sewage effluents is gaining the attention of sanitary engineers, governmental agencies and private companies involved in the design and operation of sewage treatment facilities. These systems appear to be more attractive where climate is conducive for rapid growth and in areas with low-cost land availability.

Nutrient assimilative capacity of aquatic plants is often the major criterion in selecting a plant for water treatment. Although this section presents data on the nutrient assimilative capacity of many floating aquatic plants, the major emphasis will be placed on water hyacinth, one of the more extensively studied floating macrophytes.

The nutrient assimilative capacity of floating macrophytes is affected by chemical composition of the water, wastewater characteristics, nutrient loading, sediment characteristics, climatic conditions, age of the plant, plant density, harvesting frequency, biochemical transformations in the water and underlying sediment, and physico-chemical environment at the sediment-water-root interface. Nutrient assimilation by floating plants is directly related to growth rate, standing crop, and tissue composition. Wide variability in growth and tissue composition are found among floating aquatic macrophytes (Table 2). The growth potential of floating macrophytes depends to a great extent on their vertical growth capability. The ability of water hyacinth to achieve substantial vertical development affords this plant a strong competitive advantage in natural systems. Low tissue N and P values are characteristic of plants grown in natural waters (lakes and streams), while high tissue N and P values represent plants cultured in nutrient-enriched waters (sewage effluents, anaerobic digester effluents).

Critical levels of nutrients needed to achieve maximum growth and nutrient uptake have not been established for all aquatic plants. Water hyacinth growth rate was shown to be directly proportional to the N and P concentrations of the water, up to 10 mg N L^{-1} and 1.1 mg P L^{-1} (Reddy, 1987) (Figure 2). However, nutrient assimilation increased with N and P concentrations up to 40 mg N L^{-1} and 10 mg P L^{-1}. This indicates that aquatic plants possess significant capacity to store nutrients in their tissue, although stored nutrients may not influence growth after a certain level of accumulation (Ower et al., 1981).

TABLE 2. Growth and nutrient (N and P) content of selected floating macrophytes.

Plant	Biomass		Tissue Composition	
	Standing crop	Growth rates	N	P
	Mg (dw) ha^{-1}	Mg ha^{-1} yr^{-1}	-----g kg^{-1}-----	
Eichhornia crassipes (water hyacinth)	20.0-24.0	60-110	10-40	1.4-12.0
Pistia stratiotes (water lettuce)	6.0-10.5	50- 80	12-40	1.5-11.5
Hydrocotyle sp. (pennywort)	7.0-11.0	30- 60	15-45	2.0-12.5
Alternanthera sp. (alligator weed)	18.0	78	15-35	2.0- 9.0
Lemna spp. (duckweed)	1.3	6- 26	25-50	4.0-15.0
Salvinia spp.	2.4- 3.2	9- 45	20-48	1.8- 9.0

Many aquatic plants appear to prefer NH_4^+ over NO_3^- when both ions are present in the water (Nelson et al., 1981; Reddy and Tucker, 1983; Oki et al., 1985). Ammonium can both inhibit the formation of NO_3^- reductase in aquatic plants (Joy, 1969) and prevent the assimilation of NO_3^- by plants which display high levels of NO_3^- reductase activity.

Plant morphology is altered by the concentration of nutrients in the water, particularly N (Reddy and Tucker, 1983; 1985). Nitrogen concentration in the water has been inversely related to root length of water hyacinth. High shoot/root ratios are characteristic of plants cultured in nutrient-enriched waters, while low shoot/root ratios are found in plants cultured in nutrient-poor waters. Translocation of nutrients varies with plant shoot/root ratios. Using ^{15}N as a tracer for inorganic N in the growth medium, up to 85% of the added ^{15}N was translocated into the photosynthetic plant parts (leaves and petioles) of water hyacinths with high shoot/root ratios, while only 73% was translocated into leaves and petioles of water hyacinths with low shoot/root ratio (Figure 3).

Floating aquatic plants have the capability to assimilate large quantities of trace elements. Some of these trace elements are essential for plant growth. The demand for these elements can be increased when plants are cultured in wastewaters containing high levels of macronutrients. For example, water hyacinths cultured in NO_3^--rich water exhibited chlorosis, even though N was present at adequate levels and, upon addition of Fe-EDTA, the chlorosis symptoms disappeared (Reddy, 1983). Water hyacinths and other aquatic plants can readily absorb heavy metals such as Cu, Zn, Pb, Cd, Hg, and Ni (Wolverton and McDonald, 1975a,b; Tatsuyama et al., 1979; Cooley et al., 1979; Muramoto and Oki, 1983). Many

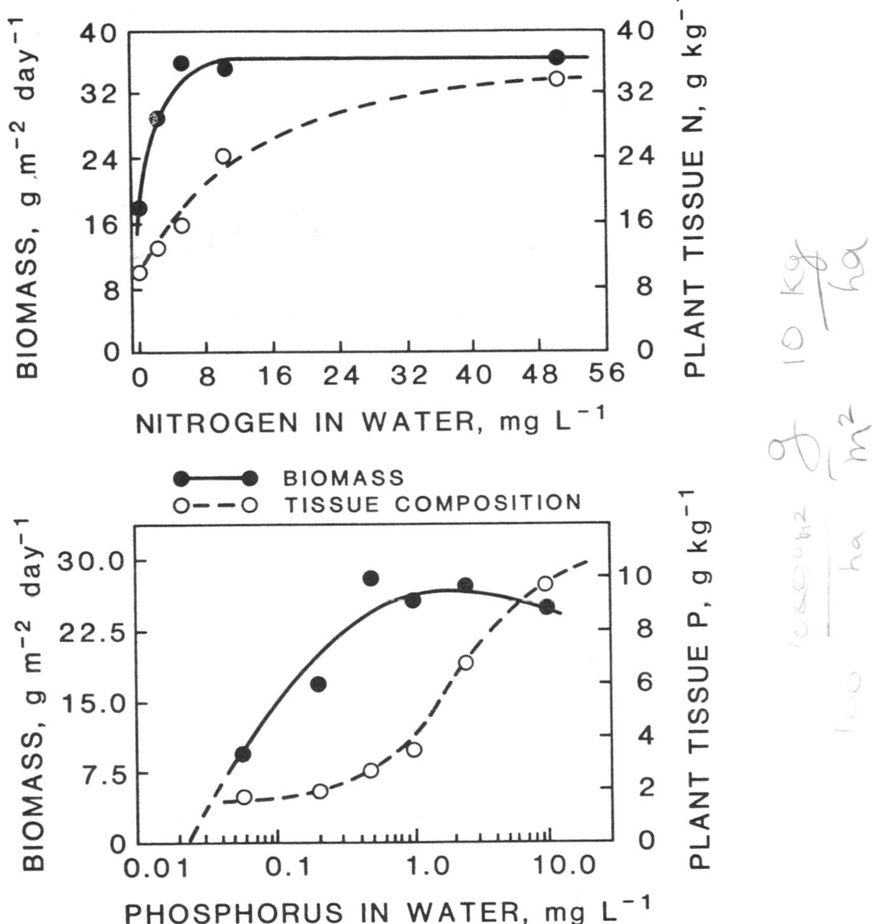

FIGURE 2. Relationship between N and P concentration of the culture medium, and biomass yield and nutrient storage in water hyacinths (Reddy, 1987).

of these studies were conducted on a short-term basis; therefore, maximum storage capabilities of heavy metals cannot be evaluated using these data.

Plant tissue nutrient content can be affected by plant density. For example, when water hyacinths were cultured in N-limited water, plant tissue N content decreased from 30 g kg^{-1} to 8 g kg^{-1} in about 4 wk of growth and remained at this level for a period of 14 wk (Figure 4). During this growth cycle, plant biomass increased from 125 g (dw) m^{-2} to 3000 g (dw) m^{-2}, causing substantial competition for nutrients. Maintenance of tissue N

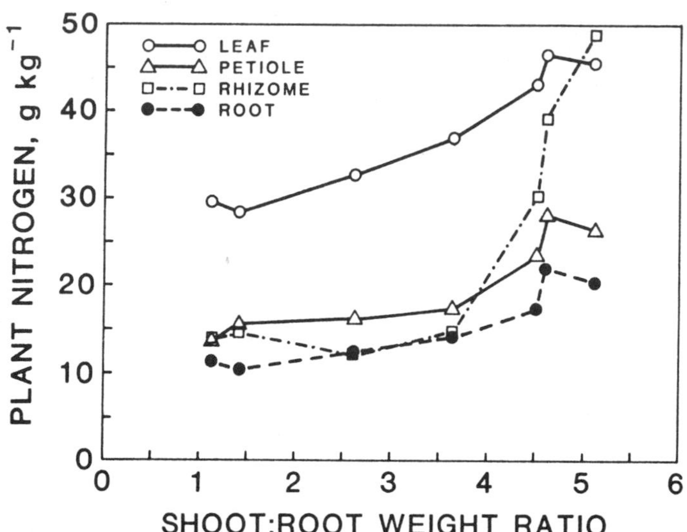

FIGURE 3. Effect of water hyacinth shoot:root weight ratio on distribution of N in various plant parts (Reddy, 1987; unpublished results).

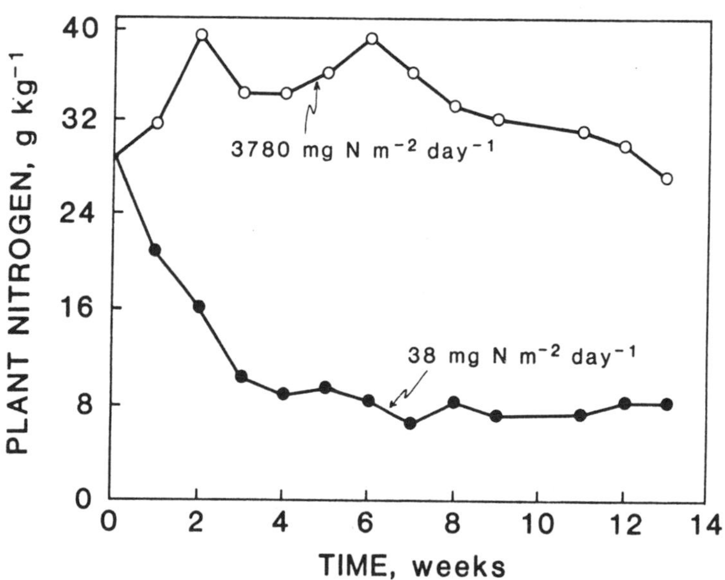

FIGURE 4. Effect of water hyacinth plant density on N accumulation in the plant tissue (Reddy, 1987; unpublished results).

content at 8 g kg^{-1} suggests that internal nutrient cycling such as biological N_2 fixation and detritus decomposition are additional sources of N to plants. At high N loading rates, however, plant tissue N was not affected by plant density.

Nitrogen and P storage in floating macrophytes is related to the standing crop of biomass. Plants characterized by high biomass per unit area have the potential to store a maximum amount of nutrients (Table 3). For example, standing crop of water hyacinth can reach 30 Mg (dw) ha^{-1}, thus resulting in a maximum storage of 900 kg N ha^{-1} and 180 kg P ha^{-1}. Plants with a low standing crop of biomass per unit area typically have low nutrient storage capabilities. Storage of nutrients in floating aquatic plants is short-term because of rapid turnover. If plants are not harvested, the dead tissue will decompose rapidly and release nutrients into the water. Frequent harvesting of the biomass is necessary to avoid losses of nutrients.

Although storage of nutrients is short-term, many aquatic plants have high nutrient uptake rates. Maximum N removal was found to be 5850 kg N ha^{-1} yr^{-1} for water hyacinths, as compared to 1200 kg N ha^{-1} yr^{-1} for duckweed (Table 3). High nutrient removal rates by plant uptake can only be achieved by frequent harvesting of plants.

EMERGENT MACROPHYTES

Herbaceous emergent macrophytes are widely distributed on the shoreline of lakes and streams, and in wetlands. Many of these plants are perennial, and have a high capacity for biomass production, offering great potential for nutrient storage (Dykyjova and Veber, 1978; Dykyjova et al., 1971,1972). Depending on location and climate, the number of species present can be

TABLE 3. Standing crop (storage) of N and P, and rate of plant uptake, for selected floating macrophytes.

Plant	N		P	
	Storage	Uptake	Storage	Uptake
	kg ha^{-1}	kg ha^{-1} yr^{-1}	kg ha^{-1}	kg ha^{-1} yr^{-1}
Eichhornia crassipes	300-900	1950-5850	60-180	350-1125
Pistia stratiotes	90-250	1350-5110	20- 57	300-1100
Hydrocotyle umbellata	90-300	540-3200	23- 75	130- 770
Alternanthera philoxeroides	240-425	1400-4500	30- 53	175- 570
Lemna minor	4- 50	350-1200	1- 16	116- 400
Salvinia rotundifolia	15- 90	350-1700	4- 24	92- 450

large (Terry and Tanner, 1984). Emergent macrophytes commonly found in freshwater marshes and wetlands, include Typha sp., Phragmites sp., Scirpus sp., Juncus sp., and Panicum sp. These species have been studied by several researchers for their potential to treat wastewater (Lakshman, 1979; Gersberg et al., 1984).

Emergent macrophytes can be used for water treatment by using 1) natural stands in wetlands for disposal of treated wastewater and 2) selected emergent macrophytes in artificial wetlands. The former are usually unmanaged and are used as sites for discharging previously treated wastewater (Dolan et al., 1981). Artificial systems may be either managed by plant harvesting or left unmanaged (Gersberg et al., 1984; Seidel, 1976; Wolverton, 1982). The goal of the latter type of system is usually secondary or tertiary treatment.

The nutrient assimilative capacity of emergent macrophytes is affected by wastewater composition, loading rate, water depth, sediment characteristics, O_2 transfer capability of the plants into the root zone, biochemical and physico-chemical processes functioning at the root-water-sediment interface, plant density, cultural practices such as harvesting, and climate.

Emergent macrophytes have the capability to grow in a wide range of substrates and in a wide variety of wastewaters. These factors and their interactive effects can result in a wide range of nutrient compositions in the plant tissue. In wetland systems used for wastewater treatment, nutrients are supplied from 1) internal sources such as the decomposition of soil organic matter, biological nitrogen fixation, and decomposition of detritus tissue; and 2) external sources such as wastewater and rainfall. Concentrations of nutrients in plants growing in natural stands can provide base-line estimates of nutrient assimilation, but these concentrations can vary greatly with the age of the plant and the time of sampling.

Nitrogen and P concentrations in emergent macrophytes exhibit wide inter- and intra-specific variability (Table 4). Low tissue N levels are found in plants analyzed at maturity or cultured in nutrient-limited systems, while high tissue N concentrations reflect plants cultured in nutrient-enriched systems or plants analyzed at early stages of growth.

Nutrient content of emergent macrophytes is high (>25 g kg^{-1} of tissue) in young plants but, as the plants approach maturity, tissue nutrient content decreases (Boyd, 1970). During the same period, total nutrient storage in the plant tissue increases. These trends were clearly demonstrated for N and P content of Typha latifolia growing in natural wetlands (Figure 5). Some nutrients, such as N and K, can further be lost at maturity, since amounts of dead foliage increase with time (Boyd, 1970).

Soil fertility and water composition can also affect the plant tissue N content (Table 5). Nutrient levels of Typha latifolia were influenced by soil type (Boyd and Hess, 1970).

TABLE 4. Typical N and P concentrations in emergent macrophytes.

Plant	Standing crop	Annual yield	Tissue Composition N	Tissue Composition P
	-Mg ha^{-1}-	Mg ha^{-1} yr^{-1}	------g kg^{-1}------	
Typha (cattail)	4.3-22.5	8-61	5-24	0.5-4
Juncus (rush)	22.0	53.3	15	2
Scirpus (bulrush)	--	--	8-27	1-3
Phragmites (reed)	6-35	10-60	18-21	2-3
Eleocharis (spike rush)	8.8	25.6	9-18	1-3
Saururus cernuus (lizard's tail)	4.5-22.5	--	15-25	1-5

TABLE 5. Nutrient storage capability of Typha latifolia cultured in various types of systems. (Dykyjova, 1978; Pratt and Andrews, 1980; Ogwada, 1983).

Nutrient	Shoots	Rhizomes & roots	Total
	-----------------g m^{-2}-----------------		
Nutrient Medium (Non-limiting nutrients)			
N	53.5	102.7	156.2
P	11.2	26.3	37.5
K	59.2	59.2	118.4
Ca	25.7	11.6	37.6
Mg	28.5	11.1	39.6
Organic Soil			
N	30.8	35.2	66.0
P	3.4	6.3	9.7
K	14.1	30.5	44.5
Shallow Ponds With Drainage Water			
N	13.4	4.2	17.6
P	1.2	0.3	1.5
K	15.3	3.0	18.3
Ca	10.7	4.3	15.0
Mg	1.6	1.0	2.6

This was attributed to variations in the amount of plant-available nutrients at different sites. In many soils, major plant nutrients (N and P) may limit plant growth. Upon additions of these nutrients, either through wastewater or fertilizer, growth rate and tissue nutrient content increase (Cary and Weerts, 1984; Ulrich and Burton, 1985; Reddy and Portier, 1987).

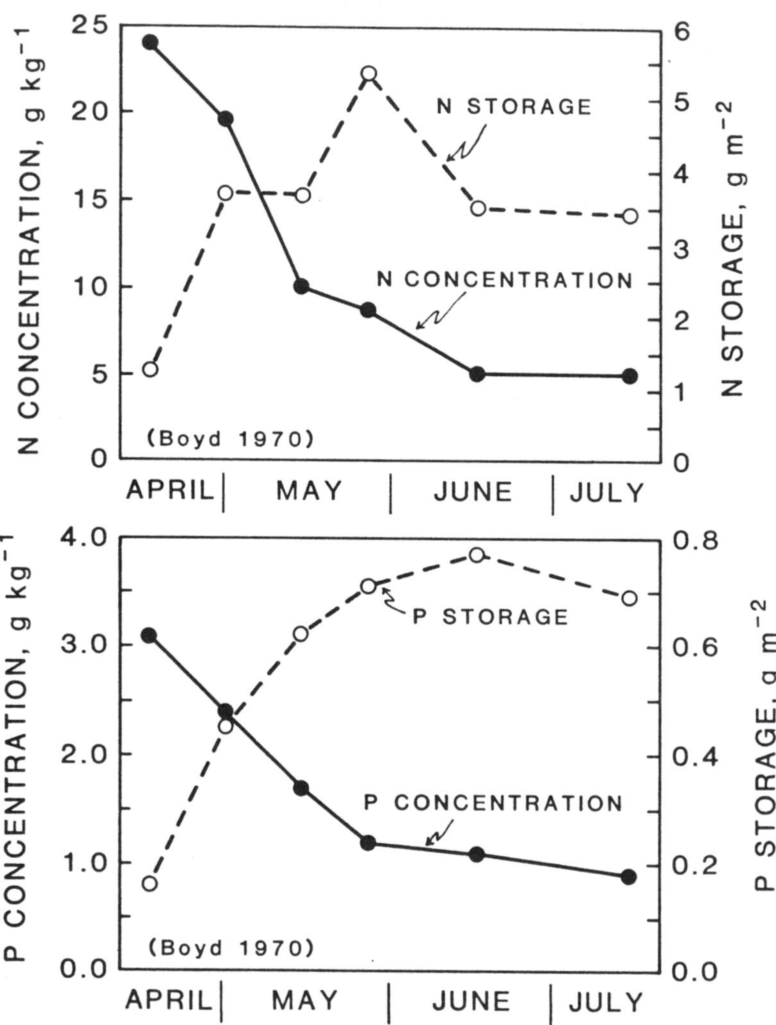

FIGURE 5. Relationship between tissue N and P concentrations and total uptake by Typha latifolia (Boyd, 1970).

Very limited information is available on the critical nutrient levels for maximum growth and nutrient uptake of emergent macrophytes. For perennial plants, critical nutrient levels can be affected by age of the plant, soil fertility and environmental conditions. Nutrient availability can also affect plant morphology. Root growth of Typha sp. was inversely related to plant-available N (Bonnewell and Pratt, 1978). Similarly, Ulrich and Burton (1985) observed that N fertilization increased aboveground growth of Phragmites australis and decreased root/shoot ratios from 2.2 to 0.75. Although P fertilization increased shoot growth, it had little or no effect on root/shoot ratio (Ulrich and Burton, 1985).

Data on nutrient storage and uptake by selected emergent macrophytes show maximum storage of nutrients was in the range of 200 to 1560 kg N ha^{-1} and 40 to 375 kg P ha^{-1} (Table 6). More than 50% of the nutrients were stored in below-ground portions of the plants, which may be difficult to harvest to achieve effective nutrient removal. Emergent macrophytes have more supportive tissue than floating macrophytes, and thus greater potential for storing the nutrients over a longer period. Frequent harvesting may not be necessary to achieve maximum nutrient removal, although harvesting aboveground biomass once a year may improve the overall nutrient removal efficiency.

FORESTED WETLAND PLANTS

Forested wetlands, or swamp forests, are characterized by periodically flooded or saturated soils for significant periods of time during the life cycles of the trees (Lugo, 1984). Forested wetlands may occur as hydrologically discreet stands or they may be located along the interface of aquatic and terrestrial systems, e.g. on river floodplains and lake fringes. Hydroperiod in forested wetlands, which varies considerably among sites, is the major factor in determining community type. Flooding is seasonal in many forested ecosystems and nearly permanent in others, where dry periods occur only during severe droughts. Regardless of hydroperiod, floodwater must be absent for a sufficient duration to permit germination and survival of seedlings for perpetuation of the community.

The most frequently occurring wetland trees in temperate regions are cypress (Taxodium distichum) and tupelo (Nyssa sp.), both of which are distributed over wide geographic and hydrologic

TABLE 6. Standing crop (storage), and rate of plant uptake of N and P, for selected emergent macrophytes.

Plant	N		P	
	Storage	Uptake	Storage	Uptake
	kg ha^{-1}	kg ha^{-1} yr^{-1}	kg ha^{-1}	kg ha^{-1} yr^{-1}
Typha (cattail)	250-1560	600-2630	45-375	75-403
Juncus (rush)	200- 300	800	40	110
Scirpus (bulrush)	175- 530	125	40-110	18
Phragmites (reed)	140- 430	225	14- 53	35

ranges (Conner and Day, 1982). Other commonly occurring wetland trees include red maple (Acer rubrum), cottonwood (Populus heterophylla), American elm (Ulmus americana), holly (Ilex sp.), water oak (Quercus nigra), sweet bay (Magnolia virginiana, birch (Betula sp.), ash (Fraxinus sp.) and white cedar (Thuja occidentalis). Understory development is dependent on canopy coverage and hydroperiod. A variety of shrubs and small trees, e.g. fetter bush (Lyonia lucida), willow (Salix sp.), button bush (Cephalanthus occidentalis) and wax myrtle (Myrica cerifera), often occur in swamp forests.

In forested wetlands, as in emergent macrophyte marshes, sediment plays a major part in removal of N and P from floodwaters. Swamp forest sediments, which range from silt and clay in floodplain systems to peat in poorly flushed acid soils, generally serve as efficient N and P traps. Denitrification is an important N sink, providing permanent removal of N from the system (Patrick et al., 1976).

Unlike herbaceous macrophytes, trees provide long-term storage of nutrients in the form of wood. However, not all of the annual nutrient uptake of trees is immobilized in woody tissue. A significant amount of biomass is returned to the forest floor by litterfall (leaves and dead wood). The turnover time for leaf biomass is usually one year, whether leaves are dropped in pulses by deciduous trees or gradually throughout the course of the year by evergreen trees. Nutrients contained in dead leaves are either leached back into the floodwater and sediment interstitial water, released through decomposition, or permanently incorporated into the sediment by accretion (peat formation).

The nutrient storage capability of trees is dependent upon the net production of wood. Although the net primary productivity of forested wetlands is high in relation to other forested ecosystems, it is not comparable to that of many floating and emergent macrophyte systems. Net primary productivity (NPP) in undisturbed forested wetlands is in the range of about 600 to 1200 g m^{-2} yr^{-1} (Conner and Day, 1976). Net primary productivity of a cypress swamp receiving wastewater effluent was substantially higher, on the order of 1900 g m^{-2} yr^{-1} (Nessel and Bayley, 1984). Stem wood production accounts for about 44% of total NPP in a cypress swamp (Schlesinger, 1978) and for about 51% of that in a bottomland hardwood swamp (Conner and Day, 1976).

Nitrogen and P concentrations are significantly lower in wood than in herbaceous plant tissue (Table 7). Tissue nutrient concentrations in wetland trees are highly dependent upon site fertility, due to sediment type, hydrology or wastewater addition; hence, concentrations vary considerably. Because growth rates and nutrient concentrations are lower in woody species, the rates of N and P assimilation are significantly less for woody plants than for herbaceous plants. Reported total (gross) uptake rates of N and P in forested wetlands ranged upward to about 26.6 and 15.0 kg ha^{-1} yr^{-1}, respectively (Table 8), substantially lower than for

TABLE 7. Concentration of N and P in various species of wetland trees.

Tree species	Leaves N	Leaves P	Stem Wood N	Stem Wood P	Reference
	g kg^{-1}				
Taxodium distichum	0.14	0.01	0.024	0.001	Schlesinger, 1978
T. distichum	--	0.5-2.6	--	0.03-0.06	Brown, 1981
T. distichum var. *nutans*	15-18	1.3-1.7	--	--	DeBusk, 1984
Nyssa sylvatica	19.3	1.01	1.38	0.22	Reynolds et al., 1979
N. sylvatica var. *biflora*	20-24	1.3-2.0	--	--	DeBusk, 1984
Acer rubrum	18.3	1.05	1.68	0.22	Reynolds et al., 1979
A. rubrum	10-22	1.5-2.6	--	--	DeBusk, 1984
Magnolia virginiana	19.1	0.90	4.13	0.30	Reynolds et al., 1979
M. virginiana	22-25	1.2-2.0	--	--	DeBusk, 1984

TABLE 8. Net plant uptake of N and P in forested wetlands.

Plant community	Plant Uptake N	Plant Uptake P	Reference
	kg ha^{-1}	yr^{-1}	
Alluvial cypress swamp	--	8.7	Mitsch et al., 1979
Cypress swamp receiving wastewater	--	15.0	Nessel and Bayley, 1984
Cypress swamp receiving wastewater	213.0	23.0	DeBusk, 1984
Cypress swamp	--	3.3	Schlesinger, 1978
Cypress dome	10.4†	0.2†	Dierberg, 1980
Cypress dome receiving wastewater	26.6†	1.1†	Dierberg, 1980
Floodplain forest	--	0.7†	Brown, 1981

†Net storage in wood only.

productive aquatic macrophytes such as water hyacinth. Due to both the magnitude of leaf drop and the high N and P concentrations in leaves as compared to wood, a substantial portion of N and P uptake is recycled in litterfall. As a result, net assimilation of N and P in wood is only a small fraction of gross uptake. For example, net annual uptake of P was less than 10% of gross uptake for an alluvial cypress swamp in Illinois (Mitsch et al., 1979).

Potential nutrient storage capacity of forested wetlands is comparable to that of herbaceous wetlands, due to the tremendous standing crop of biomass. Aboveground biomass in various communities in the Great Dismal Swamp, for example, was estimated to range from 19.6 kg m^{-2} in a maple-black gum community to 34.5 kg m^{-2} in a cypress strand (Dabel and Day, 1977).

Standing crop of N and P in the aboveground portions of various forested wetland sites ranged from 815 to 996 kg N ha^{-1} and from 25 to 86 kg P ha^{-1} (Table 9). Significant nutrient storage also occurs in below-ground biomass (Nessel and Bayley, 1984), but estimates for this component are difficult to obtain for many sites.

Although forested wetlands have the capability for long-term storage of nutrients, nutrient uptake rate of trees is probably insignificant in a system used for wastewater treatment. Consequently, the role of plant uptake in nutrient removal from floodwaters is apparently greatly reduced in forested wetlands compared to herbaceous wetlands.

SUMMARY

Plant uptake plays an important role in the removal of nutrients, especially P, from wastewater in aquatic plant-based plants or above-water biomass affords complete removal from the treatment systems. Floating and emergent macrophytes provide relatively rapid nutrient uptake. Subsequent harvesting of whole plants or abovewater biomass affords complete removal from the system. In forested wetlands, tree biomass provides long-term nutrient storage, eliminating the need for management; however,

TABLE 9. Standing crop of N and P in forested wetlands. Values represent aboveground storages only, unless noted otherwise.

Plant community	Standing Crop N	Standing Crop P	Reference
	---kg ha^{-1}---		
Hardwood swamp	815	86	Reynolds et al., 1979
Floodplain forest	--	33	Brown, 1981
Cypress dome	--	25	Brown, 1981
Cypress dome receiving wastewater	--	48	Brown, 1981
Cypress swamp	996	46	Schlesinger, 1978
Cypress swamp receiving wastewater	1219	86	DeBusk, 1984
Cypress swamp receiving wastewater	--	40	Nessel and Bayley,
	--	120†	1984

†Above- and below-ground storage.

the net nutrient uptake rate is substantially lower than that of either floating or emergent macrophytes.

Maximum nutrient storage potentials (standing crop) reported for emergent macrophytes were 2630 kg N ha^{-1} and 403 kg P ha^{-1}, compared with 900 kg N ha^{-1} and 180 kg P ha^{-1} for floating macrophytes and 996 kg N ha^{-1} and 120 kg P ha^{-1} for forested wetland trees. Maximum nutrient uptake rates are achieved by floating macrophytes, although consistently high uptake rates are encountered only in managed (harvested) systems. Maximum N and P uptake rates were approximately 5850 and 1125 kg ha^{-1} yr^{-1}, respectively, for floating macrophytes (*Eichhornia crassipes*). In contrast, maximum net N and P uptake rates for emergent macrophytes and forested wetlands were 2630 kg N ha^{-1} yr^{-1} and 403 kg P ha^{-1} yr^{-1}, and 26.6 kg N ha^{-1} yr^{-1} and 15.0 kg P ha^{-1} yr^{-1}, respectively.

Plant uptake and storage of nutrients in aquatic and wetland wastewater treatment systems typically have been quantified for mass balance purposes using values from single measurements or averages of various unrelated measurements. Because plant growth and nutrient content exhibit high temporal variability, in terms of season and plant age, frequent and systematic monitoring of these parameters is a necessary prerequisite to accurate quantification of nutrient uptake and storage.

Future research on this topic should include basic studies of plant uptake and storage of nutrients in wastewater treatment systems, and factors which affect these processes. Research of a broader scope to further examine the role of plants in nutrient removal is also needed.

ACKNOWLEDGMENTS

Florida Agricultural Experiment Stations Journal Series No. 7762. Supported in part by the funds provided through a cooperative project between the University of Florida, IFAS, Gainesville, FL, and the Gas Research Institute, Chicago, IL.

REFERENCES

Bagnall, L. O. 1986. Harvesting systems for aquatic biomass. p. 159-173. *In* W. H. Smith (ed.) Biomass Energy Development. Plenum Press, NY.

Bagnall, L. O. 1987. Water hyacinth biomass cropping systems. II. Harvesting and handling. *In* W. H. Smith and J. Frank (ed.) Methane from Biomass - A Systems Approach. Elsevier Appl. Sci. Publ., England (in press).

Bonnewell, V., and D. C. Pratt. 1978. Effects of nutrients on productivity and morphology of *Typha angustifolia* x. *latifolia*. Minnesota Acad. Sci. 44:18-20.

Boyd, C. E. 1969. Vascular aquatic plants for mineral nutrient removal from polluted water. Economic Bot. 23:95-103.

Boyd, C. E. 1970. Production, mineral accumulation and pigment concentrations in Typha latifolia and Scirpus americanus. Ecol. 51:285-290.

Boyd, C. E., and L. W. Hess. 1970. Factors influencing shoot production and mineral nutrient levels in Typha latifolia. Ecol. 51:296-300.

Brown, S. 1981. A comparison of the structure, primary productivity, and transpiration of cypress ecosystems in Florida. Ecol. Monogr. 51:403-427.

Cary, P. R., and P. G. Weerts. 1984. Growth and nutrient composition of Typha orientalis as affected by water temperature and nitrogen and phosphorus supply. Aquat. Bot. 19:105-118.

Conner, W. H., and J. W. Day, Jr. 1976. Productivity and composition of a baldcypress-water tupelo site and a bottomland hardwood site in a Louisiana swamp. Am. J. Bot. 63:1354-1364.

Conner, W. H., and J. W. Day, Jr. 1982. The ecology of forested wetlands in the southeastern United States. p. 69-87. In B. Gopal, R. E. Turner, R. G. Wetzel, and D. F. Whigham (ed.) Wetlands Ecology and Management. Proc. First Inter. Wetlands Conf., Sept. 10-17, 1980, New Delhi, India.

Cooley, T. N., D. F. Martin, W. C. Durden, Jr., and B. D. Perkins. 1979. A preliminary study of metal distribution in three water hyacinth biotypes. Water Res. 13:343-348.

Dabel, C. V., and F. D. Day. 1977. Structural comparisons of four plant communities in the Great Dismal Swamp, Virginia. Bull. Torr. Bot. Club 104:352-360.

Dean, J. V., and D. D. Biesboer. 1986. Factors affecting nitrogen cycling in a freshwater marsh: Uptake of ^{15}N-ammonium by Typha latifolia L. (Typhaceae) and oxidation-reduction potentials of submerged soils. Am. J. Bot. (in press).

DeBusk, T. A., L. O. Williams, and J. H. Ryther. 1983. Removal of nitrogen and phosphorus from wastewater in a water hyacinth-based treatment system. J. Environ. Qual. 12:257-262.

DeBusk, W. F. 1984. Nutrient dynamics in a cypress strand receiving municipal wastewater effluent. M.S. Thesis. Univ. of Florida, Gainesville. 103 pp.

Dierberg, F. E. 1980. The effects of secondary sewage effluent on the water quality, nutrient cycles and mass balances, and accumulation of soil organic matter in cypress domes. Ph.D. Diss. University of Florida, Gainesville. 286 pp.

Dolan, T. J., S. E. Bayley, J. Zoltek, Jr., and A. J. Hermann. 1981. Phosphorus dynamics of a Florida freshwater marsh receiving treated wastewater. J. Appl. Ecol. 18:205-219.

Dykyjova, D. 1978. Determination of energy content and net efficiency of solar energy conversion by fishpond helophytes. p. 216-220. In D. Dykyjova and J. Kvet (ed.) Pond Littoral Ecosystems. Springer-Verlag, New York.

Dykyjova, D., and K. Veber. 1978. Experimental hydroponic cultivation of helophytes. p. 181-192. In D. Dykyjova and J. Kvet (ed.) Pond Littoral Ecosystem. Springer-Verlag, New York.

Dykyjova, D., P. J. Ondok, and D. Hradecka. 1972. Growth rate and development of root/shoot ratio in reedswamp macrophyte grown in winter hydroponic cultures. Folia Geobot. Phytotax., Praha. 7:259-268.

Dykyjova, D., K. Veber, and K. Priban. 1971. Productivity and root/shoot ratio of reedswamp species growing in outdoor hydroponic culture. Folia Geobot. Phytotax., Praha. 6.

Gersberg, R. M., B. V. Elkins, and C. R. Goldman. 1984. Use of artificial wetlands to remove nitrogen from wastewater. J. Water Pollut. Contr. Fed. 56:152-156.

Good, B. J., and W. H. Patrick, Jr. 1987. Root-water-sediment interface processes. In K. R. Reddy and W. H. Smith (ed.) Aquatic Plants for Water Treatment and Resource Recovery. Magnolia Publishing, Inc. (in press).

Joy, K. W. 1969. Nitrogen metabolism of Lemna minor. II. Enzymes of nitrate assimilation and some aspects of their regulation. Plant Physiol. 44:849-853.

Lakshman, G. 1979. An ecosystem approach to the treatment of wastewaters. J. Environ. Qual. 8:353-361.

Lugo, A. E. 1984. A review of early literature on forested wetlands in the United States. p. 7-15. In K. C. Ewel and H. T. Odum (ed.) Cypress Swamps. Univ. of Florida Press, Gainesville, FL.

Mitsch, W. J., C. L. Dorge, and J. R. Wiemhoff. 1979. Ecosystem dynamics and a phosphorus budget of an alluvial cypress swamp in southern Illinois. Ecology 60:1116-1124.

Muramoto, S., and Y. Oki. 1983. Removal of some heavy metals from polluted water by water hyacinth (Eichhornia crassipes). Bull. Environ. Contam. Toxicol. 30:170-177.

Nelson, S. G., B. D. Smith, and B. R. Best. 1981. Kinetics of nitrate and ammonium uptake by the tropical freshwater macrophyte Pistia stratiotes L. Aquaculture 24:11-19.

Nessel, J. K., and S. E. Bayley. 1984. Distribution and dynamics of organic matter and phosphorus in a sewage-enriched cypress swamp. p. 262-278. In K. C. Ewel and H. T. Odum (ed.) Cypress Swamps. Univ. of Florida Press, Gainesville, FL.

Ogwada, R. A. 1983. Growth, nutrient uptake and nutrient regeneration by selected aquatic macrophytes. M.S. Thesis. University of Florida, Gainesville, FL.

Oki, Y., K. Nakagawa, and K. R. Reddy. 1985. Uptake and translocation of ^{15}N in water hyacinth. Proc. 10th Asian-Pacific Weed Sci. Soc. Conf. p. 317-324.

Ower, J., C. F. Cresswell, and G. C. Bate. 1981. The effects of varying culture nitrogen and phosphorus levels on nutrient uptake and storage by the water hyacinth Eichhornia crassipes (Mart) Solms. Hydrobiologia 85:17-22.

Patrick, W. H., R. D. DeLaune, R. M. Engler, and S. Gotoh. 1976. Nitrate removal from water at the water-mud interface in wetlands. U.S. Environmental Protection Agency. EPA 600-3-76-042. p. 79.

Pratt, D. C., and N. J. Andrews. 1980. Cattails (*Typha* spp.) as an energy source. p. 43-62. *In* Symp. Energy from Biomass and Wastes IV (Symp. Chairman D. L. Klass). Inst. Gas Technol., Chicago, IL.

Reddy, K. R. 1983. Fate of nitrogen and phosphorus in a waste-water retention reservoir containing aquatic macrophytes. J. Environ. Qual. 12:137-141.

Reddy, K. R. 1984. Nutrient transformations in aquatic macrophyte filters used for water purification. *In* Proc. on Future of Water Reuse. Am. Water Works Assoc. 2:660-678.

Reddy, K. R. 1987. Water hyacinth biomass cropping system: I. Production. *In* W. H. Smith and J. Frank (ed.) Methane from Biomass - A Systems Approach. Elsevier Publ. (in press).

Reddy, K. R., and W. F. DeBusk. 1985. Nutrient removal potential of selected aquatic macrophytes. J. Environ. Qual. 14:459-462.

Reddy, K. R., and K. M. Portier. 1987. Nitrogen utilization by *Typha latifolia* L. as affected by temperature and rate of nitrogen utilization. Aquat. Bot. (in press).

Reddy, K. R., and D. L. Sutton. 1984. Water hyacinth for water quality improvement and biomass production. J. Environ. Qual. 13:1-8.

Reddy, K. R., and J. C. Tucker. 1983. Growth and nutrient uptake of water hyacinth. I. Effect of nitrogen source. Econ. Bot. 37:236-246.

Reddy, K. R., and J. C. Tucker. 1985. Growth and nutrient uptake of pennywort as influenced by nitrogen concentration of the water. J. Aquat. Plant Mangmt. 23:35-40.

Reddy, K. R., F. M. Hueston, and T. McKim. 1985. Biomass production and nutrient removal potential of water hyacinth cultured in sewage effluent. J. Solar Eng. 107-128-135.

Reddy, K. R., D. L. Sutton, and G. E. Bowes. 1983. Biomass production of freshwater aquatic plants in Florida. Soil & Crop Sci. Soc. Fla. Proc. 42:28-40.

Reddy, K. R., K. L. Campbell, D. A. Graetz, and K. M. Portier. 1982. Use of biological filters for agricultural drainage water treatment. J. Environ. Qual. 11:591-595.

Reynolds, P. E., K. G. Carlson, T. W. Fromm, K. A. Gigliello, and R. J. Kaminski. 1979. Phytosociology, biomass, productivity and nutrient budget for the tree stratum of a southern New Jersey hardwood swamp. p. 123-139. *In* W. E. Frayer (ed.) Forest Resources Inventories: Workshop Proceedings, Vol. II. July 23-26, 1979, Colorado State Univ., Ft. Collins, CO.

Schlesinger, W. H. 1978. Community structure dynamics and nutrient cycling in the Okefenokee cypress swamp-forest. Ecol. Monogr. 48:43-65.

Seidel, K. 1976. Macrophytes and water purification. p. 109. In J. Tourbier and R. W. Pierson (ed.) Biological Control of Water Pollution. Univ. of Pennsylvania Press, Philadelphia, PA.

Stowell, R., R. Ludwig, J. Colt, and G. Tchobanoglous. 1981. Concepts in aquatic treatment system design. J. Environ. Eng. 107:919-940.

Tatsuyama, K., H. Egawa, H. Yamamoto, and M. Nakamura. 1979. Sorption of heavy metals by the water hyacinth from the metal solutions. II. Some experimental conditions influencing the sorption. Weed Res. (Japan) 24:260-263.

Terry, W. S., and G. W. Tanner. 1984. Mineral concentration within freshwater marsh plant communities. J. Freshwater Ecol. 2:509-518.

Ulrich, K. E., and T. M. Burton. 1985. The effects of nitrate, phosphate and potassium fertilization on growth and nutrient uptake patterns of Phragmites australis (CAV) Trin. Ex Steudel. Aquat. Bot. 21:53-62.

Wolverton, B. D. 1982. Hybrid wastewater treatment system using anaerobic microorganisms and reed (Phragmites communis). Econ. Bot. 36:373-380.

Wolverton, B. C., and R. C. McDonald. 1975a. Water hyacinth and alligator weeds for removal of lead and mercury from polluted waters. NASA Tech. Memo. No. TM-X-72723. Natl. Space Tech. Lab., Bay St. Louis, MS.

Wolverton, B. C., and R. C. McDonald. 1975b. Water hyacinths and alligator weeds for removal of silver, cobalt and strontium from polluted waters NASA Tech. Memo No. TM-X-72727.

ROOT-WATER-SEDIMENT INTERFACE PROCESSES

B. J. Good
Louisiana Geological Survey
Louisiana State University
Baton Rouge, Louisiana 70803

W. H. Patrick, Jr.
Laboratory for Wetland Soils and Sediments
Center for Wetland Resources
Louisiana State University
Baton Rouge, Louisiana 70803

ABSTRACT

Selected properties of the sediment-water, root-sediment, and the root-water interfaces; and some sediment processes not necessarily restricted to the water interface affect the functioning of aquatic plant systems. The sediment-water interface can be an important site for nitrification-denitrification reactions. The high diffusive resistance and O_2 demand of sediments limit the oxidized portion to a relatively thin layer which overlies the remaining reduced sediment. The oxidized layer is conducive to nitrification, while the reduced layer below favors denitrification. Reactions involving P are also discussed in light of oxidation-reduction reactions of sediments. At the root-sediment interface of flood-adapted plants, there is frequently a situation analogous to the oxidized sediment layer: the rhizosphere is oxidized while the surrounding sediment is reduced. Nitrification-denitrification reactions, and Fe oxidation and P occlusion at the root surface are frequently important phenomena there. In addition to O_2, the exudation of carbohydrates, enzymes, and other compounds into the rhizosphere make this an important site of methane formation, N_2 fixation and H_2S oxidation. The root-water interface has perhaps received less study than the other two, yet the potential application of such knowledge to wastewater management is enormous. Factors affecting N and P removal from wastewater systems are briefly discussed in relation to root-water interface processes.

Keywords: Nitrification, denitrification, phosphorus, rhizosphere, wastewater treatment.

ISBN 0-941463-00-1

INTRODUCTION

Wastewater is frequently introduced into aquatic or wetland environments (e.g., Brinson et al., 1984; Reddy and Sutton, 1984; Richardson, 1985). For this reason, there is much interest and on-going research into the chemical transformations in these wetlands. Three interface systems are of particular importance because of the potential for the development of aerobic-anaerobic transition properties: 1) the sediment-water, 2) the root-sediment, 3) and the root-water interfaces. The first two of these interfaces have been studied fairly intensively, and the third represents an area of importance needing further research. This paper will briefly discuss characteristics of these three interfaces that are known to affect the levels of selected elements in wastewater.

WATER-SEDIMENT INTERFACE PROCESSES

The amount of free pore space of the soil determines the rate at which O_2 from the atmosphere can diffuse into the soil and replenish that which is consumed (Henderson and Patrick, 1982). When an upland soil is flooded, the first noticeable change is in the composition of the pore space. In a well-drained mineral soil, approximately half the total volume is occupied by pore space. Half of this volume is occupied by air -- the remainder being mostly water (Patrick et al., 1973). In flooded soils and sediments, on the other hand, the rate of O_2 diffusion is reduced by 4 orders of magnitude. Thus, the major effect of water is to severely impede the movement of O_2 into the system.

Several chemical components of a sediment are affected by anoxia, and are of critical importance to water-sediment interface processes. After the air is displaced with water, O_2 is rapidly depleted. Subsequent to this, facultative then obligate anaerobic bacteria proliferate, and reduce a series of terminal electron acceptors. Nitrate is reduced when the redox potential reaches about 220 mV (assuming neutral pH). Manganic manganese is then reduced at about 200 mV, ferric iron at 120 mV, sulfate from -75 mV to -150 mV, and CO_2 between -250 to -300 mV (Gambrell and Patrick, 1978).

Usually, in a biologically active sediment, the consumption of O_2 is much greater than its supply rate. This often results in the formation of 2 distinct zones: an aerobic or oxidized surface layer into which O_2 can penetrate before it is all consumed, and a reduced layer below this. The oxidized surface layer is often yellowish-brown due to the ferric iron compounds, and below this is the more greyish zone characteristic of ferrous iron which is indicative of anoxic conditions (Figure 1).

Nitrification-denitrification reactions can play a valuable role in wastewater treatment. The oxidized sediment layer is an important site for nitrification, an oxidation process in which NH_4^+ is converted to nitrate by _Nitrosomonas_ and _Nitrobacter_

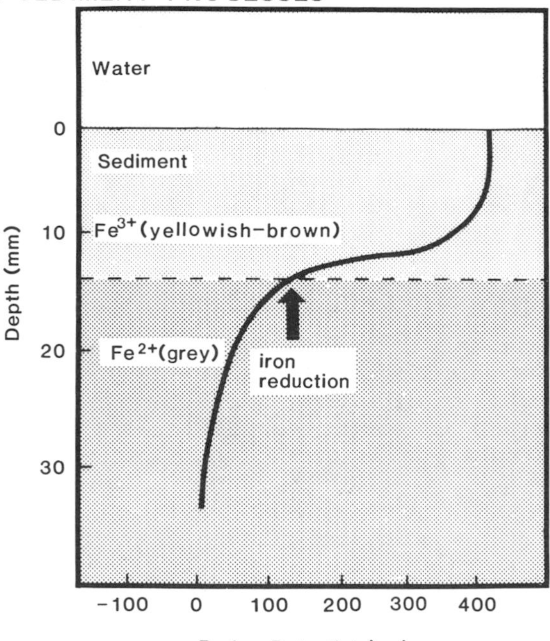

FIGURE 1. Relationship between redox potential profiles and the oxidized layer of a flooded soil. After Patrick and DeLaune (1972).

bacteria. Denitrification is a reduction process that utilizes NO_3^- as a terminal electron acceptor for microbial respiration under anaerobic conditions and effectively removes the NO_3^- by converting it into gasesous forms such as N_2O and N_2. The nitrification process in the oxidized layer sets up a concentration gradient, and the NH_4^+ from the reduced zone diffuses into the upper, oxidized layer. The NO_3^- formed in the oxidized zone will likewise diffuse in response to a concentration gradient into the reduced sediment and become available for denitrification and loss from the system. The overall process is rate limited by the diffusion rate of NH_4^+ from the reduced to the oxidized zone, and by NH_4^+ oxidation in the aerobic layer (Reddy et al., 1980). Nitrate will not accumulate in the oxidized layer because it diffuses to the reduced zone as rapidly as it is formed and is denitrified. For a thorough review of these processes see Reddy and Patrick (1984).

Phosphorus is another element of concern to those involved with wastewater management. It does not undergo valence reactions, but its chemistry is inextricably tied up with that of Fe, and consequently with the oxidation-reduction and pH status of the soil. It has been shown that reduced soils exchange P with the soil solution much more readily than oxidized soils: presumably because upon reduction, ferric hydroxides are transformed to gel-like, hydrated ferrous hydroxides, which have more sorption sites and have more capacity to sorb and release orthophosphate-P (Khalid et al., 1977; Patrick and Khalid, 1974). Aluminum is also a determinant of the P chemistry in wetland systems. In a study of several freshwater wetland ecosystems, the capacity to absorb P was predicted better by concentrations of extractable amorphous aluminum (r = 0.929) and iron (r = 0.621) than by organic matter, extractable Ca, or pH (Richardson, 1985).

ROOT-SEDIMENT INTERFACE PROCESSES

The root-sediment interface can also play an important role in aerobic-anaerobic chemical reactions. Upland plants get their O_2 from the soil by diffusion, while in wetland plants the O_2 reaching the root system must come from the aerial part of the plant. In a typical cross section through a wetland plant root, aerenchyma is quite evident (Figure 2). Oxygen movement within plants is dependent upon tissue having the property of relatively low resistance to gaseous diffusion. Aerenchyma is the most common and thoroughly studied tissue having this property, although there are other means of gaseous diffusion in plants.

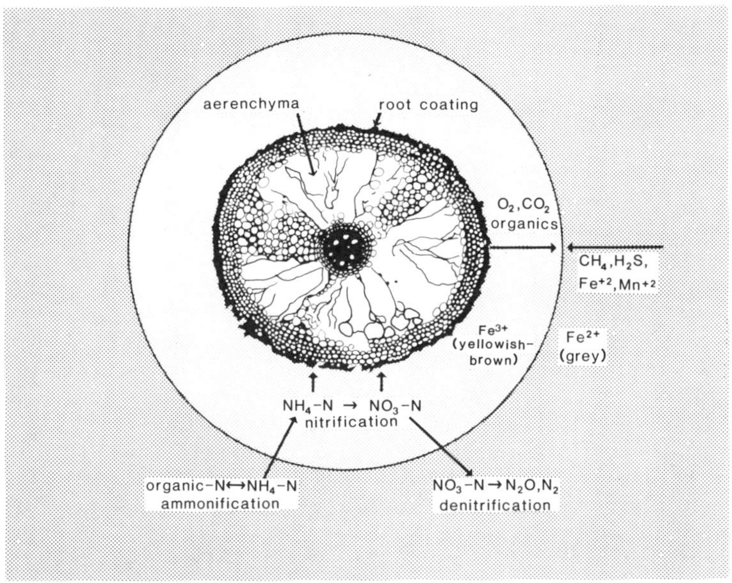

FIGURE 2. Cross section of an oxidizing root growing in a reduced sediment. The oxidized rhizosphere is depicted, along with some processes that occur as a result of this aerobic-anaerobic interface. After Mendelssohn and Postek (1982).

For example, Raskin and Kende (1985) documented that air can diffuse to the root system via an external, cuticular system.

Oxygen has a two-fold importance to roots growing under reduced conditions. Rhizosphere oxidation ameliorates soil toxins such as H_2S, and reduced Fe and Mn (Armstrong, 1972; Gambrell and Patrick, 1978; Ponnamperuma, 1965); and it is also necessary for aerobic respiration. Aerobic respiration nets 36 moles of adenosine triphosphate per mole of glucose as compared to the two moles yielded by lactic acid or alcohol fermentation. Considering the difference in efficiency, one major school of thought contends that the most important determinant of flood tolerance is the ability of a plant to aerate the roots under flooded conditions (Armstrong, 1978).

The importance of aeration as an adaption to an anoxic root environment is also suggested by the fact that the diffusion characteristics of roots usually correspond to flood tolerance. Jensen et al. (1967) measured the root permeability and O_2 diffusion rates of intact _Hordeum vulgare_, _Oriza sativa_, and _Zea mays_ plants using ^{18}O analysis by mass spectrophotometry. From their determinations of longitudinal diffusional coefficients and surface permeability of O_2 in these three species, they developed a model to predict the partial pressure of O_2 as a function of distance along the root. Their predictions were in agreement with the known relative tolerances to anaerobiosis of these species: _O. sativa_ > _Z. mays_ > _H. vulgare_.

Some of the O_2 that diffuses into wetland roots leaks out into the rhizosphere and creates an aerobic layer similar to the one formed at the sediment-water interface (Figure 2). One indication is the commonly observed oxidation of Fe on the roots of wetland species grown under waterlogged conditions (Figure 2). The reduced forms of Fe and Mn from the anaerobic soil surrounding the roots are soluble, but the oxidized forms are not (Gambrell and Patrick, 1978). Thus, when Fe^{+2} and Mn^{+2} are oxidized in the rhizosphere they tend to precipitate onto or near the root surface (Bacha and Hossner, 1977) and in some instances within epidermal and cortical cells (Chen et al, 1980; Green and Etherington, 1977).

The oxidation of Fe^{+2} at the root-sediment interface has been reported in the literature for many species including: _Fraxinus pennsylvanica_ (Good and Patrick, 1986; Good et al., 1986), _Phalaris_ sp., _Phleum pratense_, _Lotus corniculatus_ (Bartlett, 1961), _Pinus contorta_ Dougl. (Sanderson and Armstrong, 1984), _Erica cinerea_ (Jones and Etherington, 1972), _Oriza sativa_ L. (Green and Etherington, 1977; Ponnamperuma et al., 1955), _Spartina alterniflora_ (Medelssohn and Postek, 1982), and _Typha latifolia_ (Taylor et al., 1984). Oxidation of manganous manganese (Mn^{2+}) and H_2S (Armstrong, 1972; Jones, 1972; Jones and Etherington, 1972; Takijima, 1965), and sorption of P (Good and Patrick, 1986), Ni, Al, As, and Zn (Good et al., 1986) on oxidizing roots under anaerobic soil conditions have also been reported.

In a comparative study of the effects of flooding on two bottomland hardwood tree species (Good and Patrick, 1986), P was apparently affected by Fe oxidation. The more flood-tolerant of the two species studied, *Fraxinus pennsylvanica*, was able to maintain an oxidized rhizosphere under flooded soil conditions while the other species, *Quercus nigra*, was not. The amount of P in the root coating of flooded *F. pennsylvanica* increased by a factor of 4, apparently as a result of P sorption onto ferric oxyhydroxide. Consistent with the idea of P removal at the root surface, the leaf tissue in the flooded *F. pennsylvanica* exhibited a decrease in P by a factor of 2. Phosphorus levels changed very little in the flooded *Q. nigra* root coatings or leaf tissue. Soil pH can also influence P uptake, but this too is probably related to Fe-P interactions (Jugsujinda and Patrick, 1977).

Some of the biochemical processes that occur at the root-sediment interface are potentially important for water quality control. In the case of nitrification-denitrification, the same processes occur here as at the water-sediment interface. Ammonium in the anaerobic soil zone diffuses to the rhizosphere in response to a concentration gradient and NH_4^+ not taken up by the root is oxidized to NO_3^- utilizing O_2 in the rhizosphere that comes down through the plant. The NO_3^- not taken up diffuses back into the anaerobic zone where it is denitrified as N_2 and nitrous oxide. In the case of eelgrass (*Zostera marina*), a submersed macrophyte, of the O_2 produced by photosynthesis and transported to the roots, 50-60% of this is released from the plant. Consequently, NH_4^+ is oxidized to NO_3^- in the rhizosphere and denitrification ensues (IIzumi and Hattori, 1980).

Smith and Tiedje (1979) presented evidence that although the rhizosphere is an important site of nitrification-denitrification, under conditions where NO_3^- concentrations were relatively low, root uptake of NO_3^- precluded increased rates of denitrification; but if NO_3^- levels were high, increased rates of denitrification may be observed. In some instances, N losses can be less in planted than in corresponding non-planted soil treatments. For example, Buresh et al. (1981) found that *Spartina alterniflora* systems effectively compete with nitrifiers and denitrifiers for available N and assimilate most of the NH_4^+ before denitrification. Smith and DeLaune found that in a flooded *Oriza sativa* (Smith and DeLaune, 1984a) system fertilized with urea and in a flooded *Spartina alterniflora* (Smith and DeLaune, 1984b) system fertilized with NH_4^+, nitrification-denitrification reactions in the planted systems exceeded those of nonplanted systems only for the first few days. This implied that nitrification-denitrification reactions in the oxidized rhizospheres caused a significant increase in N loss only while the N levels remained high. Increased nitrification-denitrification reactions attributable to rhizosphere processes after large doses of NH_4^+ are illustrated in Table 1 (Reddy and Patrick, 1986). Although a direct measurement of denitrification would require measurement of the gaseous end

TABLE 1. Mass balance of added $^{15}NH_4$ in flooded Crowley silt loam planted with rice. From Reddy and Patrick (1986). Mean values of eight replications.

N-fraction	With rice	Control	With rice	Control
	--mg ^{15}N/soil core--		---% of added ^{15}N---	
Soil:				
Inorganic N	6.1	251.1	1.8	73.9
Organic N	51.4	73.4	15.1	21.6
Total soil N	57.5	324.6	16.9	95.5
Plant:				
Shoots	165.9	--	48.8	--
Roots	56.3	--	16.6	--
Total plant N	222.2	--	65.4	--
Total N recovered	279.6	324.6	82.2	95.5
N unaccounted for	60.4	15.4	17.8	4.5

products, the "unaccounted for" N serves as a good indicator of denitrification rates.

The root-soil interface is also an important locus for biological N_2 fixation. Nitrogen fixation in association with rice has been found to be higher in flooded than dryland conditions, apparently because the aerobic-anaerobic transition zone of the rhizosphere provides a favorable environment for N_2 fixing bacteria (Barraquio et al., 1982)

Sulfide oxidation is another significant root-sediment interface process. Hydrogen sulfide can build up to phytotoxic levels under flooded soil conditions. Some wetland plants overcome this problem through a symbiotic relationship with bacteria of the genus Beggiatoia. This genus of filamentous, colorless, gliding bacteria is worldwide in distribution and found chiefly within semi-anaerobic environments. These bacteria are capable of oxidizing H_2S to S intracellularly. The elemental S is presumably further oxidized to H_2SO_4 which has been observed to accumulate in the medium of Beggiatoa (Hollis, 1979).

Beggiatoa is a unique symbiont characterized by H_2S and catalase dependence under natural conditions. It occupies a niche in the interface between anaerobic and aerobic organisms, i.e. H_2S producing bacteria such as Desulfovibrio spp., and higher plant roots (Hollis, 1979). The distribution and abundance of Beggiatoa in soils is probably very important in determining the distribution of S^{-2} diseases in rice, and is also likely to be an important determinant of naturally occurring wetland plant species endemic to swamps and marshes (Joshi and Hollis, 1977).

Methanogenesis is another process influenced by root exudates at the root-sediment interface. Cicerone and Shetter (1981) found that the principle means of CH_4 transport from the point of origin in the paddy soil to the atmosphere is through the rice plants themselves. Likewise, Hozapfel-Pschorn et al. (1986) found that more than 90% of the CH_4 produced in a rice paddy field was transported through the rice plants. Although the root exudates stimulated an increase in CH_4 production, only 23% of it was emitted due to oxidation of CH_4 at the root-sediment interface. Weed species in these fields oxidized 95% of the CH_4 stimulated by the roots, and thus did not emit any to the atmosphere (Holzapfel-Pschorn et al., 1986).

In the case of the yellow water lilies (*Nuphar luteum*), Dacey and Klug (1979) determined that of the total CH_4 escaping from Duck Lake, Michigan, 50% or more found its way to the surface via lily pads. Of several categories of species studied including fresh water rooted, fresh water unrooted, and rooted saltwater and brackish water plants, the only group that produced methane in appreciable quantities was the fresh water rooted type (Sebacher et al., 1985). Sulfate reduction precludes methanogenesis in saltwater sediments.

ROOT-WATER INTERFACE PROCESSES

Although the processes occurring at the root-water interface are not well understood, one would expect to find many of the same processes that characterize the water-sediment and root-sediment interfaces. Oxygen and organic substances likely diffuse from the root surface into O_2 depleted water and create an aerobic-anaerobic interface conducive to nitrification-denitrification reactions and N_2 fixation. However, significant differences are also likely. For example, water hyacinth (*Eichhornia crassipes*) can deplete the O_2 in the area of their roots and thus create zones that favor denitrification (Reddy, 1981). In addition, an aqueous rhizosphere would likely be more sensitive to root induced changes in pH and O_2 status than a rhizosphere in soil or sediment. The dynamic nature of the aqueous rhizosphere may prove to be valuable for those concerned with wastewater management because it could permit more rapid and precise control over nutrient removal reactions.

Nitrogen and P removal are frequently important objectives in wastewater management. Plant-induced influences on water pH and rhizosphere aeration can have important consequences in this regard. In a water hyacinth sewage treatment operation, 40 to 92% of the incoming N was lost, apparently through denitrification (DeBusk et al., 1983). Reddy (1983) compared the N and P removal for floating, emergent, and submerged aquatic macrophytes. The floating aquatic plants removed the most N (Table 2). However, the floating macrophytes had less influence on the culture solution pH and were less effective in P removal than the other systems studied (Table 3). In the other systems, the pH increased to nine during the afternoons which evidently resulted in loss of P due to precipitation with Ca compounds.

In addition, as in the two interface systems already discussed, the chemistry of P at the root-water interface is

TABLE 2. Mass balance of added ^{15}N in four types of reservoir systems, with a wastewater detention period of 27 d. From Reddy (1983). Mean values of four subsamples from one treatment replication.

Reservoir system	Water	Sediment	Plant	N unaccounted for
		% of added $^{15}NH_4$-N		
Pennywort	0.0	8.9	67.3	23.8
Water hyacinth	3.4	8.5	41.2	46.9
Cattail-Elodea	0.1	8.0	43.8	48.1
Control (algae)	21.0	20.9	4.6	53.5
		% of added $^{15}NO_3$-N		
Pennywort	0.0	6.2	13.0	80.8
Water hyacinth	11.5	5.9	39.3	43.3
Cattail-Elodea	0.1	28.5	23.8	47.6
Control (algae)	35.8	30.9	4.3	28.9

TABLE 3. Mass balance of P in four types of reservoir systems, with a wastewater detention period of 27 d. From Reddy (1983). Mean values from four subsamples from two treatment replications.

Reservoir system	P in the Water		P Removed from System	
	Soluble	Insoluble	Plant	Unaccounted for
	-----------------	% of added P	-----------------	
Pennywort	27.6	13.7	64.5	-5.8
Water hyacinth	27.5	36.5	28.6	7.4
Cattail-Elodea	29.3	11.1	4.4	55.2
Control (algae)	4.5	4.8	3.4	87.3

governed to a large extent by coprecipitation reactions involving Fe and Al. Pritchard et al. (1984) found that in nutrient solutions in which *Trifolium repens* was cultured, P sorption was significantly influenced by Fe and Al. Their observations were "consistent with the formation of extra-cellular Fe-P and Al-Fe-P complexes."

In a system containing emergent and floating macrophytes, each of the three interface systems discussed in this report would be represented: sediment-water, root-sediment, and root-water. More research in this area is needed in order to fully exploit the potential that exists for wastewater management. Species having desired properties can be grown in polyculture or in a series of ponds in order to enhance treatment efficiency (Reddy and DeBusk,

1985). In addition, many sediment characteristics and water parameters can be manipulated so as to enhance waste removal. As the interactive effects of plants, water, and sediment become better understood, the potential that exists for the development of more cost-effective treatment systems will become a reality.

REFERENCES

Armstrong, W. 1972. A re-examination of the functional significance of aerenchyma. Physiol. Plant 27:173-177.

Armstrong, W. 1978. Root aeration in the wetland condition. p. 269-297. In D. D. Hook and R. M. M. Crawford (ed.) Plant Life in Anaerobic Environments. Ann Arbor Science, Ann Arbor, MI.

Bacha, R. E., and L. R. Hossner. 1977. Characteristics of coatings formed on rice roots as affected by iron and manganese additions. Soil Sci. Am. J. 41:931-935.

Barraquio, W. L., M. R. DeGuzman, M. Barron, and I. Watanabe. 1982. Population of aerobic heterotrophic nitrogen-fixing bacteria associated with wetland and dryland rice. Applied Env. Microbiology 43:124-128.

Bartlett, R. J. 1961. Iron oxidation proximate to plant roots. Soil Sci. 92:539-543.

Brinson, M. M., H. D. Bradshaw, and E. S. Kane. 1984. Nutrient assimilative capacity of an alluvial floodplain swamp. J. Applied Ecol. 21:1041-1057.

Buresh, R. J., R. D. DeLaune, and W. H. Patrick, Jr. 1981. Influence of *Spartina alterniflora* on nitrogen loss from marsh soil. Soil Sci. Soc. Am. J. 45:660-661.

Chen, C. C., J. B. Dixon, and F. T. Turner. 1980. Iron coatings on rice roots: Morphology and models of development. Soil Sci. Soc. Am. J. 44:1113-1119.

Ciceronne, R. J., and J. D. Shetter. 1981. Sources of atmospheric methane: Measurements in rice paddies and a discussion. J. Geophysical Research 86:7203-7209.

Dacey, J. W. H., and M. J. Klug. 1979. Methane efflux from lake sediments through water lilies. Science 203:1253-1255.

DeBusk, T. A., L. D. Williams, and J. H. Ryther. 1983. Removal of nitrogen and phosphorus from wastewater in a water hyacinth-based treatment system. J. Env. Qual. 12:257-262.

Gambrell, R. P., and W. H. Patrick, Jr. 1978. Chemical and microbiological properties of anaerobic soils and sediments. p. 375-423. In D. D. Hook and R. M. M. Crawford (ed.) Plant Life in Anaerobic Environments. Ann Arbor Science, Ann Arbor, MI.

Good, B. J., and W. H. Patrick, Jr. 1986. Gas composition and respiration of water oak (*Quercus nigra* L.) and green ash (*Fraxinus pennsylvanica* Marsh.) roots after prolonged flooding. Plant Soil 97:419-427.

Good, B. J., S. P. Faulkner, and W. H. Patrick, Jr. 1986. Evaluation of green ash root responses as a soil-wetness indicator. Soil Sci. Soc. Am. J. 50:1570-1575.

Green, M. S., and J. R. Etherington. 1977. Oxidation of ferrous iron by rice (Oriza sativa L.) roots: A mechanism for waterlogging tolerance. J. Exp. Bot. 28:678-690.

Henderson, R. E., and W. H. Patrick, Jr. 1982. Soil aeration and plant productivity. Handbook of Agricultural Productivity. CRC Press. p. 51-69.

Hollis, J. P. 1979. Ecology of Beggiatoa. Acta Phytopathologica Academiae Scientiarum Hungaricae 14:419-439.

Holzapfel-Pschorn, A., R. Conrad, and W. Seiler. 1986. Effects of vegetation on the emission of methane from emerged paddy soil. Plant Soil 92:223-233.

IIzumi, H., and A. Hattori. 1980. Nitrate and nitrite in interstitial waters of eelgrass beds in relation to the rhizosphere. J. Exp. Mar. Ecol. 47:191-201.

Jensen, C. R., L. H. Stolzy, and J. Letey. 1967. Tracer studies of oxygen diffusion through roots of barley, corn, and rice. Soil Sci. 103:23-29.

Jones, H. E. 1972. Comparative studies of plant growth and distribution in relation to waterlogging. VI. The effect of manganese on the growth of dune and slack plants. J. Ecol. 60:141-146.

Jones, H. E., and J. R. Etherington. 1972. Comparative studies on plant growth and distribution to waterlogging. V. The uptake of iron and manganese by dune and dune slack plants. J. Ecol. 60:131-139.

Joshi, M. M., and J. P. Hollis. 1977. Interaction of Beggiatoa and rice plant: detoxification of hydrogen sulfide in the rice rhizosphere. Science 195:179-180.

Jugsujinda, A., and W. H. Patrick, Jr. 1977. Growth and nutrient uptake by rice in a flooded soil under controlled aerobic-anaerobic and pH conditions. Agron. J. 69:705-710.

Khalid, R. A., W. H. Patrick, Jr., and R. D. DeLaune. 1977. Phosphorus sorption characteristics of flooded soils. Soil Sci. Soc. Am. J. 41:305-310.

Mendelssohn, I. A., and M. T. Postek. 1982. Elemental analysis of deposits on the roots of Spartina alterniflora Loisel. Amer. J. Bot. 69:904-912.

Patrick, W. H., Jr., and R. D. DeLaune. 1972. Characterization of the oxidized and reduced zones in flooded soil. Soil Sci. Soc. Am. J. 36:573-576.

Patrick, W. H., Jr., and R. A. Khalid. 1974. Phosphate release and sorption by soils and sediments: Effects of aerobic and anaerobic conditions. Science 186:53-55.

Patrick, W. H., Jr., R. D. DeLaune, and R. M. Engler. 1973. Soil oxygen content and root development of cotton in Mississippi River alluvial soils. Bull. No. 673, Louisiana Agric. Exp. Stn.

Ponnamperuma, R. N. 1965. Dynamic aspects of flooded soils and the nutrition of the rice plant. p. 295-328. In The Mineral Nutrition of the Rice Plant. John Hopkins Press, Baltimore, MD.

Ponnamperuma, F. N., R. Bradfield, and M. Peech. 1955. Physiological disease of rice attributable to iron toxicity. Nature 175:265.

Pritchard, M. W., J. Lee, J. Dunlopp, and J. R. Sedcole. 1984. Effects of aluminum and micro-nutrients on the sorption of phosphorus by Trifolium repens L. cv. 'Grasslands Huia' from nutrient solutions during plant induced pH changes. Plant Soil 81:389-402.

Raskin, I., and H. Kende. 1985. Mechanism of aeration in rice. Science 228:327-329.

Reddy, K. R. 1981. Diel variations in physico-chemical parameters of water in selected aquatic systems. Hydrobiologica 85:201-207.

Reddy, K. R. 1983. Fate of nitrogen and phosphorus in a wastewater retention reservoir containing aquatic macrophytes. J. Env. Qual. 12:137-141.

Reddy, K. R., and W. F. DeBusk. 1985. Nutrient removal potential of selected aquatic macrophytes. J. Env. Qual. 14:459-462.

Reddy, K. R., and W. H. Patrick, Jr. 1984. Nitrogen transformations and loss in flooded soils and sediments. p. 273-309. In CRC Critical Reviews in Environmental Control, Vol. 13. CRC Press, Inc.

Reddy, K. R., and W. H. Patrick, Jr. 1986. Fate of fertilizer nitrogen in the rice root zone. Soil Sci. Soc. Am. J. 649-651.

Reddy, K. R., and D. L. Sutton. 1984. Water hyacinths for water quality improvement and biomass production. J. Env. Qual. 13:1-8.

Reddy, K. R., W. H. Patrick, Jr., and R. E. Phillips. 1980. Evaluation of selected processes controlling nitrogen loss in a flooded soil. Soil Sci. Soc. Am. J. 44:1241-1246.

Richardson, C. J. 1985. Mechanisms controlling phosphorus retention capacity in freshwater wetlands. Science 228:1424-1427.

Sanderson, P. L., and W. Armstrong. 1984. The responses of conifers to some of the adverse factors associated with waterlogged soils. New Phytol. 85:351-362.

Sebacher, D. I., R. C. Harriss, and K. B. Bartlett. 1985. Methane emissions to the atmosphere through aquatic plants. J. Env. Qual. 14:40-46.

Smith, C. J., and R. D. DeLaune. 1984a. Effect of rice plants on nitrification-denitrification loss of soil nitrogen under greenhouse conditions. Plant Soil 39:287-290.

Smith, C. J., and R. D. DeLaune. 1984b. Influence of the rhizosphere of Spartina alterniflora Loisel. on nitrogen loss from a Louisiana gulf coast salt marsh. Env. Exp. Bot. 24:91-93.

Smith, M. S., and J. M. Tiedje. 1979. The effect of roots on soil denitrification. Soil Sci. Soc. Am. J. 43:951-955.

Takijima, Y. 1965. Studies on the mechanism of root damage of rice plants in the peat paddy fields (Part 2). Status of roots in the rhizosphere and the occurrence of root damage. Soil Sci. Plant Nutr. 11:20-27.

Taylor, G. J., A. A. Crowder, and R. Rodden. 1984. Formation and morphology of iron plaque on the roots of *Typha latifolia* L. grown in solution culture. Amer. J. Bot. 71:666-675.

THE HYDRODYNAMICS OF WETLAND WATER TREATMENT SYSTEMS

R. H. Kadlec
Wetland Ecosystem Research Group
Department of Chemical Engineering
The University of Michigan
Ann Arbor, Michigan 48109-2136

ABSTRACT

The water budget and water regime of a wetland are the key features to which water quality wetland functions can be connected. The processes of water addition and water removal determine storage status in the wetland as a function of season and environmental factors. The processes of precipitation and evapotranspiration are opposing interactions with atmospheric water. Stream flow in and out of a given wetland ecosystem provides points for ready measurement of incoming and outgoing material. Recharge and discharge phenomena connect the wetland with underlying aquifers. Runoff from surrounding upland areas across the perimeter of the wetland forms another possible input or output for the water pool within the wetland. Within the wetland, there are strong responses to wastewater additions. Overland flow is frequently the mode of interest, and results of several studies are given. Underground flow is discussed and compared to other flow processes. Overall water budgets are presented, and compared to more detailed, spatially distributed, dynamic budgets. The base case is the natural wetland receiving municipal wastewater.

Key words: Evapotranspiration, overland flow, budgets, wetland, wastewater.

INTRODUCTION

Natural and constructed wetlands are used for advanced wastewater treatment in many locations. The water budget forms the basis for interpreting water quality and biological response of the ecosystem. Such systems differ from pristine wetlands in the controllable addition of significant quantities of wastewater.

Discussion of flows and content of the water within a wetland must focus upon a defined system. For this purpose, that system

ISBN 0-941463-00-1

will be taken as the water sheet within the wetland. It is considered separate and distinct from the stationary components of the wetland ecosystem--the soils and vegetation. The seasonal fluctuations of all components of the water budget for a given wetland system are also of great importance. Wet and dry, frozen and unfrozen, and warm and cold seasonal behavior, when coupled with the differences in water regime within the wetland give rise to strong influences on processes involving water-borne substances. These variations influence the vegetative cover, the types and abundance of invertebrates, and the use of the wetland by birds and animals. Most importantly, total inputs and outputs of many materials of interest vary strongly with the above factors. Consequently, water quality samples are seasonally variable, and total quantities depend on a firm knowledge of the water budget.

When wastewater is discharged to the surface of a wetland it flows away, creating a dynamic mound about the discharge point. The depth of this mound depends upon the hydrological characteristics of the wetland. Without man-made structures, faster flow accompanies deeper surface water. Therefore each wetland system will have a hydraulic capacity, which could change rapidly in response to rain or other hydrological factors. Depth limits will be determined by the tolerance of wetland vegetation and by consideration of operating factors such as residence time. Depth and velocity will also affect the ability of the wetland to remove pollutants from the surface waters. Hydrology of the wetland site is therefore crucial to the understanding of the treatment processes which occur.

The basis for this review of general principles is a series of studies conducted at Houghton Lake, Michigan, over the period 1972-1986, complemented by results from other sites.

The community of Houghton Lake, located in the central lower peninsula of Michigan, has a seasonally variable population, averaging approximately 5,000. A sewage treatment plant was built in the early 1970s to protect the large shallow recreational lake. Wastewater from this residential community is collected and transported to two aerated lagoons, which provide initial treatment. Sludge accumulates on the bottom of these lagoons, below the aeration pipes. Effluent is then stored in a 12 ha pond for summer disposal, resulting in depth variation from 0.5 m (fall) to 3.0 m (spring). The final disposal is to a 700 ha peatland. The water is distributed across the width of the peatland through small gated openings in the discharge pipe. Each of the 100 gates discharge approximately 100 m^3 d^{-1}, under typical conditions, and the water spreads slowly over the peatland. The branches are not used equally, depending on operational goals, but distribution has been about equal on average over six years.

The wetland is flow-through, with complete vegetation cover. The water table fluctuates from spring high water (depth about 25 cm) to summer low water (dry to 5 cm). The two dominant cover types were 950 ha of sedge-willow (*Carex* spp. and *Salix* spp.) and 140 ha of leatherleaf - bog birch (*Chamaedaphne calyculata* and *Betula pumila*). There were lesser amounts of cattail (*Typha* spp.) (13 ha) and alder edges (*Alnus rugosa*) (24 ha). Further descriptions may be found in Wentz (1976) and Chamie (1975). Small, natural water inflows occur on the north and east margins of the wetland. Overland flow proceeds from northeast down a 0.02% gradient to a stream outlet (Deadhorse Dam) and beaver dam seepage outflow (Beaver Creek), both located 3 km from the discharge. Wastewater adds to the surface sheet flow.

The general framework for the following discussion is given in Figure 1. Subsequent sections describe the component processes, and synthesize these in the form of budget equations.

EVAPORATION AND TRANSPIRATION

Water losses to the atmosphere from wetlands are a combination of evaporation and transpiration by emergent macrophytes. The wetland surface may be permanently or periodically saturated, with periods of shallow standing water. A variable fraction of the surface area may be occupied by open water. The soil surface may be bare or covered with a litter layer which forms an effective mulch.

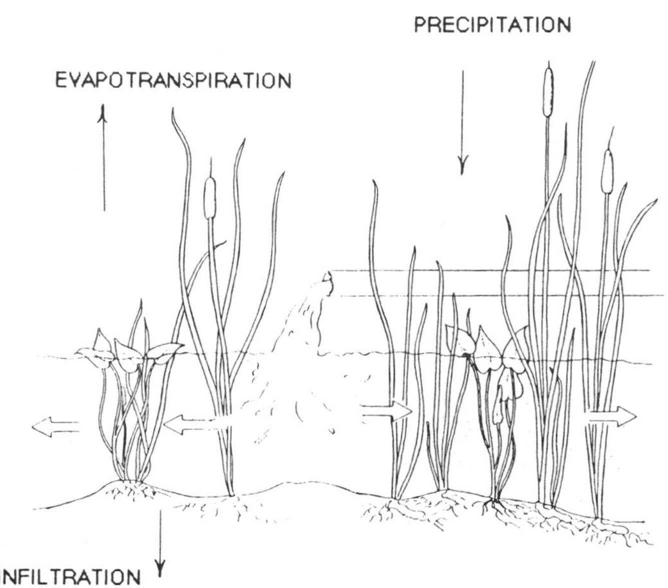

FIGURE 1. Establishing the water budget.

This complexity would appear to lead to widely disparate water losses, but in fact does not. Two factors cause a narrow range of values: the energy from vaporization must come from the sun; and many wetlands are normally saturated, and thus are capable of realizing their full evaporation potential. The meteorological factors which modify the solar energy utilization for vaporization are well known: wind, relative humidity, temperature and cloud cover.

The term transpiration is used to denote water losses to the atmosphere from the vegetation, while evaporation refers to losses from the soil and water surfaces. In combination, these are termed evapotranspiration, and all are on an areal basis. Pan evaporation refers to losses from containers of various sizes in various environments.

The Houghton Lake data set is presented by Kadlec et al. (1986), and in more detail by Scheffe (1978).

Table 1 gives pan evaporation from open and shaded areas, together with evapotranspiration from the same localities. Free surface (pan) evaporation is strongly influenced by shading, which is dependent on the cover type. The order is increasing canopy density, except for alder, which provides more shade than sedge. The greatest loss is from the most open cover (meadow), the least from the most dense (leatherleaf). Some of the effect is due to wind and humidity differences, as indicated by the 1979 data from pans placed in unshaded areas. Data for evapotranspiration show much reduced variation with cover type. The transpiration component apparently utilizes the radiation blocked from the evaporative surface. Individual species measurements of transpiration may be combined with standing crop data to estimate the areal transpiration (Table 2). These estimates are high for sedge-willow and low for leatherleaf-bogbirch, probably because of the variability of standing crop from plot to plot. Further, the mosses under the leatherleaf have not been included.

TABLE 1. Effects of cover type and shading on June pan evaporation and evapotranspiration at Houghton Lake (mm d^{-1}) peatlands.

	Meadow	Sedge	Cattail	Leatherleaf	Alder
			Pan Evaporation		
1976	6.20	5.50	4.85	3.50	4.60
1979 open	5.54	2.83	3.83	3.60	--
1979 shaded	--	1.83	2.33	1.33	--
			Evapotranspiration		
1976	--	4.75	--	4.58	--
1978	--	4.08	--	--	--

TABLE 2. Effect of cover type on transpiration at Houghton Lake peatland (Scheffe, 1978).

Species	Water loss	Cover Type: Sedge Willow		Cover Type: Leatherleaf Bog Birch	
	$g\ g^{-1}\ d^{-1}$	$g\ m^{-2}$	$mm\ d^{-1}$	$g\ m^{-2}$	$mm\ d^{-1}$
Sedge	26.4	225	6.0	20	0.5
Willow	22.9	31	0.7	--	--
Bog Birch	21.6	--	--	57	1.2
Leatherleaf	12.6	--	--	107	1.4
Total		256	6.7	184	3.1

A number of predictive equations have been developed to allow estimation of evapotranspiration in wetlands. Solar radiation, wind, relative humidity, soil temperature, air temperature, and cover type are all recognized as controlling factors, but the more useful predictive techniques are usually those which use only the meteorological measurements which are commonly available. The more popular general methods do not account for variation in transpiration between plant species. Reviews of the major techniques currently in use, have been presented by Chang (1968), Knisel (1976) and Scheffe (1978).

The Penman (1948,1956) method utilizes more of the meteorological data which is commonly available from weather stations. Specifically, data on air temperature, duration of bright sunlight, air humidity, and wind speed are included with empirical constants to produce estimates of evapotranspiration from vegetated surfaces. Based in part upon an energy balance, this method involves relatively complicated calculations. Computer programs have been developed to facilitate its use (Messem, 1975). Mathematically the Penman equation can be represented by:

$$e = \frac{(\Delta Q_n + \gamma_1)\ (P_o - P_a)\ f(v)}{(\Delta + \gamma_1)} \qquad [1]$$

$$\text{and } f(v) = 0.35(0.5 + v/160) \qquad [2]$$

where Q_n is the net solar radiation, Langleys
P_o is the vapor pressure of water at the mean daily temperature, torr
P_a is the partial pressure of water vapor, torr
v is the wind velocity at a height of 2 meters, km d^{-1}
Δ is the slope of the water vapor pressure curve, at the mean daily temperature
γ_1 is the psychrometer constant maintaining consistent

Equation 2 expresses the functional dependence of evaporation upon wind speed, with empirically determined constants. Chang (1968) and Knisel (1976) consider this method to be among the most accurate for estimation of evapotranspiration. Determination of Q_n may pose some difficulty, averaging about 55% of measured incident solar radiation for various cover types.

Empirical methods have proven useful, although site-specific. For example, the Christiansen equation (Christiansen and Low, 1970) was used effectively at a Carson City site (Kadlec et al., 1986):

$$E = K R' C_s C_t C_w C_h C_t C_c \qquad [3]$$

where:
R' = incoming radiation
C_s = sunshine percentage coefficient
C_w, C_h, C_t = coefficients for wind, humidity and temperature, with linear functions of wind, relative humidity, and temperature, respectively
C_c = a monthly coefficient, which accounts for heat storage and crops/vegetation
K = a constant

However, the same constants may not be used at the Houghton Lake site.

It is clear that more data are required before wetland evapotranspiration can be understood and quantified. For example, the presence of vegetation can create both positive and negative changes in water loss. Shading can cause water conservation, whereas transpiration can provide a parallel path and enhance loss of water as noted by Bernatowicz et al. (1976). As wetland water management practice increases, definitive information must be available to achieve the desired goals.

PRECIPITATION AND WATERSHED INPUTS

There are significant impacts of rain events on wetland hydrology (Figure 2), notably for early September, when several days of rain added about 5 cm to the water depth. Rain also causes increases in runoff from the surrounding watershed, thus amplifying the effect of the rain event. The wetland is effective in storing this added water, but does show immediate release of a small fraction (Figure 3).

Calculations involving rainfall have two attendant difficulties: the watershed model and the stochastic nature of the precipitation events. Watershed inputs are significant at Houghton Lake in the early spring months (Kadlec, 1978), but no watershed model has been developed. Runoff is therefore data input used in the wetland hydrology model. Rainfall may be a data input, for after-the-fact calculations. However, a double stochastic prediction reproduces historical frequencies reasonably well (Parker, 1974). Following Eagleson (1970), Weibull

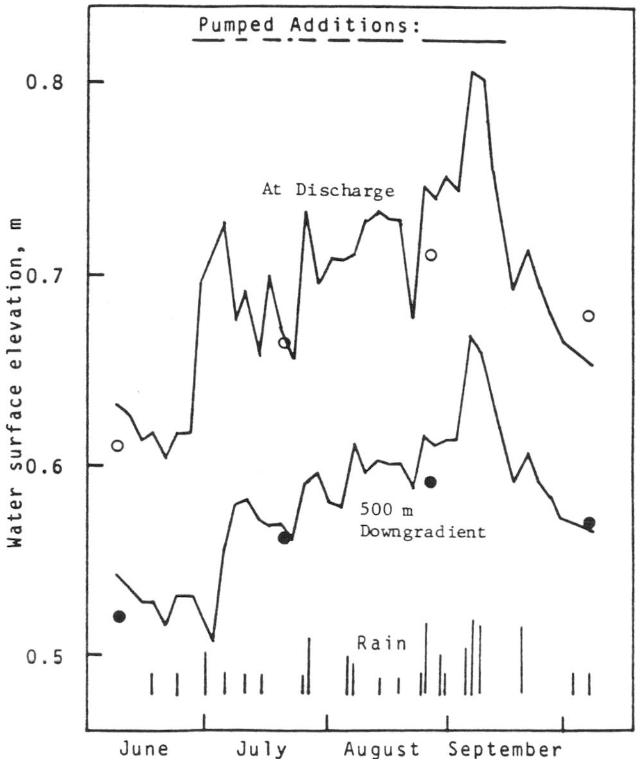

FIGURE 2. Houghton Lake Peatland water surface elevations, Points represent data: lines are computed. The pumping rate is 10,000 m^3 d^{-1}.

distributions of times between rains, and of the rain, are combined with a logarithmic distribution of rain amount.

OVERLAND FLOW

The rate at which water can flow across a wetland is controlled by the ground slope, water depths, type of vegetation, and by the degree and type of channelization. The flow is not only related to water depth by the water balance equation, but also by an appropriate expression which relates the water velocity to driving forces (hydraulic gradient) and resistances.

Typical water depths in a wetland may range from a few cm to about 1 m. Spatial variations in depth within a wetland are largely due to changes in the elevation of the underlying soil. The water pool is relatively flat with very small surface

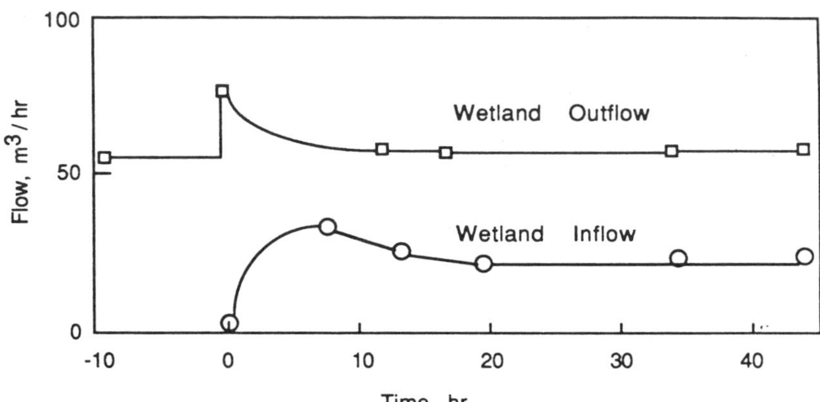

FIGURE 3. Response of the Houghton Lake wetland to a 0.84 cm rain, from -2 to 0 h.

gradients. Wastewater, introduced to the wetland, will spread from the discharge points, and if the irrigation rate is sufficiently high, a shallow mound of water will form. Properly applied, this mound will not exceed about 10 cm, but the height will be determined by the discharge rate and piping configuration and the factors mentioned above.

The water will move away from the discharge through the wetland vegetation, which presents an obstruction to flow. This vegetative mat comprises a doubly porous medium, with plant stems and litter forming fine-scale porosity, while hummocks, islands and channels cause a coarse-scale porosity (Figure 4).

The movement of surface waters through wetlands is characterized by very slow velocities, which result in developing streamline flow. Considering the momentum balance under these conditions, the inertial and acceleration terms are negligible with respect to frictional and gravitational effects. Flow therefore proceeds at the rate at which gravitational forces are just counter-balanced by frictional drag forces.

Although a great deal of work has been done on overland flow (e.g., Woolhiser and Liggett, 1967), most researchers have not addressed the problem of point or line water discharges. These geometries are the common approach to wastewater irrigation in wetlands. The functional dependence of water velocity upon depth and gradient in wetlands has been reported by Kadlec et al. (1981) for the Houghton Lake wetland. This dependence is briefly restated here.

The Manning equation for uniform flow in an open channel is often adapted to other situations:

$$v = 1/n \quad h^{2/3} S^{1/2} \qquad [4]$$

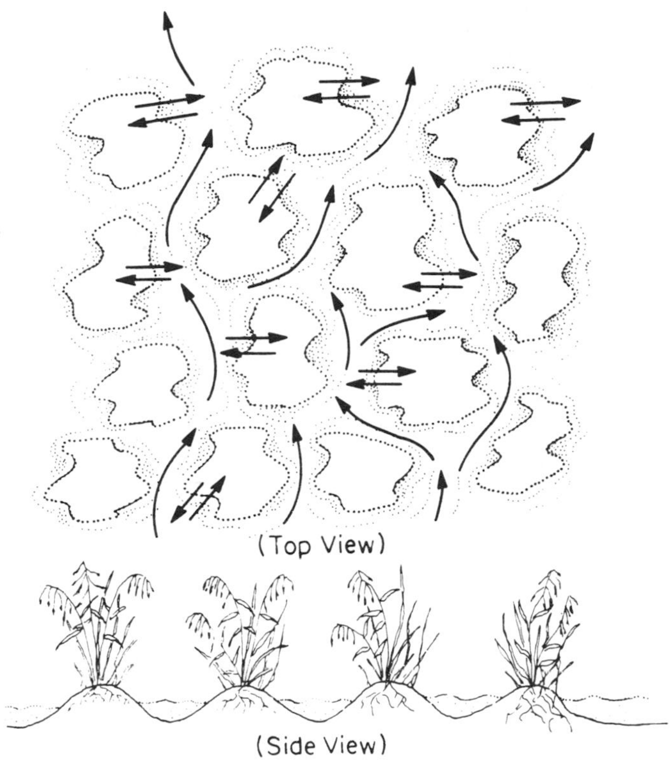

FIGURE 4. Wetland surface water flow is impeded by porous clumps of vegetation and hummocks.

where
v = velocity, m s^{-1}
h = depth, m
S = slope, m m^{-1}
n = coefficient, s $m^{-1/3}$

Figure 5 illustrates these quantities. In the wetland, the entire 'channel' is not available for flow, but only a fraction ϕ. However, the actual velocity is usually not available; rather, just the volume flow rate, width and depth. It is then necessary to modify the formula:

$$v_s = 1/n_e \; h^{2/3} \; S^{1/2} \tag{5}$$

where
v_s = $Q/wh = v\phi$ = superficial velocity, m s^{-1}
n_e = effective coefficient, S $m^{-1/3}$
Q = volumetric flow, m^3 s^{-1}
w = width, m

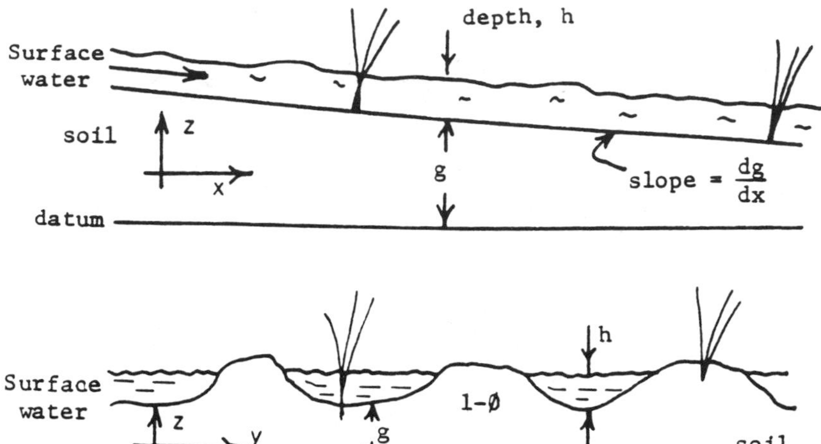

FIGURE 5. Flow configuration for a peatland ecosystem. From Hammer and Kadlec, 1983.

Then the open channel and effective coefficients are related by:

$$n_e = n/\phi \qquad [6]$$

Manning n-values have been determined by a few investigators for wetlands (Table 3). There is reasonable uniformity among

TABLE 3. Manning's n-values for wetlands (for depth approximately 15 cm).

Location	Cover Type	n-Value
Houghton Lake, MI (ϕ=0.13)	Sedge/Cattail	0.7
Great Sippewissett, MA (Burke and Stolzenbach, 1983)	Spartina	0.3
Chandler Slough, FL	Hyacinth	0.7
(Shih, et al., 1979)	Mixed	0.7
(Shih and Rahi, 1982)		
South Florida Conservation Areas (Corps. of Eng., 1954)	--	1.3
Soil Conservation Service Predictive Procedure (French, 1985)	Cattail/Shrub	0.2

disparate sites, but the only predictive procedure available for wetlands gives low values.

There are strong dependencies of n on flow depth and vegetation characteristics. Shih and Rahi (1982) showed a sharp decrease in n with increasing depth, and a sharp increase with vegetation density. Other investigators (Chen, 1976) have shown that n depends on slope (S) for flow over grass. Consequently, the flow may be more appropriately described by an empirical form:

$$v = \alpha h^{\beta} S^{\gamma} \quad [7]$$

When $\beta = 0$ and $\gamma = 1$, this is equivalent to Darcy's Law; and where $\beta = 2/3$ and $\gamma = 1/2$, it yields Manning's equation. For the Houghton Lake site, $\beta = 2$ and $\gamma = 1$ gave good results (Kadlec et al., 1981; Hammer and Kadlec, 1986).

UNDERGROUND FLOWS

Subsurface flow is generally believed to follow Darcy's law, which in one dimension is:

$$v = - k\, \partial P/\partial x \quad [8]$$

where k = hydraulic conductivity, m s^{-1}
P = pressure, m of water
x = distance, m

Depending on the soil medium, this flow may or may not be important. Comparative k values (Table 4) for several soils revealed that they vary over nine orders of magnitude. Further, Dooge (1975) has shown that k depends on direction of flow in peat soils, with vertical conductivities being only half of lateral conductivity.

Lateral gradients in wetlands are typically very low, ca. 10^{-4}; whereas vertical pressure differences may be much greater, on the order of unity. Consequently, underground lateral flow may usually be safely ignored, except where the treatment system is

TABLE 4. Conductivities, gradients and flows.

Medium	Hydraulic conductivity	Lateral flow ($\partial h/\partial x = 10^{-4}$)	Vertical flow ($\partial h/\partial x = 1$)
	----------	m d^{-1}	----------
Surface vegetation	300,000	30	--
Coarse gravel	100	0.01	100
Sand	10	0.001	10
Peat	0.1	10^{-5}	1
Clay	0.001	10^{-7}	0.001
Phragmites root zone (Kickuth)		($\partial h/\partial x = 10^{-2}$)	
	100	1.0	--

designed for this purpose (Kickuth, 1984) with high gradients and high conductivities.

Vertical flows--recharge, discharge, infiltration--may well be important. At Houghton Lake, the wetland is sealed underneath by a thick clay layer which permits virtually no vertical flow (Haag, 1979). At the opposite extreme, a wetland constructed on mine tailings at Cobalt, Ontario infiltrated so rapidly that no water could be maintained in downstream sections (Miller and Young, 1985).

Portions of the Houghton Lake wetland are subject to dry-out, even when wastewater is being added. Under drought conditions, wastewater forms a mound with an area such that evaporation equals pumping. When this occurs, capillary suction in the soil plays an important role in determining pressure gradients. At saturations of less that 50%, suction can reach several m of water (Figure 6), and move water laterally and vertically in the soil to achieve a saturation balance.

OVERALL WATER BUDGETS

In order to accurately assess the assimilative performance of a wetland, a complete water budget must be prepared. All points of influx and efflux must be identified and the flows estimated

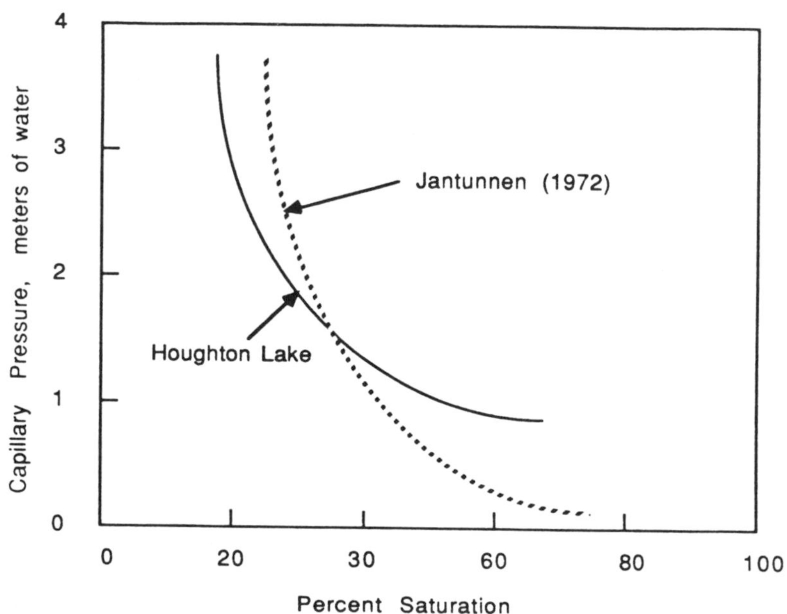

FIGURE 6. Capillary pressure as a function of percent saturation for peat.

throughout the year. Similarly, precipitation and evapotranspiration must be quantified. This water budget, when combined with measurements of nutrient concentrations, can provide a complete picture of the wetland treatment system performance. Concentration values at the inlet and outlet of any system are only part of the picture, and can be misleading if the inflow and outflow of water are not identical. If not taken into account, infiltration, dilution of wastewater by flowing surface waters or by rain, or concentration of solids due to evapotranspiration can confuse the interpretation of system performance.

The annual water budget of any region in a wetland can be expressed as an unsteady-state material balance of the form:

$$Q_i - Q_o + A + P - E - I = \Delta M \qquad [9]$$

where Q_i = flow in, m^3
Q_o = flow out, m^3
A = wastewater additions, m^3
P = precipitation, m^3
I = downward infiltration or discharge (-I) through the soil, m^3
M = aboveground water accumulation, m^3

Surface water depth, denoted as h, can be related directly to the accumulation term, ΔM, so long as there is standing water

$$h = (M/s\phi_s) \qquad [10]$$

where h = water depth, m
s = surface area of region, m^2
ϕ_s = fraction of wetland volume, aboveground, available for water storage, dimensionless.

Should the aboveground water accumulation become negative, no surface water exists. Under these conditions the soil is no longer saturated. Due to the hygroscopic nature of peat and typical wetland organic substrates, it is generally impossible to measure the elevation of the below ground water table by usual techniques.

Closure on the wetland water budget is necessary before the performance of an existing system can be meaningfully evaluated. Inflows and outflows must be identified and measured. Precipitation figures are normally available from official weather records. Evapotranspiration can be estimated, using techniques which were discussed previously. Infiltration flows can be estimated by examination of soil borings and determination of the permeability of underlying soils. Such flows can more often be determined only by the discrepancy in closure on the water balance.

Similarly the water budget is essential to prediction of new system performance. In this case, future inflows must be estimated and precipitation predicted from historical weather data. Infiltration/percolation can only be estimated by examining soil cores. Outflows will be system dependent and can be predicted by estimating both the expected evapotranspiration and the rate of overland water flow.

A 100 ha area has been used as the system for overall water balances at Houghton Lake (Figure 7). Based on eight years of data, virtually all wastewater added to the system found its way overland and out (Table 5).

RESIDENCE TIME

The rates at which nutrients and other solutes can be removed from the surface waters will dictate the permissible rate of water passage through the system. The period available for treatment is termed the residence time of the system. Wastewater can be exposed to the wetland ecosystem in various ways. If a small area is surrounded by a dike or other enclosure to maintain a captive water pool, wastewater can be treated batchwise (Lakshman, 1980). The treatment site is flooded, and the water held until the desired effluent quality is achieved. The area can then be drained, releasing the treated water and refilled with a fresh charge. The water residence time for such a process is easily defined. However, as with most large-scale processes, it is often convenient to employ a continuous flow system and an analogous residence time can be defined. The actual residence

FIGURE 7. Porter Ranch Peatland Houghton Lake, Michigan.

TABLE 5. Houghton Lake peatland summer water budgets, in thousands of m^3, for a 100 ha zone.

	P-E	A	Q_i	Q_o	ΔM	Pool
1978	80	240	0	135	185	140
1979	-4	384	18	333	65	153
1980	-137	407	0	304	-34	172
1981	99	455	30	558	26	172
1982	-51	404	20	386	-13	169
1983	-110	485	132	487	20	170
1984	-24	546	73	602	-7	170
1985	44	379	0	347	76	160
TOTAL	-103	3300	273	3152		

time τ, for a flow system is

$$\tau = \frac{\text{volume of the surface water}}{\text{volumetric flow rate of surface waters}} \qquad [11]$$

In general the volumetric flow will vary from one point in the wetland to another due to rain, evaporation or stream flows. If these changes are not extreme, an average flow rate will often suffice, otherwise smaller portions of the wetland can be considered separately. For a rectangular wetland with a linear discharge along one side,

$$\tau = \phi\, hwz/Q = z/v \qquad [12]$$

where
- ϕ is the void fraction of the wetland for water flow
- h is the surface water depth, m
- w is the width
- z is the distance from the point of wastewater discharge, m
- Q is the average surface water flow rate, $m^3\ s^{-1}$
- v is the true velocity of surface waters (average), m s^{-1}.

This actual residence time is difficult to obtain accurately, due to the lack of information on wetland void fractions. Small-scale obstructions due to vegetation are a factor in determining the void fraction, but even more difficult to assess are the contributions due to large-scale channelling. In addition, the void fraction is undoubtedly a function of water depth. Values of ϕ for the Houghton Lake treatment site have been estimated to be about 0.1 - 0.3 for shallow water sedge meadows, and to approach 1.0 for deep, open water areas.

In absence of better data, it may be preferable to define a superficial velocity, v_s, and superficial residence time, τ_s:

$$v_s = Q/hw \qquad [13]$$

$$\tau_s = hwz/Q = z/v_s \qquad [14]$$

While lacking intrinsic information about the topography and hydrology of the wetland, the superficial residence time can sometimes be of use in examining data after a single site under varying water depths and flows. At any rate, care must be taken not to confuse the significance and applicability of the actual and superficial values.

If the data in Table 5 are used to compute a superficial residence time, the result is $\tau_s = 50$ d. However, field measurements of actual velocities indicate $\tau = 5$ d, the difference being due to porosity (ca. 15%) and the directions of water flow (most water traverses only half the area).

There is a clear need to address the details of water movement inside the budget zone.

DETAILED WATER MOVEMENT

Hydrological models of wetlands have been reviewed by Mitsch et al. (1982). They describe three basic types, 'ecosystem' models and 'regional' models which simply account for water inventory, and 'hydrodynamic transport' models which describe stream flow and storm runoff. None of these approaches are adequate to describe overland flow of a thin water sheet impeded by wetland vegetation. Consequently, Hammer and Kadlec (1986) developed a spatial model for wetland surface water dynamics.

Flow proceeds at the rate at which gravitational and pressure forces are just counterbalanced by frictional drag forces. A velocity correlation and a mass balance are required under these circumstances. We chose as a control volume a depth sufficient to contain the upper water surface (or equivalent piezometric surface if underground). Then for constant density:

$$\partial(\phi_s h)/\partial t = -\partial/\partial z\ (hv) + P - E + A - I \qquad [15]$$

where the vector quantities have only two lateral components.

A one-dimensional representation of the wetland surface has been selected for simplicity. To work with a rigorous two-dimensional model of surface water flows would present a significantly larger calculative task. Such sophistication is unwarranted for several reasons. First, for many natural wetlands, such as the Porter Ranch site, water flow is essentially one-dimensional. If the wetland simulation axis is chosen to correspond to the direction of maximum ground surface gradient, great simplification is possible. Secondly, the purpose of this hydrology model is to provide, in part, for simulation of new wetland/wastewater sites. It is anticipated that constructed wetlands will dominate over natural sites for this use. Such man-made systems will stress simple geometries for good water distribution and hydrological control--thus a one-dimensional theme would normally be followed (e.g., ditches or long, narrow cells).

Equation (7) for the Houghton Lake site may be written:

$$v = \alpha\, h^2\, (-\partial h_w/\partial z) \qquad [16]$$

where h_w = water elevation; m
= h-g

Combining (15) and (16) for constant width and porosities gives:

$$\phi_s\, \partial h/\partial t = \partial/\partial z\, (\alpha h^3\, \partial h_w/\partial z) + P - E + A \qquad [17]$$

where, for this site, I=0. This equation has two parameters: porosity ϕ_s and vegetation conductivity, α. Input site data are topography (g) and water additions (P-E, A). Watershed inputs enter as boundary conditions on this differential equation.

Computer solution of this water balance is required (Hammer, 1984).

Capabilities of the hydrology model to predict responses to short-term events were determined (Figure 8). The initial start-up of the Porter Ranch irrigation system occurred on August 8, 1978. The depth of surface water near the discharge point was measured continuously. The simulator accurately predicted water levels both above and below the ground surface and predicted level changes due to rain events (as on August 2nd) and variation in the wastewater pumping schedule.

The model is relatively insensitive to the flow and porosity parameters. The effects of errors in precipitation and evapotranspiration are easily visualized; and, given good meteorological data, will not present a problem. The model is, however, quite sensitive to inflows and outflows and their timing.

Pumped additions present no major difficulty, with 1 caveat. Water levels could not be adequately modeled using averaged weekly or monthly irrigation rates. Daily values taken from the pumping log were needed to produce the proper shape and depth for the water sheet. Boundary flows are important, but in some cases their effect diminishes with distance from the boundary, since interior processes then dominate. Likewise, the effect of an error in a boundary flow diminishes with elapsed time from the point of error. These observations in general match those of other investigators (Kadlec, 1983; Gardner et al., 1980). It is reiterated that infiltration flows were not present at the studied site, nor completely tested in the simulator.

SUMMARY

All components of the water balance are important. Each process is fairly well understood, but may not be easily quantified at a particular site. Rain events have the obvious effect of raising water levels in wetlands. The wetland slowly releases rainwater. Excessive depths are not normally caused by rain but dry-out may occur in natural wetlands. A wetland is often part of a larger watershed, which funnels runoff to the wetland.

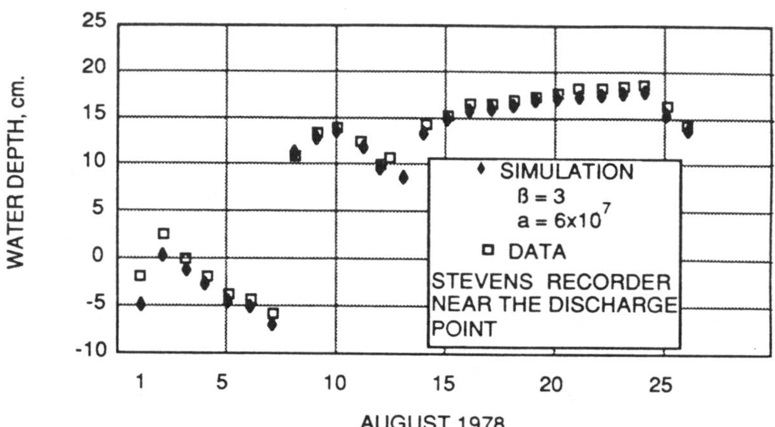

FIGURE 8. Simulation of the 1978 start-up for the Porter Ranch treatment Facility. (From Hammer and Kadlec, 1986).

Water losses to the atmosphere are a combination of evaporation and transpiration by emergent macrophytes. The energy for vaporization must come from the sun, which narrows the range of observed values. Temperature is the other major factor.

The rate at which water can flow across a wetland is controlled by the ground slope, water depth, vegetation type, channelization, and constructed structures. The Manning equation needs modification to deal with wetland flows, and porosity effects must be properly accounted for.

Overall water budgets are useful in accounting for waterborne substances on a monthly or yearly basis. Errors may be large, and assistance from tracer budgets is necessary. Closure on the overall water budget is necessary to evaluate system performance.

The dynamic, distance-variable nature of water processes requires a complex model to describe phenomena. Even the simple concept of residence time requires detailed knowledge of internal processes. These include below-ground phenomena, such as capillary pressure and soil anisotropy. Because of the dynamic nature of flows and depths, and because of distance variability, 'black box' models will not work for the time scales of interest for water chemistry and water biology. A partial differential equation is unavoidable. The information required to use these includes: daily precipitation and evapotranspiration and additions, flow and storage porosities, and infiltration rule, and the wetland boundary flows. The complex interactions between biota, soils and water are driven first and foremost by the hydrology of the wetland. Much of the work to date has stopped short of providing quantitative and definitive answers to questions involving nutrient cycling, sediment transport and pollutant removal because of our inability to accurately measure water movement in wetlands.

REFERENCES

Bernatowicz, S., S. Leszczynski, and S. Tyczynska. 1976. The influence of transpiration by emergent plants on the water balance in lakes. Aquat. Bot. 2:275-288.

Burke, R. W., and K. D. Stolzenbach. 1983. Free surface flow through salt marsh grass. MIT Sea Grant Report MITSG 83-16, Cambridge, MA.

Chamie, J. P. M. 1975. The effects of simulated sewage effluent upon decomposition, nutrient status and litterfall in a central Michigan peatland. Ph.D. Thesis. The Univ. of Michigan, Ann Arbor.

Chang, J. J. 1968. Climate and agriculture: An Ecological Survey. Aldine Publishing Co., Chicago, IL. 304 pp.

Chen, C. 1976. Flow resistance in brood shallow grassed channels. J. Hydr. Div., ASCE, 102:307-322.

Christiansen, J. E., and J. B. Low. 1970. Water requirements of waterfowl marshlands in northern Utah. Utah Division of Fish and Game, Publication No. 69-12.

Corps of Engineers. 1954. Central and Southern Florida Project: Part IV, Section 7 - Design Memorandum, Interim Report on Evaluation of Manning's n in Vegetated Areas. Serial No. 32, Jacksonville, FL.

Dooge, J. 1975. The water balance of bogs and fens. In Hydrology of Marsh-Ridden Areas. UNESCO Press, Paris.

Eagleson, P. S. 1970. Dynamic hydrology. McGraw-Hill, New York.

French, R. H. 1985. Open-channel hydraulics. McGraw-Hill, New York.

Gardner, R. H., D. D. Huff, R. V. O'Neill, J. B. Mankin, J. Carney and J. Jones. 1980. Application of error analysis to a marsh hydrology model. Water Resour. Res. 16:659-664.

Haag, R. D., Jr. 1979. The hydrogeology of the Houghton (Lake) Wetland. M.S. Thesis. The Univ. of Michigan, Ann Arbor.

Hammer, D. E. 1984. An engineering model of wetland/wastewater interactions. Ph.D. Thesis. The Univ. of Michigan, Ann Arbor.

Hammer, D. E., and R. H. Kadlec. 1983. Design principles for wetland treatment systems. Report EPA-600/2-83-026 to USEPA, NTLS PB83-188722; U.S. Dept. of Commerce, Springfield, VA.

Hammer, D. E., and R. H. Kadlec. 1986. A model for wetland surface water dynamics. Water Resources Research (accepted).

Jantunen, H. 1972. Drainage experiments on ErCS-Peat in the laboratory. 4th Int. Peat Cong. Proc., Otaniemi, Finland.

Kadlec, J. A. 1983. Water budgets for small diked marshes. Water Resour. Bull. 19:223-229.

Kadlec, R. H. 1978. Wastewater treatment via wetland irrigation: Hydrology. In C. B. DeWitt and E. Soloway (ed.) Wetlands

Ecology, Values and Impacts. Institute for Environmental Studies, Univ. of Wisconsin.

Kadlec, R. H., R. B. Williams, and R. D. Scheffe. 1986. Evaporation and transpiration in arid and temperate climates. Proc. Int. Conf. on Wetlands, Charleston, SC.

Kadlec, R. H., D. E. Hammer, I.-S. Nam, and J. O. Wilkes. 1981. The hydrology of overland flow in wetlands. Chemical Engineering Communications 9:331-334.

Kickuth, R. 1984. The root-zone process in practice. Landschaft and Stadt 16:3.

Knisel, W. H., Jr. 1976. Methods of estimating evaporation and evapotranspiration. In S. H. Kunkle and J. L. Thames (ed.) Hydrological Techniques for Upstream Conservation. FAO of the United Nations, Rome, Italy.

Lakshman, G. 1980. A demonstration project at Humboldt to provide tertiary treatment to the municipal effluent using aquatic plants. Progress Report, Saskatchewan Research Council. SRC Pub. No. E-820-13-1-E-80.

Messem, A. B. 1975. A rapid method for the determination of potential transpiration derived from the Penman Combination Model. Agricultural Meteorology 14:369-384.

Miller, G. and M. Young. 1985. The use of cattail marshes to treat sewage in northern Ontario. Ont. Min. of Env. Internal Report.

Mitsch, W. J., J. R. Taylor, and C. Madden. 1982. Models of North American freshwater wetland. Int. J. Ecol. Environ. Sci. 51:109-140.

Parker, P. E. 1974. A dynamic ecosystem simulator. Ph.D. Thesis. The Univ. of Michigan, Ann Arbor.

Penman, H. L. 1948. Natural evaporation from open water, bare soil, and grass. Proc. R. Soc. Lond. 93:120-145.

Penman, H. L. 1956. Estimating evaporation. Trans. Amer. Geophys. Union 37:43-48.

Scheffe, R. D. 1978. Estimation and prediction of summer evapotranspiration from a northern wetland. M.S. Thesis. The Univ. of Michigan, Ann Arbor.

Shih, S. F. and G. S. Rahi. 1982. Seasonal variations of Manning's roughness coefficient in a subtropical marsh. Trans. ASAE 25:116-119.

Shih, S. F., A. C. Federico, J. F. Milleson, and M. Rosen. 1979. Sampling programs for evaluating upland marsh to improve water quality. Trans. ASAE 22:828-833.

Wentz, W. A. 1976. The effects of simulated sewage effluents on the growth and productivity of peatland plants. Ph.D. Thesis. The Univ. of Michigan, Ann Arbor.

Woolhiser, D. A., and J. A. Liggett. 1967. Unsteady, one-dimensional flow over a plane - the rising hydrograph. Water Resour. Res. 3:753-771.

NUTRIENT DYNAMICS IN WETLANDS

J. A. Kadlec
Department of Fisheries and Wildlife
Utah State University
Logan, Utah 84322-5211

ABSTRACT

Processes affecting nutrient dynamics in wetlands can be placed in two categories: 1) processes of import and export, and 2) processes within the wetland. For most nutrients, import or export processes involve the movement of water, making a knowledge of hydrology an essential prerequisite. Carbon, O_2 and N enter and leave wetlands as gases, complicating the cycles of those elements. Occasionally, animal movements result in substantial net import or export of nutrients. Processes within wetlands can be physical-chemical, such as adsorption; microbiological such as decomposition; or macrobiological such as plant uptake. Changes in nutrient content of any single component of the wetland ecosystem involve many of these processes. For example, sediments are often suspected of playing a key role in nutrient cycling, but so many of the processes above are involved that careful analysis is needed to elucidate the important dynamics.

Wastewater application to wetlands usually involves substantial quantities of water, thereby altering the hydrology of the system and all aspects of nutrient cycles connected to the hydrological processes. Increased nutrient supplies via waste-water addition can result in increased storage, either temporary or long term, in ecosystem components, or they can increase rates of transfer among components or flow through the system.

Keywords: Nitrogen, phosphorus, hydrology, cycling, budgets.

INTRODUCTION

This paper provides an overview of the important features of nutrient dynamics in wetlands. To restrict the scope to a manageable level, the nutrient elements considered will be N and P, although occasionally other elements are also discussed to illustrate key points. A more difficult problem is posed by the term "wetlands", which includes a very diverse set of biotic systems, ranging from arctic tundra to tropical mangrove swamps

ISBN 0-941463-00-1

and from tidal salt marshes to prairie potholes to desert spring marshes, and a whole host of other kinds of wetlands. It would not be possible, in one brief paper, to even describe all the different kinds of wetlands, much less discuss the nutrient dynamics of each. However, I believe the nutrient dynamics of these systems determine their major biotic features. Thus, different kinds of wetlands will be viewed as the result of differences in basic nutrient dynamic processes.

The conceptual approach for this analysis will be the idea of mass balance. Basically, changes in the amount of material in the wetland, or for any of its subdivisions, are the result of differences between inputs and outputs. This method of analysis can be used at a wide variety of sizes of study units, from the whole wetland to individual organisms, and time scales from years to hours. To implement this approach, it is necessary to specify clearly the study unit or units, often called compartments; all the inputs and outputs; and the time scale of interest.

In the first part of this review, I shall consider the whole ecosystem the unit of study and consider inputs and outputs at that level, usually for the time period of a whole growing season or a year. These mass balances are sometimes referred to as annual budgets (Phillips, 1977) but I prefer the term input-output budget (LaBaugh, 1986). The value of such an approach is two-fold: 1) input-output budgets explain much of the variation among wetland ecosystems; and 2) input-output budgets provide the essential framework within which we can study internal mass balances of ecosystem compartments (LaBaugh, 1986).

Within the framework of input-output budgets, we will consider the internal structure and processes of wetland ecosystems. Here there are several units of study, or compartments, for which inputs, outputs, and storages are of interest. The array of processes involved in the inputs and outputs at this level of resolution is larger than at the whole system level.

Finally, we will consider the impacts of added quantities of water and nutrients on the transfer processes and storages of nutrients in wetland ecosystems.

INPUT-OUTPUT BUDGETS

At the whole wetland or ecosystem level, most elements enter and leave by water transport (Figure 1). The major exceptions are inputs of airborne dry particulates (dust), and both inputs and outputs of gaseous forms of N, O_2 and CO_2. Sometimes there are outputs of other gases, notably H_2S, CH_4, NH_3 and other volatile hydrocarbons.

Because water transport is so important to inputs and outputs of N, P, and K at this level, good water budgets are essential to good nutrient balances (Carter et al., 1979; LaBaugh, 1986). The terms of the general water balance equation, given below, vary in their importance in different kinds of wetlands (Novitski, 1978):

$$P + SWI + GWI = ET + SWO + GWO + \Delta S$$

where:
- P = precipitation on wetland surface
- SWI = surface water inflow
- GWI = ground water inflow
- ET = evapotranspiration
- SWO = surface water outflow
- GWO = ground water outflow
- S = change in storage

Each of the sources of water are likely to be very different in chemical composition, so the nutrient supply to a wetland depends on which source(s) dominates. For example, streams and river (SWI) may be high in particulates and nutrients, whereas GWI usually will be low in particulates. Water loss by evapotranspiration (ET) leaves the nutrients in the residual water in the wetland, leading to evaporative concentration of dissolved and suspended materials. Outflows of both surface water and ground water are initially similar chemically in unstratified wetlands, but ground water is more likely to interact with sediment particles and change rapidly as it flows through the pore spaces. If, as sometimes happens (Anderson and Munter, 1981), ground water flow reverses from out of to into a wetland, the material recently removed from the wetland water body may be returned to it.

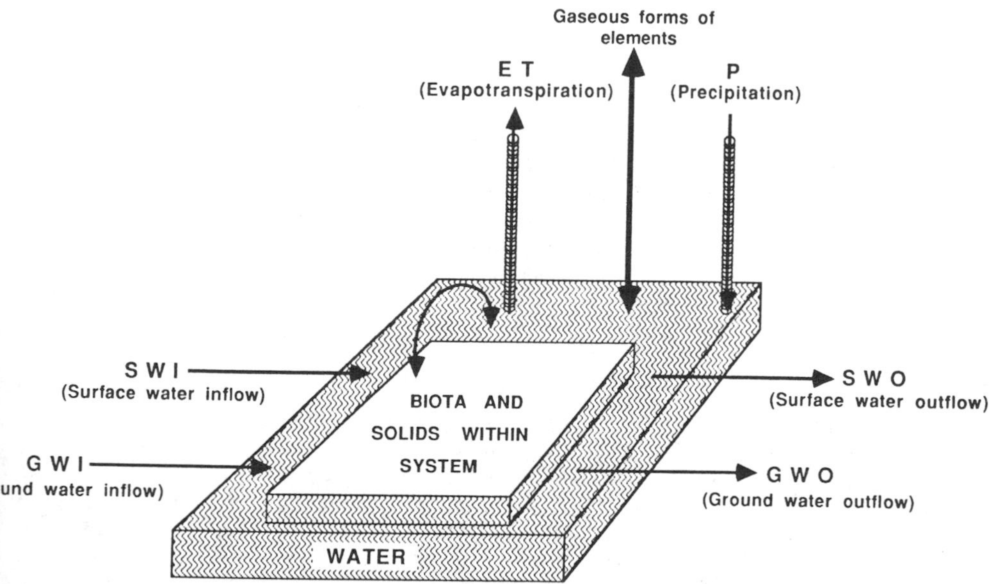

FIGURE 1. Schematic representation of material balance process (arrows) at whole system level.

Obviously, different combinations and volumes of these inflows and outflows will result in very different nutrient supplies and retentions within the wetland. In fact, I believe the major wetland types are defined primarily by these relationships. For example, tidal marshes are partly the result of saline SWI and SWO, but details of marsh plant zonation depend on the interaction with fresh SWI and GWI. Very unproductive bogs are essentially totally dependent on precipitation (P) for their nutrient supply (Moore and Bellamy, 1974) and are called ombrotrophic, which literally means "rain fed". Most of these bogs occur in closed basins in cool, damp regions with low ET and thus lose most of their water through GWO. An otherwise similar wetland, but with substantial SWI or GWI, is likely to have a richer nutrient supply (Heinselman, 1970), leading to a more productive peatland called a fen. Wetlands on the borders of lakes or rivers obviously have the potential for large SWI and SWO terms, but many also have important GWI terms. Often these waters are high in nutrients, leading to productive wetland systems ranging from cattail (*Typha* spp.) marshes (Klopatek, 1978) to tropical "sudd" or floating *Papyrus* mats (Gaudet, 1979) to wooded swamps (Mitsch et al., 1979). In semi-arid to arid regions, low P and high ET lead to increasing ion concentrations and inland saline (sometimes called alkaline) wetlands.

Wetlands also differ depending on the variation of inputs and outputs over time. Because wetlands are almost always shallowly flooded, many of the common marsh plants - for example cattail - are adapted to periodic decreases in water level, perhaps to the point of no surface water at all during dry periods. A change to constant water levels is ultimately detrimental to such plants, and others will take their place. This may be primarily due to the effects of the water itself, but simultaneous changes in nutrient relationships probably also occur.

Input-output nutrient budgets may consider the whole wetland as a unit or, as in Figure 1, separate the surface water from the other components of the wetland. The approach adopted in Figure 1 is useful if the system is manipulated to make major changes in hydrology. In either case, the emphasis is clearly on relationships between inputs and outputs and not on internal processes.

Input-Output Processes

The processes of water movements involved in nutrient transport are well understood but their measurement often involves substantial errors (Winter, 1981; LaBaugh and Winter, 1984), not infrequently about 10-20%. Because nutrient mass balances require that these uncertain water volumes be multiplied by uncertain chemical concentrations, there is obviously a potential for even higher errors in calculations of the mass of nutrients being transported (LaBaugh, 1986). And when the calculations involve determining a term by difference, not infrequently the ground water component, all the error is accumulated in the ground water term. Unfortunately, in this situation there is no way to assess the accuracy of any term in the mass balance equation - the equation automatically balances! A "worst case" analysis, based on statistical estimates of variability in both water volumes and nutrient concentrations, leads to the conclusion that nutrient mass balances at the input-output level could be useless in the sense that all interpretations of the data are within the realm of being reasonably probable. In contrast, an analysis of variability among mass balances for major ions (e.g., Na^+, Cl^-, Ca^{++}, Mg^{++}, K^+, and SO_4^{2-}) for replicated, controlled, small diked marshes (Kadlec, 1986b) showed standard errors on the order of 5-10%. Although that indicates substantial variability, it is lower than would be expected solely on the basis of measurement errors in the water volumes involved.

Other than water transport, the major processes affecting nutrient input-output budgets are: 1) atmospheric inputs of particulates and 2) gas exchanges with the atmosphere. Particulate inputs, or dry fall, are highly variable both by geographic region and by time (Swank, 1984). Commonly they are measured in combination with inputs via precipitation. Such combined inputs can be major parts of nutrient budgets for aquatic systems even in relatively non-industrialized regions (Wetzel, 1975). Kadlec (1986b) found that in Manitoba marshes, atmospheric inputs of total N and total P were about one half of the input via surface water.

At the input-output level, two gas exchange processes are important in N cycling: N_2 fixation and denitrification. Nitrogen fixation converts N_2 from the atmosphere to NH_4^+. Most wetland and aquatic systems fix N_2 according to numerous assays by the acetylene reduction technique (e.g., Moore and Bellamy, 1974; Hemond, 1983). It is very difficult to extrapolate from those studies to estimates of the amount of N_2 fixed by an entire wetland, either net or gross. A few studies report apparent net N_2 fixation for a whole wetland: 1.0 g N m^{-2} yr^{-1} for Louisiana salt marsh (DeLaune et al., 1976), 56.7 g N m^{-2} yr^{-1} for tropical papyrus (Gaudet, 1979) and 6.1 g N m^{-2} yr^{-1} for salt marsh (Kaplan et. al., 1979).

Denitrification converts NO_3^--N to N_2 via several intermediate steps (Harter, 1966) in an anaerobic environment. According to Patrick et al. (1976), this process seems to be very important to wetlands, including wetland rice culture. Efforts to fertilize wetland rice, or adding NO_3 for other reasons, in by far the majority of cases results in a rapid disappearance of the added N, presumably being denitrified to N_2. NO_3^- is rarely abundant in wetlands and both Hemond (1983) and I (1986a) have concluded that it exists only ephemerally in wetlands. Rates of denitrification, if these observations are correct, depend on conditions suitable for the bacteria involved, but seem to increase with increasing NO_3^- so that NO_3^--N is converted almost as fast as it is added. As in the case of N_2 fixation, however, estimates of total N lost by denitrification from a whole wetland are rare. Generally, the literature gives only net values; that is, either net gain or loss of N by the combination of fixation and denitrification and sometimes some other processes as well. For example, DeLaune et al. (1976) estimate a net loss through denitrification of 2 g N m^{-2} yr^{-1} for Louisiana salt marsh, Andersen (1974) 30-32 g N m^{-2} yr^{-1} for shallow lakes, and Kaplan et al. (1979) report a net loss of 7.3 g N m^{-2} yr^{-1} and a gross loss of 13.3 g N m^{-2} yr^{-1} for Massachusetts salt marsh.

Ammonia volatilization is another potential pathway for N loss from wetlands, but it is more poorly known than denitrification. It has been found to be substantial from some small, shallow saline prairie lakes (Murphy and Brownlee, 1981) but there are few data from wetlands. Hemond (1983) suggested that 90 mg N m^{-2} yr^{-1} was an order of magnitude estimate for Thoreau's Bog.

Other gas exchanges at the whole system level are of O_2, CO_2, and H_2S, CH_4, and probably some other organic compounds. These are or can be important to ecosystem function and possibly, at least in the case of H_2S, to global cycles, but a consideration of these is beyond the scope of this paper.

Nutrient Storage

Because wetlands often occur in basins or other landforms characterized by long term sediment or organic matter accumulation (or both), they tend to be sites of nutrient accumulations or storage. The ecological or management significance of net storage varies from area to area and time to time depending on site specific hydrology and ecosystem characteristics.

INTERNAL NUTRIENT CYCLE

Input-output nutrient budgets provide the basic framework within which internal nutrient cycles function in aquatic ecosystems. Hydrologically, wetlands systems are intermediate between lake and stream systems in many respects. Lakes are characterized by relatively high volume to sediment surface area ratios and relatively slow water turnover times, often leading to emphasis on depth as a factor governing the characteristics of the lake. In contrast, streams tend to have lower volume to sediment surface area ratios, but water flow leads to an emphasis on a directional longitudinal structure and concepts such as spiralling (Webster and Patten, 1979) which relate flow to water-sediment interactions. Wetlands have low water volume to sediment surface area ratios and often short to moderate water turnover times (there are some major exceptions, such as bogs) like streams, but often lack the strong flow patterns of streams. Consequently, wetlands have neither the strong vertical (depth) or horizontal organization of lakes or streams. However, they do have predominantly horizontal structure which may be important to some ecosystem processes (Nelson and Kadlec, 1984). In some, perhaps most, cases the horizontal structure is poorly organized, leading to severe problems in sampling and understanding overall system behavior. Thus, while the basic processes by which nutrients are cycled within wetlands are undoubtedly the same as those in lakes or streams, it seems unlikely that their relative importance is the same in these three major types of aquatic ecosystems. Further, given the great variation in hydrology among wetlands, I think we should expect to see similar variation in patterns of internal nutrient cycling. With these concepts in mind, I first will discuss the general features of internal cycles in a generalized wetland and then look at how altered water and nutrient loadings might impact them.

Compartments

The way in which the wetland ecosystem is divided for study into compartments depends on the kind of wetland, the objectives of the analysis, and some practical considerations; it is always to some degree arbitrary. A simple breakdown is diagrammed in Figure 2. It has 6 major compartments, namely macrophytes, epiphytes, algae, water, organic sediments, and combined litter and associated microorganisms compartment. The arrows in Figure 2

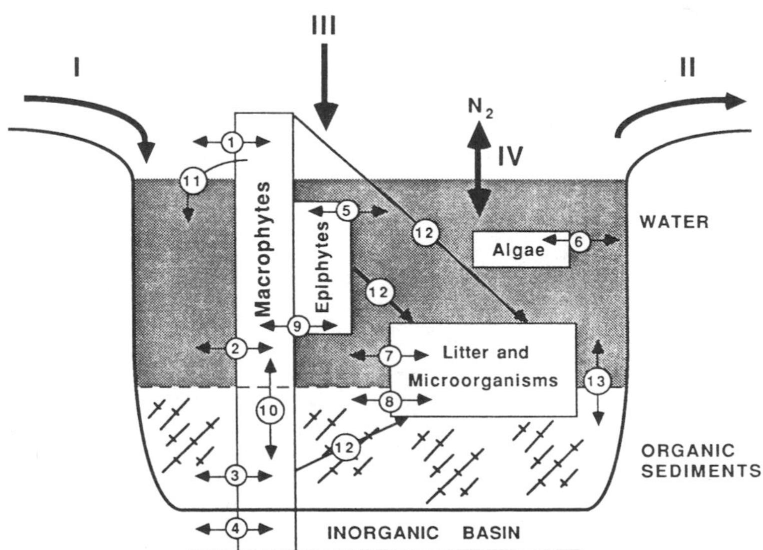

FIGURE 2. Diagrammatic representation of the major components and flows of biomass and nutrients in a hypothetical wetland. Numbers designate processes discussed in text.

represent an assortment of flows and processes by which nutrients and biomass are transferred among compartments. They will be discussed in the next section.

Several of the compartments in Figure 2 could be sub-divided and other compartments could be added - notably absent are animals of any kind. The macrophyte compartment could be divided into four or five separate compartments such as submersed plants (e.g., pondweeds, _Potamogeton_ spp.), floating plants (e.g., duckweeds, Lemnaceae), emergent plants (e.g., cattail); rooted plants with floating leaves (e.g., water lilies, _Nuphar_ spp.), and perhaps one or more kinds of woody plants (e.g., willows, _Salix_ spp.). The assortment of processes or "arrows" associated with each of these different kinds of plants would be different. For example, for emergent plants, such as cattail, arrow 2, exchange with water is much less than it is for a submersed pondweed. The process of sub-dividing components could be carried to greater detail, at least to considering plant species separately and perhaps even to considering different sizes of a single species [e.g., cypress trees (_Taxodium distichium_)] individually.

The epiphyte compartment (Figure 2) is heterogeneous assemblage of small organisms--plants, animals, bacteria, etc. It is rarely, if ever, possible to separate these organisms into separate compartments in the field and often it is difficult to treat them separately from plants on which they occur. Nevertheless, in terms of the animal component of wetlands the periphyton may be a key basic food resource (Nelson and Kadlec, 1984). Consequently, I show this assemblage as a separate compartment, thereby revealing one of my biases!

The importance of algae in freshwater wetlands has been widely neglected (Hosseini and van der Valk, in press; Wetzel, 1975). This may be because in contrast to lakes, the phytoplankton--small, free-floating algae--are less conspicuous and productive than the visually dominant macrophytes. However, 3 forms of algae often contribute substantially to wetland primary (biomass) production. These are the epiphytes, growing attached to plants; the epipelon, growing on or in the surface layers of the litter and bottom sediments; and the filamentous algae that sometimes form extensive mats. Investigations of these forms of algae in freshwater wetlands are just beginning, but some studies have shown that one or more of these forms sometimes may be as important as submersed plants in wetland primary production (G. Robinson, pers. comm.), and presumably therefore also in nutrient cycling. Because algae have much shorter life spans than most macrophytes, standing crops are likely to be lower and the uptake and release of nutrients more rapid.

The litter and microorganisms compartment (Figure 2) consists of fallen dead plant (and animal) material and a complex group of organisms involved in reducing that material to decay-resistant organic residues that comprise the organic sediments. The organisms range from some large invertebrates such as crayfish, snails, and immature insects (e.g., midge larvae, Tendipedidae) to bacteria and fungi. Light conditions permitting, this is also the site of substantial algal activity. Because decomposition is so important in releasing nutrients for reuse, this may be a key compartment in terms of nutrient cycling. Some recent studies (Gallagher, 1978; Murkin and Kadlec, 1986) suggest modifying our view of litter in wetlands to include root and rhizome remains. Much of the biomass of emergent plants such as cattail is actually below ground. Roots and rhizomes often equal and may exceed the aboveground leaves and stems in terms of weight per unit area. Although the below ground tissues of, for example cattail and reed (*Phragmites australis*), live two or three years (Fiala, 1973) in contrast to 1 growing season or less for aboveground tissues (Smith and Kadlec, 1985), it still seems probable that there is a substantial below ground litter compartment (Figure 2).

Many important processes which convert, store, and release nutrients occur inside the litter compartment. The net results of these processes is the progressive conversion of large pieces of plant debris to smaller and smaller particles. Depending on current and wave action, this material may be sorted vertically or horizontally, giving rise to spatial patterns of fine and coarse material. Consequently, the contents of this compartment (like the plants that are its predominant origin) are often not homogeneous throughout a wetland.

In Figure 2, water is shown as a compartment physically distinct from both organic sediments and the inorganic basin. Actually, the surface water is continuous with pore water in the sediments and ground water flowing into or out of the basin. The continuity is reflected in a variety of chemical gradients important to nutrient cycling. Because the volume of surface water in many wetlands is usually quite small, concentrations of dissolved nutrients often are markedly affected by small changes in either input-output or internal cycling processes. Conversely, increases in water level, perhaps because of some man-made alterations in hydrology, can greatly affect water volume and therefore the storage capacity for dissolved or suspended forms of nutrients. Thus, physical changes in the size of this compartment can not be neglected in considering mass balances of nutrients.

The organic sediment compartment also is rarely as distinct as indicated in Figure 2. It may be very small or absent in all or parts of some wetlands, depending primarily on wind and wave action and decomposition rates. However, most wetlands show some organic accumulation and the vast areas of peatlands, about 230 million ha (Moore and Bellamy, 1974) testify to the importance of this component in many wetlands. The organic material ranges from very finely divided amorphous material to large pieces of wood which have become buried. Indeed, the distinction between litter and organic sediments is largely arbitrary; litter is in the early stages of decomposition and sediments in the late stages. The upper layers of the sediment and litter may contain 94-99% of the total N and P present in some wetlands (Brock et al., 1983).

Processes

General processes of nutrient cycling (Figure 2) can be considered in several categories. First, there are those that transfer nutrients directly into or out of the wetland, discussed earlier and designated by the Roman numerals in Figure 2. Second, there are processes which involve ionic or molecular transfers from one compartment to another, sometimes with a change in state (Arrows 1-9, 11, and 13). Third, nutrients incorporated in biomass are transferred as the biomass changes from living (or standing dead) to litter (arrows 12). Finally, macrophytes transport nutrients up from roots to leaves and back down to below ground tissues (arrow 10). Nitrogen is a special, more complicated case of this generalized pattern which will be discussed in more detail later. Figure 2 is, of course, a substantial simplification and many of the arrows actually represent a whole set of processes. A discussion of some of the major processes follows.

In Figure 2, arrows 1-4 represent processes by which macrophytes take up and release nutrients. Arrow 1 indicates exchange with the atmosphere of primarily CO_2 and O_2 and is included primarily for completeness. Wetland plants with aerial leaves, such as trees, shrubs, and emergents (e.g., cattail, water hyacinth) have access to atmospheric CO_2 and there is little reason to consider potential C limitation. On the other hand, totally submersed plants must rely on dissolved CO_2 and HCO_3^- as C sources, as do most kinds of algae. Hence for these plants there is a possibility of C limitation, especially in soft water (low bicarbonate) systems. I know of no documented case.

Nutrient exchanges between macrophytes and surface water (arrow 2) have been and are the subject of much debate (e.g., Carignan and Kalff, 1980). Obviously, submersed non-rooted plants (e.g., coontail, *Ceratophyllum* spp.) and free-floating plants such as duckweeds and water hyacinth (*Eichhornia crassipes*) must obtain their nutrients from the water. The controversy has centered on rooted plants (Sculthorpe, 1967). Submersed rooted plants (e.g., pondweeds) could conceivably take up nutrients from the sediment via roots (arrows 3 and 4) or directly from the water via underwater leaves which often appear adapted for such absorption. Early thinking emphasized leaf uptake but both leaf and root uptake (arrows 3 and 4) have now been demonstrated for many species (Hutchinson, 1975). However, emergent plants such as cattail and some bulrushes (e.g., *Scirpus acutus*) are structurally very similar to terrestrial plants (Sculthorpe, 1967) and nutrient uptake by leaves or stems from the water is not likely to be a major process.

Rooted plants not only extract nutrients from the sediments, but they also release nutrients from senescing and sometimes living tissues to water, both surface and interstitial. Hence arrows 2, 3, and 4 are 2-way; nutrients do move both directions. Depending on internal movements (arrow 10), the net effect may be to move nutrients from the root zone up to the water, the so-called nutrient pump effect. McRoy et al. (1972) estimated eelgrass (Zostera marina) transported 62 mg P m^{-2} d^{-1} from sediments to water by this process. In contrast, Twilley et al. (1985) found little evidence of translocation out of water lily (Nuphar luteum) rhizomes in spring or into the rhizomes in fall.

The community of epiphytic organisms interchange nutrients both with surface water (arrow 5) and with the plants upon which they grow (arrow 9). Because the epiphytes include microscopic plants, animals, bacteria, and perhaps fungi, the interchanges are complex. A current controversy debates the existence of plant-ephiphyte interchanges. One school of thought considers the plant merely a surface for attachment of the epiphytes (e.g., Cattaneo and Kalff, 1979) while others maintain nutrients released by the macrophytes benefit the epiphytes (Wetzel, 1983). Operationally, it is often difficult to separate the epiphytes from the macrophytes, making interchanges 2 and 5 indistinguishable.

Algal populations are characterized by rapid multiplication ("birth") and death rates, resulting in rapid turnover of biomass and nutrients, usually on the time scale of days. Thus, nutrients are used, released, and reused very rapidly. However, the total quantity involved may not be large and the total storage quite small. Nevertheless, in terms of nutrients taken up or released per unit time (arrow 6), this may be one of the most active portions of wetland nutrient cycling.

Interchanges between the litter-microorganisms compartment and surface water (arrow 7) and sediments (arrow 8) are associated primarily with the breakdown and decomposition of the litter. Nutrients are released in these processes, but some, notably N, may be actively accumulated (van der Valk and Davis, 1978; Marrinucci and Bartha, 1982). The inference is that micro-organisms, probably bacteria, take up inorganic N from the water in the process of breaking down complex organic compounds in the litter. Studies of the decomposition process have concentrated on the breakdown of aboveground plant parts, but there must be a substantial below ground component (Gallagher, 1978). Data on the below ground decomposition is slim and circumstantial. As noted earlier, the simple fact that much macrophyte biomass is below ground implies a significant contribution to litter within the sediments. In an experiment involving killing macrophytes with deep water, Murkin and Kadlec (1986) found an increase in bottom dwelling invertebrates and inferred this was a response to increased below ground litter. In the same marshes, Kadlec (1986a) showed increases in pore water N and P consistent with release from decomposition of below ground macrophyte litter. This evidence is admittedly circumstantial, but suggests that studies of death and decomposition of below ground plant structures would be useful. We do know that this below ground environment is often anaerobic and highly reducing (Wetzel, 1975). Chamie (1976) studied decomposition of aboveground plant parts (leaves and stems) placed in this environment in a peatland and found it to be very slow. We need to know if the same is true for roots and rhizomes in other kinds of wetlands.

Nutrients are physically leached (literally, washed out) from standing live and dead macrophytes (arrow 11, parts of arrows 1-8). For example, nutrients are washed from tree leaves (Mitsch et al., 1979). Leaching may be responsible for part of the loss of nutrients from submersed leaves. At senescence, cells in plant tissues die and soluble compounds are readily washed out of aerial parts by rainfall and by ambient water for submersed parts. Thus, an often substantial (2.2 g P m^{-2} yr^{-1}, Klopatek, 1975; 18-23% of detritus, Brock, 1984) of the nutrient, especially P and K, content of plant tissues is released very rapidly after death; perhaps within a few days (Nelson, 1982). Because of this rapid loss, detention of nutrients in plant tissues is predominantly short term, ranging from days for algae to one growing season for most leaves, to perhaps several years for underground parts of emergent macrophytes. Nutrients incorporated in woody tissue of trees and shrubs may be stored for many years.

Nutrients retained in dead plant and animal tissues are physically transferred to the litter and microorganism compartment 9 (arrows 12) by processes such as leaf fall, stem breakage, water-logging and sinking. The seasonality of these transfers depends on the species. Deciduous leaves are added to litter in the fall predominantly, as are leaves and stems of annual plants and many submersed macrophytes (e.g., pondweeds). Leaves of some emergents, such as cattail, remain standing even after dying in fall and are not added to litter until the next spring (Davis and van der Valk, 1978). Stems of the common reed (*Phragmites australis*) are very sturdy and remain standing as long as three years. These differences among plants in time and rate of litter fall probably have some effect on nutrient regeneration rates, especially because leaching is likely to be most important when litter enters the water. However, decomposition processes are a function of microorganism activity and therefore are more likely to be controlled by moisture and temperature, among other factors, and be most active during the summer after the material enters the submersed litter compartment.

The last general process shown in Figure 2 is arrow 13, the interchange between sediments and surface water. As in many of the previous interchanges discussed, this is a very complex set of processes. Two major phenomena are involved: sedimentation and ion exchanges across the mud-water interface. The factors controlling ion exchange are complex, but they are known in substantial detail because of the importance of these ion transfers in lakes (c.f. Wetzel, 1975). DeLaune et al. (1976) summarize many of these processes in salt marshes. Of key importance is the sharp transition between aerobic and anaerobic conditions at the boundary between mud and water. In lakes, this boundary may move up and down seasonally, but in wetlands it may move diurnally and sometimes be quite variable horizontally depending on vegetation (Nelson and Kadlec, 1984). Because several key transformations of both N and P depend on the position and variability of the gradient between oxidizing and reducing conditions, these relationships will be discussed in more detail when the specifics of the N and P cycles are considered.

For wetlands with major inputs of surface water (SWI of the water balance equation) sedimentation can be a very important process (Boto and Patrick, 1979). Wetlands associated with rivers often are major sites of sediment deposition. For example, Herron (1985) found as much as 50,000 Mg of suspended solids were removed by a 66 km^2 wetland from 1.2 x 10^9 m^3 of river flow at the Bear Lake National Wildlife Refuge. Approximately 72 Mg of P in particulate form was also removed, or about 43% of all P entering the wetland in that year.

The Nitrogen Cycle

Nitrogen is perhaps the most complex of the nutrient cycles. As an example, Figure 3 shows the results of Hemond's (1983) detailed study of the N cycle in Thoreau's Bog in Massachusetts. Of key importance are bacteria which convert N from organic to inorganic forms and from one inorganic form to another. N_2 fixation, mineralization, denitrification and reduction of NO_3^- to NH_4^+ are important microbially mediated processes in wetlands. Bacterial conversion of NH_4^+ to NO_3^-, nitrification, requires an aerobic environment and is important in terrestrial soils. Its importance in wetlands depends on the presence of adequate O_2. In Thoreau's Bog, Hemond (1983) did not quantify nitrification.

All of the bacterially mediated conversions are sensitive to sediment redox potential (a measure of aeration). Wetland sediments often are anaerobic and highly reducing, so generally the net result of these processes is an accumulation of NH_4^+, as in Thoreau's Bog. Denitrification apparently is important in wetlands, but requires anaerobic conditions and a source of NO_3^-, which is formed in aerobic environments. Close juxtaposition of aerobic and anaerobic conditions in time (Reddy and Patrick, 1976) or space presumably favors conversion of NO_3^- to N_2. Therefore, the sharp transition of anaerobic to aerobic at the sediment-water interface, discussed earlier, is a logical site for rapid denitrification. However, Hemond's (1983) studies on Thoreau's Bog did not indicate a large loss of N through denitrification under natural conditions.

In Thoreau's Bog there is no water inflow, making atmospheric deposition and fixation the only sources of N_2. The system conserved N_2, with relatively small quantities lost through run-off, denitrification and NH_3 volatilization.

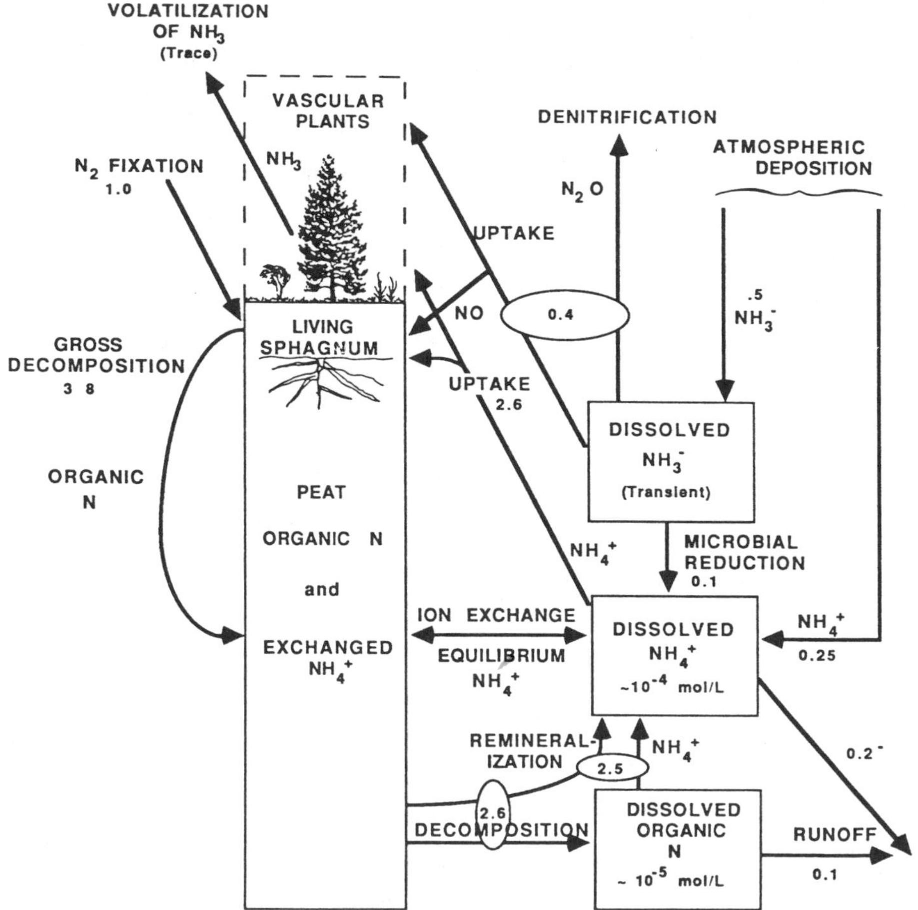

FIGURE 3. Proposed mean annual budget for N_2 in Thoreau's Bog, in g m^{-2} (from Hemond, 1983).

The Phosphorus Cycle

Because P does not exist in gaseous forms, most of the key parts of the P cycle are contained in Figure 2. However, the sediment-water interactions involving P are very complex and extensively involve Al, Fe, S and $CaCO_3$ and oxidation-reduction processes. These are detailed in most standard texts in limnology (e.g., Wetzel, 1975) and I will only look at some key features, as I see them, for wetlands. Probably the most important basic fact is that PO_4^{3-} ions are removed from solution by several chemical reactions involving F^{3+}, Ca^{++}, and Al^{3+} in an oxidized environment. Conversely, inorganic P is released into solution in a reduced environment, at rates ranging from 1-20 mg P m^{-2} d^{-1} (Theis and McCabe, 1978). Consequently, dissolved inorganic P (DIP) should be, and is, much more abundant in anaerobic sediment pore water than in aerated surface water (Kadlec, 1986a; Wetzel, 1975). Mechanisms for transferring DIP from pore water to surface water include molecular diffusion, turbulent mixing in shallow waters, and activities of sediment inhabiting animals. Because molecular diffusion is comparatively very slow, turbulent mixing is likely to be much more important in the shallow waters of wetlands, except in areas protected from wind, waves, and currents, e.g., within dense beds of emergents. Transfer of sediment DIP to the overlying water is much more rapid when the transition from anaerobic to aerobic occurs above the sediment. Because O_2 demand is often high in wetlands, anaerobic conditions throughout the water column are not uncommon, especially at night when temperatures are high. For example, strong winds associated with summer thunderstorms sometimes cause turbulent mixing of organic sediments into the entire water column, resulting in totally anaerobic conditions in all the wetlands in an area (personal observation). Consequently, in wetlands the transfer of DIP from sediments to surface water probably occurs at intervals ranging from daily to monthly as a result of various processes affecting O_2 concentrations. It also varies with the kind of vegetation, as dense emergents or floating species, such as duckweeds affect O_2 levels in the water column (Dvorak, 1969; Lewis and Bender, 1961; Reddy, 1981). The importance of macrophytes in the P cycles also has been recognized in lakes, where the littoral regions with their associated plants often dominate the P cycle (Wetzel, 1975).

Because P is often a limiting nutrient for plants and because a variety of physical and chemical process tend to remove it from aerated surface waters, inorganic P usually occurs in very low concentrations in fresh-water lakes (Wetzel, 1975) and some ponds (Olness et al., 1979b) and probably marshes. On the other hand, the processes discussed above tend to result in high levels of DIP in many wetlands. Therefore, wetlands are variable in how they cycle and store P depending on specific details of hydrology, water depth, sediment types, and kinds of vegetation.

IMPACTS OF WASTEWATER APPLICATIONS TO WETLANDS

Wastewater application to wetlands usually involves substantial quantities of water, thereby altering the hydrology of the system and all aspects of wetland vegetation and nutrient cycles connected to the hydrological processes. Thus just the application of more water will change the wetland. This kind of change probably should be considered natural and normal, for almost all wetlands undergo water level fluctuations depending on climatic variations, tides, lake seiches, river flows, etc. Whether or not the change is considered desirable or undesirable is a human judgement and beyond the scope of this discussion. For example, in our studies at the Delta Marsh in Manitoba (Batt et al., 1983) we have experimentally raised and lowered water levels in replicated diked marshes and thereby markedly affected vegetation and nutrient cycling. Raising the water levels 1 m almost eliminated the macrophytes, converting the marsh to open ponds in which algae were the main primary producers. As a result, nutrient storage in plants was smaller and turnover more rapid, dissolved N and P increased in interstitial water, but nutrient concentrations in the surface water were not changed (Kadlec, 1986a). Because we eliminated surface water outflow, the hydrology was greatly different (J. A. Kadlec, 1983). Water loss was by evaporation or seepage with nutrients lost only in the latter. The seepage was largely through dikes and a sandy ridge and actually involved mostly surface water and accompanying nutrient concentrations (J. A. Kadlec, 1983,1986a,1986b, and unpub.). Evaporative water loss was replaced by pumping surface water from the adjacent marsh into the experimental diked areas. This pumped water and rainfall were the major sources of water and nutrient impacts. A condensed version of the results is given in Table 1. Chloride is a conservative ion; that is, it does not enter actively in biological processes. These marshes are, although inland, mildly brackish because they were, in post-glacial time, part of a closed basin which concentrated salts by evaporation. Pumping water from the adjoining marsh into the diked marshes to replace evaporation led to very large input of Cl^-, 7.32 Mg ha^{-1}. This was very consistent among the marshes, as indicated by a small s.e. Evaporative concentration led to a substantial increase in stored Cl during the open water season and a similar amount was lost as seepage output. Nevertheless, there was a small but statistically significant source within the wetland, as indicated by the 0.83 Mg ha^{-1} net change in the mass balance. I have argued elsewhere (Kadlec, 1986b) that in this case this represents diffusion of Cl from the sediment into the surface water.

The forms of N and P (Table 1) differ from Cl^- in that atmospheric inputs were more important. Changes in storage of suspended N and P were negative, indicating net loss in surface water, presumably as a result of settling of the suspended materials pumped into the marshes. The marshes were a net sink for suspended N and a net source for TDN, possibly indicating conversion of suspended to dissolved forms. A similar pattern is seen for P, but the gain in TDP is not significant so the evidence for conversion is not as strong. The major forms of N and P available for plant growth, NH_4^+ and SRP, demonstrated an approximate balance of the growing season budgets because the balance terms are not statistically different from 0. We know that both of these nutrients are actively cycled within the marshes, but viewed in total for whole growing season, there was

TABLE 1. Input-output nutrient budgets during flooding for eight diked marshes in the Marsh Ecology Research Program complex, Delta Marsh, Manitoba. Means and s.e. (in parentheses).

	Inputs		Output	Change in	
	Pumped	Atmospheric	(seepage)	storage[+]	Balance[++]
Chloride (Mg ha^{-1})	7.32 (0.64)	0.01[+++]	4.55 (0.39)	3.62 (0.17)	-0.83 (0.19)
NH_4-N (kg ha^{-1})	1.23 (0.15)	3.27	1.09 (0.13)	2.76 (0.57)	+0.65 (0.61)
TDN (kg ha^{-1})	17.92 (1.69)	9.30	16.18 (1.51)	27.39 (1.14)	-16.36 (0.86)
Suspended N (kg ha^{-1})	10.30 (0.83)	2.78	1.67 (0.38)	-0.72 (0.39)	+12.13 (0.75)
Total N (kg ha^{-1})	28.22 (2.37)	12.08	26.67 (1.36)	17.86 (1.78)	-4.23 (1.15)
SRP (g ha^{-1})	85 (28)	623	341 (111)	882 (220)	-515 (316)
TDP (g ha^{-1})	570 (60)	735	793 (162)	1162 (217)	-650 (376)
Suspended P (g ha^{-1})	1360 (120)	390	280 (70)	-90 (20)	+1570 (120)
Total P (g ha^{-1})	1930 (180)	1130	1070 (240)	1070 (240)	+920 (410)

[+]Stored in the water column in dissolved or particulate form, as appropriate.

[++]A negative means a net source in which outputs exceeded inputs minus change in storage. A positive means a net sink in which outputs were less than inputs minus change in storage.

[+++]Calculated from same data for all eight marshes, so no s.e. possible.

no net change not accounted for by inputs, outputs, and change in storage. For both SRP and NH_4^+ output was much less than input, but the difference was merely the amount stored in the surface water--concentrations did increase along with an increase in water volume.

In summary, just increasing water inputs, with natural nutrient concentrations, will have effects on wetlands. In the case described, the amount of water was very large, with corresponding large impacts on vegetation. Nutrient cycling changed in several ways, and in the short term led to increases in storage of N and P in the surface water. The same pattern persisted in the growing season of a second year of flooding (1982).

Nutrients

Wastewater application to wetlands usually involves high levels of added nutrients as well as water. If my introductory arguments about the importance of hydrology and nutrient dynamics in controlling the kind of wetland that will occur in a given site were valid, then we should predict that wastewater application will often result in a change to a different kind of wetland. And in some cases, this certainly seems to have happened (R. H. Kadlec, 1983; Valiela et al., 1985; Bayley et al., 1985).

For a consideration of the details of the impacts on a wetland of sewage application, I return to Figure 2. Sewage application will involve an increase in the volume and concentration of process I, water inflow. Let's assume that this inflow has high concentrations of NO_3^-, NH_4^+, SRP and K^+, and suspended particulates with high N and P levels. Note that these inputs are to the surface water. Therefore the first responses are expected to involve processes originating in surface water. Process II, water flow out, both surface and subsurface, will increase unless added depth of flooding also increases the area flooded sufficiently to permit added evapotranspiration equal to the added inflow. However, an increased volume of outflow is most likely, and even if concentrations do not change, the mass of nutrients leaving will be higher and could be a problem for a receiving lake or stream. Process IV, N_2 exchange with the atmosphere might change dramatically. Most studies of denitrification in wetlands (e.g., Patrick et al., 1976, van Kessel, 1978) in fact involve adding NO_3^-, precisely what is happening in our hypothetical case. Denitrification then should increase as a function of NO_3^- added (Patrick et al., 1976) until the process is limited by some other resource, presumably C (Richardson and Nichols, 1985; van Kessel, 1978).

Rapid responses within the system might involve processes represented by arrows 2, 5, 6, 7, and 13 and also involve an increase in storage in the water compartment. Increases in storage can involve either an increase in size of the compartment or an increase in nutrient concentration within it, or both. Rapid responses should be fostered if the processes are physical or chemical or if they involve organisms which have rapid rates of growth and reproduction. Thus, the first responses to nutrient addition should involve movement to the sediments (13), increased rates of uptake and growth of algae (6) and epiphytes (5), and immobilization, especially of P, by uptake by the microorganisms associated with litter (7) (Richardson and Nichols, 1985). Only a few macrophytes fit the fast response and water nutrient source criteria, but duckweeds and water hyacinth are prime examples; hence their usefulness in treatment systems. Of the storages resulting from these rapid responses, algae, epiphytes, and microorganisms have short life spans and turnover nutrients very rapidly, so these are primarily temporary storages. However, if nutrients sediment rapidly (e.g., arrow 12) and are buried in anaerobic deposits, the storage may be much longer.

A portion of the rapid uptake of added nutrients by the sediments is due to adsorption. Adsorption is a function of exchange capacity of sediment particles. It may be rapid in the short term, but in the long term continued nutrient additions will saturate the capacity unless new unsaturated sediments are being added, either via water inflow (arrow I) or via litter breakdown. The quantity of a particular ion, say PO_4^-, adsorbed depends on an exchange equilibrium with the dissolved phase (e.g., Khalid et al., 1982; Olness et al., 1979a; Avnimelech et al., 1983). Chemical precipitation and coprecipitation are other sediment processes which can be effective in removing added ions, especially PO_4^-, in some wetlands. Generally, these processes involve Fe, Al, or Ca (Richardson, 1985; Khalid et al., 1982) and depend on the oxidation state of sediments. In general, anaerobic sediments tend to release more P than aerobic sediments (DeLaune et al., 1976; Theis and McCabe, 1978). This suggests that maintaining adequate dissolved O_2 is important to P removal from surface waters.

An important part of the sediment-water interaction under the conditions postulated is the sedimentation of particles carrying nutrients. The particles may be inorganic or organic and the nutrients may be incorporated within the particle or held by surface phenomena. Because wetland surface waters tend to be shallow with little wave or current action, settling out of particulates is an important process and often a major route of nutrient transfer to the sediments (Herron, 1985; Boto and Patrick, 1979).

Although submersed and floating macrophytes can rapidly take up added nutrients in the surface water, they generally lack large amounts of structural tissues so that breakdown at senescence is rapid and complete. This results in release back to the water of most of the nutrients; thus these plants function mainly as short-term storages unless they are harvested.

Rooted emergent macrophytes, such as cattail, and wetland trees and shrubs will tend to respond more slowly to added nutrients because of the time needed for the nutrients to be transferred to the root zone (Neely and Davis, 1985) by the variety of processes outlined in Figure 2. Because these plants have more structural tissue, and the woody species have perennial aboveground parts, storage of nutrients in these plants is for longer periods of time. They also are physically larger and constitute a much larger storage compartment than other kinds of plants. Nevertheless, the amount of nutrient that can be stored is quite limited in comparison to the amounts added in most cases (Brinson, 1985).

Recalling my earlier prediction that water and nutrient additions will change the vegetation of wetlands, it should also be obvious that some of those changes will alter the nutrient storage capability of plants, limited though it is in most cases. Many woody species do not tolerate increased depths or duration of flooding, so a wooded wetland could be converted to an herbaceous - cattail - wetland with accompanying changes in nutrient storage (R. H. Kadlec, 1983). Low biomass, low nutrient sedge-grass systems might convert to higher biomass, higher nutrient cattail systems. This actually seems quite common (R. H. Kadlec, Michigan, pers. comm.).

If a wetland is considered solely from the point of view of a long term nutrient retention system, we can simplify our conceptualization significantly (Figure 4). Operationally, the litter, sediment and associated microorganism are an inseparable unit, although there are distinct gradients with depth. Macrophytes function primarily as uptake and transfer mechanisms unless there is a harvest. Interchanges between water and sediments (including plant mediated processes and sedimentation) are of major importance. For N only, exchanges with the atmosphere are probably critical in determining the net function of the system. A review of the literature, perhaps as exemplified by this volume, indicates that successful uses of wetlands as nutrient removal systems have involved situations in which one or more of these key interchanges was enhanced by the effluent additions.

Research Needs

The need for studies of nutrient cycling in wetlands with known hydrology is widely recognized but still rarely if ever achieved (LaBaugh, 1986). Further, because annual variation in hydrology and chemistry is substantial, long term studies are necessary to avoid erroneous conclusions based on infrequent events.

In general, the processes by which water and nutrients are transported, transformed, and stored in wetlands are not likely to be different from those in lakes, streams, and uplands. However, because of differences in the physical environment such as water depth and permanence, water flow rates, temperatures, etc., the rates at which these processes operate may be quite different in wetlands. Consequently, I believe there is a need for detailed investigations of internal nutrient cycling processes in wetlands. The major emphasis, in my opinion, should be at the level of field (as opposed to lab) microcosms. The field microcosm concept allows for control of hydrology while still approximating most aspects of the natural wetland. Coupling such research with appropriate laboratory and open ecosystem studies should increase our understanding of these processes in wetlands.

I continue to be convinced that the litter and sediments are the key components of wetland ecosystems. In most, but not all, wetlands, the sediments are primarily organic, representing the resistant residue of decay processes. Although the rate of disappearance of plant fragments and accompanying inorganic nutrient release has been studied extensively, much less attention has been given to the fine particulates and dissolved organic fractions produced by decomposition. Further, as I pointed out earlier, there is very little information about the fate of the large amount of below ground biomass. Against this background of limited knowledge there is an impressive list of potentially important functions of litter and sediment organic matter: 1) the proportion of organic matter in the sediment controls bulk density, a key physical characteristic related to nutrient availability (Gosselink et al., 1984); 2) the accumulation of

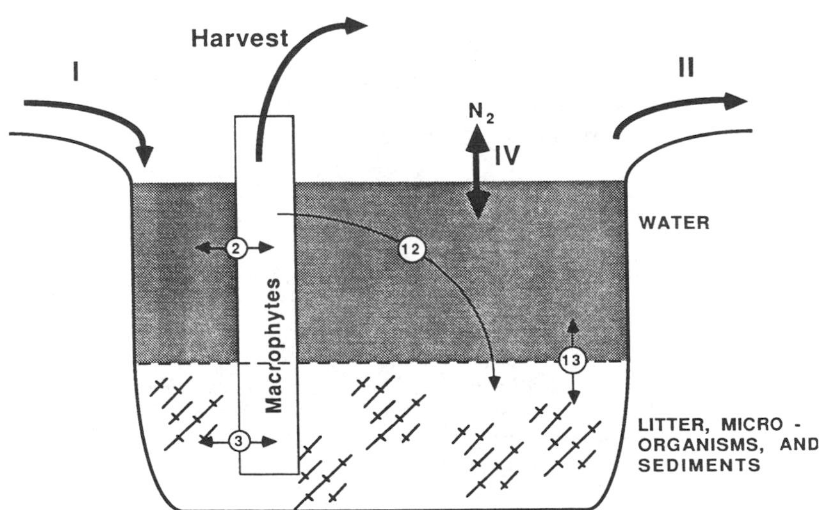

FIGURE 4. Diagrammatic representation of major components and processes involved in nutrient removal from inflowing water.

organic matter seems to be detrimental to the growth of some macrophytes (Barko and Smart, 1983); 3) decomposition rates determine nutrient release rates and may predict macrophyte growth (Carignan, 1985; Chapin et al., 1978); 4) the sediment is the ultimate storage of nutrients (Richardson and Nichols, 1985), but it may represent only a very small fraction of the organic matter originally deposited; 5) sediment nutrients may represent 94-99% of the total in the system, but very little of that is in a form available for plants; 6) plants may extract as much as 1000 times the "available" P in the sediment for growth needs in one season (Barko and Smart, 1980) suggesting that the processes (not well known) of converting "total" to "available" P in the sediment may control plant growth; and 7) water currents and waves may redistribute sediments, leading to major alterations of nutrient accumulation patterns. Quite clearly, we need to know a great deal more about litter and sediments in wetlands.

Another neglected area of wetland nutrient dynamics is the role of algae. Both Herron's (1985) work and ongoing studies at the Delta Marsh in Manitoba (G. Robinson, pers. comm.) suggest algae are more important in wetlands than has generally been appreciated. They may be an important pathway for nutrient movements from water to sediments.

REFERENCES

Andersen, V. J. M. 1974. Nitrogen and phosphorus budgets and the role of sediments in six shallow Danish lakes. Arch. Hydrobiol. 74:528-550.

Anderson, M. P., and J. A. Munter. 1981. Seasonal reversals of groundwater flow around lakes and the relevance to stagnation points and lake budgets. Water Resour. Res. 17:1139-1150.

Avnimelech, Y., M. Yamamoto, and R. G. Menzel. 1983. Evaluating the release of soluble components from sediment. J. Environ. Qual. 12:86-91.

Barko, J. W., and R. M. Smart. 1980. Mobilization of sediment phosphorus by submersed freshwater macrophytes. Freshwater Biol. 10:229-238.

Barko, J. W., and R. M. Smart. 1983. Effects of organic matter additions to sediment on the growth of aquatic plants. J. Ecol. 71:161-175.

Batt, B. D. J., P. J. Caldwell, C. B. Davis, J. A. Kadlec, R. M. Kaminski, H. R. Murkin, and A. G. van der Valk. 1983. The Delta Waterfowl Research Station - Ducks Unlimited Canada marsh ecology research program. p. 19-23. In H. Boyd (ed.) First Western Hemisphere Waterfowl and Waterbird Symposium. Edmonton, Alberta, 25-28 May, 1982. Can. Wildl. Serv., Ottawa, Ont., Canada.

Bayley, S. E., J. Zoltek, Jr., A. J. Hermann, T. J. Dolan, and L. Tortora. 1985. Experimental manipulation of nutrients and water in a freshwater marsh: Effects on biomass decomposition, and nutrient accumulation. Limnol. Oceanogr. 30:500-512.

Boto, K. G., and W. H. Patrick, Jr. 1979. Role of wetlands in the removal of suspended sediments. p. 479-489. In P. E. Greeson, J. R. Clark, and J. E. Clark (ed.) Wetland Functions and Values: The State of Our Understanding. American Water Resources Assoc., Minneapolis.

Brinson, M. M. 1985. Management potential for nutrient removal in forested wetlands. p. 405-416. In P. J. Godfrey, E. R. Kaynor, S. Pelczarski and J. Benforado (ed.) Ecological Considerations in Wetlands Treatment of Municipal Wastewaters. Van Nostrand Reinhold Co., New York.

Brock, T. C. M. 1984. Aspects of the decomposition of Nymphoides peltata (Gmel.) O. Kuntze (Menyanthaceae). Aquat. Bot. 19:131-156.

Brock, T. C. M., M. C. M. Bongaerts, G. J. M. A. Heijnen, and J. H. F. G. Heijthuijsen. 1983. Nitrogen and phosphorus accumulation and cycling by Nymphoides peltata (Gmel.) O. Kuntze (Menyanthaceae). Aquat. Bot. 17:189-214.

Carignan, R. 1985. Nutrient dynamics in a littoral sediment colonized by the submersed macrophyte Myrrophyllum spicatum. Can. J. Fish. Aquat. Sci. 42:1303-1311.

Carignan, R., and J. Kalff. 1986. Phosphorus sources for aquatic weeds: water or sediments? Science 207:987-989.

Carter, V., M. S. Bedinger, R. P. Novitski, and W. O. Wilen. 1979. Water Resources and Wetlands. p. 334-376. In P. E. Greeson, J. R. Clark, and J. E. Clark (ed.) Wetland Functions and Values: The State of Our Understanding. American Water Resources Association, Minneapolis, Minnesota.

Cattaneo, A., and J. Kalff. 1979. Primary production of algae growing on natural and artificial aquatic plants: A study of interactions between epiphytes and their substrate. Limnol. Oceanogr. 24:1031-1037.

Chamie, J. P. M. 1976. The effects of simulated sewage effluent upon decomposition, nutrient status, and litter fall in a central Michigan peatland. Ph.D. Diss., Univ. Michigan, Ann Arbor.

Chapin, F. S. III, R. J. Barsdale, and D. Barel. 1978. Phosphorus cycling in Alaskan coastal tundra: A hypothesis for the regulation of nutrient cycling. Oikos 31:189-199.

Davis, C. B., and A. G. van der Valk. 1978. The decomposition of standing and fallen litter of Typha glauca and Scirpus fluviatilis. Can. J. Bot. 56:662-675.

DeLaune, R. D., W. H. Patrick, Jr., and J. M. Brannon. 1976. Nutrient transformations in Louisiana salt marsh soils. Louisiana State Univ. Center for Wetland Research, Sea Grant Publication LSU-T-76-009. 38 pp.

Dvorak, J. 1969. Horizontal zonation of macrovegetation, water properties, and macrofauna in a littoral stand of Glyceria aquatica (L.) Wahlb, in a pond in south Bohemia. Hydrobiologia 35:17-30.

Fiala, K. 1973. Growth and production of underground organs of _Typha angustifolia_ L., _Typha latifolia_ L., and _Phragmites communis_ Trin. Pol. Arch. Hydrobiol. 20:59-66.

Gallagher, J. L. 1978. Decomposition processes: Summary and recommendations. _In_ R. E. Good, D. F. Whigham, and R. L. Simpson (ed.) Freshwater Wetlands: Ecological Processes and Management Potential. Academic Press, New York.

Gaudet, J. J. 1979. Seasonal changes in nutrients in a tropical swamp: North Swamp, Lake Naivasha, Kenya. J. Ecology 67:953-981.

Gosselink, J. G., R. Hatton, and C. S. Hopkinson. 1984. Relationship of organic carbon and mineral content to bulk density in Louisiana marsh soils. Soil Sci. 137:177-180.

Harter, R. D. 1966. The effect of water levels on soil chemistry and plant growth of the Magee Marsh Wildlife Area. Ohio Game Monographs No. 2, Ohio Division of Wildlife, Columbus. 36 pp.

Heinselman, M. L. 1970. Landscape evolution, peatland types and the environment in the Lake Agassiz Peatlands Natural Area, Minnesota. Ecological Monographs 40:235-261.

Hemond, H. F. 1983. The nitrogen budget of Thoreau's Bog. Ecology 64:99-109.

Herron, R. C. 1985. Phosphorus dynamics in Dingle Marsh, Idaho. Ph.D. Diss., Utah State Univ., Logan. 153 pp.

Hosseini, S. M., and A. G. van der Valk. 1986. The impact of prolonged flooding on filamentous algae in a freshwater marsh. Symposium on Freshwater Wetlands and Wildlife, Charleston, S. Carolina, March 24-27 (in press).

Hutchinson, G. E. 1975. A treatise on limnology. Vol. III. Limnological Botany. Wiley, New York.

Kadlec, J. A. 1983. Water budgets for small diked marshes. Water Resour. Bull. 19:223-229.

Kadlec, J. A. 1986a. Effects of flooding on dissolved and suspended nutrients in small diked marshes. Can. J. Fish. Aquat. Sci. 43:1999-2008.

Kadlec, J. A. 1986b. Input-output nutrient budgets for small diked marshes. In press, Can. J. Fish. Aquat. Sci. 43:2009-2016.

Kadlec, R. H. 1983. The Bellaire Wetland: Wastewater alteration and recovery. Wetlands 3:44-63.

Kaplan, W., I. Valiela, and J. M. Teal. 1979. Denitrification in a salt marsh ecosystem. Limnol. Oceanogr. 24:726-734.

Khalid, R. A., W. H. Patrick, Jr., and M. N. Nixon. 1982. Phosphorus removal processes from overland flow treatment of simulated wastewater. J. Water Pollut. Control Fed. 54:61-69.

Klopatek, J. M. 1975. The role of emergent macrophytes in mineral cycling in a freshwater marsh. p. 367-393. _In_ Mineral Cycling in Southeastern Ecosystems. U.S. Energy Research and Development Administration, Washington, D. C.

Klopatek, J. M. 1978. Nutrient dynamics of freshwater riverine marshes and the role of emergent macrophytes. p. 195-216.

In R. E. Good, D. F. Whigham, and R. L. Simpson (ed.) Freshwater Wetlands: Ecological Processes and Management Potential. Academic Press, NY.

LaBaugh, J. W. 1986. Wetland ecosystem studies from a hydrologic perspective. Water Resour. Bull. 22:1-10.

LaBaugh, J. W., and T. C. Winter. 1984. The impact of uncertainties in hydrologic measurement on phosphorus budgets and empirical models for two Colorado reservoirs. Limnol. Oceanogr. 29:322-339.

Lewis, W. M., and M. Bender. 1961. Effect of a cover of duckweeds and the alga Pithophora upon the dissolved oxygen and free carbon dioxide of small ponds. Ecology 42(1):

Marinucci, A. C., and R. Bartha. 1982. A component model of decomposition of Spartina alterniflora in a New Jersey salt marsh. Can J. Bot. 60:1618-1624.

McRoy, C. P., R. J. Barsdate, and M. Nebert. 1972. Phosphorus cycling in an eelgrass (Zostera marina L.) ecosystem. Limnol. Oceanogr. 17:58-67.

Mitsch, W. J., C. L. Dorge, and J. R. Wiemhoff. 1979. Ecosystem dynamics and a phosphorus budget of and alluvial cypress swamp in southern Illinois. Ecology 60:1116-1124.

Moore, P. D., and D. J. Bellamy. 1974. Peatlands. Springer-Verlag, NY.

Murkin, H. R., and J. A. Kadlec. 1986. Responses by benthis macroinvertebrates to prolonged flooding of marsh habitat. Can J. Zool. 64:65-72.

Murphy, T. P., and B. C. Brownlee. 1981. Ammonia volatilization in a hypertrophic prairie lake. Can. J. Fish. Aquat. Sci. 38:1035-1039.

Neely, R. K., and C. B. Davis. 1985. Nitrogen and phosphorus fertilization of Sparganium eurycarpum Engelm. and Typha glauca Godr. stands. I. Emergent plant production. Aquat. Bot. 22:347-361.

Nelson, J. W. 1982. Effects of varying detrital nutrient concentrations on macroinvertebrates abundance and biomass. M. S. Thesis, Utah State Univ., Logan. 85 pp.

Nelson, J. W. and J. A. Kadlec. 1984. A conceptual approach relating habitat structure and macroinvertebrate production in freshwater wetlands. Trans. North American Wildlife and Natural Resources Conf. 49:262-270.

Novitski, R. P. 1978. Hydrologic characteristics of Wisconsin's wetlands and their influence on floods stream flow, and sediment. In P. E. Greeson, J. R. Clark, and J. E. Clark (ed.) Wetland Functions and Values: The State of Our Understanding. Am. Water Resour. Assoc., Minneapolis, Minnesota.

Olness, A., W. W. Troeger, G. D. Pardue, and R. R. Huckleberry. 1979a. Phosphorus in a model pond study: I. Sediment selection and preparation. Hydrobiologia 63:11-15.

Olness, A., W. W. Troeger, R. R. Huckleberry and G. D. Pardue. 1979b. Phosphorus in a model pond study: II. Sediment fertility and water concentrations. Hydrobiologia 63:99-104.

Patrick, W. H., Jr., R. D. DeLaune, R. M. Engler, and S. Gotoh. 1976. Nitrate removal from water at the water mud interface in wetlands. U.S. E.P.A., Ecological Research Series EPA-600/3-76-042, Corvallis, Oregon, 80 pp.

Phillips, G. L. 1977. The mineral nutrient levels in three Norfolk broads differing in trophic status, and an annual mineral content budget for one of them. J. Ecol. 65:447-474.

Reddy, K. R. 1981. Diel variations of certain physico-chemical parameters of water in selected aquatic system. Hydrobiologia 85:201-207.

Reddy, K. R., and W. H. Patrick, Jr. 1976. Effects of frequent change in aerobic and anaerobic conditions on redox potential and nitrogen loss in flooded soil. Soil Biol. Biochem. 8:491-495.

Richardson, C. J. 1985. Mechanisms controlling phosphorus retention capacity in freshwater wetlands. Science 228:1424-1427.

Richardson, C. J., and D. S. Nichols. 1985. Ecological analysis of wastewater management criteria in wetland ecosystems. p. 351-391. In P. J. Godfrey, E. R. Kaynor, S. Pelczarski and J. Benforado (ed.) Ecological Considerations in Wetlands Treatment of Municipal Wastewaters. Van Nostrand Reinhold Co., New York.

Sculthorpe, C. D. 1967. The biology of aquatic vascular plants. St. Martins Press, New York. 610 pp.

Smith, L. M., and J. A. Kadlec. 1985. A comparison of marsh plant loss estimates in production techniques. Amer. Midl. Nat. 114:393-395.

Swank, W. T. 1984. Atmospheric contributions to forest nutrient cycling. Water Resourc. Bull. 20:313-321.

Theis, T. L., and P. J. McCabe. 1978. Phosphorus dynamics in hypereutrophic lake sediments. Water Res. 12:677-686.

Twilley, R. R., L. R. Blanton, M. M. Brinson, and G. J. Davis. 1985. Biomass production and nutrient cycling in aquatic macrophyte communities of the Chowan River, North Carolina. Aquat. Bot. 22:231-252.

Valiela, I., J. M. Teal, C. Cogswell, J. Hartman, S. Allen, R. van Etten, and D. Goehringen. 1985. Some long-term consequences of sewage contamination in salt marsh ecosystems. p. 301-316. In P. J. Godfrey, E. R. Kaynor, S. Pelczarski, and J. Benforado (ed.) Ecological Considerations in Wetlands Treatment of Municipal Wastewaters. Van Nostrand Reinhold Co., New York.

van Kessel, J. F. 1978. Gas production in aquatic sediments in the presence and absence of nitrate. Water Res. 12:291-297.

Webster, J. R., and B. C. Patten. 1979. Effects of watershed perturbation on stream potassium and calcium dynamics. Ecol. Monogr. 49:51-72.

Wetzel, R. G. 1975. Limnology. Saunders, Philadelphia. 743 pp.

Wetzel, R. G. 1983. Attached algal-substrata interactions: Fact or myth, and when and how? p. 207-215. In R. G. Wetzel (ed.) Periphyton of Freshwater Ecosystems. Dr. W. Junk, The Hague.

Winter, T. C. 1981. Uncertainties in estimating the water balance of lakes. Water Resour. Bull. 17:82-115.

EFFECTS OF ATMOSPHERIC CARBON DIOXIDE ENRICHMENT UPON THE STOMATAL CONDUCTANCE AND EVAPOTRANSPIRATION OF AQUATIC MACROPHYTES

M. G. Anderson
Climatology Laboratory
Arizona State University
Tempe, Arizona 85287

S. B. Idso
USDA-ARS
U.S. Water Conservation Laboratory
Phoenix, Arizona 85040

ABSTRACT

The evapotranspiration characteristics of water hyacinth, water lily, water fern, and cattail were established during a four year investigation of advective energy exchange as a function of peripheral canopy exposure and stomatal conductance. Total water loss decreased by 10% (E/E_o = 0.90) compared to an identical open water surface for water lily and water fern. Short to medium height water hyacinth displayed similar E/E_o ratios for relatively extensive surface coverages where peripheral exposure was minimal; but tall hyacinth and cattail yielded E/E_o values near 1.45. Steady-state porometer measurements indicated a 50% reduction in stomatal conductance with a 20% decrease in transpiration per unit leaf area for a mean doubling of ambient CO_2 levels. Water hyacinth biomass production increased by 36% and water use efficiency doubled for a similar doubling of the atmospheric CO_2 content. The combination of the studies indicates that floating or emergent species with leaves near the water surface will experience decreased transpiration in future higher CO_2 atmospheres, while substantial biomass increases on the taller floating or emergent species will provide greater surface exposure and possibly result in equivalent transpiration.

Keywords: Advection, canopy structure, aerodynamic resistance, stomatal conductance, evapotranspiration.

ISBN 0-941463-00-1

INTRODUCTION

Investigations of evapotranspiration (E) by aquatic macrophytes have been conducted for nearly a century, yielding contradictory results. Using small, exposed canopies of various species, Otis (1914), Penfound and Earle (1948), Timmer and Weldon (1967), and Rogers and Davis (1972) all found the vegetation's presence increased open water evaporation (E_o) from 200-400%. However, during the same period other investigators found much smaller increases or reductions employing small plant canopies positioned within large natural stands of similar vegetation (Young and Blaney, 1942; Migahid in Penman, 1963; Van der Weert and Kamerling, 1972; Bernatowicz et al., 1976). These latter researchers reasoned that small, exposed canopies were subject to unnatural irradiation and advection (the horizontal flux of sensible heat) and that they were unrepresentative of the vegetation's natural state. Indeed, several descriptive terms have been proposed for the phenomenon, including "oasis effect" (Shaw, 1967), "border effect" (Van der Weert and Kamerling, 1974), and "clothes-line effect" (Linacre, 1976). Nevertheless, the relationship between consumptive use coefficients for these species relative to a canopy's peripheral surface area and its evapotranspiration rate remains essentially unspecified.

The mean CO_2 content of the earth's atmosphere has steadily risen from a pre-industrial concentration of about 265 $\mu L\ L^{-1}$ (Schneider, 1983; Wigley, 1983) to its current mean value near 350 $\mu L\ L^{-1}$. It is also projected to continue to increase, reaching some 600 $\mu L\ L^{-1}$ around the middle of the next century (National Research Council, 1983). Atmospheric CO_2 is a very effective antitranspirant. In a recent review, Kimball and Idso (1983) found that doubling the atmospheric CO_2 content decreased the transpiration rates of 18 terrestrial plant species by an average of 34%. Atmospheric CO_2 also stimulates photosynthesis and plant growth (Lemon, 1983), thus plant water use efficiency (biomass produced per unit of water transpired) should also be increased (Rosenberg, 1981). In fact, a doubling of plant water use efficiency has been experimentally demonstrated for both agronomic and forest species by Rogers et al. (1983).

MATERIALS AND METHODS

E and E_o of similar-sized vegetated and open water bodies, respectively, were examined during four growing seasons (1982-1985). Pairs of galvanized metal tanks of 0.4, 0.5, 1.1, and 2.3 m diameter were recessed into the ground on an outdoor plot at the U.S. Water Conservation Laboratory (USWCL), Phoenix, Arizona, in 1981. Each of the 0.6 m deep tanks was outfitted with a single external stilling well and fully water-proofed with silicon sealant. The tanks were compared for uniformity of water loss and leakage.

Water hyacinths [Eichhornia crassipes (Mart) Solms] were introduced into one-half of these metal tanks in March, 1983, joining water lily (Nymphea marliac carnea) which had been transplanted 1 yr earlier in a 2.3 m diameter tank. Hyacinth vigor was maintained with a modified Hoagland solution 2 (Johnson et al., 1957). The solutions of the large tanks were replaced on a monthly basis while the smaller tanks were replenished at 2 wk intervals. Plant heights above water level were measured weekly at numerous positions on each canopy and averaged to obtain a single value.

The first water hyacinth atmospheric CO_2 enrichment under open field conditions was conducted in the fall of 1983. The details of the gas supply and sampling systems, procedures, and porometer measurements have been previously described in detail (Idso et al, 1984a,b). In brief, new plants were collected and established in two 1.1 m diameter tanks containing fresh nutrient medium. One of these tanks was outfitted with the gas enrichment apparatus while both were equipped with atmospheric sampling devices. Steady-state porometer measurements were made every 20 min throughout the day for several days at a particular CO_2 concentration on the enriched and ambient canopies. The canopy conditions were switched (i.e., ambient becoming enriched and vice-versa) to eliminate any bias existing between the canopies. Several days were allotted when an ambient canopy became enriched to permit the plants to acclimate to their new conditions.

In 1984, larger vegetated and open water ponds of 3.4, 4.3, 5.4, and 11.4 m diameter were constructed by placing one piece sheets of 0.76 mm thick chlorinated polyethylene into and over 0.6 m tall earth berm rings of the appropriate dimensions. The 3.4 m ponds were equipped with a single internal stilling well, the 4.3 and 5.4 m ponds with two, and the 11.4 m ponds with three such wells to ensure accurate water level measurements. All ponds except the 11.4 m pair were monitored for uniformity of water loss. Subsequent analysis of data has indicated that none of the ponds experienced leakage.

In early July water hyacinths were introduced into one-half of the 3.4, 5.4, and 11.4 m ponds, along with water fern (Azolla pinnata) on the 4.3 m pond, and grown to full canopy cover. Plant height measurements were performed every three to four weeks as in the 1983 study. By mid-August, the water hyacinths were over 0.60 m tall, growing eventually to a height of 0.81 m which presented a new range of surface area relationships.

In order to study the effects of atmospheric CO_2 enrichment on evapotranspiration and water use efficiency in water hyacinth, four pairs of 1.1 m diameter stock tanks were recessed into the ground on an open-field site at Phoenix, Arizona. Four open-top, clear-plastic-wall CO_2 enrichment chambers identical in design but slightly reduced in size from those described by Kimball et al. (1983) were constructed around the stock tank pairs. By means of the CO_2 supply, distribution and sampling systems described by

Kimball et al. (1983), we established and maintained season-long mean 24 h CO_2 concentrations of approximately 500, 650 and 900 μL L^{-1} in three of the chambers, leaving one chamber to represent open-field CO_2 concentrations.

The details of plant introduction and maintenance, evapotranspiration and biomass measurements have been described previously (Idso et al., 1985) and therefore will not be repeated. Briefly, the plants were fed frequently to maintain a healthy condition with daily water level measurements taken from stilling wells and weekly biomass assessments. Presumably hampered by a lack of sufficient nutrients, the 900 μL L^{-1} treatment grew at about the same rate as the plants in the 650 μL L^{-1} treatment. Thus, no further reference will be made to this highest CO_2 treatment.

In the spring of 1984, mature cattails (*Typha latifolia*) were dug from a local lake and transplanted into soil within a 2.3 m diameter tank at the U.S. Water Conservation Laboratory site. A dense stand was eventually established in the summer of 1985 through frequent feedings with the full strength nutrient solution. In fall, water hyacinths were collected from a local pond and then quickly nurtured to over 0.6 m height in the 2.3 and 1.1 m diameter ponds so direct comparison of daily water loss rates could be observed between the two species.

Leaf diffusion resistance measurements for the 2.3 m stands of cattail and water hyacinth were made in the fall of 1985, utilizing a steady-state porometer according to the procedures listed in Idso et al. (1982). On 10 d during this period, half-hourly measurements of leaf diffusion resistance were made from sunrise to sunset. Each data point thus obtained was determined from three abaxial and three adaxial measurements taken on or near the peripheral surface of the sunward side of each canopy, and then the same procedure was followed on the opposite side. The conductance at the top of the cattail canopy was found to be essentially equal to the mean overall conductance of the hyacinths canopy. However, the conductance values dropped approximately linearly to zero near the bottom of the canopy. Thus, three measurements on each side of the cattail canopy were taken at approximately 0.2, 1.0, and 1.8 m down the canopy's peripheral surface.

Daily evaporative water losses from all vegetated and open water surfaces were determined from water level readings taken just after sunrise with a standard, Lory Type-C hook-gauge, accurate to 0.1 mm, throughout the four growing seasons. The tanks holding the hyacinth, water lily, and cattail canopies at the USWCL site were refilled on a daily basis after each set of measurements. The larger ponds at the ASU Research Park could be refilled only twice weekly, since water delivery occurred only once per week from the site's supply source, an adjacent canal. A 18.9 m^3 grain bin provided the mid-week refill. No evaporation measurements from any of the tanks or ponds were recorded for days having precipitation, because rainfall interception was found to differ between the plant and water surfaces. All data were obtained from lush, luxuriant stands of vegetation.

RESULTS AND DISCUSSION

The results of the 1983 water hyacinth evapotranspiration vs. canopy size study are presented in the upper half of Figure 1. The vegetated surface area was calculated as the sum of a canopy's ceiling surface (neglecting total leaf area) and the area comprised of the canopy's circumference multiplied by the height of the vegetation. Plant heights in this study ranged from 0.06-0.36 m. As the breadth of an individual canopy (i.e., tank diameter) increased, the vegetative/open water surface area ratio approached unity and daily E/E_o approached a y-axis intercept value less than 1.00. This indicates that a large expanse of relatively short water hyacinths would actually reduce the evaporation from an expansive body of water. Twelve E/E_o

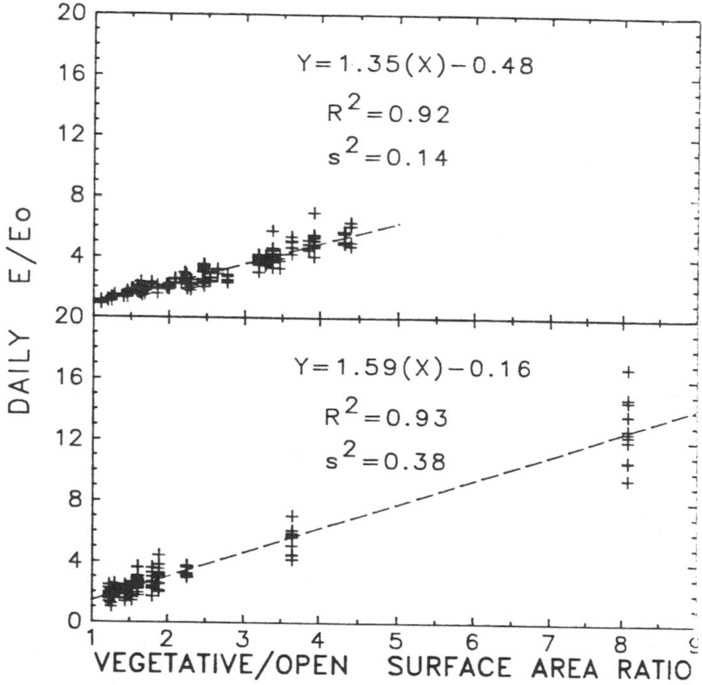

FIGURE 1. The ratio of 24 h totals of evaporation from canopies of water hyacinth, ranging in height from 0.06-0.36 m in the upper half, and 0.63-0.81 m in the lower half, to similar totals of evaporation from similar-sized open water tanks vs. the ratio of total exposed vegetative surface area to exposed open water surface area.

measurements less than 1.00 were collected during April from a 0.06 m tall, 2.3 m diameter hyacinth canopy and its open surface counterpart.

The lower half of Figure 1 contains the results from the taller hyacinths (0.63-0.81 m) and the larger canopies in the 1984 study. E/E_o again decreases with increasing pond diameter. However, the regression line indicates that the ratio will be greater than 1.00 (i.e., the vegetation's presence will increase evaporation). The regression's y-axis intercept value of 1.43 is in good agreement with the 44 and 48% evaporation increases reported in Van der Weert and Kamerling's (1974) water hyacinth study conducted with tanks of 0.6 m plants located within a natural stand of similar vegetation which fully removed advection from the experimental plants' peripheral canopy exposure.

So why did we get an intercept value less than 1.00 from our 1983 experiment with short hyacinths? According to aerodynamic resistance theory (Thom and Oliver, 1977), short plant canopies generate less atmospheric turbulence than tall canopies. Therefore, the short canopies would possess greater aerodynamic resistance to evaporation than a tall canopy of equivalent size. The much greater variance in the tall canopy evaporation data lends considerable support to this theory.

Additional evidence for stomatal regulation of evaporation from vegetative canopies transpiring at the potential rate was obtained from the water lily and water fern experiments. Measurements indicated an average 10% reduction in evaporation when these flat, floating water plants were present. Furthermore, daily E/E_o values less than unity were obtained from the water lily and water fern data during 83 and 85% of their study periods, four seasons and one season, respectively. These reductions are similar to those reported by Otis (1914) for water lily (i.e., E/E_o ratios of 0.86 and 0.89 in two different years), the 20% reduction reported by Diara and Van Hove (1984) for water fern, and the reductions reported by Seybold (1930) for common duckweed (*Lemna minor* L.).

Further meshing of surface geometry and stomatal conductance effects was developed from our 1985 study of evaporation from water hyacinth and cattail canopies. The cattail evaporation data were not originally compatible with the linear relationship found between E/E_o and the vegetative to open water surface area ratio derived from the water hyacinth data (Figure 2). However, the results of our stomatal conductance measurements indicated that the mean stomatal conductance of the peripheral surface area of the cattail canopy was only 28% as great as that of the water hyacinth canopy. Thus, the peripheral vegetative surface area of the cattail canopy was multiplied by the factor 0.28 and a new "equivalent" vegetative/open water surface area ratio was calculated. With this adjustment, the cattail data could then be described by the linear regression obtained for the water hyacinths. Following this relationship to a canopy with minimal

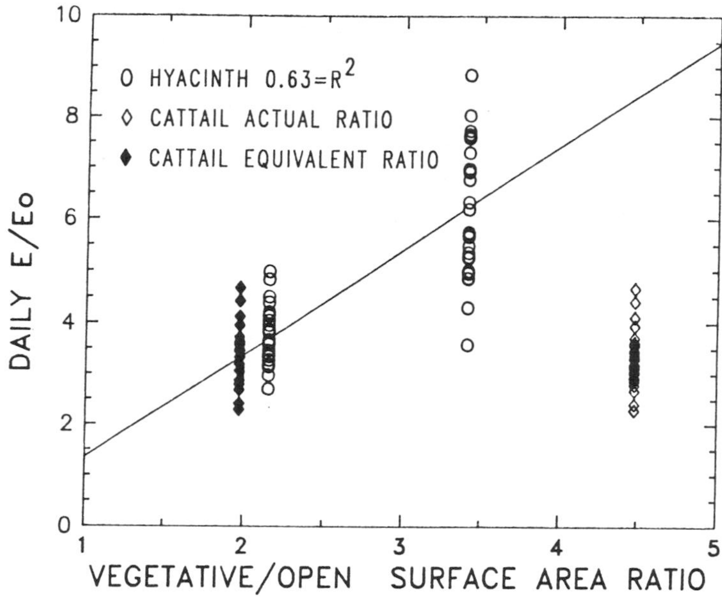

FIGURE 2. The ratio of 24 h totals of evaporation from tall water hyacinth and cattail canopies to similar totals of evaporation from similar-sized open water tanks vs. the actual vegetative/open water surface area ratio for water hyacinth and both the actual and the "equivalent" ratios for cattails.

peripheral exposure, these data gave the same intercept result as those of our 1984 study, with the cattail canopy result matching the 40% increase determined by Young and Blaney (1942).

Dramatic reductions in water hyacinth stomatal conductance were obtained for initial increases in CO_2 concentration in our 1983 study. The mean mid-day conductance fell to 50% of its ambient-condition value at 550 $\mu L\ L^{-1}$ CO_2. Reduction in actual water loss was not as great as the reduction in stomatal conductance. Stomatal closure reduced evaporative cooling and increased internal leaf temperatures producing a greater driving force for transpiration. This decreased the effect of the lower stomatal conductances and yielded a 27% reduction in evapotranspiration from the CO_2-enriched canopy for a mean doubling of the ambient CO_2 concentration.

The maximum growth rates of water hyacinth correlated well with the degree of atmospheric CO_2 enrichment in our 1984 experiment, yielding a 36% increase in productivity for a 300 to 600 $\mu L\ L^{-1}$ doubling of the atmospheric CO_2 content during a four week period of maximum growth. Plant height also increased linearly with rising CO_2 concentration which caused all treatments to exhibit increasing water losses during the study. It has been shown that for small-diameter water bodies, transpirational water loss rates rise dramatically as plant height increases (McDonald and Hughes, 1968). Thus, to correct for this "oasis effect" of our small-diameter tanks we adjusted the transpirational water losses from the 500 and 650 μL L^{-1} CO_2 treatments to what they would have been if the plants in those treatments had all been of the same height each week as the plants in the ambient CO_2 treatment. This adjustment yielded around a 20% evapotranspiration reduction for a mean doubling of the ambient CO_2 concentration.

Using the weekly height-adjusted transpiration and corresponding biomass production results, we computed the mean plant water use effficiencies of the ambient, 500 and 650 μL L^{-1} treatments and plotted them against the mean daylight CO_2 concentrations. This procedure indicated that for a 300 to 600 μL L^{-1} doubling of the atmospheric CO_2 there was a 115% increase in the water use efficiency of the water hyacinths.

CONCLUSIONS

Canopy surface geometry plays a dominant role in evaporation studies on short and tall aquatic macrophytes. The additional advective energy supplied to the canopy's peripheral exposure and not to the open water surface is highly related to the vegetative/ open water surface area ratio. The atmospheric turbulence generated above the plant canopy can influence the vegetation's evaporative rate. A short, extensive hyacinth canopy produces only a minor perturbation of the adjacent atmosphere and the vegetation's stomatal diffusion resistance is able to negate the relatively minor consequent influx of energy resulting in an evaporation reduction or an amount equivalent to E_o. However, the turbulent influx of advective energy caused by tall, extensive hyacinth and/or cattail canopies overpowers the vegetation's internal resistance and the evaporative rate (as compared to open water) increases by some 40%. In the case of water lily and water fern, no peripheral exposure exists, precluding any additional influx of energy and resulting in evaporative reduction. Hence, short or flat, floating or emergent aquatic macrophyte stomata display regulation of evaporation even at the "potential" rate.

Further research must be conducted before anything definitive can be claimed on this account for the tall hyacinths and cattails. However, it should be noted that the cattails do regulate transpiration through their stomata at different locations along the reed. In effect, only the top quarter of the cattail reed transpires appreciably despite the fact that stomatal counts exhibited little variation or size differences overall.

The results of our atmospheric CO_2 enrichment of water hyacinth indicate that this floating aquatic plant behaves much like many terrestrial plants with respect to its transpirational and growth responses to atmospheric CO_2 enrichment. Indeed, we found that as with previously studied agronomic and forest species, the efficiency with which water hyacinth utilizes water in the production of biomass essentially doubles with a 300 to 600 $\mu L\ L^{-1}$ doubling of the atmospheric CO_2 content. Similar responses may therefore be anticipated for cattail, water lily, and water fern. If so, the future higher atmospheric CO_2 concentration will reduce the evaporative loss from water bodies inhabited by the latter two species a further 20%. Unlike these flat, floating species, hyacinth and cattail alter their canopy structure with increasing biomass. If the CO_2's growth stimulus is expressed in plant height alone, it will increase the amount of peripheral surface exposure and atmospheric turbulence. The resulting greater driving force for evaporation should negate the stomatal closure response and yield the same evaporative loss for these species in higher CO_2 atmospheres. However, the CO_2 growth responses could also occur horizontally or in combination with augmented plant height. The prior situation would decrease evaporation since less peripheral exposure would exist upon the canopy. In the latter case, however, the resulting effect upon evaporation would depend on whether the plants reached the critical height where atmospheric turbulence supercedes all other influences.

ACKNOWLEDGMENT

The authors wish to thank Lenore Murphy for her valuable assistance in the typing of this paper.

REFERENCES

Bernatowicz, S., S. Leszczynski, and S. Tyczynska. 1976. The influence of transpiration by emergent plants on the water balance in lakes. Aquat. Bot. 2:275-288.

Diara, H. F., and C. Van Hove. 1984. Azolla, a water saver in irrigation rice fields? Developments in Plant and Soil Sci. 13:115-118.

Idso, S. B., R. J. Reginato, and J. W. Radin. 1982. Leaf diffusion resistance and photosynthesis in cotton as related to a foliage temperature based water stress index. Agric. Meteorol. 27:27-34.

Idso, S. B., P. J. Pinter, Jr., R. J. Reginato, and K. L. Clawson. 1984a. Stomatal conductance and photosynthesis in water hyacinth: Effects of removing water from roots as quantified by a foliage-temperature-based plant water stress index. Agric. For. Meterol. 32:249-256.

Idso, S. B., B. A. Kimball, and K. L. Clawson. 1984b. Quantifying effects of atmospheric CO_2 enrichment on stomatal conductance and evapotranspiration of water hyacinth via infrared thermometry. Agri. For. Meteorol. 33:15-22.

Idso, S. B., B. A. Kimball, and M. G. Anderson. 1985. Atmospheric CO_2 enrichment of water hyacinths: Effects on transpiration and water use efficiency. Water Resourc. Res. 21:1787-1790.

Johnson, C. M., P. R. Stout, T. C. Broyer, and A. B. Carlton. 1957. Comparative chlorine requirements of different species. Plant Soil 8:337-353.

Kimball, B. A., and S. B. Idso. 1983. Increasing atmospheric CO_2: Effects on crop yield, water use and climate. Agric. Water Manage. 7:55-72.

Kimball, B. A., J. R. Mauney, G. Guinn, F. S. Nakayama, P. J. Pinter, Jr., K. L. Clawson, R. J. Reginato, and S. B. Idso. 1983. Effects of increasing atmospheric CO_2 on yield and water use of crops. p. 196-233. U.S. Water Conservation Laboratory Ann. Rept. U.S. Dept. of Energy Series, Response of Vegetation to Carbon Dioxide, No. 021.

Lemon, E. R. (ed.). 1983. CO_2 and plants. AAAS Selected Symp. 84, Westview Press, Boulder, CO.

McDonald, C. C., and G. H. Hughes. 1968. Studies of consumptive use of water by phreatophytes and hydrophytes near Yuma, Arizona. U.S. Geological Survey Prof. Paper 486-F:F15-F17.

National Research Council (U.S.). 1983. Changing Climate. National Academy Press, Washington, D.C.

Otis, C. H. 1914. The transpiration of emersed water plants: Its measurements and its relationships. Botanical Gazette 58:457-494.

Penfound, W. T., and T. T. Earle. 1948. The biology of the water hyacinth. Ecological Monographs 18:447-472.

Penman, H. L. 1963. Vegetation and hydrology. Commonwealth Bureau of Soil Science (Great Britain). Technical Communication 53:64-65.

Rogers, H. H., and D. E. Davis. 1972. Nutrient removal by water hyacinth. Weed Sci. 20:423-428.

Rogers, H. H., J. F. Thomas, and G. E. Bingham. 1983. Response of agronomic and forest species to elevated atmospheric carbon dioxide. Science 220:428-429.

Rosenberg, N. J. 1981. The increasing CO_2 concentration in the atmosphere and its implication on agricultural productivity. I. Effects on photosynthesis, transpiration and water use efficiency. Climatic Change 3:264-279.

Schneider, S. H. 1983. The problem of "pre-industrial" CO_2 concentration -- an editorial. Climatic Change 5:311-313.

Seybold, A. 1930. Die pflanzliche transpiration. I. U. II. Ergeb. Bio. 5:29.

Shaw, R. R. (ed.). 1967. Ground level climatology. American Assoc. for the Advancement of Science, Pub. No. 86, Washington, D.C. 395 pp.

Thom, A. S., and H. R. Oliver. 1977. On Penman's equation for estimating regional evaporation. Quart. J. Royal Meteorol. Soc. 103:345-357.

Timmer, C. E., and L. W. Weldon. 1967. Evapotranspiration and pollution of water by water hyacinth. Hyacinth Control J. 6:34-37.

van Bavel, C. H. M. 1966. Potential evapotranspiration: The combination concept and its experimental verification. Water Resources Res. 2:455-467.

Van der Weert, R., and G. E. Kamerling. 1974. Evapotranspiration of water hyacinth (*Eichhornia crassipes*). J. Hydrol. 22:201-202.

Wigley, T. M. L. 1983. The pre-industrial carbon dioxide level. Climatic Change 5:315-320.

Young, A. D., and H. F. Blaney. 1942. Use of water by native vegetation. State of California Dept. of Public Works, Division of Water Resources, Bulletin No. 50.

GROWTH AND PHOTOSYNTHETIC CHARACTERISTICS OF WATER HYACINTH IN CO_2 ENRICHED GREENHOUSES

J. Roy
Laboratoire de Physiologie Ecologique
Centre Emberger, CNRS, BP 5051
34033 Montpellier Cedex
FRANCE

B. Landon
Spie Batignolles
33 quai de Dion-Bouton
92814 Puteaux Cedex
FRANCE

A. Larigauderie
Laboratoire de Physiologie Ecologique
Centre Emberger, CNRS, BP 5051
34033 Montpellier Cedex
FRANCE

J. Brochier
Agronome Consultant
14 Rue du Chateau
34160 Castrie
FRANCE

ABSTRACT

Growth experiments showed that the maximum growth rate of water hyacinth [Eichhornia crassipes (Mart) Solms] was obtained at a CO_2 concentration as high as 10,000 µL L^{-1} (ppm), where the rate was twice that at 500 µL L^{-1}. The photosynthetic response to CO_2, light intensity, temperature and humidity was investigated on plants grown at atmospheric (340 µL L^{-1}) and elevated (10,000 µL L^{-1}) CO_2 concentrations. Photosynthetic rate at high CO_2 concentration was 57 µmol CO_2 m^{-2} s^{-1} compared to 35 µmol CO_2 m^{-2} s^{-1} for plants grown at 340 µL L^{-1}. The reduction of photosynthetic capacities by long term exposure to CO_2 was low (15%). Saturating light intensity was 1500 to 2000 µmol (photon) m^{-2} s^{-1} when measured at 340 µL L^{-1} CO_2 and above 2000 when measured at high CO_2 concentration. Photosynthesis was slightly affected by

ISBN 0-941463-00-1

leaf temperature in the range 22 to 40°C and not at all by water vapor deficit in the range 0.7 to 2.4 KPa (85 to 50% RH).

Keywords: CO_2 enrichment, growth rate, photosynthetic efficiency, light saturation, greenhouses.

INTRODUCTION

Water hyacinth [Eichhornia crassipes (Mart) Solms] is considered as the eighth worst weed in the world, obstructing navigation in many tropical and subtropical countries (Holm et al., 1977). But it is also an agricultural and industrial resource, used in water treatment systems (Hayes et al., 1987) and providing methane, cattle feed, paper pulp or compost (Monsod, 1987). A doubling of the atmospheric CO_2 concentration is envisaged for the next century (Trabalka, 1985). Knowing the photosynthetic and growth responses of water hyacinth to elevated CO_2 concentrations is then crucial to predicting how natural populations and water treatment systems will be affected. Such information is also required to assess the benefit of a CO_2 enrichment when water hyacinths are grown in greenhouses, e.g. for protein production (Brochier et al., 1985) or for wastewater treatment in regions with winter frost (Doersam, 1987).

A short-term exposure to elevated CO_2 concentration results in a large increase in photosynthetic rate for species with the C_3 photosynthetic pathway (Kramer, 1981; Cure, 1985). The long-term effect of elevated CO_2 is generally a lesser increase or no change in photosynthetic rate (Oechel and Strain, 1985). The overall response of crops, grown with no resource limitation by CO_2, is expected to be a 33% increase in agricultural yield for a doubling of the current CO_2 concentration (Kimball, 1983).

We investigated the effects of long term CO_2 enrichment on water hyacinth growth with a range of CO_2 concentrations and compared the leaf photosynthetic characteristics of plants grown at atmospheric versus 10,000 $\mu L\ L^{-1}$ (ppm) CO_2. These experiments are part of a program run by Spie Batignolles, a public work company, with the purpose of using heat and CO_2 from industrial smokes to produce high protein forage (Brochier et al., 1985).

MATERIALS AND METHODS

A single clone of water hyacinth collected at the botanical garden of Lyon, France was used in the study. For the growth experiments, plants were grown in five adjacent minigreenhouses (1 m^2 of growing area, 1.45 m^3 of air each) which were independently regulated for CO_2 and temperature. The same nutrient solution (Coic and Lesaint 1975 type with 250 mg N L^{-1} added as NO_3^-, NH_4^+ and urea) was allowed to flow through all five greenhouses. Plant density in each greenhouse was 47 plants m^{-2}.

For the photosynthetic experiments, plants were grown in tanks (11.2x5.5x0.6 m) filled with the nutrient solution previously described. Plants were grown in summer under two CO_2 levels: 1) outside at atmospheric concentration, 340 μL L^{-1} CO_2 mean day and night temperatures 25 to 35°C and 15 to 20°C respectively, mean photosynthetically active radiation PAR 43 mol m^{-2} d^{-1} and 2) in a greenhouse at CO_2 concentration of 10,000 μL L^{-1}, mean daily maximum and minimum temperatures 37°C and 18°C respectively, mean PAR 27 mol m^{-2} d^{-1}. Plants were grown under these conditions several months before transferring into the laboratory prior to gas exchange measurements. The last fully expanded leaf of a ramet was enclosed in a 23 cm diameter cuvette made of plexiglass (Figure 1). The open gas exchange system was comparable in principle to the system described by Winner and Mooney (1980). Two cuvettes were run simultaneously. Concentration and uptake of CO_2 were measured with infrared gas analyzer (Analytical Development Company) in absolute and differential mode. The

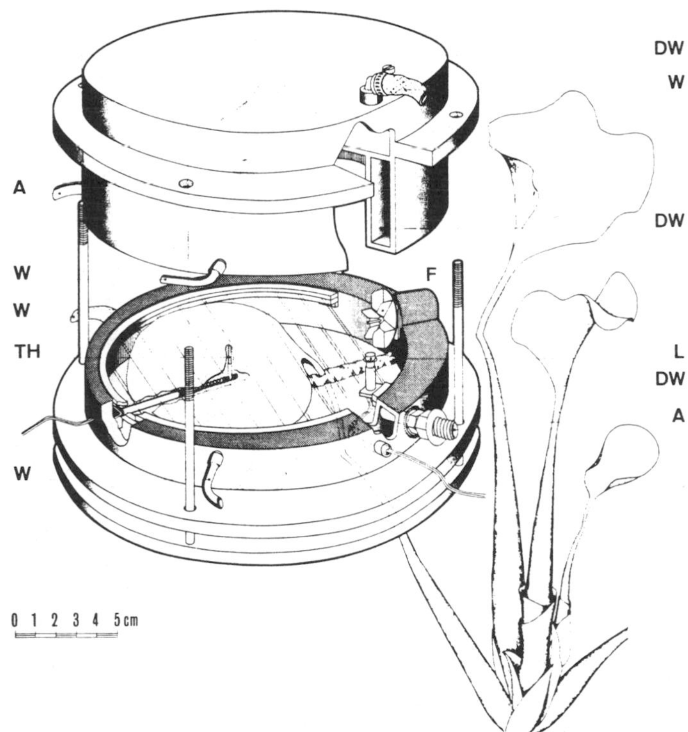

FIGURE 1. Expanded view of the assimilation chamber. It consists of three parts: the bottom in which the petiole is sealed, the surrounding wall with a fan (F), a light sensor (L) and a thermistor (TH), and finally the lid. The lid and the surrounding wall were double jacketed to allow temperature control by water circulation. W: water pipes. A: air pipes.

relative humidity of airstream leaving and bypassing the cuvettes was measured with two thin film capacitance type sensors (Testoterm). Illumination was provided by 1000 W metal halide lamps (HPIT 1000, Philips). Silicon photovoltaic cells, calibrated against a quantum sensor (LI 1905, LI-COR), measured PAR inside the cuvettes. Leaf temperature was measured with a thermistor positioned on the lower leaf surface. An Apple II computer calculated the values of the gas exchange parameters in real time (according to the procedure of von Caemmerer and Farquhar, 1981) and controlled the analyzers calibration and the gasflow switching unit.

RESULTS

Growth Response to CO_2 Enrichment

For plants grown under low light (in winter), maximum growth rate was obtained at CO_2 concentrations between 8,000 and 16,000 $\mu L\ L^{-1}$ with a rate twice the rate at 500 $\mu L\ L^{-1}$ (Figure 2). For plants grown under high light (summer), maximum growth rate was obtained at 8,000 $\mu L\ L^{-1}$. In all the experiments, the change in growth rate in response to CO_2 concentration came mainly from a change in the number of new ramets. Since young ramets always

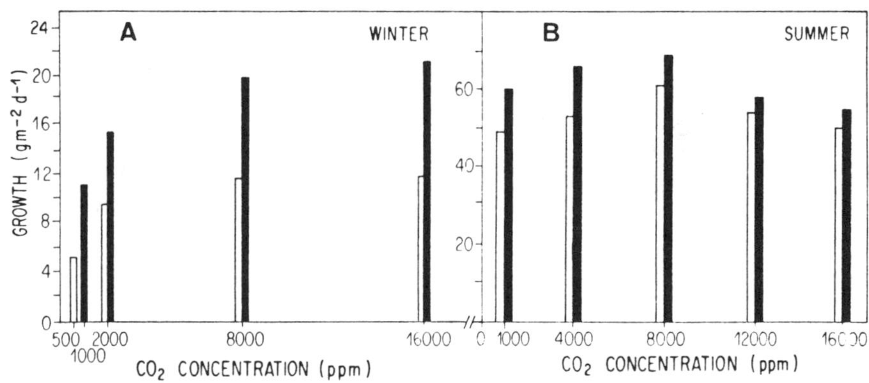

FIGURE 2. Effect of CO_2 concentration on growth rate. Open and solid histograms are two sets of experiments. (A) open and solid histograms respectively: Radiant energy 7.9 and 6.9 MJ m^{-2} d^{-1}; Solution temperature 25 and 25°C; Air temperature min 12 and 12°C, max 33 and 32°C; Length 35 and 18 d. (B) open and solid histograms respectively: Radiant energy 21.7 and 22.1 MJ m^{-2} d^{-1}; Solution temperature min 27.5 and 27.5°C; Air temperature min 15 and 14°C, max 38 and 39°C; Length 26 and 14 d. All plants were grown at 8,000 $\mu L\ L^{-1}$ CO_2 before the experiment except for (A) open histogram, for which plants were previously grown at 16,000 $\mu L\ L^{-1}$.

have a low number of leaves, the mean number of leaves per plant decreased as CO_2 increased.

Response of Photosynthesis to Intercellular CO_2

Photosynthetic rate doubled when ambient CO_2 concentration was raised from 340 to 1,000 µL L^{-1} but then decreased (Figure 3a). Plants grown at 10,000 µL L^{-1} CO_2 showed a typical response to CO_2 with a saturation plateau at high CO_2 (Figure 3b). At CO_2 concentrations below 1,000 µL L^{-1}, photosynthetic rate was 15% lower than the plants grown at atmospheric CO_2. However, the differences were not significant (t test, P=0.05). The mean photosynthetic rate for low and high CO_2 levels were 63.1 ± 3.7 and 57.1 ± 2.8 µmol (CO_2) m^{-2} s^{-1}, respectively.

Response of Photosynthesis to Photon Flux Density

Plants grown at atmospheric and high CO_2 levels were saturated between 1,500 and 2,000 µmol (photon) m^{-2} s^{-1} when measured at 330 µL L^{-1} CO_2, and were saturated above 2,000 µmol m^{-2} s^{-1} when measured at 1,200 µL L^{-1} CO_2 (Figure 4). Quantum yield was not statistically different between plants grown at high or low CO_2 (P=0.05), but measurements at high CO_2 increased quantum yield by 47%.

Response of Photosynthesis to Temperature

Water hyacinth has a large range of optimal leaf temperatures for photosynthesis (Figure 5). Growth under high CO_2 conditions

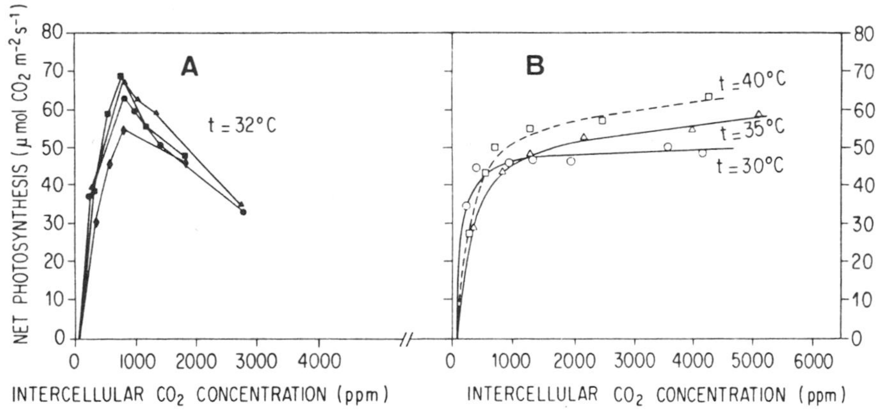

FIGURE 3. Response of net photosynthesis to intercellular CO_2 in plants grown at atmospheric CO_2 (A) or at 10,000 µL L^{-1} (B). Different symbols represent different plants. conditions during measurements: Leaf temperature (T) as indicated on the figure, photon flux density (e) 2,000 µmol m^{-2} s^{-1}, vapor pressure deficit (VPD) 1-1.5 KPa.

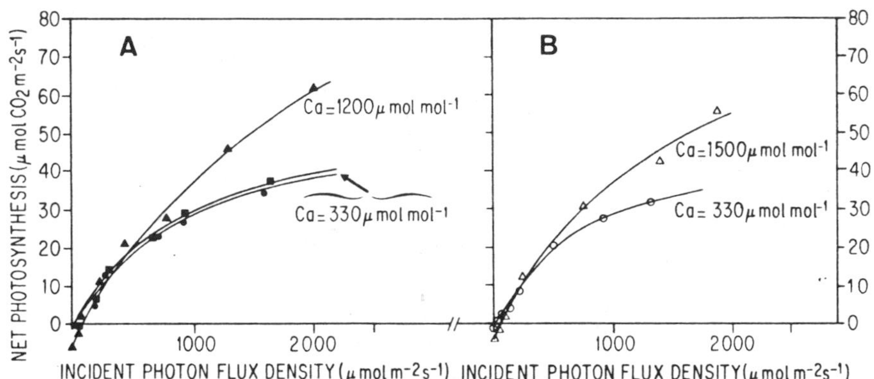

FIGURE 4. Response of net photosynthesis to photon flux density in plants grown at atmospheric (A) or 10,000 µL L^{-1} CO_2 (B). Different symbols represent different plants. Conditions during measurements: CO_2 concentration (Ca) as indicated on the figure, T = 32°C, VPD = 1-1.5 KPa.

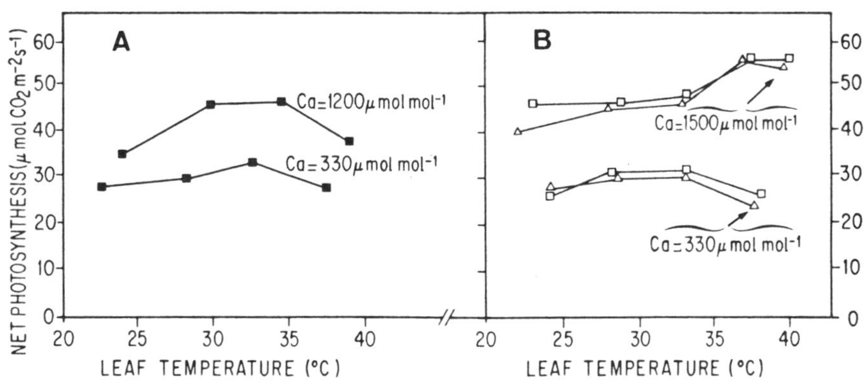

FIGURE 5. Response of net photosynthesis to leaf temperature in plants grown at atmospheric (A) or 10,000 µL L^{-1} CO_2 (B). Different symbols represent different plants. The same leaves were measured one day at the low CO_2 concentration and the following day at the high CO_2 concentration. Conditions during measurements: Ca as indicated on the figure, E = 2,000 µmol m^{-2} s^{-1}, VPD = 1-1.5 KPa.

seems to enlarge this range and to displace the optimum toward higher temperatures when the measurements are conducted at high CO_2 (Figure 5b).

Response of Photosynthesis and Stomatal Conductance to Water Vapor Pressure Deficit (VPD)

Photosynthesis and stomatal conductance of plants grown at high CO_2 were measured at different VPD (Figure 6). Photosynthesis was unaffected over the range tested (from 85 to 50% relative humidity). Stomatal conductance was not affected by VPD except at VPD higher than 2 KPa when measurements were run at atmospheric CO_2 concentration. Measurements under high CO_2 (4,300 $\mu L\ L^{-1}$) increased photosynthesis by 50% and decreased stomatal conductance by 90%, resulting in a very large increase of water use efficiency.

DISCUSSION

Photosynthetic Characteristics

The inhibition of water hyacinth photosynthesis by high CO_2 seems to be related to the relative availability of C and light during growth: it occurred for plants grown during summer at atmospheric CO_2 (high light, low CO_2), plants grown at 10,000 $\mu L\ L^{-1}$ but shaded (low light, high CO_2), plants grown during winter

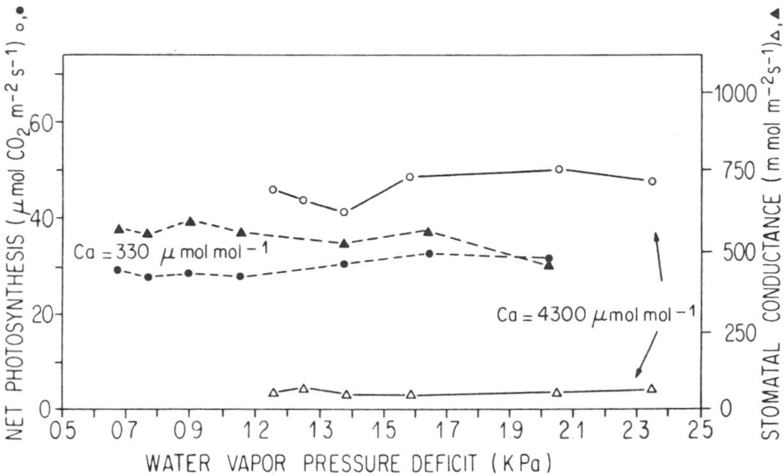

FIGURE 6. Response of net photosynthesis and stomatal conductance to vapor pressure deficit in plants grown at 10,000 $\mu L\ L^{-1}$ CO_2. The same leaf was measured one day at the low CO_2 concentration and the following day at the high CO_2 concentration. Conditions during measurements: Ca as indicated on the figure, E = 2,000 $\mu mol\ m^{-2}\ s^{-1}$, T = 32°C, VPD = 1-1.5 KPa.

at 6,000 μL L^{-1} (low light, high CO_2) but not for plants grown during summer at 10,000 μL L^{-1} CO_2 (high light, high CO_2). Woo and Wong (1983) also described such an inhibition linked to growth conditions (low light and N levels) and modulated by measurement conditions (temperature and O_2 partial pressure). They suggested that this inhibition affects both electron transport and Rubisco carboxylase activity.

Plants grown at high CO_2 levels had photosynthetic rates 15% lower than plants grown at atmospheric CO_2. A reduction of photosynthetic capacities by long term exposure to elevated CO_2 concentrations is widely reported (Wulf and Strain, 1982, Delucia et al., 1985; Oechel and Strain, 1985). In some cases, photosynthetic rate of plants grown and measured at high CO_2 is lower compared to plants grown and measured at atmospheric CO_2 concentration (Raper and Peedin, 1978; Wong, 1979; Hicklenton and Jolliffe, 1980). The decrease in photosynthesis in the high CO_2 plants is not the result of stomatal limitations. It is accompanied by starch accumulation (Madsen, 1968; Delucia et al., 1985). The mechanisms of photosynthetic inhibition correlated to starch accumulation are not resolved (Neales and Incoll, 1969; Sasek et al., 1985). This inhibition is reversible (Sasek et al., 1985; Combe and Kobilinsky, 1985), suggesting that strong sinks for photosynthesis near its theoretical capacity. In water hyacinth, the unusually high photosynthetic rate maintained under high CO_2 growth conditions (58% higher than the rate of plants at atmospheric CO_2 concentration) is probably due to active sinks for photosynthates (high leaf and ramet production rate, indeterminate growth).

Photosynthetic Basis of High Biomass Production

Water hyacinth grown outside (in Florida) with nutritive solution yield 88 to 106 Mg ha^{-1} yr^{-1} (DeBusk et al., 1981; Reddy and DeBusk, 1984). Potential production in a temperature controlled greenhouse with CO_2 enrichment is estimated at 200 Mg ha^{-1} yr^{-1} (Brochier et al., 1985). For comparison, temperate crops produce an average of 22 to 29 Mg ha^{-1} yr^{-1} and sugar cane (C_4), 66 Mg ha^{-1} yr^{-1} (Hall, 1980). Photosynthetic characteristics described in our study provide some physiological basis for the high biomass production of water hyacinth. Photosynthetic rate of plants grown and measured at atmospheric conditions was about 35 μmol m^{-2} s^{-1}. This rate is high compared to other C_3 plants. The range for C_3 and C_4 cultivated grasses is 13-21 and 31-50 μmol m^{-2} s^{-1} respectively (Korner et al., 1979). Published photosynthetic rates for water hyacinth are lower than ours. Avadhni et al. (1983) found 2.4 μmol m^{-2} s^{-1}; Knipling et al. (1970) (cited by Sale et al., 1985), 10.2; Patterson and Duke (1979) 21.5. Photosynthetic rate at light saturation is linearly related to N content of the leaf (Field and Mooney, 1986). Therefore the low strength of the nutrient solution (0.1 Hoagland) used by Patterson and Duke may explain the low photosynthetic rate they obtained.

CO_2 enrichment (8,000 μL L^{-1}) resulted in a doubling of water hyacinth growth rate (Figure 2). Anderson and Idso (1985) found a 36% increase between 350 and 700 μL L^{-1}. This increase in biomass production results from an increase in leaf area due mainly to a higher rate of daughter ramet production (Landon, 1986), as well as an increase in photosynthetic rate (Figure 3). The high photosynthetic rate of plants under high CO_2 comes from a 1.5 times greater quantum yield (a similar increase was found by Ehleringer and Bjorkman (1977) on Encelia californica) as well as from a relatively low inhibition by starch accumulation. Measurements of photosynthesis under saturating light and CO_2 were run eight hours a day for two days without observing any decrease in photosynthetic rate (Larigauderie, 1985). Petioles were also found to photosynthesize. Their photosynthetic rate was 10% of the lamina's rate when provided with a similar light level (Larigauderie, 1985).

In conclusion, this study revealed: 1) low inhibition of photosynthesis by long term exposure to CO_2; 2) high light level to saturate photosynthesis; 3) low sensitivity of photosynthesis to temperature; and 4) low sensitivity to ambient air relative humidity.

REFERENCES

Brochier, J., B. Landon, and J. L. Noyer. 1985. Culture de plantes aquatiques en milieu controle pour la production de proteines. Evaluation de la productivite de la jacinthe d'eau (Eichhornia crassipes). Comp. Rend. Acad. Agric. France 71:467-479.

von Caemmerer, S., and G. D. Farquhar. 1981. Some relationships between the biochemistry of photosynthesis and the gas exchange of leaves. Planta 153:376-387.

Coic, Y., and C. Lesaint. 1975. La nutrition minerale et en eau des plantes en horticulture avancee. Document technique S.C.P.A. 23, 22 pp.

Combe, L, and A. Kobilinsky. 1985. Effet de la fumure carbonee sur la photosynthese de radis (Raphanus sativus) en serre en hiver. Photosynthetica 19:550-560.

Cure, J. D. 1985. Carbon dioxide doubling responses: a crop survey. p. 99-116. In B. R. Strain and J. D. Cure (ed.) Direct Effects of Increasing Carbon Dioxide on Vegetation. US Dept. of Energy (DOE/ER-0238), Washington, DC.

DeBusk, T. A., J. H. Ryther, M. D. Hanisak, and L. D. Williams. 1981. Effects of seasonality and plant density on the productivity of some freshwater macrophytes. Aquat. Bot. 10:133-142.

Delucia, E. H., T. W. Sasek, and B. R. Strain. 1985. Photosynthetic inhibition after long-term exposure to elevated levels of atmospheric carbon dioxide. Photosynthesis 7:175-184.

Doersam, J. 1987. Use of water hyacinths for the polishing of secondary effluent at the city of Austin hyacinth greenhouse facility. In K. R. Reddy and W. H. Smith (ed.) Aquatic Plants for Water Treatment and Resource Recovery. Magnolia Publishing, Inc., Orlando, Florida.

Ehleringer, J., and O. Bjorkman. 1977. Quantum yield for CO_2 uptake in C_3 and C_4 plants. Plant Physiol. 59:86-90.

Field, C., and H. A. Mooney. 1986. The photosynthesis-nitrogen relationship in wild plants. p. 25-55. In T. J. Givnish (ed.) On the Economy of Plant Form and Function. Cambridge Univ. Press, Cambridge.

Hall, D. O. 1980. Biological and agricultural systems: an overview. p. 1-30. In A. San Pietro (ed.) Biochemical and Photosynthetic Aspects of Energy Production.. Academic Press, New York.

Hayes, T. D., H. R. Isaacson, D. P. Chynoweth, K. R. Reddy, and R. Biljetina. 1987. Water hyacinth systems for water treatment. In K. R. Reddy and W. H. Smith (ed.) Aquatic Plants for Water Treatment and Resource Recovery. Magnolia Publishing Inc., Orlando, FL.

Hicklenton, P. R., and P. A. Jolliffe. 1980. Carbon dioxide and flowering in *Pharbitis nil* Choisy. Plant Physiol. 66:13-17.

Holm, L. G., D. L. Plucknett, J. V. Pancho, and J. P. Herberger. 1977. The World's Worst Weeds. Distribution and Biology. University Press of Hawaii, Honolulu. 609 pp.

Idso, S. B., B. A. Kimball, and M. G. Anderson. 1985. Atmospheric CO_2 enrichment of water hyacinths: effects on transpiration and water use efficiency. Water Resour. Res. 21:1787-1790.

Kimball, B. A. 1983. Carbon dioxide and agricultural yield: an assemblage and analysis of 430 prior observations. Agron. J. 75:779-788.

Korner, Ch., J. A. Scheel, and H. Bauer. 1979. Maximum leaf diffusive conductance in vascular plants. Photosynthetica 13:45-82.

Knipling, E. B., S. H. West, and W. T. Haller. 1970. Growth characteristics, yield potential and nutritive content of water hyacinth. Proc. Soil and Crop Sci. Soc. Fla. 30:51-63.

Kramer, P. J. 1981. Carbon dioxide concentration, photosynthesis and dry matter production. Bioscience 31:29-33.

Landon, B. 1986. Etude de la reponse de la jacinthe d'eau (*Eichhornia crassipes* (Mart) Solms) a trois composantes de l'environement en condition de culture intensive sous serre: temperature de la solution nutritive, temperature de l'air, teneur en CO_2 de l'atmosphere ambiante. These de docteur ingenieur. ENSAM Montpellier, France. 215 pp.

Larugauderie, A. 1985. Ecophysiologie des echanges gazeux chez *Eichhornia crassipes* (Mart) Solms (jacinthe d'eau): Reponse aux fortes teneurs en CO_2. These de troisieme cycle. USTL Montpellier, France. 110 pp.

Larigauderie, A., J. Roy, and A. Berger. 1986. Long term effects of high CO_2 concentration on photosynthesis of water hyacinth

(Eichhornia crassipes (Mart) Solms). J. Exp. Bot. 37: (in press).

Madsen, E. 1968. Effect of CO_2 concentration on the accumulation of starch and sugar in tomato leaves. Physiol. Plant. 21:168-175.

Monsod, G. G., Jr. 1987. Water hyacinth biomass a valuable resource for agriculture and industry. In K. R. Reddy and W. H. Smith (ed.) Aquatic Plants for Water Treatment and Resource Recovery. Magnolia Publishing Inc., Orlando, FL.

Neales, T. F., and I. D. Incoll. 1969. The control of leaf photosynthesis rate by the level of assimilate concentration in the leaf: a review of the hypothesis. Bot. Rev. 34:107-125.

Oechel, W. C., and B. R. Strain. 1985. Native species responses to increased atmospheric carbon dioxide concentrations. p. 117-154. In B. R. Strain and J. D. Cure (ed.) Direct Effects of Increasing Carbon Dioxide on Vegetation. (DOE/ER-0238) US Department of Energy, Washington DC.

Patterson, D. T., and S. O. Duke. 1979. Effect of growth irradiance on the maximum photosynthetic capacity of water hyacinth [Eichhornia crassipes (Mart.) Solms]. Plant and Cell Physiol. 20:177-184.

Raper, C. D., Jr., and G. Peeding. 1978. Photosynthetic rate during steady state growth as influenced by carbon dioxide concentration. Bot. Gaz. 139:147-149.

Reddy, K. R., and W. F. DeBusk. 1984. Growth characteristics of aquatic macrophytes cultured in nutrient rich water. I. Water hyacinth, water lettuce and pennywort. Econ. Bot. 38:229-239.

Sale, P. J., P. T. Orr, G. S. Shell, and D. J. C. Erskine. 1985. Photosynthesis and growth rates in Salvinia molesta and Eichhornia crassipes. J. Appl. Ecol. 22:125-137.

Sasek, T. W., E. H. DeLucia, and B. R. Strain. 1985. Reversibility of photosynthetic inhibition in cotton after long-term exposure to elevated CO_2 concentration. Plant Physiol. 78:619-622.

Trabalka, J. R. (ed.) 1985. Atmospheric Carbon Dioxide and the Global Carbon Cycle (DOE/ER-0209). US Dept. of Energy, Washington DC. 235 pp.

Winner, W. E., and H. A. Mooney. 1980. Ecology of SO_2 resistance. I. Effects of fumigations on gas exchange of deciduous and evergreen shrubs. Oecologia 44:290-295.

Woo, K. C., and S. C. Wong. 1983. Inhibition of CO_2 assimilation by supraoptimal CO_2: Effect of light and temperature. Aust. J. Plant Physiol. 10:75-85.

Wong, S. C. 1979. Elevated atmospheric partial pressure of CO_2 and plant growth. Interactions of nitrogen nutrition and photosynthetic capacity in C_3 and C_4 plants. Oecologia 44:68-74.

Wulff, R. D., and B. R. Strain. 1982. Effects of CO_2 enrichment on growth and photosynthesis in Desmodium paniculatum. Can. J. Bot. 60:1084-1091.

THE EFFECT OF MIXING AND AERATION ON THE PRODUCTIVITY OF MYRIOPHYLLUM HETEROPHYLLUM MICHX. (WATER MILFOIL) DURING AQUATIC WASTEWATER TREATMENT

P. M. Kozak and P. L. Bishop
Department of Civil Engineering
Durham, New Hampshire 03824

ABSTRACT

The transport of CO_2, bicarbonate (HCO_3^-) and essential nutrients across the stagnant boundary layer can significantly affect the rate of plant photosynthesis. Mixing can decrease the thickness of this layer and increase the chances of nutrients encountering active uptake sites along the plant surfaces. Approximately 4.0 g of *Myriophyllum heterophyllum* (initial plant wet weight) were exposed to 0, 30, 50 and 70% primary effluent and one of two possible mixing/aeration treatments in 1 L batch culture flasks. The two mixing treatments included mixing by aeration and mechanical mixing without aeration. Reynolds numbers were essentially the same with either treatment, indicating similar degrees of mixing. Plant productivity was greatest in the 50% wastewater mechanically mixed flasks. There was a linear decrease in plant productivity with increasing wastewater concentrations in the aerated flasks. The differences between the mechanically mixed and aerated treatments were significant at the 0.05 level. Mixing was necessary to enhance plant productivity in a submerged macrophyte aquatic treatment system, and mechanical mixing may be preferable to aeration as the form of mixing.

Keywords: Wastewater treatment, aquatic plants, photosynthesis, submersed plant.

INTRODUCTION

The removal of nutrients from wastewater by aquatic plants involves a number of complex interactions within the physicochemical environment (Reddy, 1983). Some of these interactions include the effects of dissolved O_2 and other soluble gases, light, photoperiod, sediment, electric and magnetic fields, hydrostatic pressure, salinity, heavy metals, pH, and the uptake of various macro- and micronutrients.

ISBN 0-941463-00-1

The transport of CO_2, HCO_3^-, and essential nutrients across the stagnant boundary layer surrounding the leaves of submerged macrophytes can significantly affect the rate of photosynthesis by the plant. Mixing can be used to decrease the thickness of this layer and increase the chances of nutrients encountering active uptake sites along the plant surfaces. Aeration significantly increased the productivity of Elodea nutalli grown in a batch culture system (White, 1984). The primary objective of this research was to evaluate the effects of mass transfer by mixing, and CO_2 enhancement by aeration on the productivity of the submerged plant species, Myriophyllum heterophyllum.

MATERIALS AND METHODS

One liter flasks containing approximately 4 g of initial plant wet weight were exposed to 0, 30, 50 and 70% primary wastewater effluent concentrations, and one of 2 possible mixing/aeration treatments. The zero percent wastewater solution was a 10% (v/v) modified Hoaglands nutrient solution.

At the beginning of each experiment, approximately 4 g of healthy plant material, started from apical cuttings, were gently tied with nylon string to glass stirring rods (oriented so roots were down and apices were up) and placed into each experimental flask. Each flask was then filled with 10% (v/v) modified Hoaglands nutrient solution or 30, 50, or 70% wastewater concentrations, subjected to one of two possible mixing/aeration treatments and placed randomly on shelves inside a controlled environment chamber (21°C; 16 h light/8 h darkness). Batch culture solutions were collected and replaced with the appropriate wastewater solution every 96 h during a 16 d productivity experiment. Sample alkalinity was determined by titration of 100 mL samples to pH 4.3 with 0.2 N H_2SO_4.

The mixing/aeration treatment was achieved by pumping compressed air, at the rate of 0.43 $m^3 h^{-1}$ through 1.3 cm diameter tubing inserted through parafilm covering each flask. Mechanical mixing/non-aeration was achieved by placing flasks covered with parafilm on a shaking table (approximately 78 rpm, stroke length 2.5 cm).

Productivity was determined for each of the experimental flasks after 16 d. The plants were removed from each flask, wet weights determined, and oven dried at 65°C for 36 h in tared aluminum dishes. After cooling to room temperature the dried plants were weighed. A standard curve for productivity [g (dry wt) $m^{-2} d^{-1}$)] was prepared to allow conversion of plant wet weight to dry weight. Plant productivity was estimated by taking the difference between the initial and final dry weight, divided by surface area (total light penetrating surface area).

RESULTS

A methylene blue dye study was conducted to quantify, and then equalize, the rate of mixing in the two systems. The mixing/aeration treatment was completely mixed after 1 min. The mechanically mixed/non-aerated treatment was completely mixed at between 1 and 5 min. Since productivity was measured over a 16 d period, the mixing rates of the two treatments could essentially be considered to be equal. Both mass transfer and CO_2 were enhanced by the mixing/aeration treatment. The mechanically mixed/non-aerated treatment resulted in the enhancement of mass transfer, while CO_2 was limited by the lack of aeration.

The results of the productivity experiment (Figure 1) showed that plant productivity was at least twice as great in the mechanically mixed flasks as in the aerated flasks with 30, 50 and 70% wastewater concentrations. For the experiment run 9/12/84 - 9/28/84, plant productivity was greatest in the 50% wastewater, mechanically mixed flasks (1.02 ± 0.40 g m^{-2} d^{-1}). The plant productivity in the 30 and 70% wastewater, mechanically mixed flasks were 0.98 ± 0.14 and 0.67 ± 0.34 g m^{-2} d^{-1}, respectively. The 30 and 50% wastewater, aeration treatments resulted in lower plant productivity at 0.75 ± 0.18 and 0.20 ± 0.06 g m^{-2} d^{-1}, respectively. Negative plant productivity was measured for both mixing treatments with Hoaglands nutrient solution, and for the 70% wastewater aeration treatment. The variation in plant productivity due to mixing was significant at the 0.05 level. The variation in plant productivity due to wastewater concentrations was also significant at the 0.05 level. Interaction between mixing and wastewater concentration did not have a significant effect upon plant productivity.

For the experiment run 10/26/84-11/11/84, plant productivity was greatest in the 30, 50 and 70% wastewater mechanically mixed treatment flasks (1.36 ± 0.14, 1.25 ± 0.10 and 1.50 ± 0.06 g m^{-2} d^{-1}, respectively). There was a linear decrease in plant productivity with increasing wastewater concentrations in the aerated flasks. Plant productivity in the 30, 50 and 70% wastewater aerated treatment flasks measured 0.95 ± 0.22, 0.59 ± 0.11 and 0.31 ± 0.41 g m^{-2} d^{-1}, respectively. The lowest plant productivity was measured in the treatment flasks containing Hoaglands nutrient solution (Figure 1). The variation in plant productivity was due to mixing alone. The effect of wastewater concentration on plant productivity was not significant at the 0.05 level. The effect of interaction between mixing and wastewater concentrations was also not significant.

DISCUSSION

Mixing can decrease the thickness of the stagnant boundary layer surrounding the leaves of submerged aquatic plants, and increase the chances of nutrient transport to the plant. Limited transport of CO_2 and HCO_3^- to the guard cells located on the leaves

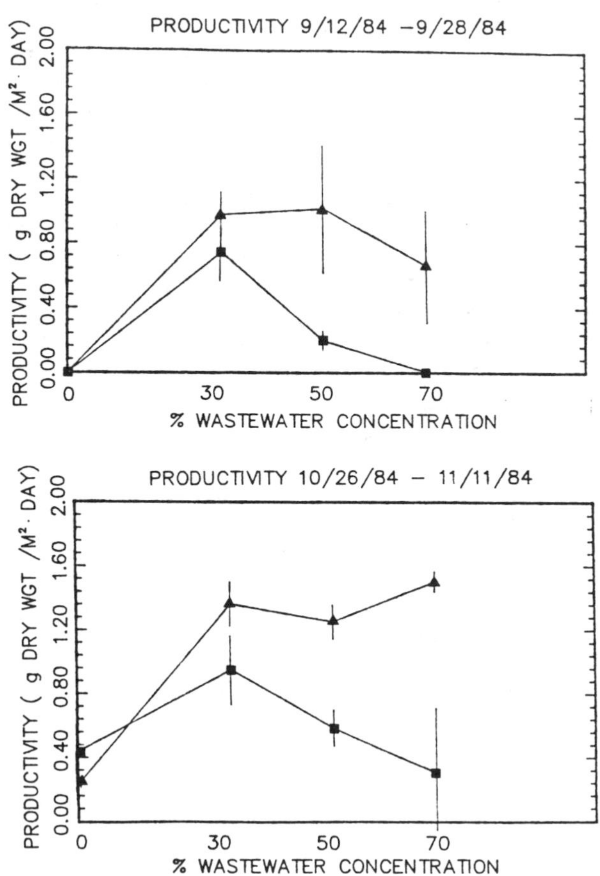

FIGURE 1. Myriophyllum heterophyllum productivity after 16 d. Zero percent wastewater is modified Hoaglands solution (Johnson et al., 1957). ▼ = mixing by aeration; ■ = mechanical mixing. Data represent means of three replicates ± S.E.

of submerged aquatic plants can lead to a reduction in plant photosynthesis (Smith and Walker, 1980). Uptake of inorganic C can only occur if the inorganic C travels through the water and hits an active uptake site along the plant surfaces (Raven, 1981). Mixing greatly increases the chances of inorganic C, and other nutrients, hitting these active uptake sites.

Westlake (1965) found that the maximum rate of photosynthesis in turbulent water was six times greater than that measured in static water for the aquatic plant _Ranunculus pseudofluitans_. Photosynthesis increased rapidly as water velocity increased, with the rate of increase dropping at higher velocities. Mixing has also been shown to affect metabolic rates in the marine kelp, _Macrocystis pyrifera_. Wheeler (1980) reported that the photosynthetic output of _Macrocystis pyrifera_ could be increased by a factor of 300% after increasing the surrounding water velocity from 0 to 4 cm s^{-1}.

To gain greater insight into the understanding of CO_2 fixation by aquatic plants and associated bacteria, all total alkalinity measurements were divided into 4 possible contributing inorganic species according to the equation:

$$\text{Total Alkalinity} = C_t\ (\alpha_1 + 2\alpha_2) + K_w/[H]-[H]$$

The four possible C species include total inorganic C (C_t), carbonic acid (H_2CO_3*), HCO_3^- and carbonate (CO_3). The H_2CO_3* component is really a combination of the CO_2 and H_2CO_3 in a system, but is often considered equal to the CO_2 alone because the concentration of CO_2 is many magnitudes greater than that of H_2CO_3 in an aqueous medium.

The speciation of total alkalinity in treatment flasks containing 50% wastewater is shown in Figures 2 through 5. Total alkalinity dropped in the 50% wastewater/aerated flasks on days 12 and 16, and this was reflected by a drop in HCO_3^- as the C source for photosynthesis (Figure 2). In the mechanically mixed treatment flasks, total alkalinity did not decrease greatly, with CO_2 being the preferred C source (Figure 3). In the control flasks lacking plants, either aerated (Figure 4) or mechanically mixed (Figure 5), CO_2 appeared to be the preferred C source.

These results support literature reports concerning the preference of submerged plants for HCO_3^- over CO_2 under high O_2 conditions. If O_2 and CO_2 compete for the same enzyme, and for the same ribulose diphosphate substrate, this could explain why _Myriophyllum heterophyllum_ switched over to using HCO_3^- in the aerated/wastewater treatment flasks ("supersaturated" O_2 conditions). Although _Myriophyllum heterophyllum_ may be capable of using CO_2 and/or HCO_3^- ions as a C source, it may be that CO_2 is more preferred for optimum photosynthesis and productivity.

As would be expected, the mixing/aeration treatments at all wastewater strengths resulted in increased dissolved O_2 concentrations within the flasks, with levels often greater than 9.0 mg L^{-1}. High O_2 levels have been reported inhibitory for photosynthesis in a number of submerged aquatic plants (Salvucci and Bowes, 1983; Lloyd et al., 1977). Net photosynthesis in _Myriophyllum spicatum_ was inhibited by 21% O_2 (Salvucci and Bowes, 1983). The fact that photosynthesis is inhibited in submerged aquatic plants when O_2 levels are high could explain why plant productivity was significantly greater in the mechanically mixed treatment flasks as compared to the aerated treatment flasks.

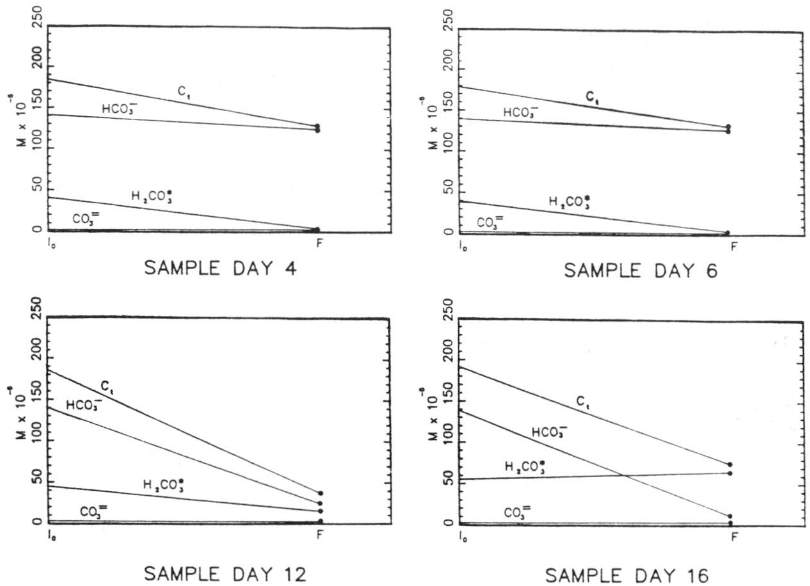

FIGURE 2. Speciation of alkalinity (M x 10^{-5}) in flasks with Myriophyllum heterophyllum and 50% wastewater/mixing by aeration. I_o = initial concentration, F = final concentration.

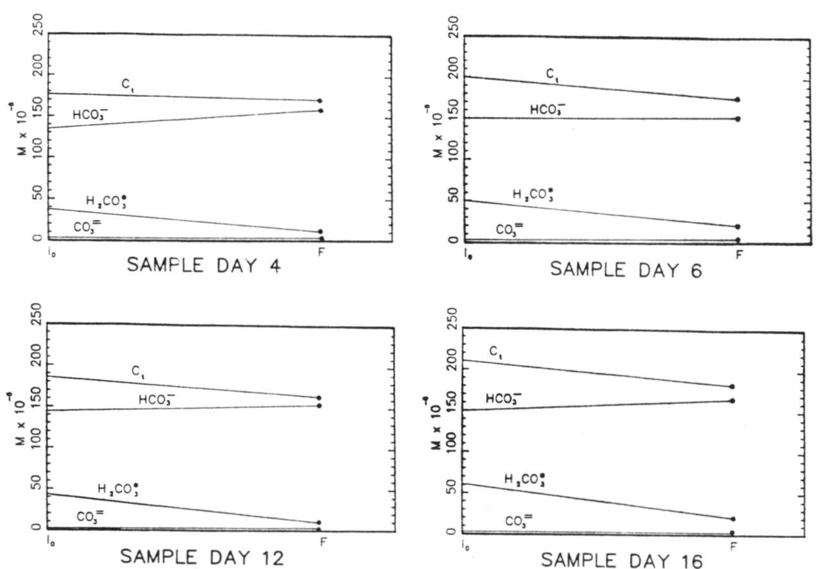

FIGURE 3. Speciation of alkalinity (M x 10^{-5}) in flasks with Myriophyllum heterophyllum and 50% wastewater/mechanical mix. I_o = initial concentration, F = final concentration.

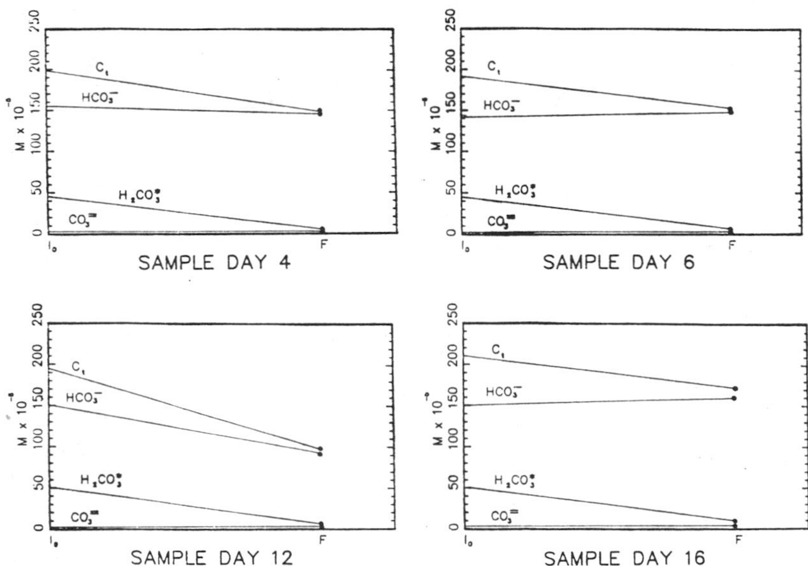

FIGURE 4. Speciation of alkalinity (M x 10^{-5}) in control flasks with 50% wastewater/mixing by aeration. I_o = initial concentration, F = final concentration.

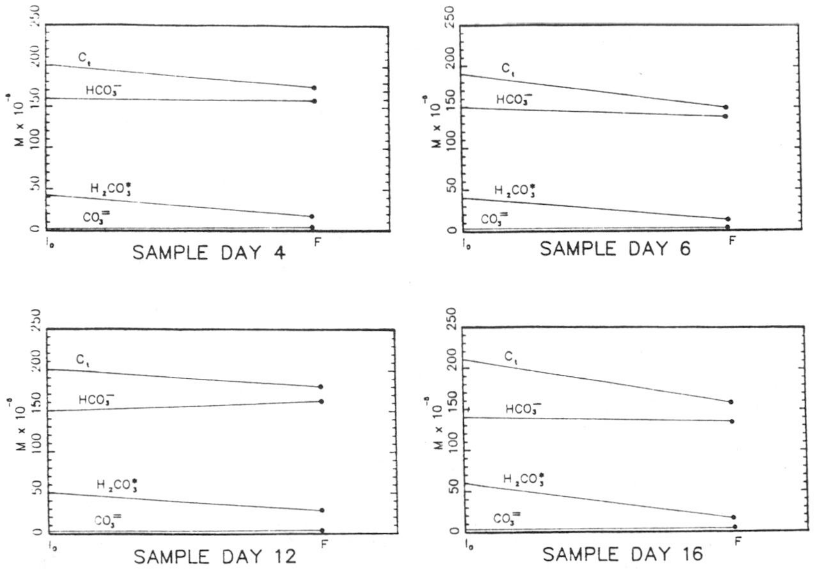

FIGURE 5. Speciation of alkalinity (M x 10^{-5}) in control flasks with 50% wastewater/mechanical mix. I_o = initial concentration, F = final concentration.

This research indicates that mixing is necessary to enhance plant productivity in a submerged macrophyte aquatic treatment system, and that mechanical mixing may be preferable to aeration for systems utilizing *Myriophyllum heterophyllum*.

REFERENCES

Barko, J. W., and R. M. Smart. 1981. Comparative influences of light and temperature on the growth and metabolism of selected submerged freshwater macrophyte. Ecol. Monographs 5:219-235.

Best, E. P., and K. E. Mantai. 1978. Growth of *Myriophyllum*: Sediment or lakewater as a source of N and P. Ecology 59:1075-1080.

Denny, P. 1972. Sites of nutrient absorption in aquatic macrophytes. J. Ecol. 60:819-829.

Lloyd, N., D. Canvin, and J. Bristow. 1977. Photosynthesis and photorespiration in submerged aquatic vascular plants. Canadian J. Bot. 55:3001-3005.

Raven, J. 1981. Nutritional strategies of submerged benthic plants: The acquisition of C, N and P by rhizophytes and haptophytes. New Phytologist 88:1-30.

Reddy, K. R. 1983. Fate of nitrogen and phosphorus in a wastewater retention reservoir containing aquatic macrophytes. J. Environ. Qual. 12:137-141.

Salvucci, M. E., and G. Bowes. 1983a. Two photosynthetic mechanisms mediating the low photorespiratory state in submersed aquatic angiosperms. Plant Physiol. 73:488-496.

Salvucci, M. E., and G. Bowes. 1983b. Ethoxyzolamide repression of the low photorespiratory state in two submersed angiosperms. Plants 158:23-34.

Smith, F., and N. Walker. 1980. Photosynthesis by aquatic plants: Effects of unstirred layers in relation to assimilation of CO_2 and HCO_5 and to carbon isotopic discrimination. New Phytologist 86:245-259.

Stephenson, M., G. Turner, P. Pope, J. Colt, A. Knight, and G. Tchobanoglous. 1980. The environmental requirements of aquatic plants. Publ. 65-Appendix A, California State Water Resources Control Board, CA.

Westlake, D. F. 1963. Comparison of plant productivity. Biol. Rev. 38:385-425.

Westlake, D. F. 1965. Some basic data for investigation of the productivity of aquatic macrophytes. Me. Inst. Ital. Hydrobiol. 18(supp.):229-248.

Wheeler, W. 1980. Effect of boundary layer transport on the fixation of carbon by the great kelp *Macrocystis pyrifera*. Marine Botany 56:103-110.

White, H. 1984. Temperate climate aquaculture treatment of wastewater. M.S. Thesis. University of New Hampshire.

PRODUCTIVITY AND PHOTOSYNTHETIC CHARACTERISTICS OF ELODEA NUTTALLII GROWN IN AQUATIC TREATMENT SYSTEMS

T. T. Eighmy, L. S. Jahnke, and P. L. Bishop
University of New Hampshire
Durham, NH 03824

ABSTRACT

Macrophyte productivity and photosynthesis affect nutrient removal and nutrient transformations in aquatic treatment systems. These processes were investigated for *Elodea nuttallii* grown in wastewater in continuous flow reactors in greenhouse systems designed to provide advanced secondary treatment of primary effluent under temperate conditions. Net productivities usually ranged from 0.0 to 4.5 g (dry wt) m^{-2} d^{-1}. The total N and total P content of *E. nuttallii* was high [up to 73 and 23 mg g^{-1} (dry wt), respectively]. Diurnal changes in reactor water column constituents indicated that both CO_2(aq) and HCO_3^- were used during photosynthesis. Oxygen electrodes were used to assess photosynthetic response to photon fluence rate (PFR), pH, and inorganic C concentration (C_T). The macrophyte was adapted to the low C_T, high O_2 photorespiratory conditions in the reactors. It had a low Γ (44 µL L^{-1}), low K_m [CO_2] (96 µM), high Vmax [C_T] (162 µmoles mg Chl^{-1} h^{-1}) and high chlorophyll concentrations [2.8 mg Chl g^{-1} (wet wt)]. RUBISCO was the predominant carboxylating enzyme (160 µmoles mg Chl^{-1} h^{-1}), though the macrophyte also possessed significant β-carboxylase activity (PEPcase = 24 µmoles mg Chl^{-1} h^{-1}, PEPckase = 14 µmoles mg Chl^{-1} h^{-1}). Carbonic anhydrase (CA) was present in low concentrations (14 EU mg Chl^{-1}). These results indicate that *E. nuttallii* makes use of both a C concentrating mechanism and C_4 acid metabolism to adapt to low C_T conditions in the reactors. *E. nuttallii* is thus well suited for use in temperate climate aquatic wastewater treatment systems.

Keywords: Elemental composition, carbon uptake, carboxylation, low photorespiration state, HCO_3^- use.

INTRODUCTION

Aquatic macrophytes play an important role in promoting both nutrient transformations and nutrient removal in aquatic macrophyte-based aquatic treatment systems. The macrophytes

ISBN 0-941463-00-1

promote nutrient transformations by acting as a biologically active substratum for epiphytic microbial heterotrophs and nitrifiers. The heterotrophs and nitrifiers can utilize photosynthetically derived O_2 to oxidize organic C to CO_2 and NH_4^+ to NO_3^-. Dark plant respiration can then reduce dissolved oxygen (DO) levels in the reactors so that denitrification occurs and N (as N_2, N_2O, or NO) is evolved from the system.

When macrophytes are productive, N and P are removed from the reactor to support cell synthesis. Plant nutrient uptake and harvest typically removes 40-60% of the N and 30-50% of P which is applied to the treatment system (DeBusk et al., 1983; Reddy and Sutton, 1984; Reddy and DeBusk, 1985). Nutrient removal by plant uptake is indirectly related to the photosynthetic activity of the macrophyte. An energized plasmalemma, manifested in a proton and charge difference across the plasmalemma, requires ATP hydrolysis and proton extrusion at the plasmalemma ATPase to drive cotransport and mediated passive uniport nutrient transport systems (Raven, 1984). Mitochondrially derived ATP is the source of ATP; its manufacture ultimately requires photosynthetic C fixation. Consequently, understanding factors which influence macrophyte photosynthesis and productivity is important to promote nutrient transformations and removal in aquatic treatment systems.

Extensive research has been conducted on the productivity (DeBusk, et al., 1981,1983; Reddy and DeBusk, 1984) and photosynthetic characteristics (Bowes, 1985; Lucas, 1983; Raven, 1984) of tropical aquatic macrophytes yet little research has been conducted on temperate macrophytes grown in aquatic treatment systems. The results presented here indicate that the temperate macrophyte *Elodea nuttallii* is a photosynthetically robust macrophyte which is well adapted to photorespiratory conditions in aquatic treatment systems and is well suited for use in temperate climate wastewater treatment systems.

MATERIALS AND METHODS

Elodea nuttallii (Planch.) St. John or "waterweed" (Hydrocharitaceae) was obtained locally and grown for two years in 120 L reactors (1 m^2 surface area) under continuous flow conditions (θ = 2.6 to 4.6 d) in a greenhouse. The reactors were fed 100% primary effluent and diffused air completely mixed the reactors. Standing crops were generally maintained at 2.5 kg (wet wt) m^{-2} by harvesting every two to four weeks.

Net productivities were determined from changes in biomass wet weight over time. Total N (TN) and total P (TP) contents were determined from alkaline (TN) and acid (TP) persulfate digestion techniques and autoanalysis (Eighmy, 1986). Reactor water column pH, total alkalinity (TA), DO, temperature, and various constituents of C_T (CO_2 (aq), HCO_3^-, CO_3^{2-}) were determined by standard methods (APHA, 1980) and published equilibria relationships. PFR was determined with a Lambda Li-Cor LI-185 quantum photometer.

Oxygen electrode studies were used to assess the effects of PFR, pH, and C_T on photosynthetic O_2 evolution. The methods used were similar to those of Van et al. (1976). Γ_{PFR} and Γ were determined by interpolation. Total chlorophyll (Chl) was determined according to Inskeep and Bloom (1985). Carbonic anhydrase (CA, EC 4.2.1.1), D-ribulose-1,5-bisphosphate carboyxylase-oxygenase (RUBISCO, EC 4.1.1.39) in its activated form, and the β-carboxylase phosphoenolpyruvate carboxylase (PEPcase, EC 4.1.1.31) were assayed according to the methods of Van et al. (1976) and Salvucci and Bowes (1981,1983a,b). The β-carboxylase phosphoenolpyruvate carboxykinase (PEPckase, EC 4.1.1.49) was assayed according to the methods of Kremer and Kuppers (1977) and PEPckase activity was corrected for PEPcase activity.

RESULTS

The macrophytes were grown in reactors receiving full strength primary effluent. Typical chemical characteristics of the primary effluent and the *Elodea* reactor water are shown in Table 1. The net productivities in three reactors containing *E. nuttallii* over the two year period are shown in Figure 1. The effects of diurnal photosynthetic and respiratory activity on water column chemical constituents is shown in Figure 2. Various productivity and photosynthetic characteristics of *E. nuttallii* grown in the reactors are shown in Table 2. Most of the analyses and assays were conducted in the fall of 1985 when the macrophyte was productive.

DISCUSSION

These results indicate that *E. nuttalli* is a photosynthetically versatile macrophyte which is tolerant of the

TABLE 1. Characteristics of the primary effluent and of the water in the *Elodea* reactors (Eighmy, 1986).

Constituent	Primary effluent	Reactors
Temp (°C)	11.0 - 26.5	10.0 - 29.5
pH	6.4 - 8.1	6.1 - 9.6
Alkalinity, as $CaCO_3$ (mg L^{-1})	80.0 - 214.0	12.0 - 113.0
DO (mg L^{-1})	0.2 - 3.1	0.5 - 15.5
BOD_5 (mg L^{-1})	91.8 - 142.5	2.7 - 30.0
NH_4-N (mg L^{-1})	10.1 - 27.2	0.1 - 16.0
NO_2-N + NO_3-N (mg L^{-1})	0.0 - 0.08	0.0 - 6.7
Total N (mg L^{-1})	13.4 - 29.9	0.5 - 24.1
PO_4-P (mg L^{-1})	1.3 - 3.4	0.1 - 2.3
Total P (mg L^{-1})	2.7 - 6.9	0.2 - 4.2

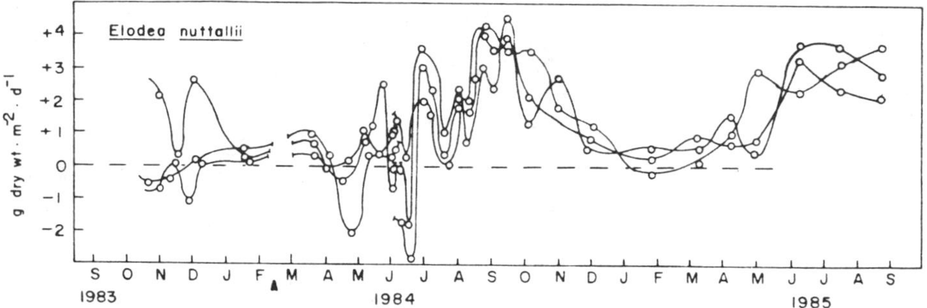

FIGURE 1. The effect of season on the net productivity of E. nuttallii.

TABLE 2. Productivity and photosynthetic characteristics of E. nuttallii grown in an advanced wastewater treatment system.

Characteristic	E. nuttallii	Range in aquatic macrophytes†
Productivity [g (dry wt) m^{-2} d^{-1}]	0.0 - 4.5	0.0 - 59.0
Tissue TN [mg g^{-1} (dry wt)]	35.0 - 73.0	8.0 - 54.0
Tissue TP [mg g^{-1} (dry wt)]	11.0 - 23.0	1.0 - 26.0
TN/TP	1.9 - 3.7	2.5 - 17.0
PFR saturation (μE m^{-2} s^{-1})	1000	200.0 - 2000.0
Γ_{PFR} (μE m^{-2} s^{-1})	31	15.0 - 100.0
Γ (μL CO_2 L^{-1})	44	13.0 - 150.0
Total Chl (mg Chl g^{-1} (wet wt)	2.8	0.5 - 1.5
K_m [CO_2] (μmoles)	96	64.0 - 175.0
Vmax [C_T] (μmoles mg Chl^{-1} h^{-1})	162	51.0 - 280.0
CA (EU mg Chl^{-1})	14	70.0 - 960.0
RUBISCO (μmoles mg Chl^{-1} h^{-1})	160	27.0 - 154.0
PEPcase (μmoles mg Chl^{-1} h^{-1})	24	5.0 - 330.0
RUBISCO/PEPcase	6.6	0.5 - 76.9
PEPckase (μmoles mg Chl^{-1} h^{-1})	14	0.0 - 0.2

†Eighmy, 1986.

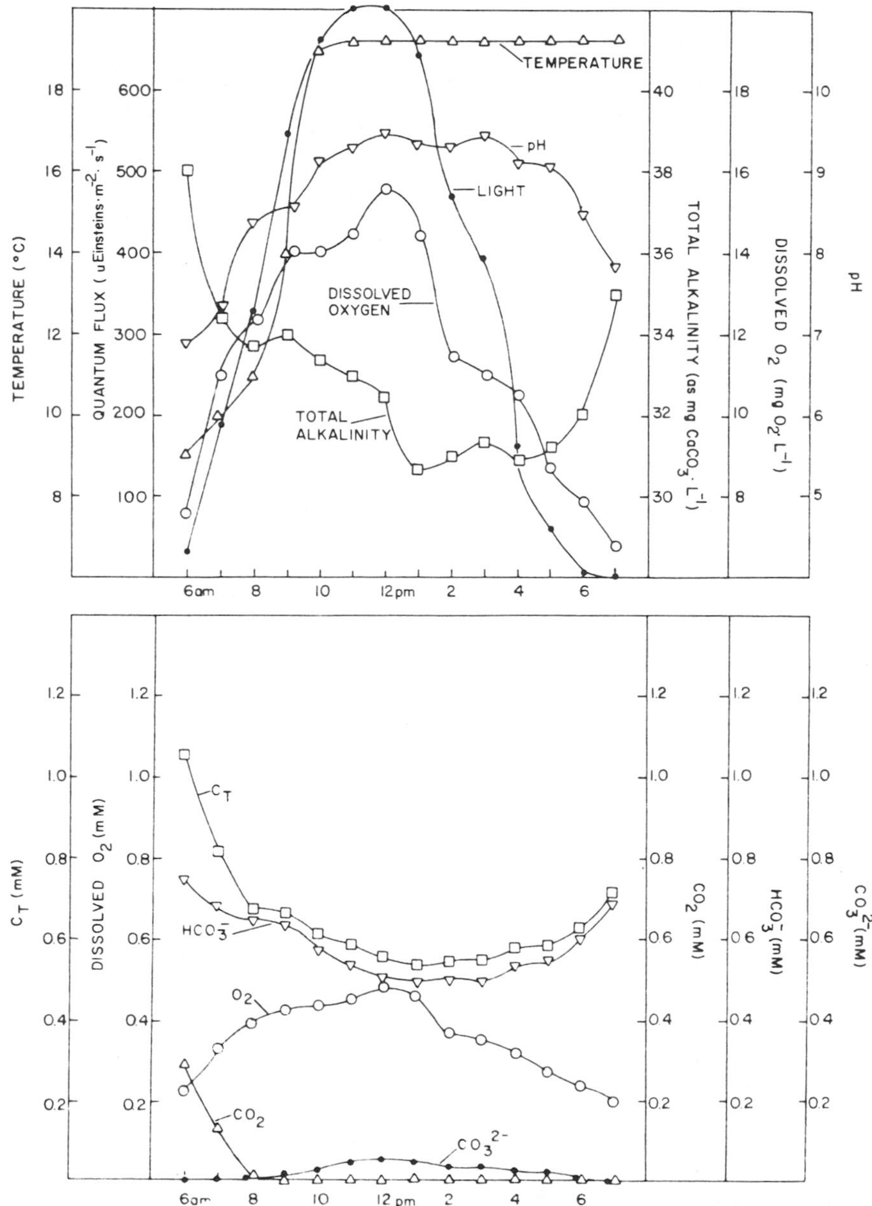

FIGURE 2. Diurnal changes in C_T, DO, pH, temperature, and incident PFR. The reactor contained 2.5 kg wet weight of *E. nuttallii*.

nutrients and organic C present in primary effluent. The plant systems were usually capable of providing advanced secondary treatment under hydraulic, organic, and nutrient loading conditions similar to those used for Eichhornia crassipes-based systems (Eighmy, 1986).

Elodea nuttallii was usually productive year round (Figure 1). Low productivities were observed in the spring when temperature, photoperiod, and maximum noontime PFR levels were close to their minimum values. The maximum productivities exhibited by E. nuttallii occurred in the summer and early fall when growth conditions were optimal. The productivity of E. nuttallii [0-4.5 g (dry wt) m^{-2} d^{-1}] was less than those reported for tropical submergent and floating macrophytes grown under nutrient enriched conditions. Eichhornia crassipes, Hydrilla verticillata, Hydrocotyle umbellata, and Pistia stratiotes exhibit productivities which range from 2 to 56 g (dry wt) m^{-2} d^{-1} (DeBusk et al., 1981; Reddy and DeBusk, 1984). Elodea nuttallii is physiologically a cold-adapted macrophyte with lower light and temperature growth optima than tropical submergent and floating aquatic macrophytes (Kunii, 1981) which may explain its comparatively lower productivity.

The TN and TP content of E. nuttallii were significantly higher than the critical growth-limiting concentrations reported by Gerloff (1975) for submergent macrophytes. The TN [35-73 mg g^{-1} (dry wt)] and TP [11-23 mg g^{-1} (dry wt)] content of E. nuttallii was higher than typical values for tropical or temperate macrophytes grown under nutrient enriched conditions (Reddy and DeBusk, 1985). These data indicate that E. nuttallii was exhibiting nutrient luxury consumption. The low productivity, high N and P content, and robust photosynthetic activity (see below) suggest that much of the metabolic energy generated by chloroplast and mitochondrial electron transport was coupled to N and P acquisition and storage rather than biomass production.

The photosynthetic activity of E. nuttallii had a pronounced affect on C_T, DO and pH in the reactors (Figure 2). Similar observations have been made by Pokorny et al. (1984) for Elodea canadensis, by Laing and Browse (1985) for Egeria densa, and by Van et al. (1976) for Hydrilla verticillata. CO_2(aq) and HCO_3^- were both removed during photosynthesis. CO_2(aq) was quickly removed from the reactor water column as light levels increased. HCO_3^- was removed more gradually. E. nuttallii exhibited a low light compensation point (Γ_{PFR} = 31 μE m^{-2} s^{-1}). Light saturated photosynthetic O_2 evolution began at 1000 μE m^{-2} s^{-1}. These characteristics are similar to ones reported for aerial portions of heterophyllous submergent macrophytes which are sun adapted (Salvucci and Bowes, 1982).

Aquatic macrophytes vary, on a seasonal basis, their CO_2 compensation point (Γ) in response to photorespiratory conditions (Holaday et al., 1983). The decrease in Γ is attributable to an adaptive increased ability to accumulate inorganic C so that carboxylation is favored over oxygenation at RUBISCO (Raven, 1984). This adaptation is mediated by (1) an hypothesized CA-associated inorganic C active transport system or (2) by the use of β-carboxylases which incorporate HCO_3^- into C_3 precursors to form C_4 acids which can be subsequently decarboxylated as an indirect source of CO_2 (Salvucci and Bowes, 1981,1983b).

Myriophyllum is thought to employ an inducible CA-associated inorganic C transporter when subjected to photorespiratory conditions; it typically has high RUBISCO and low PEPcase activity (RUBISCO/PEPcase > 9.0) as well as high CA activity (Salvucci and Bowes, 1983b). The precise mechanisms of transport and the nature of the inorganic C specie which is transported are not known. *Hydrilla* tends to utilize β-carboxylases as the predominant carboxylating enzyme and HCO_3^- as the principal inorganic C specie to be fixed; its RUBISCO/PEPcase ratio drops below 1.0 when it adapts to photorespiratory conditions (Salvucci and Bowes, 1983b) However, both adaptions are ethoxyzolamide repressible suggesting that CA is somehow involved in both adaptive mechanisms (Salvucci and Bowes, 1983a,b).

Elodea nuttallii exhibited Γ, K_m [CO_2], Vmax [C_T], and Chl values similar to aquatic macrophytes which have been subjected to low C_T, high DO conditions and have adapted to a low photorespiratory state (Salvucci and Bowes, 1981; 1982; 1983a,b). The low CA activity and high RUBISCO/PEPcase ratio in *E. nuttallii* indicates that the macrophyte employed both *Hydrilla*-like and *Myriophyllum*-like adaptive mechanisms to concentrate inorganic C. The macrophyte had high RUBISCO activity (160 μmoles mg Chl^{-1} h^{-1}) which indicates that CO_2 is the preferred C source for carboxylation. The presence of low, but significant activity of β-carboxylases indicates that HCO_3^- may indirectly serve as a source of CO_2 (via C_4 decarboxylation). PEPckase was active in *E. nuttallii*; it is usually found in brown algae. This enzyme can also serve as a C_4 decarboxylase (Raven, 1984). The low activity of CA suggests that extracellular conversion of HCO_3^- to CO_2 (or vice versa) is minimal and that HCO_3^- and CO_2 cross the plasmalemma without interconversion. Recently, we have presented evidence which shows that *E. nuttallii* employs an active transport system to concentrate HCO_3^- internally (Eighmy et al., 1986). Thus, *E. nuttallii* uses both CO_2(aq) and HCO_3^- in its adaptive low photorespiratory state though the precise intracellular fate of HCO_3^- remains to be elucidated. These adaptive characteristics are important when photosynthetic activity and biomass levels are high in aquatic treatment systems and C_T is consequently limiting to photosynthesis.

Elodea nuttallii is thus an excellent candidate for use in temperate climate aquatic treatment systems. *E. nuttallii*-based systems provide advanced secondary treatment capabilities. The macrophyte accumulates high levels of N and P. It is also photosynthetically robust and well suited for the low C_T, high DO conditions found in the system . An understanding of its productivity and photosynthetic characteristics has helped to elucidate why this macrophyte performs well in aquatic treatment systems.

ACKNOWLEDGMENT

Research supported by the National Science Foundation (CEE-8209851).

REFERENCES

APHA. 1980. Standard methods for the examination of water and wastewater. 15th ed. APHA, NY.

Bowes, G. 1985. Pathways of CO_2 fixation by aquatic organisms. p. 187-210. In W. J. Lucas and J. A. Berry (ed.) Inorganic Carbon Uptake by Aquatic Photosynthetic Organisms. Am. Soc. Plant Physiol., MD.

DeBusk, T. A., L. D. Williams, and J. H. Ryther. 1983. Removal of nitrogen and phosphorus from wastewater in a water hyacinth-based treatment system. J. Environ. Qual. 12:257-262.

DeBusk, T. A., J. H. Ryther, M. D. Hanisak, and L. D. Williams. 1981. Effects of seasonality and plant density on the productivity of some freshwater macrophytes. Aquat. Bot. 10:133-142.

Eighmy, T. T. 1986. An investigation of aquatic macrophyte-based aquatic wastewater treatment systems for temperate climates. Doctoral Dissertation, University of New Hampshire.

Eighmy, T. T., L. S. Jahnke, and W. R. Fagerberg. 1986. Evidence for bicarbonate active transport in *Elodea nuttallii*. In J. Biggins (ed.) VII International Congress on Photosynthesis, Providence, RI, Aug. 9-14 (in press).

Gerloff, G. C. 1975. Nutritional ecology of nuisance aquatic plants. EPA-660/3-75-027.

Holaday, A. S., M. S. Salvucci, and G. Bowes. 1983. Variable photosynthesis/photorespiration ratios in *Hydrilla* and other submersed aquatic macrophyte species. Can. J. Bot. 61:229-236.

Inskeep, W. P., and P. R. Bloom. 1985. Extinction coefficients of chlorophyll a and b in N,N-dimethylformamide and 80% acetone. Plant Physiol. 77:483-485.

Kremer, B. P., and U. Kuppers. 1977. Carboxylating enzymes and pathways of photosynthetic carbon assimilation in different marine algae-evidence for the C_4 pathway? Planta 133:191-196.

Kunii, H. 1981. Characteristics of the winter growth of detached *Elodea nuttallii* (Planch.) St. John in pond Ojaga-ike, Japan. Aquatic Bot. 18:239-247.

Laing, W. A., and J. Browse. 1985. A dynamic model for photosynthesis by an aquatic plant, *Egeria densa*. Plant Cell Environ. 8:639-649.

Pokorny, J., J. Kuet, J. P. Ondok, Z. Toul, and I. Ostry. 1984. Production-ecological analysis of plant community dominated by Elodea canadensis Michx. Aquat. Bot. 19:263-292.

Raven, J. A. 1984. Energetics and transport in aquatic plants. A. R. Liss, Inc., NY.

Reddy, K. R., and W. F. DeBusk. 1984. Growth characteristics of aquatic macrophytes cultured in nutrient enriched water: Water hyacinth, watter lettuce, pennywort. Econ. Bot. 38:229-239.

Reddy, K. R., and W. F. DeBusk. 1985. Nutrient removal potential of selected aquatic macrophytes. J. Environ. Qual. 14:459-462.

Reddy, K. R., and D. L. Sutton. 1984. Water hyacinths for water quality improvement and biomass production. J. Environ. Qual. 13:1-8.

Salvucci, M. E., and G. Bowes. 1981. Induction of reduced photo-respiratory activity in submersed and amphibious aquatic plants. Plant Physiol. 67:335-340.

Salvucci, M. E., and G. Bowes. 1982. Photosynthetic and photorespiratory responses of the aerial and submersed leaves of Myriophyllum brasiliense. Aquat. Bot. 13:147-164.

Salvucci, M. E., and G. Bowes. 1983a. Ethoxyzolamide repression of the low photorespiration state in two submersed angiosperms. Planta 158:27-34.

Salvucci, M. E., and G. Bowes. 1983b. Two photosynthetic mechanisms mediating the low photorespiratory state in submersed aquatic angiosperms. Plant Physiol. 73:488-496.

Van, T. K., W. T. Haller, and G. Bowes. 1976. Comparison of the photosynthetic characteristics of three submersed aquatic plants. Plant Physiol. 58:761-768.

LEAD UPTAKE BY THE WATER HYACINTH

C. Heaton, J. Frame, and J. K. Hardy
Department of Chemistry and Center for Environmental Studies
The University of Akron
Akron, Ohio 44325

ABSTRACT

Factors influencing uptake of lead(II) (PbII) by the water hyacinth, (Eichhornia crassipes), were examined. Two phases of uptake were observed for the concentration range evaluated (0.01-1000 mg L^{-1}). The initial, rapid uptake phase of about 4 h is followed by a slower, near linear phase extending past 24 h. Stirring the solution enhanced uptake, suggesting that Pb removal is in part diffusion limited. In the range of 4-8, pH has little effect on uptake whereas outside this range, uptake is reduced. Increased solution volume or rootmass results in more metal being removed by the plant. The presence of strong complexers blocks the initial rapid uptake phase as does the presence of Zn(II), Cd(II), Hg(II), and Fe(III). Strong complexers can also strip a portion of any Pb already removed from solution by the plant.

Keywords: Heavy metals, Pb uptake, aquatic plants.

INTRODUCTION

Lead is one of 129 chemical species currently on the United States Environmental Protection Agency's list of Priority Pollutants (Keith and Telliard, 1977) with a recommended maximum discharge level of 0.05 mg L^{-1}. Previous investigations of Pb uptake have shown that Pb is removed from its environment and translocated to upper body parts of the plants (Chigbo et al., 1982; Wolverton and McDonald, 1978). To date, however, no extensive evaluation as to the effects of concentration, pH, complexers or other factors which may effect uptake of Pb by the plant have been published. Previous work in this laboratory has investigated these effects on Cd and Zn uptake along with the effects of rootmass, solution volume, and solution stirring (Hardy and O'Keeffe, 1985; Hardy and Raber, 1985; O'Keeffe and Hardy, 1984). This work parallels these earlier studies.

ISBN 0-941463-00-1

MATERIALS AND METHODS

Lead uptake was monitored by assaying the exposure solution at regular intervals by atomic absorption spectroscopy using a Perkin-Elmer 4000 spectrometer equipped with an HGA 2200 graphite furnace. Water hyacinths were grown both outdoors and in the laboratory. In the laboratory, plants were grown using a combination of fluorescent (40 watt) and incandescent (100 watt) lights (16 h light cycle). All plants were maintained in half-strength Hoagland's solution (Hoagland and Arnon, 1950) at pH 7.

Plants from 2 to 3 wk of age with a dry weight of about 1 g were used. All experiments were performed in the laboratory at a constant temperature (22°C) and relative humidity (50%). Individual plants were initially rinsed with deionized water to remove any nutrient that might be transferred and then placed in 500 mL bottles containing 400 mL of the solution to be evaluated. At appropriate periods, the solution volume was adjusted to maintain constant volume, briefly stirred and a 1 mL sample removed for analysis. Any unused sample was returned to the solution. Each effect was monitored by altering a single factor in the solution and noting variations in uptake as compared to a control. Experiments were in triplicate to account for variations.

Stirring was evaluated using a magnetic stirrer and a 2.5 cm circular stir bar. The stirrer was set at the lowest setting. Solution pH was adjusted using HNO_3 or KOH and for evaluation of metal ion competition, NO_3^- salts of all metals were used.

RESULTS

Uptake at Various Concentrations

Plants were exposed to Pb concentrations ranging from 0.01 to 1000 mg L^{-1} which revealed two phases for Pb uptake (Figure 1). The first phase is rapid, extending through the first 4 h. The second, slower phase is near linear. As the initial concentration is increased, the rate of the initial phase decreases though the total metal removed at any time increases. At 100 and 1000 mg L^{-1}, plant damage became evident within 24 h of exposure. For this reason, all other experiments were at 10 mg L^{-1} and typically limited to 24 h.

Effect of Stirring

Earlier work with Cd and Zn showed that stirring of the exposure solution enhanced initial uptake rates for these metals. A large increase in the initial uptake rate is observed, but beyond this phase, the rates of uptake are comparable to an unstirred solution (Figure 2). This increase indicates that the initial uptake phase is, in part, diffusion limited.

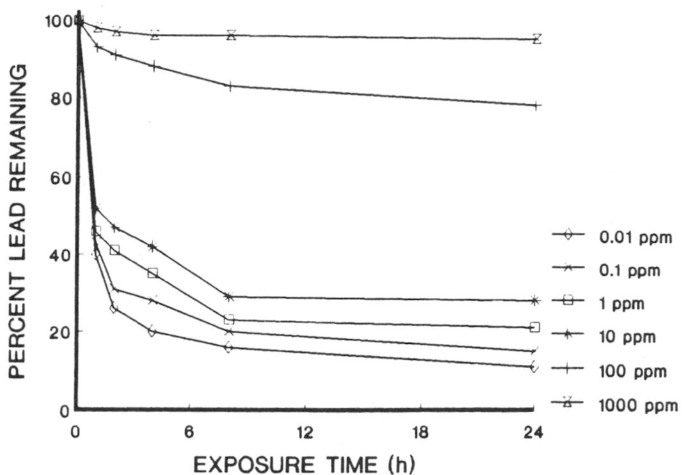

FIGURE 1. Lead uptake at varying exposure concentrations, mg L^{-1}.

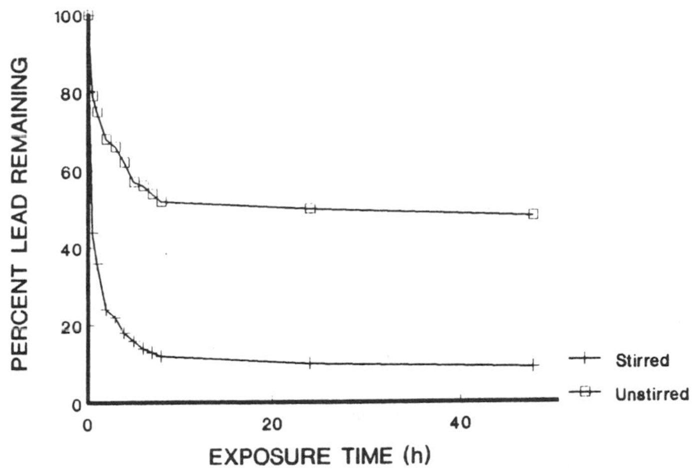

FIGURE 2. Effect of stirring on Pb uptake.

Effect of pH

A set of plants were immersed in unbuffered solutions ranging in pH from 3-9. Measures of the percent Pb remaining as a function of pH at 24 h of exposure (Figure 3) showed pH to have little effect over the range of 4-8. The pH of each solution was measured after 24 and 48 h of exposure and it was observed that the plants tended to adjust the pH of their environment to about 7 within 48 h.

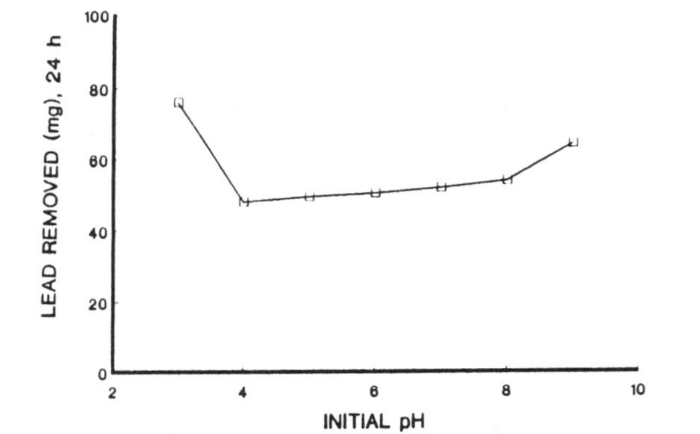

FIGURE 3. Effect of pH on Pb uptake, 24 h of exposure.

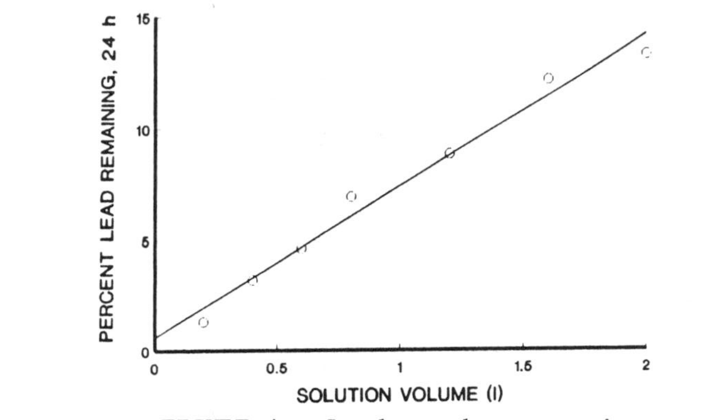

FIGURE 4. Lead uptake at various solution volumes.

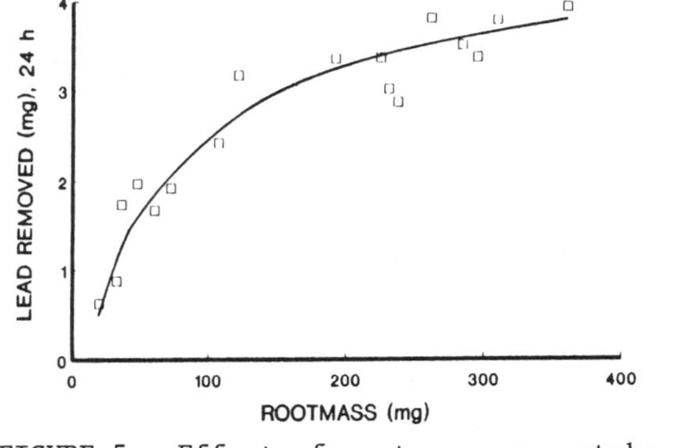

FIGURE 5. Effect of root mass on uptake, 24 h exposure.

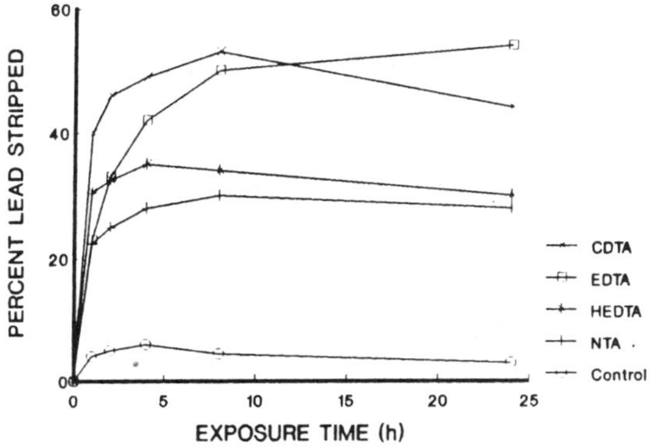

FIGURE 6. Stripping effect.

Solution Volume

Uptake was monitored in solution volumes ranging from 200-2000 mL to determine how the 4 mg Pb upper limit for earlier studies was affecting uptake. In each case, single plants were placed in each solution. Increased solution volume resulted in a near linear increase in the total Pb removed at 24 h of exposure (Figure 4).

Rootmass

A series of 15 plants with apparent differences in rootmass were selected and exposed to 10 mg Pb L^{-1} for a period of 24 h. At the end of this time, the roots were removed, dried at 100°C and weighed. The results (Figure 5) show that as rootmass increases over a range of 25-310 mg, the amount of Pb removed also increases. The total amount of Pb that can be removed from these solutions is 4 mg which might explain why the line bends over at higher rootmass values.

Effect of Competing Metal Ions on Uptake

Two studies were conducted to determine if Pb uptake could be hindered by the presence of other metal ions. Initially, a set of solutions containing 10 mg Pb L^{-1} and a 10-fold molar excess of competing metal ions (Table 1) were produced, assuming that any effect on Pb uptake would be readily apparent under these conditions. Zinc, Fe, Hg and Cd each caused a reduction in Pb removal. Other metal species had little or no effect. The uptake of each of the competing ions was also determined at 48 h. To further investigate the blocking of Pb uptake, the effect of various Zn concentrations was evaluated. Zinc was used because it is an essential trace nutrient and had the greatest effect on Pb uptake. Zinc to Pb molar ratios of 100:1, 10:1, 1:1, 0.1:1, and

TABLE 1. Effect of competing metal ions on Pb removal at 24 and 48 h of exposure.

Competing ion	Concentration	% Decrease in Pb^{2+} 24 h	% Decrease in Pb^{2+} 48 h	% Competing ion removed
	---mg L^{-1}---			
Ni^{2+}	29	1.0	-0.2	30.1
Co^{2+}	29	0.5	0.2	14.5
Cu^{2+}	29	-2.0	3.3	55.2
Mg^{2+}	12	0.0	3.4	19.4
Cd^{2+}	54	25.0	25.6	70.2
Hg^{2+}	97	28.9	29.5	20.9
Fe^{3+}	27	35.3	27.9	43.4
Zn^{2+}	31	51.0	53.6	16.7
Pb^{2+}	10	--	--	72.4

0:1 were used (Table 2). Uptake rates for the Zn-Pb combined solutions yielded results comparable to the initial Pb concentration studies which seem to indicate that uptake is a function of the total Pb and Zn concentrations and that the plant is unable to distinguish between the two species.

Effect of Complexers on Uptake

Lead solutions (10 mg L^{-1}) were prepared which contained a 10-fold excess of one of the following complexers: NTA, HEDTA, EDTA, and CDTA (log K formation 11.34, 15.5, 17.88, and 20.24, respectively). Plants were then exposed to these solutions. The presence of strong complexers effectively eliminated the rapid uptake phase though the metal is still removed from solution (Table 3). The effect of various concentrations of EDTA was then evaluated. Table 4 lists the percent Pb remaining at 24 h for various EDTA:Pb ratios which shows that increasing the concentration of the complexer further reduces the overall rate of Pb removal. To determine if Pb initially removed could be stripped from the plant, plants were initially exposed to 10 mg Pb L^{-1} for 24 h and then transferred to a solution containing the same concentration of complexer as in the first study. A plot of percent Pb stripped vs. exposure time (Figure 6) indicated that up to 55% of the Pb initially removed can be stripped within 8 h in

TABLE 2. Effect of Zn on Pb uptake.

Zn:Pb ratio†	% Pb remaining, 24 h
100:1	88.5
10:1	62.3
1:1	26.0
0.1:1	24.7
0:1	24.4

†Molar ratio of Zn to Pb in solution, 10 mg Pb L^{-1}.

TABLE 3. Effect of complexers on Pb uptake.

Complexer†	% Pb Remaining 2 h	4 h	24 h	48 h
CDTA	99.7	95.2	95.0	92.4
EDTA	99.3	99.0	84.7	84.5
HEDTA	99.5	98.6	91.8	87.9
NTA	96.5	95.0	93.1	92.6
Control	78.2	67.1	15.3	15.0

†10-fold molar excess of a single complexer, 10 mg Pb L^{-1} Pb, pH = 7.

TABLE 4. Effect of EDTA on Pb uptake at 24 h, 10 mg Pb L^{-1}.

EDTA:Pb ratio	% Pb Remaining
100:1	97.6
10:1	95.0
1:1	89.2
0.1:1	60.0
0:1	54.7

the case of CDTA. However, this is followed by a slow reabsorption of the metal similar to the slow uptake phase observed in Figure 1.

DISCUSSION

The results presented agree well with earlier work with Cd and Zn (Hardy and O'Keeffe, 1985; Hardy and Raber, 1985; O'Keeffe and Hardy, 1984). As with these metals, Pb uptake is a biphasic, concentration process. The series of studies indicate that Pb, Cd and Zn uptake by the plant were very similar and the plant may not be able to distinguish between them. The fact that the rapid uptake phase decreases with increased Pb concentrations would seem to indicate the saturation of sites on the root. At low concentrations, initial uptake is rapid and cannot be eliminated by stirring suggesting that this phase is diffusion limited. The competing metal studies indicate that Pb uptake can be hindered by certain metal ions but not all. This would seem to indicate the presence of a specific site for Zn/Cd/Pb uptake. More complex studies show that it is not only possible to hinder Pb uptake but that up to half of the metal can be stripped from the plant. The fact that only a fraction of the Pb initially removed from solution can be stripped out suggests that the metal is translocated into the plant.

REFERENCES

Chigbo, F. E., R. W. Smith, and F. L. Shore. 1982. Uptake of arsenic, cadmium, lead and mercury from polluted waters by the water hyacinth. Environ. Pollut., Ser. A, 31-6.

Hardy, J. K., and D. H. O'Keeffe. 1985. Cadmium uptake by the water hyacinth: Effects of root mass, solution volume, complexers and other metal ions. Chemosphere 14:417-426.

Hardy, J. K., and N. B. Raber. 1985. Zinc uptake by the water hyacinth: Effect of solution factors. Chemosphere 14:1155-1166.

Hoagland, D. R., and D. I. Arnon. 1950. The water culture method for growing plants without soil. Calif. Agric. Exp. Stn. Circ. 347.

Keith, L. H., and Telliard. 1977. Priority pollutants I-A prospective view. Environ. Sci. & Tech. 13:416-420.

O'Keeffe, D. H., and J. K. Hardy. 1984. Cadmium uptake by the water hyacinth: Effects of solution factors. Environ. Pollut., Ser. A, 34:133-137.

Wolverton, B. C., and R. C. McDonald. 1978. Water hyacinth sorption rates of lead, mercury and cadmium. NASA ERL Report No. 170.

ABSORPTION OF ^{59}FE BY WATER HYACINTHS

R. A. Wills
School of Chemical Engineering
Oklahoma State University
Stillwater, Oklahoma 74078-0537

S. S. Pierson
P. O. Box 9347
Casper, Wyoming 82609

ABSTRACT

Radio-labeled ^{59}Fe was used to determine the distribution and uptake rates of Fe in water hyacinth (Eichhornia crassipes) roots, stems, and leaves in combination. While the experiments were run in both a batch and a continuous mode of operation, only the continuous mode is described. Discussion is made with respect to uptake rates, and alternative analytical techniques to verify the scintillation counting. Uptake rates varied from 0.14 to 1.3 mg Fe g^{-1} h^{-1} for plant combinations (whole plants).

Keywords: Heavy metal, water hyacinths, ^{59}Fe, absorption, isotope.

INTRODUCTION

Water hyacinth plants were studied for uptake of metals as a potential means of cleaning up some Fe-contaminated water sources in Oklahoma. Some of the most extensive water hyacinth research has been conducted by Wolverton and McDonald (1975). Their work on metal uptake began with studies on uptake of Cd and Ni by water hyacinth. Hyacinths were exposed to solutions containing cadmium chloride and nickel nitrate in concentrations from 0.92-6.1 mg L^{-1} water. Based on observed uptake levels and assuming an optimum growth rate of 60 g (dry wt) m^{-2} d^{-1}, 1 ha could remove 300 g metal d^{-1} (Wolverton et al., 1975). Maximum uptake levels observed were 0.176 g of Pb and 0.15 g of Hg from a static water system kg^{-1} of dry plant material (Wolverton and McDonald, 1975).

In a continuous system Wolverton and McDonald concluded that metals readily became chelated in the presence of organic chemicals that were also discharged into the system (Wolverton and McDonald, 1977).

ISBN 0-941463-00-1

Muramoto and Oki (1983) observed water hyacinth grown in solutions of low levels of Cd, Hg and Pb. Maximum levels of metals found in plants were 0.393 g Cd, 13.9 g Pb, and 2.34 g Hg, per kg^{-1} dry weight of plant material (Muramoto and Oki, 1983). Tatsuyama et al. (1977) studied uptake of Pb, Cd and Cu by the water hyacinth. Tokunga et al. (1976) reported hyacinths can be used for uptake of various concentrations of Cd. Adsorption of the Cd onto the hyacinth roots was significant. Total content of Cd in the roots and leaves by adsorption and absorption was 331-2420 mg and 20.5-1010 mg kg^{-1} (dry wt), respectively (Tokunga et al., 1976). Rosas et al. (1981) has reported hyacinths to concentrate, into the plant, Cd as high as 1000 to 10,000 times the concentration in their water. Low and Lee (1981) have examined water hyacinth absorption of cyanide. Wolverton and McDonald (1978) have studied metal uptake by hyacinths with combinations of metals. Chigbo et al. (1979) and Wolverton and McDonald (1975,1977) have studied the simultaneous absorption of different metals by water hyacinth.

With respect to tracer materials, McDonald (1981) exposed seven plant species to cesium, strontium, and cobalt. Cooley et al. (1978) have studied uptake rates of Mn, Fe and P by using radioactive elements. O'Keeffe et al. (1984) studied uptake of Cd of water hyacinth using a radio-tracer (Cd-109) by exposing plants to Cd concentrations ranging from 8.7 x 10^{-6} 8.65 g kg^{-1}. Their results show that hyacinths "could purify a 1000 mg L^{-1} incoming Cd concentration down to 0.000001 mg L^{-1}."

Various radio-tracer materials such as Cs, Sr, Co, Mn, Fe, P and Cd have been expanded to water hyacinth (Cooley et al., 1978; McDonald, 1981; O'Keeffe et al., 1984). O'Keeffe et al. (1984) postulated that water hyacinth should be able to reduce a 1000 mg L^{-1} incoming Cd concentration down to at least 0.000001 mg L^{-1} in a flow-through system.

MATERIALS AND METHODS

The experimental setup (Figure 1) operates in a continuous mode. The feed tank is a 680 L livestock water tank, coated with an epoxy paint and lined with plastic. The constant head reservoir was a 38 L glass aquarium. Both the feed tank and the constant head reservoir were covered with a N blanket. The N blanket was used to prevent atmospheric O_2 from reacting with the Fe in solution before the solution entered the process tanks. This reaction would cause ferric hydroxide to precipitate and the pH of the solution to become lower. The process tanks consisted of four 38 L glass aquaria in series, connected by plastic tubing. Each tank held approximately 32 L. The effluent stream flowed into a reservoir which was emptied daily.

The temperature of the process and feed tanks was controlled by heating tapes glued to the tanks. The temperature was maintained at 24 $\pm$ 1°C. The lighting cycle was 12 h on--12 h off.

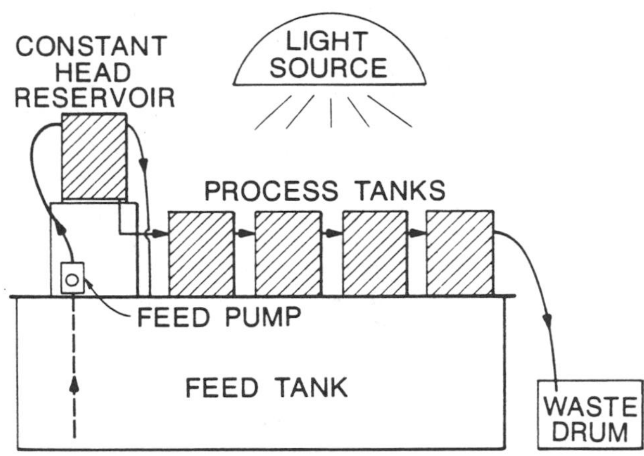

FIGURE 1. Experimental apparatus.

The lighting levels averaged 3000 ft candles over the process tanks. The flow rate through the process was set at 16 L d^{-1} with a residence time of 8 d.

Iron Solution

The feed tank was filled with 400 L of tap water, and heated to 24°C. The water was acidified to pH 5.0 with hydrochloric acid. Certified grade ferrous sulfate heptahydrate (796.4 g) was dissolved into the feed tank with extensive stirring, resulting in a uniform concentration of 400 mg Fe^{2+} L^{-1}.

The radioisotope ^{59}Fe was used to monitor Fe concentrations in both plant tissue and water of the system. One millicurie of ^{59}Fe was obtained from New England Nuclear as ferrous sulfate in a 0.05 M H_2SO_4 solution. The radioactive solution, approximately 1 mL, was dissolved into 1 L of acidified distilled water (pH 5.0) along with subsequent rinsings. This was added to the feed tank with extensive stirring. The cover was placed over the feed tank and the N blanket was initiated.

Plants

The water hyacinth plants used in this experiment were grown in a nutrient solution consisting of tap water and commercially available fertilizers in sealed livestock water tanks in an environmental chamber. Fresh plants of the small and medium biotypes, 500 g (wet wt), were placed in each tank of both biotypes ranged from 2.5 to 6.5 cm.

Sampling Techniques

The Fe solution was sampled twice daily corresponding with the lighting cycle of 12 h on--12 h off. The Fe sampling was monitored at the influent, tank 1, tank 2, tank 3, tank 4, and the effluent. The tanks were all sampled at the middle of the tank approximately 2.5 cm below the surface of the solution. The effluent was sampled from the receiving bucket. For all effluent samples, 0.5 mL was removed. The 0.5 mL sample was placed in a plastic Nalgene filmware tube along with 9.5 mL of Packard Insta-Gel liquid scintillation cocktail solution for counting in a Beckman liquid scintillation counter Model LS 7000.

Plant samples were removed from the process tanks as whole plants and allowed to drain for approximately one minute. Two or three plants were lightly wrapped in aluminum foil. Two or three more plants were divided into roots, stems, and leaves and the combined portions wrapped lightly in foil. The plant samples were dried at 103°C for 48 h.

The dried samples were ground first in a blender and then in a Wiley mill. A 0.1 mg sample was placed in a 100 mL beaker with 4 mL of nitric acid and digested for 8 h on a hot plate. One mL of 30% hydrogen peroxide was carefully added to the heated mixture and again after an additional hour. The mixture continued digesting for 1 h after the second addition of hydrogen peroxide.

The solution was transferred to a volumetric flask and diluted with distilled water to 5.0 mL until no solid material was visible. For liquid scintillation analysis, 0.5 mL of the digested sample was placed in a filmware tube along with 9.5 mL of Insta-Gel.

Plant samples were also analyzed in a Hach Chemical Company DR/2 colorimetric spectrophotometer. Ten to twenty µL of the digested sample were diluted to 25 mL into a sample cell. A prepackaged amount of Hach "ferrover" reagent was then added to the sample cell. After the sample cell was mixed, it was placed in the spectrophotometer. Iron content in mg L^{-1} was read from the Fe scale provided.

Three replicates were analyzed for each sampling period by colorimetric spectrophotometry. Four replicates were analyzed for each sampling period by liquid scintillation counting.

RESULTS AND DISCUSSION

No immediate effect on the water hyacinth was noticed on plants placed in the Fe solution (400 mg Fe^{+2} L^{-1}); however visible changes were noticed within 12 h. After 1 d of exposure, a ferric hydroxide coating on the roots became visible. Some of the leaf tips were slightly curled (yellow and/or brown) and the curled portions appeared dry and brittle. At 3 d of exposure, the ferric hydroxide coating on the roots was noticeably thicker. The leaves that had previously shown phytotoxic effects were curling, shrinking and turning brown down to the water lines. By 5 d of exposure, the ferric hydroxide coating on the roots was thicker. About two thirds of the leaves exhibited signs of stress. Finally, at 7 d of exposure, the root structure appeared unchanged. All parts of the plants exhibited phytotoxic effects of the harsh environment. Over half of the leaves appeared dead.

It was assumed that the ^{59}Fe was completely and evenly mixed into the solution. Furthermore, the ^{59}Fe was assumed to react chemically and physically the same as the bulk Fe.

The background levels of Fe in plants not exposed to the Fe solution were measured to be less than 0.5 mg g^{-1} dry wt whole plant. The background activity of hyacinths was not different from incidental background activity as analyzed by liquid scintillation counting.

Figures 2 and 3 represent Fe concentration increasing in plant tissue with time as analyzed by colorimetric spectrophotometry and liquid scintillation for roots, and whole plant. The results are presented as vertical bars through the high and low concentration points at each observation time. The data for each observation were replicates from the same samples.

To alleviate variations in relative proportions of plant parts sampled, a model plant was reconstructed from the analyzed portions. This typical plant was assumed to be, on a dry weight basis, 30% roots, 60% stems, and 10% leaves. These values were summed for the metal content of roots, stems, and leaves at each of the sampling times (Figure 4).

Different results were obtained with both analytical techniques (Figures 2 and 4). The liquid scintillation counting analysis provided consistently lower values of Fe content than the colorimetric spectrophotometry analysis.

The relatively low values obtained by the liquid scintillation counting analysis may have been the results of impurities in the sample placed in the cocktail solution, which

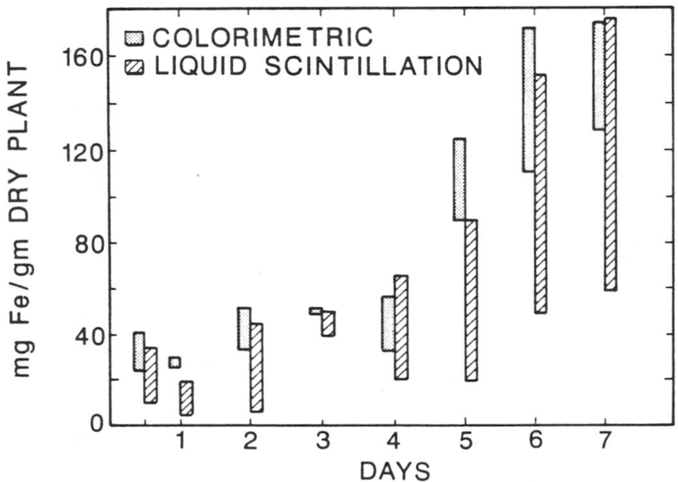

FIGURE 2. Accumulation of iron in the roots.

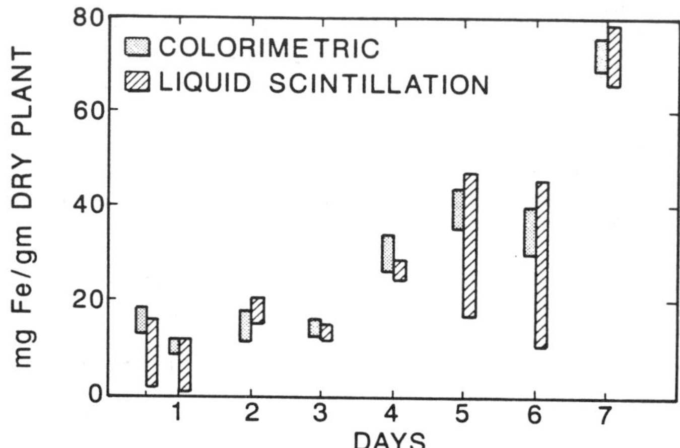

FIGURE 3. Accumulation of iron in whole plants.

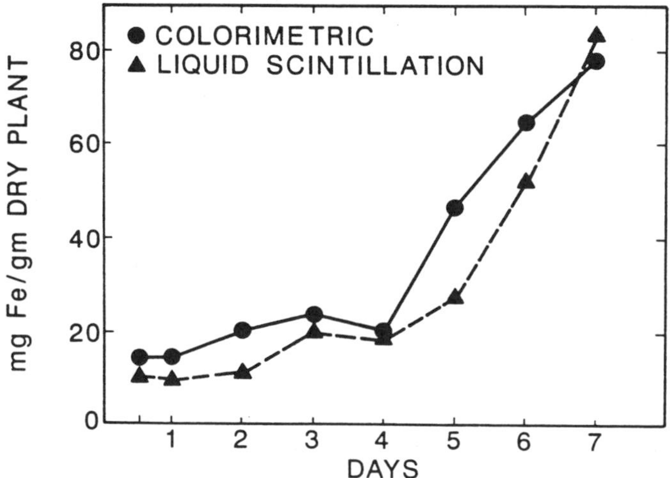

FIGURE 4. Accumulation of iron for a reconstructed whole plant.

causes a reduction in the number of counts per minute reported by the liquid scintillation counter.

The data obtained by either technique did not fit a perfect linear correlation, with the scintillation method having more scatter than the colorimetric method. This was thought to be due to many factors. First, the pH of the Fe solution dropped steadily throughout the experiment. The rates of both nutrient and toxin uptake by water hyacinths are partially dependent on the pH of the solution. Secondly, the plants sampled at a given time were harvested from only one aquarium for each of the eight sampling periods. Third O'Keeffe et al. (1984) suggest that a limited number of sites are available for cation exchange on the root structure. As these sites are saturated, a time lag occurs, that corresponds to the metal being translocated into the plant and reactivating the site. O'Keeffe observed hyacinths placed in a Cd solution for 48 h, transferred to a fresh nutrient solution for 48 h, then returned to the Cd solution for 48 h. At the first exposure to the Cd solution, a biphasic rate of uptake was observed. In the fresh nutrient solution, no Cd was released to the solution from the plant. At the second exposure to Cd solution, the plants exhibited the same biphasic uptake rate as the first exposure. This may indicate a "cycling" in the uptake rates, dependent upon the rates of saturation of cation exchange sites and subsequent translocation.

The Fe solution used in this experiment was chosen to chemically approximate the major characteristics of Tar Creek water. The N blanket over the liquid surfaces in the feed tank and the constant head reservoir was not completely effective at preventing the precipitation of ferric hydroxide before entering the process tanks. The concentration of Fe, and the pH, dropped steadily throughout the duration of the experiment, indicating that the precipitation reaction was occuring steadily. Iron concentration dropped from approximately 400 mg L^{-1} to 320 mg L^{-1} through the time of the experiment. Corresponding to the change in Fe concentration, pH dropped from approximately 4.3 to 2.8. Note the low pH probably contributed to the phytotoxicity but the authors feel that this was not the sole effect.

Most of the change in the Fe concentration and the pH can be attributed to the ferric hydroxide precipitation reaction. As the precipitation reaction progressed, ferric hydroxide was deposited in the feed tank, and in the constant head reservoir. In the process tanks, ferric hydroxide adhered to the tubing, and sides and bottom of the tanks. Although the Fe concentration dropped throughout the experiment, a significant change in concentration between the influent and effluent streams at any one time did not develop over the time frame of the experiment.

The effects of the water hyacinth on the Fe solution were complex. Iron in solution (Fe^{+2}) adhered to the roots of plants. Hyacinths pumped O_2 into the water which oxidized iron in solution and on the roots. Iron was absorbed into the root structure and translocated to the green parts of the plant.

The levels of Fe accumulated at 7 d exposure were unexpectedly high for all parts of the plant. The plants visually appeared dead, yet a surge of metal uptake appears to have occurred. Ashton et al. (1980) observed that dead plant material will leach out absorbed ions very quickly. From this, it would be expected that the curves of Fe accumulation with time would peak, then drop off quickly. Apparently, this peak was not reached. Further research to determine levels of Fe accumulated at 8, 9, 10 d or until this peak is reached would provide a better understanding of this process.

REFERENCES

Ashton, P. J., W. E. Scott, and D. J. Steyn. 1980. The chemical control of the water hyacinth [Eichhornia crassipes (Mart) Solms]. Prog. Wat. Tech. 12:865-882.

Chigbo, F. E., M. Clark, L. Thompson, and F. Shore. 1979. Simultaneous absorption of cadmium, lead, arsenic and mercury by water hyacinths. J. of the Mississippi Acad. of Sci. 24:13-31.

Cooley, T. N., M. H. Gonzalez, and D. F. Dean. 1978. Radio-manganese, -iron, -phosphorus uptake by water hyacinth and economic implications. Econ. Bot. 32:371-378.

Low, K. S., and C. K. Lee. 1981. Cyanide uptake by water hyacinth [Eichhornia crassipes (Mart) Solms]. Pertanika 4:122-128.

McDonald, R. C. 1981. Vascular plants for decontaminating radioactive water and soils. NASA Technical Memorandum TM-X-72740, August 1981.

Muramoto, S., and Y. Oki. 1983. Removal of some heavy metals from polluted water by water hyacinth (Eichhornia crassipes). Bull. of Environ. Contam. and Toxicol. 30:170-177.

O'Keeffe, D. H., J. K. Hardy, and R. A. Rao. 1984. Cadmium uptake by the water hyacinth: Effects of solution factors. Environ. Pollut. (Series A) 34:133-147.

Rosas, I., N. Baez, R. Belmont, and E. Gomez. 1981. "Eichhornia crassipes como un indicador de la presencia de cosmio." Rev. Geofiscia 12.

Tatsuyama, K., H. Edawu, and T. Yamagishi. 1977. Sorption of heavy metals by the water hyacinth from the metal solutions. Zasso Kenkyu 22:27-32.

Tokunga, T., N. Furuta, and M. Morimoto. 1976. Accumulation of cadmium in Eichhornia crassipes Solm. The J. of Hygienic Chemistry 22:234-239.

Wolverton, B. C. 1975. Water hyacinths for removal of cadmium and nickel from polluted water. NASA Tech. Memo. X-72721, February, 1975.

Wolverton, B. C., and R. C. McDonald. 1975. Water hyacinths and alligator weeds for removal of lead and mercury from polluted waters. NASA Tech. Memo. X-72723, April, 1975.

Wolverton, B. C., and R. C. McDonald. 1977. Wastewater treatment utilizing water hyacinths [Eichhornia crassipes (Mart) Solms]. Presented at the 1977 National Conference on Treatment and Disposal of Industrial Wastewater Residues, Houston, Texas, April 26-28, 1977.

Wolverton, B. C., and R. C. McDonald. 1978. Water hyacinth sorption rates of lead, mercury, and cadmium. NASA Tech. Memo. TM78-26715.

Wolverton, B. C., R. C. McDonald, and J. Gordan. 1975. Bio-conversion of water hyacinths into methane gas. Part I. NASA Tech. Memo. X-72725, July, 1985.

STUDIES ON EFFICACY OF EICHHORNIA CRASSIPES (MART) SOLMS IN REMOVING HEAVY METALS FROM AQUATIC MEDIUM AND THEIR EFFECTS ON THE PLANT TISSUES

K. Jamil, P. V. R. Rao, and M. Z. Jamil
Regional Research Laboratory
Hyderabad 500 007
INDIA

ABSTRACT

Laboratory studies were conducted to evaluate the efficacy of water hyacinth in removing Cu^{2+}, Fe^{2+}, Cd^{2+}, Zn^{2+} and Cr^{6+} from the aquatic medium. Histological studies on the petiole and leaf sections demonstrated that the extent of damage varied with each metal or a combination of metals. Water hyacinths also demonstrated an ability to neutralize acidic solutions with pH values ranging from 4.8 to 7.4.

Keywords: Histological studies, heavy metals, plant tissues, wastewater.

INTRODUCTION

Recent research on water hyacinths (*Eichhornia crassipes*) ability to remove heavy metals from waste effluents has received considerable attention in recent years (Cooley and Martin, 1977, Cooley et al., 1979; Haider et al., 1981; Mohammaud, 1984; and Jamil et al., 1985). The plant's role in combating aquatic pollution has led us to investigate the response of the plant to heavy metal uptake, tolerance, and transport in various tissues. The objective of this study was to determine the effects of water hyacinth on pH of aquatic mediums containing heavy metals.

MATERIALS AND METHODS

Experimental Procedures

Water hyacinths were grown outdoors and in the laboratory. For each study, plants described as Type III were used. The plants were thoroughly cleaned and placed in various heavy metal ion solutions, and acidic and alkaline solutions of known concentration. Cross sections of roots and petioles of the

ISBN 0-941463-00-1

treated and control plants were made at different time intervals and the preparations were examined for histological damage in different tissues of plants, by phase contrast microscopy.

Preparation of Tissues for Histological Studies

Portions of the roots, petioles and leaves about 1-2 cm in length were cut and fixed in Carnoy's fluid (ethylalcohol and acetic acid in 3:1 ratio). After fixing the tissues for 1-2 h, thin sections of about 1-2 cell thickness were cut. These sections were then stained with 0.5% safronin and dehydrated with different grades of alcohol and fixed in glycerine. Slides were prepared by sealing these sections with Canada bolsom or DPX. Going through clearing agent had to be omitted as the sections tended to shrink and precipitate was formed. These sections were then examined under microscope and observations were recorded.

Preparation of Heavy Metal Solutions

Stock solutions of 4000 mg L^{-1} of heavy metals were prepared by dissolving copper nitrate, cadmium sulphate, zinc chloride, ferric chloride and potassium dichromate in distilled water. Working solutions were prepared from the stock either individually or as mixtures of various combinations such as Cu^{2+} + Zn^{2+} + Fe^{3+}, Cu^{2+} + Cd^{2+}, Cd^{2+} + Cr^{6+} in 1:1 ratios. Nitric acid (strong acid) acetic acid and benzoic acid (weak acids) and sodium carbonate solutions of varying pH were used. The initial pH of all the solutions was measured and subsequent pH change was recorded at regular intervals after placing the plants in the medium.

RESULTS

Effect of Water Hyacinth on pH of Organic Acids (Acetic and Benzoic Acid)

Water hyacinths placed in organic acid solutions of pH 3.5 showed deletorious effects on the plant morphology resulting in the eventual death of the plants. But the plants placed in the acid with pH 4.02 and 4.20 appeared to be affected slightly,

TABLE 1. Effect of water hyacinth on pH (a) acetic acid (b) benzoic acid.

Time (h)	pH						
	Control	a	b	a	b	a	b
0	6.34	3.54	3.50	4.21	4.05	5.28	4.65
1	6.61	3.60	3.72	4.24	4.31	5.32	4.87
24	7.26	3.70	3.88	4.52	6.00	6.79	6.67
48	7.10	3.72	3.88	4.53	6.36	6.79	6.67
72	7.15	4.15	4.42	6.45	6.86	7.25	7.00

acetic acid at pH 4.2 showed more harmful effects than those placed in benzoic acid of the same pH. Measurements of the pH levels indicated that water hyacinth plants growing in either acidic or alkaline water had a tendency to change the pH towards neutrality.

Effect of Water Hyacinth on pH of Nitric Acid (Strong Acid)

Nitric acid of pH 3.0 and 3.6 (Table 2) had toxic effect on the plant vigor and growth. Mortality of the plants was observed within a week. Plants placed in nitric acid medium of higher pH i.e. 5.7 were better survivors, however, wilting of the plants was observed after a week in the acidic medium.

Water Hyacinth's Effect on Individual Metal Ions

Water hyacinth plants were able to raise the pH of the medium (Table 3). Fe^{3+} ion solutions which had a very low hydrogen ion concentration, exhibited maximum toxic effects on the plants, whereas the other metal ions Cu^{2+}, Cd^{2+} and Zn^{2+} did not affect the plant morphology and growth continued. The plants exhibited a capacity to raise the pH of the medium in which they were placed.

Water Hyacinth's Effect on Mixture of Metal Ions

Mixtures of (1:1) Cu^{2+} + Cd^{2+} + Cr^{6+}, Cu^{2+} + Zn^{2+} ions did not affect plant vigor, growth and morphology as in the case of individual ions (Table 4). The plants also raised the pH of the medium in which they were placed. However, Cu^{2+} + Fe^{2+} mixture had a toxic effect on the plant, causing severe leaf and stem damage.

TABLE 2. Effect of water hyacinth on pH on nitric acid (strong acid).

Time	pH			
(h)	Control	1	2	3
0	7.16	3.05	3.65	5.75
1	7.57	3.24	3.80	6.06
2	7.70	3.06	3.80	6.98
3	7.26	3.06	3.80	6.00
4	7.10	3.28	3.84	6.02
5	7.07	3.30	3.86	6.18
6	7.13	3.30	3.85	6.18
24	7.16	3.10	4.15	6.26
48	7.30	3.60	4.94	6.63
72	7.20	3.40	4.94	6.63
144	7.50	4.29	5.30	6.75

TABLE 3. Changes in pH of metal ion solutions with water hyacinth, concentration = 5 mg L^{-1}.

Time (h)	pH				
	Cu^{2+}	Cd^{2+}	Zn^{2+}	Fe^{2+}	Control
0	6.01	4.10	4.02	3.27	6.78
0.5	6.19	4.10	4.15	3.28	--
1	6.19	4.10	4.15	3.28	--
2	6.26	4.10	4.35	3.35	6.77
3	6.26	4.10	4.38	3.35	--
4	6.26	4.10	4.51	3.35	6.55
5	6.26	5.95	4.58	3.38	--
6	6.26	5.95	4.70	3.40	--
24	6.37	6.24	5.48	3.39	6.79
48	6.52	6.32	5.96	3.53	--
72	6.53	6.50	6.15	3.60	6.78
96	6.60	6.70	6.28	3.64	--
120	6.60	7.02	6.34	3.60	6.79

TABLE 4. Water hyacinth's effect on mixture of metal ions.

Time (h)	Concentration ratio 1:1				
	pH				
	Cu^{2+}+ Zn^{2+}	Cu^{2+}+ Fe^{2+}	Cu^{2+}+ Cd^{2+}	Cd^{2+}+ Cr^{6+}	Control
0	3.12	2.67	5.91	5.15	6.79
1	3.16	2.69	5.92	5.18	--
2	3.33	2.69	5.92	5.15	6.81
3	3.33	2.69	5.92	5.17	--
4	3.81	2.82	5.94	5.45	6.86
5	4.05	3.10	5.92	5.35	--
6	4.05	3.10	5.92	5.35	6.83
24	4.30	3.33	5.92	5.40	--
48	4.72	3.32	6.39	5.81	6.90
144	5.94	3.30	6.74	6.30	6.82

Water Hyacinth's Effect on Alkaline (Na_2CO_3) Solution

The effect of water hyacinth on Na_2CO_3 solution is presented in Table 5. The plants placed in a medium of pH 10.0 did not survive for long. Wilting was observed within 3 d and mortality was observed within a week. The water hyacinth plants slightly lowered the pH of the medium in which they were placed. The pH values came closer towards neutrality. The growth and vigor of the plants continued to be normal.

Effect of Heavy Metals on the Plant Tissues

Histological examination of the petiole and leaf sections of water hyacinth plants treated with individual and mixtures of

TABLE 5. Water hyacinth's effect on alkaline Na_2CO_3 solution.

Time (h)	pH			
	Control	1	2	3
0	7.73	8.66	9.05	10.01
1	7.75	8.34	7.78	9.90
2	7.59	8.23	8.78	9.85
3	7.32	8.18	8.58	9.85
4	7.32	8.03	8.58	9.85
5	7.30	8.10	8.46	9.85
6	7.45	8.11	8.40	9.90
24	6.94	7.64	7.68	9.78
48	6.66	7.48	7.58	10.01
72	6.99	7.56	7.51	9.78

heavy metals showed interesting results. The uptake of the metal ions and its transport through xylem to other parenchymatous tissues was observed at various time intervals. The plants appeared to have deposits of heavy metals in the hypodermal cells, stellate tissue, collenchyma, parenchyma and epidermal cells. Six hours after heavy metal treatment, it was observed that starch granules diminished and raphides were knocked off from the plant tissues. A thickening of vascular bundles was also observed. Those plants which were not affected by acidic pH conditions did not show visible morphological damage, however, internally the calcium oxalate structures (raphides) were considerably reduced.

DISCUSSION

The pH buffering ability of water hyacinth has been noted earlier. Measurements of the initial and final pH levels indicated that water hyacinth plants growing in either acid or alkaline water had a tendency to change the pH towards neutrality. Except Cu^{2+} (6.01) all the other heavy metal ion solutions, like Cd^{2+}, Zn^{2+} and Fe^{3+} are initially highly acidic with 4.10, 4.02 and 3.27 pH respectively. The hydrogen ion which is present in aqueous systems markedly influences living systems. It is known that some relationship between respiration and water uptake along with the diurnal periodicity in root pressure has been taken as a proof for a mechanism more directly dependent on metabolism. Water hyacinth gradually raised the pH of its medium over a period of time indicating a possible physiological adjustment. Maximum adjustment of pH was brought about by the plant within 48 h in all the experiments. In case of Fe solutions the plant could not neutralize the highly acidic solution and succumbed to it. Death occurred after a week. This could be due to the oxidative stress caused by Fe. Sohal et al. (1985) have reported the oxidative stress of Fe in animal systems. When mixtures of heavy metal solutions were used the efficiency of water hyacinth plants in neutralizing the pH of Cu^{2+} containing solutions remained the same with all the three combinations (Cd^{2+}, Zn^{2+} and Fe^{3+}). Cu^{2+} in the mixtures appeared to have antagonistic effect on Zn^{2+} and Fe^{3+} and no effect on Cd^{2+} neutralization. Cr^{6+} also demonstrated antagonistic effect on Cd^{2+} neutralization. The plant's efficiency in neutralizing the three different acid solutions varied. Between acetic acid and nitric acid, the variation is less, but for benzoic acid it is more than that of the other two. However, Eichhornia plants were more efficient in neutralizing the heavy metal solutions than pure acidic or alkaline solutions. Neutralizing capacity of the plant was found to be more for Zn^{2+} solution followed by Cd^{2+} and Cu^{2+}. This may be due to the more rapid uptake of Zn^{2+} than of Cd^{2+} and Cu^{2+}.

Toxicity of the heavy metal ions is known to depend chiefly on the activation of vital enzymes and the heavy metal sensitivity of enzymes is element specific and the avoidance mechanisms offer protection which can be very effective (Larcher, 1980). Jamil et al. (1983) reported the inhibition of calcium oxalate precipitation and the raphide reduction in water hyacinth plants treated with heavy metals. It is likely that calcium is released into the medium due to the reduction of raphides which may be responsible for neutralizing the pH of the medium. An increase in the K^+ concentration in the formic acid containing medium after growing water hyacinth plants is reported by Rajan et al. (1983). Dehydrogenases present in the roots may remove hydrogen and act as electron transferring agents thus contributing to the neutralization of the medium.

ACKNOWLEDGMENTS

We are thankful to our Director (RRL-H) for providing facilities and we acknowledge the help and suggestions of Dr. G. Thyagarajan for this investigation.

REFERENCES

Cooley, T. N., and D. F. Martin. 1977. Factors affecting the distribution of trace elements in aquatic plant water hyacinth. J. Inorg. Nucl. Chem. 39:1893-1896.

Cooley, T. N., D. F. Martin, W. C. Durden, and B. D. Perking. 1979. A preliminary study of metal distribution in three water hyacinth biotypes. Water Res. 13:343-348.

Haider, S. Z., K. N. A. Malik, and M. M. Rahnan. 1981. Pollution control by water hyacinth and determination of its tolerance index. J. Bangladesh Academy of Science 5:105-107.

Jamil, K., V. Vinay Kumar, and G. Thyagarajan. 1983. Histological damage of Eichhornia crassipes due to heavy metal uptake. Proceedings of the International Conference on Water Hyacinth. Feb. 7-11, Hyderabad, India. Commonwealth Sciences Council, Vol. I. p. 237-242.

Jamil, K., M. Z. Jamil, P. V. R. Rao, and G. Thyagarajan. 1985. The role of water hyacinth in abating aquatic pollution. Pollut. Res. 4:67-75.

Larcher, W. 1980. Physiological Plant Ecology. 2nd ed. Translated by M. A. Biederman-Torson Springer Verlag, Berlin, Aeidelberg, NY. p. 192.

Mohammaud, W. I. 1984. Level of zinc, manganese, iron and cadmium in three species of seegram from aquata (Jordan). Aquat. Bot. 20:179-183.

Rajan, V. R., E. Marayya, Ch. Rao, and B. B. Raju. 1983. Treatment of formic acid effluent using water hyacinth. Proceedings of the International Conference on Water Hyacinth. Feb. 7-11, Hyderabad, India. Commonwealth Science Council, 2:664-675.

Sohal, R. S., R. G. Allen, K. J. Farner, and R. K. Newton. 1985. Iron induced oxidative stress and may alter the rate of aging in the housefly, Musca domestica. Mechanisms of Aging and Development 32:33-38.

DISTRIBUTION AND ACCUMULATION OF ZINC IN TYPHA LATIFOLIA

G. Blake
Laboratoire d'Ecologie
Universite de Savoie
B.P. 1104, 73011 Chambery
FRANCE

J. Gagnaire-Michard
Centre d'Etudes Nucleaires de Grenoble, D.R.F.
Laboratoire de Biologie Vegetale
Avenue des Martyrs, 38041 Grenoble
FRANCE

B. Kirassian
Agence Francaise pour la Maitrise de l'Energie
Service Biomasse
27 rue Louis Vicat, 75015 Paris
FRANCE

P. Morand
Centre de Recherche en Ecologie Marine et Aquaculture
C.N.R.S. L'Houmeau
Case 5-F 17 137, Nieul-sur-Mer
FRANCE

ABSTRACT

The distribution and accumulation of $^{65}Zn(ZnCl_2$ and Zn-EDTA) in *Typha latifolia* was studied under controlled conditions. The concentration of Zn in the culture medium decreased rapidly during the first 10 d. The top 2.5 cm layer of the sediment became enriched with Zn; highest concentrations were found in the roots, especially in superficial roots which contained 150 to 1400 mg kg^{-1}, accounting for up to 75% of added Zn. Differences in the incorporation and migration of $ZnCl_2$ compared to Zn-EDTA in various parts of the plant were also demonstrated.

Keywords: Metal, zinc, *Typha latifolia*, sediments, cattails.

ISBN 0-941463-00-1

INTRODUCTION

In the last ten years, macrophytes have been studied extensively with regard to their use as indicators of pollution (Beeftink et al., 1982; Empain, 1976; Taylor and Crowder, 1983) and as water purifiers (Blake and DuBois, 1982; Tourbier and Pierson, 1976; Seidel et al., 1978). These investigations, however, often did not fully consider the physiological mechanisms involved in the exchange of chemical substances in these species, leading to inadequate interpretation of results.

Zinc (Zn) is an element that is increasingly contaminating the natural environment and originates from such sources as mines, industrial wastewater, fertilizers, dyes, tires, oil, etc. In particular, the contamination of water may occur via direct pollution of water bodies, by precipitation, and through surface runoff. The toxic effect of Zn on aquatic plants has been demonstrated several times, particularly in the fresh water plant *Elodea canadensis*, where Brown and Rattigan (1979) found that photosynthetic activity was reduced when Zn concentrations in the environment exceeded 8 mg L^{-1}.

Typha latifolia appears to be able to absorb and tolerate high levels on Zn (McNaughton et al., 1974). This plant grows very rapidly and possesses a large capacity for assimilating mineral compounds (Blake et al., 1984); we therefore selected it for studying Zn assimilation.

METHODS

Typha latifolia plants, grown in a pollution free site, were individually taken from the clay at the end of winter. Principal stems were cut with 20 cm of rhizome, cleaned, the roots scarred and the cut part sealed with putty. The plants were transplanted into small polythene containers in a growth chamber (sun-like lighted with a 14-10 h photoperiod), at the Centre for Nuclear Studies (C.E.A.) in Grenoble.

The underground part of the macrophyte was immersed in liquid medium Hoagland solution (per liter: $Ca(NO_3)\ 4H_2O$, 0.95 g; KNO_3, 0.3 g; KH_2PO_4, 0.03 g; NH_4NO_3, 0.16 g; $MgSO_4$, 0.49 g, H_3BO_3, 0.286 mg; $MgCl_2\ 4\ H_2O$, 0.14 mg; $CuCl_2\ 2H_2O$, 0.08 mg ; $FeSO_4\ 7\ H_2O$, 28 mg ; Fe-EDTA, 58.5 mg) and, depending on the series, with or without washed sand sediment (Table 1). The volume of the solution was maintained throughout the experiment and its composition adjusted weekly. The pH was controlled during the experiments--in presence of sediments, the levels were: 7.1 $\pm$ 0.1 for the series n° 1 and 7.3 $\pm$ 0.1 for series n° 2; whereas in hydroponic culture, the pH level was near 5.5. The redox potential was also measured, it showed constant values for the experiments and vertical distribution ranged from 150 to 400 mV.

There were three series of experiments. In each of eight small tanks containing radioactive ^{65}Zn, in some the Zn was as

TABLE 1. Treatments studied to evaluate Zn translocation in *Typha latifolia* (S = with sediment; H = hydroponic).

Conditions	Zn shape	Zn	Liquid volume (1)	Specific activity	Number of containers
		mg L^{-1}		µci mg Zn^{-1}	
S (control)	$ZnCl_2$	0.1	10	--	1
H (control)	$ZnCl_2$	0.1	20	--	1
Preliminary					
H	$ZnCl_2$	1.0	20	10.0	2
H	$ZnCl_2$	10.0	20	10.0	1
H	Zn-EDTA	1.0	20	10.0	2
H	Zn-EDTA	10.0	20	10.0	1
S	$ZnCl_2$	1.0	10	10.0	2
Series I					
S	$ZnCl_2$	10.0	10	3.0	3
S	Zn-EDTA	10.0	10	4.2	3
H_1	$ZnCl_2$	10.0	20	1.5	1
H_1	Zn-EDTA	10.0	20	2.1	1
Series II					
S	$ZnCl_2$	10.0	10	3.4	3
S	Zn-EDTA	10.0	10	3.7	3
H_2	$ZnCl_2$	12.4	20	15.0	1
H_2	Zn-EDTA	14.0	20	18.0	1

Zinc chloride ($ZnCL_2$) while in others Zn was complexed with a metal chelator EDTA (Zn-EDTA). Chelated Zn is less accessible thus making experimental conditions closer to natural ones than when the metal is absorbed or complexed with different compounds. The preliminary experiments allowed us to observe physiological aspects of the exchanges inside the plant. In this series, controls without Zn were also included. In the two following series, the *Typha* sp. cultures were maintained.

The Zn was labelled with ^{65}Zn, as in other experiments (Baudin, 1977). Each experimental tank received 100 mL of the Zn solution (mixed radioactive and stable Zn). The concentrations of the Zn at the beginning of the experiment were 0.1, 1 and 10 mg kg^{-1}. A sheet of polythene placed on the bottom and sides of each pot permitted the measurement of Zn absorbed on the inner surfaces. The radioactivity (γ) of the different biological samples or of the surrounding media was measured by a sodium iodide detector. A correction which allows for the radioactive decay was systematically applied. The results are expressed in mg L^{-1} of Zn (both radioisotope and carrier) relative to the dry weight of the analyzed material.

RESULTS AND DISCUSSION

Removal of Zinc from the Culture Medium

The sediment was the most important medium for the removal of introduced Zn. Removal was considerable in the first few days of the experiment, and greater for $ZnCl_2$ than the EDTA complex of Zn (Figure 1). Removal of Zn from the two sources, i.e. $ZnCl_2$ and Zn-EDTA, followed the equation shown below:

$$C = C_o \ (1 + t/a)^n$$

where: $14 < a < 27$ $ZnCl_2$; $777 < a < 59{,}000$ Zn-EDTA; $-0.71 < n < -0.53$ $ZnCl_2$; $-127 < n < -4$ Zn-EDTA.

The decrease in Zn in the culture medium was more regular and linear than in experiments without sediments. In fact, experiments with sediments showed a more rapid decrease in concentration as a result of precipitation and adsorption of Zn by sediments. With $ZnCl_2$, only 20% of the metal was found in the culture medium after 10 d.

The capacity of sediments to accumulate heavy metals has been studied previously (Forstner and Wittmann, 1979; Forstner and Salomons, 1981) and the important role of sediments in this study is evident from the results presented in Figure 1. The gradient distribution of Zn in the sediments showed that a major proportion

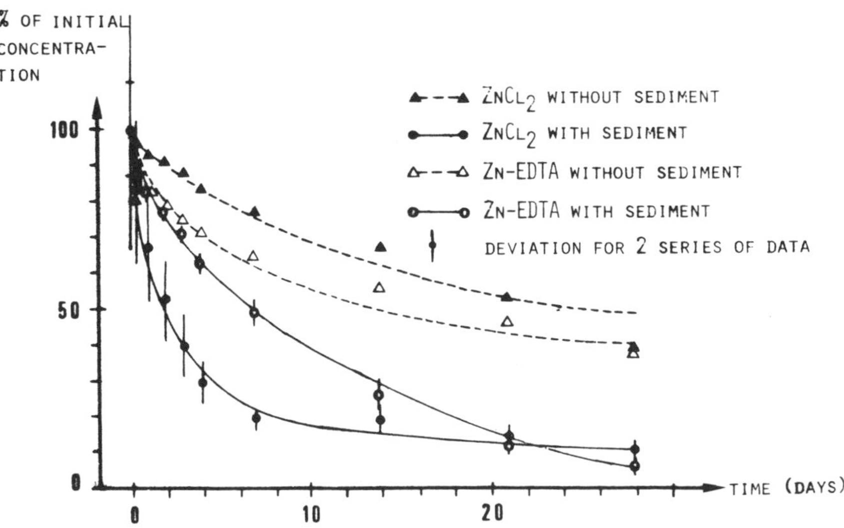

FIGURE 1. Disappearance elimination of Zn from the culture medium containing Typha latifolia.

was found at the surface of the sediment. These data also show that the distribution of the metal depends on the form of applied Zn. A greater proportion was detected at the sediment-water interface when $ZnCl_2$ was added. The top 0.2 cm of sediment had a concentration 2.5 higher than the sediment at 0.2-1.0 cm.

In the case of Zn-EDTA, Zn remained for a longer period in the culture medium and a greater percentage of Zn (33-53%) was extracted with NH_4^+-acetate, indicating a labile pool. This exchangeable fraction of Zn may represent the quantity that can be released in the sediments by percolating water (Duchaufour, 1960).

Distribution of Metal in Typha Latifolia

At the end of experiments, the concentration of ^{65}Zn in the different parts of plants (rhizomes, young or old leaves, roots) (Figure 2). The underground plant parts were the most enriched with Zn, especially the superficial root system directly exposed to metal concentration of sediments. Bristow (1975) has shown the particular role of these roots in the metabolism of the whole plant. After one month of contact with sediment (initial concentration of Zn in the medium was 10 mg kg^{-1}), we measured 200 mg kg^{-1} (Zn introduced as Zn-EDTA) and 1400 mg kg^{-1} (Zn introduced as $ZnCl_2$) in the roots (Series 1). Decreasing concentrations were found in the following order: roots > rhizomes and immersed parts of leaves > aerial leaves.

The leaves of the main plant retained more than 50% of the accumulated metal in this segment of the plant (Figure 2). The exterior leaves of the main plant (particularly the submerged parts) accumulated the highest levels of Zn. These plant parts were more active during the time when the Zn concentration was high in the culture medium. In other words, these old leaves contained a greater percentage of membranes in the composition of the organic matter and these elements retained the metal. In contrast, the new plants had highest levels of Zn in the inner and younger leaves which had not fully developed by the time of Zn additions. This distribution was due to the exchange of Zn by rhizomes from the older parts to the younger ones.

When Zn-EDTA was used, the transfer of metal from the roots to the leaves was more significant, but the total amount of Zn assimilated by the plant decreased. The increase of Zn in the culture medium (1 to 10 mg L^{-1}) resulted in a smaller increase in the concentration of the metals inside the different segments of *Typha latifolia* (Table 2). Under these experimental culture conditions, the biomass density of the plant was low, 1600 g m^{-2} and 1300 g m^{-2} for $ZnCl_2$ and Zn-EDTA, respectively (Tables 3a and 3b). As for the distribution of the metal in the plant, the percentage of Zn-EDTA of the young and old leaves is more important (43%) than the percentage of Zn introduced as $ZnCl_2$ (25%) (Table 3b).

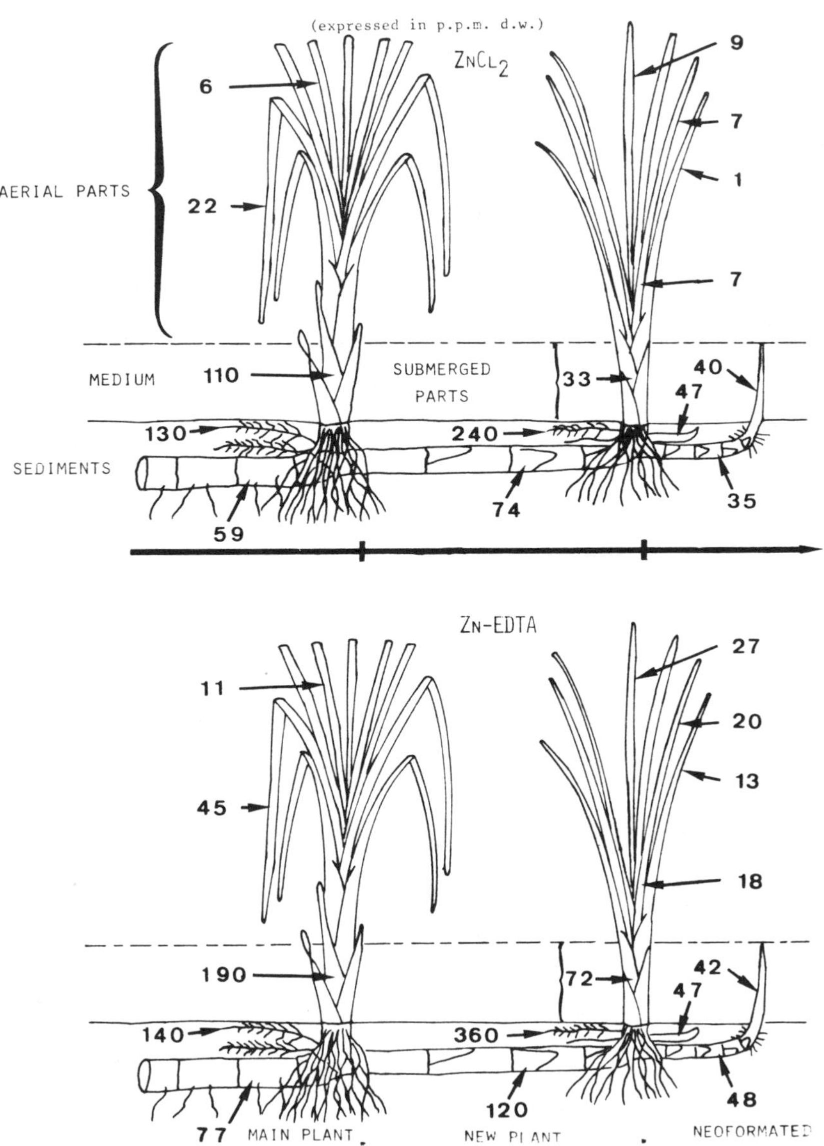

FIGURE 2. Distribution of Zn in plants (Series II).

TABLE 2. Comparative increases of concentrations of Zn in plants/initial concentration in culture medium.

		Main Plant		New Plant		
Zn Compound	Concentration	Roots	Rhizome	Roots	Rhizome	Leaves
		-----μg Zn g^{-1} of tissue (dry wt)-----				
Zn Chloride	1 mg L^{-1} (A)	650	100	2500	390	68
	10 mg L^{-1} (B)	2400	270	3600	1800	250
	Ratio (B)/(A)	3.7	2.7	1.4	4.6	3.7
Zn-EDTA	1 mg L^{-1} (C)	310	26	380	200	30
	10 mg L^{-1} (D)	1000	80	1500	1100	350
	Ratio (D)/(C)	3.2	3.1	3.9	5.5	11.7

TABLE 3a. Culture of *Typha latifolia* on sediment with Zn chloride.

	Biomass			Total Zn Uptake		
	g $plant^{-1}$	g m^{-2}	% of total	mg $plant^{-1}$	mg m^{-2}	%
Main plant leaves	22.46 ±0.07	641.7 ±2.1	39.7 ±0.1	0.36-0.84	16.5	20
Submerged parts of leaves	2.93 ±0.03	83.6 ±0.7	5.2 ±0.04	0.24-0.42	9.4	12
New plant leaves	6.67 ±0.07	190.3 ±1.7	11.8 ±0.1	0.10-0.18	3.9	5
Submerged parts of Main plant	2.23 ±0.03	63.6 ±0.7	3.9 ±0.04	0.07-0.12	2.7	3
underground parts	12.29 ±0.06	351.2 ±1.4	21.7 ±0.1	0.56-1.50	26.9	33
New plant	15.18 ±0.10	433.7 ±2.3	26.8 ±0.1	0.79-1.48	33.7	42
Underground parts with new organs	5.21 ±0.04	149.0 ±0.09	9.2 ±0.05	0.15-0.23	5.3	6
TOTAL	56.69 ±0.30	1616.9 ±7.5		1.81-4.0	81.0	

CONCLUSIONS

The experiments conducted in this study on the incorporation of ^{65}Zn by *Typha latifolia* in simplified ecosystems have shown that the uptake of the metal depends on the form in which it is introduced. The removal of Zn from water was more rapid for the chloride form than for Zn-EDTA, because of the precipitation and adsorption of $ZnCl_2$ on sediment particles.

The sediments were the major components for this removal. As Zn tended to accumulate in the first centimeters of the sediments of aquatic systems, it was logical to use this rooted macrophyte

TABLE 3b. Culture of Typha latifolia on sediment with Zn-EDTA.

	Biomass			Total Zn Uptake		
	g plant^{-1}	g m^{-2}	% of total	mg plant^{-1}	mg m^{-2}	%
Main plant leaves	12.70 ±0.06	513.7 ±2.7	40.5 ±0.2	0.53-1.10	32.3	34
Submerged parts of leaves	2.10 ±0.02	84.9 ±1.0	6.7 ±0.07	0.25-0.55	15.9	17
New plant leaves	5.34 ±0.06	215.9 ±2.1	17.0 ±0.2	0.10-0.25	7.2	8
Submerged parts of leaves	1.37 ±0.02	55.2 ±0.7	4.4 ±0.06	0.06-0.15	4.0	4
Main plant underground parts	5.49 ±0.03	222.2 ±1.2	17.5 ±0.09	0.30-0.59	19.3	21
New plant	7.82 ±0.06	316.8 ±2.2	25.0 ±0.2	0.64-1.11	35.4	37
Underground parts with new organs	3.82 ±0.03	154.8 ±1.0	12.2 ±0.08	0.16-0.24	7.4	8
TOTAL	31.35 ±0.21	1268 ±8.2		1.57-3.05	94.2	

(with numerous superficial roots) to remove it. The quantity of metal removed from the system by the aboveground segments of the plants (after one year of culture) remained low in comparison to the high concentration of metal in the roots and the rhizomes (200 to 1400 mg kg^{-1} for an initial concentration of 10 mg L^{-1} in culture medium).

Since 25 to 30% of the Zn potentially could be released from the decomposed leaves in the first days of immersion (Blake, 1979; Blake et al., 1984), it is necessary to cut and harvest the plant, as this technique allows the export of 25 to 42% of the Zn accumulated in Typha latifolia and prevents the leaching of the metal from decaying organic matter. With regard to stabilized populations, the biomass density of the leaves was low, compared to the biomass of underground parts.

ACKNOWLEDGMENTS

This work was supported by the French Ministere of Environment (contract 82107). The authors sincerely thank Dr. Ray Barlow for critical reading of the manuscript.

REFERENCES

Baudin, J. P. 1977. Transfert du zinc 65 dans un ecosysteme saumatre (l'etang de Citis). These Doct. 3eme Cycle, Univ. Aix-Marseille. 165 pp.

Beeftink, W. G., J. Nieuwenhuize, M. Stoeppler, and C. Mohl. 1982. Heavy-metal accumulation in salt marshes from the western and eastern Scheldt. Sci. Total Environ. 25:199-223.

Blake, G. 1979. Decomposition of macrophytes with uniformly C 14 labelled plant material. Arch. Hydrobiol. 85(3):326-335.

Blake, G. 1985. Les macrophytes lacustres: Production et decomposition. These d'Etat de l'Univ. de Grenoble, 2 vol.

Blake, G., and J. P. DuBois. 1982. L'epuration des eaux par les plantes aquatiques. AFEE. 103 pp.

Blake, G., J. Gagnaire-Michard, and B. Kirassian. 1984. Accumulation du zinc (65 Zinc) par une macrophyte: *Typha latifolia*. Sc. de l'eau 3:241-248.

Bristow, J. M. 1975. The structure and function of roots in aquatic vascular plants. p. 221-236. *In* J. G. Torrey and D. T. Clarkson (ed.) The Development and Function of Roots. Academic Press.

Brown, B. T., and B. M. Rattigan. 1979. Toxicity of soluble copper and other metal ions to *Elodea canadensis*. Environ. Pollut. 20:303-313.

Duchaufour, P. 1960. Precis de Pedologie, Masson. 482 pp.

Empain, A. 1976. Les bryophytes aquatiques utilises comme traceurs de la contamination en metaux lourds des eaux douces. Mem. Soc. R. Bot. Belg. 7:141-156.

Forstner, U., and W. Salomons. 1981. Trace metal analysis on polluted sediments. Delft Hydraulics Lab Publ. N° 248. p. 1-13.

Forstner, U., and G. T. W. Wittmann. 1979. Metal pollution in the aquatic environment. Springer, Berlin Heidelberg. New York. 486 pp.

McNaughton, S. J., T. C. Folsom, T. Lee, F. Park, C. Price, D. Roeder, J. Schmitz, and C. Stockell. 1974. Heavy metal tolerance in *Typha latifolia* without the evolution of tolerance races. Ecology 55:1163-1165.

Seidel, K., H. Happel, and G. Graue. 1978. Contributions to revitalization of water. Stiftung Limnologische Arbeitsgruppe Dr. C. V. Seidel , Meersburg, West Germany.

Taylor, G. J., and A. A. Crowder. 1983. Uptake and accumulation of heavy metals by *Typha latifolia* in wetlands of the Sudbury, Ontario region. Can. J. Bot. 61:63-73.

Tourbier, J., and R. W. Pierson. 1976. Biological control of water pollution. University of Pennsylvania Press, Philadelphia, PA. 211 pp.

REMOVAL OF COPPER AND LEAD USING A THIN-FILM TECHNIQUE

F. E. Dierberg
Department of Environmental Science and Engineering
Florida Institute of Technology
Melbourne, Florida 32901

T. A. DeBusk
Reedy Creek Utilities Co., Inc.
Lake Buena Vista, Florida 32830

N. A. Goulet, Jr.
Department of Environmental Science and Engineering
Florida Institute of Technology
Melbourne, Florida 32901

ABSTRACT

Lead (Pb) and copper (Cu) were continuously injected for two months into raceways containing pennywort (Hydrocotyle umbellata L.) growing on a thin film (4 cm) of secondarily treated sewage effluent. These metals were applied at high loading rates [2250 mg Cu d^{-1} (2.5 mg L^{-1}) and 900 mg Pb d^{-1} (1.0 mg L^{-1})] and at a short residence time (~10 h). Approximately 69% of the 14.0 g Cu m^{-2} and 85% of the 4.9 g Pb m^{-2} applied were removed, with effluent concentrations averaged 839 µg Cu L^{-1} and 149 µg Pb L^{-1}. Metals associated with the plant-detritus complex in the metals-amended raceways, which were 1000 fold more concentrated than in the control raceways, accounted for all of the metals removed. It is likely that higher reductions could be achieved in a thin film system by using lower loading rates and/or longer residence times.

Keywords: Nutrient film technique, lead, copper.

INTRODUCTION

The thin-film, or nutrient film technique, employs vascular plants grown in shallow raceways through which a thin layer of wastewater is passed (Jewell et al., 1983). The plants develop a dense root mat which effectively filters out suspended solids, particulate BOD_5 and nutrients from the wastewater. Particulate and soluble BOD_5 are also stabilized by bacteria which colonize

ISBN 0-941463-00-1

the root tissues. Thin-film systems may also be effective in removing heavy metals from wastewaters. Metals have been found to be taken up by vascular plants growing in aqueous solutions. Wolverton and McDonald (1975a,b,1976) reported that the aquatic plants water hyacinth (*Eichhornia crassipes*) and alligator weed (*Alternanthera philoxerides*) could assimilate Pb, Hg, Ag, and Co from river water solutions amended with these elements. Metals which are absorbed may accumulate in plant tissues at concentrations considerably higher than that found in the aqueous medium (Sutton and Blackburn, 1971). Periodic plant harvest would provide an ultimate means of removing these metals from the treatment systems.

Because thin-film treatment systems are a relatively new concept, a short-term study was conducted to evaluate the ability of this system to remove heavy metals from wastewater. Copper and lead were chosen because they are among the metals found at highest concentrations in sewage sludge, with copper occurring at about twice the concentration of lead (Fricke et al., 1985). These metals were spiked into secondary treated sewage effluent and their concentrations measured after flowing through a thin-film treatment system containing a cold tolerant aquatic macrophyte, pennywort (*Hydrocotyle umbellata*). The effect of metals on growth of pennywort was also evaluated.

MATERIALS AND METHODS

Pilot Facilities

Experimental technique was similar to the one described by Dierberg et al. (1987). Four wooden raceways, each 7.32 m long, 1.22 m wide, and 0.15 m deep, were lined with fish grade PVC sheeting (10 mil thickness). After stocking with pennywort each raceway received approximately 900 L d^{-1} of secondary effluent before chlorination from the Reedy Creek Improvement District wastewater treatment plant near Orlando, Florida. Effluent depth ranged from 3.3 - 4.2 cm with a detention time of 8 to 10 h. All four raceways were left undisturbed for two weeks to develop full stands of pennywort. The sewage was then amended in the following manner: raceways 1 and 2 each received approximately 2.5 mg L^{-1} of Cu and 1.0 mg L^{-1} of Pb; raceways 3 and 4 remained unamended of any toxic compounds (control).

The metal stocks were delivered to a 7.4 L mixing chamber by multiple channel Masterflex (Model 7567) peristaltic pumps. After mixing with the continuous flowing sewage for 12 min, the solutions were discharged in a 3 min period into the raceways via a perforated distribution pipe which ran the width of the raceway. Traversing the raceway, effluent eventually drained into a stand pipe which was routed back to the sewage treatment plant. Characteristics (yearly averages) of the secondary treated sewage effluent were BOD_5 = 6.0 mg L^{-1}; NO_3-N = 6.9 mg L^{-1}; NH_4-N = 0.9 mg L^{-1} and TP = 3.1 mg L^{-1}.

Operation and Monitoring

Facility operation included twice daily measurement (and adjustment if necessary) of flow rates for both sewage and metals. Copper and Pb from each raceway were sampled twice weekly at the influent (~0.5 m from the distribution pipe) and effluent ends by using a hand-held Nalgene pump. In addition, stock solutions were sampled when replaced with fresh solutions (11 d intervals). Samples were refrigerated immediately, acidified in the lab and kept at 4°C until digestion, which was usually within three weeks of sample collection.

Primary productivity of the pennywort in each raceway was obtained semi-monthly by weighing the contents of each of six plastic mesh baskets (0.0645 m^2) arranged equidistant from each other along the longitudinal axis of the raceway. Dry weights were determined at the beginning and end of the 60 d period (January 14-March 14 1986) and the data were used to calculate daily primary productivity.

Analytical Methods

Analysis for Pb and Cu was conducted on either a Perkin Elmer Model 603 or Model 306 Atomic Absorption Spectrophotometer equipped with a HGA 2100 graphite furnace. Injection volumes were 20 µL. Agreement between experimental and stated EPA reference samples average 91 ± 5% (N = 5) for Cu and 97 ± 2% (N = 4) for Pb. Spike recoveries (added when samples were acidified in the lab) averaged 98 ± 6% (N = 13) for Cu and 101 ± 9% (N = 14) for Pb.

The pennywort, microbial mat, and detritus were also analyzed at the end of the experimental period. Whole plants and detritus were collected by cutting out sections of the plant/root mat (consisting of lamina, rhizomes, petioles, roots, microbes and detritus) from the influent, middle, and effluent sections of the four raceways. Because of the phytotoxic effects of Cu on the pennywort, much of the material collected consisted of dead plant tissues. The unwashed sections were dried in an 80°C oven for four days, and individually pulverized (Waring blender) for analysis. Two g of the pulverized plant were digested for one week using a hot HNO_3 matrix and analyzed by atomic absorption spectroscopy. A National Bureau of Standard (SRM #1573 - Tomato Leaves) was analyzed for Cu and Pb in order to determine percent recovery of the metals. Recoveries ranged from 70% for Pb to 83% for Cu. Concentrations of each metal analyzed in the pennywort were adjusted to account for the percent recoveries of the standard reference material.

RESULTS AND DISCUSSION

Removal of Copper and Lead

The daily mass contaminant loadings to each raceway were based on the measured stock metal concentration and the average daily flow rate of the stock solution. The daily mass loadings at the front end (0.5 m distant from the distribution pipe) and effluent end of each raceway were calculated by multiplying the average metal concentration from two successive samplings (twice weekly) by the daily average flow rate of the sewage. The sewage flow rate at the effluent end was assumed to equal the flow at the front end minus 14 L d^{-1}, to adjust for evapotranspiration (T. DeBusk, unpublished). The daily mass loadings for the inflow, front end, and effluent end of each raceway were then added for the 60 d exposure period and divided by the area of the raceway (8.924 m^2) to arrive at an areal loading rate.

Duplicate raceways yielded nearly the same percent removals for the same metal: 67 and 71% of the added Cu (13.1 and 14.9 g m^{-2}), and 85 and 85% of the added Pb (4.6 and 5.2 g m^{-2}), for raceways 1 and 2, respectively (Table 1). Both Cu and Pb leaving the metal-spiked raceways were considerably higher (435 x for Cu and 35 x for Pb) than the mass released from the control raceways (nos. 3 and 4, Table 1).

The concentration data for the head end of each metal-spiked raceway (Figure 1) reveal an increase in metal concentration (reduction in removal rate) after day 28, despite the relatively constant influent metal loading. The timing of the onset of the decreased removals at the head end of each raceway corresponded to a noticeable negative effect one or both metals were having on the pennywort. Even the effluent end concentrations began increasing above the limits of 1000 μg L^{-1} for Cu and 150 μg L^{-1} for Pb toward the end of the experiment, indicating failure of the thin film system to continue to reduce these metals to their prior levels. As a result, concentrations of both metals leaving the spiked raceways during the 60 d exposure period were high: 149 $\pm$ 98 μg Pb L^{-1} and 839 $\pm$ 270 μg Cu L^{-1}; control raceway concentrations were only 4.6 $\pm$ 8.3 μg Pb L^{-1} and 1.8 $\pm$ 2.6 μg Cu L^{-1}.

TABLE 1. Mass loadings and removals in duplicate raceways amended with metals (raceways 1 and 2) and in duplicate control raceways (raceways 3 and 4) for the 60 d exposure period.

Metal	Raceway number	Inflow	Front end†	Effluent end	% Removal
		g m^{-2}			
Copper	1	13.12	8.33	4.35	66.8
	2	14.92	8.10	4.35	70.8
	3	--	0.05	0.01	--
	4	--	0.05	0.01	--
Lead	1	4.57	2.70	0.70	84.7
	2	5.15	2.56	0.77	85.0
	3	--	0.06	0.02	--
	4	--	0.06	0.02	--

†0.5 m distant from distribution pipe.

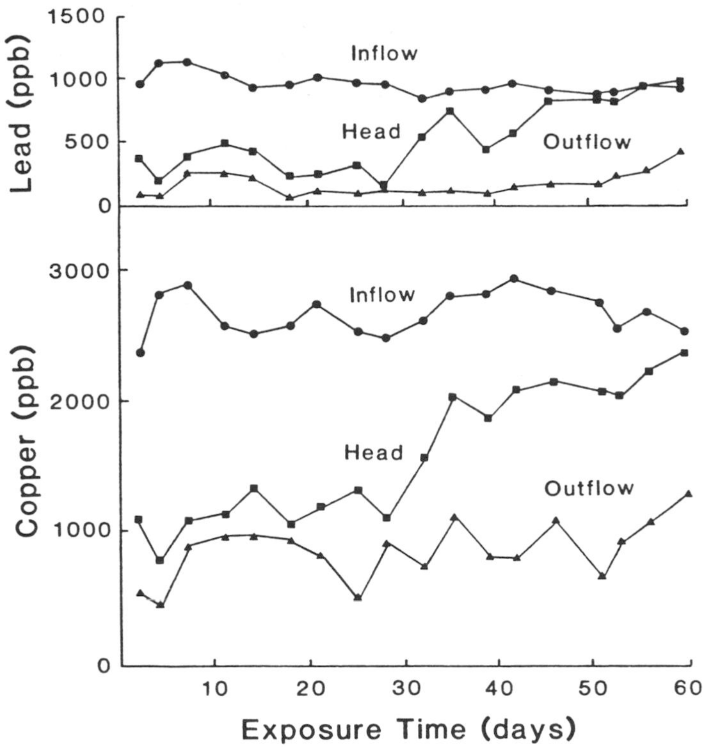

FIGURE 1. Raceway performance for Cu and Pb during the 60 d exposure period. The circles represent the influent concentrations pumped to raceways 1 and 2; the squares represent the concentrations at the front end of raceways 1 and 2 (0.5 m distant from the distribution pipe); the triangles represent the concentrations at the effluent end leaving raceways 1 and 2.

Metal concentrations associated with total biomass of live and dead plants decreased with distance from the input source in each metal raceway (Table 2). Average concentrations ranged from 19,424 to 27,338 mg Cu kg^{-1} and 8,309 to 8,739 mg Pb kg^{-1} in the plant-detritus complex of the metals-amended raceways. This represented a concentration in excess of one thousand times higher than what was found associated with the plants growing in the control raceways. Copper and lead concentrations within water hyacinths after short uptake experiments (1 d to 14 d) were 1452 μg Cu^{2+} g^{-1} root dry wt (Sutton and Blackburn, 1971) and 176 μg Pb^{2+} g^{-1} plant dry wt (Wolverton and McDonald, 1975a). In the present 60 d study, it was not known how much of the metals were

TABLE 2. Concentrations of Cu and Pb (μg metal g^{-1} dry wt) associated with live and dead pennywort plants at the head, middle and end of the two metals-receiving (nos. 1 and 2) and two control (nos. 3 and 4) raceways.

	1	2	3	4
Concentration of Cu in plant + detritus complex, μg g^{-1}				
Head	24,460	34,892	30.6	35.7
Middle	19,784	23,024	25.5	14.9
End	14,149	24,101	15.7	13.1
Mean	19,424	27,338	24.0	21.7
S.D. ±1	±5,156	±6,595	±7.6	±12.6
Plant & detritus uptake & sorption (g m^{-2})	9.44	14.60	0.017	0.015
Loading minus leaving (g m^{-2})	8.77	10.57		
% agreement	93%	72%		
Concentration of Pb in plant + detritus complex, μg g^{-1}				
Head	11,318	12,464	5.7	8.7
Middle	9,885	9,456	8.5	3.0
End	4,871	3,152	4.6	2.0
Mean	8,739	8,309	6.3	4.6
S.D. ±1	±3,438	±4,728	±2.0	±3.6
Plant & detritus uptake & sorption (g m^{-2})	4.25	4.44	0.004	0.003
Loading minus leaving (g m^{-2})	3.87	4.38		
% agreement	91%	99%		

taken up by the plant and how much may have been adsorbed or precipitated outside the plant. The plant-microbe-detritus complex accounted for all of the metals removed in raceways 1 and 2 (Table 2), based on the simple input-output mass balances in Table 1. Agreement between the metals associated with the plant-microbe-detritus complex and those removed in the raceways differed by <10% for three of the four metal-raceway combinations.

Effects of Model Toxicants on the Thin-film System

The pennywort in the metals-receiving raceways did not exhibit toxic effects until about half-way through the experiment, when the plants became spindly and chlorotic, resulting in a thinning of the above-water petioles and laminae. These conditions continued until the end of the study. Further batch studies where each metal was added singularly and in combination revealed Cu was the metal responsible for the toxic effect on the pennywort.

The literature is replete with short-term (e.g., 4 h to 14 d) batch studies indicating that the particular plant used (e.g., water hyacinth) can take up large quantities of metals without major detriment to the plant (Wolverton and McDonald, 1975a,b, 1976; Sutton and Blackburn, 1971; O'Keeffe et al., 1984; Hardy and O'Keeffe, 1985; Hardy and Raber, 1985; Everard and Denny, 1985). This investigation would have yielded similar results if the experiment had been terminated prior to the fourth week when toxic effects and decreased removal efficiency became noticeable. These results point to the need of testing biological treatment systems under realistic conditions (i.e., continuous, long-term exposures using appropriate loading rates and residence times) before serious consideration is given to using these systems to treat toxic wastes.

Contrary to expected low values, dry weight productivity of the stressed pennywort plants in the metals receiving raceways were higher than the control plants (4.1 and 5.6 g dry wt m^2 d^{-1} vs. 2.0 and 4.1 g dry wt m^2 d^{-1}). This is an artifact created by a roughly 2-fold increase in the dry weight of the live plant tissues, caused by the uptake of heavy metals. The ash weights for the plants sampled from the head, middle, and effluent end of each raceway receiving metals averaged 30.7 and 35.9% of the total dry wt, compared to 16.9 and 17.1 % for the control raceways. In contrast to the dry weight, the wet weight of the plants actually decreased during the study period from 8.4 to 8.1 kg m^{-2} in raceway 1 and from 10.5 to 8.9 kg m^{-2} in raceway 2, while that of the control plants increased from 8.0 to 11.5 kg m^{-2} and from 9.2 to 11.9 kg m^{-2} in raceways 3 and 4, respectively, indicating that the organic plant biomass was decreasing because of metal toxicity. If the experiment had been continued, it is likely that further pennywort die-off and decomposition would have occurred.

The slow growth of the pennywort obviated the need to harvest the plants during the study. However, in an operational system in which the plant-detritus complex contains most of the metals originally in the wastewater, periodic harvest of the plants would be necessary. Utilization or disposal schemes would subsequently have to take into account the high metals concentration of the plant material.

CONCLUSIONS

The thin film pennywort system removed Cu and Pb at average rates of 161 and 69 mg m^{-2} d^{-1}, respectively, over a 60 d period. The high loading of Cu ultimately proved toxic to the plants, and a subsequent decline in treatment efficiency occurred after one months's operation. Lower metal loadings to such thin-film systems would likely reduce the concentration of metals in the effluent stream, and also reduce phytotoxic effects. The high recovery of metals in the plant-detritus complex demonstrates that plant harvest would be required to provide an ultimate means of metal removal from the system.

ACKNOWLEDGMENTS

This research was supported by a Small Business Innovation Research grant to Aqua Chem Analyses, Inc., from the Department of Energy, Contract No. DE-AOD5-85ER80259. The second author was supported by the Gas Research Institute, Chicago, Illinois.

REFERENCES

Dierberg, F. E., N. A. Goulet, Jr., and T. A. DeBusk. 1987. Removal of two chlorinated compounds by a thin film technique. J. Environ. Qual. (in press).

Everard, M., and P. Denny. 1985. Flux of lead in submerged plants and its relevance to a freshwater system. Aquat. Bot. 21:181-193.

Fricke, C., C. Clarkson, E. Lomnitz, and T. O'Farrell. 1985. Comparing priority pollutants in municipal sludge. Biocycle 26:35-37.

Hardy, J. K., and D. H. O'Keeffe. 1985. Cadmium uptake by the water hyacinth: Effects of root mass, solution volume, complexers and other ions. Chemosphere 14:417-426.

Hardy, J. K., and N. B. Raber. 1985. Zinc uptake by the water hyacinth: Effects of solution factors. Chemosphere 14:1155-1166.

Jewell, W. J., J. J. Madras, W. W. Clarkson, H. Delancey-Pompe, and R. M. Kabrick. 1983. Wastewater treatment with plants in nutrient films. Project Summary EPA-600/S2-83-067, United States Environmental Protection Agency ERL, Ada, Oklahoma.

O'Keeffe, D. H., J. K. Hardy, and R. A. Rao. 1984. Cadmium uptake by the water hyacinth: Effects of solution. Environ. Pollut. Ser. A34:133-147.

Sutton, D. L., and R. D. Blackburn. 1971. Uptake of copper by water hyacinth. Hyacinth Control J. 9:18-20.

Wolverton, B. C., and R. C. McDonald. 1975a. Water hyacinths and alligatorweed for removal of lead and mercury from polluted waters. NASA Technical Memorandum Report, Report No. TM-X-72723. Bay St. Louis, Mississippi.

Wolverton, B. C., and R. C. McDonald. 1975b. Water hyacinths and alligatorweed for removal of silver, cobalt, and strontium from polluted waters. NASA Technical Memorandum Report, Report No. TM-X-72723. Bay St. Louis, Mississippi.

Wolverton, B. C., and R. C. McDonald. 1976. Water hyacinths (*Eichhornia crassipes*) for removing chemical and photographic pollutants from laboratory wastewaters. NASA Technical Memorandum Report, Report No. TM-X-72731. Bay St. Louis, Mississippi.

EFFECTS OF POSITIONAL ISOMERISM ON THE UPTAKE OF MONOSUBSTITUTED PHENOLS BY THE WATER HYACINTH

D. H. O'Keeffe, T. E. Wiese, and M. R. Benjamin
Department of Chemistry
The University of Michigan-Flint
Flint, Michigan 48503

ABSTRACT

Synthetic phenolic compounds are known to arise from the coking of coal, gas works and oil refineries, chemical and pesticide plants, dye manufacturing plants and other sources. When present in aquatic ecosystems they represent toxic environmental pollutants. We are investigating how the water hyacinth (Eichhornia crassipes) takes up and metabolizes (detoxifies) such compounds. Here we present the results of studies regarding how this aquatic macrophyte deals with the positional isomers (o, m, p) of several monosubstituted phenols (chloro, methyl, nitro). The quantity of each phenol taken up from 25-50 mg L^{-1} solutions as a function of time was determined using high performance liquid chromatography. The uptake process is associated with both the particular substituent and with the isomeric form. Methyl- and chlorophenols are taken up more rapidly than the nitrophenols; and, in general, the relative removal rate of the isomers is para >> meta > ortho. The observed toxicity of the phenols increases with increasing removal rate. The uptake of p-chloro- and p-methylphenol is very rapid (5-6 h) while for meta-nitrophenol it is extremely slow (50% removed in 300 h). Phenol itself is completely removed in 30 h under similar conditions.

Keywords: monosubstituted phenols, toxic organics, uptake.

INTRODUCTION

The water hyacinth [Eichhornia crassipes (Mart) Solms] has been shown to bioconcentrate many metal ions from water including Pb, Cd, Hg, Cu, Zn, and Cr (Chigbo et al., 1982; Cooley and Martin, 1977; Kay et al., 1984; Muramoto and Oki, 1983). Much work continues on the mechanisms of uptake (O'Keeffe et al., 1984; Hardy and O'Keeffe, 1985; Hardy and Raber, 1985; Heaton et al., 1986) and translocation (Chigbo et al., 1982). Uptake of organic

ISBN 0-941463-00-1

compounds has received considerably less attention. The removal from solution of a few herbicides (Bingham, 1978; Bingham and Shaver, 1977) mirex, toxaphene (Smith and Shore, 1978; Smith et al., 1977), and mevinphos (Wolverton, 1975) has been briefly examined. Water hyacinths have been reported to take up phenol (Wolverton and McKown, 1976) and a simple water hyacinth-based unit for the removal of phenol from solution has been designed (Vaidyanathan et al., 1983). This chemical and a myriad of synthetic phenolic compounds are common environmental pollutants (DeWalle et al., 1982) arising from the coking of coal, gas works and oil refineries, chemical and pesticide plants as well as dye manufacturing plants (Buikema et al., 1979). When present in aquatic ecosystems they represent a toxic threat to most plant and animal life. Our purpose was to determine the extent to which the water hyacinth is capable of taking up and metabolizing (detoxifying?) this class of environmental pollutants.

MATERIALS AND METHODS

Water hyacinths were grown in the laboratory using a combination of incandescent (60 W) and fluorescent (40 W Sylvania Gro-Lux) lighting (14 h light cycle). Plants were maintained (changed weekly) in half strength Hoagland's solution (pH 7). Under these conditions growth (vegetative) was rapid and flowering did not occur. Mature plants of about 1 g (dry wt) and about 3 wk of age were used for all studies.

Individual plants were placed in 500 mL amber bottles containing Hoagland's solution or deionized water (400-450 mL) with 25 mg L^{-1} and 50 mg L^{-1} of phenolic compound (o-, m- and p-isomers of chlorophenol, methylphenol and nitrophenol). Control samples consisted of bottles containing the phenolic compounds in Hoagland's solution or deionized water. Each study was done at least in triplicate. At regular time intervals a 1 mL aliquot was withdrawn and analyzed for the amount of phenolic compound remaining in solution. Since the plant evapotranspiration rate is high (about 50 mL d^{-1}), additional Hoagland's solution or deionized water was added to maintain volume.

The phenolic compounds were determined by high performance liquid chromatography (Beckman Altex Model 420 system employing an Hitachi Model 100 UV-VIS Spectrophotometer equipped with an Altex Flow Cell for peak detection). Aliquots were filtered free of all particulates (0.45 μ nylon filter) and chromatographed on a 20 cm by 4.6 mm I.D. reversed-phase C-18 column (Hewlett-Packard or Whatman) or on a cyano column (Fisher Scientific). The mobile phase was methanol:water (50:50 v v^{-1} or 60:40 v v^{-1}) sometimes containing 1% glacial acetic acid. A flow rate of 1 mL min^{-1} was used and the detection wavelength was either 280 or 270 nm depending upon the phenolic compound being studied.

RESULTS

Water hyacinths were exposed to 50 mg L^{-1} solutions of the isomeric forms (o,m,p) of chloro-, methyl-, and nitrophenols. Each of these compounds was removed from deionized water or Hoagland's solution by water hyacinths at a different rate (Table 1). The p-chloro- and p-methylphenols are removed from solution very rapidly (data not shown). Neither compound could be detected in solution after about a 12 h exposure. All of the other phenolic compounds are taken up by the water hyacinth but at much slower rates. The times required for the 50% decrease of the m- and o- isomers of the chloro and methylphenols were ~25-30 h and ~40-50 h, respectively. In general, the nitrophenols were removed from solution at slower rates as indicated in Table 1. Plants were also exposed to 25 mg L^{-1} solutions of each of these phenolic compounds. Their disappearance as a function of time was similar to that at the higher concentration.

Kinetic analysis of the uptake data suggests that removal of the phenolic compounds from solution is a first order process (Table 1). The calculated correlation coefficients range from a high of 0.99 (m-chlorophenol) to lows of 0.96 (o-, p-nitrophenols). While it is apparent that additional experiments are required, the trends in the kinetic data regarding positional isomerism and substituent identity were reasonably consistent. The uptake rates of the chloro- and methylphenol isomers decrease in the order p>>m>o. This order was reversed in the case of the nitrophenol isomers (o>m>p). The kinetic data also indicated that, in general, the rates at which the three phenolic compounds were removed from solution decrease in the substituent order $-CH_3 > -Cl > -NO_2$. The p-methyl ($t_{1/2}$ = 1.1 h) and p-chlorophenols

TABLE 1. Rate and toxicity data from phenolic compound uptake experiments.

Phenolic compound	First order rate constant (h^{-1})	Correlation coefficient	$t_{1/2}$ (h)	Time (h) for leaf damage
Methylphenol				
para-	0.610	0.99	1.1	<1
meta-	0.031	0.98	23	~72
ortho-	0.013	0.98	53	~96
Chlorophenol				
para-	0.310	0.98	2.3	<1
meta-	0.029	0.99	24	~72
ortho-	0.017	0.99	41	~96
Nitrophenol				
para-	0.0062	0.96	112	-3
meta-	0.0120	0.97	60	~24
ortho-	0.0150	0.96	48	>96

($t_{1/2}$ = 2.3 h) were the most rapidly taken up by the water hyacinths. p-Nitrophenol appears to be the most slowly removed from solution ($t_{1/2}$ = 112 h) followed by m-nitrophenol ($t_{1/2}$ = 60 h).

The most obvious toxic effect noted when water hyacinth plants were exposed to the chloro-, methyl- and nitrophenols (25-50 mg L^{-1}) was the on-set of lower leaf wilting (dehydration). The extent of the toxicity of the isomers of each monosubstituted ($-CH_3$, -Cl, $-NO_2$) phenolic compound decreased in the order p>>m>o. Approximate exposure times resulting in observable leaf damage closely paralleled the rates of uptake of the chloro- and methyl-phenols as indicated in Table 1. Plants exposed to p-methyl and p-chlorophenol exhibit this toxic effect in less than 1 h. The $t_{1/2}$ values for the removal of these phenolic compounds indicated that substantial uptake occurred within this first hour of exposure (Table 1). The m- and o- isomers of these two phenolic compounds were clearly much less toxic to the plants since obvious leaf damage was observed only after ~72 and ~96 h respectively, which is consistent with their slower rates of uptake. The opposite correlation between toxicity and uptake was noted when plants were exposed to the nitrophenols (Table 1). The p- isomer was the most slowly removed from solution ($t_{1/2}$ = 112 h) but it is the most toxic. The ortho isomer is the most rapidly taken up ($t_{1/2}$ = 48 h) but little, if any, toxic effects are noted after four days.

Each plant was transferred to fresh Hoagland's solution when most (after about three halflives) of each phenolic compound had been removed. The 50 mg L^{-1} solutions of each phenolic compound invariably proved lethal to the plants. However, all of the plants exposed to 25 mg L^{-1} solutions survived and vegetatively produced new plants within 1-2 wk.

With exposure of water hyacinths to p-chloro- and p-methyl-phenol, the solutions and the plant roots developed color. Both the p-chloro- and p-methylphenol solutions initially became a pale yellow color (~2 h). Thereafter the p-chlorophenol solution turned light brown (~6 h), and then a medium brown (~12 h). The p-methylphenol solution turned light orange (~4 h), and then pinkish orange (~12 h). The roots of plants exposed to p-chlorophenol for 24 h were noticeably dark brown, while those of plants exposed to p-methylphenol were orange. Solid material (polymeric?) was present in solutions of both phenolic compounds after 24 h and was retained on 0.45 μ nylon filters. The filtrate usually had much less color.

Solutions of o- and p-nitrophenol were initially yellow in color and some color was present even after several days exposure to water hyacinths. Solutions of the o- and m- isomers of chloro- and methylphenols and m-nitrophenols were clear and colorless throughout their exposure to water hyacinth plants. All plant roots retained their normal appearance as well.

DISCUSSION

Water hyacinth was able to remove significant quantities of the monosubstituted phenolic compounds investigated in this study and may become an important treatment option. The positional isomers of the chloro-, methyl- and nitrophenols investigated here were taken up at different rates and had different toxicities (Table 1). These data provide further evidence that these factors are controlled, partially at least, by differences in the plant's ability to metabolize each of these molecules (O'Keeffe et al., 1987) and were consistent with those obtained from studies of phenol, di- and trihydroxybenzene uptake by and toxicity to the water hyacinth (O'Keeffe et al., 1987).

Polyphenol oxidase (PPO) enzymes present in root tissue are at least partially responsible for the metabolism (oxidative) since these apparently ubiquitous plant Cu oxidases are known to metabolize mono- and diphenols (Mayer and Harel, 1973; Vamos-Vigyazo, 1981). Preliminary enzyme assay data indicates the presence of substantial PPO activity in cell-free supernatants obtained from root tissue. Commercial PPO from mushroom and the enzyme present in the cell-free supernatant both rapidly oxidize p-chloro- and p-methylphenols and yield products having the same brown and orange colors observed during the uptake of these phenols (Colles and O'Keeffe, unpublished results). The use of the mushroom enzyme to remove phenol from wastewater has already been suggested (Vedralova et al., 1980). Seidel has also demonstrated that bulrush (Scirpus) takes up phenolic compounds and that metabolism occurs (Seidel, 1963,1965,1966,1967,1976). Stom and co-workers have suggested that selected hydrophytes eliminate exogenous phenols via oxidative metabolism involving polyphenol oxidases (Stom and Roth, 1981; Stom et al., 1980a,b,c, 1981). We are continuing to examine this metabolic process and others which may be involved in the water hyacinth's ability to function as an effective biological pollution control option.

ACKNOWLEDGMENTS

The authors thank Daniel Kennedy and Julie Poliskey for help in performing some of the experiments. Financial support included Faculty Research and Development Grants from The University of Michigan-Flint and a grant from the State of Michigan Research Excellence and Economic Development Fund (administered by The Project for Urban and Regional Affairs, The University of Michigan-Flint).

REFERENCES

Bingham, S. W. 1973. Improving water quality by removal of pesticide pollutants with aquatic plants. Office of Water Resources Research (PB219389). 94 pp.

Bingham, S. W., and R. L. Shaver. 1977. Diphenamid removal from water and metabolism by aquatic plants. Pest Biochem. Phys. 7:8-15.

Buikema, A. L., Jr., M. J. McGinniss, and J. Cairns, Jr. 1979. Phenolics in aquatic ecosystems: A selected review of recent literatue. Marine Environ. Res. 2:87-181.

Chigbo, F. E., R. W. Smith, and F. L. Shore. 1982. Uptake of arsenic, cadmium, lead and mercury from polluted waters by the water hyacinth _Eichhornia crassipes_. Environ. Pollut. Ser. A 27:31-36.

Cooley, T. N., and D. F. Martin. 1977. Factors affecting the distribution of trace elements in aquatic plants. J. Inorg. Nuc. Chem. 39:1893-1896.

DeWalle, F. B., D. A. Kalman, R. Dills, D. Norman, E. S. K. Chian, M. Giabbai, and M. Ghosal. 1982. Presence of phenolic compounds in sewage, effluent and sludge from municipal sewage treatment plants. Water Sci. Tec. 14:143-150.

Hardy, J. K., and D. H. O'Keeffe. 1985. Cadmium uptake by the water hyacinth: Effects of root mass, solution volume, complexers and other metal ions. Chemosphere 14:417-426.

Hardy, J. K., and N. B. Raber. 1985. Zinc uptake by the water hyacinth: Effects of solution factors. Chemosphere 14:1155-1166.

Heaton, C., J. Frame, and J. K. Hardy. 1986. Lead uptake by _Eichhornia crassipes_. Tox. Env. Chem. 11:125-136.

Jana, S., and M. A. Chouduri. 1984. Synergistic effects of heavy metal pollutants and senescence in submerged aquatic plants. Water, Air and Soil Poll. 21-1:351-357.

Kay, S. H., W. T. Haller, and L. A. Garrard. 1984. Effects of heavy metals on water hyacinths [_Eichhornia crassipes_ (Mart.) Solms]. Aquat. Toxicol. 5117-128.

Low, K. S., and C. K. Lee. 1981. Copper, zinc, nickel and chromium uptake by "Kangkong Air" (Ipomea Aquatica Forsk). Pertanika 4:16-20.

Mayer, A. M., and E. Harel. 1979. Polyphenoloxidases in plants. Phytochem. 18:193-215.

Muramoto, S., and Y. Oki. 1983. Removal of some heavy metals from polluted water by water hyacinth (_Eichhornia crassipes_). Bull. Env. Cont. Tox. 39:170-177.

O'Keeffe, D. H., J. K. Hardy, and R. A. Rao. 1984. Cadmium uptake by the water hyacinth: Effects of solution factors. Environ. Pollut. Ser. A 34:133-147.

O'Keeffe, D. H., T. E. Wiese, S. R. Brummet, and T. W. Miller. 1987. Uptake and metabolism of phenolic compounds by the water hyacinth (_Eichhornia crassipes_). _In_ Recent Advances in Phytochemistry, Vol. 21. (in press).

Seidel, K. 1963. On phenol accumulation and phenol reduction in water plants. Naturwissenschaften 50:452-453.

Seidel, K. 1965. Phenol reduction in water by Scirpus lacustris L. during a 31-month investigation. Naturwissenschaften 52:398.

Seidel, K. 1966. Purification of surface water by higher plants. Naturwissenschaften 53:289-297.

Seidel, K. 1967. Mixotrophy in Scirpus lacustris L. Naturwissenshaften 54:176-177.

Seidel, K. 1976. Macrophytes and water purification. p. 141-149. In J. Tourbier and R. W. Pierson (ed.) Biological Control of Water Pollution. Univ. of Penn. Press.

Smith, R. W., and F. L. Shore. 1978. Water hyacinths for removal of Mirex from Water. J. Miss. Acad. Sci. Supp. 23:22.

Smith, R. W., W. Van Zandt, and F. L. Shore. 1977. Water hyacinths for removal of Toxaphene from water. J. Miss. Acad. Sci. Supp. 22:20.

Stom, D. I., and R. Roth. 1981. Some effects of polyphenols of aquatic plants: I. Toxicity of phenols in aquatic plants. Bull. Env. Cont. and Tox. 27:332-337.

Stom, D. J., S. S. Timofeeva, and S. N. Souslov. 1981. Some methods of phenol elimination from sewage waters. Part 1: biodestruction by the vegetable homogenates. Acta Hydrochim. Hydrobiol. 9:433-445.

Stom, D. J., S. S. Timofeeva, N. F. Kashina, L. J. Bielykh, S. N. Souslov, V. V. Boutorob, and M. S. Apartzin. 1980a. Methods of analyzing quinones in water and their application in studying the effects of hydrophytes on phenols. Part 3: Phenol Elimination under the action of aquatic plants. Acta Hydrochim. Hydrobiol. 8:223-230.

Stom, D. J., S. S. Timofeeva, N. F. Kashina, L. J. Bielykh, S. N. Souslov, V. V. Boutorov, and M. S. Apartzin. 1980b. Methods of analyzing quinones in water and their application in studying the effects of hydrophytes on phenols. Part 4: Accumulation of exogenic phenols, localization of endogenic phenols and o-diphenol oxidase in Nitella cells. Acta Hydrochim. Hydrobiol. 8:231-240.

Stom, D. J., S. S. Timofeeva, N. F. Kashina, L. J. Bielykh, S. N. Souslov, V. V. Boutorov, and M. S. Apartzin. 1980c. Methods of analyzing quinones in water and their application in studying the effects of hydrophytes on phenols. Part 5: Elimination of Carcinogenic Amines from Solutions under the Actino of Nitella. Acta Hydrochim. Hydrobiol. 8:241-245.

Vamos-Vigyazo, L. 1981. Polyphenol oxidase and peroxidase in fruits and vegetables. CRC Crit. Rev. Food Sci. and Nutr. 15:49-127.

Vedralova, E., Z. Pechan, and J. Duchon. 1980. Removing phenol from wastewaters by oxidation to Melanin with mushroom polyphenoloxidase. Coll. Czech. Chem. Comm. 45:623-627.

Wolverton, B. C. 1975. Aquatic plants for removal of mevinphos from aquatic environment. NASA Tech. Mem. TM-X-72720.

Wolverton, B. C., and M. M. McKown. 1976. Water hyacinths for removal of phenols from polluted waters. Aquat. Bot. 2:191-201.

Validyanathan, S., K. M. Kavadia, M. G. Rao, S. Basu, and S. P. Mahajan. 1983. Removal of phenol using water hyacinth in a continuous unit. Intern. J. Env. Studies 21:183-191.

WASTEWATER TREATMENT IN A WETLAND FILTER - EFFECTS OF VARYING APPLICATION FREQUENCY ON NITROGEN REMOVAL

H.-B. Wittgren and K. Sundblad
Department of Water in Environment and Society
Linkoping University
Linkoping, SWEDEN

ABSTRACT

Field lysimeter experiments were carried out with reed sweetgrass, _Glyceria maxima_ (Hartm.) Holmb., planted in loamy sand. From April to October, in the year after planting, the lysimeters received 70 mm wk^{-1} (weeks 1-5) and 140 mm wk^{-1} (weeks 6-29) of wastewater from a facultative pond. The wastewater was applied to lysimeters with different frequencies during weeks 6-29: 14, 7, 2 and 1 surface irrigation occasions per week. The lysimeters were harvested twice, when 29, 30, 32 and 24 g N m^{-2} were removed with the biomass. Based on input and leachate data, N removal was equal to 58, 62, 73 and 77% for lysimeters receiving from 14 to 1 irrigation(s) per week, respectively.

At the second harvest, N-recovery in _G. maxima_ was considerably higher in the lysimeter receiving 12 irrigations (15 g N m^{-2}) than in the others. More aerated soil conditions in lysimeters receiving the frequent irrigations resulted in increased competition from terrestrial species. When the lysimeter was irrigated with 140 mm in one application it is highly probable that ponding created a high demand for N as an electron acceptor.

Keywords: Application frequency, field lysimeter, nitrogen removal, reed sweetgrass (_Glyceria maxima_), wastewater, wetland filter.

INTRODUCTION

The use of aquatic plants for wastewater treatment and resource recovery in cold regions like Sweden is limited by the climate. In wetlands, however, plants are combined with the capacity of soil for filtration, sorption and some biological activity which also functions in winter. Hence, wetlands should be systems capable of year round wastewater treatment in cold regions.

ISBN 0-941463-00-1

Reed sweetgrass, Glyceria maxima (Hartm.) Holmb., is an emergent macrophyte which has a high nutrient uptake capacity, high biomass production and is possible to use as fodder or for biogas production. The grass is often dominant in littorals of eutrophic waters in Sweden as well as in central Europe (Hejny & Husak, 1978), and shows a high capacity to adapt nutrient uptake to availability (Dykyjova, 1978). Earlier in Sweden, the species was transplanted to wetlands as fodder for cattle (Lohammar, 1955). The maximum aboveground biomass varies between 600 and 2600 g (dw) m^{-2} in climatic regions similar to Sweden (Kvet & Husak, 1978; Westlake, 1966).

Patrick & Wyatt (1964) showed that N losses through denitrification from soils under alternately submerged and dry conditions exceeded those from soils under either permanent submergence or a constant moisture content between field capacity and wilting point. However, with heavy application of secondary treated sewage water to soil columns (Lance & Whisler, 1972) and fields with reed canarygrass, Phalaris arundinacea L. (Linden et al., 1981) rather long (more than one week) application-drying cycles were required to significantly remove N through denitrification.

In this study, field lysimeters planted with Glyceria maxima (wetland filters) received wastewater from a facultative pond with different (twice a day to once a week) application frequencies. The purpose was to see if the different application schedules could produce significant differences in N removal.

EXPERIMENTAL DESIGN AND METHODS

This study was conducted at the Slaka facultative pond close to the city of Linkoping, Sweden, during 1985. This region has a mean annual temperature of 6°C. The mean temperature of the coldest month (Feb.) is -4°C., and for the warmest (July) 17°C. The annual mean precipitation is 510 mm.

Four rubber basins (3 x 4 m) were placed in the ground. Each basin was equipped with a drainage loop (diameter 50 mm) connected to an outflow pipe at the bottom. The outflow pipes were connected to a well equipped with tipping buckets. The basins were filled with the loamy sand of the site, after removal of the main root layer and mixing. The mixed soil contained 3% clay, 13% silt, 59% fine sand and coarser material. The average organic matter content was 2.0% of dw (loss on ignition), the average Kjeldahl N content 0.06% of dw and the average soil pH (H_2O) was 5.9. The soil depth in the beginning of the study was 0.75 m.

For wastewater application, each lysimeter was equipped with four PVC-pipes (diameter 25 mm) with five 5 mm holes drilled in each pipe. The pipes were placed on plastic strips on the soil surface with the holes pointing downwards to create a self-draining system.

The lysimeters were planted with reed sweetgrass, Glyceria maxima (Hartm.) Holmb., in the summer of 1984. Application of wastewater from the facultative pond commenced in March 1985. Wastewater was applied three times a week with 10+10+15 mm each week in March, followed by 20+20+30 mm weekly until the 15th of May. After that, the load was increased to 140 mm per week and applied with different frequencies. Lysimeter I got 10 mm twice a day, II 20 mm once a day, III 70 mm twice a week and IV 140 mm once a week (less during the latter part of the study; see Results and Discussion). The irrigation rate was always 4 mm min^{-1}. This application schedule resulted in ponding of lysimeters III and IV for 1-2 and 2-3 d, respectively, while I and II were never ponded. The wastewater application was continued until the end of October. The average chemical composition of the applied wastewater is given in Table 1.

The leachate volume from each lysimeter was measured quantitatively with tipping buckets. The accumulated volume was read once a week. Grab samples of leachate were taken once a week at maximum leaching rate. Wastewater samples were taken at the same occasion. Samples were analyzed for: pH, BOD, COD and conductivity according to standard methods (APHA, 1980); NO_3+NO_2-N (cadmium reduction method) and NH_4-N (gas diffusion method) by flow injection analysis using an automated FIA star 5020 (Tecator AB, Hoganas, Sweden); total-N as NO_3-N after alkaline oxidation with peroxodisulphate according to Swedish standard methods; (Swedish Standardization Board, 1976); and total-P as PO_4-P after acidic oxidation with peroxodisulphate. PO_4-P was analyzed by flow injection analysis with the molybdate stannous chloride method.

The grass was harvested twice, leaving a 7 cm stubble, in the middle of June and in the beginning of August. Six diagonally arranged squares (0.5 x 0.5 m) in each lysimeter were sampled. All green shoots in each square were counted and the harvested biomass weighed. In addition, the rest of the G. maxima biomass in each lysimeter was cut quantitatively for determination of total aboveground biomass. In August, the harvested biomass was separated into G. maxima and other species.

Subsamples from each square were cut into pieces, dried (55°C) and ground (mesh size 1 mm). Kjeldahl-N and loss on ignition (600°C for 2 h) were determined on each sample of G. maxima. Other species were analyzed as one pooled sample from each lysimeter. Water content was determined after drying at 105°C. Total harvested biomass and the amount of N removed with the crop were calculated for each lysimeter using the mean values of water and Kjeldahl-N contents.

Soil samples were collected in May and November from two depths, 0-15 and 15-30 cm. Five samples were taken from each depth in all lysimeters. The soil was dried (55°C), sieved (mesh size 2 mm) and analyzed for Kjeldahl-N and loss on ignition (600°C for 2 h).

TABLE 1. Average chemical composition of applied wastewater and leachate from the lysimeters. Standard deviations are shown in brackets. (Apr.-Oct. 1985).

	Wastewater		Lysimeter Leachate				
	Number of determinations	Value	Number of determinations	I	II	III	IV
pH	29	7.9 (0.4)	29	6.2 (0.2)	6.2 (0.2)	6.3 (0.2)	6.2 (0.3)
Conductivity ($mS\ cm^{-1}$)	28	0.94 (0.11)	29	0.66 (0.15)	0.65 (0.15)	0.66 (0.15)	0.65 (0.15)
COD ($mg\ O_2\ L^{-1}$)	29	274 (76)	19⁺	40 (10)	44 (14)	45 (12)	78 (50)
BOD ($mg\ O_2\ L^{-1}$)	4⁺⁺	130 (45)	7⁺⁺	2.5 (1.0)	2.0 (0.6)	4.9 (2.1)	3.9 (1.1)
Total-N ($mg\ L^{-1}$)	29	29.2 (6.2)	29	11.3 (6.6)	10.6 (7.1)	7.5 (4.4)	6.5 (5.9)
NH_4-N ($mg\ L^{-1}$)	29	16.7 (8.0)	20	0.6 (0.1)	0.5 (0.1)	0.8 (0.5)	1.2 (0.3)
NO_3+NO_2-N ($mg\ L^{-1}$)	14	<0.5	29	10.0 (6.8)	9.4 (7.2)	5.8 (4.5)	4.2 (6.5)
Total-P ($mg\ L^{-1}$)	28	10.4 (1.9)	5	0.08 (0.03)	0.07 (0.01)	0.13 (0.05)	0.19 (0.06)

⁺Weeks 1-19. ⁺⁺Weeks 20-29.

RESULTS AND DISCUSSION

Water Balance

There were no significant differences in leachate volume between lysimeters I, II and III (ANOVA, $p>0.1$). The average evapotranspiration during the period with 140 mm wk^{-1} irrigation (weeks 6-29), assuming no change in the soil water content, was 14 mm wk^{-1}. The average precipitation during the same period was 15 mm wk^{-1}.

Decreased leaching from lysimeter IV was observed from the end of June. After termination of the study a leak was found just above the soil surface. Consequently, less wastewater percolated through the lysimeter than intended. The actual wastewater application to lysimeter IV, after it started to leak, was calculated as follows with the assumption that the evapotranspiration was not affected by the decreased load:

Load IV = Load (I,II,III) - Average leachate (I,II,III) + leachate IV

The total wastewater application (week 1-29) to lysimeter IV was calculated to be 85% of the application to the other lysimeters.

Nitrogen

The lowest total-N concentrations in the wastewater were recorded during the summer (Figure 1). The decline was accompanied by a shift in relative importance from NH_4-N to organic-N. In the summer, with a heavy algal bloom, organic-N made up for more than 50% of the total-N, whereas the opposite was true during the spring and autumn. NO_3+NO_2-N was always below 0.5 mg L^{-1}.

Determination of NO_3-N concentrations in the leachate after an irrigation occasion showed that they were independent of time of sampling. Hence, grab samples appeared to be representative for the whole week in which they were taken. A decreased number of irrigation occasions per week was accompanied by lower total-N concentrations in the leachate after harvests and during the autumn (Figure 1). In the leachate from lysimeter I and II, NO_3^- was the dominant ion, with NH_4-N never exceeding 1 mg L^{-1} (Table 1). In lysimeter III, NO_3^- was also dominant, but NH_4-N concentrations increased from below 1 mg L^{-1} during the summer to 1.8 mg L^{-1} at the end of October. In lysimeter IV, NO_3+NO_2-N concentrations were below 0.5 mg L^{-1} during most of the summer and up to October, whereas NH_4-N concentrations were below 1 mg L^{-1} in April and May and between 1 and 2 mg L^{-1} from June to the end of October.

Average recovery of N in harvested biomass (Table 2) was calculated from the individually sampled squares. It is difficult to generalize from these results, since they are based on one growing season only. Part of the heterogeneity within each

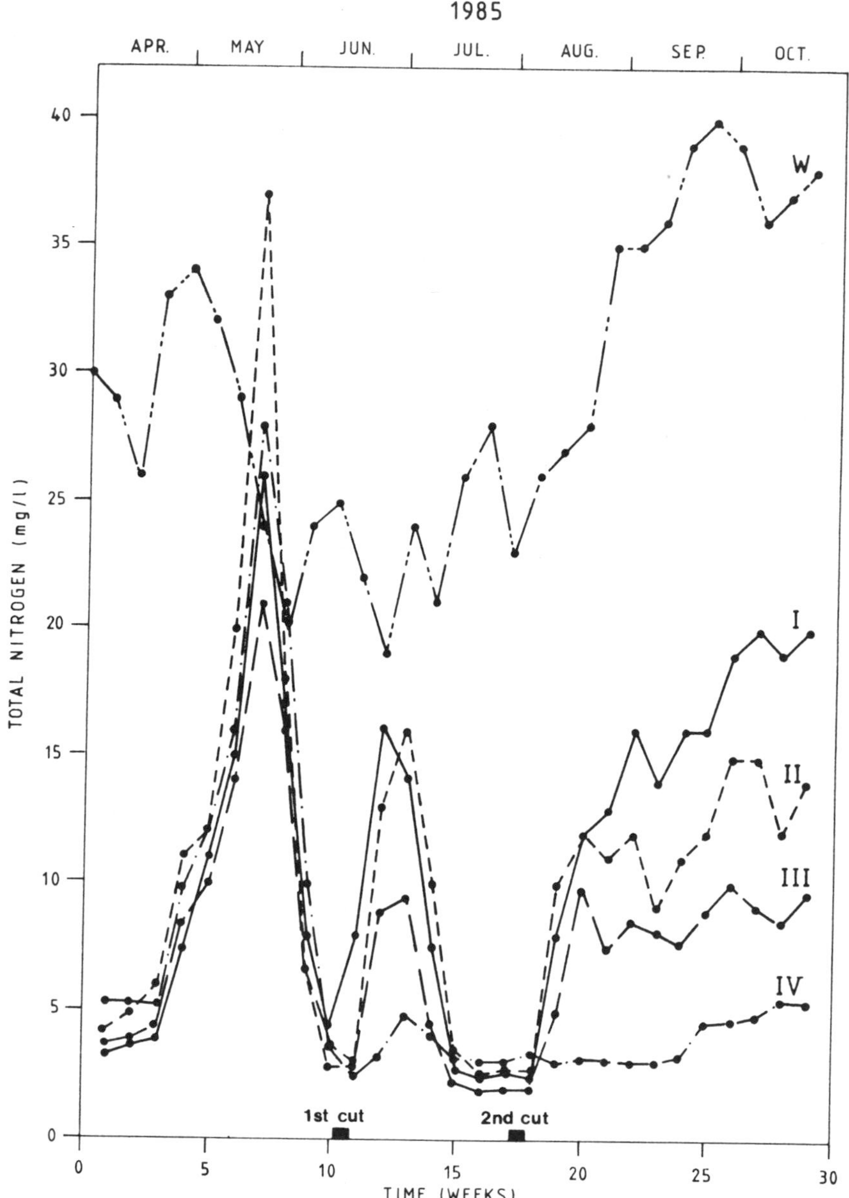

FIGURE 1. Total N concentrations in wastewater (W) and leachate from lysimeters with Glyceria maxima. The lysimeters received wastewater with identical (Week 1-5: 20+20+30 mm wk^{-1}) and different application frequencies (Week 6-29: I = 14x10 mm wk^{-1}, II = 7x20 mm wk^{-1}, III = 2x70 mm wk^{-1} and IV = 1x140 mm wk^{-1}. Due to leakage, lys. IV received less than 140 mm wk^{-1} from week 12 and on).

TABLE 2. Average dry weight, N-concentration and N-recovery of the harvested biomass, based on six sampled squares/lysimeter. Standard deviations are shown in brackets.

Harvest month	Lysimeter I	Lysimeter II	Lysimeter III	Lysimeter IV
Glyceria maxima	Biomass, g m^{-2}			
June	502 (134)	694 (138)	589 (94)	501 (85)
Aug.	436 (191)	380 (225)	570 (89)	292 (182)
Other Species Aug.	124	129	64	56
Glyceria maxima	N-concentration, mg g^{-1}			
June	28 (2)	28 (3)	30 (2)	26 (2)
Aug.	22 (3)	25 (3)	27 (3)	23 (1)
Other Species Aug.	28	30	28	29
Glyceria maxima	N-recovery, g m^{-2}			
June	14 (4)	20 (6)	18 (4)	13 (3)
Aug.	9.4 (3.3)	9.6 (5.8)	15 (3)	6.8 (4.4)
Other species Aug.	3.4	3.9	1.8	1.6
Total	27	34	35	21

lysimeter might have been a remaining effect of the transplantation in 1984. Nevertheless, in August the amount of N removed with the harvested *G. maxima* was significantly higher in lysimeter III than in lysimeter IV (students t-test, $p<0.05$). In addition, the short irrigation intervals in lysimeter I and II seemingly favored other species, all of which were terrestrial. Nitrogen removal by harvested biomass, when calculated from the total harvested biomass (Table 3), is a better estimation of N actually removed from the lysimeters than are the figures based on the squares only (Table 2), since these do not include growth differences along the edges.

No significant changes in soil N content were detected except in the upper 15 cm of lysimeter I. The N content in this layer increased from 0.053% of dw in May to 0.080% of dw in November (ANOVA, $p<0.01$).

Using water flow and N concentrations, the input and leaching of total-N during the study were calculated (Table 3). Nitrogen removal by the wetland filter was equal to 58, 62, 73, and 77% for lysimeters I to IV, respectively. If only the period from the first cut was considered (weeks 10-29), N removal was 59, 67, 77 and 87%, respectively. This period is more relevant when

TABLE 3. Total N input, leachate and removal with harvested biomass (*Glyceria maxima* + other species) for wastewater irrigated lysimeters (Apr. - Oct. 1985).

	Lysimeter			
	I	II	III	IV[++]
Application frequency[+] (irrigation occasions/week)	14	7	2	1
Input (g N m^{-2})	106	106	106	91
Leachate (g N m^{-2})	44	40	29	21
Harvest[+++] (g N m^{-2})	29	30	32	24

[+]May 15 - Oct. 23. Identical frequencies before that.
[++]Due to leakage lysimeter IV got less wastewater than the others.
[+++]Based on the total harvested biomass in each lysimeter.

considering effects caused by the different application frequencies which probably had minor influence on N concentrations in leachate during the spring peak in May. However, the N leached during this peak made a large contribution to the total amount of N in leachate during the study, especially in lysimeter IV where 46% of leached N appeared during weeks 4-8. The peak might be partially explained by the increased wastewater load. Most likely, however, the main reason was leaching of N produced by a rapid spring mineralization of organic N when the soil temperature increased.

Although denitrification losses are a probable explanation for the differences in N removal between the lysimeters, other possible processes include: NH_3 volatilization, microbial assimilation, NH_4^+ adsorption to clay and plant uptake. The pH of the wastewater averaged 7.9 which is high enough to allow significant NH_3 volatilization. In fact, the lower N concentrations in the applied wastewater during the summer might be explained by NH_3 volatilization from the facultative pond. In the lysimeters, ponding should promote volatilization which would consequently increase in importance from I to IV, similar to denitrification. However, opinions about the importance of NH_3 volatilization in systems like ours are clearly divergent (Craswell and Vlek, 1983). If significant losses through volatilization occurred, it should have been most important after cutting of the grass, when there is no foliar adsorption (Denmead et al., 1976). In addition, increased wind exposure after harvest and fairly high temperatures in summer promotes volatilization.

Microbial assimilation of N is favored by aerobic conditions and might account for part of the observed increase in soil N content in lysimeter I. Adsorption of NH_4^+ ions to clay probably was not important for net removal of N since the soil clay in the lysimeters was low (3%).

Plant N uptake, accounted for by the harvested biomass, was clearly depressed in lysimeter IV compared to the other three. This lysimeter received 10% less N than the others between the harvest occasions, but this could not account for the low recovery in the second harvest. After harvest, the increase in total-N concentration in leachate was negligible, whereas in the other lysimeters it increased substantially. This suggests that gaseous losses of N were even more important in lysimeter IV than what is obvious from input and leachate data. The restriction of the O_2 supply by ponding possibly resulted in a higher demand for NO_3^- as an electron acceptor than as a nutrient source in this lysimeter.

The highest N recovery in G. maxima was achieved with two applications per week. Recovery was similar to that reported with two cuts of other forage grasses irrigated with wastewater (Marten et al., 1980). Higher application frequencies, as in lysimeter I and II, probably resulted in more aerated soil conditions and increased competition from terrestrial species, as well as a higher leaching of N.

Other Parameters

The pH in leachate (Table 1) from all the lysimeters increased slightly during the study (6.0 to 6.5). Conductivity also increased (0.38 to 0.88). In both cases, the observed increases were probably a reflection of the fairly high values for the applied wastewater.

The COD increase in leachate (Table 1) over time was moderate in lysimeter I (25 to 53), II (27 to 65) and III (24 to 63), but it was considerable in IV (28 to 190). Analysis of BOD during the last part of the study revealed that BOD made up for only a small portion of the leached COD. The high COD may have originated from wastewater components as well as organic matter leached from the soil.

Phosphorus removal was almost complete in all lysimeters (Table 1). The differences in runoff concentrations, however, followed the expected increase in anaerobiosis going from lysimeter I to IV.

CONCLUSIONS

Short time scheduling of wastewater application was of crucial importance for N removal in a wetland filter. Two applications per week were optimal for efficient renovation and high N recovery in harvested biomass. However, if a more treated wastewater and lower application rates are used, the effects of different application frequencies might not appear (Linden et al., 1981). The sharp peak of NO_3^- in runoff in May suggests that it is worthwhile to interrupt the wastewater application for some weeks between snow melt and substantial plant growth. Applying wastewater all year round will substantially reduce the recovery rate, since large amounts of N will be applied during periods with no plant growth.

ACKNOWLEDGMENTS

Prof. Thomas Rosswall and Prof. Ulrik Lohm are gratefully acknowledged for critical reading of the manuscript. We thank Bo Thuner for skillful technical assistance and Tekniska Verken i Linkoping AB for valuable cooperation. This work was supported by grants from the Carl Trygger Foundation and the Valdemar & Emmy Gustavsson Foundation.

REFERENCES

A.P.H.A., American Public Health Association. 1980. Standard methods for the examination of water and wastewater. 15th ed. A.P.H.A., Washington, DC.

Craswell, E. T., and P. L. G. Vlek. 1983. Fate of fertilizer nitrogen applied to wetland rice. In J. R. Freney and J. R. Simpson (ed.) Gaseous Loss of Nitrogen From Plant-Soil Systems, Developments in Plant and Soil Sciences 9:237-264. Martinus Nijhoff/Dr. W. Junk Publishers, The Hague.

Denmead, O. T., J. R. Freney, and J. R. Simpson. 1976. A closed ammonia cycle within a plant canopy. Soil Biol. Biochem. 8:161-164.

Dykyjova, D. 1978. Nutrient uptake by littoral communities of helophytes. In D. Dykyjova and J. Kvet (ed.) Pond Littoral Ecosystems, Ecological Studies 28:257-277. Springer-Verlag, Berlin.

Hejny, S., and S. Husak. 1978. Higher plant communities. In D. Dykyjova and J. Kvet (ed.) Pond Littoral Ecosystems, Ecological Studies 28:23-64. Springer-Verlag, Berlin.

Kvet, J., and S. Husak. 1978. Primary data on biomass and production estimates in typical stands of fishpond littoral plant communities. In D. Dykyjova and J. Kvet (ed.) Pond Littoral Ecosystems, Ecological Studies 28:211-215. Springer-Verlag, Berlin.

Lance, J. C., and F. D. Whisler. 1972. Nitrogen balance in soil columns intermittently flooded with secondary sewage effluent. J. Environ. Qual. 1:180-186.

Linden, D. R., C. E. Clapp, and J. R. Gilley. 1981. Effects of scheduling municipal wastewater effluent irrigation of reed canarygrass on nitrogen renovation and grass production. J. Environ. Qual. 10:507-510.

Lohammar, G. 1955. The introduction of foreign water plants, with special reference to conditions in northern Europe. Proceedings of the International Association of Theoretical and Applied Limnology 12:562-568.

Marten, G. C., W. E. Larson, and C. E. Clapp. 1980. Effects of municipal wastewater effluent on performance and feed quality of maize vs. reed canarygrass. J. Environ. Qual. 9:137-141.

Patrick, W. H., and R. Wyatt. 1964. Soil nitrogen loss as a result of alternate submergence and drying. Soil Sci. Soc. Am. Proc. 28:647-653.

Swedish Standardization Board. 1976. Determination of nitrogen compounds in water. Oxidation with peroxodisulphate. SIS 028131. Swedish Standardization Board, Stockholm, Sweden.

Westlake, D. F. 1966. The biomass and productivity of *Glyceria maxima*. I. Seasonal changes in biomass. J. Ecol. 54:745-753.

NITRIFICATION, DENITRIFICATION, AND AMMONIA DIFFUSION IN A CATTAIL MARSH

J. S. Lorenz and D. D. Biesboer
Department of Botany
University of Minnesota
St. Paul, Minnesota 55108

ABSTRACT

The role of nitrification, denitrification and NH_4^+ diffusion in soils was studied to determine the availability of N for cattail growth in marsh soils. Five soils were examined. Ammonium diffusion from deep placement showed counter-diffusion coefficients of 0.193 and 0.207 $cm^2\ d^{-1}$ for two of the soils. Short-term (16 h) nitrification of applied NH_4^+ in the five soils yielded rates that varied from not detectable to 1.37 $\mu M\ g^{-1}\ h^{-1}$ under ideal aeration conditions. Denitrification rates varied from 0.022 to 0.139 $\mu M\ N_2O\ g^{-1}\ h^{-1}$ for the five soils. For two soils, addition of sucrose increased NO_3^- reduction significantly, indicating C limitation.

Keywords: Nitrogen, acetylene inhibition, floating mat.

INTRODUCTION

Interest in the use of freshwater wetlands for biomass energy production has been growing because of the disappearance of inexpensive domestic energy. The high productivity of cattails (*Typha* sp.) and their adaptability to a wide variety of wetlands make cattails a prime candidate for energy farming (Garver et al., 1983).

Application of fertilizer N to cattail stands has been shown to increase their production of biomass, principally because N is a growth-limiting nutrient in cattail paddies (Biesboer, 1984; Bonnewell and Pratt, 1978). However, gains in productivity from application of N to cultivated or natural stands of cattails must be weighed against the large cost and potentially high rate of denitrification of these fertilizers. Wastewater N may be an affordable source, providing N for the crops, while renovating wastewater.

Most of the research concerning nitrification and denitrification in flooded soils has been done on rice paddies

Aquatic Plants for Water Treatment and Resource Recovery
K.R. Reddy and W.H. Smith (Eds.)

ISBN 0-941463-00-1

(Reddy and Patrick, 1984; Savant and DeDatta, 1982). While seasonal temperatures and some soil characteristics may differ between cattail marshes and submerged rice soils, the processes leading to nitrification and denitrification are similar. The purpose of this study was to determine for several soils from cattail marshes the rate potentials for NH_4^+ diffusion, nitrification, and denitrification.

MATERIALS AND METHODS

The five soils used in this study were gathered from three sites: a floating mat from Carlos Avery Wildlife Management Area (Biesboer, 1984); a sapric peat and loamy sand from a river floodplain near Aitkin, Minnesota; and two layers of a hemic peat soil, one excavated to 0.76 m and one unexcavated from a minerotrophic fen near Zim, Minnesota (Garver et al., 1983). All soil samples were put into jars with enough water to saturate them, transported to the lab on ice, and stored at 2°C until use. Selected characteristics of these five soils are listed in Table 1.

The acetylene (C_2H_2) inhibition method was used to measure short-term denitrification (Yoshinari et al., 1977). Acetylene inhibits the reduction of the N_2O to N_2 during denitrification. The N_2O is measured chromatographically and is representative of denitrification. Soil was mixed with enough distilled water to make a slurry and 60 mL of slurry was added to 125 mL flasks. Potassium nitrate was added to the flasks at a concentration of 0, 20, and 100 μg N g^{-1} dry wt soil. For the floating mat, the loamy sand, and the unexcavated soils, all of which showed low rates of denitrification in preliminary tests, 400 μg sucrose g^{-1} soil was

TABLE 1. Characteristics of five cattail marsh soils.

Soil[+]	Nitrate[++]	Ammonium	Cation exchange capacity	pH[+++]	Ash %
	-------μg g^{-1}-------				
FM	0	83	0.64	5.90	27.0
SP	10	4	1.13	5.20	59.8
LS	7	0	0.37	5.95	90.2
ZN	50	12	1.00	5.00	18.0
ZX	0	92	0.95	4.90	9.3

[+]Soil abbreviations: FM = floating mat soil from Carlos Avery Wildlife Management Area; SP and LS = sapric peat and loamy sand soils from Aitkin, Minnesota; ZN and ZX = unexcavated and excavated hemic peat soils from Zim, Minnesota.

[++]These concentrations vary greatly with season and with aeration status of the soils.

[+++]pH in 0.01 M $CaCl_2$.

added to flasks containing 100 µg of N g^{-1} to determine if denitrification was C limited. Four replications were used for each NO_3^- and sucrose treatment.

The flasks were sealed with serum stoppers, evacuated to -25 cm Hg, and flushed with Ar. Evacuation and flushing were repeated once. Ten percent of the headspace volume was removed and replaced with acetylene. A 0.5 mL gas sample was withdrawn by syringe from each flask at 0, 2, 4, 7.5, 11 and 23 h. The samples were injected into a HP 5840A gas chromatograph fitted with a Porapak Q column (100 C) to separate N_2O from CO_2 and C_2H_2. A thermal conductivity detector set at an operating temperature of 175 degrees was used to quantify N_2O.

The short-term nitrification procedure was adapted from Sarathchandra (1978). For each soil, six 250 mL flasks containing 100 g slurry were prepared with 100 μg^{-1} dry wt (estimated) N added as $(NH_4^+)_2SO_4$. The flasks were put on a shaker for 1 h. At the end of that time, 2 flasks of each soil were assayed for NH_4^+, and NO_3^-+NO_2^- (Keeney and Bremner, 1966). Flasks were weighed empty, after extraction, and after oven drying at 90°C. The weights were used to calculate µM NO_3^-, and g dry wt for each sample. At 17 to 41 h the remaining pairs of flasks were assayed in a similar fashion.

Ammonium diffusion was measured in the Aitkin sapric peat and loamy sand by constructing columns of 5 cm diameter PVC pipe. A rubber stopper was placed in the bottom of each column and sealed with a 1:1 mixture of paraffin and petroleum jelly (Reddy et al., 1980). One-hundred-fifty g of saturated soil with 330 µg N g^{-1} as $(NH_4^+)_2SO_4$ was added. A filter paper was placed in the column to mark the top of the amended soil. One-hundred-fifty grams of saturated unamended soil was added to top. The columns were incubated for four days under Ar to prevent nitrification. Then the columns were extruded and 0.8 cm slices transferred to 125 mL flasks. These samples were extracted with KCl and assayed for NH_4^+ as in the above experiment. From the data, a concentration profile was made and a diffusion constant D calculated (Phillips and Brown, 1964).

RESULTS

Two measures of potential denitrification for the five soils are shown in Table 2. The value shown to the right of "0 µg g^{-1}" for each soil is the NO_3^- present in that soil before any amendment. In Table 2 the column under "Denitrification" shows the maximum rate of denitrification that was sustained for 4 h. The rates of denitrification at 100 µg NO_3-N g^{-1} of soil were, in descending order, sapric peat, unexcavated hemic peat, floating mat, loamy sand, excavated hemic peat. The loamy sand and unexcavated hemic peat soils showed an increase in rate with the addition of 400 µg g^{-1} sucrose, while the floating mat soil failed to respond to sucrose amendment (Table 2). The constant K for

TABLE 2. Denitrification in soils amended with NO_3^- and sucrose. Values are means of four replicates.

Soil[+]	Added NO_3^- and (sucrose)	Actual NO_3^-	Denitrification	K	K^1	Regression coefficient
	-----μg g^{-1}-----		μM N_2O g^{-1} h^{-1}	h^{-1}	d^{-1}	
SP	0	10	T.			
	20	31	0.121			
	100	113	0.148	0.058	0.738	(0.996)
ZX	0	0	0			
	5	4	0.017			
	20	17	0.050			
	100	86	0.071	0.029	0.502	(0.996)
ZN	0	50	0.139			
	20	67	0.162			
	100	136	0.167	0.034	0.539	(0.999)
	100 (400)	136	0.218	0.055	0.721	(0.990)
CA	0	0	0			
	20	21	0.021			
	100	103	0.105	0.026	0.455	(0.950)
	100 (400)	103	0.109	0.023	0.425	(0.907)
LS	0	7	0.022			
	100	107	0.023	0.004	0.085	(0.979)
	100	107	0.047	0.010	0.207	(0.998)
	0 (400)	7	0.030			

[†]Soil abbreviations: FM = floating mat soil from Carlos Avery Wildlife Management Area; SP and LS = sapric peat and loamy sand soils from Aitkin, Minnesota; ZN and ZX = unexcavated and excavated hemic peat soils from Zim, Minnesota.

for each soil in this experiment were calculated from the first 11 h of each assay using the equation of Stanford et al. (1975). The rate constant K represents the proportion of the remaining NO_3^- denitrified in an hour. The accompanying constant R is a regression coefficient for the slope. The value K_1 listed in Table 2 is the conversion of K to a per day basis.

Figure 1a shows the production of N_2O over time for the loamy sand soil from Aitkin with and without the addition of NO_3^- and sucrose. The rate of N_2O production at 0 μg g^{-1} does not differ significantly from the rate of production after the addition of NO_3^- to the soil. The addition of 400 μg g^{-1} sucrose significantly raised the production of N_2O from the soil (P = 0.001 level) at 7.5 h, but this rate decreased slowly after this time. Addition of both NO_3^- and sucrose caused N_2O production to continue and increase throughout the assay.

The effect of 0, 5, 20, and 100 μg g^{-1} NO_3^- on the time course of denitrification in the unexcavated hemic peat soil from Zim was

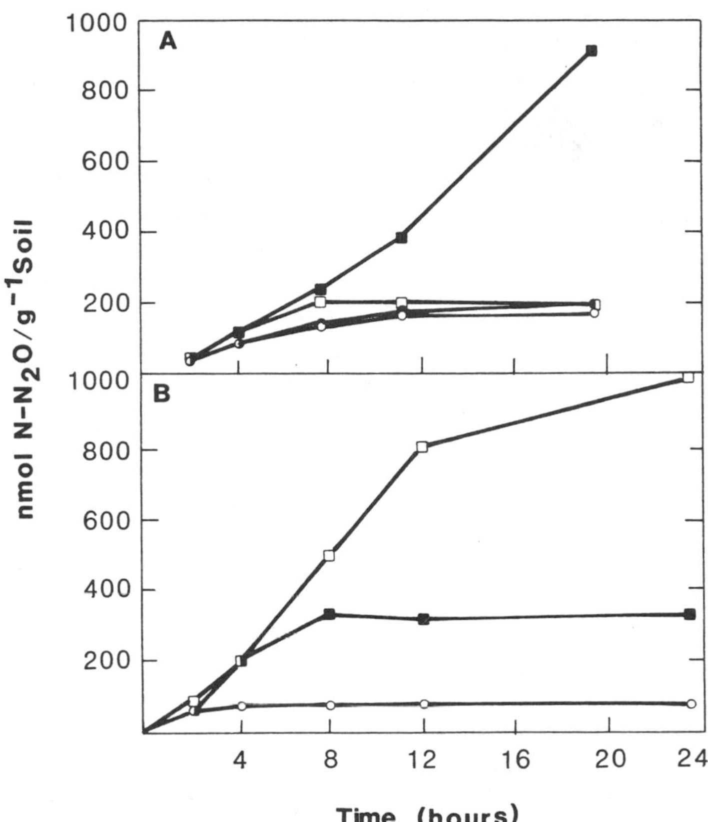

FIGURE 1A. Time course of denitrification (N_2O evolution) in the loamy sand soil at four NO_3^- and sucrose amendments. Each point represents the mean of four replicates. ● = 100 μg g^{-1} NO_3-N, ■ = 400 μg g^{-1} sucrose, □ = 100 μg g^{-1} NO_3-N + 400 μg g^{-1} sucrose, ○ = no soil amendment.

FIGURE 1B. Time course of denitrification (N_2O evolution) in the excavated hemic peat soil at four NO_3^- amendments. Each point represents the mean of four replicates. No amendment of the soil showed no activity. ○ = 5 μg g^{-1} NO_3-N, ■ = 20 μg g^{-1} NO_3^-, □ = 100 μg g^{-1} NO_3^-.

determined (Figure 1b). Production of N_2O ranged from 0.0 μM g^{-1} h^{-1} at 0 μg NO_3-N g^{-1} to 0.071 μM g^{-1} h^{-1} at 100 μg NO_3-N g^{-1}.

Figure 2 shows the NO_3^- production expressed as a natural log and plotted against time. Results from the three soil amendments of Carlos Avery Soil produced three similar regression lines from which were calculated a doubling-time for nitrifying activity of 1.20 ± 0.07 d and an initial nitrification rate of 0.002 ± 0.0006

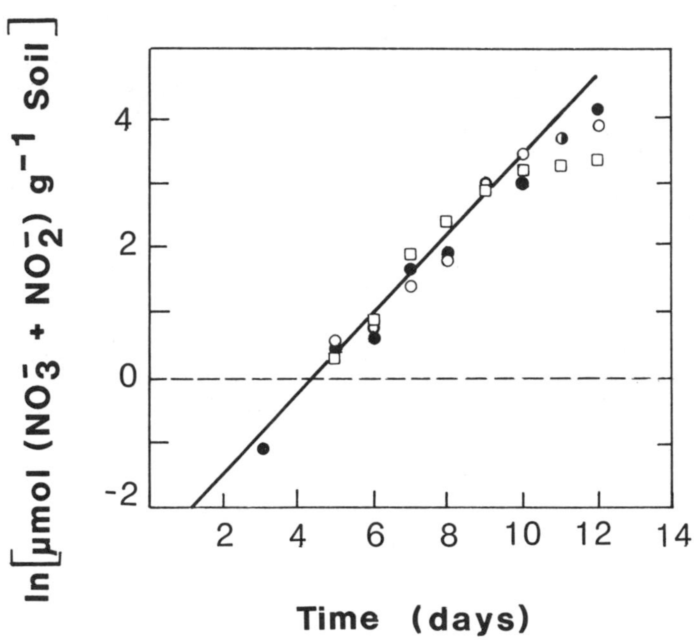

FIGURE 2. Natural log graph of nitrification (NO_3^- production) in the floating mat soil at three NH_4^+ concentrations. The regression line yields a doubling time for nitrifier activity of 1.20 ± 0.088 d and an initial rate of nitrification of 0.002 ± 0.0006 μM g^{-1} h^{-1}. ● = 140 μg g^{-1} NH_4-N, ○ = 420 μg g^{-1} NH_4-N, □ = 700 μg g^{-1} NH_4-N.

μM g^{-1} h^{-1}. During the assay, the total inorganic N (NO_3^-, NO_2^-, and NH_4^+) increases by an average of 19.0 μM g^{-1} over 12 d. This result probably demonstrates mineralization due to the accelerated organic matter breakdown during aerobic agitation (Reddy and Patrick, 1975).

The rate of short-term nitrification for the five tested soils showed the unexcavated hemic peat soil from Zim to have the highest rate with 1.37 μM g^{-1} h^{-1}, followed by the sapric peat and loamy sand soils from Aitkin with a rate of 0.85 μM g^{-1} h^{-1} and 0.28 μM g^{-1} h^{-1}, respectively (Table 3). The floating mat and excavated hemic peat soils showed no detectable nitrification after 41 h. As shown above for the floating mat soil, this does not rule out low level nitrification in these soils.

The distribution of 330 μg NH_4-N g^{-1} in diffusion columns for the sapric peat and loamy sand soils after incubation for four days is shown in Figure 3. The apparent counter diffusion coefficients calculated for these soils were 0.207 and 0.193 cm^2

TABLE 3. Short term nitrification in soil slurries amended with NH_4-N.

Soil	NH_4^+ added	O_2	Nitrification 16 h	40 h
	-----μg g^{-1}-----		μg N g^{-1} h^{-1}	μg N g^{-1} h^{-1}
FM⁺	197	6.3	N.D.⁺⁺	N.D.
SP	98	5.9	0.85	1.22
LS	103	7.0	0.28	0.42
AX	101	5.4	N.D.	N.D.
ZN	136	6.3	1.37	1.94

⁺Soil abbreviations: FM = floating mat soil from Carlos Avery Wildlife Management Area; SP and SL = sapric peat and loamy sand hemic peat soils from Aim, Minnesota.

⁺⁺N.D. = not detectable.

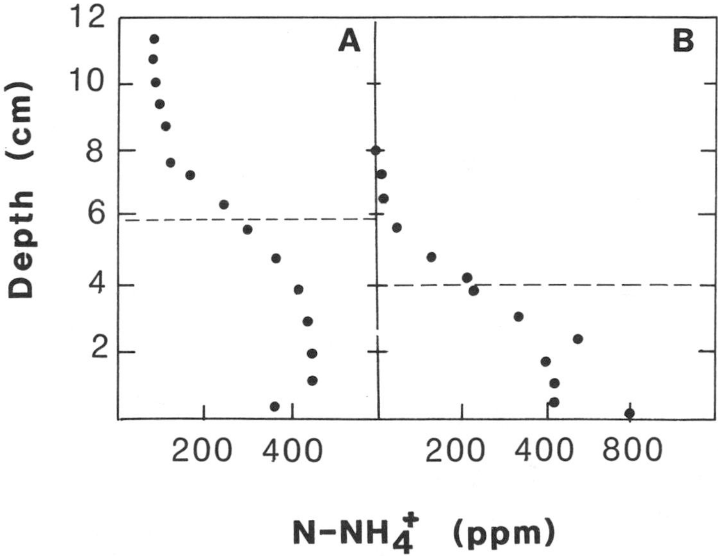

FIGURE 3. Profiles of NH_4^+ diffusion columns of sapric peat (A) and loamy sand (B) soils after four days incubation under Ar. The dashed line represents the original boundary between unamended soil (top) and soil amended with 330 μg g^{-1} NH_4-N (bottom).

d^{-1}, respectively. This represents diffusion of NH_4^+ from a zone of high concentration to a zone of low concentration under flooded conditions. The NH_4^+ concentrations at the extreme ends of the column are assumed to be unchanged during the experimental period.

Attempts to quantify diffusion in the floating mat soil were unsuccessful due to the difficulty of sectioning this extremely fibrous soil.

DISCUSSION

In this study the rate of NO_3^- diffusion was omitted from consideration as a limiting factor for denitrification in marsh soils. Ammonium diffusion should proceed more slowly than NO_3^- diffusion in a flooded soil because adsorption of NO_3^- in soils is virtually zero at pH 5.5, while NH_4^+ is strongly held on cation exchange sites. Reddy et al. (1980) found the NO_3^- diffusion coefficient for Crowley silty loam to be roughly nine times the NH_4^+ diffusion coefficient, and also eliminated it as a limiting factor in N loss.

The nitrification rate of the five soils sampled in this study are comparable to those found elsewhere. Sarathchandra (1978), in 16 h assays on New Zealand soils found a nitrification rate of 0.00 - 3.31 μg g^{-1} h^{-1}. Stojanovic and Alexander (1958), using a soil perfusion apparatus, had an average first day NO_3^- production rate of 17.35 μM g^{-1} d^{-1} (0.72 μM g^{-1} h^{-1}). Reddy et al. (1980), working with flooded rice paddy soils, found much lower rates, 1.10 to 2.77 μM g^{-1} d^{-1}, which they attributed to low pH of their soils (4.9 to 6.8) and the low O_2 content in their assays. Reddy et al. (1980) preincubated soil slurries by stirring and bubbling with air for 6 d. Their assay was run in shallow flats with a slurry depth of 1 cm. Soil O_2 level was maintained by diffusion. Our assays approximate the potential for nitrifying activity under ideal aeration. In addition they represent the per gram potential of the entire 15 cm soil profile and not just the oxidized layer.

There is much debate in the scientific literature over how to derive and interpret denitrification rates from raw data. Steele et al. (1984) used C_2H_2 inhibition of N_2O reductase in soils in a short assay (8 h) and derived zero-order rate constraints from their data of between 0.18 and 1.83 μg g^{-1} h^{-1} (0.006 to 0.065 μM N_2O g^{-1} h^{-1}). Since they added no C source or NO_3^-, they derived steady rates that depended on the release rate of oxidizable C from the organic matter. The assays at 0 μg g^{-1} NO_3^- and sucrose yielded rates of denitrification ranging from zero for the two submerged soils, the floating mat and the excavated hemic peat, which have no NO_3^-, to 0.022 μM g^{-1} h^{-1} for the loamy sand and 0.139 μM g^{-1} h^{-1} for the unexcavated hemic peat soil (Table 2). These last two soils were the most highly oxygenated and contained 7 and 50 μg g^{-1} NO_3^-, respectively. Both proved to be C limited with the loamy sand responding to both C and NO_3^- additions (Figures 1a,b).

Reddy et al. (1980) determined that denitrification rates of soils amended with 100 μg g^{-1} NO_3^- were best described by a first-order rate constant. Their soils produced rate constants of 0.315

and 0.520 per day (fraction denitrified). These values are comparable to the constants (K1) determined for our soils at 100 $\mu g\ g^{-1}$ NO_3-N that ranged from 0.085 d^{-1} for the loamy sand soil to 0.738 d^{-1} for the sapric peat soil with C amendment.

The diffusion constants for the sapric peat and loamy sand soils (Figure 3) of 0.207 and 0.193 $cm^2\ d^{-1}$, respectively, were similar to those for saturated paddy soils as determined by Reddy et al. (1980) of 0.059 to 0.216 $cm^2\ d^{-1}$, but much lower than those determined for marine sediments by Krom and Berner (1980) of 0.850 $cm^2\ d^{-1}$, adjusted for NH_4^+ adsorption. The diffusion of cations in organic soils is greatly affected by compaction, which increases both the distance cations must travel in diffusing from one point to another and the contact cations make with the cation exchange sites. Differences in compaction may mean that an artificial column of soil may have a diffusion constant for NH_4^+ that varies significantly from the diffusion constant of the same soil in an undisturbed soil profile.

The present study was designed to give preliminary information on how the rates of NH_4^+ diffusion, nitrification, and denitrification are affected by the addition of N to marsh soils; and to determine how N might be applied to cattail paddies to control fertilizer losses. Efforts to slow N loss center on methods to slow nitrification by 1) slowing diffusion of NH_4^+ to the upper oxidized zones of the soil by deep placement of fertilizer, and 2) lessening the diffusion O_2 into the soil by keeping the soil well-flooded.

ACKNOWLEDGMENT

This research was funded by the Biological Energy Coordinating Office, Department of Botany, University of Minnesota, St. Paul, Minnesota.

REFERENCES

Biesboer, D. D. 1984. Nitrogen fixation associated with natural and cultivated stands of _Typha latifolia_ L. (Typhaceae). Amer. J. Bot. 71:505-511.

Bonnewell, V., and D. C. Pratt. 1978. Effect of nutrients on productivity and morphology of _Typha angustifolia_ x _latifolia_. J. Minnesota Acad. Sci. 44:18-20.

Buresh, R. J., M. E. Casselman, and W. H. Patrick, Jr. 1980. Nitrogen fixation in flooded soil systems, a review. Adv. Agron. 33:149-192.

Garver, E. G., D. R. Dubbe, and D. C. Pratt. 1983. Adaptability of _Typha_ spp. to various wetland soil conditions for bio-energy productions. p. 263-276. _In_ C. H. Fuchsman and S. A. Spigarelli (ed.) Proceedings of the International Symposium on Peat Utilization. Bemidji State University, Bemidji, Minnesota.

Keeney, D. R., and J. M. Bremner. 1966. Determination and isotope-ratio analysis of different forms of nitrogen in soils: 4. Exchangeable ammonium, nitrate, and nitrite by direct-distillation methods. Soil Sci. Soc. Am. Proc. 30:327-328.

Krom, M. D., and R. A. Berner. 1980. The diffusion coefficients of sulfate, ammonium and phosphate ions in anoxic marine sediments. Limnol. Oceanogr. 25:327-328.

Phillips, R. E., and D. A. Brown. 1964. Ion exchange diffusion II. Calculation and comparison of self- and counter-diffusion coefficients. Soil Sci. Soc. Am. Proc. 28:758-763.

Reddy, K. R., and W. H. Patrick, Jr. 1975. Effect of alternate aerobic and anaerobic conditions on redox potential, organic matter decomposition and nitrogen loss in a flooded soil. Soil Biol. Biochem. 7:87-94.

Reddy, K. R., and W. H. Patrick, Jr. 1984. Nitrogen transformations and loss in flooded soils and sediments. CRC Critical Reviews in Environ. Control 13:273-309.

Reddy, K. R., W. H. Patrick, Jr., and R. E. Phillips. 1980. Evaluation of selected processes controlling nitrogen loss in a flooded soil. Soil Sci. Soc. Am. J. 44:1241-1246.

Sarathchandra, S. U. 1978. Nitrification activities of some New Zealand soils and the effect of some clay types on nitrification. New Zealand J. Agr. Res. 21:615-621.

Savant, N. K., and S. K. DeDatta. 1982. Nitrogen transformations in wetland rice soils. Adv. Agron. 35:241-302.

Stanford, G., R. A. VanderPol, and S. Dzienia. 1975. Denitrification rates in relation to total and extractable soil carbon. Soil Sci. Soc. Am. J. 39:284-289.

Steele, K. W., P. M. Bonish, and S. U. Sarathchandra. 1984. Denitrification potentials and microbiological characteristics of some northern North Island soils. New Zealand J. Agri. Res. 27:525-530.

Stojanovic, B. J., and M. Alexander. 1958. Effect of inorganic nitrogen on nitrification. Soil Sci. Soc. Am. J. 86:525-530.

Yoshinari, T., R. Hynes, and R. Knowles. 1977. Acetylene inhibition of nitrous oxide reduction and measurement of denitrification and nitrogen fixation in soil. Soil Biol. Biochem. 9:177-183.

NITROGEN CYCLING IN AN INTEGRATED "BIOMASS FOR ENERGY" SYSTEM

K. K. Moorhead and K. R. Reddy
Central Florida Research and Education Center
University of Florida, IFAS
Sanford, Florida 32771

D. A. Graetz
Soil Science Department
University of Florida, IFAS
Gainesville, Florida 32611

ABSTRACT

Nitrogen cycling in three components of an integrated "biomass for energy" system, water hyacinth production, anaerobic digestion of hyacinth biomass, and recycling of digester effluent and sludge were evaluated.

Biomass production of water hyacinth under field conditions was 0.7 to 28.3 g (dry wt) m^{-2} d^{-1}. Assimilation of added N by water hyacinth was 51% under field conditions and up to 89% during greenhouse experiments. Net mineralization of plant organic ^{15}N during anaerobic digestion was 35 and 70% for water hyacinth plants with low (10 g N kg^{-1}) and high (35 g N kg^{-1}) N content, respectively. Approximately 20% of the ^{15}N was recovered in the digested sludge, and the remaining was recovered in the effluent.

Addition of water hyacinth to soil resulted in decomposition of 39 to 50% of the added C for fresh plant biomass and of 19 to 23% of the added C for digested biomass sludge. Only 8% of the added ^{15}N in digested sludge was mineralized to NO_3-N despite differences in initial N content (27 and 39 g N kg^{-1} dry sludge). In contrast, 3 and 33% of the added ^{15}N in fresh biomass with low and high N content, respectively, was recovered as NO_3-N.

Plant assimilation of N from digester effluent recycled 21 to 38% of the initial plant biomass ^{15}N placed in the digester. Total N recovery by sludge and effluent recycling in the integrated "biomass for energy" system was 41 to 58% of the initial plant biomass ^{15}N. The remaining ^{15}N was lost from the system during anaerobic digestion and effluent recycling.

Keywords: Water hyacinth, anaerobic digestion, N mineralization, digester effluent, digested sludge.

ISBN 0-941463-00-1

INTRODUCTION

An integrated "biomass for energy" system was developed using water hyacinth for wastewater treatment and for total resource recovery (Chynoweth et al., 1983). In this system, water hyacinths were used to recover nutrients from wastewater. The biomass produced was then harvested and processed through anaerobic digestion to produce CH_4. The waste by-product generated during this process must be disposed of, or preferably utilized, in an environmentally-safe manner. The waste by-product contains digested biomass sludge and effluent. The digested sludge, applied to soil, can be used as a fertilizer source, whereas the effluent can be recycled in water hyacinth ponds to produce additional biomass and for nutrient recovery (Hanisak et al., 1980; Atalay and Blanchar, 1984). This type of integrated system provides low cost water treatment and total resource recovery.

The objectives of this study were to determine 1) plant productivity and N assimilation of water hyacinths grown in nutrient-enriched and limited systems, 2) N mineralization during anaerobic digestion of water hyacinth biomass, 3) the potential of water hyacinth to grow in anaerobic digester effluents for N recovery, and 4) N mineralization during decomposition of fresh and digested water hyacinth added to soil.

MATERIALS AND METHODS

Water Hyacinth Productivity and N Assimilation

Water hyacinth productivity and N assimilation were evaluated under field and greenhouse conditions. The field study was conducted in two reservoirs at the University of Florida's Central Florida REC research farm in Zellwood, FL. The reservoirs were 7.6 m by 61 m, with a water depth of 0.6 m. Both reservoirs were filled with water from nearby Lake Apopka, sectioned into four equal areas for replication, and stocked with water hyacinth.

A total of eight 0.25-m^2 cages (Vexar mesh screen connected to 5 cm diameter PVC pipe) were stocked with water hyacinths at an initial density of 16 kg (fresh wt) m^{-2}. The cages were placed within the four replicated areas of each reservoir. One reservoir was fertilized monthly by broadcasting a granular 10-4-10 fertilizer, to add 100 kg N ha^{-1} from October 1981 to February 1982, and 50 kg N ha^{-1} from March 1982 to September 1982. The second reservoir contained Lake Apopka water with no added nutrients, to serve as a control.

Plant productivity and N assimilation were monitored at monthly intervals for one year. The cages were removed from each section, drained for 5 min, and weighed. Three plants were removed for analyses and the cages were stocked to initial plant density and replaced in the reservoirs.

The greenhouse studies were conducted at the University of Florida, Gainesville, FL, to evaluate water hyacinth assimilation of added $^{15}NO_3$-N or $^{15}NH_4$-N. The plants were grown in 0.25-m^2 microcosm tanks with a 20 cm water depth. Initial plant density was 10 kg (fresh wt) m^{-2} and ^{15}N was added at a concentration of 20 mg N L^{-1}. Plants were removed for analyses after 28 d.

Anaerobic Digestion of Water Hyacinth

Water hyacinths, with either high or low tissue N content, were anaerobically digested in 55-L batch digesters at 35°C. Water hyacinths with a high N content (35 g N kg^{-1}) were obtained from the wastewater treatment plant of the Reedy Creek Utility Company, Inc., at Walt Disney World near Orlando, FL. Water hyacinths with a low N content (10 g kg^{-1}) were grown in tap water at Sanford, FL. Both types of hyacinths were grown in $^{15}(NH_4)_2SO_4$ for two weeks, frozen and chopped to 1.6 mm length using a Hobart T 215 food processor.

The digesters received 4.7 kg (fresh wt) of the ^{15}N labeled water hyacinths; 2.5, 5, or 10 L of inoculum from digesters containing water hyacinth as feedstock; and 210 g $NaHCO_3$ to stabilize digester pH. At the end of the digestion period, each digester was thoroughly mixed and the total contents were passed through a 1.00-mm fiberglass screen to separate the digested biomass sludge from the effluent.

Waste Recycling

Screened digester effluent was used as a growth media for water hyacinths. Six plants were placed in 10 L of undiluted or diluted effluent in containers having a surface area of 0.051 m^2. Plant productivity and N assimilation were evaluated after 22 d.

The digested biomass sludges and fresh water hyacinths were freeze-dried and mixed with 50 g surface-soil samples of a Kendrick fine sand (Arenic paleudult) at a rate of 10 Mg ha^{-1}. The soil/residue mixtures were incubated for 90 d at 27°C with a moisture content equivalent to 0.01 MPa. Carbon mineralization was determined by CO_2 evolution into 0.1 $\underline{M}$ NaOH traps followed by titration with acid after reaction with saturated $BaCl_2$. Nitrogen mineralization was determined at 30, 60 and 90 d by analyzing for inorganic N (NH_4-N and NO_3-N).

Analytical Methods

Ammonium and NO_3-N of water and digester samples were determined by steam distillation followed by titration with standard acid (A.P.H.A., 1980). Plant samples were oven-dried at 70°C and ground to pass a 0.84-mm screen of a Wiley Mill. Plant, water, and soil organic N were determined by Kjeldahl digestion followed by steam distillation (Nelson and Sommers, 1972,1973, 1975). Soil samples were extracted with 2 $\underline{M}$ KCl and analyzed for inorganic N by steam distillation (Keeney and Nelson, 1982). The ^{15}N analyses of plant, water or soil samples were conducted on a Micro Mass 602 spectrometer. Plant growth and uptake of nutrients by hyacinth were expressed on dry weight basis, unless specified otherwise.

RESULTS AND DISCUSSION

Nitrogen cycling in an integrated "biomass for energy" system was evaluated for two types of water hyacinth plants: 1) plants growing in nutrient-enriched waters representing wastewater treatment systems (sewage and digester effluents, animal wastes or agricultural drainage water), and 2) plants growing in nutrient-limited systems representing natural waters receiving low external N inputs.

Water Hyacinth Productivity and N Assimilation

A wide range of productivity (5 to 64 g m^{-2} d^{-1}) has been reported for water hyacinths growing in nutrient-enriched waters (Boyd, 1976; Hanisak et al., 1980; Reddy et al., 1985). Water hyacinth productivity was influenced by ambient air temperature, solar radiation and water nutrient composition. Monthly biomass yields during the one year field study were 0.7 to 28.3 g m^{-2} d^{-1} for plants growing in eutrophic Lake Apopka water with added fertilizer. Approximately 51% of the added fertilizer N was assimilated by plants. Total ^{15}N assimilation by water hyacinths ranged from 57 to 72% of added NO_3-N and 70 to 89% of added NH_4-N during 28 d of the greenhouse study. Reddy and Tucker (1983) established preferential NH_4-N assimilation by water hyacinth when both NH_4-N and NO_3-N were supplied in equal amounts.

Growth rates of 2 to 29 g m^{-2} d^{-1} have been reported for water hyacinths in natural waters of central and south Florida (Yount and Crossman, 1970; DeBusk et al., 1981). Monthly biomass yields during the one year field study were $<$ 0 to 14.7 g m^{-2} d^{-1} for plants growing in eutrophic Lake Apopka water without added fertilizer.

Water hyacinths growing in nutrient-enriched media generally have a N content of 30 to 40 g N kg^{-1} (Boyd, 1976; Wolverton and McDonald, 1979; Reddy et al., 1985). Nitrogen cycling during anaerobic digestion and waste recycling for plants with a high N content (35 g kg^{-1}) is shown in Figure 1.

Plants growing in nutrient-limited systems generally have a low N content. Nitrogen cycling during anaerobic digestion and waste recycling for plants with a low N content (10 g kg^{-1}) is shown in Figure 2. In addition to a low N content, the shoot/root dry weight ratio decreased as nutrient availability decreased (Reddy, 1984). The shoot/root ratio of plants with a low N content was 1.6, compared to 4.2 for plants with a high N content.

Anaerobic Digestion of Water Hyacinth

Mineralization of plant organic ^{15}N to NH_4-N was the primary N transformation during anaerobic digestion of water hyacinth.

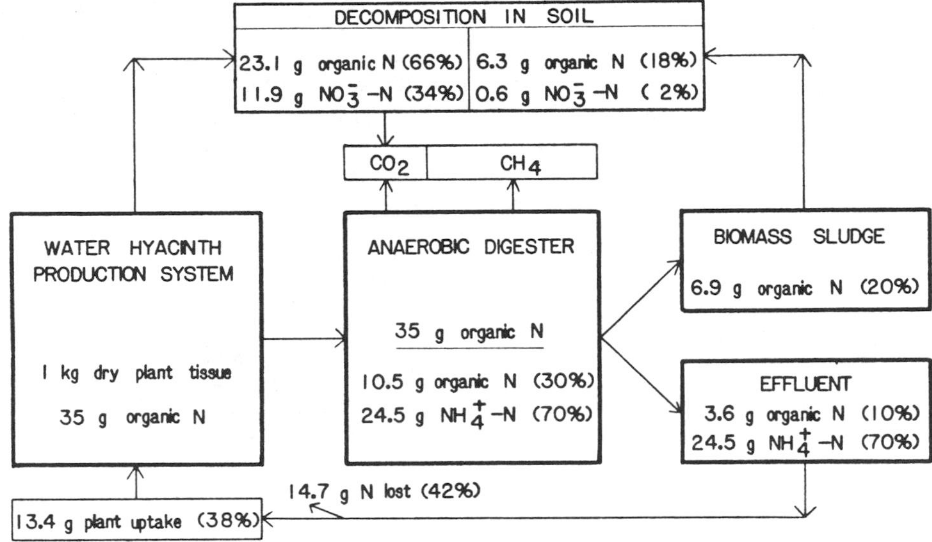

FIGURE 1. Nitrogen cycling during anaerobic digestion and waste recycling of water hyacinth plant tissue with a high N content. Numbers in parentheses are percentages of the initial 35 g N placed in the anaerobic digester.

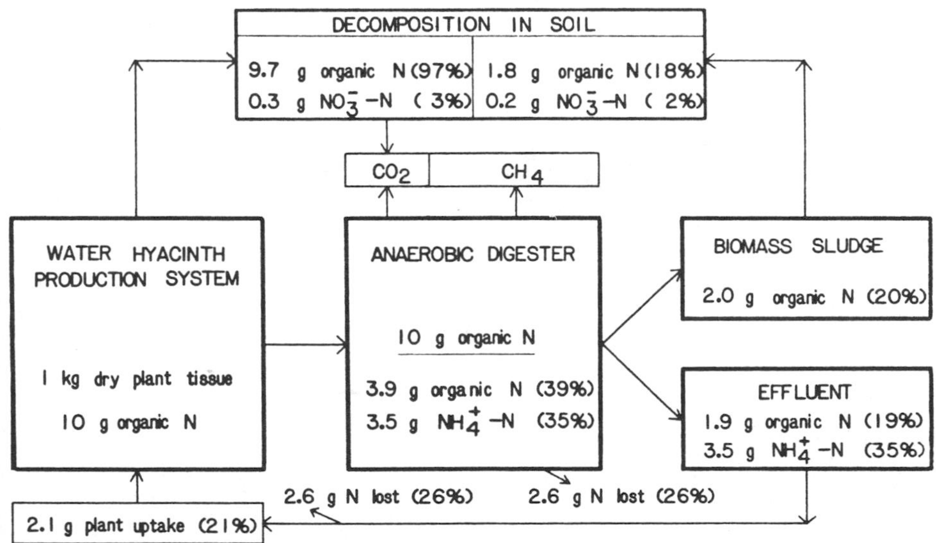

FIGURE 2. Nitrogen cycling during anaerobic digestion and waste recycling of water hyacinth plant tissue with a low N content. Numbers in parentheses are percentages of the initial 10 g N placed in the anaerobic digester.

Approximately 70% of the plant organic ^{15}N for plants with a high N content was mineralized to $^{15}NH_4$-N (Figure 1). Total ^{15}N recovered in digester sludge and effluent was ~100%, which agreed with results of Hashimoto et al. (1980) and Field et al. (1984).

Only 35% of the plant organic ^{15}N placed in the digester was recovered as NH_4-N for plants with a low N content (Figure 2). However, 26% of the initial ^{15}N was lost during anaerobic digestion. The remaining ^{15}N was recovered as organic N. One possible N-loss mechanism during anaerobic digestion is volatilization of NH_3-N, which requires prior mineralization of organic N to NH_4-N.

Waste Recycling

The two digested sludges contained 20% of the initial ^{15}N placed in the digester (Figures 1 and 2). The sludges were resistant to decomposition in soil and 19 to 23% of the sludge C was evolved as CO_2 during 90 d of incubation. Eight percent of the sludge ^{15}N was mineralized to NO_3-N at 90 d. This represented 2% of the initial ^{15}N placed in the digester (Figures 1 and 2). The remaining sludge ^{15}N was recovered as soil organic N, which appeared to be resistant to decomposition. The C and N mineralization rates were similar to those reported for anaerobically digested and composted sewage sludge (Miller, 1974; Tester et al., 1977). A low decomposition rate of sludge added to soil was attributed to loss of the more readily-decomposable C constituents during anaerobic digestion. The similar CO_2 evolution and N mineralization rates of the two digested sludges cannot be attributed to initial N content (27 and 39 g N kg^{-1}).

Fresh water hyacinth biomass from nutrient-enriched systems decomposed rapidly in soil. Almost 50% of the biomass C was evolved as CO_2 during 90 d. Over one-third of the organic ^{15}N was mineralized to NO_3-N (Figure 1). Rapid decomposition of the fresh biomass suggests blending this material with the digested sludge to enhance the decomposition of the sludge.

Fresh water hyacinth biomass from nutrient-limited systems also decomposed rapidly in soil, with 39% of the biomass C being evolved as CO_2 during 90 d of incubation. However, only 3% of the plant organic ^{15}N was mineralized to NO_3-N (Figure 2). Any N mineralized during the decomposition of this plant material was rapidly immobilized by the microbial population.

Undiluted and diluted effluent from digested plants with a high N content were used as nutrient sources to produce additional water hyacinth biomass and for evaluation of potential N recovery. Plants growing in undiluted effluent did not survive the combination of high electrical conductivities (EC = 4.3 to 5.3 dS m^{-1}) and NH_4-N concentrations (161 to 289 mg N L^{-1}). However, diluting the digester effluent provided medium which stimulated water hyacinth growth. The diluted effluent had EC values ranging from 0.7 to 2.3 dS m^{-1} and NH_4-N concentrations of 23 to 104 mg N L^{-1}. The highest yield of water hyacinth was observed in diluted effluent having an NH_4-N concentration of 65 mg N L^{-1} and an EC of 1.6 dS m^{-1}.

Undiluted effluent from digested plants with a low N content were recycled directly to a water hyacinth production system. Plants survived in undiluted effluent due to low NH_4-N concentrations (24 to 87 mg N L^{-1}), although ECs were high (EC = 5.6 to 6.7 dS m^{-1}). The salt concentrations were higher than those reported for water hyacinth survival by Haller et al. (1974).

Plant assimilation of N from undiluted and diluted effluent recycled 21 to 38% of the initial ^{15}N placed in the digester (Figures 1 and 2). Nitrogen loss during effluent recycling accounted for 26 to 42% of the initial ^{15}N. Possible N-loss mechanisms during effluent recycling included algal assimilation and NH_3-N volatilization.

Total ^{15}N recovery by sludge and effluent recycling was 41 to 58% of the initial ^{15}N placed in the digester. The remaining ^{15}N was lost during anaerobic digestion and during effluent recycling in the water hyacinth production systems. Hanisak et al. (1980) determined that 65% of (liquid and sludge) N in diluted effluent from anaerobically digested water hyacinth could be reassimilated by water hyacinths.

An integrated system of wastewater renovation through biomass production, anaerobic digestion of the biomass to produce CH_4, and recycling of the digester waste to produce additional biomass is environmentally appealing. Research is needed to improve upon the recovery of nutrients in digester effluent and sludge. The optimum dilution of digester effluent for maximizing water hyacinth yields needs to be established.

ACKNOWLEDGMENTS

This paper reports results from a joint program between the Institute of Food and Agricultural Sciences (IFAS) of the University of Florida and the Gas Research Institute (GRI), entitled "Methane from Biomass and Waste". Florida Agricultural Experiment Stations Journal Series No. 7713.

REFERENCES

A.P.H.A. 1980. Standard Methods for the Examination of Water and Wastewater. 20th Edition. Amer. Publ. Health Assoc. Washington, DC.

Atalay, A., and R. W. Blanchar. 1984. Evaluation of methane generator sludge as a soil amendment. J. Environ. Qual. 13:341-344.

Boyd, C. E. 1976. Accumulation of dry matter, nitrogen, and phosphorus by cultivated water hyacinths. Econ Bot. 30:51-56.

Chynoweth, D. P., D. A. Dolene, B. Schwegler, and K. R. Reddy. 1983. Wastewater reclamation and methane production using water hyacinth and anerobic digestion. Presented at the 10th Energy Technology Conference. Washington, DC.

DeBusk, T. A., J. H. Ryther, M.D. Hanisak, and L. D. Williams. 1981. Effects of seasonality and plant density on the productivity of some freshwater macrophytes. J. Environ. Qual. 10:133-142.

Field, J. A., J. S. Caldwell, S. Jeyanayagam, R. B. Reneau, Jr., W. Kroonte, and E. R. Collins, Jr. 1984. Fertilizer recovery from anaerobic digesters. Trans. ASAE 27:1871-1881.

Haller, W. T., D. L. Sutton, and W. C. Barlowe. 1974. Effects of salinity on growth of several aquatic macrophytes. Ecology 55:891-894.

Hanisak, M. D., L. D. Williams, and J. H. Ryther. 1980. Recycling the nutrients in residues from methane digesters of aquatic macrophytes for new biomass production. Resource Recovery Conser. 4:313-323.

Hashimoto, A. G., Y. R. Chen, V. H. Varel, and R. L. Prior. 1980. Anaerobic fermentation of agricultural residues. _In_ M. Shuler (ed.) Utilization and Recycle of Agricultural Wastes and Residues. CRC Press, Inc., Boca Raton, FL.

Keeney, D. R., and D. W. Nelson. 1982. Nitrogen-Inorganic Forms. _In_ A. L. Page (ed.) Methods of Soil Analysis. Part 2. 2nd. Edition. Agronomy 9. ASA, Madison, WI.

Miller, R. H. 1974. Factors affecting the decomposition of an anaerobically digested sewage sludge in soil. J. Environ. Qual. 3:376-380.

Nelson, D. W., and L. E. Sommers. 1972. A simple digestion procedure for estimation of total nitrogen in soils and sediments. J. Environ. Qual. 1:423-425.

Nelson, D. W., and L. E. Sommers. 1973. Determination of total nitrogen in plant materials. Agron. J. 65:109-112.

Nelson, D. W., and L. E. Sommers. 1975. Determination of total nitrogen in natural waters. J. Environ. Qual. 4:465-468.

Reddy, K. R. 1984. Water hyacinth (_Eichhornia crassipes_) biomass production in Florida. Biomass 6:167-181.

Reddy, K. R., and J. C. Tucker. 1983. Productivity and nutrient uptake of water hyacinth, _Eichhornia crassipes_. I. Effect of nitrogen source. Econ. Bot. 37:237-247.

Reddy, K. R., F. M. Hueston, and T. McKim. 1985. Biomass production and nutrient removal potential of water hyacinth cultured in sewage effluent. J. Solar Energy Eng. 107:128-135.

Tester, C. F., L. J. Sikora, J. M. Taylor, and J. F. Parr. 1977. Decomposition of sewage sludge in soil: I. Carbon and nitrogen transformations. J. Environ. Qual. 6:459-463.

Wolverton, B. C., and R. C. McDonald. 1979. Energy from aquatic plant wastewater treatment sytems. NASA/NSTL. Tech. Memorandum TM-X-72733. Natl. Space Technol. Lab., Louis, MS.

Yount, J. L., and R. Crossman. 1970. Eutrophication control by plant harvesting. J. Water Pollut. Control Fed. 42:173-183.

EVIDENCE FOR DENITRIFICATION IN ARTIFICIAL WETLANDS

E. Stengel, W. Carduck, and C. Jebsen
Institut for Biotechnologie III
Kernforschungsanlage Julich GmbH.
Postfach 1913, D-5170 Julich
FEDERAL REPUBLIC OF GERMANY

ABSTRACT

Artificial wetland systems were investigated for their ability to remove NO_3^- from ground- and tap water by two main mechanisms; i.e., assimilative uptake in biomass and dissimilative reduction to N_2O and N_2. The occurrence of high N_2O levels after addition of acetylene enriched water gave a strong indication of the denitrification process.

Keywords: Artificial wetland, denitrification, wastewater, aquatic plants.

INTRODUCTION

Worldwide, we are faced with the problem of a continuous increase of NO_3^- concentrations in ground- and surface waters. This is due to the application of excessive amounts of N fertilizers to arable land (Obermann, 1982). When reconditioning such waters to drinking waters, it is necessary to eliminate the NO_3^- to acceptable levels. The high cost of conventional methods, such as ion exchange or reverse osmosis, and handling problems with the arising salt concentrates, gave the stimulus to search for less expensive methods with less impairment to the environment and suitability for smaller municipalities.

To recondition NO_3-contaminated water to drinking water, we started with investigations on artificial wetlands as part of a two-component system. Such a system should work as follows: NO_3^--contaminated groundwater is pumped into an artificial wetland with horizontal flow and after 1-3 d of retention time, the water is then returned to the aquifer via an infiltration well. After about two months of retention in the aquifer, the water is pumped into a water works and subjected to the usual treatment.

The following processes are expected to function in an artificial wetland during NO_3^- removal. These include 1) photosynthetic production of organic matter creates a reduction

ISBN 0-941463-00-1

potential; 2) in the rhizosphere part of the organic matter is released, either by root exudation or by decay of plant organs (if necessary, allochthonous organic matter can be supplied to the water stream); 3) dissolved organic matter in the root horizon is partially utilized for bacterial denitrification; and 4) residual organics enter the groundpassage so that further denitrification can take place.

In principle, two main processes of NO_3^- removal are functioning in artificial wetlands: 1) assimilation of NO_3^- into biomass (roots, rhizomes of higher plants, and bacteria); and 2) dissimilation via bacterial denitrification.

From the average matter balance of reed (Phragmites australis) (see Schierup, 1978 and Westlake, 1982), one can estimate that the rate of NO_3^- removal through bacterial denitrification is about 10 times higher than by incorporation of NO_3^- into the higher plants, assuming that the whole autochthonously produced organic matter could serve as energy sources for denitrification (Stengel, 1986). To a large extent, this is possibly the case in the tropics with permanent high O_2 consumption and low O_2 supply in the root zone.

MATERIALS AND METHODS

Most measurements and experiments were carried out in an outdoor artificial wetland unit, consisting of a flat basin (about 1.5 m wide, 8 m long, 0.4 m deep; total surface area, 10 m^2) made of polyurethane foam profiles and lined with 0.8 mm PVC. A longitudinal baffle divided the container in such a way that a U-shaped channel (0.6 m in width) of 16 m length resulted. The channel was filled up to the rim with gravel, i.e. quartzite pebbles, 3-8 mm in diameter, equipped with 10 vertical sampling tubes enabling water samples to be taken at various distances from the inlet. In 1983, young plants of Phragmites australis (reed) were planted into the gravel, and in 1985 and 1986, when a dense stand had developed, measurements were taken (Stengel, 1986).

Local tap water containing 30 $\pm$ 2 mg L^{-1} NO_3^- was continuously supplied at the inlet by means of a pump (Seybert and Rahier), usually at a rate of 30 L h^{-1}. Gas chromatographic analyses of N_2O, acetylene and ethylene were performed after Barrenstein et al. (1983), Bergersen (1980) and Carduck (1986).

The hydraulic properties of the unit were determined by supplying a solution containing 110 mg L^{-1} of KNO_3 as a tracer. As implicated by the increase of conductivity, the tracer front reached the middle of the channel after 10 h and the outlet after 17.5 h. A steady-state was reached 35-40 h after the beginning of the tracer experiment.

RESULTS AND DISCUSSION

Efficient denitrification depends especially on two prerequisites: availability of organic matter as the energy source, and sufficient by low O_2 tension in the root zone. From the biomass dynamics of Phragmites and the O_2 concentrations in an artificial wetland studied at Julich in the course of one year (Figure 1), we can conclude that the aforementioned principal conditions are partially fulfilled, even in a temperate climate, although O_2-saturated NO_3^--containing water was constantly pumped into the horizontal filter. Hence, denitrification could be expected to take place in the artificial wetland, at least to some extent and during the growth period.

The decrease in O_2 concentration between the inlet and the outlet of an experimental wetland filter was steep and substantial from April - October and only slight during the winter months (Figure 1). The strong seasonal variability of the longitudinal O_2 profiles becomes more salient when one plots only the inclination of the O_2 curves for the first 3 m of the artificial wetland (Figure 2). The initial rates of O_2 consumption thus obtained appeared to be an exponential function of temperature (Figure 3).

Comparing the N balance for Phragmites (Esteves, 1978) with our data (Figure 4), we noted that the measured rates of NO_3^- removal exceeded the normal range of N uptake in macrophytes by far, at least during summertime in the last third of our wetland filter (Stengel, 1986). This was taken as a first clue for the correctness of the basic assumption according to which denitrification should play a major role in the intensive NO_3^- removal by an artificial wetland.

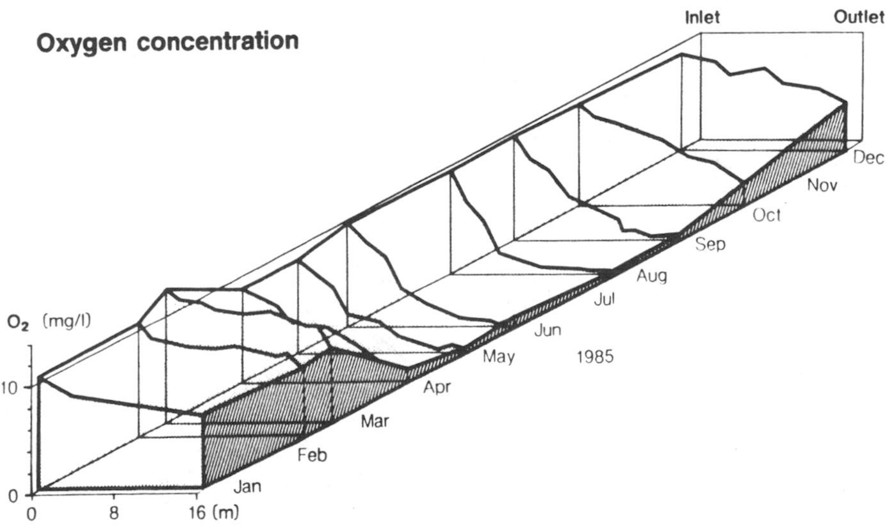

FIGURE 1. Oxygen profiles in an artificial wetland during the year 1985.

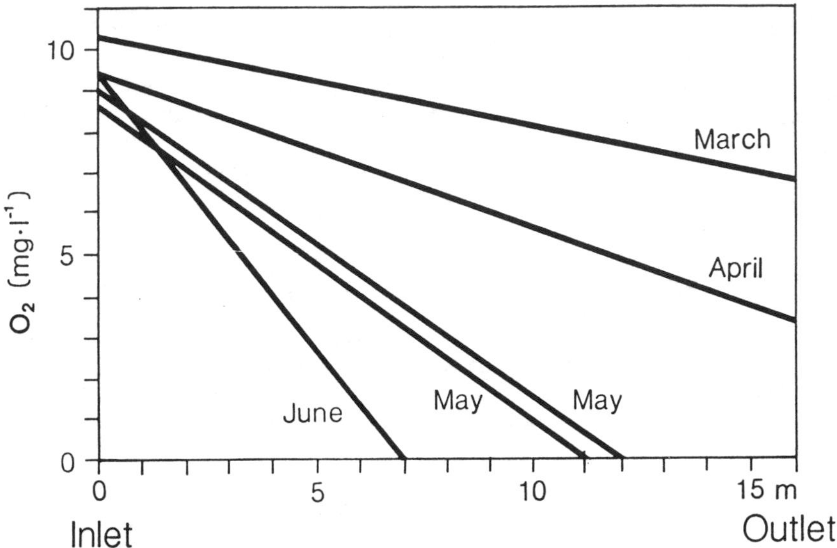

FIGURE 2. Initial slope of O_2 concentration profiles (0-3 m from inlet) on selected days.

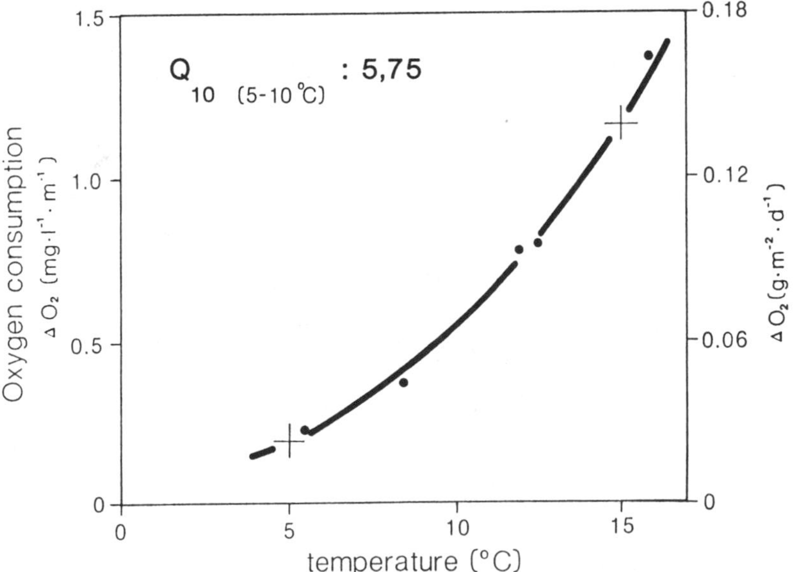

FIGURE 3. Relation of O_2 decrease to temperature in the first 3 m of an artificial wetland.

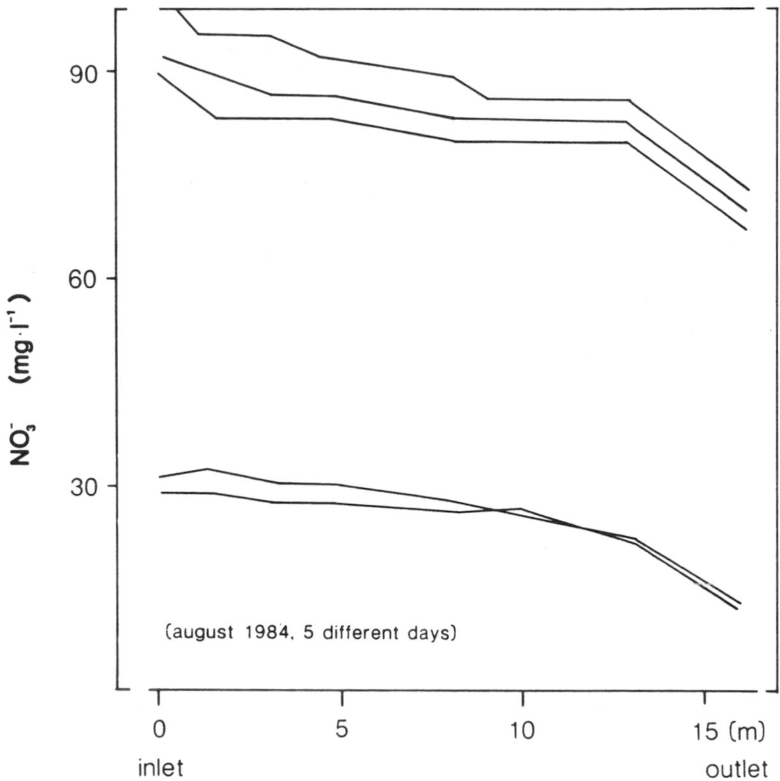

FIGURE 4. Nitrate-profiles along artificial wetlands with higher and lower NO_3^- loading in summer 1984.

As the most direct evidence that might be obtained in situ, we considered an application of the acetylene blockage technique (Fedorova et al., 1973). This method relies on the inhibition of the reduction of nitrous oxide (N_2O) to N_2 by acetylene (Payne, 1981). Consequently, there should be a rise of N_2O concentration in stoichiometric relation to the NO_3 reduced, as soon as acetylene is administered appropriately. In contrast to most of the tests of denitrification rates described in literature (e.g., Kaspar, 1982; Christensen and Sorensen, 1986), we injected the appropriate amounts of acetylene into the water stream under normal operational conditions. The usefulness of this approach was confirmed by the results obtained in a small greenhouse unit with Cyperus alternifolius (Carduck, 1986). The studies reported in this paper were conducted in an outdoor artificial wetland (see Materials and Methods). Tap water saturated with acetylene entered the artificial wetland channel over 50.5 h at a steady-rate of about 0.25 L h^{-1} where it was mixed in the stream of tap water (30 L h^{-1}) so that an initial acetylene concentration of approximately 8 mg L^{-1} resulted. After 50 h the longitudinal profiles of acetylene, N_2O, O_2 were determined (Figure 5). A significant reduction of NO_3^- concentration was detected from 5 m behind the inlet onwards, being more intense over the last third of the wetland channel, where O_2 concentration dropped below 2 mg L^{-1}. The profile of N_2O concentration shows that the formation of N_2O starts only in the zone where O_2 concentration in the free water is below 3 mg L^{-1}. Similar to the results of Carduck (1986), we noted in our outdoor studies that the formation of N_2O-N correlated to about 80% to the decrease in NO_3-N.

The concentration of ethylene which might have been formed by direct reduction of acetylene stayed always below our detection limit of 0.01 mg L^{-1}. This shows that the metabolization of the inhibitor remained insignificant.

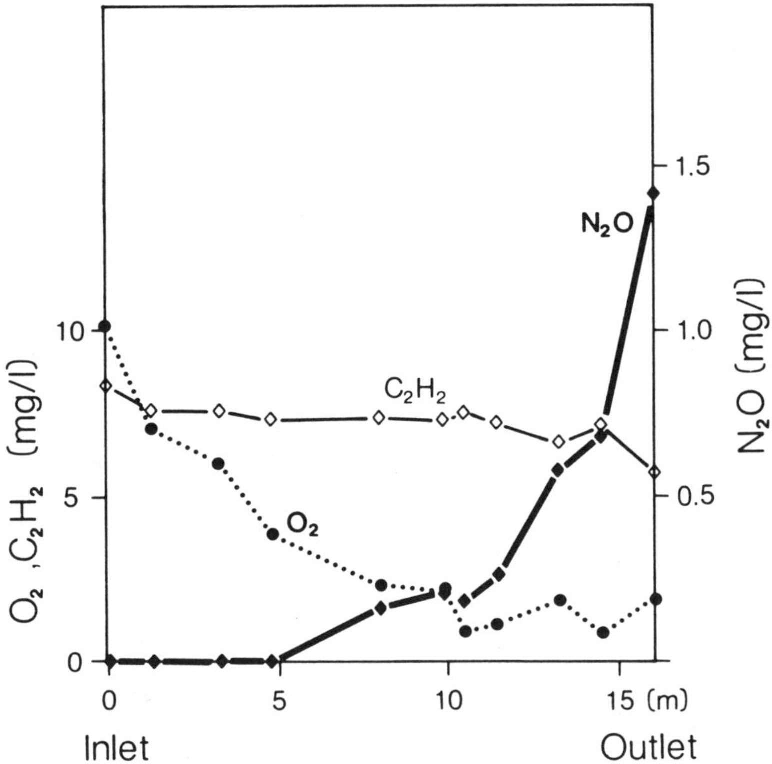

FIGURE 5. Profiles of N_2O, acetylene and O_2 after approximately 50 h of continuous dosage of acetylene-enriched water in an artificial wetland (18.6.1986).

CONCLUSIONS

Results presented show that artificial wetlands have a significant potential for NO_3 removal from groundwater. In the temperate zone an input of allochthonous organic matter is necessary to maintain sufficient NO_3^- removal rates during winter time (Stengel, 1986) Acetylene blockage method was successfully employed to determine denitrification in artificial wetlands. For the first time, the acetylene blockage technique has been used to prove denitrification in an artificial wetland without changing the operation mode of the system. The production of N_2O after dosage of acetylene enriched water proves that in a part of the experimental unit denitrification has taken place. The amount of the proved N_2O-N corresponds to 75-90% of the decrease in NO_3-N. Results obtained from these small experimental units encourage to application of this method to larger systems for the differentiation of assimilative and dissimilative NO_3^- reduction.

REFERENCES

Barrenstein, A., W. Eckrich, and P. Obermann. 1983. Weiterentwicklung einer gaschromatographischen Methode zur Bestimmung von Gasen im Wasser. Vom Wasser 60:85-93.

Bergersen, F. J. 1980. Methods for Evaluating Biological Nitrogen Fixation. John Wiley & Sons, Ltd., New York.

Carduck, W. 1986. Direkter Nachweis der Denitrifikation im Wasserpflanzen-Boden-Filter mittels Acetylenblockadetechnik. Diplomarbeit an der Ruhr Universitat Bochum.

Christensen, P. B., and J. Sorensen. 1986. Temporal variation of denitrification activity in plant-covered, littoral sediment from Lake Hampen, Denmark. Appl. Environ. Microbiol. 51:1174-1179.

Esteves, F. D. A. 1978. Die Bedeutung der aquatischen Makrophyten fur den Stoffhaushalt des Schohsees. Dissertation, Christian-Alberts-Universitat, Kiel.

Fedorova, R. I., E. I. Milekhina, and N. I. Ilyukhina. 1973. Evaluation of the method of "gas metabolism" for detecting extraterrestrial life. Identification of nitrogen-fixing organisms. Izv. Akad. Nank.SSSR Ser. Biol. 6:797-806.

Kaspar, H. F. 1982. Denitrification in marine sediment: Measurement of capacity and estimate of _in situ_ rate. Appl. Environ. Microbiol. 43:522-537.

Obermann, P. 1982. Hydrochemische/hydromethanische Untersuchungen zum Stoffgehalt von Grundwasser. 2. Auflage. Besondere Mitteilungen zum Deutschen Gewasserkundlichen Jahrbuch. Nr. 42 (edited by Vereinigung Deutscher Gewasserschutz e.v. in Bonn).

Payne, W. J. 1981. Denitrification. John Wiley & Sons, New York.

Schierup, H.-H. 1978. Biomass and primary production in a Phragmites communis Trin. swamp in North Jutland, Denmark. Verh. Intern. Verein. Limnol. 20:94-99.

Stengel, E. 1986. Perspektiven der Nitrateliminierung in kunstlichen Feuchtbiotopen. In Sammelband des Symposiums "Grundlagen und Praxis naturnaher Klarverfahren - 10 Jahre Othfresen" vom 31.01 - 01.02.1985. Lehrstuhl fur Okochemie der Gesamthochschule Kassel.

Westlake, D. F. 1982. The primary productivity of water plants. In J. J. Symoens, S. S. Hooper, and Compere (ed.) Studies on Aquatic Vascular Plants. Publ. by the Royal Botanical Society of Belgium, Brussels.

A THREE COMPARTMENT NITROGEN MODEL OF A WATER HYACINTH WASTEWATER TREATMENT SYSTEM

W. H. Zachritz II
Air Force Engineering and Services Center
Environmental Engineering Branch
Tyndall Air Force Base
Panama City, Florida 32403

R. B. Jacquez
Department of Civil Engineering
New Mexico State University
Las Cruces, New Mexico 88001

ABSTRACT

A three compartment water hyacinth model capable of predicting effluent concentrations of NH_4-N, NO_3-N, and organic N (ORG-N) was developed and tested. The model uses a system of ordinary differential equations solved by a fourth-order, Runge-Kutta estimation technique with a 0.1 time step interval to simulate the system. The model was programmed in Basic A using an IBM PC microcomputer.

A rate optimization program was used to calibrate the model using field derived data as a baseline. Residual error ($\overline{E}$) and residual mean square ($\hat{\sigma}^2$) were used to test the closeness of the fit of the data for each N compartment. The results of two simulations are presented. The first simulation, using literature derived rate constants, indicates that the residual errors for the NH_4-N, NO_3-N, and ORG-N compartments were 5.63 mg L^{-1}, 0.83 mg L^{-1}, and 3.36 mg L^{-1}, respectively. The second simulation, using the rates generated from the optimization program, resulted in an improved fit of the data as indicated by lower residual errors of 2.26 mg L^{-1}, 0.40 mg L^{-1}, and 1.90 mg L^{-1} for the same N compartments. The residual mean square data indicated a similar pattern of fit.

Keywords: Water hyacinth model, microcomputer, nitrogen, residual error, simulation.

ISBN 0-941463-00-1

INTRODUCTION

Water hyacinth tertiary treatment systems are usually designed on a detention time basis with little regard for the removal dynamics of specific nutrients. There is a very real need to develop models that can simulate a water hyacinth treatment system both for design purposes and for day-to-day control of the treatment operation. Investigators have used logistic (Stewart et al., 1984) or Monod (Weber and Tchobanoglous, 1985) structured models to describe NH_4^+ removal in water hyacinth systems. Other hyacinth modeling efforts used total N removal functions as part of a larger model to predict biomass (Mitsch, 1976; Lorber et al., 1983). The purpose of this paper is to present a three compartment water hyacinth model designed to predict effluent concentrations of NH_4-N, NO_3-N, and ORG-N.

MODEL PROCESSES

The flow of material into and out of each of the three N compartments is shown in Figure 1. This figure does not show loading of N into or out of compartments due to fluid flow, but does show the generalized transformation assumed for the proposed hyacinth model. This simplified hyacinth ecosystem structure uses both biological processes (mineralization, plant uptake or growth, denitrification, and nitrification) and physical processes (sedimentation and volatilization) to describe the flow of N. Several complex processes such as nitrification, denitrification, and net loss of organic material were simplified to avoid adding additional model compartments.

The model, as structured, has 11 daily inputs, 7 rates, and 5 rate controlling subroutines. Material loss and gain from a compartment is indicated by a negative or positive sign, respectively, and all N species are given in units of N to simplify material flow. The model is a system of ordinary differential equations solved by using a fourth-order, Runge-Kutta technique with a 0.1 time step a complete mix system was assumed. The model was programmed in Basic A using an IBM PC microcomputer.

Organic Nitrogen

Compartment 1 (Figure 1) describes the process of ORG-N flow in the hyacinth system. Process gains include inflow, QI/V (not shown in Figure 1), of ORG-N attributed to biomass resulting from plant uptake of NH_4-N (rate R21) and uptake of NO_3-N (rate R31). The plant uptake process equations use a Monod structure. The proposed model structure is designed to predict effluent concentrations of ORG-N and the influences of hyacinth biomass as reflected as modifications (not shown in Figure 1) to plant uptake rates as previously shown by Mitsch (1981). Process losses from this compartment include the ORG-N effluent flow, QE/V, and two first-order expressions, R12 and R1S, which describe losses due to decomposition and losses to the sediment, respectively.

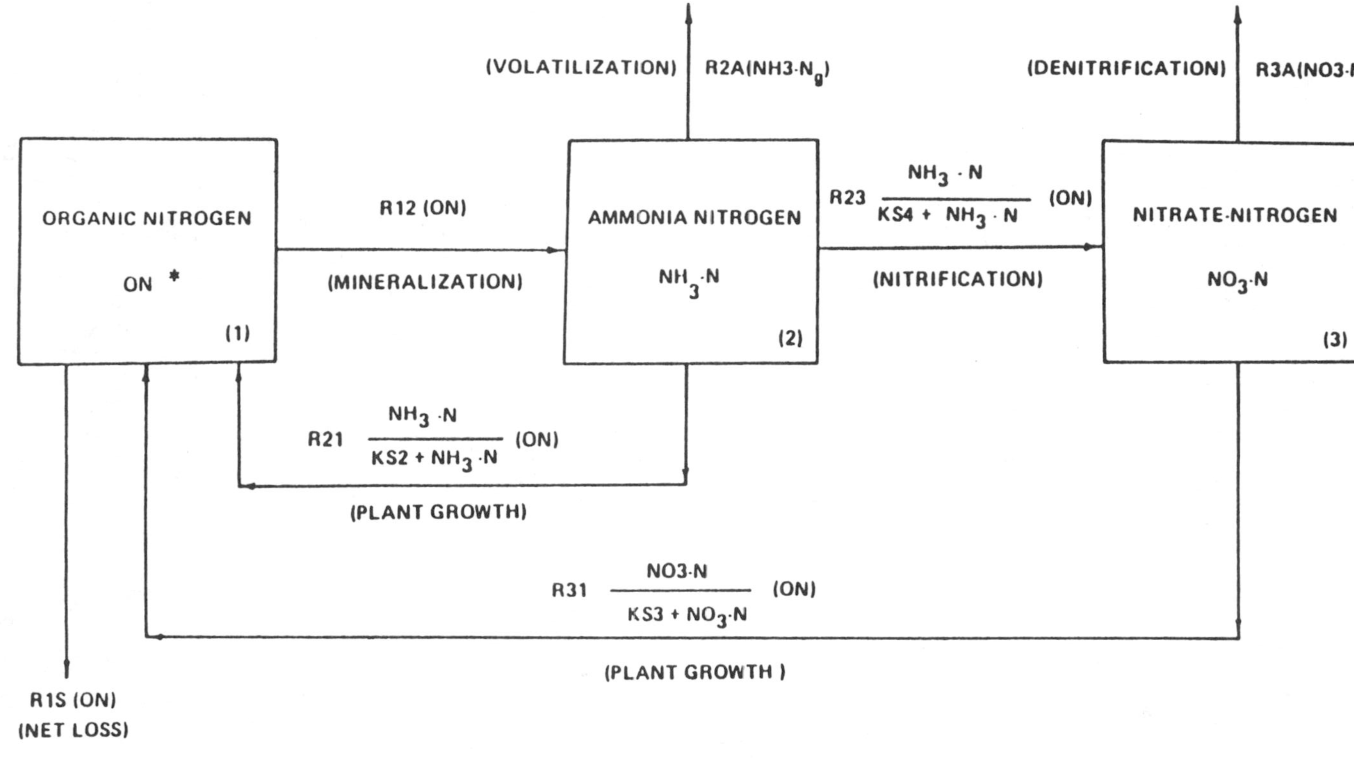

FIGURE 1. Three compartment N model of the water hyacinth wastewater treatment system.
*Note: ON = ORG-N (Zachritz, 1985).

Ammonia Nitrogen

The NH_4-N compartment process inputs, compartment 2 (Figure 1), include the inflow, QI/V (not shown), and the decomposition of organic material (R12). Process losses for this compartment include outflow, QE/V, plant uptake of NH_4-N (R21), conversion of NH_4-N to NO_3-N by nitrification (R23), and a first-order emperically derived expression for the volatilization of NH_4-N from the system (R2A). The nitrification process shown is similar to structures proposed by Weber and Tchobanoglous (1985) and Parker et al. (1976) and is limited by the concentration of dissolved O_2 and NH_4-N. The rate of volatilization is a function of the depth of the pond, the temperature, and the system pH. Temperature effects on the biological functions are controlled by the Q_{10} expression. Plant uptake rates (R21 and R31) are controlled by temperature functions described by Mitsch (1981) and Lorber et al. (1984).

Nitrate Nitrogen

The NO_3-N compartment losses (Figure 1), include the outflow, QE/V, of NO_3-N, the first-order expression for denitrification (R3A), and plant uptake of NO_3-N (R31). Inputs to the compartment include the inflow of NO_3-N, QI/V, and NO_3-N produced via nitrification from the NH_4-N compartment.

MODEL TESTING

Models that contain several rate parameters describing nonlinear functions are extremely difficult to optimize due to the complexity of the required calculations, the nonsignificance of a model with many rate parameters, and the lack of available software to fit the specialized needs. Past efforts of modeling complex systems by indicating the goodness of fit by descriptive terms, in this study a simple optimization procedure was used. Two simulations were performed to compare the general fit of model predicted values to observed field derived data. Field data was obtained from a pilot plant operated over a period of two years as part of an evaluation of a 2-stage polyculture wastewater treatment system by Zachritz (1985). Other aspects of the model were also tested such as rate sensitivity, model stability, and model expression complexity. Only the results of the optimization simulations are reported here.

For the first model simulation, initial rate constants were approximated from literature values. The second simulation used the literature reported values as a starting point and an optimization program incremented all rates for each compartment by 10% for a set of 20 iterations of the model. Each iteration used a high and a low NH_4-N value to test the validity of the parameters at these two levels of NH_4-N loading. When the rate values appeared to give a good fit of the data, the complete data set was run through the model and the resulting output was compared with observed data. If any of the three N compartment predicted values did not appear to fit the data well, additional simulations were performed by incrementing the rates controlling the NH_4-N or other compartments by 10% until a better fit was obtained. In this way the rates were "fine tuned" and then tested on the whole data set as previously mentioned. Residual error ($\overline{E}$) or the average residual as defined in equation 1 and residual mean square ($\hat{\sigma}^2$) as defined in equation 2 were used to determine the "closeness of fit" of the predicted data.

$$\overline{E} = \Sigma(y_i - \hat{y}_i)/n \qquad [1]$$

$$\hat{\sigma}^2 = \Sigma(y_i - \hat{y}_i)^2/n-1 \qquad [2]$$

The results of the initial simulation for NH_4-N using the literature rate values (Figure 2a) indicate a general fit of the observed and predicted values. These rates appear to cause the model to consistently over-predict effluent NH_4-N concentrations with a calculated $\overline{E}$ of 5.63 mg L^{-1} ($\hat{\sigma}^2$ = 42.12). The second simulation using optimized rates (Figure 2b) indicates an improved fit of the data with an average residual error of 2.26 mg L^{-1} ($\hat{\sigma}^2$ = 12.06). For both simulations, the variations between the initial sample runs at low NH_4-N loadings and the later sample runs with higher NH_4-N loadings appeared to be very similar.

The initial simulation for the NO_3-N compartment (Figure 3a) indicates a good pattern of fit of the observed and predicted data values with days 1-10 appearing to have a closer fit of the data than the later sample days (17-45). The calculated $\overline{E}$ value for this first simulation was 0.83 mg L^{-1} ($\hat{\sigma}^2$ = 1.87). The second simulation (Figure 3b) with a calculated $\overline{E}$ of 0.40 mg L^{-1} ($\hat{\sigma}^2$ = 1.23), appeared to result in a better fit of the observed data than the first simulation. The overall variation of the data appeared less for this second simulation than in the first, but the pattern of variation appeared to be about the same.

The first simulation run for the ORG-N compartment (Figure 4a) indicates a high degree of variability at both high and low NH_4-N loading. Organic N generated from a water hyacinth treatment system can consist of a variety of materials including bacterial solids, detritus, macroinvertebrates, and hyacinth root fragments. Production of these sources in the effluent can be affected by many physical processes and thus, effluent ORG-N could be more stochastic in nature than either the NO_3-N or NH_4-N compartments. The calculated E value for the first simulation was 3.36 mg L^{-1} ($\hat{\sigma}^2$ = 21.18). The second simulation indicates a closer fit of the data particularly in sample days 1-10. The calculated $\overline{E}$ for this simulation was 1.90 mg L^{-1}($\hat{\sigma}^2$ = 8.83).

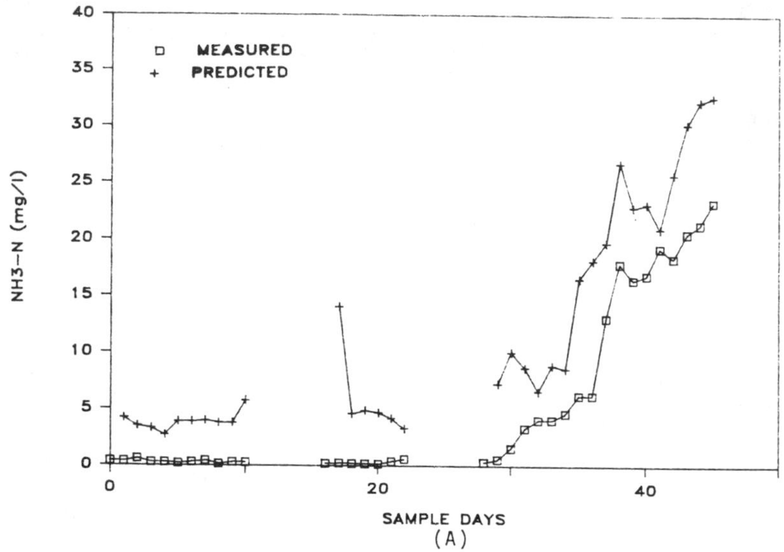

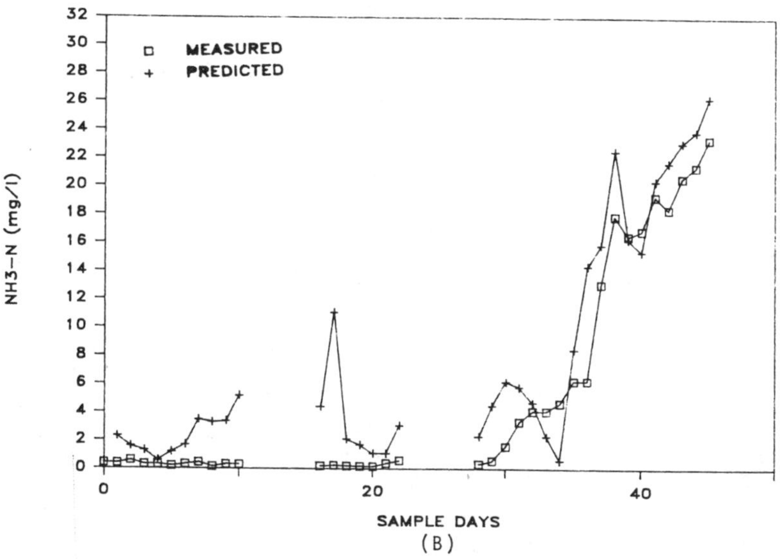

FIGURE 2. Comparison of model predicted and measured NH_4-N effluent concentrations for Simulation 1 (A) and Simulation 2 (B) (Zachritz, 1985).

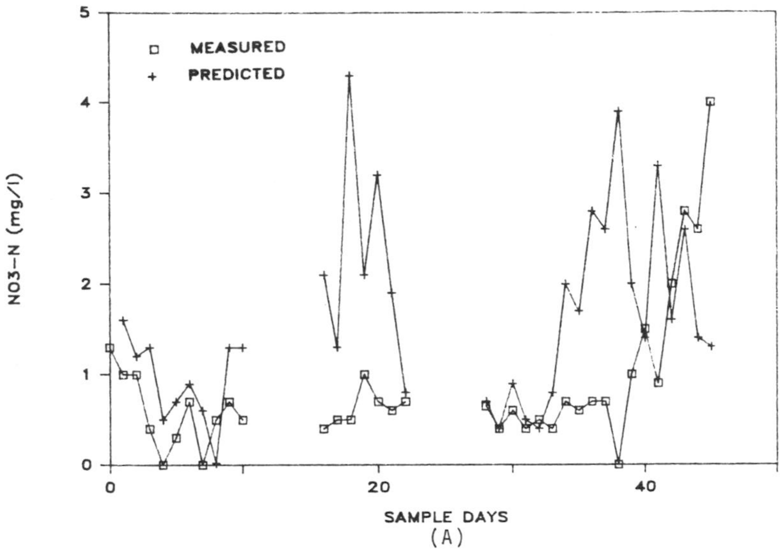

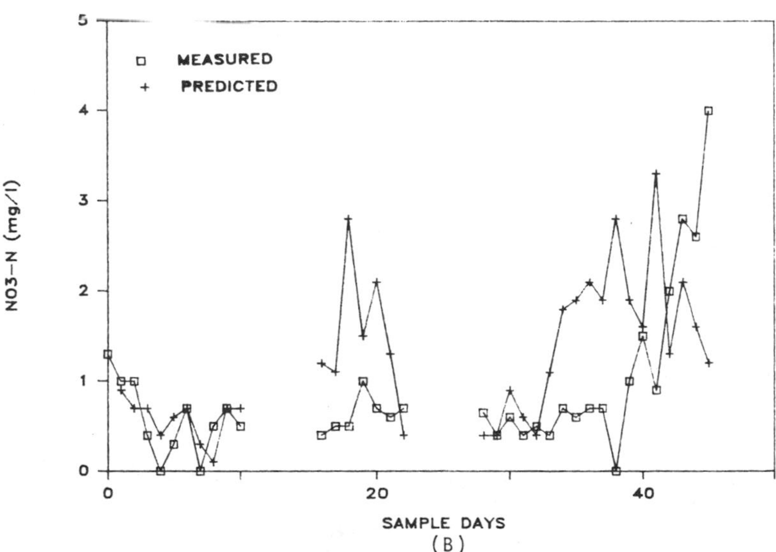

FIGURE 3. Comparison of model predicted and measured NO_3-N effluent concentrations for Simulation 1 (A) and Simulation 2 (B) (Zachritz, 1985).

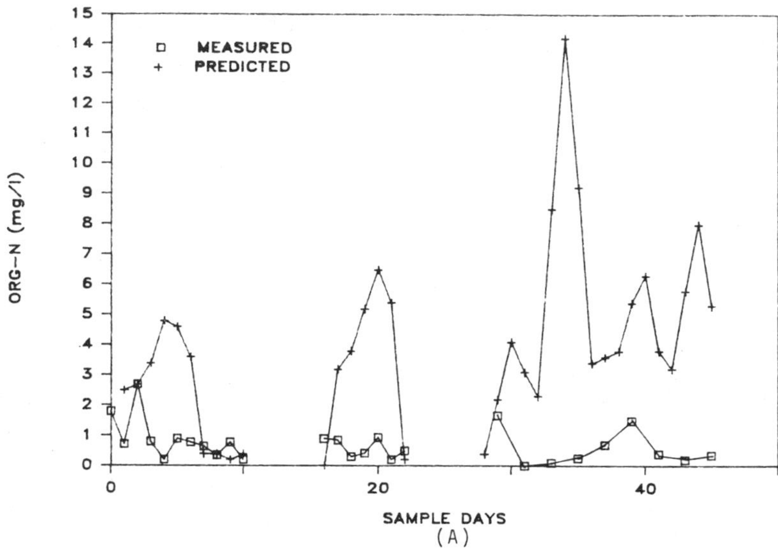

(A)

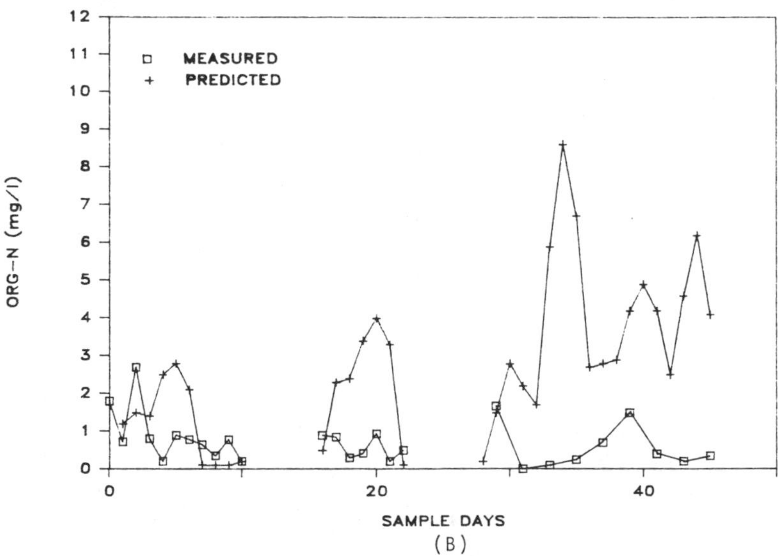

(B)

FIGURE 4. Comparison of model predicted and measured organic N effluent concentrations for Simulation 1 (A) and Simulation 2 (B) (Zachritz, 1985).

SUMMARY

A three compartment water hyacinth model capable of predicting effluent concentrations of NH_4-N, NO_3-N, and ORG-N was developed on a microcomputer and tested using a simple optimization routine. The optimization simulations resulted in lower calculated residual errors and residual mean square values for all three N compartments than the initial simulation using literature derived rates values.

REFERENCES

Lorber, M. N., J. W. Mishoe, and K. R. Reddy. 1984. Modeling and analysis of water hyacinth biomass. Ecol. Modelling 24:61-77.

Mitsch, W. J. 1976. Ecosystem modeling of water hyacinth in Lake Alice, Florida. Ecol. Modelling 2:69-89.

Parker, D. S., R. W. Stone, R. J. Stenquist, and G. Culp. 1975. Process design manual for nitrogen control. U.S. EPA, Technology Transfer, Washington, DC.

Stewart III, E. A., D. L. Haselow, and N. M. Wyse. 1984. A practical model for water hyacinth based wastewater management-design and operation. Water Reuse Symp., San Diego, CA.

Weber, A. S., and G. Tchobanoglous. 1984. Rational design parameters for ammonia conversion on water hyacinth treatment systems. J. Water Pollut. Control Fed.

Zachritz II, W. H. 1985. Modeling the nitrogen dynamics of a water hyacinth-Azolla-freshwater prawn polyculture wastewater treatment system. Ph.D. Dissertation, New Mexico State University.

NOMENCLATURE

DO = dissolved oxygen, mg L^{-1}
$\overline{E}$ = average residual or residual error, mg L^{-1}
Ks2 = half saturation constant for NH_4-N uptake, mg L^{-1}
Ks3 = half saturation constant for NO_3-N uptake, mg L^{-1}
Ks4 = half saturation constant for nitrification, mg L^{-1}
Ks5 = half saturation DO constant for nitrification, mg L^{-1}
NH_4-N = ammonia nitrogen concentration, mg L^{-1}
NO_3-N = nitrate nitrogen concentration, mg L^{-1}
ORG-N = organic nitrogen concentration, mg L^{-1}
QI = influent flowrate, L d^{-1}
QE = effluent flowrate, L d^{-1}
R1S = rate of ammonification d^{-1}
R12 = rate of ammonification, d^{-1}
R2A = rate of ammonia volatilization, d^{-1}
R21 = rate of plant uptake of ammonia, d^{-1}
R23 = rate of nitrification, d^{-1}
R3A = rate of denitrification, d^{-1}

R31 = rate of plant uptake of nitrate, d^{-1}
t = time, d
V = system volume, L
$\hat{\sigma}^2$ = residual mean square
y = observed value
$\hat{y}$ = predicted value

EFFECT OF THREE GROWTH REGULATORS ON GROWTH AND NUTRIENT UPTAKE OF EICHHORNIA CRASSIPES [MART] SOLMS

E. M. D'Angelo and K. R. Reddy
Central Florida Research and Education Center
University of Florida, IFAS
Sanford, Florida 32771

ABSTRACT

A greenhouse study was conducted to determine the effectiveness of three growth regulating hormones on growth and nutrient uptake of water hyacinths [Eichhornia crassipes (Mart) Solms]. Water hyacinths responded to high concentrations of gibberellic acid (GA_3) (1.00 mg L^{-1}) with yield increases up to 71% over control. Yields were lower when plants were cultured in benzyladenine (BA) and Promalin (50% GA_4A_7 and 50% N-[phenylmethyl]-IH-purine-6-amine=N-[PMA]/GA_4A_7). Yields increased up to 33% over control in hyacinths treated with low concentrations of BA (0.01 mg L^{-1}). Hyacinths responded to increasing concentrations of GA_3 and N-(PMA)/GA_4A_7, with increased length to width (L/W) ratios of newly formed petioles and decreased leaf area. High concentrations of both chemicals ($\geq$1.00 mg L^{-1}) induced profuse inflorescence production and decreased vegetative multiplication. Hyacinths responded to increasing concentrations of BA and N-(PMA)/GA_4A_7 with increased shoot to root weight ratios, resulting from root hair loss. Lower concentrations of BA increased L/W ratios of petioles, increased leaf area, and increased vegetative multiplication, but BA did not inhibit float formation or affect inflorescence production. Percent dry weight increased with increasing concentrations of growth regulators at concentrations less than 1.00 mg L^{-1}. Nitrogen and P uptake was directly proportional to hyacinth productivity.

Keywords: Morphology, biomass yields, gibberellic acid, cytokinin.

INTRODUCTION

Several studies have considered the use of growth regulators to control the growth of water hyacinths. Pieterse and Roorda (1982) and Joyce and Haller (1984) showed that gibberellic acid

ISBN 0-941463-00-1

enhanced the sensitivity of hyacinths to 2,4-dichlorophenoxyacetic acid (2,4-D). Pieterse (1976) showed that GA_3 inhibited float formation and vegetative multiplication, leaving plants unstable and submerged. However, none of the studies report the effect of growth regulators on biomass yields and nutrient uptake of water hyacinths.

The purpose of this study was to determine the effects of GA_3, a cytokinin (BA), and a cytokinin/gibberellic acid mixture (N-[PMA]/GA_4A_7), on the growth and nutrient uptake of water hyacinth cultured in nutrient-enriched water.

MATERIALS AND METHODS

Growth and nutrient uptake of water hyacinths treated with growth regulators were monitored under greenhouse conditions for eight weeks during March and April of 1986.

Individual, healthy, and preweighed hyacinth plants (float type), obtained from the Walt Disney World water treatment facility, were cultured in 12 L tubs (0.062 m^2 surface area) containing 10% Hoagland solution and micronutrients applied as liquid fertilizer (Nutrispray, Sunniland, Chase and Co., Sanford, FL) (Fe=4 mg L^{-1}; Mo=0.02 mg L^{-1}; B=0.04 mg L^{-1}; Cu=0.2 mg L^{-1}; Mn=1.5 mg L^{-1}; S=3 mg L^{-1}) with varying concentrations of 3 growth regulators (GA_3, BA, N-[PMA]/GA_4A_7, Abbott Laboratories, Chicago, IL). Each treatment was set up in a randomized block design with three replications. Water in each tub was replaced weekly with fresh medium containing growth regulators.

Growth parameters were measured after 28 d. For each plant, roots and shoots were separated and fresh weight was determined after draining for 5 min, and dry weight after oven drying at 70°C for 48 h. Total number of daughter plants and inflorescences per tub were recorded. Three petioles and laminae of newly formed shoots per treatment were used to calculate petiole L/W ratios and leaf area. Total Kjeldahl N and P in the plant tissue were determined using standard methods (A.P.H.A., 1980).

RESULTS

Biomass Yields

The growth rate of water hyacinths was significantly influenced by growth regulator treatment. Productivity was highest in hyacinths treated with high concentrations of GA_3 (1.00 mg L^{-1}), with increases up to 71% over control (Figure 1). Yields were much lower for plants treated with high concentrations of BA and N-(PMA)/GA_4/A_7. Productivity increased up to 33% over control for hyacinths treated with low concentrations of BA (0.01 mg L^{-1}).

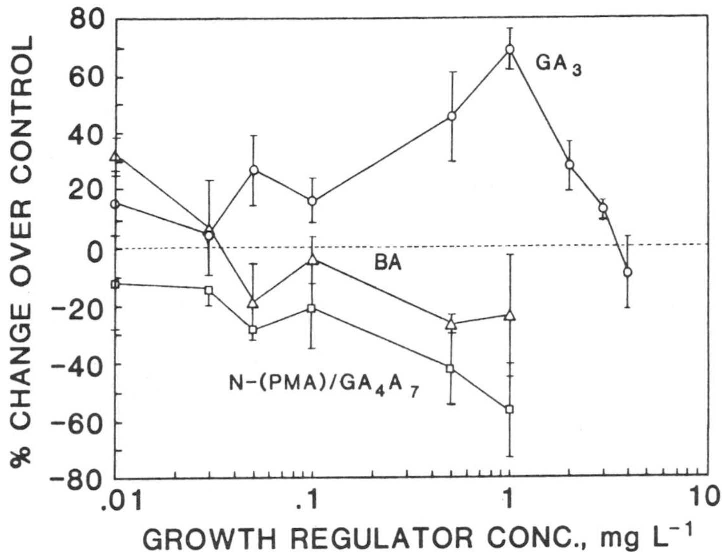

FIGURE 1. The effect of three growth regulators on the biomass yield of water hyacinths, March and April 1986.

Morphological Parameters

The L/W of petioles increased with increasing concentrations of GA_3 and N-(PMA)/GA_4A_7 (Tables 1a,b and 2), with inhibition of float formation evidenced by hyacinths treated with concentrations as low as 0.03 - 0.05 mg L^{-1}. At the highest GA_3 concentration tested (4.0 mg L^{-1}), the L/W of petioles was over nine times greater than for the control (Table 1b). At the highest N-(PMA)/GA_4A_7 concentration tested (1.00 mg L^{-1}), petiole widths decreased to under 1.00 cm. The L/W of petioles did not significantly change for hyacinths treated with BA, and float formation was not inhibited (Table 3). Leaf area increased up to 67% for hyacinths treated with low concentrations of BA (0.01 mg L^{-1}), but decreased at higher concentrations. Leaf area gradually decreased with increasing concentrations of GA_3 and N-(PMA)/GA_4A_7 (Tables 1a and 2).

Shoot/root dry weight ratios increased with increasing BA and N-(PMA)/GA_4A_7 (Tables 2 and 3). At maximum concentrations (>0.50 mg L^{-1}), both chemicals caused root hair loss, resulting in shoot/root weight ratios almost two times greater than for the control. GA_3 did not have large effects on shoot/root weights of water hyacinth (Tables 1a,b). Dry weight ratios increased with increasing growth regulator concentration, but decreased at GA_3 concentrations greater than 2.00 mg L^{-1} (Tables 1a,b, 2, and 3).

TABLE 1a. Effect of GA_3 on the morphology of water hyacinths cultured in nutrient-enriched water, March 1986.

Parameter	GA$_3$ concentration mg L^{-1}						
	0.00	0.01	0.03	0.05	0.10	0.50	1.00
Petiole L/W ratio	6.1a†	4.9a	9.8bc	6.1a	9.0b	12.4c	16.9d
Leaf area (cm^{-2})	80.6a	83.9a	71.5ab	62.3b	64.9b	37.3c	37.5c
Shoot/root weight ratio	5.0b	5.9a	5.3ab	4.9b	5.9a	4.9b	5.2ab
% Dry matter	6.9a	8.6b	8.3c	9.0d	8.8e	9.9f	10.3g
No. of daughter plants/tub	11a	10ab	10ab	10ab	9bc	8c	8c

†Values with the same letter suffix are not significant at P=0.05.

TABLE 1b. Effect of GA_3 on the morphology of water hyacinths cultured in nutrient-enriched water, April 1986.

Parameter	GA$_3$ concentration, mg L^{-1}			
	0.00	2.00	3.00	4.00
Petiole L/W ratio	4.3a†	27.6b	27.7b	38.9c
Shoot/root weight ratio	4.0a	3.3ab	3.7ab	3.8ab
% Dry matter	5.5a	5.6b	5.2c	4.6d
No. of daughter plants/tub	16a	16a	13a	13a
No. of inflorescence/tub	0a	8b	15b	24c

†Values with the same letter suffix are not significant at P=0.05.

TABLE 2. Effect of N-(PMA)/GA_4A_7 on the morphology of water hyacinths cultured in nutrient-enriched water, March 1986.

Parameter	N-(PMA)/GA$_4$A$_7$ concentration, mg L^{-1}						
	0.00	0.01	0.03	0.05	0.10	0.50	1.00
Petiole L/W ratio	4.9a†	5.2a	6.5a	11.4b	12.5b	19.3c	28.6d
Leaf area (cm^2)	81.3a	81.9a	71.4a	56.0b	51.4b	22.8c	25.7c
Shoot/root weight ratio	4.3a	4.4a	4.0a	4.5a	4.7a	6.3b	8.4c
% Dry matter	5.6a	5.7b	5.5c	5.3d	5.9e	6.4f	6.8g
No. of daughter plants/tub	12ab	10a	10a	11ab	13b	11ab	5c
No. of inflorescences/ tub	0a	0a	0a	0a	1a	10b	12b

†Values with the same letter suffix are not significant at P=0.05.

TABLE 3. Effect of BA on the morphology of water hyacinths cultured in nutrient-enriched water, March 1986.

Parameter	BA concentration, mg L^{-1} 0.00	0.01	0.03	0.05	0.10	0.50	1.00
Petiole L/W ratio	4.2a†	4.4a	6.2a	5.6a	6.2a	4.8a	4.5a
Leaf area (cm^2)	46.5a	77.6b	56.2a	48.4a	42.3ac	35.0ac	24.2c
Shoot/root weight ratio	4.5a	6.0ab	5.4a	5.3a	5.8ab	8.2c	7.5bc
% Dry matter	5.8a	6.6b	6.2c	5.7a	6.0d	6.4e	8.3f
No. of daughter plants/tub	12a	12a	14ab	16b	17b	17b	15ab

†Values with the same letter suffix are not significant at P=0.05.

High concentrations of GA_3 and N-(PMA)/GA_4A_7 inhibited vegetative multiplication and induced profuse flowering of hyacinths (Tables 1a,b and 2). Daughter plant production increased up to 42% over that of the control for hyacinths treated with BA concentrations of 0.10 - 0.50 mg L^{-1} (Table 3). Inflorescence production was not observed for plants treated with BA.

Nutrient Uptake

Uptake of N and P followed trends similar to those of plant biomass yields (Table 4). Nutrient uptake was highest for hyacinths treated with high GA_3 (1.00 mg L^{-1}) and low BA (0.01 mg L^{-1}) concentrations. Nutrient uptake was much lower for plants treated with high concentration of N-(PMA)/GA_4/A_7.

DISCUSSION

The results with E. crassipes support the conclusion that GAs and cytokinins affect the growth of aquatic plants by altering their morphology (Sprent, 1968; Pieterse, 1976; Widyanto, 1978; Joyce and Haller, 1984; Klich et al., 1985).

The most typical and striking plant response to GA treatment was plant elongation, limited to younger tissues which were actively growing. Elongation reduced self-shading of GA_3 treated hyacinths, thereby maximizing biomass yields and nutrient uptake even with decreased leaf area. The anatomical basis for elongation effects (increases in height, L/W of petiole, float loss) may be attributed to both cell elongation and increased cell division (Jacobsen, 1977). Cell elongation is a result of alterations in the orientation of microfibrils in the epidermal cell walls (Takeda and Shibaoka, 1981) and cell wall plasticity (Adams et al., 1975) by GAs. Increased cell division is the

TABLE 4. Effect of three growth regulators on the nutrient uptake of water hyacinth cultured in nutrient-enriched water, March 1986.

Concentration	N			P		
	GA_3	BA	PRO	GA_3	BA	PRO
$mg\ L^{-1}$			$mg\ m^{-2}\ d^{-1}$			
0.00	660a†	454bc	549a	127ab	73ab	99a
0.01	858bc	617a	468abc	156bc	101a	95ab
0.03	771ab	515b	484ab	122a	86ab	90ab
0.05	833abc	413bc	446abc	146abc	69b	80abc
0.10	819abc	496b	458abc	131ab	79ab	82abc
0.50	908bc	388bc	340bcd	155bc	66b	64bc
1.00	1005c	375c	225d	176c	65b	54c

PRO = N-(PMA)/GA_4A_7
†Values with the same letter suffix are not significant at P=0.05.

result of the enhancement of DNA transcription (i.e. synthesis of RNA) by activating RNA polymerase and increasing DNA template availability (Tomi et al., 1983) by GAs. GAs also function in flower production by acting as specific flowering stimuli and by diverting nutrients to apical meristem at the expense of structural tissues and vegetative branch buds (Ross et al., 1984), thereby reducing biomass yields and vegetative multiplication at high application rates. GA_4A_7 is more potent than GA_3 in reallocating nutrients to terminal buds and also serves as a morphogenic function in sexual differentiation (Ross et al., 1984).

At low concentrations, the cytokinins most striking effects are induction of cell division, promotion of tissue differentiation (Horgan, 1984), and branching (Sprent, 1968) resulting in increased leaf area, biomass yields, nutrient uptake and vegetative multiplication. Cytokinins act by controlling transcription of DNA and regulating chloroplast RNA metabolism, as well as nuclear and cytoplasmic metabolism (Jacobsen, 1977). High concentrations of cytokinins are growth inhibitory (Tasseron-de Jong and Veldstra, 1971). BA is known to inhibit elongation and promote thickening of stems by lateral cell expansion after altering the orientation of microfibrils in cell walls (Sprent, 1968; Takeda and Shibaoka, 1981). In studies by Sprent (1968) with peas, reduced root growth and shoot height resulted when high BA concentrations were applied to roots. When high concentrations of cytokinins were applied to hyacinth roots, root hair loss and reduced shoot height occurred, resulting in decreased shoot/root weight ratios.

Recent research efforts have been directed toward finding effective and inexpensive ways to optimize yields of aquatic plants for nutrient removal and resource recovery. The response of hyacinths to high concentrations of GA_3 (1.0 mg L^{-1}) resulted in decreased vegetative multiplication, with concomitant features including increased biomass yields and nutrient uptake. Response of hyacinths to low concentrations of BA (<0.03 mg L^{-1}) resulted in such features as increased leaf area, biomass yields, vegetative multiplication, and nutrient uptake, but did not inhibit float formation or affect flower production. In some plants, BA can delay senescence (Osborne, 1967; Sprent, 1968), increase starch accumulation in cells (Tasseron-de Jong and Veldstra, 1971), and increase the tolerance of plants to adverse temperature conditions (Fuller et al., 1972). Water hyacinths did not respond favorably to N-(PMA)/GA_4A_7 treatment.

ACKNOWLEDGMENTS

This paper reports results from a project that contributes to a cooperative program between the Institute of Food and Agricultural Sciences (IFAS) of the University of Florida and the Gas Research Institute (GRI) entitled 'Methane from Biomass and Waste'.

REFERENCES

A.P.H.A. 1980. Standard methods for the examination of water and wastewater. 15th ed. American Public Health Assoc., Washington, D.C.

Adams, P. A., M. J. Montague, M. Tepfer, D. L. Rayle, H. Ikuma, and P. B. Kaufman. 1975. Effects of gibberellic acid on the plasticity and elasticity of Avena stem segments. Plant Physiol. 56:757-760.

Fuller, H. J., Z. B. Carothers, W. W. Payne, M. K. Balbach. 1972. The Plant World. Holt, Rinehart, and Winston, Inc., NY.

Horgan, R. 1984. Cytokinins. p. 53-70. In M. B. Wilkins (ed.) Advanced Plant Physiology. Pitman Publishing, London.

Jacobsen, J. V. 1977. Regulation of Ribonucleic Acid Metabolism by Plant Hormones. Ann. Rev. Plant Physiol. 28:537-564.

Joyce, J. C., and W. T. Haller. 1984. Effect of 2,4-D and gibberellic acid on water hyacinths under operational conditions. J. Aquat. Plant Mgt. 22:75-78.

Klich, M. G., M. B. Mujica, and O. A. Fernandez. 1985. The effect of gibberellic acid on the buoyancy of Spirodela intermedia W. Koch. Aquat. Bot. 21:63-69.

Osborne, D. J. 1967. Hormonal regulation of leaf senescence. Symp. Soc. Ex Biol. 21:305-322.

Pieterse, A. H. 1976. Inhibition of float formation in water hyacinth by gibberellic acid. Nature 260:423-424.

Pieterse, A. H., and F. A. Roorda. 1982. Synergistic effect of gibberellic acid and chloroflurenol on 2,4-D with regard to water hyacinth control. Aquat. Bot. 13:69-72.

Ross, S. D., M P. Bollman, R. P. Pharis, and G. B. Sweet. 1984. Gibberellin A_4/A_7 and the promotion of flowering in Pinus radiata. Plant Physiol. 76:326-330.

Sprent, J. I. 1968. The effect of Benzyladenine on the growth and development of peas. Planta 78:17-24.

Takeda, K., and H. Shibaoka. 1981. Effects of gibberellin and colchicine on microfibril arrangement in epidermal cell walls of *Vigna angularis* Ohwi et Ohashi epicotyls. Planta 151:393-398.

Tasseron-DeJong and H. Veldstra. 1971. Investigations on cytokinins. I. Effect of 6-Benzylaminopurine on growth and starch content of *Lemna minor*. Physiol. Plant 24:235-238.

Tomi, H., Y. Sasaki, and T. Kamikubo. 1983. Stimulation of in vitro RNA synthesis by DNA-loosely bound proteins treated with GA_3. Plant and Cell Physiol. 24:1087-1092.

Widyanto, L. S. 1978. The effect of GA_3 on the growth of water hyacinth (*Eichhornia crassipes* [Mart] Solms). Proc. 6th Asian-Pacific Weed Sci. Soc. Conf. 1:269-273.

ABSTRACTS

CO_2 ENRICHMENT INCREASES BIOMASS PRODUCTION OF WATER HYACINTH.

W. Spencer and G. Bowes (Department of Botany, University of Florida, Gainesville, Florida 32611).

Water hyacinth (Eichhornia crassipes [Mart.] Solms) plants were grown in environmental chambers at ambient and enriched CO_2 levels (330 and 600 μL CO_2 L^{-1}, respectively). Daughter plants (ramets) produced in the enriched CO_2 showed a 39% greater dry weight gain than those at ambient CO_2, but the original mother plants did not. The CO_2 enrichment increased the number of leaves per ramet, total ramet leaf area, and the leaf area index, but it did not increase leaf size or the number of ramets formed. The elevated CO_2 initially increased the net photosynthetic rate of the mother plant by 40%, but this was not maintained as the plants adapted to the higher CO_2 level. After 28 days in elevated CO_2 as compared to ambient, ribulose bisphosphate carboxylase activity was 40% less, soluble protein 49% less, and chlorophyll 26% less; whereas starch content was 40% greater. It appears that with CO_2 enrichment, the temporary increase in net photosynthesis produced larger ramets with greater leaf area index. After adaptation, the greater total ramet leaf area more than compensated for the lower net photosynthetic rate found on a unit leaf area basis, and resulted in a sustained improvement in dry weight gain. Apparently, factors other than an increase in individual leaf photosynthetic efficiency can lead to an increase in biomass productivity.

SOME RELATIONSHIPS DURING NATURAL ON SITE PHOTOSYNTHESIS PROCESS.

Y. Deleu (Ministry for Public Health and Family, 14, Juliett Wytsmanstreet, B-1050 Brussels, BELGIUM).

The paper describes some results occurring during sunny periods into river water. These results were collected over five to 10 years, depending on the river, via a prototype automatic water quality monitoring (AWQM) network, installed over a great variety of rivers, under the point of view of their polluted character. Strong relationships between solar radiation and oxygen evolution have been found and they were attributed to photosynthetic processes occurring in the water phase. Aside of effect of sunny days over water temperature, mitigated effects of

ISBN 0-941463-00-1

the photosynthesis have been constated over other parameters such as pH, redox potential, conductivity, and turbidity. Attempts have been made to find trivial and evoluted relationships between sun and the measured parameters, particularly between sun quantas and oxygen molarity. This work demonstrates the high ability of a AWQM network in describing natural processes, even if no satisfying mathematical relation can be expressed. Such expression actually needs more data volume than available, due to the relative scarcity of true sunny days in the country.

ELEMENTAL ACCUMULATION IN THE SALT MARSH RUSH, *JUNCUS ROEMERIANUS*, GROWN IN SIMULATED AND ENRICHED WASTEWATER. L. N. Eleuterius (Gulf Coast Research Laboratory, East Beach Drive, Ocean Springs, Mississippi 39564).

The salt marsh rush, *Juncus roemerianus*, is an excellent plant species to be used in the treatment of wastewater. Experimental evidence indicates that the total elemental content of mature plants can be increased over 10 times the norm for individual concentrations of plants of similar age growing under pristine conditions. Some K elements increased 20 times over the norm. Certain elements are accumulated in direct proportion to the concentration in the nutrient solution in which the plants were grown, while others are not. Immature plants increased in biomass, and elemental concentrations increased with age. Mature plants reach a threshold in biomass, but elemental concentrations continue as a luxury consumption. The upper limit of uptake of most elements is unknown, but the extremely high concentrations indicate an unusually high uptake capacity. Some ecotypes of *Juncus roemerianus* have an extremely high tolerance to sea salts. Populations of these naturally occurring ecotypes occur under hypersaline conditions of 300 ppt. Certain elements are toxic to *Juncus roemerianus* in relatively high concentrations; however, the tolerance is much greater than that reported for most vascular plants. A brief overview of how *Juncus roemerianus* should be grown, prior to use in a wastewater system, will be given.

REMOVAL OF PHENOLS FROM WATER BY DUCKWEED (LEMNACEAE). P. H. Templet and M. Valez (Louisiana State University, Institute for Environmental Studies, 47 Atkinson Hall, Baton Rouge, Louisiana 70803).

The absorption of phenol and 2-chlorophenol from water by duckweeds (Lemnaceae) was investigated in a controlled manner. The rate at which the organic compounds were removed from water by a known amount of duckweed was determined for three different concentrations of phenol and with three different amounts of duckweed for 2-chlorophenol. The duckweed removed phenol from water at a rate which is dependent on the phenol concentration and averages 107 μg phenol removed h^{-1} g^{-1} duckweed for the first 48 h at 10 ppm initial concentration of phenol in water. The removal rate for 2-chlorophenol was investigated at a lower initial concentration (2.3 ppm) and the removal rate was slower and a function of the quantity of duckweed present even when normalized to a constant duckweed level. The rate increased for the first four to six days and averaged 33 μg chlorophenol removed d^{-1} g^{-1} duckweed at the sixth day. The results support the hypothesis that duckweeds can be used to feasibly remove phenols and chlorophenols from water and offer the possibility of biological treatment of polluted waters.

EFFECTS OF CHANGES IN SEDIMENT pH AND REDOX POTENTIAL RESULTING FROM INPUTS OF STORMWATER RUNOFF ON THE STABILITY OF METAL-SEDIMENT ASSOCIATIONS IN A HARDWOOD WETLAND. H. H. Harper III, M. P. Wanielista (University of Central Florida, P. O. Box 25000, Orlando, Florida 32816), and E. H. Livingston (Florida Department of Environmental Regulation).

The movement and fate of heavy metal inputs (Cd, Zn, Mn, Cu, Al, Fe, Pb, Ni, and Cr) from stormwater runoff were investigated in a 3 ha hardwood wetland near Sanford, Florida. Stormwater inputs were monitored over a one year period. Core samples were collected to a depth of 20 cm in the flow path and in isolated control areas to characterize the accumulation and attenuation of heavy metals. Sediment samples were carried through a series of sequential extraction procedures to examine the type of chemical associations binding metals to the sediments. An apparatus was built which allowed sediment to be incubated under various conditions of redox potential and pH to investigate the importance of redox potential and pH on metal-sediment stability. Groundwater monitoring wells were installed in the flow path and in the control area. Sediment metal concentrations in both the flow path and control areas were highest near the surface and declined rapidly with increasing depth. Most metal species were found to be tightly bound to Fe/Mn oxides and organic matter in relatively stable associations. Redox potential was less important than pH in regulating the release of metals from sediments. The inputs of stormwater generally resulted in higher levels of both pH and redox potential which increased metal stability when compared to the control area.

THE TREATMENT OF LANDFILL LEACHATE UTILIZING ON SITE LIVING FILTER TECHNOLOGY. R. L. Lavigne and P. L. M. Veneman (University of Massachusetts, Stockbridge Hall, Amherst, Massachusetts 01003).

Research was undertaken to develop a mathematical model for the on site treatment of landfill leachate using a low technology "living filter" system. Greenhouse growth chambers were used to test the assumption that microbial degradation of leachate would follow first order kinetics for substrate utilization. Sixteen batch reactors seeded with reed canarygrass (P. arundinacea L.) were operated with residence times ranging from 2 hours to 12 days. A first-order model for Total Organic Carbon (TOC) was tested for goodness of fit, and rate constants were determined for different modes of operation. Peat soils were analyzed before and after treatment for cation exchange capacity (CEC), and exchanged leachate ions were identified by atomic adsorption spectrophotometry. Microbes were identified and enumerated at three depths within the peat beds, so that modes of metabolic activity could be better understood. Plug flow modeling is being used to verify rate orders and constants evaluated in the batch experiment. A pilot scale demonstration site will be constructed at a newly lined landfill in western Massachusetts.

UPTAKE OF COPPER AND IRON FROM POLLUTED WATER BY DUCKWEED (LEMNA MINOR AND SPIRODELA POLYRHIZA SPECIES). S. K. Jain, P. Vasudevan and N. K. Jha (Indian Institute of Technology, New Delhi 110 016, INDIA).

The uptake of copper and iron by duckweed (*Lemna minor* and *Spirodela polyrhiza*) was investigated in model solutions enriched with 1.0, 2.0, 4.0 and 8.0 ppm of these two metal ions. The solutions in contact with the weed were changed every other day for each concentration of the metal ions and the old solutions were analyzed for metal ion content. Copper concentration remaining in water after the plant growth ranged from 0.10-0.51, 0.18-1.13, 0.47-2.01 and 1.19-4.32 ppm corresponding to solutions initially containing 1.0, 2.0, 4.0, and 8.0 ppm of copper. The iron content in the residual water was 0.12-0.30, 0.16-0.41, 0.30-0.72 and 1.40-6.63 ppm corresponding to solutions initially containing 1.0, 2.0, 4.0, and 8.0 ppm of iron. The metal content in the weed increased with time as well as initial concentration.

REMOVAL OF SOME HEAVY METALS FROM POLLUTED WATER BY AZOLLA PINNATA. S. K. Jain, P. Vasudevan and N. K. Jha (Indian Institute of Technology, New Delhi 110 016, INDIA).

Azolla pinnata was studied for pollution control from model solutions of iron and copper and mixture of these two metal ions. Initial concentration of metal ions were varied from 1.0-8.0 ppm. The solutions in contact with the weed were changed every other day for each concentration and the old solutions were analyzed for metal ion content. Iron remaining in water after the plant growth ranged from 0.11-0.05, 0.17-0.10, 0.28-0.15, and 1.20-2.75 ppm corresponding to solutions initially containing 1.0, 2.0, 4.0, and 8.0 ppm of iron respectively. Copper concentration in the residual water ranged 0.09-0.51, 0.15-1.13, 0.36-1.53 and

0.84-2.83 ppm corresponding to solutions initially containing 1.0, 2.0, 4.0, and 8.0 ppm copper. The metal content in the weed varies with time as well as initial concentration.

RELATIONSHIP BETWEEN THE STANDING CROP OF MACROPHYTES AND NUTRIENT REMOVAL EFFICIENCY IN WASTEWATER WETLAND.

J. R. Williams, Jr. (U.S. Environmental Protection Agency, Lockhead, Las Vegas, Nevada 89114) and R. A. Gearheart (Humboldt State University, California).

Recently a great deal of interest has developed in the use of wetlands for the treatment of wastewater. A combination of physical, chemical and biological factors have been identified for nutrient removal in wetlands. The principal factors suggested to date are: sedimentation, precipitation, adsorption, bacterial-algal metabolism, and macrophytic metabolism. During a two year study (1981-1983) of a wastewater wetland, the role of macrophytic metabolism in nutrient removal rates was determined. A mass balance was developed for ammonia, nitrate-nitrogen, ortho-phosphate and aquatic macrophyte peak standing crop. In the study years there was a net release of ortho-phosphate, and a net uptake of both ammonia and nitrate-nitrogen from the wetland. During 1981 the standing crops for the aquatic macrophytes was significantly, (Mann-Whitney U, = 0.05), higher than 1982. But the removal rate for inorganic nitrogen was half the 1982 value (10 vs. 20 percent). The loading rates used in this study did not present a phosphorus limiting condition for the macrophytes. The inorganic nitrogen removal rate was not dependent on the standing crop of the major taxa of aquatic macrophytes. In this artificial marsh, there was no leaf litter in the start-up year of 1981. The leaf litter which accumulated in the marsh by 1982 provided habitat for microbial populations. The metabolic activity of the periphytic microbes was a major factor in the nutrient removal rates. Consequently, the common marsh management practice of burning accumulated leaf litter or removal of detrital debri is expected to have adverse effects on the capacity of a wetland to act as a nutrient nitrogen form. In fact, enhanced nutrient removal rates and increased storage potential may be obtained after an accumulation of leaf litter has occurred.

HEAVY METAL REMOVAL FROM AQUEOUS SOLUTION BY WATER HYACINTH.

S. R. Hunter (26430 Chapel Hill Dr., North Olmsted, Ohio 44070).

The use of _Eichhornia crassipes_ commonly known as water hyacinths has, in recent years, become a topic of serious interest to scientists and engineers. The hyacinths have the potential of becoming a solution to the growing problem of water pollution control. As industries continue to grow and dump chemicals, which collect in lakes and streams, it is important to control the amounts of toxic and heavy metals affecting nature and surrounding wildlife. With the possibility of using water hyacinths, it is necessary to determine the maximum levels of metals and waste that the hyacinth plants are capable of absorbing. The following research and experimentation has been conducted to ascertain the applicability of hyacinth-based treatment on current water pollution issues. The experiment includes exposing mature water hyacinths to lead, copper, and chromium solutions. At frequent intervals throughout the duration of the testing period, samples were collected of each variable and control. By determining the reductions in the molar concentrations of the metallic solutions, conclusions will be made regarding the feasibility of operating hyacinth treatment plants. It is intended that, as research and experimentation continue, as well as the growth of current larger operations, the potential of water hyacinth treatment will become a reality.

SEASONAL CHANGES AND DISTRIBUTION OF MINERAL NUTRIENTS IN DIFFERENT ORGANS OF THE TWO VARIETIES OF PISTIA STRATIOTES L. A. S. Reddy (Nizam College, Hyderabad 500 001, A. P., INDIA) and P. N. Rao (Nagarjuna University, Guntur, INDIA).

Seasonal changes in total N, P, K, Ca, Mg, Na and crude protein in the two varieties of Pistia stratiotes L. viz., P. stratiotes var. cuneata Engl. and P. stratiotes var. spathulata Engl. were analyzed from the natural populations of a perennial pond (80°27' East & 16°11' North) in the state of Andhra Pradesh, India. Maximum concentration of these elements was during summer and minimum during rainy and early winter seasons. Similarly, the crude protein showed a maximum 22.94% and 35.75% and a minimum of 15.06% and 22.94% in these two varieties, respectively. The variety spathulata accumulates higher percentage of nutrients from the substratum than the variety cuneata. The magnitude of these nutrients in both the varieties was in order: N>K>Ca>Mg>P>Na. A comparison is made with certain other aquatic macrophytes and also with some species useful as fodders. Accumulation of N, P, K, Ca, Mg and Na in different plant organs of the two varieties were surveyed from populations growing in eutrophic and non-eutrophic ponds. The cations and anions accumulated more in the leaves followed by rhizomes and stolons and their amounts are higher at the eutrophic pond than at the non-eutrophic pond. This study also suggests that the water lettuce (P. stratiotes) reduces the nutrient pollution and is useful as a cattle feed.

EFFECT OF LIGHT INTENSITY ON THE BIOMASS PRODUCTION AND SPORULATION IN NINE CULTURES OF THE AQUATIC NITROGEN FIXING FERN AZOLLA. S. Kannaiyan (Tamil Nadu Agricultural University, Coimbatore 641 003, Tamil Nadu, INDIA).

Azolla is a genus of small aquatic fern that floats in water and assimilates atmospheric N in association with N-fixing blue green alga - *Anabaena azollae* that lives in the cavities present in the upper leaf lobes of *Azolla* as symbiont. Application of *Azolla* biofertilizer as green manure or as dual culture have been shown to increase the grain yield of rice equivalent to 30-40 kg N ha^{-1}. The influence of light intensity on the growth and sporulation in nine Azolla cultures was investigated and presented. *Azolla* cultures *viz*. *A*. *caroliniana* WT-V, *A*. *mexicana* BRGL, *A*. *pinnata* GP-BY, *A*. *pinnata* - SK-I, *A*. *pinnata* - SK-CI, *A*. *microphylla* - BR-GI, *A*. *filiculoides* - BR-H, *A*. *nilotica* TLH and A. sp - ST-SI were inoculated in IRRI(-)NO_3 medium and grown at 180 $\mu E\ m^{-2}\ s^{-1}$ (log light) and 380 $\mu E\ m^{-2}\ s^{-1}$ (high light). The temperature was maintained at 26+1°C throughout the period of the study.

WATER POLLUTION REMOVAL BY THREE HELOPHYTIC CULTURES IN COMPARISON WITH A LAGOON SYSTEM UNDER THE SAME TEMPERATE CLIMATE. M. Radoux (Foundation Universitaire Luxembourgeoise, 140 - B6700 Arlon, BELGIUM).

The aim of this research is to compare the depurative efficiency of different helophytic artificial cultures supplied with the same domestic and rural wastewater under the same temperate climate. The study, realized on a small scale, compares the depurative efficaciousness of three macrophytic plantations (*Typha latifolia*, *Iria pseudacorus*, *Epilobium hirsutum*) in comparison with a lagoon system (without plants). The experimental plant at Viville (Arlon, Belgium) is fitted for maximum reliability and precision in the evaluation of depurative efficiencies. Retention time of water for these experiments is rather short: maximum 6 m^2/E.H., hydraulic load. During two complete successive years, precise evolution of purification capacities for C.O.D., suspended matter, total N and total P is presented in different ways, taking rainfall and evapo-transpiration also into account. Development of aerial macrophytic biomass is also presented and its probable relation with water pollution removal is discussed.

HEAVY METAL TOLERANCE OF CERTAIN AQUATIC PLANTS. K. Ilangovan (Bharathidasan University, Tiruchirapalli 620 023, INDIA) and M. Vivekanandan (Washington State University).

Eichhornia crassipes, *Marsilea* spp., and *Salvinia* spp. growing in highly polluted water polluted by residential wastes as well as mineral oils were observed, to study the effect of heavy metals on the aforementioned plants. These same plant species introduced in areas highly polluted by toxic heavy metals showed remarkable accumulation of Cd, Pb, Al, Cu, Cr, and Zn in the various plant parts like leaves and roots. Plants grown in unpolluted water were considered as control. Significant amounts of Pb and Zn accumulated in the leaf, and increased amounts of Zn, Cd, and Cr were also found in the root system. From this preliminary study concluded that aforementioned aquatic plants were considered as efficient heavy metal filters in the aquatic environment. It is almost impossible to treat the industrial effluents chemically to make them non-toxic and acceptable for agricultural purposes since the removal of heavy metals by chemical treatment are too expensive, these plants can be utilized as a viable alternative for treatment of industrial effluents as well as residential wastes.

PART IV
AQUATIC PLANT MANAGEMENT

BIOMASS PRODUCTION AND YIELDS OF AQUATIC PLANTS

T. A. DeBusk
Reedy Creek Utilities Co., Inc.
Lake Buena Vista, Florida 32830

J. H. Ryther
Division of Applied Biology
Harbor Branch Oceanographic Institution, Inc.
Ft. Pierce, Florida 33450

ABSTRACT

A diversity of aquatic plants, including unicellular algae, macroscopic algae and freshwater macrophytes, is currently being utilized for wastewater treatment and resource recovery applications. Biomass yields of many aquatic species, both micro and macroscopic, have been found to equal or exceed those of the most productive terrestrial crops. Although certain aquatic plants are cultured as food crops, aquatic plant biomass is more typically used for fiber products, chemical production, livestock feed, and conversion to CH_4 or alcohol. This paper describes maximum short term and annual yields of some of the more productive micro and macroscopic aquatic species, with consideration given to the quality and potential uses of the biomass, culture methods, and problems encountered in cultivation.

Keywords: Primary productivity, freshwater macrophytes, microalgae, seaweeds.

INTRODUCTION

With the exception of a few freshwater macrophytes and marine macroalgae, used for food or for their polysaccharide gums, aquatic plants are not conventional crop species cultivated and harvested or even gathered from wild populations by man. To the contrary, they more often have been regarded with disfavor, as weeds that choke waterways, decay on beaches, and impart unpleasant odors, tastes, and colors to aquatic habitats. Prior to the mid-1970's, data on the biomass production potential of aquatic plants were limited to growth studies in natural systems, such as the extensive work on freshwater macrophytes performed by Boyd (1969a,b, 1971). However, interest in the conversion of

Aquatic Plants for Water Treatment
and Resource Recovery
K.R. Reddy and W.H. Smith (Eds.)

ISBN 0-941463-00-1

plant biomass to methane (CH_4) during the last decade led to the evaluation of the yields of a number of productive aquatic species. Aquatic plants seemed ideal for this purpose, since preliminary studies showed that many aquatic species are productive, and are easily converted to CH_4 via anaerobic digestion. Moreover, such plants grow in areas not used by man for other purposes.

Also during the past two decades, increasing demands for algal polysaccharide gels (agar, carrageenin, alginic acid) and diminishing stocks of the seaweeds that have traditionally supplied that market have led to research, development, and in a few cases, commercialization of seaweed culture systems for producing such products. Biomass yields of the seaweeds grown in such systems are, of course, a key element in the economic success of such ventures, so yield data for that particular form of aquatic plant production have been carefully documented.

Finally, the aspect of aquatic plant cultivation that has received by far the most attention for the longest period of time is that involving the unicellular algae. Research in this area began with the continuous laboratory cultures of Ketchum and Redfield (1938), followed by that of Myers and Clark (1949), and Cook (1951). The landmark publication of the Carnegie Institution (Burlew, 1953) summarized the then current state-of-the-art of mass unicellular algae culture and stimulated great interest internationally on the subject. Studies were also initiated at about this time on the use of unicellular algae for wastewater treatment (Oswald et al., 1953), and human food (Tamiya, 1959).

The following discussion summarizes existing information on the yields of aquatic plants, including unicellular algae, macroalgae (seaweeds), and freshwater macrophytes. Where possible, data presented will be the result of long-term, large-scale studies. Unless specified, biomass yields reported in this paper are on a dry weight basis.

Unicellular Algae

Most culture systems in which microalgae are grown are similar in design and operation, involving the use of shallow (0.1 to 0.5 m), well mixed reservoirs provided with CO_2 and other nutrient enrichment. These systems are usually operated semi-continuously, with instantaneous harvest of a portion of the culture and its replacement (i.e., dilution) with fresh medium every one to several days.

Yields from the outdoor mass culture of unicellular algae on a world-wide basis over the 25 year period since the Carnegie Institute report of 1953 were summarized by Goldman (1979). Eighteen examples cited in that paper are reproduced here (Table 1). Sustained yields (over 27-365 d) for microalgae cultures were found to range from 2 to 27 g m^{-2} d^{-1}, with an average of 13 g m^{-2} d^{-1}. Some of the higher yields reported in Table 1 (Shelef et al., 1973) include bacteria and other non-algal

TABLE 1. Summary of world-wide programs for mass culturing of microalgae up to 1978 (from Goldman, 1979).

Location	Species	Culture system size (m^2) Unit	Total	Operation*	Best yields (duration) $g\ m^{-2}\ d^{-1}$ (d) Maximum	Average	References
USA, MA	Chlorella	56	56	N,F,SC	11 (10)	2 (52)	Burlew, 1953
Japan	Chlorella	3	14	N,F,SC	28 (3)	16 (27)	Morimura et al., 1955
Japan	Tolypothrix	5	5	N,F,SC	?	6 (?)	Watanabe et al., 1959
USA, CA	Green algae	2700	2700	W,F,C,	?	?	Oswald, 1969
Israel	Chlorella	4	4	N,F,SC	16 (27)	12 (35)	Mayer et al., 1964
Germany	Scenedesmus	80	320	N,F,SC	28 (?)	10 (?)	Soeder, 1976
Czechoslovakia	Scenedesmus	900	900	N,F,SC	19 (10)	12 (89)	Vendlova, 1969
Romania	Scenedesmus	50	50	N,F,SC	30 (10)	23 (62)	Vendlova, 1969
USA, CA	Scenedesmus	1000	1000	TD,F,C	35 (10)	10 (70)	Beck et al., 1969
Israel	Chlorella	300	300	W,F,C	60 (30)†	27 (30)‡	Shelef et al., 1973
USA, FL	Diatoms	4	8	WSW,M,C	25 (15)		Goldman et al., 1975
USA, MA	Diatoms	180	1080	WSW,M,C	10 (7)		D'Elia et al., 1977
Mexico	Spirulina	?	200,000	B,F,SC	20 (?)	10 (?)	Durand-Chastel, 1977
Israel	Green algae	120	270	W,F,C	35 (30)	15 (365)	Shelef et al., 1978
Thailand	Spirulina	87	609	N,F,SC	18 (?)	15 (?)	Soeder, 1976
Japan	Chlorella	?	11,500	N,F.SC	?	21 (365)‡	Tsukada et al., 1977
Taiwan	Chlorella	500	180,000	N,F,SC	35 (7)	18 (365)‡	Shurtleff, pers. comm.
USA, CA	Micractinium	2700	27,000	W,F,SC	12 (31)	9 (77)	Benemann et al., 1978

*N = artificial nutrients; W = wastewater; WSW = wastewater-seawater mixture; B = brine; TD = agricultural tile drainage; F = freshwater algae; M = marine algae; SC = semi-continuous harvest; C = continuous harvest.

†Included non-algal solids from wastewater.

‡Algae grown on combined CO_2 and organic substrates.

solids from the wastewater in which the algae were grown, and none of the yield data are corrected for ash content.

Although the yields described in Table 1 are quite high, to date it has not been possible to culture over any sustained period of time any target species selected for its food, fuel, or chemical value. Often, the organism cultured has been a contaminant that has invaded cultures of other organisms, achieved dominance, and persisted. The few species that have been maintained in a large, outdoor mass culture system include the freshwater species *Scenedesmus* and *Chlorella*, and the marine species *Phaeodactylum* and *Tetraselmis*.

Weissman and Goebel (1986) recently found that *Scenedesmus* and other "weed species" of green algae, the adventitious contaminants that usually out-compete and dominate mass freshwater algal cultures, are actually not able to tolerate the high concentrations of dissolved O_2 and/or the high pH and low pCO_2 levels that are characteristic of dense algal cultures, and that their yields are consequently self limiting. It is therefore perhaps unfortunate that *Scenedesmus* has been the deliberate or accidental object of so much of the earlier mass culture efforts.

Extremely high yields (25-40 g m^{-2} d^{-1}) were recently obtained from some of the small centric diatoms (*Cyclotella*, *Chaetoceros*) that had been isolated by subcontractors supported by the Solar Energy Research Institute (SERI) Aquatic Species Program. These species appear less sensitive to high density-related environmental stress (high pO_2, high pH, low pCO_2) than the green algae, though the test systems utilized were small (1.4 m^2) and the duration of the experiments short (20-40 d) (Weissman and Goebel, 1986).

In one of the few marine studies reported recently in the literature, Laws et al. (1986) described yields over a five month period of the green flagellate *Tetraselmis suecica*, grown in a shallow, well mixed flume system in Hawaii, that averaged 28 g m^{-2} d^{-1}. These cultures were semi-continuous, with harvests which varied every 2, 3, or 4 d. For some unexplicable reason, the yield from day 2 to day 3 was much higher than that for the other time intervals (i.e., days 0-1, 1-2, or 3-4), reaching as high as 60-70 g (ash-free dry wt) m^{-2} d^{-1}, and making the average for the 30 d run with the 3 d harvest regime 41.3 g (afdw) m^{-2} d^{-1}, considerably higher than any other reported sustained unicellular algal culture yields.

A number of photosynthetic models have been developed to predict the maximum sustainable yield of unicellular algae in outdoor mass culture (Van Orschat, 1955; Shelef, 1978; Goldman, 1979). These models have generally placed a ceiling on light-limited potential algal productivity of 30-40 g m^{-2} d^{-1}. In practice, however, long-term, large scale yields of unicellular algae have seldom averaged more than half of that potential.

Such chronic, unresolved problems as species control, predation, culture systems design and operation, and environmental stress have, in fact, resulted in there being few if any examples of long-term (one year or more), large-scale (1 ha or more) unialgal cultures from which to cite sustained yield data. The state-of-the-art is still essentially in the same, small-scale, experimental stage that it was 35 or more years ago, when unicellular algae led the field of aquatic plant productivity. Perhaps the greatest advance in recent years has been the isolation of some new species of unicellular algae, as part of the SERI Aquatic Species Program, that show considerably more promise for mass algal culture than most of the old, traditional species that have been grown more by chance than by design.

Macroscopic Algae (Seaweeds)

Because seaweeds are not widely used, a well developed and established technology for their large-scale commercial cultivation does not exist. There are exceptions to be found, however, in southeast Asia and the Orient, where a few species are grown for food or their chemicals. The most important of these are: (1) *Porphyra* (nori) culture in Japan, (2) *Laminaria* (kelp) culture in China, (3) *Eucheuma* farming in the Philippines, and (4) *Gracilaria* culture in Taiwan. The biology of the respective species and their cultivation technology have been described in detail in reviews by Bardach et al. (1972), Hansen et al. (1981), and Tseng (1981).

Several species of the red alga genus *Porphyra* have been grown as a highly-prized food since the seventeenth century in Japan, where it is commonly known as "nori." In 1978, 60,000 ha of sea surface were used to produce 21,150 dry metric tons of nori with a value of 540 million U.S. dollars, by far the most economically important seaweed crop in the world (Tseng, 1981).

The productivity or yield of *Porphyra* is not usually given in the literature that describes its cultivation. A rough estimate (Bardach et al., 1972) placed mean production at 0.75 Mg ha^{-1} yr^{-1} (0.2 g m^{-2} d^{-1}). Productivity estimated from the production data given in the preceding paragraph is 0.35 Mg ha^{-1} yr^{-1}. Both figures are probably conservative and higher yields are undoubtedly achieved, but apparently either the species and/or the culture method employed do not lend themselves to high levels of production.

The small kelp *Laminaria japonica* is indigenous to the cold-water environment of Hokkaido, the northern island of Japan, from which some 3000 dry tons yr^{-1} were formerly exported to China. Now it is grown in over 18,000 ha of China's coastal waters with a production in 1979 of more than 275,000 dry tons worth some 300 million U.S. dollars. Kelp yields in Tsingtao, where the growing season is 230 d, average 12 Mg ha^{-1} yr^{-1} (5.2 g m^{-2} d^{-1}). In the colder Dalien region, where the season is perhaps one month longer, kelp yields of 20 Mg ha^{-1} yr^{-1} have been reported (Tseng, 1981).

Eucheuma is a multiple-branched, fleshy red alga used for its contained polysaccharide, carrageenin. Originally harvested from wild stocks in Southeast Asia, such supplies were cut off in the 1950's and led to the development of cultivation methods for the species by the joint efforts of Marine Colloids, Inc. (Rockland, Maine), M. S. Doty (Univ. of Hawaii), and the Philippines Bureau of Fisheries and Aquatic Resources. Using six months of harvest data (1971-1972), Parker (1974) estimated annual production of Eucheuma at a pilot farm on Tapaan Island, Philippines to be 13 Mg ha^{-1} yr^{-1}.

In 1962, cultivation of the red seaweed Gracilaria began in southern Taiwan. The alga is either used locally, or following preliminary processing, is shipped to Japan for the extraction of the polysaccharide, agar. The bulk of the production of this alga occurs from June through December, with yields ranging from 12 to 20 Mg and averaging about 14 Mg ha^{-1} yr^{-1} (Shang, 1976).

Excluding the Japanese Porphyra cultivation, where quality of the product is paramount and yield is of secondary importance, the three other major seaweed culture industries in the world, though involving different species and very different culture methods, produce remarkably similar average yields of 13-16 Mg ha^{-1} yr^{-1} (3.6-4.4 g m^{-2} d^{-1}). Considering the fact that these are young (15-30 yr) and technologically rather simple industries, such yields are rather impressive.

Within the last decade, considerable work has been conducted in the United States toward maximizing the productivity of numerous macroalgae, the two most prominent of these being Gracilaria spp. and the giant kelp, Macrocystis pyrifera. Through the use of frequent harvest, continuous agitation and a rapid water exchange, annual mean Gracilaria yields of 127 Mg ha^{-1} yr^{-1} (34.8 g m^{-2} d^{-1}) were attained in small tank cultures in Florida (Lapointe and Ryther, 1978). Gracilaria yields under non-energy intensive, pond culture conditions (no agitation, low water exchange) averaged less than 5 g m^{-2} d^{-1}, very similar to the Gracilaria yields obtained from similar culture methods in Taiwan.

The giant kelp, Macrocystis pyrifera, is the largest known alga and one of the world's largest plants, attaining a length in excess of 50 m. Although a number of cultivation techniques have been attempted for this plant in California, none have substantially improved long term yields over those which are attained in natural kelp stands [i.e., 8-20 Mg ha^{-1} yr^{-1} (2.2-5.5 g m^{-2} d^{-1})] (Neushal and Harger, 1984).

Emergent Freshwater Macrophytes

Emergent freshwater macrophytes have long been considered among the most productive of aquatic plants (Westlake, 1963), largely due to the favorable environmental conditions of the habitats in which they occur. Wetland sediments generally contain adequate nutrients to support rapid plant growth. In addition, atmosphere-leaf gas (CO_2) exchange by plants occurring in moist environments is rarely limited by water stress-induced stomatal closure.

Observations of natural stands of emergent macrophytes lends support to the concept that such plants are potentially attractive biomass crops. Many emergent species, such as cattail, soft rush, and reed, occur in dense, monospecific stands, at standing crops exceeding 2 kg m^{-2} (Boyd, 1971). Leaf area indices (LAI) of such stands are often as high as 10 (Andrews and Pratt, 1978), which suggests efficient solar radiation capture. Cattail (*Typha* sp.), papyrus (*Cyperus papyrus*), and water willow (*Justicia americana*) are among emergents whose short-term productivity in natural stands approaches or exceeds 20 g m^{-2} d^{-1} (Table 2).

For most aquatic macrophytes, the photosynthetic pathway, or mechanism by which CO_2 is initially fixed in leaf mesophyll cells has not been determined (Garrard and Van, 1982). Plants in which CO_2 is initially incorporated as a four C compound (C_4 plants) possess physiological characteristics (lower CO_2 compensation points, reduced rates of photorespiration) which may enable them to produce biomass at a faster rate than plants which initially incorporate CO_2 as a three C compound (C_3 plants). However, the importance of C_3 or C_4 metabolism to biomass production in aquatic

TABLE 2. Biomass yields of emergent macrophytes in natural and cultivated stands.

Species	Yield, g m^{-2} d^{-1}			Reference
	Location	Max	Avg.	
	Natural Stands			
Typha latifolia	USA, S.E.	52.6^t	---	Penfound 1956
Cyperus papyrus	Africa		22.9 (12)	Westlake 1963
Justicia americana	USA, S.E.	31.1^s	---	Boyd 1969a
Juncus effusus	USA, S.E.	14.6^s	---	Boyd 1971
Nupar advena	USA, E.	---	5.7^s (*)	Whigham & Simpson 1976
	Cultivated Stands			
Typha latifolia[2]	USA, N.	40.0^t	17.7 (5)	Pratt & Andrews 1980
Phragmites australia[3]	USA, FL	---	25.9^s (12)	Batterson 1984
Colocasia esculenta[4]	USA, FL	---	5.2^t (9)	O'Hair et al. 1982
Ipomoea aquatica[4]	USA, FL	---	8.3^t (8)	Snyder et al. 1981

s = shoot yield; t = total plant yield.
[1]Duration in months. [2]Peat substrate. [3]Sewage sludge substrate.
[4]Muck substrate.
*7-month growing season assumed.

environments has not been established, since many productive emergent species, such as cattail and soft rush (Juncus effusus), are thought to be C_3 species (Reddy et al., 1983).

Attempts at maximizing yields of emergents through the optimization of culture practices are fairly recent. Soil type, nutrient additions, planting density, and harvesting frequency are all parameters which have been investigated for improving plant yields. However, to date such studies have been conducted with relatively few species. The plant which has been studied most intensively is cattail, a ubiquitous emergent which occurs both in tropical and temperate regions. In Minnesota, Pratt and Andrews (1980) reported a maximum growth rate of 40 g m^{-2} d^{-1} for cattail cultivated on peat, with yields over a 5 month growing season averaging 17.7 g m^{-2} d^{-1}. These investigators proposed cultivating cattail as an energy crop for conversion to CH_4.

In Sweden, the common reed, Phragmites australis, is both farmed and harvested wild in order to provide a fuel source for heating (Graneli, 1984). Dry culms from this plant are collected during the winter and directly combusted. Studies suggest common reed may be even more productive than cattail. Batterson (1984) reported annual shoot yields of 25.9 g m^{-2} d^{-1} for P. australis cultivated on secondary domestic wastewater effluent in Florida (Table 2).

Although dry matter production by cattail and reed is rapid, the shoots of these plants are fibrous, with a wide C:N ratio. Polisini and Boyd (1972) noted that emergent species which occur at high standing crops (and which are typically very productive) produce shoot tissues of low nutritional value relative to species which form less dense stands. Hence, some pretreatment (cellulose hydrolysis, N additions) of shoot tissues may be necessary if they are to be utilized as a CH_4 digester feedstock. It may also be prudent to harvest the tissues of such species young, when concentrations of macronutrients and other constituents (chlorophyll, carotenoids) in the shoots are highest (Boyd, 1969b).

Productivity of emergent macrophytes is usually estimated by measuring changes in standing crop biomass over time. However, because of their rooted habit, it is often difficult to accurately assess the total biomass yield of emergent plants. For many species, the production of underground root and rhizome tissues may equal or exceed that of the aboveground standing crop. Andrews and Pratt (1978) found the ratio of underground (root+rhizome) tissues to shoot tissue of cattail to vary from 0.2 to 1.0 during the growing season. In his study with the common reed, Batterson (1984) estimated that shoot tissues represented only 25% of the total standing crop. Notations are made in Table 2 as to whether the yields presented for each species represent shoot, or whole plant biomass increases.

Although herbivore utilization of emergent macrophytes is typically slight, the loss of tissues to senescence and decomposition may reduce the harvestable yield in a plant stand. Such losses are probably greatest in tropical regions, where environmental conditions favor continuous, year-round biomass production and leaf turnover, as well as rapid decomposition (Tieszen, 1982). Rates of detritus production and decomposition must therefore be considered in order to accurately assess the net yield of emergent macrophytes. In managed stands, tissue losses can be minimized by continuous harvest, a practice which helps maintain a standing crop of young, actively growing shoots.

The products for which emergent macrophytes can be utilized depend largely on the tissue type available. Cattail shoots are of considerable importance throughout third world countries for products such as baskets, floor mats, sandals, and paper (Morton, 1975). Such products, for which the nutritional value of the plant tissues is of little or no consequence, are probably the most appropriate use for shoots of cattail, reed, and similar species (e.g., rushes). In contrast, rhizomes of emergent species often contain relatively high levels of soluble carbohydrates (Pratt, 1978), and are thus of greater nutritive value than shoots. In natural stands, particularly in temperate regions, the rhizome tissues perform a storage function, allowing the plant to survive during the winter season when shoots are dead or dormant. These underground tissues are much more suitable than shoots for conversion to fuels such as CH_4 or alcohol. However, roots and rhizomes of cultivated emergents are often not utilized due to the difficulties encountered in harvesting the underground tissues.

Colocasia esculenta (wetland taro) is one such productive aquatic crop which would probably be utilized more extensively if harvesting of the rhizomes (corms) were not so difficult. O'Hair et al. (1982) reported average annual yields of 1.1 and 5.2 g m^{-2} d^{-1}, respectively, for corms and total biomass of this plant. The corms of *Colocasia* are currently utilized for several food products (most notably, poi), and the plant foliage could potentially be utilized for conversion to CH_4.

Another productive emergent plant cultivated as a food crop is *Ipomoea aquatica* (water spinach). *Ipomoea* grows rapidly, is easy to harvest, and is used widely as a food and feed crop in S.E. Asia. An average yield of 8.3 g m^{-2} d^{-1} during an 8 month period was reported for this species in south Florida (Snyder et al., 1981). Although popular as a vegetable among people of Asiatic origin, the cultivation of *Ipomoea* in Florida is prohibited because of its potential for infesting natural waterways.

Floating-leaved aquatic macrophytes, such as spatterdock (*Nuphar* sp.), water lilies (*Nymphaea* spp.), lotus (*Nelumbo* spp.), and watershield (*Brasinea* sp.), can be considered emergent species in that the plants are rooted in the sediment with the foliage at least partially exposed to the atmosphere. With the exception of water lilies and lotus, which are occasionally grown as ornamentals, the floating-leaved species are not commonly cultivated. Although yield data for these plants in cultivation are not available, observations of natural populations indicate that their maximum standing crop biomass (<1 kg m^{-2}) and productivity (Table 2) are low relative to many other emergent macrophytes.

The same characteristics which allow emergent macrophytes to thrive in flooded or poorly drained soils make them suitable candidates for treating wastewaters. Most emergents have some ability to oxidize their rhizosphere (Armstrong, 1964; Teal and Kanwisher, 1966); this can enhance survival in wastewaters which contain a high O_2 demand. In addition, many emergent species can assimilate large quantities of wastewater nutrients to support their rapid growth.

Floating Freshwater Macrophytes

Studies conducted within the last decade have demonstrated that yields of many floating macrophytes equal or exceed those of the most productive emergent species (Reddy and DeBusk, 1984). Floating plants utilize atmospheric CO_2 as a C source, but, unlike emergents, floating species depend on the aqueous medium to provide all other plant nutrients. Sediments may augment floating plant nutrition only indirectly, through nutrient release into the water column.

Probably the most productive aquatic plant in cultivation, and the most successful aquatic weed in terms of its adventive spread, is the water hyacinth (Eichhnoria crassipes). Water hyacinth often forms dense standing crops in natural systems (2 kg m^{-2}), and possesses a high leaf area index (ca 8; Knipling et al., 1970). The morphological characteristics of water hyacinth plants vary considerably in response to changing light and temperature, and interspecific and intraspecific competition. Center and Spencer (1981) noted that such canopy fluctuations enable this species to maximize solar energy capture while minimizing respiratory losses incurred by supportive (non-photosynthetic) tissues.

Although water hyacinth, which is considered a C_3 plant, is quite productive, its growth rate in natural stands is rapid only during periods of colonization (Center and Spencer, 1981). Once a dense mat is formed, net productivity is reduced due to plant crowding and self-shading; tissue synthesis at high standing crops (>2 kg m^{-2}) serves primarily to replace older tissues as they senesce and decompose. Under cultivation, water hyacinth is harvested frequently in order to maintain the standing crop within a range most conducive to rapid plant growth.

Extensive studies have been conducted with floating species such as water hyacinth, water lettuce (Pistia stratiotes), and pennywort (Hydrocotyle umbellata) on the manipulation of standing crop to enhance biomass yields. Reddy and DeBusk (1984) reported optimum densities for water hyacinth, water lettuce, and pennywort of 0.5-2.0, 0.2-0.7, and 0.25-0.65 kg m^{-2}, respectively. Maximum short term yields of these same species cultured on nutrient media were 64.4, 40.0, and 29.7 g m^{-2} d^{-1}, with long-term yields (greater than 6 months) in central Florida averaging 27.1, 14.2, and 10.9 g m^{-2} d^{-1}, respectively (Table 3). In frequently harvested stands where young plants predominate, estimates of productivity based on standing crop changes (such as the above) are fairly accurate. For example, detritus sloughing was found to account for less than 10% of total biomass production by water

TABLE 3. Biomass yield of some floating and submersed macrophytes cultivated in central and south Florida.

Species	Medium[1]	Yield, g m^{-2} d^{-1} Max	Avg.[2]	Reference
		Floating: large-leaved		
Eichhornia crassipes	N	--	24.2 (12)	DeBusk et al. 1981
	N	64.4	27.1 (10)	Reddy & DeBusk 1984
	A	45.9	---	Reddy & Bagnall 1981
	PS	41.7	---	Reddy et al. 1983
Pistia stratiotes	N	29.0	14.2 (7)	Tucker & DeBusk 1981
	N	40.0	---	Reddy & DeBusk 1984
Hydrocotyle umbellata	N	29.7	15.9 (4)	Ryther 1979
	N	18.3	10.3 (12)	Reddy & DeBusk 1984
		Floating: small-leaved		
Salvinia rotundifolia	N	13.9	8.8 (12)	Reddy & DeBusk 1985
	PS	10.0	8.8 (2)	Reddy et al. 1983
	SS	9.6	6.4 (2)	Reddy et al. 1983
Lema minor	N	12.0	3.8 (10)	Reddy et al. 1983
	SS	8.4	4.5 (14)	Reddy et al. 1983
Spirodela *polyrhiza*	N	5.9	3.4 (4)	Ryther 1979
Azolla caroliniana	N	7.9	2.9 (10)	Reddy et al. 1983
	PS	8.2	---	Reddy et al. 1983
	SS	6.5	---	Reddy et al. 1983
		Submersed		
Hydrilla verticillata	N	10.4	4.2 (12)	DeBusk et al. 1981
Elodea densa	N	12.9	2.8 (10)	Reddy et al. 1983

[1]Media: N=nutrient medium; PS=primary domestic wastewater effluent; SS-secondary effluent; A=agricultural drainage water.
[2]Duration in months.

hyacinth cultured at a standing crop of 1 kg m^{-2} in a wastewater treatment system in Florida (DeBusk et al., 1983).

Both water lettuce and water hyacinth are killed by prolonged exposure to sub-freezing temperatures; year-round outdoor cultivation of these species is therefore possible only in tropical and subtropical regions. Recent studies have shown that pennywort is slightly more cold tolerant, and produces biomass at approximately the same rate during both winter and summer in central Florida (Reddy and DeBusk, 1984). Currently, cultivation of these large-leaved floating macrophytes is limited to wastewater treatment applications; utilization of the biomass for fuels or other products is of secondary economic importance.

The small-leaved floating plants, such as water fern (*Salvinia rotundifolia*), mosquito fern (*Azolla caroliniana*), and the duckweeds (*Lemna* and *Spirodela* spp.) are noted for their rapid specific growth rate, which can exceed 25% d^{-1} (DeBusk et al., 1981; Reddy and DeBusk, 1985). However, these species demonstrate only slight vertical canopy development, and are therefore inefficient at capturing solar radiation where they occur at a high standing crop. Annual yields of the small-leaved plants typically average only 4-8 g m^{-2} d^{-1} (Table 3) because of the low densities (0.01 to 0.24 kg m^{-2}) at which rapid frond division occurs (Reddy and DeBusk, 1985).

Duckweeds have been cultivated, albeit not extensively, for the treatment of domestic and agricultural wastewaters (Hillman and Culley, 1978). However, because of their lower yields, nutrient removal by these plants is not as great as that of the more productive large-leaved floating species (Reddy and DeBusk, 1985). The nutritive value of duckweeds cultivated on domestic and agricultural wastewaters is often high, with the plant biomass commonly utilized as a livestock feed (Culley and Epps, 1973).

Salvinia molesta, like the water hyacinth, is a particularly aggressive aquatic weed in natural systems. However, few data on yields of this plant in cultivation are available. In a domestic wastewater treatment facility in Queensland, Australia, maximum short term yields of 9.4 g m^{-2} d^{-1} were reported for this species (Finlayson et al., 1982). It is worth noting that maximum yields of most floating plants have been attained using formulated media, rather than in wastewater (Table 3). Wastewaters may be deficient in micro- or macronutrients, contain toxic substances, or possess a high electrical conductivity or O_2 demand. Any of these factors may be inhibitory to plant growth. Yields of *S. molesta* cultivated in an artificial nutrient medium, rather than wastewater, may therefore be higher than those reported herein.

Azolla is unique among floating macrophytes in that plants of this genus can grow in waters deficient in N. When combined N is absent from the aqueous medium, *Azolla* spp. can obtain N from a N-fixing alga (*Anabaena azollae*) contained within its fronds (Peters et al., 1980). *Azolla* spp. are grown as a green manure in rice fields in S.E. Asia (Lumpkin and Plucknett, 1982), and may have some application for removing contaminants from wastewaters deficient in N.

Changes in standing crop of floating species are much easier to quantify than for emergents. All plant components (foliage, roots, and rhizomes) of floating species may be collected with equal ease. Each of the floating species listed in Table 3 reproduces primarily by the production of vegetative offshoots. The ease with which floating species can be stocked and harvested accounts to a large extent for the popularity of plants such as the water hyacinth for use in wastewater treatment applications.

Submersed Freshwater Macrophytes

Biomass production by submersed macrophytes is generally considered to be lower than that of emergent and floating species (Westlake, 1963). Productivity of submersed plants is limited by environmental constraints (low light levels, slow diffusion rate of CO_2 in the aqueous medium) and, in some instances, physiological characteristics of the plants themselves. Garrard and Van (1982) noted that the activity of carboxylase enzymes in many submersed species is low. Reddy et al. (1983) reported that some submersed macrophytes are capable of varying their photorespiration mode in response to environmental conditions, and thus seem to belong neither to the C_3 nor C_4 category of plants.

A few submersed species, such as hydrilla (*Hydrilla verticillata*), are noxious weeds which interfere with man's utilization of waterways. Although hydrilla is probably one of the most productive submersed species, prior studies have shown that relative to floating and emergent plants, hydrilla neither occurs at a high standing crop (0.9 kg m^2 at maximum) (Bowes et al., 1979), nor is it overly productive (Table 3). Hydrilla is a serious problem in waterways primarily because most of its biomass is concentrated in the top meter of the water column. In addition, *Hydrilla*, like most other submersed species, is difficult to control by either mechanical or chemical means.

Few studies have been conducted on the long-term yields of submersed species in natural systems. Westlake (1963) reported average annual yields of 2.5 g m^{-2} d^{-1} for *Ceratophyllum demersum* in a eutrophic lake in Sweden. Because man's utilization of submersed species is minimal, cultivation of these plants has been limited to the small-scale production of ornamental plants for the tropical fish industry. In Florida, maximum yields of hydrilla and *Elodea densa* species, which are periodically sold as "bunch plants" for freshwater aquaria, were 10.4 and 12.9 g m^{-2} d^{-1}, respectively (Table 3). The nutritional requirements of most submersed species are not well known, although it is thought that most, but not all, macronutrients can be assimilated from either the water column or sediment (Barko, 1982).

Oxygen which collects within the lacunae of submersed macrophytes may assist in holding the plants upright in the water column. Some submersed species thus require little structural material, and their nutritive value is high. Cellulose contents of shoot tissues of Ceratophyllum sp., Eichhornia crassipes, and Typha latifolia were reported to be 27.9, 28.2, and 33.2% of dry weight, respectively. Respective crude protein concentrations for these same species were 21.7, 17.1, and 10.3% (Boyd, 1974). Most submersed macrophytes would probably make a suitable ingredient for livestock feed or as feedstock for conversion to CH_4.

DISCUSSION

Despite the great morphological and physiological diversity among aquatic plants, each of the plant types discussed in the present paper (i.e., microalgae, seaweeds, freshwater macrophytes) are capable of producing large quantities of biomass. However, high yields are typically attained by only a few species of each type, and under specific culture conditions.

What factors, then, contribute to high yields for an aquatic species? First, an aquatic plant must efficiently utilize solar radiation and inorganic C in converting light energy to chemical energy. Of the terrestrial crops, C_4 plants such as corn and sugar cane are considered to perform this conversion most efficiently since energy is not "wasted" on photorespiration. Similarly, microalgae or seaweeds which can efficiently assimilate C at low CO_2 concentrations and high pH levels, conditions which often occur in intensive algal cultures, are thought to have a competitive advantage over those species whose photosynthetic rate decreases at high pH. However, for many aquatic species, the relationship between their photosynthetic pathway and productivity is not clear. Many of the most productive species, such as the water hyacinth, do not appear to fix C by the most efficient mechanism.

Although reasonably efficient light energy conversion by the individual plant is requisite for high yields, of equal or perhaps greater importance is the efficiency of light capture per unit area by the entire crop. Many aquatic plants, such as duckweeds and phytoplankton, exhibit a specific growth rate, or doubling time, on the order of a few days or even less. However, studies with phytoplankton (Goldman and Ryther, 1975), seaweeds (Ryther et al., 1977) and freshwater macrophytes (DeBusk et al., 1981) have shown that high yields result only when a rapid specific growth rate is coupled with a moderate to high standing crop. In sparse plant stands, specific growth rates may be high, but crop yields will be low since not all of the incident solar radiation is utilized. In overly dense stands, crop yields may be low due to the reduced specific growth rates caused by self-shading and overcrowding.

The ability of a plant to grow rapidly in dense stands is largely a function of canopy architecture. Highest yields by freshwater macrophytes are typically attained by species which have a high leaf area index, and a minimum of structural or support tissue. Similarly, when microalgae and macroalgae, which possess little or no non-photosynthetic tissues, are cultured in well-mixed tanks (to reduce self-shading), their yields can be quite high.

Some means of vegetative propagation is an additional characteristic shared by most productive aquatic plants. Most of the phytoplankton, seaweeds and freshwater macrophytes discussed herein have the capacity for reproducing vegetatively, either indefinitely or for prolonged periods of time. This characteristic is advantageous, particularly for plants grown in tropical regions, because the crop density can be maintained at a relatively high or "optimum" level through the use of frequent harvest. Production time is therefore not lost due to replanting or reseeding.

Most environmental constraints to aquatic plant biomass production are related to light and nutrition. The growth of submersed plants, for example, is often limited by light or C availability. Light utilization by cultures of submersed species (e.g., microalgae, macroalgae) is typically improved by mixing, a process by which the plants are kept suspended and in motion in the water column. Mixing or agitation may also improve C utilization through the breakdown of diffusion barriers, although supplemental C additions or pH control is often necessary. Management of nutrients (e.g. C, N, P) in submersed plant cultures is critical both to support high yields of the target organism and to prevent takeover of the system by competing species. Cultivation of submersed species in high yield systems is therefore often difficult and costly. Fortunately, many submersed plants contain valuable constituents (e.g., agar), whose product value may be sufficiently high to justify their intensive cultivation.

In marked contrast with the submersed species, many floating and emergent freshwater macrophytes provide high yields with little or no crop management. Productive species in these groups typically possess high leaf area indices, and their foliage is exposed to direct sunlight and atmospheric CO_2. Periodic harvest is often the only management practice required in cultivated stands of emergent and floating plants. However, the biomass produced, particularly in emergent plant stands, may be of the poorest quality (lowest product value) of all the plant groups discussed herein.

How do yields of microalgae, macroalgae and freshwater macrophytes compare to the most productive terrestrial plants? Maximum short-term yields of terrestrial crops such as corn, sugar cane, napier grass, and sorghum range from 38 to 52 g m^{-2} d^{-1}. The maximum reported sustained yield for a terrestrial species is by a sugar cane crop in Texas, for which an average annual yield of 30.7 g m^{-2} d^{-1} was reported (Bassham, 1980). Such yields are remarkably similar to those attained by the most productive aquatic species (e.g., water hyacinth). Yields of aquatic plants will undoubtedly improve in the future as cultivation technologies become more sophisticated. As with terrestrial crops, research on aquatic biomass production and tissue quality enhancement will be directed primarily towards those plants of greatest economic importance.

ACKNOWLEDGMENTS

Research by the senior author on the use of aquatic macrophytes for biomass production and wastewater treatment is currently supported by the Gas Research Institute, Chicago, Illinois.

REFERENCES

Andrews, N. J., and D. C. Pratt. 1978. Energy potential of cattails (Typha spp.) and productivity in managed stands. J. Minn. Acad. Sci. 44:5-8.

Armstrong, W. 1964. Oxygen diffusion from the roots of some British bog plants. Nature 204:801-802.

Bardach, J. E., J. H. Ryther, and W. O. McLarney. 1972. Aquaculture. Wiley-Interscience, NY. 868 pp.

Barko, J. W. 1982. Influence of potassium source (sediment vs. open water) and sediment composition on the growth and nutrition of a submersed freshwater macrophyte (Hydrilla verticillata (l.f.) Royle). Aquat. Bot., 12:157-172.

Bassham, J. A. 1980. Energy crops (energy farming). p. 147-172. In A. San Pietro (ed.) Biochemical and Photosynthetic Aspects of Energy Production. Academic Press.

Batterson, T. R. 1984. Biomass and gasification potential of Phragmites australis (Cav.) Trin. ex Steu. Report to Gas Research Institute, Chicago, IL, #8237. 12 pp.

Beck, L. A., W. J. Oswald, and J. C. Goldman. 1969. Nitrate removal from agricultural tile drainage by photosynthetic systems. Presented at American Society of Civil Engineers, Second National Symp. on Sanitary Engineering Research, Development, and Design. Cornell University, Ithaca, NY, July 15, 1969.

Benemann, J. R., J. C. Weissman, D. M. Eisenberg, B. L. Koopman, R. Grebol, P. Kaski, R. Thompson, and W. J. Oswald. 1978. An integrated system for solar energy conversion using sewage grown algae. Final Report. San Engr. Res. Lab., Univ. Calif., Berkeley.

Bowes, G., A. S. Holaday, and W. T. Haller. 1979. Seasonal variation in the biomass, tuber density, and photosynthetic metabolism of Hydrilla in three Florida lakes. J. Aquat. Plant Manage. 17:61-65.

Boyd, C. E. 1969a. Vascular aquatic plants for mineral nutrient removal from polluted waters. Econ. Bot. 23:95-103.

Boyd, C. E. 1969b. Production, mineral accumulation, and pigment concentrations in Typha latifolia and Scirpus americanus. Ecol. 51:287-290.

Boyd, C. E. 1971. The dynamics of dry matter and chemical substances in a Juncus effusus population. Amer. Midland Naturalist 86:28-45.

Boyd, C. E. 1974. Utilization of aquatic plants. p. 107-111. In Aquatic Vegetation and Its Use and Control. D. S. Mitchell (ed.) Paris, Unesco.

Burlew, J. S. (ed.). 1953. Algal culture from laboratory to pilot plant. Carnegie Inst. of Washington, Publ. No. 600, Washington, D.C. 357 pp.

Center, T. D., and N. R. Spencer. 1981. The phenology and growth of water hyacinth (Eichhornia crassipes [Mart.] Solms) in a eutrophic north-central Florida lake. Aquat. Bot. 10:1-32.

Cook, P. M. 1951. Chemical engineering problems in large-scale culture of algae. Eng. Proc. Develop. 43:2385-2389.

Culley, D. D., and E. A. Epps. 1973. Use of duckweed for waste treatment and animal feed. J. Water Pollut. Control Fed. 45:337-347.

DeBusk, T. A., L. D. Williams, and J. H. Ryther. 1983. Removal of nitrogen and phosphorus from wastewater in a water hyacinth-based treatment system. J. Environ. Qual. 12:257-262.

DeBusk, T. A., J. H. Ryther, M. D. Hanisak, and L. D. Williams. 1981. Effects of seasonality and plant density on the productivity of some freshwater macrophytes. Aquat. Bot. 10:133-142.

D'Elia, C. F., J. H. Ryther, and T. M. Losordo. 1977. Productivity and nitrogen balance in large-scale phytoplankton cultures. Water Res. 11:1031-1040.

Durand-Chastel, H. 1977. The Spirulina algae. In D. O. Hall and P. M. Vignais (ed.) European Seminar on Biological Solar Energy Conversion Systems. (Collection of Abstracts). May 9-12, 1977, Grenoble-Autrans, France.

Finlayson, C. M., T. P. Farrell, and D. J. Griffiths. 1982. Treatment of sewage effluent using the water fern Salvinia. Water Research Foundation of Australia, Report #57. 64 pp.

Garrard, L. A., and T. K. Van. 1982. General characteristics of freshwater vascular plants. In Handbook of Biosolar Resources, Vol. 2, Chap. 10. Publ. CRC Press., Inc.

Goldman, J. D. 1979. Outdoor algal mass cultures. I. Applications. Water Res. 13:1-19.

Goldman, J. C., and J. H. Ryther. 1975. Nutrient transformation in mass cultures of marine algae. J. Env. Eng. Div., ASCE 101:351-364.

Goldman, J. C, J. H. Ryther, and L. D. Williams. 1975. Mass production of marine algae in outdoor cultures. Nature 254:594-595.

Graneli, W. 1984. Reed (Phragmites australis Cav. Trin. ex Steu.) as an energy source in Sweden. Biomass 4:183-209.

Hansen, J. E., J. E. Packard, and W. T. Doyle. 1981. Mariculture of red seaweeds. Calif. Sea Grant College Prog. Publ. T-CSGCP-002. 42 pp.

Hillman, W. S., and D. D. Culley, Jr. 1978. The uses of duckweed. Am. Sci. 66:442-451.

Ketchum, B. H., and A. C. Redfield. 1938. A method for maintaining a continuous supply of marine diatoms in culture. Biol. Bull. 75:165-169.

Knipling, E. G., S. H. West, and W. T. Haller. 1970. Growth characteristics, yield potential, and nutritive content of water hyacinths. Proc. Soil & Crop Sci. Soc Fla. 30:51-63.

Lapointe, B. E., and J. H. Ryther. 1978. Some aspects of the growth and yield of Gracilaria tikvahiae in culture. Aquaculture 15:185-193.

Laws, E. A., S. Taguchi, J. Hirata, and L. Pang. 1986. High algal production rates achieved in a shallow, outdoor flume. Biotech. and Bioeng. 28:191-197.

Lumpkin, T. A., and D. L. Plucknett. 1982. Azolla as a green manure: Use and management in crop production. Westview Press, Boulder, CO.

Mayer, A. M., U. Zuri, Y. Shain, and H. Ginzburg. 1964. Problems of design and ecological considerations in mass culture of algae. Biotechnol. Bioengr. 6:173-190.

Morimura, Y., T. Nihei, and T. Sasa. 1955. Outdoor bubbling culture of some unicellular algae. J. Gen. Appl. Microbiol. 1:173-182.

Morton, J. F. 1975. Cattails (Typha spp.) - Weed problem or potential crop? Econ. Bot. 29:7-29.

Myers, J., and L. B. Clark. 1949. Culture conditions and the development of the photosynthetic mechanism. II. An apparatus for the continuous culture of Chlorella. J. Gen. Physiol. 28:103-112.

Neushul, M., and B. W. W. Harger. 1984. Studies of biomass yield from a nearshore macroalgal test farm. J. Solar Eng. 107:93-96.

O'Hair, S. K., G. H. Snyder, and J. F. Morton. 1982. Wetland Taro: A neglected crop for food, feed, and fuel. Proc. Fla. State Hort. Soc. 95:367-374.

Oswald, W. J. 1969. Current status of microalgae from wastes. Chem. Engr. Prog. Symp. Ser. 65:87-92.

Oswald, W. J., H. B. Gotaas, H. F. Ludwig, and V. Lynch. 1953. Algal symbiosis in oxidation ponds. Sewage Indust. Wastes. 25:692-705.

Parker, H. S. 1974. The culture of the red alga genus Eucheuma in the Philippines. Aquaculture 3:425-439.

Penfound, W. T. 1956. Primary production of vascular aquatic plants. Limnol. Oceanogr. 1:92-101.

Peters, G. A., T. B. Ray, B. C. Mayne, and R. E. Toia, Jr. 1980. Azolla-Anabaena association: morphological and physiological studies. p. 293-309. In W. E. Newton and W. H. Orme-Johnson (ed.) Nitrogen Fixation. Vol. II. Univ. Park Press, Baltimore, MD.

Polisini, J. M., and C. E. Boyd. 1972. Relationships between cell-wall fractions, nitrogen, and standing crop in aquatic macrophytes. Ecol. 53:484-488.

Pratt, D. C. 1978. Cattails as an energy source. Final report to Minnesota Energy Agency on Alternative Energy Research. 49 pp.

Pratt, D. C., and N. J. Andrews. 1980. Cattails as an energy source. p. 43-62. In D. L. Klass (ed.) IGT Symposium on Energy from Biomass and Wastes IV. Jan. 21-25, 1980.

Reddy, K. R., and L. O. Bagnall. 1981. Biomass production of aquatic plants used in agricultural drainage water treatment. p. 660-681. In 1981 International Gas Res. Conf. Proc. Govt. Inst., Inc., Rockville, MD.

Reddy, K. R., and W. F. DeBusk. 1984. Growth characteristics of aquatic macrophytes cultured in nutrient enriched water: I. water hyacinth, water lettuce, and pennywort. Econ. Bot. 38:229-239.

Reddy, K. R., and W. F. DeBusk. 1985. Growth characteristics of aquatic macrophytes cultured in nutrient-enriched water: II. Azolla, duckweed, and Salvinia. Econ. Bot. 39:200-208.

Reddy, K. R., D. L. Sutton, and G. Bowes. 1983. Freshwater aquatic plant biomass production in Florida. Proc. Soil & Crop Sci. Soc. Fla. 42:28-40.

Ryther, J. H. 1979. Cultivation of macroscopic marine algae and freshwater aquatic weeds. Rept. to U.S. Dept. Energy Contr. No. EY-76-S-02-2948. 74 pp.

Ryther, J. H., J. A. DeBoer, and B. E. Lapointe. 1977. Cultivation of seaweeds for hydrocolloids, waste treatment, and biomass for energy conversion. Proc. 9th Int. Seaweed Symp., Santa Barbara, CA, August 20-27, 1977. A. Jensen and J. R. Stein (ed.) Sci. Press, Princeton. p. 1-16.

Shang, Y. C. 1976. Economic aspects of Gracilaria culture in Taiwan. Aquaculture 8:1-7.

Shelef, G., M. Schwartz, and H. Schnecter. 1973. Prediction of photosynthetic biomass production in accelerated algal-bacterial wastewater treatments systems. p. 181-189. In S. H. Jenkins (ed.) Advances in Water Pollution Research, Pergamon Press, Oxford.

Shelef, G., R. Moraine. T. Berner, A. Levi. and G. Oron. 1978. Solar energy conversion via algal wastewater treatment and protein production. p. 657-675. In D. O. Hall, J. Coombs, and T. S. Goodwin (ed.) Proc. 4th Int. Cong. Photosynthesis. The Biochemical Society, London.

Snyder, G. H., J. F. Morton, and W. G. Genung. 1981. Trials of Ipomoea aquatica, nutritious vegetable with high-protein and nitrate-extraction potential. Proc. Fla. State Hort. Soc. 94:230-235.

Soeder, C. 1976. The use of microalgae in nutrition. Naturwissenschaften 63:131-138.

Tamiya, H. 1959. Role of algae as food. Proc. Symp. Algology, pp. 379-389. UNESCO, New Delhi, India.

Teal, J. M., and J. W. Kanwisher. 1966. Gas transport in marsh grass, *Spartina alternaflora*. J. of Expt. Bot. 17:355-361.

Tieszen, L. L. 1982. Biomass accumulation and primary production. *In* J. Coombs and D. O. Hall (ed.) Techniques in Bioproductivity and Photosynthesis. Pergamon Press, Oxford, England.

Tseng, C. K. 1981. Commercial cultivation in biology of seaweeds. C. S. Lobban and M. J. Wynne (ed.) Monogr. 17, pp. 680-741. Univ. of Calif. Press.

Tsukada, O., T. Kawahara, and S. Miyachi. 1977. Mass culture of *Chlorella* in Asian countries. p. 363-365. *In* A. Mitsui, S. Miyachi, A. San Pietro, and S. Tamura (ed.) Biological Solar Energy Conversion. Acad. Press, NY.

Tucker, C. S., and T. A. DeBusk. 1981. Productivity and nutritive value of *Pistia stratiotes* and *Eichhornia crassipes*. J. Aquat. Plant Manage. 19:61-63.

Van Orschot, J. L. P. 1955. Conversion of light energy in algal cultures. Med. Van. Lund. Wang., Nederland. 55:225-277.

Vendlova, J. 1969. Les problemes de la technologie de la culture des algues sur une grande echelle dans les installations au dehors. Annali Microbiol. 19:1-12.

Watanabe, A., A. Hattori, Y. Fujita, and T. Kiyohara. 1959. Large scale culture of a blue-green alga, *Tolypothrix trenuis*, utilizing hot spring and natural gas as heat and carbon dioxide sources. J. Gen. Appl. Microbiol. 5:51-57.

Weissman, J. C., and R. P. Goebel. 1986. Production of liquid fuels and chemicals by microalgae. Final subcontract Rept., Cont. No. XK-3-03135 to Solar Energy Research Inst., Golden, CO.

Westlake, D. F. 1963. Comparisons of plant productivity. Biol. Rev. 38:385-425.

Whigham, D. F., and R. L. Simpson. 1976. The potential use of freshwater tidal marshes in the management of water quality in the Delaware River. *In* J. Tourbier and R. W. Pierson (ed.) Biological Control of Water Pollution. Univ. of Pennsylvania Press.

HARVESTING AND HANDLING OF BIOMASS

L. O. Bagnall
Agricultural Engineering Department
University of Florida, IFAS
Gainesville, Florida 32611

C. E. Schertz
Agricultural Engineering Department
University of Minnesota

D. R. Dubbe
Bio-Energy Coordinating Office
University of Minnesota

ABSTRACT

Wastewater aquacultural systems based on emergent or floating aquatic macrophytes appear to be technically and economically feasible. For maximum effectiveness, efficiency and economy of production, design of cultural and harvesting systems must be coordinated. Harvesting machinery and system design depends on plant type and size, waterbody geometry, cultural practices and end use. Because there is considerable flexibility in how aquatic plants can be harvested and there is not a large body of established practices, techniques and sequencing of operations are still exploratory. However, some system models are being devised. Several experimental, developmental and commercial systems are in operation and harvesting costs for the various types of systems can be estimated. Basic and applied research and development are needed to improve the productivity and efficiency of harvesting systems.

Keywords: Aquaculture, aquatic plants, wastewater, harvesting machinery, cultural methods.

WASTEWATER AQUACULTURAL SYSTEMS

Use of wastewater for production of a commercial biological product requires careful management to optimize removal of pollutants and production of a biomass product. This balance of management extends to the design and operations of the harvesting

ISBN 0-941463-00-1

system so that biological and mechanical productivity are optimized.

Artificial environments designed to treat wastewater can include enhancements that simplify harvester design and operation, such as regular geometric shapes, long runs, minimum turns, uniform depth, no obstructions and easy access. Wastewater is likely to be at least slightly more corrosive than natural waters and should be treated as a bio-hazard with regard to operator contact.

Aquatic plant communities used for wastewater treatment are usually monocultures, or nearly so. Accommodating the characteristics of a single plant species or type simplifies the design of a harvesting system. If operations management can be predicted accurately, the size, stage of growth and areal biomass can be accurately estimated, further simplifying design.

Use of the harvested product will specify the type and degree of pre-processing required. Some, and perhaps all, of the pre-processing may be done within the harvesting system. The pre-processing required for most efficient handling may be greater than that required for the end use.

HARVESTING SYSTEM CONSTRAINTS AND DESIGN CRITERIA

Aquatic plant harvesting systems must operate effectively, efficiently and economically in difficult environments. The environment presents constraints on harvesting system design. Design criteria are based on the process to be accomplished and the constraints surrounding the operation.

Constraints

The constraints on harvesting system design can be defined as they relate to wastewater operation, plant types, and end use of the plants.

Wastewater-Related Constraints. The equipment must be made with corrosion-resistant materials, using corrosion-minimizing construction techniques. The design must also minimize exposure of the operator and mechanics to direct contact with the wastewater, suggesting complete, reliable mechanical handling of the biomass throughout the system with a minimum of transfers. Machinery should also be readily cleaned to minimize transfer of pollutants from site to site.

The harvesting system must be adapted to the type of site in which it will be used. A harvesting system for a natural or quasi-natural site will be more complex to design, build and operate and more rugged in construction than a system for a properly designed artificial site.

The harvesting system will impact the environment in and around the waterbody in which it operates. Sediments may be raised from the bottom. Detritus and filter floc may be shaken or broken from the plants. Machine access may increase bank erosion. Transfer of wet plant material from the water to the land may create a bog around the transfer site. Some of these factors can be countered by suitable design of artificial sites and by proper system operation. Others may have to be treated as separate, additional problems. Legal/institutional constraints related in design and operation include: 1) health-related limitations, present and likely to be imposed, on products produced on wastewater, and 2) the health and safety requirements of operating personnel.

Plant-Related Constraints. Aquatic harvesters interact with the plants in ways that not only affect productivity and efficiency of the harvesting system, but also affect long-term productivity of the crop. Some mechanical disturbance of some aquatic plant communities increases productivity, e.g. a clean water hyacinth mat edge reproduces and grows slowly, whereas a broken edge or small distributed mats will grow or fill in rapidly. However, excessive mechanical disturbance may damage plants and create sites for insect infestation or disease infection.

The most productive aquatic species reproduce vegetatively, so a substantial residue of biomass must be left after harvest for continued production of the crop. Harvesting systems must be designed to leave this residue or provision must be made in the cultural system for replanting, usually at greater cost. For example, the perennial cattail plant depends on nutrients and carbohydrates stored in the rhizome system for overwinter survival and early season growth and stand vigor. If rhizomes are harvested, it appears that productivity will not return to preharvest rates until the second year following harvest, thus precluding annual rhizome harvests (Pratt et al., 1986). Additionally, a sufficient number of rhizomes (perhaps 20%) need to be left in the field for stand regeneration. Seasonal patterns in nutrient uptake and carbohydrate storage also restrict harvesting options by determining the time of year and physical conditions under which harvesting will occur (Pratt et al., 1985). In water hyacinth systems, at least 50% of the biomass should be left as reproductive stock.

Plants with large, tough or woody structures will require harvesting equipment with strong mechanical components. Plants rooted in the hydrosoil or with large, entangled masses will require harvesters with front-end cutting mechanisms. Rotating components should be protected from being wrapped by plant stems.

In polycultural plant communities the harvesting system will either have to be selective or adapted to simultaneously handle the differing characteristics of the plants present.

Utilization-Related Constraints. End use of the plants may place constraints on the harvesting system, particularly the pre-processing component. Composting usually works best on a coarsely-chopped product whereas finely-chopped biomass digests more effectively. If specific plant parts must be harvested or separated in the harvest, the harvester will probably be more complicated.

Design Criteria

Design criteria are based on the constraints surrounding the operation, construction requirements and the process to be accomplished.

Constraints. In most wastewater aquaculture systems, water is relatively shallow, so draft must be small or, if the water is extremely shallow, flotation must be high. Because soil density and moisture are variable in emergent plant systems, and the destruction of soil/rhizome integrity accompanying rhizome harvesting, equipment traction and flotation are critical considerations in harvester design. In systems with narrow channel widths, the principal machinery never enters the water, thus reach must be adequate to assure that all parts of the water surface can be harvested.

Swath width of the harvesting equipment must be great enough to assure an adequate capacity while operating at a reasonable speed. Minimum working swath width of floating plant harvesters should seldom be smaller than 1.2 m, to prevent dominance of edge effects on the swath. Maximum width should be limited primarily by transportation requirements through channels or over the road.

Mechanical criteria. Mechanically, the harvesting system must be reliable and durable enough to withstand years of abuse in a hostile environment, either by strength of construction or by load-limiting mechanisms. Drive systems must be simple, flexible and easily maintained. Effects of weather and climate on system performance should be imperceptible, because wastewater continues to flow in hot, cold, wet, dry, windy or calm weather.

Because biomass is usually a low-value crop, the system must be inexpensive to own and operate, must be reliable and easy to maintain. It must be efficient, to minimize energy inputs, and nearly automatic, to minimize labor input.

Mechanisms. Operations in an aquatic harvesting system may include cutting, gathering, elevating, draining, chopping, over-water transport and over-land transportation (Bagnall, 1986).

The usual cutting mechanism for harvesting aquatic biomass is a modified reciprocating mower. Modification usually consists of use of stub guards or opposed sickle sections so that no "dead" components are present for the plants to wrap on, slow drive frequencies (<100 cpm) consistent with low forward speed, location and protection of drives to prevent wrapping of plant material, and flexible support to prevent damage due to contact with obstructions. High-speed, impact cutters are generally inappropriate due to energy losses of high-speed components in the water. High-speed, fixed, towed blades have been tried for submersed plants but generally have not been adopted because of control and energy considerations. Various types of uprooters and tillers have been used on submersed and emergent plants, primarily to remove the rootstock or rhizomes from the soil, either for extension of control, in the case of hydrilla or Eurasian watermilfoil, or for collection of a significantly greater quantity of high quality biomass, in the case of cattails.

Most aquatic plants float, either naturally or after they have been cut. Some species slowly float to the surface, remain there until decomposed or waterlogged, then sink. The plants are gathered while floating at or near the surface, usually by raking elements that extend into the water from above the surface so that the plants are engaged and captured before they can be swept from the path of the gatherer by water currents generated by the gatherer.

Plants may be elevated from the water in batches or in a "continuous" stream. Batch elevation is usually done by modified dragline buckets, clamshells or backhoes, but may be done by specialized machinery similar to the buckrakes used in hay-making on the plains. Continuous elevation is usually done with some type of chain conveyor, the lower end of which is immersed so that the plants can be floated onto it. The most common type of elevating chain is flat-wire-belt, which has excellent traction and drainage characteristics. High-speed rubber or fabric belts are not used because of poor traction on plants and drive pulleys and poor drainage. Mechanisms similar to gathering mechanisms can be used to elevate, but they are not as effective or efficient as chain conveyors.

Preliminary drainage is usually done during the elevating operation, but residual drainage will continue for at least 5 minutes after plants are removed from the water so provision must be made throughout the initial part of the handling system to drain surface water. If plants are finely chopped and injected into a pipeline transportation system immediately after harvesting, the surface water will be contained and act as a diluent/lubricant.

Aquatic plants can be transported in the water, supported by their own buoyancy, but are often difficult to contain and move in that way. Elevation and movement on a barge is more controllable, but requires more expensive equipment. Movement over-water in a flexible, floating pipeline has been tried, but was unsuccessful due to plugging, bursting and range limitations.

Chopping reduces the volume and intractability of the plant mass and produces a product better suited to handling and processing. In order to maximize the benefits of chopping, it should be done as soon as possible after elevating from the water. Intact water hyacinth plants have a bulk density of about 80 kg m^{-3}, whereas finely chopped water hyacinth has a bulk density as high as 960 kg m^{-3} (Stewart, 1972).

Overland transportation has usually been in batches by truck. Belt and chain conveying systems have been used for short runs. Finely-chopped water hyacinths have been pumped several hundred meters by progressive cavity pumps with little or no supplementary water.

MODEL SYSTEMS

Aquatic plant harvesting systems may be described by the way their components are organized or by the sequence of operations. By describing commonalities of systems, they can be analyzed as mechanical or mathematical models.

Components of harvesting systems may be organized in a variety of sequences, as shown in Figure 1. Cutting or otherwise separating from the hydrosoil is the first operation in harvesting emergent and submersed plants. All types of aquatic plants may be separated from entanglement with other plants sometime prior to being elevated from the water.

Gathering may precede or follow over-water transportation but must precede elevation from the water. Drainage must follow or occur concurrently with elevation, while chopping optionally follows elevation. Overland transportation follows elevation from the water, but may precede or follow chopping.

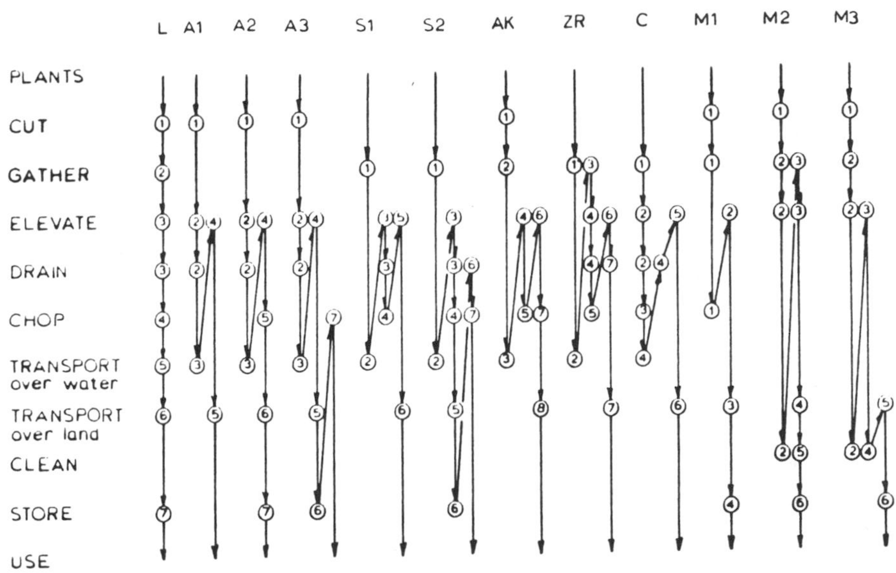

FIGURE 1. Organization of harvesting system functions and components.

Harvesting systems may be described by at least 2 typologies: batch vs. continuous and mobile vs. immobile. In actual operating systems the distinctions are sometimes blurred by changes in the way the stream is handled as it moves through the system.

A batch harvesting system is one in which defined lots of plants are removed from the water in individual, repetitive actions, such as by dragline buckets. A continuous harvesting system is one in which a more-or-less continuous stream of plants is removed from the water by a continuing action, such as a conveyor. A system which harvests in batches may stream the material for chopping and/or transportation operations. A system which harvests a continuous stream may batch the harvested plants for transportation.

A mobile harvesting system is one in which a complex harvesting machine moves to the plants, gathers, elevates and perhaps chops them, then transports them to shore or transfers them to a separate transporter. An immobile system is one in which the complex elevating/chopping machinery is located at a fixed shore site and the plants are gathered and transported in the water by relatively simple auxiliary devices. A hybrid within this typology is a system in which plants are gathered from a wide area into a confined pool by simple devices, then harvested from the pool by complex harvesters of limited range which directly discharge the product into the land transportation system (Bagnall, 1986).

EXPERIMENTAL AND COMMERCIAL HARVESTING/HANDLING SYSTEMS

Some commercial harvesting systems are available, most of which have been designed for weed control. Many weed control systems are unsuited for biomass harvesting because of limited capacity and high operating costs. Experimental harvesting systems appear from time to time, usually in conjunction with development of experimental biomass or waste treatment systems (Bagnall, 1975,1982,1983,1986).

Floating Aquatic Plant Systems

Floating plants of interest in wastewater biomass systems include water hyacinth, water lettuce, hydrocotyle and duckweed. Water hyacinth, water lettuce and hydrocotyle are of similar size and have similar harvesting characteristics. Floating aquatic plants are reputed to be easy to harvest. They are free-floating and can be gathered and moved in the water. They also disperse readily by wind and current and, although they have very high real densities, are extremely bulky.

Immobile systems. Immobile systems are most commonly used for floating plants because the plants can be readily moved with only their own buoyancy for support and are commonly so bulky that the required barges in mobile systems would be economically prohibitive.

Modified construction equipment is often used in aquatic weed removal operations, making additional use of equipment already available to control agencies. These could be applied to biomass systems, but capacity and efficiency are usually low, and capital and operating costs high.

Dragline "hyacinth buckets" have been extensively used to remove water hyacinth from canals, rivers and impoundments where they have become a nuisance. They can reach up to 30 m and where maintenance roads are available, they can move to the hyacinths. Often the hyacinths are moved to the dragline at a fixed site by current or airboats equipped with pusher rakes. Backhoe removal of water hyacinth is similar to dragline removal in that an available machine with a special-purpose attachment is used. The reach of the backhoe is not as great as that of the dragline, but the cycle is faster. Clamshell buckets have been modified by attaching tined bars to extend the width and apparent opening of the clamshell, allowing it to trap and lift a larger load. Operation and capacity are similar to those of the dragline.

The harvester used at the water hyacinth wastewater treatment system at Walt Disney World is an extension of the modified clamshell type of harvester. The clamshell, instead of hanging on a cable on the end of a long boom, is supported directly on the end of a relatively short, hydraulically-operated truck-mounted boom. The clamshell is rotated and closed hydraulically. While having the limitations of this class of system, it has the advantage of selective harvest; colonies of plants within a pond can be selectively removed to optimize maturity, distribution or other factors. The capacity of the system is more than adequate for the small pond area to which it is applied but the concept is not readily adapted to large systems.

Conveyors have been used to harvest water hyacinth since the early 20th century, when the U.S. Army Corps of Engineers used large conveyors to remove water hyacinth which blocked navigation in streams, canals and lakes in the Southeastern United States (Tabita and Woods, 1963; Wunderlich, 1963).

Small chain-and-flight conveyors, usually over 1.2 m wide and with a chain speed of about 0.5 m s^{-1}, have been designed and built to harvest water hyacinth in biomass production and waste treatment systems. One such conveyor was observed to harvest over 14 Mg h^{-1} with hand feeding and removal of the harvested product. Theoretical capacities of these machines are much higher, but actual capacity is limited by inability to supply a continuous stream to the harvester and remove the product as fast as it is delivered.

Sarasota Weed and Feed built a series of three developmental water hyacinth harvesters during the 1970's. The first consisted of a forage harvester modified so that a specialized gatherer/ elevator could feed into it from the side opposite the drawbar. The specialized elevator was inefficient and the capacity of the chopper was too low, but the machine incorporated most of the basic elements of a complete system. The second harvester was a 3 m wide flat-wire-belt elevator with a feeding reel. Water hyacinth were supplied to the elevator by a airboat with a pusher rake. A cross-conveyor and flail chopper were added as an integral part of the harvesting system. In tests conducted by the Florida Game and Fresh Water Fish Commission, it harvested 20 Mg h^{-1}, with a peak hour of 40 Mg h^{-1} (Phillipy and Perryman, 1972). The third harvester was another 3 m wide flat-wire-belt elevator with a feeding reel. It was mounted on a truck chassis so that it could be readily moved from site to site. It had no chopper, but the cross conveyor fed directly into an elevating conveyor which loaded a truck.

An Aquamarine shore conveyor was modified by attaching an elevating conveyor laterally to its horizontal leg. The elevating conveyor was made of closely spaced conduit supported and driven by chains. A small, fixed feeding reel fed water hyacinth onto the conveyor and airboats supplied water hyacinth to the harvester.

A water hyacinth harvesting system was installed by the University of Florida on a 0.4 ha pond at the field laboratory at Zellwood (Figure 2). It consisted of a 6 m wide rake manipulated by four shore-based winches, a takeout conveyor and a flail chopper. The rake (Figure 3) gathered the plants and moved them to the 6 m wide takeout conveyor (Figure 4), which moved them laterally in a 0.6 m wide stream and elevated them into the chopper. The chopped plants were elevated into storage or transportation. Highest observed capacity of the system was 2 Mg h^{-1}, but it is being modified to improve its performance.

Immobile systems are especially sensitive to the interactions of the plants with the wind, water and machinery. In order to optimize these systems, research is being conducted to determine these interactions. Mechanical characteristics of plants in the water are being determined with several sizes of compression frames in order to predict the capacities of systems and to determine how and to what extent capacity can be increased by application of a modest force (Sivakumaran and Bagnall, 1984). Hydrodynamic drag is the major force encountered in gathering and in-water movement of aquatic plants. It is also the force which introduces movements about the vertical and horizontal axes which cause mats of plants to pile, spill or disengage from the gathering and in-water transportation devices. Preliminary data suggest that drag force increases proportionally to the square of the speed and is not greatly affected by mat horizontal geometry (Bagnall, 1984). Vertical distortion of the mat greatly increases drag. Aerodynamic forces may carry floating plants far across a lake, but are small relative to the hydrodynamic and mechanical forces usually encountered in aquatic plant systems. Ultimately, in order to be most useful, the mechanical, hydrodynamic and aerodynamic properties must be integrated into a model which can

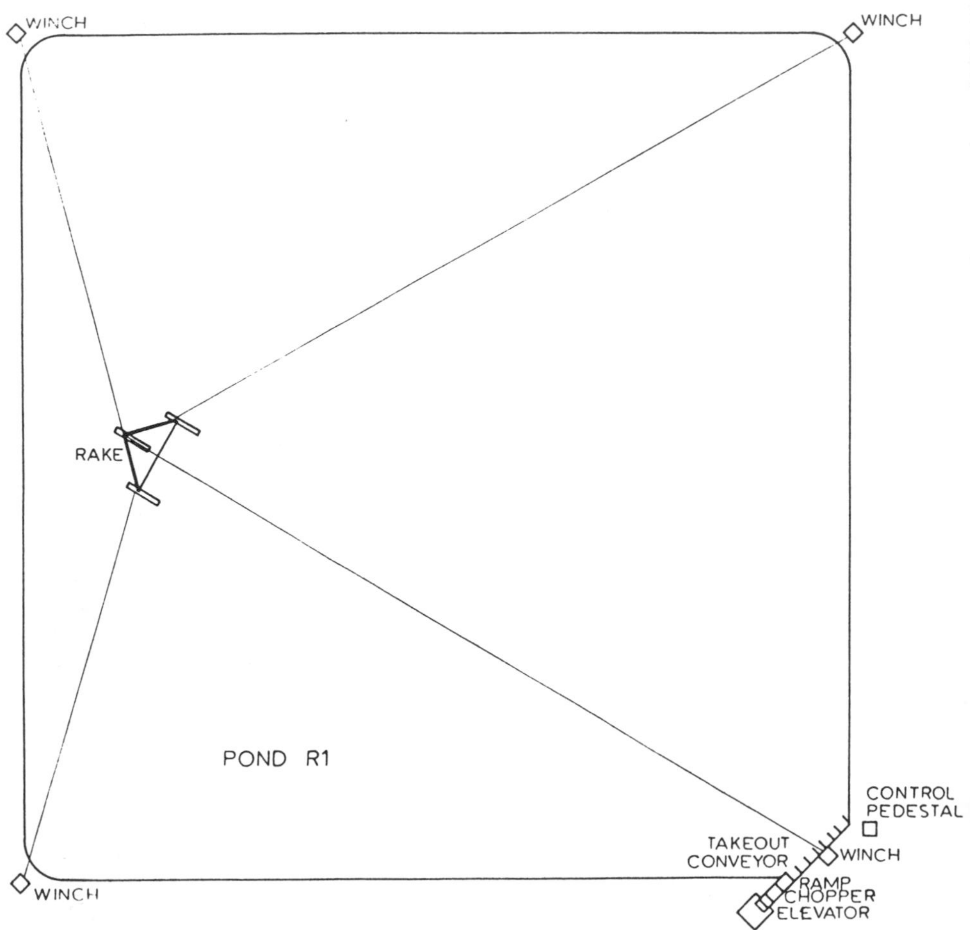

FIGURE 2. Schematic diagram of IFAS hyacinth harvesting system located on pond R1 at Zellwood.

be used to predict the total response of matted plants within a system.

Mobile systems. Mobile systems are seldom used on water hyacinth because the great bulk of the plants make their use uneconomical. Systems designed for submersed aquatic plants are occasionally used in experimental or emergency floating plant operations where there is no readily available alternative.

The Aquamarine Aqua-trio, a submersed plant harvesting system, has been used to harvest floating aquatic plants. Its capacity is limited by the bulk of the plants that must be transported over-water.

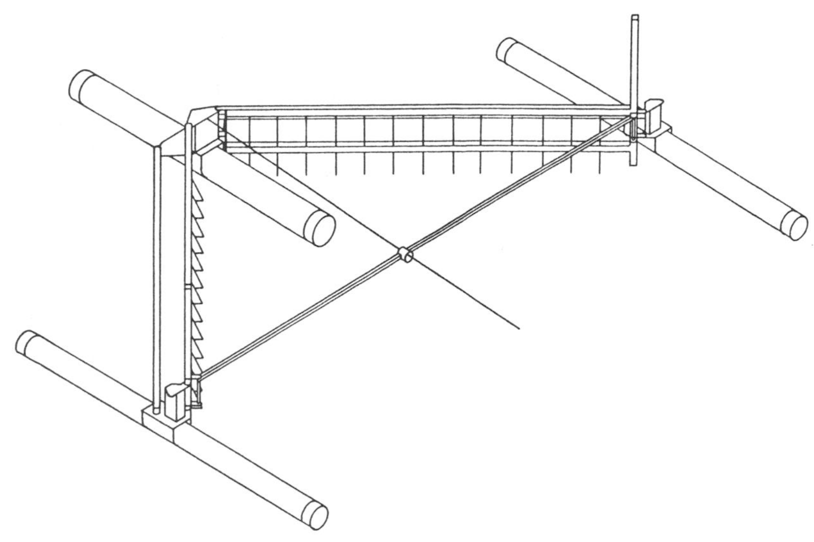

FIGURE 3. Laterally-folding rake use in IFAS hyacinth harvesting system located on pond R1 at Zellwood.

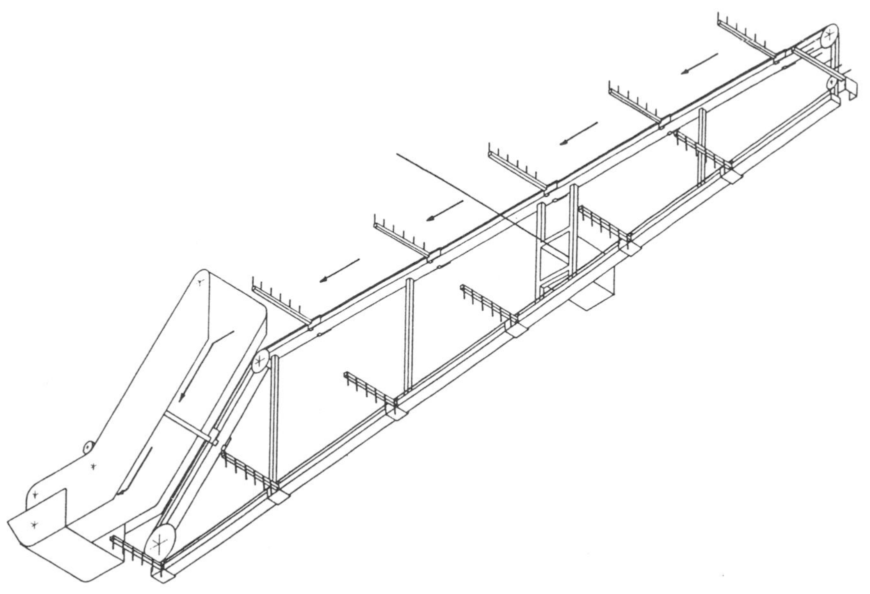

FIGURE 4. Takeout conveyor used in IFAS hyacinth harvesting system located on pond R1 at Zellwood.

Two combined harvester/choppers were designed and built in the University of Florida's Agricultural Engineering Department. Combine 1 (Bagnall, 1986) consisted of a 30 cm wide chopper and a 90 cm wide screw/reel gatherer mounted on a 90 cm wide barge. The gatherer gathered a 90 cm wide swath and fed it rearward and upward into the feed rolls of the cylinder/shearbar chopper which was mounted with its feed axis 45° above horizontal. The chopped product dropped into a chain-and-flight drag conveyor which elevated it and dropped it onto the deck. In field tests it harvested water hyacinth at an average rate of 716 kg h^{-1} and a specific energy requirement of 50 kJ kg^{-1}. Combine 2, shown in Figure 5, was based on combine 1, but harvests a 2.4 m swath and feeds it through a 1.2 m wide flail chopper. The reduced convergence, lower elevating angle, looser coupling and absence of outrigger pontoons should improve its performance substantially over combine 1.

Hybrid systems. Amasek, Inc., of Cocoa, Florida, has built a harvesting system for use in conjunction with their wastewater treatment/resource recovery systems. It consists of a water tractor and a gatherer/chopper. The water tractor is supported and propelled by cleated plastic drums and is used to break and

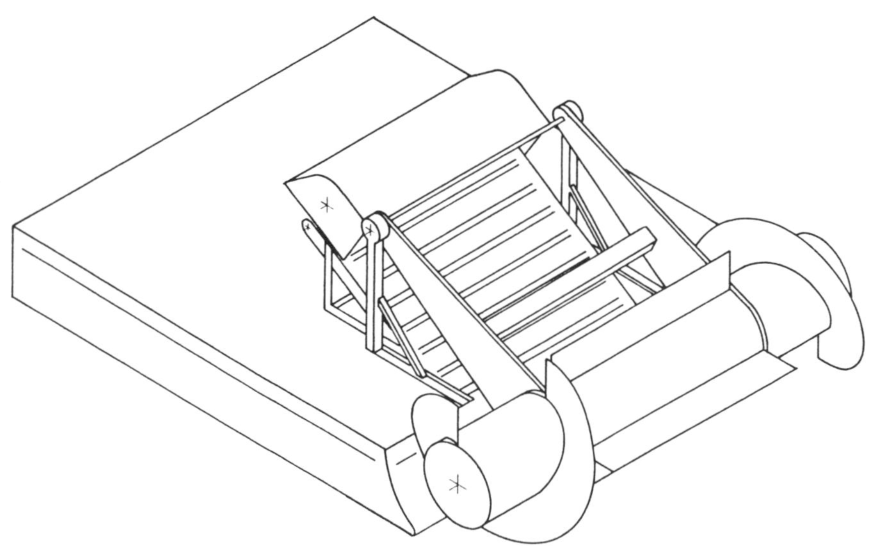

FIGURE 5. Water hyacinth combined harvester-chopper 2.

gather mats of water hyacinth to feed into the gatherer/chopper. The gatherer/chopper consists of an extended pool feeding system, a coarse hog/chopper, an elevator, a fine chopper and a progressive cavity pump. Reported capacity is 20 Mg h^{-1} and the product is pumped from the system to whichever end use is intended with little supplementary water.

Emergent Aquatic Plant Systems

The high yield potential and attractive chemical composition of cattail (*Typha* spp.) make it an attractive energy crop for wet marginal lands. In Minnesota, total annual yields (dry wt) equivalent to 30 Mg ha^{-1} have been demonstrated in field trials (Andrews and Pratt, 1978). Approximately 50% of the cattail plant is comprised of a below ground rhizome system located in the top 30 cm of soil. The rhizome system contains 40% starch and sugar at the end of the growing season (Pratt et al., 1981) making rhizomes an attractive feedstock for alcohol production. The aboveground leafy portion of the plant is largely cellulose and can be gasified or burned.

Possible harvesting scenarios for cattail which are currently being evaluated include: (1) shoot biomass only, harvested annually, (2) shoot biomass only, harvested semiannually, and (3) shoot biomass harvested annually and combined with rhizome biomass harvested biennially.

At the University of Minnesota, a flail chopper was modified for harvesting cattail leaves. The 1 m wide, hydraulically-driven chopper was mounted on the front toolbar of a Seiga Amphibious Transporter which was adapted to function as a Mobile Research Platform (MORP). This leaf harvesting system is shown in Figure 6. The delivery conveyor from the flail chopper was an enclosed single chain flight conveyor adapted to the configuration of the MORP. The delivery conveyor received harvested cattail leaf material directly from the flail rotor which did the blowing and throwing, in addition to the cutting and shredding. The harvested leaves were collected in a transportation/weighing bin mounted on the MORP. The bin was provided with a cam action to lower it onto the scale for weighing, and lift it off for transport. A pan was attached immediately behind the flail head to collect the gathering loss material as it was thrown from the rear of the flail. The gathering loss which was not cut or that which hit the ground at a point beneath the rotor was not collected.

The flail harvester worked satisfactorily for leaf harvesting. The flail cut and shredded the leaf material into pieces ranging in size up to 20 cm in length with predominant lengths being 10 to 20 cm. The rotor throwing and blowing in conjunction with the flight conveyor delivered the cut material to the transport bin in most situations. However, in extremely wet conditions, particularly if the rotor had been inadvertently lowered and encountered free water or extremely wet soil, the

FIGURE 6. Flail harvester with delivery conveyor and transport bin in use in the harvest of cattail leaf material. (Exit end turn down not installed.)

conveyor plugged. Also, depending on stiffness of the soil support structure for the stalks, the front pusher bar on the flail head would sometimes bend the stalks forward before being encountered by the flail knives, resulting in the stalks not springing back sufficiently after being initially cut to establish a "low" cut or low stubble. Crop losses collected in the gathering loss pan ranged from 2 to 6% of the net harvested yield in one series of tests and 5 to 11% in another series. Moisture content, leaning of stalks, wind direction, stalk rigidity, stalk support, and stalk density influenced the gathering loss level.

Power to the flail rotor ranged from 3.7 to 8.6 kW. The specific energy input to the rotor ranged from 9 to 26 kJ kg^{-1} of dry leaf material, or from 0.05 to 0.13% of the energy content of the material, assuming an energy content of 18.6 MJ kg^{-1} of dry matter.

The concept of digger blade and rod-chain conveyor for the harvest of cattail rhizome was evaluated using a modified potato harvester (Schertz et al., 1982; Pratt et al., 1983). Modifications included addition of the following: (1) two 61 cm rolling, powered coulters, one on each side of the digger blade, (2) clearance above the rod-chain conveyor to allow a 35 cm mat of the rhizome-soil material to pass freely through the machine, (3) two 2.4 m long by 30 cm wide metal skis to provide support for the harvester, (4) low-speed, high-torque hydraulic motor for powering the rod-chain conveyor, (5) hydraulic system for controlling the depth of cut, (6) mechanical linkage for adjusting the angle of inclination of the rod-chain conveyor, and (7) a simple horizontal draft link for towing. The rhizome harvester was towed by the MORP. The schematic of this experimental rhizome harvest system is shown in Figure 7.

At a speed of 1 km h^{-1} and a cutting depth of 25 cm, the average draft force was 13.5 kN and maximum force was 14.5 kN. Unit draft was 8.6 N cm^{-2}. Power required by the rod-chain conveyor depended on height and loading. Maximum hydraulic power to the rod-chain conveyor was 7.5 kW.

Rhizome-soil material was processed with a rotary tumbler and water flush system. The rotary tumbler was a 76 cm diameter by 1.7 m long horizontal cylinder with hardware cloth on the cylindrical surface, rotated about its longitudinal axis by a variable-speed hydraulic drive. The tumbler contained internal, radial, longitudinal vanes which lifted the mass of material as the tumbler rotated. Water was supplied by a perforated pipe and dispersed by an expanded metal mesh above the cylinder. The rotary tumbler is shown in Figure 8. Rotational speed of the tumbler was adjusted so that the material was carried up the side of the tumbler cylinder but fell away shortly before it reached the top. Excessive rotational speed caused the material to cling to the surface and not fall free as it went over the top. The configuration was sized to permit batch processing of samples. Samples were inserted, end plates were installed, and the rotation and water flush were started. Soil material was washed through the screened surface of the tumbler and separated rhizomes were removed from the tumbler.

The rotary tumbler with water flush successfully separated rhizomes from soil. The lifting, dropping, tumbling action in combination with the water flushing effectively dislodged soil from the rhizome mat, effecting a clean separation. The only soil type tested was sandy peat. Test showed that 29 to 45 kg samples of rhizomes and soil could be separated adequately with less than 30 s of tumbling and a water flush of 9 to 16 L s^{-1}. Mesh opening and radial vane size and frequency also affected performance.

Figure 9 shows in schematic form a concept for the harvest of rhizomes, including gathering by means of the digger blade, transport by means of the rod-chain conveyor and separating by means of the rotary tumbler and water-bath separator.

Submersed Aquatic Plant Systems

Submersed plants have such low production rates that they are not seriously considered as biomass crops but only serve special functions, e.g. re-aeration and absorption of specific chemicals, in wastewater treatment systems. The Aquamarine and Limnos systems are typical of submersed plant harvesting systems. The

FIGURE 7. Rotary tumbler being prepared for test processing of sample of cattail rhizome-soil matrix.

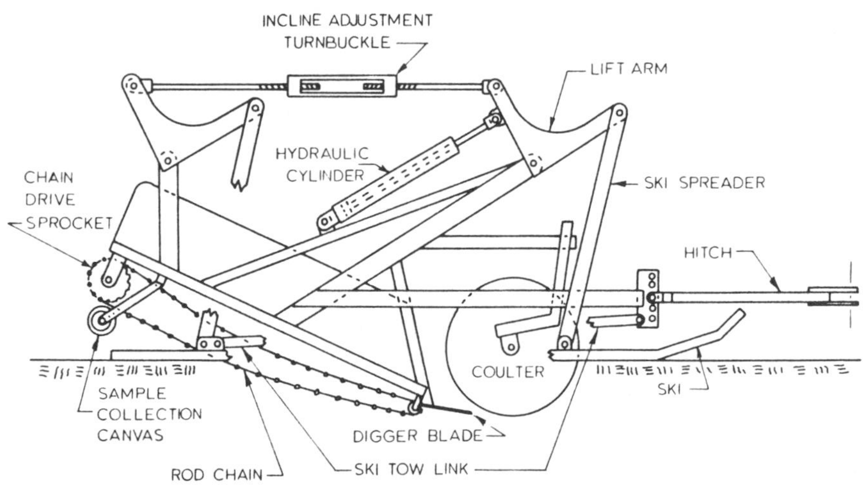

FIGURE 8. Schematic diagram of final configuration of rhizome harvester.

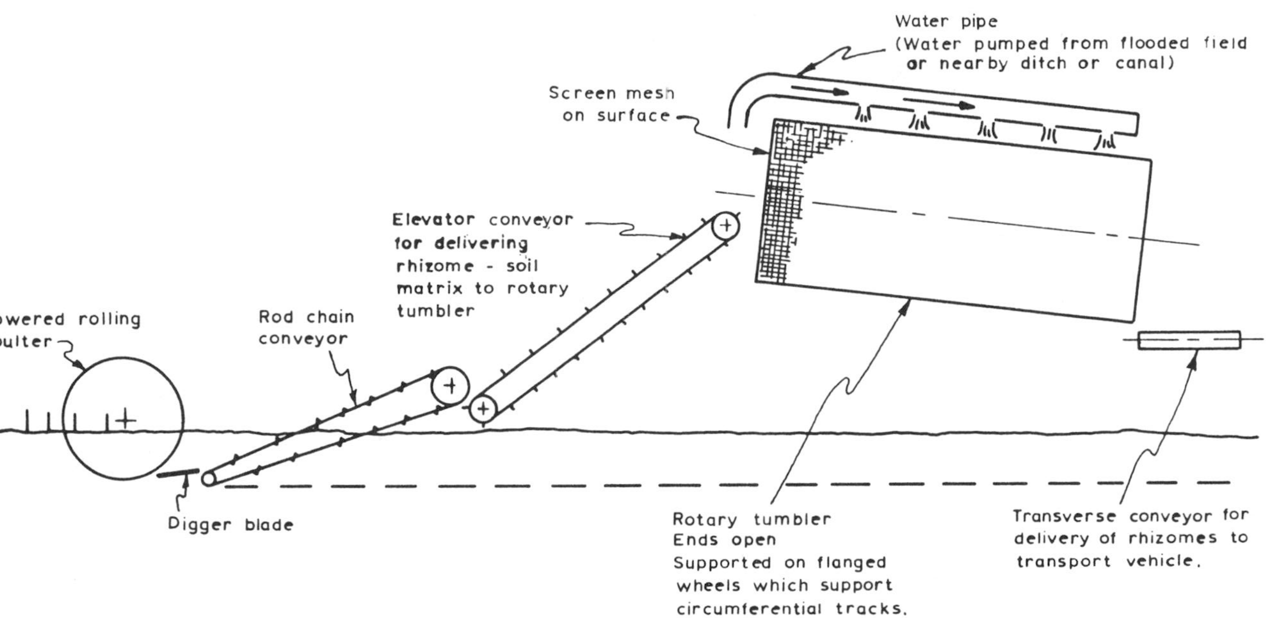

FIGURE 9. Schematic concept for full harvest and processing of cattail rhizomes.

Aquamarine system has been widely used on a wide variety of plant types, including floating and emergent plants.

The Aquamarine harvesting system is the most widely used aquatic plant harvesting system. It consists of a harvester, a transporter and a shore conveyor. The harvester consists of a set of reciprocating cutters mounted in front of a flat-wire-belt elevator, a live-bottom holding barge and a discharge conveyor. The transporter is a live-bottom holding barge and a discharge elevator. The holding barge capacity ranges from 6 to 28 m^3. Under good operating conditions, the system can harvest 0.4 ha h^{-1} of submersed plants. In water hyacinth, the harvester can be filled in a few seconds, but the transport and unloading cycle time is usually in excess of 10 min, even with short hauls. The harvester has worked most successfully in water hyacinth when used as a stationary harvester, supplied by a pusher boat and discharging directly and continuously to a conveyor system.

The Limnos harvester was also designed for submersed plants, but has been tested briefly in water hyacinth. The system consists of a cutter boat, a gatherer/mill and a transportation barge. The cutter boat is not needed in water hyacinth. The gatherer/mill consists of a pair of gathering wheels rotating about nearly-vertical axes, an elevating conveyor and a large hammermill. A 6 m wide swath of plants is gathered and fed onto the 1.8 m wide elevator, which feeds it into the hammermill. The milled product is discharged downward into the transportation barge. The barge carries the milled product to a shore site and pumps it into a pipeline. The fine water hyacinth fibers are extremely difficult to mill and productivity can be expected to be very low.

ECONOMICS OF HARVESTING/HANDLING

Costs of harvesting affect the economic feasibility of wastewater aquaculture/resource recovery operations (Bagnall and Hentges, 1979). These costs are often attributed only to the resource recovery aspect of the system even though nutrient removal and maintenance aspects of harvesting also determine effectiveness of wastewater treatment.

Elements of Cost

The cost of harvesting is made up of capital and operating costs. Evaluation of these components, especially as systems are being developed, gives insight into which development efforts may most greatly effect the greatest reduction in total system cost.

Capital cost, important in itself, also affects subsequent costs throughout the life of the system. In some cases, especially where capital or foreign exchange are limited, capital cost may be a serious obstacle to installation of a system. Usually, however, capital cost amortization by interest and depreciation is the more important concern. Some capital cost must be attributed to every operating hour or dry ton of biomass that passes through the system. In estimating the distribution of capital cost, the expected life and capacity of the system must be estimated.

Annual maintenance and repairs are assumed to be proportional to first cost, modified by class of machinery and age.

Labor cost is primarily dependent on the number of people required to operate the system and the hourly rate that they are paid. Labor is often a major cost because most systems require relatively large crews. As systems become more reliable and performance more predictable, more of the functions can be automated and labor requirements reduced.

Energy required to operate harvesting systems is usually small relative to the energy content of the biomass being moved through it. Primary energy consumers in the system are size reducers and transportation. When mechanism performance and reliability have been enhanced, serious efforts will be made to reduce energy inputs.

Siting and transportation may vary widely. For a machine system which will remain at one site throughout its useful life, this cost will consist of site maintenance. Biomass harvesting sites can bury themselves in plant residue and wornout machinery which attract many types of vermin and interfere with ongoing operations. Systems that will be moved periodically will require means of transportation, site preparation, and loading and unloading which, combined, may be a major cost of operation.

Removing biomass from the water is only the beginning of the acquisition and processing sequence. Even if the digester or other processing system is on-site, equipment, energy and labor will be required to get it from the shore to the end use. If the processing site is an appreciable distance from the harvest site, the handling costs may exceed the harvesting costs.

Capacity or productivity of the harvesting/handling system must be commensurate with the production and utilization systems with which it is associated. Cost per unit of production should be a major criterion in the selection of a system. There should be economies of scale in a properly designed system.

Example

A typical modern 20 to 50 Mg h^{-1} harvesting system with an initial cost of \$100,000 and an expected life of 5 yr will cost about \$24,000 per yr to own. Repairs and maintenance will cost about \$15,000 per year. Usually this type of system will require a crew of 3 people. If the crew is paid a total of \$18 per hour, works year round and has a fringe benefit rate of 15%, labor cost is \$43,056 per year. Energy will cost about \$0.12 per Mg of fresh plant material harvested. Site maintenance or moving costs may vary widely, but for the purpose of this example are assumed to be \$7,000 per year. If capacity of the system is 25 Mg h^{-1}, the system is operated 200 d yr^{-1} and availability is 80%, the system will harvest 24,000 Mg yr^{-1}. Harvesting cost will be \$5.00 Mg^{-1}, 35% of which will be for labor, 20% for capital, and 15% for repairs and maintenance. If these estimates are accurate, the obvious way to reduce cost is to automate the system.

FUTURE RESEARCH, DEVELOPMENT AND COMMERCIALIZATION

Harvesting system capacity has been stalled at about 20 Mg h^{-1} for over a decade. Multiple systems are one, expensive, solution. The limitations of component and system design and operation need to be overcome to arrive at a more efficient, economical solution. Analysis of the pre-processing/ transportation interaction is one important component of the problem. Another is analysis of the machine/water/plant interactions, which will include properties determination.

ACKNOWLEDGMENTS

Some of the work reported herein was supported by the joint program between the University of Florida's Institute of Food and Agricultural Sciences and the Gas Research Institute titled "Methane from Biomass and Waste." The authors acknowledge the assistance of J. M. Simpson, F. Waltz, and J. R. Petrell in conducting some of the research and development upon which this paper is based.

REFERENCES

Andrews, N. J., and D. C. Pratt. 1978. The potential of cattails (Typha spp.) as an energy source: Productivity of managed stands. J. Minn. Acad. Sci. 44(2):5-8.

Bagnall, L. O. 1975. Crimper-type water hyacinth harvester. Florida Department of Natural Resources. 49 pp.

Bagnall, L. O. 1982. Aquatic plant harvesting and harvesters. Proceedings of the Conference on Strategies for Aquatic Weed Management. Gainesville, Florida. p. 37-41.

Bagnall, L. O. 1983. Development of a water hyacinth biomass combine. ASAE Paper 83-5038. Am. Soc. Agric. Eng. 16 pp.

Bagnall, L. O. 1984. Hydrodynamic properties of water hyacinth. ASAE Paper 84-5030. Am. Soc. Agric. Eng. 11 pp.

Bagnall, L. O. 1985. Biomass harvesters: A new challenge for equipment designers. Agric. Eng. 66(9):16-17.

Bagnall, L. O. 1986. Harvesting systems for aquatic biomass. p. 259-273. In W. H. Smith (ed.) Biomass Energy Development. Plenum Press, New York.

Bagnall, L. O., and J. F. Hentges, Jr. 1979. Processing and conservation of water hyacinth and hydrilla for livestock feeding. p. 367-374. In J. E. Breck, R. T. Prentki, and O. L. Loucks (ed.) Aquatic Plants, Lake Management, and Ecosystem Consequences of Lake Harvesting. University of Wisconsin.

Garver, E. G., D. R. Dubbe, and D. C. Pratt. 1983. Adaptability of Typha spp. to various wetland soil conditions for bio-energy production. Paper presented at the International Symposium on Peat Utilization. Bemidjim Minnesota, October 1983.

Phillipy, C. L., and J. M. Perryman. 1972. Mechanical harvesting of water hyacinth (Eichhornia crassipes) in Gant Lake Canal, Sumter County, Florida. Fla. Game and Fresh Water Fish Commission, Tallahassee.

Pratt, D. C., D. R. Dubbe, and E. G. Garver. 1985. Energy from biomass in Minnesota: Part 1: Wetland biomass production. Final report to Minnesota dDepartment of Energy and Economic Development and the Legislative Commission on Minnesota's Resources, August 1985.

Pratt, D. C., N. J. Andrews, R. L. Glass, and R. E. Lovrien. 1981. Production of wetland energy crops in Minnesota - an update. p. 158-175. In Proc. of Biomass Workshop sponsored by Midwest Universities Energy Consortium.

Pratt, D. C., D. R. Dubbe, E. G. Garver, and C. Schertz. 1986. Typha spp. biomass production: Evaluation of management practices. Annual report to Herbaceous Biomass Program, U.S. Dept. of Energy, March 1986.

Schertz, C., D. R. Dubbe, and D. C. Pratt. 1983. Harvesting cattail (Typha spp.) rhizomes as an alternative feedstock for alcohol production: Modifications of potato harvester. Final Report to Dept. of Energy - Alcohol Fuels Division. 19 pp.

Sivakumaran, K., and L. O. Bagnall. 1984. In-situ mechanical properties of water hyacinth. ASAE Paper 84-5029. Am. Soc. Agric. Eng. 18 pp.

Stewart, J. S. III. 1972. Energy and flow requirements for chopping water hyacinths. ME Thesis. University of Florida, Gainesville.

Tabita, A., and J. W. Woods. 1963. History of hyacinth control in Florida Hyacinth Control J. 1:19-22.

Wunderlich, W. E. 1963. History of water hyacinths control in Louisiana. Hyacinth Control J. 1:14-18.

BIOMASS CONVERSION OPTIONS

D. P. Chynoweth
Bioprocess Engineering Research Laboratory
Agricultural Engineering Department
University of Florida, IFAS
Gainesville, Florida 32611

ABSTRACT

Biological conversion processes are more suitable than thermal conversion processes for extraction of energy and fuels from aquatic plants because of high energy requirements for dewatering aquatic feeds to levels suitable for thermal conversion. Anaerobic digestion has received more attention than alcohol and other fermentations for conversion of aquatic plants to chemicals because of lack of need for feed pretreatment and pure culture maintenance and ease of recovery and wide potential use of the methane (CH_4) product. This paper presents a systematic approach for evaluation of the suitability of aquatic feedstocks for anaerobic digestion, selection of the best reactor design and operating conditions for conversion, process scaleup, and process integration with a total wastewater reclamation and energy recovery system. Studies conducted with water hyacinth are used to illustrate inter- and intra-feedstock variability, effects of pretreatment on conversion yields and rates, performance of several conversion reactor options, and data needs supplied only in a scaled-up experimental test unit. The economics of conversion is discussed in context of a total aquaculture energy conversion system.

Keywords: Aquatic biomass, anaerobic digestion, methane, wastewater treatment, biological treatment.

OVERVIEW OF BIOCONVERSION

The focus of this conference is on use of aquaculture for wastewater reclamation and conversion of resulting plants to useful products. This paper describes conversion options with emphasis on fermentation to methane (CH_4).

Several aquaculture systems are under various stages of development and implementation for wastewater reclamation, including lagoons, shallow channels, and non-ponded hydroponic

Aquatic Plants for Water Treatment
and Resource Recovery
K.R. Reddy and W.H. Smith (Eds.)

ISBN 0-941463-00-1

systems (Tchobanoglous et al., 1979; Reed et al., 1980; Reddy and DeBusk, 1984; 1985). Lagoons and channels provide the environment for growth of a variety of plants which may be classified as photosynthetic bacteria, microalgae, submergent macrophytes, and emergent macrophytes. Although most research on these systems has been conducted with freshwater plants, comparable marine systems should be feasible. The use of non-ponded hydroponic systems such as nutrient film technology may also employ herbaceous and woody species which are not normally associated with aquaculture (Fannin et al., 1982; Reddy and DeBusk, 1985). Feedstocks available for conversion may therefore include sludges generated in primary treatment (prior to aquaculture systems) and a broad spectrum of species covering the entire amount of the category referred to as biomass. The majority of work in this field has been on freshwater aquatic plants which will be the focus of this paper.

Biomass generated from aquaculture systems may be used directly or in modified forms for fertilizer and animal feed or as a feedstock for extraction of or conversion to fuels or chemicals (Table 1). Of these options, conversion to useful energy forms has received widest attention and is the subject of this paper. Other options are addressed elsewhere in this book (Lakshman, 1987). Energy conversion processes potentially available for aquatic plants include thermal, e.g. combustion and thermal gasification, and biological, e.g. alcohol fermentation and biogasification. Most aquatic plants have a high water content (about 95%) and can only be dewatered economically to about 80%. Because of high energy requirements associated with dewatering completely to reach high temperatures, thermal processes are not generally considered feasible for aquatic feeds. Conversion of these feeds is therefore usually limited to biological processes.

Conventional pure-culture mediated fermentation for conversion of biomass to ethanol and other chemicals has received wide attention and is discussed elsewhere in this book (Lakshman, 1987). These processes are not economical because of high costs related to pretreatment (saccharification), pure culture maintenance, and separation of products from dilute solutions.

TABLE 1. Uses of aquatic plants.

Animal Feeds
Fertilizers
Extraction of chemicals (or chemical precursors)
Feedstock for thermal conversion processes
Feedstock for biochemical processes
- Methane
- Alcohol fuels
- Chemicals

This paper focuses on the most widely applied conversion process for high moisture feedstocks, biogasification (or anaerobic digestion). The advantages of this process over thermal or other biological processes are:

1) high moisture feeds can be processed
2) no pretreatment is required for degradation
3) pure culture maintenance is not required
4) product gas is easily separated from the medium
5) product gas is primarily methane and CO_2 with traces of H_2S
6) product gas is useful with varied stages of purification and scales
7) process economics are good at small and large scales

Microbial Ecology of Methanogenesis

Microbial methanogenesis is a natural process occurring in anaerobic environments such as ocean and lake sediments and animal digestive tracts. Harnessing and optimizing this process for decomposition of wastes and biomass into useful fuels is being actively pursued. Methanogenic decomposition (Figure 1) is a process occurring only under strict anaerobic conditions where

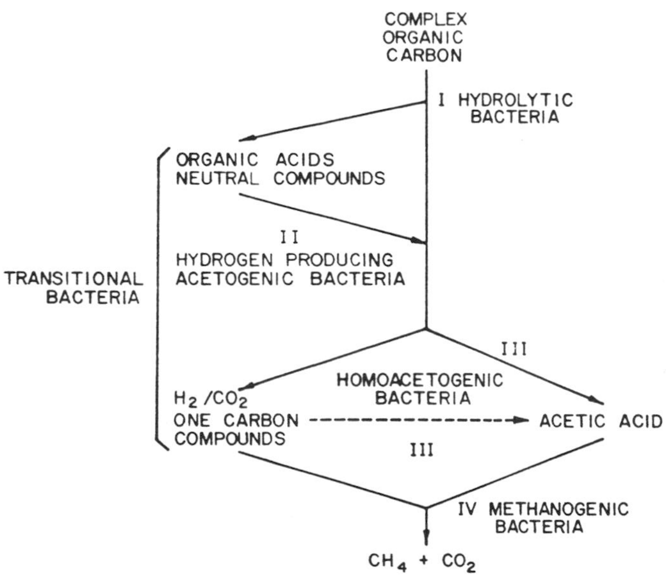

FIGURE 1. Categories of metabolically distinct bacteria in the CH_4 fermentation (Chynoweth and Isaacson, 1987).

mixed populations of bacteria decompose organic matter to CO_2 and CH_4. Methanogenesis traditionally has been considered a two-step process involving acid-forming bacteria which hydrolyze and ferment organic compounds (i.e., carbohydrates, lipids, and proteins) to fermentation products such as organic acids, alcohols, neutral compounds, H_2, and CO_2, and CH_4-forming bacteria that convert these fermentation products to CH_4 and CO_2. As knowledge of methanogenic bacteria has accumulated, it has become apparent that their natural substrates are restricted primarily to acetate, H_2, and CO_2, and a separate group of bacteria, the H_2-producing acetogenic bacteria convert hydrolysis and fermentation products to acetate, H_2, and CO_2. In many cases, H_2 and acetate have been shown to inhibit the acetogenic bacteria (Chynoweth and Isaacson, 1987). Consequently, the balanced fermentation is dependent upon constant removal of these products by the methanogenic bacteria. More recently, a fourth group of bacteria has been identified in the fermentation, the homoacetogenic bacteria, which ferments a wide spectrum of compounds such as H_2, CO_2, and formate to acetate (Chynoweth and Isaacson, 1987). The significance of this group in the overall fermentation is currently not known. Removal or inhibition (Figure 2) results in backup of electron flow resulting in fermentation products other than CH_4 and CO_2 (Chynoweth and Isaacson, 1987). Our laboratory is investigating exploitation of these aberrant paths of electron flow for conversion of biomass to alcohol and other chemicals by the mixed fermentation.

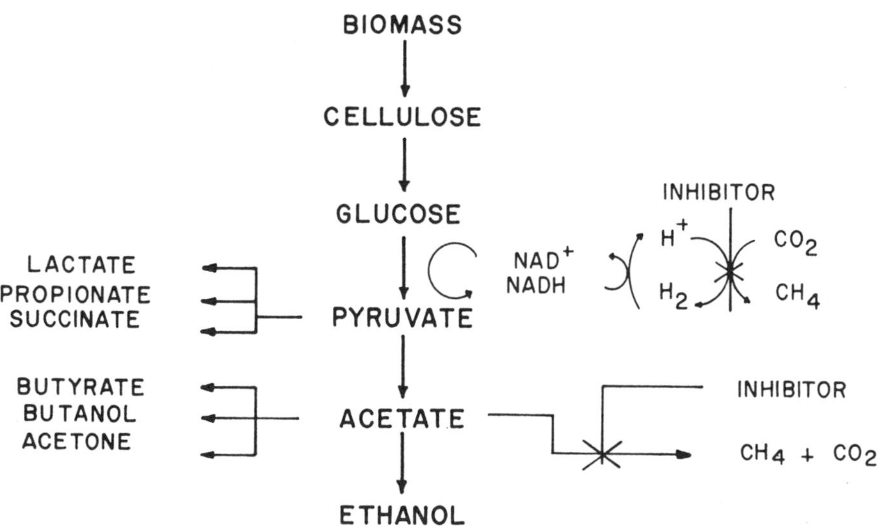

FIGURE 2. Diversion of CH_4 fermentation to liquid fuels.

During the past 10 years, literature on the microbiology and biochemistry of methanogenic bacteria has increased exponentially with isolation of several new species and development of more rapid techniques for study. Beginning with the discovery of interspecies H_2 transfer in 1967 (Bryant et al., 1967), several species of H_2-producing acetogenic bacteria have been isolated (Boone and Mah, 1987). Although the overall niches of these microbial groups are beginning to unveil, it is important to realize that knowledge of the physiology, metabolism, and genetics of these organisms is in its infancy. Hydrolytic bacteria are the least studied organisms in the CH_4 fermentation even though hydrolysis is apparently the overall rate-limiting step in many of the methanogenic environments. With the exception of the rumen, knowledge of the microbial ecology of methanogenesis in anaerobic environments, including anaerobic digesters, is superficial.

Overview of Anaerobic Digestion Process

A generalized scheme (Figure 3) for the anaerobic digestion process based on CH_4 fermentation shows that upon harvest or collection, biomass or wastes are chopped and ground for size reduction, and possibly subjected to some kind of pretreatment to enhance biodegradation. In a continuously-fed stirred tank reactor (CSTR) the feed is either added directly or as a slurry at a typical loading rate of 1.6 kg m^{-3} d^{-1} and a hydraulic retention time of 15 to 20 d. In this reactor, which is usually operated at a mesophilic temperature of 35°C, a mixed population of bacteria effect conversion of about 50% of the organic matter (volatile solids) to CH_4 and CO_2, at a mole percent ratio of 60:40. This is equivalent to a CH_4 yield of 0.25 m^3 kg^{-1} volatile solids (VS) added and a CH_4 production rate of 0.4 vol vol^{-1} culture-day. Solids in the effluent may be settled in an anaerobic secondary digester and recycled (directly or following posttreatment), processed as fertilizer or animal feed, or subjected to thermal conversion. Supernatant may be recycled, used as fertilizer, animal feed supplement, or processed into a form suitable for disposal. Product gas can be utilized directly or treated to remove CO_2 and traces of H_2S.

The above refers to a conventional digester system that might be found in a domestic wastewater treatment plant. Methane yields from this process are limited by the fact that only a fraction of the organic matter in the feed can be hydrolyzed under anaerobic conditions. Process rates are limited by the slow growth rates of methanogenic bacteria for conversion of soluble feed constituents and hydrolysis rates of particulate feed components. Research to overcome these limitations is therefore focusing on methods of increasing solids and microorganism retention in the reactor and pretreatment to improve biodegradability.

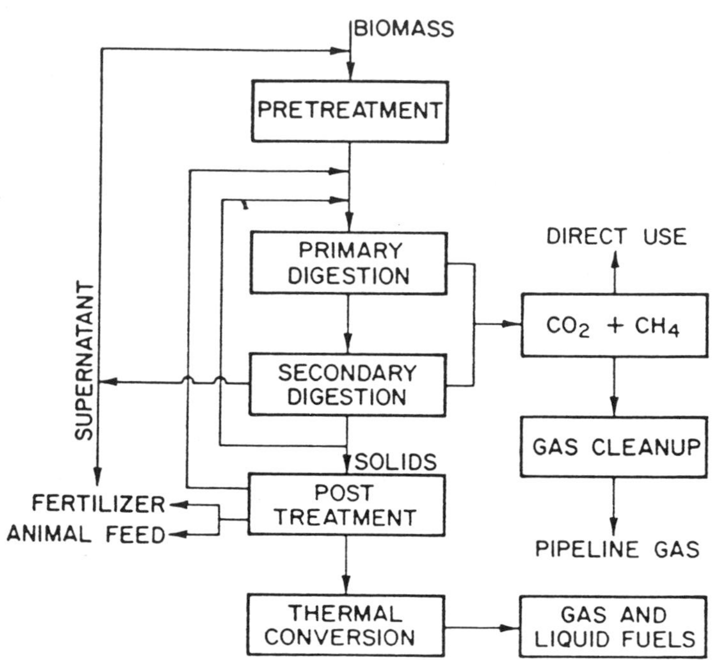

FIGURE 3. Anaerobic digestion process scheme (Chynoweth, 1981).

Process Evaluation

The major criteria used to evaluate performance of anaerobic digestion of different feeds or new digester reactor designs are CH_4 yield, CH_4 production rate, reduction in organic matter, culture stability, thermal efficiency, and process economics. Methane yield is the quantity of CH_4 produced relative to the quantity of organic matter added, and is usually reported as m^3 kg^{-1} (SCF lb^{-1} VS) ash-free dry weight added. Methane production rate refers to the quantity of CH_4 generated in volumes of CH_4 per volume of active reactor per day. Organic reduction efficiency is an important performance parameter because it directly influences methane yield and is inversely related to the quantity of process residues requiring further processing or disposal. This parameter is determined by a process materials balance in terms of organic matter reduction. Certain combinations of feedstocks and operating conditions may result in microbial population imbalance and related reduction or failure of digester performance. This condition is characterized by reduced gas production, increased volatile acids concentration, and reduced pH. Finally, process evaluation must consider energy balances and economics relative to the overall biomass production or waste collection and treatment system. These criteria and the factors influencing them are outlined briefly below.

Factors Limiting Yields

In any anaerobic digestion process that is not inhibited or kinetically limited, two major factors affecting CH_4 yields are feedstock composition and inoculum characteristics. The composition of the biodegradable organic compounds can, for example, influence CH_4 yield in that reduced compounds such as fats and protein produce a higher percentage of CH_4 than oxidized compounds such as sugars. Ultimate CH_4 yields, however, are influenced principally by the biodegradability of the organic components. Certain natural organic compounds such as lignin, for example, are refractory to decomposition under anaerobic conditions even at long residence times. This explains why organic matter accumulates in lake sediment and as fossil fuels such as peat, oil, and coal. This refractory property is related to the lack of enzymes in anaerobic bacteria and an O_2 requirement by many enzymes to carry out the initial hydrolytic reactions. It has also been established that certain compounds can complex with others rendering them resistant to anaerobic decomposition. For example, lignin affects decomposition of cellulose in this manner (Jerger and Tsao, 1987). A variety of physical, chemical, and biological treatment techniques are under consideration for improvement of biodegradability. Because most of these techniques were developed for improvement of animal digestibility or conversion of biomass to ethanol, research on application of these methods for anaerobic digestion has been minimal.

Lack of decomposition of certain components of feed substances may be attributed to the absence of organisms capable of their degradation (rather than the inherent refractory nature of the compounds). It is generally thought that for most types of organic wastes and biomass, a viable inoculum can be developed from any environment in which anaerobic methanogenic decomposition of a mixture of organic compounds is occurring naturally; for example, anaerobic sewage digesters, anaerobic lake sediments, or animal feces. However, there is disagreement on this point. It might be expected that an inoculum adapted for a long period of time on a substrate would give improved performance over an unadapted inoculum.

Factors Limiting Kinetics

Process kinetics reflected as CH_4 production rate are important to design and operation of anaerobic digesters since rapid rates permit higher loadings or smaller reactor size. A number of mathematical models have been developed to predict kinetics of various digester designs (Chen and Srivastava, 1987).

Most of these are based on the Monod model for continuous culture of bacteria. Representative CH_4 production rates for various feeds and operating conditions range typically from 0.5 to 5 vol vol^{-1} of active reactor per d for particulate feeds to over 10 vol vol^{-1} d^{-1} for soluble feeds. In general, higher rates result in reduced CH_4 yields. Rates of most CSTR digesters with low hydraulic retention times are limited by the activity of methanogenic bacteria. Adjustment of design or operation to remove this limitation may result in a hydrolysis-limited system. Major factors affecting the kinetics of the anaerobic digestion process are feed concentration, temperature, nutrients, mixing, particle size, toxic feed components, and feeding frequency.

Reactor Options

Development and design of new and innovative digestion schemes should have the goals of maximizing CH_4 yields and optimizing production rates, increasing process stability, decreasing processing energy requirements, and decreasing processing energy requirements, and decreasing digester costs through simplification of design and operation. From the previous discussion it can be surmised that optimization of yields can be best achieved through selection of biodegradable feeds, pretreatment, and development and optimization of inoculum. Optimum process kinetics without sacrifice in yields may be achieved by schemes with long retention of microorganisms and solids, thermophilic temperature, minimum particle size, non-limiting nutrient levels, continuous feeding, and absence of toxic feed components.

Optimization of anaerobic digestion for high yields and rates may not be consistent with obtaining the highest net energy output and best economics. For example, higher temperatures, particle size reduction, and heat pretreatment are all factors that may increase yields and rates, but may result in overall reduction in net output process energy and increased process cost.

It is becoming apparent that in most applications the conventional stirred tank reactor is not the optimum configuration for anaerobic digestion. Limitations of this reactor include: 1) washout of unreacted solids and active microorganisms at higher loadings, 2) difficulty in achieving complete mixing, 3) energy requirements associated with mixing, and 4) disruption of microbial consortia by mixing. Several innovative digester configurations are under development with the objectives of increasing CH_4 yields and production rates, increasing process stability and net energy output, and simplifying design and operation and improving economics.

No single reactor design or set of operating conditions is suitable for all applications. Major factors influencing design and operating conditions include:

- Chemical characteristics of feed
- Concentration of feed biodegradable matter

. Concentration of feed particulate solids
. Density of raw and digested feed
. Scale of application
. Continuity of feed availability
. Desired product (methane yield or VS reduction)

The major criterion for selection of reactor design is feed particulate solids concentration (Table 2). For soluble feeds such as hyacinth juice, attached film reactors are most suitable because of high retention of microorganisms and high rates at low temperatures (reduced energy requirements for heating water in such feeds). Feeds with low concentrations of particulate solids require reactors which have longer solids retention than liquid retention in order to conserve microorganisms and feed solids at high loadings. Reactors that accomplish this are the CSTR with solids recycle and non-mixed reactors which convert solids via passive settling or flotation. Digestion of high solids feeds requires reactors which minimize water addition and reduce mass transport problems related to transport of substrates to and products away from the sphere of influence of the bacteria. Thermophilic occasionally-stirred reactor and two-phase leaching bed attached film reactor are options for these types of feeds. These reactor configurations are illustrated in Figure 4.

Approach to Anaerobic Digestion Process Development

A systematic approach for determination of the suitability of a feedstock for anaerobic digestion and development of the optimum process design and operating conditions is outlined in Table 3. Proximate and ultimate analyses are conducted to establish theoretical yields, energy content, nutrient levels, and solids, water, and ash content. Feeds are subject to an anaerobic

TABLE 2. Reactor options for biomass conversion.

Biomass type	Example	Reactor options
Soluble (<2% solids)	Water hyacinth juice	Anaerobic filter Fluidized bed Expanded bed Upflow anaerobic sludge blanket
Low solids (2-10% solids)	Whole water hyacinth	CSTR with solids recycle non-mixed vertical flow reactor
High solids (>10% solids)	Hyacinth solids	CSTR Leaching bed Attached film reactor

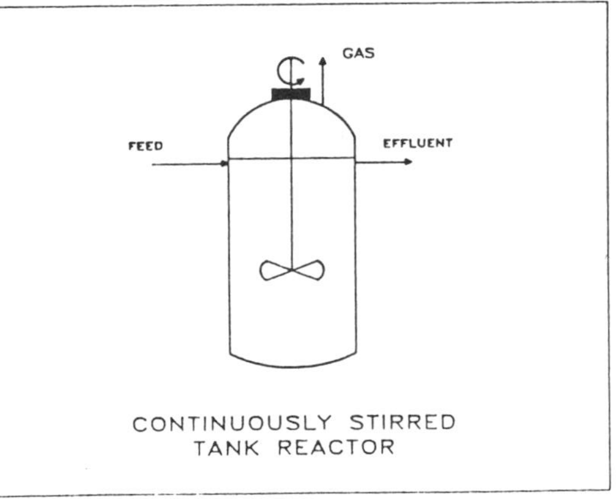

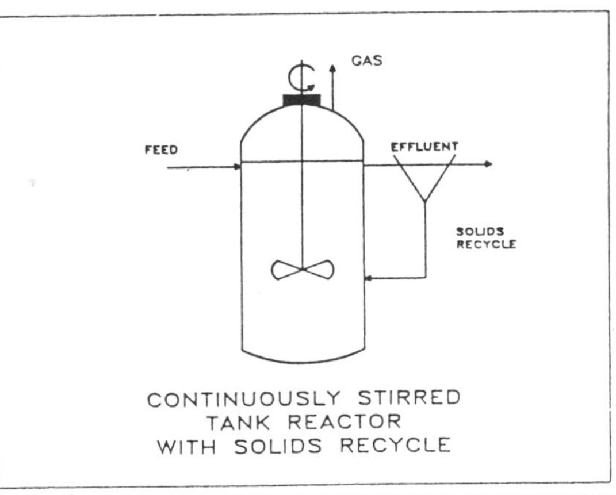

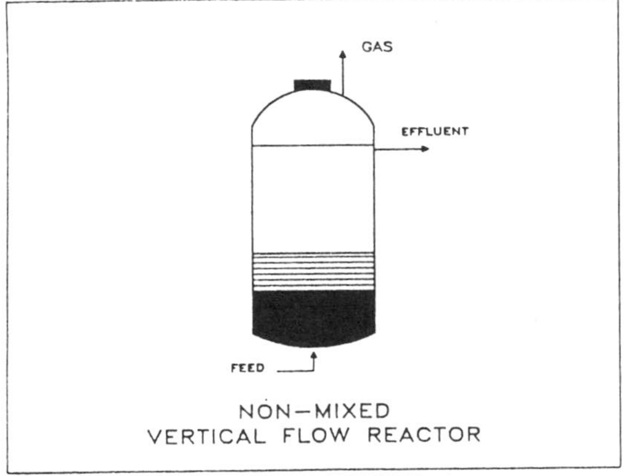

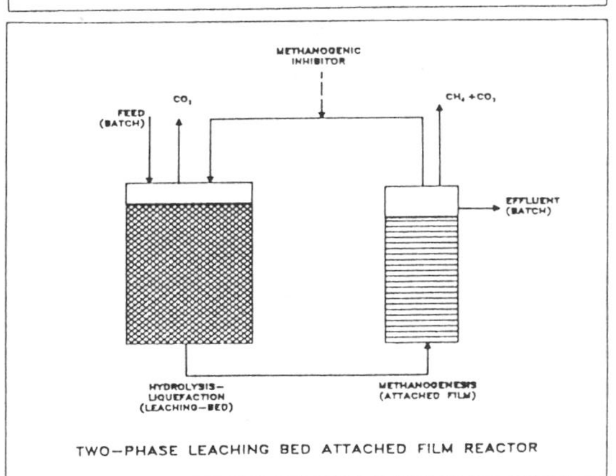

FIGURE 4. Reactor configurations for anaerobic digestion.

TABLE 3. Approach to anaerobic digestion process development.

Chemical and physical feed analysis
Anaerobic biogasification potential
- feed variation
- process variable evaluation
- pretreatment
Bench-scale process development
- conventional CSTR
- unconventional
- model development
Automated data acquisition and process control
Process scale-up
- experimental test unit (ETU)
- demonstration
Microbial support studies

biogasification potential (ABP) assay (Owens et al., 1979) to determine ultimate biodegradability and relative rates. The assay may be employed to estimate inter- and intra-species variability, effects of pretreatment options on biodegradability, and presence of toxic feed components.

Conventional CSTR digester kinetic experiments are conducted to serve as a baseline for comparison of advanced digester designs. Feed composition, ABP data, and total system considerations are employed to select one or more advanced digester designs for evaluation. Related to this bench-scale testing is input of data into various models ranging from those that predict overall performance to detailed research-level models. A preliminary systems analysis is employed to determine if process scale-up is warranted. The next step is design, construction and operation of a pilot-scale system large enough to evaluate feed processing and materials flow through the digester. This reactor along with other components of the systems provide data for a decision to proceed to the demonstration and/or commercial scale.

PROCESS EVALUATION AND DEVELOPMENT FOR AQUATIC PLANTS

Feed Properties

The chemical and physical properties of several biomass/waste feedstocks (Table 4) with significant differences in solids content require different reactor types be employed for these feeds. In general, aquatic feeds may be lumped into a category containing low concentrations of suspended solids. These data also show that wide differences in C/N and C/P occur amongst

TABLE 4. Characteristics of prototype biomass feeds (Chynoweth et al., 1983; Fannin et al., 1986).

	Hyacinth	Sludge	Kelp	Sorghum	Poplar
Total solids, %	4.2	4.8	12	34	87
Volatile solids, % TS	82	95	60	92	99
C/N	13	13	14	84	145
C/P	55	84	96	700	988
Stoichiometric yield, L g^{-1} VS added	0.54	0.69	0.53	0.47	0.53
Ultimate methane yield, L g^{-1} VS added	0.33	0.64	0.43	0.40	0.31

species. However, for Macrocystis (Table 5), the C/N ratio and content of organic matter (e.g. mannitol) may vary with growth conditions. When these ratios are high (greater than 15 and 75, respectively), they can significantly reduce the rate and stability of the fermentation (Chynoweth et al., 1981). Reactor design and operation options can overcome or reduce these limitations. Results of ABP assays of several biomass species (Jerger and Tsao, 1987) show that wide interspecies differences in yields and rates may be attributed to differences in organic makeup (Figure 5, Table 4). Note that the ABP yield is always lower than the theoretical yield, indicating that a fraction of the organic matter is refractory to anaerobic degradation. Intraspecies variability in biodegradability is illustrated in Figure 6. Two samples of hyacinth harvested from secondary and tertiary ponds exhibited similar rates but different yields. The biodegradability of different plant parts may influence harvesting methods. Yields and rates of conversion of hyacinth roots and shoots were similar (Chynoweth et al., 1983). Biomass may be

TABLE 5. C-to-N ratios and mannitol concentrations of different lots of Macrocystis pyrifera (Fannin et al., 1981; Fannin et al., 1982; Fannin et al., 1983).

Lot. No.	C/N	Mannitol, % dry wt.
47	14.9	5.18
48	13.4	9.06
49	32.7	23.9
50	14.7	8.27
53	14.9	21.4
54	11.7	15.4
59	17.4	18.7

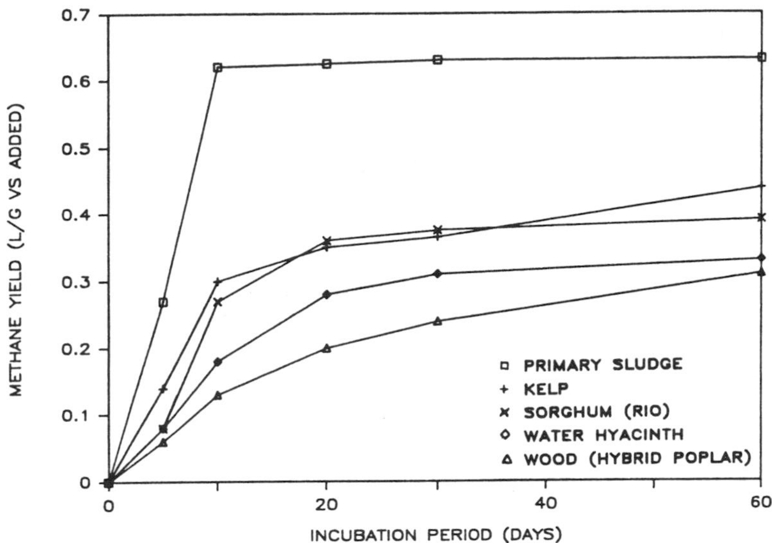

FIGURE 5. Biogasification of prototype biomass feedstocks (Jerger and Tsao, 1987).

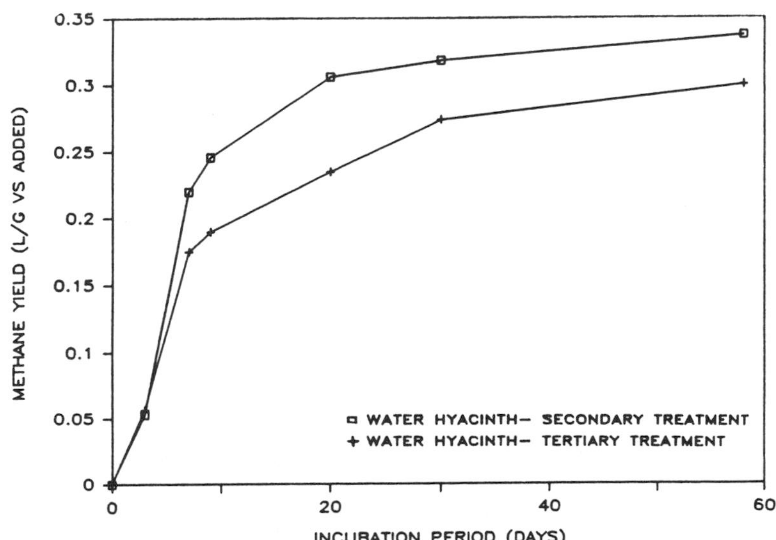

FIGURE 6. Comparison of CH_4 yields from water hyacinth used for secondary and tertiary wastewater treatment (ABP Assay) (Chynoweth et al., 1983).

pretreated to improve biodegradability. Of three methods tested, only alkaline pretreatment increased biodegradability of hyacinth (Table 6). In general, this and other types of pretreatment are not economic for overall systems for production of CH_4 from biomass.

The ABP assay may also be employed to evaluate the affects of applied pesticides on biomass conversion. Kelthane (employed for pest control on hyacinth) is inhibitory (Figure 7) to the CH_4 fermentation, however the organisms showed evidence of acclimation to the inhibitory concentration tested after about 20 d.

TABLE 6. Effect of pretreatment on the anaerobic biogasification potential of water hyacinth (Chynoweth et al., 1983).†

Treatment	Methane yield, L g⁻VS added		
	Control	Experimental	% increase
Particle size reduction			
(wet ball milling to 3 μm)	0.33	0.31	0
Steam (30 min. 690 kPa, 164°)	0.32	0.32	0
Sodium hydroxide			
5% of VS, 35°C, 72 h	0.32	0.32	2
50% of VS, 35°C, 24 h	0.32	0.36	15

†All data based on 60-d ABP assay.

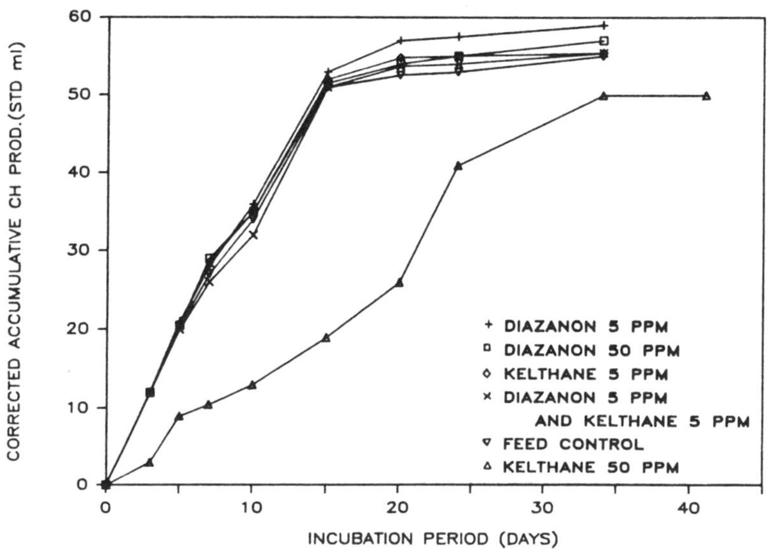

FIGURE 7. Effect of pesticides (diazanon and kelthane) on the biogasification potential of water hyacinth (Biljetina et al., 1986).

Bench-Scale Process Development

Performance of a conventional CSTR digester receiving low solids feeds typical of aquatic biomass deteriorates at loadings below those that would be economic for a commercial process (Chynoweth et al., 1982). Factors causing this reduced performance were listed above.

In order to overcome these limitations, the non-mixed vertical flow reactor (NMVFR) was developed and evaluated initially for digestion of kelp (Fannin et al., 1983). This reactor (Figure 4) is non-mixed and solids are concentrated either by passive settling or enhanced solids flotation. In either mode of operation, feed solids and organisms are concentrated resulting in an approximate 3-fold higher solids than hydraulic residence time. The improved performance of this reactor over the CSTR for conversion of hyacinth/sludge blend is illustrated in plots of CH_4 yield and CH_4 production rate versus loading (Figures 8 and 9) (Biljetina et al., 1987).

Separate digestion of juice and solids provides the potential for further improvement of conversion of high moisture feedstocks. In this process, juice (containing 20% of the organic matter) is separated from the solids and digested in an ambient temperature attached film digester. The solids are digested in a two-phase

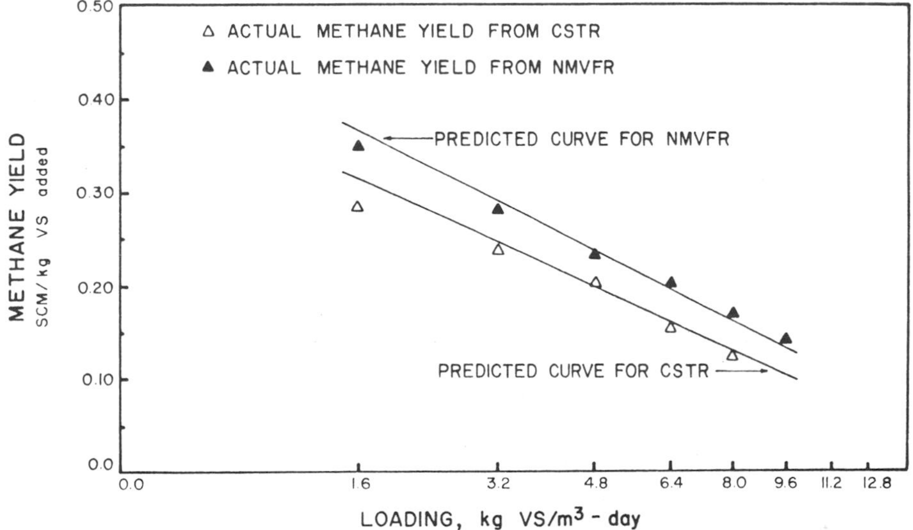

FIGURE 8. Comparison of CH_4 yields in terms of loading for 3:1 blend in NMVFR and CSTR using first order kinetic model (Biljetina et al., 1986).

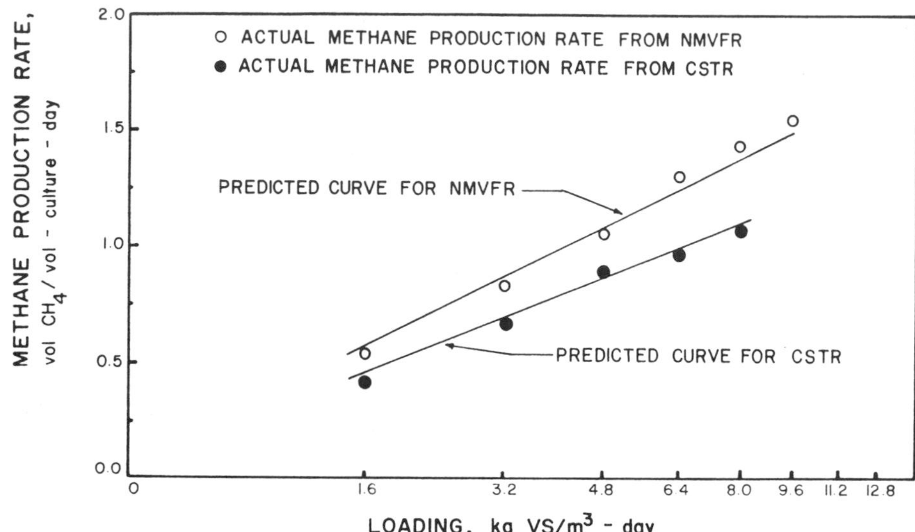

FIGURE 9. Comparison of CH_4 production rate in terms of loading for 3:1 blend in NMVFR and CSTR using first order kinetic model (Biljetina, 1986).

leaching bed attached film digester using the same attached film digester used for juice conversion. This process has the following advantages over the NMVFR:

- Highly reactive high water content juice can be digested in a low residence time ambient temperature attached film reactor
- Ambient temperature digestion of juice eliminates major process energy requirement
- Lowly reactive low water solids can be digested in a high residence time heated digester

Juice and solids fractions of hyacinth exhibited significant differences in reactivity (Figure 10); they accounted for 20% and 80%, respectively, of the potential CH_4 yield from hyacinth (Chynoweth et al., 1983). Experiments to evaluate separate digestion of juice and solids are in progress at the bench scale.

Process Scaleup

Pilot-scale testing of a conversion process that seems feasible at the bench-scale is essential to prevent costly errors in design at the demonstration or commercial scales. The objectives of pilot-scale units are:

- verification of laboratory observations
- testing of selected feed processing and digester configurations

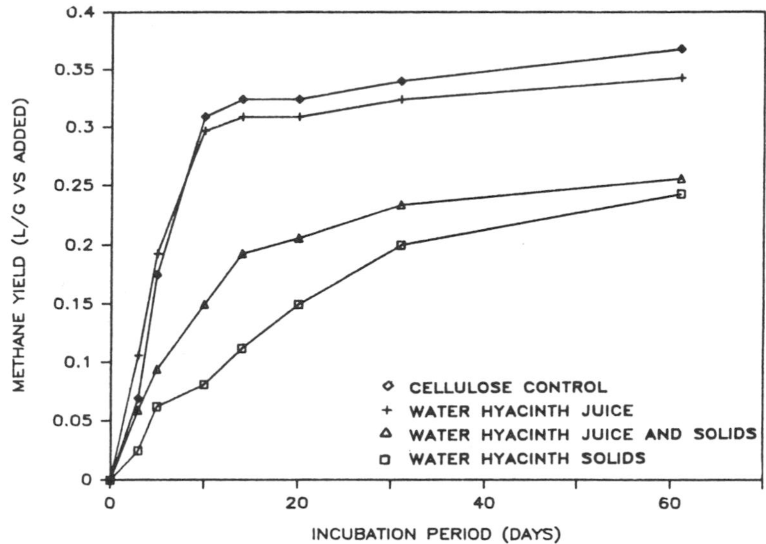

FIGURE 10. Anaerobic biogasification potential of hyacinth juice, solids, and reconstituted plants (Fannin et al., 1986).

- field-scale evaluation of physical, chemical, and biological unit operations
- determination of analytical and process control requirements
- compilation of preliminary information on maintenance and operating problems, equipment safety, and scale-up effects
- obtain a valid data base for systems and economic analysis

Such a pilot-scale digester was designed, constructed, and is in operation at Walt Disney World Resort Complex to test the commercial feasibility of the non-mixed vertical flow reactor for digestion of hyacinth/sludge (Biljetina et al., 1987). The performance of this 4 m^3 digester has been successful (Table 7). The improved performance can be attributed in increased solids residence time resulting from solids concentration achieved by downflow feeding and enhanced flotation of solids. This digester system is ready for further scaleup. The advantages of this solids concentrating reactor (SOLCON) are: 1) higher conversion efficiency; 2) higher CH_4 yield and production rate; 3) smaller digester volume; 4) more stable performance; and 5) higher net energy (no mixing). Details of its operation and performance are described elsewhere in this book (Biljetina et al., 1987).

Engineering Analysis

Evaluation of process energy requirements is critical to selection of digester designs and operating conditions.

TABLE 7. Comparison of performance of ETU (non-mixed vertical flow reactor) and conventional CSTR digesters receiving hyacinth-sludge blend (1:1 dry solids basis)† (Biljetina et al., 1987).

	CSTR	ETU
Culture volume, m^3	0.05	3.9
Hydraulic residence time, d	11	11
Solids residence time, d	11	30
Methane yield $m^3\ kg^{-1}$ organic added	0.40	0.45
Methane production rate vol. CH_4 vol^{-1} reactor-d	1.3	1.4
Methane conc. vol. %	63	64

†Temperature, 35°C; feed solids conc., 3.8%; organic loading, 3.2 kg m^{-3} d.

Conventional digesters can require 50% or more of the product energy for operation. Although such an analysis is highly site specific, a general assessment reported by Ghosh (1981) indicated that the major process requirement (Table 8) is feed heating. This factor is quite significant for high moisture feeds such as aquatic species. The most effective steps in reducing process energy requirements are to: 1) decrease feed water content; 2) decrease digester operation temperature; 3) increase ambient temperature; 4) minimize heat loss; and 5) employ heat exchange.

TABLE 8. Energy requirements for conventional anaerobic digestion† (Ghosh, 1981).

Component	% of product energy required
Feed heating	22-25
Heat loss	7-8
Mixing and pumping	2-3
Misc. utilities	2-3
Total	33-39

†Mesophilic, 35°C; CSTR loading, 1.6 kg m^{-3} d^{-1}; feed solids conc., 5% CH_4 yield, 0.31 $m^3\ kg^{-1}$ VS; feed temp., 15°C; ambient temp., -8°C and 3°C, air and ground temps. respectively, no heat exchange assumed.

A summary of the economics of anaerobic digestion employing the SOLCON process in an overall hyacinth wastewater treatment scheme is summarized in Table 9. The anaerobic digestion operation represents only 12% of the capitol cost and 3% of the operating cost of the total system. High costs associated with feed production and harvesting and sludge disposal suggest that emphasis should be placed on high conversion yields rather than high conversion rates.

TABLE 9. Capital and O&M costs for the major components of an integrated water hyacinth/anaerobic digestion facility for a 500,000 population (Hayes et al., 1987).

Systems component	Costs (1985 $10 million)	
	Capitol	Annual O&M
Wastewater	11.9	1.0
Water hyacinth harvesting	4.1	0.9
Anaerobic digestion	2.8	0.2
Sludge disposal	3.9	0.3
Gas cleanup	1.3	0.3
Total	24.0	2.7

CONCLUSIONS

Anaerobic digestion conversion to CH_4 is one of the more attractive conversion options for utilization of aquatic biomass. This is related to the ability of this process to economically process high-moisture feeds, lack of requirement for pretreatment, pure culture maintenance, ease of product separation, and wide use for product. Attractive reactor designs include one that concentrates solids and microorganisms and another that involves separate digestion of juice and solids.

Following is an outline of research needs for anaerobic digestion of this class of feedstocks:

- Evaluation of new species
- Determination of compositional characteristics influencing biodegradability
- Determination of effects of growth and harvest conditions on composition
- Advanced digestion development
    - Reactor design and optimization
    - Modeling
    - Process evaluation
    - Automated data acquisition and process control
    - Microbial community structure

ACKNOWLEDGMENTS

The author wishes to acknowledge the Gas Research Institute for research contracts to the Institute of Gas Technology and University of Florida which led to concepts and data presented in this paper.

REFERENCES

Biljetina, R., V. J. Srivastava, D. P. Chynoweth, and T. D. Hayes. 1987. Anaerobic digestion of water hyacinth and sludge. In K. R. Reddy and W. H. Smith (ed.) Aquatic Plants for Water Treatment and Resource Recovery, Magnolia Publishing Inc., Orlando, FL.

Biljetina, R., D. P. Chynoweth, V. J. Srivastava, J. A. Janulis, A. Razik, and S. Smallwood. 1986. Biogasification of Walt Disney World Biomass Waste Blend. Final Report for GRI Contract 5082-223-0567 to IGT.

Boone, D. R., and R. A. Mah. 1987. Transitional bacteria. In D. P. Chynoweth and H. R. Isaacson (ed.) Anaerobic Digestion of Biomass, Elsevier Applied Science Publishers, Ltd., London. (in press).

Bryant, M. P., E. A. Wolin, M. J. Wolin, and R. S. Wolfe. 1967. *Methanobacillus omelianskii*, a symbiotic association of two species of bacteria. Arch. Mikrobiol. 59:20-31.

Chen, Y. R., and V. J. Srivastava. 1987. Kinetics and modeling. In D. P. Chynoweth and H. R. Isaacson (ed.) Anaerobic Digestion of Biomass. Elsevier Applied Science Publishers, Ltd., London. (in press).

Chynoweth, D. P. 1981. Microbial conversion of biomass to methane. Proc. of the Eighth Ann. Energy Tech. Conf., Washington, DC. pp. 1281-1305.

Chynoweth, D. P., S. Ghosh, and D. L. Klass. 1981. Anaerobic digestion of kelp. p. 315-338. In O. R. Zaborsky and S. Sofer (ed.) Biomass Conversion Processes for Energy and Fuels, Chapter 18. Plenum Press, New York.

Chynoweth, D. P., S. Ghosh, M. P. Henry, and V. J. Srivastava. 1982. Kinetics and advanced digester design of water hyacinth and primary sludge. In Biotech. Bioeng. Symp. No. 12. pp. 381-398.

Chynoweth, D. P., D. E. Jerger, J. R. Conrad, A. Razik, V. Srivastava, S. Ghosh, M. P. Henry, and S. P. Babu. 1983. Gasification of land-based biomass. IGT Project No. 30564 Final Report, Chicago.

Chynoweth, D. P., and H. R. Isaacson (ed.). 1987. Anaerobic digestion of biomass. Elsevier Appl. Sci. Publ., Ltd., London. (in press).

Fannin, K. F., V. J. Srivastava, and D. P. Chynoweth. 1983. Unconventional anaerobic digester designs for improving methane yields from sea kelp. In Symposium Papers: Energy from Biomass and Wastes IV, sponsored by Institute of Gas Technology, Lake Buena Vista, FL.

Fannin, K. F., V. J. Srivastava, J. R. Conrad, and D. P. Chynoweth. 1981. Marine biomass program: Anaerobic digester systems development. IGT Project 65044 Annual Report, Chicago.

Fannin, K. F., V. J. Srivastava, J. D. Mensinger, and D. P. Chynoweth. 1983. Marine biomass program: Anaerobic digestion systems development and stability study. IGT Project No. 30558. Final Report for Gas Research Institute, GRI Contract 5083-226-0773 to IGT.

Fannin, K. F., V. J. Srivastava, J. Menisinger. J. R. Conrad, and D. P. Chynoweth. 1982. Marine biomass program: Anaerobic digester systems development. IGT Projects 65044 and 30547 Final Reports, Chicago.

Fannin, K. F., V. J. Srivastava, D. P. Chynoweth, D. E. Jerger, J. R. Conrad, and J. D. Mensinger. 1986. Biological gasification of renewable resources. Final Report for GRI Contract 5083-226-0773 to IGT.

Ghosh, S. 1981. Net energy production in anaerobic digestion. Paper presented at Energy from Biomass and Wastes V, Institute of Gas Technology, Orlando, Florida.

Handley, L. L., L. S. Carey, J. L. Lopez, J. M. Sutja, H. T. Abdel-Shafy, and S. B. Colley. 1986. Gravel bed hydroponics for wastewater renovation and biomass production. p. 287-302. In W. H. Smith (ed.) Biomass Energy Development. Plenum Press, New York.

Hayes, T. D., H. R. Isaacson, K. R. Reddy, D. P. Chynoweth, and R. Biljetina. 1987. Water hyacinth systems for water treatment. In K. R. Reddy and W. H. Smith (ed.) Aquatic Plants for Water Treatment and Resource Recovery, Magnolia Publishing Inc., Orlando, FL.

Jerger, D. E., and G. T. Tsao. 1987. Feed composition. In D. P. Chynoweth and H. R. Isaacson (ed.) Anaerobic Digestion of Biomass. Elsevier Applied Science Publishers, Ltd., London. (in press).

Jewell, W. J., J. J. Madras, W. W. Clarkson, H. DeLancey-Pompe, and M. Kabrick. 1983. Wastewater treatment with plants in nutrient films. Final Report to U.S. EPA.

Lakshman, G. Biomass utilization options. 1987. In K. R. Reddy and W. H. Smith (ed.) Aquatic Plants for Water Treatment and Resource Recovery. Magnolia Publishing Inc., Orlando, FL.

Owens, W. F., D. C. Stuckey, L. Y. Healy, Jr., J. B. Young, and P. L. McCarty. 1979. Bioassay for monitoring biochemical methane potential and anaerobic toxicity. Water Research 13:485-492.

Reddy, K. R., and W. F. DeBusk. 1984. Growth characteristics of aquatic macrophytes cultured in nutrient-enriched water. I. Water hyacinth, water lettuce, and pennywort. Econ. Bot. 38:225-235.

Reddy, K. R., and W. F. DeBusk. 1985. Growth characteristics of aquatic macrophytes cultured in nutrient-enriched water. II. Azolla, duckweed, and salvinia. Econ. Bot. 38:200-208.

Reed, S., R. Bastian, and W. Jewell. 1980. Engineering assessment of aquaculture systems for wastewater treatment: An overview. In Aquaculture Systems for Wastewater Treatment/MCD-68, General Services Administration, Denver, CO. Document No. EPA 430/9-80-007, p. 1.

Tchobanoglous, G., R. Stowell, R. Ludwig, J. Colt, and A. Knight. 1979. The use of aquatic plants and animals for the treatment of wastewater: An overview. In Aquaculture Systems for Wastewater Treatment/MCD 67. General Services Administration, Denver, CO, Document No. EPA 430/9-80-006, p. 35.

WASTEWATER TREATMENT USING FLOATING AQUATIC MACROPHYTES: CONTAMINANT REMOVAL PROCESSES AND MANAGEMENT STRATEGIES

T. A. DeBusk
Reedy Creek Utilities Co., Inc.
P. O. Box 40
Lake Buena Vista, Florida 32830

K. R. Reddy
Central Florida Research and Education Center
University of Florida, IFAS
Sanford, Florida 32771

ABSTRACT

Shallow ponds containing the floating aquatic macrophytes water hyacinth, pennywort and water lettuce are gaining widespread use for removing contaminants from wastewaters. This paper presents some of the optimization techniques for floating aquatic macrophyte (FAM) treatment systems which affect both cost and efficiency of contaminant removal. In unmanaged FAM systems, N is removed from wastewater by plant uptake, microbial immobilization, and nitrification-denitrification reactions. Suspended solids are removed by settling, and organic matter (BOD_5) is oxidized by bacteria present in the root zone, water column and sediment. Phosphorus removal fluctuates with plant growth, senescence and decomposition, as well as with microbial immobilization and chemical precipitation. Plant harvest, a management practice common to many FAM systems used for domestic wastewater treatment, is requisite for P removal and may improve N and BOD_5 removal. Removal of heavy metals from wastewaters can also be accomplished when plants are harvested. Although provisions for biomass utilization or disposal are required in harvested FAM systems, operating costs for crop management and harvest may be offset in part by product revenues. Other FAM system management practices which may be implemented to maximize pollutant removal include: 1) manipulation of the pond environment (e.g., with aeration, recirculation) to increase chemical, biological, or physical contaminant-removing processes; 2) increasing warm-season plant yields/contaminant removal (e.g., by utilizing foliar applications of nutrients and plant growth hormones); and 3) increasing cool-

Aquatic Plants for Water Treatment
and Resource Recovery
K.R. Reddy and W.H. Smith (Eds.)

ISBN 0-941463-00-1

season plant yields/contaminant removal (by the use of polyculture systems, sprinklers, or enclosures). In temperate and subtropical locations where effluent quality requirements do not vary seasonally, area requirements of FAM systems will be dictated by wintertime performance. Hence, the optimization of cool-season contaminant removal should be the primary management goal for such systems.

Keywords: Aquaculture, nitrogen processes, carbon processes, harvesting frequency, optimization.

INTRODUCTION

The use of aquatic macrophytes for treating wastewaters has been the subject of considerable research during the past two decades. Engineering analyses have shown that, in some locations, the cost of secondary and advanced domestic wastewater treatment can be reduced by utilizing aquatic macrophyte-based systems rather than conventional treatment methods (Duffer, 1982). Although emergent and submersed plants have been examined for use in aquatic macrophyte systems, floating macrophytes (e.g., water hyacinth) are the plants most commonly used for wastewater treatment in warm climates.

Factors which contribute to the popularity of floating macrophytes for wastewater treatment applications include: 1) the high productivity of several of the large-leaved floating plants (Reddy and DeBusk, 1984); 2) the ease with which floating plants can be stocked and harvested; and 3) the high nutritive value of floating plants relative to that of many emergent species (Boyd, 1974).

Floating aquatic macrophytes are typically cultured in shallow ponds or raceways through which wastewater is passed with a long retention time. Floating plants are stocked in the ponds and, in some systems, are periodically harvested in order to maintain a young, viable crop. Unfortunately, the apparent simplicity of design and operation of floating aquatic macrophyte-based systems (FAMS) has obviated for many wastewater engineers the need for research on system optimization. This problem is exacerbated by the fact that even a poorly designed FAM system can satisfactorily remove many wastewater contaminants. However, the mechanisms for contaminant removal in these systems may be complex, involving physiological characteristics of the plants and biological and physicochemical reactions in the pond environment (Reddy, 1983). Consequently, even though FAMS have been utilized for wastewater treatment for at least two decades, techniques for optimizing contaminant removal have not been developed.

In this paper we describe some of the mechanisms by which wastewater contaminants are removed, and we discuss management practices which can be implemented in order to maximize treatment efficiency in FAM systems.

PLANT SELECTION

Plant Growth Characteristics

Water hyacinth (Eichhornia crassipes), water lettuce (Pistia stratiotes), and pennywort (Hydrocotyle umbellata) are productive, large-leaved floating macrophytes which exhibit mean annual growth rates in excess of 10 g m^{-2} d^{-1} in central Florida (Reddy and DeBusk, 1984). These species are capable of assimilating large quantities of nutrients during periods of rapid growth. Growth rates are dependent on environmental factors such as temperature, solar radiation, and nutrient availability, as well as competition for resources (e.g., light, and nutrients) among plants within the floating mat (Center and Spencer, 1981).

Nutrient uptake by aquatic macrophytes is a function of both productivity and tissue nutrient concentration of the plants. Typically, productivity is highest and tissue nutrient concentrations are lowest during warm periods of the year (Tucker and DeBusk, 1981). In wastewaters of domestic origin, plant tissue nutrient concentrations vary seasonally by only about 30%, whereas productivity may vary by an order of magnitude during the year. Productivity, therefore, is the primary factor dictating nutrient uptake rates in high-nutrient wastewaters. For plants cultured in wastewaters of inconsistent flow or composition, such as agricultural drainage water, plant tissue concentrations may vary by as much as 400% and can thus be of equal importance to productivity in determining nutrient uptake rates.

Nutrient uptake rates vary among floating species due to interspecific differences in productivity and elemental composition. During the summer in central Florida, productivity and nutrient uptake of the three large-leaved floating macrophytes decreases in the order: water hyacinth, water lettuce, and pennywort (Table 1) (Reddy and DeBusk, 1985). Although rates of N and P uptake by water hyacinth and water lettuce drop sharply during the winter, nutrient uptake by pennywort is approximately the same during both warm and cool seasons. Among the three species, N and P uptake during the winter months is greatest by pennywort (Table 1).

TABLE 1. Nitrogen and phosphorus uptake by floating aquatic macrophytes during summer and winter in central Florida (Reddy and DeBusk, 1985).

Plant	Nitrogen		Phosphorus	
	Summer	Winter	Summer	Winter
	uptake, g m^{-2} d^{-1}			
Water hyacinth	1.30	0.25	0.24	0.05
Water lettuce	0.99	0.26	0.22	0.07
Pennywort	0.37	0.37	0.09	0.08

Recent studies have shown that productivity of floating macrophytes is strongly influenced by plant standing crop, with high yields (and rapid nutrient uptake) occurring only when the plants are maintained within a certain density range (DeBusk et al., 1981; Reddy and DeBusk, 1984). If the standing crop biomass exceeds the optimum range for growth (i.e., 0.5-2.0, 0.25-0.65, and 0.2-0.7 kg m^{-2} for water hyacinth, pennywort and water lettuce, respectively), new tissue synthesis serves merely to replace senescing or decaying plant material, and no net increase in plant biomass (or nutrient uptake) occurs. Floating macrophytes can be maintained at an optimum standing crop for growth by periodic harvesting.

Plant Detritus

In FAM-based wastewater treatment systems, old or senescing plant tissues are continuously sloughed from the floating mat. The quantity of such tissues produced, and the rate at which they decompose, are important both to sedimentation and nutrient cycling within the FAM system. The water hyacinth is the only floating macrophyte for which measurements of detritus production and decomposition in wastewater treatment systems have been conducted. In a harvested water hyacinth system used for advanced domestic wastewater treatment, sediment was estimated to accrue at a rate of 1.2 cm yr^{-1} (T. A. DeBusk and F. E. Dierberg, unpublished), and N and P accumulated in the sediment at rates of 11 and 1 mg m^{-2} d^{-1}, respectively (DeBusk et al., 1983). When plant harvest was not practiced, the dry matter sedimentation rate and sediment N and P accrual rates increased by about 50%.

Even under non-harvested conditions, the rate at which water hyacinth-derived sediment accumulates is slow. This is largely due to the labile nature of the tissues when the plants are cultured in a high-nutrient medium such as domestic wastewater. Losses of dry matter, N and P from decomposing aerial tissue of water hyacinth in secondary domestic effluent are shown in Table 2. Water lettuce and pennywort are similar to the water hyacinth in tissue composition (Reddy and DeBusk, 1985), so it is likely that sediment buildup and immobilization of nutrients beneath stands of these species is also slow.

CONTAMINANT REMOVAL PROCESSES

Carbon

Organic carbon in wastewaters, which is typically measured as five day biochemical oxygen demand (BOD_5), is utilized by bacteria in FAM systems as an energy source and for cell synthesis. These bacteria inhabit microenvironments in the sediment, the plant root zone, and may also be dispersed throughout the water column. Aerobic bacteria utilize O_2 as an

TABLE 2. Loss of dry matter, N and P from decomposing water hyacinth tissues (rhizomes, stolons, petioles and laminae) incubated in secondary domestic wastewater (DeBusk et al., 1983).

Time	Dry wt. remaining	Observed wt. of N as % of initial wt.	Observed wt. of P as % of initial wt.
days		%	
0	100.0	100.0	100.0
7	26.0	19.9	5.9
14	15.3	12.9	3.5
28	5.0	2.9	0.9
49	3.0	1.7	0.6
77	4.0	2.1	0.8
120	1.1	0.9	0.4

electron acceptor in the breakdown of substrate C, whereas facultative anaerobic bacteria utilize oxidized inorganic compounds such as NO_3 and SO_4 as electron acceptors. Our recent studies have shown that electron acceptor availability is often the factor limiting organic C removal in FAM systems used for secondary wastewater treatment (Reddy and DeBusk, unpublished).

Previous studies have shown that dense mats of floating plants can reduce O_2 concentrations in the water column (Reddy et al., 1983). Although diffusion is indeed inhibited by the presence of a floating plant mat, the plants themselves contribute O_2 to the water column via transport through the leaves, stems, and roots. Oxygen thus transported, if not consumed during root respiration, can enter the water column and be utilized by aerobic bacteria for the oxidation of organic C. Little is known of this O_2 "pumping" process by plants, although recent research has shown that common floating macrophytes differ in their ability to oxidize their rhizosphere. Pennywort, for example, transports O_2 2.5 times as rapidly (per unit weight of root tissue) as water hyacinth, which in turn transports O_2 four times more rapidly than water lettuce (Table 3).

Oxygen can also be supplied to the wastewater by mechanical aeration. However, the shallow depths of most floating aquatic

TABLE 3. Oxygen transport by three floating macrophytes (Moorhead and Reddy, 1986).

Plant	O_2 transport†
	mg O_2 g^{-1} h^{-1}
Pennywort	3.5 ± 1.8
Water hyacinth	1.2 ± 1.2
Water lettuce	0.3 ± 0.1

†O_2 transport per g of root tissue per unit time, x, s.d.

macrophyte-based treatment systems may preclude the development of cost-effective aeration practices. It is likely that wastewater pretreatment, or increased detention time in conventional activated-sludge aeration chambers, would be the most effective means of removing carbonaceous or nitrogenous BOD_5 (i.e., nitrification enhancement) in the wastewater prior to its introduction into the FAM system.

Nitrogen and Phosphorus

Although large quantities of N can be removed by plant uptake and harvest, nitrification-denitrification reactions are more often the dominant N sink in FAM systems (Stowell et al., 1981; DeBusk et al., 1983). Nitrification of wastewater ammonium can occur in the oxidized root zone of floating macrophytes systems. This nitrification process may be enhanced beneath stands of plants which transport large quantities of O_2, such as pennywort. Nitrate-N, thus formed, diffuses into reduced microenvironments in the pond system, where it is utilized as an electron acceptor by facultative anaerobic bacteria and lost from the system as nitrogen gas. Both native wastewater C and plant detritus can be utilized by these bacteria as a C source. Denitrification rates in excess of 1 g m^{-2} d^{-1} have been reported in FAM systems (Stowell et al., 1981).

Losses of N from FAM systems via ammonia volatilization, a process common in ponds containing rapidly photosynthesizing submersed plants, are probably slight (Reddy, 1983). The dense plant mats formed by most floating macrophytes block light penetration into the water column, thereby limiting photosynthesis of submersed macrophytes or microalgae. Consequently, the wastewater pH in (domestic) FAM systems remains close to neutral, and wastewater ammonium is present primarily in the non-volatile, ionized (NH_4^+) form.

Phosphorus can be removed from the wastewater in FAM systems by microbial assimilation, precipitation with divalent and trivalent cations, or adsorption onto clays or organic matter. However, most studies of FAM systems have shown that plant uptake and harvest is the only reliable long-term P-removal mechanism.

Both N and P can also be temporarily immobilized in plant detritus which accumulates as sediment in FAM systems. However, due to the labile nature of most floating species, most of the N and P contained in the sloughed plant tissues is quickly mineralized (Table 2).

MANAGEMENT STRATEGIES

The goals of FAM management are to improve system reliability and to reduce capital (e.g., land) and operating (energy consumption) costs. These goals can be best accomplished by evaluating, and then optimizing the mechanisms which influence contaminant removal in FAM systems. A thorough appraisal of FAM capabilities, as well as of external factors such as land costs and climate, will lead to the successful implementation of FAMS as a secondary or advanced wastewater treatment process (Figure 1).

Domestic Wastewater: Carbon Removal

Loading Rate. BOD_5 loading rates ranging from 56 to 560 kg ha^{-1} d^{-1} have been tested in FAM systems. In a recent review, Stowell et al. (1981) noted that mass BOD_5 removal generally increases with influent BOD_5 loading. Indeed, removal rates as high as 300 to 400 kg BOD_5 ha^{-1} d^{-1} have been observed under conditions of high BOD_5 loading (T. A. DeBusk, unpublished). However, effluent wastewater BOD_5 concentrations from such highly loaded systems rarely fall below 60 mg L^{-1}. To obtain final effluent concentrations of 30 mg L^{-1} or less, influent loadings typically cannot exceed 100 to 160 kg ha^{-1} d^{-1}. With the FAM technology currently available, at least 3.6 ha are required to treat 3,800 m^3 d^{-1} of primary domestic effluent to secondary standards (BOD_5 and SS below 30 mg L^{-1}).

Two inexpensive management parameters which show promise for increasing organic C removal efficiency in FAMS are the step loading and recirculation of wastewater. Results from a study conducted in San Diego, CA, showed that most of the BOD_5 removal in a plug-flow water hyacinth channel occurs in the first quarter

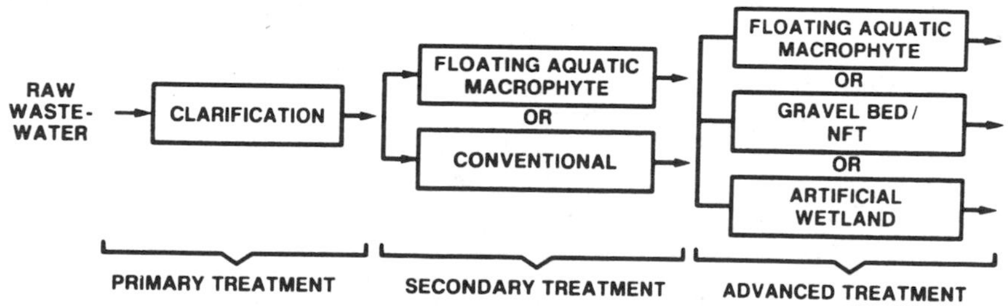

FIGURE 1. Integration of FAM, conventional and wetland systems for domestic wastewater treatment.

of the system (T. Chadwick, Black and Veatch, personal communication). The implementation of step-loading (that is, the addition of wastewater at various points along the length of the channel) may increase the assimilation capacity of the system. Additional studies in California indicate that the dilution of high BOD_5 influent wastewater with recirculated effluent may also improve system performance (G. Tchobanoglous, Univ. of California Davis, personal communication).

Several characteristics make FAMS attractive candidates for providing secondary treatment of domestic wastewater. Unlike conventional treatment systems, FAMS provide oxidation of organic matter and particle settling within one pond or basin. Moreover, studies conducted to date suggest that no removal (and hence, no treatment or disposal) of sludge is required in FAMS. Sediment accumulation in a 0.1 ha water hyacinth wastewater treatment channel at the WALT DISNEY WORLD Resort Complex was found to average only 0.6 cm yr^{-1} over a three year operational period. This channel received an average organic loading of 400 kg BOD_5 ha^{-1} d^{-1}. However, when FAMS are utilized to treat oxidation or retention pond effluents which contain large amounts of algal solids, sludge deposits may have to be removed at intervals of one to two years (R. Dinges, Austin, TX, personal communication).

Plant Species. BOD_5 reduction is greatest in systems containing plants which efficiently oxidize their rhizosphere, such as pennywort. In a nine month study of harvested FAM systems, we found that BOD_5 removal by pennywort and pennywort-water hyacinth polycultures averaged 89% and 91%, respectively, whereas BOD_5 removal by a water hyacinth monoculture averaged only 83%. We feel that pennywort's superior O_2-pumping ability, along with its relatively high cold tolerance, make it the preferred species for use in secondary treatment systems. Other macrophytes should also be examined for their O_2-transport capability.

Plant Harvest. Plant harvesting is a management practice often utilized in FAMS. Harvesting may enhance C removal in secondary treatment systems by reducing BOD_5 associated with the detritus and soluble organic compounds produced by senescing plant tissues. However, plant harvest entails high operating and capital costs, which are currently not matched by revenues generated from macrophyte-based products. The effect of harvest on C removal in both monoculture and polyculture FAMS should therefore be carefully evaluated.

System Design. Shallow, rectangular ponds with a high length to width ratio are usually proposed for FAMS so that short-circuiting of wastewater within the system can be reduced. The use of baffles and influent distribution manifolds may maximize contaminant retention times and improve treatment. A study by Stowell and Tchobanoglous (unpublished) demonstrated that the optimum depth for water hyacinth systems used for secondary domestic wastewater treatment is between 0.5 and 0.7 m. As mentioned above, systems in which wastewater is introduced at a number of locations, as well as those plumbed for effluent recirculation, may provide the highest C removal efficiency.

Mechanical aeration has been proposed as a means of improving carbonaceous BOD_5 removal, promoting nitrification, and reducing odors and mosquitoes in FAMS. However, at the shallow depths at which most FAMS are operated, the O_2 transfer efficiency of diffuse aeration systems is poor. Paddlewheel aerators, such as those used in the fish aquaculture industry, may be more appropriate for improving water quality in FAMS (C. Boyd, Auburn Univ., personal communication).

Problems. Injury to the plant crop by arthropods (e.g., the water hyacinth weevils, Neochetina spp.) has proven to be a major problem in water hyacinth-based treatment systems, particularly those located in Florida. Pest problems may be mitigated by harvesting infested plants, or through the use of FAM polycultures. All floating macrophytes are, of course, attacked by pests, but the cultivation of several species in a treatment pond helps to prevent widespread, debilitating infestations.

Mosquitoes frequently breed in FAMS which receive a high organic load. Mosquitofish can be used to consume larvae in areas of the system which are not completely anoxic. However, other mosquito control measures must be implemented in regions where the BOD_5 concentration exceeds approximately 60 mg L^{-1}.

Depending on the elemental composition of the wastewater, odors may also develop in those FAMS which receive a high organic load. The step loading and recirculation strategies proposed by the California investigators may alleviate both odor and mosquito problems.

Domestic Wastewater: Nitrogen Removal

Loading Rate. Area requirements of FAMS used for the removal of N from secondary domestic effluent are greater than those required for C removal from primary effluent. Nitrogen removal rates from 2.0 to 20 kg N ha^{-1} d^{-1} have been reported (Stowell et al., 1981; DeBusk et al., 1983). Assuming a removal rate of 10 kg N ha^{-1} d^{-1}, approximately 6 ha are required to reduce the concentration of 3,800 m^{-3} d^{-1} of secondary effluent from 20 mg L^{-1} to 3 mg L^{-1}. The two dominant N sinks in FAMS are nitrification-denitrification, and plant uptake and harvest. No relationship between N loading and mass removal has been established.

Plant Species. Although the water hyacinth has been utilized extensively for removal of N from secondary effluent, recent findings suggest that other floating macrophytes efficiently promote N transformations and removal. For example, nitrification is probably the process limiting to N removal in non-harvested FAMS in which the influent wastewater N is primarily

NH_4^+. Nitrification may be enhanced by the presence of plants such as pennywort, which efficiently transport O_2 into the water column. Nitrate produced beneath stands of pennywort may subsequently be removed via denitrification in anoxic regions of the system.

Pennywort can also improve the cool season N removal in a FAMS. In a routinely harvested system in central Florida, pennywort monocultures and pennywort-water hyacinth polycultures were found to remove 55% more N than water hyacinth monocultures from December through February (Clough, DeBusk and Reddy, unpublished). Of systems tested to date, water hyacinth-pennywort polyculture systems appear most promising for providing consistent, year round N removal in subtropical regions.

Plant Harvest. High N removal rates have been documented for water hyacinth-based treatment systems operated without plant harvest (DeBusk et al., 1983; Hauser, 1984), particularly for those which receive a nitrified wastewater. However, if a valuable product can be produced from the plant material, continuous harvest should be practiced in order to stimulate plant growth. Similarly, plants seriously damaged by arthropod pests should be removed from the system. The floating macrophyte standing crop plays an important role in influencing biochemical removal mechanisms, and also acts as a large storage reservoir of nutrients. Dense water hyacinth mats, for example, may contain as much as 600 kg N ha^{-1}. Treatment efficiency of the FAM can be seriously impaired if extensive damage to the floating mat is incurred.

System Design. As with FAMS used for secondary treatment, the configuration of ponds used for N removal should be such that short circuiting is reduced. The optimum depth for N removal is unknown. A strategy in which nitrified effluent is recirculated into high BOD_5 sections of the system (e.g., secondary treatment ponds) may accelerate removal of both BOD_5 and N. The BOD_5 would serve as the C source, and NO_3 as the electron acceptor for denitrification. The mixing of primary and secondary domestic effluents in a FAMS may also improve BOD_5 and N removal.

Mechanical aeration may be used to enhance nitrification, but, as was noted for C removal, the cost effectiveness of this practice is unknown.

Problems. Mosquitofish can control mosquito larvae effectively in systems used for removing N from secondary domestic effluent. Occasional plant harvest may facilitate access by the fish to larvae which develop in extremely dense sections of plants. The harvesting of infested plants, or the use of polyculture systems, can also reduce the impact of arthropod pests in FAM N removal systems.

Domestic Wastewater: Phosphorus Removal

Loading Rate. As noted previously, plant uptake and harvest is the only consistent P removal mechanism in FAMS. The area requirement for the removal of P from secondary effluent in FAMS is high since, relative to N and K, P is stored in macrophyte tissues at low concentrations. Phosphorus removal rates for FAMS range from about 0.5 to 5.0 kg ha^{-1}, with the area requirement for reducing the concentration of 3,800 m^{-3} d^{-1} of secondary effluent from 10 mg L^{-1} to 1 mg L^{-1} being roughly 13 ha. As with N, it is not known whether P removal is affected by P loading to the system.

Plant Species. Because of its high productivity at warm temperatures, the water hyacinth is the plant of choice for P removal in tropical regions. In cooler regions, the use of a pennywort-water hyacinth polyculture will improve winter season P removal.

Plant Harvest. Because P uptake is directly related to plant growth, routine plant harvest is requisite in FAMS used for P removal. For water hyacinth systems, considerable technology has been developed for plant harvesting, processing and utilization. Harvesting and utilization practices have not been refined for polyculture systems which contain water lettuce and pennywort.

System Design. FAMS used for P removal should incorporate pond designs which reduce wastewater short-circuiting, and which are also amenable to the use of plant harvesting and processing equipment. The optimum water depth for P removal is unknown.

If waste load allocations for the receiving water can be met by seasonal operation of the FAMS, management practices should emphasize the acceleration of plant growth during the warm season. If necessary, foliar or aqueous applications of micronutrient solutions should be used to correct growth-limiting nutrient deficiencies in the wastewater. Similarly, in some instances it may be possible to increase plant yields by the use of growth hormones. We found water hyacinth productivity to be increased by as much as 45% with foliar applications of the hormone gibberellic acid (GA_3). This yield stimulation was most pronounced during May and June, when conditions of temperature and light were favorable for growth (DeBusk and Reddy, unpublished). Although growth hormones are not overly expensive, their effects on plant growth and morphology are dramatic and not fully understood. Further research on the effects of GA_3 and other hormones on increasing plant yields and P uptake is therefore warranted.

If a year round effluent quality (concentration) requirement for P must be met, the optimization of P removal during the cool season is of critical importance since system area requirements will be dictated by wintertime performance. The misting of water hyacinth foliage is one means of reducing damage and improving yields following freeze events. During a two-week period following a severe freeze (24°F), we found that productivity of misted and non-misted plants averaged 12.3 and 5.8 g m^{-2} d^{-1}, respectively. It may therefore be useful to incorporate misting systems (using pond effluent wastewater, for example) at some facilities.

Problems. The intensive harvesting which is required in FAMS used for P removal can mitigate certain operational problems. Damage by arthropod infestations can be minimized by removing infected plants. In addition, the open water areas caused by harvest probably facilitates the predation of mosquito larvae by fish.

A major problem in FAMS used for P removal lies in the seasonal fluctuation in plant growth and P uptake. An export of P from FAMS can occur during periods of poor plant growth, particularly if the standing crop is damaged by arthropods or sub-freezing temperatures.

Non-domestic Wastewaters

A number of contaminants can be removed from non-domestic wastewaters using FAM systems, provided that the wastewater supports plant growth. Many process or industrial facilities which generate wastewaters have existing treatment-pond or canal systems which can be modified to support floating macrophytes. Unmanaged, or non-harvested, FAMS may be appropriate for providing contaminant removal from many such wastewater streams. For example, many process wastewaters in Florida, although not covered by strict effluent standards for total N and P, must meet effluent unionized-ammonia levels of 0.02 mg L^{-1} because of the toxic effects of this compound on aquatic organisms. A FAM system can lower total N concentrations by nitrification-denitrification reactions, and also reduce diel pH fluctuations. Both factors combine to sharply reduce unionized-ammonia concentrations.

Non-harvested FAM systems can also be utilized to remove toxic organic compounds (e.g., phenols) from wastewaters. Organic compounds may be metabolized by the microflora that proliferate on the roots of the floating plants, or assimilated by the plants and then metabolized to harmless end products. In addition, a spectrum of metals, including copper, chromium and lead, have been found to be assimilated and concentrated in tissues of macrophytes such as water hyacinth and pennywort (Wolverton et al., 1976; F. Dierberg, unpublished). Plant harvest is required to provide the ultimate removal of metals from the macrophyte system.

CONCLUSIONS

FAM systems, particularly those utilizing the water hyacinth, have been proven successful enough that design and operational data are being marketed commercially. Although FAM technology has apparently evolved to a full-scale operational level, there is a paucity of reliable design criteria for these systems. As a consequence, most FAM systems employ similar, but non-optimized, design and management strategies. Advancements in plant harvesting and processing are the only area in which visible progress has been made over the past decade. FAM system management parameters which require further evaluation include: mechanical aeration or wastewater pretreatment, effluent recirculation, plant growth hormones, contaminant loading strategies, water depth, and plant species. It should also be noted that the utility of a particular management practice will vary for each wastewater contaminant, a fact which is typically ignored in current FAM designs.

ACKNOWLEDGMENTS

Research by the senior author on biomass production and wastewater treatment by aquatic macrophytes is currently supported by the Gas Research Institute, Chicago, Illinois. Florida Agricultural Experiment Stations Journal Series No. 7714.

REFERENCES

Boyd, C. E. 1974. Utilization of aquatic plants. p. 107-114. In D. S. Mitchell (ed.) Aquatic Vegetation and Its Use and Control. Paris, Unesco.

Center, T. D., and N. R. Spencer. 1981. The phenology and growth of water hyacinth (Eichhornia crassipes [Mart.] Solms) in a eutrophic north-central Florida lake. Aquat. Bot. 10:1-32.

DeBusk, T. A., M. D. Hanisak, L. D. Williams, and J. H. Ryther. 1981. Effects of seasonality and plant density on the productivity of some freshwater macrophytes. Aquat. Bot. 10:133-143.

DeBusk, T. A., L. D. Williams, and J. H. Ryther. 1983. Removal of nitrogen and phosphorus from wastewater in a water hyacinth-based treatment system. J. Environ. Qual. 12:257-262.

Duffer, W. R. 1982. Assessment of aquaculture for reclamation of wastewater. p. 349-367. In E. Joe Middlebrooks (ed.) Water Reuse. Ann Arbor Science Publishers.

Hauser, J. R. 1984. Use of water hyacinth aquatic treatment systems for ammonia control and effluent polishing. J. Water Pollut. Control Fed. 56:219-225.

Moorhead, K. K., and K. R. Reddy. 1986. Oxygen transport by selected aquatic plants (submitted for publication).

Reddy, K. R. 1983. Fate of nitrogen and phosphorus in a waste-water retention reservoir containing aquatic macrophytes. J. Environ. Qual. 12:137-141.

Reddy, K. R., P. D. Sacco, D. A. Graetz, K. L. Campbell, and K. M. Portier. 1983. Effect of aquatic macrophytes on physico-chemical parameters of agricultural drainage water. J. Aquat. Plant Manage. 21:1-7.

Reddy, K. R., and W. F. DeBusk. 1984. Growth characteristics of aquatic macrophytes cultured in nutrient enriched water: I. Water hyacinth, water lettuce and pennywort. Econ. Bot. 38:229-239.

Reddy, K. R., and W. F. DeBusk. 1985. Nutrient removal potential of selected aquatic macrophytes. J. Environ. Qual. 14:459-462.

Stowell, R., R. Ludwig, J. Colt, and T. Tchobanoglous. 1981. Concepts in aquatic treatment design. pp. 919-940. Proc. Am. Soc. Civ. Eng., Vol. 107, Bo EE5, October 1981.

Tucker, C. S., and T. A. DeBusk. 1981. Seasonal growth of *Eichhornia crassipes* (Mart.) Solms: Relationship to protein, fiber and available carbohydrate content. Aquat. Bot. 11:137-141.

Wolverton, B. C., R. M. Barlow, and R. C. McDonald. 1976. Application of vascular aquatic plants for pollution removal, energy, and food production in a biological system. *In* J. Tourbier and R. W. Pierson, Jr. (ed.) Biological Control of Water Pollution. University of Pennsylvania Press.

EFFECT OF NITROGEN/PHOSPHORUS RATIO OF THE CULTURE MEDIUM ON GROWTH AND NUTRIENT REMOVAL BY WATER HYACINTH

D. M. Knoll
Lee and Ro Consulting Engineers and
San Diego State University
1017 San Bernardino
Spring Valley, California 92077-4627

ABSTRACT

The N and P disappearance rate and relative growth rate of *Eichhornia crassipes* was studied and modeled in growth chamber experiments. Nitrogen and P treatments were adjusted to produce specific N:P ratios at limiting concentrations. Static, steady-state experiment data, using 20 different N:P ratios at low N (1-16 mg L^{-1}) and low P (1-8 mg L^{-1}) concentrations, were utilized in multiple-regression analysis and analysis of variance to determine whether the solution N or P, N:P ratio or the value of the N and P concentration product ([N]x[P]) produced a significant ($p \geq 0.05$) treatment effect. Relative growth rate was predicted ($p \geq 0.05$) by [N], N:P and [N]x[P]. Relative growth rate = 0.09 + 0.007 [N] - 0.005 N:P - 0.006 [N]x[P]. Nitrogen concentration predicted ($p \geq 0.05$) N disappearance rate. Nitrogen disappearance rate = 1.32 + 0.209 [N]. Phosphorus disappearance rate is predicted ($p \geq 0.05$) by [P] and [N]. Phosphorus disappearance rate = 0.213 + 0.042 [N] + 0.077 [P]. Disappearance uptake rate correction factors were determined to obtain uptake rates directly from disappearance rate.

Keywords: Aquaculture wastewater treatment, mathematical modelling.

INTRODUCTION

Wolverton (1979) suggested that there may be problems in utilizing only water hyacinth to achieve nutrient levels that approach the EPA secondary discharge levels of 3 mg N L^{-1} and 1 mg P L^{-1}. While the N:P ratio for raw municipal wastewater is approximately 6:1, it drops to 3:1, due to denitrification, by the end of secondary treatment. Because the N:P ratio in water hyacinth tissue is approximately 6:1 (Gossett and Norris, 1970),

Aquatic Plants for Water Treatment
and Resource Recovery
K.R. Reddy and W.H. Smith (Eds.)

ISBN 0-941463-00-1

there is insufficient N in secondarily treated wastewater to counterbalance the available P and to meet EPA standards for secondary discharge. As water hyacinth absorbs N and P, N in domestic wastewater is depleted prior to P, thus resulting in unacceptable levels of P in the effluent.

The objective of this study was to determine the effect of N:P ratio of the nutrient medium on productivity and nutrient removal by water hyacinth.

MATERIALS AND METHODS

Two nutrient ratio terms are used in this study. The N:P ratio is the mass of N relative to the mass of P (e.g. 1:1 or 3:1). In this study, a N:P concentration ratio is the actual concentration (mg L^{-1}) of N and P expressed as a ratio (e.g. 3:3 or 9:3, mg L^{-1}:mg L^{-1}).

Nitrogen and P disappearance rate and relative growth rate were measured in static experiments under a controlled environment with day and night temperatures held constant at 35°C and 20°C, respectively, and relative humidity ranging from 40 to 70%. Artificial light (500 µE m^{-2} s^{-1}) was supplied by 10 Cool White high output flourescent tubes during a 12 h light period. Individual, uniform plants were collected from the City of San Diego Aquatic Treatment Pilot Plant. For one week prior to experimental use, plants were incubated in 10% Van de Elst's nutrient solution (Bergmann, 1958) to gain nutrient equilibrium. Algal contamination was minimized by changing the solution frequently and maintaining high plant density.

The 20 N:P concentration ratios used in this study were produced by varying the amounts of potassium nitrate, ammonium sulfate (two parts NO_3 to one part NH_4) and calcium hydrophosphate within the 10% Van de Elst's solution. Each experiment maintained a constant, steady-state (less than 10% change in nutrient concentration) environment with three replications of each N:P concentration ratio and random trials.

Three plants were randomly selected from each equilibrium batch, placed in 3-L containers and placed randomly within the growth chamber with constant air-stone aeration. Every 2 d of the 14 d experiment, the fresh weight of each plant was determined and the nutrient solutions were replenished to their original levels with deionized water because of evapotranspiration. After replenishment, each container had 50 mL removed for chemical analysis. Samples were analyzed for NO_3, NH_4 and PO_4 using the Technicon Autoanalyzer (Technicon, 1982). After the nutrient solution was sampled, each container was emptied, cleaned of any algae, refilled with 3 L of nutrient solution and sampled. Control basins were maintained without plants. One plant was randomly selected in each container, harvested and weighed at the end of the experiment. Plants were dried at 70°C to obtain a consistent dry weight and homogenized to pass a 20-mesh screen.

Dried plant matter was analyzed for total Kjeldahl N (TKN) and total P (TP) by digestion and Technicon Autoanalyzer II method. Results from TKN and TP were used in calculation of uptake rates to be used for correlation to disappearance rate. Data reduction and statistical analyses by least squares linear multiple regression and regression analysis of variance were utilized to test for treatment effect of the following independent variables; N and P concentration, the interaction predictor ([N]x[P]) and N:P ratio. The statistical data collected were used to develop simple mathematical models for N and P disappearance rate and relative growth rate.

RESULTS AND DISCUSSION

When [P] was held constant, relative growth rate increased with increasing [N] (Figure 1). The highest relative growth rate (0.139 $g\ g^{-1}\ d^{-1}$) was at N:P concentration ratios of 8:4 and 16:4. The lowest relative growth rate was at 1:8 N:P concentration ratio (0.075 $g\ g^{-1}\ d^{-1}$). Statistical analysis indicated that [N] had a significant ($p \geq 0.05$) correlation with relative growth rate. N:P ratio and [N]x[P] were significantly ($P \geq 0.05$), but negatively correlated with growth rate, while [P] was not significantly related to growth rate and therefore not included in the regression model.

Relative Growth Rate = 0.09 + 0.007 [N] - 0.005 N:P - 0.0006 [N]x[P] where R^2 = 0.61, adjusted for 4 degrees of freedom, total variability (R^2 value) is reduced by the addition of [N] (45%), [N]x[P] (12.5%) and N:P ratio (3.7%). [P] was statistically not significant but appears to produce an inhibitory influence in concentrations of 8 mg P L^{-1}.

With [P] held constant, N disappearance rate was generally higher with increasing [N] (Figure 2). The N:P concentration ratios of 8:4 and 16:4 produced the highest and similar disappearance rates of 3.0 and 2.92 mg N $plant^{-1}\ d^{-1}$. Statistical analysis indicated that only [N] was significant ($p \geq 0.01$) in predicting N disappearance rate. N:P ratio, [P] and [N]x[P] were not significant and therefore not included in the regression model. Nitrogen disappearance rate = 1.32 + 0.209 [N] where: R^2 = 0.65, adjusted for 4 degrees of freedom. Total variability in the prediction is reduced by 63% by the addition of [N] in the analysis. Phosphorus disappearance rate was generally higher with the increase in both [N] and [P] (Figure 3). N:P concentration ratio of 16:4 produced a rate of 0.95 mg P $plant^{-1}\ d^{-1}$. The lowest rate was found at a concentration ratio of 1:1 (0.18 mg P plant d^{-1}). Statistical analysis indicated that [P] ($P \geq 0.005$) and [N] ($P \geq 0.025$) were significant in predicting P disappearance rate. N:P ratio and [N]x[P] were weakly significant ($p \geq 0.1$) and therefore not included in the regression model. Phosphorus disappearance rate = 0.213 + 0.04 [N] + 0.077 [P] where: R^2 = 0.77, adjusted for 4 degrees of freedom.

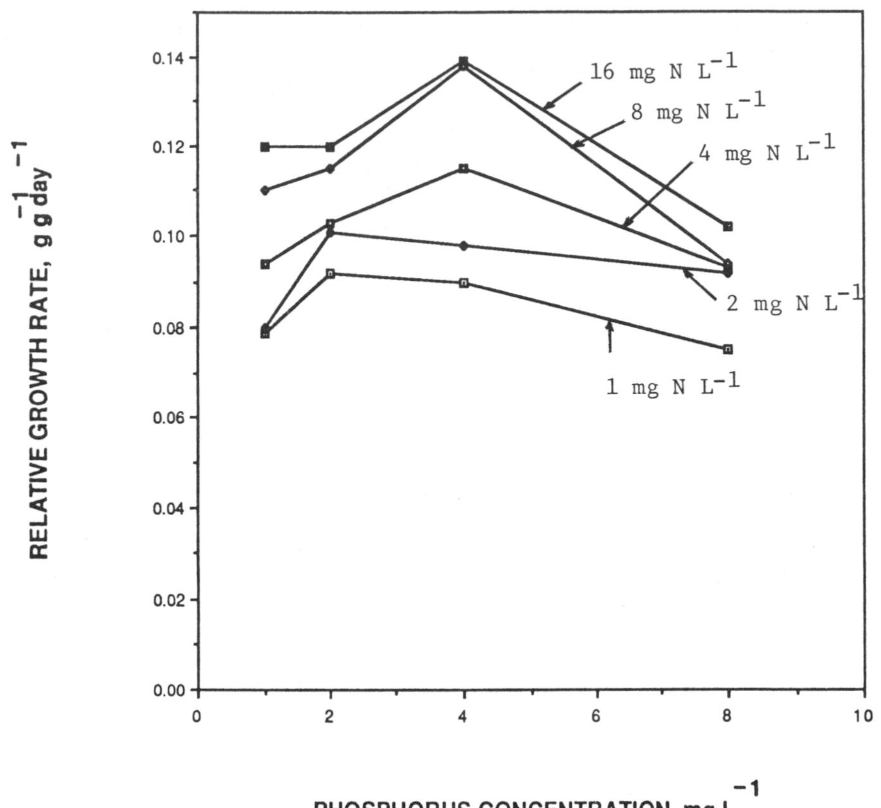

FIGURE 1. Relative growth as a function of external P concentration with N concentration varied at 1, 2, 4, 8 and 16 mg N L^{-1}.

Total variability is reduced with the addition of [P] (68%) and [N] (10%). The P disappearance results were consistent with N in that neither N:P ratio nor [N]x[P] predictors were significant.

In this study, N and P disappearance rates accounted for 82% of the actual uptake rate determined by tissue analysis. Control conditions (without plants) accounted for 17-19% and 20-28% of the lost nutrients for N and P, respectively. This mass balance indicates a disappearance-uptake rate correction factor of 0.82.

The N and P disappearance regressions produced results which are comparable to those reported in the literature. In testing these models, two previous studies were utilized: Sato and Kondo (1981) and Rodgers and Davis (1972). The latter study reported removal rates of 4.7, 11.0 and 17.8 mg N $plant^{-1}$ d^{-1} and 1.1, 2.0

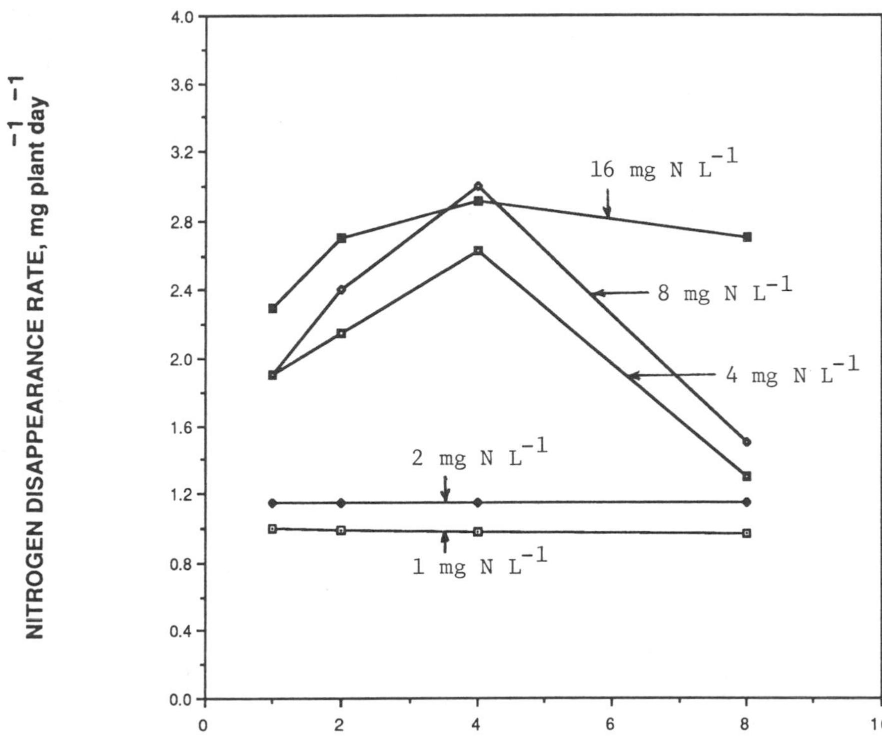

FIGURE 2. Nitrogen disappearance rate as a function of external P concentration with N concentration varied at 1, 2, 4, 8 and 16 mg N L^{-1}.

and 3.0 mg P $plant^{-1}$ d^{-1} for N and P concentrations of 22, 55 and 110 mg L^{-1} and 3, 7.5 and 15 mg L^{-1}, respectively. The model predictions with disappearance-uptake rate correction factor were 4.82, 10.46 and 19.86 mg N $plant^{-1}$ d^{-1} and 1.15, 2.54 and 4.84 mg P $plant^{-1}$ d^{-1}. The model predictions fall within 98, 95 and 90% of the N removal rates and 96, 79 and 62% of the P. Sato and Kondo reported an uptake rate of 13.1 kg N ha^{-1} d^{-1} and 2.7 kg P ha^{-1} d^{-1} under optimal conditions of 50 mg N L^{1} and 13.8 mg P L^{-1}. Assuming a plant density of 1.62 x 10^{6} plants per ha (Penfound and Earle, 1948), their rate is 8.08 mg N $plant^{-1}$ d^{-1} and 1.66 mg P $plant^{-1}$ d^{-1}. Model plus correction factor prediction is 9.55 mg N $plant^{-1}$ d^{-1} and 2.79 mg P $plant^{-1}$ d^{-1} which fall within 85 and 60% of the reported values.

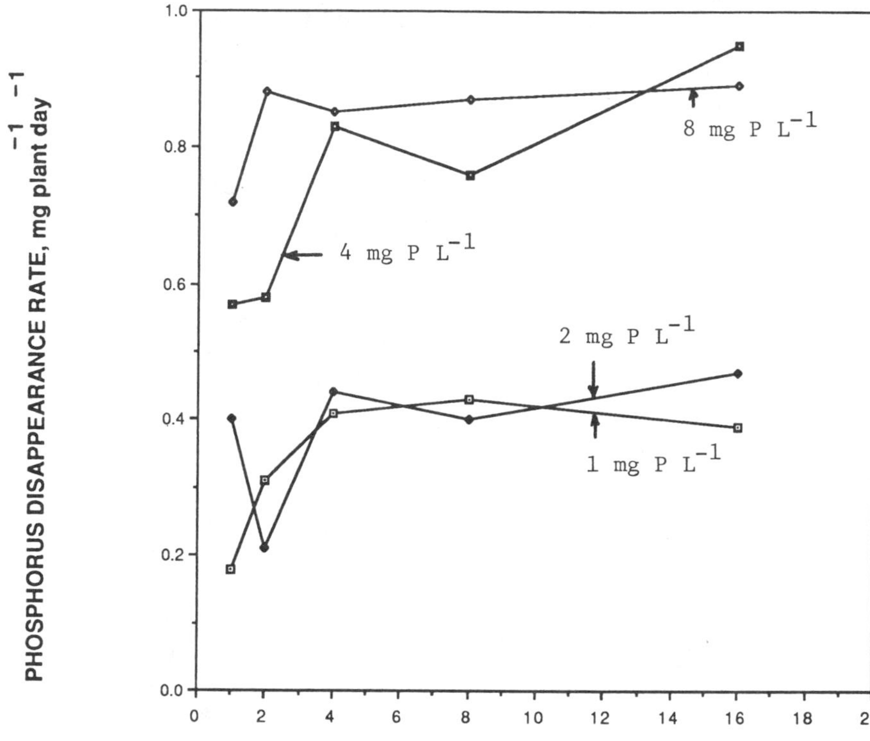

FIGURE 3. Phosphorus disappearance rate as a function of external N concentration with P concentration varied at 1, 2, 4 and 8 mg P L^{-1}.

This high correlation with previous literature under non-growth chamber conditions show that these models may be utilized to predict the uptake of water hyacinth under wastewater treatment conditions where plants are in a steady-state environment due to N and P availability along the pond gradient. Utilization of disappearance rates allows determination of uptake rate without tissue analysis. Engineers, by use of these models, may determine nutrient removal from easily obtained data. Validation of growth chamber models to wastewater treatment conditions has not been conducted and therefore these predictions should be applied with caution.

REFERENCES

Bergmann, W. 1958. Methoden zur ermittlung der mineralischen bendurfnisse der pflanzen. In W. Ruhland (ed.) Encyclopesidia of Plant Physiology, Vol IV. Springer Verlag, Berlin.

Gossett, D. R., and W. E. Norris, Jr. 1970. Relationship between nutrient availability and content of nitrogen and phosphorus in tissues of the aquatic macrophyte, Eichhornia crassipes (Mart) Solm. Hydrobiologia 38:15-28.

Penfound, W. T., and T. T. Earle. 1948. The biology of the water hyacinth. Ecological Monographs 18:447-472.

Rodgers, H. H., and D. E. Davis. 1972. Nutrient removal by water hyacinths. Weed Sci. 20:423-428.

Sato, H., and T. Kondo, 1980. Biomass production of water hyacinth and its ability to remove inorganic minerals from water. I. Effect of the concentration of culture on the rates of plant growth and nutrient uptake. Japan J. of Ecol. 31:257-267.

Technicon. 1982. Technicon autoanalyzer II bulletins. Technicon Industrial Systems. Tarrytown, New York.

Wolverton, B. C. 1979. Engineering design data for small vascular aquatic plant wastewater treatment systems. Aquaculture Systems for Wastewater Treatment Seminar Proceedings and Engineering Assessment. Environmental Protection Agency, USA.

BIOMASS PRODUCTION OF WATER HYACINTH CULTURED IN AN AQUACULTURE SYSTEM IN JAPAN

Y. Oki and K. Ueki
Institute for Agricultural and Biological Sciences
Okayama University
Kurashiki 710
JAPAN

ABSTRACT

The purpose of this research was to develop cultural methods for maximum yields of water hyacinth [Eichhornia crassipes (Mart.) Solms), and to determine the effect of environmental factors on biomass yields. Water hyacinths were grown in Okayama prefecture, located in the southwestern part of Japan, in two types of culture systems: 1) tanks, 4 m^2 in area and 0.5 m in depth, and 2) water hyacinth cultivation pond for wastewater treatment, ca. 55 m^2 in area and 0.5 m in depth. A maximum yield of 63.4 Mg (dry wt) ha^{-1} during May to November was obtained in a tank with nutrient-rich waters when plant density was adjusted to the original density of 10 kg (fresh wt) m^{-2} by harvesting excess plants at intervals of 4 wk. Initial plant density and the harvesting frequency affected the biomass yield. Significant relationships were observed between growth rates of water hyacinth and air temperature, water temperature and solar radiation from July to December, but not from May to November.

Keywords: Water hyacinth (Eichhornia crassipes), harvesting, plant density, biomass.

INTRODUCTION

Annual productivity of water hyacinths in natural waterways of Japan during the months of May through October is about 20 Mg ha^{-1} yr^{-1} (Oki and Nakagawa, 1981). Mechanical removal is the most popular method of controlling this weed in Japan. Utilization of this weed has been considered an important part of the weed management. Currently in Japan, several research projects are in progress to evaluate the potential use of water hyacinth for water treatment, animal feed, and for biogas production. The purpose of this research was to develop cultural

ISBN 0-941463-00-1

methods to obtain optimum biomass yields of water hyacinth, and to determine the effect of environmental factors on biomass yield.

MATERIALS AND METHODS

Water hyacinths were cultured in Okayama prefecture, located in the southwestern part of Japan, in two types of culture systems.

Experiment 1

Water hyacinths were cultured outdoors in four 2000 L steel tanks (4 m^2 surface area). Tanks were drained, washed with water and refilled weekly with 40 mg L^{-1} of 16-16-16 (N-P_2O_5-K_2O) fertilizer. This was equivalent to 6.4 mg N L^{-1}, 2.8 mg P L^{-1} and 5.3 mg K L^{-1}. An initial plant density of 10 kg (fresh wt) m^{-2} (Treatment B,C,F and G) or 15 kg (fresh wt) m^{-2} (treatment A,D and E) was used in each tank (Table 1). Plant density in each tank was adjusted to the original density by harvesting excess plants every 1-4 wk. The standing crop was measured once a week, and plant samples were obtained from harvesting excess plants, that were allowed to dry for 48 h at 70°C for dry weight determination. Throughout the study period, air temperature, water temperature and solar radiation were recorded.

TABLE 1. Culture methods of water hyacinth cultured in tanks.

Treatment	Initial density	Period of investigation	Interval of harvest	Aeration
	(kg m^{-2})†		----wk----	
A	15	July 21-Dec 8, '82 (140 d)	2	Non-aerated
B	10	July 21-Dec 8, '82 (140 d)	2	Non-aerated
C	10	July 24-Dec 11, '82 (140 d)	1	Non-aerated
D	15	May 7-Nov 5, '83 (182 d)	2	Non-aerated
E	15	May 7-Nov 5, '83 (182 d)	4	Non-aerated
F	10	May 11-Nov 9, '83 (182 d)	4	Non-aerated
G	10	May 6-Nov 4, '83 (182 d)	4	Aerated

†Fresh weight.

Experiment 2

The pilot-plant scale system, constructed for the treatment of domestic waste, consisted of a stabilization pond, a catalytic oxidation pond and the water hyacinth cultivation pond. The water hyacinth cultivation pond received effluent from the oxidation pond. This system was designed to treat 20 m^3 d^{-1} of wastewater. The cultivation pond has a surface area of 55 m^2, divided into eight segments, with each of the four segments operating in series. The operation began in May 1983, with an initial plant density of 0.6 kg (fresh wt) m^{-2} used in each pond segment and ran through November 1983. Within 40 d, there was approximately 100% plant coverage. Every two weeks after 100% plant coverage, the standing crop was measured and the amount over the target weight was harvested. The target weight in Treatment 1 was 10 kg (fresh wt) m^{-2}, and in Treatment 2 was 15 kg (fresh wt) m^{-2}. Plant samples were collected, allowed to dry for 48 h at 70°C. Through the study, air temperature, water temperature and solar radiation were recorded, and these climatic data were accumulated every two weeks.

RESULTS AND DISCUSSION

Experiment 1

Biomass yield and growth rates of water hyacinth cultured for 140-182 d were affected by the changes in cultural methods (Table 2). Productivity of water hyacinth was highest in Treatment G. Biomass yields from May to November were 6.34 kg (dry wt) m^{-2} yr^{-1} in Treatment G, where plants were maintained at constant density of 10 kg (fresh wt) m^{-2}. Biomass yields were significantly increased when plants were cultured under aerated conditions

TABLE 2. Comparison of yield and growth rate of water hyacinth cultured in tanks.

Treatment	Total increment†		Yield†		Average growth rate
	Fresh wt	Dry wt	Fresh wt	Dry wt	
	kg m^{-2}				g m^{-2} d^{-1}
A	49.4	2.87	64.4	3.89	22.80
B	49.3	2.85	59.3	3.55	22.60
C	21.8	1.24	31.8	1.78	9.90
D	96.2	5.22	111.2	6.06	32.73
E	89.4	5.02	104.4	5.85	29.55
F	99.5	5.38	109.5	5.94	32.62
G	110.2	5.78	120.2	6.34	35.23

†Values represent 140 d in Treatment A,B and C, and 182 d in Treatment D,E,F and G, respectively.

compared to non-aerated treatment (Treatment F). Aeration maintained average dissolved O_2 level at 5 mg L^{-1}. Reddy et al. (1983) reported that initial plant density and harvesting frequency affected the biomass yields. Our results indicate that water hyacinths maintained at a density of 15 kg (fresh wt) m^{-2} would require harvesting every two weeks, while plants maintained at a density of 10 kg (fresh wt) m^{-2} need harvesting once every four weeks. In both treatments, after two and four weeks the standing crop reached 30 kg (fresh wt) m^{-2} which was the maximum density of exponential biological growth (Oki and Nakagawa, 1981). DeBusk et al. (1981) found the optimum stocking density for productivity of water hyacinth based on weekly harvests was 1000 kg (dry wt) m^{-2} (approximately 20 kg fresh wt m^{-2}), but from the viewpoint of reduction of labor, an optimum plant density in the range of 10 to 15 kg (fresh wt) m^{-2} was found to have the highest yields.

The relationships between climatic conditions and fresh weight increases of water hyacinth are shown in Table 3. Significant positive relationships ($P<0.95$) were observed in Treatments A,B and C in data obtained July to December, 1982, while correlation coefficients were lower in Treatment D,E,F and G where data were obtained from May to November, 1983. In Florida, significant positive relationships ($P<0.95$) were observed between growth rates and solar radiation (Reddy et al., 1983b), and ambient air temperature (Knipling et al., 1970). However, in Japan, if the culture period includes May and June, productivity of water hyacinths can be more influenced by the cultural techniques used than the climatic conditions.

TABLE 3. Correlation coefficients (r) between climate conditions and increment of fresh weight of water hyacinth cultured in tanks.

	Increment of Fresh Weight (kg/m²/2 wk)						
	Treatment						
	A (N=10)	B (N=10)	C (N=19)	D (N=13)	E (N=6)	F (N=6)	G (N=6)
Accumulated solar radiation (MJ m^{-2})	0.730†	0.768†	0.486†	0.517	0.638	0.862	0.807†
Accumulated air temp. (C°.day)	0.901‡	0.941‡	0.524†	0.508	0.492	0.452	0.391
Accumulated water temp. (C°.day)	0.882‡	0.925‡	0.474†	0.483	0.511	0.454	0.304

†,‡Significant difference at 5% and 1% level, respectively.

Experiment 2

The average concentrations of plant available nutrient in the secondary sewage effluent used to culture water hyacinths in this period are in Table 4. The last pond (D) showed a reduction of 72% of inorganic N and 53% ortho-P from the sewage effluent over nutrients in the first pond (A). Also, the amount of water hyacinth harvested from the first pond (A) was 110 kg (fresh wt) m^{-2} in Treatment 1 and 107 kg (fresh wt) m^{-2} in Treatment 2 compared with 70 kg (fresh wt) m^{-2} and 63 kg (fresh wt) m^{-2} from the last pond (D), respectively. In the case of Experiment 2, the yields of Treatment 1 maintained at constant density of 10 kg (fresh wt) m^{-2} by harvesting every two weeks were higher than those of Treatment 2 maintained at density of 15 kg (fresh wt) m^{-2} by the same harvesting frequency. Biomass yields of Pond A were approximately the same value compared to those of Treatment D-F in Experiment 1 in spite of low nutrient level in water. These results indicate that flowing water is more effective to increase biomass yields than stagnant water.

Correlation coefficients between climatic conditions and increment of fresh weight of water hyacinth cultured in cultivation ponds are shown in Table 5. The results indicate a significant relationship between air and water temperature and the growth rate, and no relationship between solar radiation and growth rate due to low standing crops of water hyacinth and the higher solar radiation in May and June in Japan.

TABLE 4. Comparison of water quality, yield and growth rate of water hyacinth cultured in ponds used for wastewater treatment (207 d).

	Treatment†	Segments of Cultivation Pond			
		A	B	C	D
Water quality (mg L^{-1})					
Total-N	1&2	3.56	2.26	1.87	1.47
Inorg.-N	1&2	2.97	1.66	1.26	0.84
Total-P	1&2	0.99	0.73	0.61	0.47
PO_4-P	1&2	0.86	0.64	0.53	0.40
Yield					
(kg fresh wt m^{-2} 207 d^{-1})	1	109.9	97.8	79.9	70.3
	2	107.0	90.3	75.2	63.2
Yield					
(kg dry wt m^{-2} 207 d^{-1})	1	5.44	4.51	3.96	3.63
	2	5.08	4.35	3.76	3.30
Average growth rate					
(g dry wt m^{-2} d^{-1})	1	23.79	21.93	19.16	17.87
	2	22.81	19.29	15.73	14.41

†Treatment 1: Maintain plant density of 10 kg fresh wt m^{-2}.
Treatment 2: Maintain plant density of 15 kg fresh wt m^{-2}.

TABLE 5. Correlation coefficients (r) between climate conditions and increment of fresh weight of water hyacinth cultured in cultivation ponds for wastewater treatment.

		Increment of Fresh Weight ($kg\ m^{-2}$ 2 wk) Segments of cultivation pond			
		A (N=13)	B (N=13)	C (N=13)	D (N=13)
Treatment 1	Accumulated solar radiation ($MJ\ m^{-2}$)	0.614†	0.434	0.403	0.156
	Accumulated air temp. (C°.day)	0.879‡	0.815‡	0.660†	0.361
	Accumulated water temp. (C•.day)	0.826‡	0.741‡	0.591†	0.268
Treatment 2	Accumulated solar radiation ($MJ\ m^{-2}$)	0.521	0.600†	0.546	0.114
	Accumulation air temp. (C°.day)	0.771‡	0.774‡	0.708‡	0.331
	Accumulated water temp. (C°.day)	0.718‡	0.711‡	0.683‡	0.229

†,‡Significant difference at 5% and 1% level, respectively.

Based on the results of the present study, the following conclusions can be drawn: 1) plant densities and harvesting frequency have significant effects on biomass yield. The optimum plant density to achieve maximum growth of water hyacinths was found to be in the range of 10-35 kg (fresh wt) m^{-2}; and 2) though water hyacinth growth is driven by climatic conditions (solar radiation, air and water temperature), it also depends on cultural practices and the nutrient status (level and flow) in the water.

ACKNOWLEDGMENTS

The authors are grateful to Drs. K. Nakagawa and I. Aoyama, Okayama University and Dr. Y. Tomihisa, Prefectural Agricultural Experiment Station, for their suggestions and supporting this work.

REFERENCES

DeBusk, T. A., J. H. Ryther, M. D. Hanisak, and L. D. Williams. 1981. Effects of seasonality and plant density on the productivity of some freshwater macrophytes. Aquat. Bot. 10:133-142.

Knipling, E. B., S. H. West, and W. T. Haller. 1970. Growth characteristics, yield potential, and nutritive content of water hyacinth. Proc. Soil Crop Sci. Soc. Fla. 30:51-63.

Oki, Y., and K. Nakagawa. 1981. Dynamics of water hyacinth population in natural water area. Special Research Project on Environmental Science. p. 115-140.

Reddy, K. R., D. L. Sutton, and G. Bowes. 1983a. Freshwater aquatic biomass production in Florida. Soil and Crop Sci. Soc. Fla. Proc. 42:28-40.

Reddy, K. R., F. M. Hueston, and T. McKim. 1983b. Water hyacinth production in sewage effluent. In Symp. Proc. Energy from Biomass and Wastes 7, Inst. Gas. Tech., Chicago. p. 135-167.

DENSITY REQUIREMENTS TO MAXIMIZE PRODUCTIVITY AND NUTRIENT REMOVAL CAPABILITY OF WATER HYACINTH

W. F. DeBusk and K. R. Reddy
Central Florida Research and Education Center
University of Florida, IFAS
Sanford, Florida 32771

ABSTRACT

Water hyacinth (Eichhornia crassipes [Mart] Solms) cultures were grown in nutrient medium (40 mg N L^{-1} and 6 mg P L^{-1}; hydraulic retention time of 7 d) at four different plant densities in order to evaluate density requirements for water hyacinth-based wastewater treatment and biomass production systems. Net productivity, nutrient removal and plant morphology were significantly affected by plant density. During the 8-month study period (May - December), net productivity averaged 24.0, 32.6, 37.8 and 33.9 g (dry wt) m^{-2} d^{-1} for plants grown at mean densities of 238, 472, 867 and 1130 g m^{-2}, respectively. Removal of inorganic N from the water increased with plant density, while P removal was greatest at intermediate density. Mean inorganic N removal rate ranged from 1351 to 2316 mg N m^{-2} d^{-1}, while removal of ortho-P ranged from 328 to 378 mg P m^{-2} d^{-1}. Plant uptake accounted for 56 to 78% of inorganic N removal and for 73 to 91% of P removal. Shoot length and leaf area were significantly increased at higher plant densities, in response to increased competition for light.

Keywords: Biomass, wastewater treatment, aquatic macrophytes.

INTRODUCTION

Water hyacinth (Eichhornia crassipes [Mart] Solms) grows prolifically in tropical and sub-tropical waters around the world. Water hyacinth has been recognized in recent years for its potential role in water quality improvement (Cornwell et al., 1977; Wolverton and McDonald, 1979; Reddy et al., 1982), biogasification (Shiralipour and Smith, 1984), feed production (Bagnall et al., 1974) and a multitude of other uses. Although several integrated water hyacinth-based systems are now in operation, there remains a paucity of available information on the

Aquatic Plants for Water Treatment
and Resource Recovery
K.R. Reddy and W.H. Smith (Eds.)

ISBN 0-941463-00-1

optimization of management parameters. Parameters such as plant density, retention time and depth must be properly manipulated in accordance with the specific design criteria of the system; e.g. removal of nutrients, BOD, metals or organics, or biomass production.

The objectives of this study were to evaluate plant growth and N and P removal as a function of plant density in a nutrient non-limited water hyacinth system, and to determine the effect of plant density on plant morphology and chemistry.

MATERIALS AND METHODS

The study was implemented at the University of Florida's Central Florida Research and Education Center (IFAS) in Sanford during the months of May through December, 1983. Water hyacinth plants were grown in 1000 L outdoor concrete tanks with 1.7 m^2 of water surface and 0.6 m water depth. Water and nutrients were supplied to the tanks on a batch-feed basis, with a detention time of one week. At the end of each week the tanks were drained and the water and nutrients replaced with fresh medium. Macronutrients were added in the form of inorganic fertilizer at the following rates (mg L^{-1}): NH_4-N = 21, NO_3-N = 21, PO_4-P = 6, K = 46, Fe = 8, Ca = 78, and Mg = 29. Iron and other micronutrients were supplied as Fe-EDTA and Nutrispray, respectively.

Water hyacinth cultures were initially stocked at four levels of plant density (3 reps.): 4, 8, 16 and 24 kg fresh wt m^{-2}, equivalent to 150, 350, 700 and 1000 g dry wt m^{-2}. Standing crop of biomass was measured by weighing the plants in a large basket after draining for 5 min; each tank was then re-adjusted to its initial plant density.

Standing-crop measurements and plant harvests were performed weekly during the active growing season, May through October, and bi-weekly for the duration of the study. Net productivity of water hyacinth was calculated from the incremental increase in dry weight and expressed as g m^{-2} d^{-1}. Percent dry weight was determined from fresh and oven-dry weights of plant subsamples.

Water samples were taken from each tank at the beginning and end of each week, corresponding to day 0 and day 7 of nutrient-medium residence time, during the period of May through October. All water samples were analyzed for NH_4-N, NO_3+NO_2-N, and soluble reactive P (USEPA, 1979). Whole-plant samples were collected from each tank at the time of harvest. Plant samples were dried at 70°C for 72 h, ground in a Wiley Mill, and digested in test tubes on a block digestor for N (semi-micro Kjeldahl digestion; Bremner and Mulvaney, 1982) and P (nitric-perchloric acid digestion; Jackson, 1958) determinations. Subsequent analyses for N and P were performed by autoanalysis using the previously referenced NH_4^+ and SRP techniques.

RESULTS AND DISCUSSION

Weekly harvesting of water hyacinth cultures to their respective starting densities effectively maintained standing crops within four nearly contiguous ranges of plant density. Average standing crops at the time of harvest were ca. 320, 600, 1000 and 1250 g (dry wt) m^{-2}, respectively, for the initial densities of 150, 350, 700 and 1000 g m^{-2}. The overall density range represented in the experimental cultures was approximately 200 to 1500 g m^{-2}. Full coverage of plants occurred at 500-600 g m^{-2} density, therefore plants growing at higher densities were considered space-limited.

Dry matter content of plant tissue did not vary significantly with plant density or season. Mean dry weight fractions were 3.9, 4.4, 4.5 and 4.2%, respectively, at lowest to highest plant density. Average net productivity of water hyacinth during the 8-month study period was highest in the density range of 800 to 1125 g m^{-2} (Table 1). Growth rates during the period May 15 through December 15 averaged 24.0, 32.6, 33.9 and 37.8 g m^{-2} d^{-1} at 150, 350, 1000, and 700 g m^{-2} starting densities, respectively. Similar results were reported in previous studies by DeBusk et al. (1981) and Reddy and DeBusk (1984), both of which concluded that maximum growth occurred at about 1000 g m^{-2}.

Although net productivity in terms of biomass per unit area increased with plant density between 150 and 1125 g m^{-2}, specific growth rate (SGR) exhibited a concurrent decrease, ranging in value from 0.079 to 0.025 d^{-1} at minimum and maximum densities, respectively (Table 1). Specific growth rate, or percent increase per day, is commonly, and most appropriately, utilized as a measure of aquatic plant growth in unconfined natural stands. However, because SGR is, by definition, density-dependent, it may be misleading when used as an expression of productivity in high-density cultures.

Net productivity was subject to significant monthly variation, although similar growth trends were observed for all

TABLE 1. Average daily productivity and specific growth rates (SGR), during the May-December study period, of water hyacinth cultures maintained at four distinct levels of plant density. Productivity values followed by the same letter are not significantly different for P = 0.05.

Mean plant density range	Net productivity	SGR
----g m^{-2}----	--g m^{-2} d^{-1}--	-d^{-1}-
150 - 320	24.0 a	0.079
350 - 600	32.6 b	0.060
700 - 1000	37.8 c	0.039
1000 - 1250	33.9 b	0.025

levels of plant density (Figure 1). Maximum growth occurred during the month of July, when net productivity averaged 29.8, 38.0, 41.8 and 51.1 g m^{-2} d^{-1} in the 150, 350, 1000 and 700 g m^{-2} cultures, respectively. Minimum plant growth was observed during November and December, with average productivity ranging from 15.1 to 21.4 g m^{-2} d^{-1} at 150 and 1000 g m^{-2} starting densities, respectively. The maximum short-term (1 wk growth period) biomass increase measured during the study period was 64.1 g m^{-2} d^{-1} at 700 g m^{-2} starting density, during the month of July.

The pattern of monthly growth fluctuations was similar to those evidenced by temperature and solar radiation, during the period May through December (Figure 1). Net productivity at the two lower densities was significantly ($P < 0.05$) correlated with solar radiation, while productivity at all densities was significantly correlated ($P < 0.01$) with mean temperature. Maximum growth for all levels of plant density occurred during the months of highest temperature, rather than during periods of highest solar radiation. This may indicate that temperature, rather than light, is the primary growth-limiting factor in nutrient non-limited water hyacinth cultures.

Numerous changes in plant morphology and chemical composition occurred in response to plant density. Increased

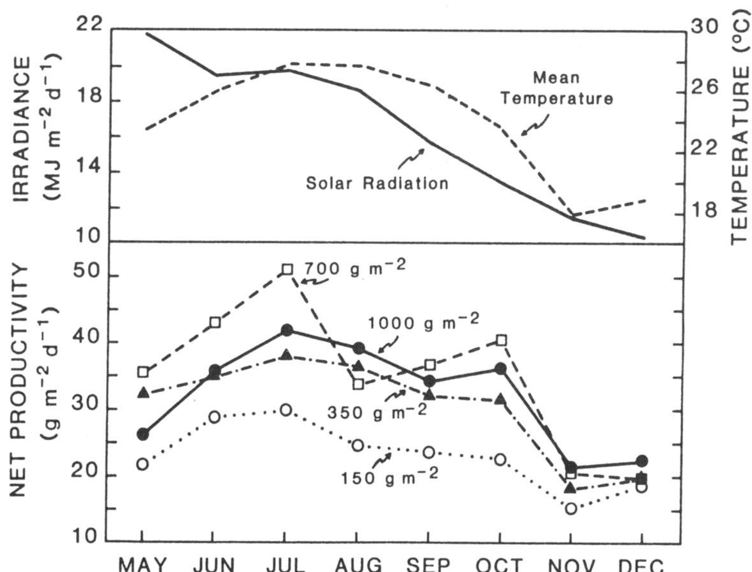

FIGURE 1. Monthly variation in net productivity of water hyacinth cultured at four levels of plant density, and corresponding trends in temperature and solar radiation, during the months of May through December. Data points represent mean daily values during each month.

shoot length at high plant densities reflected basic changes in the growth habit of water hyacinth in response to density-induced stress (Table 2). Mean shoot lengths, measured in July, were 37.1, 47.0, 65.4 and 74.0 cm at 150, 350, 700 and 1000 g m^{-2} starting densities, respectively. Actual plant heights at the two lower densities were less than the shoot lengths because of the spreading growth habit of the plants. Root length, on the other hand, did not increase significantly with plant density, due to the high availability of nutrients in the water.

In addition to increased plant height, a significant increase in lamina size was observed between the 350 and 700 g m^{-2} cultures (Table 2). Mean lamina size ranged from 73.6 to 78.2 cm^2 at low densities and 135.6 to 152.6 cm^2 at high densities. Although lamina size increased significantly with plant density, no significant change in the number of leaves per plant was observed (Table 2). Leaf area index (LAI) increased with plant density, as a result of increased lamina size as well as greater number of plants per unit area. LAI values ranged from 1.4 at the lowest plant density to 8.4 at the highest density (Table 2).

Tissue concentrations of N and P decreased at higher plant densities, resulting from the accelerated production of fibrous, supportive tissue with high C:N and C:P ratios. Average

TABLE 2. Morphological and chemical characteristics of water hyacinth plants grown at four distinct density levels under nutrient non-limiting conditions. Measurements were made during the active growing season (July). Values represent mean ± standard deviation.

Parameter	n	Plant density range (g m^{-2}) 150-320	350-600	700-1000	1000-1250
Shoot length (cm)	30	37.1± 6.8	47.0± 8.1	65.4± 8.8	74.0± 10.3
Root length (cm)	30	13.3± 4.3	13.8± 4.0	17.1± 4.8	18.2± 4.3
Lamina size (cm^2)	53	73.6±41.6	78.2± 2.2	135.6±76.1	152.6± 69.7
No. leaves/ plant	30	8.4± 2.8	8.3± 2.4	9.2± 3.4	8.8± 2.8
Leaf area index (m^2 m^{-2})	3	1.4± 0.03	2.0± 0.02	6.2± 0.02	8.4± 0.01
Tissue N conc. (g kg^{-1})	30	39.5± 4.7	37.1± 4.0	35.1± 4.5	33.3± 3.6
Tissue P conc. (g kg^{-1})	30	9.2± 1.0	9.0± 1.3	8.0± 1.0	8.3± 1.3

concentrations of N ranged from 33.3 to 39.5 g kg^{-1}, while tissue P levels ranged from 8.0 to 9.2 g kg^{-1}.

The observed density-induced changes in plant morphology were indicative of the competitive strategy of water hyacinth to maximize photosynthetic efficiency (Boyd and Scarsbrook, 1975; Center and Spencer, 1981).

Inorganic N (NH_4^+ + NO_3^-) removal, determined by mass balance, increased with plant density, ranging from 1351 to 2316 mg N m^{-2} d^{-1} during the period May - October (Figure 2). Most of the observed N removal was attributed to plant uptake, although a substantial fraction was due to other processes. Plant uptake of N, calculated from growth and tissue concentration data, ranged from 1037 mg N m^{-2} d^{-1} at 150 g m^{-2} starting density to 1503 mg N m^{-2} d^{-1} at 700 g m^{-2}. The relative importance of plant uptake decreased at higher plant densities, accounting for only 56% of the total inorganic N removed at 1000 g m^{-2} starting density.

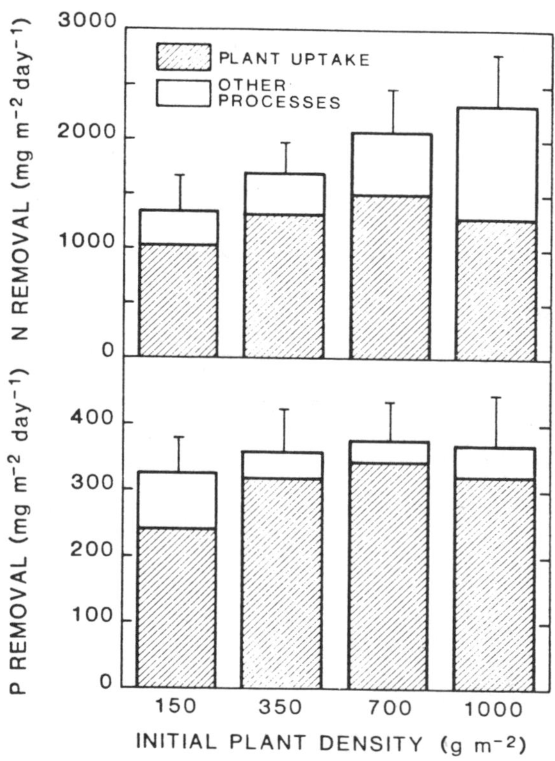

FIGURE 2. Plant uptake and total removal of inorganic N and P in water hyacinth cultures maintained at four distinct plant density ranges. Data points represent mean daily values for the period May - October, 1983. Initial N and P concentrations in the water (changed weekly) were 42 and 6 mg L^{-1}, respectively.

Other processes probably contributing to N removal were nitrification-denitrification reactions in the water and rhizosphere; volatilization of NH_3 which would be dependent on pH and the amount of exposed water surface; and assimilation by micro- and macro-invertebrates. Since sediment was not incorporated into the growth tanks, N losses by adsorption of NH_4-N and denitrification were not considered.

Removal of P from the water was not significantly affected by plant density (Figure 2). The mean rate of P removal during May - October (maximum growth period) ranged from 328 to 378 mg P m^{-2} d^{-1} for starting densities of 150 and 700 g m^{-2}, respectively. Plant uptake accounted for 73 to 91% of the total P removal. Uptake rates ranged from 241 mg P m^{-2} d^{-1} at 150 g m^{-2} to 344 mg P m^{-2} d^{-1} in the 700 g m^{-2} cultures. The balance of P removal was probably a result of chemical precipitation, caused by the high concentrations of Ca and Mg in the water and, to a lesser extent, by microbial assimilation. Removal of P would also have been significantly enhanced on a short-term basis had sediments been present.

CONCLUSIONS

Results of this study indicate that maximum productivity of water hyacinth in high-nutrient cultures occurs at moderately high plant densities, ca. 1000 g dry wt m^{-2}. This would suggest that management of a water hyacinth system for maximum biomass production would involve frequent harvesting to maintain optimum plant density. This management strategy would also appear to be most suitable for maximum P removal, which depends largely upon plant uptake and, consequently, upon high growth rates. It is probable that frequent harvesting results in a higher plant quality for biogasification or feed production; i.e. higher nutrient and lower fiber content. Maximum N removal, however, would be achieved through infrequent harvesting, due to the enhancing effect of various biochemical processes.

Other factors must be considered, however, when results from a controlled study are extrapolated to a large-scale managed system. For example, harvesting and handling costs may preclude frequent harvesting in some cases. On the other hand, an infrequent or no-harvest approach to system management may lead to other, more serious problems, most notably disease and insect damage. Thus, a successful management plan must begin with the basic concepts determined through controlled studies and incorporate intensive system monitoring and evaluation in the operational phase.

ACKNOWLEDGMENTS

This paper reports results from a project that contributes to a cooperative program between the Institute of Food and Agricultural Sciences (IFAS) of the University of Florida and the

Gas Research Institute (GRI) entitled "Methane from Biomass and Waste." Florida Agricultural Experiment Stations Journal Series No. 7710.

REFERENCES

Bagnall, L. O., J. A. Baldwin, and J. F. Hentges. 1974. Processing and storage of water hyacinth silage. Hyacinth Control J. 12:73-79.

Boyd, C. E., and E. Scarsbrook. 1975. Influence of nutrient additions and initial density of plants on production of water hyacinth _Eichhornia crassipes_. Aquat. Bot. 1:253-261.

Bremner, J. M., and C. S. Mulvaney. 1982. Nitrogen-total. p. 595-624. _In_ A. L. Page (ed.) Methods of Soil Analysis, Part 2: Chemical and Microbiological Properties. ASA, SSSA, Madison, WI. 1159 pp.

Center, T. D., and N. R. Spencer. 1981. The phenology and growth of water hyacinth (_Eichhornia crassipes_ [Mart] Solms) in a eutrophic north-central Florida lake. Aquat. Bot. 10:1-32.

Cornwell, D. A., J. Zoltek, Jr., C. D. Patrinely, T. deS. Furman, and J. I. Kim. 1977. Nutrient removal by water hyacinth. J. Water Pollut. Control Fed. 49:57-65.

DeBusk, T. A., J. H. Ryther, M. D. Hanisak, and L. D. Williams. 1981. Effects of seasonality and plant density on the productivity of some freshwater macrophytes. Aquatic Bot. 10:133-142.

Jackson, M. L. 1958. Soil Chemical Analysis, p. 498. Prentice-Hall, London.

Reddy, K. R., and W. F. DeBusk. 1984. Growth characteristics of aquatic macrophytes cultured in nutrient-enriched water: 1. Water hyacinth, water lettuce, and pennywort. Econ. Bot. 38:229-239.

Reddy, K. R., K. L. Campbell, D. A. Graetz, and K. M. Portier. 1982. Use of biological filters for agricultural drainage water treatment. J. Environ. Qual. 11:591-595.

Shiralipour, A., and P. H. Smith. 1984. Conversion of biomass into methane gas. Biomass 6:85-94.

U. S. Environmental Protection Agency. 1979. Methods for chemical analysis of water and wastes. U. S. Environmental Protection Agency, Cincinnati, OH.

Wolverton, B. C., and R. C. McDonald. 1979. Upgrading facultative wastewater lagoons with vascular aquatic plants. J. Water Pollut. Control Fed. 51:305-313.

MODELING OF THE HYDROMECHANICAL CHARACTERISTICS OF WATER HYACINTH

R. J. Petrell and L. O. Bagnall
Agricultural Engineering Department
University of Florida, IFAS
Gainesville, Florida 32611

ABSTRACT

To aid in the design of more efficient harvesters, the compressive characteristics of the water hyacinth were determined at loading rates up to 0.5 m s^{-1}. Hyacinths were contained in a 9.29 m^2 frame-like structure that contained force measurement devices. Effects of plant size and structural composition on compressive forces were tested, and the resulting curves cross over each other at the point on the graph of a specific area of 0.02 m^2 kg^{-1} and a force/unit width of 180 N m^{-1}.

Keywords: Water hyacinth, hydrodynamic, compressive properties.

INTRODUCTION

Water hyacinths (Eichhornia crassipes) are harvested to control their propagation in natural waterways and in sewage treatment plants as part of the water treatment system. In any hyacinth harvesting system, the plants must reach land in order to be further processed or disposed of. One way of performing the transport is by towing or by pushing a mat of plants. Often, however, when the mats are dragged, the plants start to jam up against the containing device. Bogart (1949) described the mechanisms of the formation of the jams as a combination of accretion in area and a rolling-under action that increases the vertical dimensions of the mat. Of consequence of the jam, towing forces increase and at times, the mat rolls under the containing device and escapes. An efficient hyacinth harvester, then, depends on simple equipment that is based on the hydromechanical characteristics such as the drag forces and the elastic properties of a given population of hyacinths; however, the physical characterization of aquatic plants is still inadequate to predict the performance of large towing or dragging systems. The

Aquatic Plants for Water Treatment
and Resource Recovery
K.R. Reddy and W.H. Smith (Eds.)

ISBN 0-941463-00-1

objective of this research was to present the compressive characterization of a large mat of hyacinth plants.

In the area of solid mechanics, the following investigations have been recorded. Bagnall (1974) found the ultimate strengths of water hyacinth stems to be 752 mPa in axial tension, 193 mPa in axial compression and 3 mPa in lateral double shear. Also, the bulk mechanical properties of the water hyacinth were determined (Bagnall, 1982). The frictional coefficients of chopped water hyacinth were found to be related to the type and condition of the material surface (Mekvanich and Bagnall, 1978).

MATERIALS AND METHODS

A test rig was designed and constructed for the investigation. The 3 by 3 m compression frame consisted of a moving rake carried along a pair of tubular rails and a similar fixed rake. Rake tines on 20 cm centers, extended 30 cm below the rake tube and 38 cm above. The moving rake was driven by chains on each rail which in turn, were driven by a hydraulic motor or a modified automotive winch. Force and motion were transmitted from the chain to the rake through a rake support carriage with load cells and parallel linkages. The signals from the load cells and from the position-sensing potentiometer were recorded on a Campbell Scientific CR7 data logger that was equipped with "Burst mode" software.

After each test, five plants were characterized by shoot height, root length, mass, root/shoot ratio, and total length (Table 1). All the plants inside of the frame were also weighed and the weight was divided by the area of the frame in order to determine the standing areal density of the hyacinth mat.

TABLE 1. Average values and [standard deviations] of the physical properties of the plants that populated the hyacinth mats tested.

Loading speed $m\ s^{-1}$	Overall length m	Root length m	Shoot length m	Root: shoot ratio	Mass kg	Areal density $kg\ m^{-2}$
0.1	0.53 [0.06]	0.048 [0.02]	0.48 [0.042]	0.095 [0.038]	0.174 [0.058]	10
0.1	0.538 [0.05]	0.048 [0.008]	0.49 [0.049]	0.098 [0.0255]	0.144 [0.05]	10.13
0.1	0.588 [0.095]	0.082 [0.027]	0.5 [0.074]	0.15 [0.039]	0.174 [0.064]	5.96
0.13	0.89 [0.1]	0.4 [0.095]	0.48 [0.052]	0.83 [0.24]	0.323 [0.1]	26.1
0.34	0.85 [0.12]	0.41 [0.08]	0.43 [0.07]	0.95 [0.18]	0.28 [0.12]	21.07
0.5	Same values as for 0.34 $m\ s^{-1}$					

Plants with the long roots were found at the IFAS field laboratory at Zellwood and the shorter rooted plants were tested at the Walt Disney World Sewage Treatment plant, Kissimmee, FL.

The data from the data logger were passed to the computer and graphed. The independent variable is specific area and the dependent variable, force per unit width of mat. Specific area is defined as:

$$A = A_t/M \qquad [1]$$

where A = specific area, $m^2\ kg^{-1}$
A_t = area within frame at time, t
M = total mass of hyacinths inside the test frame.

Specific area was chosen as the independent variable to compensate for differences in initial areal standing densities of the hyacinth mats.

The data was regressed to the form:

$$F = b + m \times \ln A \qquad [2]$$

where F = force/width of mat, $N\ m^{-1}$
A = specific area
b,m are coefficient of regression.

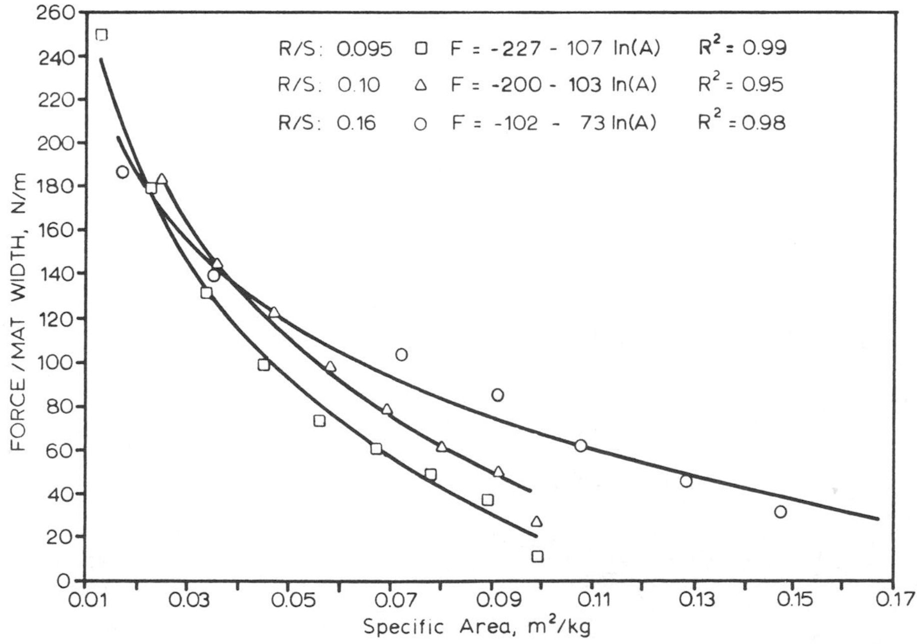

FIGURE 1. Effect of root/shoot ratio (R/S) on compressive characteristics of 3 m^2 water hyacinth mats. Compression speed: 0.1 $m\ s^{-1}$.

RESULTS AND DISCUSSION

The compressive characteristics of two different populations of water hyacinth mats are presented in Figure 1. One population had slightly longer roots than the other. As the root/shoot ratio of the plants in a mat increased, the force required to compress the mat increased.

The effect of varying loading speed on the compressive characteristics is still inconclusive (Figure 2). The plants used in the three tests shown were of similar root to shoot ratios, but were bigger than those plants used in the other experiments. The conclusion can be drawn that loading rate has a very different role as compared to root length in the hydrodynamics of water hyacinths. Further testing will be required to be able to determine the exact function of the loading rate.

The coefficients of determination (r^2) were nearly all greater than 0.9 but in one case the correlation was 0.78. The lower value was due to a larger than normal force required to initiate the compression.

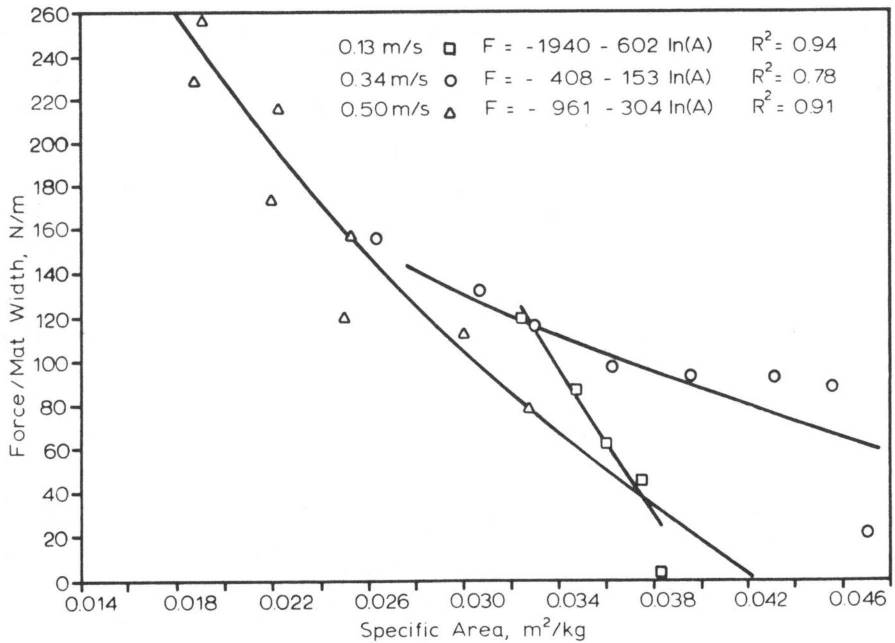

FIGURE 2. Effect of compression speed on compressive characteristics of 3 m^2 water hyacinth mats. Root/shoot ratio: 0.84 - 0.95.

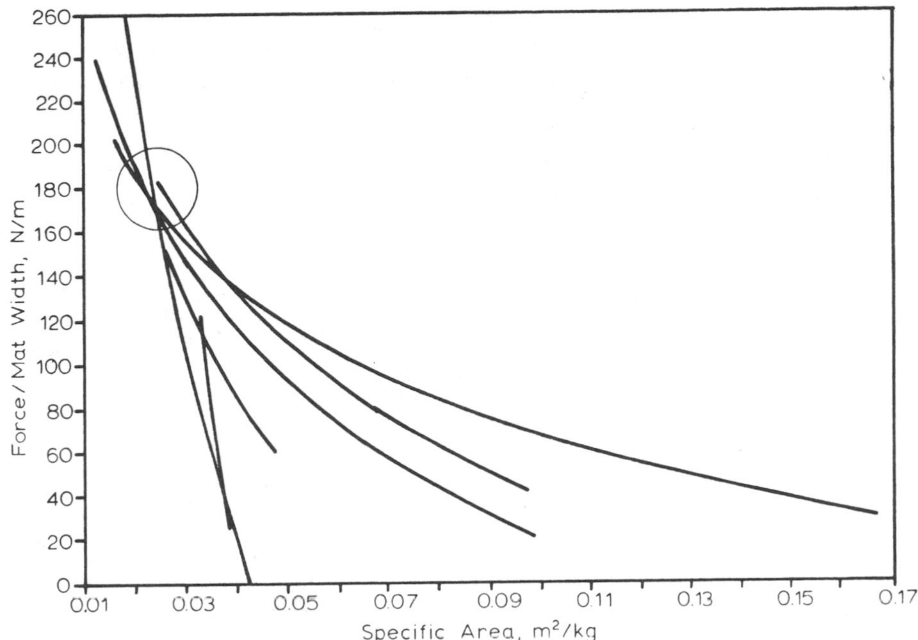

FIGURE 3. Compressive characteristics of 3 m^2 water hyacinth mats at all observed speeds and root/shoot ratios, showing convergenge at 0.025 m^2 kg^{-1} and 180 N m^{-1}.

Finally, for all the loading speeds and root to shoot ratios, the various force vs. specific area curves converged at around 0.025 m^2 kg^{-1} and 180 N m^{-1} (Figure 3). This point could be related to the "jamming" point or the point when the vertical displacement of the mat increases.

CONCLUSIONS

The larger the root/shoot ratio the plants have in a given mat, the greater will be the force required to gather the plants together.

The characteristic compressive curves of force versus mat displacement fit equations for exponential curves.

ACKNOWLEDGMENTS

The authors gratefully acknowledge the assistance given by personnel of the Disney World Water Hyacinth Sewage Treatment Center and to J. Petrell, technician and sister to R. Petrell in helping collect our data.

REFERENCES

Bogart, D. B. 1949. The effects of aquatic weeds on flow in Everglades canals. Proc. Soil Sci. of Fla. 9:32-52.

Bagnall, L. O. 1974. Mechanical properties of mature water hyacinth stems. Presented at the SE Regional ASAE Meeting, Memphis, TN.

Baganll, L. O. 1982. Bulk mechanical properties of water hyacinth. J. Aquat. Plant Manage. 20:49-53.

Mekvanich, K., and L. O. Bagnall. 1984. Friction coefficients of chopped water hyacinth. ASAE Paper 78-3554. St. Joseph, MI.

BIOMASS PRODUCTION IN A NON-POINT SOURCE WETLAND

E. B. Henson
University of Vermont
Burlington, Vermont 05405

ABSTRACT

Munsons Flat is a 265 ha lake margin wetland that was designated as a nonpoint example, and should therefore be less productive than nutrient enriched wetlands. An intensive study was made in 1976 to evaluate the distribution and biomass production of the vegetation. Five line transects totaling c600 m of transect, more than 160 quadrat samples, and biometry of individual plants were used to estimate net annual biomass production.

Distribution of vegetation was not uniform, and different species dominated along each transect. *Equisetum*, *Sparganium*, *Sagittaria* and *Scirpus* were the dominant plants in the marsh. *Phalaris* and *Scirpus* yielded 484 and 455 g m^{-2} yr^{-1} respectively. Six dominant plants together accounted for about 1,200 g m^{-2} yr^{-1} in net production. The low production of this wetland is attributed to the short growing season, the diversity of plants in the wetland, and to a relatively low level of nutrients.

Keywords: Primary production, Lake Champlain, *Equisetum*, *Phalaris*, *Sagittaria*, *Scirpus*, *Sium*, *Sparganium*.

INTRODUCTION

This paper contributes to our knowledge of the net biomass production of a lake-margin riverine embayment type wetland bordering Lake Champlain. Since the area receives no sewage discharge, and only a minor amount of non-point agricultural discharge, this wetland was used as an example of non-point drainage by the U.S. Environmental Protection Agency (1974). It also represents conditions in mid-northern latitudes, just below 45° N.

The results represent a portion of the study to evaluate nutrient relations in adjacent wetlands as related to potential lake-level regulation (Henson and Potash, 1977). Dr. Milton Potash, Linda Canina and Thomas Gutowski made significant contributions to this study.

Aquatic Plants for Water Treatment
and Resource Recovery
K.R. Reddy and W.H. Smith (Eds.)

ISBN 0-941463-00-1

DESCRIPTION OF THE STUDY AREA

Munsons flat (Figure 1) is located 16 km north of Burlington, Vermont, on the eastern margin of Lake Champlain (Henson, 1978). It is described as a partially enclosed lake-margin riverine bayhead wetland. The wetland occupies a bowl-shaped depression that opens to Lake Champlain through a narrow opening in a rocky ridge through which the main effluent stream drains into the lake. It is fed by four streams that have a combined catchment area of 103.9 Km^2. Malletts Creek, the largest, meanders through the wetland emptying into Lake Champlain in a channel cut through a rock ridge. The vegetation of the wetland is comprised of a non-homogeneous mosaic of stands of mixed species, with dominance of any one species being localized (Bogucki et al., 1978).

STRATEGY OF EVALUATING BIOMASS PRODUCTION

The research was approached along three directions so that the results would merge into a unified estimate of plant net

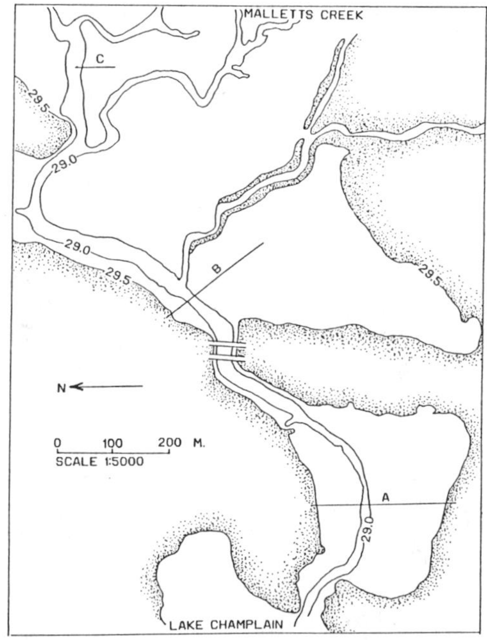

FIGURE 1. Map of Munsons Flat wetland. The 29.0 contour defines the margins of the channels, and the 29.5 m defines the margin of the wetland during ordinary summer lake level with stippled area indicating land. Transects A, B, and C are located.

production. These three directions include: a) transect analyses, where approximately every 10 d a measured transect was observed, documenting species (or genus) distributions for each meter of the transect; b) quadrat samples, where designated areas along each transect were measured quantitatively to determine the density of the plants in the specific area of the transect; and c) biometry, data on the weights of each plant found in the quadrats were determined. With this design, data would be available concerning the relative abundance of the plants in different parts of the wetland, their quantitative abundance, and the growth characteristics of each species or genus.

Considering the non-homogeneous dispersal of plants in this wetland, five transects (Figure 1) were established to include as many areas of dominant vegetation as feasible. Regression analyses of the increase in biomass and density of each dominant plant through the growing season were used to estimate the net production of each plant, and by summation, the net production of the wetland. It was not possible to obtain sufficient data for an appraisal of biomass production for every plant growing in the wetland, but by considering the dominant plants, underestimation is minimal.

METHODS

Five transects were established (Figure 1). Transect A was situated near the opening to Lake Champlain (AN north of Malletts Creek, 70 m, and AS south of the Creek, 150 m long). Transect BS (184 m) was in the middle of the wetland; Transect BN a short extension north of Malletts Creek. Transect BS extended from a sloping grain field to Malletts Creek channel and represented the open marsh of this wetland. Transect C, 71 m long, was near the bayhead end of this wetland, bordering a swamp forest.

Field studies were conducted from May through November of 1976. Julian days were used for regression analyses, with day 400 falling on April 29, 1976.

At approximately 10 d intervals, line transect observations were made along a calibrated line. Records were made of each plant observed in each meter of the transect (Table 1). This provides an index of relative presence along the transect.

Quadrat samples were also collected in the emergent zones, the mixed zones, and the floating/submergent zones. Three quadrats (1978 cm^2 each) were collected from each zone. All plants enclosed in the quadrats were counted, and the data converted into number of plants and grams per square meter.

The observers collected three specimens of each species found in the quadrat, roots and all, from the general area when possible. The collected plants were labeled as to location and tentative identification, and taken to the laboratory.

All plants were washed with tap water to remove as much of the soil and attached algae as possible. They were then spread

TABLE 1. Most common wetland plant genera encountered in Munson Flat transects in 1976. Values are average number of plants observed per 10 m of transect. The number of quadrat sets sampled that included the plants is given for comparison.

Plant	Transect				Quadrats	
	AN	AS	B	C	Avg.	Totals
Equisetum sp.	6.46	1.19	6.17	3.14	4.24	53
Sparganium eurycarpum	1.34	7.47	2.11	0.26	3.73	40
Sagittaria spp.	1.51	1.48	7.10	3.25	3.34	69
Ceratophyllum demersum	3.89	2.23	0.65	1.91	2.89	25
Scirpus fluviatilis	1.23	3.21	6.52	0.10	2.72	51
Polygonum amphibium	2.49	1.79	0.26	3.86	2.10	11
Potomogeton Berchholderi	2.43	1.52	2.00	2.03	2.00	29
Sium suave	0.89	2.88	1.75	2.41	1.98	35
Eleocharis robbinsii	3.54	2.51	1.13	--	1.80	13
Anacharis canadensis	2.43	1.01	0.37	1.19	1.67	24
Phalarus arundinacea	0.40	2.07	1.74	1.45	1.42	40
Acorus calamus	1.63	1.05	1.03	0.20	0.98	6

out over laboratory benches for drying. Within a day, the plants were examined and identified using Muenscher (1944) or Fasset (1960) and by consulting with specialists in the Botany Department.

The plants were air dried. Bulky stems of certain plants such as *Sparganium* were cut open to retard mold or decomposition. As pointed out by Westlake (1963), air drying is a source of error, but specimens were retained on the bench until they were considered dry. During this process the plants were dissected into the component parts of roots, stems, leaves, and any fruiting bodies. After drying, the anatomical parts were weighed on a triple-beam balance.

Typically, there were three specimens of each species collected for each quadrat. The air dry weights (ADW) of the three specimens were averaged, and those results are used in the biomass analyses.

Estimates of biomass production of each species were made by plotting the mean total air dried weight (ADW), the mean below ground weight (BGW), and the aboveground weight (AGW) against time.

Aquatic macrophytes grow rapidly in spring and early summer followed by a decreasing growth rate, reaching a maximum or peak biomass in middle summer. This is a characteristic sigmoid growth (Westlake, 1965; Wetzel, 1983). This period is followed by a decline in biomass as respiration exceeds production, or by dieback.

In practice, however, sampling schedules and variability of sampling results are not sensitive enough to detect the exponential growth phase, and in most instances the biomass growth is approximated by linearity.

Each of the dominant species of plants were analyzed from the quadrat data in order to derive an evaluation of the changes in density of the plants during the growing season. Since the objective of this study is to appraise the net biomass production in the total marsh, all quadrat data from each transect and for each sampling data were pooled and examined, and for each plant species the mean numbers per square meter for each day were calculated. A value of zero was given for those quadrats where the plant in question was not encountered.

Regression results of mean plant weight against time were combined with the regression results of mean abundance against time. The net result is a curve of average daily biomass of the plant per square meter of the total marsh area.

RESULTS

The results presented are based on 490 mean weight values of plant species in quadrat samples collected from 5 transects. This represents analyses of nearly 1,500 plant specimens. Munsons Flat is described as a wetland of mixed species, with 35% of the area consisting of emergent vegetation (Bogucki et al., 1978). Over thirty species of plants were identified from the transects, with few that can be considered dominant, and many species of submergents. The most common plants found in each transect for all days of the growing season of 1976 are listed in Table 1. Values are the average number of encounters for each plant along an average 10 m of transect. Plant distribution in this wetland was non-uniform (Table 1). A test of proportionality indicated that all emergent plants were adequately represented in the quadrat sampling (Table 1) except *Polygonum* and *Acorus*, two genera not included in the present discussion because of insufficient data.

Total Air Dry Weight

The dry weight data (Table 2) may be considered to be at least 5% heavier than oven dried weight (Westlake, 1963) because of residual moisture in the air dried specimens. *Sparganium* was the bulkiest plant and *Equisetum* the lightest included in this study. Average weights for the entire growing season (Table 2) showed the average aboveground weight ranged from 58% of total weight for *Scirpus* to 87% for *Polygonum*.

ADW Regression Analyses

The mean air dry weights for plants with sufficient data were plotted against time and most plots suggested linearity. The regression analyses for seven dominant plants are summarized (Table 3) where N is the number of days used for the regression.

TABLE 2. Seasonal mean values of total air dried weight (ADW) of seven dominant genera of plants in Munson Flats, 1976. N is the number of days where mean values were used in the calculations. BGW is below ground weight (roots), AGW is the aboveground weight. Weight values in grams.

Plant	N	ADW	BGW	AGW	%AGW
Equisetum	20	2.49	0.6	1.9	77.9
Sparganium	16	14.20	2.9	11.3	79.7
Scirpus	14	9.85	4.1	5.7	58.1
Sagittaria	22	3.79	0.9	2.9	76.5
Sium	16	2.87	1.0	1.9	65.5
Phalaris	18	4.93	1.3	3.6	73.8
Polygonum	5	16.80	2.2	14.6	86.9

TABLE 3. Analyses of growth of biomass (ADW) of selected genera in Munson Flat, 1976. The time for the independent variable is Julian days. N = number of quadrat sets in the analyses, r = the coefficient of correlation, b = regression constant (= g m^{-2} d^{-1}), a = the intercept, D_o = day when ADW is zero, and the data. The average weights are given in Table 2.

Plant	N	r	b	a	D_o	Date
Equisetum	20	0.87	0.051	-22.1	434	June 2
Sparganium	11	0.52	0.115	-42.1	366	March 26
Scirpus	16	0.50	0.086	-31.8	370	March 30
Sagittaria	22	0.65	0.066	-28.0	423	May 22
Sium	16	0.71	0.055	-23.9	454	June 22
Phalaris	18	0.35	0.024	-6.8	284	Jan 4
Polygonum	5	0.84	0.819	-409.1	500	Aug 7

The mean values for each day may have been derived from a single quadrat to as many as seven quadrat means. The constants (a and b) for the linear equation are given in the table, with the Julian day (D) being the variable. The slope (b) is the mean biomass production rate in g m^{-2} d^{-1}. The value D_o is the day that the projected ADW is zero. With the exception of the reed canarygrass (Phalarus), the dormant vegetation of reserves starts growing between March 26 and June 22. This is reasonable since the ice melts and the bottom warms at this time of year. The starting date for the reed canarygrass is an artifact of the regression (weakest regression coefficient), but does reflect the fact that this grass is one of the first plants to appear in early spring. The choice was to take a constant mean for the analyses, or to go with the trend. The latter course has been followed.

Table 4 presents the results of regression analyses for mean plant density (No. of plants m^{-2}) of all quadrats for each sampling day. The mean density and standard deviation of the plants for the entire season are listed (Table 4), as well as the constants for the regression equation. The correlation coefficient in all instances is low (Table 4), and for most of the plots made there was wide scatter because of the large amounts of variation between transects and between adjacent quadrats. For two of the genera the regression is negative, suggesting a density decrease as the season progressed.

The last step in the analysis was to combine the two regressions by multiplying the ADW for a plant from the first equation by the mean density of the plant in the second equation. The product is the mean biomass in g m^{-2} (Figure 2).

Sagittaria and *Equisetum*, two plants with negative regressions for density, generate biomass curves that reach a peak in late July followed by declining biomass (Figure 2). The others show constantly increasing biomass curves with different slopes. For these plants the curve would be deflected downwards as biological conditions (as maturity) are completed, and environmental conditions (light, temperature) lead to senescence.

Maximum biomass production for *Sagittaria* and *Equisetum* is determined to be at the day of inflection. This was August 7 for *Sagittaria* and August 2 for *Equisetum*. The peak productions data for the other plants is designated as being August 17. That date was chosen because the growth plots for the individual species indicated lower values of ADW, and field observations indicated dieoff beyond that date. The initial date of growth (D_o, Table 3) was obtained by regression.

TABLE 4. Regression analyses of mean density of plants through the growing season in Munson Flats in 1976. N is the number of days where mean abundance data were obtained. The mean abundance (No. m^{-2}) for the season, and the standard deviation. The Correlation Coefficient, and the constants for linear regression are shown in the last three columns.

Plant	N	Mean	St. D.	r	b	a
Equisetum	23	9.01	10.28	-0.260	-0.106	60.49
Sparganium	17	7.60	7.54	0.135	0.135	-15.72
Sagittaria	27	11.85	20.61	-0.148	-0.123	71.34
Scirpus	20	29.40	47.20	0.145	0.321	-125.95
Sium	23	2.03	2.25	0.034	0.003	0.57
Phalaris	21	62.63	65.90	0.315	0.944	-392.52

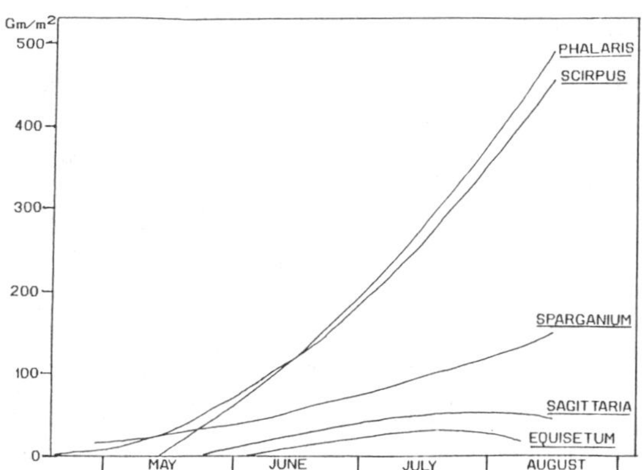

FIGURE 2. Plot of the calculated net dry weight biomass production of five dominant plants in Munsons Flat, 1976. Values in g dry wt m^{-2}.

From these analysis, net biomass production was as follows:

Equisetum	25.23 g m^{-2} yr^{-1}	0.41 g m^{-2} d^{-1}
Sparganium	145.28 "	1.01 "
Sagittaria	49.70 "	0.65 "
Scirpus	455.27 "	3.25 "
Sium	8.59 "	0.15 "
Phalaris	483.72 "	2.75 "
Total	1,167.79 g m^{-2} yr^{-1}	8.22 g m^{-2} d^{-1}

DISCUSSION

This paper contributes information on net biomass production for a non-point northern latitude marsh. Six dominant species had an average seasonal production rate of 1.37 g m^{-2} d^{-1} dry weight. The dominant plants analyzed yielded a net production of 12 Mg ha^{-1} yr^{-1}. Since these six species represented most of the emergent species in the marsh, that value is a conservative estimate of the level of production for this marsh. If all of the other plants contributed 60% of this value, the total marsh production would be approximately 19 Mg ha^{-1} yr^{-1}.

This marsh, therefore, has low production compared with other data available. Wetzel (1965) reviewed biomass production data for fertile northern latitude wetlands, and concluded that the range was between 20 and 45 Mg ha^{-1} yr^{-1}. Whigham et al. (1978) show that net production of middle Atlantic freshwater tidal wetlands produce between 10-35 Mg ha^{-1} yr^{-1}. Thus, according to those standards, Munsons Flat is one of the lowest producers.

The low production of this marsh can be attributed to the high latitude, large species diversity in the marsh, low density of plants, and low nutrient levels in the area.

ACKNOWLEDGMENTS

This paper was part of an environmental impact study sponsored by the International Joint Commission. Munsons Flat (44° 34' N., 73° 11' W) is located in the Town of Colchester, Chittenden County, in the State of Vermont.

REFERENCES

Bogucki, D. J., and G. K. Gruendling. 1978. Remote sensing to identify, assess, and predict ecological impact on Lake Champlain wetlands. U.S. Dept. Int., Off. Water Res. and Tech., Proj. C-6075, 191 pp., maps.

Fassett, N. C. 1960. A manual of aquatic plants. Univ. Wis. Press, Madison. 405 pp.

Henson, E. B. 1978. Ecology of a Lake Champlain wetland transect. Verh. Internat. Verein. Limnol. 20:507-509.

Henson, E. B., and M. Potash. 1977. Support data (biological production and nutrient studies) for the reports to the International Joint Commission on the Regulation of Lake Champlain. Rep. to Environ. Impact Committee, Int. Champlain-Richelieu Board. 58 pp.

Muenscher, W. C. 1944. Aquatic plants of the United States. Comstock Publ. Co., Ithaca, NY. 374 pp.

U.S. Environmental Protection Agency. 1974. EPA national eutrophication survey. Report on Lake Champlain, New York and Vermont, EPA Regions I and II, Working Paper No. 154. Pacific Northwest Environmental Res. Lab., Corvallis, Oregon. 206 pp.

Westlake, D. F. 1963. Comparison of plant productivity. Bio. Rev. 38:385-429.

Westlake, D. F. 1965. Some basic data for investigations of the productivity of aquatic macrophytes. Mem. Ist. Ital. Idrobiol. 18(Suppl.):229-248.

Wetzel, R. G. 1983. Limnology. Saunders College Publ. Co. 2nd ed. 767 pp.

Whigham, D. F., J. McCormick, R. E. Good, and R. L. Simpson. 1978. Biomass and primary production in freshwater tidal wetlands of the middle Atlantic coast. pp. 3-20. In R. E. Good, D. F. Whigham, and R. L. Simpson (ed.) Freshwater Wetlands. Academic Press.

THE EFFECT OF HYDRAULIC RETENTION TIME AND DUCKWEED CROPPING RATE ON NUTRIENT REMOVAL FROM DAIRY BARN WASTEWATER

A. J. Whitehead, K. V. Lo, and N. R. Bulley
Dept. of Bio-Resource Engineering
University of British Columbia
Vancouver, B.C., CANADA

ABSTRACT

The effect of hydraulic retention time and duckweed cropping rate on nutrient removal from dilute dairy manure was investigated. A combination of Lemna minor and Spirodela polyrhiza was cultured in 8-L, 8.5 cm deep, plastic channels in a glasshouse. Hydraulic retention times of 7, 10, 20 and 40 d were used. The plants were cropped daily at rates of 5%, 10%, 20% and 30% of the 940 cm^2 water surface area per day. The highest sustainable nutrient removal efficiencies were obtained at 20 d HRT and 10% d^{-1} cropping. Under these conditions the duckweed N and P removal rates were 404 mg N m^{-2} d^{-1} and 84 mg P m^{-2} d^{-1}, representing 30% and 25% of the respective nutrient loading rates. The 30% d^{-1} cropping rate was not sustainable due to algal competition. The results suggest that the contribution of duckweed to N and P removal is maximized by increasing the cropping intensity in proportion to the nutrient loading rate.

Keywords: Duckweed, cropping rate, hydraulic retention time, nutrient removal, dairy manure, laboratory-scale.

INTRODUCTION

The use of aquatic plants as functional components of wastewater lagooning systems can be an effective means of improving effluent quality (N.A.S., 1976; E.P.A., 1978). The duckweeds are promising species for seasonal use at higher latitudes (O'Brien, 1980). In nutrient-rich environments, the Lemnaceae exhibit rapid growth rates, have a high protein content, and have no significant pests (Hillman and Culley, 1978). Duckweed growth rate can be enhanced by maintaining the population density below a critical level, above which crowding inhibition occurs (DeBusk et al., 1981). Little published information is available on the treatment effectiveness of managed (i.e.,

ISBN 0-941463-00-1

cropped) rather than batch (e.g. Said et al., 1979) wastewater loading. This paper reports on the results of laboratory experiments to study the effect of duckweed harvesting intensity and hydraulic retention time on nutrient removal from simulated dairy barn wastewater.

MATERIALS AND METHODS

The treatment combinations are summarized in Table 1. The experiment was carried out in a controlled environment glasshouse (18-28°C) under natural illumination (49°N latitude), during August and September, 1985.

Each experimental unit consisted of a plastic tub (33 cm long, 29 cm wide, 16 cm deep), modified to provide a U-shaped channel with a length to width ratio of approximately 4.5:1. Wastewater was continuously pumped for 12 h each day to the channels using a peristaltic pump. The hydraulic retention times were approximately 7, 10, 20 and 40 d. The overflow level was set to maintain a working volume of 8 L, at a depth of 8.5 cm.

The experimental "wastewater" was prepared from fresh dairy cow manure mixed with urine, collected from the U.B.C. Dairy Unit. The manure was diluted 8:1 with tap water and successively passed through No. 10 and No. 50 standard mesh screens (2 mm and 0.295 mm square openings, respectively), and then stored at 4°C prior to use.

The species used were *Lemna minor* and *Spirodela polyrhiza*. Each channel was stocked initially with 20 g of duckweed, 10 g of each species. Cropping entailed daily removing all the plants from within floating plastic frames which were placed on the duckweed mat. The wet biomass was centrifugally dewatered, and the fresh weight determined. Dry matter was measured after drying the duckweed to constant weight in a 70°C oven. Water samples were collected twice weekly and stored in plastic bottles at 4°C for up to one week prior to analysis.

Both water and duckweed samples were analyzed for Total Kjeldahl Nitrogen (TKN) and total phosphorus (TP) after digestion in concentrated sulfuric acid, according to the method of Schumann et al. (1973). Water samples were also analyzed for NO_3^- plus NO_2^- (reported as NO_3-N) and total ammonia (NH_3-N). All chemical measurements were determined colorimetrically using a Technicon Autoanalyzer II. The pH was measured periodically with a pH meter.

RESULTS AND DISCUSSION

Influent and Effluent Quality

Over 60% of the TN consisted of organic N (Table 1). Effluent nutrient concentrations were in all treatments lower than in the influent, with the exception of organic-N. The high

TABLE 1. Influent and effluent nutrient concentrations.

Treatment	HRT[+]	Cropping rate	NH_3-N	NO_2+NO_3-N	Total-N	Total-P
	-d-	% area d^{-1}	-------mg L^{-1} ± % variability[++]	-------		
Mid Summer (Aug 13-Sept 4)						
Influent			65.5 ±8.2%	2.25 ±11.1%	186.8 ±12.7%	63.1 ±26.9
A	7	10	15.05 ±63.0%	1.15 ±24.3%	169.8 ±9.3%	58.9 ±19.5%
B	10	20	7.42 ±60.3%	1.08 ±26.8%	154.2 ±11.1%	55.2 ±22.7%
C	20	30	3.22 ±49.2%	0.9 ±35.0%	141.4 ±9.7%	53.6 ±18.2%
D_1	20	10	2.09 ±54.1%	1.20 ±8.8	129.9 ±13.6%	52.9 ±18.5%
E	7	30	14.7 ±52.3%	1.17 ±28.2%	159.3 ±9.8%	55.3 ±26.7%
Late Summer (Sept 7-Sept 26)						
Influent			64.10 ±12.3%	1.58 ±7.6%	194.5 ±14.0%	68.8 ±24.6%
D_2	20	10	16.51 ±32.0%	1.27 ±8.7%	110.6 ±9.6%	36.1 ±37.5%
F	20	10	13.41 ±21.0%	1.41 ±12.2%	115.3 ±15.9%	39.8 ±51.3%
G	20	0	16.7 ±21.4%	1.32 ±9.0%	111.5 ±15.4%	37.3 ±50.9%
H	20	5	16.4 ±17.0%	1.37 ±9.1%	111.8 ±14.7%	37.8 ±45.4%
I	40	5	12.3 ±25.5%	1.37 ±8.9%	108.2 ±17.6%	38.0 ±44.6%

[+]Hydraulic residence time.
[++]Standard deviation, as % of mean.

variability of effluent inorganic N species and TP (Table 1) was due to a gradual increase in their concentrations over time. The pH ranged from 7.6 to 8.2 units, and showed no marked changes during the study.

Duckweed Growth and Yield

Only one treatment, D, (20 d HRT and 10% cropping), was able to maintain a dense duckweed mat throughout the 43 d of the experiment. Treatments E and C, both cropped at 30% d^{-1}, could only sustain a duckweed mat for the first 14 d. Similarly, treatments A and B could only sustain cropping (at 10% and 20%, respectively) for 21 d. Harvesting was discontinued once the population density no longer appeared to be effective in limiting algal growth. When dense algal growth occurred, it interfered with normal duckweed development by growing over and submerging the fronds, or by occupying space into which the mats would have expanded. The collapse of duckweed populations in C and E was the result of over-harvesting (Table 1). The collapses in A and B appear to have been due to both a reduction in the availability of solar energy (cloudy weather) and successful competition by algae. The failed treatments did not recover after cessation of cropping, and new treatments were therefore initiated (Table 1).

Growth rates during the start-up phase (days 1-3) were always greater than during subsequent periods. The range of sustainable growth rates was 0.10-0.54 g g^{-1} d^{-1}, with the 43 d average for treatment D being 0.31 g g^{-1} d^{-1} (Table 2). The highest steady state growth rates were obtained from the treatments receiving the highest nutrient loading. The difference in growth rates in treatment D, before and after day 21 probably reflects changes in the availability of solar energy. The mean daily solar radiation during days 0-21 was 21.0 $\pm$ 3.9 MJ m^{-2} d^{-1}, compared to 11.5 $\pm$ 4.4 MJ m^{-2} d^{-1} during days 27-43 (Environment Canada, 1985).

The crop growth rate (CGR) at steady state ranged among treatments from 1.07 g m^{-2} d^{-1} to 5.78 g m^{-2} d^{-1}, with the average from the longest-lived duckweed population (Treatment D) being 3.29 g m^{-2} d^{-1} (Table 2). The highest CGR obtained was 18.1 g m^{-2} d^{-1} during the start-up phase of treatment C. Mean annual yields of 12-15 g m^{-2} d^{-1} have been reported by Culley et al. (1981) in Louisiana (approximately 30°N latitude). Rejmankova (1981, in Culley et al., 1981) measured CGRs of 3.14 g m^{-2} d^{-1} in fishponds and 7.09 g m^{-2} d^{-1} in harvested outdoor tanks in Czechoslovakia (approximately 50°N).

Duckweed N content ranged from 3.5% to 10.9% on a dry weight basis, while P content ranged from 0.7% to 3.3% (Table 2). Treatment D yielded removal rates via duckweed equivalent to 404 mg N m^{-2} d^{-1} and 84 mg P m^{-2} d^{-1}. The nutrient concentrations were generally higher than those reported for duckweed grown on nutrient-rich waters (N.A.S., 1976; N.R.C., 1983). Since, in the present experiment algae was not separated from the cropped duckweed, algal biomass (N.R.C., 1981) probably contributed

TABLE 2. Duckweed productivity and nutrient content.

Treatment	Interval	Relative growth rate	Yield	Nutrient Content++ N	P	Crude protein+++
	---d---	$g\ g^{-1}\ d^{-1}$+	$g\ m^{-2}\ d^{-1}$	----%----		
A	1-3	0.89	9.4	10.7	3.1	66.8
	5-21	0.54	5.8			
B	1-3	1.23	13.1	10.9	3.3	68.1
	5-21	0.51	5.4			
C	1-3	1.70	18.1	10.4	3.2	65.0
	5-14	0.40	4.3			
D	1-3	0.63	6.7	10.1	2.9	63.1
	5-23	0.40	4.2			
	31-42	0.22	2.3	8.2	2.0	51.3
E	1-3	1.33	14.1			
	5-14	0.54	5.8	10.9	2.9	68.1
F	27-43	0.24	2.6	8.0	1.9	50.0
H	27-43	0.123	1.3	8.0	1.8	50.0
I	27-43	0.101	1.1	7.9	2.7	49.4

+Slope of linear regression equation of cumulative dry matter yield versus time.
++Nutrient content as measured at end of experiment.
+++TKN x 6.25.

significantly to the N content of the duckweed harvested during the mid summer interval.

Nutrient Removal Efficiency

The optimum treatment combination, D, yielded mass removal efficiencies of 97.0% for NH_3-N, 58.8% for NO_3-N, 45.6% for Total-N and 21.0% for Total-P, over the whole experimental period. The removal efficiency for both forms of inorganic N was positively correlated with HRT. Cropping rate appeared to have a greater effect on NO_3^- than on NH_3 removal, particularly at the longer HRTs. The lower NO_3^- removal efficiencies may have been due to nitrification taking place at the expense of NH_4. The highest total N removal efficiencies, 32.7% during mid summer and 47.2% during late summer, were obtained from treatments D and I, respectively. The highest P removals were 21.1% during mid summer and 42.0% during late summer, from treatments D and G, respectively. At low HRT (7-10 d), N and P removals increased with increasing cropping rate, while at long HRT (20-40 d), N and P removal increased with decreasing cropping rate.

The duckweed harvest accounted for a maximum of 58.3% and 36.6% of the influent TN and TP, respectively over the mid summer interval. Total duckweed N plus effluent N were found, during this period, to exceed total measured influent N. Similarly, total P output mass exceeded input P, though to a lesser extent than N. This may be due to nutrient import via insects, and microbial N fixation (Zuberer, 1982). During the late summer, duckweed harvest accounted for a maximum of 18.3% and 21.3% of the influent N and P, respectively. Nitrogen uptake efficiency during mid summer increased with increasing HRT but was not significantly affected by cropping rate. Phosphorus uptake also increased with HRT and, at $\leq$10 d HRT, was positively correlated with cropping rate. These results suggest that the contribution of duckweed to nutrient removal was limited by the growth rate.

CONCLUSIONS

Cropping rate is likely to be more manageable than HRT in full scale systems. The results of this study show that under conditions of high nutrient loading (7-10 d HRT) increasing the cropping rate resulted in improved nutrient removal. At lower nutrient loading rates (20-40 d HRT), decreasing the cropping rate was desirable. The trends suggest that, at some point between 10 and 20 d HRT, the factor limiting duckweed growth rate changed from crowding to nutrient availability and duckweed/water contact time. It might be inferred that increasing the time interval between harvests may, therefore, be beneficial at low nutrient loading rates.

Apparently all three parameters, HRT, solar radiation and nutrient loading, may serve as preliminary guides for adjusting the cropping rate. For nutrient removal purposes, the contribution of duckweed would appear to be greater at the upstream (nutrient-rich) end of a treatment system, where growth rate is limited only by climate and/or genetics. Thus, high treatment efficiencies might not be attainable from duckweed culture for polishing purposes at the relatively nutrient poor end of a treatment stream.

Use of these laboratory results in the design of a large scale system should be with caution due to the brief duration of the experiment, the relatively shallow water depth, as well as the absence of wind and grazing animals. Outdoor pilot-scale studies are necessary before design and operational guidelines can be developed for duckweed wastewater treatment systems.

ACKNOWLEDGMENTS

The assistance of the U.B.C. Plant Science Department and the staff of the Horticulture Greenhouse, as well as Jarnal Virdi and Jet Blake, is gratefully acknowledged.

REFERENCES

Culley, D. D., E. Rejmankova, and J. Kvet. 1981. Production, chemical quality and use of duckweeds (Lemnaceae) in aquaculture, waste management and animal feeds. (Priveleged communication, rough draft in review, 1981, World Mariculture Society).

DeBusk, T. A., J. H. Ryther, M. D. Hanisak, and L. D. Williams. 1981. Effects of seasonality and plant density on the productivity of some freshwater macrophytes. Aquat. Bot. 10:133-142.

Environment Canada. 1985. Monthly radiation summary. August and September, 1985. Atmospheric Environment Service. Environment Canada, Ottawa.

Environmental Protection Agency. 1979. Aquaculture systems for wastewater treatment - seminar proceedings and engineering assessment. EPA 430/9-80-006. 485 pp.

Hillman, W. S., and D. D. Culley, Jr. 1978. The uses of duckweed. Am. Sci. 66:442-451.

National Academy of Sciences. 1976. Making aquatic weeds useful: Some perspectives for developing countries. Washington, D.C. 175 pp.

National Research Council (U.S.). 1981. Food, fuel, and fertilizer from organic wastes. National Academy Press, Washington, D.C. 154 pp.

National Research Council (U.S.). 1983. Underutilized resources as animal feedstuffs. National Academy Press, Washington, D.C. 253 pp.

O'Brien, W. J. 1980. Engineering assessment of aquatic plant systems for wastewater treatment. p. 63-80. In Aquaculture Systems for Wastewater Treatment - An Engineering Assessment. EPA 430/9-80-007.

Oron, G., D. Porath, and L. R. Wildschut. 1986. Wastewater treatment and renovation by different duckweed species. J. Environ. Eng. 112:247-263

Said, M. Z. M., D. D. Culley, Jr., L. C. Standifer, E. A. Epps, R. W. Myers, and S. A. Boney. 1979. Effect of harvest rate, waste loading and stocking density on the yield of duckweeds. Proc. World Maricul. Soc. 10:789-780.

Schumann, G. E., M. A. Stanley, and D. Knudsen. 1973. Automated total nitrogen analysis of soil and plant samples. Proc. Soil Sci. Soc. Am. 37:480-481.

Wolverton, B. C., and R. C. McDonald. 1975. Water hyacinth for upgrading sewage lagoons to meet advanced wastewater treatment standards: Part I. NASA Tech. Memorandum TM-X-72729, October 1975. 9 pp.

Zuberer, D. A. 1982. Nitrogen fixation (acetylene reduction) associated with duckweed (Lemnaceae) mats. Appl. Environ. Microbiology 43:823-828.

BIOLOGICAL FLOCCULATION OF MICROALGAE GROWN ON ANAEROBIC DIGESTER EFFLUENT

B. Koopman
Department of Environmental Engineering Sciences
University of Florida
Gainesville, Florida 32611

E. P. Lincoln
Agricultural Engineering Department
University of Florida, IFAS
Gainesville, Florida 32611

H. Kang and S.-I. Lee
Department of Environmental Engineering Sciences
University of Florida
Gainesville, Florida 32611

ABSTRACT

Microalgae were grown in a high-rate pond treating anaerobically digested swine waste. Mature cultures from the high-rate pond were isolated in flow-mixed, secondary ponds, where bioflocculation took place. Algae removals of up to 90% were obtained by gravity sedimentation of flocculent cultures. Operational variables that were tested included flow mixing velocity, waste loading to the secondary ponds and waste pretreatment. The effect of algal species composition was also monitored.

Keywords: Algae removal, anaerobic digestion, animal waste, bioflocculation, microalgae.

INTRODUCTION

Bioflocculation, the exopolymer-mediated formation of cellular aggregates, is a potentially economical process for harvesting microalgae. It has been induced in ponds treating domestic wastewater through either continuous flow mixing of the primary pond (Oswald et al., 1978; Eisenberg et al., 1981) or isolation of primary pond effluent in a flow mixed, secondary pond (Koopman et al., 1981; Eisenberg et al., 1981). Lincoln and Koopman (1986) applied continuous flow mixing to a high-rate,

ISBN 0-941463-00-1

primary pond treating settled swine waste. With the onset of continuous circulation, bioflocculating Micractinium sp. appeared and eventually dominated the culture. These algae remained until the source of medium was changed to anaerobic digester effluent, whereupon a nonflocculent population of Chlorella sp. became dominant and persisted until termination of the experiment. Lincoln and Koopman (1986) subsequently transferred mature culture medium, dominated by Synechocystis, from an unmixed high-rate pond treating anaerobic digester effluent to a flow mixed, secondary pond. Following the transfer, essentially complete bioflocculation of the algal population occurred within the secondary pond.

The first objective of the present study was to determine if culture medium dominated by Chlorella and Monodus could be bioflocculated in flow mixed, secondary ponds. Synechocystis might be a special case in that it is inhibited by flow mixing (Lincoln et al., 1984) whereas other microalgae such as Chlorella and Micractinium are favored by agitation (Azov et al., 1980). The second objective was to evaluate the effects of flow mixing velocity, waste loading to the secondary pond and waste pretreatment on bioflocculation.

MATERIALS AND METHODS

Flushed swine waste was pumped to a 15 m^3 steel settling tank. After 24 h sedimentation, the settled waste (supernatant) had an average chemical oxygen demand (COD) of 27.0 $\pm$ 12.9 kg m^{-3} and average total Kjeldahl-nitrogen (TKN) of 1.72 $\pm$ 0.71 kg m^{-3}. Settled waste was fed to a 20 m^3 fixed bed reactor (FBR). The FBR consisted of a polyolefin shell filled with cypress chips. Its loading rate (empty bed volume basis) ranged from 0.30-1.92 kg volatile solids (VS) m^{-3} d^{-1} and averaged 1.08 kg VS m^{-3} d^{-1}. FBR effluent had average COD and TKN concentrations of 17.3 $\pm$ 9.5 and 1.68 $\pm$ 0.64 kg m^{-3}, respectively. Excess effluent flows from the digestion system, as well as flushed waste not pumped to the settling tank, were discharged to a 1200 m^2 anaerobic lagoon which in turn overflowed to a 800 m^2 facultative pond.

The algal system consisted of a 600 m^2 high-rate pond and two 170 m^2 secondary ponds, each having a race track configuration. The clay-lined high-rate pond was flow mixed at 20 cm s^{-1} for three 30 min periods each week, coinciding with the times of waste loading. Its primary waste input was FBR effluent, at a rate averaging 0.55 m^3 d^{-1}. In addition, facultative pond effluent was used to refill the high-rate pond after its medium was transferred to the secondary ponds. Operating depth ranged from 0.2-0.5 m. The secondary ponds were identical concrete lined channels. They were flow mixed at 19 cm s^{-1} except when mixing velocity was the variable under consideration. They also received a moderate loading of FBR effluent (0.08-0.19 m^3 d^{-1}, depending on season) unless waste loading was the variable under consideration. Operating depth ranged from 0.35-0.46 m.

The experimental procedure was to fill the secondary ponds with mature culture medium and monitor selected parameters while bioflocculation took place. Degree of bioflocculation was assessed on the basis of settleable solids production and algae removal efficiency. Settleable solids were determined by retaining a sample of culture medium in a 1 L Imhoff cone over a 24 h period in the absence of light. Algae removal efficiency was calculated by comparing the initial chlorophyll a concentration of the sample to the chlorophyll a concentration of a 150 mL supernatant sample taken at the end of the 24 h settling period. Chlorophyll a was determined by extraction into boiling 90% methanol (Talling and Driver, 1963). Algal composition of the cultures was determined by weekly microscopic examination. Numbers of each genus were recorded as cell counts per Whipple grid at 400x magnification. Relative abundance for each genus was estimated by multiplying cell number by the cell volume relative to Chlorella, which was assigned unit volume. COD and VS were analyzed according to APHA (1980), methods 508A and 209E, respectively. TKN was determined according to method 00625 of US EPA (1974).

RESULTS

Flow-mixing velocities of 14 cm s^{-1} in one secondary pond (C-1) and 30 cm s^{-1} in the other secondary pond (C-2) were employed during Exp. 1. Chlorella and Monodus were co-dominant initially and remained so throughout the experiment. The production of settleable matter was greater in C-2 (Figure 1, left). A maximum settleable solids volume of 53 mL L^{-1} was measured in C-2 medium, compared to 10 mL L^{-1} in C-1 medium. Algae removals by sedimentation were similar in both cultures through day 14, after which they became significantly greater in C-2 (max. 56% vs. 36%). In Exp. 2, the flow mixing velocities employed were 30 cm s^{-1} in C-1 and 14 cm s^{-1} in C-2. Synechocystis was dominant initially, but declined to less than 12% of the initial counts within 2 wk. Chlorella was dominant in both cultures by the end of the experiment. Settleable solids increased progressively in C-1, reaching a maximum of 14 mL L^{-1}, but remained near zero in C-2 (Figure 1, right). Algae removal by sedimentation was also greater in C-1 (max. 44% vs. 35%).

Throughout Exp. 3, culture medium in C-1 was loaded with 0.45 m^3 FBR effluent three times weekly whereas the same medium in C-2 received no waste loading. The algal communities in both ponds consisted almost exclusively of Chlorella and Monodus throughout the experiment. Both cultures became visibly flocculent after one week. Production of settleable matter was similar for the first three weeks, then became somewhat greater in C-2 than in C-1 (max. 54 vs. 40 mL L^{-1}) (Figure 2, left). Algae removals in media from the two ponds were nearly equal throughout the experiment, reaching maxima of 32-33%. In Exp. 4, culture medium initially

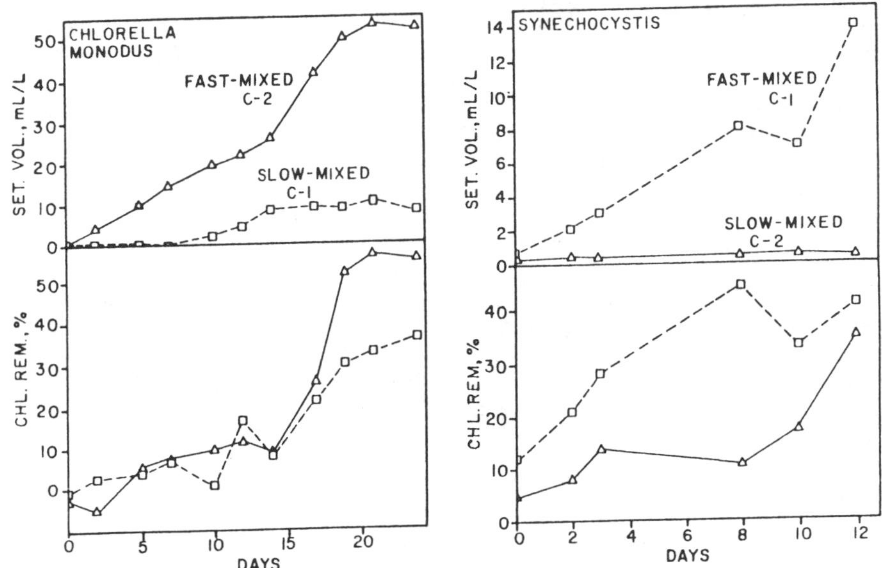

FIGURE 1. Effect of flow mixing velocity on algal bioflocculation in secondary ponds. Left - Experiment 1; right - Experiment 2.

dominated by Synechocystis was subjected to waste loading (0.5 m^3 FBR effluent twice weekly) in C-2. The same medium in C-1 was not loaded. The medium in C-2 became visibly flocculent after 6 d, whereas macroscopic flocs were not visible in the C-1 medium. Microscopic examinations showed the flocs in C-2 medium to have diameters on the order of hundreds to thousands of microns and to consist almost exclusively (approx. 95%) of Synechocystis cells. Smaller flocs ($\leq$100 µm in diam) were observed microscopically in C-1 medium. Synechocystis counts increased initially, then declined in both cultures. The extent of decline was somewhat greater in C-2 medium than in C-1 medium (terminal counts of 52 vs. 73 cells/grid). Synechocystis was still the dominant genus in both cultures at the end of the experiment. Production of settleable matter was greater in the waste-loaded culture, as shown in Figure 2 (right). Maximum settleable volumes were 35 mL L^{-1} in C-2 and 4.5 mL L^{-1} in C-1. Algae removals were initially similar, but became significantly greater in the waste loaded culture after 20 d. Maximum removals in C-2 and C-1 media were 43% and 31%, respectively.

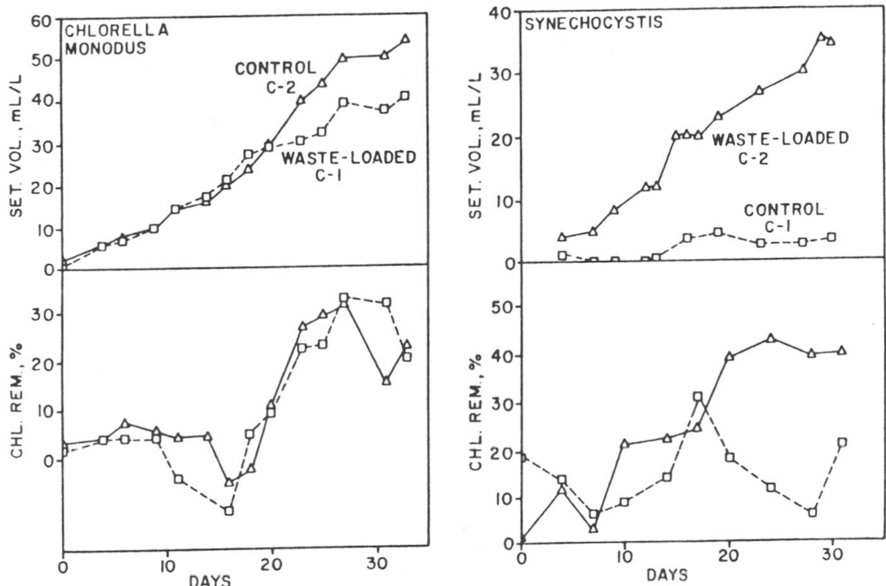

FIGURE 2. Effect of waste loading on algal bioflocculation in secondary ponds. Left - Experiment 3; right - Experiment 4.

The design of Exp. 5 involved addition of settled waste to C-1 and FBR effluent to C-2. The waste volume added was 0.3 m^3 three times weekly. Chlorella and Monodus were co-dominant in the culture medium initially. The undigested waste had a stimulatory effect on Chlorella and also sustained a relatively high population of the purple sulfur bacterium, Thiopedia rosea. Relative proportions of Chlorella and T. rosea decreased in C-2 during the experiment. Settleable matter production and algae removals were greater in the pond loaded with FBR effluent (Figure 3, left). Maxima for these parameters in C-2 medium were 29 mL L^{-1} and 42%, respectively. Maximum settleable solids and algae removal in C-1 medium were 15 mL L^{-1} and 14%, respectively.

In Exp. 6, FBR effluent was applied to C-1 and C-2 at average rates of 0.072 and 0.217 m^3 d^{-1}, respectively. Synechocystis was dominant initially. Counts of this alga declined throughout the experiment, ending near zero. A limited regrowth of Chlorella and Monodus occurred. Extensive bioflocculation was observed in both ponds. Flocs appeared to be more numerous in C-1 than C-2, but settleable solids were almost identical in the 2 ponds (Figure 3, right), reaching a maximum of 29 mL L^{-1}. Algae removals were also very similar, except near the end of the trial. A greater maximum removal was attained in C-1 medium (90%) than in C-2 medium (74%).

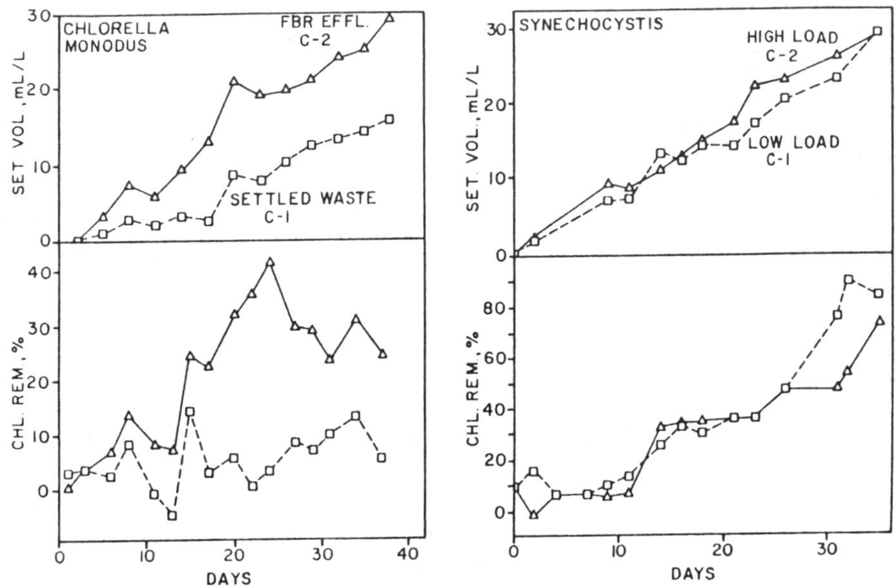

FIGURE 3. Effect of waste pretreatment and waste loading rate on algal bioflocculation in secondary ponds. Left - effect of waste pretreatment, Experiment 5; right - effect of waste loading rate, Experiment 6.

DISCUSSION

Algal genera of both the Chlorophyceae and Cyanophyceae (Ankistrodesmus, Chlorella, Micractinium, Scenedesmus, Synechocystis) were previously identified in bioflocculating waste grown cultures (McKinney et al., 1971; Koopman et al., 1978; Oswald et al., 1978; Eisenberg et al., 1981; Lincoln et al., 1984; Lincoln and Koopman, 1986). In the present study, bioflocculation of genera from the Cyanophyceae, Chlorophyceae and Chrysophyceae was successfully induced. It thus appears that bioflocculation as a harvesting technique is applicable to a wide spectrum of algae production systems.

Among Synechocystis, Chlorella and Monodus, the former genus had the greatest tendency to bioflocculate. Maximum algae removals obtained when Synechocystis was dominant were as high as 90% and averaged 59%, whereas maximum removals averaging 43% and ranging up to 56% were observed when Chlorella and Monodus were dominant. More biomass could be recovered from the latter cultures, however. Maximum settleable solids in the Chlorella and Monodus cultures were almost double those in cultures dominated by

Synechocystis (avg. of 45 mL L^{-1} vs. 26 mL L^{-1}). This is a consequence of the higher densities to which Chlorella and Monodus grew in the high-rate pond.

Doubling the flow mixing velocity increased settleable matter production five- to nine-fold and enhanced algae removals by 20-36%. It is likely that enhanced particle interactions and the bridging of exocellular polymers between cells contributed to this effect. Also, larger flocs can be maintained in suspension at higher levels of turbulence.

If bacteria play a role in algal bioflocculation, as suggested by Eisenberg et al. (1981), it should be beneficial to provide organic substrate to the secondary pond. The results from this study were mixed, with highly positive as well as neutral to slightly negative effects of waste loading observed. This implies that the issue is more complicated than simply promoting the growth of more bacteria in the culture. Other factors, such as the type of bacteria stimulated, must also be considered. This is exemplified by the results of Exp. 5, where the undigested waste stimulated phototrophic bacteria that did not physically interact (flocculate) with the microalgae.

REFERENCES

APHA. 1980. Standard Methods for the Examination of Water and Wastewater, 15th ed. Am. Pub. Health Assoc., Washington, D.C.

Azov, Y., G. Shelef, R. Moraine, and A. Levi. 1980. Controlling algal genera in high-rate wastewater oxidation ponds. p. 245-253. In G. Shelef and C. J. Soeder (ed.) Algae Biomass. Elsevier/North-Holland Biomedical Press, Amsterdam.

Benemann, J. R., B. L. Koopman, D. C. Baker, J. C. Weissman, and W. J. Oswald. 1977. Systems analysis of bioconversion with microalgae. p. 101-126. In Proc. Symp. Clean Fuels from Biomass and Wastes. Inst. Gas Technol., Orlando, Florida, January 25-28, 1977.

Eisenberg, D. M., B. Koopman, J. R. Benemann, and W. J. Oswald. 1981. Algal bioflocculation and energy conservation in microalgal sewage ponds. Biotechnol. Bioengng. Symp. No. 11. p. 429-448.

Koopman, B., R. Thomson, R. Yackzan, J. Benemann, and W. Oswald. 1978. Investigation of the pond isolation process for microalgae separation from Woodland's waste pond effluents. San. Engng. Res. Lab., Univ. of Calif., Berkeley, CA. SERL Report No. 79-1.

Koopman, B., J. R. Benemann, and W. J. Oswald. 1981. In-pond separation of algae from treated effluents. p. 434-442. In F. M. Saunders (ed.) Proc. 1981 National Conf. on Environ. Engrg. Am. Soc. Civil Engrs., Atlanta, GA.

Lincoln, E. P., and B. Koopman. 1986. Bioflocculation of microalgae in mass cultures. Beiheft Zur Nova Hedwigia 83:207-211.

Lincoln, E. P., B. Koopman, and T. W. Hall. 1984. Control of a unicellular, blue-green alga, Synechocystis sp., in mass algal culture. Aquaculture 42:349-358.

McKinney, R. E., R. J. Sherwood, V. N. Wahbeh, and D. W. Newport. 1971. Ahead: Activated algae? Water Wastes Engng. 8:51.

Oswald, W. J., E. W. Lee, B. Adan, and K. H. Yao. 1978. New wastewater treatment method yields a harvest of saleable algae. WHO Chron. 32:348-350.

Talling, M., and D. Driver. 1963. Some problems in the estimation of chlorophyll a in phytoplankton. In Proc. Conf. Productivity Meas., Marine and Fresh Water. U.S. Atomic Energy Commission. Report TID-7633.

US EPA. 1974. Methods for chemical analysis of water and wastes. U.S. Environ. Prot. Agency, Washington, D.C.

DEVELOPMENT OF AN ADVANCED ANAEROBIC DIGESTER DESIGN AND A KINETIC MODEL FOR BIOGASIFICATION OF WATER HYACINTH/SLUDGE BLENDS

V. J. Srivastava, K. F. Fannin, and R. Biljetina
Institute of Gas Technology
3424 S. State Street
Chicago, Illinois 60616

D. P. Chynoweth
Agricultural Engineering Department
University of Florida, IFAS
Gainesville, Florida 32611

T. D. Hayes
Gas Research Institute
8600 W. Bryn Mawr Avenue
Chicago, Illinois 60631

ABSTRACT

A comprehensive laboratory-scale research program was conducted to develop and optimize the anaerobic digestion process for producing methane (CH_4) from water hyacinth (*Eichhornia crassipes*) biomass and sludge blends. This study focused on digester design and operating techniques, which gave improved CH_4 yields and production rates over those observed using conventional digesters. The final digester concept and the operating experience was utilized to design and operate a larger-scale experimental test unit (ETU) at Walt Disney World, Florida. This paper describes the novel digester design, operating techniques, and the results obtained in the laboratory. The paper also discusses a kinetic model which predicts CH_4 yield and production rate, and digester effluent solids as a function of retention time. This model was successfully utilized to predict the performance of the ETU.

Keywords: Process development; process kinetics; aquatic plants; wastewater treatment; non-mixed vertical flow reactor, methane.

ISBN 0-941463-00-1

INTRODUCTION

This paper describes laboratory-scale research on biological gasification of water hyacinth/sludge blends, which enabled the development of a digester design and operating techniques that resulted in improved CH_4 yields and production rates over those obtained from conventional methods. The final digester concept and the operating experience was utilized to design and operate a large-scale experimental test unit (ETU) at Walt Disney World, Florida.

The system concept (Figure 1), employs water hyacinth ponds used for secondary and tertiary treatment after the sewage effluent had been subjected to primary treatment (removal of settleable solids). Collected primary sludge which consists of settleable solids, and harvested water hyacinth biomass are added as a blend to the anaerobic digester where a portion of the organic matter is converted to CH_4 and CO_2. Digester residue solids may be posttreated to improve biodegradability and recycled to the digester or used for land fertilization.

This scheme not only requires less energy than conventional wastewater treatment, but it has the potential for net energy production as well as the production of a higher-quality effluent. The process solves a waste disposal problem, reduces gas requirements for wastewater treatment, and adds gas as a process product to the overall gas supply.

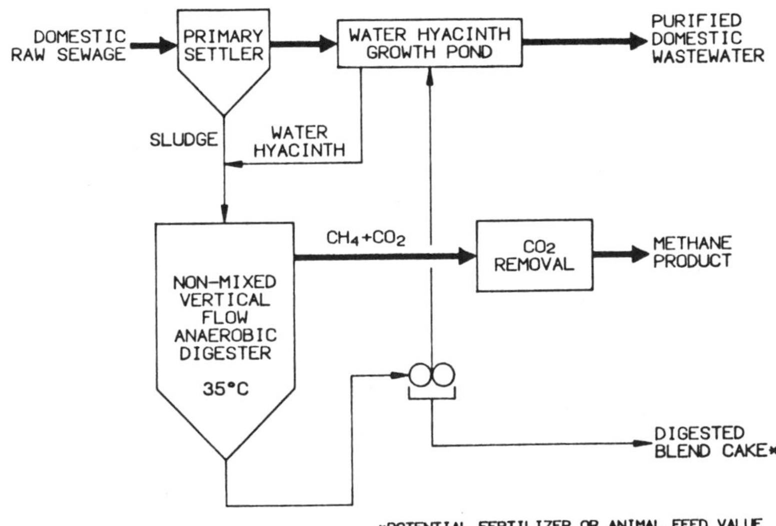

FIGURE 1. Schematic diagram of integrated water hyacinth domestic wastewater treatment and digestion system.

BIOGASIFICATION PROCESS DEVELOPMENT

Anaerobic digestion was selected as the process for energy conversion of water hyacinth and primary sludge blend because it produces CH_4 as the principal product and the process is suitable for feedstocks with a high water content. The overall objective of the laboratory research conducted at the Institute of Gas Technology (IGT) was to develop an advanced digester concept and a data-base for the design and operation of a large-scale ETU for the biogasification of water hyacinth and primary sludge and its integration with the hyacinth wastewater reclamation facility at the Community Waste Research Facility (CWRF) located at the Walt Disney World (WDW) Resort Complex in Florida. The specific objectives of the process development work included 1) determination of gasification characteristics of water hyacinth, primary sludge, and hyacinth/sludge blends under baseline conditions of anaerobic digestion; 2) evaluation of the effects of blend ratios on anaerobic digestion; 3) advanced anaerobic digestion studies on different blends of hyacinth and sludge; 4) kinetic analyses of anaerobic digestion on blends of hyacinth and sludge; 5) application of the kinetic model to predict the effects of digester design and operating conditions on the CH_4 formation efficiency (yield) and rate; and 6) design, construction, and operation of an ETU using different blends of hyacinth and sludge.

MATERIALS AND METHODS

Digester Design

One continuously stirred tank reactor (CSTR) and two advanced anaerobic digester designs, which promote higher solids than hydraulic retention times (HRT's), were evaluated under this program. The first advanced digester was the continuously stirred tank reactor with solids recycle (CSTR/SR), in which a fraction of the effluent solids was separated and recycled into the reactor. This process has been practiced commercially as the anaerobic contact process, but has previously been used primarily for retention of microorganisms during digestion of soluble feeds. This application for particulate feeds also results in increased residence time of unreacted solids. The second advanced digester design under evaluation was the upflow non-mixed vertical flow reactor (NMVFR), which is a modification of the upflow anaerobic sludge blanket digester widely studied and applied to anaerobic digestion of soluble feeds. This process* is different in that the feeds contain higher concentrations of non-homogeneous particulate matter, and the bed is not expanded and contains both unreacted solids and microorganisms. The culture was recirculated twice a day to keep the top layer of the digester wet for

*IGT has filed a patent application for this process.

efficient solids degradation. This reactor concept was first applied to sea kelp in IGT's laboratory (Fannin, 1983). It exhibited the highest performance observed for mesophilic digestion of non-homogeneous particulate feeds of 12% total solids (CH_4 yield as high as 0.37 SCM kg^{-1} VS added, and a CH_4 production rate as high as 3.3 vol vol^{-1} d^{-1}).

Start-Up

Digesters were inoculated from a 50 L stock culture maintained at 35°C and fed once a week at a loading rate of 0.4 kg VS m^{-3} d^{-1}. This culture, originally started from a municipal high-rate digester, was adapted to water hyacinth by feeding a blend of water hyacinth and primary sludge for over a two year period.

Feeding

All digesters were fed once a day. Before feeding, gas production was measured at atmospheric pressure, and room temperature and barometric pressure were recorded. The effluent volume at a specified loading rate was withdrawn, and the temperature and pH of this effluent were measured and recorded. An effluent volume at a specified loading rate was withdrawn, and the temperature and pH of this effluent were measured and recorded. A feed volume equal to that withdrawn was added to the digester.

Digester Sampling and Monitoring

Digester performance was evaluated regularly by monitoring digester gas production, pH, volatile acids, alkalinity, NH_4-N, and gas component analysis. Gas production, digester temperature, and pH were determined daily. Gases were analyzed at least once a week to evaluate digester performance. Digester effluents were sampled for volatile acids, alkalinity, and NH_4-N on a weekly basis, and for total and volatile solids, total suspended solids, soluble and total C, as required, during stable performance. These samples were analyzed immediately or were preserved as described in Standard Methods (American Public Health Association, 1981) (in capped polyethylene or polypropylene bottles placed in a freezer). Selected preserved samples were analyzed as rapidly as possible to delineate trends in the digestion process and to clarify unusual digester performance.

Raw feeds and digester feed slurry effluents were analyzed for total and volatile solids, heating value, elements, organics, and anaerobic biogasification potential (ABP) as required for feed characterization, and mass balance calculation. Procedures and methods used for these calculations and analyses have been discussed in an IGT report (Chynoweth, 1983).

RESULTS AND DISCUSSION

Chemical and Biological Characteristics of Feeds

Two types of feeds were utilized for these studies, either separately or as blends: water hyacinth and primary sludge. Proximate and ultimate analyses were conducted on these feeds for the purpose of experimental set-up, material balances, calculation of theoretical yields, estimation of nutrient availability for bioconversion, and determination of feed variability between samples. The ABP assay was also conducted on these feeds to determine the ultimate biodegradability.

Analyses of water hyacinth and primary sludge feeds showed that they contained low solids and ash contents. The typical heating value for water hyacinth was 19.5 MJ kg^{-1} VS, which is in the range normally observed for herbaceous biomass: 19.2 to 19.7 MJ kg^{-1} VS. The heating values for sludge was high and ranged from 25.8 to 29.3 MJ kg^{-1} VS. Carbon-to-N and C/P ratios were within ranges previously found to be non-limiting for biogasification. The typical ultimate CH_4 yields as determined by ABP assays were 0.27 and 0.62 SCM kg^{-1} VS added for water hyacinth and primary sludge, respectively. These yields account for 52% and 90% of the stoichiometric CH_4 yield and represent an upper expected level anticipated from anaerobic digestion studies.

Baseline Digestion (CSTR) Studies

Several experiments were conducted to evaluate the performance of water hyacinth and sludge, and blends of these feeds, under conditions of conventional anaerobic digestion. Such experiments provide a data base that can be compared to those obtained in this and other laboratories on various feedstocks. These studies also provide a basis for comparison of performances with that of unconventional advanced digestion studies with this feedstock. These baseline studies were conducted in a CSTR operated at 35°C, a loading rate of 1.6 kg VS m^{-3} d^{-1} and an HRT of 15 d. The results of these experiments have been previously described (Lee, 1981). Methane yields of 0.19, 0.52, and 0.28 SCM kg^{-1} VS added were reported for water hyacinth, sludge, and a 3:1 blend of hyacinth/sludge which corresponds to volatile solids reductions of 42%, 72%, and 53%, respectively, and CH_4 recovery of 70%, 79%, and 84%, respectively, of ultimate yields determined by ABP assay. All three digesters exhibited stable performance with almost negligible concentrations of volatile acids in the effluent.

ADVANCED ANAEROBIC DIGESTION STUDIES

The objectives of this work was to evaluate the performance of two advanced digestion systems (CSTR/SR and NMVRF) and to select one for further experimentation to provide a data base for the design and operation of the ETU.

Several experiments were conducted at three different loading rates (1.6, 1.9, and 2.7 kg VS m^{-3} d^{-1}) with CSTR/SR and NMVFR digesters. A CSTR was also operated to provide baseline data. The results (Table 1) obtained with a 3:1 blend of water hyacinth and primary sludge showed that both the CSTR/SR and the NMVFR outperformed the CSTR at all three loading rates by an average of 25% (Table 2). However, the performance of the CSTR/SR was not better than the NMVFR, which unlike the CSTR/SR, did not employ any mechanical mixing or a solids separation unit. Considering the simplicity in design and operation of the NMVFR and its superior performance with other particulate feedstocks, (such as sea kelp, Fannin, 1983), the NMVFR digester design was selected as a prototype for the ETU development.

Several additional experiments were conducted at different loading rates and with two different water hyacinth-to-sludge ratios to develop a broad data base for the ETU operation. These results (Table 2) clearly showed that CH_4 yields were 15% to 30% higher in the NMVFR than in the CSTR and performance was more stable as indicated by higher pH and lower volatile acids concentration in the digester (Chynoweth, 1984).

TABLE 1. Comparison of CH_4 yields from 3:1 hyacinth/sludge blend in CSTR, CSTR/SR, and NMVFR digesters (35°C).

	Loading, kg VS m^{-3} d^{-1}		
	1.6	1.9	2.7
Anaerobic digesters	CH_4 Yield, SCM kg^{-1} VS added		
Continuously stirred tank reactor (CSTR)	0.28	0.24	0.24
Continuously stirred tank reactor/ solids recycle (CSTR/SR)	0.34	0.34	0.29
Upflow solids reactor (NMVFR)	0.35	0.33	0.38

TABLE 2. Comparison of CH_4 yields from a CSTR and an NMVFR receiving 3:1 hyacinth/sludge blend (dry weight basis).

Loading	CH_4 Yield	
	------SCM kg^{-1} VS added------	
kg VS m^{-3} d^{-1}	CSTR	NMVFR
1.4	0.28	0.35
1.9	0.24	0.34
2.7	0.24	0.28
3.2	0.23	0.27
4.8	0.20	0.23
6.4	0.16	0.21

PROCESS KINETICS AND MODELING

Prediction of process performance in terms of CH_4 yield and CH_4 production rate is generally essential to the effective design and operation of a large-scale anaerobic digestion facility. Two well-established kinetic models were evaluated for their ability to predict performance on bench-scale CSTR and NMVFR digesters receiving two different blends of hyacinth and sludge: the Monod and Standard First Order. Both models were modified to a form that describes the dependence of CH_4 yield and production rate on loading.

The first order kinetic equation (Equation 1) (Figure 2), applied by other researchers to anaerobic digestion (Doyle, 1983; Pfeffer, 1979; McFarlane, 1985), was found to be statistically more accurate than the Monod model (Srivastava, 1986) for predicting the actual performance of the CSTR and the NMVFR receiving hyacinth/sludge blends. Experiments providing volatile solids reduction and CH_4 yields as a function of loading provide data needed for this model. The pertinent equations for the model are shown below.

<u>First Order Kinetic Model</u>

$$-rs = K\ S \qquad [1]$$

where: $-rs$ = reaction rate, $g^{-1}\ d^{-1}$
K = reaction rate constant, d^{-1}
S = effluent substrate concentration, $g\ L^{-1}$

<u>Rate Constant Determination</u>

$$So/S = K \qquad [2]$$

where: So = influent substrate concentration, $g\ L^{-1}$
= hydraulic retention time, d

<u>Process Efficiency (E)</u>

$$E = (So - S)/So \qquad [3]$$

<u>Methane Yield (Ym)</u>

$$Ym = \alpha\ (K\ )/(1+ K\ ) \qquad [4]$$

where: α = CH_4 yield coefficient, L CH_4 g^{-1} substrate

<u>Methane Production Rate (Rm)</u>

$$Rm = L\ Ym = \alpha\ (K\ )\ L/(1 + K\ ) \qquad [5]$$

where: L = loading rate, g VS ρ $culture^{-1}\ d^{-1}$

Using Equation 2 as a basis for plotting So/S versus θ, the substrate utilization rate constant (K) can be determined. This first order model was rearranged (that is, addition of CH_4 yield coefficient in the process efficiency equation, Equation [3]), and substitution of the value of So from Equation [2] to develop Equations [4] and [5], which describe CH_4 yield and production rate as a function of HRT (and loading rate for feeds of fixed solids concentration). Unlike the Monod model, this model is not dependent upon a known value for feed biodegradability, which is more useful in field applications where feed biodegradability could vary considerably.

Using performance data published earlier (Biljetina, 1985; Srivastava, 1986), kinetic constants (K and α) were determined for digestion of a 3:1 hyacinth/sludge blend in the CSTR and NMVFR, and a 2:1 blend in the NMVFR. It was assumed that due to continuous mixing caused by the gas production and twice-a-day culture recirculation, the NMVFR was closer to the CSTR than to the plug flow reactor. The effect of longer solids than hydraulic retention time in the NMVFR (and lower endogenous respiration and cell maintenance energy requirements) was exhibited in higher values of α for the NMVFR than for the CSTR (Table 3).

Using the constants shown in Table 3, theoretical plots of CH_4 yield and CH_4 production rate versus loading were developed, as shown in Figure 2-4. Actual laboratory data are also shown in these figures for comparison purposes.

These plots show that the first order kinetic model can be used to predict digester performance of hyacinth/sludge in both the CSTR and NMVFR, and that the performance of the NMVFR was better than that of the CSTR. The predictability of the first order model was also verified with the actual data obtained from the pilot-scale ETU, as shown in Table 4. A major limitation of the first order model, however, is that it does not describe conditions resulting due to microorganisms washout at lower HRT's. However, in practice, this is not a limitation because digesters would not be operated under those conditions.

CONCLUSIONS

We concluded from these results and those presented in other publications (Fannin, 1983; Chynoweth, 1983; Biljetina, 1986) that the NMVFR (operated both in upflow and downflow modes) is superior to the CSTR and the CSTR/SR, as evidenced by its improved gas

TABLE 3. Kinetic parameters for anaerobic digestion of hyacinth/sludge blends in CSTR and NMVFR using first order kinetics.

	NMVFR		CSTR	
Feed type	α CH_4 g^{-1} VS converted	K d^{-1}	α CH_4 g^{-1} VS converted	K d^{-1}
3:1 WH/PS	0.532	0.095	0.460	0.088
2:1 WH/PS	0.548	0.121	--	--

α = methane yield coefficient; K = reaction rate constant.

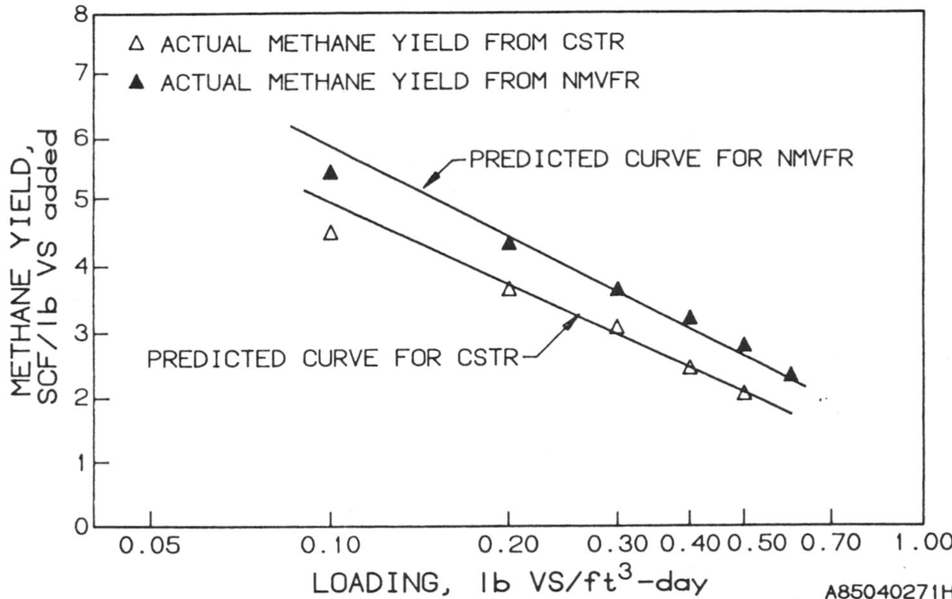

FIGURE 2. Comparison of CH_4 yields in terms of loading for 3:1 blend in the NMVFR and the CSTR using the first order kinetic model.

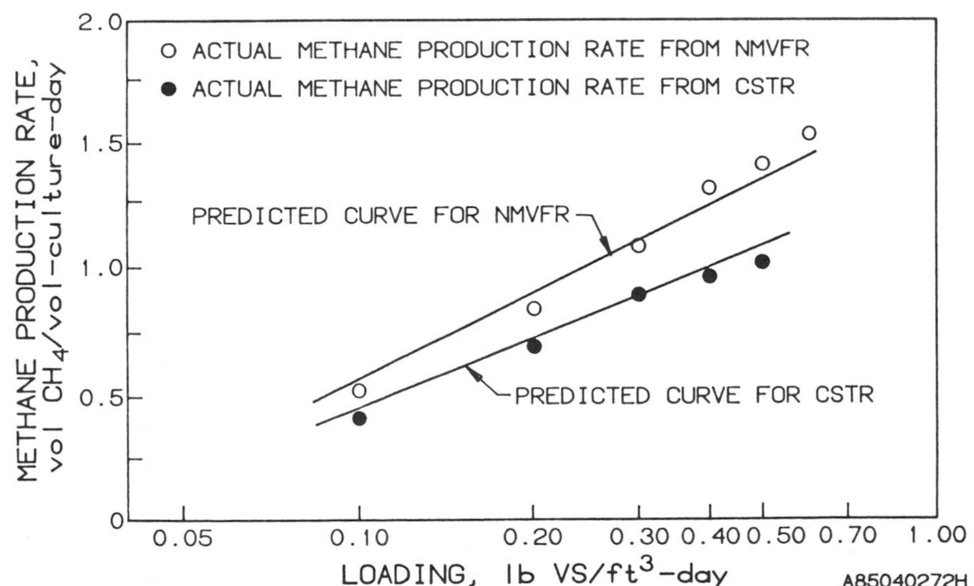

FIGURE 3. Comparison of CH_4 production rate in terms of loading for 3:1 blend in the NMVFR and the CSTR using the first order kinetic model.

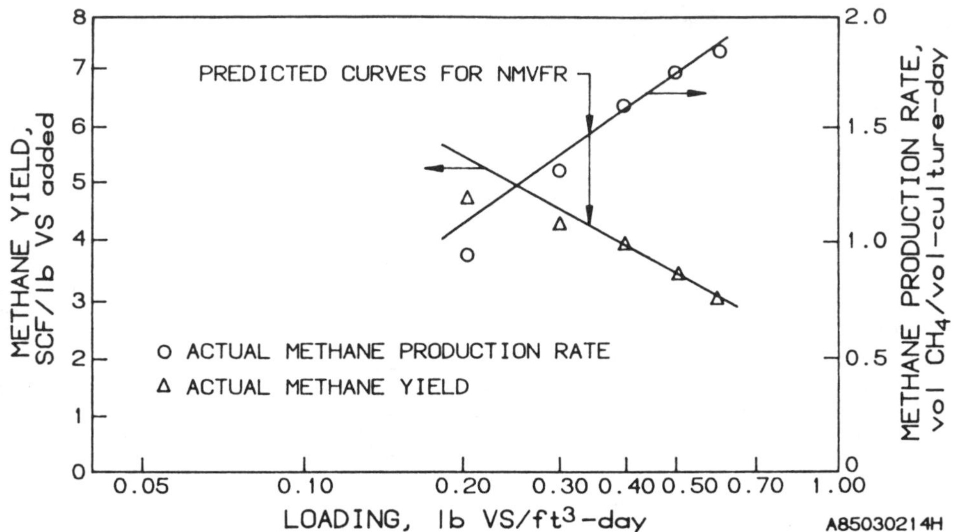

FIGURE 4. Predicted CH_4 yields and production rates in terms of loading for 2:1 blend in the NMVFR using the first order kinetic model.

TABLE 4. Comparison of predicted and actual CH_4 yields from the ETU.

Hyacinth/Sludge ratio	Loading rate	Methane Yield	
		Predicted value, (first order model)	Actual value from Etu
	kg VS m^3 d^{-1}	--------SCM kg^{-1} VS added--------	
2:1	3.2	0.31	0.29
1:1	2.9	0.44	0.44
0.8:1	2.9	0.44	0.44
2.1:1	3.2	0.37	0.37
2.1:1	5.0	0.31	0.31

production and sludge volume reduction, simplicity in design and operation, and overall stable digestion. Results obtained from the laboratory-scale digesters were sufficient in providing a data base for a successful design and operation of the pilot-scale ETU, suggesting that the digester design and operation, and the kinetic model were scaleable. We believe that, like the first step scale-up from the laboratory-scale to the pilot-scale, results from the pilot-scale ETU will successfully provide the bases for scale-up to a large-scale demonstration or commercial-scale system operation in the late 1980's.

ACKNOWLEDGMENTS

The authors acknowledge the Gas Research Institute for the primary support of this research under Contracts 5081-323-0463, 5083-226-0773, and 5082-223-0567 to the Institute of Gas Technology. They also acknowledge the technical services of D. E. Jerger, J. R. Conrad, and J. D. Mensinger.

REFERENCES

American Public Health Association. 1981. Standard Methods for the Examination of Water and Wastewater, 15th ed, Washington, D.C.

Biljetina, R., V. J. Srivastava, D. P. Chynoweth, and T. D. Hayes. 1987. Anaerobic digestion of water hyacinth and sludge. In K. R. Reddy and W. H. Smith (ed.) Aquatic Plants for Water Treatment and Resource Recovery. Magnolia Publishing Inc., Orlando, Florida.

Biljetina, R., D. P. Chynoweth, V. J. Srivastava, J. Janulis, A. Razik, and S. Smallwood. 1985. Biogasification of Walt Disney World Biomass Waste Blend. Annual Report for GRI Contract 5082-223-0567.

Chynoweth, D. P., K. F. Fanin, V. J. Srivastava, D. E. Jerger, J. R. Conrad, and J. D. Mensinger. 1984. Biological gasification of renewable resources. Annual Report for GRI, Contract No. 5083-226-0773, November 1984.

Chynoweth, D. P., D. E. Jerger, J. R. Conrad, A. Razik, V. J. Srivastava, S. Ghosh, M. P. Henry, and S. Babu. 1983. Gasification of land-based biomass. Final Report for GRI, Contract No. 5081-323-0773, November 1984.

Doyle, O. P., J. D. O'Malley, E. C. Clausen, and J. L. Gaddy. 1983. Kinetic improvement in the production of methane from cellulosics residues. Symposium papers: Energy from Biomass and Wastes VII, Institute of Gas Technology, Chicago.

Fannin, K. F., V. J. Srivastava, J. D. Mensinger, and D. P. Chynoweth. 1983. Marine biomass program: Anaerobic digestion system development and stability study. Final Report, GRI Contract No. 5082-225-0687, June 1983.

McFarlane, P. N., and J. T. Pfeffer. 1985. Biological conversion of biomass to methane. Report for SERI, No. SERI/TR-98357-1.

Pfeffer, J. T. 1979. Domestic refuse as a feed for digesters. Paper presented at The First International Symposium on Anaerobic Digestion, University College, Cardift, Wales, September 1979.

Srivastava, V. J., and D. P. Chynoweth. 1986. Kinetic analysis of biogasification of biomass/waste blend and its engineering significance. 1986. Paper presented at Energy from Biomass and Wastes X, Washington, DC, Institute of Gas Technology, April 7-11, 1986.

ANAEROBIC DIGESTION OF WATER HYACINTH AND SLUDGE

R. Biljetina and V. J. Srivastava
Institute of Gas Technology
Chicago, Illinois 60632

D. P. Chynoweth
Agricultural Engineering Department
University of Florida, IFAS
Gainesville, Florida 32611

T. D. Hayes
Gas Research Institute
Chicago, Illinois 60631

ABSTRACT

The Institute of Gas Technology has been operating an experimental test unit at the Walt Disney World wastewater treatment plant to demonstrate the conversion of water hyacinth and sludge to CH_4 in a solids concentrating digester. Results from two years of operation have confirmed earlier laboratory observations that this digester achieves higher CH_4 yields and solids conversion than those observed in continuous stirred tank reactors. Methane yields as high as 0.49 m^3 kg^{-1} volatile solids added have been obtained during steady-state operation on a blend of water hyacinth and sludge.

Keywords: Biogasification, wastewater treatment, digester design, aquatic plants, biological conversion.

INTRODUCTION

The Gas Research Institute (GRI) has been sponsoring a biomass waste blend gasification project at the Institute of Gas Technology (IGT) since June 1979 to establish the technical and economic feasibility of integrating a biogasification process with a wastewater treatment system using water hyacinth at the Community Waste Research Facility (CWRF) located at the Walt Disney World (WDW) Resort Complex. The use of water hyacinth for secondary and tertiary treatment of domestic sewage sludge has been investigated (Del Fosse, 1977; Cornwall et al., 1977). To

ISBN 0-941463-00-1

further evaluate water hyacinth wastewater treatment, five 0.1 ha ponds and a number of smaller vaults were constructed at the CWRF (Hayes et al., 1987). Data obtained, thus far, at the CWRF indicate that the ponds, which treat both primary and secondary effluents at retention times from 3 to 24 d, reduce biological oxygen demand (BOD) and suspended solids by 70% to 90%. A hyacinth-based wastewater treatment process, therefore, can meet secondary treatment standards while providing an additional source of biomass for CH_4 generation.

The prolific growth of hyacinth and the relatively high biodegradability make it a very suitable feedstock for biological conversion to CH_4. Laboratory-scale research by IGT since 1979 has provided information on feed properties, biodegradability, nutritional requirements, kinetics and has led to the development of a new digester for the conversion of water hyacinth/sludge mixtures (Chynoweth et al., 1982,1983; Ghosh et al., 1980). This digester, which is essentially non-mixed, is designed to concentrate solids and thus provides higher solids retention at any given hydraulic residence time. Loading studies in this digester in the range of 1.6 to 6.5 kg volatile solids (VS) m^{-3} d^{-1} indicated that CH_4 yields were 15% to 20% higher and performance was more stable than in the continuously stirred tank reactor (CSTR).

Bench-scale units do not offer the opportunity to duplicate the various field operating conditions encountered in a full-scale hyacinth/sludge gasification system. Also, a laboratory system does not permit evaluation of the major unit operations and processes under actual conditions of feed availability, variability of feed characteristics, and other operating conditions that are difficult to simulate with small-scale equipment. Perhaps more importantly, a laboratory system does not allow concerted operation of all major processes and subsystems, which is vital to the development of an integrated and reliable biogasification system.

These limitations lead to locating a larger-scale biogasification experimental test unit (ETU) at the water hyacinth treatment and growth channels being evaluated at the CWRF. In this ETU, water hyacinth plants harvested from the treatment channels are mixed with sludge removed in the primary wastewater clarifiers and fed to a digester for the production of CH_4 and waste reduction. Design and installation of the ETU was completed in 1983 and a two year biogasification program on water hyacinth/ sludge mixtures was subsequently completed. To verify the laboratory observations and to provide data for scale-up and economic assessment of an integrated water hyacinth based wastewater treatment and biogasification concept were the program objectives.

PROCESS DESCRIPTION

The ETU (Figure 1) was installed on a pad between the experimental wastewater treatment channels at the CWRF. A description of the various processing areas is provided in Figure 2.

Water Hyacinth Preparation

Water hyacinths are harvested from the wastewater treatment channels and are transported to a chopper, which cuts the plants into approximately 5 cm pieces. The chopped plants are subsequently fed to a grinder that reduces the plants to a particle size as low as 0.2 cm. The ground plants are stored in a tank equipped with a mixer. The storage tank is also insulated and cooled to prevent appreciable degradation of the plant material prior to digestion.

Over 182 Mg (wet) of hyacinth were processed through this section during the two year operating period. Initial grinding and pumping tests indicated that water hyacinth up to 0.6 cm in size could be pumped in 5 cm transfer lines without dilution by water. Seasonal variation of water hyacinth quality and composition were minor and had no noticeable effect on digester operations. Even frost damaged plants were easily processed and did not affect performance. Seasonal variation of water hyacinth total solids and volatile solids concentration are presented in Table 1; a typical chemical analysis is in Table 2. A preliminary energy evaluation indicates that less than 2% of the plant energy production (CH_4 equivalent) is required for the water hyacinth

FIGURE 1. Experimental test unit.

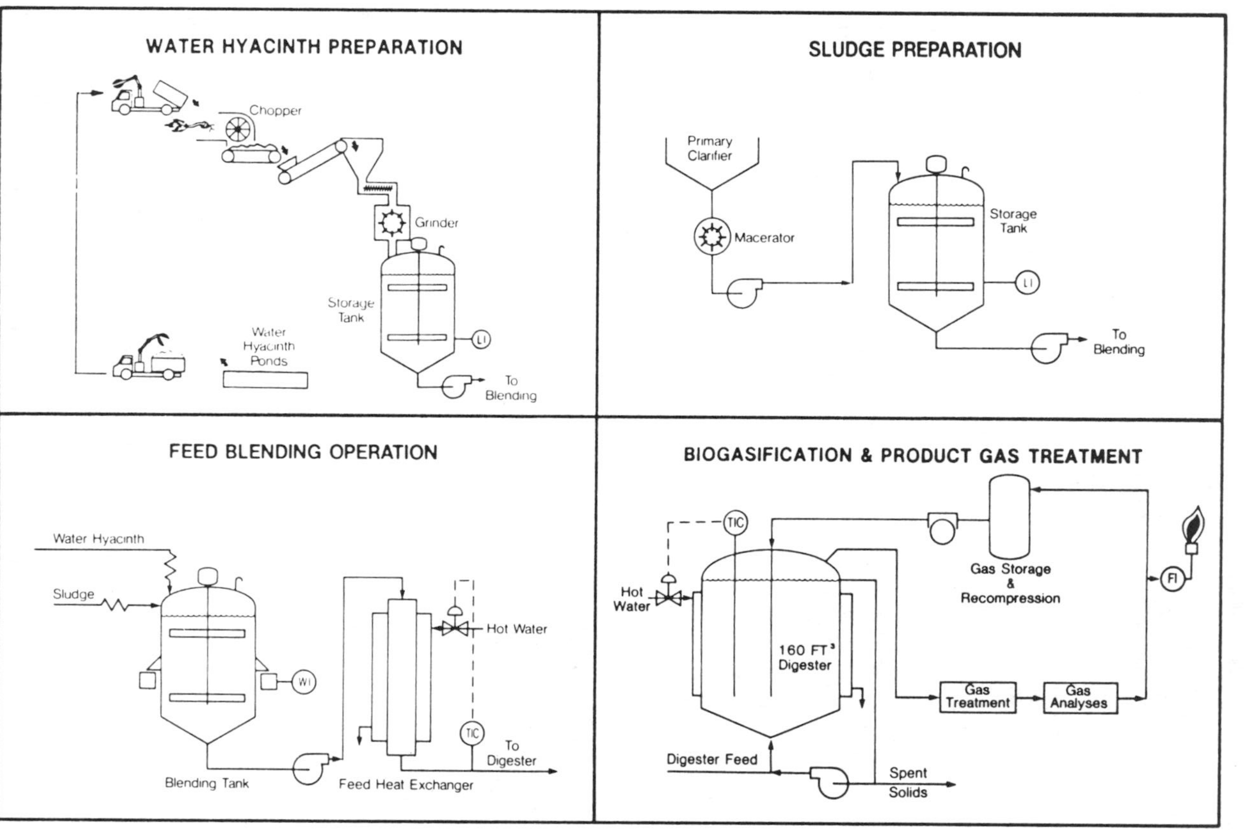

FIGURE 2. Description of the ETU facility.

chopping and grinding operation and as a unit operation is readily scaleable to larger operations.

Sludge Preparation

Sludge is obtained from the primary clarifiers at the wastewater treatment plant. This requires coordination with a full-scale operating plant. The timing and methods of withdrawal from the clarifiers has to be carefully controlled to ensure the transfer of representative and consistent sludge quantities. The

TABLE 1. Seasonal variation of water hyacinth total solids and volatile solids concentration.

	Water Hyacinth			
	Total solids, wt %		Volatile solids, wt % TS	
Month	1984	1985	1984	1985
January	--	4.8	--	84.5
February	--	5.0	--	85.8
March	5.4	4.8	85.5	82.1
April	5.4	4.8	83.6	84.4
May	4.7	5.2	82.2	84.4
June	5.4	5.3	85.5	84.6
July	--	5.4	--	86.8
August	--	5.1	--	85.5
September	5.4	4.9	86.5	86.1
October	5.7	5.2	85.5	86.4
November	5.6	4.8	85.3	79.8
December	4.8	4.4	84.5	80.3
Average	5.3	5.0	84.8	84.2
Standard Deviation	0.4	0.3	1.4	2.3

TABLE 2. Typical chemical analysis and heating value for the water hyacinth feed material.

Ultimate Analysis, wt % (dry basis)	
Carbon (total)	43.80
Hydrogen	5.39
Nitrogen	3.73
Sulfur	0.81
Oxygen (by difference)	33.05
Ash	13.22
Total	100.00
Gross Calorific Value, KJ kg^{-1} VS	17,778
Phosphorus Content, wt % (dry basis)	0.73
Ammonia Nitrogen Content, mg L^{-1} (after grinding)	440

sludge is first passed through a macerator to reduce any plastic and other foreign objects to less than 0.3 cm size before being pumped 225 m in a 7.5 cm underground line to a storage tank. A return line allows sludge to first be recycled through these lines to ensure fresh sludge addition to the ETU facility.

This section uses conventional treatment plant equipment and designs, and therefore is also readily scaleable to larger operations. Energy and manpower requirements are not significant.

During the two year operating period the primary sludge solids concentration was lower and fluctuated more than expected. However, this is probably due to the theme park location and is not typical of other municipal locations where concentrations are much more stable at 5 to 6 weight percent. Seasonal data for the sludge solids and volatile solids are given in Table 3. A typical chemical analysis is provided in Table 4.

Feed Blending Operation

Water hyacinth and sludge are blended at the ratios expected from an integrated commercial operation. Based on the water hyacinth growth rates of 56 to 112 Mg (dry wt) ha^{-1} yr^{-1} and channel detention times of three to six days, the water hyacinth to sludge solids weight ratio varies between 2:1 and 1:1 during the year.

In the ETU, the water hyacinth and sludge are blended in a water-cooled tank supported on load cells for weight measurement of the daily feed quantities added to the digester. Automatic timers control feed to the digester at regular intervals and a heat exchanger is provided for preheat of the feedstream. One of

TABLE 3. Seasonal variation of sludge total solids and volatile solids concentration.

Month	Total Solids, wt %		Volatile Solids, wt % TS	
	1984	1985	1984	1985
January	--	3.8	--	91.1
February	--	3.3	--	90.5
March	--	4.1	--	91.2
April	4.0	3.8	91.0	90.4
May	3.8	2.8	91.2	91.0
June	4.4	3.0	91.0	90.5
July	4.0	3.4	89.8	91.7
August	4.2	3.7	82.2	90.2
September	3.7	3.2	87.4	90.0
October	4.2	3.9	88.9	90.4
November	3.8	4.8	90.8	91.5
December	3.8	3.0	91.1	91.1
Average	4.0	3.6	89.3	90.8
Standard Deviation	0.2	0.6	2.9	0.5

TABLE 4. Typical chemical analysis and heating value for the WDW sludge feed material.

Ultimate Analysis, wt % (dry basis)	
Carbon (total)	53.05
Hydrogen	7.41
Nitrogen	3.12
Sulfur	0.38
Oxygen (by difference)	26.42
Ash	0.62
Total	100.00
Gross Calorific Value, kJ kg^{-1} VS	22,650
Phosphorus Content, wt % (dry basis)	0.45
Ammonia Nitrogen Content, mg L^{-1} (as received)	220

the most important considerations at this stage of the development is the accurate determination of solids feed quantities to allow material balance closures and validation of experimental data. This system provided excellent measurement accuracies of 1% to 2% and recalibrations showed that the system maintained its measurement accuracies. Very tight C balances were subsequently calculated around the digester. All balances were better than 100 $\pm$ 10%.

Biogasification and Product Gas Treatment

Biogasification of the water hyacinth/sludge mixture occurs in a 4.5 m^3 digester having a height to diameter ratio of 2:1. The maximum feed rate to the digester is 1 Mg d^{-1} of mixed feed containing 5% solids. During the two year operating period the digester was operated as a non-mixed, vertical flow reactor. Start up and operation of the digester provided significant insight into the distribution of solids, pH, volatile acids, and other parameters within the digester during operation with sludge and water hyacinth/sludge blends in the non-mixed mode. These observations were previously not possible in the smaller laboratory reactors. Measurement and analysis of these critical parameters have allowed refinements in operating procedures and have resulted in further performance improvements for this reaction system when compared to conventional stirred tank reactors.

One of the most important observations was that solids distributed differently for sludge and water hyacinth/sludge blends. The blend ratio also affected solids distribution. This led to changes in the operating procedure, and dictated the feed and withdrawal points in the digester for maximum solids retention. Initial operation introduced the feed material into the bottom of the reactor and allowed material to overflow from one of the upper digester nozzles to the waste tank. This procedure was developed under the assumption that solids would settle to the bottom. However, samples taken every foot of reactor height revealed that the water hyacinth/sludge blend had a tendency to accumulate higher solids concentrations at the top of the digester. This was confirmed for both 2:1 and 1:1 water hyacinth/sludge blend ratios.

These observations along with volatile acid and pH profile data led to the development of the solids concentrating (SOLCON) digester. This digester is fed from the top and withdraws and partially recirculates some of the culture from the bottom nozzles of the digester. This concept maximizes solids retention times and conversion for the water hyacinth/sludge blends. No nutrient addition or pH control is required for stable digester operation. Some typical solids, volatile acid and pH profiles in the SOLCON digester are in Figure 3.

In addition, for water hyacinth/sludge blends periodic recirculation (3 to 4 h daily) of the upper portion of the digester culture volume is desirable and ensures degradation of the floating plant fraction. A special nozzle was effective in distributing the recirculated culture. The nozzle is available commercially and can readily be adapted to large-scale digesters.

Product gas treatment consists of a complete gas conditioning, storage, and handling system. A conventional house gas meter provided accurate readings during the two years of service. Calibration checks showed that the meter measured daily gas production with an accuracy of 1% to 2%. The reed switch counter on the gas meter was replaced with a microswitch to ensure reliable remote recording of the gas measurement. Gas quality is primarily determined by spot samples and gas chromatography. All pertinent data are continuously recorded on strip charts located on a main control panel.

Daily analyses of gas composition, effluent pH, volatile acids, total and volatile solids, and weekly analysis of total and volatile suspended solids and alkalinity are completed in a field laboratory trailer. Other analyses are conducted at IGT's laboratory in Chicago. Periodically, samples for daily and weekly analyses were sent to IGT to verify the results obtained at the ETU sentinels for the ETU digester. One 50 L unit is operated using the same blend as fed to the ETU digester, one 50 L unit receives pure water hyacinth and one 5 L unit is operated on pure sludge.

RESULTS

Experimental operation of the ETU began in January 1984. After a brief shake-down period, operation was begun with water hyacinth/sludge (WH/SL) blends in the upflow mode (Figure 4). Loading rates to the digester were controlled at 3.2 kg VS m^{-3} d^{-1} and an 11 d hydraulic retention time. Performance data were

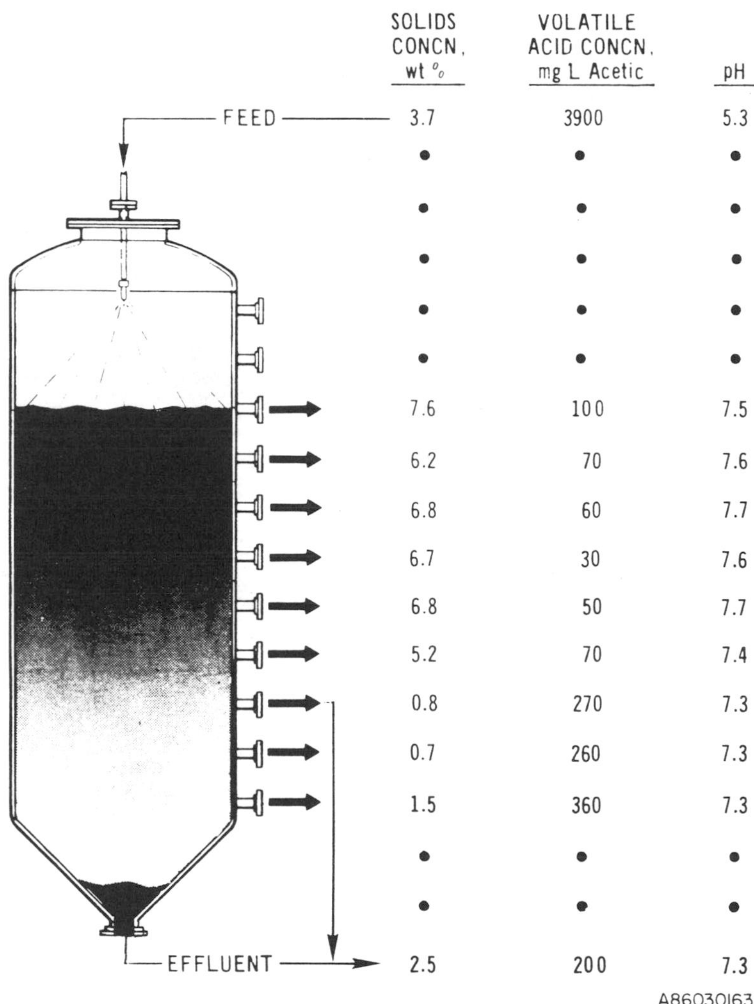

FIGURE 3. Digester profile for water hyacinth/sludge blend.

collected around the digester during two steady-state periods. One using a 2:1 WH/SL blend and one using a 1:1 WH/SL blend. Based on the solids distribution in the digester, operation was then switched to the downflow mode. Performance data were collected during four different steady-state periods. One studied long-term effects and one raised the loading rate to 4.9 kg VS m^{-3} d^{-1} and a seven day hydraulic retention time. The performance data for the six periods are summarized in Table 5.

Despite constantly changing operating conditions to establish a data base at different blend ratios and loading rates, the

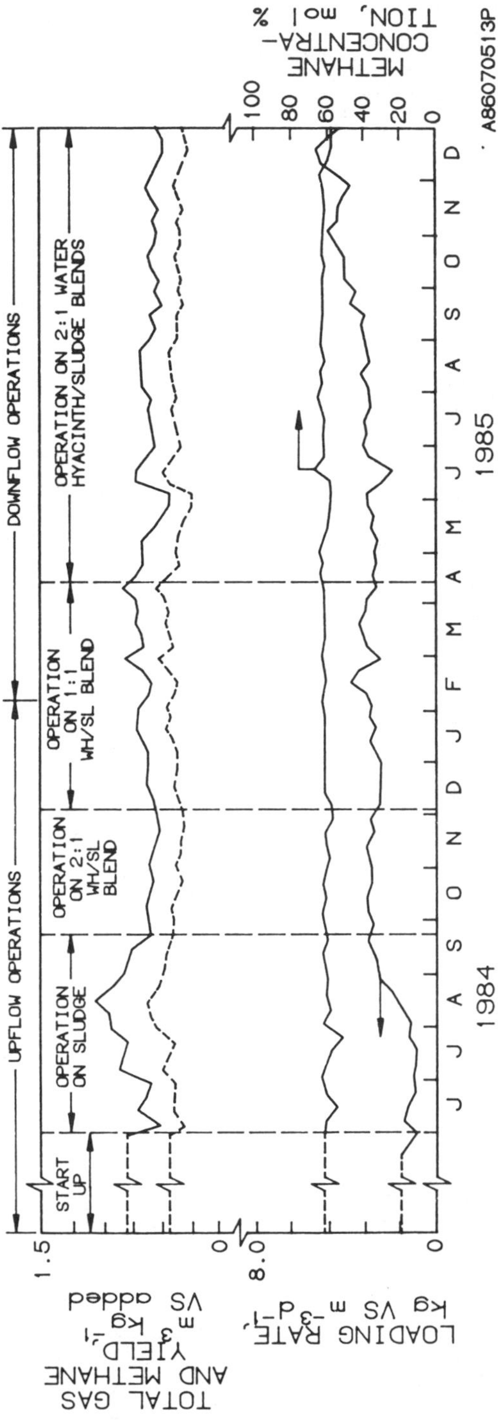

FIGURE 4. Biogasification ETU performance data water hyacinth/sludge blends.

digester operation was uninterrupted and always stable during 18 months of data collection. Hyacinth/sludge blends were converted to CH_4 at high rates and efficiencies. During operation on a 1:1 blend CH_4 yields averaged 0.49 m^3 kg^{-1} fed to the digester. This conversion exceeds 90% of the maximum biodegradable yield. Furthermore, in all cases the SOLCON digester outperformed the continuous stirred tank reactors operated at the site. As illustrated by Figure 5, the results obtained at a loading rate of 3.2 kg VS m^{-3} d^{-1} and different blend and flow configurations.

CONCLUSION

The improved performance in the SOLCON digester is primarily the result of higher solids retention (20 to 30 d) relative to the hydraulic retention time. In addition, net-energy recovery is also higher because continuous stirring of the reactor content is not required. Therefore, this digester produces 15% to 20% more CH_4 and results in smaller digester designs. During the two year operating campaign sufficient data were collected and a kinetic model (Srivastava, 1986) established to allow confident scale-up to larger commercial operations. In addition, independent studies by an engineering firm indicate that if the performance of the ETU

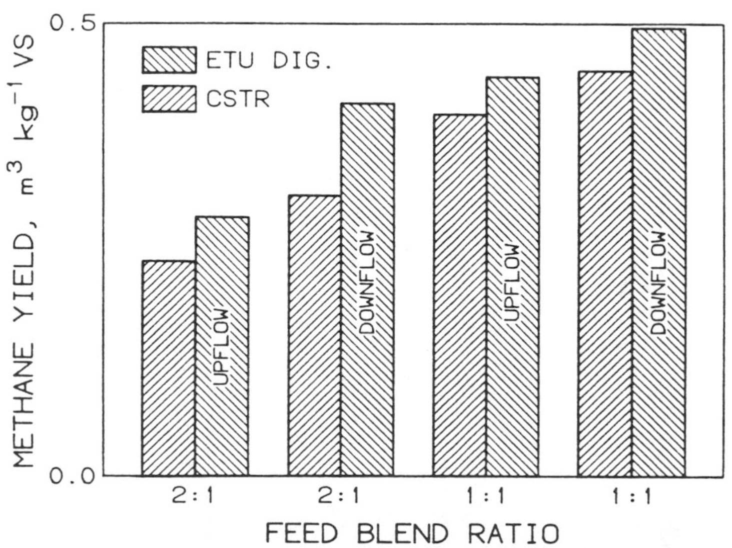

FIGURE 5. Performance comparison of CSTR and ETU digesters (3.2 kg VS m^{-3} d^{-1} loading rate).

TABLE 5. ETU steady-state performance data.

Performance Period	1	2	3	4	5	6
Date	11/5-12/2/84	1/21-2/10/85	3/25-4/21/85	8/5-9/1/85	9/2-9/29/85	12/16-1/12/86
Duration	4 wk	3 wk	4 wk	4 wk	4 wk	4 wk
Operating Mode	Upflow	Upflow	Downflow	Downflow	Downflow	Downflow
Digester Feed Characteristics						
Avg. Blend Ratio WH/PS, TS wt ratio	2:1	1:1	1:1	2:1	2:1	2:1
Avg. Solids Content, wt %	4.5	3.6	3.8	3.7	3.8	4.4
Avg. Volatile Solids Conc., wt % TS	84.6	87.1	85.5	85.6	86.5	83.2
Avg. Volatile Acids Content, mg L^{-1} acetic	3600	2600	3400	3900	2800	5000
pH	--	5.2	5.2	5.3	5.4	5.3
Avg. Alkalinity, mg L^{-1} $CaCO_3$	--	1900	3400	2900	3000	3860
Avg. NH_3-N Content mg L^{-1}	390	340	730	580	450	570
Digester Operating Conditions						
Daily Loading Frequency	1	1	1	1	1	1
Avg. Daily Loading Rate, kg VS m^{-3}	3.2	3.2	3.2	3.2	3.2	4.9
Culture Volume, m^3	3.8	3.8	3.8	3.8	3.8	3.8
Avg. Temperature, °C	35	35	35	35	35	35
HRT, d	12	11	11	11	10	7
SRT, d	21	17	30	24	25	13

TABLE 5 (cont'd.)

Performance Data						
Total Gas Yield, $m^3\ kg^{-1}$ VS added	0.47	0.69	0.76	0.65	0.59	0.50
Methane Content, vol. %	60	63	64	63	63	59.1
Methane Yield, $m^3\ kg^{-1}$ VS added	0.28	0.43	0.49	0.41	0.37	0.30
Methane Yield, $m^3\ kg^{-1}$ organic matter added[+]	0.26	0.39	0.44	0.36	0.34	0.25
Percent of Maximum Biodegradable Yield[++]	63	84	92	86	83	62
Methane Production Rate, vol vol^{-1} culture d^{-1}	0.9	1.3	1.5	1.3	1.2	1.5
Carbon Conversion, wt %	40	59	62	55	51	42
Carbon Balance, wt %	98	105	103	108	99	94
Effluent Quality Data						
Avg. Solids Content, wt %	3.02	1.96	1.91	2.52	2.35	2.64
Avg. Volatile Solids Conc., wt % TS	74.5	78.0	75.1	74.6	77.3	73.0
Avg. Volatile Acids Content, mg L^{-1} acetic	2800	600	1100	200	100	2330
pH	7.3	7.2	7.2	7.3	7.3	7.1
Avg. Alkalinity, mg L^{-1} $CaCO_3$	6000	4700	5200	4800	4200	5240
Avg. NH_3-N Content, mg L^{-1}	870	850	1100	750	760	870

[+]Standard volatile solids (VS) determination does not account for volatile acids (VA).

[++]As measured by bioassays and based on a value of 0.3 $m^3\ kg^{-1}$ Org. for WH and 0.6 $m^3\ kg^{-1}$ Org. for WDW SL.

can be duplicated at the community scale, CH_4 can be produced from the SOLCON digester for less than \$2.00 GJ^{-1} for populations of over 100,000.

ACKNOWLEDGMENTS

The authors acknowledge the Gas Research Institute support of this work under GRI Contract No. 5082-223-0567. We further acknowledge our field scientists, Ahmad Razik and Susan Smallwood, for their diligence and skill in operating the ETU. In addition, we appreciate the interest and assistance of employees of WDW and Reedy Creek Utility Company in preparing feedstock for the ETU system.

REFERENCES

Chynoweth, D. P., S. Ghosh, M. P. Henry, and V. J. Srivastava. 1982. Kinetics and advanced digester design for anaerobic digestion of water hyacinth and primary sludge. Biotech. Bioeng. Symp. 12:381-398.

Chynoweth, D. P., B. Schwegler, D. A. Dolenc, and K. R. Reddy. 1983. Wastewater reclamation and methane production using water hyacinth and anaerobic digestion. Proc. Tenth Annual Energy Technology Conf., Washington, DC, p. 1293-1303.

Cornwall, D. A., J. Zobtek, C. D. Patrinely, C. O. Furman, and J. I. Kim. 1977. J. Water Pollut. Control Fed. 49:57.

Del Fosse, E. S. 1977. Water hyacinth biomass yield potentials. p. 73-99. In Symposium Papers, Clean Fuels from Biomass and Wastes. Institute of Gas Technology, Orlando, FL.

Ghosh, S., M. P. Henry, and D. L. Klass. 1980. Bioconversion of water hyacinth-coastal Bermuda grass-MSW-sludge blends to methane. Biotechnol. Bioeng. Symp. 10:163.

Hayes, T. D., H. R. Isaacson, K. R. Reddy, D. P. Chynoweth, and R. Biljetina. 1987. Water hyacinth systems for water treatment. In K. R. Reddy and W. H. Smith (ed.) Aquatic Plants for Water Treatment and Resource Recovery. Magnolia Publishing, Inc., Orlando, FL.

Srivastava, V. J., K. Fannin, R. Biljetina, D. P. Chynoweth, and T. D. Hayes. 1987. Development of an advanced anaerobic digester design and a kinetic model for biogasification of water hyacinth/sludge blends. In K. R. Reddy and W. H. Smith (ed.) Aquatic Plants for Water Treatment and Resource Recovery, Orlando, FL.

ENERGY RECOVERY FROM AQUATIC BIOMASS IN A THERMOCHEMICAL REACTOR

R. S. Butner, D. C. Elliott, and L. J. Sealock, Jr.
Pacific Northwest Laboratory
Richland, Washington 99352

ABSTRACT

A series of experiments has been conducted to study the conversion of water hyacinths and macrocystis kelp to gaseous and liquid energy products in a catalytic thermal reactor. Treatment of the water hyacinths and kelp at 400-450°C in the presence of nickel and alkali catalysts resulted in moderate yields of medium-heating value (9.2-11.1 MJ std m^{-3}) gas. The gas was composed primarily of H, CO_2, CH_4 and other light hydrocarbon gases. Treatment of the same materials at lower temperatures (350°C) with the addition of an alkali catalyst only resulted in the production of both water soluble and water-insoluble organic material. Analysis of the resulting oils indicates that their chemistry is significantly different from oils produced by treating other ligno-cellulosic feedstocks (i.e., wood) under similar conditions. These differences have practical implications with regards to the utilization of the oils.

Keywords: catalytic gasification, liquefaction, gasification, hydrocarbon, kelp, water hyacinth.

INTRODUCTION

The experiments have been conducted in a 1 L batch autoclave reactor. The feedstocks are utilized at their native moisture contents (90-95 wt %). The reactor operates at elevated pressures to permit thermal treatment without prior drying of the biomass. The reactor is being developed by Pacific Northwest Laboratory (PNL) to investigate a process for the thermal conversion of high-moisture biomass feedstocks to CH_4 and liquid fuels.

Because of the high moisture content of aquatic species (typically 90-95 wt % moisture), energy recovery from these species has been carried out almost exclusively via biological processes, principally anaerobic digestion of the plant to produce CH_4. While this method has been used to produce relatively high yields of CH_4 from wet biomass, problems of incomplete conversion,

ISBN 0-941463-00-1

low rates of conversion (relative to thermochemical processes) and excessive sensitivity to feed variations and/or contamination still exist. These problems are sufficiently far from resolution that investigation of thermochemical processing options for high-moisture biomass appears to be warranted.

MATERIALS AND METHODS

Two aquatic species have been tested in the high-moisture biomass gasifier. Samples of these two species were obtained from field researchers studying the production and utilization of the feedstocks. A fresh-water species (water hyacinth) was provided by the University of Florida and had been grown at the Reedy Creek water treatment facility adjacent to Walt Disney World. The hyacinths were wrapped in several layers of plastic and shipped frozen. The sample consisted of whole plants which were rinsed of mud and debris prior to use. Macrocystis kelp (giant brown kelp) was provided by researchers at the University of California at Santa Barbara. The kelp was shipped frozen from a collection point near Santa Barbara, California. Prior to shipping, it had been allowed to drain, but was otherwise untreated. The samples were stored in plastic wrapping at approximately -10°C.

Moisture content, ash content, and calorific content of the feedstocks were determined using standard laboratory procedures. Characterization of these feedstocks are presented in Table 1. The feedstocks were also analyzed for organic and elemental constituents (Table 2). The values were determined using a Perkin Elmer Elemental analyzer.

TABLE 1. Characterization of feedstocks.

	Moisture content (% of total wt)	Ash content (% of dry wt)	Heating value (MJ/dry kg)
Hyacinths	94.9	15.3	18.0
Kelp	88.9	38.4	16.6
Sorghum	77.0	7.9	18.7

TABLE 2. Composition of feedstocks (all values in wt % of dry, ash-free feedstock).

	Water hyacinths	Kelp	Sorghum
Carbon	51.7	43.2	50.7
Hydrogen	6.8	6.4	6.6
Nitrogen	6.6	1.9	0.2
Oxygen	34.8	48.5	42.5

The feedstocks were also subjected to Inductively Coupled Argon Plasma spectrometry (ICP) for determination of inorganic constituents (principally from the ash components). The results of these analyses do not include such ash components as chlorine, bromine, etc. (Table 3).

Two types of conversion experiments (liquefaction and gasification) were performed on each of the feedstock. All of the experiments were carried out in a 1 L stirred autoclave batch reactor equipped for remote sampling of contents at high pressure and temperatures. The experimental apparatus and procedures have been reported in previous publications (Butner et al., 1985a).

A series of gasification experiments were carried out at 400 and 450°C. Under normal conditions, approximately 30 min were required to bring the reactor and contents from 250°C to 400°C. Approximately 220-330 g of biomass (at 3-10 wt % solids content) were used for each experiment. For these particular experiments, an alumina-supported hydrogenation catalyst (Harshaw Ni-1404-T) was employed along with reagent grade sodium carbonate. Catalyst concentrations are listed in the discussion of results. The reactor was operated at the autogenic pressure of the system, which was typically 30.9-34.4 MPa (4500-5000 psig). Each gasification experiment lasted for 1 h, measured from the time when the reactor contents reached the desired temperature.

After each gasification experiment the reactor contents were cooled, collected, and analyzed. The water remaining in the reactor was typically discolored slightly, and in some instances had a small amount (less than 1 g) of black or dark brown liquid floating on top as a separate phase. Mass recovery during these experiments was typically around 90%.

Liquefaction experiments were carried out in the same reactor used for gasification with reaction conditions summarized in Table 4. Carbon monoxide was charged to the reactor prior to heating, and no samples were taken during heating. Liquefaction experiments were carried out at 350°C for 30 min.

TABLE 3. Element analysis of feedstocks (values are wt % of dry feedstock).

	Water hyacinth	Kelp	Sorghum
Aluminum	0.06	0.01	0.06
Calcium	1.26	1.11	0.40
Iron	0.11	0.01	0.12
Magnesium	0.21	0.57	0.14
Phosphorus	0.57	0.23	0.10
Potassium	0.81	6.05	1.85
Nickel	0.19	not reported	0.02
Sodium	0.91	2.65	0.02
Silicon	0.70	0.04	2.04
Strontium	0.01	0.05	0.00

TABLE 4. Summary of liquefaction experiments.

	Water hyacinths	Kelp	Sorghum
Alkali concentration (g g^{-1}) biomass solids)	0.024	0.323	0.075
Initial CO pressure (MPa)	4.8	5.7	5.4
Insoluble material (g g^{-1} dry ash-free feedstock)	0.082	0.111	0.045
Oil yield (g oil g^{-1} dry ash-free feedstock)	0.26	0.14	0.27
Acetone soluble (wt %)	43.4	77.1	45.9
MeCl soluble (wt %)	56.6	22.9	54.1

After the reactor contents were cooled, the gas in the autoclave was vented through a wet-test meter to determine its final volume and collected for analysis by GC. The reactor was found to contain two liquid phases and some suspended solids. The upper (light) phase consisted of a dark, oil-like material which was mostly soluble in acetone or methylene chloride. The lower (heavy) phase consisted primarily of water which exhibited varying degrees of discoloration. Both phases were saved, and the reactor components were rinsed with acetone to collect residual oil which adhered to the metal surfaces. The aqueous phase was acidified with HCl to pH 3.5-4 and solvent extracted with methylene chloride to remove and water-soluble organics. The solvent was stripped under vacuum from the organic products, which were then weighed to determine yield (Table 4). Analysis of the oils was performed in a gas chromatograph equipped with a mass selective detector (GC/MS). Elemental analyses were also performed to determine C, H, N and O contents of the oils.

RESULTS AND DISCUSSION

Liquefaction experiments conducted for the two aquatic species showed oil yields to be typical of experiments performed with more conventional, lignocellulosic materials (Table 4). In the gasification experiments performed using both kelp and water hyacinths as feedstocks, the CH_4 yield from each of the feedstocks was converted to an equivalent CH_4 yield by calculating the volume of CH_4 required to produce the energy available from the total product gas, which is quite high in H content (Table 5).

The catalyst loadings employed for the gasification experiments were selected arbitrarily and are not optimum levels. As a result, gasification results show modest yields of CH_4, along with relatively low C conversion to other gas products. In contrast, gasification of other high-moisture materials under similar conditions has resulted in appreciably higher C conversions (Butner et al., 1985b). A possible reason for the

TABLE 5. Results of gasification experiments.

	Water hyacinth		Kelp		Sorghum
	(400°C)	(450°C)	(400°C)	(450°C)	(400°C)
Ni catalyst[1] concentration	0.30	0.52	0.15	0.20	0.23
Alkali concentration	0.62	0.71	0.31	0.27	0.00
C[2] conversion	29.6	61.3	68.7	89.0	98.2
CH_4 yield[3]	0.039	0.102	0.075	0.090	0.247
CH_4 yield[4]	2.8	7.3	5.5	6.4	17.6
Equivalent[5] CH_4 yield	0.115	0.262	0.156	0.192	0.319
HHV[6] of product gases	8.9	11.1	10.6	10.4	13.5
Gas Composition[7]					
H_2	41.9	48.0	30.1	35.2	26.8
CO_2	48.7	39.2	53.8	49.8	45.3
CH_4	8.1	11.4	13.5	13.0	26.6
Ethane/Ethylene	1.3	1.3	3.0	2.0	1.1
CO	0.0	0.0	0.1	0.0	0.2

Notes

[1]Catalyst concentrations are presented in g of catalyst per g of dry biomass solids.

[2]Carbon conversion is based on wt % of total C converted to gaseous products.

[3]Expressed in normal m^3 dry ash-free kg^{-1} of biomass.

[4]Expressed in wt % of dry, ash-free feedstock.

[5]Equivalent CH_4 yield is based on the calorific equivalent of the produced gas yield, expressed in normal m^3 dry ash-free kg^{-1} of biomass.

[6]Higher heating values (HHV) are expressed in MJ std m^{-3}.

[7]All gas composition data in in dry vol%.

poorer conversion of the aquatic feedstocks, is the relatively high ash content of both feedstocks, particularly kelp. Experience with the high-moisture reactor system has demonstrated that the presence of basic alkali and/or alkaline earth salts tends to reduce CH_4 production. The explanation for this reduction in yield is possibly related to redirection of reaction pathways by these salts to favor production of CO_2 and H_2 via the water gas shift reaction (Sealock et al., 1985). The data (Table 5) appears to support this explanation since the gases produced from water hyacinth and kelp both exhibit high concentrations of H (approximately 21-48 vol% for hyacinth, 20-37 vol% for kelp).

The high concentration of H present in these gases results in a product gas having a HHV of 8.9-11.2 MJ m^{-3}. When the gas yields for these medium-energy gases are equated to their CH_4 equivalents (on a calorific basis), yields of 0.1-0.26 std m^3 dry ash-free kg^{-1} are observed, which is closer to those obtained via anaerobic digestion. Further experiments carried out with no added alkali and higher loadings of nickel would be expected to result in significantly higher yields of CH_4.

Analysis of the liquid products by GC/MS reveals that there are several dozen different components to the oils, only a portion of which can be readily identified. Only 25-35 wt% of the recoverable oil is represented on the GC trace; the remainder of the oil is either too heavy (too large in molecular weight) or too polar to be volatilized in the GC oven. This value compares to values of 50-80 wt% of the recovered oil from typical wood oils.

The aquatic plant-derived oils also exhibit many other differences relative to other biomass-derived oils. While the aquatic oils are somewhat higher in H/C and O/C ratios, the most significant difference may be in the markedly higher amounts of N present in the aquatic oils (Table 6). Identification of several GC/MS peaks indicates that much of the N is situated as the heteroatom in heterocyclic compounds. These same N compounds are virtually non-existent in wood-derived oils.

The oils also contained relatively high concentrations of straight chain hydrocarbons in the C_{14}-C_{18} range. Phenolic compounds have also been identified, with ethyl phenol being a major component. The current understanding of the chemical mechanisms involved suggests that these phenolics can be generated both from lignin pyrolysis products and also as alkali-catalyzed condensation products from cellulose pyrolysis.

The presence of N compounds in the oils derived from aquatic species is certainly not unexpected. Previous workers have shown that water hyacinths are relatively high in N. However, the location of the N within the ring structure of the oils rather than in side groups does have some interesting implications for their potential use.

The targeted use of biomass-derived liquids is fuel use. Because N heterocyclics are known to be strong autooxidants (Ghassemi et al., 1984) and are suspected NO_x formers in combustion environments (Robinson and Evin, 1983), fuel use of the N containing oils derived from aquatic plants would require a substantial degree of N removal. While hydrotreating process research has advanced to the point where these compounds can be treated to remove much of the N, extracting the N from the ring generally requires a fairly complex catalytic scheme. Relatively

TABLE 6. Composition of biomass-derived oils (all values in wt % of oil).

	Water hyacinths	Kelp	Sorghum	Albany wood oil
Carbon	76.3	74.2	75.9	77.5
Hydrogen	9.9	8.9	8.7	7.9
Nitrogen	8.9	4.0	1.7	0.1
Oxygen	7.9	12.1	13.6	14.1

high consumption of H is required and compounds with a high degree of saturation are produced (Shabtai and Oblad, 1985). These characteristics are not desirable from a fuel performance and economy standpoint.

An alternative to the use of these liquids for fuel is to find applications where the N heteroatom may be chemically useful. Some of the compounds which have been detected in the biomass-derived oils are of industrial interest as both intermediates and end products. The relatively high value of these products has prompted a further investigation of the potential for isolating the materials from the complex mixture of compounds which are present in the oils.

REFERENCES

Butner, R. S., L. J. Sealock, Jr., and D. C. Elliott. 1985a. Development of water slurry gasification systems for high-moisture biomass. Biotechnology and Bioengineering, Symposium #15. John Wiley and Sons, New York, NY. p. 3-16.

Butner, R. S., L. J. Sealock, Jr., and D. C. Elliott. 1985b. Gasification of high-moisture biomass feedstocks. Proceedings of the 17th Biomass Thermochemical Conversion Contractor's Meeting, Minneapolis, MN. PNL-SA-13571. Pacific Northwest Laboratory, Richland, WA.

Ghassemi, M., A. Panahloo, and S. Quinlivan. 1984. Physical characteristics of some widely used petroleum fuels: A reference data base for assessing similarities and differences between synfuels and petroleum products. Energy Sources 7:377-401.

Robinson, E. T., and C. G. Evin. 1984. Commercial scale hydrotreating of shale oil. In S. A. Newman (ed.) Shale Oil Upgrading and Refining. Butterworth Publishers, Boston, MA.

Sealock, L. J., D. C. Elliott, and R. S. Butner. 1985. Development of an advanced water-gas shift conversion system. Final Report #PNL-5468 (DOE/MC/80871-1906).

Shabati, J. S., and A. G. Oblad. 1985. Hydrodenitrogenation of coal-derived liquids and related N-containing compounds. In Volume V Final Report, Chemistry and Catalysis of Coal Liquefaction: Catalytic and Thermal Upgrading of Coal Liquids and Hydrogenation of CO to Produce Fuels. W. H. Wiser, principal investigator. Contract No. AC22-79ET 14700, #DOE/ET/14700-TI-Vol. 5. NTIS, Springfield, VA.

APPLICATION OF WATER HYACINTHS FOR TREATMENT OF DOMESTIC WASTEWATER, GENERATION OF BIOGAS AND ORGANIC MANURE

V. R. Joglekar and V. G. Sonar
Shivsadan Griha Nirman Sahakari Society Ltd.
Sangli, Maharashtra, INDIA

ABSTRACT

With rapid urbanization of thousands of Indian towns, an urgent need was felt to evolve a financially self sustaining system for recycling of domestic wastewater to produce purified water, biogas and organic manure. The basic data required to design such a system was rate of hyacinth growth on wastewater, degree of purification of water achieved, the quantity of biogas obtained from the harvested biomass and the organic manure resulted thereafter. Hence, a research project was established at Sangli to obtain this data.

It was observed that 5.8 Mg wet hyacinth (5% dry matter) could be harvested every day from 1 ha of hyacinth pond, 0.9 m deep, without reducing the parent stock of plants. This system was able to treat 1250 m^3 d^{-1} of wastewater, delivering 1120 m^3 d^{-1} of treated water, the loss of 10% being attributed to evapo-transpiration and seepage losses. In the process, BOD and COD were reduced from 187 and 280 to 20 and 80 mg L^{-1}, respectively. The daily harvested biomass would yield one million k cal of energy by way of biogas. The yearly manure yield was 212.5 Mg with N, P and K values of 19.4, 5.7 and 41.5 mg g^{-1}.

Keywords: Water hyacinth, wastewater treatment, biogas, organic manure.

INTRODUCTION

Disposal of city sewage has presently become a serious problem in the safeguarding of public health. Similarly, energy, both for domestic and industrial consumption, is facing a number of difficulties such as rising costs and erratic supply. On account of rapid industrialization and an increase in the city population, conventional methods of disposal for city waste are no longer useful. The water hyacinth, which grows luxuriantly on the city wastewater, is now looked upon as an instrument for removal

Aquatic Plants for Water Treatment
and Resource Recovery
K.R. Reddy and W.H. Smith (Eds.)

ISBN 0-941463-00-1

of pollution and also as a non-conventional energy source. The potential use of water hyacinth based systems has been summarized by Wolverton and McDonald (1976), Mosse and Chagas (1983), Nath et al. (1983), Reddy (1984), and Reddy and Sutton (1984).

Shivsadan Society at Sangli (India) has undertaken a composite research project entitled "Domestic Wastewater Treatment, Biogas Generation and Manuring Plant" which is sponsored by the Department of Non-conventional Energy Sources, Ministry of Energy, Government of India. It visions the cultivation of water hyacinths on domestic wastewater for removal of pollution, regular harvesting and mastication of water hyacinths to feed biogas digesters and finally sun drying of outflowing spent slurry to produce organic manure (Figure 1).

MATERIALS AND METHODS

Purification of Sewage Water

Ten ponds, each measuring 7.3 x 7.3 x 0.9 m, were constructed by prefabricated method using bricks and reinforced cement concrete (RCC) panels. The raw sewage was drawn from Sangli Municipal Oxidation Lagoons into these ponds to raise a perennial crop of water hyacinths. The ten ponds were divided into two sets, each set comprising of five ponds (1 to 5 and 6 to 10) which were interconnected in series. This enabled two sets of observations to be carried out simultaneously. When the surface area of all the ponds was fully covered by water hyacinths, experiments were conducted by flowing measured volumes (16.8-42 m^3 d^{-1}) of wastewater successively through the ponds. The outflow water was measured and pumped into municipal irrigation system. The water samples at the inflow and outflow were collected and analyzed for selected physical, chemical and biological parameters (Table 1). Using standard methods (APHA, 1981) the cellulose, hemicellulose and lignin were determined as per DST-MACS Laboratory Manual (Godbole, 1984).

Biomass Production

Water hyacinth biomass yields were also measured in the ponds. Each pond was stocked with 100 kg (fresh wt) hyacinth plants which were allowed to grow to cover the entire surface area of the ponds. Thereafter, the biomass harvested every day from the successive pond (making a full rotation in 10 d) was weighed and recorded.

Biogas Production

The daily harvested and weighed biomass was mechanically processed with fresh water to get a workable slurry which was stored in a sump and subsequently fed by gravity into three anaerobic digesters viz. single-stage, two-stage, and three-stage.

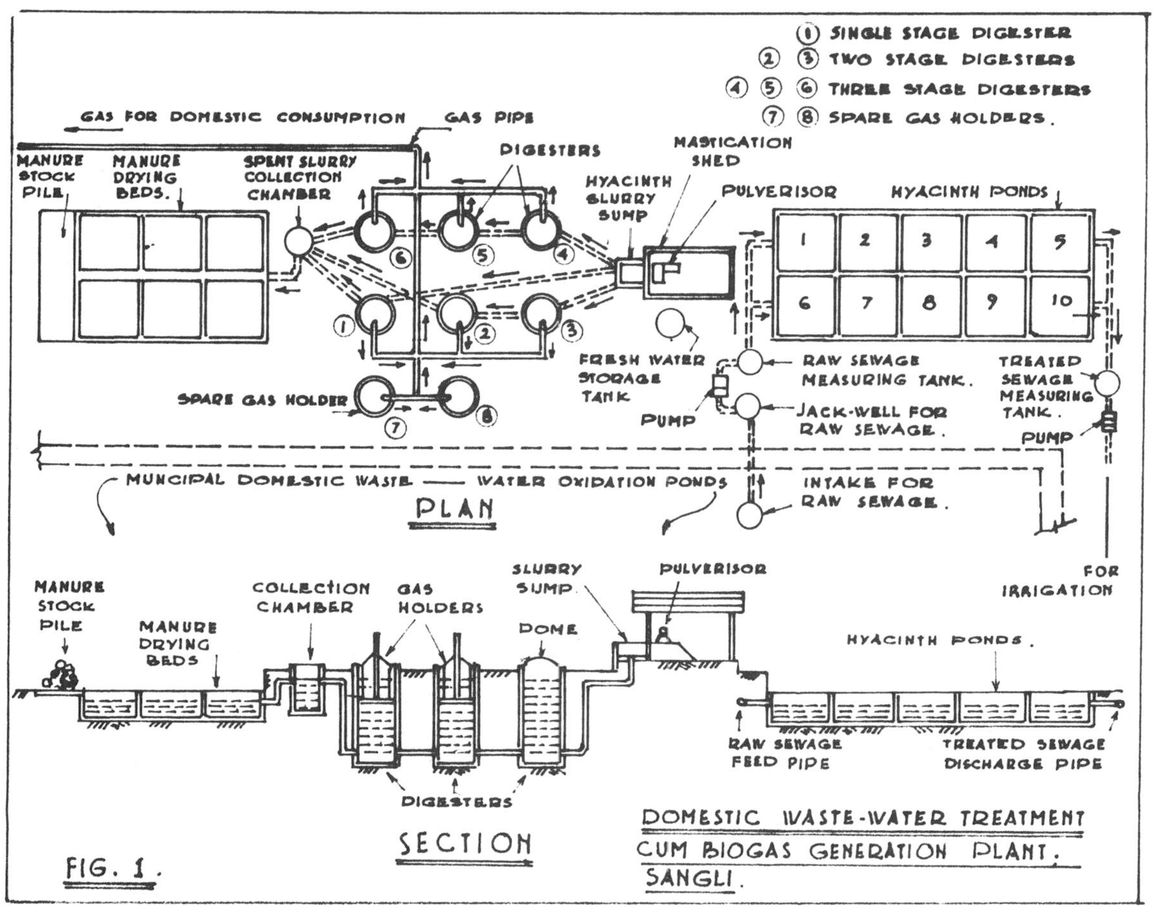

FIG. 1. DOMESTIC WASTE-WATER TREATMENT CUM BIOGAS GENERATION PLANT, SANGLI.

TABLE 1. Effect of growth of water hyacinth on sewage water. Except for pH and MPN all the values are in mg L^{-1}.

Parameter	Before treatment	After treatment	% change
Physical			
pH	7.5	7.1	--
Turbidity	352	5.0	98.6
Total solids	1470	1350	8.2
Total dissolved solids	820	670	18.3
Total suspended solids	190	220	--
Chemical			
DO	<0.1	8.2	--
COD	280	80	71.4
BOD	187.5	20	89.3
Total Kjeldahl's N	22.5	2.5	88.9
Total P	5	2.5	50
Total Organic C	36	15.6	56.7
Total hardness	388	352	9.3
Chlorides	150	124	17.3
Na	140	152	--
Ca	33	30	9.1
K	29	18.6	35.9
Biological			
Standard plate count mL^{-1}	1340×10^8	117×10^8	91.3
MPN 100 mL^{-1}	>2400	>2400	--

In the case of a single-stage system, the digester resembled a Khadi and Village Industries Commission digester with a floating gas holder at the top. In the two-stage system, the primary digester was covered by a fixed dome and the secondary digester by a floating gas holder. Both digesters were interconnected by pipe. In the three-stage system, the first digester was provided with a fixed dome, the second and the third with floating gas holders and they were interconnected by pipes. The digesters and the connecting pipes were of RCC prefabricated construction and the domes and the gas holders were of mild steel. Each digester had a holding capacity of 19.6 m^3. Two spare floating gas holders were provided to store the surplus gas. The biogas generated was measured and supplied to individual customers for cooking through the network of high density polyethylene pipes.

Organic Manure

The spent slurry from all three digesters was collected in a common chamber from where it was discharged into six manure drying beds, each measuring 7.3 x 7.3 x 0.6 m. Their construction was similar to the hyacinth ponds. After 2-3 months, the semi-dried manure was transferred to the stockyard for field applications.

RESULTS AND DISCUSSION

Growth of Water Hyacinth and Purification of Wastewater

When 50% surface area of the water hyacinth biomass in successive ponds was harvested every day for two months, the biomass in each pond was reduced over time. At about 35% harvest level, over harvest also occurred and biomass decreased. Therefore, about 25% of the biomass was harvested daily for six months and it was concluded that nearly 5.8 Mg wet wt hyacinth biomass could be harvested every day from 1 ha hyacinth pond, 0.9 m deep, without reducing the parent stock of plants.

The flow rate of 33.6 m^3 d^{-1} through one set of five ponds was found to be optimum to achieve maximum pollution removal (Table 1). Notably, BOD and COD values were reduced by as much as 89% and 70% respectively. Likewise, a one ha hyacinth pond would treat nearly 1250 m^3 d^{-1} of wastewater delivering nearly 1120 m^3 d^{-1} of treated water suitable for agricultural and industrial use. The loss of water varying from 5 to 16% depending upon the season was attributed to the evapotranspiration and seepage losses.

Generation of Biogas

It was observed that 5.8 Mg of water hyacinth biomass, if digested anaerobically with a retention period of 60 d, would yield about 185 m^3 biogas having a 60% CH_4 content and 1 million k cal fuel value. Seasonal variations were observed in the rate of biogas generation within a range of 13.4 to 100.6 L kg^{-1} of biomass used with an average value of 32 L kg^{-1} (Table 2).

TABLE 2. Relationship of water hyacinth biomass used and biogas produced.

Period	Total biomass used per month in kg	Total biogas generated per month in m^3
October 1983	1,150	43.81
November	600	40.76
December	2,550	60.32
January 1984	4,800	64.25
February	1,600	58.96
March	1,900	64.47
April	2,500	68.59
May	2,575	85.44
June	2,600	82.88
July	NA	NA
August	900	90.53
September	1,672	73.31
Total	22,847	733.33

NA = not available.
Biogas generated per kg of biomass used: 32 L.

Production of Organic Manure

The spent slurry from the digesters was allowed to dry on the composting beds. The resulting manure was given to the Institute of Applied Research and Development in Agriculture at Sangli for field trials. Detailed aspects of application of this manure on various crops are being studied. The water hyacinth based organic manure is rich in N, P and K (Table 3), which is comparable to any farm yard compost manure and therefore one could expect a beneficial effect on crop yields.

TABLE 3. Chemical composition of water hyacinth and spent slurry.

Parameter	Percent Dry Weight Basis	
	Water hyacinth	Spent slurry
Total solids	4.0	2.29
Volatile solids	83.3	57.00
C	48.3	33.06
N	3.37	1.94
P (as P_2O_5)	1.00	0.57
K (as K_2O)	5.14	4.15
Cellulose	9.00	5.00
Hemicellulose	8.18	1.77
Fat	2.1	ND
Lignin	3.0	ND

ND = Not determined.

ACKNOWLEDGMENTS

Shivsadan Society is grateful to DNES, Ministry of Energy, Government of India for funding this research project and the Sangli Municipal Council for providing facilities in setting up the project.

REFERENCES

American Public Health Association. 1985. Standard methods for the examination of water and wastewater. 16th ed. American Public Health Association, Washington, DC.

Godbole, S. H. 1984. Edited DST-MACS Training Course Laboratory Manual. Published by Maharashtra Association for the Cultivation of Science, Pune - 411 004, India.

Mosse, R. A., and J. M. Chagas. 1984. Utilization of water hyacinth in the tertiary treatment of domestic sewage. p. 635-646. In G. Thyagarajan (ed.) Proceedings of the International Conference on Water Hyacinth. Hyderabad, India, Feb. 7-11, 1983.

Nath, K. J., S. V. Ram Rao, Sunanda Nair, and R. H. Gilman. 1984. Low cost wastewater treatment with water hyacinth. p. 655-663. In G. Thyagarajan (ed.) Proceedings of the International Conference on Water Hyacinth. Hyderabad, India, Feb. 7-11, 1983.

Reddy, K. R. 1984. Water hyacinth (Eichhornia crassipes) biomass production in Florida. Biomass 6:167-181.

Reddy, K. R., and D. L. Sutton. 1984. Water hyacinth for water quality improvement and biomass production. J. Environ. Qual. 13:1-8.

Wolverton, B. C., and R. C. McDonald. 1975. Bioconversion of water hyacinths into methane gas and fertilizers. NASA Technical Memorandum (USA) No. TM-X72725.

GROWTH CHARACTERISTICS OF DUCKWEEDS AND THEIR POTENTIAL USE AS ORGANIC FERTILIZERS IN HONG KONG

M. L. So
Biology Department
Hong Kong Baptist College
224 Waterloo Road
HONG KONG

ABSTRACT

Three species of duckweeds, *Spirodela polyrhiza*, *Lemna minor*, and *Wolffia arrhiza*, were grown in monocultures and mixed cultures to determine their growth rates for a period of 42 d. All species exhibited a sigmoid growth curve when grown in monoculture, but in mixed cultures, *Lemna minor* outgrew the other two. *Spirodela polyrhiza* was totally inhibited whereas the growth of *Wolffia arrhiza* was reduced by 40-50%. Duckweeds, when dried, were tested for their potential use as a fertilizer to grow Chinese flowering cabbage (*Brassica parachinensis* Bailey). Results showed a more than three-fold increase in yield over control plots.

Keywords: *Lemna*, *Spirodela*, *Wolffia*.

INTRODUCTION

Even though farming in Hong Kong is limited to 9% of its land area, the territory produces almost 35% (74,000 Mg d^{-1}) of the vegetables together with 54% (420 Mg d^{-1}) of the live poultry and 18% (1782 d^{-1}) of the live pigs consumed by its 5.5 million people. Farms in Hong Kong are very small (0.05-0.1 ha) compared with those in rural China and are often managed by a family of 4-5 members. Crops are usually grown in strips of soil measuring 10 m x 1 m with a space of 1 m in between. These spaces may be dry or water-filled ditches depending on the types of crops grown. In these ditches, several species of duckweeds are found in great abundance, requiring considerable labor for their periodic removal.

Recent investigations into the possibility of using aquatic weeds for wastewater treatment (Cornwell et al., 1977; Oron et al., 1986), as a biofeed (Gaigher et al., 1984), and as a source of protein (Bhanthumnavin, 1977), have developed a renewed interest in the economic importance of these plants. Several have

Aquatic Plants for Water Treatment
and Resource Recovery
K.R. Reddy and W.H. Smith (Eds.)

ISBN 0-941463-00-1

reported on the high productivity of aquatic plants (Ingemarsson et al., 1984), tolerance to high salt concentration (Haller, 1974) and high nutrient content (Porath et al., 1979). Short term (3 d) growth (Mestayer et al., 1984) and long term growth (> year) (Reddy and DeBusk, 1985) studies of various aquatic macrophytes have determined their growth responses under varying conditions. Several species of duckweeds in Hong Kong co-exist in the same waterways, and which particular species is dominant depends largely on the nutrient levels in the water. Recently, Oron et al. (1986) showed that Lemna generally replaced Spirodela if they were grown together, while Wolffia grew well in a mixed culture with other duckweeds. This paper was an attempt to document the growth characteristics of three duckweed species, namely S. polyrhiza, L. minor and W. arrhiza, in mono and mixed cultures. The second objective was to evaluate the potential of these duckweeds used as organic fertilizer for the growth of the Chinese flowering cabbage, B. parachinensis.

MATERIALS AND METHODS

Three species of duckweeds, S. polyrhiza, L. minor and W. arrhiza, were collected from the waterways in the New Territories. They were washed and stocked outdoors in a concrete tank (2 m^2) containing tap water and a small amount of fresh cattle manure. A total of 40 plants of each species were stocked separately into tanks which allowed ample space for growth during the experimental period of 42 d. All tanks were filled with half-strength Hutner's solution and the pH was adjusted to 6.5

Once a week, the old solutions were replaced with a fresh medium containing macronutrients and micronutrients and the pH was adjusted to ensure normal growth. At weekly intervals, the duckweeds were skimmed from the tanks and their fresh weights recorded and then they were carefully returned to their respective tanks and allowed to continue growth. The process was repeated until no further change in fresh weight was obtained.

Since a number of Brassica species are commonly used as vegetables in Hong Kong, the most common species, B. parachinensis, was selected for this experiment. It also has the advantage of having a short growing period of 30 to 40 d. Pots were filled with 10 kg sieved soil (sand:clay, 9:1). Seeds of B. parachinensis were germinated in seed beds and later transplanted into pots, each containing four seedlings. Twelve pots were used and they were treated as follows: control (no duckweed or fertilizer added), dried duckweed added, (6.5, 9.9, 13 and 16.4 g, equivalent to 100, 150, 200 and 250 g respectively of fresh duckweeds) and fertilizer added (20% N, 5% P_2O_5, 10% K_2O). Another pot trial was done using sandier soil for comparison. Duckweed or fertilizer application was repeated once a week and continued until the time of harvest. The duckweed used was mainly L. minor.

After 30 d, the whole plants were harvested and washed free of soil. The plant height was measured and the fresh weight and dry weight of each plant were recorded. Since Brassica is not temperature specific for maximum growth during the year, this experiment was conducted in Spring of 1986.

RESULTS AND DISCUSSION

Growth Curves for Single Cultures

All growth curves (Figure 1) showed the typical three phases, i.e. 1) initial lag phase, 2) linear growth phase where exponential growth occurred and 3) declining phase where the growth rate declined. Linear growth began after three weeks and all species exhibited rapid growth, climbing to a maximum within the next two weeks. Lemna continued rapid growth even when the tank was completely covered with the daughter fronds. But in Spirodela, growth was rather gradual and the log phase was not as steep as that in Lemna and it also took much longer to double (7 d).

In Wolffia, the smallest of all the duckweed species, growth also followed the same general trend. Space should not be a problem because of its microscopic size but it still exhibited the

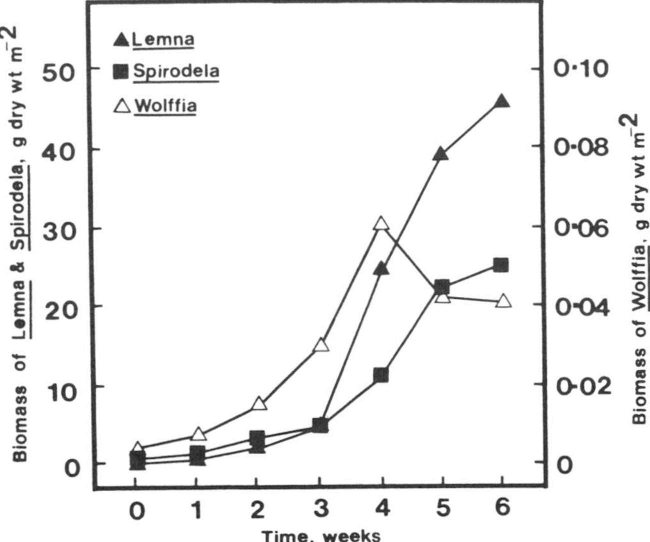

FIGURE 1. Growth curves of three duckweed species in single cultures.

normal sigmoid curve. Bhanthumnavin (1971) reported that this little flowering plant could serve as a potential source of inexpensive protein in the South East Asian countries. Its protein content was estimated to be several times greater than that of the local crops and it also produced more dry matter than traditional crops grown in Thailand. In view of its extremely short doubling time (4 d), the prospect of Wolffia being used to help solve food problems in developing countries seems promising. Wolffia is usually found in any available space between Lemna and Spirodela and it adheres closely to them. When comparing the three species in single cultures, Lemna showed the highest growth rate of 2.77 g m^{-2} d^{-1} (Table 1).

Growth Curves for Mixed Cultures

Lemna Minor and Wolffia Arrhiza. In a mixed culture of Lemna and Wolffia (Figure 2a), the growth of Lemna was much the same as when it was grown in the single culture. In Wolffia a similar growth pattern was also observed but it increased fairly slowly and never reached a peak as observed when grown alone. Even the maximum weight achieved when grown with Lemna was only about 15% of that when grown singly. Clearly, Wolffia was strongly inhibited in the presence of Lemna. Its population declined to almost its original level, but Lemna was observed to maintain vigorous growth.

Spirodela Polyrhiza and Lemna Minor. In single cultures, growth of Spirodela or Lemna followed that of a typical sigmoid curve. However, when mixed (Figure 2b), Lemna grew excellently and even more vigorously than when grown alone, reaching a slightly higher biomass of 50.14 g m^{-2} at the end of six weeks. In Spirodela, for reasons yet unknown, the population peaked on the second week and then quickly declined and finally all died. Death coincided with the rapid growth of the Lemna fronds. Evidently, some kind of inhibition must be present that completely prevented Spirodela from competing directly with Lemna. This was also observed in the natural conditions when Lemna and Spirodela were found together. The former invariably dominated and the

TABLE 1. Maximum growth rate of duckweeds in single and mixed cultures.

Culture	Growth Rate		
	Lemna (L)	Spirodela (S)	Wolffia (W)
	g (dry wt) m^{-2} d^{-1}		
Single	2.78	1.58	0.0038
Lemna & Wolffia	4.49	--	0.0007
Lemna & Spirodela	4.31	0.76	--
Spirodela & Wolffia	--	0.63	0.0094
Mixed	2.27	1.94	0.0038

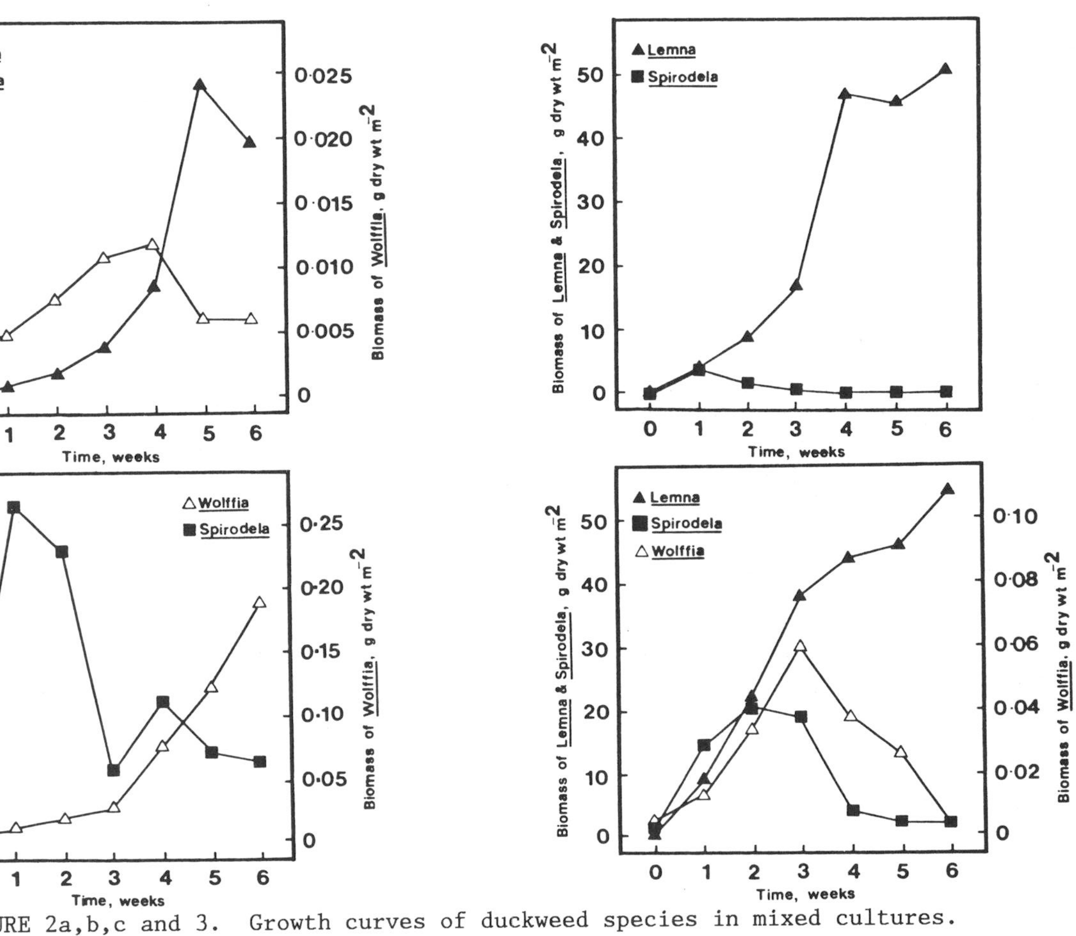

FIGURE 2a,b,c and 3. Growth curves of duckweed species in mixed cultures.

latter was only found as islands scattered among the pool of Lemna.

Wolffia Arrhiza and Spriodela Polyrhiza. When the two comparatively inferior species of duckweeds were grown together, even though Spirodela began with its big fronds, it could not compete with the microscopic sized Wolffia (Figure 2c). Wolffia grew as though it were in a single culture and its weight rose steadily during the six weeks of vigorous and uninhibited growth. It did even better than when it was grown alone, reaching a biomass twice as much as in the single culture. This might be due to the presence of some substance liberated by Spirodela, stimulating the growth of Wolffia.

Spirodela, Lemna and Wolffia. When all three species were grown together, Lemna was the one which showed the most uninhibited or even stimulated growth (Figure 3). Lemna growth was much the same as when it was grown alone or mixed with either of the other duckweeds. Furthermore, a higher biomass within the same growth period was reached and it could probably have continued its increase. According to Reddy and DeBusk (1985), the growth of Lemna usually peaked at week 4 during the summer and week 6 during the winter in Florida, USA. The results of the present study were much in agreement with their findings as the experiments were conducted during the period when the temperatures ranged between 24°C and 30°C. Spirodela peaked at week 3 and then decreased gradually until it reached a level similar to the initial population. Complete death did not occur as when grown with Lemna. Wolffia on the other hand, did not thrive; it started well, peaked at week 3, and then declined in growth.

In the natural waters, especially in the ditches of the farmlands in Hong Kong, the dominant species of duckweed is Lemna minor. Spirodela is only found together with Lemna in some of the ditches and as Lemna usually outgrows it, the population of the former will dwindle and remain low. Wolffia is not as common as Lemna and is only found in some ditches. Scarcity is probably due to the pH of the water which was measured to range from 8.2 to 8.8 whereas the pH of the water where Lemna or Lemna plus Spirodela occur is found to range between 6.4 to 7.4. Spirodela is sensitive to high pH. Thus, different duckweed species can colonize different habitats, making use of nutrients available for their growth.

Duckweeds Used as Organic Fertilizers

The addition of duckweed to soil improved crop yield (Table 2) significantly with a two-fold increase in Chinese flowering cabbage at the lowest duckweed application (fresh weight equivalent of 100 g per 10 kg soil). The crop yield with chemical fertilizer added did not exceed those with the highest duckweed application. Both lots showed a more than three-fold increase over that of the control. At the lowest amount of duckweeds

TABLE 2. Effect of duckweeds added to soil on yield of whole plants of Chinese flowering cabbage.

Treatment	Avg. Plant Ht. (cm)		Fresh Weight		Dry Weight	
	S	M	S	M	S	M
Control	14.9	21.3	7.0±0.7	11.7±1.6	1.1±0.1	1.4±0.3
Duckweed added						
100 g	30.9	33.3	23.0±2.6‡	24.4± 2.4‡	2.6±0.4‡	2.6±0.2‡
150 g	33.4	32.6	29.6±5.1‡	37.3± 5.9‡	3.1±0.5‡	3.5±0.8‡
200 g	39.7	36.1	47.8±2.8‡	37.8± 7.8‡	4.6±0.7‡	3.6±0.9‡
250 g	37.6	34.5	45.4±3.7‡	37.9±10.9‡	3.7±0.6‡	3.6±0.8‡
Fertilizer	28.9	35.1	22.9±1.6‡	39.5± 7.0‡	2.0±0.4†	3.8±0.9‡

†Significant at 1% level of probability when compared with the control.

‡Significant at 0.1% level of probability when compared with the control.

applied, dry weight of the cabbage plants showed a 50% increase over that of the control.

Results were greater from the sandy soil with the same treatments than from the sand/clay soil (Table 2). There was a striking difference between the yield from duckweed treated soil and that with the fertilizer added. When compared with the control, a three-fold increase in fresh weight was observed even with the lowest duckweed application. The weight increase of plants grown with 200 g and 250 g duckweeds was calculated to be more than six times that of the control. Those grown with fertilizer added showed the same yield as with the lowest duckweed application. Perhaps, fertilizer added would be wasted because the nutrients would leach from the high porosity sandy soil. The yield was only 56% that of the sand/clay soil with fertilizer added. This also shows that decomposing duckweeds can serve as organic fertilizer for plant growth and as a soil conditioner, increasing soil-water retention and providing a substrate for microorganisms.

The harvestable dry duckweed biomass available from each ditch (area 10 m^3) is about 400 g which is enough to support the growth of at least 40 Chinese flowering cabbage for a period of 30 d. As pointed out by Flores et al. (1983), _Lemna_ and _Wolffia_ species tested in the Chinampa zones in Mexico were found to be the most likely candidates to be used as organic fertilizer.

Ironically, the blooming of duckweeds in waterways is due to the heavy application of chemical fertilizers in farms. If the applications were reduced, the waterways may not suffer eutrophication and severe clogging since the natural ecological balance could be maintained with its diversity of fish, snails, worms and other invertebrates. In rural China where nightsoil is used extensively, the waterways are almost free of these weeds. However, because of the labor involved in collecting nightsoil and pig manure, farmers in Hong Kong may not be willing to stop using chemical fertilizers and duckweeds will still be found. But the duckweeds can still serve as a partial substitute for chemical fertilizer and help maintain soil structure.

ACKNOWLEDGMENTS

I wish to thank the Hong Kong Baptist College for providing the facilities for this study and Mr. S. S. Chan and Mr. M. T. To for technical assistance.

REFERENCES

Bhanthumnavin, K. 1971. Wolffia arrhiza as a possible source of inexpensive protein. Nature 232:495.

Cornwell, D. A., J. Zoltek, Jr., C. D. Patrinely, T. des Furman, and J. I. Kim. 1977. Nutrient removal by water hyacinths. J. Water Pollut. Control Fed. 49:57-65.

Flores, A. Q., M. G. M. Arce, and A. L. Helgueras. 1983. Potential use of some hydrophytes as organic fertilizer in the Chinampa zone in Xochimilco Mexico. Biotica (Mex.) 7:631-633.

Gaigher, I. G., D. Porath, and G. Granoth. 1984. Evaluation of duckweed Lemna gibba as feed for Tilapia in a rectangular unit. Aquaculture 41:235-244.

Haller, W. T. 1974. Effects of salinity on growth of several aquatic macrophytes. Ecology 55:891-894.

Ingemarsson, B., L. Johansson, and C. M. Larsson. 1984. Photosynthesis and nitrogen utilization in exponentially growing nitrogen-limited cultures of Lemna gibba. Physiol. Plant 62:262-269.

Mestayer, C. R., D. D. Culley, Jr., L. C. Standifer, and K. L. Koonce. 1984. Solar energy conversion efficiency and growth aspects of the duckweed, Spirodela punctata (G.F.W. Mey) Thompsom. Aquat. Bot. 19:157-170.

Oron, G., D. Porath, and L. R. Wildschut. 1986. Wastewater treatment and renovation by different duckweed species. J. Environ. Eng . Div., ASCE 112:247-263.

Porath, D., B. Hepher, and A. Koton. 1979. Duckweeds as an aquatic crop: Evaluation of clones for aquaculture. Aquat. Bot. 7:273-278.

Reddy, K. R., and W. F. DeBusk. 1985. Growth characteristics of aquatic macrophytes cultured in nutrient-enriched water: II. Azolla, duckweed, and salvinia. Econ. Bot. 39:200-208.

BIOMANIPULATION OF AQUATIC MACROPHYTES IN LAKE CANDIA (N. ITALY)

G. Galanti and P. Guilizzoni
C.N.R. Istituto Italiano di Idrobiologia
28048, Pallanza, ITALY

ABSTRACT

Research on aquatic food web biomanipulations of a small shallow Lake Candia in Northern Italy provided a framework for harvesting the very dense populations of water chestnut (*Trapa natans*) and reed (*Phragmites australis*) in the lake. Runoff and precipitation are the sole contributors of nutrients to the lake. Since municiple effluents have been diverted, harvesting 50% of the emergent and floating macrophyte biomass will remove a quantity of 120 kg P, which is well above the external P load (70 kg) now received annually.

Keywords: *Trapa natans*, harvesting, *Phragmites*, phosphorus.

INTRODUCTION

The small, shallow and eutrophic Lake Candia is under study with the aim of manipulating its dense macrophyte and fish populations. Located near the city of Turin in Northern Italy, Lake Candia is an important recreational and natural resource, that has been experiencing problems due to the increasing nuisance of aquatic macrophytes. The dominant species are represented by the reed *Phragmites australis* (Cav.) Trin. ex Steud. and the water chestnut *Trapa natans* L., which form a dense belt, up to 100 m wide all around the lake. Other species of aquatic plants also present include *Typha angustifolia* L., *Ceratophyllum demersum* L., *Nymphaea alba* L., and *Nuphar luteum* L. (Badino et al., 1982-83).

Since the diversion of the municipal sewage of the Village of Candia Canavese, runoff and precipitations have been the sole contributors of nutrients to the lake (Durio et al., 1983). This situation gives us the opportunity to practice lake biomanipulation *sensu* Shapiro (1979), which includes interventions on the fish community and removal of nutrients from the system through a harvesting program. Here only this latter aspect is addressed. Although there is a vast number of papers available on the biology

Aquatic Plants for Water Treatment
and Resource Recovery
K.R. Reddy and W.H. Smith (Eds.)

ISBN 0-941463-00-1

of macrophytes and their potential for improving water quality (Galanti and Guilizzoni, 1985; Rodhe et al., 1979; Westlake, 1968) this is probably the first attempt at lake management in Italy using this approach.

Recently Loucks (1985) has questioned the effectiveness of aquatic plant harvesting and it is clear that a number of questions still remain to be answered, especially on short and long term effects (Carpenter and Adams, 1977; Nichols, 1974). However, as noted by Yount and Crossman (1970) we "feel that large-scale harvesting from natural waters can be expected to reduce the productivity of those waters, and probably reverse the trend toward hypertrophy", especially when coupled with fish management.

MATERIALS AND METHODS

Morphological, chemical, and biological characteristics of Lake Candia are shown in Figure 1 and Tables 1 and 2). The distribution map of Lake Candia macrophytes (*P. australis* and *T. natans*) during summer 1985 were obtained by infrared aerophotogrammetry and topographic measurements with radar. Biomass was chosen as the method of measuring the effect of harvesting.

Plant material was collected quantitatively from 6 experimental areas harvested by the Rolba Aquamarine 400 and immediately weighed for wet biomass determination. Samples were dried at 105°C and at 500°C, respectively for total dry weight and organic weight estimates. Carbon and N in plant tissues were determined with a CHN analyzer, while plant tissues for P content analysis were dry-ashed according to the method of Jackson (1958) and then analyzed for reactive orthophosphate P (Murphy and Riley, 1962).

RESULTS AND DISCUSSION

From ground and aerial photography it has been estimated that *T. natans* and *P. australis* cover areas of 19 and 14 ha respectively. An echo-sounding survey indicated that water chestnut grows in water at depth of up to 2.5 m in a rich organic mud. Maximum biomass, found in early September for water chestnut, was about 80 Mg (fresh wt) ha^{-1} (Table 3).

TABLE 1. Main morphometric characteristics of Lake Candia.

Surface (km^2)	1.4
Area of drainage basin (km^2)	6.9
Shore line (km)	5.7
Volume ($m^3 \times 10^6$)	5.4
Max. depth (m)	6.5
Mean depth (m)	3.8
Theoretical renewal time (yr)	2.3

FIGURE 1. Aerial photograph of Lake Candia.

TABLE 2. Main chemical and biological characteristics of Lake Candia.

Anoxic condition below 4-5 m depth
Bottom NH_3 concentration of 131-1706 µg L^{-1} (annual range)
$N\text{-}NO_3$ concentration of 0-284 µg L^{-1} (annual range along the water column)
$P\text{-}PO_4$ concentration of 0-54 µg L^{-1} (annual range along the water column)
Total-P concentration of 3-141 (annual range along the water column)
Total chlorophyll concentration of 6.6-42.7 µg L^{-1} (annual integrated values)

Phosphorus inputs:

Runoff (kg yr^{-1})	69
Precipitation (kg yr^{-1})	10
Internal loading	Unknown (expected high)
Cyanobacteria (mainly *Microcystis aeruginosa*)	75% of total phytoplankton community
Filter-feeder cladocerans dominated by:	*Ceriodaphnia quadrangula*, *Bosmina longirostris* & *Daphnia hyalina*
Coarse fish overstocking	Rudd (*Scardinius erythrophthalmus*) Catfish (*Ictalurus melas*)

TABLE 3. Biomass, organic matter and nutrients (dry weight basis) in *Trapa natans* of Lake Candia during the growing season of 1985.

Date	Dry weight kg ha^{-1}	Organic Matter %	Organic Matter kg ha^{-1}	Nitrogen %	Nitrogen kg ha^{-1}	Phosphorus %	Phosphorus kg ha^{-1}
6/28	1740	90.1	1570	3.12	54	0.21	3.7
8/5	4710	81.9	3860	2.69	127	0.23	10.8
8/22	7150	84.6	6050	2.11	151	0.17	12.2
9/12	7890	87.4	6900	1.89	149	0.15	11.8
9/25	3890	85.9	3340	2.40	93	0.21	8.2
10/21	1450	86.2	1250	2.19	32	0.17	2.5

Concentrations of organic matter, N and P are slightly higher at the beginning of growth (o.m. = 90%; N = 3.12%; P = 0.21% on a dry weight basis). The N and P tissue content (kg ha^{-1}) follows the seasonal trend of biomass reaching maximum values in August (Table 3). A sharp decrease in nutrient content is then observed because of the rapid decay from the second half of September through October.

On the basis of data on plant distribution and production (a study on reed is in progress), and taking the biological information into account, the full-scale harvesting program planned for 1986 will remove at regular intervals along the lacustrine perimeter 50% of the aerial part of reed and the same percentage of water chestnut. The projected harvesting program will optimize goals such as maintenance of cover for fish, nutrient removal, encouragement of desirable species, and enhancement of recreational potential. The purpose is also that of safeguarding the important ecological role played by the aquatic vegetation in this ecosystem and improving the aquatic bird species diversity.

The quantity of plant tissue and N and P removable in the harvests (Table 4) of aquatic vegetation amply exceed the external loading (ca. 70 kg P yr^{-1}; Durio et al., 1983). Moreover, the removal of a large quantity of organic biomass from the littoral zone means that plants are not available to deplete O_2 supplies and release nutrients for new plant growth (Jewell, 1971; Peterson et al., 1974).

No short-term detrimental effects following the preliminary harvesting experiments carried out in 1985, were observed in terms of water nutrient enrichments and algae development; whereas an increase of biomass of the submersed species _Ceratophyllum demersum_ seems quite evident.

Studies on plant biomass utilization are still in progress, and we are considering the use of _Trapa_ tissues as fertilizer, as litter for earthworms (_Anellida_) and afterwards, the use of the high nutrient-rich organic matter ("compost") resulting from their activity, for gardening and agricultural purpose. Hopefully, livestock feed, cellulosic materials and paper (these latter from the fibrous stems of reed) will also be produced and used locally.

TABLE 4. Potential removal of organic matter, N and P by harvesting.

	P. australis	_T. natans_
Vegetation cover, ha	16	20
Harvesting area, ha	10	10
Timing of harvesting	Jan-Feb	Aug-Sep
Biomass (fresh wt), Mg	120	600
Biomass (dry wt), Mg	90	60
Biomass (org. wt), Mg	80	50
Nitrogen, kg	700	1400
Phosphorus, kg	20	100

ACKNOWLEDGMENTS

This research has been partially supported by the E.E.C. Environmental Research Program (Contract No. ENV-748-1 (SB).

REFERENCES

Badino, G., R. Camoletto, G. Dal Vesco. 1982-83. Popolamenti fanerogamici del bacino di Candia e assetto idrobiologico del lago. Rev. Valdostaine d'Hist. Naturelle 36-37:43-125.

Carpenter, S. R., and M. S. Adams. 1977. Environmental impacts of mechanical harvesting of submersed vascular plants. Center for Biotic Systems, Institute for Environmental Studies, IES Report 27, Univ. of Wisconsin-Madison. 30 pp.

Durio, P., D. Mori, G. C. Perosino. 1983. Aspetti limnologici del Lago di Candia. Riv. Piem. St. Nat. 4:137-169.

Galanti, G., and P. Guilizzoni. 1985. Nutrient uptake by a floating leaved aquatic plant (*Trapa natans* L.) Verh. Internat. Verein. Limnol. 22:2943-2946.

Jackson, M. L. 1958. Soil chemical analysis. Prentice Hall.

Jewell, W. J. 1971. Aquatic weed decay. J. Water Pollut. Control Fed. 43:1457-1467.

Loucks, O. L. 1985. Looking for surprise in managing stressed ecosystems. Bio Sciences 35:428-432.

Murphy, J., and J. P. Riley. 1962. A modified single solution method for the determination of phosphate in natural waters. Anal. Chem. Acta. 27:31-36.

Nichols, S. A. 1974. Mechanical and habitat manipulation for aquatic plant management. A review of techniques. Tech. Bull. No. 77 Dept. Nat. Resour., Madison, Wisconsin, 34 pp.

Peterson, S. A., W. L. Smith, and K. W. Malveg. 1974. Full-scale harvest of aquatic plants: nutrient removal from a eutrophic lake. J. Water Pollut. Control Fed. 46:697-707.

Rodhe, W., G. E. Likens, and C. Serruya (ed.). 1979. Lake metabolism and management. Arch. Hydrobiol. Beih., 13.

Shapiro, J. 1979. The need for more biology in lake restoration. *In* Lake Restoration. EPA 440/5-79-001. U.S. Government Printing Office, Washington, D.C.

Westlake, D. F. 1968. The biology of aquatic weeds in relation to their management. Proc. 9th Br. Weed Control Conf. p. 372-379.

Yount, J. L., and R. A. Crossman, Jr. 1970. Eutrophication control by plant harvesting. J. Water Pollut. Control Fed. 42:173-183.

DUCKWEED CULTURE FOR REDUCTION OF AMMONIA, PHOSPHORUS AND SUSPENDED SOLIDS FROM ALGAL-RICH WATER

S. M. Koles, R. J. Petrell, and L. O. Bagnall
Agricultural Engineering Department
University of Florida, IFAS
Gainesville, Florida 32611

ABSTRACT

Lemna gibba and Spirodela punctata were cultured in outdoor ponds between October 1984, and July 1985, on algae-rich wastewater. The maximum productivity was 280 g m^{-2} d^{-1} (fresh wt), with an average productivity of 87 $\pm$ 0.054 g m^{-2} d^{-1}. Total P, TSS, and NH_4^+ concentrations at pH 7 to 7.5 decreased exponentially with time, while NH_4^+ concentrations at pH 7.5 to 8.0 decreased linearly with time.

Keywords: Lemna, Spirodela, biomass, production.

INTRODUCTION

The use of aquatic plants for wastewater treatment has received increased attention in recent years. Because of high N and P tissue concentrations and rapid growth rates, large quantities of nutrients can be removed from wastewater by the plants.

Duckweed (family Lemnaceae) grows rapidly and has high nutrient uptake rates. In addition, duckweed is cold tolerant and less sensitive than other aquatic plants to high nutrient stress, droughts, pests and diseases (Dinges, 1982). Duckweed waste treatment systems have been examined for dairy waste lagoons (Culley et al., 1981); raw domestic wastewater (Oron et al., 1984); secondary effluent (Harvey and Fox, 1973; Sutton and Ornes, 1975, 1977); waste stabilization ponds (Wolverton, 1979) and fish culture systems (Rakocy and Allison, 1984). Nutrient removal efficiencies varied widely but were higher than for control channels having no duckweed cover.

A duckweed culture system was evaluated for removal of ammonia (NH_4^+) and phosphorus (P), reduction of total suspended solids (TSS) and biomass production in algae-rich wastewater. This culture system was unique in that the wastewater to be

ISBN 0-941463-00-1

treated consisted of effluent from an algae culture unit and was therefore at high pH and contained high NH_4^+ and P concentrations. The specific objectives were: 1) to determine NH_4^+, P and TSS removal rates, and 2) to determine the compatibility of wastewater treatment and biomass production.

MATERIALS AND METHODS

Local strains of *Lemna gibba* and *Spirodela punctata* were cultured in earthen ponds at the University of Florida Swine Research Unit between October 1984, and July 1985. The ponds were 4.9 m by 24.4 m and ranged during the experiments from 0.3 to 0.9 m in depth. The ponds were divided into sections with floating PVC pipes to maintain even density distributions and to prevent wind disruption and loss of duckweed through water over flow standpipes.

Wastewater was supplied to the ponds from an experimental algae production unit where *Chlorella* was cultured on anaerobically digested swine waste (Koopman et al., 1987, this volume). At irregular intervals, subject to the completion of the *Chlorella* experiments, effluent from the algae ponds was introduced into the duckweed ponds. Because of the irregularity of the nutrient loadings to the duckweed ponds, additional nutrients were obtained from an anaerobic lagoon containing a culture of *Thiopedia rosea*, a purple photosynthetic bacterium. The *Thiopedia* culture lagoon received anaerobically digested swine waste as well as direct loadings from the swine culture operation. Algae culture effluent entered the ponds at pHs exceeding 9 and and NH_4^+ concentrations exceeding 100 mg L^{-1}. Loading rates of algae culture effluent to the ponds were on the average 1:3 to 1:4. After dilution of the influent with the pond water and well water during periods of drought, NH_4^+ concentrations were generally less than 40 mg L^{-1}. The residence times of the wastewater in the ponds, depending on its strength, were from 2 to 4 weeks.

Water samples were collected after nutrient additions and at weekly intervals. Samples were stored at 2°C until analysis for total P, NH_4^+, total Kjeldahl N (TKN), TSS, total solids, and pH. Water analysis was according to standard analytic methods (APHA, 1975).

Duckweed was harvested biweekly or restocked periodically to maintain a fresh density of 1.25 kg m^{-2}. Standing crop densities were estimated by weighing drained duckweed removed from 1 m^2 area from each of three to five sections of the pond. The sectional densities were averaged to determine the total pond density. Excess duckweed was removed at each harvest to return the ponds to approximately 1.25 kg m^{-2} fresh weight. This density was found to give maximum production for biweekly harvests in prior experiments while maintaining a sufficient cover to prevent algae infestations.

Relative growth rates were computed according to Porath et al. (1979) and Rejmankova (1975):

$$RGR = \ln (Den2/Den1)/N$$

where RGR = the relative growth rate, d^{-1}
Den1 = the estimated pond density after the previous harvest, kg m^{-2}
Den2 = the standing crop density, kg m^{-2}
N = number of days between harvests

Den1 was estimated from

$$Den1 = [(Den2b*Area) - Wharvest]/Area$$

where Den1 = final density from the previous harvest, kg m^{-2}
Den2b = standing crop density from the previous harvest, kg m^{-2}
Area = pond surface area, m^2
Wharvest = kg of duckweed harvested

Productivity was computed from (DeBusk et al., 1981):

$$Prod = Den1 * RGR$$

where Prod = productivity, kg m^{-2} d^{-1} fresh wt

RESULTS AND DISCUSSION

Biomass Production

Average relative growth rates for the ponds were 0.089 ± 0.055 d^{-1} fresh wt while average productivities were 0.087 ± 0.054 kg m^{-2} d^{-1} fresh wt. The maximum productivity obtained for the system was 0.280 kg m^{-2} d^{-1} fresh wt but this high production level could not be maintained. Decreases in the RGR were noted within 3 to 4 d after additions of algae or anaerobic lagoon water, but the duckweed recovered to previous growth rates 7 to 10 d after the water additions. Decreases in the RGR were also noted when NH_4^+ concentrations dropped below 6 mg L^{-1}. These decreases in the growth rate continued until nutrients were added to the ponds. Large die-offs of duckweed were attributed to 1) increases in the pond NH_4^+ concentrations to above 50 mg L^{-1}, especially at pHs greater than 8; 2) extended periods of subfreezing weather; 3) addition of NH_3 gas to the pond water to increase NH_4^+ concentrations; 4) contamination from overflow of a facultative lagoon; and 5) low NH_4^+ concentrations (below 3.5 mg L^{-1}) at high standing crop densities (1.84 kg m^{-2}).

Bitcover and Sieling (1951) experienced poor growth of S. polyrhiza at 46 mg NH_4-N L^{-1} for pHs between 5 and 8 and found 92 mg NH_4-N L^{-1} was toxic to the duckweed. Reduced growth was noted for L. minor for concentrations of 1 mg NO_3-N L^{-1} (White, 1936) but minimum N concentrations for sustained growth of duckweed have not been extensively researched. The duckweed culture at the

Swine Unit was adapted to high nutrient water and therefore became N limited at higher concentrations than expected. Cold temperature tolerances vary with duckweed species. During the experiments, the lowest temperatures were below 0°C and occurred at night. Cold weather lasted for two weeks and during it one pond remained frozen for three days; however, most of the L. gibba in the pond survived. S. polyrhiza ceases to grow at temperatures below 7°C (Jacobs, 1947) while L. minor shows some growth to temperatures of 1°C (Harvey and Fox, 1973).

Nutrient Removal

Since nutrient concentrations in the ponds did not reach the same level with each nutrient water addition, the data were compiled into composite graphs by time shifting data points. Regression equations for reductions in nutrient concentrations are summarized in Table 1. Ammonia concentrations decreased exponentially with time for the pH range of 7 to 7.5 for both Lemna and Spirodela. For the Lemna culture at pH 7.5 to 8.0, NH_4^+ concentrations decreased linearly with time. At pH 7.5 to 8.0 NH_3 volatilization contributes to N losses and may be responsible for the different curve. P concentrations and TSS concentrations also decreased exponentially. P removal from the ponds was observed to cease whenever NH_4^+ concentrations fell below 3.5 mg L^{-1}.

EPA discharge limits for tertiary wastewater treatment require NH_4^+ concentrations to be less than 5 mg L^{-1} and P concentrations to be below 1 mg L^{-1}. Total suspended solids should not exceed 10 mg L^{-1} (0.001%). Using the regression equations, 98 d are required to reduce total P from 40 mg L^{-1} to 1 mg L^{-1}, assuming no further additions of P into the system and sustained NH_4^+ concentrations. Reduction of NH_4^+ from 40 mg L^{-1} would require 40 to 46 d at pH 7 to 7.5 and 31 d at pH 7.5 to 8.0. Reduction of TSS from 500 to 10 mg L^{-1} would require 26 d. Exponential declines with time were observed for NH_4^+ and TP concentrations for L. minor for domestic wastewater (Harvey and

TABLE 1. Regression equations for nutrient removal curves.

1) NH_4^+, Lemna gibba, pH 7-7.5	
$NH_4\text{-N (mg L}^{-1}) = 36.11\ e^{-0.0523}\ t$	$r^2 = 0.962$
where t = time in days	
2) NH_4^+, Spirodela punctata, pH 7-7.5	
$NH_4\text{-N (mg L}^{-1}) = 22.07\ e^{-0.0444}\ t$	$r^2 = 0.993$
3) NH_4^+, Lemna gibba, pH 7.5-8	
$NH_4\text{-N (mg L}^{-1}) = 46.96 - 1.1384\ t$	$r^2 = 0.977$
4) Phosphorus	
$P\ (\text{mg L}^{-1}) = 40.81\ e^{-0.0376}\ t$	$r^2 = 0.953$
5) Suspended solids	
$TSS\ (\%) = 0.0491\ e^{-0.1512}\ t$	$r^2 = 0.941$

Fox, 1973) and for TP using S. polyrhiza (Sutton and Ornes, 1977). TSS concentrations vs. time closely followed exponential declines for various species of duckweed grown on dairy waste lagoons (Culley et al., 1973). Decreases in NH_4^+ concentrations in the effluents (0.0444 to 0.0523 d^{-1}) were lower than those achieved by Harvey and Fox (1973) (0.155 to 0.214 d^{-1}). Total P concentrations also decreased more slowly for these duckweed cultures (0.0376 d^{-1}) than decreases reported by Harvey and Fox (1973) (0.077 to 0.137 d^{-1}) but were similar to decreases achieved by Sutton and Ornes (1977) (0.0428 d^{-1}). Total suspended solids decreased faster in the effluents (0.151 d^{-1}) than for dairy waste lagoons (0.0484 d^{-1}) (Culley et al., 1978) but decreased similarly to reductions reported by Wolverton (1979) (0.167 d^{-1}). Harvey and Fox (1973) performed their treatment studies in indoor aquaria at optimum temperature and light levels for the duckweed, which may account for the higher decreases in nutrient concentrations.

CONCLUSIONS

Duckweed can be used to effectively treat high pH, NH_4^+, and TSS wastewater provided 1) the NH_4^+ concentration of the duckweed pond does not exceed 50 mg L^{-1} after dilution of the influent; 2) the pH of the duckweed pond remains below 8 through dilution or buffering; and 3) water temperatures do not remain below freezing for more than a few days. Nutrient removal rates are slow, and therefore long retention times are necessary to reduce nutrient concentrations to EPA discharge limits for tertiary treatment. P reduction to 1 mg L^{-1} may require supplemental addition of N. Biomass production was not optimal since growth rates decrease with falling NH_4^+; however, some biomass will be produced as a byproduct of the treatment process.

REFERENCES

American Public Health Association (APHA). 1975. Standard methods for the examination of water and wastewater. APHA, New York.

Bitcover, E. H., and D. H. Sieling. 1951. Effect of various factors on the utilization of nitrogen and iron by Spirodela polyrhiza (L.) Schleid. Plant Physiol. 26:290-303.

Culley, D. D., Jr., J. H. Gholson, T. S. Chisholm, L. C. Standifer, and E. A. Epps. 1978. Water quality renovation of animal waste lagoons utilizing aquatic plants. LSU Ag. Exp. Station, Baton Rouge, LA.

Culley, D. D., Jr., E. Rejmankova, J. Kvet, and J. B. Frye. 1981. Production, chemical quality, and use of duckweeds (Lemnaceae) in aquaculture, waste management, and animal feeds. J. World Mariculture Soc. 12:27-49.

DeBusk, T. A., J. H. Ryther, M. D. Hanisak, and L. D. Williams. 1981. Effects of seasonality and plant density on the productivity of some fresh water macrophytes. Aquat. Bot. 10:133-142.

Dinges, R. 1982. Natural systems for water pollution control. Van Nostrand Reinhold, New York.

Fitzgerald, G. P. 1969. Some factors in the competition or antagonism among bacteria, algae, and aquatic weeds. J. of Phycology 5:351-359.

Harvey, R. M., and J. L. Fox. 1973. Nutrient removal using *Lemna minor*. J. Water Pollut. Control Fed. 45:1928.

Jacobs, D. L. 1947. An ecological life-history of *Spirodela polyrhiza* (greater duckweed) with emphasis on the turion phase. Ecological Monograph 17:437-469.

Koopman, B., E. P. Lincoln, H. Kang, and S.-I. Lee. 1987. Biological flocculation of microalgae grown on anaerobic digester effluent. *In* K. R. Reddy and W. H. Smith (ed.) Aquatic Plants for Water Treatment and Resource Recovery. Magnolia Publishing Inc., Orlando, FL.

McClay. 1976. The distribution of duckweed *Lemna perpusilla* in a small southern California lake: An experimental approach. Ecology 55:262-276.

Oron, G., L. R. Wildschut, and D. Porath. 1984. Wastewater recycling by duckweed for protein production and effluent renovation. Water Sci. Tech. 17:803-817.

Porath, D., B. Hepher, and A. Koton. 1979. Duckweed as an aquatic crop: Evaluation of clones for aquaculture. Aquat. Bot. 7:273-278.

Rakocy, J. E., and R. Allison. 1981. Evaluation of a closed recirculating system for the culture of tilapia and aquatic macrophytes. Bio-Eng. Symp. Fish Cult. 1:296-307.

Rejmankova, E. 1975. Comparison of *Lemna gibba* and *Lemna minor* from the production ecological viewpoint. Aquat. Bot. 1:423-427.

Sutton, D. L., and W. H. Ornes. 1975. Phosphorus removal from static sewage effluent using duckweed. J. Environ. Qual. 4:367-370.

Sutton, D. L., and W. H. Ornes. 1977. Growth of *Spirodela polyrhiza* in static sewage effluent. Aquat. Bot. 3:231-237.

White, H. L. 1936. The interaction of factors in the growth of *Lemna*. VIII. The effect of nitrogen on growth and multiplication. Annals Bot. 50:403-417.

Wolverton, B. C. 1979. Engineering design data for small vascular aquatic plant wastewater treatment systems. p. 179-192. *In* EPA Aquaculture Systems for Wastewater Treatment - Seminar Proc. and Engineering Assessment. EPA 430/9-80-006, Washington, D.C.

MODEL WATER HYACINTH AND PENNYWORT SYSTEMS FOR THE SECONDARY TREATMENT OF DOMESTIC WASTEWATER

K. S. Clough and T. A. DeBusk
Reedy Creek Utilities, Co., Inc.
P. O. Box 40
Lake Buena Vista, Florida 32830

K. R. Reddy
Central Florida Research and Education Center
University of Florida, IFAS
Sanford, Florida 32771

ABSTRACT

Water hyacinth (Eichhornia crassipes) and pennywort (Hydrocotyle umbellata) were cultured in central Florida in 1000 L batch-fed tanks which received primary sewage effluent at a 3.5 d detention period. Biomass production and water quality were measured from March 1985 through March 1986 in monocultures and in a polyculture of the two species. Maximum warm-season (March-November) biomass yields and nitrogen (N) and phosphorus (P) removal were observed in tanks containing water hyacinth, whereas maximum cool-season (December-February) plant growth and nutrient removal occurred in tanks containing pennywort. Plant uptake generally accounted for 20% of the N and 60% of the P removed from the wastewater. Typical BOD_5 reductions in the primary wastewater effluent varied from 70 to 90% during the study, with highest BOD_5 removal observed in tanks containing pennywort. The pennywort-water hyacinth polyculture was the most effective of the systems tested in removing BOD_5 and nutrients from wastewater during both warm and cool seasons.

Keywords: Aquatic macrophytes, nutrient removal, BOD_5 removal, productivity.

INTRODUCTION

Interest in the use of aquatic plants for wastewater treatment has prompted studies on the productivity and nutrient-uptake potential of a number of floating macrophytes (Boyd, 1969; Reddy and DeBusk, 1985). Most such studies have focused on the water hyacinth (Eichhornia crassipes), a productive

ISBN 0-941463-00-1

macrophyte which has been utilized extensively for providing secondary and advanced treatment of domestic wastewaters. Although water hyacinth yields are high, averaging 25 g dry wt m^{-2} d^{-1} in central Florida (DeBusk et al., 1981), growth of this plant in subtropical and temperate regions is poor during the winter months. A native species found throughout the southeast U.S. which shows promise as an alternative winter crop for floating macrophyte-based wastewater-treatment systems is pennywort (*Hydrocotyle umbellata*). Reddy and DeBusk (1984) reported that the growth rate of pennywort exceeds that of water hyacinth during January and February in central Florida. However, the ability of pennywort to treat wastewaters has not been evaluated. The present study examines seasonal rates of biomass production in water hyacinth and pennywort culture systems, and the capability of these systems to reduce BOD_5 and nutrient concentrations of primary domestic wastewater effluent.

METHODS

This study was conducted from March 1985 through March 1986 at the WALT DISNEY WORLD Resort Complex Community Waste Research Facility, Lake Buena Vista, Florida. Water hyacinth and pennywort were cultured in 1000 L batch-fed tanks (1.7 m^2 surface area, 0.5 m depth) which received primary sewage effluent at a 3.5 d retention period. The following treatments were established in duplicate tanks: 1) a water hyacinth monoculture (WH); 2) a pennywort monoculture (PW); 3) a WH + PW polyculture; and 4) tanks in which no macrophytes were stocked (NM). Water hyacinth and pennywort were stocked at an initial standing crop of 10 kg wet wt m^{-2}, and were weighed and harvested back to this density semimonthly. Plant samples were collected monthly from each tank and analyzed for N and P composition (Jackson, 1958). Influent and effluent water samples were collected from tanks weekly, and analyzed for BOD_5, NO_3 + NO_2-N (APHA, 1980), NH_4-N, TKN and TP (US EPA, 1979).

RESULTS AND DISCUSSION

The major goal of the present study was to determine the effect of season on biomass production and wastewater treatment potential of water hyacinth and pennywort in central Florida. Productivity and water quality data were therefore grouped into cool or winter (December-February), and warm or summer (March-November), seasons. Minimum air temperatures during the "cool season" months averaged 11°C or less.

The nitrogen (TKN) concentration of the primary domestic effluent used for this study varied seasonally, from 30.4 mg L^{-1} during the warm season to 40.1 mg L^{-1} during the cool months. Total P concentrations were relatively constant during the year, averaging 7.2 mg L^{-1}. Other (annual mean) characteristics of the influent wastewater were as follows (in mg L^{-1}): BOD_5, 191; NH_4, 18.1; NO_3, 0.7; dissolved oxygen, 0.7; and pH, 6.4.

Biomass production of water hyacinth was higher than that of pennywort during the warm season (Table 1). Maximum short-term yields of 30.1 and 24.3 g dry wt m^{-2} d^{-1} were observed in the water hyacinth and polyculture systems during the spring. In contrast, growth peaks for pennywort (13.6 g dry wt m^{-2} d^{-1}) occurred both in June and in January. Plant productivity in our tanks was lower than the maximum rate reported for cultivated stands of these species in central Florida [e.g., 64.4 and 29.7 g dry wt m^{-2} d-1 for water hyacinth and pennywort, respectively (Reddy and DeBusk, 1984; Ryther, 1979)]. The low yields in the present study were probably due to the inhibitory effect of high BOD_5 in the influent wastewater on plant growth.

Pennywort was more productive than water hyacinth during the cool season (Table 1). Pennywort also exhibited little or no damage following two freeze events, during which aerial water hyacinth tissues were seriously damaged. Plant productivity in the polyculture was lower during the cool than in the warm season, with water hyacinth accounting for most of the plant growth during the warm season, and pennywort contributing to the bulk of the polyculture yields during the cool season (Table 1).

TABLE 1. Mean productivity and elemental composition of water hyacinth and pennywort cultured in primary domestic wastewater during warm and cool seasons.

	Productivity	Tissue Concentration	
		N	P
	g dry wt m^{-2} d^{-1}	-------g kg^{-1}-------	
	Warm Season: March-November		
WH	16.5	36.9	9.6
PW	7.1	41.7	11.4
WH + PW	14.5	40.0	9.8
	Cool Season: December-February		
WH	6.3	45.6	11.8
PW	6.9	47.9	13.1
WH + PW	5.4	45.5	12.3
	Annual Mean		
WH	14.2	38.9	10.1
PW	6.9	43.1	11.9
WH + PW	11.5	41.3	10.4

WH = water hyacinth monoculture; PW = pennywort monoculture; WH + PW = water hyacinth and pennywort polyculture.

BOD_5 removal exceeded 75% in all treatments during the warm season, with highest removal rates occurring in the tanks containing pennywort (Table 2). Although BOD_5 removal efficiency declined during the cool season, the PW and WH + PW treatments provided better than 80% removal of organic matter in the winter months. Mass BOD_5 removal in the pennywort treatment during the year averaged 253 kg ha^{-1} d^{-1}, a relatively high removal rate in comparison to the removal rates (50-150 kg ha^{-1} d^{-1}) typically obtained in water hyacinth systems (Stowell et al., 1981).

Tissue N and P concentrations of both water hyacinth and pennywort were high during this study, primarily due to the high nutrient concentrations of the primary wastewater culture medium. Tissue nutrient concentrations of both species were highest during the winter. Previous studies have shown that tissue N and P levels of the water hyacinth are reduced or "diluted" during the summer due to high warm season productivity, as well as morphological (increased stem length) and proximate composition (increased structural carbohydrate concentrations) changes (Tucker and DeBusk, 1981).

TABLE 2. Mean BOD_5 removal from primary domestic wastewater in macrophyte systems during warm and cool seasons.

	BOD_5 reduction (%)	
	Mean	Range
	Warm Season: March-November	
WH	81.2	64.9 - 94.1
PW	88.9	83.3 - 98.0
WH + PW	89.0	76.5 - 96.7
NM	77.5	70.7 - 83.0
	Cool Season: December-February	
WH	73.0	66.7 - 78.7
PW	85.4	83.5 - 86.7
WH + PW	81.9	72.7 - 87.0
NM	59.0	54.3 - 63.9
	Annual Mean	
WH	79.1	64.9 - 94.1
PW	88.0	83.3 - 98.0
WH + PW	87.2	72.7 - 96.7
NM	71.5	54.3 - 83.0

Average BOD_5: warm season, 192 mg L^{-1}; cool season, 189 mg L^{-1}; annual mean, 190 mg L^{-1}.

WH = water hyacinth monoculture; PW = pennywort monoculture; WH + PW = water hyacinth and pennywort polyculture; NM = no macrophytes.

Uptake of nutrients by water hyacinth and pennywort, calculated as dry matter yield multiplied by tissue N or P concentration, varied similarly with plant productivity. Water hyacinth plants removed an average of 617 mg N and 159 mg P m^{-2} d^{-1} during the summer, but only 288 mg N and 75 mg P m^{-2} d^{-1} during the winter. In contrast, maximum nutrient uptake rates by pennywort occurred in the winter. Respective N and P uptake rates by this species averaged 300 mg N and 79 mg P m^{-2} d^{-1} during the warm season, and 336 mg N and 97 mg P m^{-2} d^{-1} during the cool season.

Total percent reductions in wastewater N and P, which includes plant uptake plus other system nutrient sinks, are presented in Table 3. Although the maximum percent reduction in nutrient concentrations averaged only 33%, these data do not imply that higher removal efficiencies cannot be obtained in macrophyte-based treatment systems. Wastewater retention time and tank sizes in the present study were selected to provide efficient organic matter removal (secondary treatment) from the primary effluent, at an area requirement of 2.4 ha per 3,800 m^3 d^{-1}. For nutrient removal, or advanced wastewater treatment, the macrophyte system area requirement is about three to five times greater.

TABLE 3. Warm and cool season N and P removal by macrophyte systems receiving primary domestic wastewater.

	N			P		
	Total⁺	Plant⁺⁺	Other⁺⁺⁺	Total	Plant	Other
	% removal					
	Warm Season: March-November					
WH	30	11	19	27	12	15
PW	25	6	19	15	6	9
WH + PW	30	5	25	26	6	20
NM	27	--	--	10	--	--
	Cool Season: December-February					
WH	21	4	17	8	6	2
PW	33	5	28	10	8	2
WH + PW	34	2	32	13	3	10
NM	19	--	--	-2	--	--
	Annual Mean					
WH	27	9	18	23	11	12
PW	27	5	22	14	6	8
WH + PW	31	4	27	23	5	18
NM	24	--	--	6	--	--

⁺% reduction in primary wastewater after 3-5 d detention.
⁺⁺Calculated from productivity and tissue elemental composition.
⁺⁺⁺Nutrient sinks other than plant uptake.

Maximum warm season N and P removal was obtained in tanks containing water hyacinth (WH and WH + PW treatments). The pennywort monoculture was less effective for nutrient removal during this period. Plant uptake accounted for more than 50% of the warm season nutrient removal observed in the WH tanks. In the pennywort tanks, plant uptake accounted for 66% of the P removal but only 32% of the N removal. Warm season N removal in tanks containing no plants was almost as great as that in tanks containing water hyacinth, although P removal in the former treatment was poor.

During the cool season, the treatments containing pennywort (PW and WH + PW) were more effective than the WH and NM treatments in removing N and P. With the exception of P in the WH and PW treatments, plant uptake was not the primary nutrient sink during the winter. Nitrogen removal in the NM treatment was comparable to that in the WH treatment, although no P removal occurred in the tanks without macrophytes during the cool season.

A number of N-removal mechanisms occur in macrophyte ponds which receive domestic wastewater. Nitrification-denitrification reactions often occur in systems containing floating macrophytes such as water hyacinth and pennywort. Denitrification rates in excess of 1000 mg m^{-2} d^{-1} have been reported, and this process is commonly the dominant N sink in macrophyte-based wastewater treatment systems (Stowell et al., 1981). In contrast, NH_3 volatilization was probably responsible for the bulk of the N removal from the wastewater in the NM treatment. Volatilization is stimulated at high pH, which occurs as a result of rapid photosynthesis by microalgae in the water column (Reddy, 1983). Indeed, short term measurements conducted with clear plastic chambers fitted with acid traps revealed NH_3 volatilization rates of 1.43 mg N m^{-2} h^{-1} in the NM treatment, but only 0.03 mg N m^{-2} h^{-1} in tanks containing water hyacinth. Microalgal systems can thus remove N at rates comparable to those obtained in floating macrophyte systems, although removal rates of BOD_5, P, and suspended solids (data not shown) in the former are relatively poor.

CONCLUSIONS

A major constraint to the use of water hyacinth ponds for treating wastewaters in subtropical and temperate climates has been the poor performance of these systems during the winter. Successful winter operation of water hyacinth treatment systems often necessitates a doubling of pond area in order to obtain contaminant removal rates comparable to those achieved in the summer months. The present study demonstrates the utility of culturing pennywort, a plant which is more cold tolerant than water hyacinth, in floating macrophyte treatment systems. Pennywort, grown either in a monoculture or in a polyculture with water hyacinth, removes larger amounts of wastewater N and P than water hyacinth monocultures during the winter in central Florida. Systems containing pennywort also provide greater BOD_5 removal efficiency than water hyacinth monocultures during both warm and cool seasons.

ACKNOWLEDGMENTS

This paper reports results from a project that contributes to a cooperative program between the Institute of Food and Agricultural Sciences (IFAS) entitled "Methane from Biomass and Waste." Florida Agricultural Experiment Stations Journal Series No. 7709.

REFERENCES

American Public Health Association. 1980. Standard methods for the examination of water and wastewater. 15th ed. American Public Health Association. Byrd Prepress, Springfield, VA.

Boyd, C. E. 1969. Vascular aquatic plants for mineral nutrient removal from polluted waters. Econ. Bot. 23:95-103.

DeBusk, T. A., M. D. Hanisak, L. D. Williams, and J. H. Ryther. 1981. Effects of seasonality and plant density on the productivity of some freshwater macrophytes. Aquat. Bot. 10:133-143.

Jackson, M. L. 1958. Soil Chemical Analysis, p. 498. Prentice-Hall, London.

Reddy, K. R. 1983. Fate of nitrogen and phosphorus in a waste-water retention reservoir containing aquatic macrophytes. J. Environ. Qual. 12:137-141.

Reddy, K. R. and W. F. DeBusk. 1984. Growth characteristics of aquatic macrophytes cultured in nutrient enriched water: I. Water hyacinth, water lettuce, and pennywort. Econ. Bot. 38:229-239.

Reddy, K. R. and W. F. DeBusk. 1985. Nutrient removal potential of selected aquatic macrophytes. J. Environ. Qual. 14:459-462.

Ryther, J. H. 1979. Cultivation of macroscopic marine algae and freshwater aquatic weeds. Rept. to U.S. Dept. of Energy. No. E4-76-5-02-2948. 74 pp.

Stowell, R., R. Ludwig, J. Colt, and G. Tchobanoglous. 1981. Concepts in aquatic treatment system design. p. 919-940. Proc. Am. Soc. Civ. Eng. Vol. 107, Bo. EE5, October 1981.

Tucker, C. S. and T. A. DeBusk. 1981. Seasonal growth of *Eichhornia crassipes* (Mart.) Solms: Relationship to protein, fiber and available carbohydrate content. Aquat. Bot. 11:137-141.

U. S. Environmental Protection Agency. 1979. Methods for chemical analysis of water and wastes. U. S. Environmental Protection Agency, Cincinnati, OH.

AQUATIC PLANT MANAGEMENT IN ORANGE COUNTY, FLORIDA

E. R. Pershe, K. V. Setaram, and R. A. Baird
Orange County Environmental Protection Department
2002 E. Michigan Street
Orlando, Florida 32806

ABSTRACT

Orange County, Florida has over 1,000 ponds and lakes which are susceptible to aquatic plant and weed infestations. Over the past 13 years, the County has employed various methods of generating revenues for weed control programs. Water hyacinths and hydrilla are the primary exotics which are controlled. Control methodologies include use of contact and systemic herbicides, grass carp and mechanical harvesting. Costs for weed control range from \$85 to \$2,000 per ha.

Keywords: Hyacinths, hydrilla, grass carp, costs, nutrients, harvesting.

INTRODUCTION

In the semitropical climate of Florida, lakes and other bodies of water offer a welcome habitat for various types of grasses and aquatic plants. Most aquatic plants in moderate amounts perform a highly useful function by removing soluble and suspended pollutional matter to produce water of high quality. In the urban sectors of Orange County, stormwater runoff flushes pollutants from streets and excess nutrients from fertilized lawns to receiving waters. Many of the lakes are prized for recreation and for their beauty.

Orange County has about 1,000 lakes within an area of some 2,600 km^2, ranging in size from 0.4 to 12,500 ha (Florida Board of Conservation, 1969). In the early 1970's, many of the lakes became infested with aquatic plants and weeds. Weed control programs became necessary in order to restore and maintain the lake values. These programs have evolved from modest, experimental beginnings to a magnitude of effort requiring an annual expenditure of about \$500,000.

This paper discusses the practical aquatic weed control programs used in Orange County and presents useful information for those planning or involved with such programs.

Aquatic Plants for Water Treatment
and Resource Recovery
K.R. Reddy and W.H. Smith (Eds.)

ISBN 0-941463-00-1

DEVELOPMENT OF CONTROL PROGRAMS

Prior to 1970, problems with aquatic weeds in the County's lakes and waterways were minimal and of no great concern. However, with the opening of Disney World in 1971, the County began to experience rapid development in both the commercial and residential sectors (East Central Florida Regional Planning Council, 1986). Much of the initial growth took place around lakes which soon became enriched with pollutional matter and nutrients and, subsequently, infested with massive amounts of aquatic plants.

The need for control programs to rid the waterways of the pest plants, became clear; however, funding for such programs was a major obstacle to their implementation. Recognizing the seriousness of the problem and the need for prompt action, state and federal agencies provided the financial impetus for developing and implementing control programs, at least for those lakes used by the general public. This was done by grants and subsidies.

The initial program proved to be successful and became the forerunner of present day programs. Today, Orange County's aquatic plant and weed control program for public lakes is jointly funded by the U.S. Army Corps of Engineers. The Corps pays 70% of the cost, and Orange County pays the balance of the cost and administers the program.

As time passed, homeowners in other developments around private or privately controlled lakes wanted weed control programs for their lakes. To fund these programs, the County established special municipal service taxing units (MSTU) which require approval by vote or petition of the residents of MSTU areas. Taxes collected by an MSTU can be utilized only for the purpose specifically designated by the MSTU. At the present time there are 19 active MSTU's in Orange County which fund weed control programs.

In unusual situations where a lake is quite large or control is needed for a group or chain of lakes, the State of Florida establishes navigation districts to generate revenues for control programs. At the present time, Orange County manages navigation control districts for Lake Conway and The Windemere chain of lakes. These systems have a total water area of approximately 2,500 ha (Florida Board of Conservation, 1969).

In addition to the County's weed control programs, some municipalities within the County, such as Orlando, Winter Park and Maitland, also manage weed control programs or have contracted for such services.

Virtually all of the County's weed control programs are managed by the Orange County Environmental Protection Department (OCEPD). The OCEPD maintains a staff of aquatic biologists and weed control specialists to carry out various control program functions. Supporting facilities and equipment include laboratories, harvesting and chemical application equipment, several types of boats, and transportation vehicles.

WEED CONTROL METHODOLOGIES

Although Orange County's weed control programs have been in existence for several years and its personnel have acquired much practical experience, cut-and-dried procedures are seldom employed. This is because each lake's weed control problem is looked upon as having specific needs to achieve long term goals.

In some cases, an integrated approach utilizing a combination of control techniques is required; in others, a single method or technique may be the best to use. The selection of specific control measures is always carefully considered in light of long term objectives. These control methods are also discussed with lakeside property owners to obtain their input and support before the final control plan is adopted and implemented. In some cases, property owners select a method of control they feel is more suitable for their lake, contrary to the advice of OCEPD personnel. This selection may be motivated by cost or by a desire to use a type of control that seems to be more appropriate for the lake. Quite often chemical herbicides are avoided because of bad publicity about chemical usage that is entirely unrelated to a weed control program.

In the majority of cases, the nuisance plants are either water hyacinths, *Eichhornia crassipes*, or hydrilla, *Hydrilla verticillata*. Weed control programs are primarily directed to control these pests although other types of plants are usually also involved. Because hyacinths have received favorable attention regarding their ability to remove pollutants from wastewater (Reddy, 1984), some lakeside residents often oppose their control and removal because they feel that hyacinths will purify their lake of pollution and not cause any problems. These people do not understand that unless a portion of the hyacinths is removed at frequent intervals, death and decay of the plants will release nutrients back to the water thereby causing or exacerbating a nuisance problem (Joyce, 1985).

The methods of aquatic plant and weed control that have been successfully used in Orange County include the uses of: 1) chemical herbicides, 2) grass carp, and 3) mechanical harvesters.

The choice of a particular method or combination of methods depends upon results from a preliminary survey of lake conditions and how the choice fits with long term lake management goals. If weeds are dispersed in a few areas around a lake, chemical usage or mechanical harvesting may be employed. If the plant growths are massive and spread more or less uniformly throughout the entire lake, either grass carp or herbicides, or a combination of the two, may be employed.

In the vast majority of cases, herbicide application is both the quickest and most efficient method of control. However, there is little doubt that the most cost effective method for long term control of hydrilla is through the use of grass carp. Small lakes and ponds that receive high inputs of nutrients and would require heavy doses of chemicals to control vegetation are the best candidates for this method of control.

Although biological methods of control other than fish, e.g., flea bettles, stem borer moths, and thrips, have been employed extensively and quite effectively throughout Florida over the last 15 yr, these methods are not being used by the OCEPD at this time.

FIELD PROCEDURES

Prior to specifying any control methodology for aquatic weed control in a lake, a survey of the water body is conducted to locate the areas where control is actually needed. Surface plants such as hyacinths are easily located. Submersed plants may also be located if the water is clear and the depth is not too great. When clarity is poor or the depth is great, a weed hook is dragged from a boat to obtain samples of the plants and determine the extent of their growth.

When large lakes or bodies of water are surveyed, scuba divers riding water sleds are towed over the lake to locate plant growths. When a plant infested area is found, the boat is stopped and the divers inspect the area more thoroughly. All information about plant growths is plotted on a map of the lake. The lake's aquatic weed problems are then evaluated, lake management goals are set, and the treatments deemed best suited to correct the weed problem are selected.

Herbicide Application

When chemical treatment is selected as the control method, the areas requiring control are computed from the survey map for the lake and the amount of herbicide that must be applied is calculated. An application for a permit to use the herbicide is then submitted to the Florida Department of Natural Resources. When the permit is issued, the necessary quantity of herbicide solution is prepared in strict conformance to the manufacturer's instructions and loaded onto an airboat for dispensing.

For relatively small areas, the application is carried out by handspraying the herbicide solution over the water surface. For large areas, strings of marker buoys are set to serve as guides for treatment application runs. Herbicide application in such cases is normally accomplished by a 2 m long distribution manifold with three discharge nozzles fastened to the bow of the boat. Runs are then made back and forth over the area until covered.

In general, both contact and systemic herbicides are used to control aquatic plants. Systemic herbicides are generally more effective than the contact type although the latter is very useful in controlling submersed vegetation.

For submersed plants, Diquat, (9,10-dihydro-8a,10a-diazoniaphenanthrene-2A), Aquathol, (dipotassium salt of endothall), and Sonar, (fluridone) (Weed Science Society of

America, 1983), are the herbicides of choice. Diquat and Aquathol are contact herbicides which kill plants quickly although the effectiveness of the application usually is only of short duration. Rodeo, (glyphosate) (Weed Science Society of America, 1983), is used primarily to control aquatic grasses and other ditchbank species. Water hyacinths normally are kept under excellent control through the use of 2,4-D Amine, (dimethylamine salt of 2,4-D) (Weed Science Society of America, 1983).

Sonar is a systemic herbicide that has proven to be particularly effective in controlling hydrilla. A single application has been found to keep hydrilla under control for a period of two years or more. Sonar prevents hydrilla from synthesizing carotenoid thereby allowing sunlight to destroy the plant's pigment active in its photosynthetic processes. Eventually the plant turns white and dies. Because Sonar exerts its maximum impact on hydrilla, other less sensitive and more desirable plants and replantings can establish themselves in the areas vacated by the destroyed hydrilla.

In some instances, a gradual release of herbicide to submersed plants is desired for persistent application. This can be accomplished by applying the herbicide in pellet form using a simple hopper and spreader device. The pellets are dropped among the plants where they dissolve slowly over a long time period. The persistence of the release makes the herbicide more effective than if it were applied as a one-time application in solution form.

An important part of a lake weed control program is the restoration of desirable plant species after the undesirable plants have been removed or brought under control. Replanting with such aquatic plants as *Nitella* spp. will restore and maintain water quality and provide suitable habitats for fish and other forms of aquatic life.

By using herbicides that are nontoxic to humans, adhering carefully to manufacturers' instructions, and following good sanitation practices, OCEPD personnel have not encountered any harmful health effects since the inception of the weed control program. As a check on the health of personnel, all persons working with herbicides are required to have a blood analysis every two or three years.

Grass Carp

Weed eating grass carp have proved to be a highly effective means of keeping aquatic plants under control in Orange County lakes. The white amur, *Ctenopharngodon idella*, is a triploid carp that has been used for this purpose. During their life span, these fish grow to large size often weighing from 16 to 18 kg and attaining lengths up to 1 m and longer. Although carp are highly effective in controlling hydrilla, they also consume many desirable plant species as well (Sutton, 1985). If too many carp are stocked in a lake, they may cause the complete loss of all aquatic macrophytes and establish a very undesirable planktonic-alga regime resulting in perpetual blooms of blue-green algae. This occurred in Lake Holden in Orange County. When grass carp are to be used for control purposes, the State Game & Fresh Water Fish Commission is consulted to determine how many fish are necessary for control purposes (Callahan and Osborne, 1983).

Mechanical Harvesting

Mechanical harvesting of aquatic weeds is being done at only one lake in Orange County, Lake Jessamine. An Altosar Model H2500 harvesting machine is used for this purpose. It is a large piece of equipment that is difficult to launch and retrieve from lakes. Because of frequent breakdowns and long waits for replacement parts, this machine has been very costly to keep in service.

Although the removal of hydrilla and other nuisance weeds by harvesting is immediate, it is difficult to keep plant growth under control very long because the plants regrow so rapidly. Under normal conditions, hydrilla can grow up to 8 cm d^{-1} (Haller, 1978). Because fragments of plant cuttings frequently escape the harvester's weed collecting mechanism and can root and grow wherever they migrate, mechanical harvesting often serves to exacerbate a weed problem in a lake. Harvesting is best employed where instant relief of the plant infestation is of paramount importance, such as in a navigation canal, and where chemical application would be impractical (Sassic, 1982).

COSTS FOR CONTROL PROGRAMS

Accurate costs for control programs are difficult to determine because manpower, equipment depreciation, travel time, and other cost factors are not detailed for specific weed control projects. In general, herbicide application costs, which include only chemicals and labor, are estimated to range from $85 to $620 per ha of treated lake area. Mechanical harvesting is roughly estimated to cost about $2,000 per ha. This does not include equipment costs and repair costs.

Triploid grass carp provided by the State Game and Fresh Water Fish Commission vary in cost from $6 to $8 per fish depending on the size of the fish. Usually about 5 to 12 fish per ha of lake area are adequate for control purposes.

SUMMARY

The ability to control nuisance aquatic plants and weeds in lakes and waterways in Orange County enables County residents to enjoy the recreation and beauty afforded by these facilities at a reasonable cost.

Over the years, experience has shown that care and caution must be exercised when planning weed control programs. Almost all aquatic plants will serve to improve the quality of water in a lake, however, even the most desirable native species can become a nuisance if allowed to grow to such an extent as to restrict navigation and create unsightly conditions.

The policy of the OCEPD is to manage lakes and waterways under its jurisdiction using the least amount of control necessary to preserve recreational and esthetic values. Although there probably always will be some fear that the use of herbicides could cause injury to the aquatic environment, it has been demonstrated that intelligent and carefully planned usage of herbicides can safely and effectively control infestations of aquatic plants without adversely affecting water quality (Morris and Jarman, 1981; Schreiner, 1980).

REFERENCES

Callahan, J. L., and J. A. Osborne. 1983. Comparison of the grass carp and the hybrid grass carp. Aquatics 5:10-15.

East Central Florida Regional Planning Council. 1986. Council Quarterly, 2nd Quarter. 27 pp.

Florida Board of Conservation. 1969. Florida lakes: Part III Gazetteer. Div. of Water Resources, Tallahassee, FL. 145 pp.

Haller, W. T. 1978. Hydrilla: A new and rapidly spreading aquatic weed problem. Cir. S-245. Univ. of Florida, IFAS, Gainesville, FL. 13 pp.

Joyce, J. C. 1985. Benefits of maintenance control of water hyacinth. Aquatics 7:11-13.

Morris, K., and R. Jarman. 1981. Evaluation of water quality during herbicide applications to Kerr Lake, OK. J. Aquat. Plant Mgt. 19:15-18.

Reddy, K. R. 1984. Nutrient removal potential of aquatic plants. Aquatics 6:15-16.

Sassic, N. M. 1982. Harvesting: The future of aquatic plant control. Aquatics 4:14-16.

Schreiner, S. P. 1980. Effects of water hyacinth on the physiochemistry of a South Georgia Pond. J. Aquat. Plant Mgt. 18:9-12.

Sutton, D. L. 1985. Management of hydrilla with triploid grass carp. Aquatics 7:11-17.

Weed Science Society of America. 1983. Herbicide handbook--5th ed. 309 W. Clark St., Champaign, IL 61820. 515 pp.

USE OF AQUATIC BIOMASS AS A FOOD SOURCE THROUGH MUSHROOM CULTIVATION

G. S. Gujral, R. Bisaria, and P. Vasudevan
Centre for Rural Development and Appropriate Technology
Indian Institute of Technology
New Delhi 110 016, INDIA

ABSTRACT

The use of aquatic weeds like water hyacinth (Eichhornia crassipes), lotus (Nelumbo nucifera), and water chestnut (Trapa bispinosa) as an indirect source of human food through the cultivation of the edible mushroom Pleurotus sajor-caju was studied. Water hyacinth supported the best mushroom growth followed by lotus and water chestnut. Their biological efficiencies in terms of dry fruit bodies per day substrate utilized were 8.46, 7.48, and 5.61%, respectively. A preferential utilization of the polysaccharides over the lignin was observed in all the substrates used.

Keywords: Aquatic weeds, Pleurotus sajor-caju, biological efficiency, lignocellulose degradation.

INTRODUCTION

Aquatic plants are often characterized as weeds because of their prolific growth. In recent years, aquatic plant biomass has been put to a number of applications such as in animal feed, soil additives, fuel, water treatment systems and for materials like fiber, pulp and chemicals. Their use as a source of human food through the cultivation of edible mushrooms like Pleurotus sajor-caju has been investigated and presented in this paper. Since P. sajor-caju, the oyster mushroom, is easily cultivated on a host of ligno-cellulosic materials (NAS, 1981; Madan and Gujral, 1983; Bisaria, 1984), this species was tried using aquatic weeds as the substrates.

MATERIALS AND METHODS

The Pleurotus sajor-caju (Fr.) Singer culture used in the study was obtained from the Forest Research Institute, Dehradun (India). Three aquatic plants abundantly growing in the region

ISBN 0-941463-00-1

were used as substrates. These were water hyacinth (*Eichhornia crassipes*), lotus (*Nelumbo nucifera*) and water chestnut (*Trapa bispinosa*). The sun dried substrates (400 g each) were finely chopped and pasteurized in hot water (60-70°C) for about an hour and subsequently transferred to cold water. The wet substrates were mixed with 8% spawn and 1% g (pulse) powder and the spawned substrates were filled in polythene bags following the method of Pal and Thapa (1979). The use of polythene bags help not only in reducing the cost of production but also facilitates a cheap and easy method of cultivation for the rural masses. The spawned bags were kept in a well ventilated hut under a temperature range of 10-25°C and a relative humidity of 80-90%. The bags were opened after 15 d when the mycelium had covered the substrate. Within 5-7 d of opening, pin-heads of mushrooms appeared on all sides of the substrate blocks. These young mushrooms attained the normal size in 3-4 d when the first flush of mushrooms was harvested from each of the bags. The second crop appeared after an interval of 7-10 d and thereafter a third crop was harvested. The crops were harvested in definite flushes and no selective harvesting was undertaken. Substrates were lightly watered twice a day during the fruiting stage. The yields from all the substrates were compared and their biological efficiency (BE) was calculated using the relation

$$BE\% = \frac{\text{weight of dry mushrooms harvested}}{\text{weight of dry substrate used}} \times 100$$

Substrate Analysis

Cellulose, hemicellulose and lignin of the dry substrates were analyzed using the method of Datta (1981). The samples were fractionated sequentially and the weight losses during each fractionation step gave the weight fraction of water soluble material, hemicellulose, cellulose and lignin.

RESULTS AND DISCUSSION

The maximum yield (fresh wt) from the three flushes from three replicates of each substrate (Table 1) was obtained on water hyacinth (0.98 kg kg^{-1} dry substrate) followed by lotus (0.86 kg kg^{-1} dry substrate) and water chestnut (0.6 kg kg^{-1} dry substrate). All the three substrates thus supported the growth of *Pleurotus sajor-caju*. The percentage conversion of dry substrate to dry fruit bodies of mushroom was indicated by the biological efficiency. The dry matter of the fruit bodies varied from 8.57-9.35% (Table 1) and the biological efficiency was 8.46, 7.48 and 5.61% for water hyacinth, lotus and water chestnut, respectively. A higher yield in case of water hyacinth is probably due to its soft nature. In general, the first flush of fruit bodies gave a higher yield than the subsequent flushes.

Analysis of cellulose, hemicellulose and lignin content in the aquatic substrates before and after cultivation of *P.*

TABLE 1. Average production and biological efficiency of fresh fruit bodies of *Pleurotus sajor-caju* on different substrates.

Substrate†	Average yield: 1st flush	2nd flush	3rd flush	Total	Yield	% dry matter	BE‡
	g	g	g		$g\ g^{-1}$		%
Eichhornia crassipes	260	105	30	395	0.98	8.57	8.46
Nelumbo nucifera	220	80	45	345	0.86	8.68	7.48
Trapa bispinosa	150	70	20	240	0.60	9.35	5.61

†400 g dry weight of each substrate was used.

‡BE = biological efficiency = g/100 g dry substrate.

TABLE 2. Degradation of cellulose, hemicellulose and lignin contents of substrates as a result of *Pleurotus sajor-caju* cultivation.

Substrate	Cellulose: Before growth	Cellulose: After growth	Cellulose degradation	Hemicellulose: Before growth	Hemicellulose: After growth	Hemicellulose degradation	Lignin: Before growth	Lignin: After growth	Lignin degradation
	%	%	%	%	%	%	%	%	%
Eichhornia crassipes	32.3	26.0	19.5	26.0	22.5	13.4	10.2	9.6	5.8
Nelumbo nucifera	32.8	28.5	13.1	28.0	24.5	12.5	10.8	9.5	12.0
Trapa bispinosa	34.0	27.0	20.5	26.5	24.0	9.4	14.5	12.0	17.2

sajor-caju revealed that the mushroom utilized all the three major components of the substrates (Table 2). The percent degradation of each component varied with the substrate. There was a preferential utilization of polysaccharides (cellulose and hemicellulose) over the lignin fraction. Water chestnut shows a higher percent degradation of lignin (17.2%) as compared to water hyacinth (5.8%) or lotus (12%). However, these results indicate that *P. sajor-caju* is a ligno-cellulolytic fungus capable of converting cellulosic and lignin wastes of aquatic weeds into edible food. The capability of *P. sajor-caju* to degrade these major components of lignocellulosic residues has also been demonstrated by other workers (Zadrazil, 1977; Kandaswamy and Ramasamy, 1978).

In conclusion, it appears that aquatic weeds which are otherwise a nuisance could be profitably utilized for cultivation of edible mushrooms like *Pleurotus*. Besides serving as a food source, the cultivation process also helps in degradation of lignocellulosic components making them prone to a number of chemical and biochemical reactions including their use in animal feed. This utilization aspect could be commercialized thus giving value added products.

REFERENCES

Bisaria, R. 1984. Utilization of agro-residues through cultivation of mushroom *Pleurotus sajor-caju* (Fr.) Singer. Ph.D. Thesis, Indian Institute of Technology, New Delhi, India. 209 pp.

Datta, R. 1981. Acidogenic fermentation of lignocellulose acid yield and conversion of components. Biotechnol. Bioeng. 23:2167-2170.

Kandaswamy, T. K., and K. Ramasamy. 1978. Effect of organic substances with different C:N ratio on the yield of *Pleurotus sajor-caju*. Ind. Mushroom Sci. 1:423-427.

Madan, M., and G. S. Gujral. 1983. Cultivation of *Pleurotus sajor-caju* on *Saccharum munja* residues - A new substrate. Conf. Advances in Fermentation '83, London, Sept. 21-23, 1983 (abstract).

National Academy of Sciences. 1976. Making aquatic weeds useful: Some perspectives for developing countries. National Academy Press, Washington, DC. 174 pp.

National Academy of Sciences. 1981. Food from wastes. p. 142-157. *In* Food, Fuel and Fertilizer from Wastes. National Academy Press, Washington, DC.

Pal, J., and C. D. Thapa. 1979. Cultivation of Dhingri (*Pleurotus sajor-caju*) made easy. Ind. J. Mushrooms 5(1,2):17-20.

Wolverton, B. C., and R. C. McDonald. 1976. Don't waste waterweeds, New Scientist 71:318-220.

Zadrazil, F. 1977. The conversion of straw into feed by basidiomycetes. Europ. J. Appl. Microbiol. 4:273-281.

IMPACT OF PATHOGENS ON AQUATIC PLANTS USED IN WATER TREATMENT AND RESOURCE RECOVERY SYSTEMS

R. Charudattan
Plant Pathology Department and
Center for Aquatic Plant Research
University of Florida, IFAS
Gainesville, Florida 32611

ABSTRACT

Diseases caused by living or nonliving agents can become a serious constraint to the use of aquatic plants in water treatment and resource recovery systems. Pathogens that cause infectious diseases are numerous and their impacts vary from a slight reduction in plant productivity to plant death. Generally, pathogens become problematic in intensive plant monocultures and in natural populations subject to abiotic stresses or imbalances induced by man. Monocultures of genetically uniform and clonally propagated aquatic macrophytes are especially vulnerable to disease epidemics. Moreover, biotic stresses, such as insect pest pressure, and abiotic factors, such as low nutrient availability or nutrient imbalance, can compound the damage caused by plant pathogens.

Although most pathogens can be controlled effectively with disinfectants or pesticides, these methods may not be legal, practical, or cost-effective in systems of aquaphyte culture. Removal of infected plants followed by restocking with pest-free, healthy plants and short-term propagations in which plants are harvested before epidemic onset are two economical and practical ways to minimize disease intensity. Alternatively, a polyculture consisting of co-culturable plant species may be used to reduce disease losses. Polyculture, through its interference with the spatial and temporal spread of diseases, will have a disease-reducing effect.

Keywords: *Cercospora rodmanii*, *Eichhornia crassipes*, water hyacinth, diseases, epidemic, pests.

INTRODUCTION

When a plant species is repeatedly grown in large numbers, whether as a farmer's crop or in water treatment and resource

Aquatic Plants for Water Treatment
and Resource Recovery
K.R. Reddy and W.H. Smith (Eds.)

ISBN 0-941463-00-1

recovery systems, it is likely to be attacked at some point by plant diseases caused by biotic or abiotic agents. However, there are ways to minimize or even prevent the adverse impacts of diseases. During the last 16 years, my colleagues and I have studied infectious diseases of aquatic plants in an attempt to identify biological control agents for noxious weeds like water hyacinth, hydrilla, pistia, Eurasian milfoil, and alligatorweed (Zettler and Freeman, 1972; Freeman, 1977; Charudattan, 1984). I have studied several significant pathogens of aquatic plants from around the world. A brief account of the nature of biotic pathogens, their effects on aquatic plants, and suggest ways to minimize the impacts of diseases is presented here mainly to aquaphyte culturists. Abiotic diseases, such as nutrient deficiencies and pollution damage, which can be controlled by remedying the causes, are outside the scope of this article.

Plant pathogens are numerous and omnipresent. Many are highly specific to one or a few closely related plant species while several others are nonspecific. If the ecoclimate is suitable for growing a certain type of plant in a region, those conditions are also likely to be generally favorable for certain types of pathogens present around the plant. Among pathogens (Table 1), the most important are the fungi, bacteria, viruses, and nematodes. Of these, fungi are the most important because they are the more frequently encountered pathogens, include a great number and variety of genera and species, and often possess immense destructive capacity. However, bacteria, viruses, and nematodes are not incapable of destroying plant cultures or causing significant economic damage. In fact, serious plant losses do occur from bacterial, viral, and nematode diseases. Typically, a plant can be a host to several different types of

TABLE 1. Biotic causal agents of infectious diseases of plants.

Agents	Some Common Types of Symptoms
Fungi	Spots, lesions, rots, blights, mildews, pustules, wilting
Bacteria	Spots, lesions, rots
Viruses and viroids	Mosaics, spots, stripes, sterility, stunting, deformation, abnormal growths
Nematodes	Galls, abnormal growths, reduced root system
Mycoplasmas	Scorching, wilting
Protozoa	Wilting, steady decline
Algae	Scab-like growth on aerial parts
Insects	Galls, abnormal growths
Parasitic plants	Parasitism of host plant, parasite often obvious, plant decline

pathogens. For example, water hyacinth is reported to be susceptible to nearly 144 pathogens (Charudattan, 1984), the most important of which are listed in Table 2. Other aquatic plants are similarly susceptible to a variety of pathogens.

SYMPTOMS

The disease symptoms often give clues to the nature of the causal agent, particularly when they occur on the visible portions of floating and rooted aquatic plants. Symptoms on aerial parts are usually distinct and are uncomplicated by the water soaking and permeation that accompany infections on submerged portions. Fungal diseases are commonly characterized by spots, lesions, rotting, pustules, and mildews of the leaves and stems. Roots are often rotted and produce wilting of the entire plant. The affected tissues may turn yellow (chlorotic) or brown, and consist of partially or fully dead (necrotic) areas. Often the pathogen itself is visible as moldy growth or spores. Bacterial damage is

TABLE 2. Virulent pathogens of water hyacinth and their effects on the plant.† (Charudattan, 1984)

Pathogen	Type of damage	Potential impacts
Acremonium zonatum	Zonate leaf spot	A slight loss of productivity
Alternaria eichhorniae	Leaf blight	Moderate to severe loss of productivity
Aquathanatephorus pendulus	Plant blight	Severe loss of productivity; plant death
Bipolaris oryzae	Leaf blight	Severe loss of productivity; plant death
Cercospora rodmanii and C. piaropi	Leaf spots	Moderate to severe loss of productivity; gradual plant decline
Helminthosporium bicolor	Leaf lesions	Moderate to severe loss of productivity
Marasmiellus inoderma	Plant blight	A slight loss of productivity
Myrothecium roridum	Leaf spots	Severe loss of productivity; plant death; potential for mycotoxin contamination
Uredo eichhorniae	Pustules	Moderate to severe loss of productivity
Xanthomonas campestris	Lesions, spots, and rots	Severe loss of productivity; death of insect-damaged plants

†All of these pathogens are fungi except Xanthomonas, which is a bacterium.

typified by water soaking associated with rots, lesions, or spots which may be chlorotic or necrotic. Virus symptoms vary from necrotic or chlorotic spots and streaks to mosaics, lesions, various types of anomalous growths on leaves and stems, and tissue malformations. Nematodes usually cause galls and deformations on leaves, stems, and roots. An infected plant may die quickly from the disease itself, but more commonly it may expire gradually from the disease or from secondary factors complicating the disease. The type of symptoms, therefore, is always the first criterion for deciding the cause of the disease.

EFFECTS OF PATHOGENS

Pathogens can produce effects ranging from minor problems of cosmetic nature to serious loss of plant productivity measurable as reductions in growth rates, reproduction, and regeneration capacity. Under severe disease condition, mortality and losses in plant stands can occur. In some cases, the presence of pathogens in an area may preclude the establishment of a plant culture. Since different pathogens can affect different parts of the plant (roots, shoots, foliage, flowers, and fruits), the severity of damage, the organ affected, and the importance of these organs to the survival and reproduction of the plant will determine the seriousness of the disease.

The loss of productivity resulting from a pathogen can be illustrated with the following example. Cercospora rodmanii is a fungal pathogen that induces a debilitating leaf spot disease of water hyacinth (Freeman and Charudattan, 1984). Under certain conditions, the fungus can severely limit water hyacinth growth, and under severe disease stress, the plant may be killed (Freeman and Charudattan, 1984; Charudattan et al., 1985). Loss of leaf productivity, reduction in biomass, and a diminution of regeneration capacity have been recorded in this host-pathogen system (Charudattan et al., 1985). Thus, even a leaf spot disease can slow plant productivity and significantly reduce the biomass or standing crop. Furthermore, in combination with other biotic stresses, such as insect pressure, and abiotic factors, such as low nutrient input or nutrient imbalance (which might be frequent in effluent waters), pathogens can become more of a threat to the operation of water treatment and resource recovery systems.

The effects of diseases on aquatic plants can be further elucidated with the examples of pathogens listed in Table 2. The type of damage, upon which symptom descriptions are based, indicates the immediate effects of the pathogen, whereas the potential impact refers to the effects over time, which are quantifiable on individual plants or on the community as a whole. It should be clear from these examples that while all of these pathogens can be quite damaging to water hyacinth populations, some, such as Aquathanatephorus pendulus, Bipolaris oryzae, and Cercospora spp., are more threatening than others. A determination of which of the pathogens will be potentially destructive to an aquaphyte culture system should therefore be based on the biology and pathology of the organisms present and their capacity to upset the production goals of the system. If the pathogen is of the less threatening type, no control actions may be necessary; a slight loss in productivity may outweigh the cost of control in this case.

FACTORS THAT PROMOTE DISEASE DEVELOPMENT

How do diseases develop and what are the key ingredients that contribute to a disease epidemic? In order for a disease to develop, there must be a susceptible host, a virulent pathogen, and favorable environmental conditions conducive for disease development (Holcomb, 1982). Generally, pathogens survive in nature in the form of resting structures such as spores and specialized cells which constitute the primary inoculum. Assuming that an aquatic macrophyte is susceptible to one or more of the virulent pathogens present naturally and the primary inoculum necessary to start the infection is present in sufficient quantity and quality, the arrival of the conducive environmental conditions generally will trigger the epidemic(s). Among the conditions, temperature that is optimal for the pathogen's growth and infection and the availability of sufficient periods of abundant moisture on plant surfaces are most important. The growth, reproduction, and infection of pathogenic microorganisms are temperature-related. Likewise, critical moisture levels and moisture periods are required for their germination, growth, and infection. The occurrence of extended warm and moist periods during the growing seasons, especially at night when the drying effects of the sun are absent, is therefore very congenial for disease development.

Additionally, several man-made practices promote disease development by favoring one or more of the key ingredients of the disease (Cowling, 1978). For example, intensive cultivation of genetically uniform plants tends to promote disease epidemics by providing the pathogen with a vast supply of susceptible sites for infection while enhancing maximum rates of reproduction and further spread. Deliberate or accidental dissemination of pathogens during plant propagation can also cause disease outbreaks. Also, improper fertilization, irrigation, and propagation practices can lead to disastrous levels of disease. For instance, excessive amount of fertilizers, particularly N, can cause a profusion of tender new growth that may be more susceptible to disease than older tissues. Overhead irrigation can leave an inordinate amount of free moisture or prolong moist periods on aerial surfaces, providing the pathogen an opportunity to germinate and infect the plant. If the propagation methods call for repeated cutting, pruning, or culling of the plants, such practices may contribute to physiological stress and susceptibility of the plant to disease. With aquaphytes, a similar situation can occur if they are heavily grazed by herbivores. Hence, in certain cases it may be necessary to control the herbivores, such as insects, to maintain a disease-free crop.

Of the key components of disease, one that is most relevant to us is the host. Assuming that aquatic plants for water treatment and resource recovery systems will be obtained from natural field sources or multiplied from "seed nurseries," the genetic quality of the stocking plants becomes an important consideration. The genetic diversity of most aquatic plants are poorly understood (Barrett, 1982). Nonetheless, in general, members of a native flora can be expected to have a diverse genetic background, whereas immigrant species, because of their passage through "genetic bottlenecks," are likely to be more genetically homogeneous (Barrett, 1982). Moreover, the majority of aquatic plants have very dominant vegetative reproductive modes. It is recognized that clonally propagated plants, due to their narrow genetic diversity, are more vulnerable to attacks by biotic agents than sexually reproducing plants (Burdon and Marshall, 1981). Thus, monocultures of genetically uniform, clonally propagated aquaphytes are likely to be more vulnerable to disease epidemics and therefore the dangers from pathogens should not be underestimated in systems of aquaphyte culture.

Monocultures are risky for another reason. The presence of a large number of potentially susceptible plants in an area offers a continuous target for the pathogen both in time and space. At a given time, the supply of susceptible hosts is unlimited when the hosts are in close proximity, and the pathogen is able to move easily from infected plants to neighboring uninfected plants (Augspurger and Kelly, 1984). Any degree of discontinuity among susceptible plants may help in slowing the spread of the pathogen and the disease (Leonard, 1969).

MINIMIZATION OF PATHOGENS' IMPACTS

How may plant pathogens be effectively managed in water treatment and resource recovery systems? Table 3 is a compilation of the methods than can be used for managing pathogens and minimizing the impacts of diseases. The most common method of suppression is with pesticides such as fungicides, bactericides, and nematicides to control, respectively, fungal, bacterial, and nematode pathogens. Insecticides may be used to reduce populations of disease-transmitting insects with some beneficial results. However, although most pathogens can be controlled effectively in this manner, the use of pesticides may not be legal, practical, or cost-effective in systems of aquaphyte culture. Few pesticides are registered for use against aquatic macrophytes, and therefore special permits may be required for their use. On the other hand, a general purpose disinfectant,

TABLE 3. Ways to control or prevent pathogens from attacking plants used in water treatment and resource recovery systems.

1. Use of a plant stock that is genetically diverse and resistant to diseases.
2. Propagation of stocking plants under phytosanitary conditions.
3. Avoiding the use of infected plants for stocking.
4. Use of general purpose disinfectants to sterilize water and hydrosoil in which the pathogen can survive and multiply.
5. Maintenance of a balanced nutrient regime to maximize plant productivity without promoting excessive amount of tender and susceptible tissues.
6. Use of propagation and harvesting methods that do not cause stress to the plant.
7. Use of pesticides to prevent or eliminate pathogens and pathogen-transmitting insects.
8. Avoiding overhead irrigation and excessive moisture on the foliage.
9. Prompt removal of infected plants and restocking the system with healthy plants.
10. Cultivation of different species of plants on a rotational basis.
11. Use of short-term cultures to minimize the incidence and spread of pathogens.
12. Use of a polyculture of different plant species to introduce spatial discontinuity among plant types in the system.

such as chlorine or methyl bromide, may be used, in accordance with federal and local regulations, to treat water or hydrosoil, if elimination of pathogens through sterilization is the goal.

The least costly and a logical approach to the control of diseases is through the removal of infected plants followed by restocking with pest-free, healthy plants. In this respect, short-term propagation, in which plants are harvested before an epidemic sets in, is also a way to manage diseases. Because disease damage is more likely when plants are grown under a heavily crowded condition, short-term propagation can offer a solution to the crowding problem that may result from the overproduction of the culture system. However, while short-term propagation may be acceptable in systems aimed at biomass recovery, it may be undesirable when plants need to be maintained for long periods, as in filtration and sedimentation systems. Alternatively, one type of aquatic plant may be grown in rotation with another, as in the crop rotation methods used in land-based agriculture.

Another option is to replace monoculture with a spectrum of aquatic plants chosen to produce an assemblage of species that are complementary to one another in growth, life cycle, and other desired characteristics. In the event of the decline of a dominant species, another member of the spectrum will fill the void, assuring continued operation of the system. Such polycultures tend to slow the spread of the disease and minimize disease epidemics because of several inter-related factors. Firstly, since diseases are more serious when host plants are heavily crowded (Augspurger and Kelly, 1984), the mixture of plant species in a polyculture serves to disperse individual species and increase the distance between susceptible sites available for infection. Secondly, with reduced crowding, the efficiency of the spatial spread of the pathogen within the polyculture is reduced. Thirdly, in the absence of pathgoen pressure, individual components of the polyculture can better cope with interspecific plant competition. Finally, with the overall reduction in disease due to the above factors, the amount of pathogen's inoculum available for further infections is reduced. This is turn will increase the time needed for future disease development and slow the progress of the disease.

Without intervention, a polyculture of aquaphytes is likely to turn into a mixture consisting of highly clumped distribution of individual plant species rather than a uniform mixture of the component species. Even so, it has been shown that under comparable population densities, the rate of disease increase could be actually slower when a plant in a mixture is distributed in a clumped manner rather than homogeneously (Burdon, 1982). Thus, polyculture has an influence on the spatial and temporal aspects of disease, can slow the spread of the pathogen, and help minimize the damaging effects of the disease on the component plant species. Overall, a polyculture may offer stability and operational efficiency to the water treatment and resource recovery systems.

ACKNOWLEDGMENTS

Florida Agricultural Experiment Stations Journal Series No. 7912.

REFERENCES

Augspurger, C. K., and C. K. Kelly. 1984. Pathogen mortality of tropical tree seedlings: Experimental studies of the effects of dispersal distance, seedling density, and light conditions. Oecologia 61:211-217.

Barrett, S. C. H. 1982. Genetic variation in weeds. p. 73-98. In R. Charudattan and H. L. Walker (ed.) Biological Control of Weeds with Plant Pathogens. John Wiley, New York.

Burdon, J. J. 1982. The effect of fungal pathogens on plant communities. J. of the British Ecological Soc. 82:99-112.

Burdon, J. J., and D. R. Marshall. 1981. Biological control and the reproductive mode of weeds. J. Appl. Ecol. 18:649-658.

Charudattan, R. 1984. Role of Cercospora rodmanii and other pathogens in the biological and integrated controls of water hyacinth. p. 834-859. In G. Thyagarajan (ed.) Proceedings of the International Conference on Water Hyacinth. United Nations Environment Programme, Box 30552, Nairobi, Kenya.

Charudattan, R., S. B. Linda, Marjan Kluepfel, and Y. A. Osman. 1985. Biocontrol efficacy of Cercospora rodmanii on water hyacinth. Phytopathology 75:1263-1269.

Cowling, E. B. 1978. Agricultural and forest practices that favor epidemics. p. 361-381. In J. G. Horsfall and E. B. Cowling (ed.) Plant Disease: An Advanced Treatise. Vol. II. How Disease Develops in Populations. Academic Press, New York.

Freeman, T. E. 1977. Biological control of aquatic weeds with plant pathogens. Aquat. Bot. 3:175-184.

Freeman, T. E., and R. Charudattan. 1984. Cercospora rodmanii Conway, a biocontrol agent for water hyacinth. Florida Agricultural Experiment Stations Technical Bulletin 842, Institute of Food and Agricultural Sciences, Gainesville, Florida. 18 pp.

Holcomb, G. E. 1982. Constraints on disease development. p. 61-71. In R. Charudattan and H. L. Walker (ed.) Biological Control of Weeds with Plant Pathogens. John Wiley, New York.

Leonard, K. J. 1969. Factors affecting rates of stem rust increase in mixed plantings of susceptible and resistant oat varieties. Phytopathology 59:1845-1850.

Zettler, F. W., and T. E. Freeman. 1972. Plant pathogens as biocontrols of aquatic weeds. Annual Review of Phytopathology 10:455-470.

ABSTRACTS

DISTRIBUTION, PRODUCTION, GROSS COMPOSITION AND MANAGEMENT OF SOME DOMINANT AQUATIC WEEDS IN KASHMIR.

V. Kaul (University of Kashmir, Srinagar 190 006, Kashmir, INDIA).

The shallow water bodies situated at 1587-2180 m in the valley of Kashmir are heavily infested by macrophytes though those at higher altitudes (3000-4000 m) with rocky basins and low prevailing water temperatures support only planktonic life. The appreciable biomass produced year after year is mainly used as food by varied aquatic fauna, feeding the livestock, as green manure and for nutrient stripping from polluted waters. The hydrological factors represent the chief milieu of conditions governing the occurrence and growth of various plant species, while soil type and nutrient composition of water seem to have little value. Water depth and turbidity are important factors in the colonization of submerged types. The standing crop and production values determined for various species reveal tall growing emergents to be highly productive (4.25-17.5 of g m^{-2} d^{-1}), contributing 50% of the total macrophytic biomass at times, against the lowest production values for low-growing and ground-layer emergents (1.44-3.11 g m^{-2} d^{-1}). Determination of six essential inorganic nutrients in 18 species revealed *Sparganium erectum* and submerged species locking up maximum percentage of all the nutrients particularly nitrogen and phosphorus. The mineral locking on per hectare basis was found to be maximum in emergents, obviously because of their higher biomass. Among the rooted - floating leaf types *Potamogeton natans* and *Nelumbium nucifera* were responsible for 72-89% locking up of nutrients of this life-form class. The association of *Ceratophyllum demersum*, *Potamogeton lucens* and *Myriophyllum spicatum* locked up 77-96% of nutrients from submerged nutrient pool. An examination of 15 dominant species for crude protein, fat and calorific value showed *Marsilea quadrifolia*, *Nelumbium nucifera* and *Lemna* spp. as rich in protein content, *Nelumbium nucifera* in fat and energy value and *Scirpus lacustris* in carbohydrate. Nutrient stripping through a regulated harvest on a sustained basis of the weeds for varied utilitarian purposes as a check against high mineralization of these water bodies is discussed in the text.

Aquatic Plants for Water Treatment and Resource Recovery
K.R. Reddy and W.H. Smith (Eds.)

ISBN 0-941463-00-1

BIOLOGICAL TREATMENT OF WASTEWATERS USING ALGAE AND PHOTOTROPHIC BACTERIA.

M. A. Aziz (National University of Singapore, Kent Ridge 0511, SINGAPORE).

Increasing demand for feed protein combined with the progressive enforcement of environmental legislations throughout the world and growing public interest for the abatement of water pollution from various wastewater discharges has encouraged a number of engineers and scientists around the world to consider both the technological and economic feasibility of biological wastewater treatments using algae and phototrophic bacteria. Some investigations have been made of the various factors involved in using aquatic plants for wastewater treatment with an objective of resource recovery over the past few years. These studies have revealed some very interesting facts. But still it remains to be a dynamic subject for further investigations.

The author conducted pilot plant studies of the biological treatment of both municipal and industrial wastewaters from pig farms, meat packing and dairy plants using algae and phototrophs. The results of these studies have been found to be very encouraging. Results show that the municipal wastewater and the wastewaters from the pig farms, meat packing and dairy plants can be treated by using algae and phototrophs, and moreover, the treated water can be well utilized as liquid fertilizer. Animal feed (protein) recovered from algal ponds is found quite substantial. In addition to being an effective wastewater treatment method with resource recovery, it has the following merits compared with other existing conventional methods: 1) High BOD loading rate (3-8 kg BOD m^{-3} d^{-1}); 2) Less space required; 3) Effective utilization of microbial mass produced as by-product; 4) Easy to maintain as the microbial flora simplified and widely adapted. In this paper, the author first critically discusses the fundamentals of the biological wastewater treatment using algae and phototrophic bacteria, and then he reports the findings of the pilot plant studies carried out on the wastewater from domestic and industrial sources.

POTENTIAL IMPACTS OF PHYTOPHAGOUS INSECTS ON AQUATIC MACROPHYTES USED IN RESOURCE RECOVERY SYSTEMS.

K. H. Haag (University of Florida, Entomology Department, Bldg. 339, Gainesville, Florida 32611) and G. R. Buckingham (ARS-USDA, Florida).

There are a number of phytophagous insects which are potential pests of aquatic plants used in resource recovery systems in the U.S. They include native insects as well as introduced biological control agents. Water hyacinth is attacked by the moths *Sameodes albiguttalis* and *Bellura densa*, and by the weevils *Neochetina eichhorniae* and *N. bruchi*. Waterlettuce is readily fed upon by the moth *Samea multiplicalis* and the aphid

Rhopalosiphum nympheae. The chrysomelid beetle *Pseudolampsis guttata*, the weevil *Stenopelmus rufinasus*, and the moth *Synclita obliteralis* are all known to feed on water fern. Species of duckweed are attacked by the weevil *Tanysphyrus lemnae*. Cattail is frequently attacked by the moth *Simyra henrici*. Several species of caterpillars in the genus *Spodoptera* are often found feeding on a variety of aquatic plants. Many of these insects, as well as closely related species, also attack aquatic plants throughout the world. In many cases, environmental constraints preclude the use of chemical control measures against pest insects. While there are potential biological control agents for a number of these insect species, no research has been done on the feasibility of their use. Among those agents are bacterial and fungal pathogens, protozoans, pathogenic nematodes, and parasitic flies and wasps.

NEEDS AND METHODS OF CONTROL OF THE HYACINTH WEEVILS, *NEOCHETINA EICHHORNIA* AND *NEOCHETINA BRUCHI* ON WATER HYACINTH BASED TREATMENT SYSTEMS.

D. L. Haselow (Amasek, Inc., 3708 North U.S. 1, Cocoa, Florida 32926).

The hyacinth weevils *Neochetina eichhornia* and *Neochetina bruchi* were introduced in Florida to control "wild" stands of hyacinths in 1972. Since that time, their populations have increased substantially, and their impacts upon reduction of the growth of hyacinths within the state's waters have deleterious impacts upon crop health and system performance. Control of weevils in these situations is critical. Experiences gained by Amasek indicate that effective control can result from a proper initial stocking, a well directed harvesting program, and the use of the pesticide Sevin during serious outbreaks. Continuous monitoring of weevil populations is mandatory to ensure early detection of developing outbreaks. Also, understanding the life cycle and general behavior of the weevil is necessary. Operational guidelines are presented regarding methods of detection and control, as well as a review of available information regarding control and a discussion of potential nonpesticide type controls and research needs.

MOSQUITO AND MOSQUITOFISH RESPONSES TO LOADING OF WATER HYACINTH WASTEWATER TREATMENT PONDS.

B. A. Wilson, K. R. Townsend (California Department of Health Services Vector Surveillance and Control Branch), and T. H. Anderson, Jr. (Black & Veatch Engineers - Architects, California).

Mosquito production and mosquitofish survival were monitored at two California water hyacinth wastewater treatment projects. The aquatic plant systems, all of a similar configuration, received effluent from seven treatment trains incorporating conventional and innovative primary and secondary processes. Mosquitoes were produced in all water hyacinth ponds. Production was higher in wastewater which had primary treatment only. B.O.D. loading rates ranged from 1.8-68.1 kg ha^{-1} d^{-1}. At rates from 10-40 ppd ha^{-1}, Gambusia mosquitofish populations increased in harvested or aerated ponds. Fish frequented the influent end, where the wastewater entered the ponds. Gambusia appeared to control the potential nuisance in this situation (Roseville, 1981 through 1982). In ponds loaded at 185-296 ppd ha^{-1}, mosquitofish avoided the influent halves of the ponds, where >96% of the mosquito larvae were found. No reduction of mosquito production by the fish was evident. Repeated applications of chemical control were mandated by the local health department (San Diego, 1984-1985). Loading rates of >272 ppd ha^{-1} for one month coincided with loss of dissolved oxygen and loss of the mosquitofish populations throughout these aerated, harvested ponds.

TREATMENT OF ANAEROBIC DIGESTER EFFLUENT BY WATER HYACINTH (EICHHORNIA CRASSIPES [MART] SOLMS).

D. A. Graetz, P. A. Krottje and R. A. Nordstedt (University of Florida, Soil Science Department, Gainesville, Florida 32611).

Integrated "Energy from Biomass" systems which produce CH_4 via anaerobic digestion may use aquatic plants such as water hyacinth both as a feedstock and as a means of "cleaning-up" digester effluent. Effluent from anaerobic digesters often contains high levels of readily-available nutrients and is not suitable for direct disposal to a water body. The objective of this study was to evaluate utilization of digester effluent as a source of nutrients to produce additional biomass for CH_4 generation and concurrently provide a mechanism for water treatment. Water hyacinth were grown in 90 L microcosms at an initial stocking rate of 10 kg wet weight m^{-2} surface area. Effluent obtained from anaerobic digesters using swine manure as feedstock was added to the microcosms at rates to provide 0, 300, and 600 kg inorganic N ha^{-1} approximately every 20 days. At the end of each 20 day period, water hyacinth were harvested back to the initial stocking rate and water samples were taken for analyses. Water hyacinth yield averaged 7 Mg dry weight ha^{-1} per harvest period for both the 300 and 600 kg N ha^{-1} application rates. Plant nitrogen content was 2.64 and 3.92%, respectively. For each harvest period, approximately 71% and 50% of the added inorganic N was taken-up by the plants at the high and low application rates, respectively. Excellent growth rates (32 g m^{-2} d^{-1}) were obtained and no adverse effects on plant growth were observed at either application rate. Nitrogen (inorganic) removal from the effluent was >99% for both application rates during the summer, however, during periods of slower plant growth, percentage N removal was less (90%) at the higher application rate. Results suggest that if properly managed with regard to harvesting and application rates, this system could produce additional biomass for CH_4 generation and also provide effective treatment of the effluent.

APPLICATION OF WATER HYACINTHS FOR UPGRADING EXISTING WASTEWATER TREATMENT FACILITIES -- TWO CASE STUDIES. N. Wyse and N. Morrison (Amasek, Inc., 3708 North U.S. 1, Cocoa, Florida 32926).

One specific application for water hyacinth based treatment systems in Florida and areas with similar climates is their use in upgrading and, in some cases, expanding the capacity of existing treatment facilities. Throughout Florida many fixed film systems (e.g. trickling filters) remain as inexpensive, and operationally reliable methods of reducing BOD_5 and suspended solids. With more stringent effluent standards it is often required that these systems be upgraded to facilitate not only additional removal of BOD_5 and solids but also nitrogen and phosphorus. By using existing polishing ponds, or by constructing new ponds, and using these ponds to support a managed hyacinth crop, it is often possible to quickly bring a facility into compliance at a modest cost. Operational and cost data for two such systems are presented. The first system is a 1.4 MGD trickling filter system operated by the City of Orlando, for the U. S. Navy at their NTC McCoy Annex. Using City forces, 0.6 ha of lagoons were constructed on site. Hyacinths grown in these lagoons combined with alum addition, have resulted in upgrading from secondary to the necessary advanced treatment standards. This resulted in the upward rerating of the plant capacity. The second system is the City of Melbourne's David B. Lee System where an interim upgrading of nitrogen and phosphorus control was needed. Using the existing 4.9 ha of polishing ponds to support a hyacinth system, the system was brought into compliance within less than four months.

OPERATIONS OF A HARVESTING AND PROCESSING SYSTEM USED IN CONJUNCTION WITH A DESIGN WATER HYACINTH BASED ADVANCED WASTEWATER TREATMENT SYSTEM AND AN ANAEROBIC DIGESTION SYSTEM. F. Hueston and E. A. Stewart III (Amasek, Inc., 3708 North U.S. 1, Cocoa, Florida 32926).

A thirty acre lagoon system designed specifically for the cultivation of water hyacinth for the removal of additional quantities of N and P from advanced wastewater effluent was constructed at the City of Orlando's 90,840 m^3 d^{-1} Iron Bridge Facility. The system's design was developed to accommodate effective harvesting and processing using Amasek's Model 101 harvesting/processing system in association with a 95 m^3 anaerobic digester. Operational data is reviewed to determine cost effectiveness and system reliability. A review of the digester design is presented as to its effectiveness in handling fibrous products. The harvesting system consists of a shore mounted unit which working in concert with a water borne unit, gathers, chops, and conveys through pumping the harvested hyacinths, delivering them as a slurry directly to the digester system. The digester is a mesophilic down flow system with a designed detention time of thirty days. The digester is step fed from an equalization tank which receives the hyacinth harvest directly from the field. The system generates a 60% CH_4 biogas at an estimated rate of 0.34 m^3 kg^{-1} vs. The unique down-flow design serves to improve solids retention time while optimizing substrate utilization.

MACROPHYTE PRODUCTIVITY FOR HARVESTING NUTRIENT SOURCE IN TROPICAL WATERS. R. S. Ambasht and Shardendu (Banaras Hindu University, Varanasi 221 005, INDIA).

This paper concerns the case study of productivity of a pond in the Banaras Hindu University campus, Varanasi, in terms of biomass increments (monthly, seasonal, and annual) and nutrient contents of harvestable parts. Twelve macrophyte species distributed in four zones were harvested at 30-day intervals. The dry organic matter increments, and N and P contents of plants have been analyzed (in relation to water nutrient analysis), standing crop biomass ranged from 194.97 g m^{-2} in May to 610.83 g m^{-2} in September in emergent zone, from 71.52 g m^{-2} in March to 106.50 g m^{-2} in June for rooted floating zone, from 177.86 g m^{-2} in June to 327.94 g m^{-2} in October for free-floating zone, and from 26.05 g m^{-2} in June to 45.78 g m^{-2} in August in submerged zone. The mean annual nutrient concentration in harvestable parts were 5.976 mg g^{-1} N and 0.578 mg g^{-1} P in emergent zone, 13.830 to 17.994 mg g^{-1} N and 0.621 to 0.931 mg g^{-1} P in rooted floating zone, 13.623 to 30.560 mg g^{-1} N, 0.538 to 1.77 mg g^{-1} P in floating zone, and from 19.00 to 19.677 mg g^{-1} N and 0.980 to 1.054 mg g^{-1} P in submerged zone were recorded. Thus, the freshwater bodies, which otherwise are only used as sinks of pollutants, have been assessed as potential source of nutrients through harvest of macrophytes for the purpose of fodder supplements, biofertilizers, and other economic purposes.

USE OF DUCKWEED FOR WASTEWATER TREATMENT AND RECYCLING. G. Oron and D. Porath (Ben-Gurion University of the Negev, Kiryat Sde-Boker, 84990 ISRAEL).

Outdoor experiments conducted in mini-ponds of 40 L each, showed that duckweed plants can be used for wastewater treatment and recycling. *Lemna gibba* was found to be the most preferable among the species examined. Optimal duckweed yield was obtained under a retention time of 5 to 10 days and effluent depth of 20 to

30 cm. The duckweed yield (dry basis) was between 10 to 15 g m^{-2} d^{-1} with a crude protein content of around 30%. The treated wastewater is at an acceptable quality for reuse for agricultural irrigation.

INDUSTRIAL AND LARGE-SCALE DUCKWEED SYSTEMS FOR WASTEWATER TREATMENT. V. Ngo and D. Hogen (The Lemna Corporation, 7800 Main Street N. E., Minneapolis, Minnesota 55432).

The Lemna Corporation has developed a U.S. Patented technology to grow and harvest duckweeds for industrial wastewater treatment and generation of high-protein biomass for animal feedstuffs. We believe our first 10 ha impoundment site in Minnesota is the first major commercial application of duckweed treatment and biomass generation in the U.S. Lemna has successfully managed to operate this facility as a tertiary treatment for a cheese manufacturing plant. The harvested biomass has over 35% protein by dry weight and full complements of minerals. Several major U.S. feed companies, including Cargill, are conducting extensive feeding tests on Lemna materials. We are actively planning and designing other similar facilities for various industries in need of better wastewater treatment throughout the U.S. Due to Lemna's efficiency in wastewater treatment and high-yield high-protein biomass, we are seeking to expand the applications of our technology to municipal wastewater treatment, non-point source pollution abatement, lake quality improvement, hazardous waste reduction and protein production in various parts of the world.

WATER HYACINTH BIOMASS A VALUABLE RESOURCE FOR AGRICULTURE AND INDUSTRY. G. G. Monsod, Jr. (Non-Waste Tech, 5657 Fountain Avenue, Los Angeles, California 90028).

This paper is presenting an integrated manufacturing concept in low-cost automation, utilizing water hyacinth biomass as raw materials for different kinds of products in agriculture and industry. Thirteen years of research and development has succeeded on converting the water hyacinth biomass as a valuable resource, thus producing an array of patented recycled by-products such as the controversial pulp. Pulping tests indicated that the pulp is a good material for specialty paper. Particle board, textile yarn, protein flour, animal feeds for poultry and livestock, and insecticide produced from this hydrophyte were proven feasible. This project was investigated by the National Aeronautics and Space Administration in the Philippines and among others, NASA validated the paper process. British and Japanese experts likewise confirmed the process as viable for various kinds of paper. Experiments from the formulated hyacinth extract for control of rancidity in coconut flour and a curing agent for food and leather tanning are on-going. A managed biomass production and novel multi-processing techniques of aquatic weeds into useful products are envisioned to be a major breakthrough in aquatic plant technology.

PROGRESS IN THE EFFLUENT COLLECTION AND PROCESSING OF WATER HYACINTHS INTO VIABLE BY-PRODUCTS. E. A. Stewart III and E. L. Keesling (Amasek, Inc., 3708 North U.S. 1, Cocoa, Florida 32936).

A paper presenting the development of three products -- compost, biogas, and livestock feed -- will be included as part of the session. Pictures of the Iron Bridge Digester complete with description of design and function will be presented. Description, photographs, and product samples of Amasek cattlefeed operation production facility will be included. Also, samples of vermicomposit and a description of the process will be presented. A video of the harvesting system operation will be part of the session, and if possible, we would like to display our harvesting equipment at the conference.

UTILIZATION OF WATER HYACINTH AS A ROUGHAGE FOR RUMINANTS. A. M. Elserafy, M. M. Shoukry, S. Mansour, A. A. Zaki, M. A. Elashry, H. M. Khattab, and H. S. Soliman (AinShams University, Cairo, EGYPT).

A four year research project was sponsored by the USDA-ARS and conducted in Egypt to evaluate water hyacinth plants (WH) when fed to ruminants as hay (WHH) or silage (WHS). Parameters for that evaluation included: chemical analysis, in vitro, in situ, in vivo nutrients digestibilities (NDG), N balance, and animal performance trials using local sheep, goats, and water buffalo steers. The results obtained during the project indicated that, firstly, chemical composition of WH depends upon the "fertility" of water it was harvested from (location) within a location, however, crude fiber, ADF, and ADL content of WH leaves or stems were similar. Secondly, in vivo NDG, retained N and daily live-weight gains of sheep decreased ($P<0.05$) when a control berseem-hay was replaced by 75 or 100% WHH, but no difference was found at the 25 or 50% replacement levels. Thirdly, intakes (g DM/0.75 kg) and NDG and WHH or WHS were greater ($P<0.01$) in buffalo steers than in either sheep or goats; addition of 1% urea to WHS increased ($P<0.05$) intake and NDG. It was concluded that in Egypt, it is feasible to process WH as sun-dried hay, to ensile it as silage mixed with other feeds, and to utilize these feed-forms as roughages for ruminants.

STUDIES ON WATER LETTUCE AS FEED SUPPLEMENT IN BROILER RATION. T. E. Ekpenyong and M. K. G. Sridhar (University of Ibadan, P.M.B. 1017, Uyo, Cross River State, NIGERIA).

Hubbard day old chicks were fed with water lettuce (*Pistia stratiotes* L.) at 5, 10, and 15% level supplemented in basal diet. They were compared with birds fed on normal diet. During the 12 week period, there were no statistically significant differences in total feed intake and weight gain between the control and the experimental groups. The carcass quality, fat deposits in various tissues, mortality, and blood composition revealed no significant differences. This study revealed that water lettuce can be supplemented in poultry feeds up to 10% level without any adverse effects on the health of the broilers.

VOLUNTARY INTAKE AND DIGESTIBILITY OF COMPLETE DIETS CONTAINING VARYING LEVELS OF CATTAIL (*TYPHA LATIFOLIA* L.). BY SHEEP AND CATTLE. Z. Mir (Agriculture Canada, Melfort, Box 1240, Melfort, Saskatchewan S0E 1A0, CANADA) and G. Lakshman (Saskatchewan Research Council, CANADA).

Cattail (CATT) hay (9.3% crude protein) was incorporated with crested wheatgrass (*Agropyron crestatum*) hay (CWG) (8.4% crude protein) into the following complete diets: 1. 100% CWG, 2. 75:25 (CWG:CATT), 3. 50:50 (CWG:CATT), 4. 25:75 (CWG:CATT), 5. 100% CATT. Dry matter disappearance in the rumen, determined by using nylon bag technique in rumen-fistulated cattle, were significantly ($P < 0.05$) reduced for diets 3, 4 and 5. Voluntary intake and digestibility trial data, obtained with 30 wethers in a completely randomized block design, indicated that dry matter intake was highest ($P < 0.05$) and lowest ($P < 0.05$) for diet 1 and 5 at 1.4 and 0.7 kg d^{-1} respectively. Wethers were able to gain or maintain their body weight, with satisfactory intake, only with diet 1, 2, and 3. Apparent digestibilities of dry matter, energy, crude protein and acid detergent fibers were reduced ($P < 0.05$) by inclusion of cattail in the diets. Voluntary intake data, obtained from 3 cattle in a 3 x 3 Latin square design, were 10.3, 8.4 and 6.4 kg/d for diet 1, 2 and 3 respectively. Results from these experiments provide evidence that optimum use of cattail as animal feed would occur only when their inclusion level is less than 50% of a medium quality complete diet.

LIQUEFACTION OF SEA-GRASS WITH ACETIC ACID FOR CONVERSION TO CRUDES. F. Taner (C.U., Arts and Sciences, Chemistry Department, Adana, TURKEY).

Sea-grass, *Z. marina*, has been dragged by the tides in Mediterranean Sea to the shore in great deal during the summer months. In this study, aqueous slurries of the sea-grass (20% by weight) has been treated to be liquefied with acetic acid (10% by weight of the sea-grass) at 150, 200, 250, and 300°C in a high pressure autoclave for one hour. The solid-oil yield, the amount of soluble fraction of solid-oil in H_2SO_4 (72% by weight), the calorific values of solid-oil phases, and also oil yield: acetone and benzene extract of solid-oil, of sea grass have been determined. It was found that the oil yield of sea grass is about 100% at low temperatures and pressures. The liquefaction of aquatic plants for conversion to crudes requires not as much as high pressure and temperatures for liquefaction of ligno-cellulosic wastes.

OZONIZATION OF AQUEOUS LAYERS OBTAINED FROM THE LIQUEFACTION OF SEA-GRASS. H. Boztepe and F. Taner (C.U., Arts and Sciences, Chemistry Department, Adana, TURKEY).

The sea-grass, *Z. marina*, obtained from the coast of the Mediterranean Sea has been treated to be liquefied with acetic acid, and water. Solid-oil and aqueous layers have been separated with filtering. The aqueous layers hence obtained have been subjected to ozonization. During ozonization the ozonized samples driven out from the reactor at particular intervals have been analyzed in terms of BOD_5, and COD values. The changes in BOD_5, and COD values with ozonization time and ozone doses have been determined. It was found that removal of COD of aqueous layers in some amount is possible, very dependent on ozonization dose and ozonization time.

HARVESTING GLYCERIA MAXIMA: EFFECTS ON RHIZOME GROWTH AND STORAGE OF CARBOHYDRATES. K. Sundblad and K. Robertson (Linkoping University, Linkoping S-58183, SWEDEN).

This study aimed at elucidating the general effects of harvesting on the growth of *Glyceria maxima*. A simple experimental design including control, one harvest (plot I) and two harvests (plot II) was used in a natural stand. The N removal was higher in plot II than in plot I, 12.1 g N m^{-2} and 8.0 g N m^{-2} respectively, while the total harvest averaged 560 and 596 g dw m^{-2}. The biomass of young rhizomes in plot II was approximately half of that in control plot two and four weeks after harvest, implying a depressed rhizome growth. A reduced translocation of carbohydrates to the rhizomes in plot II, compared with control, was indicated by a lower concentration of soluble carbohydrates in rhizomes during four weeks after harvest. At the end of the growing season, the standing crop of rhizomes was 380 g m^{-2} in plot II and 725 g m^{-2} in control plot. In the subsequent spring, the N content of the grass was lower in harvested plots, whereas there was no significant differences in standing crop. This indicates that harvesting non-fertilized *Glyceria maxima* primarily affects the quality of the biomass, rather than the productivity. The implication of these results on estimation of harvest intervals, when using Glyceria maxima for wastewater treatment, are discussed.

NEW POTENTIAL USES FOR LIGNIN. D. Feldman, M. Lacasse and L. M. Beznaczuk (Concordia University, Montreal, Quebec, H3G 1M8 CANADA).

Lignin is a renewable resource, readily available from the pulp industry, which has the potential of being utilized as a basic raw material. In spite of many years of development effort however this potential has not been fully realized. In this paper, the present state of knowledge regarding the macromolecular structure of lignin is briefly described, and some new areas of application are reviewed; graft copolymers based on lignin, lignin - thermosetting polymer systems, and lignin - elastomer systems.

SOIL IMPROVEMENT OF RICE CROP FIELD THROUGH WATER HYACINTH COMPOST-A QUANTITATIVE STUDY. A. Gupta and R. S. Ambasht (Banaras Hindu University, Varanasi 221 005, INDIA).

Water hyacinth (Eichhornia crassipes L.) is a cosmopolitan aquatic weed of worst nuisance value. This study concerns composting this weed for six to eight weeks in the warm tropical climate of Varanasi (Bangalore method developed by IARI- New Delhi) and then its treatment in different dosages (5 t ha^{-1}, 10 t ha^{-1}, 15 t ha^{-1}) to paddy crop fields before seedling transplant was done. At fortnightly intervals, the soil physico-chemical properties and paddy crop growth performance were measured in compost treated and control (untreated) fields. The water holding capacity, cation exchange capacity, organic carbon, total N, available P, K, Ca, and Na contents showed considerable increase with increasing compost dosages. The growth performance of paddy plants also increased progressively with E. crassipes compost quantity in all aspects such as shoot length, leaf area index, chlorophyll and carotene contents, biomass of entire plants, organic matter production including grain yield. So far no adverse side effect of this compost has been noticed. E. crassipes which is a fast growing noxious weed has the ability to take in lots of nutrients from eutrophic and polluted water bodies, and if harvested, this could be a good source of reducing pollution load of ponds and lakes, eradicating weed menace, and increasing much needed rice production in the tropics.

AN APPROACH TOWARDS THE RECOVERY OF RESOURCES THROUGH AZOLLA CULTURE. D. P. Kushari, A. Sinhababu, and M. Chakravorty (Burdwan University, Burdwan 713 104, W. B., INDIA).

Azolla pinnata is an important agri-horticultural resource for biofertilizer, fodder, etc. In an 11 week growth period in sewage enriched water, the fresh biomass (g m^{-2}) increased from 5 to 148.00 during the six weeks. Though the growth still increased, the rate of increase was reduced. This trend of growth promotion was closely associated with the chlorophyll, N, P, and K contents of plant tissue. Plant cultured in tap water quickly deteriorated and turned into pinkish leading to senescence in contrast to sewage cultured plants. Along with the increased production, a change in water quality was remarkable. The available P concentration was reduced from 66.00 to 28.00 mg l^{-1}, the pH of the medium gradually changed to a more alkaline range and the dissolved oxygen concentration got depleted considerably from 13.49 to 8.00 mg L^{-1}, particularly after the development of a thick mat. The nutrients of leaf leachate of Pongamia pinnata after natural upwelling from deep soil strata promoted the growth of azolla. Leachate from juvenile leaves showed most effectiveness in undiluted condition while the leachate from mature and senescent leaves were most effective in four times diluted condition. Thus, the findings may be integrated to develop a model for the culture of azolla in sewage-enriched water under the canopy of a suitable tree for the recovery of resources from enriched water and leaf leachate.

PART V
SYSTEMS EVALUATION

NATURAL AND ARTIFICIAL WETLAND ECOSYSTEMS: ECOLOGICAL OPPORTUNITIES AND LIMITATIONS

C. J. Richardson and J. A. Davis
School of Forestry and Environmental Sciences
Duke University
Durham, North Carolina 27706

ABSTRACT

Available data suggest that natural and artificial wetlands offer some opportunity for removal or processing of certain nutrients, suspended solids, and BOD. Phosphorus removal efficiency, however, can quickly decrease from more than 90% to as low as 30% in a few years, depending on wetland type, loading rate, and season of application. The capabilities and weaknesses of both natural and artificial wetlands to filter, transform, and store nutrients are discussed along with an analysis of the mechanisms controlling nutrient cycling and retention of N and P. A series of management guidelines based on ecological principles are presented for the selection and potential utilization of natural wetlands for effluent treatment as well as the impacts of using wetland systems for wastewater.

Keywords: Nitrogen, phosphorus, impacts, wastewater, marsh, swamp.

INTRODUCTION

In the past two decades, interest has increased in the U.S. concerning discharge of treated municipal wastewater into wetlands, as evidenced by the large number of discharge and research sites in the U.S. (Richardson and Nichols, 1985), the unprecedented Florida regulations supporting this practice (Fla. Dept. of Environ. Regul., 1986) and a new EPA Handbook entitled Freshwater Wetlands for Wastewater Management (EPA, 1983).

In this paper, we have selected and analyzed data from representative research sites which includes the use of both natural and artificial wetlands for the discharge of treated municipal wastewater. The research in the U.S. has focused primarily on the use of natural ecosystems while European studies

Aquatic Plants for Water Treatment
and Resource Recovery
K.R. Reddy and W.H. Smith (Eds.)

ISBN 0-941463-00-1

have stressed the development of artificial wetlands. We have utilized specific case studies to address the following questions:

1. What is the institutional framework which controls the utilization of the natural wetlands as discharge sites for treated wastewater?
2. Which ecological processes enhance or limit the treatment of wastewater in terms of N and P removal?
3. Do wetlands efficiently remove N and P (case studies of natural wetlands)?
4. Are wetlands a sink for N and P?
5. What are the major wastewater impacts on wetlands?
6. What major types of artificial wetlands have been designed as treatment systems?
7. What are realistic loading criteria for natural wetlands?

Finally, we utilize the available information to develop general management guidelines. For an extensive ecological analysis of wetlands and wastewater, including management guidelines, see Richardson and Nichols (1985), and Godfrey et al. (1985).

BACKGROUND AND ANALYSES

Institutional Framework

Wetlands are considered to be surface waters of the United States, and are therefore under the jurisdiction of the Clean Water Act. A primary objective of the Act is to assure that designated in-stream uses and natural processes are maintained and protected. Wetlands in the U.S., therefore, cannot be degraded by a wastewater discharge. They must be considered as receiving systems, and not as treatment systems (Dodd et al., 1986).

The Clean Water Act (1972,1977) requires all states to develop a systems of classifications and standards to protect the best uses of their surface waters. Each discharger of wastes to surface waters is required to obtain a NPDES permit which specifies the allowable pollutant loading. Effluent limitations contained in NPDES permits are either technically and economically achievable, or water-quality based, reflecting treatment levels required to protect water quality standards. Many states have set technology based limits (secondary treatment) for wetland dischargers, because there is no proven method of predicting wastewater assimilation in wetlands as a basis for water-quality based limits.

Ecological Processes

Wetlands have key ecological features which have led many in the past 10 years to investigate their potential in providing advanced treatment of secondary wastewater (Godfrey et al., 1985).

Long retention times and an extensive amount of sediment surface area in contact with the flowing water provide for effective removal of particulates (e.g. Boto and Patrick, 1979). The sediment surfaces are also where most of the microbial activity affecting water quality occurs, including oxidation of organics and processing of nutrients (Chan et al., 1982). Wetlands are known to be capable of assimilating organic loadings which are an order of magnitude greater than nutrient loadings (EPA, 1985; Stowell et al., 1981). Although most research done across the country on wetlands discharge has focused on nutrient assimilation, treatment plant design and performance are typically based on the removal of O_2 demanding constituents. To date, research has indicated that impacts due to organic loadings are relatively small in wetlands receiving secondary wastewater (Bastian and Reed, 1979; Godfrey et al., 1985).

The impact and assimilation of nutrients, however, is of primary concern, both in the wetland and in downstream systems susceptible to eutrophication (Richardson, 1985). Nutrient removal is of immediate concern even though statewide standards often do not exist for many nutrient forms because nutrient additions may be the key to adverse ecological effects (i.e., eutrophication of receiving waters).

Nutrient Pathways. Though nutrient cycling has received a great deal of attention, flux rates for any specific element in any specific wetland cannot easily be predicted based on existing information, especially under high loading conditions. However, the hydrological characteristics of wetlands provide almost ideal conditions for a process such as denitrification.

Denitrification is performed by bacteria which use NO_3^- in place of free O_2 as an electron acceptor in anaerobic respiration. Organic C compounds, which are abundant in wetland sediments and surface waters, serve as proton donors. The end products of denitrification are N_2O and N_2, which are gases and consequently leave the wetland ecosystem permanently (Hemond, 1983; Richardson and Nichols, 1985). Under favorable temperature and pH, the main limit on the amount of N processed is simply the availability of the NO_3^- substrate. Denitrification can have an indirect effect on NH_4^+ levels. When O_2 is available, bacteria convert NH_4^+ to more oxidized forms, NO_2^- and NO_3^-. This occurs in surface layers of water or sediments exposed to the atmosphere. Nitrate produced in the aerobic layer can diffuse to deeper anaerobic layers where it can be denitrified. A lack of O_2 in the surface water, therefore, can limit denitrification (Gambrell and Patrick, 1978). This fact has important implications for design of wetlands discharge systems, as will be discussed later.

Phosphorus distribution has been studied in a range of wetland ecosystems, including riverine swamps (e.g. Mitsch et al., 1979; Kuenzler et al., 1980) and fens (Richardson and Marshall, 1986). The largest standing stock, by far, accounting for about 90% of total P in the ecosystem, is in the sediments (Richardson et al., 1976). Most of the remaining P is present in above- and belowground wood, while very small amounts are present in leaves, the litter layer, and in surface water. Significant internal storage of P, therefore, would primarily depend on accumulation in sediments and plant biomass. Nitrogen storage occurs primarily in these same compartments. Wetland plants take up significant amounts of N and P during the growing season but most of this is returned to the water column in the fall (Richardson and Nichols, 1985). The net effect of emergent vegetation is to transfer nutrients from the soil to the water (Nichols, 1983). Limited amounts of N and P are stored on a long-term basis in the wood of trees in riverine swamps, when compared to the soil compartment (Brinson et al., 1981).

Phosphate and NH_4^+ can be adsorbed to exchange sites in the soil (Richardson, 1985). Dierberg and Brezonik (1985) have shown in laboratory trials that swamp sediments are capable of immobilizing substantial amounts of P over many months of loading. Gradually, however, the soil binding sites become saturated, and release of nutrients can occur when surface water concentrations are low (Richardson and Marshall, 1986). The total amount of soil adsorption of these elements depends on soil composition and other factors such as redox potential and pH (Ponnamperuma, 1972). The magnitude of P retention capacity has been shown to vary considerably among wetland types (Richardson, 1985). For example, swamp sites in Maryland with mineral soils (high amorphous Al and Fe) were shown to have the highest P retention capacity, bogs with low Al and Fe retained little P.

Early Projects

The first pilot wetlands discharge projects to be thoroughly studied were at Houghton Lake, MI (Richardson et al., 1976; Kadlec et al., 1979; Tilton and Kadlec, 1979) and Gainesville, FL (Ewel and Odum, 1984). The considerable influence of these two projects is illustrated by the fact that EPA Region IV's first recommendations for loading criteria (EPA, 1985) are very heavily based on these studies. The issue which must be addressed as far as other states are concerned is the extent to which the results of these studies can be extrapolated to other wetland types. Close examination of design features and ecological characteristics of these projects makes it clear that only cautious inferences can be made.

Gainesville, FL (Cypress Dome). Pilot studies done at the University of Florida at Gainesville provide a good example demonstrating why even performance data from apparently pertinent pilot projects cannot simply be accepted at face value in trying to predict water quality in proposed wetlands discharge systems. These studies were conducted in a unique type of wetland common in Florida known as cypress domes. These ecosystems have much in common with flood plain swamps, but have one very significant difference relating to wastewater assimilation. Most of the flow in a cypress dome exists as groundwater after percolation through organic sediments and underlying sand and clay soils (Ewel and Odum, 1979). High nutrient removal efficiencies of cypress domes (Dierberg and Brezonik, 1984) reflect filtration and adsorption by clay soils. Reductions of N, P, and BOD were less than 33% in the surface waters of these domes, while reductions to background levels were found in groundwater outflow. In riverine swamps this removal mechanism cannot operate because outflow is typically 95% as surface runoff and only 5% as groundwater (Winner and Simmons, 1977).

Houghton Lake, MI (Fen). The second widely cited project involved the discharge of treated wastewater into a shrub/sedge (*Carex* spp.) fen in Houghton Lake, MI (Tilton and Kadlec, 1979). This project had an elaborate pretreatment system, which consisted of: two aeration ponds in series; a 11.7 ha holding pond with sufficient capacity for nine months storage (wastewater was only released during the summer); and another 189 m^3 (50,000) gallons holding pond to allow dechlorination and provide a storage buffer between the transfer pump at the sewage plant and the irrigation pump at the marsh edge (Kadlec et al., 1979). If funds were available to install this sort of system in many states, with a detention time of nine months, there would be little need for designation of a wetlands discharge because the water would likely meet the stringent effluent limits associated with a stream discharge. Also, the size of the wetland (700 ha) greatly exceeds the average acreage (16-20 ha) utilized for discharge sites. This along with a moving front of N and P (Kadlec, 1985; Richardson and Marshall, 1986), suggests that the lack of output of N and P is mainly related to size and not efficiency.

Tilton and Kadlec (1979) describe research in the summers of 1976 and 1977. In 1976, the treatment system was new, and very little N and P were actually released into the wetland (see Table 1). In this year a gated pipe was used to distribute the wastewater. Nutrient removal was quite good, with greater than 95% removal of NO_3+NO_2-N and TDP, but only 77% removal of NH_4. In 1977, pretreatment was not as thorough and a point discharge replaced the gated pipe. Nutrient removal efficiency dropped, and a lower hydraulic loading (11.7 cm wk^{-1} versus 21.8 cm wk^{-1}) was required to achieve comparable removal efficiency. Even with a lighter hydraulic load, P removal fell to 67%, while overall removal of all inorganic forms of N fell to 82%. After five years, a 19.6 ha test area was shown to have only a 37% P removal efficiency (Richardson, 1985).

Swamp Studies

Tar Swamp, NC (Tupelo/Cypress Swamp). A few wetlands discharge projects have utilized southeastern swamps. One small-scale, but highly informative, study was done in the coastal plain of North Carolina, in the Tar River floodplain in Pitt County (Brinson et al., 1981,1984).

The study was conducted in small enclosed chambers on the swamp floor, which received a variety of nutrient amendments over a 46 wk period. Removal efficiencies from this set of experiments are summarized in Table 1. The authors point out that the removal efficiency of 57% for NO_3^- is most likely a severe underestimate. Estimates of leakage from the chambers were based on P dynamics, a "conservative" element with no pathways to the atmosphere. While this estimate is accurate for P, NO_3^- additions were probably denitrified before leakage could occur. There was little evidence of NO_3^- accumulation in surface waters, indicating that the denitrification capacity of the system had not been approached. Therefore, a more accurate statement would be that all of the available NO_3^- in the chambers was denitrified. On the other hand, both NH_4^+ and P surface water concentrations responded to additions. The removal efficiency listed for P is most accurate, and that of NH_4^+ is somewhat low (because of the nitrification/-denitrification pathway).

Other important conclusions reached in Brinson's study concerned the seasonal dynamics of nutrient processing. Nitrate and P assimilation were basically unaffected by seasonal changes in the swamp. Ammonium levels, however, were influenced by seasonal changes. Ammonium concentrations in surface and sub-surface waters and the exchangeable fraction of sediment were well above controls, and surface water levels fluctuated a great deal with season. Optimal NH_4^+ assimilation was only attained if drydown occurred. Absence of a summer drydown period severely restricted the nitrification/denitrification sequence from occurring. If summer drydown did not occur with wastewater additions, NH_4^+ could accumulate to unacceptably high levels.

Wildwood, FL (Tupelo/Cypress). A full scale swamp discharge was studied in Wildwood, FL (Boyt et al., 1977). This town had released secondarily treated wastewater into a tupelo/cypress swamp for 20 years. The researchers report very effective removal of N and P based on concentration data, but reductions on a mass loading basis were only calculated for P. Phosphorus retention by these calculations was 87%. The important thing to note about this apparently successful project is that the hydraulic loading was very small - 0.2 cm wk (200 ha receiving 567 M^3 day (0.15 MGD). Nutrient mass loadings were also very small.

Pottsburg Creek, FL (Tupelo/Cypress Swamp). Pottsburg Creek Swamp near Jacksonville, Florida, was also the site of a 206 ha research project (Winchester and Emenheiser, 1983). Secondary effluent had been released to the swamp since 1967. In 1983, the discharge rate was 2,650 m^3 d^{-1} (0.7 MGD). The authors determined that an area of only 61 ha was effective in nutrient assimilation because of dry conditions. Areal loadings of N and P listed in Table 1 were reported in Knight et al. (1985). Nitrogen removal was effective at 87%, while 55% of the added P was retained.

TABLE 1. Loading data and removal efficiencies for wetland wastewater studies.

Project (yr of study) reference	Hydraulic loading ($cm\ wk^{-1}$)		Mass loadings (input/output, $g\ m^{-2}\ yr^{-1}$)		Percent retention	
	Wastewater	Other	Nitrogen	Phosphorus	Nitrogen	Phosphorus
Houghton Lake (1) MI (1976) Tilton and Kadlec (1979)	21.9	--	NO_3+NO_2 1.6/0.01 NH_4 0.3/0.07	TDP 1.7/0.09	NO_3+NO_2 99 NH_4 77	TDP 95
Houghton Lake, (2) MI (1977) Kadlec et al. (1979)	11.8	--	$NO_3+NO_2+NH_4$ 17.9/3.22	TDP 17.9/5.9	$NO_3+NO_2+NH_4$ 82	TDP 67
Tar Swamp, NC Brinson et al. (1981)	NA	NA	NO_3 48.6/20.9 NH_4 58.0/29.7	PO_4 49.4/21.8	NO_3 57** NH_4 49	PO_4 56
Wildwood, FL Boyt et al. (1977)	0.2	1.6	--	TP 0.9/0.11	--	TP 87
Pottsburg Creek, FL Knight et al. (1985)	2.1	5.6	TN 16.6/2.6	TP 8.4/3.7	TN 87	TP 55
Basin Swamp, FL Tuschall et al. (1981)	3.4	--	TN 13.8/4.3	TP 7.4/4.8	TN 69	TP 36

TABLE 1 (cont'd.)

Project (yr of study) reference	Hydraulic loading ($cm\ wk^{-1}$)		Mass loadings (input/output, $g\ m^{-2}\ yr^{-1}$)		Percent retention	
	Wastewater	Other	Nitrogen	Phosphorus	Nitrogen	Phosphorus
Reedy Creek, FL Knight et al. (1985)	13.6	--	TN 72.6/9.2	TP 16.8/16.8+	TN 87	TP net release
Waldo, FL Nessel (1978)	--	6.1	--	TP 4.3/2.1	--	TP 51
Bellaire, MI (1) (1980) Kadlec (1983)	2.3	7.1	DN 22.5/5.5	TP 4.2/1.5	DN 75	TP 65
Bellaire, MI (2) (1981) Kadlec (1981)	2.3	7.1	DN 10.3/2.0	TP 2.47/3.08	DN 81	TP -27
Eagle Lake, IA Davis et al. (1981)	NA	4.9	NO_3 20.9/2.98 NH_4 0.91/0.20	PO_4 0.35/0.28	NO_3 86 NH_4 78	TP 20

**This value is a severe underestimate because it assumes a leakage of 43% of the applied nitrate. In reality, nearly all of the added nitrate must have been denitrified.

Basin Swamp, FL (Cypress Strand). Basin Swamp is a cypress strand, a type of cypress wetland where water flows through the ecosystem during at least part of the year (Tuschall et al., 1981; Lemlich and Ewel, 1984). Basin Swamp has been receiving wastewater effluent from the City of Jasper since 1914. Since 1972, the effluent has received secondary treatment. The average daily flow 1,136 m^3 d^{-1} (0.3 MGD) contributes 21-61% of the total water volume of the flooded portion of the swamp. A total of 24 ha receives the wastewater. Nitrogen was effectively reduced to background levels. Less effective removal of P was attributed to the fact that P is not the limiting nutrient for plant growth in the swamp. In actual fact, soil P adsorption is probably the controlling factor for this system, not plant uptake.

Reedy Creek, FL (Cypress, Pine Swamp). Reedy Creek is a project that has been in operation at the Disney World complex for eight years. About 7,570 m^3 d^{-1} (2 MGD) of secondary effluent is discharged into a 41 ha, somewhat artificial wetland area consisting of cypress, pine and bay trees (Hyde et al., 1984). Nitrogen is assimilated in this system, but a net release of P occurs. This can be explained by the sandy substrate in the wetland (R. Kohl, per. comm.).

Waldo Cypress Strand, FL (Cypress Strand). The Waldo Strand had received effluent from a large community septic tank for over 40 years when Nessel (1978) reported a study of P cycling in the ecosystem. This cypress wetland is different from a typical southeastern riverine swamp in that infiltration into groundwater is a major route for water leaving the ecosystem. As discussed before, this infiltration facilitates soil removal, and explains the long term effectiveness of this wetland in terms of P assimilation.

Bellaire, MI (White Cedar Swamp). A forested palustrine wetland in Bellaire, MI, was the site of informative research by Kadlec (1983). Data from two consecutive years are given in Table 1 that illustrate an interesting trend in long term nutrient assimilation. Nitrogen removal in these two years was practically constant, actually showing a slight increase in the succeeding year. Phosphorus retention, however, shows a dramatic change on a mass loading basis in 1981 - an actual net release (Richardson, 1985). Phosphorus had been retained in the first five years of the study. This net release, after six years, demonstrates what has been termed "aging" of a wetland receiving wastewater (Kadlec, 1985). Phosphorus is primarily retained in wetlands by sorption to the soil. After six years, the Bellaire soils apparently became saturated with P and P was released. Laboratory studies of sorption capacity of the Bellaire soils also predicted that P retention would be low (Richardson, 1985).

It is interesting to note that this net release of P is not reflected in the concentration data (Table 1). This anomaly can be explained in the terms of a large dilution effect in this wetland (Kadlec, 1983). The author states that approximately 2/3 of the concentration reduction of the early years of this project can be attributed to simple dilution. This dilution effect distorts the meaning of performance data based solely on surface water concentrations, and is the reason that mass loadings are the focus of our analysis.

Eagle Lake, Iowa (Prairie Pothole). Finally, the results of research in a freshwater marsh (a prairie pothole) receiving agricultural runoff is given simply as further evidence of the trends indicated by the other studies (Davis et al., 1981). Ammonium and P loadings were low, yet 80% of the P passed through the ecosystem as compared to only 22% of the NH_4^+ (Table 1). Nitrate loading in this runoff was high, but outputs showed a decrease of 86%, probably due to high denitrification rates.

Wetlands: A Sink for N and P?

Results shown in Table 1 are very difficult to generalize upon in a quantitative way. Mass loadings are spread over a wide range. Hydraulic data are not always complete, and hydrology data do not always match well with the loading data. Unreported features of the water budget, such as percentage exiting the ecosystem as surface flow, further frustrates interpretation. Discharges to these wetlands have also been made for different lengths of time, a critical feature particularly for P retention (Richardson, 1985). Also, soil composition undoubtedly varies among these sites, and certainly influences both P and N adsorption.

Some qualitative conclusions, however, about wetland transformation, and assimilation of different forms of N and P can be reached based on this data set and the known nutrient pathways in wetlands discussed earlier. First, N removal for water is consistent and substantial over a range of loading rates. Removal efficiency is generally 75% or more on a mass loading basis (Figure 1a). Nitrate is always more efficiently processed than NH_4^+, when these forms are specified. Denitrification is the obvious explanation for NO_3^- transformation, achieving continued processing even after many years of wastewater addition.

Ammonium and P retention are both largely dependent on sorption to soils. Soils provide a finite and reversible sink for these forms, and retention efficiency is dependent on a complex of factors: water contact with the soil, soil composition, length of time of discharge, etc. Phosphorus retention is widely variable in these projects because of the variability in these factors among wetland types. For example, Richardson (1985) has shown that P retention is related directly to amorphous Al and Fe content and the amount of Al and Fe is low in bogs and high in some swamps. Figure 1b shows the % retention of P for each study. In contrast to N removal efficiency, P removal varies greatly, including two instances where a net release occurs. It has also

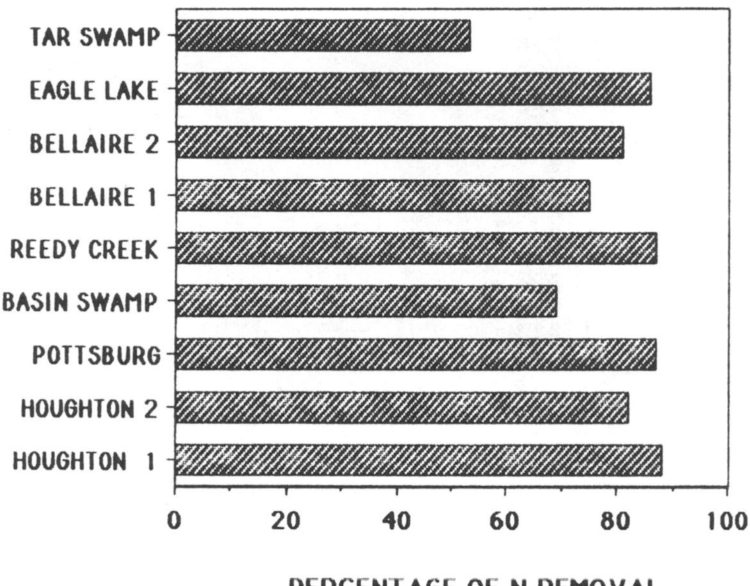

FIGURE 1a. Nitrogen removal efficiencies in selected pilot projects.

been shown that high initial removal rates of P by freshwater wetlands will be followed by large exports of P within a few years (Richardson, 1985). A graph (Figure 2a) showing log-transformed nitrogen mass inputs and outputs for the projects listed in Table 1. The data were log transformed to correct for the deviation of the distribution from normality. A line where input equals output is given as a visual reference. When values are below this line the wetland might be thought of as a sink or efficient transformer for N. Outputs above the equal line would mean that the wetland is a source of N. The regression line for these nine data sets has an R value of 0.96 and a p-value of 0.0002. This indicates that N output is directly and significantly related to N input.

An input/output graph for P based on the data in Table 1 is shown in Figure 2b. The R value of 0.88 and a p-value of 0.0007 for this regression also indicate a significant result, though the relationship between input and output for P is not as strong as it was for N. Furthermore, the regression line for the P data is much closer to being coincident with the line where input=output (Figure 2b), indicating that net removal of P is not as substantial as that for N. Several of the wetlands are a source for P.

These input/output analyses are based on limited amounts of data, so the quantitative relationships they suggest are not

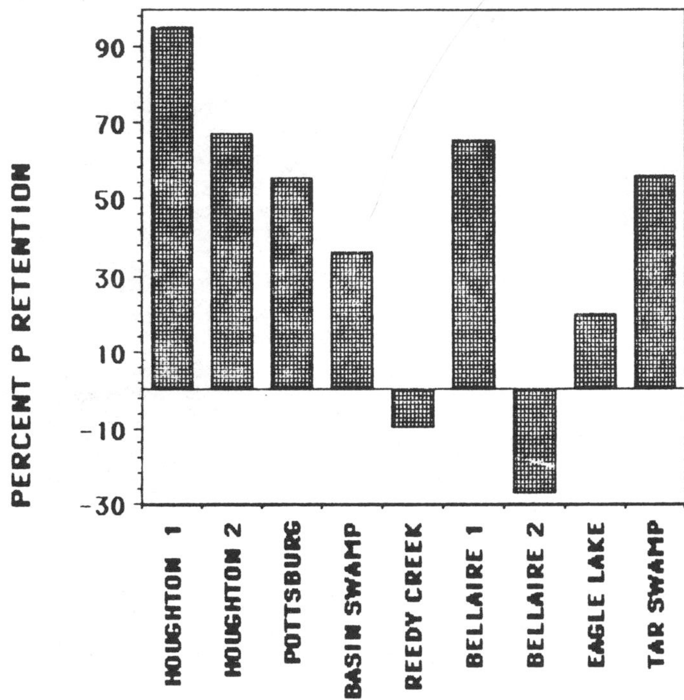

FIGURE 1b. Phosphorus retention efficiencies in selected projects.

necessarily absolute, but other authors have reported similar results for N and P. Kelly and Harwell (1985) presented a summary of input/output studies of N and P in wetland and terrestrial ecosystems and reached essentially the same conclusions reached here. Their review covered both "unaltered" ecosystems and ecosystems receiving artificial nutrient subsidies. Nitrogen additions to terrestrial and wetland ecosystems did not change the relationship between inputs and outputs seen in unfertilized ecosystems. Added N inputs were accompanied by corresponding increases in N outputs. A regression based on this admittedly limited data set, gave a general relationship in systems receiving nutrient additions: the output of N via water flow (runoff and groundwater) is expected to be about 43% of the input over an input range of 4 g m^{-2} yr^{-1} to 40 g m^{-2} yr^{-1}. Knight (1986) analyzed data on N mass removal rates at seven marsh and swamp discharge projects in Florida. A linear regression of N removal on input yielded an R^2 of 0.94 and a predicted removal efficiency of 78% over a range of average annual inputs from 14 to 82 g m^{-2} yr^{-1}. Knight (1986) concludes that removal of N by natural wetlands is not only very efficient but also very predictable.

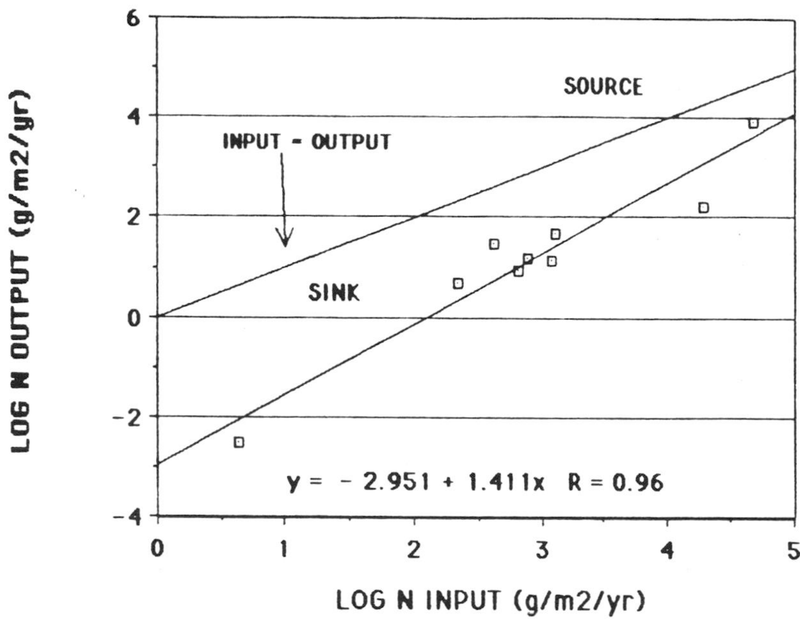

FIGURE 2a. Nitrogen mass loading: output as a function of input.

A similar analysis of P by Kelly and Harwell (1985) led to quite different conclusions. Terrestrial and wetland ecosystems do not behave similarly, nor is there a linear relationship for either type of ecosystem in terms of P output as a function of increasing P input. Terrestrial systems are much better at retaining P than wetlands. The authors also note broad variation in P retention in wetlands. A comparison of P retention efficiency among wetland types and a terrestrial ecosystem showed that wetlands do not conserve P as efficiently as terrestrial ecosystems (see Figure 3, in Richardson, 1985). Phosphorus removal at loading rates of 180 kg P ha^{-1} yr^{-1} is generally around 30% (Knight et al., 1985; Richardson and Nichols, 1985).

These studies indicate that natural wetlands can be expected to process significant amounts of N, and can be managed to assimilate even more. Phosphorus retention is highly variable, and highly dependent on the characteristics of the wetland ecosystem involved and the loading rates. Design and management of wetlands discharges can greatly influence N processing, but P retention will largely be determined by the natural ecological features (primarily soil type) of a chosen site. The consistency of N removal in natural wetlands is a reflection of the irreversible pathway by which removal takes place, and the uniformity of the denitrification process among various wetlands

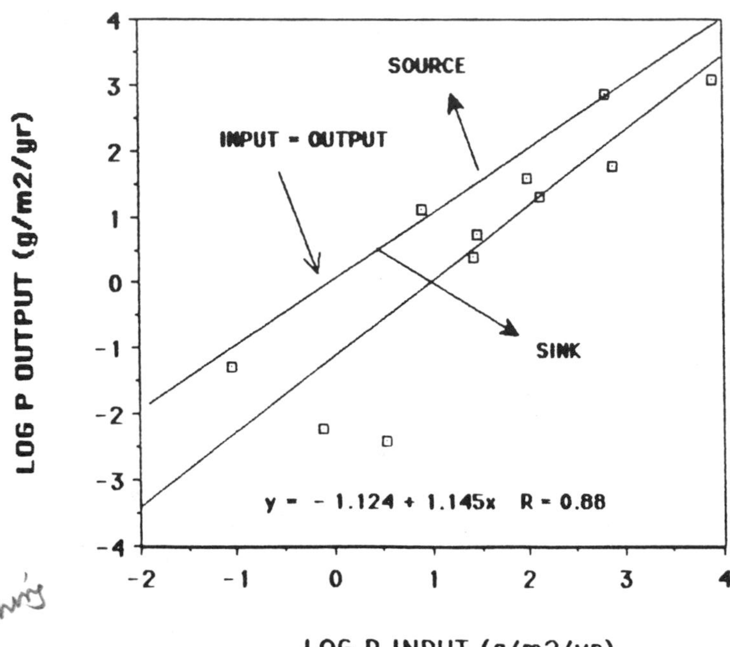

FIGURE 2b. Phosphorus mass loading: output as as a function of input.

and wetland types. The analyses do show that more data is needed, especially for predicting P retention capacity. Important factors that need to be accounted for in data collection on P retention capacity include mass loading, hydraulic loading, length of time of the discharge, soil type, soil adsorption capacity, and route of water outflow from the ecosystem.

Collectively, the data in Table 1 and the previous discussions, and literature (Brinson et al., 1981; Ewel and Odum, 1984; Godfrey et al., 1985; Richardson, 1985; Richardson and Marshall, 1986; Richardson and Nichols, 1985) suggest that wetland types are low level P sinks and efficiently process N. Wetlands often do contain vast stores of nutrients, i.e. N, P, K, and C but this has slowly been collected over hundreds, and in the case of peatlands, thousands of years. This reservoir of nutrients has often been misinterpreted to indicate that these ecosystems have high annual nutrient retention capacity. In actual fact, wetlands are often better transformers of nutrients (i.e. inorganic to organic forms or organic to gaseous states) than annual net retainers. They apparently have a high capacity to transform inorganic N to N_2 or N_2O.

Wastewater Impacts

Effective Area. The EPA Handbook (EPA, 1985) raises the issue of an "effective" wetland area, or zone of influence of applied wastewater. Even in an artificial wetland with a constant hydroperiod, areas near the discharge point or points are most influenced. Some areas may not come into contact with wastewater at all because of flow patterns.

Some wetlands, however, have a hydroperiod which complicates matters tremendously, ranging from complete drydown in summer to several feet of standing water in winter. The effective area of a discharge, therefore, can vary from a few constantly inundated hectares of heavy wastewater influence in summer, to a large area in winter when dilution is at its peak and the influence of the wastewater is minimal. The most severe impacts of a wetlands discharge could be expected in the summer zone of influence (SZI).

There are 3 main ways in which a wetland can be stressed by wastewater additions: 1) an increased in the duration of flooding; 2) contaminants present in the wastewater; and 3) mechanical impacts of wastewater distribution. Impacts caused in each of these ways would be most severe in the SZI, and decreased in severity with distance from this area. A summary of the ecological impacts due to wastewater discharge into wetlands is shown in Table 2.

TABLE 2. Summary of ecological impacts due to wastewater discharge into wetland ecosystems.

Stress caused by wastewater loading	Effects on wetland ecosystem
Increase in duration of flooding	. elimination of all but the most flood-tolerant plants
Wastewater contaminants	
Nutrients	. increased growth of dominant plants
	. increased growth of nuisance plants in surface waters
	- diurnal O_2 depletion
	. change in species composition in surface waters (toxic species)
	- reduced secondary productivity due to unpalatable primary production
	. NH_4^+ toxicity to aquatic animals
BOD	. inhibition of tree regeneration
	. alterations in the benthic community
Mechanical stress	. plant mortality (from spray irrigation)
	. erosion of substrate
	. channelization

Stress

Hydroperiod. Wetlands, by definition, exist because they are periodically flooded. Hydroperiod has been shown to be the fundamental natural factor determining distribution of wetland plant communities (Conner et al., 1981). They found that a regime of permanent flooding prevented recruitment of even the flood-tolerant species. In the SZI, the most significant hydrologic impact of wastewater addition would be the drastic alteration to a regime of year-round flooding. This would probably eliminate all but the most flood tolerant wetland species which would be intolerant of continual flooding, especially around the fringes of the wetland. Extended flooding duration will also severely restrict tree regeneration. Even cypress, which are extremely flood tolerant, are known to require a drawdown period for seedling germination (Deghi, 1984). Deghi (1984) suggests, however, that seedlings grown in nurseries can be planted in swamps to mitigate this problem in wetland discharges.

Wastewater Contaminants. Wastewater contaminants will also have their greatest impacts in the SZI. The SZI will, obviously, be centered around the wastewater discharge points. This area will be exposed to the highest concentrations of pollutants throughout the year, because some amount of processing will occur to lessen concentrations before water flows off of this area. Furthermore, in summer, the wastewater will be receiving little or no dilution. In fact, pollutants may become further concentrated as water is lost through evapotranspiration in these warm months (Wharton and Brinson, 1979).

Nutrients. Nitrogen and P in secondary effluent are known to have impacts on receiving wetlands. These impacts are not necessarily adverse. Since these elements are essential plant nutrients, one effect of wastewater discharge is to increase plant growth, from trees to phytoplankton (Table 2). However, the plant diversity of the impact area will decrease significantly (Richardson et al., 1976).

A number of studies have examined the effect of nutrient additions on the growth of dominant wetland plant species, often to determine if plant uptake is a significant retention pathway. Research has shown that plant uptake of N and P is relatively insignificant because nutrients are returned to the water column by litterfall and leaching (Nichols, 1983; Richardson and Marshall, 1986). Wastewater effluent has been shown to increase cypress growth rates (Nessel, 1978; Brown, 1981; Lemlich and Ewel, 1984).

Nutrient additions have also been shown to affect vegetative growth in surface waters, however, having profound effects on water quality and wetland food chains. For example, Ewel and Odum (1979) report that sewage additions to a cypress dome caused the development of a thick layer of duckweed, up to 5 cm thick in some areas and covering nearly the entire dome. This duckweed layer caused O_2 concentrations to drop to zero in the center of the dome. Most fish populations were eliminated, amphibian reproductive success was reduced, insect populations associated with the water's surface were altered, and numerous changes in the food chains associated with these organisms resulted. Duckweed proliferates under such conditions because of its remarkable ability to utilize increased concentrations of P. Duckweed can accumulate up to 2% of its dry weight as P (Ewel and Odum, 1979).

Stimulation of algal growth has also been demonstrated in several cases. At Houghton Lake, algal production was "massive" within 20 m of the outfall, even under relatively light nutrient loading (Kadlec, 1981). Attached algae were visible near the standpipe. Several species appeared in dense blooms in the application area, including *Microspora* spp. and *Cladophora* spp. which were rare in the wetland prior to wastewater discharge (Richardson and Schwegler, 1986). Significant increases in filamentous algal production and gross productivity occurred in the application area in comparison to control sites. At the end of the growing season, approximately 4.3 g N m^{-2} and 0.96 g P m^{-2} were immobilized in *Cladophora* algal biomass. Algal growth temporarily immobilized 3.0% of N and 1.0% of P added as sewage effluent (Richardson and Schwegler, 1986). At the end of the growing season these nutrients were returned to the wetland water column.

Kadlec (1983) describes similar surface water problems at the Bellaire wetland. "The surface waters in the vicinity of the discharge could not be regarded as pleasant. Fungi and blue green algae were prevalent on several occasions, and on others *Sphaerotilus* bacteria and mosquito larvae were observed." It is interesting to note that one year after discharge was ceased, conditions had already improved. This was attributed to the disappearance of standing water from an area that had been continually flooded.

Schwartz and Gruendling (1985) did a more precise study of the phytoplankton in the Stevens Brook wetland, a secondary effluent discharge site in Vermont. An eightfold increase in phytoplankton biomass was reported compared to a control wetland. Furthermore, species composition in the Stevens Brook wetland was predominantly green algae, euglenoids, and blue-green algae. The control wetland supported primarily diatoms. The authors make the important point that blue-green algae often seem unpalatable to consumers. The increase in gross primary production caused by increased nutrient inputs is not consumed, but simply passes through the wetland.

Stinner (1984) reported an interesting example of another situation in which the effects of nutrient additions on wetlands can be studied. For at least nine years, thousands of nesting wading birds have concentrated nutrient resources in the 84 ha Macks Island Rookery of Okefenokee Swamp. This has resulted in annual input of total P of 11 g m^{-2} yr^{-1}. A mat of *Lemna* spp., which is rare in most of Okefenokee Swamp has developed over the water surface in this area.

Algal blooms and duckweed layers adversely impact aquatic animal populations and alter food chains. Unfortunately, blooms can be expected in the immediate area of a discharge. Algal growth in a swamp discharge would be highest in the SZI, especially if NH_4^+ levels were allowed to build up. Ammonia is a preferred nutrient form for algae.

Ammonia is also known to be toxic to freshwater aquatic life (EPA, 1976). Toxicity is caused by the un-ionized form of NH_4^+. The concentration of un-ionized NH_3 in water is dependent on both pH and temperature. Normally, in wetland waters with acidic pH, relatively high levels of NH_3 can be tolerated by aquatic life. In the SZI, however, high concentrations of N and P would promote the growth of algae. This growth would be accompanied by a rise in pH, and lower concentrations of NH_3 would cause toxicity. In the permanently flooded area of a wetlands discharge, therefore, NH_3^+ toxicity is a potential hazard.

BOD: anaerobic stress. Anaerobic stress is normal in wetlands, but increased impacts due to prolonged anaerobic stress in wastewater discharges in wetlands have been documented (Godfrey et al., 1985). Increased organic loading and algal growth both contribute to O_2 depletion. Effects of this stress are realized in both plants and animal communities. Once again, these stresses would be greatest in the SZI, where dry down is prevented.

Anaerobic stress would accelerate impacts on flood intolerant trees in the SZI. Guntenspergen and Stearns (1985) point out that anaerobic environments involve a large respiratory cost to plants. Discharge of primary and raw wastewater in Basin Swamp (Lemlich and Ewel, 1984), as an example, decreased growth even in the extremely flood-tolerant pond cypress. Secondary effluent, however, enhanced growth over controls. The negative impacts of raw and primary effluent were attributed to extensive reducing conditions and formation of toxic compounds.

Extreme anaerobic conditions also would aggravate the effects of prolonged hydroperiod on tree regeneration in swamps. Anaerobic conditions have been shown to inhibit growth of both cypress (Deghi, 1984) and tupelo (Harms, 1973; Deghi, 1984) seedlings.

Another effect of extended anaerobic conditions would be alterations in the benthic community. Brightman (1984) reports a decrease in both abundance and diversity in a cypress dome. Schwartz and Gruendling (1985) obtained similar results in Stevens Brook. The increase in algal production caused by a wetlands discharge without a corresponding increase in benthic abundance, once again, suggests organic export from the wetland.

Mechanical stress. Mechanical stresses due to wastewater distribution in wetlands are seldom discussed. The only release methods tested in wetlands that appear in the literature are single point discharges, multiple point discharges, and spray irrigation. Both multiple point and spray discharges were used in the Bellaire wetland with disastrous consequences (Kadlec, 1983). Spray irrigation destroyed canopy and understory plants wherever the spray reached them. Multiple point discharges in succeeding years led to exposure of tree roots within the discharge area, presumably through erosional processes. Uprooting and death followed. After this "near-total destruction of the canopy," there was immediate invasion by weedy species, cattail and smartweed. Channelization, also undesirable (Kuenzler et al., 1977), can result from wastewater application. Channelization in a wetland discharge area would result in less efficient processing of pollutants, and would necessitate the use of larger wetland areas for treatment.

Artificial Wetlands

The utilization of artificial wetlands for water treatment is based, in principle, on optimizing the treatment features of natural wetland ecosystem processes (e.g. high denitrification rates) and minimizing such limitations as large acreage requirements, and low P removal, etc. In addition, artificial wetlands offer several additional advantages compared to natural wetlands including site selection, flexibility in sizing, fewer user conflicts with conservation goals, and most importantly, control over the hydraulic pathways and retention time. During the past two decades, a number of artificial wetland systems have been developed in both the U.S. (Small, 1976; Sloey et al., 1978; Bastian and Reed, 1979; Godfrey et al., 1985), and Europe (Seidel, 1976; Lewis et al., 1982; Greiner and de Jong, 1984). These systems utilize many types of aquatic and semi-aquatic vegetation in some form of pond, ditch or lagoon system. Many specific examples of these systems have been presented in other papers of this volume so we will not dwell on the specific design of any particular system but rather present an overall ecological analysis of the systems. Notably, in warmer areas of the world, floating aquatic plants like water hyacinth have been utilized to absorb nutrients and function as a biofiltration system (Bastian and Reed, 1979). Excellent examples of this approach are reported in this volume or are found in Finlayson et al. (1982), Wolverton and McDonald (1979), and Bastian and Reed (1979), and thus are not repeated here.

Artificial wetland treatment ecosystems generally follow one of the following 4 designs: 1) artificial marshes, 2) treatment ditches (sewage farm), 3) infiltration ponds, and 4) root zone beds. We have selected representative case examples of each of these treatment approaches and compared them in terms of general design, treatment capabilities and limitations.

Artificial Marshes. One of the most intensively studied artificial marsh ecosystems is in Listowel, Ontario, Canada.

Since 1979, a year-round experimental sewage treatment system consisting of five separate marsh systems has been utilized to test pretreatment guidelines (conventional lagoon, complete-mixed air) system configuration, hydraulic loading rates, detention times and the capacity of the artificial marshes to renovate wastewater (Wile et al., 1985; Herskowitz, 1986). A summary analysis of results from the two best marsh designs (channelized) covering the 1980-84 period shows an increased removal for marsh system 3 which received lagoon pre-treated influent (Table 3) (Ontario Ministry of the Environment, 1985). Variations in retention times, and loading rates, along with seasonal drops in dissolved O_2 and temperature, were responsible for the variability in the contaminant removal. The suggested reason for the increased efficiency in marsh 3 versus 4 (Table 4) is apparently related to the reduced influent concentrations from the lagoon. In general, large reductions in SS and BOD_5 were achieved on a year-round basis with summer removal being the highest. These data show a reduction in the soluble retention capacity during the four years which appeared to be related to cumulative phosphorus loadings (Figure 3). The decline was much higher in system 4 which received the highest P loading levels. The report also concludes that low summer sediment redox in system 3 (-36 to -319) and system 4 (-4 to -284) was measured in the sediments during the time of P release and this may have contributed to increased solubilization of P and the lack of retention (Patrick and Khalid, 1974). Total P retention averaged 46% and 79% in systems 3 and 4, respectively. Elevated NH_4^+ levels were reported in the winter and summer and the levels were sufficient to be toxic to aquatic life. Inadequate O_2 levels (summer) and the low water temperatures (winter) apparently reduced nitrification levels and prevented the transformations of NH_4^+ to N_2.

TABLE 3. Marsh System 3: Channelized marsh receiving lagoon effluent (Listowel, Canada) (4 year average, 1980-84) (Ontario Ministry of the Environment, 1985).

Constituent	4 Yr Average		Removal	
	Influent	Effluent	Average	Annual range
	--------mg L^{-1}--------		-----------%-----------	
SS	22.8	9.2	60.5	(40 to 75)
BOD_5	19.6	7.6	59.4	(56 to 63)
TP	1.0	0.5	46.0	(39 to 53)
SRP	0.37	0.26	9.3	(-12 to 59)
TKN	12.0	6.1	43.1	(32 to 59)
NO_3+NO_2	0.25	0.23	28.9	(12 to 53)
NH_3	7.2	3.8	38.8	(31 to 51)
Un-NH_3	0.13	0.01		
H_2S	1.8	1.0		
Un-H_2S	1.31	0.65		

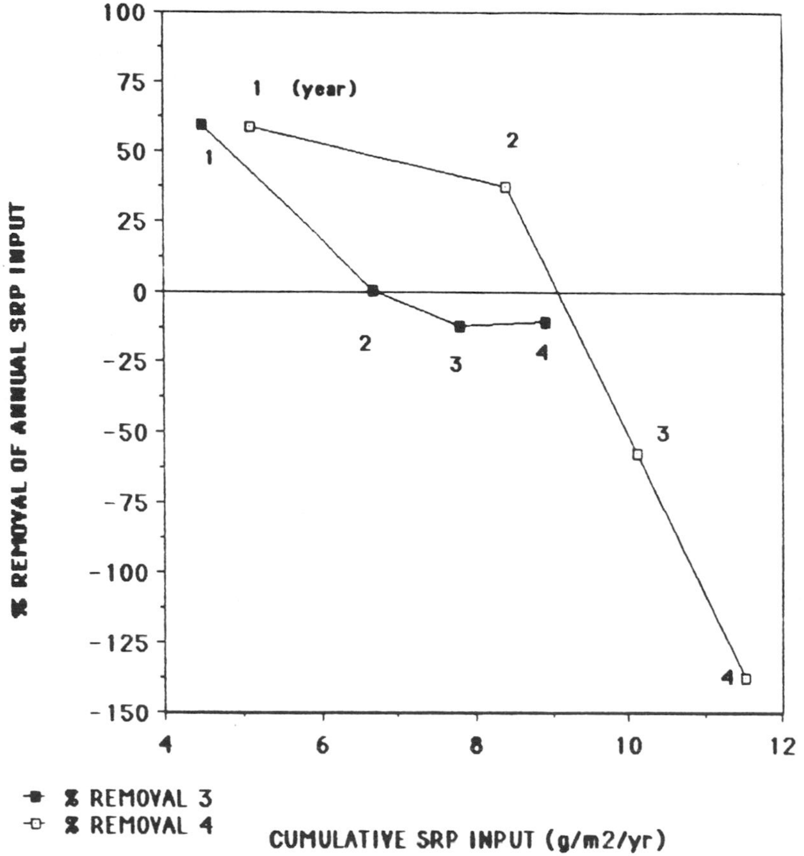

FIGURE 3. Cumulative soluble P loadings and percent removal (Ontario Ministry of the Environment, 1985).

The percentage of N and P removed by harvesting from 1982-84 in the Typha, even with multiple harvests, ranged from 9.6% to 3.8% for P and 9.1% to 5.7% for N. This low removal of nutrients (on average 6%) does not seem to justify the design and harvest costs and certainly demonstrates that aboveground plant assimilation is not a primary contributor to nutrient removal in these marsh systems. This has also been shown to be the case for natural wetland ecosystems (Richardson and Marshall, 1986). Plants apparently provide a favorable environment for bacterial assimilation and some degree of soil aeration. The degree of soil adsorption and bacterial activity are limited by hydraulic conductivity and aeration (Kickuth, 1984).

Results from this study lead the researchers to conclude that pre-treatment utilizing a partial-facultative aeration cell must be done so as to reduce BOD, SS and P input to 1.0 mg L^{-1} TP.

TABLE 4. Marsh System 4: Channelized marsh receiving aeration cell effluent (Listowel, Canada) (4 year average, 1980-84) (Ontario Ministry of the Environment, 1985).

Constituent	4 Yr Average Influent	4 Yr Average Effluent	Removal Average	Removal Annual range
	mg L^{-1}		%	
SS	111.1	8.0	92.6	(90 to 94)
BOD_5	56.3	9.6	81.6	(78 to 88)
TP	3.2	0.6	79.1	(76 to 84)
SRP	0.40	0.34	-24.8	(-138 to 59)
TKN	18.7	8.7	47.9	(41 to 55)
NO_3+NO_2	0.38	0.21	58.9	(41 to 71)
NH_3	8.6	6.1	22.5	(5 to 35)
Un-NH_3	0.07	0.02		
H_2S	0.2	1.3		
Un-H_2S	0.13	0.81		

They recommended an aeration cell 3 to 4 m in depth with an average retention time of 30 d to reduce NH_4^+ and H_2S levels. For a detailed analyses of this site see Herskowitz (1987).

Treatment Ditches (Sewage Farms) and Infiltration Ponds

Treatment ditch and infiltration pond research in the Flevoland polder and in the Lauwersmeer area of the Netherlands has focused on the use of these artificial wetlands for the treatment of low levels of wastewater primarily from recreation sites during the summer (Greiner and de Jong, 1984). Sewage farms are usually planted with reeds or bulrushes and infiltration ponds only with reeds. Reeds can maintain themselves under both wet (water depth 0.5 m) and dry conditions and develop deep roots and a large bottom surface area. Bulrushes are not able to compete with other aquatic plants (e.g. cattail) and the competitors must be removed periodically.

The treatment design for these systems is based on the following principles: a) reeds form a substrate for micro-organisms which can breakdown pollutants (20-40 reed or bulrush stems per m^2), b) absorption of nutrients by microorganism and plants, and c) reeds promote soil permeability and ensure air supply to and in the soil (Greiner and de Jong, 1984). A schematic view of a treatment ditch system is given in Figure 4. The ditches are 0.2 to 0.4 m deep (water level) and are 3 m in width. On average, about 1 ha of surface area is needed to treat 100 m^3. A combination sewage farm/infiltration pond consisting of a preliminary settling distribution ditch system and four infiltration ponds was tested during the 1970's (Figure 5). The soil was a medium-fine sand with 1.3% sludge, Fe of 2.9 mg g^{-1}, Al and Ca content of 2.7 and 11.5 mg g^{-1} dry matter, respectively.

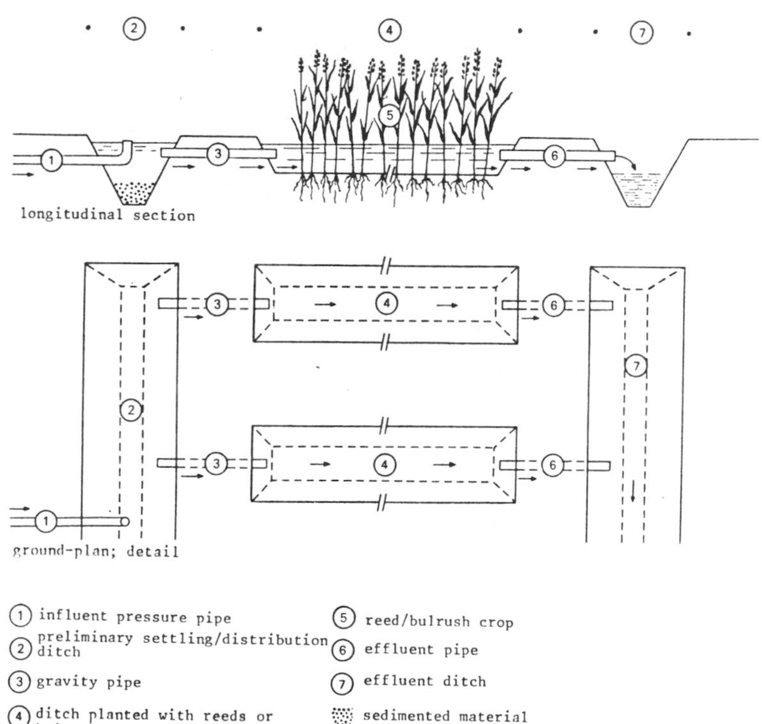

FIGURE 4. Schematic ground-plan and longitudinal section of a planted sewage farm (from Greiner and de Jong, 1984).

The permeability of the profile was 2 to 3 m per 24 h period. The wastewater was discharged in the preliminary settling/distribution ditches. After settling, the water was fed every 3 or 4 days into one of the compartments. Because of the low loading rates and the fact that there are four ponds, each pond is dry for a period of 10 to 11 days. The wastewater flows through the soil filter to a drainage system 0.55 m beneath the ground to a ring drain. From this drain some of the water is recirculated to the settling ditches by windmill if needed or is released if water quality is adequate.

The purification of wastewater in terms of BOD, COD, total N and P as a function of residence time is shown in Figure 6. Net purification is the gross purification less the seepage of 9 mm per 24 h period (Greiner and de Jong, 1984). A residence time of six days or more results in a 96% reduction in suspended soils

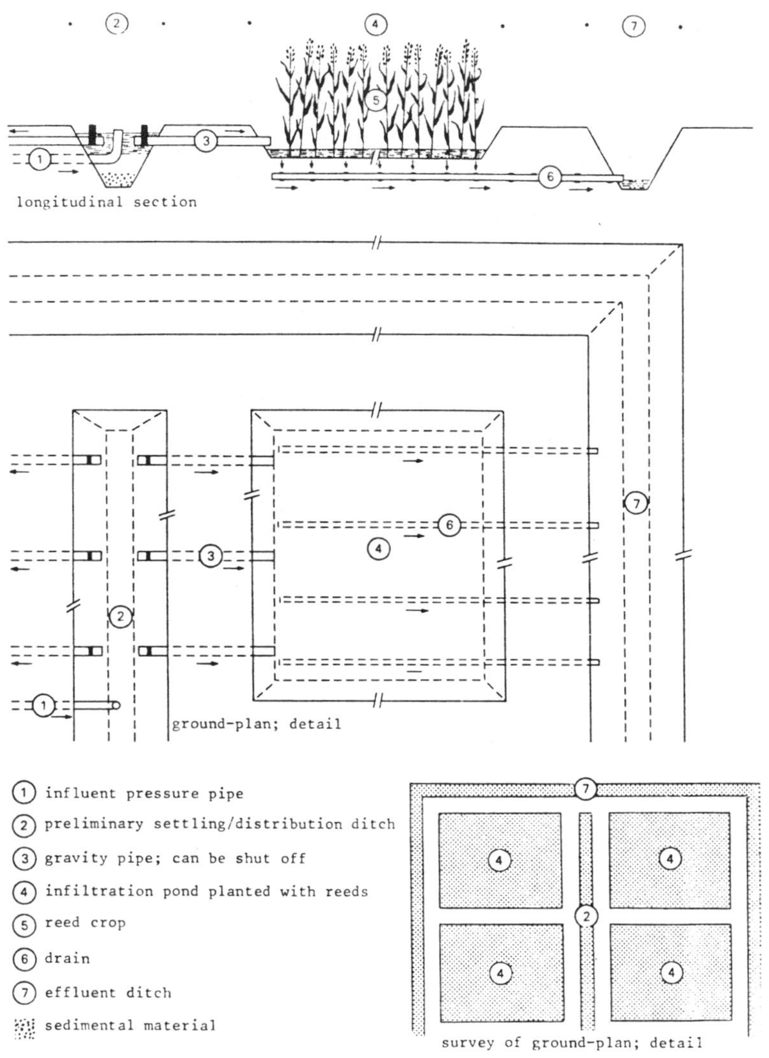

FIGURE 5. Schematic ground-plan and longitudinal section of a planted infiltration pond (from Greiner and de Jong, 1984).

(e.g. 260 mg L^{-1} influent versus 9.8 mg L^{-1} effluent). The bacteriological water quality is reported to reach a 99.9% purification level (Greiner and de Jong, 1984).

The extent of N and P removal was reported to decrease during the latter part of the summer as plant uptake decreased (Greiner

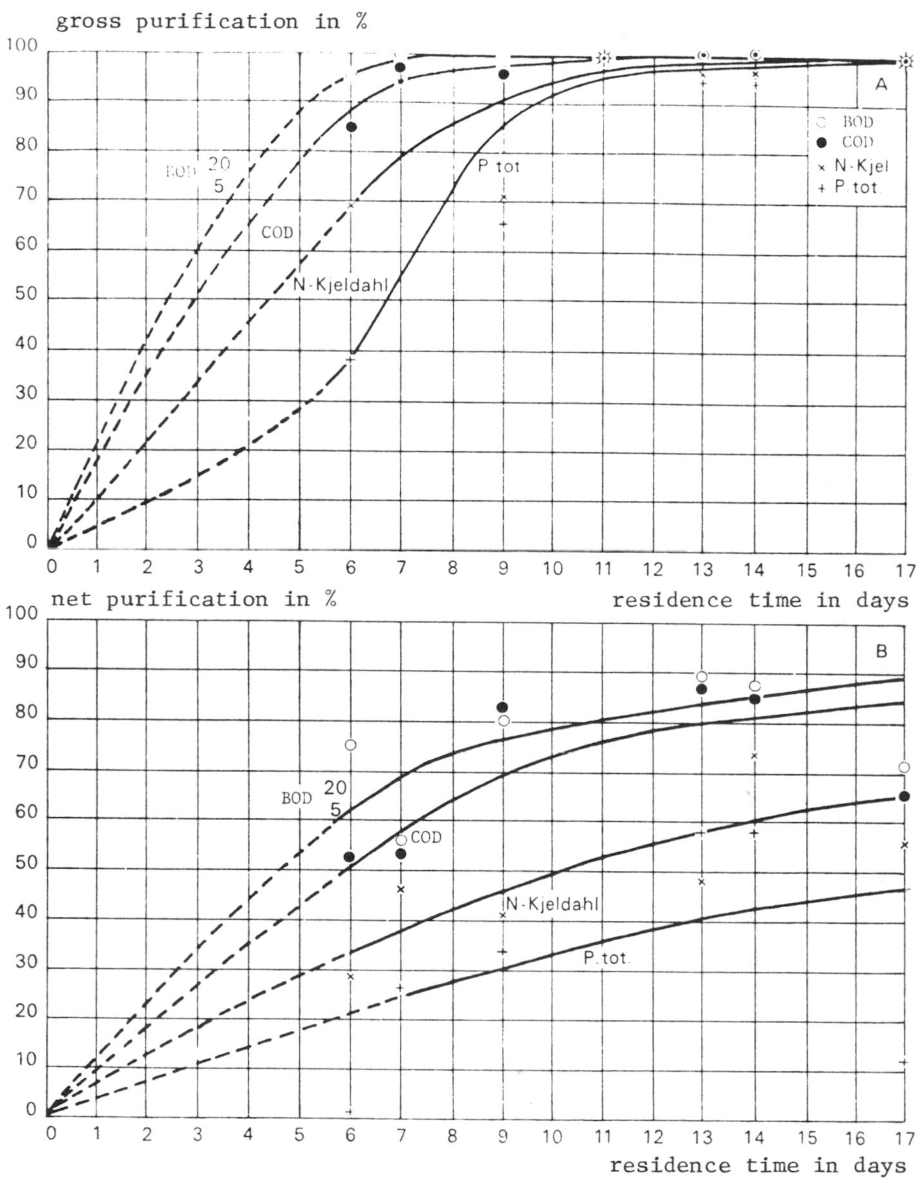

FIGURE 6. Percentage purification with regard to BOD, COD, total phosphorus (as PO_4) and nitrogen (as N) as a function of the residence time in an experimental pond planted with bulrushes (from Greiner and de Jong, 1984).

and de Jong, 1984). They noted that a 3 to 5 yr old crop of bulrushes can sequester 300 to 500 kg N ha^{-1} and 50 to 75 kg P ha^{-1} during the growing season. Harvesting of above-ground parts can result in the removal of 150 to 300 kg ha^{-1} of N and 20 to 40 kg ha^{-1} of P. Results from an experimental pond in 1969 show that 29% of the introduced N and 24% of the P loading can be removed by harvesting above-ground plants (Table 5). About one-third of both N and P are not accounted for in the plants or outflow. It is suggested that the difference is stored in microorganisms and bottom sediments or in the case of N, denitrification released a large portion of N to the atmosphere. No measurements of N release or N and P storage in the soil were reported. Treatment results for a sewage farm/infiltration pond for the period from 1976 to 1980 showed that the % reduction for ammonium-N was 91% (influent 65 mg L^{-1}: effluent 5.6 mg L^{-1}), Kjeldahl-N was 91% (influent 94 mg L^{-1}: effluent 10.4 mg L^{-1}). BOD 98% (influent 317 mg L^{-1}: effluent 7 mg L^{-1}) and total P 75% (influent 20.7 mg L^{-1}: effluent 5.1 mg L^{-1}) (Greiner and de Jong, 1984).

These data suggest that this type of system if properly designed and not overloaded can significantly remove or process N and BOD as well as remove a large mass of P.

Root Zone Method

The Root Zone Method (RZM) for wastewater treatment was developed by Reinhold Kickuth in West Germany and is described in detail by Cooper and Boon (1987). The system is engineered to maximize microorganism activity in the rhizosphere. Prepared soil is used as a rooting/filtration/adsorption system and the soil beneath is impermeable (see Figure 1, Cooper and Boon, 1987). The key feature reported for this system is that *Phragmites* rhizomes create a porous soil structure and high hydraulic conductivity. This point, however, has been disputed by a number of researchers in West Germany (Bucksteeg, 1985). They claim that the high conductivity reported by Kickuth's RZM is off by an order of magnitude and that this increases the required treatment area to 11 to 33 m^2 per population equivalent not the 2 to 3 reported by Kickuth (1984). They also question nutrient retention capacity,

TABLE 5. Nutrient removal (kg ha^{-1}) from an experimental bulrush and reed pond in Holland (Greiner and de Jong, 1984).

	Kjeldahl-N	%	Total P	%
Loading	1004	100	167	100
Outflow	128	13	32	19
Bulrush	290†,220‡	29,22	40,40	24,24
Difference	366	36	55	33

†aboveground, ‡belowground.

especially P, and suggest that a realistic analysis of this system has never been done.

The first pilot plant for the RZM was in the community Liebengurg-Othfresen near Goslar (Winter, 1985). The area was a wetlands habitat as of 1962 and was previously supplied with iron ore mine waste. The site was a loamy soil with a clay substrate. In 1981, an additional RZM system was constructed with an area of 1.5 ha for a 5,000 population equivalent. The removal capacity by the RZM at Othfresen in 1977 is shown in Table 6. The 1977 removal rates for all the variables was in excess of 87% but an overloaded state in 1983 resulted in reduced N removal (Winter, 1985).

It is difficult to assess the efficiency of the RZM due to the lack of published data. This system appears to have great promise but the actual design criteria and costs relative to a standard treatment system have not been worked out. The proposed research presented by Cooper and Boon (1987) and the current work in Denmark should provide answers in the next few years.

Loading Guidelines

Critical features of a wetlands discharge are assimilation and processing of N and P (key constituents of secondary effluent) and prevention of adverse impacts on receiving ecosystems. Discussion of discharge loading limits for wetlands have been based primarily on nutrient assimilation, because adverse impacts are not expected at these loadings. Stresses on wetlands receiving effluent have not been thoroughly studied, however, especially on a long-term basis. Possible ecological impacts would be related not only to average annual loadings of water and nutrients, but also depend heavily on distribution methods and disruption of natural seasonal variation.

The great diversity of wetland types makes the idea of generic wastewater loading limits inappropriate. This diversity was evident even in the limited sample of projects reviewed in this paper. The pressing need for discharge guidelines has forced some scientists to make cautious recommendations based on the data that has been collected. Some of the published guidelines, the

TABLE 6. Removal capacity by the Root Zone Method at Othfresen, 1977 (Winter, 1985).

Constituent	Inflow	Outflow	%
--mg L^{-1}--			
BOD_5	488 ± 133	18 ± 7	96
COD	377 ± 45	44 ± 7	87
TN	82 ± 17	5 ± 2	94
TP	16.3 ± 3.0	0.3 ± 0.3	98

source, the recommended loading, and a description of the basis of each recommendation are presented in Table 7. The rates presented here have all been converted to cm wk^{-1} for direct comparison.

EPA (1985) suggests two loading rates as a conservative basis for initiating system design. One of these is 2.54 cm wk^{-1}, the rate used in the cypress domes at Gainesville. As mentioned above, this rate was dictated by mechanical reasons for sludge buildup near the single outfall into the cypress dome, not reasons relating to nutrient removal.

The other suggested rate is 1.5 cm wk^{-1}, equivalent to the waste produced by 60 people spread over 1 ha. This rate is suggested in Nichols (1983) and Richardson and Nichols (1985) for 50% removal of N and P. This estimate was based on a very limited data set including one swamp, a cypress dome, and seven other wetlands including two fens, four marshes and an Irish bog.

Other loading guidelines were published a few years ago, beginning with Kadlec and Tilton (1979). They recommended a rate of 2.5 cm wk^{-1}, based on consideration of natural precipitation input into typical natural wetlands and their capacity for wastewater assimilation. They point out that waste assimilation depends on the level of contamination of incoming water coupled with residence time and contact between the added wastewater and the wetland substrate.

Tchobanoglous and Culp (1980) reviewed available literature and remarked on the great confusion that exists in the reporting of performance data. In most cases, the data are so confounded in a statistical sense that little or no usable information can be derived. Also, there is no standardization regarding the basis on which performance data are reported. Further, they add that data for most of the natural systems are extremely site specific and should not be generalized. The authors reported that reliable prediction of natural wetland treatment of secondary effluent is not possible, and concluded that 12-24 ha are needed for removal of solids and organics, but noted that larger areas may be required for N and P removal. Because wetland climatology, hydrology, geology and biology are so site specific they believe that pilot studies at each location may be necessary to establish proper loading rates.

Stowell et al. (1981) discuss design of artificial treatment systems utilizing aquatic plants. These are highly managed, unnatural systems. The performance data for individual parameters are instructive, however, as indications of optimal removal efficiencies in wetlands.

The general consensus that 2.5 cm wk^{-1} as a conservative basis for design is at least not contradicted by the data in Table 1. Clearly, 2.5 cm wk^{-1} was not determined precisely from data. The projects with 2.5 cm wk^{-1} loadings - Pottsburg Creek, Basin Swamp, and Bellaire - show the same pattern seen over the entire range of loading rates. Nitrogen is removed in each case, and P retention is erratic, and decreases with time. The best reason

TABLE 7. Summary of published guidelines for hydraulic loading of wastewater into wetlands.

Author	Loading rate	Rationale
Kadlec & Tilton (1979)	2.5 cm wk^{-1}	"2.5 cm or so per week...is not unreasonable from the viewpoint of the natural precipitation input to a typical wetland." Will provide adequate treatment of nutrients and suspended solids.
Richardson & Nichols (1985)	0.76-2.90 cm wk^{-1} 16-150 cm yr^{-1}	Estimated from (Nichols, 1983) (for 50% to 75% removal of N & P) and (Kadlec & Tilton, 1979)
Stowell et al. (1981)	BOD 261 cm wk (112 kg ha^{-1})	Based on BOD removal from secondary effluent (30 mg L^{-1}) and 80% removal efficiency. Artificial systems.
	N 26.2 cm wk^{-1} (11.2 kg ha^{-1})	Based on N removal from secondary effluent (30 mg L^{-1}). Preliminary guideline.
	P <20.9 cm wk^{-1} (2.2 kg ha^{-1})	Based on P removal from secondary effluent (7.7 mg L^{-1} P removal rates decrease in winter months when releases of P to the wastewater are not uncommon.
Tchobanoglous (1980)	10.9-21.8 cm wk^{-1} (12-24 ha·3785 m^3 d^{-1})	Based on literature & Culp review. "Even with these quantities of land, N & P removal is uncertain and may require larger areas of significant removal.
EPA (1985)	2.5 cm wk^{-1} or 1.5 cm wk^{-1} (60 people ha^{-1})	"Two hydraulic loading rates governing wastewater flows to wetlands often are used as guidelines. One is the application rate of 2.5 cm wk^{-1} over the area of the wetland and the other is 60 people ha^{-1}. The latter...is intended more as a determinant for nutrient removal; nonetheless, it addresses hydraulic loading."

for using this loading rate is that it doesn't call for unrealistically large tracts of wetland for wetlands discharge. At a 2.5 cm wk^{-1} loading, 103 ha are required for a 3785 m^3 d^{-1} discharge. A loading of 5 cm wk^{-1} would, of course, halve the land requirement.

CONCLUSIONS

The literature and the information in this paper suggests that wetland designs for wastewater discharge should be conservative. There is a tremendous economic incentive to invest as little money as possible into wetlands discharge systems because of the savings that can be realized relative to other means of advanced treatment. There is still too little data from natural systems, however, to allow confident predictions of the performance of wetlands in terms of treatment or the effects of wastewater on receiving ecosystems. Exploitation of this untested technology could lead to disastrous results in ecosystems where recovery from long-term damage could take many decades (Kadlec, 1985; Godfrey et al., 1985; Richardson and Nichols, 1985). The uncertainty associated with this technology should be taken into account in the design of wetlands discharge systems. For these reasons, artificial wetlands may have greater potential than natural wetlands as treatment systems.

In summary we can conclude that:

1. Wetland types differ greatly in their ability to store and release nutrients.
2. Wetlands can be a source or sink depending on the nutrient and season.
3. Wetlands are an efficient filter for suspended solids and organic matter.
4. Wetlands are efficient transformers for N.
5. Soil adsorption chemistry (Al, Fe) and microbial activity are the key to storing P.
6. Many wetlands do not have the potential for high levels of nutrient storage.
7. Wetland discharge systems should be designed to utilize conservative loading rates, adjusted to seasonal variations in wetland hydrology.
8. Wetlands that are threatened or endangered ecosystems should not be used for wastewater discharge.
9. Monitoring of wetland discharges should be extensive and include biological information, hydrologic data, and water nutrient budgets.
10. Artificial wetlands may have greater potential than natural wetlands as treatment systems, because they have,
    a. lower area requirements.
    b. better hydrologic control.
    c. good removal of BOD, SS and N,
    d. low P removal capacity, unless water infiltrates soil and aeration is increased, but

e. annual plant storage of nutrients is low due to dieback and mineralization.

11. Pre-treatment of effluent is often required.
    a. Al (alum) or Fe to remove P.
    b. aeration to decrease BOD, SS
12. Research is needed on:
    a. loading designs.
    b. soil infiltration and nutrient sorption capacity.
    c. root zone methodology.
    d. cumulative loading impacts.

REFERENCES

Bastian, R. K., and S. C. Reed. 1979. Aquaculture systems for wastewater treatment. U.S. EPA 430/90-80-006 Environmental Protection Agency, Washington, DC. 485 pp.

Boto, K. R., and W. H. Patrick, Jr. 1979. Role of wetlands in the removal of suspended sediments. p. 479-489. In P. E. Greeson, J. R. Clark, and J. E. Clark (ed.) Wetland Functions and Values: The State of Our Understanding. AWRA Tech. Pub. No. TPS 79-2, Minneapolis, MN.

Boyt, F. L., S. E. Bayley, and J. Zoltek, Jr. 1977. Removal of nutrients from treated municipal wastewater by wetland vegetation. J. Water Pollut. Control Fed. 49:789-799.

Brightman, R. S. 1984. Benthic macroinvertebrate response to secondarily treated wastewater in north-central Florida cypress domes. pp. 186-196. In K. C. Ewel and H. T. Odum (ed.) Cypress Swamps. Univ. of Florida Press, Gainesville, FL.

Brinson, M. M., H. D. Bradshaw, and E. S. Kane. 1981. Nitrogen cycling and assimilative capacity of nitrogen and phosphorus by riverine wetland forests. Report No. 167, Water Resources Research Institute of the University of North Carolina, Raleigh, NC.

Brinson, M. M., H. D. Bradshaw, and E. S. Kane. 1984. Nutrient assimilative capacity of an alluvial floodplain swamp. J. Appl. Ecol. 21:1041-1057.

Brinson, M. M., H. D. Bradshaw, R. N. Holmes, and J. B. Elkins, Jr. 1980. Litterfall, stemflow, and throughfall nutrient fluxes in an alluvial swamp forest. Ecology 61:827-835.

Brown, S. 1981. A comparison of the structure, primary productivity and transpiration of cypress ecosystems in Florida. Ecological Monographs 51:403-427.

Bucksteeg, K. 1985. Initial experience of the root zone process in Bavaria. In Symposium at The Technical University of Darmstadt.

Chan, E., T. A. Bursztynsky, N. Hanzsche, and Y. J. Litwin. 1982. The use of wetlands for water pollution control. EPA 600/2-82-086. USEPA, Municipal Environmental Research Laboratory, Cincinnati, OH.

Conner, W. H., J. G. Gosselink, and R. T. Parrondo. 1981. Comparison of the vegetation of three Louisiana swamp sites with different flooding regimes. Amer. J. Bot. 68:320-331.

Cooper, P. F., and A. G. Boon. 1987. The use of Phragmites for wastewater treatment by the root zone method: The UK approach. In K. R. Reddy and W. H. Smith (ed.) Aquatic Plants for Water Treatment and Resource Recovery. Magnolia Publishing Inc., Orlando, FL.

Davis, C. B., J. L. Baker, A. G. van der Valk, and C. E. Beer. 1981. Prairie pothole marshes as traps for nitrogen and phosphorus in agricultural runoff. In B. Richardson (ed.) Selected Processings of the Midwest Conference on Wetland Values and Management. Freshwater Society, Navarre, MN.

Deghi, G. S. 1984. Seedling survival and growth rates in experimental cypress domes. p. 141-144. In K. C. Ewel and H. T. Odum (ed.) Cypress Swamps. University of Florida Press, Gainesville, FL.

Dierberg, F. E., and P. L. Brezonik. 1984. The effect of wastewater on the surface water and groundwater quality of cypress domes. p. 83-101. In K. C. Ewel and H. T. Odum (ed.) Cypress Swamps. University of Florida Press, Gainesville, FL.

Dierberg, F. E., and P. L. Brezonik. 1985. Nitrogen and phosphorus removal by cypress swamp sediments. Water, Air, and Soil Pollut. 24:207-213.

Dodd, R. C., J. A. Davis, and M. Kerr. 1986. The use of wetlands for wastewater management: An update. Presented at 1986 Triangle Conference on Environmental Technology, University of North Carolina, Chapel Hill.

Environmental Protection Agency. 1976. Quality Criteria for Water. USEPA, Washington, DC.

Environmental Protection Agency. 1983. Freshwater wetlands for wastewater management: Phase I report. EPA 904/10-84-128. Region IV, Atlanta, GA.

Environmental Protection Agency. 1985. Freshwater wetlands for wastewater management handbook. EPA 904/9-85-135. Region IV, Atlanta, GA.

Ewel, K. C., and H. T. Odum. 1979. Cypress domes: Nature's tertiary treatment filters. p. 103-114. In W. E. Sopper and S. V. Kerr (ed.) Utilization of Municipal Sewage Effluent and Sludge on Forest and Disturbed Land. Penn State Univ. Press, University Park, PA.

Ewel, K. C., and H. T. Odum. 1984. Cypress Swamps. University of Florida Press, Gainesville, Florida.

Finlayson, C. M., J. P. Farell, J. D. Griffiths. 1982. Treatment of sewage effluent using the water fern Salvinia. Water Res. Found. of Aust. Tech. Rep. No. 57.

Florida Department of Environmental Regulation. 1986. Notice of proposed rulemaking: Rule Chapter 17-6, Wastewater Facilities. Florida Administrative Weekly, January 3, 1986. Tallahassee, FL.

Gambrell, R. P., and W. H. Patrick, Jr. 1978. Chemical and microbiological properties of anaerobic soils and sediments. p. 375-423. In D. D. Hook and R. M. M. Crawford (ed.) Plant Life in Anaerobic Environments. Ann Arbor Sci. Pub. Inc., Ann Arbor, MI.

Godfrey, P. J., E. R. Kaynor, S. Pelczarski, and J. Benforado (ed.). 1985. Ecological Considerations in Wetlands Treatment of Municipal Wastewaters. Van Nostrand Reinhold Co., New York, NY.

Greiner, R. W., and J. de Jong. 1984. The use of marsh plants for the treatment of wastewater in areas designated for recreation and tourism. RIJP Report No. 225. Lelystad, Netherlands.

Guntenspergen, G. R., and F. Stearns. 1985. Ecological perspectives on wetland systems. p. 69-97. In P. J. Godfrey, E. R. Kaynor, S. Pelczarski, and J. Benforado (ed.). Ecological Considerations in Wetlands Treatment of Municipal Wastewater. Van Nostrand Reinhold Company, New York, NY.

Harms, W. R. 1973. Some effects of soil type and water regime on growth of tupelo seedlings. Ecology 54:188-193.

Hemond, H. F. 1983. The nitrogen budget of Thoreau's Bog. Ecology 64:99-109.

Herskowitz, T. 1987. Listowel artificial marsh project. Ministry of Canada. In K. R. Reddy and W. H. Smith (ed.) Aquatic Plants for Water Treatment and Resource Recovery. Magnolia Publishing, Inc., Orlando, FL.

Hyde, H. C., R. S. Ross, and F. Demgen. 1984. Technology assessment of wetlands for municipal wastewater treatment. EPA 600/2-84-154. USEPA, Cincinnati, OH.

Kadlec, R. H. 1981. How natural wetlands treat wastewater. In B. Richardson (ed.) Selected Proceedings of the Midwest Conference on Wetland Values and Management, June 17-19, 1981. St. Paul, MN. Freshwater Society, Navarre, MN.

Kadlec, R. H. 1983. The Bellaire Wetland: Wastewater alteration and recovery. Wetlands 3:44-63.

Kadlec, R. H. 1985. Aging phenomena in wetlands. p. 338-350. In P. J. Godfrey, E. R. Kaynor, S. Pelczarski, and J. Benforado (ed.) Ecological Considerations in Wetlands Treatment of Municipal Wastewater. Van Nostrand Reinhold Co., New York, NY.

Kadlec, R. H., and D. J. Tilton. 1979. The use of freshwater wetlands as a tertiary wastewater treatment alternative. CRC Critical Reviews in Environmental Control 9:185-212.

Kadlec, R. H., D. L. Tilton, and B. R. Schwegler. 1979. Wetlands for tertiary treatment: A three year summary of pilot scale operations at Houghton Lake. RANN Grant AEN 75-08855, Univ. of Michigan, Ann Arbor, MI.

Kelly, J. R., and M. A. Harwell. 1985. Comparisons of the processing of elements by ecosystems. I. Nutrients. p. 137-157. In P. J. Godfrey, E. R. Kaynor, S. Pelczarski, and

J. Benforado (ed.) Ecological Considerations in Wetlands Treatment of Municipal Wastewater. Van Nostrand Reinhold Co., New York, NY.

Kickuth, R. 1984. Das Wurzelraumverfahren in der Pravis. Landsch Stadt. 16:145-153.

Knight, R. L. 1986. Florida effluent wetlands - total nitrogen. WTRDS No. 1. CH2M Hill, Gainesville, FL.

Knight, R. L., R. H. Winchester, and J. C. Higman. 1985. Carolina Bays - feasibility for effluent advanced treatment and disposal. Wetlands 4:177-203.

Kuenzler, E. J., P. J. Mulholland, L. A. Ruley, and R. P. Sniffen. 1977. Water quality in North Carolina coastal plain streams and effects of channelization. Report No. 127, Water Resources Research Institute of the University of North Carolina, Raleigh, NC.

Kuenzler, E. J., P. J. Mulholland, L. A. Yarbro, and L. A. Smock. 1980. Distribution and budgets of carbon, phosphorus, iron and manganese in a floodplain swamp ecosystem. Report No. 157, Water Resources Research Institute of the University of North Carolina, Raleigh, NC.

Lemlich, S. K., and K. C. Ewel. 1984. Effects of wastewater disposal on growth rates of cypress trees. J. Env. Qual. 13:602-604.

Lewis, R. F., L. Banks, and S. F. Davis. 1982. Wastewater treatment by rooted aquatic plants in sand and gravel trenches. p. 1-28. In Abwasserrenigang mit hi ife Von Wasserpflanzen. Hornburg-Harburg Technical University.

Mitsch, W. J., C. L. Dorge, and J. R. Wiemhoff. 1979. Ecosystem dynamics and a phosphorus budget of an alluvial cypress swamp in southern Illinois. Ecology 60:1116-1124.

Nessel, J. K. 1978. Phosphorus cycling, productivity, and community structure in the Waldo cypress strand. p. 750-801. In H. T. Odum and K. C. Ewel (ed.) Cypress Wetlands for Water Management, Recycling, and Conservation, Fourth Annual Report. Center for Wetlands, University of Florida, Gainesville, FL.

Nessel, J. K., K. C. Ewel, and M. S. Burnett. 1982. Wastewater enrichment increases mature pondcypress growth rates. For. Sci. 28:400-403.

Nichols, D. S. 1983. Capacity of natural wetlands to remove nutrients from wastewater. J. Water Pollut. Control Fed. 55:495-505.

Ontario Ministry of The Environment. 1985. Town of Listowel. Artificial Marsh Project. Project No. 128RR.

Patrick, W. H., Jr., and R. A. Khalid. 1974. Phosphate release and sorption by soils and sediments: Effects of aerobic and anaerobic condition. Science 186:53-55.

Ponnamperuma, F. N. 1972. The chemistry of submerged soils. Adv. Agron. 24:29-96.

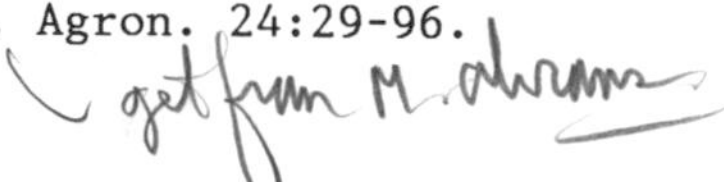

Richardson, C. J. 1985. Mechanisms controlling phosphorus retention capacity in freshwater wetlands. Science 228:1424-1427.

Richardson, C. J., and P. E. Marshall. 1986. Processes controlling movement, storage, and export of phosphorus in a fen peatland. Ecological Monographs 56:279-302.

Richardson, C. J., and D. S. Nichols. 1985. Ecological analysis of wastewater management criteria in wetland ecosystems. p. 351-391. In P. J. Godfrey, E. R. Kaynor, S. Pelczarski, and J. Benforado (ed.). Ecological Considerations in Wetlands Treatment of Municipal Wastewater. Van Nostrand Reinhold Co., New York, NY.

Richardson, C. J., and B. R. Schwegler. 1986. Algal bioassay and gross productivity experiments using sewage effluent in a Michigan wetland. Water Res. Bull. 22:111-120.

Richardson, C. J., J. A. Kadlec, A. W. Wentz, J. M. Chamie, and R. H. Kadlec. 1976. Background ecology and the effects of nutrient additions on a central Michigan wetland. p. 77-117. In M. W. Lefor, W. C. Kennard, and T. B. Helfgott (ed.) Proc. Third Wetland Conf. Report No. 26. Institute of Water Resources, University of Connecticut.

Schwartz, L. N. 1987. Regulation of wastewater discharge to Florida wetlands. In K. R. Reddy and W. H. Smith (ed.) Aquatic Plants for Water Treatment and Resource Recovery. Magnolia Publishing Inc., Orlando, FL.

Schwartz, L. N., and G. K. Gr-uendling. 1985. The effects of sewage on Lake Champlain wetland. J. Freshwater Ecol. 3:35-46.

Seidel, K. 1976. Macrophytes and water purification. p. 109-122. In J. Tourbier and R. W. Pierson (ed.) Biological Control of Water Pollution. Univ. of Penn. Press, Philadelphia, PA.

Sloey, W. E., F. L. Spangler, and C. W. Felter. 1978. Management of freshwater wetlands for nutrient assimilation. p. 321-340. In R. E. Good, D. F. Whigham, and R. L. Simpson (ed.) Freshwater Wetlands: Ecological Processes and Management Potential. Academic Press.

Small, M. 1976. Marsh/pond sewage treatment plants. p. 197-213. In D. L. Tilton, R. H. Kadlec, and C. J. Richardson (ed.) Freshwater Wetlands and Sewage Effluent Disposal, Univ. of Michigan, Ann Arbor, MI.

Smith, R. G., and E. D. Schroeder. 1985. Field studies of the overland flow process for the treatment of raw and primary treated municipal wastewater. J. WPCF 57:785-794.

Stinner, D. H. 1984. Nutrient enrichment and effects in Macks Island Rookery: Preliminary results. p. 343-352. In A. D. Cohen, D. J. Casagrande, M. J. Andrejko, and G. R. Best (ed.) The Okefenokee Swamp: Its Natural History, Geology, and Geochemistry. Wetland Surveys, Los Alamos, NM.

Stowell, R., R. Ludwig, J. Colt, and G. Tchobanoglous. 1981. Concepts in aquatic treatment system design. J. Env. Eng. Div., Processings of the ASCE 107, No. EE5.

Tchobanoglous, G., and G. L. Culp. 1980. Wetland systems for wastewater treatment. p. 13-42. In S. C. Reed and R. K. Bastian (ed.) Aquaculture Systems for Wastewater Treatment: An Engineering Assessment. EPA 430/9-80-007. Washington, DC.

Tilton, D. L., and R. H. Kadlec. 1979. The utilization of a freshwater wetland for nutrient removal from a secondary treated wastewater effluent. J. Env. Qual. 8:328-334.

Tuschall, J. R., P. L. Brezonik, and K. C. Ewel. 1981. Tertiary treatment of wastewater using flow-through wetland systems. In Proc. Nat'l Conf. ASCE, July 1981, Atlanta, GA.

Wharton, C. H., and M. M. Brinson. 1979. Characteristics of southern river systems. p. 32-40. In R. R. Johnson and J. F. McCormick (tech. coords.) Strategies for Protection and Management of Floodplain Wetlands and Other Riparian Ecosystems. Publ. GTR-WO-12, U.S. Forest Service, Washington, DC.

Wile, I., C. Miller, and S. Black. 1985. Design and use of artificial wetlands. p. 26-37. In P. J. Godfrey, E. R. Raynor, S. Pelczarski, and J. Benforado (ed.) Ecological Considerations in Wetlands Treatment of Municipal Wastewaters.

Winchester, B. H., and T. C. Emenheiser. 1983. Dry season wastewater assimilation by a north Florida hardwood swamp. Wetlands 3:90-107.

Winner, M. D., Jr., and C. E. Simmons. 1977. Hydrology of the Creeping Swamp watershed, North Carolina. USGS Water Resources Investigation 77-26. UGS, Raliegh, NC.

Winter, M. 1985. Municipal plant at Othfresen. Root zone - Sewage Treatment Plants after Kickuth. B. Ronsch (ed).

Wolverton, B. C., and R. C. McDonald. 1979. The Water Hyacinth: from Prolific Pest to Potential Provider. Ambio 8:2-9.

PUBLIC HEALTH ISSUES OF AQUATIC SYSTEMS USED FOR WASTEWATER TREATMENT

S. B. Krishnan
Office of Environmental Engineering Technology
U. S. Environmental Protection Agency
Washington, D.C. 20460

J. E. Smith
Center for Environmental Research Information
U.S. Environmental Protection Agency
Cincinnati, Ohio 45268

ABSTRACT

The potential health effects arising from the use of aquatic plants for wastewater treatment and resource recovery are examined, and a critical evaluation of these effects made. The contaminants of concern from a public health viewpoint are divided into the categories of pathogens and chemical substances. The pathogens include bacteria, viruses, protozoa, and helminths; the chemical substances include organics, trace elements, and nitrates. For each contaminant of concern the types and levels commonly found in municipal wastewater are briefly reviewed. A discussion of the levels, behavior, and route of potential human exposure, i.e., aerosols, surface soil and plants, subsurface soil and groundwater, and epidemiology of major contaminants are then briefly reviewed. The uncertainties and risks involved in using aquatic plants for wastewater treatment are addressed and methods of reducing them are presented. Other public health areas such as disease vectors, nuisance organisms, aquatic vascular plants, and viruses are discussed. The degree of pretreatment provided and the public health impact on biological components of ecosystem are also presented.

Keywords: Waste treatment, aquatic systems, public health, occupational hazards, mitigative measures.

INTRODUCTION

The most common types of aquatic systems used for waste treatment and recycling considered here involve algae, macrophyte and fish culture. Recycling of wastes to add nutrients to and

ISBN 0-941463-00-1

improve the protein production in aquaculture ponds is an ancient practice and has been employed for centuries in China and other Asian countries, Egypt and in European monasteries during the middle ages. In recent years in the U.S.A., there has been an increased interest in these systems and in the development of sound design criteria for their use as alternative wastewater treatment processes. While there is interest in utilizing such systems, where appropriate, there are also some public health concerns.

Some major benefits regarding aquatic treatment systems relate to economics, recycle and reuse of water and wastewater constituents, energy conservation, and use of natural processes. Vegetation harvested from these systems has been investigated as a fertilizer/soil conditioner after composting, animal feed, and a source of methane (CH_4) when anaerobically digested. Most concerns associated with such systems relate to potential public health effects, land requirements, and public acceptance.

In this paper, the potential public health effects arising from aquatic systems that are used for waste treatment are examined and an appraisal of these affects is made. The agents of concern from a public health point of view such as pathogens, heavy metals and trace organics are briefly reviewed for their behavior, route of potential exposure and mitigative measures. Guidelines for level of pathogens, organics and heavy metals, as proposed by national/international bodies are presented and needs for additional work are identified.

BY-PRODUCTS OF AQUATIC WASTEWATER TREATMENT SYSTEMS

The by-products of aquatic wastewater treatment systems may include unicellular algae, aquatic macrophytes, invertebrates and even finfish in both marine and freshwater systems. The hygienic quality of these products depends on the particular wastewater used. In some cases, these products may be worked and consumed directly by people (e.g. finfish, prawns), used as feed or feed-additives for animals (e.g. algae and brine shrimp), processed for valuable extracts (e.g. agar from seaweeds), or put to other uses (e.g. bait).

Harvested biomass could be used in the production of livestock feed, compost, soil amendments or methane gas. All of these uses, however, have limited application for economic reasons. It is very unlikely that a production system will be developed in the near future which would approach paying for the treatment of wastewater (Crites et al., 1979).

In Israel, the algal/bacterial float from waste stabilization ponds is processed to serve as a feed protein source for poultry and fish. Its market value, when added to that of the clarified effluent in this water short areas allows the system to show a substantial cost advantage over other wastewater treatment systems (Shelef et al., 1978).

PUBLIC HEALTH CONCERNS

The agents of concern from a health effects viewpoint can be divided into the three broad categories of pathogens, heavy metals and trace organics. The pathogens include pathogenic bacteria, viruses, protozoa and helminths. The heavy metals include Cd, Cr, Cu, Pb, Ni and Zn. Trace organics include synthetic organic chemicals, especially chlorinated hydrocarbons.

Pathogens

The public health concerns potentially depend upon pathogen-host relationships and possible transmission routes for excreta related infections (IRCWD, 1985). Pathogen characteristics, anthropological factors and the biology of the human host must interact in a rather complex manner to render possible the transmission of surviving pathogens to a human host and to cause an infection in that host (Figure 1).

The major paths for the transmission of disease are: direct contact with applied wastewater, aerosol transport, the food chain, and improperly treated drinking water. Research has been conducted on transmission of parasitic diseases to animals and man by means of land application of municipal wastewater and sludge (Pahren, 1980). A significant study completed at the San Angelo, Texas, wastewater irrigation site (Weaver et al., 1978) indicated that parasites did not increase in cattle that grazed on wastewater irrigated pastures during the period of the study. These results are similar to those reported earlier in Poland (Patyk, 1958; Jankiewicz, 1972) and in Australia (Evans et al., 1978). Feeding wet algal slurry from stabilization ponds to livestock, could lead to animal infection by the beef tapeworm *Taenia saginata*, and *Salmonella* spp. for cattle; and *Salmonella* spp. for poultry.

In a study conducted in Denmark (Grunnet and Moller, 1978), the decrease in initial concentration of certain biological indicators (*Ascaris suum*, *Salmonella typhimurium*, and coliphages) and pathogens with time were measured on grass, hay, and in silage contaminated by irrigation of grassland with domestic sewage. On standing crops and in hay (stored at 20°C) the named organisms except coliform bacteria and *Ascaris suum* eggs, showed a fast die-off, reaching zero in about 40 days. The number of coliform organisms dropped within 3 days to a basic level and the reduction was parallel to the decrease in the number of *E. coli*. The *Ascaris* eggs were only reduced in 120 days by about 50%.

In silage, the pH dropped to 4 within the first 10-14 days due to the growth of lactobacilli, but prior to this drop in pH, a growth of *E. coli*, coliform bacteria, and *Salmonella typhimurium* took place, and the concentration increased to 10^8 from 10^3 organisms/gram. This phase was followed by one of a rapid decline reaching zero in about 40 days after the ensiling. As expected, concentration of *Ascaris* eggs remained about the same during the five months of observation.

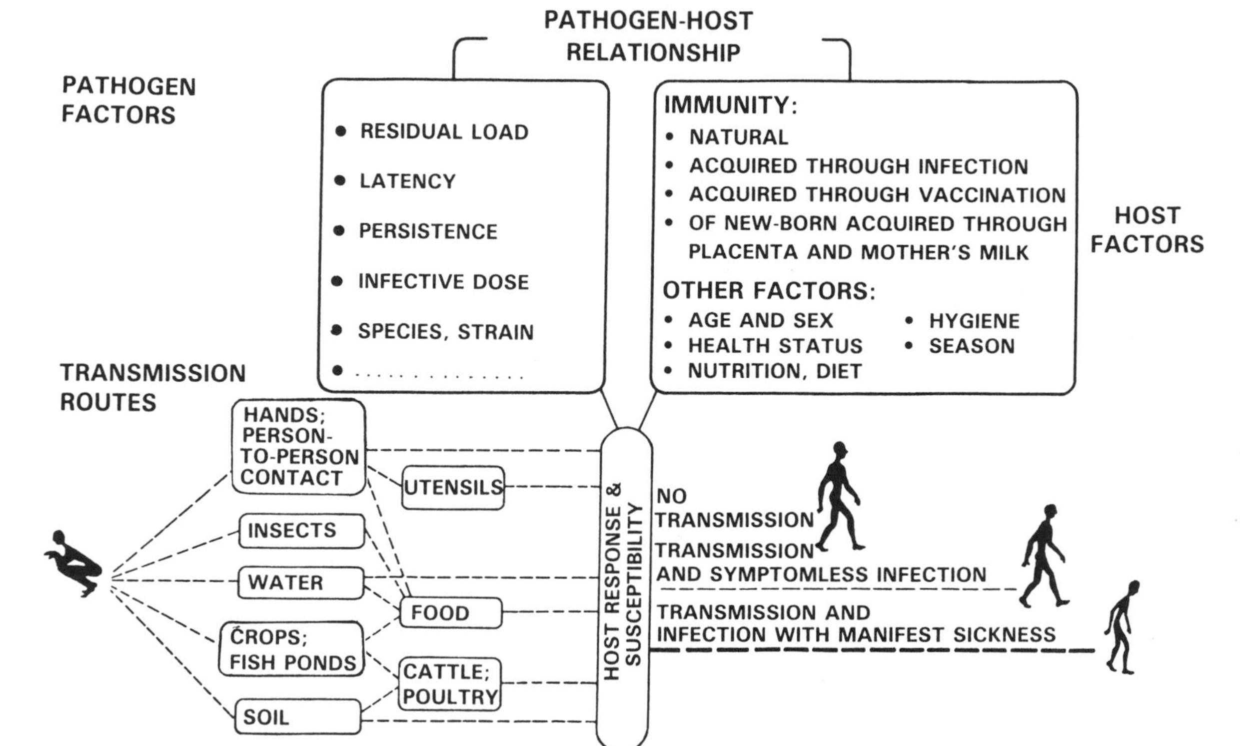

FIGURE 1. The pathogen-host relationship and possible transmission routes for excreta-related infections.

As bacteria and viruses present in domestic sewage used in agriculture are usually eliminated within 40 days, they represent only a minor problem which can be solved by appropriate quarantine periods. Helminth eggs, thus constitute the factor which potentially limits reuse of domestic sewage in agriculture. Furthermore, silage should not be used during the first six weeks after ensiling due to the initial regrowth of enteric bacteria.

Fish grown in aquatic treatment systems may contain pathogens in their muscle, organs, and intraperitoneal fluid and potentially pose a public health problem when consumed directly by humans. The suitability of tertiary wastewater treatment ponds for aquaculture has been evaluated (Phelps, 1985) in terms of fish production (silver carp) and the significance of bacteria in the wastewater and fish. Net production of fish grown in this system was 1309 kg ha^{-1} yr^{-1}. Fecal coliforms and fecal streptococci were commonly found in both the water and fish. Certain bacterial colony types such as *Klebsiella pneumoniae* were more common in water than fish, while others such as *Aernomonas hydrophila*, were common in fish. *Streptococcus faecalis* was the most common fecal streptococcus from both water and fish. There is a potential for worker exposure to pathogens when depurating the fish grown in wastewaters containing high concentrations of microorganisms.

Because sewage contains pathogenic agents, there is a potential for infection or illness when exposed to domestic wastewater or aerosols from treatment facilities. Based on several comprehensive investigations reported (Pahren and Jakubowski, 1981) it can be said that people who have been exposed to microorganisms from the wastewater treatment processes generally do not become infected or ill. This is essentially due to concern for fish handling, but in reality sewage treatment plant workers would be at a higher risk and this group has not been demonstrated to have greater than average health problems.

Heavy Metals

Heavy metals are of concern in aquatic treatment systems because of plant uptake and possible toxicity to plants or their consumers, and possible migration to ground or surface waters. While most heavy metals can lead to adverse effects if present above certain concentrations, cadmium causes the most concern from a human health point of view. The concentration of heavy metals greatly depends on the type or amount of industrial wastes contributed to the wastewater system. In wastewaters of domestic origin only, the concentration of heavy metals is usually very low. Also, adequate pretreatment of industrial wastes can reduce the concentration of heavy metals to acceptable levels.

Trace Organics

Municipal and industrial wastewaters contain variable concentrations of synthetic organic compounds in addition to valuable plant nutrients. There is a growing concern over contamination of the environment by synthetic organics. This has led to recent but limited studies of organics in sewage sludges (Naylor and Loehr, 1982; Overcash, 1983). The research base on fate of municipal wastewater and sludge-borne organics is extremely limited. Likewise, uncertainties as to the health effects and threshold exposures of these compounds has made the evaluation of risk from exposure to wastewater and sludge organics difficult.

A work group on trace organics in sludge met in Las Vegas, Nevada in November 1985, to assess the current state of knowledge of the potential trace organics problem associated with land application of municipal sewage sludges. They concluded (Jacobs, 1986, personal communication, Michigan State Univ., Lansing, MI) that major assimilative pathways for organic chemicals applied to the soil-plant system include adsorption, volatilization, degradation, leaching and plant uptake; that many organics are strongly adsorbed to soil organic matter and/or undergo degradation, reducing the potential for plant uptake or leaching. In general, risk assessments appear to suggest that most sludge organics will not increase the health risk to animals and humans, based on their relative toxicities and anticipated loadings to soil at agronomic or low sludge application rates.

A working group on the Risk to Health of Chemicals in Sewage Sludge Applied to Land organized by the World Health Organization (WHO), Regional office for Europe (WHO, 1985) concluded that the information on identified organic pollutants in sludge and their pathways to man is limited; that the concentrations reported in the literature appear to be low, and almost always below 10 mg kg^{-1} dry solids; that the most significant route of organic pollutants from sludge is to grazing animals, transfer through food crops is negligible; and that the contribution to total human intake of identified organic pollutants resulting from sludge application to land is minor and is unlikely to cause adverse health effects. The work group also recommended that more information should be obtained on the following for the organic chemicals of significance to health in sludge: organic soils pollutant content of sludge, fate and behavior of persistent organic chemicals, improved methods for the extraction and preparation for analysis and broad-spectrum tests related to effects on human health (such as enzyme inhibition and mutagenicity tests) to overcome the practical problems of analysis posed by the large number of organic pollutants in sludge.

Vectors

A possible serious public health problem associated with aquatic wastewater treatment systems is the potential for production of mosquitoes which might transmit diseases like encephalitis. Also, when wetlands are used for wastewater treatment, they can provide wildlife habitats; food for birds and animals through vegetation especially in winter. *Clostridium botulinum* which is often found in wetlands under anaerobic conditions, and causes avian botulism could possibly be impacted by wastewater addition although this vector does not cause botulism in humans.

INTERNATIONAL ORGANIZATIONS EXPERIENCE

The World Health Organization (WHO), the World Bank and International Reference Centre for Waste Disposal (IRCWD) have developed and are continuing to develop information on the health aspects of night soil and sludge use in agriculture and aquaculture (Edwards, 1985; IRCWD, 1985; Blum and Feachem, 1985; and Feachem et al., 1980). A list is provided in Table 1 of pathogens that are potentially spreadable through the use of excreta in aquaculture, illness they cause and intermediate hosts, if any. The results suggest that the use of raw night soil in aquaculture has been associated with transmission of *Clonorchis* and *Fasciolopis* infection. While studies which examine the risks of using treated night soil in aquaculture are lacking, there is some evidence that introducing the use of treated night soil in agriculture lowers the risk of helminthic infections among people previously using raw night soil.

Consumption of Contaminated By-Products

Fish do not apparently suffer from infections caused by enteric bacteria and viruses that cause disease in warm-blooded animals -- humans and livestock. It is generally believed, however, that fish carry human pathogens passively in their intestines and on their body surfaces. Recent work in Israel has revealed the rather startling fact that both enteric bacteria and viruses are able to penetrate various fish tissues (Buras et al., 1982). The concentration of microorganisms in the water determines their presence in fish tissues, and there appears to be a threshold concentration in pond water below which microorganisms do not penetrate into fish muscle. The threshold concentration of viruses appears to be an order of magnitude less than that for bacteria. There is little danger of disease incidents resulting from eating well cooked fish or vegetables since heat destroys pathogens. It should be stressed that the consumption of raw, partially cooked, or improperly preserved products, could lead to a serious health hazard.

Certain parasitic helminths may be transmitted through recycling excreta in aquaculture systems since their life cycles include aquatic organisms like fish, crabs, or aquatic macrophytes, and intermediate hosts. However, many helminths have a restricted geographical distribution and infections would likely occur only in areas in which they are endemic. The liver fluke diseases are frequently transmitted where fish are eaten raw or partially cooked. Both liver flukes and schistosomes can be

TABLE 1. Important infectious disease agents with potential for spread by the use of excreta in aquaculture (IRCWD, 1985).

Agent	Illness	Intermediate host(s)
VIRUSES		
Enteroviruses	Diarrhoea, respiratory disease, polio	None
Hepatitis A	Infectious hepatitis	None
Rotavirus	Diarrhoea	
BACTERIA		
Campylobacter jejuni	Diarrhoea	None
Pathogenic *Escherichia coli*	Diarrhoea or dysentery	None
Salmonella spp. (non-typhoid)	Diarrhoea	None
Salmonella typhi	Typhoid fever	None
Shigella spp.	Diarrhoea or dysentery	None
Vibrio spp. (?)†	Cholera or diarrhoea	None
PROTOZOA		
Entamoeba histolytica	Diarrhoea or dysentery	None
Giardia lamblia	Diarrhoea	None
HELMINTHS		
Cestodes		
Diphyllobothrium latum	Fish tapeworm infection	Freshwater copepod and freshwater fish
Trematodes		
Clonorchis sinensis	Bile duct infection	Freshwater snail and freshwater fish
Fasciola hepatica	Liver fluke infection	Amphibious snail and aquatic vegetation
Fasciolopsis buski	Intestinal fluke infection	Amphibious snail and aquatic vegetation
Opisthorchis spp.	Bile duct infection	Freshwater snail and freshwater fish
Schistosoma spp.	Schistosomiasis	Snail

†Considerable uncertainty surrounds the ecology of these organisms.

controlled by keeping vegetation on pond dikes under control to discourage the reproduction of the snails, an intermediate host. The cultivation of macrophytes for human and animal feed fertilized with excreta is common in Asia. The metacercariae of Fasciolopis liver fluke, attach to various aquatic macrophyte species which, if eaten raw or partially cooked, can lead to fluke infections.

Potential health hazards associated with the reuse of algae grown in wastewater ponds depend upon the type of reuse. If the algae are fed to cattle, the major concern will be Taenia saginata, Salmonella spp., and Mycobacterium tuberculosis. If they are fed to chickens, the major concern may be Salmonella. If the algae are consumed by people, thorough disinfection prior to packaging and marketing could be necessary.

Enteric bacteria and viruses survive for considerably shorter periods in sea water than in freshwater, although the survival of protozoan and helminth ova in the two environments is similar. Helminth ova tend to settle down to the bottom and intermediate hosts of most helminth parasites would not occur in sea water. Shellfish such as oysters and mussels, can concentrate enteric bacteria and viruses in their tissues, and outbreaks of polio, hepatitis A, and diarrheal disease have all been related to the consumption of shellfish from water polluted with raw wastewater. Furthermore, Vibrio parahaemolyticus, which causes acute gastroenteritis, has frequently been isolated from marine fish, shellfish, crabs and prawns.

The reuse of wastewater containing toxic chemicals such as heavy metals and various organics can lead to their accumulation by cultivated organisms, which thus constitute a threat to public health. However, levels of heavy metals and pesticides in fish grown in sewage stabilization ponds have generally been reported to be within acceptable limits.

Occupational Hazards

A possible health hazard exists for workers involved in excreta collection and reuse, but there is little epidemiological evidence. Workers can accidentally swallow pathogens or carry them home on their clothing or bodies. A specific occupational hazard from excreta use could be schistosomiasis, but this is only likely in areas where the disease is endemic and the necessary intermediate snail host is present in the pond. Helminth diseases, particularly Schistosoma japonicum, have been related to excreta reuse. Eggs can survive in feces for more than one week so that if fresh excreta is applied to a pond containing certain amphibious snail hosts, the snails may become infected. Larvae are released into the water following development within a snail and can bore into human skin to infect pond workers. The avoidance of using fresh excreta can control the disease in areas where the helminth disease is endemic. Storage of excreta for two weeks renders it free of Schistosoma eggs.

As mentioned previously, the intraperitoneal fluid of fish has been found to have high levels of bacteria and viruses. This is an important finding from a public health point of view since the fluid comes into direct contact with the handler when fish are gutted, creating a potential source of infection. Perhaps the most significant health hazard, which is generally overlooked, is the danger from handling and preparing contaminated products. In practice, however, it is equally likely that the fish can become infected after harvesting and during handling, processing and transportation. The major known fish-associated outbreaks of salmonellosis in animals and man have been associated with contamination of food products after harvesting.

The Engelberg Meeting of Experts (IRCWD, 1985)

About a year ago, a group of experts concerned with public health met in Engelberg, Switzerland to discuss the health aspects of excreta and wastewater use in agriculture and aquaculture. This meeting was sponsored by the World Bank/United Nations Development Programme (UNDP), WHO/United Nations Environment Programme (UNEP) and IRCWD. The meeting primarily reviewed comprehensive and critical literature on the epidemiological, microbiological, sociological, and technical aspects of these practices. Based on these reviews (Shuval et al., 1985; Blum and Feachem, 1985; and Cross and Strauss, 1985) the group developed a methodology for assessing the health risks associated with the use of untreated excreta and wastewater in agriculture and aquaculture. The assessment suggests that the amount of excess infection and disease caused by various classes of pathogens is in the following order of descending magnitude; intestinal nematode infections (*Ascaris*, *Trichuris*, and the hookworms), bacterial infections and viral infections (including rotavirus diarrhea and hepatitis A). It was unanimously agreed that this assessment and the detailed epidemiological and microbiological data from which it is derived, provide a sufficient basis for the revision of current international guidelines as detailed in WHO Technical Report No. 517, 1973, and formulation of firm operational guidelines on the public health aspects of excreta and wastewater use. This assessment not only provides a basis for operational guidelines to be used immediately by project planners and policy makers, but also highlights areas of uncertainty and associated research priorities.

MITIGATIVE MEASURES

Pathogen Control

It would be ideal to cultivate aquatic organisms with excreta following its treatment to eliminate all pathogenic organisms. Unfortunately prior waste treatment to achieve complete pathogen destruction would seldom be feasible from an economic or even technical point of view in many parts of the world. However, certain procedures should be followed to reduce to an absolute minimum the chances of any public health hazard due to wastewater reuse and by-product use. The destruction of excreted pathogens is principally achieved by a combination of time outside the human host and temperature. Extraintestinal environmental conditions that are important in pathogen attenuation are sunlight, high dissolved oxygen and high pH; natural inactivation processes are very complex. Our knowledge of enteric virus inactivation is limited, but attenuation is expected to occur rapidly in the tropical areas.

Night soil, septage, or primary sewage sludge should never be added to a waste recycling system without storage for at least two weeks to eliminate any liver fluke or schistosome ova, in areas where these parasites are a problem. Since cesspool and secondary sludges are at least partially digested, they may be recycled without further storage, because any liver fluke and schistosome ova will have been destroyed. However, sludges, and effluents from sludge digesters, are still likely to contain significant densities of enteric bacteria and viruses.

Activated sludge and trickling filters are not highly effective technologies by themselves for pathogen removal from sewage, but a well designed system of stabilization ponds is highly effective. A minimum of three ponds with a minimum total detention time of 20 d will produce an effluent that is either completely pathogen free or with only low concentrations of enteric bacteria and viruses; pathogenic helminths and protozoa will have been completely destroyed. It is fortunate that stabilization ponds are both low cost and appropriate wastewater treatment technologies for warm climates and developing countries.

Vector Control

The following measures are taken at a constructed wetland system which receives secondary effluent (Demgen and Nute, 1979) to avoid occurrence of avian botulism: avoiding anaerobic conditions in the wetland by keeping the water circulating and maintaining the depth at less than 1 m, removing floating organic debris which collects behind weirs, using steep-sided levees and adjustable weirs to control water levels, and conveying water by pipelines instead of channels.

Mosquito breeding problems can generally be avoided by providing open water areas subject to wind action which also provide easy access to mosquito larvae predators such as Gambusia afinish. Control measures considered along with fish populations include parasitic nematodes and monomolecular alcohols (Paterson, 1975).

ASSESSMENT OF STATE OF KNOWLEDGE AND GUIDELINES RECOMMENDATION

Other papers in this conference have identified three major areas or systems for using aquatic plants in waste treatment and/or resource recovery. They include natural wetlands, constructed wetlands and wetlands which use aquatic plants for resource recovery. Public health concerns relative to these aquatic systems include the fate of pathogens, vector organisms, heavy metals, and trace organics; and these are addressed here.

Guidelines proposed here are the result of a critical review of published information and related experiences with aquaculture, land treatment of wastewater and sludge and the use of wastewater and sludge in agriculture. They reflect a general consensus of experts in these fields. The treatment requirements for wastewater prior to its utilization are based on the method of wastewater application, the degree of public contact with the site, receiving stream water quality considerations and the disposition of the crops.

The public health and water quality goals and requirements for the three aquatic systems are listed in Table 2.

In the natural wetland area, many industrialized countries are moving towards a policy of nondegradation of existing water quality. Inherent in this policy is the requirement for a high degree of treatment. The aquatic plants system's emphasis is on recovery of resources present in the waste. It is desirable, therefore, to minimize contaminants/pollutants, which have no obvious resource value. In the case of the constructed wetland, the system's principal purpose is to provide cost effective wastewater treatment.

The public health implications of wastewater recycling in wetlands have not been fully evaluated for all wetland types. A number of factors intervene in a complex manner to define the likelihood that a potential risk will result in measurable human disease or infection. These include the excreted pathogen load and the organisms' latency, ability to multiply and persistence; the infective dose of the organisms; presence of any necessary intermediate hosts; the immunity and behavior of the potential human recipient; and ultimately the recipient's risk of illness to infection and consideration of alternative routes of transmission. Potential adverse impacts include increasing the threat of waterborne disease via surface or groundwater contamination and increasing the incidence of insect-, bird-, or mammal-vectored diseases. Even though the soil profile retains a substantial amount of viruses and bacteria, it is not a failsafe system (Wellings, 1975). Wetlands receiving wastewater that interconnect with other bodies of water like lakes and streams, could potentially transmit bacteria and viruses. Concern has also been expressed over the possible implication of eastern encephalitis (EE) viruses in swamps receiving sewage because of the possible increase in bird and mosquito populations associated with EE (Davis, 1975).

TABLE 2. Goals and requirements of aquatic systems.

A. Natural Wetlands (Water Quality Limited)	
Goals	. Protect and/or upgrade existing water quality
	. Provide recreational use
	. Provide a higher level of treatment
Requirements	. Need adequate degree of treatment
	. In U.S.A. this requirement is regulated by state law
B. Aquatic Plant Systems Specifically Designed for Waste Treatment and Resource Recovery (Product Quality Limited)	
Goals	. Recover resources from wastewater
	. Grow animal/human foods (fish; plants)
	. Treat wastewater
	. Provide an advanced level of wastewater treatment
Requirements	. Pollutant concentrations limited by needs for health of plants and/or animals being grown and their later use as food for animals or humans
	. Effluent limits at point of discharge to receiving stream
	. Standards for recreational water should be met
	. Occupational standards should be met
C. Artificial Wetlands (Wastewater Treatment Capability Limited)	
Goals	. Treat wastewater
	. Grow crops for non-food chain consumption
Requirements	. Occupational standards
	. Concern about quality of by-products recovered
	. Regulation at point of discharge to stream
	. Concern about cost, climate and treatment efficiencies

Discharging high levels of bioavailable metals to an ecosystem in which they can be circulated and accumulated should be avoided. Other aspects of wastewater discharges to wetlands remain uncharacterized. An example is the persistence of nitrate which results in contamination of drinking water supplies and especially presents potential toxicity problems for infants (methemoglobinemia). However, while data exist to indicate the potential for public health problems arising from wetland discharges, no incidences of disease resulting directly from such discharges have been identified.

The risks to public health associated with aquatic treatment systems are probably not higher than those for conventional treatment, when any animals or plants grown are not used for human consumption and potential vector problems are controlled. The potential public health hazards of direct consumption of unprocessed organisms grown with exposure to municipal wastewater are very serious and complicated. Their use for animal feeds may be possible if the residues of heavy metals, trace organics, and pesticides meet acceptable levels.

Natural Wetlands

It is necessary to consider the existing quality of the receiving stream: is it being used to grow shellfish, other fish or plants for human consumption, is it being used for recreational purposes - that include body contact sports, is it dissolved oxygen or nutrient limited? What are the state's water quality criteria or NPDES requirements for such a water body? All these factors influence the level of wastewater treatment required before a wastewater treatment plant effluent is discharged into a natural wetland. It is known that some natural wetlands are currently receiving the effluents from primary treatment plants.

Criteria for biological pollutants in situations where shellfish are harvested for human consumption or the waters are used for recreational activities are listed in Table 3. In this situation total coliforms and fecal coliforms are surrogate measurements for the presence of many microbial forms. If a stream is dissolved oxygen limited, near eutrophic and used for body contact sports, the wastewater would likely require secondary treatment, nutrient removal and disinfection.

Guidance for the loading of metals is more difficult. EPA Region IV (1985) has recommended maximum concentrations for trace metals in real aimed water used for irrigation and these are given in Table 4. Obviously since this is from an irrigation recommendation, any dilution would have to be considered. Recommendations for organics and other pollutants are harder to make. Nearly all the information available for volatile organic chemicals, synthetic organic chemicals/pesticides etc. is from

TABLE 3. Criteria for biological pollutants (USEPA, 1986b).

	Total coliforms	Fecal coliforms
Protection of shellfish (most common value cited by authorities)	<70 MPN 100 mL^{-1} (mean value)	<14 MPN 100 mL^{-1} <10% samples >43 MPN 100 mL^{-1} (median values)
Primary contact recreational waters (most common value cited by authorities)	---	< a geometric mean of 200 100 mL^{-1} 10% over 30 days of 400 100 mL^{-1}
State of Maryland non-restricted recreational use and near shellfish areas	2.2 100 mL^{-1} (7-day median)	---

the work being done to arrive at guidelines for drinking water quality. Some of these appear below in Table 5.

Aquatic Plant Systems Specifically Designed for Waste Treatment and Resource Recovery

The emphasis here is on recovery of resources contained in the wastewater and production of a food for animal or human consumption. A benefit of the system is more complete wastewater treatment. Guidance on the recommended maximum concentrations for trace metals in reclaimed water used for irrigation is available in Table 4. The microbiological quality guidelines for treated wastewater reuse in agriculture (IRCWD, 1985) are shown in Table 6. For wastewater use in aquaculture, it is felt that less stringent standards may be acceptable. The guidelines are tentative and technically feasible. The quality guideline for restricted irrigation (fruit trees, pasture) implies a removal >99% of helminth eggs, mainly to protect the health of agricultural workers. A two-cell wastes stabilization pond, when they are operated at sufficiently high temperatures, readily achieves this removal.

The guidelines for unrestricted irrigation of wastewater (edible crops, sports fields and public parks) comprise the same requirement for helminth eggs as that of restricted irrigation of wastewater and a minimum geometric mean concentration of 1000 fecal coliforms per 100 mL. The latter recommendation implies a very high level of removal of fecal bacteria (5-6 log 10 units or >99.999%). Its purpose is to protect the health of the consumers of crops, principally vegetables. This is readily achievable in a properly designed series of waste stabilization ponds (Shuval et al., 1985). For the range of temperatures normally encountered in tropical areas, a series of four 5 d detention ponds will normally produce an effluent of this quality as shown in Figure 2.

It is difficult to give any guidance with regard to the presence of other contaminants including organics.

Artificial Wetlands

These systems provide treatment of wastewater and/or production of non-food crops. The degree of treatment required at these constructed wetlands depends on the effluent limitations for wetland discharges. The wetland could be designated as effluent limited or water quality limited depending on the assimilative capacity of the receiving body of water. If the wetland is designated as effluent limited, secondary treatment would be appropriate. If the classification of wetland is water quality limited, specific attention to the parameters such as nutrients should be given to comply with effluent limitations.

When crops are grown in these wetlands, guidelines on bacteria, viruses, and trace metals described in the previous sections apply.

TABLE 4. Recommended maximum concentrations for trace metals in reclaimed water used for irrigation.

Constituent	Long-term use+ (mg L^{-1})	Short-term use++ (mg L^{-1})	Remarks	Typical concentrations in secondary treated municipal wastewater+++ (mg L^{-1})
Aluminum	5.0	20.0	Can cause nonproductivity in acid soils, but soils at pH 5.5 to 8.0 will precipitate the ion and eliminate toxicity.	--
Arsenic	0.10	2.0	Toxicity to plants varies widely, ranging from 12 mg L^{-1} for Sudan grass to less than 0.05 mg L^{-1} for rice.	0.002
Beryllium	0.10	0.5	Toxicity to plants varies widely, ranging from 5 mg L^{-1} for kale to 0.5 mg L^{-1} for bush beans.	--
Boron	0.75	2.0	Essential to plant growth, with optimum yields for many obtained at a few-tenths mg L^{-1} in nutrient solutions. Toxic to many sensitive plants (e.g., citrus plants) at 1 mg L^{-1}.	--
Cadmium	0.01	0.05	Toxic to beans, beets and turnips at concentrations as low as 0.1 mg L^{-1} in nutrient solution. Conservative limits recommended.	0.01
Chromium	0.1	1.0	Not generally recognized as essential growth element. Conservative limits recommended due to lack of knowledge on toxicity to plants.	0.09
Cobalt	0.05	5.0	Toxic to tomato plants at 0.1 mg L^{-1} in nutrient solution. Tends to be inactivated by neutral and alkaline soils.	--
Copper	0.2	5.0	Toxic to a number of plants at 0.1 to 1.0 mg L^{-1} in nutrient solution.	0.05

TABLE 4 (cont'd.)

Constituent	Long-term use⁺ (mg L^{-1})	Short-term use⁺⁺ (mg L^{-1})	Remarks	Typical concentrations in secondary treated municipal wastewater⁺⁺⁺ (mg L^{-1})
Fluoride	1.0	15.0	Inactivated by neutral and alkaline soils.	--
Iron	5.0	20.0	Not toxic to plants in aerated soils, but can contribute to soil acidification and loss of essential P and molybdenum.	--
Lead	5.0	10.0	Can inhibit plant cell growth at very high concentrations.	0.02 to 0.02
Lithium	2.5	2.5	Tolerated by most crops at up to 5 mg L^{-1}; mobile in soil. Toxic to citrus at low doses--recommended limit is 0.075 mg L^{-1}.	--
Manganese	0.2	10.0	Toxic to a number of crops at a few-tenths to a few mg L^{-1} in acid soils.	0.05
Molybdenum	0.01	0.05	Not toxic to plants at normal concentrations in soil and water. Can be toxic to livestock if forage is grown in soils with high levels of available molybdenum.	--
Nickel	0.2	2.0	Toxic to a number of plants at 0.5 to 1.0 mg L^{-1}; reduced toxicity at neutral or alkaline pH.	0.2
Selenium	0.02	0.02	Toxic to plants at low concentrations and to livestock if forage is grown in soils with low levels of added selenium.	--
Tin, Tungsten and Titanium	--	--	Effectively excluded by plants; specific tolerance levels unknown.	--

TABLE 4 (cont'd.)

Constituent	Long-term use⁺ (mg L^{-1})	Short-term use⁺⁺ (mg L^{-1})	Remarks	Typical concentrations in secondary treated municipal wastewater⁺⁺⁺ (mg L^{-1})
Vanadium	0.1	1.0	Toxic to many plants at relatively low concentrations.	--
Zinc	2.0	10.0	Toxic to many plants at widely varying concentrations; reduced toxicity at increased pH (6 or above) and in fine-textured or organic soils.	0.3

⁺For water used continuously on all soils. ⁺⁺For water used for a period of up to 20 years on fine-textured neutral or alkaline soils. ⁺⁺⁺Depends upon extent of disinfection.
Sources: U.S. EPA (1980) and data from North Carolina and California.

TABLE 5. Drinking water standards (US EPA, 1986a).

Constituent	US EPA Standards		WHO⁺		Canadian recommended maximum acceptable levels	US FDA bottled water standards
	Primary MCL's	Secondary MCL's	Health significance	Aesthetic quality		
	mg L^{-1}					
Organics						
Aldrin	---	---	0.00003	---	0.0007	---
Benzene	0.005	---	0.010	---	---	---
Benzo[a]pyrene	---	---	0.00001	---	---	---
Carbaryl	---	---	---	---	0.07	---

TABLE 5 (cont'd.)

Constituent	US EPA Standards Primary MCL's	US EPA Standards Secondary MCL's	WHO+ Health significance	WHO+ Aesthetic quality	Canadian recommended maximum acceptable levels	US FDA bottled water standards
	mg L^{-1}					
Carbon tetrachloride	0.005	---	0.003	---	---	---
Chlordane	---	---	0.0003	---	0.007	---
Chlorobenzenes	---	---	ngvs	ngvs	---	---
Chloroform	---	---	0.030	---	---	---
Chlorophenols	---	---	ngvs	ngvs	---	---
DDT	---	---	0.001	---	0.03	---
Diazinon	---	---	---	---	0.014	---
1,2-Dichloroethane	0.005	---	0.100	---	---	---
1,1-Dichloroethylene	0.007	---	0.0003	---	---	---
p-Dichlorobenzene	0.75	---	---	---	---	---
Dieldrin	---	---	0.00003	---	0.0007	---
Endrin	0.0002	---	---	---	0.0002	0.0002
Foaming agents (detergents)	---	0.5	---	There should be no foaming	---	---
Heptachlor	---	---	0.0001	---	0.003	---
Heptachlor expoxide	---	---	0.0001	---	0.003	---
Hexachlorobenzene	---	---	0.00001	---	---	---
Lindane	0.004	---	0.003	---	0.004	0.004
Methoxychlor	0.1	---	0.030	---	0.1	0.1
Methyl parathion	---	---	---	---	0.0007	---
Nitrilo-triacetic acid	---	---	---	---	0.05	---
Parathion	---	---	---	---	0.035	---
Pentachlorophenol	---	---	0.010	---	---	---

TABLE 5 (cont'd.)

Constituent	US EPA Standards: Primary MCL's	US EPA Standards: Secondary MCL's	WHO[†]: Health significance	WHO[†]: Aesthetic quality	Canadian recommended maximum acceptable levels	US FDA bottled water standards
	mg L^{-1}					
Phenols	---	---	---	---	0.002	0.001
Polynuclear aromatic hydrocarbons (PAH's)	---	---	---	---	---	---
Tetrachloroethylene	---	---	0.010	---	---	---
Total trihalomethanes	0.10	---	ngvs	---	0.35	0.10
Toxaphene	0.0005	---	---	---	0.005	0.005
Trichloroethylene	0.005	---	0.030	---	---	---
1,1,1-trichloroethane	0.20	---	---	---	---	---
2,4,6-trichlorophenol	---	---	0.010	---	---	---
Vinyl chloride	0.001	---	---	---	---	---
2,4-D	0.1	---	0.1	---	0.1	0.10
2,4,5-TP Silvex	0.01	---	---	---	0.01	0.01
Total Pesticides	---	---	---	---	0.1	---

[†]World Health Organization.

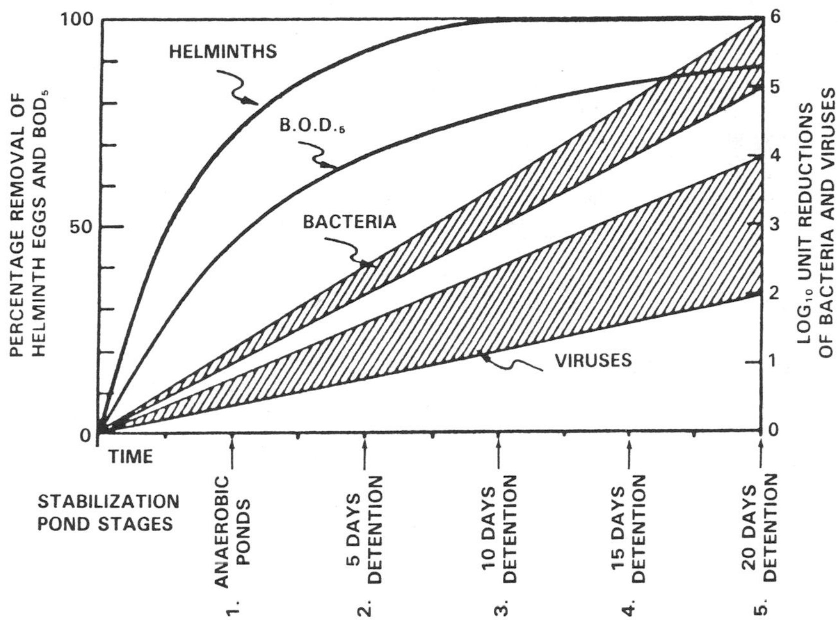

FIGURE 2. Generalized removal curves for BOD, helminth eggs, excreted bacteria and viruses in waste stabilization ponds at temperatures above 20°C (after Shuval et al., 1985).

TABLE 6. Tentative microbiological quality guidelines for treated wastewater reuse in agricultural irrigation (1).

Reuse process	Intestinal nematodes (2) (geometric mean no. of viable eggs per liter)	Faecal coliforms (geometric mean no. per 100 mL)
Restricted irrigation (3) Irrigation of trees, industrial crops, fodder crops, fruit trees (4) and pasture (5)	≤ 1	Not applicable (3)
Unrestricted irrigation Irrigation of edible crops, sports fields, and public parks (6)	≤ 1	≤ 1000 (7)

(1) In specific cases, local epidemiological, sociocultural, and hydrogeological factors should be taken into account, and these guidelines modified accordingly.

(2) Ascaris, Trichuris and hookworms.
(3) A minimum degree of treatment equivalent to at least a 1-day anaerobic pond followed by a 5-day facultative pond or its equivalent is required in all cases.
(4) Irrigation should cease two weeks before fruit is picked, and no fruit should be picked off the ground.
(5) Irrigation should cease two weeks before animals are allowed to graze.
(6) Local epidemiological factors may require a more stringent standard for public lawns, especially hotel lawns in tourist areas.
(7) When edible crops are always consumed well-cooked, this recommendation may be less stringent.

ACKNOWLEDGMENTS

Appreciation is extended to Mr. G. Schultzberg, Division of Environmental Health, World Health Organization, Geneva, Switzerland who generously provided the information on International Organizations Experience in aquaculture. Special thanks are due Mr. James Basilico, Office of Environmental Engineering Technology Demonstration, U.S. Environmental Protection Agency for critically reviewing and offering constructive comments. Any opinions, findings and or recommendations expressed in this paper are those of the authors and do not necessarily reflect the view of the U.S. EPA.

REFERENCES

Blum, D., and R. G. Feachem. 1985. Health aspects of nightsoil and sludge use in agriculture and aquaculture, Part III, An epidemiological perspective. Report No. 05/85, November, International Reference Center for Waste Disposal (IRCWD), Duebendorf, Switzerland.

Buras, N., B. Hepher, and E. Sandbank. 1982. Public health aspects of fish culture in wastewater. Final Report. IDRC sponsored program.

Crites, R. W., M. J. Dean, and H. L. Selenick. 1979. Land treatment vs AWT - How do costs compare? Water and Wastes Engineering 16:16-19.

Cross, P., and M. Strauss. 1985. Utilization of excreta in agriculture and aquaculture. Part. I: Existing practices and beliefs. Part II: Pathogen survival. IRCWD, Duebendorf, Switzerland.

Davis, H. 1975. Distribution of mosquito species among four cypress domes. In H. T. Odum and K. C. Ewel (ed.) Cypress Wetlands for Water Management Recycling and Conservation. Second Annual Report. Center for Wetlands, Univ. of Florida, Gainesville, FL.

Demgen, F. C., and J. W. Nute. 1979. Wetlands creation using secondary treated wastewater. Proceedings - Vol. I of the Water Reuse Symposium. March, Washington, D.C. p. 729-739.

Edwards, P. 1985. Integrated resource recovery, aquaculture: A component of low cost sanitation technology. World Bank Technical Paper Number 36, April, World Bank, Washington, D.C.

Evans, K. J., I. G. Mitchell, and B. Salau. 1978. Heavy metal accumulation in soils irrigated by sewage and effect in the plant-animal system. International Conference on Developments in Land Methods of Wastewater Treatment and Utilization. October, Melbourne, Victoria, Australia. p. 24/1-24/14.

Feachem, R. G., D. J. Bradely, H. Garelick, and D. Duncan Mara. 1980. Appropriate technology for water supply and sanitation; Health aspects of excreta and sullage management. A State of the Art Review, World Bank, December, Washington, D.C.

Grunnet, K., and J. Moller. 1978. Changes in biological parameters on grass, hay and in silage following irrigation with domestic sewage. International Conference Developments in Land Methods of Wastewater dTreatment and Utilization. October, Melbourne, Victoria, Australia. p. 9/1-9/9.

International Reference Center for Wastes Disposal. 1985. Health aspects of nightsoil and sludge use in agriculture and aquaculture. IRCWD News, No. 23, December. 18 pp.

Jankiewicz, L. 1972. Survival of Ascaris eggs on soils irrigated with communal sewage, Zesz. nauk. A.R. - Wroc. Melioracje, XV, No. 90, p. 61-66. In Critical Review and Assessment of Polish Literature on Sewage Irrigation, Institute of Meteorology and Water Management (Wroclaw, Poland), Technical Interim Report No. 1 on Project JB-5-532-24, Dec. 1977, Abstract No. 193. p. 275-276.

Naylor, L. M., and R. C. Loehr. 1982. Priority pollutants in municipal sewage sludge Part II. Biocycle, November/December. p. 37-42.

Overcash, M. R. 1983. Land treatment of municipal effluent and sludge; specific organic compounds. p. 199-231. In A. L. Page, T. L. Gleason III, J. E. Smith, Jr., I. K. Iskandar, and L. E. Sommers (ed.) Utilization of Municipal Wastewater and Sludge on Land. Univ. of California, Riverside, CA.

Pahren, H. R. 1980. Overview of the problem. p. 1-5. In G. Bitton, B. L. Damron, G. T. Edds, and J. M. Davidson (ed.) Sludge - Health Risks of Land Application. Ann Arbor Science Publishers, Ann Arbor, MI.

Pahren, H. R., and W. Jakubowski. 1981. Health aspects of wastewater aerosols. 10th International Conference, IAWPR, Ontario, Canada. Water Science and Technology 13:1091-1096.

Paterson, J. J. 1975. Penetration and development of the mermittrid nematode *Reesimetis nielseni* in eighteen species of mosquitos. Nematology 7:297-210.

Patyk, S. 1958. Worms eggs in Wroclaw sewage and on meadows and pastures irrigated with municipal sewage. Wiad. parazyt. 4, f. 5/6, p. 479-481. In Critical Review and Assessment of Polish Literature on Sewage Irrigation, Institute of Meteorology and Water Management (Wroclaw, Poland), Technical Interim Report No. 1 on Project JB-5-532-24, Dec. 1977, Abstract No. 205. p. 288-289.

Phelps, R. P. 1985. Bacteria of public health significance associated with fish reared in treated wastewater. September. EPA 600/1-85-012.

Shelef, G., R. Moraine, A. Messing, and A. Kanarek. 1978. Improving stabilization ponds efficiency and performance. International Conference on Developments in Land Methods of Wastewater Treatment and Utilization. October, Melbourne, Victoria, Australia. p. 30/1-30/16.

Shuval, H. I., A. Adin, B. Fattal, E. Rawitz, and P. Yekutiel. 1985. Health effects of wastewater reuse in agriculture, World Bank studies in water supply and sanitation. The World Bank, Washington, D.C.

U.S. Environmental Protection Agency, Region IV, Atlanta, GA. 1985. Freshwater Wetlands for Wastewater Management Environmental Assessment Handbook.

U. S. Environmental Protection Agency. 1986a. Compilation of the status of USEPA rule making related to MCLGs and MCLs under the safe drinking water act, as of June 1986.

U.S. Environmental Protection Agency. 1986b. Design manual - municipal wastewater disinfection. EPA/625/1-86/021.

Weaver, R. W., N. O. Dronen, B. G. Foster, F. C. Heck, and R. C. Fehrmann. 1978. Sewage disposal on agricultural solids: Chemical and microbiological implications, Vol. II: Microbiological implications. Prepared for U.S. Environmental Protection Agency, RSKERL, Ada, OK.

Wellings, F. M., A. Lewis, L. Mountain, and V. Pierce. 1975. Demonstration of virus in ground water after effluent discharge onto soil. Appl. Microbiol. 29:751-757.

WHO. 1985. The risk to health of chemicals in sewage sludge applied to land. Report of a WHO Working Group. WHO Regional Office for Europe, Copenhagen, Denmark. Waste Management and Research 3:251-278.

ECONOMICS OF AQUATIC WASTEWATER TREATMENT SYSTEMS

R. W. Crites and T. J. Mingee
Nolte and Associates
Sacramento, California 95814

ABSTRACT

Aquatic plants have been used to treat municipal wastewater at a growing number of locations. The economics of these aquatic wastewater treatment systems are explored in this paper. Costs are included for hyacinth treatment systems and for constructed wetlands systems.

Design criteria from a number of case studies are examined. The variations in type of system and design detention time are analyzed. Specific costs of aquatic treatment systems at Sannon Beach, Oregon; Gustine, California; Incline Village, Nevada; and Orlando, Florida; are compared. Capital costs for constructed wetlands ranged from \$170 to \$410 per $m^3\ d^{-1}$. These costs compare favorably to the typical cost range of \$800 to \$1,000 per $m^3\ d^{-1}$ for secondary treatment.

Keywords: Costs, water hyacinths, wetlands, case studies, design criteria.

INTRODUCTION

The two types of aquatic wastewater treatment systems that have produced the most interest are the water hyacinth (Middlebrooks, 1980) and the created wetlands (Reed et al., 1980). The artificial or created wetland systems have had a wider geographical development (Reed et al., 1984).

The economics of these two types of aquatic treatment systems depend partly on the hydraulic detention time and hydraulic loading rate. Capital costs depend on the cost of land and earthwork costs. Typical values for detention time and loading rate are presented in Table 1.

The costs of typical 3,785 $m^3\ d^{-1}$, created wetlands and water hyacinth systems were compared in 1979. Energy usage of wetlands and hyacinth systems were evaluated in 1979 and found to be low compared to conventional treatment processes (Tchobanoglous and Culp, 1980). A summary of capital costs for 3,785 $m^3\ d^{-1}$ created

Aquatic Plants for Water Treatment
and Resource Recovery
K.R. Reddy and W.H. Smith (Eds.)

ISBN 0-941463-00-1

TABLE 1. Design criteria for aquatic treatment systems.

Type of system	Detention time	Depth	Loading rate
	----d----	----m----	$m^3\ ha^{-1}\ d^{-1}$
CREATED WETLANDS			
Typical	5-10	0.1-0.5	200-500
Listowel, Wile, 1985	7	0.1-0.3	200
Gearheart et al., 1984	6	0.3-0.6	500-1,000
Tchobanoglous and Culp, 1980	10	0.25	250
Gustine, CA	4-11	0.1-0.45	380
WATER HYACINTHS			
Typical	4-50	0.5-1.0	200-2,000
Middlebrooks, 1980	6-50	1.0-1.6	200-800

wetlands and water hyacinth systems is presented in Table 2. Costs are for 1986, updated from 1979 using an Engineering News-Record (ENR) construction cost index of 4290 for June 1986.

The conditions for the cost estimates in Table 2 are relatively favorable for the natural systems components. For example, the oxidation pond requires 7.2 ha and the aquatic treatment site is within 0.9 km of the oxidation pond. Capital costs in Table 2 include the entire treatment process of headworks, oxidation pond, pumping and piping to the site plus the aquatic treatment process.

There are insufficient data available on operation and maintenance costs of created wetlands or hyacinth systems from which to develop typical costs. Annual operation and maintenance of the 4.8 ha Vermontville, Michigan created wetland receiving 284 $m^3\ d^{-1}$ of oxidation pond effluent cost \$0.46 m^{-3} in 1981 (Sutherland, 1985).

TABLE 2. Capital costs of advanced secondary treatment using water hyacinths or artificial wetlands (Crites, 1979).

Item	1986 Dollars	
	Water hyacinths	Created wetlands
Capital costs†	\$1,830,000	\$1,960,000
Unit cost, \$ $m^{-3}\ d^{-1}$	483	518

†Flow = 3,785 $m^3\ d^{-1}$; wetlands area = 8 ha; hyacinth pond area = 2 ha; ENR CCI = 4290 for June 1986.

CASE STUDIES

Four case studies are presented of wetlands and water hyacinth projects. The 3 wetlands projects are:

. Cannon Beach, Oregon (natural wetland)
. Gustine, California (created marsh)
. Incline Village, Nevada (created and natural wetland)

The water hyacinth project at the Iron Bridge plant in Orlando, Florida, is also included.

Cannon Beach, Oregon

Background. Cannon Beach on the northern Oregon coast has developed a wastewater management plan that incorporates an existing wetland into an upgraded treatment plant. The preapplication treatment is accomplished in facultative ponds. The site selected for the wetland was a wooded wetland adjacent to Ecola Creek.

Description of the Treatment System. The objective of the wetlands is to provide additional removal of BOD and suspended solids (SS) to meet a summer discharge of 10 mg L^{-1} for both BOD and SS. The wetland operates from June 1 to October 31 each year. There are two 3.2 ha cells in the wetland. The current flow is 1,700 $m^3\ d^{-1}$. The effluent from the facultative lagoon averaged 28 mg L^{-1} BOD and 40 mg L^{-1} SS. The average discharge quality from the wetland for the summer of 1985 was 5 mg L^{-1} BOD and 14 mg L^{-1} SS (Jerry Minor, personal communication, July 1986). The design criteria are summarized in Table 3.

TABLE 3. Design criteria for wetlands treatment at Cannon Beach, Oregon (Demgen, 1984).

Item	Value
Effluent criteria	
BOD	10 mg L^{-1}
SS	10 mg L^{-1}
Design flow	3,444 $m^3\ d^{-1}$
Operating period	June 1 to October 31
Hydraulic loading rate	540 $m^3\ ha^{-1}\ d^{-1}$
Operating depth	0.6 m
Detention time	10.7 d
Wetland area	6.4 ha
Inlets	Multiple inlets on south side
Outlets	Single effluent outlet (summer) and multiple flood outlets (winter)

Costs. Construction on the Cannon Beach system began in July 1983 and was completed in April 1984. The construction cost for the wetland project was $580,000. Items included in the cost are a pump station and force main, earthwork to divide the wetland into two cells, influent and effluent structures, and fencing along the inlet side of the wetland. No land was purchased. The capital cost and projected operational cost of the wetland system are significantly less than alternative systems (physical/chemical treatment, phased isolation ponds, and intermittent sand filtration).

Gustine, California

Background. The City of Gustine, California, is a small agricultural town on the west side of the San Joaquin Valley. The city treats approximately 3,785 m^3 d^{-1} of wastewater of which about one-third originates from domestic and commercial sources and the remainder from three dairy products industries. The wastewater is of high strength, averaging over 600 mg L^{-1} BOD, which reflects the industrial component of the waste.

Until recently, the city's wastewater treatment plant consisted of 14 oxidation ponds operated in series which covered approximately 21.8 ha and provided about 70 d detention time. Treated effluent was discharged without disinfection to a small stream leading to the San Joaquin River.

As with many oxidation pond systems in the United States, mandatory secondary treatment levels were not achieved with any consistency. The discharge regularly exceeded the 30 mg L^{-1} SS standard and periodically violated the 30 mg L^{-1} BOD standard, both, at times, by large margins.

The city applied for and received funding under the Clean Water Act to analyze alternatives and develop a facilities plan. Alternatives included the following:

a. Treatment followed by land application (irrigation).
b. Treatment followed by reuse in the form of seasonal flooding to attract migrating water fowl for local duck clubs.
c. Oxidation pond treatment followed by effluent polishing to meet secondary treatment standards for river disposal using sand filters, microscreens, or submerged rock filters.
d. Conventional mechanical treatment to meet secondary treatment standards for river disposal.
e. Oxidation pond pretreatment followed by effluent polishing in a constructed marsh (using emergent aquatic vegetation) to meet secondary treatment standards for river disposal.

The analysis of alternatives showed the oxidation pond/constructed marsh to be the most cost-effective solution. The advantages of this alternative were that suitable land was available, the treatment method was compatible with the surrounding area (a low land area with naturally occurring aquatic vegetation and virtually no development) and the consumption of very little energy.

A one year pilot testing program using a 0.4 ha cattail marsh was initiated to develop design criteria for the system which are presented in Table 4.

Description of the Treatment System

The recommended treatment system, which is now under construction, consists of 11 of the existing oxidation ponds, operated in series, followed by 24 marsh cells each about 0.4 ha in size and operated in parallel. The operator draws wastewater which has been pretreated in the oxidation ponds from any one of the last seven ponds in series. This flexibility allows the operator to control the detention time in the ponds (28 to 54 d), to adjust the degree of pretreatment and also to avoid applying heavy concentrations of algae, which develop in the latter ponds through the summer. Pond effluent flow is split into six parts in a distribution structure and each portion of the flow is directed to a group of four marsh cells. Each of the 24 cells is 11.6 m wide, 337 m long and has an adjustable water depth of 10 to 45 cm. Levees, 3 m wide, separate the cells from one another. Flow is introduced across the width of the marsh cells at their head end and also at the one-third-of-length point. Overloading of the inlet zone of the cell is thus avoided. Effluent from each cell flows over an adjustable weir which controls water depth in the cell. The effluent is then pumped to a disinfection process prior to discharge.

TABLE 4. Design criteria for artificial marsh at Gustine, California.

Item	Value
Effluent criteria	
BOD	30 mg L^{-1}
SS	30 mg L^{-1}
Design flow	3,785 m^3 d^{-1}
Area	9.7 ha
Hydraulic loading rate	380 m^3 ha^{-1} d^{-1}
Depth	0.1-0.45 m
Detention time	4 to 11 d
Loading rate	380 m^3 ha^{-1} d^{-1}
Inlets	Head end of channels and one-third point
Outlets	Adjustable weirs

The number of cells and the variable water depth allow the operator flexibility in attaining the desired detention time in the marsh which varies from about 4 d in the summer to 11 d in the winter. This operational flexibility allows for the cells to be sequentially taken out of service each summer for vegetation management and other maintenance requirements.

Costs. Costs for the marsh system portion of the total project are summarized in Table 5. City-owned land for the Gustine project was available so that no land costs were involved. Land requirements for this system were 9.7 ha net for the area actually planted and about 14.5 ha gross for the whole marsh system including all interior cell divider levees and the outer flood protection levee.

TABLE 5. Capital costs for Gustine Marsh project.

Item	Cost, $ (August 1985)
Pond Effluent Piping (1)	192,000
Earthwork (2)	200,000
Flow Distribution Structure (3)	16,000
Flow Distribution Piping in Marsh (4)	205,000
Marsh Cell Water Level Control Structures (5)	27,000
Marsh Effluent Collection Piping (6)	83,000
Planting (7)	69,000
Paving (8)	90,000
Total	$882,000

NOTES: (1) Includes 793 m of 53 cm PVC gravity piping, five manholes, 7-pond outlet control pipes with wooden access platforms. (2) Total earthwork volume, approximately 34,400 m^3. Cost includes clearing and grubbing, extra effort to work in area of very shallow groundwater and to construct a 2 m high outer levee to enclose the marsh area and protect it from the 100 year flood. (3) A concrete structure with V-notch weirs, grating, access stairs and handrail. (4) Approximately 854 m of 20 cm PVC gravity sewer pipe, 763 m of 20 cm gated aluminum pipe, and wooden support structures with concrete base slabs for the gated pipe installed at the one-third-of-length point. (5) Small concrete structures in each cell with weir board guides and 0.6 cm mesh stainless steel screen. (6) Approximately 458 m of 10 to 38 cm PVC gravity sewer pipe plus three manholes. (7) Based on mechanical planting of bulrush and cattail rhizomes on 45 cm and 90 cm grid, respectively. Total bulrush area of about 2.4 ha; 7.2 ha for cattails. (8) Aggregate base paving of the outer levee and selected inner levees of the marsh area.

Incline Village, Nevada

Background. The Incline Village General Improvement District (IVGID) produces about 6,200 m^3 d^{-1} of secondary effluent. Located on the northeast shore of Lake Tahoe, the effluent is pumped to the eastern side of the Sierra Nevada mountains. In the summer it is used to irrigate a ranch in Jacks Valley, south of Carson City. In the winter, the effluent was discharged into the Carson River. A discharge prohibition order from the State of Nevada led to the selection of a wetlands project for wastewater management.

Description of the Treatment System. The objectives of the wetland are wastewater treatment and disposal and habitat enhancement. An existing warm water wetlands is kept separate from the created effluent wetlands. The project established an upland area of 81 ha, a created wetland of 49 ha, an overflow area of 47 ha, a floodplain area of 43 ha, and a seasonal storage area of 17 ha. The high degree of flexibility in the design should allow the operator to match climatic and percolation variations and not discharge any effluent from the system. Design criteria are presented in Table 6.

Costs. The costs of the Incline Village project are summarized in Table 7. The total construction cost of $3.3 million does not include the land acquisition cost of $950,000.

The construction of the wetlands was made difficult by shallow (1 m) groundwater, areas of peat and gypsum. Berms constructed in the peat areas had to be over-excavated and filled with rock to form a stable foundation for the berm. Dissolution of gypsum during startup resulted in the development of sink holes.

TABLE 6. Design criteria for wetlands project for Incline Village, Nevada (Robert Williams, July 1986, personal communication).

Item	Value
Effluent criteria	No discharge
Design flow	8,100 m^3 d^{-1}
Operating period	October 1 to April 15
Area	9.7 ha
Hydraulic loading rate (Created wetland only)	165 m^3 ha^{-1} d^{-1}
Operating depth	Variable 0.1 to 1 m
Detention time	6.5 months
Total area (actively used)	158 ha

TABLE 7. Capital costs for Incline Village wetland system (Robert Williams, July 1986, personal communication).

Item	Cost, $ (1984)
Mobilization and site clearing	353,000
Earthwork	867,000
Base rock and embankment protection	24,000
Pipelines	852,000
Buildings and structures	425,000
Landscaping, fencing and weather instrumentation	160,000
Total	3,284,000

Orlando, Florida

One of the largest water hyacinth treatment systems is located in Orlando, Florida, at the Iron Bridge treatment plant. The water hyacinths are used for nutrient removal in the polishing of advanced secondary effluent. The flow to the water hyacinth system is 30,280 $m^3\ d^{-1}$ and the hyacinth pond area is 12 ha. The hyacinth pond cost $1.5 million. In addition the pumps and pipelines cost $0.6 million and the digester for the harvested and chopped hyacinths cost $1.2 million (A. Stewart, 1986, personal communication, Cocoa, Florida).

SUMMARY OF CASE STUDIES

The four case studies are summarized in Table 8. Construction costs for the three wetlands projects ranged from

TABLE 8. Summary of project case studies.

Location	System type	Design flow $m^3\ d^{-1}$	Area, ha	Construction costs, $ millions	Unit cost, $ $m^{-3}\ d^{-1}$
Cannon Beach, Oregon	Existing wetland	3,440	6.5	0.58	170
Gustine, California	Created marsh	3,785	10	0.88	230
Incline Village, Nevada	Created and existing wetland	8,100	49	3.3	410
Iron Bridge Plant, Orlando, Florida	Hyacinth system	30,280	12	3.3	110
Typical secondary	Activated sludge	3,785	--	3-3.8	800-1,000

\$170 to \$410 per m^3 d^{-1} of capacity. The highest unit cost is for Incline Village which involved habitat improvement and complete containment of the applied effluent. For the hyacinth project at Orlando the unit cost is \$110 per m^3 d^{-1}. By comparison, typical secondary treatment capital costs range from \$800 to \$1,000 per m^3 d^{-1}. Costs to upgrade facultative pond effluent (as for Cannon Beach and Gustine) vary widely, but are usually less than the cost of secondary treatment alone.

REFERENCES

Crites, R. W. 1979. Economics of aquatic treatment systems. p. 475-485. In Aquaculture Systems for Wastewater Treatment: Seminar Proceedings and Engineering Assessment. U.S. EPA, EPA 430/9-80-006. Davis, California, September 1979.

Demgen, F. C. 1984. An overview of four new wastewater wetlands projects. p. 617-638. In Future of Water Reuse, Proceedings of the Water Reuse Symposium III, Volume 2, AWWA Research Foundation, San Diego, California, August 1984.

Gearheart, R. A., et al. 1984. The use of wetland treatment processes in water reuse. p. 617-638. In Future of Water Reuse, Proceedings of the Water Reuse Symposium III, Volume 2, AWWA Research Foundation, San Diego, California, August 1984.

Middlebrooks, E. J. 1980. Aquatic plant processes assessment. p. 43-62. In Aquaculture Systems for Wastewater Treatment: An Engineering Assessment, S. C. Reed and R. K. Bastian, Project Officers. U.S. EPA, EPA 430/9-80-007, June 1980.

Reed, S. C., R. K. Bastian, and W. J. Jewell. 1980. Engineering assessment of aquaculture systems for wastewater treatment: An overview. p. 1-12. In Aquaculture Systems for Wastewater Treatment: An Engineering Assessment, S. C. Reed and R. K. Bastian, Project Officers. U.S. EPA, EPA 430/9-80-007, June 1980.

Reed, S. C., R. K. Bastian, S. Black, and R. Khettry. 1984. Wetlands for wastewater treatment in cold climates. p. 962-972. In Future of Water Reuse, Proceedings of the Water Reuse Symposium III, Volume 2, AWWA Research Foundation, San Diego, California, August 1984.

Sutherland, J. C. 1985. Wetland-wastewater economics. p. 417-423. In P. J. Godfrey, E. R. Kaynor, S. Pelczarski, and J. Benforado (ed.) Ecological Consideration in Wetlands Treatment of Municipal Wastewaters. Van Nostrand Reinhold Co., New York.

Tchobanoglous, G., and G. L. Culp. 1980. Wetland systems for wastewater treatment: An engineering assessment. p. 13-42. In Aquaculture Systems for Wastewater Treatment: An Engineering Assessment, S. C. Reed and R. K. Bastian, Project Officers. U.S. EPA, EPA 430/9-80-007, June 1980.

Tchobanoglous, G., J. E. Colt, and R. W. Crites. 1979. Energy and resource consumption in land and aquatic treatment systems. p. 431-440. In Proceedings Energy Optimization of Water and Wastewater Management for Municipal and Industrial Applications Conference, Volume 2. New Orleans, Louisiana, December 1979.

Wile, I., G. Miller, and S. Black. 1985. Design and use of artificial wetlands. p. 26-37. In P. J. Godfrey, E. R. Kaynor, S. Pelczarski, and J. Benforado (ed.) Ecological Considerations in Wetlands Treatment of Municipal Wastewaters. Van Nostrand Reinhold Co., New York.

INSTITUTIONAL FACTORS AFFECTING WASTEWATER DISCHARGE TO WETLANDS

J. C. Montgomery
Office of Federal Activities
U.S. Environmental Protection Agency
Washington, DC 20002

ABSTRACT

The paper titled "EPA's Regulatory and Policy Considerations on Wetlands and Wastewater Treatment," (Davis and Montgomery, 1986) describes the key Environmental Protection Agency (EPA) programs which affect wastewater discharge to wetlands. Therefore, this paper is limited to briefly summarizing the main results of an internal EPA Task Force which was created to look at a number of legal and administrative issues concerning the discharge of wastewater to wetlands. It also offers some of the author's personal observations on these issues. A related paper, "Wastewater Management Programs and Wetlands," (R. J. Lord, 1986, USEPA, Atlanta, Georgia, unpublished results) discusses specific cases in the EPA southeastern region involving these programs and wastewater discharge to wetlands.

Keywords: Wastewater treatment, wetlands, waters of the United States, Clean Water Act, water quality standards.

INTRODUCTION

The EPA Task Force, formed in early 1985, was made up of staff level professionals from the Agency's municipal construction, water enforcement, wetlands protection, and NEPA (National Environmental Policy Act) compliance programs, as well as attorneys from the EPA Office of General Counsel. The focus was necessarily on the national requirements which regulate such discharges, rather than on local institutional requirements.

EPA's Chicago and Atlanta regions requested the formation of this task force to address policy questions which were identified in the course of preparing generic environmental impact statements (EISs) on wastewater discharges to wetlands (EPA Region 5, 1983, 1984; EPA Region 4, 1985). EPA must make decisions on such discharges as part of the construction grants and National Pollutant Discharge Elimination System (NPDES) permit programs.

Aquatic Plants for Water Treatment
and Resource Recovery
K.R. Reddy and W.H. Smith (Eds.)

ISBN 0-941463-00-1

Under the NEPA, EPA, prior to awarding a construction grant, must consider the different treatment alternatives available and assess the environmental impacts of each one. Construction grant regulations also require that alternatives be reviewed for cost-effectiveness. Under NPDES, EPA or delegated states must issue permits for municipal discharges to assure that they meet treatment limits and comply with applicable state water quality standards. EPA reviews may also be required as a result of EPA's role in implementing Section 404 of the Clean Water Act.

There is a growing interest in making use of the abilities of some natural wetlands to absorb nutrients and tolerate lower dissolved oxygen (DO) levels as a means of providing further treatment of wastewater prior to its entry into adjacent lakes or rivers, or simply as a direct means of disposal. This practice, if properly managed in appropriate wetlands, appears to be environmentally acceptable; indeed, in certain wetlands wastewater is used to maintain or expand levels of biological productivity associated with wetland systems. However, concern has also been expressed regarding the possible harmful effects of toxic materials and pathogens in wastewater, and the long-term degradation of wetlands due to increased water flow and nutrient loadings resulting from wastewater additions. The Agency is also promoting the use of "created wetlands" as a form of treatment for municipal wastewater.

PRINCIPAL FINDING

The principal finding of the Task Force was that the conceptual model which primarily views wetlands as a treatment system conflicts directly with a fundamental concept of the Clean Water Act, which makes no provision for use of natural wetlands (or any other protected water body) for treatment.

In brief, the Clean Water Act is concerned primarily with what goes into the wetland - not with what comes out of it. Obviously, the ensuing regulatory requirements introduce a number of complex considerations for planners proposing to use wetlands as treatment systems. They create limitations which would not be present if an artificial wetland were being constructed. Nevertheless, the EPA group found that 1) environmentally beneficial or acceptable wastewater discharges into wetlands can be allowed within the framework of the existing regulatory structure and still achieve significant wastewater treatment savings; and 2) there is still sufficient concern regarding the possible harmful effects of wastewater on wetlands such that they should continue to be primarily viewed as protected water bodies.

Therefore, from the overall standpoint of the regulatory structure established by the Clean Water Act, reviewing a proposed wetlands discharge is generally not much different in concept from considering discharges to other water bodies, with the exception that some wetlands may have a greater ability to tolerate lower DO and higher nutrient levels than lakes, streams or rivers.

SPECIFIC REGULATORY QUESTIONS

The principal finding discussed above guided the Task Force in addressing two key questions which had been identified by the Regions:

(1) Must municipal wastewater discharges to natural wetlands receive NPDES permits and do these dischargers have to meet the minimum technology requirement of secondary treatment and comply with applicable state water quality standards?

(2) Should the Agency alter any of its policies to promote more use of wetlands for wastewater treatment? Is there a need for expanded efforts in any other agency programs involved in this issue?

In response to the first of these questions, the Task Force concluded that the Clean Water Act clearly does not allow discharge of less-than-secondary municipal wastewater effluent into wetlands defined legally as waters of the U.S. (except possibly for Section 318 aquaculture permits). Nor does the Task Force believe that there is any good technical reason for the Agency to seek a change in this policy, pending further field experience and development of water quality criteria for wetlands. This is an important clarification since it precludes use of natural wetlands to achieve secondary levels at adjacent water bodies. However, wetlands still can be used to provide additional processing of secondarily treated wastewater prior to its entering a lake or river, thus providing an alternative to building an advanced wastewater treatment facility. Of course, such discharges must not have harmful environmental effects on the wetland.

It is also clear that discharges to wetlands must comply with applicable state water quality standards. However, at this time only one state, Florida, has developed water quality standards addressing wastewater discharge to wetlands, although Wisconsin is actively considering such standards. One state - North Carolina - has a "swamp waters" category and, for a time, South Carolina had a sub-category classification for wetlands. Some states apply the same standards to wetlands as to adjacent rivers or lakes; in these states the water quality standards which are legally applicable to wetlands may not reflect the physical, chemical and biological characteristics of these types of areas. Other states include wetlands in an "all others" category, which requires site-specific evaluation.

According to the EPA Atlanta Regional Office's Handbook (EPA Region 4, 1985) most of the states in the Southeast use provisions for site-specific water quality standards in considering wetlands discharges. These allow alternative effluent limits if the impacts on the wetland are compatible with wetland conditions. The EPA Chicago Region (EPA Region 5, 1983,1984) notes that the Great Lakes states vary widely in their resources and willingness to consider wetlands discharges on a case-by-case basis, especially if advanced polishing is an issue.

Given the considerable lack of knowledge on the fate of toxic effluents (such as heavy metals) in wetlands, the Task Force believed that their discharge into natural wetlands should be discouraged.

In response to the second question, the Task Force concluded that the lack of EPA water quality criteria for wetlands (and the absence of separate state water quality standards for wetlands in most states) is currently the most serious impediment to a consistent national policy on use of wetlands for wastewater discharge. The lack of such guidance results in state, local and EPA decision-makers having no technical frame of reference for site-specific decisions regarding wastewater application to wetlands discharge because an extensive effort to develop a separate, site-specific effluent limit may be required. They also face public concern for wetlands protection, a lack of knowledge needed to assess questions about the environmental acceptability of a wetlands discharge, and existing EPA policies which call for avoiding impacts to wetlands. Developing generic standards would reduce the effort needed to address each site-specific situation. EPA wetlands water quality criteria are also required to address a number of technical issues in this area. For example, there is concern that some wetlands may have a limited capacity for uptake of phosphorus, which may limit their potential for wastewater application where phosphorus is an issue. Such areas as identifying appropriate biological parameters (including wildlife and vegetation) for monitoring the preservation of various wetland uses and setting out the degree of change which can be allowed in wetlands (receiving wastewater discharges) also need to be included in this kind of guidance. Another area which should be addressed concerns the impact of wetlands wastewater discharges on adjacent water bodies, particularly if there is concern that the wetland will become saturated with nutrients over time. These are but a few of the many technical areas where the Agency should be developing guidance for the states and municipal wastewater dischargers.

TASK FORCE RECOMMENDATIONS

In summary, the major Task Force recommendations were:

1. The EPA needs to carry out a long-term effort to develop water quality criteria for wetlands. Related monitoring requirements will also have to be identified at the same time. The Task Force supports a recent effort by EPA in implementing and EPA/Army Memorandum of Agreement on Solid Waste Discharges to look at possible approaches to development of wetland water quality criteria which the states could use to develop appropriate water quality standards.

2. In conjunction with the development of water quality criteria, EPA should continue to make states and localities aware that discharge to wetlands of municipal wastewater effluents (which comply with applicable effluent limits and where data show that the wetlands under consideration will not be degraded) may be an environmentally sound and cost-effective alternative to be considered in planning wastewater treatment systems. The Agency should be sure that this is considered in connection with its requirements that construction grant applicants select the most cost-effective treatment alternative.
3. EPA should continue to support studies on wetlands wastewater application and should closely follow projects now in place. A research program should be developed and carried out on wastewater discharge to wetlands and in support of developing wetlands water quality standards.
4. EPA should continue to provide grant funding for the construction of artificial wetlands for wastewater treatment.
5. The Task Force agreed that the Agency should examine in more detail whether any existing provisions of the Clean Water Act (e.g. Section 318 aquaculture provisions) could be used to develop specific NPDES permits which provide for use of wetlands processes as a means of providing further improvement in water quality.

PERSONAL OBSERVATIONS

The author has two observations to add to this discussion. First, the effect of treatment plant failure and pretreatment noncompliance needs to be considered in evaluating treatment alternatives, particularly those involving wetlands discharges. In the real world treatment plants do not always operate as they are supposed to, and there is some reason to believe that a more complex regime of discharge (involving, say, seasonal variations in quantities of wastewater allowed to go into a certain wetland area) could be more subject to failure from human error. Of course this is not to say that it is always the case that a wetland would suffer more long-term damage (due to a plant failure) than a lake or river. Excess nutrient loadings might have a more severe impact on aquatic life in a river than in a wetland. However, given the fact that wetlands are often hydrologically sluggish it is reasonable to assume that excess levels of toxics would remain in them in a less diluted form over a longer period of time.

The other point worth stressing is that there is reason to be concerned with the different requirements that exist for management of a wetland treatment system, as opposed to a conventional treatment operation. A plant manager will have to be concerned with the wetland not only in terms of its ability to deliver water of a certain quality at an adjacent stream, but also with such things as maintaining species, assuring that wetland uses (such as recreation) are maintained, and making sure that nearby development does not interfere with the treatment ability of the wetland. This creates a much more demanding job of management, and there is some reason to be doubtful about the ability of small systems to assure a consistently high level of management over the lifetime of a treatment system.

REFERENCES

Davis, D. G., and J. C. Montgomery. 1987. EPA's regulatory and policy considerations on wetlands and wastewater treatment. In K. R. Reddy and W. H. Smith (ed.) Aquatic Plants for Water Treatment and Resource Recovery. Magnolia Publishing, Inc., Orlando, Florida.

EPA Region IV. 1985. Freshwater wetlands for wastewater management handbook. EPA 904/9-15-135. September 1985, Atlanta, Georgia. 493 pp.

EPA Region V. 1983. The effects of wastewater treatment facilities on wetlands in the Midwest. EPA 905/3-83-002. September 1983, Chicago, Illinois.

EPA Region V. 1984. Literature review of wetland evaluation methodologies. EPA 905/3-84-002. September 1984.

EPA. 1986. Office of Federal Activities, Unpublished Internal Report. August 1986, Washington, DC.

FLORIDA'S WASTE DISPOSAL DILEMMA: A TIME FOR INNOVATION

V. J. Tschinkel
Florida Department of Environmental Regulation
Tallahassee, Florida 32301

To set the stage, a brief overview of the situation in Florida on wastewater disposal is provided. Florida is somewhat unique environmentally, but the state certainly has similar problems with wastewater disposal as others, complicated further by its tremendous growth. Addressed also is an issue whose time has come--the concept of recycling and reuse in our planning for disposal of wastes. It is an exciting area which may bring solutions to at least some of Florida's waste disposal and water supply problems.

OVERVIEW OF WASTEWATER DISPOSAL IN FLORIDA

Florida's population more than tripled from 1950 to 1980. Another 50% increase in population is predicted for the state between 1980 and 2000. This means an estimated population of 15 million. This rapid population increase in turn leads to a need for greatly expanded sewage treatment and disposal facilities, with the inevitable massive associated capital costs. Protection of water quality and provision of adequate water supplies are also major concerns. The 1984 Environmental Protection Agency Needs Survey found that the state will need $5.3 billion more in publicly-owned treatment systems by the year 2000, with a backlog need of $2.8 billion right now.

Besides the capital and operating costs, increased wastewater effluent strains the very environment people move to Florida for in the first place. It also can threaten our tourist industry, which generates about $620 million in annual revenue. What's more, there are very limited options for disposal in Florida, because our small surface streams, lakes and estuaries are warm, shallow and slow-moving, which means they are relatively intolerant of effluent discharge and prone to eutrophication. Our high groundwater table, porous soil and the fact that we get 92% of our drinking water from groundwater supplies further limits disposal possibilities. At the least, a high degree of treatment

ISBN 0-941463-00-1

is needed; in some areas, alternative disposal methods must be employed.

Most of Florida's population growth in the past has come in the coastal area. More recently the Orlando area has also experienced a substantial population boom. Unfortunately, the areas which are growing also are areas of significant constraints for wastewater management, with high groundwater tables and lack of good receiving waters.

The financial picture, along with the constraints of population growth and environmental stress, makes it clear that we must innovate. Effluent discharge to wetlands and wastewater reuse are two methods which show promise in Florida, so those are discussed first. Then, some promising nutrient removal projects using water hyacinths are briefly reviewed.

WASTEWATER TO WETLANDS

Wastewater treatment in wetlands may prove to be of particular value in Florida, where approximately a third of the state was in wetland acreage as of the late 1970s. For this reason, water quality exemptions were adopted to provide for experimental use of wetlands for low-energy water and wastewater recycling. The exemptions were designed to encourage experiments which could lead to wider use of low-energy approaches to advanced treatment of domestic, agricultural, and industrial wastes; and to encourage the conservation of wetlands and fresh waters.

Specifically, the exemption rule provided that the Secretary of Environmental Regulation may exempt wastewater to wetlands projects from the water quality standards which otherwise would apply, provided that:

1. The discharger affirmatively demonstrates that the wetlands ecosystem may reasonably be expected to assimilate the waste discharge without significant adverse impact on the biological community with the receiving waters;
2. Granting the exemption is in the public interest and will not adversely affect public health or the cost of public health or other related programs;
3. The public is restricted from access to the waters under consideration;
4. The waters are not used for recreation;
5. The applicant affirmatively demonstrates that presently specified criteria are unnecessary for the protection of potable water supplies or human health;
6. The exemption will not interface with the designated use of contiguous waters; and
7. Scientifically valid experimental controls are provided by the applicant and approved by the department to monitor the long-term ecological effects and waste recycling efficiency.

Nine exemptions have been granted under the rule.

In addition to the water quality exemption for the experimental use of wetlands for wastewater treatment, Florida's Warren S. Henderson Wetlands Protection Act of 1984 required the Department of Environmental Regulation to establish, by rule, criteria to provide for the use of wetlands to receive and treat domestic wastewater that at a minimum has been treated to secondary standards.

The law requires that the criteria must protect the type, nature and function of the wetlands receiving the wastewater. In order to develop the rule, a wetlands work group was designated in the department, and charged with the responsibility to design a rule which would include regulation at three levels; (1) effluent limits; (2) standards within the treatment wetland; and (3) standards for discharge from the treatment wetland to downstream water bodies.

We recently adopted this new Florida regulation prescribing criteria for discharges to wetlands. Basically, the rule allows use of three categories of wetlands for disposal and treatment of domestic wastewater effluent: 1) all artificial or created wetlands; 2) all hydrologically-altered wetlands; and 3) woody or non-herbaceous unaltered wetlands. The rule prohibits the use of wetlands classified as Outstanding Florida Waters, drinking water supplies, shellfish harvesting waters, and those within a 24 h effluent travel time from a lake, estuary, lagoon, or areas of critical state concern. In addition, the rule established technology-based effluent limitations and pH requirements for wastewater discharged to wetlands, as well as design criteria for wetlands application and operation and maintenance requirements for treatment plants and effluent disposal systems which discharge to wetlands.

The idea of using wetlands to treat and recycle wastewater is not new. A 1983 United States Environmental Protection Agency study found 58 wastewater systems in Florida discharging to wetlands, or about 5% of the total number of discharges to surface waters. Most discharges had been for more than 20 years, and at least one for over 90 years. Experience has shown that wetlands can effectively filter sediments, nutrients and other pollutants. And, although there are still uncertainties which dictate caution, this can generally be done in an environmentally-sound manner, with proper monitoring. Wetlands offer great potential, especially given the constraints for discharge of treated effluent to uplands, or open water.

But now, with preparation of a new economic impact statement for our waste to wetlands rule, we have additional evidence that this alternative can indeed be economically advantageous. The economic impact statement compares the cost of wetlands treatment with various other treatment alternatives. Two alternative technologies were selected which approximate the level of N and P removal possible with wetlands treatment. They are: 1) nitrification-denitrification, with alum added to the aeration basin; and 2) spray irrigation.

Advanced secondary treatment costs were estimated for each technology. Advanced secondary treatment is required before discharge to a natural wetland, so that natural wetlands treatment will never be cheaper than secondary treatment. Use of man-made wetland only requires secondary treatment. So a discharger might very well find wetlands treatment in an artificial wetland a reasonable alternative to advanced secondary treatment.

Results were computed for various size projects, including one, 72,000, 94,625 and 189,250 m^3 d^{-1}. A wetland acquisition cost of \$4,942 ha^{-1} was assumed. For pristine wetlands, a maximum loading rate of 2.5 cm wk^{-1} is permitted; for hydrologically altered wetlands, the maximum rate is 15 cm wk^{-1}; and for artificial wetlands, there is no maximum rate.

Essentially, we found that at most project sizes, wetlands treatment is cheaper than the alternative wastewater treatment technologies to which it was compared. In order of increasing cost, artificial wetlands are the cheapest alternative, followed by advanced secondary treatment, altered wetlands, then unaltered wetlands. Benefits of wetlands treatment were computed by subtracting wetlands treatment costs from the cost of the cheapest alternative, both for advanced wastewater treatment and advanced secondary treatment.

Using this method, we found that a discharger of 10 million gal d^{-1} to an artificial wetland would enjoy a benefit of \$3.3 million a year over the cost for advanced waste treatment; at 94,625 m^3 d^{-1}, the annual benefit is \$6.8 million; a 189,250 m^3 d^{-1} discharger would benefit by \$11.6 million annually. Net benefits are positive at project sizes for all types of wetlands, indicating that wetlands treatment is often cost effective compared with advanced wastewater treatment.

Direct economic benefits could potentially accrue to many wastewater dischargers as a result of the new wetland rule. Also, indirect economic benefits appear probable since hydrologically altered wetlands may be reflooded and their biological quality and water storage capacity restored. The standards established by the rule should prevent damage to wetlands.

WASTEWATER REUSE

Through the Florida State Comprehensive Plan, as well as the State Water Use Plan and State Water Policy, the state is committed to "promote water conservation programs as well as the use and reuse of water of the lowest acceptable quality for the purposes intended."

A number of Florida communities--including Naples, Mt. Dora, Leesburg, Ocala, St. Petersburg, Orlando and Tallahassee--are using various wastewater reuse techniques to dispose of effluent. Most use spray irrigation on public access areas such as golf courses, parks, agricultural areas, lawns and citrus crops.

We have found that reuse of water generally is related to free market economic forces. Another factor, however, is lack of other environmentally suitable disposal options in some communities, making reuse the only alternative regardless of costs.

Heavy withdrawal of groundwater in some areas of Florida by agriculture, industry and urban populations has limited the available supplies. As this has happened, communities are faced with various options, including water importation, desalinization, or substitution of reclaimed water for potable water to satisfy some nonpotable needs. Water importation can lead to water wars; desalinization, although it may eventually become necessary, is expensive, but may be competitive in some areas.

These water supply factors, along with stringent wasteload allocations which prohibit discharge to surface water or require advanced waste treatment, have made reuse the only economically viable disposal option in many areas of the state. Backup is needed, however.

For this reason, the city of Tampa is evaluating the technical and economic feasibility of using reclaimed wastewater to supplement freshwater supplies during dry weather conditions. A combination of both factors--water supply and wastewater disposal needs--the city is projected to experience shortages of fresh water supplies over the next 10-15 years.

We have determined that, absent a true demand, wastewater reuse is incidental to the primary objective, which is wastewater disposal. To encourage direct reuse, the cost of disposal must be subsidized to favor reuse, or the cost of freshwater must be raised. There already are some cases where this has been done. This can either be accomplished through financial assistance, such as grants and loans, or by creating a market for reclaimed water to recover some of the costs of treatment and disposal costs from the user through regulation.

Naples, Florida, for example, is faced with regulatory objections to continued disposal of its effluent to surface waters, and public objections to deep well disposal. Consequently, the city is making a substantial effort to reuse most of its reclaimed effluent for irrigation. They will provide reclaimed water to golf courses for about two cents per 3.8 m^3. It would cost about 1.3 cents per m^{-3} to pump their own groundwater for irrigation, plus the fertilizer value of the reclaimed wastewater is estimated at 1.8 cents m^{-3}.

The city of St. Petersburg is operating a successful wastewater reuse program, through which it makes the reclaimed water accessible to residential and institutional customers for irrigation of lawns and other landscaped areas. Because federal EPA funding defrayed a large part of the capital costs, the city is able to offer reclaimed water to businesses for \$0.07 m^{-3}, and to residential customers for a flat fee of \$6 a month. The cost of potable water is \$0.24 m^{-3} from the city. Therefore, the economic benefit for customers is substantial, plus the irrigation water has nutrient value.

This program allowed the city to avoid construction of expensive advanced waste treatment facilities, and also eliminated the need for water importation projects to meet the growing demand for water from population growth. The success of St. Petersburg's program has allowed it to substitute about 26% of its dry weather water supply requirements by reclaimed water.

Some other communities in Florida which have found reuse to be the most economically-feasible alternative are: Mt. Dora, with a reuse cost of \$0.45 m^{-3} versus \$0.63 m^{-3} for advanced sewage treatment facilities; and Leesburg, \$0.39 m^{-3} for reuse, compared with \$0.46 m^{-3} for advanced secondary treatment, or \$0.54 m^{-3} to upgrade to advanced treatment.

Another encouraging sign is that we have been advised by an official of Florida's Public Service Commission that if reuse is a regulatory requirement, it can be used in a utility's rate base. In some cases, there is limited or no demand for wastewater; thus reuse would be only a disposal option, with the utility paying the entire cost.

Where this is the case, it may be necessary to provide incentives, such as creating a market for the reclaimed water, provision of government grants or low-interest loans, or allowing the utility to pass the cost of reuse on to its customers.

In Florida, and presumably in most other states, legislative appropriations for grant or low interest loan programs to enable utilities to overcome cost barriers for successful reuse programs would have to be sought. Desirable also for the state is a cap set on liability claims against the supplier, if the system is in compliance with state environmental standards.

Another option would be to establish a water use fee system with rebates which would reward reuse projects, and excess fees to be used for grants for water reuse projects. We are also convinced that any state grant or loan program established by legislation in the future should encourage use of the funds for direct reuse projects. Large users of water--such as golf courses, public landscape, industry and agriculture--should be required, as part of getting a consumptive use permit, to conduct feasibility studies on reuse.

Also, private utilities should have the same limits of liability as public utilities. Also desirable are funds for research on technological and public health aspects of water reuse. And, we should encourage mitigation of saltwater intrusion in coastal areas using direct or indirect recharge of aquifers with reclaimed water.

EXPERIMENTAL WATER HYACINTH PROJECTS

The use of water hyacinths to treat domestic wastewater has been researched heavily over the last ten years. Early research in the field was performed by the state of Texas, and was followed (1975) by National Aeronautics and Space Administration (NASA) studies in Mississippi. This research has proven complimentary for Florida conditions because of basic similarities in climate and conditions. Florida has, in the last few years, taken the lead in development of information on water hyacinth use.

Hyacinths are a "natural" candidate for wastewater treatment here, because the sunny, moist Florida climate is ideal for this tropical exotic plant.

A $500,000 project for the city of Kissimmee was funded through the department in 1984. The final report is not yet complete, but interim reports have been very encouraging. The system has worked as expected, removing N and P from sewage effluent. The hyacinths may actually treat the effluent beyond the level attainable with Advanced Wastewater Treatment (AWT) processes.

In addition, the state has provided $1.8 million over the last two years for hyacinth studies by the St. Johns River Water Management District, which is working in cooperation with the Florida Game and Fresh Water Fish Commission. Hyacinths may be used on an experimental basis to remove excess nutrients from Lake Apopka. The district governing board will decide soon whether to go forward with a proposed three year, $3 million hyacinth demonstration project, which would involve 20 ha of the lake, plus a 20 ha control site. One of the requirements for funding of the Lake Apopka restoration project is evaluation of different methods of lake recovery. Water hyacinths are used to control algae growth in the Loxahatchee River. The hyacinths live on the same nutrients as algae, and "shade out" the algae from the sunlight it needed to survive.

We should temper our optimism for hyacinth use, however with caution about problems we may face. The hyacinth system initiated last summer at the Orlando Iron Bridge regional treatment facility has uncovered several potential constraints on water hyacinth use in some parts of the state. Freezing temperatures kill the plants, wreaking havoc on a treatment system. Once the plants are killed, it takes quite a long time to reestablish them at a level sufficient for wastewater treatment. This rules out their use in north Florida. Insect attacks also destroy hyacinths if allowed to go unchecked. A fungus outbreak caused a brief shutdown at the Iron Bridge facility, and the 12 ha project had to be restocked with water hyacinths to achieve DER water quality standards.

Nevertheless, the department's position is that these problems should not discourage the use of hyacinth systems in central and south Florida, at least for 9 months per year. Also, hyacinths appear to be capable of removing some toxics such as heavy metals from wastewater discharges, so numerous industrial applications might be possible.

The biggest problem so far with hyacinth treatment appears to be economic in nature. To remove nutrients from the system, plants must be periodically harvested and disposed, but no cost-effective, environmentally safe method for final disposal of the plants currently exists. Thus, the department currently is looking for cost-effective disposal methods which could gain some level of economic return for providing a strong incentive for the use of hyacinth treatment. The plants might be recycled to produce byproducts like methane gas, compost, livestock feed, or possibly high-value extracted chemicals.

A solution to the "disposal dilemma" should make hyacinth use a very attractive, promising technology for wastewater treatment in central and south Florida. The concept could also be applied to existing treatment facilities by putting hyacinths into existing percolation ponds as is being done right now in Melbourne, Florida. While hyacinths might not always be appropriate as the primary treatment system, their use certainly deserves consideration as an added component for some wastewater treatment systems.

Use of hyacinths for wastewater treatment is considered "innovative and alternative technology" and thus receives special consideration under the current federal sewage grants program. This adds to the economic attractiveness of this energy-efficient treatment concept. The department is encouraging potential users of hyacinth treatment to evaluate prospects and limitations in terms of location-specific factors such as exact location of the facility, number of freezing or near-freezing days per year, and costs of other potentially applicable treatment technologies. While hyacinth use might be useful for some situations, it will not always be the best choice available.

The DER currently handles hyacinth projects on a case-by-case basis. As use of hyacinths for wastewater treatment increases, the department will set guidelines and rules for their future use in the state. There undoubtedly will be some pitfalls among the successes, but hyacinth treatment is too potentially valuable an option not to be explored fully.

SUMMARY

Florida's population growth creates the need for additional wastewater treatment and disposal facilities, along with the other infrastructure needs. To keep up with this growth, we are trying not only innovative funding options, but also innovative disposal methods. Our studies show wastewater reuse and wastewater discharge to artificial and natural wetlands and the use of water hyacinth treatment to be promising, both environmentally and economically. Further advancement of these treatment options and public education will also be necessary to help pave the way for wider use of innovative techniques.

TREATMENT OF ACID DRAINAGE FROM COAL FACILITIES WITH MAN-MADE WETLANDS

G. A. Brodie
Division of Fossil Hydro Power
Tennessee Valley Authority
Chattanooga, Tennessee 37402

D. A. Hammer
Division of Land and Economic Resources
Tennessee Valley Authority
Norris, Tennessee 37828

D. A. Tomljanovich
Division of Air and Water Resources
Tennessee Valley Authority
Knoxville, Tennessee 37902

ABSTRACT

A series of shallow impoundments planted with a variety of wetlands emergents was constructed in May 1985 to treat acidic drainage emanating from the toe of a fine coal refuse impoundment dike at the Tennessee Valley Authority's Fabius Coal Preparation Plant in northeastern Alabama. Flora and fauna within the wetlands (both transplants and invaders) showed rapid growth and expansion. Comparisons between the seeps and final effluent showed substantial reductions in Mn, Fe, and suspended solids during July 1985 through June 1986 and increases in pH and dissolved O_2. In December 1985, an additional 75-150 L min^{-1} of pH 3.5 water discharged into the wetlands reduced treatment efficiency, but the system gradually recovered after the acidic flow was terminated.

Keywords: Wetlands, waste treatment, coal, acid mine drainage, red water, Tennessee Valley Authority.

INTRODUCTION

Acid water drainage (pH<6, Fe>4 mg L^{-1}, Mn>2 mg L^{-1}), primarily from coal mining and processing, lowers water quality, impacts aquatic biota, and jeopardizes drinking water supplies throughout the Appalachian coal fields, western mining areas, and

ISBN 0-941463-00-1

throughout the world. A 1967 survey estimated that almost 18,000 km of rivers and streams in Appalachia were negatively impacted by acid drainage (FWPCA, 1969).

Conventional treatment technology primarily consists of grading and recontouring to reduce or divert flows and addition of alkaline solutions to elevate pH levels and chemically precipitate metallic ions. Land reforming is almost prohibitively expensive, and chemical treatment is not only expensive--coal mining companies in Appalachia spend over 1 million dollars per day (Kleinmann, personal communication)--but often requires a long-term maintenance and operational commitment. Man-made wetlands appear to offer an inexpensive, self-maintaining, long-term solution that may be applicable to small or large flow acid discharges.

Several investigators have suggested or demonstrated the effectiveness of wetlands in removing acidity, sulfate (SO_4), Fe, Mn, and other pollutants from acid mine drainage (Weider et al., 1984; Holm, 1983; Pesavento, 1984; Brodie, unpub. data). Some have described failures of demonstration wetlands to achieve desired results (Pesavento, 1984; Weider et al., 1985).

Laboratory studies have explored design and operational parameters of wetlands for acid mine drainage treatment (Gerber et al., 1985; Tarleton et al., 1984; Brodie et al., 1985). Most existing experimental or operational wetlands have adapted or simulated peat bogs with _Sphagnum_, _Polytrichum_, or _Hypnum_ mosses as the dominant vegetative species. Although generally successful in removing Fe, Mn, and some other metals from acid mine drainage, peat bogs are naturally acidic with pH values commonly between 3.2 and 4.0 (Clymo, 1984). Since a moss-dominated treatment system may not be able to achieve effluent limitations for pH, some workers have incorporated limestone neutralization into wetlands systems (Kleinmann, 1985; Holm, 1983).

Natural marsh-type wetlands, dominated by emergent plant species (_Typha_, _Scirpus_, _Eleocharis_, _Juncus_) frequently occur at acid water seeps emanating from a variety of natural and anthropogenic sources. Our field investigations suggest that many of these systems provide considerable water quality improvement. In addition, marsh-type wetlands have been used for municipal wastewater treatment for many years, resulting in design guides and publications which have application to designing and operating treatment wetlands for acid mine drainage (Hammer and Kadlec, 1983; Nichols, 1983; Hyde et al., 1982; Tchobanoglous and Culp, 1980). Preliminary design guidelines for constructing wetlands to treat acid mine drainage have also been suggested (Brooks, 1984; Pesavento, 1984).

Little work has been done on pollutant removal mechanisms of wetlands for mine drainage treatment. Physical/chemical mechanisms may include ion exchange on substrate surfaces, precipitation and sedimentation, coagulation, chemical filtration, volatilization, absorption, chelation, and sulfate reduction (Chan et al., 1982; Hammer and Kadlec, 1983).

Vegetative and microbiological mechanisms are thought to be important, if not the major factors in pollutant removal. These may include cation exchange on plant surfaces, physical filtration, uptake of pollutants through plant/substrate and plant/water interface and translocation of pollutants through plant vascular systems, uptake and immobilization of pollutants in plant litter zones, microbiological oxidation of Fe and Mn, and SO_4 reduction (Gregory and Staley, 1982; Stone, 1984; Chan et al., 1981).

Results of various treatment systems have ranged from poor to excellent, and more importantly, few systems have been studied over long time periods (Weider et al., 1984). Intuitively, we suspect these systems will provide self-maintaining water treatment for extended time periods since similar natural wetlands appear to have accomplished these functions over geological time.

SITE DESCRIPTION

Since November 1971, two coal slurry disposal ponds have existed on the 104 ha site of the Tennessee Valley Authority's (TVA) Fabius Coal Preparation Facility in Jackson County, Alabama. In 1979, the facility was mothballed. In 1984, TVA decommissioned the facility and began reclamation. Reclamation was to include mitigating seepage at the toe of the dike of Slurry Lake 2.

In 1979, the slurry lakes consisted of 17 ha of fine (minus 28 mesh) coal refuse and water impounded by a 585 m long earthen dam. The total drainage area at the primary spillway for Slurry Lake 2 was 147 ha. Runoff generally flows over the surface of exposed coal slurry and becomes strongly acidic (pH = 3.5), necessitating chemical treatment. During operations, slurry water was decanted and either treated and discharged or recirculated for process water. After operations ceased, the slurry water was pumped to a holding pond where it was treated and discharged. Seepage along the toe of the dike was identified in 1976 and subsequently monitored for flow and quality. Flows ranged from 30 to 106 L min^{-1} with total Fe averaging 80 mg L^{-1}, Mn exceeding 10 mg L^{-1}, dissolved O_2 below 2 mg L^{-1}, suspended solids exceeding 98 mg L^{-1}, and pH averaging 6.0.

MATERIALS AND METHODS

In April 1985, a marsh/pond wetlands systems was selected to treat seepage emanating from the toe of the coal slurry impoundment dam. Existing topography was surveyed and specifications developed to create the maximum practical amount of shallow water wetland and to conserve a small (10 m^2) existing wetland. Bulldozers cleared approximately 1 ha of woodlands and constructed four dikes with overflow spillways (Figure 1).

Hand clearing and felling trees perpendicular to anticipated flow patterns preserved existing wetland vegetation and reduced flow channeling or short-circuiting. In addition, seven sandbag dikes created smaller impoundments in the immediate vicinity of two known seeps and below the discharge pipe for acidic water from the slurry impoundment. Total impounded water area approximated 0.6 ha. Plants were obtained from nearby acid seeps to ensure plant populations adapted to similar edaphic and aquatic conditions.

In early June, laborers hand dug and transplanted bulrush (*Scirpus*), rush (*Juncus*), spikerush (*Eleocharis*), cattail (*Typha*), and scouring rush (*Equisetum*) from natural stands at nearby seeps into the sandbag ponds and shallow water (<0.7 m) areas of the larger ponds. Larger plants (*Typha*) and clump forming species (*Scirpus*) were spaced at 1 m^{-2} whereas those with smaller habits were planted 5-10 m^{-2}. A moss (*Philonotes*) found growing in association with *Equisetum* at a nearby seep was also planted within the sandbag pond at Seep 1.

Scirpus and *Juncus* clumps were thrown into the wetland from shore and *Typha* were individually pressed into the substrate. To stimulate new vegetative growth and to prevent wind-throw, *Typha* stems were broken over. Triple phosphate was broadcast at a rate of 505 kg ha^{-1} in August 1985.

Since donor locations were nearby and transplanting sites were inundated by impounded water, plants were transported in the bed of pick-up trucks without additional precautions against dehydration.

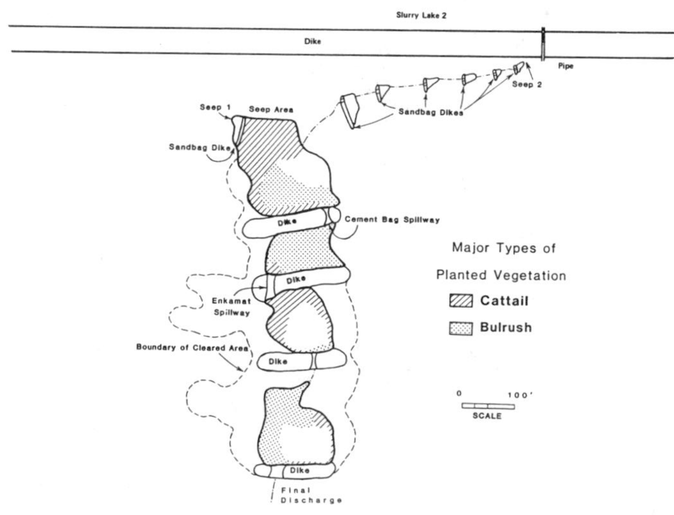

Figure 1. Slurry Lake 2 wetlands treatment system.

Weekly water sampling was initiated on July 2, 1985, and included samples from two primary seeps, 4 locations within the wetlands system, and the final discharge point. Parameters analyzed by the TVA Laboratory Branch using standard methodologies (EPA, 1979) included pH, Eh, dissolved O_2, Al, Ca, Cu, total Fe, dissolved Fe, Mg, total Mn, dissolved Mn, Zn, and total suspended solids. Monitoring was later reduced to biweekly samples for pH, Eh, DO, total Fe, total Mn, and total suspended solids since only insignificant quantities of Al, Ca, Cu, and Zn were present in seep water or discharge.

RESULTS AND DISCUSSION

After clearing and dike construction was completed, five small and two larger seeps emerged within the marsh/pond system. Before construction, these seeps had apparently discharged directly into the small stream resulting from the two previously known seeps at the toe of the dike. Three seeps occurred in Ponds 1 and 2; one large and one small seep were located in Pond 3; and two smaller seeps occurred in Pond 4.

With the possible exception of the *Equisetum*/*Philonotes* complex, vigorous growth and considerable vegetative reproduction occurred in transplanted cattail, rushes, and bulrushes. In addition, *Utricularia*, *Potamogeton*, *Carex*, *Sagittaria*, *Echinodorus*, *Cyperus*, *Bidens*, *Polygonum*, *Leersia*, and *Alisma* were accidentally introduced or naturally invaded. Density transect sampling revealed that *Typha* had become dominant over much of Pond 1, *Typha* and *Scirpus* were dominant in Ponds 2 and 3, and Pond 4 was dominated by *Scirpus*, *Eleocharis*, and *Echinodorus* by July 30. Limited success of the *Equisetum*/*Philonotes* plantings was probably caused by excessive water depth at planting sites.

Mosquitofish (*Gambusia affinis*) and fathead minnows (*Pimephales promelas*) were stocked in the ponds and within a few weeks considerable *Gambusia* reproduction was evident. Frogs and toads responded naturally as did numerous species of invertebrates.

Water quality monitoring showed significant improvement within three weeks after completion of the wetlands system. During the first year, dissolved O_2 increased to nearly 8.0 mg L^{-1}, total Fe declined to 1.1 mg L^{-1}, total Mn averaged 2.8 mg L^{-1}, and total suspended solids averaged 2.8 mg L^{-1} (Table 1).

Comparison of sample parameters from the outlet of Pond 1 with seep parameters demonstrated that most contaminant removal from water from the original two seeps occurred within Pond 1. However, because of additional seeps downstream, the final discharge would have exceeded effluent limitations (Table 2) without the additional treatment area in Ponds 2-4.

Although fluctuating slightly, values for pH, Fe, Mn, DO, and TSS in the final discharge were equal to or better than comparable values from undisturbed natural streams on the Cumberland Plateau

TABLE 1. Range and average water quality values: July 1985 through June 1986.

		Seep 1	Seep 2	Pond 1	Final discharge
pH (standard units)	Avg.	6.0	5.9	5.7	6.1
Baseline: 7.2	Range	5.7-6.4	5.6-6.5	4.5-7.0	5.1-7.2
Dissolved O_2	Avg.	0.20	3.0	5.91	7.82
(mg L^{-1})	Range			0.0-10.7	5.3-13.8
Total Fe (mg L^{-1})	Avg.	79.8	82.4	3.6	1.1
Baseline: 30.0	Range	24-140	57-103	0.6-20.5	0.4-6.8
Total Mn (mg L^{-1})	Avg.	7.74	11.51	5.1	2.8
Baseline: 9.10	Range	4.0-9.0	9.3-12	0.7-16.2	0.2-17.0
Total Suspended Solids (mg L^{-1})	Avg.	85	103	6.5	2.8
Baseline: 57	Range	33-140	54-260	1.0-19.0	1.0-9.0

TABLE 2. Effluent limitations.

Parameter	Daily Maximum	Monthly Average
Total Fe (mg L^{-1})	6.0	3.0
Total Mn (mg L^{-1})	4.0	2.0
Total Suspended Solids (mg L^{-1})	70.0	35.0
pH (standard units)	6.0-9.0	--

throughout the summer and fall. In addition, the Fe precipitate coating rocks were removed and aquatic insects and small fish became reestablished within the receiving stream.

On December 3, 1985, discharges of 75-150 L min^{-1} of pH 3.5 water from the coal slurry impoundment were initiated. By the end of December, the final discharge pH fell below 6, Mn increased to 17 mg L^{-1}, Fe increased to 7 mg L^{-1}, and the slurry lake discharge was terminated. Final effluent Fe concentrations (7 mg L^{-1}) were lower than baseline values (30 mg L^{-1}) suggesting continued Fe removal was occurring. A substantial increase in Mn (17 mg L^{-1}) over baseline levels (8 and 12 mg L^{-1}) suggested that previously deposited Mn was undergoing dissolution by acidic inflow. Comparative inflow and outflow values before and after introduction of slurry lake water are shown in Figures 2 and 3.

After cessation of the additional inflow, pH values recovered within two weeks, total Fe in the discharge was less than 2 mg L^{-1} within a month, but Mn levels remained elevated until late March 1986. Despite shocking the wetlands system by suddenly adding a relatively large quantity of highly acidic water during the nongrowing season (ice covered the ponds from January 14 to February 3), the marsh/pond system recovered the functional

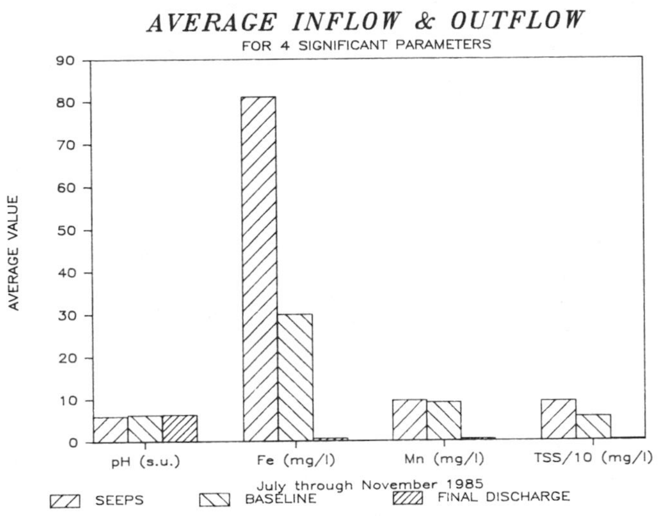

FIGURE 2. Inflow and outflow values for pH, Fe, Mn, and TSS before addition of Slurry Lake 2 low pH water.

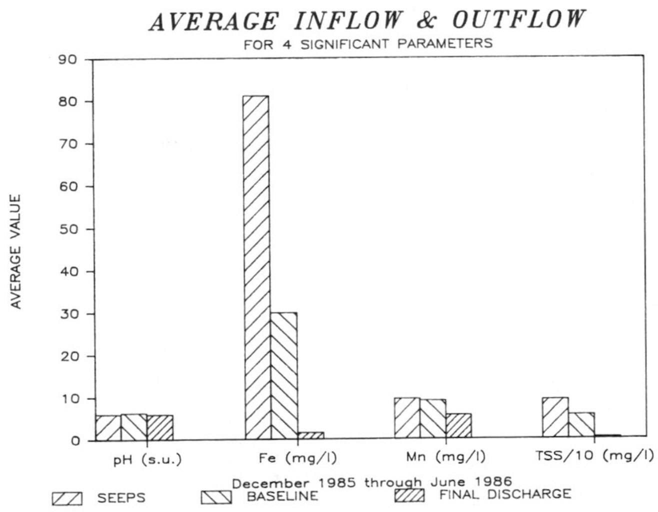

FIGURE 3. Inflow and outflow values for pH, Fe, Mn, and TSS after addition of Slurry Lake 2 low pH water.

ability to modify acidic seepage to natural stream water quality. In addition, vigorous vegetative growth and vertebrate and invertebrate populations present in April indicated that macro-biotic components of the system were not permanently damaged.

On May 21, 1986, we began releasing 2.0 L min^{-1} of slurry lake water into the wetlands system and on June 18 increased the flow to 4.0 L min^{-1}. Water quality has remained within effluent limitations and we are hopeful that gradual introduction of slurry lake water during the growing season will permit adaptation by the microscopic and macroscopic biotic components to lower pH levels. Successful treatment of the slurry lake decantation will eliminate the need for pumping and chemical treatment.

Total costs for construction of the marsh/pond wetlands system approximated $28,000. Comparable chemical treatment is estimated to cost $10,000 per year for acid seep water not including initial construction of a treatment basin or treating the slurry lake discharge. If the wetlands system continues to provide adequate treatment, it will have proven cost effective.

The competitive advantage of man-made wetlands over chemical treatment is based not only upon the immediate, short-term economics but upon the internal maintenance attributes of wetlands that suggest long-term independent functioning of stabilized systems. Reasonable assurance of relatively long-term treatment of acid water discharge by a wetlands system will overcome reluctance of regulatory agencies to approve additional applications and permit terminations.

Although a thorough understanding of the biotic factors and treatment mechanisms is probably years and substantial dollars in the future, two immediate questions for which the entire coal-related industry needs answers are: 1) What are the design criteria regarding size, configuration, depth, substrates, and vegetation types for efficient treatment wetlands; and 2) What is the capacity and longevity of a functioning system.

We have initiated a pilot scale field experiment to investigate substrate types, vegetative components, application rates, and capacities from which design criteria will be developed (Brodie et al., 1985). In addition, we have constructed five additional wetlands at the Fabius site and three wetlands systems at ash pond seeps at two TVA coal-fired steam plants.

Our results suggest that man-made wetlands dominated by emergent plant species have the capability of removing dissolved metallic ions and moderating low pH values of acid mine drainage. Using appropriate techniques, wetlands can be designed and established for a wide range of flows and contaminant levels at almost any desired location. Man-made wetlands appear to offer an inexpensive, self-maintaining, long-term alternative to conventional treatment methods.

REFERENCES

Brodie, G. A., D. A. Hammer, and D. A. Tomljanovich. 1985. Investigation of acid seepage treatment by manmade wetlands. Unpublished Proposal of Current Research, Tennessee Valley Authority.

Brooks, R. P. 1984. Optimal designs for restored wetlands. In J. E. Burris (ed.) Treatment of Mine Drainage by Wetlands. Contribution No. 264 of the Dept. of Biology, Pennsylvania State University.

Chan, E., T. Bursztynsky, N. Hantzche, and Y. Kitwin. 1981. The use of wetlands for water pollution control. Municipal Environmental Research Laboratory, EPA No. PB-83-107-466.

Clymo, R. S. 1984. Sphagnum - dominated peat bog: A naturally acid ecosystem. Phil. Trans. R. Soc. Land. B305.

Environmental Protection Agency. 1979. Methods for chemical analysis of water and wastes. Office of Res. & Dev., Cincinnati, Ohio.

Federal Water Pollution Control Administration. 1969. Stream pollution by coal mine drainage in Appalachia. U.S. Dept. of Interior.

Gerber, D. W., J. E. Burris, and B. W. Stone. 1985. Removal of dissolved iron and manganese ions by a Sphagnum Moss system. In R. P. Brooks et al. (ed.) Wetlands and Water Management on Mined Lands. Proc. of a Conf., October 1985, Pennsylvania State University.

Gregory, E., and J. T. Staley. 1982. Widespread distribution of ability to oxidize manganese among freshwater bacteria. Applied and Environmental Microbiology 44:2.

Hammer, D. E., and R. H. Kadlec. 1983. Design principles for wetland treatment systems. EPA No. PB-83-188-722.

Holm, J. D. 1983. Passive mine drainage treatment: Selected case studies. In A. Medin and M. Anderson (ed.) Proc. of the ASCE Specialty Conference, 1983, National Conference on Environmental Engineering, Boulder, Colorado.

Hyde, H. C., R. S. Ross, and F. Dengen. 1982. Technology assessment of wetlands for municipal wastewater treatment. Municipal Env. Res. Lab., EPA, Cincinnati, Ohio.

Kleinmann, R. L. P. 1985. Treatment of acid mine water by wetlands. Bureau of Mines, Information Circular No. 9027.

Nichols, D. S. 1983. Capacity of natural wetlands to remove nutrients from wastewater. J. Water Pollut. Control Fed. 55:495-505.

Pesavento, B. G. 1984. Factors to be considered when constructing wetlands for utilization as biomass filters to remove minerals from solution. In J. E. Burris (ed.) Treatment of Mine Drainage by Wetlands. Contribution No. 264 of the Department of Biology, Pennsylvania State University.

Stone, R. W. 1984. The presence of iron and manganese - oxidizing bacteria in natural and simulated bogs. In J. E. Burris (ed.) Treatment of Mine Drainage by Wetlands,

Contribution No. 264 of the Department of Biology, Pennsylvania State University.

Tarleton, A. L., G. E. Lang, and R. K. Weider. 1984. Removal of iron from acid mine drainage by Sphagnum Peat: Results of experimental laboratory microcosms. Proc. National Symposium Surface Mining, Hydrology, Sedimentology, and Reclamation. University of Kentucky.

Tchobanoglous, G., and G. L. Culp. 1980. Wetland systems for wastewater treatment. In S. C. Reed and R. K. Bastian (ed.) Aquaculture Systems for Wastewater Treatment: An Engineering Assessment. EPA 430/9-80-007.

Weider, R. K., G. E. Lang, and A. E. Whitehouse. 1984. The use of freshwater wetlands to treat acid mine drainage. In J. E. Burris (ed.) Treatment of Mine Drainage by Wetlands. Contribution No. 264 of the Department of Biology, Pennsylvania State University.

Weider, R. K., G. E. Lang, and A. E. Whitehouse. 1985. Metal removal in a Sphagnum-dominated wetland. In R. P. Brooks et al. (ed.) Wetlands and Water Management on Mined Lands Process of a Conference, October 1985. Pennsylvania State University.

EFFLUENT DISTRIBUTION AND BASIN DESIGN FOR ENHANCED POLLUTANT ASSIMILATION BY FRESHWATER WETLANDS

R. L. Knight
CH2M Hill
7201 NW 11th Place
Gainesville, Florida 32605

ABSTRACT

Since most of the assimilation processes in wetland wastewater systems are common to both constructed and natural wetlands, design criteria can be developed for one system and, with care, applied to the other. The finding that mass removal rates for carbonaceous and nitrogenous compounds are highly correlated with mass loading rates over a broad range of loadings, indicates that assimilation can be maximized by increasing the length to width ratio. The optimal length to width ratio is less than the maximum possible because of decreased residence time per interval and increased cost due to greater edge to surface area ratio. For a hypothetical constructed wetland the optimal length to width ratio was calculated to be about 2:1.

Keywords: Freshwater wetlands, pollutant assimilation, nitrogen, BOD, wastewater.

INTRODUCTION

Utilization of freshwater wetlands for wastewater assimilation is rapidly evolving from an innovative technology to an accepted alternative for reliable wastewater treatment and disposal (EPA, 1985). Both naturally occurring wetlands and constructed wetlands are being used on a limited scale throughout the United States for removal of O_2-demanding materials and nutrients. A literature search by U.S. EPA (EPA, 1984) located over 1,000 citations of published information on wastewater wetlands. Since release of that bibliography, other volumes have appeared that summarize knowledge from multiple wastewater wetland projects (Ewel and Odum, 1984; Godfrey et al., 1985; Hyde et al., 1984a,b). Some authors have begun to summarize design information for wastewater wetland systems (Hammer and Kadlec, 1983; Chan et

ISBN 0-941463-00-1

al., 1982; EPA 1985) but no comprehensive design handbook has been published.

Design criteria relative to constructed wetlands including water hyacinth systems (Hyde et al., 1984b), trenches (Wolverton et al., 1983; Gersberg et al., 1984), and thin-film techniques (Jewell et al., 1983) are more readily available than similar information for the use of natural wetlands. Since most of the processes that provide assimilation in wetlands function similarly in both constructed and natural wetlands, design criteria derived from constructed wetland systems may be applicable to the design of natural wetland treatment systems and vice versa. Major assimilation processes that are common to both natural and constructed wetlands are organic decomposition, nitrification/denitrification, volatilization, plant uptake, and soil adsorption. The ability to remove nutrients and organic matter via harvesting is the only major difference between many constructed and natural wetlands, although constructed wetlands can provide significant assimilation of both organic matter and total N without harvesting (Knight et al., 1986).

In this paper the observed relationship between loading and removal rates for organic matter and total N measured in natural or semi-natural wastewater wetlands is utilized to derive a theoretical and empirical basis for selection of optimal basin configurations and effluent distribution techniques for both natural and constructed wetlands.

MASS LOADING AND REMOVAL RATES

Loading rate and removal rate as used in this paper refer to the mass of a wastewater constituent applied or assimilated per area per time. Units are generally in g m^{-2} d^{-1}, kg ha^{-1} d^{-1}, or lb $acre^{-1}$ d^{-1}. The empirical relationship between loading and removal rate for 5 d biochemical oxygen demand (BOD_5) and total nitrogen (TN) has been found to be linear and predictable (Chan et al., 1982; Nichols, 1983; Knight et al., 1984; Knight et al., 1986). For certain loading rates between upper and lower threshold values, removal rate is linearly correlated with removal rate (Figures 1 and 2). This relationship has yielded correlation coefficients above 0.98 for data from a single system, and even when data from entirely different wastewater wetlands are compared (as in Figure 2), removal rates are still correlated to loading rates in a predictable fashion. The relationship between loading and removal rates for BOD_5 and TN are perhaps the most predictable aspect of wetland wastewater systems and can be used in the design of new systems by predicting assimilation of these key pollutants.

BASIN CONFIGURATION

The predicted output concentrations for BOD_5 for three different hypothetical wetland basin configurations having equal

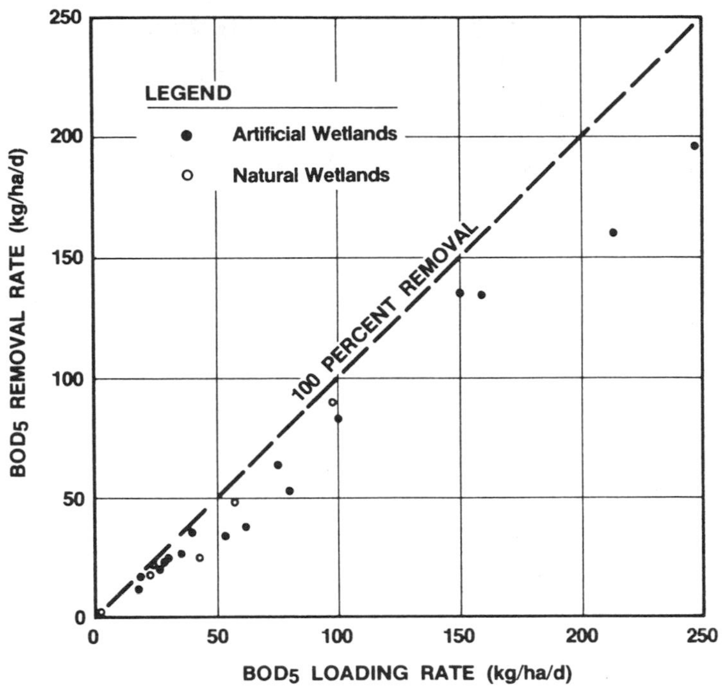

FIGURE 1. Annual average loading and removal rates for BOD_5 in freshwater wetlands (Modified from Chan et al., 1982).

effective treatment areas, input concentrations, and mass loading rates are contrasted in Figure 3. Effluent flow rate was assumed to be 4,000 m^3 d^{-1} and removal was predicted to be linear at an 80% efficiency. Note that a long, linear wetland system is predicted to have a much greater assimilation than a short, wide wetland. This remarkable difference in predicted assimilations is also applicable to total suspended solids (TSS) and TN and results from the positive correlation between mass loading and removal rates. Because the mass loading rate per increment is effectively higher in the long wetland than in the wide wetland, the pollutant mass removed in this initial increment would be expected to be higher. For pollutant assimilation, a wetland system should be as long and linear as possible to maximize utilization of the loading/removal rate phenomenon. This observation does not depend on these increments being separated into individual cells as described by Blumer (1978) for the Brookhaven marsh/pond system.

In actual wetland treatment systems output concentrations of BOD_5, TSS, and TN are never as low as those shown in Figure 3. The higher output concentrations actually measured (generally

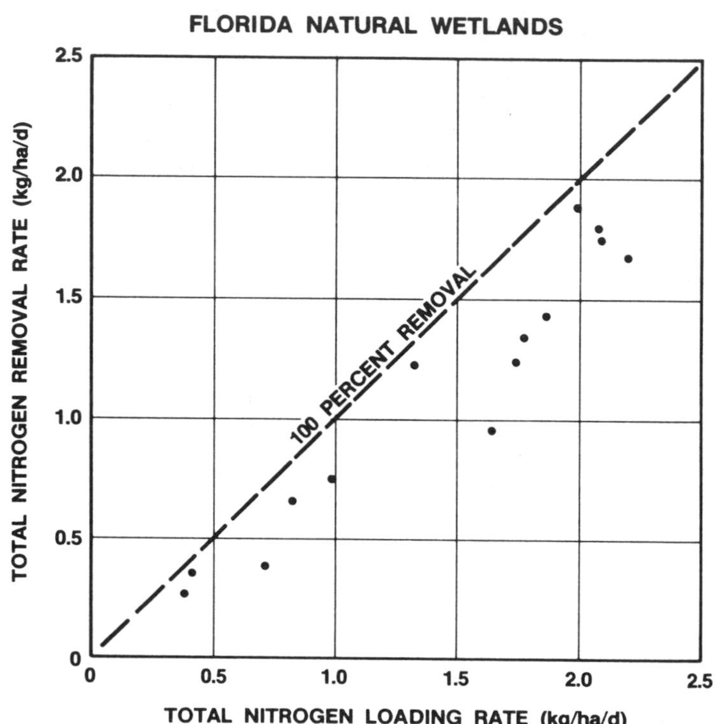

FIGURE 2. Annual average loading and removal rates for total N in Florida natural wetland wastewater systems.

between 1 to 3 mg L^{-1} for BOD_5, TSS, and TN) probably result from a phenomenon that has been observed in wetland treatment systems but not previously described. At low input concentrations for BOD_5, TSS, and TN, percent removal declines rapidly and becomes increasingly negative apparently due to natural production of organic matter and N fixation. The result of this phenomenon is that at some downstream point in a wetland treatment system, natural biological processes return as much of these non-conservative parameters to the water as they remove.

A second phenomenon observed in the natural wetland treatment system at the Walt Disney World Resort Complex in Florida is that assimilation of BOD_5, TSS and TN also drops off sharply at certain threshold residence times. Thus, effective removal rate per increment of a wetland may decline in very narrow wetlands due to the decreased residence time per linear distance as the cross-section is reduced.

For a detailed calculation of optimal basin configuration for assimilation, all three of these factors, i.e. loading rate versus removal rate, concentration versus removal rate, and residence time versus removal rate, should be considered.

For constructed wetland systems the most cost-effective length to width ratio is not determined solely by pollutant assimilation considerations. Construction cost for a wetland system is related to the amount of excavation or fill material that must be moved. For a given treatment area, excavation volume will be constant while berm length (or the area dedicated to berms in a belowground construction) is minimum for a circle and increases as the wetland becomes either longer or wider.

Optimal length to width ratio for a constructed wetland based on total cost is thus a function of both the value of the pollutant assimilation (in Figure 3) and construction cost. A number of site-specific variables such as land costs, availability and cost of fill, effluent limitations, etc., will affect the optimal size for any given system. An analysis of the optimal length to width ratio for the hypothetical wetland in Figure 3 is presented in Figure 4. The area of this wetland is assumed to be 50 ha and is enclosed by a berm with a 15 m^2 cross-sectional area. Assuming \$15 m^{-3} of fill and a berm land cost of \$10,000 ha^{-1}, the berm cost was calculated as about \$230 m^{-1}. The distribution system cost was assumed to be about \$40 m^{-1} of lineal extent and was insignificant compared to the berm cost except at the very smallest length to width ratios. Local data for costs, project life, and other factors should be utilized for design of any particular system.

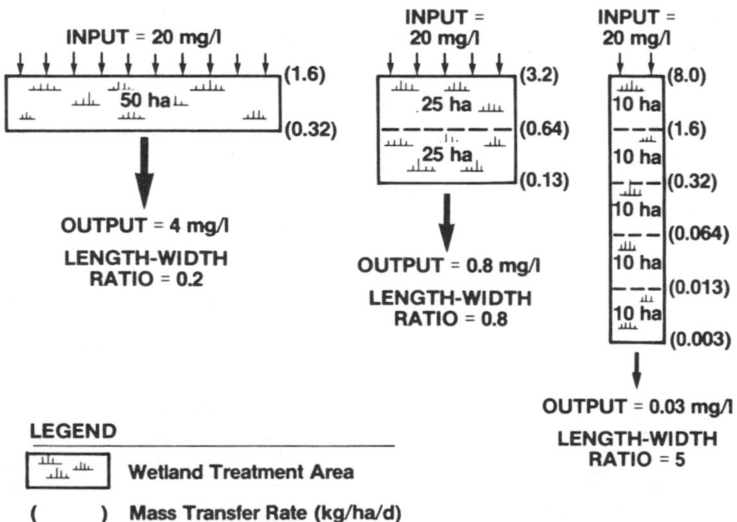

FIGURE 3. Hypothetical illustration of effect of length to width ratio on wetland BOD_5 assimilation.

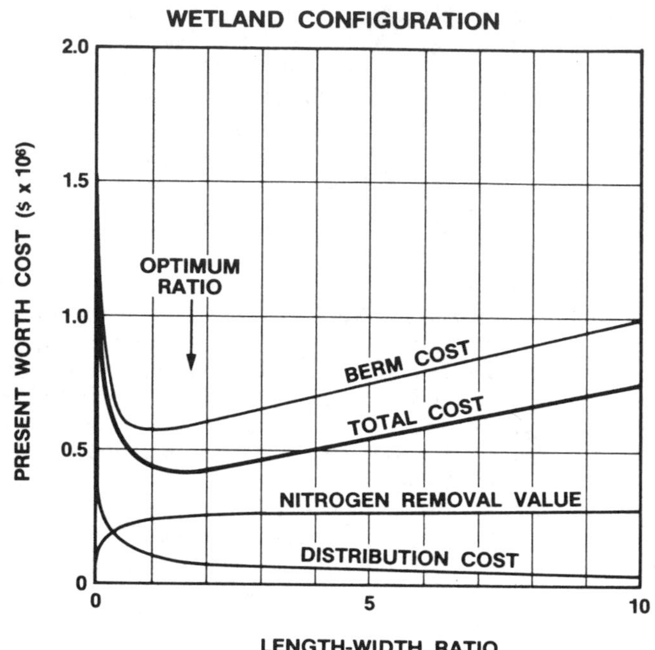

FIGURE 4. Optimization of length to width ratio for hypothetical wetland treatment system.

The value of the N assimilation potential of this hypothetical constructed wetland was estimated by the total present worth cost for TN removal in a conventional advanced treatment facility. The cost of TN assimilation capacity equal to one kg d^{-1} was estimated to be $4,400. Based on predicted TN assimilation by the wetland under differing length to width configurations the economic value of TN assimilation was calculated and is presented in Figure 4.

In order to find the total cost for differing length to width ratios the cost of the berm and the distribution system were added and the TN assimilation value was substracted to give the overall cost-effectiveness as shown in Figure 4. For this hypothetical case the optimal length to width ratio was about 2:1.

A few researchers have reported optimal length to width ratios based solely on empirical observations of assimilation. Wile et al. (1985) reported that a 75:1 ratio was significantly more effective than a 4.5:1 ratio. Stowell et al. (1985) used a 12:1 ratio in a water hyacinth system and recommended a ratio greater than 15:1. Based on his review of water hyacinth systems in Texas, Dinges (1979) recommended a ratio greater than 3:1.

This lower ratio has also been recommended by Middlebrooks and Reed (1981) and Hyde et al. (1984). Using trench systems with cattails and bulrushes Gersberg et al. (1984) recommended a ratio of 6:1. None of these researchers have reported any detailed empirical analysis documenting an optimum length to width ratio based on both assimilation and cost.

EFFLUENT DISTRIBUTION

Two types of effluent distribution configurations are generally used for input to constructed and natural wetlands. Either the effluent is released at a single point by a pipe or weir, or alternatively, the effluent is distributed linearly from a gated pipe or swale. Because of a commonly held misconception that maximizing treatment is based on maximizing distribution, some researchers have discussed applying the effluent evenly over the entire wetland treatment area. As suggested in the previous section, assimilation is maximized with a long, narrow wetland. Cost of a narrow system is also lower because a point source or very short gated pipe will effectively distribute the effluent. If a natural wetland cross section profile varies, then distribution of the effluent can be enhanced by placing a weir at the downstream end to control water depth and create a permanently wetted area.

CONCLUSIONS

One possible disadvantage of increasing assimilation by optimizing the length to width ratio for natural wetlands is that higher effective pollutant loading rates at the upstream end of the wetland will create a greater stress on the natural biota in the discharge area. A zone of greater impact has been seen near an effluent outfall line (Kadlec and Tilton, 1979) because of this higher areal loading. To minimize biotic change in a natural wetland treatment system, effluent should be distributed as evenly as possible. A trade off between maximizing pollutant assimilation and minimizing biotic change might be necessary in some systems.

REFERENCES

Blumer, K. 1978. The use of wetlands for treating wastes--wisdom in diversity? p. 182-201. In M. Drew (ed.) Environmental Quality through Wetlands Utilization. Proceedings from a Symposium Sponsored by the Coordinating Council on the Restoration of the Kissimmee River Valley and Taylor Creek-Nubbin Slough Basin, Tallahassee, Florida.

Chan, E., T. A. Bursztynsky, N. Hantzsche, and Y. J. Litwin. 1982. The use of wetlands for water pollution control. EPA-600/2-82-086.

Dinges, R. 1979. Development of hyacinth wastewater treatment systems in Texas. In R. K. Bastian and S. C. Reed (ed.) Aquaculture Systems for Wastewater Treatment. EPA 430/9-80-000.

Ewel, K. C., and H. T. Odum (ed.). 1984. Cypress wetlands. University of Florida Press, Gainesville, Florida.

Gersberg, R. M., B. V. Elkins, and C. R. Goldman. 1984. Use of artificial wetlands to remove nitrogen from wastewater. J. Water Pollut. Control Fed. 56:152-156.

Godfrey, P. J., E. R. Kaynor, and S. Pelczarski (ed.). 1985. Ecological considerations in wetlands treatment of municipal wastewaters. Van Nostrand Reinhold Co., New York, NY.

Hammer, D. E., and R. H. Kadlec. 1983. Design principles for wetland treatment systems. EPA-600/2-83-026.

Hyde, H. C., R. S. Ross, and L. Sturmer. 1984a. Technology assessment of wetlands for municipal wastewater treatment. EPA-600/2-84-154.

Hyde, H. C., R. S. Ross, and F. Demgen. 1984b. Technology assessment of wetlands for municipal wastewater treatment. EPA-600/2-84-154.

Jewell, W. J., J. J. Madras, W. W. Clarkson, H. DeLancy-Ponpe, and R. M. Kabrick. 1983. Wastewater treatment with plants in nutrient films. EPA-600/52-83-067.

Kadlec, R. H., and D. L. Tilton. 1979. The use of freshwater wetlands as a tertiary wastewater treatment alternative. Critical Reviews Environ. Control 9:185-212.

Knight, R. L., B. H. Winchester, and J. C. Higman. 1984. Carolina Bays-feasibility for effluent advanced treatment and disposal. Wetlands 4:177-203.

Knight, R. L., B. H. Winchester, and J. C. Higman. 1986. Ecology, hydrology, and advanced wastewater treatment potential of an artificial wetland in north-central Florida. Wetlands 5:167-180.

Middlebrooks, E. J., and S. C. Reed. 1981. The flowering of wastewater treatment. Water Engineering and Management. p. 51-54.

Nichols, D. S. 1983. Capacity of natural wetlands to remove nutrients from wastewater. J. Water Pollut. Control Fed. 55:495-505.

Stowell, R., S. Weber, G. Tchobanoglous, B. A. Wilson, and K. R. Townzen. 1985. Mosquito considerations in the design of wetland systems for the treatment of wastewater, Chapter 3. p. 38-47. In P. J. Godfrey, E. R. Kaynor, and S. Pelczarski (ed.) Ecological Considerations in Wetlands Treatment of Municipal Wastewaters. Van Nostrand Reinhold Co., New York, NY.

United States Environmental Protection Agency. 1984. The ecological impacts of wastewater on wetlands: An annotated bibliography. EPA-905/3-84-002.

United States Environmental Protection Agency. 1985. Freshwater wetlands for wastewater management handbook. EPA 904/9-85-135.

Wile, I., G. Miller, and S. Black. 1985. Design and use of artificial wetlands, Chapter 2. p. 26-37. In P. J. Godfrey, E. R. Kaynor, and S. Pelczarski (ed.) Ecological Considerations in Wetlands Treatment of Municipal Wastewaters. Van Nostrand Reinhold Co., New York, NY.

Wolverton, B. C., R. C. McDonald, and W. R. Duffer. 1983. Microorganisms and higher plants for wastewater treatment. J. Environ. Qual. 12:236-242.

MUNICIPAL WASTEWATER TREATMENT WITH ARTIFICIAL WETLANDS - A TVA/KENTUCKY DEMONSTRATION

G. R. Steiner and J. T. Watson
Tennessee Valley Authority
270 Haney Building
Chattanooga, Tennessee 37401

D. A. Hammer
Tennessee Valley Authority
Forestry Building
Norris, Tennessee 37828

D. F. Harker, Jr.
Commonwealth of Kentucky
18 Reilly Road
Frankfort, Kentucky 40601

ABSTRACT

Research projects on artificial wetlands have shown that they can be used to treat domestic sewage effectively. Other significant advantages over conventional treatment processes include simplicity of operation and maintenance and relatively low capital and operation costs. However, the use of artificial wetlands is neither widely known nor accepted by engineering firms and regulatory agencies. To overcome this problem, the Tennessee Valley Authority (TVA) in cooperation with the Kentucky Division of Water has implemented a project to demonstrate the feasibility and benefits of artificial wetlands sewage treatment systems. Three full-scale treatment systems will be built at small towns in Kentucky. Several design concepts will be evaluated, including the marsh-pond-meadow, the root-zone method, and the gravel marsh. Different plant species, slopes, flow rates, and engineered substrates and native soils will be used. A successful demonstration and the planned technology transfer activities will result in benefits to water resources, small communities and private developers throughout the Tennessee Valley region and nation.

Keywords: Marsh/pond/meadow, root-zone, gravel marsh, Tennessee Valley Authority, lagoons, low-tech, low-cost sewage treatment method.

ISBN 0-941463-00-1

INTRODUCTION

Treatment systems are needed which are effective, have relatively low capital and operation costs, and are simple to operate and maintain. Artificial (i.e., man-made) wetlands treatment systems have these desired characteristics. However, the use of artificial wetlands is not widely known or accepted outside the scientific community. The Tennessee Valley Authority (TVA) has implemented a project to demonstrate the feasibility and benefit of using artificial wetlands for treating municipal sewage in the Tennessee Valley region. Three full-scale sewage treatment systems will be built and tested. The project is being conducted through technical and financial assistance of TVA in cooperation with the Commonwealth of Kentucky, Division of Water. The demonstration is designed to obtain detailed information on the following factors; namely, 1) technical designs, 2) operating criteria, 3) applicability for complete and upgrade treatment, 4) treatment efficiencies, 5) unit operations data, and 6) advantages to conventional systems; including low capital cost, low operating cost, O&M simplicity, and water quality benefits.

A successful demonstration will help justify a viable low-cost, low tech, effective alternative to conventional processes. As a result, water resources, small communities, and private developers, in the Tennessee Valley Region and throughout the nation will benefit. In Kentucky alone, it is estimated that 31 communities have poorly functioning treatment plants which could be either upgraded or replaced by artificial wetlands. Also, 33 additional communities with no treatment plants potentially could use the artificial wetlands.

DESCRIPTION

The demonstration treatment systems will be built at Benton, Hardin and Pembroke, Kentucky. These artificial wetlands will either upgrade or eventually replace each town's existing treatment facility. TVA staff has provided technical guidance including conceptual designs to two consulting engineering firms (Gammel Engineering, 200 East 12th Street, Benton, KY 42025; Howard K. Bell Consulting Engineers, Inc., 102 West Second Street, P.O. Box 661, Hopkinsville, KY 42240) who are preparing the detailed engineering plans.

The Benton project will consist of modifying a two-cell, 10.5 ha lagoon system. The 4.0 second cell of the lagoon will be changed into a 3-cell artificial wetlands. The wetlands systems will receive effluent from the primary cell of the lagoon. The first wetland cell will be a gravel marsh, have subsurface flow, and planted with bulrushes. The second and third wetland cells will be surface flow marshes using the native soil, one planted with bulrushes, and the other planted with a mixture of plant species. The engineering design is summarized in Table 1 and shown in Figure 1.

TABLE 1. Benton, Kentucky, gravel and surface marshes engineering design factors.

Design Flow: 0.048 m^3 s^{-1} average
Pretreatment: Sedimentation and biochemical oxidation in 6.5 ha primary lagoon
Marsh: Secondary lagoon converted to three parallel cells, 1, 2, and 3
Design Basis: Studies by (1) Gersberg et al., Santee Water Reclamation Facility, Santee, California, and (2) Wolverton, National Space Technology Laboratories, Mississippi.
Application rate: 212 to 92 ha per m^3 s^{-1}
Total surface area: 4.4 ha
Number of cells: Three with 14,616 m^2 each
Length/width ratio: 7.6:1 each cell
Slope: 0.1%
Liner: 3.0 to 4.6 m in-situ clay

	Cell 1	Cell 2	Cell 3
Vegetation	Bulrush	Bulrush	Reeds, cattail, or mixed
Water Depth	-0.6 to +0.6 m	0 to 0.6 m	0 to 0.6 m
Substrate	46 cm of 1.9-2.5 cm gravel, and 15 cm pea gravel	native soil	native soil

Posttreatment: Disinfection (chlorination) initially. Delete if found unnecessary.

The Hardin project will consist of constructing and testing a type of subsurface flow artificial wetlands system using the root zone method. The design is based on developmental studies in West Germany, reported in information obtained from the Water Research Centre, England. The system will be sized for 0.0044 m^3 s^{-1}. Raw sewage will first be routed through part of the existing contact stabilization plant which will provide comminution and some aeration. (Aeration will be provided only due to a system convenience. It may not be needed in other systems). The substrate will consist of native soil and limestone, engineered to obtain a desired hydraulic conductivity. The plants for the root zone marsh will be reeds (Phragmites). Also, an adjacent hardwood area will be used for a 5678 m^3 storage facility to manage excess storm flows. Storm flow will be diverted to the hardwood area and then slowly released to the root zone system. The engineering design is summarized in Table 2 and shown in Figure 2.

The Pembroke project will consist of constructing and testing a marsh-pond-meadow type system. Raw sewage will first be routed through part of the existing contact stabilization plant where it

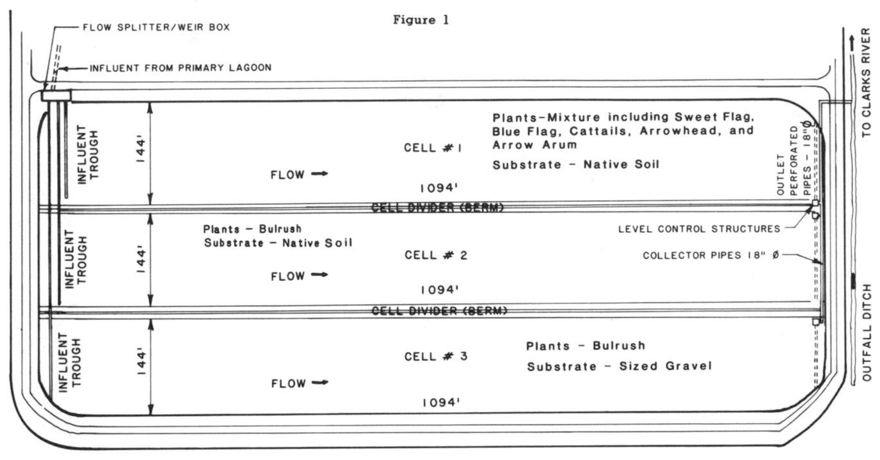

BENTON, KY.
ARTIFICIAL WETLANDS SEWAGE TREATMENT SYSTEM
ROOT ZONE AND SURFACE FLOW MARSHES

TABLE 2. Hardin, Kentucky, root zone method system engineering design factors.

Design Flow: 0.0044 $m^3\ s^{-1}$
Pretreatment: Comminution; aeration
Marsh: Four parallel root zone method beds
Design basis: Equations and guidelines by Reinhold Kickuth, Kassel University, West Germany.
Ah = 5.2 Qd (ln Co - ln Ct)
where Ah = marsh bed area, m^2; Qd = avg. flow, $m^3\ d^{-1}$; Ct = BOD of treated sewage; Co = BOD of raw sewage
Ac = Qs/Kf dH/ds
where Qs = 2 to 3 times the Dry Weather Flow rate, $m^3\ s^{-1}$; Ac = marsh bed cross-sectional area, m^2; Kf = $1 \times 10^{-3}\ m^3\ m^{-2}S$ (hydraulic conductivity); dH/ds = marsh bed slope $m\ m^{-1}$
Application rate: 135 ha per $m^3\ s^{-1}$
Total surface area: 0.6 ha
Number of cells: 4 with 1478 m^2 each
Length/width ratio: 0.33:1 each cell
Vegetation: Reeds (*Phragmites*)
Slope: 4%
Liner: 15 cm compacted clay
Water depth: +0.2 to -0.6 m

Substrate: 0.6 m of 75% topsoil and 25% #10 crushed limestone to obtain 0.1 to 0.001 cm sec^{-1} hydraulic conductivity
Hardwood Storage Facility: to store excess inflow/infiltration up to seven days until flow can be routed to marsh
Capacity: 5678 m^3
Surface area: 0.6 ha
Vegetation: Existing trees and new willow oak saplings
Water depth: 0.9 m max.
Posttreatment: Disinfection (chlorination) and/or aeration (diffused air) added later only if necessary

---

will receive comminution and some aeration. (Aeration will be provided due to a system convenience. It may not be needed in other systems). The wetlands will consist of two parallel systems each having in series a marsh, a pond, and a meadow. The marsh and meadow of one system will have a substrate of sized, crushed limestone to obtain subsurface flow. In the parallel system, plants will be established in native soil and most of the flow in the marsh and meadow should be on the surface. The engineering design is summarized in Table 3 and shown in Figure 3.

TABLE 3. Pembroke, Kentucky, marsh-pond-meadow system engineering design factors.

Design Flow: 0.0039 m^3 s^{-1}
Pretreatment: Comminution; aeration
Marsh: Two parallel systems, A and B
Design application rates: 185 ha per m^3 s^{-1}
Total surface area: 0.7 ha
Number of cells: Four with 1821 m^2 each
Length/width ratio: 8.15:1 each cell
Slope: 0.1%

	System A	System B
Substrate	Native topsoil	0.6 m sized limestone
Liner	None	15 cm compacted clay
Water depth	3 to 15 cm	-0.6 to +0.5 m
Vegetation	Cattail	Bulrush

Pond: Two parallel cells, for Marsh A and Marsh B
Total area: 4249 m^2
Total volume: 9137 m^3
Depth: 1.8 m
Liner Depth: 15 cm compacted clay
Vegetation: Duckweed
Meadow: Two parallel systems, A and B
Design application rate: 92 ha per m^3 s^{-1}
Total surface area: 0.35 ha

Number of cells: 2 with 756 m^2 each
Length/width ratio: 5.25:1
Slope: 0.1%

	System A	System B
Substrate	Native topsoil	0.6 m sized limestone
Liner	None	15 cm compacted clay
Water depth	0 to 15 cm	-0.6 to +0.2 m
Vegetation	Reed canary grass	Sedge, rush or iris

Posttreatment: Disinfection (chlorination) and/or aeration (cascades) added later only if necessary.

STATUS

Preliminary engineering designs (Table 4) for the three sites were completed in May 1986 and approved by the State in June 1986. Detailed designs have been completed and construction of the three systems tentatively will begin in fall, 1986. Demonstration monitoring will be conducted over a three to four year period. Data will be evaluated and the technology will be transferred

TABLE 4. Summary project site design factors.

Factor	Benton	Hardin	Pembroke
Artificial wetlands	Gravel marsh and surface flow marsh	Root Zone Method	Marsh-Pond-Meadow
Application rate	92 ha m^3 s^{-1}	135 ha m^3 s^{-1}	379 ha m^3 s^{-1}
Population served	5000	560-606	1000-1200
Design flow	0.048 m^3 s^{-1}	0.0044 m^3 s^{-1}	0.0039 m^3 s^{-1}
Influent	Primary lagoon effluent	Comminuted; aerated	Comminuted; aerated
Vegetation	Bulrush, reed or cattail (or mixed)	Reed	Cattail; bulrush; duck-weed; reed canary grass; and sedge, rush, or iris
Slope	0.1%	4%	0.1%
Substrate	Gravel; native soil	Crushed lime-stone mixture	Native soil; sized limestone
Liner	Native impermeable soil	Compacted clay	Native imperme-able soil
Cost, total capital	$200,000	$135,000	$172,000
Cost per m^3 d^{-1}	$0.18	$1,350	$1,910

Figure 2

HARDIN, KY.
ARTIFICIAL WETLANDS SEWAGE TREATMENT SYSTEM
ROOT ZONE METHOD SYSTEM

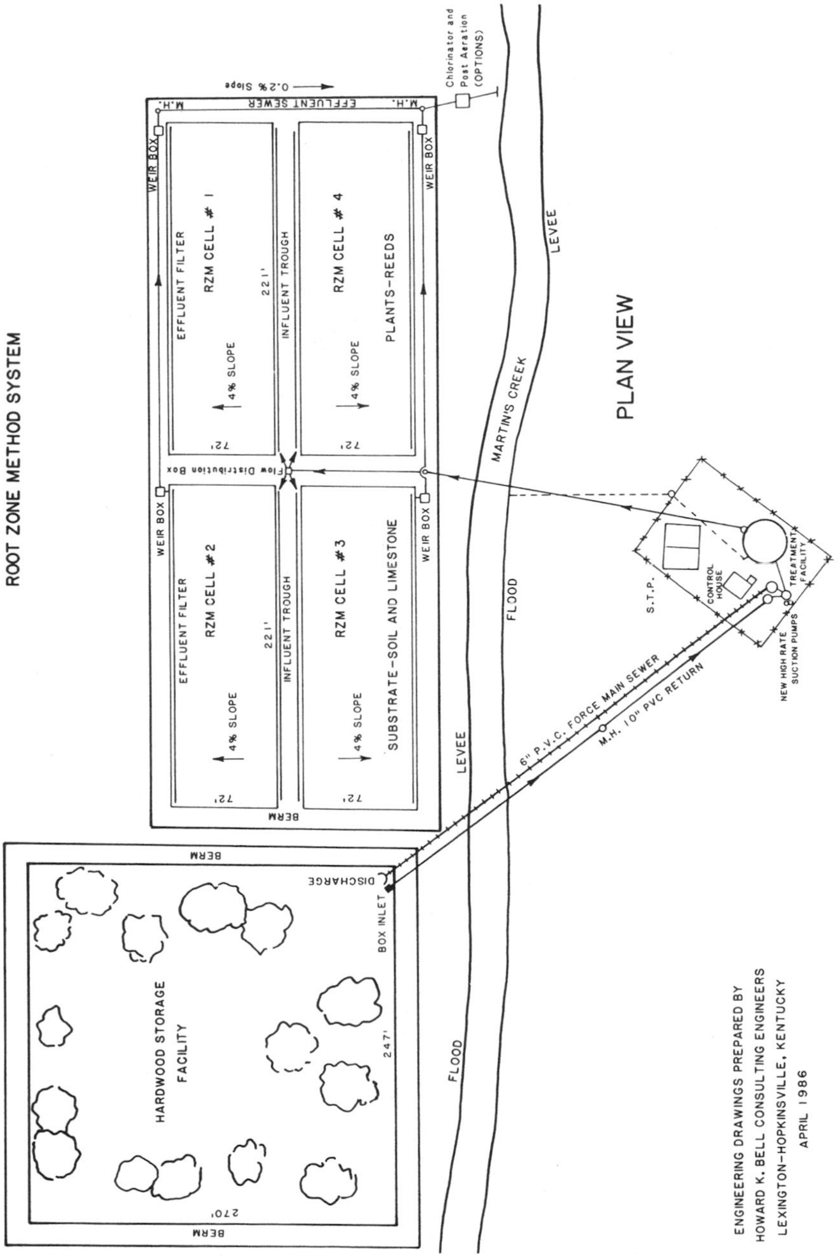

Figure 3

PEMBROKE, KY.

ARTIFICIAL WETLANDS SEWAGE TREATMENT SYSTEM
MARSH–POND–MEADOW TYPE

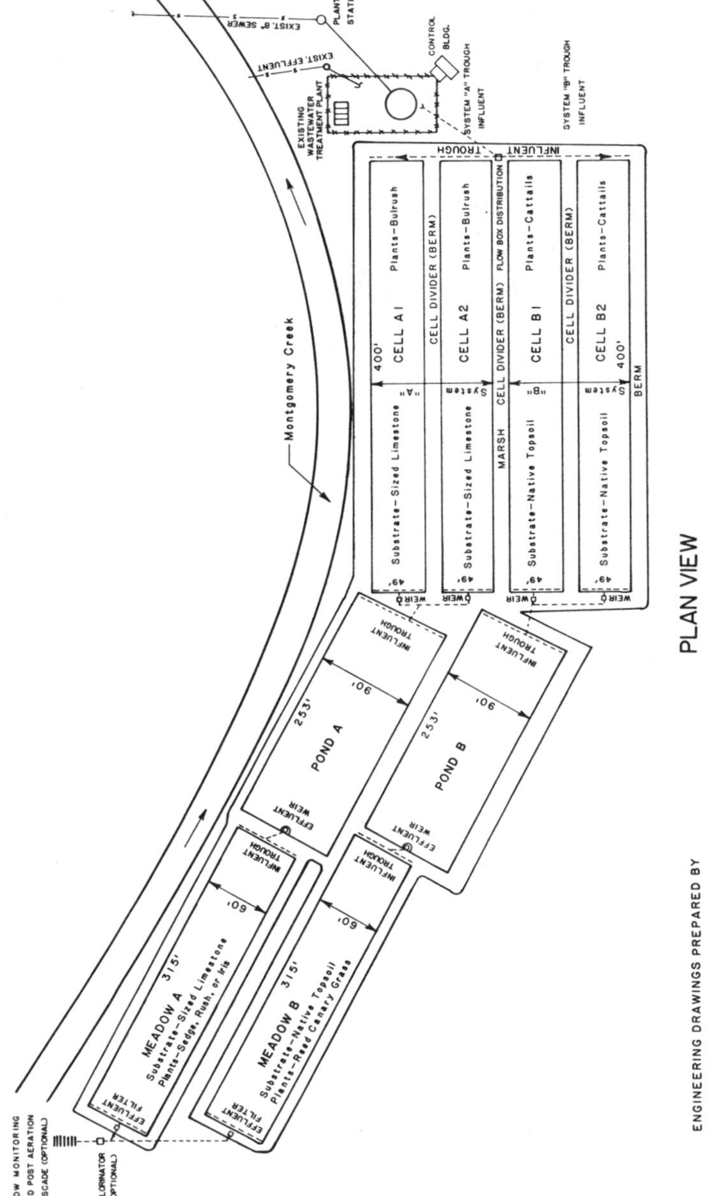

PLAN VIEW

ENGINEERING DRAWINGS PREPARED BY
HOWARD K. BELL CONSULTING ENGINEERS
LEXINGTON–HOPKINSVILLE, KENTUCKY
APRIL 1986

through periodic status reports, a final report, professional conferences, and site tours. A more detailed report may be obtained from the primary author.

REFERENCES

Boon, A. G. 1986. Report of a visit by members and staff of WRc to Germany (GFR) to investigate the Root Zone Method for treatment of wastewaters. Water Research Centre, Processes, Stevenage, Herts, England.

Gearheart, R. A., B. A. Finney, S. Wilbur, J. Williams, and D. Hull. 1984. The use of wetland treatment processes in water reuse. Future of Water Reuse, Vol. 2. AWWA Research Foundation, Denver, Colorado.

Gersberg, R. M., B. V. Elkins, S. R. Lyon, and C. R. Goldman. 1986. Role of aquatic plants in wastewater treatment by artificial wetlands. Water Res. 20:363-368.

Howard K. Bell Consulting Engineers, Inc. 1986a. Preliminary engineering study for artificial wetlands wastewater treatment facility, City of Hardin, Kentucky. April 1986, Hopkinsville, Kentucky.

Howard K. Bell Consulting Engineers, Inc. 1986b. Preliminary engineering study for artificial wetlands wastewater treatment facility, City of Pembroke, Kentucky. April 1986, Hopkinsville, Kentucky.

Small, M. M. 1977. Natural sewage recycling systems. BNL 50630. Brookhaven National Laboratory, Associated Universities, Inc., Upton, New York.

SMC-Martin, Inc. 1980. Marsh-pond-meadow sewage treatment facility. Village of Neshaminy Fall, Montgomery Township, Montgomery County, PA. SMC-Martin, Valley Forge, PA.

Watson, J. T., F. D. Diodata, and M. Lauch. 1986. Deisgn and performance of the artificial wetlands wastewater treatment plant at Iselin, Pennsylvania. In K. R. Reddy and W. H. Smith (ed.) Aquatic Plants for Water Treatment and Resource Recovery. Magnolia Publishing, Inc., Orlando, FL.

Wolverton, B. C. 1986. Artificial marshes for wastewater treatment. National Aeronautics and Space Administration, National Space Technology Laboratories, NSTL Station, MS. Presented at the First Annual Environmental Health Symposium; Water and Wastewater Issues in the North Central Gulf Coast, April 28-29, 1986, Mobile, AL.

Wolverton, B. C., and R. C. McDonald. 1982. Basic engineering criteria and cost estimations for hybrid microbial filter-reed (*Phragmites* communis) wastewater treatment concept. NASA TM-84669. National Aeronautics and Space Administration, National Space Technology Laboratories, NSTL Station, MS.

Disclaimer

The Tennessee Valley Authority makes no representation or warranty of any kind whatsoever including, but not limited to, representations or warranties, express or implied, of merchantability, fitness for use or purpose, accuracy or completeness of the information contained in this article.

IMPLEMENTATION OF AN OVERLAND FLOW/WETLANDS APPLICATION DEMONSTRATION PROJECT

T. Schanze
Camp Dresser & McKee, Inc.
Maitland, Florida 32751

ABSTRACT

The overland flow/wetlands application demonstration project will provide Orange County with a cost-effective alternative to a conventional land application system while generating useful data for FDER's determination of criteria for wetlands effluent disposal in compliance with the Warren S. Henderson Wetlands Protection Act. Because the Eastern Service Area wastewater treatment plant produces reclaimed water of AWT quality, an initial loading rate of 8.4 cm wk^{-1} has been approved, with the possibility of an increase up to 14.7 cm wk^{-1} after an initial operating period. This range of loading rates is significantly higher than the recommended conservative loading rates of approximately 2.5 cm wk^{-1} for typical secondary effluent. The project also has the long-term environmental benefit of increasing wetlands habitat.

Keywords: Wastewater, habitat improvement, water quality, overland flow, advanced wastewater treatment, dechlorination.

INTRODUCTION

Following an overland flow pilot investigation to determine the technical feasibility, an overland flow/wetlands application system was identified as a cost-effective water reuse option for the Phase III expansion of Orange County's Eastern Service Area wastewater treatment facilities (ESAWWTF). The facility uses the Bardenpho advanced biological treatment process and sand filtration to produce reclaimed water of advanced wastewater treatment (AWT) quality. Data for the period November 1984 to May 1986 indicate an average of 1.83 mg L^{-1} of total N (TN) and 0.75 mg L^{-1} of total P (TP).

The demonstration project incorporates the overland flow process for biological reduction and vegetative uptake to accomplish nutrient removal. Dechlorination and dissolved O_2 enhancement are also achieved through O_2 transfer due to extended

ISBN 0-941463-00-1

detention time and surface area. The reclaimed water then flows to natural wetlands for ultimate nutrient removal and additional cleansing before discharge to the receiving water.

PILOT INVESTIGATION METHODS

An overland flow pilot investigation was performed for a period of 10 months to determine the effects of reclaimed water on natural systems and to determine the treatment efficiency of the overland flow processes at high application rates. The pilot investigation incorporated two treatment environments at three flow rates operated simultaneously.

Two environments, consisting of a natural pine flatwoods system [pine trees (*Pinas* sp.), saw palmetto (*Serenoa repens*, wax myrtle (*Myrica cerifera*), fetterbush (*Lyonia lucida*), various grasses] and a sloped and sodded [bahiagrass (*Paspalum notatum*)] area, were exposed to application rates of 38, 76 and 114 cm wk^{-1} of reclaimed water delivered directly from the ESAWWTF chlorine contact chamber. The schedule for the first four to five months of operation consisted of continuous application for two weeks followed by several days of non-application to allow for maintenance, which consisted of mowing the sodded plots and visually inspecting the natural pine flatwoods plots. Following the initial four to five months, the system was allowed to operate continuously without maintenance mowing for the remainder of the investigation to determine the effects of continuous application on the biological quality of the test plots.

PILOT RESULTS

The results of the overland flow pilot investigation are similar to other systems operated and tested in the state of Florida (Overman et al., 1984). Although the reclaimed water produced by the ESAWWTF is of high quality, the performance of the overland flow system is effective in the reduction or enhancement of several parameters. Most notably, residual chlorine is reduced greater than 95% over a flow length of 18.3 m for an application rate of 76 cm wk^{-1} (Figure 1).

The overland NO_3+NO_2-N reduction curve (Figure 2) for the natural plots indicates definite sensitivity with regard to varying application rates. The reduction of NO_x-N for the natural plots ranged from 40% for an application rate of 114 cm wk^{-1} to 80% for an application rate of 38 cm wk^{-1}. The NO_x-N reduction curve for the grassed plots indicates less sensitivity in relation to application rates. The reduction was generally 70 to 80% over the range of application rates.

Total N reductions reflected similar trends for NO_x-N reduction in relation to the natural and grassed plots. However, the magnitudes of the percent reduction are significantly different for total N (Figure 3). Total N reductions for the

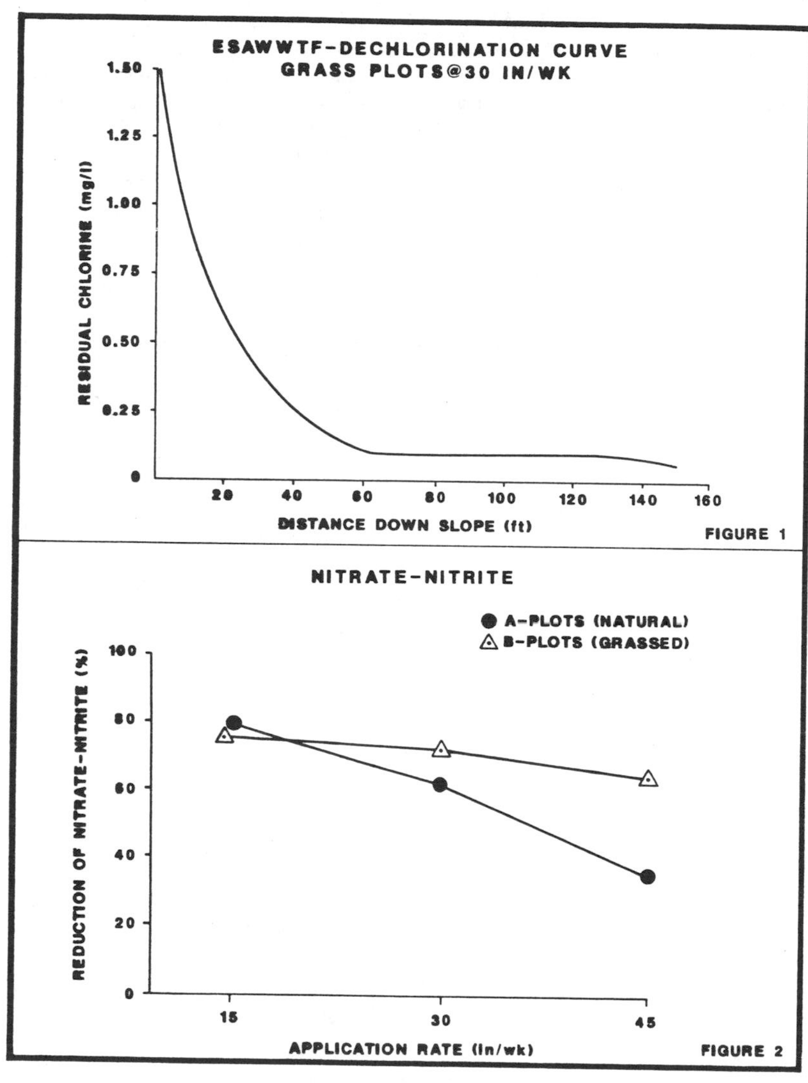

FIGURE 1

FIGURE 2

natural plots ranged between 10% for an application rate of 114 cm wk^{-1} to 34% for an application rate of 38 cm wk^{-1}, compared to the grassed plot performance which ranged between 14 and 16% reductions.

The minimal reduction of total N is largely due to the increase in organic N as the water passed through the plots. Organic N concentrations of applied waters in some instances increased 100%. Mowing and removal, or harvesting of the cover crop, in this case, bahiagrass, should have significantly increased the total N removal.

The results for reduction of total P, primarily due to plant uptake and soil adsorption (Figure 4) are consistent with the literature in that very little P removal can be expected. In fact, during some times of the year P may actually increase. The P addition experienced on the grassed plots may be due to fertilizers applied when the field was constructed in 1982.

The plant species existing on the pine flatwoods plots were largely unaffected and exhibited increased growth as compared to surrounding areas. The only species which indicated signs of stress were the wax myrtle, which began to yellow towards the end

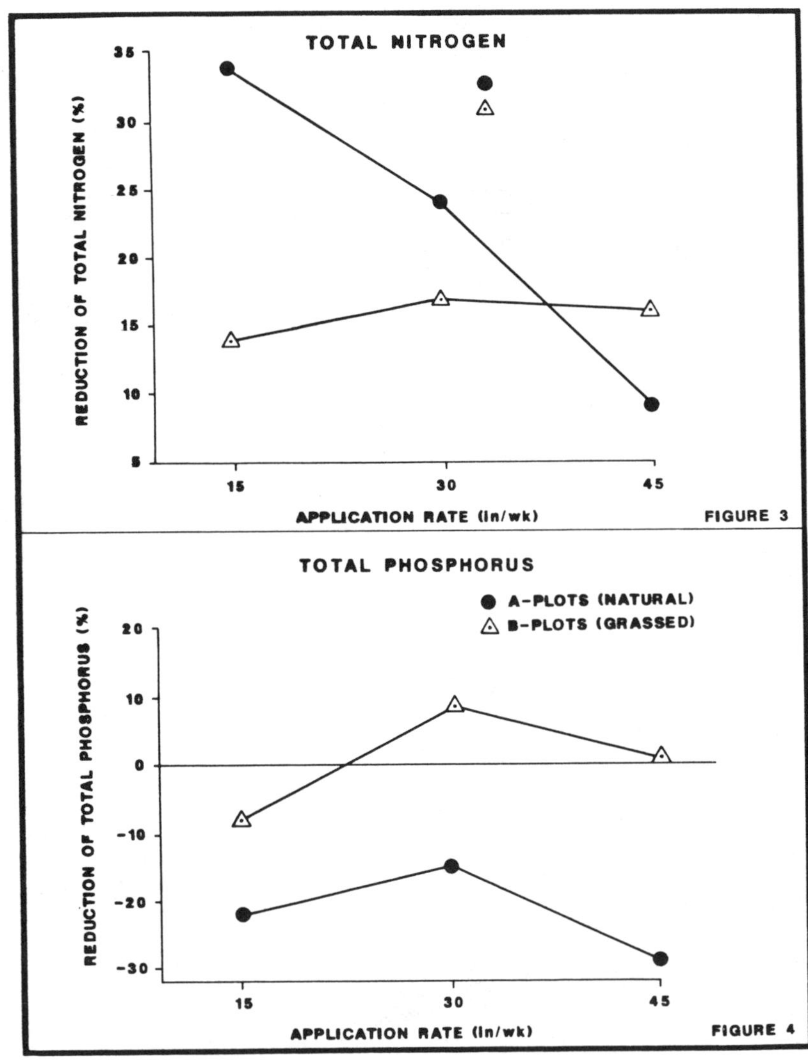

FIGURE 3

FIGURE 4

of the program when there was continuous application. In addition, cattails (Typha sp.) and sawgrass (Cladium jamaicense) encroached in areas which were cleared for isolation berms between the plots during continuous application.

Once mowing of the grassed plots ceased, cattails and dog fennel (Eupatorium sp.) proliferated all plots, with the density being greatest on the plot receiving 114 cm wk^{-1}.

REGULATORY REQUIREMENTS

Exemptions for the experimental use of wetlands (Section 17-4.243 FAC) are intended to encourage development of data on the ecological and water quality impacts of effluent discharge to wetlands to aid Florida Department of Environmental Regulation's (FDER) criteria determination process. The exemption is valid for five years, with provision for renewal based on long-term monitoring data.

Exemption from Class III water quality standards was approved for the Eastern Service Area wetlands demonstration project with the following performance stipulations:

- For the initial evaluation period, the application rate is limited to an annual average of 12,491 m^3 d^{-1} (loading rate of 8.4 cm wk^{-1}). Based on a review of the monitoring data and an assessment of the system's satisfactory performance after an initial operating period, FDER may authorize an increase up to a maximum of 23,467 m^3 d^{-1} (loading rate of 14.7 cm wk^{-1}). Hydraulic loading rates have usually been restricted to 1.2 to 2.5 cm wk^{-1} with minimum treatment requirements of secondary treatment and disinfection. Thabaraj (1982) has recommended conservative loading rates of approximately 2.5 cm wk^{-1} of "typical" secondary effluent, but research has shown that wetlands can assimilate tertiary effluent at higher loading rates (Zoltek et al., 1979). Because the ESAWWTF produces reclaimed water meeting AWT quality limits, significantly higher wetland application rates are possible.
- Reclaimed water from the ESAWWTF must not exceed an annual average of 5:5:3:1 mg L^{-1} for BOD_5, TSS, TN, and TP, respectively.
- Nutrient limits for discharge from the wetlands treatment system are a yearly total of 5319.8 kg TN and 531.9 kg TP (based on 13,248 m^3 d^{-1}). These limits are equivalent to concentrations of 1.1 mg L^{-1} TN and 0.1 mg L^{-1} TP.
- An intensive research study is required to monitor long-term effects of the wetlands application system.
- A pre-operative monitoring program to establish background water quality and biological quality and quantity is required to be performed over a two wet-season period (approximately 15 months).

Background water quality data collected to date (Table 1) include the data for Site 2 (the experimental jurisdictional wetland) and Site 5 (the control wetland which will not receive reclaimed water, but will serve as a parallel comparison to indicate effects on the wetlands as a result of regional or meteorological impacts). In comparison with the water quality data for other wetland systems in the central Florida area, the wetlands included as part of the exemption system are typical in water and biological quality as demonstrated in Table 2. With the exception of total P, the reclaimed water produced by the ESAWWTF is of better quality than the wetland ambient water.

OVERLAND FLOW/WETLANDS APPLICATION SYSTEM DESIGN

The overland flow/wetlands application site covers approximately 122 ha: approximately 61 ha of existing wetlands and 61 ha of pine flatwoods that will be converted to artificial wetlands. There are an additional 67 ha of offsite wetlands through which the reclaimed water will flow before reaching the Econlockhatchee River. The total distance from the point of discharge to the Econlockhatchee River is approximately 4.8 km.

The distribution system is designed for seven application zones to allow application rotation. Zone application rotation increases the overland flow treatment effectiveness, promotes assimilation of nutrients between loadings, and permits maintenance of the distribution system and overland flow areas. The reclaimed water will be applied to three or four active zones

TABLE 1. Comparison of experimental (Site 2) and control (Site 5) wetlands.

	TP		TN		DO		pH	
Month	Site 2	Site 5	Site 2	Site 5	Site 2	Site 5	Site 2	Site 5
	------------------mg L^{-1}					----------------		
Aug	0.27	0.48	2.14	2.59	1.24	1.12	4.4	5.0
Sep	0.17	0.20	1.69	2.12	0.80	0.61	4.5	4.5
Oct	0.22	0.22	2.11	2.11	0.54	0.80	4.5	4.6
Nov	0.27	0.16	3.65	1.90	1.74	0.96	5.2	4.8
Dec	0.17	0.28	1.47	1.70	1.25	1.14	4.3	4.4
Jan	0.06	0.05	1.11	1.54	2.00	1.14	4.1	4.1
Feb	0.31	0.27	2.35	2.70	4.70	2.10	4.4	4.4
Mar	0.20	0.20	1.12	1.60	2.19	1.96	4.2	4.4
Avg	0.21†	0.23	1.96	2.03	1.80‡	1.23	4.4	4.5

†Average TP for Site 2 without January value is 0.23 mg L^{-1}.
Average dry season TP without January value is 0.23 mg L^{-1}.
‡Average DO for Site 2 without February value is 1.39 mg L^{-1}.
Average dry season DO without February value is 1.53 mg L^{-1}.

TABLE 2. Comparison of ESA wetlands with other Central Florida wetlands (Source: Camp Dresser & McKee Inc., 1986).

Season	Site 2	Site 5	A	B	C	D	E	F	G	H	I	J
	Total P (mg L^{-1})											
Wet†	0.23	0.31	--	--	--	--	--	--	--	0.31	--	--
Dry‡	0.22	0.20	0.27	0.25	0.10	0.27	0.22	0.25	0.78	0.25	0.30	0.2
	Total N (mg L^{-1})											
Wet	1.92	2.3	--	--	--	--	--	--	--	1.18	--	--
Dry	1.97	1.93	3.33	2.47	0.63	1.79	3.95	3.85	1.88	0.85	0.80	1.4
	pH											
Wet	4.5	4.7	--	--	--	--	--	--	--	5.2	--	--
Dry	4.5	4.5	7.6	6.9	6.9	6.5	4.2	4.2	4.4	5.9	6.7	4.3
	DO (mg L^{-1})											
Wet	1.0	0.9	--	--	--	--	--	--	--	2.0	--	--
Dry	2.1	1.4	--	--	--	--	--	--	--	4.8	--	--

†Wet season includes June through September. ‡Dry season includes October through May.

A - Crown Point Swamp
B - Black Lake Swamp
C - Boggy Creek Swamp
D - Shingle Creek Swamp
E - Cypress Creek Swamp
F - Burned Swamp
G - Lake Speer Swamp
H - Wide Cypress Swamp
I - Bay Branch
J - Sulphur Creek Swamp

for two consecutive weeks. Each zone provides uniform sheet flow of the reclaimed water, with an overland flow distance of 91-182 m through a revegetated artificial wetlands before discharge to the first natural wetlands. A flow control structure will regulate the flow of reclaimed water out of the first natural wetlands. A redistribution channel will collect and convey the water from the flow control structure across the adjacent land and will allow zone application rotation.

The land adjacent to and east of the redistribution channel has been cleared and graded. This area will be planted with a variety of aquatic plants to create a second artificial wetland. The reclaimed water will be allowed to flow from the artificial wetland to the second natural wetland (a hardwood swamp), and ultimately to the Econlockhatchee River via an unnamed watercourse.

The artificial wetlands areas are incorporated into the system to provide additional treatment through plant uptake and other microbial activity, to create additional habitat for native wildlife, and to enhance the existing wetland systems through artificial expansion of those systems.

FOLLOW-UP MONITORING

A research study is required to monitor long-term ecological effects, water quality impacts on downstream waters, and waste recycling efficiency of the wetlands. Monitoring of significant chemical and biological characteristics will be conducted for the wetland systems receiving the reclaimed water and nearby control wetlands systems. The research study, which will be conducted by the University of Florida Center for Wetlands, will include the following components: 1) ecological research, 2) soil research, 3) hydraulic research, and 4) water quality research.

REFERENCES

Camp Dresser & McKee Inc. 1986. Orange County Wastewater Master Plan. Prepared for Orange County Public Utilities Division, Orlando, Florida.

Overman, A. R., and T. Schanze. 1985. Overland flow treatment of wastewater in Florida. EPA-600/2-84-163, NTIS PB85-11578, U.S. EPA, Cincinnati, Ohio.

Thabaraj, G. J. 1982. Wastewater discharge to wetlands: Regulatory aspects. Presented at the Florida Wastewater Management Seminar sponsored by the Florida Department of Environmental Regulation and the Florida Pollution Control Association, Tampa, Florida, February 26, 1982.

Zoltek, J., Jr., S. E. Bayley, A. J. Hermann, L. R. Tortora, and T. J. Dolan. 1979. Removal of nutrients from treated municipal wastewater by freshwater marshes. Final Report to the City of Clermont, Florida. University of Florida, Gainesville.

AN EXEMPTION FOR THE EXPERIMENTAL USE OF MARSHALL SWAMP FOR ADVANCED EFFLUENT RECYCLING

E. L. Melear and D. J. Homblette
Boyle Engineering Corporation
320 East South Street
Orlando, Florida 32801

R. A. Davis
City of Ocala
Ocala, Florida 32678

ABSTRACT

In recent years, there has been a major trend toward the utilization of wetlands for the treatment and/or disposal of wastewater effluent. Attention has been given to the research aspects regarding the ability of wetlands to assimilate nutrients and how they respond to modified hydrologic regimes. Another imperative consideration is the regulatory constraints that govern these activities. Existing rules, new regulations, and those under consideration, create a myriad of restrictions, controls, and guidelines that must be considered when pursuing this wastewater treatment/disposal option. This papers describes the permitting process and regulatory rules that the City of Ocala, Florida, is working with in order to develop a project that involves the discharge of treated effluent to Marshall Swamp. The regulatory process has taken more than two years and at this time is not yet complete. A tentative timetable has construction startup scheduled for the end of 1986. One of the final hurdles to meeting that schedule is permitting through the St. Johns River Water Management District (SJRWMD).

Keywords: Wetlands, experimental use, regulations, wastewater, permits.

INTRODUCTION

State and Federal regulations are an integral part of the formulation of a wastewater reuse project. This paper summarizes the regulatory process that the City of Ocala, Florida, has followed in order to implement a treated effluent discharge to the

ISBN 0-941463-00-1

Marshall Swamp. A description of the on-going background monitoring and proposed long-term research study is included.

REGULATORY ISSUES

Project Development

Consent Order. In April, 1981, the City of Ocala (City) entered into a Consent Order with the Florida Department of Environmental Regulation (FDER) for Sewage Treatment Plant No. 2 (STP No. 2). A Temporary Operating Permit (TOP) was issued on September 30, 1982, which included a Compliance Schedule to cease disposal of secondary effluent into percolation ponds and to implement a new method by September 30, 1987. STP No. 2 is located in a sinkhole prone area, and thus, the percolation ponds were not an environmentally acceptable disposal method.

Facilities Planning. The City of Ocala and Environs 201 Facilities Planning Program began in late September, 1976, as a joint effort between the City of Ocala, as "Lead Applicant," and Marion County. The draft 201 Facilities Plan was concluded in October 1977, and was revised in December 1978, to conform with review agency comments. However, it was never adopted by the City. An update of the 201 Facilities Plan was initiated in July 1984, by the City, with the purpose of generating a cost effective and environmentally sound wastewater collection, treatment and disposal plan for the area.

The alternatives evaluated in the 201 Facilities Plan included service area adjustments for the City's two wastewater treatment facilities, interceptor alignments and wastewater treatment/disposal options. Of particular interest are the disposal options for STP NO. 2: slow rate land application (spray irrigation); rapid rate land application (percolation ponds); overland flow system with discharge to wetlands; and direct surface water discharge. A cost analysis, and non-monetary and environmental evaluation was used to choose a treatment/disposal option. The existing STP No. 2 will be upgraded and expanded from 13,248 $m^3\ d^{-1}$ to 32,173 $m^3\ d^{-1}$. New preliminary treatment, primary clarifiers and anaerobic digestions system will be added, with a contact stabilization (activated sludge) system and secondary clarifiers improved and enlarged. Effluent will be pumped to an overland flow system for further treatment with the drainage being collected and then discharged into Marshall Swamp.

The City requested inclusion in the State Construction Grants Program and was notified in May 1984, that the project was ranked very high on the priority list.

Exemption. In September 1984, the selected disposal alternative was reviewed with the St. Johns District office of FDER. A Site Specific Alternative Criteria (SSAC) would have been required by FDER, but given the time constraints for both the grant program and the deadline for the Consent Order, the FDER-Tallahassee office suggested the City request an "Exemption to Provide for the Experimental Use of Wetlands for Low Energy Water and Wastewater Recycling" (Exemption) as set forth in Chapter 17-4.243(4), Florida Administrative Code (F.A.C.).

The City made a formal written request for an Exemption on October 11, 1984, and supplied additional information on December 19, 1984, as requested by FDER for their evaluation. FDER made a site visit to Marshall Swamp to inspect existing conditions shortly thereafter. the Department issued an Amended Notice of Intent to the City for an Exemption on October 16, 1985, and finalized it on February 4, 1986. The Exemption includes 15 conditions, primarily related to potential impacts on Marshall Swamp and the monitoring programs to establish background conditions and to assess the impacts of secondary effluent on the wetland.

Permits. Five major permits from four agencies were required prior to constructing the project. The primary activities requiring permits were the construction/operation of a treatment facility, discharge of the treated effluent to surface waters (Marshall Swamp), construction in and impacts on wetlands, and the management of surface water runoff from the project sites. The permitting effort was initiated in 1984 and has included extensive in-field coordination with the agency representatives. Applications currently under review are:

- U.S. Environmental Protection Agency (USEPA) National Pollutant Discharge Elimination System (NDPES) Permit,
- U. S. Army Corps of Engineers (COE) Permit for Construction Dredging and Filling in the Waters of the United States,
- FDER Permit to Construct/Operate Domestic Wastewater Treatment and Disposal Systems,
- FDER Permit for Construction Dredging and Filling in the Waters of the State of Florida, and
- SJRWMD Permit for Management and Storage of Surface Waters.

The key issues have been the mitigation of wetland losses for construction of the overland flow system and the potential impacts on water quality in the Oklawaha River and water bodies downstream from Marshall Swamp. At the present time, FDER is developing a wetland mitigation rule. Although the rule does not become effective until February 1987, FDER staff is currently reviewing permit applications based upon policies similar to the proposed rule. Uncertainty over whether forested wetlands, such as Marshall Swamp, can be effectively replaced by a new artificial system has necessitated higher ratios of created to destroyed wetlands for mitigation. This issue is not clearly defined within the SJRWMD & COE permitting processes.

The primary water quality issue is the ability of forested wetlands to assimilate P over an extended time frame. FDER recognizes the lack of a substantiated data base, and thus, granted the Experimental Exemption. Essentially, a research project has been created as a mechanism to permit effluent discharge to wetlands. If established criteria are not met by the project, then either an alternative disposal option or increased levels of treatment at the wastewater facility would be required. SJRWMD, through the surface water management permit, has taken the position there is insufficient valid scientific evidence that a forested wetland can assimilate P to the necessary levels. The agency may not grant a permit; even one with conditions addressing alternate methods of disposal and/or increased levels of treatment for nutrient removal.

While the City sought an Experimental Exemption, FDER developed and implemented a wastewater to wetland rule (Chapter 17-6.055, F.A.C.). Criteria and monitoring plans were developed for "pristine", hydrologically altered, and manmade wetlands. This rule is reflected in the conditions of the Exemption.

Access and Ownership. A third task that has involved extensive coordination was securing access to the sampling sites, obtaining long term easements within Marshall Swamp, and ownership of the overland flow site. Six land owners are involved (Figure 1). Access for the monitoring programs and easements for the pipeline are being secured from the appropriate owners. The drainage easements are those areas within Marshall Swamp that may be inundated by effluent from the overland flow system. The overland flow system site and wetland outfall areas will be purchased from Container Corporation.

WETLAND DESCRIPTION AND LOCATION

Characteristics

Project Vicinity. Marshall Swamp is an extensive freshwater mixed-hardwood swamp that encompasses approximately 2,914 ha in the floodplains of both the Dead and Oklawaha Rivers. It is bounded by sandy well-drained uplands on the west, and a sandy clay ridge, on the east. Its outlet is eastward via the Dead River to the Oklawaha. A low topographic divide separates the swamp from the Silver River on the north. The central portion of the Swamp (approximately 3,000 acres) south of the Dead River has been significantly altered by ditching and draining in the 1950's for agricultural purposes. However, the site was abandoned and has reverted back to a herbaceous/shrub marsh. The northern end has had relatively little direct impact from human activity.

The Exemption is specific to the northern portion of Marshall Swamp (Figure 1) between the Dead River along the north edge of the muck farm and Sharps Ferry Road. The general hydraulic gradient is south to the Dead River. The approximate area is 790 ha.

Hydrology. Marshall Swamp has undergone significant changes in surface hydrology due to drainage and flood control

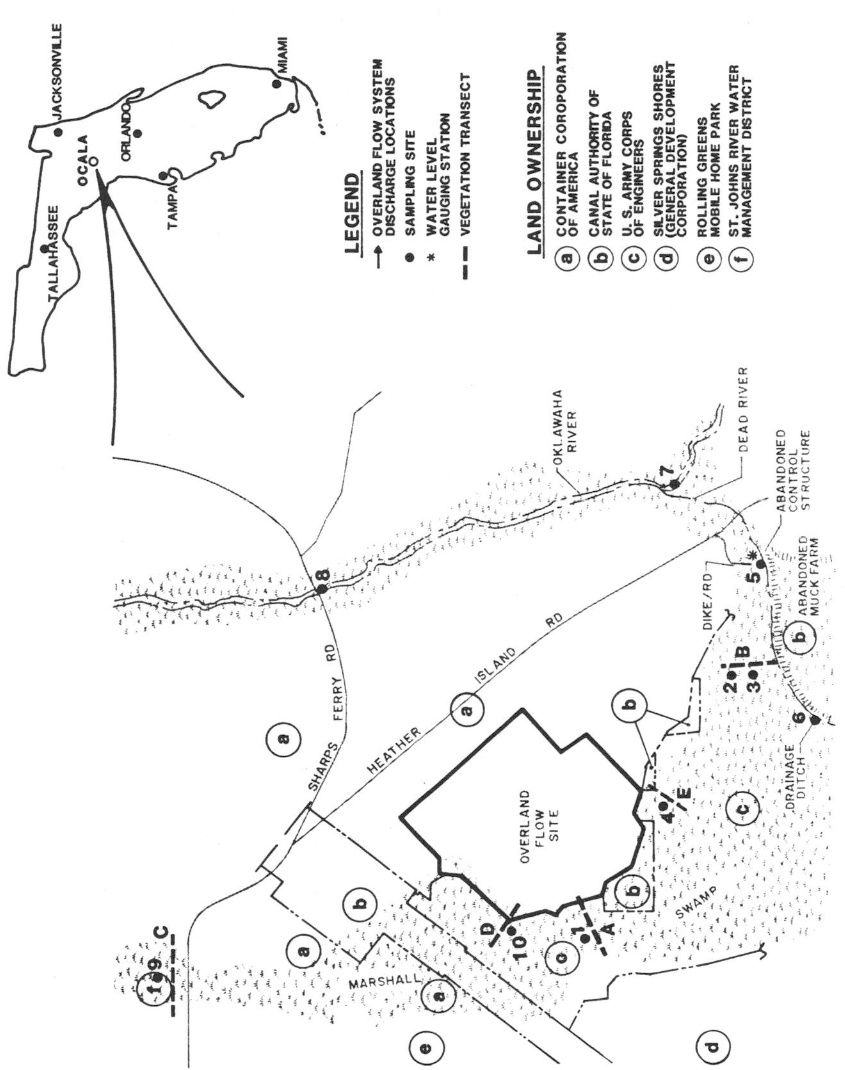

FIGURE 1. Land ownership and sampling sites.

projects in the surrounding watershed. Originally, the wetland was predominately a standing water swamp with seasonal periods of high water that temporarily inundated adjacent low areas. Over the past 90 years, dredging of the Oklawaha River for navigation and flood control purposes has lowered water levels. The Swamp contains no standing water during dry periods. Seasonal sheet flow from the uplands meanders down the gradual side slopes to shallow swales and ill-defined channels to the Dead River. Previously, the Swamp served as a storage area for hydraulic overloads from the Oklawaha River. This flushed the wetland to some extent on a regular basis as other more undisturbed swamps still experience. Construction of the dam at Moss Bluff for flood control has shifted the normal hydroperiod by approximately three months. A dike with culverts and flapgates was constructed across the Dead River to prevent backflow into the swamp during high water periods in the Oklawaha River. The structure has been abandoned for a number of years and no longer effectively prevents flow into the swamp.

Water quality. Sampling of the Dead River during December 1984, and January 1985, indicated a specific conductivity of 401-524 μmhos cm^{-1}, total P of 0.094-0.217 mg P L^{-1}, and total Kjeldahl N of 2.18-3.02 mg N L^{-1}. This data probably reflects the water quality in the perimeter ditch around the former muck farm. Monitoring of the Dead River (August and September, 1984) downstream from the backflow control structure indicated nutrient values were indistinguishable from those in background samples.

Vegetation. Marshall Swamp can generally be characterized as a freshwater swamp consisting of a combination of mixed hardwoods and cypress, with hardwood hammocks around the eastern perimeter as a transition into the upland. Prior to hydrologic alteration, the site developed as a deep swamp, with many areas dominated by cypress. With lower standing water levels during the past 20 years, the dominance has changed to species more tolerant of less inundation. The general sequence of canopy from upland into the swamp is laurel oak, swamp chestnut oak, sabal palm and loblolly pine; through sweet gum, sabal palm and ironwood; to red maple, swamp tupelo and cypress; and finally, a uniform stand of cypress.

Geology and Soils. The soils of Marshall Swamp are primarily from two associations: Bluff-martel and the Okeechobee-Terra Ceia-Tomoka. The first association is characterized by very poorly drained mineral soils, some loamy and clayey throughout, with others loamy in the upper reaches and a clay layer within 50 cm of the surface. The other association is very poorly drained organic soils. Some are organic to a depth of greater than 1.5 m, and others, only in the upper 40-100 cm with sand/loam beneath. Both are usually inundated for periods of six months or more and lack a good natural drainage system.

Control Site

The northern extremity of Marshall Swamp will be used as the control site. This area is now isolated hydrologically from the remainder of the wetland by an impervious berm (roadbed). An upland ridge separates the area from the Silver River basin further north. Previously, the flow was into Marshall Swamp proper. The only sources of water are runoff and rainfall.

The control site can generally be characterized as a freshwater swamp consisting of a combination of mixed hardwoods and cypress. Areas at lower elevations with longer hydroperiods are dominated by stands of cypress. The more mesic areas contain hardwood species that are sensitive to hydroperiods. The sequence of canopy from the upland into the swamp is sand pine, live oak, laurel oak, palmetto, and water oak through sweetgum, sabal palm, ironwood, red maple, tupelo and cypress.

The soils of the control site are the Bluff series of the Bluff-Martel Association. These soils are very poorly drained. The sandy clay loam surface layer is overlain with decayed organic debris.

BACKGROUND MONITORING PROGRAM AND RESEARCH STUDY

Objectives

The background monitoring program and the research study are required by the Exemption. The overall objectives are:

- Obtain background vegetation, water quality, soils and macroinvertebrate data,
- Monitor the wetland vegetation, water quality, soils and macroinvertebrates during discharge of secondary effluent,
- Assess the impacts, if any, upon the study area from the discharge of secondary effluent.

The data will be used to 1) develop alternative criteria for nutrients and dissolved O_2; 2) to provide supportive information for criteria in the Exemption; and 3) to assess the response of the wetland to the discharge of secondary effluent.

The background monitoring program is to be conducted over two wet seasons, commencing May 1, 1986. Only partial sampling has been done due to dry conditions in the wetland. The research study phase would not begin until initiation of the discharge of secondary effluent from the overland flow system into Marshall Swamp.

Project Description

Sample Sites. Ten sampling stations were established (Figure 1). Stations 1-4 and 10 will monitor the water quality in the wetland and the impact of effluent discharge on the ecosystems. Station 5 provides data on the overall discharge from the Swamp to the Dead River. Station 6 in the outside perimeter ditch is used to assess the contribution of nutrients from the middle portion of the Swamp. Stations 7 and 8 monitor the influence of the discharge from the Dead River upon the water quality in the Oklawaha River. The purpose of the control site (Station 9) is to provide data on naturally occurring conditions and their impact on the wetland system.

Sampling Frequency. The monitoring plan for Marshall Swamp is a combination of the plans that were developed for "pristine" and hydrologically-altered wetlands in the wastewater to wetlands rule. Routine monthly monitoring is conducted for surface water, and sediment and biota samples are collected annually. Intensive sampling is performed for three consecutive weeks during both the dormant and primary growing seasons for specified parameters to provide detailed data on the variability of the water quality and nutrient fluxes.

Sample Collection. Soil/sediment samples are used to determine the rate of nutrient and metal accumulation and the potential for their long-term storage. Since two soil associations are present, a difference in retention capacity may be found.

Elongated "line-strip" quadrats have been placed along the transects to sample and map the herbaceous understory. Tree, seedling, sapling and shrub data are collected using 15 m diameter plots adjacent to the quadrats. The plant community structure is to be evaluated annually near the end of the growing season for both herbaceous species and woody plants. Diversity and seedling-to-mature tree ratios should indicate changes in the community structure due to nutrient and hydraulic loadings. Branch and foliage samples are to be collected for plant tissue analysis of nutrient and metal contents. False-color infrared aerial photography taken just prior to senescence will be used to monitor potential floral community responses to the discharge of effluent and aid in mapping and assessing stress.

Microorganisms in the coliform and streptococci group will be used as indicators for fecal pollution, to index the degree of contamination and identify the source. Qualitative estimates of macroinvertebrate and fish populations will be made to assess the areal extent and subtle changes occurring in the mixing zones. A Shannon-Weaver index will be developed.

SUMMARY AND CONCLUSIONS

To date, more than $165,000 has been expended to obtain the Exemption for the City of Ocala and the necessary permits for the project. Resolution of issues with SJRWMD, FDER and Container Corporation are still outstanding. The annual cost of the background monitoring program is estimated to be $125,000. The background monitoring program is underway, however due to record dry conditions, there is no standing water in Marshall Swamp or the control site for water quality and macroinvertebrate sampling. The Oklawaha River is being sampled regularly.

Wetlands are a viable option for low energy wastewater reuse, but a major drawback is the myriad of regulatory constraints which often overlap and result in an extended lead time prior to project implementation. Potential applicants should be prepared to commit extensive financial resources for project design and permit coordination. A minimum of two years prior to construction is required to obtain the necessary permits. Background monitoring requirements prior to project startup could potentially add 18 to 24 months if the program is not initiated earlier in the permit process.

With the extensive and sometimes conflicting regulatory constraints and controls covering projects of this kind in Florida, strong consideration must be given to streamlining the permitting process and eliminating overlapping jurisdictions between agencies. Parallel evaluations on local, State and Federal levels may not be eliminated, but it is critical that permitting on the same governmental level be consolidated within a single agency. At the present time both the FDER and the water management districts require parallel evaluations that are costly, time consuming, and often contradictory in their results. Thus, a beneficial wetland project may be compromised and a less environmentally and economically desirable treatment/disposal option chosen.

REGULATION OF WASTEWATER DISCHARGE TO FLORIDA WETLANDS

L. N. Schwartz
Florida Department of Environmental Regulation
Tallahassee, Florida 32301

ABSTRACT

The legislative mandate of the Warren S. Henderson Wetlands Protection Act of 1984 was to provide for an alternative for the treatment of wastewater through discharge to wetlands. A rule has been adopted establishing criteria for this activity and protecting the type, nature, and function of the wetlands to be used. The strength of the rule is that is has been developed to generate information that will better allow us to evaluate the impact of wastewater discharge to wetlands and ultimately the suitability of this wastewater treatment alternative.

Keywords: Wastewater discharge, aquatic plants, design criteria, legislative mandate, water quality.

INTRODUCTION

The Warren S. Henderson Wetlands Protection Act of 1984 is Florida's first law dealing specifically with protecting the state's remaining wetland resources. Among other things, the Act expresses a legislative intent to provide for the use of certain waters that are dominated by specified plant species to receive and treat domestic wastewater that at a minimum has been treated to secondary standards [Florida Statute 403.918(4)]. In addition the Florida Department of Environmental Regulation (DER) was directed to develop a rule establishing criteria for this activity. The criteria must protect the type, nature, and function of wetlands receiving the wastewater. The Department promulgated such a wastewater to wetlands rule effective April 1986.

The rule was developed with the belief that wetland systems, if managed properly, can treat wastewater and their type, nature, and function can be protected. Nonetheless, the Department recognizes and explicitly states in the rule that the discharge of domestic wastewater effluent to wetlands is a field in which there exists limited but expanding knowledge, and as additional data become available, reevaluations will determine if revisions are

ISBN 0-941463-00-1

necessary. The rule's format includes design criteria and regulation at three levels: effluent limits; standards within the treatment wetland; and standards for discharge from the treatment wetland to downstream water bodies.

WETLAND TYPES USED FOR WASTEWATER TREATMENT

The rule specifically prohibits the use of certain wetland types for wastewater treatment. Thus, the discharge of domestic wastewater effluent cannot be permitted where the: (1) wetlands are within Outstanding Florida Waters (e.g., waters within Everglades National Park); (2) wetlands are within Class I (Potable Water Supplies) or Class II (Shellfish Propagation or Harvesting) waters; (3) wetlands are within areas designated as areas of critical state concern as of October 1, 1985 (e.g., the Green Swamp); (4) herbaceous ground cover constitutes more than 30% of the uppermost stratum of the proposed treatment wetland, unless this herbaceous ground cover is composed of 75% *Typha* sp. (cattail); and (5) discharge from the proposed treatment wetland is within an upstream annual average travel time of 24 h of a lake, estuary, lagoon, Outstanding Florida Water, or area designated as an area of critical state concern unless Water Quality Based Effluent Limits (WQBEL) have been established and can be met. These prohibitions reflect the need to provide additional protection to special waters and water bodies sensitive to eutrophication, as well as the existing uncertainty regarding the response of certain herbaceous wetlands to wastewater discharge. Therefore, most of the rule's provisions apply to the use of wetlands dominated by woody vegetation.

However, to encourage the use of impacted wetlands and the creation of additional wetland acreage designed to maximize wastewater assimilation, the rule specifies two additional wetland categories to be used for wastewater treatment. The first is hydrologically altered wetlands which are areas within the landward extent of waters of the state in which the hydrologic regime has been altered prior to October 1, 1985, by drainage works which have directly resulted in substantial and continuing encroachment by perennial upland species or nuisance exotics in any strata, and substantial and continuing reduction in water levels or change in hydroperiod. The second category is man-made or artificial wetlands which are created solely as a result of human activity, such as scraping or contouring of uplands, or the land application of wastewater. The regulatory criteria governing wastewater discharges to these two categories of wetlands are less restrictive than those applicable to unaltered woody wetlands, as will be described below.

EFFLUENT LIMITS

Under Florida's regulatory system, effluent limits exist for all surface water discharges. Wastewater, at a minimum, must be treated to secondary standards and, to the extent necessary, provide disinfection and pH control. Under the wastewater to wetlands rule, additional levels of treatment (beyond secondary) are required for discharge to all but artificial wetlands, as follows:

- effluent discharge can not exceed 19 mg L^{-1} total N (as N) as a monthly average, except that in hydrologically altered treatment wetlands it can not exceed 26 mg L^{-1} total N (as N) as a monthly average;
- effluent discharge can not exceed 2 mg L^{-1} total NH_4^+ (as N) as a monthly average;
- effluent discharge can not exceed 1 mg L^{-1} total P (as P) as a monthly average, except that in hydrologically altered treatment wetlands it shall not exceed 3 mg L^{-1} total P (as P); and
- the pH of the effluent discharging to the treatment wetland must be within the range of (1.0 $\pm$ -0.2) x the wetland background pH.

The high level of allowable total N loading is based on the high treatment of N exhibited in wetland systems. The low level of allowable total NH_4^+ loading indicates that nitrification (of NH_4^+ to NO_3^-) is required. Wetland treatment of N is primarily through the denitrification process. As indicated by the low level of allowable total P loading, there is a need for some type of pre-treatment for P since wetlands vary greatly in their capacity to remove P, and even under the best circumstances, P removal apparently is time limited. The allowable range of effluent pH is a function of the buffering capacity of the wetland system. The lower the pH in the wetland, the lower the buffering capacity, and therefore the smaller the allowable effluent pH range.

QUALITATIVE DESIGN CRITERIA

The rule requires that the discharge of domestic wastewater to treatment wetlands minimize channelized flow and maximize sheet flow of effluent over the treatment wetland. Since maximum contact of the effluent with the treatment wetland will ensure maximum wastewater assimilation, effluent distribution design in each wetland is critical. The rule further provides that the discharge must minimize the loss or dissolution of sediments due to erosion or leaching, and result in no adverse effects on endangered and threatened species.

QUANTITATIVE DESIGN CRITERIA

Hydrologic loading rates are to be designed to minimize alteration of the natural hydroperiod and to maximize the treatment wetland's assimilative capacity. Thus, a conservative annual average hydraulic loading rate of 5 cm wk^{-1} applies in unaltered wetlands regulated by the rule. In hydrologically altered treatment wetlands, the hydraulic loading rate is to be appropriately designed for the site, approved on a case-by-case basis, and not exceed 15 cm wk^{-1}. This higher hydraulic loading rate is aimed at returning historic water levels to these impacted sites.

In order to maximize the wastewater assimilation capacity in the treatment wetland, the minimum detention time of the wastewater within the treatment wetland is 14 days, unless it can be affirmatively demonstrated that a shorter detention time will provide the required level of effluent quality in the discharge from the treatment wetland. In order to maximize long-term wastewater assimilation, the loading rate of total N (as N) can not exceed 25 g m^{-2} yr^{-1}, except for hydrological altered treatment wetlands where it can not exceed 75 g m^{-2} yr^{-1}. The loading rate of total P (as P) shall not exceed 2.64 g m^{-2} yr^{-1}, except for hydrologically altered treatment wetlands where it shall not exceed 7.92 g m^{-2} yr^{-1}. As with hydraulic loading rates, nutrient loading rates in hydrologically altered wetlands must be appropriately designed for the site and approved on a case-by-case basis.

Total N loading was determined from information on seven Florida forested wetland sites receiving wastewater. The data indicates that at least 70% removal is expected at a loading rate of 25 g m^{-2} yr^{-1} of N. Since information on P assimilation is less conclusive, total P loading was determined upon the basis of a hydraulic loading of 5 cm wk^{-1} and an effluent limit of 1 mg L^{-1}. As indicated above, the hydraulic loading in hydrologically altered wetlands can triple. Therefore, nutrient loading can also triple to 75 g m^{-1} yr^{-1} and 7.92 g m^{-2} yr^{-1} for total N and total P, respectively. The wastewater to wetlands rule further requires that the effluent be given basic disinfection and then stored in holding ponds prior to discharge to the treatment wetland to provide for dechlorination and equalization of hydraulic surges.

STANDARDS WITHIN TREATMENT WETLANDS

The minimum criteria for surface waters apply in all wetlands under DER jurisidiction as waters of the state. Wetlands appropriate for wastewater discharge under the rule are Class III waters (recreation and for propagation and maintenance of a healthy, well-balanced population of fish and wildlife). The rule exempts treatment wetlands from certain general surface water criteria and Class III water criteria; all other water quality criteria continue to apply. In addition, it establishes new biological quality criteria which provide a measure of the impacts of wastewater discharge on the type, nature, and function of the wetland.

The general criteria for nutrients, pH, specific conductance, nuisance species, and turbidity are inapplicable in treatment wetlands, as are the Class III criteria for pH, transparency, and total coliforms. The rule also contains several substitute standards applicable in treatment wetlands. Dissolved O_2 levels, including daily and seasonal fluctuations, must be maintained to prevent violations of the "wetland biological quality" standards, and substances in concentrations which are chronically toxic to humans, animals, or plants can not be present.

The rule establishes four "wetland biological quality" standards. First, the flora and fauna of the treatment wetland can not be changed so as to: impair the wetland's ability to function in the propagation and maintenance of healthy, well-balanced fish and wildlife populations; or substantially reduce its ability to be effective in wastewater treatment. Second, the Shannon-Weaver diversity index of benthic macroinvertebrates can not be reduced below 50% of background levels as measured using standard techniques. Third, in a treatment wetland containing fish populations, there must be an annual analysis of covariance by species using water depth as a covariant and biomass as a dependent variable. Where significant changes from baseline data in biomass occur, the cause of the change must be investigated. A 10% decrease in the biomass of sport and commercial fish or of forage fish, or a 25% increase of rough fish, is not allowed, unless the ratio of sport and commercial fish to rough fish is maintained. Fourth, the importance value of any of the dominant plant species in the canopy and subcanopy at any monitoring station can not be reduced by more than 50% (excluding certain exotics). In addition, the average importance value of any of the dominant plant species occupying the canopy or subcanopy can not be reduced by more than 25%. Dominant plant species are defined as those species present during the baseline monitoring within the canopy and subcanopy that have a total relative importance value of at least 90%. While a biological integrity standard requiring the use of the Shannon-Weaver diversity index has been used to evaluate impacts in waters of the state under existing water quality criteria, the development of both fish and vegetation standards in wetland systems represents a new approach for evaluating changes in these areas.

The dissolved O_2 standard and the benthic macroinvertebrate, fish, and vegetation standards are inapplicable in hydrologically altered treatment wetlands. However, the rule does require enhancement of wetland biological quality. The same monitoring requirements for benthic macroinvertebrates, fish, and vegetation apply in hydrologically altered wetlands, but the data is used qualitatively to evaluate enhancement and not as a standard. In artificial wetlands, only the minimum criteria for surface waters and the Class III heavy metal standards apply, as do secondary treatment, disinfection, and pH control requirements. Also, appropriate groundwater standards apply in all treatment wetland projects.

STANDARDS FOR DISCHARGE FROM TREATMENT WETLANDS

The discharge from treatment wetlands can not cause or contribute to violations of water quality criteria in contiguous waters. The average annual total N concentrations can not exceed 3 mg L^{-1} (as N), of which no more than 0.02 mg L^{-1} (as N) can be as un-ionized NH_3. The average annual total P concentrations can be no greater than 0.2 mg L^{-1} (as P). These limits apply unless Water Quality Based Effluent Limits (WQBEL) have been established and can be met. In addition, if the maximum allowable concentrations of total N, un-ionized NH_3, or total P are exceeded in the discharge from the treatment wetland, the areal loading of these constituents must be reduced in accordance with a pre-approved alternative, which may include installation of additional control technology at the plant.

MONITORING

The wastewater to wetlands rule mandates a monitoring program to ensure compliance with water quality standards and to establish a reliable, scientifically valid data base upon which to evaluate design criteria and treatment wetland performance. The standard monitoring program, including the frequency of sampling for each parameter, is presented in Table 1. Surface water, sediment, and biota must be monitored during both the baseline (one year) and operational phase.

A minimum of two stations must be sampled in the treatment wetland for surface water parameters, along with flow measurements to provide data for a simple input/output mass balance analysis. A minimum of three biota stations must be established, with additional surface water and biota stations required if needed to determine compliance with standards both within the treatment wetland and in contiguous waters.

ADDITIONAL REQUIREMENTS

Sufficient legal interest must be obtained in the treatment wetland to provide reasonable assurance that no activities will be conducted that will adversely affect the treatment capability of the system. The adverse effects of dredging or filling on the assimilation capacity of the treatment wetland will be examined. No distribution system will be allowed that requires destruction of the wetland habitat proposed for use in wastewater treatment. Reasonable assurance that public access to the treatment wetland is restricted must be provided. The rule also establishes policy for existing wastewater to wetland discharges. All existing dischargers have five years from the rule's effective date to comply with either its provisions or all applicable water quality standards in waters of the state.

TABLE 1. Standard monitoring programs.

Parameter	Baseline Monitoring[5] Program			Operational Monitoring Program			
	Surface[1] water	Sediment[1]	Biota[2]	Effluent[3]	Surface[1] water	Sediment[1]	Biota[2]
Temperature	M			T	M		
Dissolved Oxygen	M (DI)			T	M (DI)		
pH	M	O		T	M	A	
Conductivity	M			T	M		
Cl_2 (TRC)				T			
Color	M				M		
$CBOD_5$	M			W	M		
TSS	M			W	M		
TP (as P)	M	O		W	M	A	
OP (as P)	M			W	M		
TKN (as N)	M	O		W	M	A	
NH_4 (as N)	M	O		W	M	A	
NO_3-NO_2 (as N)	M	O		W	M	A	
SO_4 (as S)	M	O		W	M	A	
S (as S)		O				A	
Fecal Coliforms	M			W	M		
Chl a	Q				Q		
Non-metallic priority pollutants	O			A	A		
Metals (Hg, Pb, Cd, Cr, Cu, Zn, Fe, Ni, Ag)	O	O		SA	SA	SA	
Flow				C			
Stage[4]	C				C		
Benthic Macroinvertebrates			Q				Q
Woody vegetation			O				A
Herbaceous Vegetation			Q				Q

TABLE 1 (cont'd.)

Parameter	Baseline Monitoring[5] Program			Operational Monitoring Program			
	Surface[1] water	Sediment[1]	Biota[2]	Effluent[3]	Surface[1] water	Sediment[1]	Biota[2]
Fish			Q				Q
Mosquitoes			Q				Q
Threatened and endangered plant and animal species list			O				A
Plant tissue analysis - Metals (Hg, Pb, Cd, Cr, Cu, Zn, Fe, Ni, Ag)			O				A
Plant tissue analysis - Nutrients - (TP, TKN)			O				A

C = continuous or hourly
DI = 48 h diurnal, maximum of 6 h intervals
O = once during baseline monitoring period
A = annually
M = monthly
Q = quarterly
SA = semi-annually
T = every 12 h
W = weekly

[1]A minimum of two stations shall be sampled in the treatment wetland; 1) at the proposed point of effluent discharge, and 2) at the point of discharge from the treatment wetland. Additional stations may be required to determine compliance with subsections 17-6.055(3) and 17-6.055(5), FAC.

[2]A minimum of three permanent stations shall be established as follows; 1) in the immediate vicinity of the point of discharge of effluent to the treatment wetlands, 2) in the approximate geographical middle of the treatment wetland, and 3) in the immediate vicinity of the point of discharge from the treatment wetland.

[3]Sampling port required just prior to point of effluent discharge to the treatment wetland.

[4]Stage used to determine flow and only required at the point(s) of discharge from the treatment wetland.

[5]Length of baseline monitoring program is one year.

BIOLOGICAL REMOVAL OF NUTRIENTS FROM WASTEWATER: AN ALGAL-FISH SYSTEM MODEL

M. E. McDonald
Natural Resources Research Institute
University of Minnesota
Duluth, Minnesota 55812

ABSTRACT

A system model using the natural assimilatory capacity of algae for nutrient removal and a phytoplanktivorous fish, *Tilapia aurea*, to remove the algae is proposed. The system consists of a high-rate algal pond followed by a series of *T. aurea* stocked ponds. The system was modeled using both a green alga, *Ankistrodesmus falcatus*, and a blue-green alga, *Anabaena flos-aquae*, as the nutrient sink. Simulations were made to determine the minimum ponding necessary to provide both a high degree of nutrient removal and approximately zero algal effluent. At fish stocking rates of 4.0 g fish L^{-1} and 6.5 g fish L^{-1} (with green and blue-green algae, respectively), 6 ponds (each with a 1 d detention time) were capable of removing 88% and 99% of the algal incorporated P (green and blue-green algal sinks, respectively) and 46% of the algal incorporated N (green alga only).

Keywords: Nutrient removal, eutrophication, algae, water quality, simulation model.

INTRODUCTION

The increasing nutrient enrichment of aquatic systems arises primarily from pollution associated with population growth, industrial development, and intensive agriculture (Oswald, 1969; Clark et al., 1977). These eutrophication causing nutrients, primarily nitrogen (N), phosphorus (P), and carbon (C), have been target substances for water pollution clean-up efforts for many years (Rohlich and Uttormark, 1972; Burdick et al., 1982). However, secondary wastewater treatment removes little N and P (Knapp, 1971; Shelef et al., 1976, 1980) and conventional advanced wastewater treatment typically requires large capital investments and consumes considerable energy (Nichols, 1983).

Aquatic Plants for Water Treatment
and Resource Recovery
K.R. Reddy and W.H. Smith (Eds.)

ISBN 0-941463-00-1

Algae blooms are one major result of eutrophication. These blooms are responsible for some taste and odor problems in drinking water supplies, for fish kills, and for reduced recreational and aesthetic value (Oswald, 1969). Because algae can effectively remove nutrients from water, they have, in part, formed the basis of waste stabilization ponds (Mara, 1975; Carpenter et al., 1976). The use of algal assimilation as a systemic means of nutrient removal from wastewater has been suggested (Oswald, 1969; Ryther et al., 1972); marine algae were found capable of removing 83-95% of the dissolved inorganic N from secondary sewage effluent and 30-60% of the P (Goldman et al., 1974a,b; Goldman and Ryther, 1975).

Use of algae for nutrient removal is attractive, since the nutrients are removed by the algae and converted directly to proteinaceous material (Goldman and Ryther, 1976). While this is simple and economically appealing, a major problem and expense is the recovery of the algae (see Gloyna and Tischler, 1981) to the required level of <30 mg L^{-1} total suspended solids (Public Law 95-217).

Some of the biological systems, which have been suggested for harvesting effluent grown algae, have shown promise (Goldman et al., 1974a,b; Nichols, 1983; Hauser, 1984). However, none appear to offer all the advantages of using an algae-grazing fish for removal. These fishes can move to areas of plentiful algae, avoid areas with adverse conditions, consume and incorporate the algal biomass directly, be relatively easily and inexpensively harvested, and be a usable protein source. Also, these fishes have not been shown to be infected by enterobacteria, carrying them passively on the gut surface and being cleared by depuration (Allen, 1976).

Of these fishes, blue tilapia (*Tilapia aurea*), can ingest and assimilate green algae (see McDonald, 1985a,b, 1987), blue-green algae (see McDonald 1985a, 1987), and detrital bacteria (Spataru and Zorn, 1978). They prefer eutrophic waters (Buntz and Manooch, 1968) and are relatively disease free (Suffern et al., 1978). They are highly tolerant of water quality extremes in dissolved O_2, salinity and NH_3 (Stickney and Hesby, 1978). At a relatively small size (>29 mm), they start to feed on plant protein (Gophen et al., 1983), assimilating up to 83% of the algal C (McDonald, 1983b).

An experimental system has been tried using *T. nilotica* in a single pond to remove algae following a high rate stabilization pond (Edwards and Sinchupasak, 1981; Edwards et al., 1981a,b). The system met with limited success (Edwards et al., 1981b), but fish production was the primary objective of the fish pond, rather than nutrient removal.

MODEL DEVELOPMENT AND ASSUMPTIONS

A model for a nutrient removal system, using a series of ponds stocked with blue tilapia following a high rate algal pond, was developed. Algal population growth when grazed by blue tilapia and the growth of blue tilapia on various algae were determined previously (McDonald, 1985b, 1987). Blue tilapia were found to grow on a green alga, *Ankistrodesmus falcatus* (McDonald, 1985b), and a filamentous blue-green alga, *Anabaena flos-aquae* (McDonald, 1987). These algae were then used in the modeling of an algal-fish nutrient removal system. Ingestion, assimilation and incorporation of algal C into fish tissue have also been determined previously (McDonald, 1985a). Blue tilapia's ingestion of *Ankistrodesmus* was 2.1×10^8 cells L^{-1} h^{-1} (at a mean fish density of 15.0 g L^{-1}) and their ingestion of *Anabaena* was 8.6×10^7 cells L^{-1} h^{-1} (at a mean fish density of 13.0 g L^{-1}). The percent algal C incorporated into growth was 24% for *Ankistrodesmus* and 46% for *Anabaena*.

Blue tilapia were assumed to incorporate nutrients from the algae in proportion to the nutrient ratio in fish tissue (17C:3N:1P for *T. mossambica*) (Tan, 1971). Using this ratio, Vallentyne's (1974) ratio of nutrients available from algae (40C:7N:1P), and algal C incorporated into fish tissue (McDonald, 1985a), the percent incorporations of N and P necessary for fish growth on *Anabaena* were calculated. Twenty-four percent of *Ankistrodesmus*'s N and 56% of its P would be incorporated into fish tissue; for *Anabaena* 46% of its N and 108% of its P would be incorporated into fish tissue. Since the calculated P requirement for blue tilapia growth was >100%, a value of 99% incorporation of P was assumed. The algal consumption by blue tilapia was assumed constant for all fish sizes and for all algal density levels greater than the fish's consumption level. At algal densities below this level, 95% of the available algae was assumed to be ingested. A 14 h daylight period was used in all calculations.

GENERAL MODEL

The model is based on simple mass balance equations for algae and nutrients in a single pond. The algal removal model is

$$E_A = I_A + G_A + C_F$$

where, E_A = algal concentration leaving the pond (cells L^{-1})
I_A = algal concentration entering the pond (cells L^{-1})
G_A = algal growth in the pond (cells L^{-1})
C_F = algal loss by fish consumption in the pond (cells L^{-1})

Effluent algal nutrient concentration was the difference between influent algal nutrient concentration and the reduction in this concentration that occurs within the pond. Reduction of influent algal nutrient concentration within the pond is due to consumption of algae by fish and nutrient retention by fish. Algal nutrient removal model is:

$$E_N = I_N - (I_N)\,(C_F(I_A + G_A)^{-1})\,(G_F)$$

where, E_N = algal incorporated nutrient concentration leaving the pond (mg L^{-1})
I_N = algal incorporated nutrient concentration entering the pond (mg L^{-1})
G_F = % of ingested algal nutrient retained in fish tissue
I_A, G_A, and C_F are as defined above.

By coupling nutrient equations and by coupling algal equations so that the effluent of one pond becomes the influent for the next pond in line, a series of ponds were simulated.

INITIAL CONDITIONS

In the model using the green alga, the algal concentration entering the initial fish pond was assumed to be 4 x 10^9 cells L^{-1} (based on densities of green algae in a high rate algal pond, Beneman et al., 1976). When Anabaena was used in the model, its influent concentration was assumed to be 3.5 x 10^9 cells L^{-1} (based on bloom density of Anabaena in a highly eutrophic pond, from Sanville et al., 1982). At high algal densities, the daily algal increase was 1.1 x 10^7 cells L^{-1} for both Ankistrodesmus (McDonald, 1985b) and Anabaena (McDonald, 1987). At low Ankistrodesmus densities ($\leq$90 x 10^7 cells L^{-1}), the daily density increase becomes 1.9 x 10^7 cells L^{-1}; at low Anabaena densities (<10^8 cells L^{-1}), the daily density increase becomes 2.9 x 10^7 cells L^{-1} (McDonald unpublished data).

The influent algal incorporated nutrient level in the first pond is based on the ratio of nutrients in algae, 40C:7N:1P:100 dry wt (Vallentyne, 1974), and dry weight values of 7.1 x 10^{-11} g $cell^{-1}$ for Ankistrodesmus and 1.6 x 10^{-10} g $cell^{-1}$ for Anabaena (McDonald, unpublished data). Thus, nutrient levels in the influent Ankistrodesmus would be 110 mg C L^{-1}, 20 mg N L^{-1}, and 3.9 mg P L^{-1}. Since Anabaena is capable of fixing N (Wetzel, 1983), only incorporated C and P were modeled. Influent Anabaena incorporated nutrient levels were calculated to be 220 mg C L^{-1} and 5.6 mg P L^{-1}.

There were four variables of interest: 1) detention time of the ponds, 2) algal removal rate (based on algal consumption by fish), 3) the number of ponds necessary to reduce the algal effluent to approximately zero, and 4) the algal nutrient reduction in the final effluent. The model was run to establish the minimum number and size of the ponds. Detention time was set at 1 d $pond^{-1}$. A fish stocking density was assumed and an algal consumption rate was calculated. The consumption rates were based on an ingestion of 2.94 x 10^9 Ankistrodesmus cells L^{-1} d^{-1} at 15.0 g fish L^{-1} and an ingestion of 1.26 x 10^9 Anabaena cells L^{-1} d^{-1} at 13.0 g fish L^{-1} (McDonald, 1985b).

RESULTS

The model was run using successive approximation and iteration for the undefined variables. Examination of the final simulation using either Ankistrodesmus (Figure 1) or Anabaena (Figure 2), showed that six ponds were required to provide a substantial reduction in algal incorporated P. When Ankistrodesmus was used as the nutrient sink at fish stocking density of 4.0 g fish L^{-1}, the model predicted that the system would reduce the algal incorporated N and P by 46% and 88% respectively (Figure 2). When Anabaena was used as the nutrient sink at a fish stocking density of 6.5 g fish L^{-1}, the P reduction was 98% (Figure 2).

SYSTEM CONSIDERATIONS

If we consider a 2650 m^3 d^{-1} inflow into this system from a high rate algal pond, a series of six 0.45 ha x 0.5 m deep ponds would be required. Blue tilapia (>29 mm) would have to be stocked at a density of approximately 600,000 fish $pond^{-1}$ with the system containing Ankistrodesmus or approximately 1,136,000 fish $pond^{-1}$ in the system containing Anabaena to achieve the simulated removals.

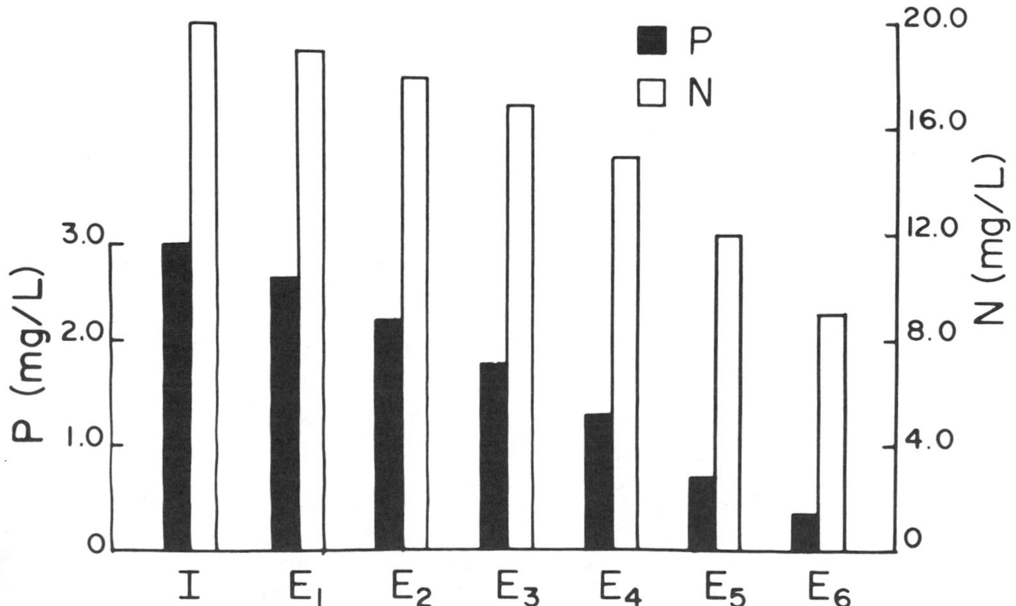

FIGURE 1. Nitrogen and P reduction in a six pond system using Ankistrodesmus as the nutrient sink and 4 g L^{-1} of fish stocked.

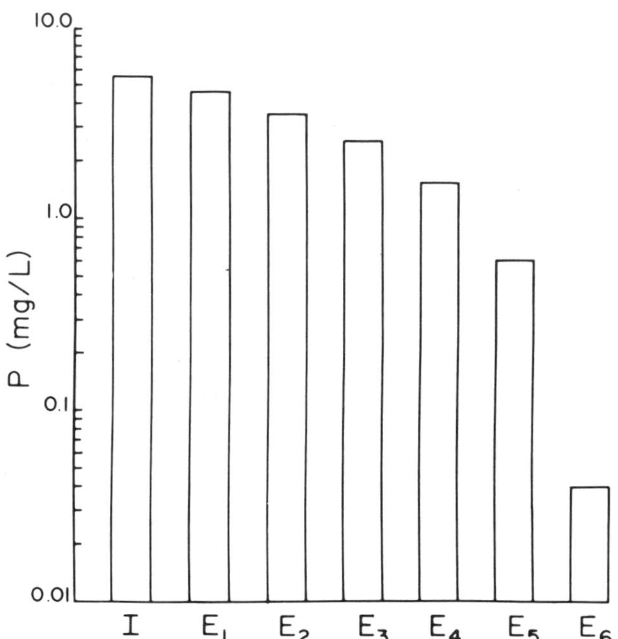

FIGURE 2. Phosphorus reduction in a six pond system using *Anabaena* as the nutrient sink and 6.5 g L^{-1} of fish stocked.

At fish biomass levels of 7.0 g L^{-1} and with a 1 d water detention time, no supplemental aeration was needed for blue tilapia in experimental ponds (Stickney and Winfree, 1983). Thus, no initial aeration of the ponds in the system would be required. However, blue tilapia's growth rate when feeding on either *Ankistrodesmus* or *Anabaena* (at the modeled levels) would be approximately 20-40 mg wet wt d^{-1} (based on McDonald 1985b, 1987), and in a more complex natural system, these fish are capable of 7 g d^{-1} growth (Armbrester, 1971). Therefore, under most conditions, it would be necessary to aerate the ponds, especially in the early mornings and on cloudy days.

Blue tilapia cannot survive temperatures below 10°C (Stickney and Hesby, 1978); thus they could only be used in more tropical climates or could only be used for part of the year in northerly climates. However, even in northerly climates the system's operation would coincide with expected periods of nuisance algal blooms. Also, in more northerly areas, if a thermal effluent was available, the system could be coupled with it for extended use.

Assuming initial costs of land acquisition and ponding were high (\$24,700 ha^{-1}) and the cost of fish for stocking was \$0.25 $fish^{-1}$, the per mg cost of nutrient removal would be <\$0.05. This does not include O and M costs, costs of supplemental aeration, harvesting costs, etc. However, this cost estimate also does not include the possible resale value of harvested fish.

Algae in this system would have the attendant problems associated with any waste stabilization pond system, e.g. fluctuations in solar radiation, temperature, O_2 depletion, and algal succession can all disrupt operation. Some of these problems could be mitigated by keeping the ponds shallow to maximize available light penetration throughout the system, lining the system with a black-colored liner to increase heat absorption and retention in more northerly climates, building the ponds so that the maximum fetch is aligned with the prevailing wind direction and/or the use of mechanical aerators, and the use of selective recycle of the high-rate pond's algal effluent into the influent of the system's ponds to maintain a desired algal species (Beneman et al., 1976). Bioaccumulation and bioconcentration of contaminants could prevent the rendering of the fish for direct human and/or livestock consumption. However, the fish could be rendered to fertilizer and applied to land, similarly to sewage sludge. If bioconcentration was sufficiently high, a widely dispersed toxicant could be concentrated into a harvestable form for possible recovery and recycling, or for more economic and efficient disposal.

CONCLUSIONS

Model simulations suggest that a blue tilapia-*Ankistrodesmus* system could reduce algal incorporated N and P by 46% and 88%, respectively; blue tilapia with *Anabaena* could remove 98% of the algal incorporated P. Since P is usually the growth limiting algal nutrient in fresh water (Wetzel, 1983), the potential high P removals by these systems may be especially useful in preventing nuisance algal blooms. These systems also have the benefits of low energy costs and recycling waste resources into a usable commodity. This system could be of most utility for industrial wastewater treatment, where waste stabilization ponds are already employed or where effluent nutrients may cause severe problems (Gloyna and Tischler, 1981), and in the treatment of sewage effluent in tropical and semi-tropical climates. While promising, much more experimentation will be needed to address the validity of the model's assumptions over a wide array of conditions before small scale pilot operations can be attempted.

ACKNOWLEDGMENTS

I thank G. T. Barthalmus, W. S. Galler, A. E. Hershey, D. Kamykowski, J. M. Miller, C. Smallwood, Jr., and several anonymous reviewers for comments on various drafts of the manuscript. I also acknowledge the Natural Resources Research Institute, University of Minnesota, for use of space and facilities during the final preparation of the manuscript. This research was performed by the author in the Depts. of Civil Engineering and Zoology, North Carolina State University, Raleigh.

REFERENCES

Allen, G. H. 1976. Recycling of wastes through aquaculture and constraints to wide application. FAO FIR:AQ/Conf/76/R, FAO, Rome. 19 pp.

Armbrester, W., Jr. 1971. The growth of caged Tilapia aurea (Steindachner) in fertile farm ponds. Proc. Ann. Conf. SE Game Fish Comm. 25:446-451.

Beneman, J. R., B. Koopman, J. Weissman, and W. J. Oswald. 1976. Biomass production and waste recycling with blue-green algae. p. 400-412. In H. G. Schlegel and J. Barnes (ed.) Microbial Energy Production. Erich Goltz KG, Gottingen.

Buntz, J., and C. S. Manooch, III. 1968. Tilapia aurea (Steindachner), a rapidly spreading exotic in south central Florida. Proc. Ann. Conf. SE Game Fish Comm. 22:495-501.

Burdick, C. R., D. R. Reifling, and H. D. Stensel. 1982. Advanced biological treatment to achieve nutrient removal. J. Water Pollut. Control Fed. 54:1078-1086.

Carpenter, R. L., M. S. Coleman, and R. Jarman. 1976. Aquaculture as an alternative wastewater treatment system. p. 215-224. In J. Tourbier and R. W. Pierson, Jr. (ed.) Biological Control of Water Pollution. Univ. of Penn. Press, Philadelphia.

Clark, J. W., W. Veissman, Jr., and M. J. Hammer. 1977. Water Supply and Pollution Control. Harper and Row, New York. 857 pp.

Edwards, P., and O. Sinchumpasak. 1981. The harvest of microalgae from the effluent of a sewage fed high rate stabilization pond by Tilapia nilotica. Part 1: Description of the system and the study of the high rate pond. Aquaculture 23:83-105.

Edwards, P., O. Sinchumpasak, and M. Tabucanon. 1981a. The harvest of microalgae from the effluent of a sewage fed high rate stabilization pond by Tilapia nilotica. Part 2: Studies of the fish ponds. Aquaculture 23:107-147.

Edwards, P., O. Sinchumpasak, V. K. Labhsetwar, and M. Tabucanon. 1981b. The harvest of microalgae from the effluent of a sewage fed high rate stabilization pond by Tilapia nilotica. Part 3: Maize cultivation experiment, bacteriological studies and economic assessment. Aquaculture 23:149-170.

Gloyna, E. F., and L. F. Tischler . 1981. Recommendations for regulatory modifications: The use of waste stabilization pond systems. J. Water Pollut. Control Fed. 53:1559-1563.

Goldman, J. C., and J. H. Ryther. 1975. Nutrient transformations in mass culture of marine algae. J. Environ. Engin. Div., ASCE 101:351-364.

Goldman, J. C., and J. H. Ryther. 1976. Waste reclamation in an integrated food chain system. p. 197-214. In J. Tourbier and R. W. Pierson, Jr. (ed.) Biological Control of Water Pollution. Univ. of Penn. Press, Philadelphia, PA.

Goldman, J. C., K. R. Tenore, J. H. Ryther, and N. Corwin. 1974a. Inorganic nitrogen removal in a combined tertiary treatment - marine aquaculture system. I. Removal efficiencies. Water Res. 8:45-54.

Goldman, J. C., K. R. Tenore, and H. I. Stanley. 1974b. Inorganic nitrogen removal in a combined tertiary treatment - marine aquaculture system. II. Algal bioassays. Water Res. 8:55-59.

Gophen, M., R. W. Drenner, and G. L. Vinyard. 1983. Cichlid stocking and the decline of the Galilee Saint Peter's Fish (Sarotherodon galilaeus) in Lake Kinnerat, Israel. Can. J. Fish. Aquat. Sci. 40:983-986.

Hauser, J. R. 1984. Use of water hyacinth aquatic treatment systems for ammonia control and effluent polishing. J. Water Pollut. Control Fed. 56:219-225.

Knapp, C. E. 1971. Recycling sewage biologically. Envir. Sci. & Tech. 5:112-113.

Mara, D. D. 1975. Proposed design for oxidation ponds in hot climates. J. Environ. Engin. Div., ASCE 100:119-139.

McDonald, M. E. 1985a. Carbon budgets for a phytoplanktivorous fish fed three unialgal populations. Oecologia 66:246-249.

McDonald, M. E. 1985b. Growth of a grazing phytoplanktivorous fish and enhanced growth of the grazed alga. Oecologia 67:132-136.

McDonald, M. E. 1987. Interactions between a phytoplanktivorous fish, Oreochromis aureus, and two unialgal forage populations. Env. Biol. Fish.

Nichols, D. S. 1983. Capacity of natural wetlands to remove nutrients from wastewater. J. Water Pollut. Control Fed. 55:495-505.

Oswald, W. J. 1969. Current status of microalgae from wastes. Chem. Eng. Prog. Symp. Ser. 65:87-92.

Rohlich, G. A., and P. D. Uttormark. 1972. Wastewater treatment and eutrophication. In G. E. Likens (ed.) Nutrients and Eutrophication: The Limiting Nutrient Controversy. ASLO Special Symposia, Vol. 1, Allen Press, Lawrence, Kansas. p. 231-243.

Ryther, J. H., W. M. Dunstan, K. R. Tenore, and J. E. Huguenin. 1972. Controlled eutrophication - increasing food production from the sea by recycling human wastes. Biosci. 22:144-152.

Sanville, W. D., C. F. Powers, G. S. Schuytema, F. S. Staym, and W. L. Lauer. 1982. Phosphorus inactivation by zirconium in a eutrophic pond. J. Water Pollut Control Fed. 54:434-443.

Shelef, G., R. Moraine, A. Meydan, and E. Sandbank. 1976. Combined algae production - wastewater treatment and reclamation systems. p. 427-442. In G. G. Schlegel and J. Barnes (ed.) Microbial Energy Production. Erich Goltz KG, Gottingen.

Shelef, G., Y. Azov, R. Moraine, and G. Oron. 1980. Algal production as an integral part of a wastewater treatment and reclamation system. p. 163-189. In G. Shelef and C. J. Soeder (ed.) Algae Biomass. Elsevier/North Holland Biomedical press, Amsterdam.

Stickney, R. R., and J. H. Hesby. 1978. Tilapia production in ponds receiving swine wastes. p. 90-101. In R. O. Smitherman, W. L. Shelton, and J. H. Grover (ed.) Culture of Exotic Fishes. Fish Culture Section, Am. Fish. Soc., Auburn, Alabama.

Stickney, R. R., and R. A. Winfree. 1983. Tilapia overwintering systems. Aquaculture Mag. 9:25-28.

Suffern, J. S., S. M. Adams, B. G. Blaycock, C. C. Coutant, and C. A. Guthrie. 1978. Growth of monosex hybrid tilapia in the laboratory and sewage oxidation ponds. p. 65-81. In R. O. Smitherman, W. L. Shelton, and J. H. Grover (ed.) Culture of Exotic Fishes. Fish Culture Section, Am. Fish. Soc., Auburn, Alabama.

Tan, Y. T. 1971. Proximate composition of freshwater fish - grass carp, Pontius gonionotus, and tilapia. Hydrobiologia 37:361-366.

Vallentyne, J. R. 1974. The algal bowl - lakes and man. Misc. Spec. Publ. 22, Dept. of Environ., Ottawa, Ontario. 185 pp.

Wetzel, R. G. 1983. Limnology. Saunders College Publ., New York. 858 pp.

WATER HYACINTH (EICHHORNIA CRASSIPES [MART] SOLMS) FOR IMPROVING EUTROPHIC LAKE WATER: WATER QUALITY AND MASS BALANCE

M. M. Fisher and K. R. Reddy
Central Florida Research and Education Center
University of Florida, IFAS
Sanford, Florida 32771

ABSTRACT

The use of water hyacinths (*Eichhornia crassipes* [Mart] Solms) as a potential method for treating eutrophic lake water was evaluated for a period of 19 months. Water from Lake Apopka, located in central Florida, was gravity fed into three 200' X 20' X 2' concrete channels stocked with water hyacinths and allowed to flow at a detention time of 36 h. One of the three channels was maintained at a constant plant density of 15-25 kg (fw) m^{-2}, with periodic harvesting. A second channel was not harvested and the remaining channel was used as a control and kept free of plants. Mean influent concentrations were 4.5 mg TKN L^{-1}, 0.3 mg TP L^{-1}, and 60 mg chlorophyll-a m^{-3}. Data on outflow water quality indicate a reduction of total N and P by approximately 60%, and of chlorophyll-a by approximately 90%. During the 19 month experimental period, 305 kg N entered the system, of which 45 kg N was recovered in plant biomass, 105 kg N accumulated in the sediment and 150 kg N was removed in the effluent. During the same period, 22 kg of P entered the system, of which 5 kg P was recovered in plant biomass, 7.5 kg P was recovered in the sediment and 8.5 kg P was accounted for in the effluent. These results indicate a positive relationship between water quality improvement and sedimentation of incoming algal biomass.

Keywords: Aquatic plants, aquaculture, water quality improvement, eutrophic lakes.

INTRODUCTION

Lake Apopka, a 12,500 ha lake located in central Florida, is currently considered highly eutrophic due to point and non-point nutrient loading from surrounding vegetable farms, citrus groves, and domestic wastewater discharges (U.S. EPA, 1979). This

ISBN 0-941463-00-1

condition presents a unique opportunity to study the effects of aquatic macrophytes on water quality improvement.

Much research in recent years has been directed at using aquatic plants for treating different types of wastewaters (Wolverton and McDonald, 1978; Reddy et al., 1982; Hauser, 1984). There have been, however, few data presented on the use of aquatic plants to improve eutrophic lake water. Increased concern over the quality of natural waters has raised the possibility of using aquatic plants for lake water renovation. In 1986, the Florida Legislature funded a 2 million dollar project which was designed to evaluate the effect of water hyacinths on water quality and sediment decomposition.

The purpose of this study was to determine the effects of several differentially-managed aquatic systems on water quality. Water hyacinths were chosen for this experiment due to their high productivity and nutrient assimilative capacity. This paper presents the results of a 19-month study on the effects of water hyacinth (Eichhornia crassipes [Mart] Solms) growth on eutrophic lake water. The study was conducted on the northern shore of Lake Apopka.

MATERIALS AND METHODS

This experiment was performed from June 1984 to December 1985 at the Zellwood field station of the Central Florida Research and Education Center, University of Florida - IFAS. Three concrete-block channels were constructed approximately 400 m from the northern shore of Lake Apopka. The channel walls were coated on the inside with an impervious mortar used to retard seepage. Channel dimensions were 61 m long by 6.1 m wide by 0.6 m deep. This resulted in a length to width ratio of 10, which was adequate to prevent short-circuiting. Each channel was supplied with lake water, gravity-fed from Lake Apopka, at an approximate flow rate of 137 $m^3 d^{-1}$. Hydraulic retention time (HRT) was 1.5 days.

Influent flow rates were checked periodically using a calibrated container and a stopwatch. Effluent flow rates were determined by measuring the height of flow over a 90° Thomson weir and applying the discharge formula as described by Simon (1981). Stage height over the weir was monitored continuously with a Leupold-Stevens Model 68F stage recorder.

Twice-weekly grab samples were taken from the influent and effluent of each channel. Composite 24 h samples were taken periodically to ensure that grab samples provided a true representation of influent and effluent composition. Mass balances were calculated by multiplying the concentration of a particular nutrient by the total volume of water.

Electrical conductivity (EC), pH, dissolved O_2, and temperature were measured weekly. Nitrate, NH_4^+-N, total Kjeldahl N (TKN), total P (TP), and soluble reactive P (SRP) were analyzed using a Technicon Autoanalyzer (A.P.H.A., 1980). Chlorophyll-a was determined by standard methods (A.P.H.A., 1980).

Plant productivity was measured by stocking 1 m^2 PVC baskets with water hyacinths, at a starting density of 15 kg (fresh wt) m^{-2}, and weighing them monthly. Six baskets were placed in each channel at approximately 10 m intervals along the length of the channel.

Two of the three channels were stocked with water hyacinths. One of these channels was periodically harvested and the other channel was not harvested. The third channel had no plants and was used to evaluate the effectiveness of the other two channels. In the channel which was harvested, plant densities were maintained in the range of 15-25 kg (fresh wt) m^{-2}.

All plant samples were dried at 70°C, ground to pass through a 20 mesh sieve, digested and analyzed for TP and TKN to determine plant uptake of N and P (Jackson, 1958).

RESULTS AND DISCUSSION

Table 1 represents the average analysis of influent water from Lake Apopka used in the experimental channels. Note that plant-available forms of N and P were quite low, with NO_3^- and NH_4^+ averaging 55 and 122 μg N L^{-1}, respectively. Soluble reactive P (roughly equivalent to ortho-P) averaged approximately 20 μg L^{-1}. Most of the N and P in Lake Apopka water is tied up in algal biomass; hence, it is unavailable for immediate plant uptake. Total Kjeldahl N and TP concentrations were quite high, averaging 4.33 and 0.29 mg L^{-1}, respectively. These concentrations reflect the high algal biomass and are indicative of a highly eutrophic lake. Average influent pH was 8.39, sometimes ranging over 9.00. High pH levels were primarily due to algal photosynthetic activity. Chlorophyll-a averaged 60 mg m^{-3}. Algal blooms in early summer occasionally resulted in chlorophyll-a values as high as 150 mg m^{-3}.

It was determined in a previous study (DeBusk et al., 1986) that water hyacinth maintained within a density range of 15-25 kg (fresh wt) m^{-2} would experience maximum growth rates under nutrient-limited conditions. The plants in the harvested channel

TABLE 1. Lake Apopka water chemistry, 1984-85.

Parameter	Units	Mean	SD±	Min.	Max.	n
Nitrate	μg N L^{-1}	55	74	0	504	153
Ammonium	μg N L^{-1}	122	89	11	570	151
TKN	mg N L^{-1}	4.33	1.25	1.81	9.43	140
Total P	mg P L^{-1}	0.29	0.14	0.032	0.86	150
pH	units	8.39	0.8	6.31	9.92	70
EC	mho cm^{-1}	381	66	185	650	72
DO	mg L^{-1}	6.04	3.0	0.87	14.02	72
Chlor. a	mg m^{-3}	60	26	10.32	197.5	73

were maintained in this density range. Plant uptake of N and P was directly related to growth rate and harvesting frequency. Biomass harvesting increased the plant uptake of N and P, as compared to no harvesting.

Average N and P removal efficiencies in the harvested channel were 54 and 63%, respectively, compared with 45 and 57%, respectively, in the unharvested channel during the 19-month study period (Figures 1 and 2). Actual removal rates showed a great deal of monthly variation, undoubtedly due to seasonal variances in plant uptake and fluctuating biological activity in the lake. Nitrogen and P removal rates for the channel without plants were 36 and 42%, respectively.

The channels stocked with water hyacinths consistently provided higher nutrient removal than the channel without water hyacinths. The difference between the two channels with different plant management strategies was less dramatic. The plants in channel 4 (the unharvested channel) were usually stressed due to overcrowding and insect damage but, although overall growth in this channel was slow, removal rates nearly equalled those of the intensively-managed channel. This was due to the ability of the water hyacinth, regardless of physiological condition, to shade out algal cells. This seemed to be the primary nutrient-removal mechanism in this system. It has been reported that an 80% coverage of the water surface with water hyacinth is sufficient to shade out suspended algae (Gee and Jenson Engineers, 1980). Chlorophyll-a removal rates were generally higher in channel 4, probably due to increased (Figure 3) shading resulting from higher plant density in this channel.

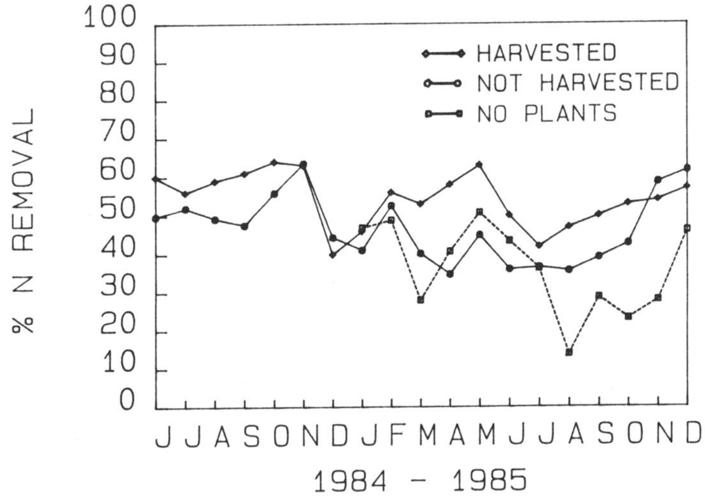

FIGURE 1. Percent reduction in mass loading of total N in experimental channels used to treat eutrophic lake water.

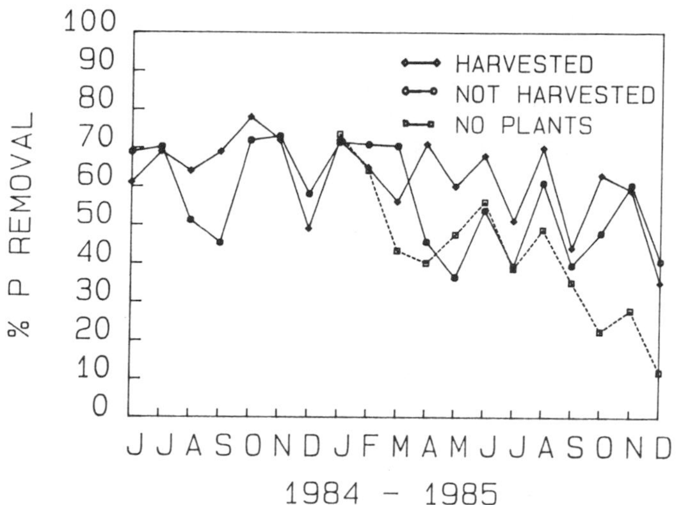

FIGURE 2. Percent reduction in mass loading of total P in experimental channels used to treat eutrophic lake water (June 1984 - December 1985).

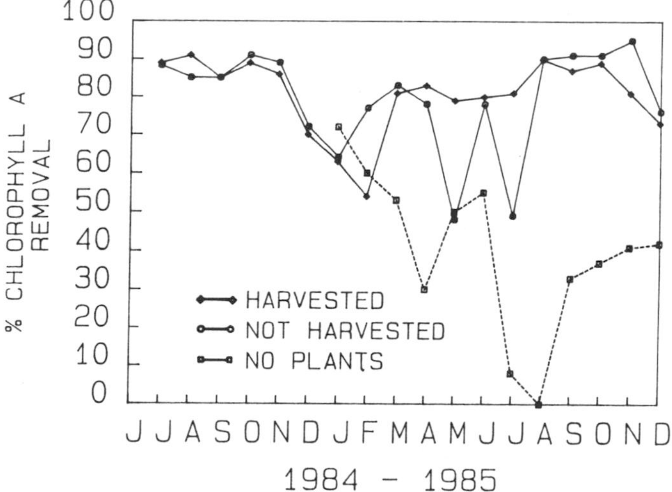

FIGURE 3. Percent reduction in mass loading of chlorophyll-a in experimental channels used to treat eutrophic lake water (June 1984 - December 1985).

The overall N budgets for the three channels showed that sedimentation of N was the dominant removal mechanism (Table 2). Thirty-three and 37% of the incoming N in the channels with

TABLE 2. Nitrogen budget for experimental channels receiving Lake Apopka water (June 1984 - December 1985).

	Channels with Plants		Channel with no plants
	Harvested	Unharvested	
	-----------% of total loading-----------		
Plant uptake	16	10	--
Sediment	33	37	39
Outflow	46	53	61
Unaccounted for	5	1	0

harvesting and without harvesting, respectively, ended up in the sediment. Only 16 and 10% of the influent N removal in the channels with harvesting and without harvesting, respectively, was due to plant uptake.

Thirty percent of the P loading into the harvested channel was recovered in the sediment, whereas 32% of the influent P turned up in the sediment for the channel with no harvesting (Table 3). Twenty-five percent of the P removal in the harvested channel was accounted for by plant uptake, whereas 13% of the incoming P removal in the unharvested channel was due to plant uptake. Plant uptake of N and P in the channel without harvesting was considerably lower due to greatly reduced growth rates.

The water hyacinths in both harvested and unharvested channels were dependent on the mineralization of N and P from the sediment to satisfy their requirements for growth. For P, such release can be as high as 5.25 to 9.18 mg P m^{-2} d^{-1} (Pollman and Brezonik, 1979). Thus, a secondary function of aquatic plants in a lake water-treatment system is removal of mineralized N and P released from the sediment.

On a large scale system such as this, it is not practical to have replicates of each treatment; therefore successive sampling dates were considered as replications.

TABLE 3. Phosphorus budget for experimental channels receiving Lake Apopka water (June 1984 - December 1985).

	Channels with Plants		Channel with no plants
	Harvested	Unharvested	
	-----------% of total loading-----------		
Plant uptake	25	13	--
Sediment	30	32	31
Outflow	36	43	58
Unaccounted for	9	12	11

CONCLUSIONS

It should be realized that the physical and chemical dynamics of a large body of water, such as Lake Apopka, are much different than the conditions under which this experiment was performed. Flow characteristics, depth, biological communities, etc., are very difficult to duplicate on a small scale.

The differences in removal efficiencies were not as dramatic as expected. Overall removal of N was 54% in the harvested channel compared to 45% in the unharvested channel and 36% in the channel with no water hyacinths. Similarly, P-removal rates were 63% in the harvested channel compared with 57% in the unharvested channel and 42% in the channel with no plants. Processes involved in the removal of N and P compounds in descending order of importance were: sedimentation, plant uptake, and nitrification-denitrification reactions in the root-zone and sediment, respectively.

If long-term crop viability is desired, some attempt should be made to regulate plant density. During the final months of this study, pennywort (*Hydrocotyle umbellata* L.) was beginning to gain a competitive advantage over the water hyacinth in the unharvested channel. This is significant, because normally water hyacinth will outcompete pennywort for both light and nutrients.

In a large-scale lake-based aquatic treatment system, effects of treatment should be monitored on a long-term basis. A technique using key water quality parameters which are converted to a scalar rating would be ideal for monitoring long-term changes (Porcella et al., 1980).

ACKNOWLEDGMENTS

This paper reports results from a cooperative program between the Institute of Food and Agricultural Sciences (IFAS) of the University of Florida and the Gas Research Institute (GRI), entitled "Methane from Biomass and Waste." Florida Agricultural Experiment Stations Journal Series No. 7711.

REFERENCES

A.P.H.A. 1980. Standard methods for the examination of water and wastewater. 15th edition. Am. Publ. Health Assoc., Washington, D.C.

DeBusk, W. F., K. R. Reddy, and J. C. Tucker. 1986. Management strategies for water hyacinth production in a nutrient-limited system. p. 275-286. In W. H. Smith (ed.) Biomass Energy Development. Plenum Publishing Corp.

Gee and Jenson Engineers. 1980. Water hyacinth wastewater treatment design manual. Prepared for NASA Laboratories, NSTL Station, Mississippi, Gee and Jenson Engineers, West Palm Beach, FL. 92 pp.

Hauser, J. R. 1984. Use of water hyacinth aquatic treatment systems for ammonia control and effluent polishing. J. Water Poll. Control Fed. 56:219-226.

Jackson, M. L. 1958. Soil chemical analysis. Prentice-Hall, London. p. 498.

Pollman, C. D., and D. L. Brezonik. 1979. Nutrient characteristics and nutrient exchange dynamics of Lake Apopka sediments. Progress Report Florida Dept. Env. Regulation. Dept. of Env. Eng. Sciences, Univ. of Florida, Gainesville, FL.

Porcella, D. B., S. A. Peterson and D. P. Larsen. 1980. Index to evaluate lake restoration. Proc. Am. Soc. Civil Engrs. 106:1151-1169.

Reddy, K. R., P. D. Sacco, D. A. Graetz, K. L. Campbell, and L. R. Sinclair. 1982. Water treatment by an aquatic ecosystem: Nutrient removal by reservoirs and flooded fields. Environ. Mgmt. 6:261-271.

Simon, A. L. 1981. Practical hydraulics. 2nd ed. New York: John Wiley & Sons.

U.S. EPA. 1979. Environmental Impact Statement: Lake Apopka Restoration Project, Lake and Orange Counties, FL. EPA 904/4-79-043.

Wolverton, B. C., and R. C. McDonald. 1978. Water hyacinth for upgrading servage lagoons to meet advanced wastewater treatment standards. Part II. NASA Technical Memo. TM-X-7230.

MODELING WATER HYACINTH PRODUCTION IN EUTROPHIC WATER

S. D. Curry and J. W. Mishoe
Agricultural Engineering Department
University of Florida, IFAS
Gainesville, Florida 32611

K. R. Reddy
Central Florida Research and Education Center
University of Florida, IFAS
P. O. Box 909
Sanford, Florida 32771

ABSTRACT

Water hyacinth (Eichhornia crassipes [Mart] Solms) growth and nutrient uptake from eutrophic lake water was modelled and incorporated into BIOMET. BIOMET is a decision support system for the production of biomass and its conversion to CH_4 gas. The water hyacinth growth model was physiologically based and driven by solar radiation and temperature. Major processes simulated in the growth model are: photosynthesis and plant productivity, respiration, and detrital production. A mass balance of N and P is maintained throughout the simulation. Major processes that are simulated in the water include diffusion-N from the sediment, uptake by the plant, inflow and outflow of nutrients, and mineralization of organic N. The model was calibrated using the data collected from water hyacinth growth in experimental channels containing sediment and water from Lake Apopka, an eutrophic lake in central Florida.

Keywords: Lake water, aquatic plants, nutrient removal, simulation, water quality, biomass.

INTRODUCTION

BIOMET (Biomass to Methane) is a decision support system for the growth and management of biomass and its conversion to CH_4 gas. A target site for this project is Lake Apopka, a central Florida lake which is highly eutrophic, as a result of nutrient loads from several adjacent sources such as drainage discharge from vegetable farms, nonpoint source runoff from citrus groves

Aquatic Plants for Water Treatment
and Resource Recovery
K.R. Reddy and W.H. Smith (Eds.)

ISBN 0-941463-00-1

and treated sewage effluent. This has created an extensive systems analysis opportunity for the development of a computer simulated water hyacinth growth model. Water hyacinth was chosen as a crop for this project because of its potential for high biomass yields and the additional benefit of wastewater cleanup (Reddy et al., 1985). The developers have attempted to keep the model simple, modelling only the major processes (Figure 1) needed to get an accurate idea of crop growth and nutrient levels in the plant.

MODEL DESCRIPTION

The water hyacinth growth model is driven by average daily temperature and solar radiation. The plant's growth is also affected by the nutrients available in the water (N and P) and the plant canopy density.

The water hyacinth growth model (Lorber et al., 1984) is based on the physiological growth equation given by:

$$DW/DT = (PG - RM)\ E - D \qquad [1]$$

where DW/DT is the change in dry weight of plant material per day, PG is the gross photosynthate on that day, RM is the respiration requirement for maintenance of plant tissue, E is the efficiency of conversion (net photosynthate to water hyacinth plant dry matter), and D is the detritus produced that day. This model assumes that water hyacinth stays in the vegetative stage of growth and phenological growth stages are not modelled. Daily photosynthate available to the plant for conversion to plant dry matter is a function of plant canopy development and light interception and stresses which are placed on the plant due to less than optimum temperature and nutrient availability.

Our focus is on the stresses produced by the limited availability of nutrients from the eutrophic water. The P function (GFP) limits plant growth when the P concentration of the plant drops below a critical level necessary for optimal growth. When stress occurs, it is defined as a function of the P concentration in the water (WATP).

$$\begin{array}{ll} GFP = [WATP/DEPTH)/(0.02 + (WATP/DEPTH)] & WATP < AMXCPP \qquad [2] \\ GFP = 1.0 & WATP = >AMXCPP \end{array}$$

where AMXCPP is the concentration of P in the plant above which no nutrient stress occurs (Reddy, 1987).

The N function (GFN) limits plant growth when the N concentration in the plant is less than a critical level necessary for optimal growth.

$$\begin{array}{ll} GFN = 0.01 & CNCP< = CNCTIS \\ GFN = CGFN \times CNCP + CIGFN & CNCTIS < CNCP < CNCLUX \qquad [3] \\ GFN = 1.0 & CNCP = >CNCLUX \end{array}$$

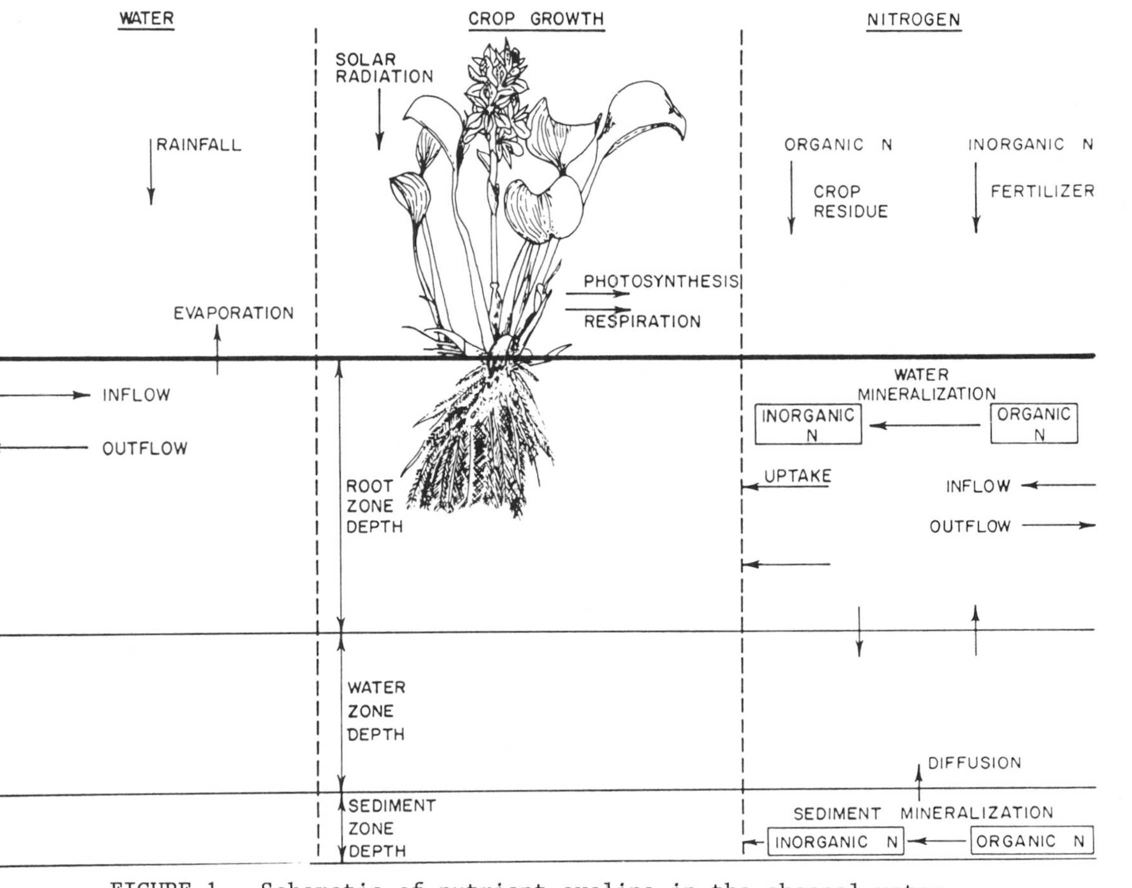

FIGURE 1. Schematic of nutrient cycling in the channel water.

where CNCP is the plant concentration of N, CNCTIS is the minimum concentration of N allowed in the tissue, CNCLUX is the concentration of tissue N above which there is not a growth stress, and CGFN and CIGFN are parameters for the N stress function.

Mass Balance of Nutrients

The functions for N and P stress necessitate the modeling of mass balance of soluble P, inorganic (NH_4^++NO_3^-), and organic N in the water.

Inputs into the water nutrient balance include nutrients in the inflow water, mineralization of organic N to inorganic N, diffusion of nutrients from the sediment, and any fertilization which occurs. Outputs are uptake by the water hyacinth, nutrients in the outflow water, and settling to the sediment of organic N (algal cells). Other means of input and output such as denitrification and volatilization were thought to be small and were not considered.

The availability of these nutrients for uptake is a critical part of the nutrient balance model. Phosphorus uptake is determined by the P stress function explained earlier and the actual concentration of P in the water. If the P concentration in the water is not sufficient to meet the needs of the plant, the P in the water is depleted and the plant concentration of P is adjusted to reflect that deficiency.

In the N water balance, plant demand is determined by the ability of water hyacinth to accumulate "luxury" concentrations of nutrients. A "luxury" concentration is a concentration greater than the amount needed to support optimal growth. In this model, N demand (UPIN) is equal to a maximum concentration of plant N less the actual N concentration in the plant.

$$UPIN = (PGAVL \times CTURN) \times CNCMAX + BIOMASS \times (CNCMAX - CNCP) \quad [4]$$

where PGAVL x CTURN is the new biomass growth for that day, CNCMAX is the maximum concentration of plant tissue N, and BIOMASS is the total tissue for the crop.

Usually in natural environments, this demand will always be greater than the available N in the water. However, stress only occurs when the plant N falls below the luxury level which is far below the maximum level as defined above. The system is assumed to be completely mixed. Inputs of organic N into the water include organic N in the inflow water and detritus decomposition. The amount of organic N in the inflow water is an input and a percentage of this input is settled to the sediment. The remaining amount is added directly to the total organic N in the channel water.

$$STLORG = INFORG \times PCTSTL/SAREA \quad [5]$$

$$ADDORG = ADDORG - STLORG \quad [6]$$

where STLORG is the organic N added to the sediment, INFORG is the organic N in the inflow water, PCTSTL is the percentage of organic which settles out, SAREA is the area of the tank, and ADDORG is the organic N which is added to the water by inflow.

Organic N is also found in the detritus formed each day. A fraction of the detrital material created each day is modelled to remain in the root zone, the remainder falls to the sediment zone where it is added to the organic N there.

Outflows of organic N occur by mineralization and loss through the outflow water. Mineralization of organic N to NH_4^+ occurs in the root zone, the water zone and the sediment zone. The rate of mineralization in the water zone and the root zone is many times faster than the sediment rate. A percentage of the organic N in the water hyacinth detrital material in addition to the organic already present in the water and sediment zone is mineralized each day. These amounts are then subtracted from the organic N totals in the root, water, and sediment zones.

Inflow of inorganic N (NH_4^+) into the water environment include inorganic N in the inflow water, transfer of N from the sediment, mineralization of organic N, and fertilization.

The amount of inorganic N in the inflow water is input and a percentage of this is added to the sediment.

$$STLNH_4 = INFNH_4 \times PCTSTL/SAREA \quad [7]$$

$$SEDNH_4 = SEDNH_4 + SEDMIN + STLNH_4 \quad [8]$$

where $STLNH_4$ is the inorganic N added to the sediment, $INFNH_4$ is the inorganic N in the inflow water, PCTSTL is the percentage of inorganic that settles to the sediment zone, $SEDNH_4$ is the total inorganic N in the sediment zone, and SEDMIN is the amount of inorganic N added to the sediment zone through mineralization of organic N. The remaining amount is added directly to the total inorganic N in the channel water ($ADDNH_4$).

$$ADDNH_4 = ADDNH_4 - STLNH_4 \quad [9]$$

A transfer coefficient is used to allow a percentage of the total inorganic N in the sediment to move into the water zone each day.

$$DIFSED = DIFRAT \times SEDNH_4 \quad [10]$$

where DIFSED is the amount of inorganic N which moves into the water zone that day, and DIFRAT is the transfer coefficient.

Fertilization of the water hyacinths can be applied on specific dates or when the N concentration in the plant reaches a critical level specified by the user. Fertilization by foliar application is modelled by assuming that 90% of the application goes directly into the plant to raise the N concentration in the plant. The remaining N is added to the water the following day.

$$FERTIL = PCTFW \times WFERTN \quad [11]$$

where FERTIL is the inorganic N added to the water zone this day due to fertilization, PCTFW is the percentage of fertilizer which is not absorbed directly by the plant, and WFERTN is the rate of fertilizer application.

In this model, an effective root zone has been created. The effective root zone represents the change in root length which occurs under varying water N concentrations. In high N concentrations, roots of water hyacinth are short and extend to approximately 1 m when N concentrations are low. Only the N present in this root zone is available for uptake each day. This prevents early depletion of N from the water when demand is high and availability is low.

RESULTS

To test the model, two experiments conducted by Reddy (1985) were simulated using measured conditions. Water hyacinths were grown in flow through channels (200' x 20') in Zellwood, Florida, throughout 1985 (Fisher and Reddy, 1987). The water in the tanks was continuous flow, gravity fed from Lake Apopka. The N and P concentrations were measured at the inlet and outlet of each tank. The volume of water flowing through the system was also measured. The crop was harvested five times during the year and crop density measured weekly. Solar radiation, minimum temperature, and maximum temperature data were collected nearby at Sanford and used in the simulation. The results of the first experiment in which no external fertilizer was added are shown in Figures 2 and 3. For the second experiment there was a foliar application of fertilizer (N and P) on days 37, 63, and 126 from planting. The results of this experiment are shown in Figures 4 and 5.

Generally, the model predicts overall growth of the water hyacinth sufficiently well. Some of the error can be explained by a freeze that occurred during the winter which damaged the crop. The model does not account for the effects of freezing temperatures. Assumptions used to simulate nutrients from the sediment may have contributed to the underprediction of growth at the beginning of the simulation and overprediction at the end. Initial conditions for simulation had no sediment zone at the start of simulation; however, sediment accumulated throughout the simulation. An increase in sedimentation or an increase in release of nutrients from the sediment would cause more initial growth and a decreased source of nutrients for growth later in the simulation.

The model tended to underpredict N concentration by about 30%. As a test, the uptake functions of the crop model were adjusted to correct this error, however in doing so, it caused an overprediction of crop growth. The reasons for this imbalance are not known; however, the crops may be adapting to its environment resulting in different growth responses for different environments. The total N taken up by the plant was approximately the same as that measured in the harvested crop. Overall the model was sufficient for evaluating the performance of a water treatment system using water hyacinths.

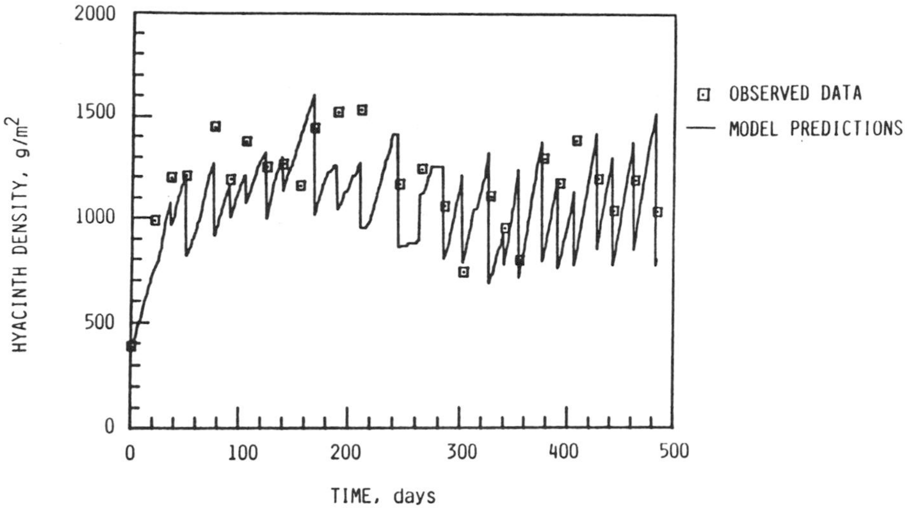

FIGURE 2. Validation of water hyacinth growth model using experimental data from Zellwood, Florida (K. R. Reddy, unpublished results).

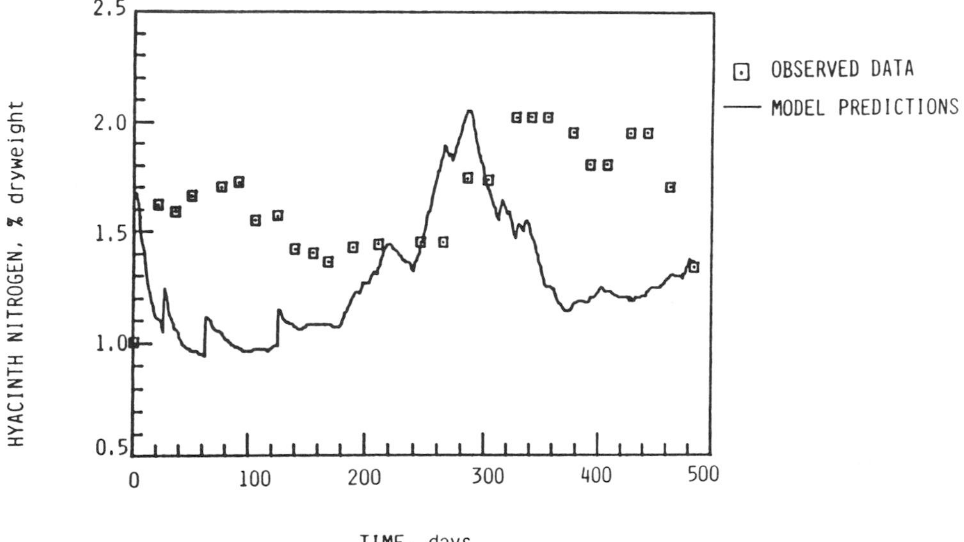

FIGURE 3. Validation of water hyacinth growth model using hyacinth N data from Zellwood, Florida (K. R. Reddy, unpublished results).

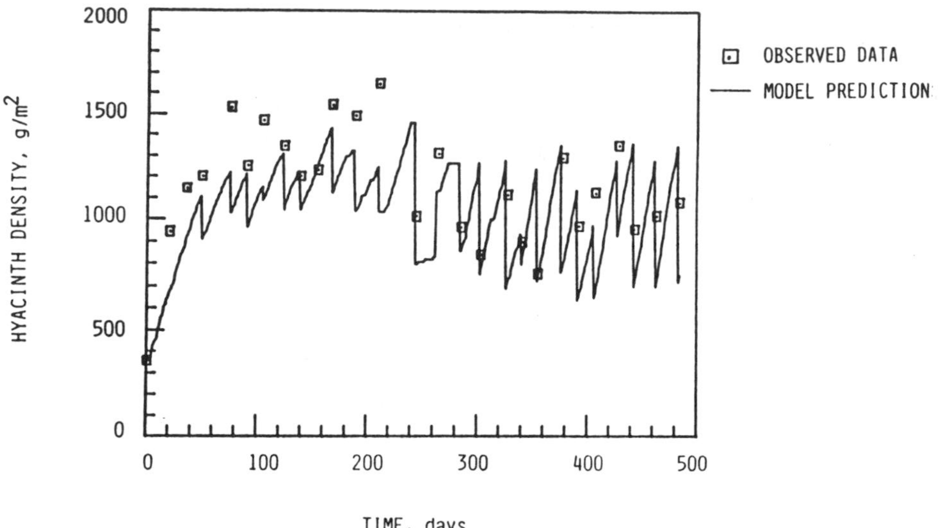

FIGURE 4. Validation of water hyacinth growth model using experimental data from Zellwood, Florida (K. R. Reddy, unpublished results).

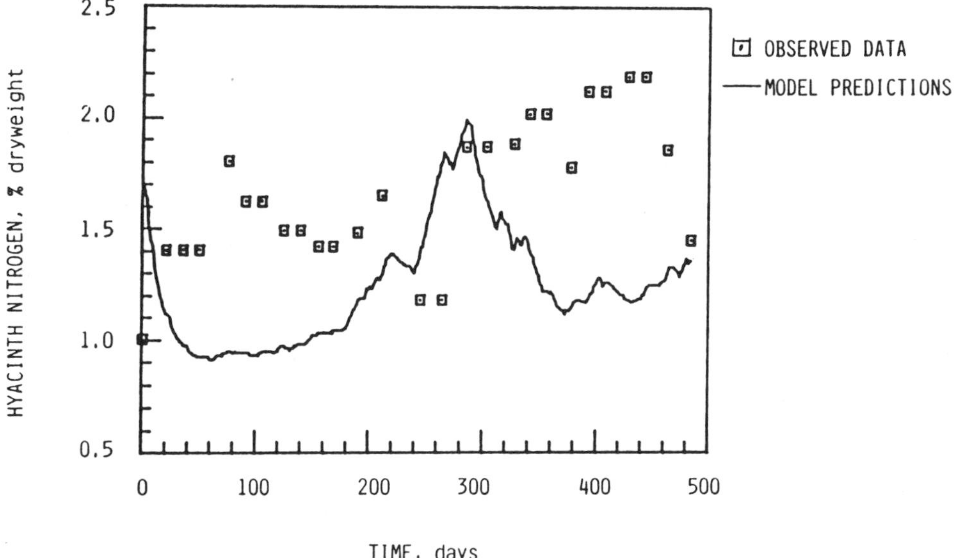

FIGURE 5. Validation of water hyacinth growth model using hyacinth N data from Zellwood, Florida (K. R. Reddy, unpublished results).

REFERENCES

Fisher, M. M., and K. R. Reddy. 1987. Water hyacinths for improving eutrophic lake water: Water quality and mass balance. In K. R. Reddy and W. H. Smith (ed.) Aquatic Plants for Water Treatment and Resource Recovery. Magnolia Publishing Inc., Orlando, Florida.

Lorber, M. N., J. W. Mishoe, and K. R. Reddy. 1984. Modelling analysis of water hyacinth biomass. Ecological Modelling 24:61-77.

Reddy, K. R. 1987. Water hyacinth [Eichhornia crassipes (Mart) Solms] biomass cropping system. I. Production. In W. H. Smith and J. Frank (ed.) Biomass for Methane - A Systematic Approach. Elsevier Appl. Sci. Publ. (in press).

Reddy, K. R., F. M. Hueston, and T. McKim. 1985. Biomass production and nutrient removal potential of water hyacinth cultured in sewage effluent. J. Solar Engr. 107:128-135.

WATER HYACINTHS FOR WASTEWATER TREATMENT IN FLORIDA: PROSPECTS AND CONSTRAINTS

G. J. Thabaraj
Florida Department of Environmental Regulation
2600 Blair Stone Road
Tallahassee, Florida 32301

ABSTRACT

Use of aquatic plants (especially water hyacinths) for the removal of plant nutrients is gaining acceptance by regulatory agencies in Florida as a potentially viable technique to supplement conventional wastewater treatment. Among the advantages claimed for this treatment technique is its ability to achieve high removals of nutrients, especially N, from effluents of secondary or advanced waste treatment plants. The prospects and constraints of water hyacinth treatment system have been evaluated on the basis of Florida's recent experience with both pilot-scale and full-scale systems treating sewage effluents. Even though hyacinth-based treatment systems seem appropriate for Florida's climate, potential constraints to be overcome include the reliability of the system to produce effluents of consistent quality under conditions of varying influent composition and ambient air temperatures, recovery of the system after any freeze damage, potential plant insect/disease problems affecting the system's performance, disposal or utilization of the biomass, and the lack of data on long-term operation of full-scale systems to serve as the basis for the design of new systems. From a regulatory agency's perspective, an adequate data base is necessary to serve as the basis of design of future treatment systems employing aquatic plants. The design criteria should include the hydraulic/nutrient loading rates, residence time, depth, plant density, optimum N/P ratio, harvesting frequency, and, more importantly, the environmentally safe and cost-effective means for disposal or utilization of the plant biomass. Site-specific pilot studies would be necessary to optimize design parameters to meet specific treatment objectives.

Keywords: Water hyacinth treatment in Florida, regulatory concerns, and water hyacinth treatment.

ISBN 0-941463-00-1

INTRODUCTION

Aquatic macrophyte systems, primarily involving water hyacinths, have recently been studied extensively in California (Hauser, 1984), Texas (Dinges, 1979), Mississippi (Wolverton and McDonald, 1979). Because of its prolific growth rate and its ability to remove large amounts of nutrients (i.e., N and P), the water hyacinth has been studied as a potential candidate for macrophyte-based treatment systems to provide tertiary or advanced treatment of sewage effluents. Even though their cool weather sensitivity is a liability for their use in year-round wastewater treatment, the relative ease of harvesting and the potential economic return from the recovery of byproducts (cattle feed, compost, methane gas, etc.) have been considered as favorable factors for the use of water hyacinths in wastewater treatment. Given its subtropical climate and relatively fewer days of freezing air temperatures, Florida would seem to offer ideal conditions for the use of water hyacinths as an economical and effective means to remove N and P from secondary, tertiary and advanced waste treatment (AWT) effluents in the state.

Similar to the principles involved in sewage treatment, the water hyacinth-based treatment system involves the same processes that occur in nature (in the receiving streams) but utilizes intensive management practices to optimize the production of biomass and hence removal of nutrients. The same environmental factors that influence the growth rate of the plant under natural conditions (e.g. air temperature, solar radiation, pH, nutrient concentration, water flow rate, detention time and plant density) also exert their effects under the more managed conditions in a treatment system. Since some of these variables are beyond human control, it is not always possible to provide an ideal environment, under field conditions, to maximize the plant growth rate and to remove nutrients in a consistent and predictable manner. It should be the goal of a managed aquatic treatment system, however, to strive for maximum removal of nutrients possible under a given set of environmental conditions.

A major impetus for the use of water hyacinth treatment systems in Florida has been the need to accomplish higher degree of nutrient removal than those achieved by conventional AWT systems (i.e., total N of 3 mg L^{-1} and total P of 1 mg L^{-1}). Treatment beyond AWT levels has been found necessary in some cases (e.g., City of Kissimmee and City of Orlando) to meet waste load allocations for surface discharge.

STATUS OF WATER HYACINTH TREATMENT IN FLORIDA

Florida has been at the forefront of pioneering work on water hyacinths (Reddy and Sutton, 1984; Stewart 1979; Cornwell et al., 1977; Clock, 1968).

These studies have progressed from laboratory-scale and pilot-scale experiments to full-scale treatment systems involving several million m^3 of effluent per day. In addition to the treatment of secondary or AWT sewage effluent, water hyacinth treatment is being employed in Florida for the treatment of wastewater from poultry processing, citrus processing and waste oil recycling facilities, drainage water from agricultural lands, and blowdown from cooling towers of a power plant that uses secondary effluents for closed-cycle cooling. Consideration is also being given to the controlled use of hyacinths to treat a hypereutrophic lake, and to remove nutrients form the drainage from the Everglades Agricultural Area prior to backpumping to Lake Okeechobee.

In addition to their propensity to absorb large amounts of nutrients, water hyacinths have been known to accumulate trace elements like heavy metals (Tridech et al., 1980; Stowell et al., 1981; Dinges, 1978) and toxic organics such as PCB's (Tridech et al., 1980). It is anticipated that, as more information from the newer facilities becomes available, there will be a growing interest on the use of water hyacinths for the treatment of nutrient-and/or toxics-laden sewage effluents or industrial wastes in Florida.

REGULATORY CONCERNS AND CONSTRAINTS

From a regulatory perspective, the issues of major concern relating to the use of water hyacinth treatment are:

- Reliability of the treatment to consistently meet discharge standards;
- Damage to the plant (and the resulting treatment upsets) caused by occasional freezing temperatures;
- Use of pesticide to control insects/disease of the plants; mosquito control;
- Nutritional status: N and P, heavy metals and toxic organics;
- Cost-effective harvesting and safe disposal or utilization of the plant biomass;
- Basis for design of new facilities, especially for those that are designed to achieve low concentrations of N and P, and,
- Permit requirements on cultivation of the plant.

Reliability

The principal issue involved in any biological treatment system is the question of treatment reliability. It is common knowledge that the efficiency of biological treatment systems is affected by variables such as the environmental conditions, the quality of effluents treated, and the frequency and severity of changes in these variables. Water hyacinth-based treatment systems, like most other biological systems, are affected by ambient air temperatures, by the composition of the growth medium (nutrients, pH, salinity, toxicity, etc.) and by pests and diseases. Therefore, it might be necessary to provide for supplemental treatment, temporary storage, or alternative disposal during periods of temporary upsets in the treatment system if the resulting effluent quality is not acceptable for discharge.

Experience has shown that water hyacinth treatment systems can be as reliable as conventional wastewater treatment systems for the removal of BOD_5, SS, and N (Stowell et al., 1981), except that the period of recovery after a major die-off, caused by environmental factors, could be much longer. Short term reliability problems may not be critical in situations where discharge limitations are based on longer-term performance (i.e. annual mass loading limits for nutrients).

Effluent Limitations Based on Mass Loadings. The wasteload allocation for Orlando's Iron Bridge Treatment Plant is based on annual mass loadings of TN and TP. Therefore, use of the water hyacinth treatment system for eight to nine months of the year to achieve the necessary mass loadings would obviate the risks involved in operating the system during the critical winter months (December through February). In situations where discharge limits are based on concentrations of N and P, it might be necessary to provide for standby storage, disposal or treatment to comply with discharge limits if temporary increases in the concentrations of these parameters, caused by transient poor performance, cannot be tolerated.

Overall Treatment Performance and Capabilities. A review of the data obtained from pilot and field-scale water hyacinth treatment systems in Florida (Amasek, 1985a,b,1986a,b; Swett 1979; DER unpublished data) shows that high N removal rates are associated with plants treating secondary effluents, and that P removal rates are variable.

Phosphorus removal efficiency was generally low and unpredictable, and attainment of low P concentrations (approaching ambient levels) was not practical without supplemental treatment. The lowest P concentration achieved, on an annual average basis, was in the range of 0.2 to 0.3 mg L^{-1} in the systems with chemical (alum) pretreatment followed by water hyacinth treatment.

It was also seen that in order to achieve low concentrations of N in the effluents (i.e. 2 mg L^{-1} or less), the areal loading rates should be low (i.e. about 3.4 kg N ha^{-1} yr^{-1}).

In summary, it can be said that it would be possible to achieve treatment levels beyond conventional AWT, if the nutrient loading rates do not exceed 3.4-4.5 kg N ha^{-1} yr^{-1} and 1.1-1.7 kg P ha^{-1} yr^{-1}. However, in view of serious N limitations at low N/P ratios typical of AWT effluents, and the likely leaching of P from the decaying biomass in the system, average P concentrations lower than 0.2 mg L^{-1} would be hard to achieve in systems treating sewage effluents.

Winter Performance

Deterioration of nutrient removal efficiency and plant die-off were noted during the winter of 1985-86 at the Iron Bridge water hyacinth treatment facility (Amasek, 1986a; DER, unpublished data). Even though the exact cause of the plant die-off is not known, it is apparent that the freezing air temperatures experienced by the system during December 1985 and January 1986 contributed to the decline in treatment efficiency. The results from a pilot study at the same location showed very little removal of N during the previous winter (Amasek, 1985a). Examination of the data from Kissimmee (Amasek, 1986b) shows that the areal removal rates for N and P are considerably reduced during the winter months.

It has been suggested that conservative design of water hyacinth treatment systems should be based on their winter performance. This might be valid for systems intended to meet concentration-based limits year-round. However, it would not be cost-effective to use winter performance as the basis of design for systems to meet annual mass loadings of nutrients to the receiving bodies of water. In order to improve winter performance cold tolerant plants such as pennywort (Hydrocotyle umbellata) can be introduced in water hyacinth-based treatment system (DeBusk and Reddy, 1987).

Insects/Disease Control

Use of Pesticides. The Florida Department of Agriculture and Consumer Services has issued an Experimental Use Permit for the application of Sevin 80S (at a maximum rate of 1-18 kg active ingredient carboryl per hectare) to three existing water hyacinth systems (Loxahatchee ECD, Iron Bridge and City of Melbourne) to control weevil populations, if controlled harvesting fails to accomplish this objective. Concentration of carboryl in the discharge from these systems is limited to less than 1.0 mg L^{-1}, with a further requirement that treated plants not be used as food or feed.

It is obvious that continued reliance on insecticides to control the weevil populations is a cause for concern, and needs satisfactory resolution. Research is being done to find a biological substitute to control the weevil in water hyacinth treatment systems.

Mosquito Control Using Fish Populations. Mosquito breeding in hyacinth ponds is a concern. The ponds should be stocked with mosquito fish (Gambusia) and clear areas should be provided to enhance its propagation.

Nutritional Status

N/P Ratio. It has been reported by several workers that the efficiency of N and P removal by a healthy water hyacinth treatment system is dependent upon the relative amounts of each nutrient present in the growth medium. The optimum ratio for N to P, based on the concentration in the tissue of healthy plants, has been reported to range from 3.6 to 6 (Reddy et al., 1985). Nutrients are removed from the growth medium in proportion to the concentration in plant tissue (Boyd, 1970). Since the N:P ratio in secondary effluents is low (less than 3), N is depleted first and becomes a limiting factor before P is reduced to low concentrations.

Low N:P ratios are typical with AWT effluents (annual average of 3 mg L^{-1} TN and 1 mg L^{-1} TP), and addition of supplemental N might be necessary to reduce P to lower levels. The efficacy of this procedure is not known. It is also not known whether bacterial competition for N (nitrification/denitrification) would occur at such low concentration levels.

Another factor that might mitigate against low levels of P in the effluents from the water hyacinth system is the potential release of P from the decaying plant tissue in the sediments (Dinges, 1979).

Toxic Substances. Despite the water hyacinth's ability to accumulate several heavy metals and toxic organics, it is adversely affected by high salinity in the growth medium and heavy accumulation of aluminum. The death of plants at the Plant City, Florida, treatment site has been attributed to discharge of industrial wastes containing high concentrations of chlorides and aluminum (Farrell, 1979).

Given the tendency of the water hyacinth to accumulate high levels of aluminum and Fe (Boyd, 1970), the practice of using aluminum and Fe salts during pretreatment to remove P should be reconsidered. It would be preferable to use supplemental chemical treatment <u>after</u> water hyacinth treatment.

Harvesting and Disposal of Biomass

Cost of hyacinth harvesting would be a potential concern, especially for small-scale systems. Costs would be influenced by the frequency of plant harvest, type of disposal of the plant biomass and the potential for byproduct recovery. The economics of mechanical harvesting and recovery of byproducts, such as methane gas and cattlefeed, will not be favorable for smaller systems.

Harvesting frequency would also be dependent on the need to control the weevil populations. Periodic harvesting of the plants might be necessary to control the density of the pests and help maintain the productivity of the plants. Harvesting creates open areas that will be conducive to algal growth resulting in an increase in suspended solids in the effluents.

Since a major portion of N is lost from the water hyacinth treatment system through bacterial nitrification and denitrification, frequent plant harvesting might not be necessary for N removal. DeBusk et al. (1983) observed a reduction of 73% total TN in the Coral Springs system under non-harvesting conditions. Denitrification accounted for 93% of such removal. Reddy (1983) suggests that nitrified effluents could lead to N limitation for water hyacinths since a significant portion of NO_3-N could be lost through denitrification.

Harvested plants should be processed and disposed of in such a manner as to prevent secondary water quality problems. Conversion to cattlefeed or compost is an attractive possibility but the economics of such conversion and payback remains an issue. Research is also being carried out by the Gas Research Institute, University of Florida, and Walt Disney World on the economic and technical feasibility of producing methane by anaerobic digestion of the water hyacinth biomass in combination with sewage sludge (Hayes et al., 1987).

Design Criteria

The specific objectives of the treatment system in terms of final effluent concentrations or loadings should be clearly defined before detailed design is undertaken. If discharge standards (mass loadings) can be met by seasonal operation of the water hyacinth treatment system, design could be based on the efficiency of treatment typical of the season of required operation. On the other hand, if the discharge standards (seasonal or year-round) are based on concentrations, the design should be conservative, taking into consideration the effects of cool weather and the need for supplemental treatment during such times of the year.

Several excellent articles have been published relating to the design parameters for the water hyacinth treatment systems (Middlebrooks, 1980; Gee & Jenson Engineers Inc., 1980; Dinges, 1979; Reddy et al., 1985; Stewart et al., 1984; Stowell et al., 1981; Tchobanoglous et al., 1979; Tchobanoglous, 1987; O'Brien, 1981; Hyde et al., 1984). Important criteria for successful nutrient removal include design (nutrient) loading rate; nutrient concentration in the influent; multiple ponds to facilitate cleaning, harvesting and maintenance; pond area, depth, detention time and recirculation. Shallow depths (0.5-1 m) and long detention times (6 days or greater) have been suggested for systems designed for nutrient removal.

In view of the numerous variables that affect the efficiency of nutrient removal, it would be necessary to perform pilot-scale experiments involving different nutrient loading rates, hydraulic retention times, depths and harvest frequencies to arrive at the optimum criteria for design to meet specific treatment objectives.

Permit Requirements

Under the authority of Section 369.25 Florida Statues, the Florida Department of Natural Resources (DNR) has classified the water hyacinth as a 'prohibited aquatic plant' (Chapter 16C-52 Florida Administrative Code). Possession of a prohibited aquatic plant requires a permit from the department. Permittees approved to culture any aquatic plant must have their facilities inspected and approved by the DNR to insure that the cultured aquatic plants will not contaminate public or private water adjacent to the permittee's facility [Section 16C-52-004(3)(C)FAC].

FUTURE PROSPECTS

Use of the water hyacinth as a natural adjunct to wastewater treatment in Florida promises to be an effective and economical alternative to meet effluent discharge limitations for nutrients and toxic elements in sewage and industrial effluents. Even though this treatment technique is subject to occasional upsets caused by uncontrollable environmental factors, such as freezing air temperatures and insect infestation, the overall treatment effectiveness is adequate to meet discharge standards based on annual mass loading limits (e.g. nutrient loadings to lakes) or to comply with seasonally applicable concentration-based limits (e.g. where temporary upsets in treatment efficiency can be tolerated).

Potential constraints to successful application of water hyacinth treatment systems would include the inability to achieve significant removals of P at low influent concentrations, disposal utilization of harvested plant biomass in a cost-effective and environmentally acceptable manner, and the need to perform a pilot study to verify the design criteria for a full-scale system. Studies underway at different locations within the state are intended to resolve these constraints, and it is hoped that the water hyacinth, long considered a nuisance, will be put to beneficial use within the confines of facilities treating sewage and industrial effluents in Florida.

REFERENCES

Amasek, Inc. 1985a. Assessment of Iron Bridge water hyacinth pilot study. Final Report Prepared for Post, Buckley, Schuh and Jernigan, Inc., Orlando, Florida.

Amasek, Inc. 1985b. Operation and performance reports of Iron Bridge regional water pollution control facility (July, August and September 1985), City of Orlando, Florida.

Amasek, Inc. 1986a. Assessment of winter time nutrient removal performances of five water hyacinth based wastewater treatment systems in Florida, study period: December 1985-February 1986. Prepared for the City of Orlando, Florida.

Amasek, Inc. 1986b. Assessment of operations: Water hyacinth nutrient removal treatment process pilot plant, City of Kissimmee. Prepared for Briley, Wild, and Associates, Inc.

Boyd, C. E. 1970. Vascular aquatic plants for mineral nutrient removal from polluted waters. Econ. Bot. 23:95-103.

Clock, R. M. 1968. Removal of nitrogen and phosphorus from a secondary sewage treatment effluent. Doctor of Philosophy Dissertation, University of Florida, Gainesville, Florida.

Cornwell, D. A., J. Zoltek, Jr., C. D. Patrinely, T. des. Furman, and J. I. Kim. 1977. Nutrient removal by water hyacinths. J. Water Pollut. Cont. Fed. 49:57-65.

DeBusk, T. A., and K. R. Redy. 1987. Wastewater treatment using floating aquatic macrophytes: Management strategies. In K. R. Reddy and W. H. Smith (ed.) Aquatic Plants for Water Treatment and Resource Recovery. Magnolia Publishing Inc., Orlando, Florida.

DeBusk, T. A., L. D. Williams, and J. H. Ryther. 1983. Removal of nitrogen and phosphorus from wastewater in a water hyacinth-based treatment system. J. Environ. Qual. 12:257-262.

Dinges, R. 1978. Upgrading stabilization pond effluent by water hyacinth culture. J. Water Pollut. Cont. Fed. 50:833-845.

Dinges, R. 1979. Development of hyacinth wastewater treatment systems in Texas. In Aquaculture Systems for Wastewater Treatment: Seminar Proceedings and Engineering Assessment." U.S. Environmental Protection Agency. EPA 430/9-80-006.

Farrell, D. H. 1979. Mortality of water hyacinth populations in the Plant City sewage treatment plant. Department of Environmental Regulation, Tampa, Florida.

Gee & Jenson Engineers, Inc. 1980. Water hyacinth wastewater treatment design manual for NASA/National Space Technology Laboratories, NSTL Station, Mississippi.

Hauser, J. R. 1984. Use of water hyacinth aquatic treatment systems for ammonia control and effluent polishing. J. Water Pollut. Cont. Fed. 56:219-226.

Hayes, T. D., H. R. Isaacson, K. R. Reddy, D. P. Chynoweth, and R. Biljetina. 1987. Water hyacinth systems for water treatment. In K. R. Reddy and W. H. Smith (ed.) Aquatic Plants for Water Treatment and Resource Recovery. Magnolia Publishing Inc., Orlando, Florida.

Hyde, H. C., R. S. Ross, and L. Sturmer. 1984. Technology assessment of aquaculture systems for municipal wastewater treatment. Municipal Environmental Research Laboratory, Cincinnati, Ohio, EPA-600/2-85-145.

Middlebrooks, E. J. 1980. Aquatic plant processes assessment. In Aquaculture Systems for Wastewater Treatment: An Engineering Assessment. U.S. Environmental Protection Agency, EPA 430/9-80-007.

O'Brien, W. J. 1981. Use of aquatic macrophytes for wastewater treatment. J. Environ. Div., ASCE 107:681-698.

Reddy, K. R. 1983. Fate of nitrogen and phosphorus in a wastewater retention reservoir containing aquatic macrophytes. J. Environ. Qual. 12:137-141.

Reddy, K. R., and D. L. Sutton. 1984. Water hyacinths for water quality improvement and biomass production. J. Environ. Qual. 13:1-8.

Reddy, K. R., F. M. Hueston, and T. McKim. 1985. Biomass production and nutrient removal potential of water hyacinth cultured in sewage effluent. J. Solar Energy Eng. 107:128-135.

Reddy, K. R., D. L. Sutton, and G. Bowes. 1983. Freshwater aquatic plant biomass production in Florida. Soil and Crop Science Society of Florida Proceedings 42:28-40.

Stewart, E. A. 1979. Utilization of water hyacinth for control of nutrients in domestic wastewater - Lakeland, Florida. In Aquaculture Systems for Wastewater Treatment. U.S. Environmental Protection Agency, EPA 430/9-80-006.

Stowell, R., R. Ludwig, J. Colt, and G. Tchobanoglous. 1981. Concepts in aquatic treatment system design. J. Environ. Eng. Div., ASCE 107:919-940.

Swett, D. 1979. A water hyacinth advanced wastewater treatment system. In Aquaculture Systems for Wastewater Treatment. U.S. Environmental Protection Agency, EPA 430/9-80-006.

Tchobanoglous, G., R. Stowell, R. Ludwig, J. Colt, and A. Knight. 1979. The use of aquatic plants and animals for the treatment of wastewater: An overview. In Aquatic Systems for Wastewater Treatment: Seminar Proceedings and Engineering Assessment. U.S. Environmental Protection Agency, Washington, D.C., EPA 430/9-80-006.

Tridech, S., A. J. England, Jr., M. Herbert, Jr., and R. F. Wilkinson. 1980. Kinetics of trace contaminant removal from secondary domestic effluent by vascular aquatic plant systems. Presented at the 53rd Annual Conference of the Water Pollution Control Federation.

Wolverton, B. C., and R. C. McDonald. 1979. Upgrading facultative waste stabilization ponds with vascular aquatic plants. J. Water Pollut. Control Fed. 51:309-313.

ABSTRACTS

CONSTRUCTION GRANT PARTICIPATION IN INNOVATIVE AND ALTERNATIVE TECHNOLOGIES.

J. Kent Kimes (Bureau of Wastewater Management and Grants, Department of Environmental Regulation, 2600 Blair Stone Road, Tallahassee, Florida 32301)

Many technologies which use aquatic plants for wastewater treatment and resource recovery may be designated as innovative or alternative technologies. Innovative and alternative technologies may receive up to 75% funding from the U.S. Environmental Protection Agency's (EPA) Construction Grant Program. There were specific provisions of the 1977 Clean Water Act (CWA) which set the tone for the EPA implementation of the I/A program. Those amendments to PL92-500 encouraged revenue producing waste management facilities; required all applicants to fully study innovative and alternative treatment options; encouraged energy conservation; and required EPA to encourage treatment techniques which will reduce total energy requirements.

The 1977 CWA provided incentives for the use of I/A technologies. While present regulations mandate the applicant to select the most cost-effective alternative during the planning of a construction project, Section 201(j) of the CWA allows EPA to participate in the innovative and alternative process option even if its costs are as much as 15% higher than the least costly conventional option. Further, the amendments increased federal grant participation from 55% to 75% for treatment works utilizing innovative or alternative processes, and has authorized EPA to pay 100% of all costs to replace innovative or alternative treatment facilities should they fail within two years after start-up.

In order to participate in the benefits as an I/A technology in the grants program the applicant must demonstrate that the project or portion of the project is innovative or alternative. While EPA has retained authority for the formal designation of I/A projects, the state transmits recommendations to EPA based on documentation received and evaluated.

According to EPA guidelines on the grants program, Construction Grants 1985 (CG-85), an alternative technology is a concept of wastewater treatment or sludge management which emphasizes conservation or eliminates the discharge of pollutants. This concept places strong emphasis on the reclaiming and reusing of wastewater and sludge constituents, energy recovery, or other environmental benefits that may contribute to reducing costs.

ISBN 0-941463-00-1

This is a very broad definition and appears to include all forms of proven treatment technologies which do not discharge to surface water.

An alternative technology is any one of a number of specifically defined processes listed below:

Effluent Treatment
- land treatment
- aquifer recharge
- aquaculture
- direct reuse (non potable)
- horticulture
- revegetation of disturbed land
- containment ponds
- preapplication treatment and storage of treated effluent

Energy Recovery
- anaerobic digestion with 90% CH_4 recovery
- self-sustaining incineration

Individual and On-site Systems
- on-site treatment
- septage treatment
- alternative collection systems for small communities

Sludge
- land application
- composting prior to land application
- drying prior to land application

Those which might utilize aquatic plants for wastewater treatment and resource recovery include but are not limited to aquaculture, direct reuse, treatment and storage prior to land application, and pre-application treatment.

An innovative technology is defined in CG-85 as significantly different from either conventional concepts of centralized treatment or alternative technologies. The most important distinction in CG-85 between alternative and innovative technologies is that alternative technologies are considered to be fully proven but may be relatively unknown because of infrequent use. An innovative technology is not a specifically defined treatment process. It is a new technology which has not been fully proven but is promising based on results from research and demonstration projects. It should be noted that in limited cases the EPA will fund demonstration projects (not research) for innovative technologies. Innovative technologies include an element of risk and a corresponding benefit which outweighs the risk.

Innovative designation may be issued upon meeting specific criteria, to insure the goal of advancing the state-of-the-art for promising new concepts. According to the 1980 EPA Innovative and Alternative Technology Assessment Manual (I/A Manual) there are two categories of projects that are candidates for designation as innovative; those identified as alternative, and those identified as conventional concepts of centralized treatment. If a project is considered alternative it may be designated as innovative if it is demonstrated to meet any one of the six criteria listed below:

- . improved operational reliability
- . improved toxics management
- . increased environmental benefits
- . improved joint municipal/industrial treatment potential
- . life cycle cost reduction of 15%
- . net primary energy reduction of 20%

However, conventional concepts of centralized treatment may be designated as innovative only after documenting the 15% life cycle cost (LCC) reduction, or the 20% net primary energy reduction criterion listed above. According to the I/A Manual the first four criteria have been established to encourage the use of new or improved applications of already proven alternative technologies. Subjective qualitative analyses would be the basis for the documentation to support a project based on one of these criteria.

The more recent regulations published in the Federal Register May 12, 1982, and February 17, 1984, define innovative technologies as those which represent a significant advancement in the state-of-the-art in terms of significant cost or energy reduction. Though the 1984 rules do include "significant environmental benefit" as a criterion in the definition, it would be difficult to demonstrate that a more expensive project would advance the state-of-the art. Basically, in order for a technology to be designated as innovative, whether a designated alternative technology or other concept, it must be demonstrated to meet the LCC or net primary energy reduction criterion.

In summary, the EPA is providing incentives, primarily through increased funding, for the use of innovative and alternative technologies in the construction grants program. The EPA must issue specific approval of I/A projects on a case-by-case basis. For more information contact your state agency delegated by EPA for administration of the construction grants program or your EPA regional office.

USE OF MAN-MADE AQUATIC SYSTEMS FOR WASTEWATER RENOVATION. C. E. Swindell, Jr. (Post, Buckley, Schuh & Jernigan, Inc., 889 North Orange Avenue, Orlando, Florida 32801).

Design criteria and costs will be compared for three man-made wetland systems and a 12 ha hyacinth lagoon. The City of Lakeland is constructing a 526.5 ha wetland system in a retired clay settling area. The system was previously dominated by *Typha* spp. and *Salix* sp. throughout. Regulatory pressure prompted the removal of *Salix* in the first cells and its replacement by grass/herbaceous species. The system will discharge to the Alfia River, a nitrogen limited river. Likewise, the City of Orlando is presently constructing a 486 ha wetland system along the middle St. Johns River. In this case, the entire system will be revegetated with over one million macrophytes. Because of its location this system is designed to provide N/P removal and a diverse habitat for wildlife. To avoid a point discharge here, the effluent will sheet flow across 243 ha of Seminole Ranch prior to entering the river. Finally, Brevard County is planning to construct a 243 ha wetland along the upper St. Johns River. The site is located on an improved pasture dotted with small, wet depressions. Testing indicates a considerable aquatic plant seed bank exists on site. Therefore, instead of planting vegetation, the seed bank will be developed to provide the aquatic vegetation for treatment of wastewater. Capital and O&M costs, treatment capacities and environmental impacts for these systems will be compared along with hyacinth lagoons. Hyacinth lagoons can maximize loading rates, facilitate harvesting and provide year-round treatment. A 12 ha hyacinth system at Iron Bridge Regional Pollution Control Facility has been operating since January 1985. Its performance will be contrasted with those projected for the wetlands above.

ACID MINE DRAINAGE ABATEMENT IN MAN-MADE WETLAND SYSTEMS. D. A. Kepler (The EADS Group, P. O. Box 684, Greenville Ave. Ext., Clarion, Pennsylvania 16214) and F. J. Brenner (Grove City College, Pennsylvania).

Preliminary results indicate that wetlands may be an effective and permanent means of abating acid mine drainage (AMD) at relatively low costs. The principal species planted in three Western Pennsylvania, man-made wetland systems in June, 1985, were *Typha latifolia*, *Equisetum arvense*, and *Scirpus validus*. These species along with *Spirogyra* spp. and *Oscillatoria* spp. and associated bacteria demonstrated in reductions in the AMD for mineral acidity at approximately 80%, total Fe at greater than 90%, total Mn and SO_4^{2-} at roughly 50% each, with a three-fold increase in pH noted. The systems were planted at *Typha* densities of 3 stems m^{-2} and became effective in treating AMD when *Typha* stem densities approached 6 stems m^2. Dry ashings displayed concentrations of Mn as high as 56,000 mg kg^{-1} of plant tissue in several species. The probable mechanisms of mineral uptake by the plants will be discussed. Factors considered in sizing the systems, such as flow and subsequent chemical loading rates, turnover rates, etc. will also be defined. Total cost of wetland construction/system averaged $4,000; compared to a projected permanent chemical treatment cost of $300,000-$400,000/system.

DESIGN OF EMERGENT AND SUBMERGENT WETLANDS FOR THE TREATMENT AND DISPERSION OF WASTEWATER EFFLUENT. P. Lombardo and P. Kozak (Lombardo & Associates, 1835 Forest Drive, Annapolis, Maryland 21401).

Maryland's Mayo Peninsula, located in Anne Arundel County 8 km south of Annapolis, is the site of an innovative wastewater management program utilizing constructed wetlands for treatment and dispersion. It is a project that will be phased over a five year period, with initial construction to begin in the fall of 1986. The Treatment System is a 0.9 MGD facility consisting of the following unit processes: sand filters, ultraviolet disinfection, emergent wetland, peat wetland, and offshore wetland. From the sand filters, effluent flows through an emergent wetland consisting of *Typha latifolia* and *Scirpus olneyi*. This freshwater wetland will serve as a back-up to the sand filters for BOD_5 and suspended solids removal, but its main function will be for N removal through denitrification. For P removal, the wastewater leaving the emergent wetland will be applied to a peat wetland. In the final step, treated effluent will be discharged into an offshore wetland located in the Rhode River of the Chesapeake Bay. The main function of the offshore site is to disperse the treated effluent. The offshore wetland is a constructed structure consisting of *Potamogeton pectinatus*, *Potamogeton perfoliatus* and *Ruppia maritima* transplants. Pre- and post-planting monitoring programs will be implemented.

MODIFIED FLOW-THROUGH EFFLUENT DISPOSAL SYSTEMS FOR FLORIDA WETLANDS. R. Johnson and C. W. Sheffield (Sheffield Engineering & Associates, Inc., 3400 S. Conway Road, Orlando, Florida 32800).

This paper addresses the use of existing wetland aquatic plant communities in freshwater wetlands in Florida, that are used as a means of effluent disposal of treated wastewater. A literature review provides background on wetland hydrology and performance of freshwater wetlands in tertiary wastewater treatment. Evaluation strategy is addressed from several points of view relevant to the effectiveness of wetlands in handling water and nutrient loads. Background projects that have been in operation in Florida over the past 20 years will be discussed. The body of the report will discuss actual projects that Sheffield Engineering & Associates, Inc. have designed and obtained D.E.R. approval and are into either the monitoring or the construction phase. A background data monitoring program is explained and depicted in graphics. System design and construction is discussed and emphasis is placed on water quality as effluent passes through the sampling stations throughout the system. Illustrations within the report graphically depict four years of background data and monthly operation data. The presentation includes slide projections that show preconstruction, construction, and post construction.

PROPOSED NATURAL WETLANDS TREATMENT SYSTEM - TOTAL CONTAINMENT. B. Burkett (Law Enforcement Center, 426 Towner Drive, Devils Lake, North Dakota 58301).

This is a proposed design of a wetlands treatment system using natural wetlands to process secondary treated water from a lagoon system for the city of Devils Lake, North Dakota. The system is designed to be a total containment system which will prevent any nutrient-rich water from reaching the large natural lake, also known as Devils Lake. The lake provides high-quality recreation and fishing activity and has an economic impact to the local economy of over $12 million per year. Continual lagoon dumps into the lake have occurred over the past 20 years adding to a heavy algal bloom and small summer fish kills on one of the lake's major bays. This is a community attempt to solve their own sources of lake degradation. The design system will dispose of effluent for approximately 10,000 people. Worst case would be to move 595.4 ha feet of secondary water during the treatment period with an application period of 200 days.

CONSTRAINTS IN A WETLAND ECOSYSTEM.

K. N. Mishra (T. D. College, Jaunpur 222 002 U.P., INDIA).

Cottage industries of woolen carpet manufacturers have covered a major portion of rural areas of India, China, Iran, and Pakistan. In India, the wetlands of rice fields, surrounding carpet industrial centers, have been receiving increasing amounts of various chemicals at extremes of pH, heavy metal chromium, dyes, and wool particles in periodic irrigations by effluents from these industries. Significant amounts of chemicals such as $(NH_4)_2SO_4$, Na_2SO_4, $K_2\ Cr_2O_7$, CH_3 COOH, Chromium (VI) and dyes at pH 4.3, and high temperature (about 80 to 90°C) are let out from (i) the dyeing of wool yarns. Effluent with caustic soda (NaOH), bleaching powder ($CaOCl_2$), and detergents at pH 10.5 come out at large scale from (ii) the processing of woolen carpets. Washing soda (Na_2CO_3), detergents, and some residues are discharged from (iii) scouring and washing of wool yarn. *Oryza sativa* Baruna variety plants were tested and studied at their critical stages for growth performance, root extension, reproductive characters, and productivity. The effluent treated plants have shown abnormal growth, less tillering with pseudotillers, reduction in photosynthetic structure with reduced productivity in comparison to that of water treated ones. Processing effluent (PE) has maximum effect than that of dying effluent (DE) and scouring effluent (SE). These enriched effluents have also deteriorated the ionic balance and the physico-chemical properties of the soil.

RESPONSE OF BENTHIC MACROINVERTEBRATES OF A SHRUB SWAMP WETLAND TO DISCHARGE OF SECONDARILY TREATED MUNICIPAL WASTEWATER.

C. Pezeshki and G. R. Best (University of Florida, Center for Wetlands, Phelps Lab, Gainesville, Florida 32611).

Benthic macroinvertebrates have been used as indicators of water quality in aquatic systems. Changes in biological oxygen demand, pH, N and P concentrations, and dissolved oxygen affect the diversity, abundance, and biomass of macroinvertebrates, either directly or indirectly by stimulation of primary productivity. The study area, a shrub swamp wetland dominated primarily by swamp or red titi (*Cyrilla racemiflora*) and black titi (*Cliftonia monophylla*), is located near Apalachicola, Florida. The area was designated as an experimental study site to assess the response to and treatment capacity of wastewater by the wetlands. As part of that study, species richness and abundance of aquatic macroinvertebrates in the wetland were determined prior to wastewater discharge in order to establish background information for the wetland (Haack, S. K., M.S. Thesis, University of Florida, 1984). Additional macroinvertebrate samples were collected at previously sampled stations, as well as at stations within 500 m of the discharge point. Data from the wastewater impacted area were compared with background data and control areas over a 12-month period. A decrease in species richness and an increase in macroinvertebrate abundance and total biomass were found in areas impacted by wastewater relative to the control areas. Invertebrate densities in the wastewater impacted areas range from 100 to 2000 individuals m^{-2} with 3-5 dominant families at control stations. Individuals of the family Chironomidae dominate wastewater impacted areas, with *Asellus* sp., *Crangonyx* sp., and Chironomidae more common in control areas. Correlations between water chemistry and macroinvertebrate data were also addressed.

ECOLOGICAL INVESTIGATION OF A POLLUTED AND A NON-POLLUTED POND AT VARANASI.

M. Sikandar and B. D. Tripathi (Banaras Hindu University, Varanasi 221 005, INDIA).

Ponds have been the major sources of bathing, washing and other domestic purposes in India since time immemorial. In and around the city of Varanasi about 100 ponds were surveyed and each were found highly polluted due to discharge of sewage and industrial toxic effluents. Pishach Mochan pond was selected for the present investigation. The physico-chemical and biological characteristics of this pond were compared with that of Sarnath pond which is regarded as a non-polluted pond. The study reveals the variation in water temperature from 20.66 ± 0.28 to 36.00 ± 0.50°C at Pishach Mochan and 17.50 ± 0.40 to 36.5 ± 0.4°C at Sarnath pond. The pH values ranged from 8.32 ± 0.05 to 9.73 ± 0.05 at Pishach Mochan pond and 6.77 ± 0.08 to 7.80 ± 0.08 at Sarnath pond. The DO values varied from 8.0 ± 0.2 to 26.8 ± 1.07 mg L^{-1} and 4.10 ± 0.90 to 9.68 ± 0.76 mg L^{-1}, the BOD values from 17.13 ± 2.04 to 49.13 ± 4.80 mg L^{-1} and 1.9 ± 0.09 to 7.97 ± 1.53 mg L^{-1}, bicarbonate alkalinity 173.33 ± 1.04 to 210.67 ± 2.47 mg L^{-1} $CaCO_3$, and 28.33 ± 1.29 to 54.50 ± 2.74 mg L^{-1} $CaCO_3$, EC values from 520.67 ± 10.26 to 800.00 $\pm$ µmhos cm^{-1} and 40.67 ± 1.95 to 131.67 ± 2.58 µmhos cm^{-1} at Pishach Mochan and Sarnath ponds respectively. The Pishach Mochan pond was highly dominated with *Microcystis* bloom and macrophytes like *Hydrilla verticillata*.

At Sarnath pond high species diversity was recorded. The dominant species observed were Hydrilla verticillata, Ceratophyllum demersum, Azolla pinnata, Morsilea quadrifolia and Aponogeton natans etc. The present investigation reveals the highly eutrophic and polluted condition of Pishach Mochan pond. This urgently needs proper management. It also provides necessary information for management practices and ecomodelling of all the ponds of Varanasi surveyed so far.

NOTES ON AQUATIC MACROPHYTES IN THE LOWER SECTION OF THE ORINOCO FLOOD-PLAIN SYSTEM, VENEZUELA. L. Sanchez and E. Vasquez (La Salle Foundation of Natural Sciences, Apdo. 51, San Felix, Edo. Bolivar, VENEZUELA).

The Orinoco River system (flood plain of 70.000 km^2) presents numerous lakes (temporary and permanent) with different shapes and water types influenced by the annual floods. Important development projects are planned in the basin (industrial and hydroelectric). Research was initiated in four lakes (lower river section) to provide baseline information regarding species composition, diversity, and cover of aquatic plants. In a first phase, a survey was made during high waters (time of maximum growth and seed production of aquatic plants). Percentages of plant cover ranged from 9 to 24.5% in these lakes. Species composition tended to be similar. Most abundant and frequent species were: Eichhornia crassipes, Paspalum repens, and Oxicaryum cubense. Others like Ludwigia helminthorriza, L. seidioides, Eleocharis sp., Salvinia auriculata, and Hymenachne amplexicaulis were less abundant. In a second phase (low waters), a general aerophoto- graphic survey was made along 120 Km of the river. From 246 lakes, 53% presented high to moderate plant cover (mainly lateral levee lakes), and 47% low to absent plant cover. A discussion is made on the ecological significance of aquatic macrophytes in tropical flood plain rivers and their potential use as food complement for cultured fishes in the Orinoco Basin.

PROFILING AN AQUACULTURE FACILITY. N. Malley and S. Pearson (Woodward-Clyde Consultants, 2504 Ellentown, LaJolla, California 92037).

Aquatic wastewater treatment facilities have received a great deal of attention during the last several years. They are appealing because of their reported low energy requirements, low cost, and simple technological approach to wastewater treatment. Aquaculture systems, however, have always been associated with the usage of rather significant amounts of land area. Efforts have been made to reduce the size of aquaculture systems by increasing efficiency and thereby reducing land requirements. Recent advances in the study of the metabolic pathways and the kinetics associated with Aquatic Treatment Systems have given us new approaches towards understanding these systems. We are finding that data based merely upon monitoring the influent and effluent of pond systems are not sufficient to evaluate and design an efficient aquatic treatment facility. Design and evaluation of a facility should instead be based upon the following: (1) characterization of the kinetic chemical equation parameters for the aquatic treatment system, and (2) the results of time-sequenced, simultaneous sampling. This two step approach to design and evaluation produces an understanding of the phenomena taking place along the length and depth of the pond system. The profiling of the San Diego Aquatic Treatment Pilot Project led to a better understanding of the chemical kinetics and metabolic pathways operating within the system. The results of the profiling study have led to a new approach to aquatic treatment pond design which promises to increase efficiency four to five times and reduce the land required for the treatment system by nearly 80%. The new pond design provides flexibility to accommodate the changing chemical and biological phenomena that take place during different times of the year and with differing waste loads. It should also facilitate the expansion of treatment facility scale.

WATER HYACINTH PRODUCTION IN EUTROPHIC LAKES FOR WATER QUALITY IMPROVEMENT AND CONVERSION TO METHANE: AN ECONOMIC FRAMEWORK FOR ANALYSIS.

C. M. Fonyo, W. G. Boggess, and C. F. Kiker (University of Florida, Department of Food and Resource Economics, Gainesville, Florida 32611).

Cultural eutrophication of surface waterbodies has become an ever increasing problem in Florida. One specific case is that of Lake Apopka which heads the Oklawaha chain of lakes in central Florida. Activities such as farming and citrus processing, in addition to sewage discharge to the lake, have led to the degradation of Lake Apopka's water quality and subsequent decline in recreational and sportfishing value. Methods to transform the lake into a valuable resource have been examined by two separate interest groups: (1) state and federal government agencies which are concerned with improving the lake's water quality, providing recreational opportunities, and creating a habitat for game fish and wildlife; and (2) the Gas Research Institute (GRI) of Chicago which has been supporting research to determine whether aquatic weeds (i.e., water hyacinths) grown in Lake Apopka may provide an economically feasible feedstock for commercial CH_4 production. The economic feasibility of a water hyacinth system for Lake Apopka is partly dependent upon the development of an effective management strategy. An optimal management strategy for water hyacinth production is defined as one which (1) maximizes the sustainable yield of water hyacinths over time while meeting the feedstock demand of the conversion facility, and (2) maximizes the removal of nutrients from Lake Apopka over time in order to improve the lake's water quality. The BIOMET (BIOmass to METhane) simulation model developed at the University of Florida was used to analyze and compare several management strategies. Decision variables which were tested include: harvest strategy, initial plant density, target yield (i.e., growing area fertilization schedule, and fertilizer application rate. Outcomes of the simulation runs were evaluated according to specific economic and environmental decision criteria. The impacts of the alternative management strategies on the long-term viability of the water hyacinth production/conversion system and its nutrient removal potential are discussed.

PART VI
RESEARCH NEEDS

RESEARCH AND DEVELOPMENT NEEDS FOR UTILIZATION OF AQUATIC PLANTS FOR WATER TREATMENT AND RESOURCE RECOVERY

INTRODUCTION

This paper presents the results of the panel discussion on research and development needs for utilization of aquatic plants for water treatment and resource recovery. The panel members were:

Sherwood C. Reed, Chairman, USA CRREL, Hanover, NH.
E. Joe Middlebrooks, Tennessee Technological University, Cookeville, TN.
John C. Corey, Savanna River Laboratory, Aiken, SC.
Carl W. Hall, National Science Foundation, Washington, DC.
William E. Odum, University of Virginia, Charlottesville, VA.
James M. Davidson, IFAS, University of Florida, Gainesville, FL.

After reviewing the presented papers and posters, each panel member prepared comments on a specific topic and then participated in the general discussion. These statements are given below in the same order as presented at the conference, followed by a general summary.

ENGINEERING STATUS E. Joe Middlebrooks

Seven years ago at Davis, California, I had essentially the same task I have in this panel, and that is to discuss some of the engineering needs of aquatic plant wastewater treatment systems. Many changes have occurred, but much remains the same. I will attempt to outline some of my principal concerns and also point out some of our gains.

One of the most promising things to come out of this conference is the presentation of the basic work being done in many locations. This research is providing useful information that will eventually lead to a description of both natural and artificial wetlands. The same is true for other plant systems.

Perhaps the greatest shortcoming of many of the systems described at this conference is the poor experimental design. There are numerous "green boxes" being operated with measurements of performance being made only at the inlet and outlet. Many of these systems are hundreds of meters in length, and a myriad of

ISBN 0-941463-00-1

reactions occur as the water passes through the system. It appears so obvious that intermediate points should be sampled, but in most cases the obvious has been ignored. We will never be able to do an engineering design of many of these systems if better data are not collected and analyzed in a way that will give engineers a relatively simple way of calculating the proper size of a system. Simple plug flow hydraulic models with a quasi-first order expression will likely be adequate for design.

Good sampling programs should be a requirement by the construction grants program and state regulatory agencies for all artificial wetland systems and other plant systems. A small expenditure at several sites around the country would result in the knowledge necessary to develop a semi-rational approach to the design of these systems.

Another limitation in many of the projects is a lack of attention to the hydraulics of the systems. A part of an extensive sampling program should include a tracer study to establish the hydraulic characteristics of the systems. Without a good hydraulic design, you know very little about a system.

Little attention has been given to optimizing the performance of the pretreatment components of the wetland and plant systems. The effluent leaving the preliminary ponds seems to be accepted without question. Tremendous improvements can be achieved in the performance of many of the pond systems described at this conference.

Another limitation in most pond designs is a poorly designed hydraulic system. I have noticed many ponds using inlet and outlet structures separated by only a few meters. There is an extensive literature base on pond systems, and I strongly encourage many of you to consult the literature and heed the advice. You can obtain a Pond Design Manual from the US EPA gratis and many helpful hints are presented therein. Pond systems fail for one or a combination of three causes: discharge of toxic substances to the pond; organic overloading; and poor hydraulic design. The last cause is the most frequently encountered problem in new systems. Multiple cell pond systems are the best option and provide a great deal of flexibility in applying light loads of algae and other organic matter to the wetland or plant systems. Nitrogen removal in the preliminary ponds should not be neglected in designing plant systems. Nitrogen removal in pond systems can be reliably predicted using formulas available in the literature.

Cost data are limited for all types of plant systems, and the costs which are available are probably of little value until the designs of the plant systems are optimized. More effort needs to be directed toward collecting cost data for each component of the wetland or plant systems. With individual component costs, it will be possible to make valid comparisons of various alternatives.

Operation and maintenance costs are extremely limited and it appears that operation and maintenance requirements for most of the systems discussed at this meeting are not fully understood. Without a commitment to proper operation and maintenance, the use of the wetland and plant wastewater treatment systems will be short-lived. Small communities are notorious for their lack of attention to the operation and maintenance of wastewater treatment systems; therefore, it is imperative that people developing these plant concepts make every effort to guarantee long-term commitments to operation and maintenance.

Greater attention needs to be focused on the physical management of the plant systems for small communities. As an example, it may or may not be feasible to burn the plant accumulation from a rock-bed-plant system. What effect does long term accumulation of biomass have on system performance? There are many, many other questions that need an answer.

PLANT-WATER-SEDIMENT PROCESSES John C. Corey

It is clear that the basic understanding in soil science is being transferred effectively to the aquatic systems discussed at this conference. Research and production knowledge from rice and other aquatic crops is being used to understand processes influencing waste management. In addition, information that is available on heavy metal uptake and plant toxicity from terrestrial systems is used to scope aquatic systems. It is obvious that if we are going to use biological systems to assist in the waste management efforts in the world, we need to fully exploit their potential by understanding the important interactions between soil, plant, and water and how to maximize the role of each component. It is quite clear that although much is known, there is a great deal to be learned about soil-plant-water interactions. Some of the areas that I feel need emphasis are the following:

1. There needs to be an improved understanding of each component of the system and the rates that important processes are conducted by these systems. We need to improve our understanding of the rates of physical, chemical, and biological processes in actual situations and techniques to enhance filtration, absorption, decomposition, and storage.
2. We need to be able to identify and quantify the rates at which detoxification occurs. This is particularly important in areas of hazardous waste. Industries will be required to utilize additional pretreatment of their waste prior to transfer to publically owned treatment works. Methodology to enhance the detoxification of this waste is sorely needed.
3. Although bacteria have been recognized as extremely important in the processing of industrial waste as well as domestic waste, their role could be enhanced through biotechnology so that the required capability to detoxify a particular hazardous waste is transferred into an organism that is ubiquitous. Efforts are underway at the present time to isolate bacteria that are capable

of enhanced waste detoxification. As soon as biotechnology is accepted by the public as a useful technique, bacteria should be engineered to handle the needs of industrial waste management.

4. Waste management sometimes only transfers the problem into a plant system or a soil system. I believe this would be better referred to as storage and in effect it is only an interim phase. We need to ask ourselves is this the best solution. If it is not, then we need to look at alternatives that would be superior to the methodology we are using.

5. We need to be able to answer to a fuller extent the "What if" questions. These include the types of questions that one gets in a public hearing when you are presenting a project to handle waste. Some of the types of questions that are asked are: What if the town doubles? What if we have process upsets? What if the N content for the design phase is really in error and it's four times the loading? What if a new industry comes to town? These are extremely important questions in the public process and it is important to be able to answer them accurately. By understanding the basic processes we will be able to give more effective answers to these types of questions.

6. There is a need to avoid problems that we have had with some of the cleanup systems that use nuisance plants. If these were sterile plants their introduction for waste management activities would be more acceptable. We have been able to develop the necessary breeding programs for agricultural products. It would be interesting to pursue some of the plant genetics work to tailor make aquatic plants capable of waste detoxification and yet unable to reproduce, therefore, averting a major threat to our waterways.

7. Programs such as these, if they are accepted by industry, must guarantee success in the cleanup. The Plant Manager is faced with state regulatory agencies. Therefore, the uncertainty factor in systems like this must be extremely low to make it acceptable to the public and to industry. We must be sufficiently knowledgeable about the systems that we will know that they work for the waste of concern.

8. I see a continuing need to meld the expertise of scientists and engineers on projects. Major strides will only be made when the various disciplines work together toward a common goal. I have seen certain projects at this conference that have had the benefits of multi-faceted approach and in these cases, successes were demonstrated. There is a place for individual progress on certain parts of the programs, but I believe that the greatest strides will be made when we work together as a team. This will require funding and I recognize that funding is difficult at the present time. However, I would like you to consider approaching certain customers that you may not have realized before were customers when you have these productive teams established. In this case, I am speaking of industries in your local area that are faced with waste management problems. Go to them and tell them what kind of a team you've assembled and what you think you can do

for the industry. I believe you will find them very receptive in many cases to what you wish to do and you may have found yourselves some funding in areas that have not been tapped to the same extent as the national sources.

RESOURCE RECOVERY Carl W. Hall

This conference exemplifies the interest of many groups in recognizing and encouraging cross-disciplinary research. Several activities of the National Science Foundation support such research, most notable of which is the Engineering Research Centers program. At the same time we recognize the importance of having strong disciplines on which to build interdisciplinary and cross-disciplinary work.

As we look ahead, even as we are experiencing today, many exciting and worthwhile research efforts will take place at the interface between fields and between external constituencies and our own fields. It has been a pleasure and an education for me to attend this conference, I've learned much; perhaps I can partly repay for those benefits by highlighting some research and development directions for the future.

I am pleased to see considerable reduction in tensions among the various interests as compared to 10 to 15 yr ago. Increased understandings by the parties involved demonstrate the lack of single answer solutions to national and international problems of water quality. Now might be an appropriate time for this and other groups to develop a strategic plan statement so that resource producers and resource users would work more rapidly toward some common goals.

A framework of reference which I published some time ago, and has been used by others, could be helpful as we attempt to aggregate the myriad of possibilities for research in resource recovery. I refer to the use of bioresources for one or more of the six F-categories: food, feed, fiber, feedstocks, fertilizer, and fuel. Food might be the highest order and fuel the lowest, from the standpoint of use and recovery. If the objective function is known, as an example, use for food, the harvesting, and handling and storage may be considerably different than the procedure for fuel. It may be necessary (or desirable) to use some of the bioresource for fertilizer. I am saying "resource recovery for what purpose?" The research and development may vary greatly depending on the use of the resources to be recovered. If a recovered product is to be used for feed, livestock feed for example, research is needed to assess the product for that use. The same applies to fertilizer, as well as the other "F's."

In my discussion I've tried to distinguish between resources removal (such as N or P from wastewater) which I'll not cover, and resource recovery. In many cases the resource recovery offers possibilities for paying for the resource removal steps. As I have listened to the papers and discussion over the past three days I have ferreted out the following research and development areas related to resource recovery:

Optimization

Need to optimize the design of the reactor in terms of biomass production, energy, economics, etc. Included would be flow control, depth of water, operational stages, and variations in design. Once a workable unit or system is assembled, considerable work is required to optimize for different operating situations and for identified objectives.

Harvesting Biomass

On several occasions mention was made of harvesting various biomass materials from different systems. I fear that in most research projects, and perhaps some development projects as well, that little thought was given up-front to the details of harvest. The cost of harvesting must be associated with the moisture content of the product, or on a dry matter basis. In agriculture, the culture has been changed to accommodate high rate mechanical harvesting. Different approaches for submerged, floating and terrestrial plants are certainly in order. Integrated harvesting and handling operations must be developed beginning in the planning stages of concept development.

Moisture Reduction

If a plant is to be used for feed, or biogas production, the moisture content may be acceptable; if it is to be burned for fuel, the product will need to be dried, preferably using solar energy; or mechanical means may be used to remove the higher moisture content. There have not been any major breakthroughs in drying (moisture removal) in recent years - we need some innovation here.

Energy

It's valuable to know how much energy is required for a certain process, or how much can be obtained from a process. The "quality" of that energy must be identified during the R&D stage. The "quality" of heat obtained from scrubbed biogas, for example, is superior to the heat obtained from burning biomass. Unfortunately, we don't have a widely acceptable method or nomenclature to remedy the situation but "energy" comes close. Use of heat recovery devices to increase system energy output, particularly for large installations, needs development. Energy balances can be very helpful in analyzing a system. The difficulty of comparing energy efficiency of systems, and the question was raised quite often by participants of this conference, is illustrated by the fact that the Joules (BTU) in the input of green plants are different in "quality" than the Joules (BTU) in the output.

Gas Quality

Considerable research and development work has been done on providing pipeline quality methane from digestion processes. Less energy intensive methods for removing carbon dioxide would be useful to more economically provide high-BTU gas from medium-BTU gas. Other materials - hydrogen, water, perhaps some CO from pyrolysis - may need to be removed. Perhaps, providing pipeline quality methane may not be needed, medium BTU gas may be quite adequate at the production site and nearby use sites.

Biomass Characteristics and Use

Research is often done with single varieties of plants whereas in practice there may be mixed plant varieties. Possibilities of utilizing and getting maximum recovery from mixed plants may need some additional attention.

Some plants may have taken up large quantities of heavy metals or toxic organics rendering them unsuitable for food, feed and perhaps fertilizer. Can these plants be readily identified as they move through? If not, devices are needed to do so. Burning for fuel may contaminate the environment and even landfill may not be acceptable.

Should plants for pharmaceutical uses be handled as a feedstock in the same way as for other uses? The issue of size reduction - chopping, grinding (which require energy) - which may be needed to improve the operation of a reactor requires additional research attention for optimization.

Liquefaction

In connection with conversion of high-moisture biomass by thermochemical gasifiers, research in methods of convection with an objective of reducing pressure in retort, overall energy, and possibly simplification are needed.

Scale Up

The efficiency of resource recovery of an operating unit may be considerably different than that from the test tube. Appropriate scaleup from test tube, to bench, to prototype must be done. In most cases, disappointments occur when one tries to go directly from test tube to plant operations. Scaleup is most important for reactor design, but applies to the whole system. It is also essential to operate the test unit under several different conditions for extended periods.

Reactor Design

Various flow configurations, temperature control, holding capacities, control variables (pH, etc.), concentration, feedstocks, stage of maturity, roughness of handling, and many more variables need to be assessed as one looks to improving resource recovery.

Separation Processes

Removal of water, concentration of substrate, possibly separation of materials in the feed stages, separation of gases from liquids, separation of one liquid from another, although not specifically mentioned by papers at this meeting merit consideration.

In summary, with resource recovery we are dealing with complicated systems involving many variables and which must meet different needs--such as environment, energy and economics. Much research and development has been done. The 18th Century was known as the Age of Enlightenment, the 19th Century as the Age of Ideology, and the 20th Century as the Age of Analysis. I suggest that the 21st Century will be known as the Age of Synthesis--and we are on our way--involving numerous subjects and fields of study and interests, all as part of complicated systems.

ECOLOGICAL CONSIDERATIONS William E. Odum

The papers at this conference have fallen generally into three categories: 1) intensively engineered systems, 2) artificial wetlands, and 3) use of natural wetlands. In each of these cases, the emphasis has been on the use of a plant-based system to treat either domestic and industrial wastewater, or storm water runoff. There are a number of interesting ecological principles which relate to these topics. Some of these ecological considerations are described below with the hope that future projects will include these from the first planning step onward.

Papers on the intensively engineered systems reported on projects in which plants such as water hyacinth, soft rush or _Phragmites_ are used in single species culture to treat wastewater. To an ecologist several questions immediately leap to mind. First, these are essentially monocultures and we have learned in studying natural ecosystems that monocultures because of their inherent ecological instability, are relatively rare. Any type of perturbation such as a disease, climatic change or insect infestation can cause a monoculture to fail suddenly and completely. In short, there are no backup species to take over in case the primary species runs into trouble.

Of course, most modern agriculture is based on using monocultures, but heavy subsidies in the forms of fertilizers, pesticides and irrigation are necessary to keep a single species from failing. In the case of engineered water treatment systems it seems advisable to attempt to research the use of multiple species. These might not require as much subsidization and might prove more stable in the long run. Problems and breakdowns with single species operations can probably be expected as commonplace.

There are other ecological considerations and lessons which might be transferred from the emerging field of agroecology to this related field of engineered plant water treatment systems. For example, a considerable amount of work has been done on plant-insect interactions in agricultural situations. Useful information concerning insect diversity (inclusion of predator insects) and experiments with different combinations of plants and insects could yield useful information for those attempting to design plant-wastewater treatment facilities.

Artificial Wetlands

There appear to be great opportunities in the future to design small to moderate sized wetlands which are built totally to treat storm water runoff, acid mine drainage, or secondary treated sewage effluent. Once again, rather than designing simple wetlands based on a single species such as cattails it would be advisable to design relatively complex systems which include multiple species of plants and some wildlife species. To do this we need to know more about succession/dominant patterns in artificial wetlands. For example, why do cattails typically dominate artificially engineered wetlands? Is it possible to design wetlands with multiple species growing in concentric rings outward from the source of water input? Questions concerning the mixture of swamps (with trees) and marsh (with grasses and sedges) for maximum treatment potential need to be addressed.

Another area related to both artificial wetlands and the intensively managed systems involves studies of sub-surface hydrology. How do we design a sediment layer which lies underneath these wetlands so that it provides the best combination of relatively high hydraulic conductivity and also a high potential for adsorption and absorption of nutrients such as P. For example, it may be possible to design subsurface layers of alternating gravels and clays to maximize both hydraulic conductivity and sorptive uptake. Many techniques are available including the use of piezometers to measure sub-surface flow rates and other aspects of sub-surface hydrology.

It is obvious that we have very few people at this meeting concerned with fish and wildlife in wetlands. It would be useful to have wildlife biologists take an interest in artificial wetlands and natural wetlands which are being used for water treatment. We need to know more about the transfer of toxic chemicals to birds and mammals. We need to know more about the role of herbivorous animals and whether it is possible to raise fur-bearing animals and other valuable species at the same time that we are treating wastewater. This area of wildlife use of wetlands is an obvious deficiency in most contemporary studies of wastewater treatment in wetlands.

Natural Wetlands

As we have heard from representatives of EPA and some of the state agencies, there is considerable concern about the use of natural wetlands for wastewater treatment. We have heard about and seen a project at Disney World where partially treated water receives its final treatment in a large cypress forest. We have heard other papers about the utility of using flooded swamp forests for wastewater treatment.

Significant questions have been raised by these papers. For example, how much alteration can a natural wetland undergo before major changes occur in its ecological structure and processes? How do we monitor an existing wetland to determine the degree of change? How long a time period is required before we understand how great potential changes may be? We have heard papers at this conference which suggest that at least 10-20 yrs may be necessary before the truly significant and long term changes have occurred.

Clearly, we need more long term studies of natural wetlands which are receiving treated wastewater. We need to monitor changes in ecological succession and changes in animal and plant communities. We need to have better methodology for monitoring these changes. It may be possible that certain types of remote sensing such as low level color infrared photography may allow us to obtain some of these answers inexpensively and over pervious intervals of time if historical photography exists.

One area in which very little knowledge appears to be available concerns the impact of storm runoff water on existing wetlands. Few studies have been directed toward this question.

In summary, it appears, from an ecological perspective, that we know relatively little about this particular field of applied science. There has been little ecological thought given to the design of intensive wastewater treatment systems which utilize plants. Attempts to design artificial wetlands are relatively recent and in many cases somewhat primitive. Few long term studies exist of natural wetlands which have received partially treated wastewater. Obviously, many interesting research opportunities are waiting to be tackled. One of the biggest problems is to attract the interest of ecologists, most of whom tend to work on pristine ecosystems and who are not too excited about working on managed or artificial ecosystems. Fortunately, the type of engineered wetlands and managed wetlands which have been discussed at this meeting provide exciting opportunties for ecologists to study both basic ecological processes and their applications. I predict that in the next decade there will be considerably more activity in this area by ecologists.

ENVIRONMENTAL ISSUES by James M. Davidson

Natural wetlands contain many biological systems which may be seriously impacted by water inputs containing significant amounts of plant nutrients and other chemicals (e.g., toxic chemicals). At the present time, considerable effort appears to be associated with the use of natural wetlands for water treatment and resource recovery with little consideration given to the nutrient impacts on flora, fauna and long term ecosystem functions. This impact on "non-target" species may be subtle and and require monitoring over extended periods of time before significant changes or deterioration is observed. Thus, the use of engineered or constructed systems may be more desirable because these ecosystems can be controlled and maintained without damage to a natural system. If natural wetlands continue to be used for water resource recovery, then extensive studies on the impact of treatment practices on non-target species and ecosystem integrity must be investigated.

At the present time, there appears to be a significant conflict between weed control in aquatic systems and the use of aquatic systems for water treatment and resource recovery. For example, a major effort is underway for the control of aquatic weeds through biological techniques. If this goal is achieved to a measurable extent, it is certain to impact systems which are growing aquatic plants for water treatment. Both state regulatory agencies and state and federal research programs must coordinate their activities in this area, and weed control scientists need to be cognizant of adverse roles of their control agents.

The potential for a serious mosquito problem should be an integral part of a water treatment and resource recovery project. There exists a number of biological control techniques as well as cultural management techniques which may be incorporated into aquatic systems to control mosquitoes to acceptable levels without pesticides. The use of pesticides for mosquito control may disrupt the ecosystem in such a way as to reduce non-target species and alter other desirable biological activities in the system.

There are several social issues which should be studied. These include not only economic questions associated with the use of aquatic plants for water treatment, but also public acceptance of the procedure. Economists and sociologists should be invited to participate in projects where appropriate. These activities should be carried out concurrently with the biological evaluation of a treatment process.

Performance standards expected from various water treatment and resource recovery systems using aquatic plants must be established. These may vary from region to region as well as for aquatic plants. Thus, a range in expected performance of a given biological system may be more appropriate than specific standards. The development of protocols for management of systems would ensure the potential for achieving specified performance standards. Both protocols and performance standards should receive increased attention, especially as our understanding of the biological system progresses.

Increased attention should be given to the utilization and/or disposal of aquatic plant material produced in association with water treatment and resource recovery. Studies involving the uptake of potential contaminants from aquatic systems should be conducted and models capable of predicting this uptake in response to chemical concentrations in the aquatic system established. The models should be mechanistic and not regression equations thus, preventing them from being site specific. Even where materials are used for methane production, the problem of digestor sludge disposal because of contaminated residues may exist.

It is suggested that fewer experiments be conducted in the future and that greater attention be given to taking more measurements (biological, physical, and chemical) within the experiments conducted. At the present time, many experiments are measuring an insufficient number of parameters making it impossible to describe the biological processes occurring in the aquatic ecosystem. By taking more measurements, the spatial and temporal variability of the ecosystem under investigation can be quantified. This would increase the potential for the development of mechanistic models and eliminate the need for multiple regression equations which are site specific. The fewer experiments must involve a multidisciplinary group of scientists interacting in taking measurements at the same site. Such an approach can lead to an understanding of important ecological functions for artificial and/or natural ecosystems and how the systems can be optimized to meet performance requirements.

SUMMARY Sherwood C. Reed

The research results presented at this conference clearly demonstrate that our confidence level with respect to the viability of aquatic plants for water treatment and resource recovery concepts has increased dramatically. It is also clear that there is still a way to go before they will be considered for general routine use. Implementation of these concepts for waste treatment will be in the hands of the engineers, the regulators, and the politicians and not usually controlled by the research and development community.

A particular concept will be "accepted" when the design engineer has some rational basis for understanding how the process works and confidence that it will work for the specific project at hand. The present data bases for many aquatic concepts are incomplete and are sometimes confusing and conflicting. As one example, there is a lack of agreement among some research groups as to the fate of N in water hyacinth systems. Is nitrification/ denitrification or plant uptake the major removal pathway? Since the choice affects both the design and operation of the system the typical design engineer is likely to avoid the concept until this, and similar, issues are resolved.

In the present situation of constrained funding it might benefit both the applied research community and the funding sponsors to try something similar to a market analysis. The key question would be "If the research is successful, what is the prospect for general utilization of the concept?" The answer, and the subsequent research, will require both a multidisciplinary approach and a clear definition of project goals. It is not possible for a single project to optimize everything, since there will be trade-offs between water quality, biomass production, nutrient removal, etc. A team approach is the only way to understand the constraints and opportunities of these complex systems and to define the research needs for a particular goal.

If wastewater treatment is the principle goal, the present answer to the key question would seem to be that constructed ("artificial") wetland and engineered systems with floating plants offer the greatest potential for general routine use. The use of natural wetlands may be technically feasible for wastewater treatment but such projects must overcome a variety of regulatory, environmental, and political constraints and their widespread use for this purpose is not considered likely. However, the long term impact of fully treated wastewater effluent and stormwater discharges on these natural wetlands will require study.

If biomass production is the principle goal, the project details will then depend on the intended final use (food, fiber, feedstock, fuel, etc.) of the harvested materials. A multi-disciplinary approach is essential to define the production, harvesting and utilization methods and the research needs for each.

Many projects may opt for the middle ground by providing acceptable water treatment with attendant resource recovery, when economically feasible. Prospects for the latter may depend to some degree on system size and this area may offer the greatest research challenge and opportunity for innovation.

It would be useful to undertake a multidisciplinary analysis of both floating macrophyte and constructed wetland concepts to define "what do we already know about the processes and what do we still need to know to allow confident design and assured performance?" The results would provide the basis for a systematic and very productive research program.

Research should also focus on both emergent and floating plants. The development of alternatives to water hyacinth could increase the geographical range and acceptability of this treatment method. The utilization of more than one plant species is also desirable. Dependence on a monoculture for waste treatment is not prudent from either the ecological or engineering point-of-view. Other issues of concern include mosquito and odor control, operation and maintenance methodology, and system costs.

Much of the conference presentation and the remarks by this panel have been directed at applied research intended to evaluate and/or develop systems for water treatment or resource recovery. This focus must not in any way diminish the critical importance of basic research on both the micro and macro levels to improve our understanding of component responses and interactions in aquatic ecosystems.

It bears repeating that a multidisciplinary approach is the key to further advancement of the use of aquatic plants for water treatment and resource recovery. At the present time, research on some of these concepts is near the end of the developmental stage. The first generation of full scale wastewater treatment systems will by necessity utilize a large safety factor to compensate for lingering uncertainties. The goal of subsequent research should be process optimization to reduce the safety factor and improve the cost effectiveness of future systems. Unfortunately, we also have research projects and full scale systems being constructed without any clear understanding of process kinetics or the interactions of internal system components. Such "green box" approaches are neither good science or good engineering. We can only advance the state-of-the-art by careful evaluation to determine how and why the system works and to identify the potential for optimization.

LIST OF REVIEWERS

The editors want to express their appreciation to the following individuals who helped review manuscripts presented in this book. Their constructive criticism has played a major role in maintaining high editorial standards of the book. In case of an oversight on our part, we extend our apologies to those reviewers whose names were not included in this list.

Abbasi, S. A., CWRDM, Kozhikode, India
Badger, P. C., Tennessee Valley Authority, Muscle Shoals, AL
Bagnall, L. O., Univ. of Florida, Gainesville, FL
Baker, C., Tennessee Valley Authority, Muscle Shoals, AL
Baker, J. T., Univ. of Florida, Gainesville, FL
Baldwin, B. L., Univ. of Florida, Gainesville, FL
Bastian, R. K., USEPA, Washington, D.C.
Bates, L., Tennessee Valley Authority, Muscle Shoals, AL
Beck, M. J., Tennessee Valley Authority, Muscle Shoals, AL
Behrends, L., Tennessee Valley Authority, Muscle Shoals, AL
Best, G. R., Univ. of Florida, Gainesville, FL
Biesboer, D. D., Univ. of Minnesota, St. Paul, MN
Bishop, L. P., Univ. of New Hampshire, Durham, NH
Bowes, G. E., Univ. of Florida, Gainesville, FL
Broder, J., Tennessee Valley Authority, Muscle Shoals, AL
Brown, M. T., Univ. of Florida, Gainesville, FL
Canfield, D. E., Univ. of Florida, Gainesville, FL
Coonrod, H. S., Tennessee Valley Authority, Muscle Shoals, AL
Corwin, D. L., U.S. Salinity Laboratory, Riverside, CA
DeBusk, T. A., Reedy Creek Utilities Co., Lake Buena Vista, FL
DeBusk, W. F., Univ. of Florida, Sanford, FL
DeLaune, R. D., Louisiana State Univ., Baton Rouge, LA
Dierberg, F. E., Florida Institute of Technology, Melbourne, FL
Dinges, R., 3404 Buck Race, Austin, TX
Dorich, R. A., DOW Chemicals U.S.A., Indianapolis, IN
Ewel, K. C., Univ. of Florida, Gainesville, FL
Gambrell, R. A., Louisiana State Univ., Baton Rouge, LA
Good, B. J., Louisiana State Univ., Baton Rouge, LA
Graetz, D. A., Univ. of Florida, Gainesville, FL
Haller, W. T., Univ. of Florida, Gainesville, FL
Hammer, D., Tennessee Valley Authority, Norris, TN
Hardy, J. K., Univ. of Akron, Akron, OH
Hayes, T. A., Gas Research Institute, Chicago, IL
Johnson, D., Solar Energy Research Institute, Golden, CO

ISBN 0-941463-00-1

Joyce, J. C., Univ. of Florida, Gainesville, FL
Kadlec, J. A., Utah State Univ., Logan, UT
Kadlec, R. H. The Univ. of Michigan, Ann Arbor, MI
Kingsley, B., Tennessee Valley Authority, Muscle Shoals, AL
Knight, R. CH2M Hill, Inc., Gainesville, FL
Kumar, N. M., USEPA, Washington, D.C.
Lakshman, G., Saskatchewan Research Council, Saskatoon, Canada
Lee, G. B., Univ. of Wisconsin, Madison, WI
Lembrechts, M. J., Univ. of Antwep, Belgium
Lemlisch, S. K., U.S. Army Corps of Eng., Jacksonville, FL
Lincoln, E. P., Univ. of Florida, Gainesville, FL
Lowe, E., St. Johns River Water Management District, Palatka, FL
Maddox, J., Tennessee Valley Authority, Muscle Shoals, AL
McCaleb, R., National Aeronautics Space Administration, NSTL, MS
McNeal, B. L., Univ. of Florida, Gainesville, FL
Miller, G. R., Black & Veatch, Kansas City, MO
Milve, T. A., Solar Energy Research Institute, Golden, CO
Mishoe, J. W., Univ. of Florida, Gainesville, FL
Moore, M., Tennessee Valley Authority, Muscle Shoals, AL
Nall, L., Florida Department of Natural Resources, Tallahassee, FL
Overman, A. R., Univ. of Florida, Gainesville, FL
Owens, L. B., USDA-ARS, Coshocton, OH
Putz, F., Univ. of Florida, Gainesville, FL
Rao, P. S., Univ. of Florida, Gainesville, FL
Robertson, D., Florida Institute of Phosphate Research, FL
Ryan, F. J., Univ. of California, Davis, CA
Schanze, T., Camp Dresser and McKee, Inc., Maitland, FL
Schwartz, L., Fla. Dept. Environ. Regulation, Tallahassee, FL
Scott, M., Oregon State Univ., Corvallis, OR
Sharitz, R., Savannah River Ecology Laboratory, Aiken, SC
Shih, S., Univ. of Florida, Gainesville, FL
Smith, C. J., Louisiana State Univ., Baton Rouge, LA
Steiner, G., Tennessee Valley Authority, Chattanooga, TN
Stewart, E. A., Amasek, Inc., Cocoa, FL
Strandberg, J. O., Univ. of Florida, Sanford, FL
Strickland, R., Tennessee Valley Authority, Muscle, Shoals, AL
Sutton, D. L., Univ. of Florida, Ft. Lauderdale, FL
Thabaraj, G. J., Fla. Dept. Environ. Regulation, Tallahassee, FL
Watson, J., Tennessee Valley Authority, Chattanooga, TN
Westmoreland, R., Tennessee Valley Authority, Muscle Shoals, AL
Wills, R. A., Oklahoma State Univ., Stillwater, OK
Wolverton, B. C., National Aeronautics Space Adm., NSTL, MS
Yousef, Y. A., Univ. of Central Florida, Orlando, FL

INDEX

D

E

F

S

T

U

V

W